C0-DXB-228

Jimmy Swaggart Bible Commentary

Mark

JIMMY SWAGGART BIBLE COMMENTARY

- » Genesis [639 PAGES 11-201]
- » Exodus [639 PAGES 11-202]
- » Leviticus [435 PAGES 11-203]
- » Numbers
  Deuteronomy [493 PAGES 11-204]
- » Joshua
  Judges
  Ruth [329 PAGES 11-205]
- » I Samuel
  II Samuel [528 PAGES 11-206]
- » I Kings
  II Kings [560 PAGES 11-207]
- » I Chronicles
  II Chronicles [505 PAGES 11-226]
- » Ezra
  Nehemiah
  Esther [288 PAGES 11-208]
- » Job [320 PAGES 11-225]
- » Psalms [688 PAGES 11-216]
- » Proverbs [320 PAGES 11-227]
- » Ecclesiastes
  Song Of Solomon [245 PAGES 11-228]
- » Isaiah [688 PAGES 11-220]
- » Jeremiah
  Lamentations [688 PAGES 11-070]
- » Ezekiel [520 PAGES 11-223]
- » Daniel [403 PAGES 11-224]
- » Hosea
  Joel
  Amos [496 PAGES 11-229]
- » Obadiah
  Jonah
  Micah
  Nahum
  Habakkuk
  Zephaniah [530 PAGES 11-230]
- » Haggai
  Zechariah
  Malachi [448 PAGES 11-231]
- » Matthew [625 PAGES 11-073]
- » Mark [606 PAGES 11-074]
- » Luke [626 PAGES 11-075]
- » John [717 PAGES 11-076]
- » Acts [832 PAGES 11-077]
- » Romans [536 PAGES 11-078]
- » I Corinthians [632 PAGES 11-079]
- » II Corinthians [589 PAGES 11-080]
- » Galatians [478 PAGES 11-081]
- » Ephesians [550 PAGES 11-082]
- » Philippians [476 PAGES 11-083]
- » Colossians [374 PAGES 11-084]
- » I Thessalonians
  II Thessalonians [498 PAGES 11-085]
- » I Timothy
  II Timothy
  Titus
  Philemon [687 PAGES 11-086]
- » Hebrews [831 PAGES 11-087]
- » James
  I Peter
  II Peter [730 PAGES 11-088]
- » I John
  II John
  III John
  Jude [377 PAGES 11-089]
- » Revelation [602 PAGES 11-090]

For prices and information please call: 1-800-288-8350
Baton Rouge residents please call: (225) 768-7000
Website: www.jsm.org • E-mail: info@jsm.org

Jimmy Swaggart Bible Commentary

Mark

World Evangelism Press

ISBN 978-1-934655-05-4

11-074 • COPYRIGHT © 2006 World Evangelism Press®
P.O. Box 262550 • Baton Rouge, Louisiana 70826-2550
www.jsm.org • email: info@jsm.org
(225) 768-8300
17 18 19 20 21 22 23 24 25 26 / EBM /12 11 10 9 8 7 6 5 4 3

All rights reserved. Printed and bound in U.S.A.
No part of this publication may be reproduced in any form or by any means
without the publisher's prior written permission.

TABLE OF CONTENTS

1. Introduction v
2. Mark 1
3. Index 595

INTRODUCTION

It is Friday morning, October 15, 2004, as I begin the rewrite on what many believe to be the most colorful of the four Gospels, the Gospel according to Mark. Mark proclaimed Christ in his beautiful down-home way, which possibly makes his Gospel easier to read than any of the others. Some have said that Mark portrays Christ as the Servant, hence, the reason for the simplicity.

The Word of God being what it is provides not only instruction, guidance, and help in all things pertaining to life and Godliness, but also provides a distinct pleasure that can be derived, in fact, from no other source. The Psalmist said it beautifully, *"How sweet are Your Words unto my taste! Yea, sweeter than honey to my mouth!"* (Ps. 119:103).

THE MESSAGE OF THE CROSS

In early spring, if I remember the season correctly, the Lord began to open up to me the Revelation of the Cross. As I've said often, it was not something new, actually that which had been given to the Apostle Paul nearly 2,000 years ago. Sadly, the Message of the Cross, which is literally the heartbeat of Christianity, at least the part of Christianity that is Biblical, has been all but lost in the last few decades. In other words, the Cross has been reduced to little more than sentimentality. This means that most Believers do not have the foggiest idea as to how to live for God. That is sad! That is tragic! But regrettably, it is also true!

In this Volume, we take every opportunity given by the Scriptural Text to present the Cross of Christ, a Message, incidentally, that will, without fail, change your life — and greatly for the better! Therefore, I would hope you would take the time to read this Volume. I believe it will be well worth your while, especially as it regards Spiritual benefit.

There is, of necessity, some repetition, as designed by the Holy Spirit, in the four Gospels; however, the repetition is never meaningless, but with purpose. I have noticed that the manner in which the Holy Spirit gave the various accounts, even though repeated in another Gospel, most of the time will give direction toward a particular Truth not found in the other accounts of the same incident. If we probe, most of the time that Truth becomes evident.

In writing Commentary on particular experiences in the Ministry of Christ, which are given two to four times in the Gospels, I very seldom refer back to previous Commentary on the same incident. I have little interest in repeating what already has been said, instead desiring that the Holy Spirit would lead us into other pastures. He almost always does!

So, I think the repetition of the four Gospels only serves to enlarge the understanding of these great Truths presented by the Holy Spirit; at least we have tried to be used in this manner.

SIMPLICITY

What makes Mark so beautiful, in my personal opinion, is its simplicity. As the Holy Spirit nudged Mark to present Christ in the Form and Ministry of the Servant, of necessity simplicity is the result. Consequently, even though it is very difficult, if not impossible, to favor one Gospel ahead of another, still, were I forced to make a choice, I suspect Mark would be my favorite. I think the beautiful, flowing simplicity has something, at least, to do with that. Mark wrote in such a way, certainly designed by the Holy Spirit, that it seems as if the Bible Student is actually present when these great Miracles were performed by Christ, or even sitting at His feet as He taught the multitudes. Mark has that wonderful capacity to make the Reader a part of what is happening. So, I suppose that's what makes this Book so grand.

THE WONDER OF THE WORD OF GOD

I love the Bible even more than I have words or

vocabulary to express. Until I began writing these Commentaries, I was reading the Bible completely through every six to ten weeks. I actually did this for years, with new Truths gleaned each and every time (Truths new to me, but not to the Word of God). Since I began to write the Commentaries, of necessity my attention has been concentrated on the particular Book which I am addressing. And yet, I never cease to be amazed at the wonder of the Word!

In my years of study of the greatest and most important subject on the face of the Earth, the Bible, I have learned that one's life will be immeasurably blessed, in every way, if one will make the Bible a lifelong project. Consequently, my encouragement to you, the Reader and Student, regarding this all-important task, is done so from a lifetime of experience. I know what the study of the Word of God will bring about in one's heart and life. As millions of others, I have experienced it! Consequently, I want every Believer to experience that of which I speak.

THE EVIL ONE

I suppose that Satan fights the Believer in this capacity as no other. Satan knows that the Word of God, if interpreted correctly, can bring about a virtual miracle in the life of the Believer. Consequently, he does everything he can to hinder that all-important spiritual progress. This is one of the reasons the Holy Spirit has moved upon me to write these Commentaries. In years of Ministry, I have had countless laymen tell me that they little read the Bible because they do not understand the Bible. Hopefully, these Commentaries will help make the Word of God easier to understand, at least for those who will take advantage of the opportunity.

Actually, the Bible is a story beginning with the Book of Genesis and concluding with the Book of Revelation. In Truth, it is a Revelation from beginning to end. That is the reason the Believer should study the Bible systematically, beginning at Genesis and going through to its conclusion. As the story was laid out in that fashion by the Holy Spirit, it should be studied in that fashion, as well! So, if, in this manner of study, I can get the Bible Student to read at least one Chapter a day in these Commentaries, I believe he will have an understanding of that particular Chapter in the Word of God which he has not previously had. I believe Truths will be brought to light that can literally change one's life, and in every capacity. The Word of God is designed to do that, and will accomplish that task if given the opportunity.

THE CROSS AND THE BIBLE

In essence, the entirety of the story of the Bible is the Story of Jesus Christ and Him crucified. In fact, the Doctrine of the Cross, that is if one would refer to the Cross as a doctrine, was formulated in the mind of the Godhead, even before the foundation of the world. Listen to what Peter said:

"Forasmuch as you know that you were not redeemed with corruptible things, as silver and gold, from your vain conversation (lifestyle) *received by tradition from your fathers;*

"But with the Precious Blood of Christ, as of a Lamb without blemish and without spot:

"Who verily was foreordained before the foundation of the world, but was manifest in these last times for you" (I Pet. 1:18-20).

Plainly, clearly, and simply, the Holy Spirit through the great Apostle tells us that the Cross of Christ is the Foundation of the entirety of the Word of God.

God, through foreknowledge, knew that He would make man and that man would Fall. So, it was decided in the high counsels of Heaven that man would be redeemed by God becoming man and dying on a Cross, so that the terrible horror of sin could be assuaged by Atonement, at least for all who will believe (Jn. 3:16).

So, this means the following: If the Doctrines of the Bible, whatever they might be, are not built squarely on the Foundation of the Cross of Christ, which was the First Doctrine formulated, actually the Foundation of all Doctrine, then, in some way, such doctrine will be specious. In fact, this is the reason for so much false doctrine — a misunderstanding of the Cross or an ignoring of the Cross. Irrespective, if the Cross of Christ is not properly understood, then nothing else will be understood quite properly, either.

THE CROSS AND THE NEW COVENANT

While the Story of the Cross is the Story of the entirety of the Bible, more particularly, the Message of the Cross is actually the entirety of the New Covenant. When the Lord gave the meaning of the Cross to the Apostle Paul, which he gave to us in his fourteen Epistles, He was literally giving the Apostle the explanation and definition of the New Covenant, that to which the entirety of the Old Covenant had ever pointed.

In this Gospel according to Mark, as stated, we will take every opportunity to present to you the rudiments of the Cross, and in every capacity, which the Lord has given unto us.

GREAT TRUTHS CONCEALED NOW REVEALED

I personally believe that the Revelation of the Cross given to me by the Holy Spirit contains Truth which the Church has not heretofore known. It doesn't mean it's new, because, as stated, it was given originally to the Apostle Paul. Perhaps I'm wrong in the statement I've just made. However, in all of my years of living for the Lord, and reading literally hundreds, perhaps thousands, of books, I have never read anywhere in all of my life the Truths that I will open up to you in this Volume.

Therefore, I believe that the material in this Commentary on *"The Gospel according to Mark"* will be some of the most revolutionary material you've ever read in your life, Truths which are 100 per cent Biblical, and obviously so, which can change your entire perspective of Christianity. I realize that's quite a statement, but I believe it to be true.

As the Psalmist, I say, *"I entreated Your favor with my whole heart: be merciful unto me according to Your Word"* (Ps. 119:58).

THE GOSPEL OF MARK

The Author of this wonderful Book is John Mark (Acts 12:12; I Pet. 5:13). It was probably written about A.D. 60, some twenty-seven years after the Resurrection and Ascension of Christ. Some believe that Mark wrote his Gospel under the direction of Peter. Ancient writers, as Irenaeus, Tertullian, St. Jerome, and others, claim Peter contributed to Mark's work. This much is obvious:

SIMON PETER

The manner in which the miracles and experiences of Christ are handled is definitely in the flavor of Simon Peter. However, even though Mark heard much about the life of our Lord from Peter, it seems also plain that he was not a mere copyist or storyteller. He also was an independent witness! He often supplies a sentence, detailing some little incident, which he only could have received from being an eyewitness.

Even though Mark's Gospel is the shortest of all the four Gospels, still, there is a unity and richness about it which quite excludes the notion that it is merely Mark relating what Peter had told him. Even though he avails himself of all the information he can procure, still, at the same time, he is an independent witness, giving, as all the sacred writers are permitted to do, the thoughts of his own mind, which the Holy Spirit moved him to communicate.

WHO IS MARK?

Who, then, was Mark? He appears to have been of the Tribe of Levi. John was his original Jewish name; Mark, his Roman prefix which was added afterward, gradually began to supercede his Jewish name. He was the son of a certain Mary who dwelt in Jerusalem. She appears to have been well known, with her house open to the friends and Disciples of our Lord. It is possible that her house may have been where our Lord *"kept the Passover"* with His Disciples on the night of His betrayal. Perhaps it also was the house where the Disciples were gathered together on the evening of the Resurrection. It was certainly the house to which Peter came when he was delivered out of prison. Actually, this house may have been the first center of Christian worship in Jerusalem after our Lord's Ascension, which would have made it the site of the first Christian Church in that city.

MARK AND PAUL

It may come as a surprise to find out that Mark was one who initially was rejected by the Apostle Paul. He accompanied Paul and Barnabas as their attendant on their first missionary journey. However, when they reached Perga, in Pamphylia (Acts 13:13), Mark left them and returned to Jerusalem. The reason for his defection is not given; but it placed an added burden on an already heavy-laden Paul and Barnabas. Consequently, whenever the second missionary journey was being planned, Barnabas desired to take Mark again, but this was rejected by Paul. Due to this, there was a temporary estrangement between Paul and Barnabas. Even though very little information is given, it seems that Paul may have been wrong in his actions, with Mark acquitting himself favorably in further activity and thus being accepted by Paul later on!

For instance, when Paul closed out the Epistle to the Colossians, which was written by him from Rome during his first imprisonment, he said at the close of that letter, *"There salute . . . Marcus, sister's son to Barnabas, (touching whom you received Commandments: if he come unto you, receive him;)"* (Col. 4:10). Quite possibly, the Christians at Colosse had heard of the temporary separation of Paul and Barnabas and its cause. It is as if the Apostle is saying, *"You have heard of the separation between Barnabas and myself on account of Mark. You will, therefore, now rejoice to know that Mark is with me, that he is a comfort to me, and that he sends Christian greetings by my hand. I have already given you directions concerning him: if he comes unto you, receive him."*

Furthermore, in his Second Epistle to Timothy, written during his second imprisonment at Rome, which was the last he wrote before his death, he said, *"Take Mark, and bring him with you; for he is profitable to me for the Ministry"* (II Tim. 4:11). This is the last notice we have of Mark in the New Testament. It is truly beautiful how the Holy Spirit correlated these events that Mark would be mentioned by the great Apostle at the very last.

OUR REACTIONS

If one fails, as Mark did, the Holy Spirit, by these actions, is telling us that the failure does not have to be permanent. As someone has said, *"It is not our actions, as important as they may be, but rather our reactions, which really proclaim what we are."* Mark overcame the failure in Pamphylia, and went on to write the second Gospel in the New Testament. What an honor! What a privilege! And what a testimony of Faith to all!

It is said by some that Mark ultimately became the Pastor of the Church at Alexandria. It is further stated that he ultimately died a martyr's death in that city, although that cannot be proven. Tradition says that his body was translated by certain merchants from Alexandria to Venice in A.D. 827. The Venetian Senate adopted the emblem of St. Mark — the lion — for their crest. It is said that when they directed anything to be done, they affirmed that it was done by the order of St. Mark.

THE SERVANT OF JEHOVAH

This second Gospel given by the Holy Spirit to Mark portrays Jesus as the Servant of Jehovah (Zech. 3:8), as Matthew had portrayed Him as King. As a result, parables and long discourses are almost entirely absent, for a servant does not teach. Though that purpose is to picture the perfect Servant, yet through that service from time to time gleams the glory of the Godhead of Christ.

In Mark, there is no genealogy given to Christ, for in a servant men seek a character and not a pedigree; hence, there is no mention of the miraculous birth of Christ or reference to His childhood at Nazareth, as in Luke; or to His preexistence and Deity, as in John; there is no Sermon on the Mount, for that became a King and not a servant; there is also no claim to authority, as, for example, in the Parable of the Tares, for the command to the reapers is omitted; here no sentence is passed upon Jerusalem or woes denounced upon the Pharisees; no bridegroom as in Matthew, Chapter 25; no Lord judging between faithful and unfaithful servants; and no king separating the nations to the right and to the left hand.

If parables and discourses are recorded, titles and actions are omitted. In Gethsemane, nothing is said about Angels; on the Cross, no promise of the Kingdom is made to the dying thief. Prior to the Ascension of Christ, there is no statement as to His having all power in Heaven and in Earth. He simply dismisses the Disciples to service and goes forth working with them as a servant.

In Mark's account, the Apostles are regarded rather as companions than servants. They never call Him *"Lord"* in this Gospel. And in His Miracles, this title is suppressed. And yet, if it would be possible to place one Gospel ahead of the other, at least in dutiful simplicity, which makes it so easy to understand, the Gospel of Mark holds that distinction.

THE BOOK OF MARK

(1) "THE BEGINNING OF THE GOSPEL OF JESUS CHRIST, THE SON OF GOD;

The exegesis is:

1. This Verse could read, *"The beginning of the Good News concerning Jesus, the Messiah, the Son of God."*

2. Consequently, the Holy Spirit begins this Book by testifying to the Kingship and Deity of Christ before setting out His Perfection as a Servant.

3. The phrase, *"The beginning of the Gospel of Jesus Christ,"* refers to the Ministry of John the Baptist, which began this Gospel. Matthew began with the ancestry and birth of the Messiah; Luke, with the birth of the Baptist; and John, with the pre-incarnate Word.

4. It is *"The Gospel of Good News."*

WHAT IS THE GOSPEL?

The Greek word for *"Gospel"* is *"Euaggelion,"* which means *"a Message of Good News"*; it was a word in common use in the First Century for good news of any kind. Mark, consequently, appropriates the word, takes it out of the current secular usage, and links it to the Message of Salvation as Good News.

As a result, the word *"Gospel"* totally refers presently to the Message of Jesus Christ and what He did for us at the Cross; it has no relationship to secular usage. Actually, this is forthright and truthful, because the *"Message of Jesus Christ"* is the only truly *"Good News"* in the world. The so-called good news claimed by the world is, in reality, simply a momentary absence of bad news.

THE ANOINTED ONE

"Jesus Christ" actually means *"Jehovah saves and is the Anointed One."* In Jesus, we have both His Deity and Humanity, and, in Christ, the Messiah of Israel. This salutation means that this Good News is not preached, at least at this stage, by Jesus Christ, but is concerning Him. In other words, all of the Good News is wrapped up totally in Him.

The phrase, *"The Son of God,"* expresses His relationship to the Father and that He is a separate and distinct Person from the Father. Jesus Christ is the Son of God by nature.

Wuest says: *"He proceeds by eternal generation from God the Father in a birth which never took place because it always was. By virtue of all this, He possesses co-eternally the same essence as God the Father."*

Mark consequently begins his Gospel by telling us what it is all about, which is *"Good News,"* and, more particularly, Who it presents as the Author of this Good News, *"Jesus Christ, the Son of God."*

GOOD NEWS

The totality of the Gospel is summed up in the phrase, as given by the Apostle Paul, *"Jesus Christ and Him Crucified"* (I Cor. 1:23). The purpose of God becoming man, the purpose of all that He did, was *"the Cross."* In other words, Jesus came to this world for one distinct purpose, to go to the Cross. Of course, every single thing He did was of vital significance. Still, the Cross was ever His destination.

When He announced to His Disciples *"that He must go unto Jerusalem, and suffer many things of the Elders and Chief Priests and Scribes, and be killed, and be raised again the third day"* the Scripture says,

"Then Peter took Him, and began to rebuke Him, saying, Be it far from You, Lord: this shall not be unto You." The Scripture then says, *"But He (Jesus) turned and said unto Peter, Get thee behind Me, Satan: you are an offense unto Me: for you savor not the things that be of God, but those that be of men"* (Mat. 16:21-23).

As is obvious here, the Disciples had many things in mind; to be sure, the Cross definitely was not one of those things. But the very idea that He was to be deterred from His primary mission of going to the Cross was attributed by the Lord to Satan, who, regrettably, used Simon Peter. This should tell us something!

THE CROSS, THE PRIMARY MESSAGE

Whenever any modern Preacher of the Gospel belittles the Cross, ignores the Cross, or fails to understand what was done there, that Preacher's direction, as evidenced here in the Word of God, can only be summed up as a direction conceived by the Evil One. Let all Preachers beware: if Simon Peter, the Prince of the Apostles, could get sidetracked as here, all of us must surely beware. It's a serious thing for our Lord to attribute that which comes out of our mouth as being of Satan. However, that's exactly what He said of Simon Peter. Thank God, Peter didn't remain in that mode, but ultimately became a proclamation of the Message of the Cross (I Pet. 1:18-20).

THE ATTACK ON THE CROSS

Perhaps one can say that presently there is a greater attack on the Message of the Cross than at any time since the Reformation. That's a serious statement, but I believe it to be true! Before the Reformation could be successfully preached, there had to be a proper understanding of the Cross. Martin Luther, the great Reformer, said, *"As one views the Cross, so one views the Reformation."* In other words, if the individual had a dim view of the Cross, they had a dim view of the Reformation. If they had a proper view of the Cross, then they were a staunch supporter of the Reformation.

As well, in the late 1800's and the early 1900's, the Cross began to be preached around the world, possibly as never before, or at least since the days of the Apostle Paul. The reason? At approximately the turn of the Twentieth Century, the Lord would pour out the Holy Spirit on this planet, even in a greater way, possibly, than even during the days of the Early Church. It was in fulfillment of Joel's great Prophecy concerning the *"former rain"* and the *"latter rain"* (Joel 2:23).

The *"former rain"* concerns the outpouring of the Spirit on the Day of Pentecost and forward throughout the time of the Early Church. Due to apostasy, the great messages of the Baptism with the Holy Spirit and Salvation by Grace began to wane until ultimately they all but died. Out of that, taking several centuries, came the Catholic Church.

The *"latter rain"* pertains to the great outpouring, which basically began, as stated, at the turn of the Twentieth Century, which has resulted in well over 100 million people being baptized with the Holy Spirit with the evidence of speaking with other tongues (Acts 2:4). However, before the great outpouring of the Holy Spirit began in these modern times, the Cross had to be preached once again in power and glory, which it definitely was. In other words, the Church had to be brought back to the Cross before this great visitation would come.

Regrettably and sadly, the Church presently is losing its way and is probably in worse spiritual condition presently than at any time since the Reformation. In fact, the modern Church falls into the following category:

"Because you say, I am rich and increased with goods, and have need of nothing; and knowest not that you are wretched, and miserable, and poor, and blind, and naked" (Rev. 3:17). The Laodicean Church properly symbolizes the modern Church.

The Message to the Churches began with Jesus standing in the *"midst of the seven candlesticks"* (Rev. 1:13), which represented the Churches. It closes with Jesus standing outside the door and knocking, saying *"If any man hear My voice, and open the door, I will come in unto Him and will sup with him, and he with Me"* (Rev. 3:20).

As the preaching of the Cross has gradually waned, with all types of false doctrine crowding it out, if one is to notice, fewer people are truly being saved presently than ever before; as well, fewer people are being baptized with the Holy Spirit than ever before, or at least since the Reformation.

The Church must come back to the Cross.

JESUS CHRIST AND HIM CRUCIFIED

What did Paul mean by the statement, *"We preach Christ crucified"* (I Cor. 1:23)? Approximately twenty-five years earlier, the Scripture says, *"Philip went down to the city of Samaria, and preached Christ unto them"* (Acts 8:5). In fact, for the first several years after the Ascension of Christ, the Disciples preached Christ, mentioning the Cross very little. There was a reason for this!

First of all, other than the fact of Jesus dying on the Cross, it was very little mentioned simply because the Disciples didn't understand exactly what the Cross meant. They also didn't understand too very much what the New Covenant meant. So they preached Christ.

It was to Paul that the meaning of the New Covenant was given, which, in effect, is the meaning of the Cross. The meaning of the Cross has to do with both our Salvation and our Sanctification. In other words, even as Paul outlined in Romans, Chapter 6, the Cross, as it refers to Sanctification, actually tells us how to live for God.

When Paul came to Christ, not understanding the Message of the Cross, because the meaning had not yet been given, he tried to live for God the only way he knew, along with all the other Disciples and Believers of that time, by trying to keep the Commandments. No matter how hard he tried, as the Seventh Chapter of Romans proclaims, he was unsuccessful. To be sure, even though virtually the entirety of the modern Church is trying to do the same thing, and I continue to speak of living for God by keeping the Commandments, the end result is the same. God has one Prescribed Order of Victory, which, in fact, He gave to the Apostle Paul, and Paul gave it to us in his Epistles. If we do not subscribe to that particular way made possible by the Cross, we will continue to live a life of defeat. You can be saved and be a Christian without understanding how to live for God, but you certainly cannot be victorious over the world, the flesh, and the Devil.

WHAT IS THE GOSPEL OF JESUS CHRIST?

In fact, the Gospel of Jesus Christ is God's Prescribed Order of Victory. It can be defined as *"Jesus Christ and Him Crucified"* (I Cor. 1:23). Paul said: *"For Christ sent me not to baptize, but to preach the Gospel: not with wisdom of words, lest the Cross of Christ should be made of none effect"* (I Cor. 1:17). In effect, this plainly tells us that the Gospel is *"the Cross of Christ."* This is the *"Good News"* that every sin debt has been paid; now the way is open for God to bless men unreservedly, that is, if they will only place their faith and trust in Christ and what Christ has done for us at the Cross.

Of course, the *"Good News"* to the unsaved person is that *"Jesus saves"*! In fact, the unsaved person doesn't have to do much to be saved, just simply call on the Name of the Lord and believe (Rom. 10:8-9, 13). But the definition of the Gospel continues, as it regards the Believer living for God. In other words, God's Prescribed Order is as follows:

THE CROSS: As a Believer, we must understand that every single thing we receive from the Lord comes to us with its Source as Christ and the Means being the Cross. Whenever the Holy Spirit through Paul began to tell us how to live for God, which refers to being victorious over the world, the flesh, and the Devil, He took us straight to the Cross, which is found in Romans 6:3-5.

No Christian can go beyond the Cross. If we go beyond the Cross, we are going beyond the great Redemption Plan. In truth, there is nothing beyond the Cross, except that which is devised by men. In effect, to try to go beyond the Cross is, in essence, saying that the Cross was insufficient and something is lacking, which we must make up ourselves. Such thinking is an insult of the highest order to the Finished Word of Christ.

No, there's nothing beyond the Cross, because there doesn't need to be anything beyond the Cross. At the Cross, Jesus paid it all, atoned for all sin, and made it possible for everything lost in the Fall to be given to us. Admittedly, we do not now have everything that we're going to have, in actuality, only the firstfruits (Rom. 8:23). The balance will be received at the Resurrection (I Cor., Chpt. 15). But, to be sure, we have enough now to live the victorious life we ought to live (Rom. 6:14). So, the Believer is to understand that not only did Salvation come to him by the means of the Cross, but power to live a sanctified life also comes exclusively by the means of the Cross.

OUR FAITH

Understanding that everything comes to us from Christ through the Cross, then our faith must be based exclusively in the Cross. In other words, the Cross of Christ must ever be the Object of our Faith. That's why Paul also said:

"But God forbid that I should glory (boast), *save in the Cross of our Lord Jesus Christ, by Whom the world is crucified unto me, and I unto the world"* (Gal. 6:14).

This means that we must not allow our Faith to have as its object anything else except the Cross of Christ. Satan will do everything within his power to push your faith away from Christ and the Cross to other things, and he doesn't too much care what those other things are, just so they aren't the Cross.

As it stands presently, the faith of most Christians does not reside in the Cross, but rather in other things. That is because the Cross is not presently understood, and, in fact, is little preached at all.

Satan will try to get you to place your faith in the quotation of Scriptures, which is good in its own right. It's not good, however, as it regards the foundation of all that God does for us. This mostly comes from the Word of Faith doctrine. It claims that, for whatever you need, you should find several Scriptures that go along with that, memorize them, and just quote them over and over. In some way, this will move God to action.

As stated, while it's very good to memorize Scriptures and to quote them, which I personally do constantly, still, that is not God's Way. The price that Jesus paid at the Cross is the Way, and the only Way. It is also very true that we should always quote the Word of God to the Devil when he comes against us; still, that is only to set him straight, exactly as Jesus did regarding the temptation in the wilderness (Mat., Chpt. 4). But it is the Cross of Christ where Satan was defeated, not our ability to memorize Scriptures, etc.

Listen again to Paul:

"Blotting out the handwriting of ordinances that was against us (the Law which we had broken), *which was contrary to us* (demanded perfection, but provided no power for us to perfect ourselves), *and took it out of the way* (satisfied the demands of the Law), *nailing it to His Cross* (the price was paid at the Cross, and at the Cross exclusively);

"And having spoiled principalities and powers (all the powers of darkness), *He* (Jesus) *made a show of them openly, triumphing over them in it"* (Col. 2:14-15).

This tells us, and in no uncertain terms, that Jesus defeated every power of darkness at the Cross, and did so by removing the means by which they hold man in captivity, which is sin (Heb. 10:12). So, it's the Cross, and the Cross alone, which must ever be the Object of our Faith, hence, Paul taking us directly to the Cross, whenever he began to open up to us the way to live for God (Rom. 6:3-5).

THE HOLY SPIRIT

Once we understand that it's the Cross where every price was paid and where every victory was won, and that the Cross must ever be the Object of our Faith, and, in fact, is the Object of our Faith, the Holy Spirit, Who works exclusively within the parameters of the Finished Work of Christ, will then work mightily upon our behalf, bringing about His Fruit within our lives (Gal. 5:22-23), which pertains to Righteousness, Holiness, and the Christlike spirit.

Concerning all that Jesus did at the Cross, He Himself said:

"If any man thirst, let him come unto Me, and drink.

"He who believes on Me, as the Scripture has said, out of his belly (innermost being) *shall flow rivers of living water."*

John, in giving this account, then said: *"But this spoke He of the Spirit, which they who believe on Him should receive"* (Jn. 7:37-39).

The idea is this: Concerning the Holy Spirit and how He works within our lives, Jesus also said, *"He* (the Holy Spirit) *will guide you into all Truth: for He shall not speak of Himself; but whatsoever He shall hear, that shall He speak: and He will show you things to come.*

"He shall glorify Me, (because it is Christ Who paid the price); *for He shall receive of Mine* (all that Jesus did for us at the Cross), *and shall show it unto you.*

"All things that the Father has are Mine (and can be ours, providing our faith is sufficiently placed in Christ and what He did at the Cross): *therefore said I, that He* (the Holy Spirit) *shall take of Mine, and shall show it* (give it) *unto you"* (Jn. 16:13-15).

The Holy Spirit doesn't work within our lives on the basis of who we are, but rather on Who Christ is, and, more particularly, what Christ has done for us. He doesn't demand much of us, only that we exhibit faith in Christ and what Christ did at the Cross. That being the case, the Holy Spirit will work mightily within our lives, giving us victory, as stated, over the world, the flesh, and the Devil. In fact, this <u>is</u> God's Prescribed Order of Victory, and His only Prescribed Order of Victory.

This is the Gospel of Jesus Christ.

(2) "AS IT IS WRITTEN IN THE PROPHETS, BEHOLD, I SEND MY MESSENGER BEFORE YOUR FACE, WHICH SHALL PREPARE YOUR WAY BEFORE YOU."

The synopsis is:

The Holy Spirit, before setting out Christ's perfections as a Servant, testifies to His Kingship and Deity.

THE PROPHETS

The phrase, *"As it is written in the Prophets,"* proclaims the Old Testament as the Word of God, and that its records were carefully preserved and handed down from generation to generation. The records are, in the language of the Psalmist, *"Forever, O LORD, Your Word is settled in Heaven"* (Ps. 119:89).

Everything that is found in the New Testament can be found somewhere in the Old Testament, which means that it is absolutely imperative for the Believer to know and understand the Old Testament. In fact, when the Holy Spirit through Paul wanted to substantiate and verify all that Christ had done and Who He was, He went to the Old Testament to prove His case, actually, the Tabernacle, hence, giving us the Book of Hebrews. In fact, if one doesn't understand the Old Testament, one cannot fully understand Who Christ is and What Christ has done for us. It's all there, in types and shadows, in the Old Testament.

The word *"Prophets"* is used in the plural because the quotation of Verses 2 and 3 comes from both Malachi and Isaiah (Mal. 3:1; Isa. 40:3). As well, it was common to combine, as here, quotations from various Prophets. Moreover, in Old Testament times, the Lord guided His people through the Ministry and the Message of *"Prophets."* While Prophets did, at times, foretell the future, most of their Ministry consisted of them being *"Preachers of Righteousness"* (II Pet. 2:5). John the Baptist, in fact, foretold very little, but yet was acclaimed by Christ as the greatest Prophet of all (Mat. 11:11).

The Ministry of the Prophet continues in the same fashion in the Church, but with one exception, and that is the Ministry of the Apostle. It is the Apostle whom the Holy Spirit uses to guide the direction of the Church, regarding Doctrine and Revelation. In fact, the hallmark of the Apostle is the Message which God gives him, placing special emphasis on a particular part of the Word of God which the Church needs. The Holy Spirit will so emphasize that Message as the Apostle delivers it to the Church that it becomes obvious that this is the way the Holy Spirit wants the Church to go.

The Scriptural reference for this is the Book of Acts and the Epistles. As the Lord gives a primary Message to an Apostle, other Preachers of the Gospel, who also are given the burden of such a Message, are themselves Apostles. This is born out by those Ministers who came up under Paul. Even though the great emphasis of Grace and Faith was given to Paul, others were given a like charge to propagate that Message, even as Timothy and others. As well, the Holy Spirit is still setting Apostles in the Church (Eph. 4:11).

THE MESSENGER

The phrase, *"Behold, I send My messenger before your face,"* is taken, as stated, from Malachi 3:1. This refers to John the Baptist. The phrase, *"Before your face,"* means that John would immediately precede Christ, in essence, preparing the way for Him. In fact, this is the reason that John the Baptist was the greatest Prophet of all! While all the other Prophets spoke of Christ, it was John who introduced Christ.

As we have also stated, John the Baptist foretold future events very sparingly, basically only saying, *"I indeed baptize you with water unto Repentance: but He Who comes after me is mightier than I, Whose Shoes I am not worthy to bear: He shall baptize you with the Holy Spirit, and with fire"* (Mat. 3:11).

The Ministry of John the Baptist burst upon Israel like a flaming meteorite, and did so after approximately 400 years of prophetic silence. In other words, from the time of Malachi to John the Baptist, there was no Prophet sent to Israel. In effect, Malachi predicted that no other Prophet would come until the one who would prepare the way for Christ (Mal. 3:1). So, when John the Baptist came on the scene, especially considering that he had such a powerful, prophetic Ministry, this should have been the evidence for the leaders of Israel to know and understand that it was time for the Messiah to come. Regrettably, they had so abused and misinterpreted the Word of God that they no longer knew what it actually did say.

THE PREPARATION

The phrase, *"Which shall prepare your way before you,"* concerns preparation for the Ministry of our Lord; the next two Verses proclaim what type of preparation. The preparation would be a demand for Repentance (Mat. 3:2). The word *"repent"* simply means that one must *"turn around"* from the wrong path which they have previously been traveling. They must come to the right path, which is the Word of God.

(3) "THE VOICE OF ONE CRYING IN THE WILDERNESS, PREPARE YE THE WAY OF THE LORD, MAKE HIS PATHS STRAIGHT."

The overview is:

Whatever the moving of the Spirit, whatever His Direction, before He does that which He desires to do, there must always be preparation, which He Himself guides and directs.

THE VOICE

The phrase, *"The voice of one crying in the wilderness,"* in the Greek actually says *"a voice,"* signifying that John was not the only *"voice"* sent to Israel, for many Prophets before him had been sent by God. In fact, the prediction of a coming Redeemer took place almost immediately after the Fall. The Lord told Satan through the serpent, *"And I will put enmity* (hatred) *between you and the woman* (this predicts that Satan would greatly hate the female gender of the human race), *and between your seed* (humanity which does not serve God) *and her Seed* (the only seed that a woman has ever had is the Lord Jesus Christ); *it* (He) *shall bruise your head* (the victory of the Cross) *and you shall bruise His heel* (the suffering of the Cross)" (Gen. 3:15).

And then, the description of the great Plan of God to redeem the human race was given in the form of the Sacrificial System, which is portrayed to us in Genesis, Chapter 4. The *"slain lamb"* would be a Type of the Son of God, Who would give His Life; the *"Altar"* was a Type of the Cross. The burning of the carcass on the Altar would typify the Judgment of God that would come upon His only Son instead of the human race. In fact, when the Law of Moses was ultimately given, the Sacrificial System, which had been paramount all the way from the time of Adam, would now become the central core of the Levitical Law (Lev., Chpts. 1-7). As well, and as stated, Prophet after Prophet foretold of His Coming (Gal. 3:16; Gen. 49:10; Isa. 7:14, etc.)

The word *"crying"* signifies that John was a strong Preacher, whose preaching was full of emotion and feeling. It came from the heart and was addressed to the heart. Even though the voice used was John's, still, it was God Who was crying out. In other words, the Heart of God was in the Message, which meant that it was delivered by a powerful anointing of the Holy Spirit, which greatly moved the people, as it was intended to do.

It was not psychology or mere emotionalism, as some modern skeptics claim, but the Holy Spirit greatly anointing the Message and the Messenger; thus, what John said was the Word of God.

THE MODERN CHURCH

Regrettably, the modern Church any more little looks to God's Prescribed Order of *"Preaching,"* which, of course, also includes Teaching; it rather resorts to other things. I speak of the modern fads of *"The Government of Twelve"* and *"The Purpose Driven Life/Church."* In those fads, the emphasis is placed on something other than the Preaching of the Gospel. These two *"fads"* have made, and are making, great inroads into the modern Church. Neither one is of the Lord; they are rather the product of *"angels of light"* (II Cor. 11:13-15).

And how do I know that?

THE CROSS MUST BE THE OBJECT OF FAITH

On her Program over SonLife Radio, Frances and those with her have taught for weeks about the fallacy of these particular fads. At a point in time, she asked me to read the book, *"The Purpose Driven Life."* I read a few pages and it quickly became obvious that the author was not preaching the Cross, but rather other things which were devised by men. Consequently, I did not read the book any further. And that's the reason why!

If the Preacher is not proclaiming the Cross as the answer for the ills of humanity, as the way to closeness to God, as the means by which victory is attained, then whatever he is preaching and proclaiming is not of God. So, I'm not going to waste my time reading false doctrine. Of course, Frances had to read it in order to properly teach the fallacy of the subject over her Program.

Now, let me address that again:

These two *"fads,"* and I continue to speak of *"The Government of Twelve"* and *"The Purpose Driven Life,"* are not preaching the Cross. That means they both are spurious.

While *"The Government of Twelve"* claims to preach the Cross, actually, they don't. (I would advise the Reader to secure our Study Guide: THE CROSS OF CHRIST, False Doctrine. In this Study Guide, we go into detail, as it regards these particular fads, plus others not mentioned; the Reader will do well to heed the teaching given therein.)

MODERN PSYCHOLOGY

This is the reason that psychology is so wrong! It is the taking of the system of this world, *"religionizing"* that system by adding a few Scriptures, and fostering it off on a gullible Christian public. Humanistic psychology is not of God, but rather the product of men; it is, in effect, the wisdom of this world, i.e., *"earthly, sensual, devilish"* (James 3:15).

Paul further addressed this by saying: *"For after that in the Wisdom of God the world by wisdom knew not God, it pleased God by the foolishness of preaching* (preaching the Cross) *to save them who believe"* (I Cor. 1:21). Paul also said, *"For Christ sent me not to baptize, but to preach the Gospel: not with wisdom of words, lest the Cross of Christ should be made of none effect"* (I Cor. 1:17).

Paul wasn't berating Water Baptism here, but rather stating that the emphasis must never be on the Ordinances of the Church, as correct as they are in their own way, but rather on the *"Cross of Christ."* That's the reason that we constantly state that the object of faith must always be the *"Cross of Christ"* (Rom. 6:3-14; 8:1-2, 11; Eph. 2:13-18; Gal. 6:14).

The only reason that I can give for Preachers advocating humanistic psychology as the answer to the ills and aberrations of man is that they simply no longer believe in Christ and what He did at the Cross. It is, pure and simple, unbelief. They simply do not believe that what Jesus did at the Cross addresses every problem of humanity, irrespective of what that problem is.

Let the Reader closely read the following:

The Holy Spirit through Simon Peter said: *"According as His Divine Power has given* unto us all things that pertain unto life and Godliness through the knowledge of Him Who has called us to Glory and Virtue:

"*Whereby are given unto us exceeding great and precious Promises: that by these you might be partakers of the Divine Nature, having escaped the corruption that is in the world through lust*" (II Pet. 1:3-4).

Now, either the Lord actually did give us "*all things*" that pertain unto life and Godliness, or else He didn't! I happen to believe that He did. The answer, as we repeatedly have stated, is found in the Cross.

THE WAY

The phrase, "*Prepare ye the way of the Lord,*" is actually given in the sense of a military command; it is a command meant to be obeyed at once. In other words, it's not a suggestion! The "*way of the Lord*" is meant not only in the sense of preparation, but also in the sense that Israel's ways must become God's Ways. In other words, "*Get back to the Bible!*"

As I write these words, I sense the Presence of the Lord, in that the Holy Spirit is admonishing America, and the world for that matter, to do accordingly. The ways of man will destroy any and all, while the "*ways of the Lord*" will bring life and prosperity. I grieve, as do all true Believers, at the efforts of man to assuage his problems by his own machinations and abilities. As always, man seems to think that he either has the answer or can find the answer in others. Never mind that all previous generations before him have failed. This generation thinks it can succeed.

However, without God there is no success! Solomon said, "*There is a way which seems right unto a man, but the end thereof are the ways of death*" (Prov. 14:12).

Let me say it again:

Irrespective as to what it might be, and no matter how many millions may accept it, if it's not "*Jesus Christ and Him Crucified,*" then it is not the right way; in effect, it is the wrong way. In other words, it will not come out to a successful conclusion, but rather the end result will be wasted lives, broken dreams, broken hearts, and ultimately the loss of the soul.

NOTES

STRAIGHT PATHS

The phrase, "*Make His paths straight,*" simply means that the ways of the Lord are "*straight,*" and that everything else is "*crooked.*" His people should be "*straight*" accordingly! The word "*straight*" has to do with a "*plumbline.*" Amos prophesied, "*Behold, I will set a plumbline in the midst of My people Israel*" (Amos 7:8). Christ is that "*Plumbline,*" with the definition of what is "*straight*" belonging to Him. As He was to Israel, He is to the Church, and to the entirety of the world, for that matter!

Any time the "*Plumbline*" is tampered with, as it is oftentimes by men, and irrespective as to how much they claim the tampering to be "*straight,*" as Israel of old, the fact remains that it is not "*straight,*" but rather "*crooked.*" That's what John was speaking of when he said, "*And the crooked shall be made straight*" (Lk. 3:5). He was speaking primarily of the crooked way of the Religious Leaders of Israel.

And when I say that the ways of these "*fads*" are not straight, I am speaking of that which is devised by men, which means they have departed from the Bible.

Let me say it again:

If it is "*straight,*" then it is "*Jesus Christ and Him Crucified*" (I Cor. 1:23). If is not "*Jesus Christ and Him Crucified,*" and that alone, then it is "*crooked.*" To be sure, the crooked way can be made straight only by coming back to the Cross, and the Cross exclusively.

ANOTHER JESUS

Paul said: "*For if he who comes preaches another Jesus, Whom we have not preached, or if you receive another spirit, which you have not received, or another gospel, which you have not accepted, you might well bear with him*" (II Cor. 11:4).

"*Another Jesus?*" "*Another spirit?*" "*Another gospel?*"

What did Paul mean by this statement?

He meant that if Jesus is preached other than by the Cross, pure and simple, it is "*another Jesus,*" meaning it's not the Jesus of the Bible. That's why he said, "*We preach Jesus Crucified*" (I Cor. 1:23).

Let the Reader understand:

Just because a Preacher mentions the Cross once in a while or even states that Jesus died on the Cross for us, this does not really constitute *"preaching the Cross."* For the Preacher to *"preach the Cross,"* which the Holy Spirit through Paul demanded, he will always proclaim the fact that every single thing we receive from the Lord comes to us exclusively by and through the Cross. It doesn't need any help, being total, complete, and absolute in its own right. In other words, Jesus paid it all.

If a Preacher understands this and preaches this, meaning he believes it, then he will leave fads alone.

(4) "JOHN DID BAPTIZE IN THE WILDERNESS, AND PREACH THE BAPTISM OF REPENTANCE FOR THE REMISSION OF SINS."

The diagram is:

Repentance is the foundation of moral intelligence. Those who refuse to submit to it can neither understand Christ nor the Book He wrote (Jn. 1:1).

WATER BAPTISM

The phrase, *"John did baptize in the wilderness,"* was similar to the type of Baptism practiced by Christians since Christ, but not altogether the same. In fact, this Baptism was connected with Israel and its acceptance of its Messiah. The word *"Baptism,"* or as given in the Greek, *"Baptizo,"* was not unknown to the Jews. It represented, or was symbolic of, the cleansing from sin which followed the Sin Offering, Trespass Offering, or Whole Burnt Offering. These ceremonial washings of Leviticus, which followed the Sacrifices, were performed by the person himself, with one exception; when Moses installed Aaron and his sons, he washed them himself (Lev. 8:6).

In fact, this is what Paul was addressing when he spoke of the Law, *"which stood only in meats and drinks and divers washings"* (Heb. 9:10). Even though these *"washings"* were practiced by the Jews, which meant they would have understood Baptism, still, the difference between the old washings, which the person performed himself, and John's Baptism is that John personally baptized his converts.

One presently must, as well, be careful that he understands John's Baptism. Matthew 3:11 unfortunately translates, *"I indeed baptize you with water unto Repentance,"* which makes it seem like Baptism is the cause of the Repentance; however, the original Greek makes it clear that John actually said, *"Repent, and be baptized because of the remission of sins."* The same holds true of Peter's words in Acts 2:38, where the same preposition is used.

Also, the word *"for"* is used in John's statement in Verse 4, and should have been translated *"because of."*

BAPTISMAL REGENERATION

These unfortunate translations have resulted in the error of *"Baptismal Regeneration,"* which means that one is saved by Water Baptism. This is gross error, and it has caused untold millions to die lost without God, hence, our somewhat extended explanation.

INFANT BAPTISM

Millions have been baptized into the Church as infants and, thereby, made to believe that such a baptism constitutes Salvation. It doesn't! Other millions, as stated, upon being baptized in water, have been led to believe that this act of baptism constitutes Salvation. It doesn't!

Let it ever be understood: men are saved, not by rituals or ceremonies, but by accepting the Lord by Faith, understanding that one is a sinner, and that Christ Alone is the Saviour. Believing on Him and what He did for us at the Cross, and doing so with one's whole heart, constitutes Salvation, which, in effect, takes place instantly. As well, it can take place anywhere — in a Church, in someone's home, in a car, on the side of a road, or anyplace (Jn. 3:16; Rom. 10:9-10, 13; Rev. 22:17). It is not so much the act of *"doing"* as it is the act of *"believing."* And the word *"believing"* means more than just giving mental assent, but rather believing with one's whole heart.

Millions believe that Jesus is the Son of God, and even that He died on the Cross, but they aren't saved. They have merely given a mental assent to these historic happenings. To believe from the heart means that one understands that he is a sinner, that he cannot save himself, and that he is, in fact, in desperate need of a Saviour, Who Alone is the Lord Jesus Christ. Jesus plainly said, *"I am the Way, the Truth, and the Life: no man comes unto the Father, but by Me"* (Jn. 14:6).

This means that anyone who tries to come to God by any manner other than the Lord Jesus Christ and what He did for us at the Cross will be looked at as a *"thief and a robber"* (Jn. 10:1). There is no such thing as baptizing one into the Body of Christ by Water Baptism or by any other ritual or ceremony, be it a baby or an adult. One comes into the Body of Christ strictly by Faith (Rom. 4:3; 5:1-2).

REPENTANCE

The phrase, *"And preach the baptism of Repentance for the remission of sins,"* means, as stated, that this all-important act is the foundation of all moral intelligence. Those who refuse to submit to Repentance can neither understand the Lord nor His Ways.

The baptism that John preached was connected with the Repentance of the individual. It actually means *"a change of mind,"* as it appears in a person who repents of a purpose he has formed or something he has done. As well, the type of *"repentance"* that John was preaching was far greater than a mere gloss or sorrow over one's wrongdoing, but was rather the Greek word *"metanoia,"* which means *"a change of mind which corresponds in a change of action consequent upon the realization that one has sinned and that sin is wrong."* In other words, the individual, upon Repentance, sees sin exactly as God sees it, not glossing over it in any fashion. He also sees himself, and says of himself, exactly what God sees and says!

However, the type of Repentance John was speaking of went even a step further. It not only addressed sin as God addressed the subject, but also it renounced all the so-called good things that one was doing, which was thought to make one righteous. So, a Repentance was demanded that renounced not only the *"bad"* but also the *"good,"* which is extremely grievous for the prideful heart, which such Repentance means to address.

That's the reason that John said, *"Bring forth therefore fruits worthy of Repentance, and begin not to say within yourselves, We have Abraham to our father"* (Lk. 3:8). He was demanding that they repent not only of their sin, but also of their dependence on who they were, the Children of Abraham. John was to *"preach"* this type of Repentance, which meant to do so with strength, power, and holy unction. The people were to have absolutely no doubt as to what he was talking about, nor a misunderstanding of what he meant.

As the Message of Repentance had to be preached as a preparation for the First Advent of Christ, it also must be preached as a preparation for the Second Advent, which definitely includes the Rapture (I Thess. 4:13-18). Even though this particular Message is desperately needed at all times, still, its proclamation at certain times, as here, is needed now more than ever. It is unfortunate that many claim the Message of Repentance is not needed presently, inasmuch as we are in the New Covenant. Those who proclaim such little know their Bible. The Messages to the Seven Churches of Asia by Christ demanded that five of them repent. One can hardly deny that these Churches were under the New Covenant (Rev., Chpts. 2-3).

THE REMISSION OF SIN

As stated, the phrase, *"For the remission of sins,"* should have been translated *"because of the remission of sins."* In other words, people were being baptized because they had already repented in their hearts, with their sins already remitted (forgiven), of which the Water Baptism was an outward act or sign. The remission of sin is part of the Salvation which God gives the believing sinner when he places his faith in the Lord Jesus. Therefore, remission of sins, as we have already stated, cannot be the result of Baptism, but rather its occasion. Baptism is the Believer's testimony to the fact that his sins are remitted.

The word *"remission"* in the Greek is *"aphesin,"* which refers to the act of putting something away. God did that at the Cross when He put away sin by incarnating Himself in humanity in the Person of His Son, stepping down from His Judgment Throne, assuming the guilt of man's sin, and paying the penalty, thus satisfying His Justice, and making possible an offer of Mercy on the basis of Justice satisfied.

When a sinner avails himself of the merits of that atoning Sacrifice, he thus puts himself within the provision God made. His sins were put away at the Cross, and he comes into the benefit of that when he believes (Jn. 3:16). His submission to Water Baptism is his testimony to the latter fact, not only that all sin has been put away, but that he has taken advantage of that fact (Wuest).

WHAT DOES IT MEAN TO
REPENT OF THE GOOD?

We made the statement some time back that a Repentance was needed that renounced not only what was *"bad,"* but also what was *"good."* What did we mean by that?

When the prideful heart is brought to the place that it admits that there is *"bad"* lodged in its very recesses, this indeed is a great victory! However, God demands more than that, that is, if it is to be True Repentance. He also demands that we repent not only of the *"bad,"* but also of the *"good."* That is where many Believers have a problem!

When we speak of repenting of the *"good,"* even as John the Baptist was addressing in his day, we are speaking presently of depending on anything other than *"Jesus Christ and Him Crucified."* This is why the Cross is so important. When one understands the Cross, he then begins to understand himself. He understands that, within himself, he cannot hope to be what God wants him to be. There is no way, by his machinations, no matter how religious they might be, that he can be brought to the place of acceptance by the Lord. Due to the Fall, mankind simply *"comes short of the Glory of God,"* and he cannot change that, no matter what he does.

In truth, untold millions are depending on their particular Denomination, or their particular Church, or particular good works they are performing, especially religious works. As we have repeatedly stated, that's

NOTES

where the object of their faith is — and that which, we might quickly add, God can never accept. Paul bluntly stated: *"I do not frustrate the Grace of God: for if Righteousness come by the Law, then Christ is dead in vain"* (Gal. 2:21).

Anything and everything that we do for the Lord which we think is *"good,"* meaning that it draws us closer to God, is *"out."* Looking at these things, as righteous as they might be in their own way, constitutes *"works,"* which God cannot accept. Everything must be strictly by Faith, which refers to Faith in Christ and His Cross (I Cor. 1:18). To be sure, good works are important; however, they must ever be the result of our walk with the Lord, and never the cause of our walk with the Lord.

The following formula will possibly be of some help:

FOCUS: Christ.
OBJECT OF FAITH: What Christ did at the Cross.
POWER SOURCE: The Holy Spirit.
RESULTS: Victory.

Now, let's turn it around and use the same formula, but in the way that it is being used presently by most of the Church.

FOCUS: Works.
OBJECT OF FAITH: Performance
POWER SOURCE: Self.
RESULTS: Failure.

THE CROSS

This is one of the reasons that the Cross is rejected. It demands that our allegiance to everything other than Christ and His Cross must be rejected out of hand. While these other things, at times, may be good in their own right, they must never be the object of our faith. To be sure, men, especially religious men, do not give up their pet devotions easily. If one has been depending on his association with a particular Denomination as a means of his spirituality, he doesn't give that up easily. The same can go for a particular Church, Preacher, doctrine, or good works, etc.

A perfect example is Cain and Abel.

CAIN AND ABEL

There was no difference in these brothers,

in that both were in desperate need of a Redeemer; however, there was an eternal difference in their Sacrifices, and that is exactly that of which I speak. They are both corrupt branches of a decayed tree, both born outside Eden, both guilty, both sinners, no moral difference, and both sentenced to death.

The words, *"by faith,"* found in Hebrews 11:4, teach that God had revealed a way of approach to Him (Rom. 10:17). Abel accepts this way, Cain rejects it. Abel's Altar speaks of Repentance, of Faith, and of the Precious Blood of Christ, the Lamb of God without blemish. Cain's altar tells of pride, unbelief, and self-righteousness.

Abel's Altar is beautiful to God's Eye and repulsive to man's; Cain's altar, beautiful to man's eye and repulsive to God's. These *"altars"* exist today; around the one, that is, Christ and His Atoning Work, few are gathered; around the other, many. God accepts the slain lamb and rejects the offered fruit; the offering being rejected, so of necessity is the offeror. Hebrews 11:4 says God *"testified over"* Abel's gifts, that is, by fire from Heaven (Lev. 9:24; Judg. 6:21; I Ki. 18:38; I Chron. 21:26).

God loves Cain, and, wishing to bless him also, He tells him that if he will make an offering similar to his brother's, it will be accepted, that the lamb for the Sin Offering was close at hand, lying at the door entrance of the Tabernacle before which the brothers were standing, adding that He would give him, if obedient, dominion over the whole Earth and dispose his brother to willingly accept that government, as He had disposed Eve (Gen. 3:16) to willingly accept subjection to Adam. This would appear to be the force of the word *"desire"* in both Passages. Amazing Grace!

Cain rejects this love, invites his brother into the field, and murders him. Adam sins against God and Cain sins against man. In their united conduct, we have sin in all its forms, and that on the very first page of human history.

Cain's religion was too refined to slay a lamb, but not too cultured to murder his brother. God's Way of Salvation fills the heart with love; man's way of salvation enflames it

NOTES

with hatred. *"Religion,"* which refers to that which is devised by man, and is always other than that which is devised by God, namely the Cross, has ever been the greatest cause of bloodshed.

Cain felt that his *"good"* should be accepted by God, but which can never be accepted by God, as the illustration amply proves! But yet the modern Church keeps trying to build an altar and there place its good works. The results presently are the same as the results in the time of Cain. The offering being rejected, the offeror is also rejected! God can only accept the offering of His Only Son, the Lord Jesus Christ. Hence, He said to Him, when He was baptized, *"This is My Beloved Son, in Whom I am well pleased"* (Mat. 3:17).

The Lord is pleased with us only as we are *"in Christ"*; this we must never forget (Rom. 8:1).

(5) "AND THERE WENT OUT UNTO HIM ALL THE LAND OF JUDAEA, AND THEY OF JERUSALEM, AND WERE ALL BAPTIZED OF HIM IN THE RIVER OF JORDAN, CONFESSING THEIR SINS."

The composition is:

In essence, this was the first genuine Move of God, at least that is recorded, since the time of Malachi, a time frame of some 400 years. Thank God, *"Happy days are here again"*!

A GREAT MOVE OF GOD

The phrase, *"And there went out unto Him all the land of Judaea, and they of Jerusalem,"* specified they were coming and kept coming! As stated, it was a genuine Move of God, as would be obvious. Naturally, the news began to be spread all over Judaea and Jerusalem concerning John the Baptist. His manner of attire, as the next verse proclaims, was somewhat different, but, above all, he spoke with the voice of a Prophet. Inasmuch as Israel had not heard such a voice in about 400 years (since Malachi), the excitement caused by John's Ministry was excitement indeed!

Since Moses, and especially since Samuel, the voice of the God-called Prophet was that which whipped Israel into spiritual line, and actually served as a liaison between God and the people. Consequently, for that voice to be stilled for some 400 years was a tragedy of unparalleled proportion. However, every action by the Lord is for Divine purpose.

There is some evidence that the Prophet Zechariah was murdered, with his Ministry taking place about 100 years before Malachi, who would be the last. To be sure, Zechariah, if, in fact, he was murdered, was not the only one to suffer such a fate. However, the cup of iniquity for Israel, at least in this respect, was filling up; therefore, the Lord purposely silenced the prophetic voice. John's Ministry, however, was of far greater significance than of any other Prophet, because his Ministry was the preparation of the coming of the Messiah, which was the greatest of all, and by far! So, this was a very special time for Israel, and the people responded accordingly, with the exception of most of the religious leaders.

With *"Jerusalem"* being specified, and it being the center of all religious activity, especially considering that the Temple was located there, the religious leaders of Israel would have been dealt with especially by the Holy Spirit, but sadly, with little favorable response. Hence, John would call them *"a generation of vipers"* (Lk. 3:7).

THE WATER COULD NOT SAVE THEM

The phrase, *"And were all baptized of him in the river of Jordan, confessing their sins,"* means that the act of Water Baptism and that of confessing sin went on at the same time. However, that means that the recipient of Baptism was not trusting in the water to save, but rather his Repentance, of which the Water Baptism was an outward sign.

As well, the confession of sin is more than a mere acknowledgment of sin in one's life. It is an agreeing with God as to all the implications that enter into the fact that one has sinned. It is looking at sin, as we have stated, from God's point of view, and acting accordingly. It means the putting away of sin. It means the determination to be done with sin.

(6) "AND JOHN WAS CLOTHED WITH CAMEL'S HAIR, AND WITH A GIRDLE OF A SKIN ABOUT HIS LOINS; AND HE DID EAT LOCUSTS AND WILD HONEY;"

NOTES

The synopsis is:

The manner in which John dressed, that which he did eat, and, in fact, everything about him were all directed by the Holy Spirit, and for purpose.

JOHN THE BAPTIST

The phrase, *"And John was clothed with camel's hair, and with a girdle of a skin about his loins,"* proclaimed, in some way, a possible imitation by John of Elijah, who also wore a rough sackcloth woven from the hair of camels (II Ki. 1:8). This garment was not made necessarily of the skin of a camel, but was a rough cloth woven of camel's hair. In a spiritual sense, it was characteristic of the doctrine which John taught, namely penitence and contempt of the world.

The phrase, *"And he did eat locusts and wild honey,"* was a diet somewhat common in that day. The *"wild honey"* was honey made by wild bees, whether in trees or the hollow of rocks. As well, the *"locusts"* were dried to a crispness in the sun and eaten with the honey.

John's garb and diet were not without spiritual significance. Israel, in a sad state of spiritual declension, had succumbed to the things that money could buy, which included luxury, finery, and idleness. Consequently, the Holy Spirit drew John's attention to the simple and austere, which was 180 degrees opposite of what the majority in Israel were presently doing. His food and clothing were meant to serve as a Message to Israel.

THE MODERN CHURCH

Looking at the modern Church, I cannot help but wonder if the similarity is not obvious! It, for the most part, has succumbed to the same evil as Israel of old. The Gospel has been twisted and turned until presently money is the priority in many, if not most, Christian circles. The *"Greed gospel"* has never had more followers and adherents; therefore, I have to wonder just how similar everything else is?

As John introduced Jesus, the Son of God brought a moving of the Holy Spirit such as Israel had never seen before, but yet was rejected out of hand. I personally believe that the Lord is about to send a Moving of the Holy Spirit on the Church and the world as they have never known before. I wonder what the reaction of the Church will be?

I fear that the spirit of deception which is already laboring mightily in the modern Church already gives us the answer to that question!

(7) "AND PREACHED, SAYING, THERE COMES ONE MIGHTIER THAN I AFTER ME, THE LATCHET OF WHOSE SHOES I AM NOT WORTHY TO STOOP DOWN AND UNLOOSE."

The synopsis is:

The dignity of Christ's Person is here declared, for John, who bowed before no Earthly king, bowed before this Servant, declaring he was not fit even to untie His sandals.

PREACHING

The short phrase, *"And preached,"* refers from the original Greek Text to strong, powerful proclamation of the Word of God, and given with deep emotion. John's manner was an authoritative delivery which must be heard and heeded.

Unfortunately, Bible preaching (I said, *"Bible Preaching"*) is little in vogue at present. This is preaching that calls men what they are: *"sinners."* It also tells them that the Wrath of God is ultimately poured out on sin and sinners (Rom. 1:18). And then it tells them that there is a Saviour, and that Saviour is exclusively the Lord Jesus Christ. As well, it is not only Jesus the Man, but Jesus the Saviour, which refers to what He did on the Cross, which makes it possible for sinful men to have righteousness imputed unto them.

This is the kind of preaching that John did. And it's the kind of preaching that Peter and Paul did, and, in fact, every true Preacher of the Gospel who has ever lived. Nothing else can honestly be called *"preaching,"* but something else entirely. That which passes presently for preaching is actually only a moral essay, which tells man how good he is, and also how he can improve himself.

Now look at those words very carefully, because that is what is presently passing for preaching. Because what is said is *"moral,"* it fools many people into believing that it's good. It isn't! In fact, there is no such thing as moral evolution. Unsaved men are lost without God, and they cannot *"good"* their way into the Kingdom of God. For the Born-Again experience to take place, the *"Blood"* must be preached. Sin must be called to account. In fact, the person must be made to feel that he's hanging over Hell on a rotten stick.

But instead, the modern Pablum that passes for preaching is actually no preaching at all. It is false, and its followers will find themselves, sadly and regrettably, in eternal Hell.

THE MIGHT OF THE MAN, CHRIST JESUS

The phrase, *"Saying, There comes One mightier than I after me,"* means not merely *"one,"* but rather *"The One."* Actually, John was speaking of the Jehovah of the Old Testament. Consequently, the people of Israel, especially the religious leaders, had absolutely no excuse for not knowing exactly Who Jesus was. John, with his powerful proclamation, introduced Him, telling exactly Who He was and what He was! Not only was this *"The One,"* but also *"The Almighty One"*!

The words, *"after me,"* proclaims the fact that Jesus would immediately follow John. In other words, John was not speaking of Someone Who was coming in the distant future, but immediately!

HUMILITY

The phrase, *"The latchet of Whose shoes I am not worthy to stoop down and unloose,"* has powerful meanings to it:

1. It meant that the majesty of the Word was shod with the sandal of our humanity — the Incarnation (Jn. 1:1-3).

2. It meant that John and his Ministry would decrease, while this *"One"* would continually increase. John was only the herald, while Jesus was the King being heralded.

3. This task of removing the shoes and washing the feet of a guest was the task performed by the slave in the household who held the lowest position in that status as a servant. So, John is telling us that one of the qualifications for being Baptized with

the Holy Spirit, as the next verse proclaims, is humility.

If John the Baptist had not had true humility, he would not have been able to have stood the *"decrease"* while the Master increased. But because he was truly humble, he bowed to the obvious Will of God.

(8) "I INDEED HAVE BAPTIZED YOU WITH WATER: BUT HE SHALL BAPTIZE YOU WITH THE HOLY SPIRIT."

The diagram is:

This is the first mention of Believers being baptized with the Holy Spirit. It all looked forward to the Cross, which would make all of this possible, and, in effect, announced at hand that which had been long predicted.

WATER BAPTISM

The phrase, *"I indeed have baptized you with water,"* is not meant to introduce a doctrine, but rather the fullness of Salvation which would be brought by Christ.

This Eighth Verse is meant to symbolize the difference between the Old Covenant and the New Covenant. There would be as much difference as between *"water"* and the *"Holy Spirit."* As is obvious, there is no comparison. One pertained to ceremony, while the other pertained to newness of life. The first was the Promise, while the second was the Performance.

THE BAPTISM WITH THE HOLY SPIRIT

The phrase, *"But He shall baptize you with the Holy Spirit,"* in effect, proclaims the fact that the Holy Spirit would move from the Temple in Jerusalem, where He had resided for about 1,500 years (Temple and Tabernacle), and would now take up residence in the heart and life of the Believer, which all would be made possible by what Jesus would do at the Cross (Jn. 14:17; I Cor. 3:16). Consequently, it has three meanings:

1. Water was the element with which John baptized. But the Holy Spirit is now the element with which Jesus baptizes. The Baptism connected with the Messiah is the act of the Holy Spirit Himself baptizing (placing) the believing sinner into Christ (Rom. 6:3-4), and thus, the Body of Christ (I Cor. 12:13). John's Baptism was Water Baptism, while the Messiah's was Spirit Baptism. It is Jesus Who makes all of this possible by what He did at Calvary, and Who is the active Agent in carrying out this work.

As well, as the Holy Spirit baptizes believing sinners into Christ at conversion, Jesus baptizes Born-Again Believers into the Holy Spirit, which is an experience separate and apart from Salvation, actually following Salvation. In fact, before Jesus can baptize a person with the Holy Spirit, that person first of all must be Born-Again (Jn. 14:17).

2. This which Jesus would do, and which He has done in millions of lives, also respects that which happened on the Day of Pentecost, when Believers were baptized with the Holy Spirit, with the evidence of speaking with other tongues, as the Spirit of God gave the utterance (Acts 2:1-4). He continues to do so exactly in that manner. There is a great difference between being *"born of the Spirit,"* of which this Passage also states, and being *"baptized with the Spirit,"* which is strongly proclaimed.

Due to this Prophecy given by John concerning the great Work of Christ, if one stops at Salvation, as important as it is, and does not go on and be baptized with the Holy Spirit, one is greatly shortchanging himself in every respect (Acts 1:4).

3. The major purpose for Salvation is that one be a habitation of the Holy Spirit. Paul said, *"In Whom you also are built together for an habitation of God through the Spirit"* (Eph. 2:22). The word *"baptize,"* referring to the Holy Spirit, means the same as *"baptize"* respecting water. It means for Him to be in you, and you to be in Him!

(9) "AND IT CAME TO PASS IN THOSE DAYS, THAT JESUS CAME FROM NAZARETH OF GALILEE, AND WAS BAPTIZED OF JOHN IN JORDAN."

The overview is:

The Ministry of the Lord Jesus Christ now begins. It would be the greatest Moving and Operation of the Holy Spirit the world had ever known.

NAZARETH OF GALILEE

The phrase, *"And it came to pass in those days, that Jesus came from Nazareth of*

Galilee," respects, as stated, the beginning of the Ministry of the Master, and the conclusion, as well, of the Ministry of John the Baptist. As John in the wilderness, so Christ respecting His city of upbringing. Nazareth was the home of Jesus for about 30 years until He was rejected (Lk. 2:39; 4:16, 28-31). He was, therefore, called *"Jesus of Nazareth."*

Nazareth lay close to several main trade routes for easy contact with the outside world, and it is thought that a Roman garrison was stationed nearby; consequently, the little town was held in contempt by strict Jews (Jn. 1:46). However, irrespective as to what Israel (especially Jerusalem) thought of Nazareth, as the wilderness concerning John, the Holy Spirit would highlight Nazareth concerning Christ. It, as well, was to make a statement concerning humility, which characterized our Lord.

THE BAPTISM OF CHRIST

The phrase, *"And was baptized of John in Jordan,"* concerned Jesus doing such to *"fulfill all Righteousness,"* and not because there had been any sin in His Life. In fact, He never sinned, not in thought, word, or deed (Mat. 3:15). John was commanded to baptize, and every Godly Israelite was commanded to be baptized. Jesus was a Godly Israelite, and was such in order to save. Hence, the obedience of Righteousness rested on them both in relation to this Baptism. But there was this difference — Righteousness brought Him there; sin brought His fellow-countrymen there.

The words, *"In Jordan,"* mean that Jesus was baptized into the river and then came up out of the water, which, in effect, lays aside the unscriptural practice of *"sprinkling."* Jesus had no sins to confess, but nevertheless took His place with the Righteous of Israel, submitting, as we have stated, to the Baptism of John. Had He not done so, He would have been misunderstood as opposing John. As well, His Personal Baptism, although having nothing to do as an outward sign of inward Repentance, as it did with all others, still, held tremendous meaning.

His going under the water signified His coming Death and Burial, with His coming out of the water signifying His coming Resurrection. As well, that symbolism proclaimed the Salvation of the Believer and that our Water Baptism symbolizes the same, with Christ serving as the example. The old man dies and is buried, symbolized by the going down into the water, and is resurrected in newness of life, symbolized by the coming up out of the water.

So, this was a far greater moment with Christ than just an act performed in order that others may see it, consequently, sanctioning John's Ministry.

(10) "AND STRAIGHTWAY COMING UP OUT OF THE WATER, HE SAW THE HEAVENS OPENED, AND THE SPIRIT LIKE A DOVE DESCENDING UPON HIM:"

The diagram is:

Jesus did not begin His public Ministry until the Holy Spirit led Him to do so, as is here illustrated.

THE OPEN HEAVEN

The phrase, *"And straightway coming up out of the water, he saw the Heavens opened,"* regards, as stated, the beginning of His Ministry, which, as would be obvious, would be the greatest Move of God the world had ever known. It would have an auspicious beginning, as this Verse and the next proclaim!

The phrase, *"He saw the Heavens opened,"* actually means that He saw the Heavens being rent asunder. The Heavens being torn asunder had to do with something being opened which had heretofore been closed. Before the Cross, there was no way that men could go to Heaven, even the Godly and the Righteous. Quite possibly the only one who ever did before the Cross was Elijah, who was translated. Concerning him, the Scripture says, *"And it came to pass, as they still went on, and talked, that, behold, there appeared a chariot of fire, and horses of fire, and parted them both asunder; and Elijah went up by a whirlwind into Heaven"* (II Ki. 2:11).

When Enoch was translated, the Scripture simply says, *"by Faith Enoch was translated that he should not see death"* (Heb. 11:5). It said nothing about Heaven. In fact, Enoch went down into Paradise, where all Believers went before the Cross. Why?

"For it is not possible that the blood of bulls and goats should take away sins" (Heb.

10:4). In other words, the Sacrificial System, consisting of the death of clean animals such as lambs, etc., could not remove the sin debt. It only covered sins, and did so unto the First Advent of Christ. Because the sin debt remained, Believers, even the Godliest, could not be taken to Heaven when they died, but went down into Paradise. Jesus described it as *"Abraham's bosom"* (Lk. 16:15-31). While they were comforted there, still, they were being held captive by Satan, even though he could not put them over into the burning side of Hell (Eph. 4:8).

THE CROSS

When Jesus died on the Cross, therefore satisfying every demand of the broken Law, and thereby satisfying the demands of a thrice-Holy God, this means that every sin was addressed, past, present, and future, meaning that it was totally atoned. That being the case, Satan no longer has control over those who have fully trusted Christ. Consequently, when Jesus died on the Cross and was put in the tomb, He went down into Paradise (Abraham's bosom). There, the Scripture says, *"He led captivity captive,"* which means that even though all of the Old Testament Saints were captives of Satan, because, as stated, the sin debt could not be taken away by animal blood, now that the price had been paid, Satan could not hold them and they were now made captives of Jesus Christ. As such, He took them out of that place and *"ascended up far above all Heavens, that He might fill all things"* (Eph. 4:10).

This means that the death of Christ on the Cross made it possible for everything to change. All the Old Testament Saints were delivered out of Paradise and taken to Heaven, where they are to this moment. As well, whenever a Believer now dies (since the Cross), the soul and the spirit instantly go to be with the Lord in Heaven, because Satan has no more legitimate claim upon them (Phil. 1:23). The *"Cross"* is what made all of this possible! Now, the Heavens are opened, because Jesus has opened them, making it possible for man to come into the very Presence of God.

Let us say it again: *"All because of the Cross"* (Eph. 2:13-18).

THE HOLY SPIRIT COMING UPON CHRIST FOR MINISTRY

The phrase, *"And the Spirit like a dove descending upon Him,"* actually should have been translated *"descending into Him."* This was the act of the Holy Spirit taking up permanent residence in the Messiah. This precipitated and made possible the Words of Christ a little later at Nazareth, *"The Spirit of the Lord is upon Me* (within Me), *because He has anointed Me . . ."* (Lk. 4:18).

Wuest says, *"This was the anointing with the Spirit for His three-fold Ministry of Prophet, Priest, and King, the dynamic power which would enable the Messiah to discharge the duties connected with these Offices."* The act of the Holy Spirit coming into Christ was also a preview of what would happen on the Day of Pentecost (Acts 2:1-4).

Even though Mark did not mention it, Luke said that Jesus was *"praying"* when *"the Heaven was opened"* (Lk. 3:21). This plainly shows us that it was not the Baptism of John which caused Heaven to open, but rather the obedience and petition of the Son of God.

THE DOVE

Exactly what is meant by the phrase, *"like a dove,"* is not known. Luke said, *"in a bodily shape like a dove,"* concerning the Holy Spirit (Lk. 3:22). Quite possibly John saw this wonderful happening, as well as others who stood nearby!

We dare not make more of this than we should, but, as well, we must not make less! It is my personal belief, although not shared by many others, that after the First Resurrection of Life, Believers in their Glorified State will be able to literally see the Holy Spirit. In effect, John the Beloved saw the Holy Spirit in his Vision, as outlined in Revelation 4:5. Admittedly, his description is beyond our pale of understanding, and, no doubt, beyond his pale of understanding as well.

Nevertheless, I think one could say, without fear of contradiction, that he did see Him. I would, consequently, assume from Mark's and Luke's descriptions that those nearby literally saw something descend from Heaven in a *"bodily shape,"* and, as Mark said it, *"like a dove,"* which referred to similarity.

SYMBOLS OF THE HOLY SPIRIT

The Holy Spirit is symbolized in several ways. They are:

1. Water: *"If any man thirst, let him come unto Me, and drink.*

"He who believes on Me, as the Scripture has said, out of his belly (innermost being) *shall flow rivers of Living Water.*

"But this spoke He of the Spirit, which they who believe on Him should receive" (Jn. 7:37-39).

2. Wind: *"And suddenly there came a sound from Heaven as of a rushing mighty wind, and it filled all the house where they were sitting. . . . And they were all filled with the Holy Spirit"* (Acts 2:2, 4).

3. Fire: *"And there appeared unto them cloven tongues like as of fire, and it sat upon each of them. And they were all filled with the Holy Spirit, and began to speak with other tongues, as the Spirit gave them utterance"* (Acts 2:3-4).

4. Dove: *"And straightway coming up out of the water, he* (John the Baptist) *saw the Heavens opened, and the Spirit like a dove descending upon* (within) *Him"* (Mk. 1:10).

5. Oil: *"You* (Jesus) *have loved Righteousness, and hated iniquity; therefore God, even Your God, has anointed You with the oil of gladness above Your fellows"* (Heb. 1:9).

The *"Water"* denotes purity; the *"Wind"* denotes power; the *"Fire"* denotes cleansing; the *"Dove"* denotes humility; the *"Oil"* denotes the anointing.

(11) "AND THERE CAME A VOICE FROM HEAVEN, SAYING, YOU ARE MY BELOVED SON, IN WHOM I AM WELL PLEASED."

The diagram is:

The Trinity is grandly expressed here. The Voice is from God the Father. The *"Son"* is the One to Whom He speaks. As well, as Verse 10 proclaims, the Holy Spirit descended upon (within) the Son.

THE VOICE FROM HEAVEN

The phrase, *"And there came a voice from Heaven,"* means that this Voice came from the rent or opened heavens. No form was seen, but a *"Voice"* was heard! Incidentally,

NOTES

"Heaven" is a place, with this Verse indicating that it has boundaries, etc. This means it is not merely a state of mind.

Chapters 21 and 22 of the Book of Revelation tell us that Heaven has at least one city, with walls and gates, with the foundations of the wall *"garnished with all manner of precious stones"* (Rev. 21:19). There is a river, streets, and trees which bear fruits. Also, many people and Angels are there (Rev., Chpts. 4-5). One could probably say that Heaven is a planet somewhere in God's vast creation. At any rate, it is a real place, but far beyond our present knowledge; however, this we do know:

The Lord is going to change this Earth into a replica of this place we call *"Heaven."* The Bible tells us so! (Rev. 21:1-3)

MY BELOVED SON

The phrase, *"Saying, You are My Beloved Son,"* means in contradistinction to all others. Even though we Believers are sons of God by adoption, still, we sustain a different relationship to the Father than does the Son. As someone has stated: Jesus is the Son of God by a birth that never was, and, in fact, always has been; therefore, He is the Son of God in a unique way that no mortal can ever hope to attain.

The word *"Beloved"* means that Jesus is infinitely precious to God the Father. This love is pulled from the Heart of God because of the preciousness of the Son. However, even though Believers are only adopted sons, still, in God's Eyes, we are His Children, and consequently *"heirs of God, and joint-heirs with Christ"* (Rom. 8:17). This means that everything Christ receives from the Father will also be given to the adopted sons.

THAT IN WHICH GOD IS PLEASED

The phrase, *"In Whom I am well pleased,"* means that the Father has always been pleased with the Son, is pleased with Him now, and will be pleased with Him forever! It is a delight that never had a beginning, because it always was; it also will never have an end. Furthermore, God is pleased with man only as man is *"in Christ"* (Jn. 14:20). This means that every single thing devised by man which purports to be spiritual can never be accepted by God. In fact, it is the Cross and the Cross alone which made it possible for our union with Christ.

This is what Paul was talking about when he said, *"Know ye not, that so many of us as were baptized into Jesus Christ* (plainly says that this Baptism is into Christ and not water [I Cor. 1:17; 12:13; Gal. 3:27; Eph. 4:5; Col. 2:11-13]) *were baptized into His Death?"* (When Christ died on the Cross, in the Mind of God, we died with Him; in other words, He became our Substitute, and our identification with Him in His Death gives us all the benefits for which He died; the idea is that He did it all for us!)

"Therefore we are buried with Him by Baptism into Death (not only did we die with Him, but we were buried with Him as well, which means that all the sin and transgression of the past were buried; when they put Him in the tomb, they put all our sins into that tomb, as well): *that like as Christ was raised up from the dead by the Glory of the Father, even so we also should walk in newness of life* (we died with Him, we were buried with Him, and His Resurrection was our Resurrection to a *'Newness of Life'*).

"For if we have been planted together (with Christ) *in the likeness of His Death* (Paul proclaims the Cross as the instrument through which all Blessings come; consequently, the Cross must ever be the Object of our Faith, which gives the Holy Spirit latitude to work within our lives), *we shall be also in the likeness of His Resurrection* (we can have the *'likeness of His Resurrection,'* i.e., *'live this Resurrection Life,'* only as long as we understand the *'likeness of His Death,'* which refers to the Cross as the means by which all this is done)" (Rom. 6:3-5).

Christ is the Source of all things, while the Cross is the Means.

(12) "AND IMMEDIATELY THE SPIRIT DROVE HIM INTO THE WILDERNESS."

The diagram is:

It is believed that this *"wilderness"* was nearby Jericho. Supposedly, John was baptizing in the Jordan near this city.

THE HOLY SPIRIT

The words, *"And immediately,"* proclaim that the first act of the indwelling of the Holy Spirit was to bring Jesus to the place of testing and temptation. The phrase, *"the Spirit drove Him into the wilderness,"* is not meant to imply a reluctance on Jesus' part to go into this place. It does speak of the Holy Spirit moving upon Him so mightily and powerfully in respect to this thing that it was almost as one would use force. It really pertained to an intense preoccupation of mind, which was set upon one thing only, and with fierce determination. Before His Ministry began, this intense testing must take place.

(13) "AND HE WAS THERE IN THE WILDERNESS FORTY DAYS, TEMPTED OF SATAN; AND WAS WITH THE WILD BEASTS; AND THE ANGELS MINISTERED UNTO HIM."

The synopsis is:

The type of temptation which Jesus underwent was of a far greater magnitude than any temptation that we undergo. And yet, He failed not even in the slightest.

PROBATION

The phrase, *"And He was there in the wilderness forty days,"* proclaims the Last Adam being in the opposite setting of the First Adam, which was Paradise. Even though Mark does not mention it, Jesus fasted the entirety of these *"forty days."* Why forty days?

Even though the Bible does not say, is it possible that Adam and Eve lived forty days in innocence in the Garden before succumbing to Satan? If so, Adam and Eve would have lived for forty days in bliss, then succumbing to Satan, while Jesus lived forty days in sheer torture and overcame Satan in every capacity, thereby doing what the First Adam did not do, and under the most difficult circumstances!

So, we must assume that the number *"forty"* is not without significance. It is God's number for probation.

TEMPTATION

The phrase, *"Tempted of Satan,"* means to be tempted constantly and vigorously during the forty days and nights. The three temptations at the end of the forty-day period, of which Matthew speaks and to which

Mark does not allude, merely indicate the additional intensity of the temptations as the period closed. The word *"tempted"* means *"to pierce or search into."* It means to discover what good or evil, power or weakness, is in a person. Since men so often break down under such a test, and consequently display the evil in them, the word *"tempt,"* in its most simple form, means to solicit a person to do evil.

During this horrible time, the entirety of the universe was looking on, which included God the Father and the Holy Angels, as well as the fallen angels and demons. In effect, this was the battle of the ages!

SATAN

The very name or designation, *"Satan,"* means *"an adversary"* or *"slanderer."* It refers to one who brings a false charge, and also those who spread the truth concerning a person, but do so maliciously, insidiously, and with hostility. A *"slanderer,"* although telling the truth, does so with the intention to destroy; consequently, to spread something negative about a fellow Believer, even if it's true, can have but one purpose, and that is to do the work of Satan. How many Believers have fallen into this trap, literally becoming emissaries of the Evil One?

Satan was once called Lucifer, seemingly the most powerful and beautiful Angel ever created by God. He served God for an undetermined period of time in Righteousness and Holiness; however, at some point, he became lifted up within himself because of his great beauty, with pride entering his heart, which was the origination of sin. He then led a revolution against God in which approximately one-third of the Angels joined with him (Rev. 12:4).

How long this battle raged before Genesis 3:1-6 is not known; however, it has been the cause of all the heartache, pain, suffering, and bloodshed in this world (Isa. 14:12-15; Ezek. 28:11-19). And yet the Bible predicts the total defeat of this Evil One, which will end, at that time, this horrible period of suffering and bloodshed, which Satan has headed up (Rev. 20:1-3, 7-10).

REDEMPTION

It is remarkable that God could speak the worlds into existence, but could not speak man's Redemption accordingly! To be sure, God had the power to do such, of that there is no question. However, the Nature and the Righteousness of God would not allow sin to be addressed in this fashion. The price must be paid in full. Therefore, to satisfy the Justice of God, the Lord had to become Man, thereby coming down to this Earth, as the Last Adam, to accomplish what the First Adam could not do. Due to the nature of the Fall of man, the victory of man through the Substitute Man, the Lord Jesus Christ, had to be in the same arena, but yet under worse circumstances.

It was the Cross, and the Cross alone, which made Redemption possible. It was there that Satan was defeated, as well as all of his minions of darkness. Paul said: *"Buried with Him in Baptism* (this refers to the Crucifixion of Christ and our part in that Crucifixion, as outlined in Rom. 6:3-5), *wherein also you are risen with Him through the Faith of the operation of God, Who has raised Him from the dead.*

"And you, being dead in your sins and the uncircumcision of your flesh, has He quickened together with Him (by the means of the Cross), *having forgiven you all trespasses;*

"Blotting out the handwriting of ordinances that was against us (the Law), *which was contrary to us* (the Law demanded perfect obedience, but gave no power to obey), *and took it out of the way* (satisfied its just demands), *nailing it to His Cross* (it was all done at the Cross);

"And having spoiled principalities and powers (in atoning for all sin, this destroyed Satan's legal right to hold man in bondage), *He made a show of them openly* (all demon powers, even Satan himself, were defeated before the entirety of the spirit world), *triumphing over them in it* (totally triumphing, in effect, addressing every single thing that man lost in the Fall)*"* (Col. 2:12-15).

Let us say it again:

The Source of every single thing we receive is the Lord and is given to us by the Means of the Cross.

WILD BEASTS

The phrase, *"And was with the wild*

beasts," is said with intention. The *"beasts"* were not wild during the time of Adam and Eve before the Fall and, therefore, no harm was feared from them; however, due to the Fall, some *"beasts"* became *"wild."* But, as we quickly add, they were subject in totality to the Lord Jesus Christ. The only answer is that these wild beasts recognized and revered their Creator and their Lord.

Paul said, concerning the Fall, *"For we know that the whole Creation* (which includes the animals) *groans and travails in pain together until now"* (Rom. 8:22). However, Isaiah prophesied long before of the time which is coming, when Satan will be locked away and Jesus will reign supreme. At that time, *"The wolf shall also dwell with the lamb, and the leopard shall lie down with the kid; and the calf and the young lion and the fatling together; and a little child shall lead them."*

He then said, *"And the cow and the bear shall feed; their young ones shall lie down together: and the lion shall eat straw like the ox"* (Isa. 11:6-7). This will take place in the coming Kingdom Age, with everything changed, and for the better.

ANGELS

The phrase, *"And the Angels ministered unto Him,"* means they strengthened Him, but not with food. Even though we are not told exactly what they did, perhaps they ministered to His Soul, only allowing Satan so much latitude.

The great Plan of God for the Redemption of the human family was more vulnerable here than it had ever been or ever would be. Satan had no chance against Christ as God; however, in Jesus the Man, Satan was offered his greatest opportunity. The efforts made against Christ by Satan were basically, irrespective of their direction, designed for one purpose. Satan attempted to get Jesus to step outside the Perfect Will of God. Had he been able to do this, he would have won the conflict.

Others claim that Jesus could not have failed; however, such thinking is unscriptural and specious. If Jesus could not fail, then, at the same time, by the very nature of such a position, He could not win. Moreover, Satan would not have wasted his time for forty days and nights attempting to do something that was impossible.

No! For Jesus to be the Last Adam, it had to be possible for Him to fail. Actually, there is no record that Jesus had any more help than any Child of God. He had the Holy Spirit, as we have the Holy Spirit (Acts 1:8). He had Angels to help Him, and we have Angels (although unseen) to help us! (Heb. 1:14).

So, Jesus met Satan exactly as the First Adam had met him, although in much worse circumstances, such as the wilderness. As well, Satan's attack against Christ was much more powerful, many times so, than against Adam in the Garden of Eden.

The First Adam failed, but the Last Adam did not fail. His defeat of Satan ensures our victory.

(14) "NOW AFTER THAT JOHN WAS PUT IN PRISON, JESUS CAME INTO GALILEE, PREACHING THE GOSPEL OF THE KINGDOM OF GOD."

The diagram is:

Now begins the greatest Ministry the world has even known, the Ministry of the Son of God, the Almighty One, God in human form. He was very God and very Man, which means *"fully God, and fully Man"*!

PRISON

The phrase, *"Now after that John was put in prison,"* concerns the ending of John's Ministry, and the beginning of Christ's; however, John wondrously and gloriously fulfilled that which he was called to do, the preparation for the Messiah. As we have stated, John's prophetic voice was the first since Malachi, a time of approximately 400 years.

Without a doubt, the people knew he was a Prophet of God, and knew that his Ministry was unique. Even though he plainly stated that One would follow him Who would be much greater, still, it seems that only a few properly understood his message — or else they understood, as the religious leaders, but would not believe it! Consequently, when he was put in prison, these religious leaders, who would later crucify Christ, would not lift a hand in his defense. Actually, they were probably very happy at the occasion of his arrest and imprisonment. Such is religion!

THE MINISTRY OF JOHN THE BAPTIST

To cut straight through to the chase, the Ministry of the Baptist was radical condemnation, as it regarded the religious leaders of Israel. In fact, he denounced these leaders as a brood of vipers, and denied that there was any value in the bare fact of descent from Abraham. A new beginning was necessary; the time had come to call out from the nation as a whole a loyal remnant who would be ready for the imminent arrival of the Coming One and the judgment which He would execute.

John thought and spoke of himself as a mere preparer of the way for this Coming One, for Whom he was unworthy, he said, to perform the lowliest service. Whereas John's own Ministry was characterized by Baptism with Water, the Coming One's Ministry would be a Baptism with the Holy Spirit and Fire.

Among those who came to John for Baptism, as is known, was Jesus, Whom John apparently hailed as the Coming One of Whom he had spoken — although later in prison, he had doubts about this identification and had to be reassured by being told that Jesus' Ministry was marked by precisely those features which the Prophets had foretold as characteristic of the Age of Restoration.

At the close of his Ministry, after he had performed his work of introducing Christ, which was his chief purpose, he aroused the suspicion of Antipas, with this man thinking that John was the leader, possibly, of a mass movement which might have unforeseen results; he also incurred this man's hostility, and still more that of Herod's second wife, Herodias, by denouncing their marriage as illicit. He was accordingly imprisoned in the Peraean fortress of Machaerus, and there, some months later, put to death.

GALILEE

The phrase, *"Jesus came into Galilee,"* specified this area as His Headquarters, which would be Capernaum by the Sea of Galilee. This was in fulfillment of Bible Prophecy. Some 800 years before, Isaiah had prophesied: *". . . beyond Jordan, in Galilee of the nations. The people who walked in darkness have seen a great Light: they who dwell in the land of the shadow of death, upon them has the Light shone"* (Isa. 9:1-2).

That Light was Jesus!

Consequently, this was the place chosen by God where His Eternal Son would carry out His Earthly Ministry. During the time of Christ, the Galilee area was bordered on the east by the Jordan River and the Sea of Galilee. On the west it did not quite extend to the Mediterranean. Its southern extension went down to the Kishon, which bordered Samaria. This was approximately 10 to 15 miles south of Nazareth.

There was actually an upper Galilee, which extended to the northern most border of Israel, and a lower Galilee, which incorporated the Sea of Galilee, Capernaum, and all the cities which ringed that lake, as well as Nazareth, etc. It was in this area where most of the Ministry of Christ was carried out.

Judah extended to the south as far as Beersheba, and included the cities of Hebron, Bethlehem, and Jerusalem, the Capital of Israel. Between Judaea and Galilee was Samaria. The Samaritans, who were somewhat half-breed Jews, were hated by the Jews proper, but were ministered to readily by Christ.

Galilee was a prosperous area, rich in olive oil and cereals, and especially fish from the Sea of Galilee.

Josephus, the Jewish Historian, said that cities ringed the eastern shore of the Lake, which teemed with fish, with the total population of lower Galilee approximately 250,000 people. It was well watered by streams flowing from the northern mountains, and possessed considerable stretches of fertile land and the limestone basins among its hills.

This, then, was the region in which Christ grew up — at Nazareth, in the limestone hills of lower Galilee. Thanks to its position, it was traversed by several major routeways of the Roman Empire, and was far from being a rural backwater region, even though its people were looked down upon by the intelligentsia of Judaea.

Its agriculture, fisheries, and commerce provided Jesus with His cultural background, and are reflected in His Parables and Teaching. Its people provided Him with His first Disciples and its dense scattering of settlements formed their first mission field.

After the Baptism of Jesus in Jordan, the forty days and nights of wilderness temptation commenced. Then He came back to Galilee, with, it seems, Andrew and Peter, two of John's Disciples, who would become His Disciples. Shortly thereafter, He would turn the water into wine at the Marriage Feast in Cana, which would be His First Miracle (Jn. 1:43).

However, the Passover at this time was drawing near; therefore, He went back into Judaea that He might present Himself in the Temple, which occasioned its first purging (Jn. 2:14). This is when Nicodemus visited Him by night, and when He began to openly preach and baptize (Jn. 3:26). Almost immediately, the Scribes and Pharisees began to burn with envy toward Him. Shortly thereafter, Jesus left Jerusalem, coming back into Galilee, which occasions this account by Mark.

THE GOSPEL OF THE KINGDOM OF GOD

The phrase, *"preaching the Gospel of the Kingdom of God,"* tells us several things:

1. PREACHING: Matthew said, *"preaching, teaching, and healing"* (Mat. 4:23; 9:35). Preaching calls *"attention"* to Truth, while teaching *"explains"* Truth. As would be obvious, the *"preaching"* of Christ was powerful, in effect, the most powerful the world had ever known. Considering that He was anointed by the Holy Spirit as no Prophet, Priest, or King had ever been anointed before Him, one can well understand how it was said of Him, *"Never man spoke like this Man"* (Jn. 7:46).

2. THE GOSPEL: This is the *"Good News,"* but even more perfectly *"The Good News that comes from God."* In effect, the world has no Good News, and that which it calls *"Good News"* is only the absence of bad news. The only *"Good News"* is the Gospel of Jesus Christ. It is the Message of *"Jesus Christ and Him Crucified."*

Due to the Fall, man is lost. Worse yet, he cannot find himself, cannot save himself, and, in effect, has no means to extricate himself from this terrible dilemma in which he now finds himself. This means that all in such a condition will die eternally lost, and, to be blunt, will burn in Hell forever and forever (Rev. 21:8).

But God didn't leave man in this dilemma. He loved His prized creation so much that God became Man and came down to this world in order to redeem man from the terrible situation in which man found himself. The price would be staggering, so great, in fact, that man, as stated, could not hope to pay such a price. But the Lord paid the price, which He did by going to the Cross, and there satisfied the claims of Heavenly Justice against man, which means that He atoned for all sin, past, present, and future, at least for all who will believe (Jn. 3:16).

To receive this glorious and wonderful *"new life,"* one only has to express faith in Christ and what Christ did at the Cross (Eph. 2:8-9). This *"more abundant life"* is not gained by works, because such works, irrespective as to what they might be, are woefully insufficient to pay the price. And due to the Fall of man, this great Salvation cannot be earned by merit, for man falls woefully short in this capacity. As stated, it can only be gained by Faith, which is possible for all (Rev. 22:17).

The fact that man can be changed from his lost condition and receive more abundant life, which means that he will live forever and forever with the Lord, and do so in Heavenly bliss, can certainly be said to be *"Good News"* (Rev., Chpts. 21-22).

3. THE KINGDOM OF GOD: The word *"Kingdom,"* as is here used, does not indicate a geographical area, but simply a realm in which a King, namely Christ, exercises His Power to act and control. In this Kingdom, Jesus did not take up any earthly political power (Jn. 18:36); however, the miracles He performed showed His authority over every competing power. But Jesus the King was rejected and crucified, as His enemies struggled to force His Kingdom out of history.

But Jesus' Death was not the end. During His days on Earth, Jesus explained what life under His rule (i.e., in His Kingdom) would be like. It is best to take most Gospel descriptions of the Kingdom of Heaven and the Kingdom of God as explanations of life in Jesus' present Kingdom.

The terms used in the Bible, *"Kingdom of Heaven"* and *"Kingdom of God,"* are similar, but yet have different meanings. The term, *"Kingdom of Heaven,"* could be said to be the *"Kingdom from Heaven,"* which more perfectly describes the Kingdom of which Jesus spoke. The term, *"Kingdom of God,"* includes everything that God originally created, with some of that creation having been corrupted by the Fall of Lucifer, etc. Ultimately, that part of the Kingdom of God will be totally and completely eliminated, with all of God's Creation once again becoming what it was before Lucifer's Fall. Chapters 21 and 22 of the Book of Revelation proclaim this grand era, which will be eternal, and which is coming.

LIFE IN THIS KINGDOM

According to His Gospel respecting the *"Kingdom of God,"* we are given powerful insights into how we can live today as Jesus' subjects and experience His Power. Because the New Birth brings us into union with Jesus and brings Jesus in a unique way into our experience here on Earth, we live in a day in which the King is present, though still disguised, one might say; however, because Jesus is present, the unmatched Power of God, through the Person of the Holy Spirit, can find supernatural expression in and through our lives (Jn. 16:7-15).

It probably can be said that the Sermon on the Mount (Mat., Chpts. 5-7) is the foundation principle of the Kingdom of God lifestyle, with the Beatitudes serving as its core. These (the Beatitudes) describe the values of a person living a Kingdom lifestyle (Mat. 5:3-12). As King, Jesus acts to transform the character of His subjects. Jesus, in the present Kingdom, is working in our inner self to change our outward behavior.

In the *"Sermon on the Mount,"* He goes on to show how we can experience this transforming power, which was brought to fruition by the Holy Spirit being made possible to all Believers by virtue of the Cross. In no way can we transform ourselves into the person we need to be, or the person we must be; however, it can be done, but only by and through Christ living and working in our lives through the Power of the Holy Spirit.

Paul said, *"I am crucified with Christ* (taking us back to Rom. 6:3-5); *nevertheless I live; yet not I, but Christ lives in me: and the life which I now live in the flesh* (everyday life and living) *I live by the Faith of the Son of God, Who loved me, and gave Himself for me.*

"I do not frustrate the Grace of God: for if Righteousness come by the Law (Law of Moses), *then Christ is dead in vain"* (Gal. 2:20-21).

"Kingdom Living" can only be brought about by and through Faith in Christ and what Christ has done for us at the Cross, which then gives the Holy Spirit latitude to work within our hearts and lives, bringing about the Righteousness and Holiness which the Holy Spirit Alone can produce, thereby making us Christlike, and, I might quickly add, ever becoming more and more like Christ, which are all made possible by the Cross (I Cor. 1:18).

RELATIONSHIP

In all of this, we focus, one might say, on our *"in secret"* relationship with the Lord, and not on visible piety (Mat. 6:1-18). We give priority to seeking God's Kingdom and Righteousness, and we trust our Heavenly Father to supply our material needs (Mat. 6:19-33). We relate to other Kingdom citizens as Brothers and Sisters and reject every claim of a right to judge or control them (Mat. 7:1-14). As well, instead of relying on human leaders, we rely on the simple Words of Jesus and commit ourselves, through the Power of the Holy Spirit, to obey them, which can only be done by our constant faith in Christ and the Cross (Mat. 7:15-27).

To have entrance into this Kingdom of God, one must be *"born again"* (Jn. 3:3, 5). The New Birth gives entrance into the Kingdom — the realm in which Jesus' Sovereign Power is translated into action on behalf of His people. And why this stress on being Born-Again? Perhaps because of the fact that when a person is Born-Again, Jesus enters his or her life, and there He takes up permanent residence through the Agency and Person of the Holy Spirit. Now, and for all time, Jesus is present in His people — in each Believer and in the corporate Body of Christ. In a mystical but real way, Jesus is present on Earth in us. He is the key to the release of the power needed to transform us and to shape the events that affect our lives according to His Will.

The Kingdom is here because Jesus is here. Because Jesus is here, the possibility of a new kind of life is laid open before us.

KINGDOM LIFE AND LIVING

Even though the Kingdom of Heaven, or the Kingdom of God, is now real in our hearts and we have, in truth, entered that Kingdom, still, it is not evident on Earth except in this capacity of the Born-Again experience.

Both the Old and New Testaments, however, proclaim a Kingdom which will not only reside in the spiritual, but the physical and material as well! In other words, there will ultimately be a material Kingdom on Earth, and Jesus will Personally rule over it. At that time, the entirety of the world will be transformed, with the *"Kingdom of God"* being realized in every facet of life: the spiritual, the academic, economic, agricultural, scientific, physical, and material. For the first time, the world and man will be seen as God originally created them.

Even though the Old Testament is full of these predictions, with Isaiah being the principle Millennial Prophet, still, Jesus Himself confirmed the Old Testament Vision of this coming Glad Day (Mat. 8:11-12; 16:28; 20:21; 25:1, 34; 26:29; Mk. 11:10; 14:25; Lk. 13:28-29; 17:20; Acts 1:6-7).

(15) "AND SAYING, THE TIME IS FULFILLED, AND THE KINGDOM OF GOD IS AT HAND: REPENT YE, AND BELIEVE THE GOSPEL."

The composition is:

The previous Verse proclaimed what was being preached, while Verse 15 proclaims what the action should be upon acceptance of such preaching — Repentance.

THE FULFILLED TIME

The phrase, *"And saying, The time is fulfilled,"* represents the most important *"time"* in history. The older order of the Law was giving place to a new one, the Kingdom of Heaven, namely, the Messianic Earth-rule of the Messiah — at least if Israel would accept Him.

However, as is known, He was rejected by Israel, which subjected the entirety of the world to a continued time of suffering and heartache, which has lasted now for nearly 2,000 years. Christ was rejected and Caesar was chosen (Jn. 19:15); consequently, the world has seen approximately 2,000 years of Caesar-rule, which has resulted in heartache, starvation, war, death, and destruction, causing untold suffering.

During this time, the Gospel of Grace and the Age of Grace, made possible by the Cross, has been brought in, with the Church, the Mystical Body of Christ, functioning in the interim between the rejection of Israel and its dispersion in A.D. 70, and its future re-gathering for the Millennial Kingdom. Then the Kingdom of God will commence on Earth, as was intended at the First Advent of Christ, but which was rejected.

The word *"fulfilled"* means that God had allotted a specific period of *"time"* before Jesus would come. This was the period between the Garden of Eden, with the first Prophecy of this coming event (Gen. 3:15), all the way to the beginning of the Ministry of Christ, a time frame of approximately 4,000 years. During this period, all the Prophets, such as Abraham, Moses, David, Isaiah, etc., spoke of this coming time.

WHY WAS THIS THE RIGHT TIME?

Of course, as would be understood, the entrance of Christ into the world, regarding His First Advent, was, as stated, the most important event in human history. Nothing else even remotely equals this, considering that Jesus Christ came to carry out the Plan of Redemption, which, in effect, was the Cross (Gal. 1:4).

We, as human beings, do not, of course, know everything in the Mind of God concerning this momentous occasion; however, there are some particulars which stand out, possibly shedding some light on the question. First of all, the entirety of the world had just about run its course, as it regarded intellectual efforts at answering the great questions of life.

Socrates had determined that there were

such things as good and evil. Plato, his student, had ascertained that, while there was good and evil, there was a great chasm between the good and the evil. Aristotle, the student of Plato, determined that there was good and evil, there was a great chasm between the two, and, moreover, man's greatest effort was not able to bridge that chasm; and, in that, he was correct.

So, at the time of Christ, the great Greek thinkers had, by and large, come and gone, and without solving anything. In other words, man had taken his intellectual abilities just about as far as they could be taken, but without any positive results. In other words, intellectually, man could not solve his dilemma. So, intellectually, the world at that time was tired, which made it ready, in a sense, for the Gospel of Jesus Christ.

Regarding material things, the great Road System of the Roman Empire made it easier to take the Gospel to the far-flung reaches of that great Empire. At the end of the first 100 years of Christianity, those roads had been utilized, to their best degree, in establishing local Churches over that part of the world.

At any rate, and whatever the reasons, the time of waiting was fulfilled, and Christ came.

THE KINGDOM OF GOD IS AT HAND

The phrase, *"And the Kingdom of God is at hand,"* meant that with the commencing of the Ministry of Christ, all those things to which the Prophets had pointed were about to be fulfilled, or at least given opportunity for fulfillment. All of it was wrapped up in Jesus.

The Kingdom of God can be further defined as God's rule over all moral intelligences willingly subject to His Will, including the Holy Angels and all Believers of all ages. This Kingdom was announced as *"at hand,"* but, as stated, was rejected.

However, to be sure, the answer to our Lord's Prayer, *"Your Kingdom come, Your Will be done on Earth, as it is in Heaven,"* will ultimately be fulfilled (Mat. 6:10).

The *"Kingdom of God,"* in a sense, was Jesus. For there to be a *"Kingdom,"* there had to be a *"King,"* and Christ was that King, even though recognized not at all by Israel. Nevertheless, if the dynasty of David had continued, which, of course, it could not, due

NOTES

to Israel being a vassal state for the last 500 years, Joseph, the foster father of Jesus, would have been the King of Israel. Due to the fact that Joseph had passed on by the time that the Ministry of Christ began, Jesus would now be King. But two things interfered with that:

First of all, Jesus did not come at this time to be the King of Israel (even though He definitely is King in the hearts of untold millions), because Israel and the world desperately needed Redemption. In other words, Israel needed a Saviour and not a King; however, it was a King she wanted and desired at that time, the very time the Messiah was supposed to come, and not a Saviour.

Concerning this time, Paul said, regarding Israel, *"For they being ignorant of God's Righteousness, and going about to establish their own Righteousness, have not submitted themselves unto the Righteousness of God"* (Rom. 10:3).

SOLOMON

The Song of Solomon is a perfect example, and meant to be by the Holy Spirit, of this of which I speak. In the love story of the *"Song,"* Solomon, the great King of Israel, the richest man on the face of the Earth, and the most powerful, woos the hand of a lovely young lady, the Shulamite; however, at the same time, she is being courted by a lowly shepherd.

Despite Solomon's grandeur and glory, lo and behold! the Shulamite accepted the hand of the lowly shepherd, thereby rejecting Solomon, the great King. The moral is this:

The Shulamite represents Israel. The King and the shepherd both represent Christ. Christ was both a King and a Shepherd. The Shulamite accepting the shepherd proclaims the fact that before Israel can have her King, she must first accept the Shepherd, which she will do immediately after the Second Coming. Then, she can have her King, but not before!

The second reason that Israel would not accept Christ was because of her gross misinterpretation of the Scriptures. She totally ignored what the Bible said about the coming Messiah, devising in her own mind that which the Messiah should be. Actually, Israel at that time did not believe that the Messiah would be God, but rather a very charismatic man, etc. Evidently, they totally ignored Isaiah's Prophecy of 7:14. So, Jesus was not at all what they were expecting, despite the fact that He fulfilled every Scripture which was predicted of Him, and in totality.

REPENTANCE

The phrase, *"Repent ye, and believe the Gospel,"* was the Message of Jesus Christ, as well as John. It was also the Message of the Apostles (Mat. 10:7-10; Mk. 6:7-13), and of all true Gospel Preachers since that time. It was not to be for Jews only, or the Early Church days only (Lk. 13:1-5; Acts 2:38-39; 3:19; 17:20; 19:8; 20:25; 28:23, 31; I Cor. 4:20).

The two words, *"repent"* and *"believe,"* may be regarded as a summary of the method of Salvation. Repentance and Faith are the conditions of admission into the Christian Covenant. Repentance has a special reference to God the Father; and Faith, to Jesus Christ, the Eternal Son. It is in the Gospels that Christ is revealed to us as a Saviour; and, therefore, we find Jesus Christ as the Object of our Faith, and, more particularly, what He did for us at the Cross, which is distinguished from the Father as the Object of our Repentance.

Repentance, of and by itself, is not sufficient — it makes no satisfaction for the Law which we have broken; and hence, over and above Repentance, there is required from us Faith in the Gospel, wherein Christ is revealed to us as a propitiation for sin, and as the only way of reconciliation with the Father.

Without Faith (believing), Repentance becomes despair, and without Repentance, Faith becomes only presumption. Join the two together, and the faithful soul instantly finds Redemption in Christ. Paul said, *"Testifying both to the Jews, and also to the Greeks, Repentance toward God, and Faith toward our Lord Jesus Christ"* (Acts 20:21).

(16) "NOW AS HE WALKED BY THE SEA OF GALILEE, HE SAW SIMON AND ANDREW HIS BROTHER CASTING A NET INTO THE SEA: FOR THEY WERE FISHERS."

The diagram is:

Christ now filled with the Holy Spirit, His Ministry begins!

THE SEA OF GALILEE

The phrase, *"Now as He walked by the Sea of Galilee,"* accounts this action as by design and purpose. This was probably near Capernaum. One can see Jesus slowly walking beside this body of water, maybe praying and meditating, which would occasion the call of Peter, Andrew, James, and John.

The Sea of Galilee is referred to by several names, *"Chinnereth"* (Num. 34:11), *"Chinneroth"* (Josh. 12:3), and, in the New Testament, as the *"Lake of Gennesaret"* (Lk. 5:1), and the *"Sea of Tiberias"* (Jn. 21:1).

The Lake is about 7 miles wide and 14 miles long. The River Jordan flows through it from north to south, and its waters are, therefore, constantly fresh. The shores of this Lake were the site of towns, such as Capernaum, which Christ chose as His Headquarters, as well as Bethsaida, and others, along with Tiberias. Today, only Tiberias remains, with the others having faded into oblivion, primarily because they little accepted the Ministry of Christ (Mat. 11:23).

THE BROTHERS

The phrase, *"He saw Simon and Andrew his brother casting a net into the sea: for they were fishers,"* denotes their occupation. Their casting the net may have been done from the shore, but, more than likely, it was from a ship close to the shore. This was not Jesus' first acquaintance with Peter and Andrew, for He had met them on the trip to Judaea, when He was baptized by John. In fact, they had been Disciples of John the Baptist, along with John the Beloved (Jn. 1:35-42).

If one is to notice, the Holy Spirit did not at all select the religious elite of Israel to be the Disciples of Christ, but instead men of humble occupation. This should portray to any and all the heart which God will use, which is seldom, if ever, the religious heart! That comes as a shock to most; however, religion and relationship with Christ are two different things altogether. Religion is man-devised, while relationship with Christ is God-devised.

(17) "AND JESUS SAID UNTO THEM, COME YE AFTER ME, AND I WILL MAKE

YOU TO BECOME FISHERS OF MEN."

The overview is:

The training will now begin!

JESUS AND THE CALL!

The phrase, *"And Jesus said unto them, Come ye after Me,"* will constitute the greatest words they would ever hear concerning their own personal lives. (As an aside, the Holy Spirit, while guiding the minds of those whom He moved to write these records, did not use an overpowering influence, so as to interfere with their own natural modes of expression. Each sacred writer, while guarded against error, has reserved to him his own peculiarities of style and expression [Spence].)

The phrase, *"Come ye after Me,"* was a simple invitation, but yet containing the meaning of being His Disciple. As stated, this was not their first encounter with Christ. As well, they no doubt had heard John's Messages, when he spoke of the One coming after him Who was mightier than he! Being dedicated to God, and even Disciples of John, they no doubt discussed long and hard among themselves that Jesus was the One of Whom John was speaking; consequently, His appeal to them was something they probably had been eagerly awaiting for a period of weeks. And now it comes, with the thrill which defies all description penetrating their hearts!

FISHERS OF MEN

The phrase, *"And I will make you to become fishers of men,"* involves a long, slow process. It is the same as when He spoke to the Church at Philadelphia, *"Him who overcomes will I make a Pillar in the Temple of My God"* (Rev. 3:12).

It was not a process that was easily arrived at, as the accounts of all four Gospels proclaim! And yet, it was arrived at, and greatly intensified by the outpouring of the Holy Spirit on the Day of Pentecost.

Someone has said:

"I can see far down the mountain, where I've wandered many years,

"Often hindered on my journey, by the ghosts of doubts and fears.

"Broken vows and disappointments, thickly strewn along the way,

"But the Spirit has led unerring, to the land I hold today."

This first admonition of Christ proclaims to one and all that priority with God is the winning of souls. All who do not know what Jesus did at Calvary, as far as those people are concerned, Jesus died in vain! (Gal. 2:21).

So, even though many other things are greatly significant, still, priority must always be the proclamation of the Gospel of Jesus Christ, to bring men into the fold, i.e., *"fishers of men."*

(18) "AND STRAIGHTWAY THEY FORSOOK THEIR NETS, AND FOLLOWED HIM."

The construction is:

This would be the greatest and most far-reaching decision ever made by anyone. It's a journey which has not concluded, even unto this moment, and will lead to glory and grandeur unparalleled!

THEY FORSOOK EVERYTHING TO FOLLOW CHRIST

The words, *"And straightway,"* mean this was done immediately! In other words, and as we have stated, this was something for which they had been waiting. The phrase, *"They forsook their nets,"* means they left the fishing business, with no idea or thought of ever returning. It was not to be, nor intended to be, a brief excursion or sabbatical from the fishing business. They left with no intention of ever coming back. This is how powerful, how far-reaching, the invitation of Christ actually is.

Of course, their understanding of Him and His Mission was limited at this time, to say the least; nevertheless, as early as this moment, they considered Him to be the Messiah, the Son of the Living God.

FOLLOWING HIM

The phrase, *"And followed Him,"* in the Greek is *"akoloutheo,"* which means *"to walk the same road."* They were intent on following Him, irrespective as to where it would lead. (It actually means to walk alongside.) Little did they know or realize that it would lead ultimately to judging the Twelve Tribes of Israel forever and also to having their names inscribed on the Foundations of the coming New Jerusalem (Mat. 19:28; Rev. 21:14).

As the Apostles of old, the modern Believer little understands the tremendous spiritual benefit in living for Christ. The rewards are so absolutely far-reaching that they beggar description! Consequently, our lives should be lived with this thought in mind, therefore doing all that is possible to serve Him as diligently as we can.

(19) "AND WHEN HE HAD GONE A LITTLE FARTHER THENCE, HE SAW JAMES THE SON OF ZEBEDEE, AND JOHN HIS BROTHER, WHO ALSO WERE IN THE SHIP MENDING THEIR NETS."

The exposition is:

James and John would now be added!

JAMES AND JOHN

The phrase, *"And when He had gone a little farther thence, He saw James the son of Zebedee, and John his brother,"* concerns two more fishermen who would become the Apostles of Christ. At this time, Christ would merely request that these would *"follow Him."* It seems that quite a number ultimately were invited to do this; however, it was only after a night spent in prayer that the actual Twelve were chosen (Lk. 6:12-16), which took place shortly thereafter.

The phrase, *"Who also were in the ship mending their nets,"* lends credence to the idea that even though they wanted and desired the call from Him, still, they were not expecting it at the moment. Their preparation, at least for now, was to continue in the fishing business.

(20) "AND STRAIGHTWAY HE CALLED THEM: AND THEY LEFT THEIR FATHER ZEBEDEE IN THE SHIP WITH THE HIRED SERVANTS, AND WENT AFTER HIM."

The overview is:

Little did they realize, at least at this time, what following Him actually meant.

THE CALL

The phrase, *"And straightway He called them,"* constitutes the *"call"* of not only James and John, but, as well, every other person He has called into His Service.

Sadly, there are too many occupying pulpits who have never received that *"call"*! Conversely, there are many who have received the *"call,"* but have failed to heed and follow; and sadly, there are many who have heard and answered the *"call,"* but have not lived up to its potential. The Ministry of the Lord Jesus Christ is not a vocation, avocation, career, or job. As here, it is a Call of God. Regrettably, far two many are in the Ministry as a career, etc. They actually have never been called of the Lord.

Some time back, I heard a political figure say that the only way to get out of the grinding poverty into which he was born in West Texas was either through politics or the Ministry. He went on to state how he had reasoned in his mind that Ministry would be the course he would take, when politics diverted his attention, with him choosing that direction instead. Thank the Lord that was the direction he chose, because the Lord certainly had not chosen him for the direction of Ministry.

Some would ask the question as to how one can be sure that one is called? The answer is not as difficult as it would seem at first. First of all, if it's possible to do anything else other than Ministry, then do it! To be sure, if one is truly called of the Lord, that *"call"* will weigh so heavily upon him (or her) that they simply will not be able to do anything else.

Nevertheless, it should be well understood that a true *"call"* from the Lord will, much of the time, ultimately result in a life of hardship, persecution, and sometimes even death! The world is not in sympathy with a true Call from God, and, sadly enough, neither is the Church. Those who are truly called of God will follow the Lord, and nothing or no one else! Sadly, some who were truly called have ceased to follow Him, and, as a result, experience no more anointing by the Holy Spirit, neither His Leading or Guidance. One cannot follow man and God at the same time!

WHAT THE CALL ACTUALLY MEANS

The reason the religious elite in Israel hated Christ so much was because those who followed Him would not follow them. The situation has little changed even unto the present. The God-called Preacher is going to make up his (or her) mind that man, and especially religious man, will strongly seek to usurp authority over the Lord. Those who call themselves *"religious leaders"* too often demand total allegiance. This also too often characterizes religious Denominations. So, the man of God will be faced with a choice; however, he must understand that he cannot serve both. *"No man can serve two masters: for either he will hate the one, and love the other; or else he will hold to the one, and despise the other"* (Mat. 6:24).

It is often found that if one truly follows the Lord, he will be ostracized by that which goes under the name of *"Church."* The *"Call"* is from the Lord; therefore, it is to the Lord that we owe total allegiance. Personally, I love my Brothers and Sisters in the Lord, and will do my best to do whatever it is they ask, providing it is Scriptural and applies to me. However, if they demand something which is not Scriptural, that I cannot follow!

ZEBEDEE

The phrase, *"And they left their father Zebedee in the ship with the hired servants,"* is peculiar to Mark concerning the *"hired servants."* This shows that Mark was an independent witness of that which we wrote. This narrative tells us that the fishing business of Zebedee was significantly larger than that of Peter and Andrew, because no mention is made of servants (other employees) in their business. Actually, there is a good possibility that Peter and Andrew worked for Zebedee.

If this is the case, then the man was left with no one but the *"servants,"* with even his sons following Christ; however, every indication is that Zebedee gladly gave up his sons and that he was rewarded greatly for his sacrifice. There is no indication whatsoever that he intended to stop them or even slow them, but actually encouraged them. He, as well, saw in Christ that which satisfies the hunger and thirst of the soul.

Zebedee was in the ship with them on the day they received the call of Jesus. Exactly what Jesus said is not registered, but more than likely it was the simple admonition, the same as to Peter and Andrew, *"Follow Me"*! The moment they looked up and saw Him, and His voice rang out to them of that clarion call, I believe the Presence of God instantly filled that ship and also their hearts.

This was a *"Call"* that had been decided a long time before; consequently, it carried far more than just the weight of invitation. Zebedee no doubt sensed and felt the tremendous import of the invitation as much as his sons. Mark does not say exactly what transpired at that moment, but Matthew did say that they *"left the ship and their father,"* meaning that they had his blessings (Mat. 4:22).

The phrase, *"And went after Him,"* means that they separated from their father and the fishing business, never to go back. The Call of God, as stated, transcends all affections, family ties, loyalties, and personal choices.

(21) "AND THEY WENT INTO CAPERNAUM; AND STRAIGHTWAY ON THE SABBATH DAY HE ENTERED INTO THE SYNAGOGUE, AND TAUGHT."

The exegesis is:

The *"teaching"* the people received from Christ was the first, more than likely, they had ever heard which was totally Biblical. What a blessing that must have been then to have been able to hear Christ Personally teach the Word of God! What great truths must have been given at that time!

CAPERNAUM

The phrase, *"And they went into Capernaum,"* did not mean immediately, but rather some time later, possibly even several days later. There is evidence that other things, such as the *"Sermon on the Mount,"* took place before the event of the deliverance of the man with an unclean spirit in the Synagogue on the *"Sabbath Day."*

The town of Capernaum was located on the northwest corner of the Sea of Galilee. It was inhabited continuously, it is said, from the First Century B.C. to the Seventh Century A.D. It seems to have been the nearest village to the River Jordan as it makes its entrance into the Lake.

On the western shore, Tiberias was the largest town closest to where the Jordan River made its exit from the Sea of Galilee, being about 5 miles distance from that site. About 2 miles north of Tiberias was Magdala, where Mary Magdalene lived. About 2 miles north of Magdala was a place called Heptapegon. Then about 2 miles further on was Capernaum. On the northeast corner of the Lake was Bethsaida, about 6 miles from Capernaum. It was in Capernaum where Jesus made His Headquarters.

It is said that a lady by the name of Egeria visited this city in A.D. 383. She was shown a Church in the little town and was told that it had been made from the house of the Apostle Peter, and the walls of this house were incorporated into it, still standing in their original form. Peter's house was probably the headquarters of Christ.

THE SYNAGOGUE

The phrase, *"And straightway on the Sabbath Day He entered into the synagogue,"* proclaims the place of worship for Jews. The importance of the synagogue for Judaism cannot be overstated. More than any other institution, it gave character to the Jewish faith. Here Judaism learned its interpretation of the Law.

Ezekiel 11:16 says, *"I have been a Sanctuary to them for a while,"* which, as interpreted by Jewish authority, meant that in world-wide dispersion, Israel would have the Synagogue as a Sanctuary in miniature to replace the loss of the Temple. Unlike the Temple, it was located in all parts of the land, and put the people in touch with their religious leaders.

In the Synagogue, there was no Altar, and prayer and the reading of the Torah (Law) took the place of the sacrifice. In addition, the prayer house performed an important social function. It was a gathering point and a meeting place where the people could congregate whenever it was necessary to take counsel over important community affairs.

The Synagogue became the cradle of an entirely new type of social and religious life and established the foundation for a religious community of universal scope. For the first time, Jewish monotheism (the worship of one God) emancipated itself in religious practice from its bonds to a specific and designated site. God was now brought to the people wherever they dwelt.

The Synagogue served a three-fold purpose of worship, education, and government of the civil life of the community. Subject to the law of the land, the Synagogue had its own government. The congregation was governed by Elders, who were empowered to exercise discipline and punish members. Punishment was by scourging and excommunication. The chief officer was the ruler of the Synagogue (Mk. 5:22; Acts 13:15; 18:8). He supervised the service to see that it was carried on in accord with tradition.

The attendant (Lk. 4:20) brought the Scrolls of Scripture for reading, replaced them in the Ark (a replica of the Ark of the Covenant), punished offending members by scourging, and instructed children to read. In fact, the primary function of the Synagogue was the popular instruction in the Law.

TEACHING

The short phrase, *"And taught,"* means, according to the Greek Scholars, that Jesus brought an extended discourse to the people that day. What He taught is not stated; however, coming from His lips, as the next Verse proves, meant that it was the greatest teaching on the things of God that the people had ever heard. What a privilege to have heard such an explanation of the Gospel!

And yet, if a Preacher knows the Word and is anointed by the Holy Spirit, it will be in the same realm as what Jesus taught, because the same Holy Spirit Who anointed then, anoints now! This is the reason that two things are imperative respecting the Preacher of the Gospel:

1. He must know the Word of God, understanding that it alone holds the answer to all things pertaining to life and Godliness (II Pet. 1:3).

2. He must seek God incessantly in order that he (or she) be a proper channel through which the Spirit of God may flow. This speaks of a strong prayer life (Acts 6:2-4).

(22) "AND THEY WERE ASTONISHED AT HIS DOCTRINE: FOR HE TAUGHT THEM AS ONE WHO HAD AUTHORITY, AND NOT AS THE SCRIBES."

The overview is:

The truth is, the religious leaders of Israel had so perverted the Law that, anymore, what the people heard was not in any capacity that which originally had been given. So when Jesus began to teach, and began to teach exactly what the Word of God said, which would have been the Old Testament, the people, for the first time, actually heard the Word of God.

DOCTRINE

The phrase, *"And they were astonished at His Doctrine,"* means they were literally *"bowled over"* at what He said and the way He said it! What they were expecting to hear, as constantly brought to them by the Scribes, etc., they did not hear, and what they hardly expected to hear, a proclamation of the Word of God, which was actually greater than had ever been delivered in human history, they did not expect.

The phrase, *"At His Doctrine,"* once again respected what He taught and the way He taught it.

What was His Doctrine?

His Doctrine was the Word of God, while the Scribes basically taught tradition. Tradition was *"the commandments of men"* (Mat. 15:9; Mk. 7:6-7). In other words, this tradition was human thought, which did not measure up to the Word of God, and, in effect, was contrary to the Word of God. Conversely, the teaching given by Christ not only agreed with the Word of God, but, in effect, was the Word of God. Thus, in the Sermon on the Mount, Jesus quoted from the Law, but put beside it His Own Words, *"But I say unto you"* (Mat. 5:22, 28, 32, 34, 39, 44; 6:25).

His justification for so doing is found in His Person. As the Spirit-anointed Messiah, the Word made flesh, He Alone could make a valid and authoritative commentary on the Spirit-inspired Word of God. Likewise, the Epistles emphasize the Person of Christ in contrast to tradition. In Colossians 2:8, Paul warns against falling prey to *"philosophy and empty deceit ... according to human tradition ... and not according to Christ."*

And yet, the Early Church was commanded to hold to the traditions which came from Christ. Paul said, *"Therefore, Brethren, stand fast, and hold the traditions which you have been taught, whether by Word, or our Epistle"* (II Thess. 2:15).

The difference was that this *"tradition"* encouraged by the Apostle Paul came from Christ, Who was, and is, God, and not man.

NOTES

Christ not only created the true tradition, but constitutes it.

CHRISTIAN TRADITION

Christian tradition, therefore, in the New Testament has three elements:

1. The facts of Christ (Lk. 1:2; I Cor. 11:23; 15:3).

2. The theological interpretation of those facts, which is the whole argument of I Corinthians, Chapter 15.

3. The manner of life which flows from them (I Cor. 11:2; II Thess. 2:15; 3:6-7).

In Jude, Verse 3, the *"Faith ... once for all delivered"* covers all three elements (Rom. 6:17). Consequently, that written by the Apostles, which constitutes the Gospels and the Epistles, claimed that its tradition was to be received as authoritative (I Cor. 11:2; II Thess. 2:15; 3:6).

Christ told the Apostles to bear witness of Him, and for several reasons:

A. Because they had been with Him from the very beginning; as such, they were to pass on what He taught them, as they did! This constitutes the four Gospels: Matthew, Mark, Luke, and John. It also includes Acts, for Luke, its writer, said, *"Forasmuch as many have taken in hand to set forth in order a declaration of those things which are most surely believed among us, even as they deliver them unto us, which from the beginning were eyewitnesses, and Ministers of the Word"* (Lk. 1:1-2).

It would also include the Books of James and Jude, I and II Peter, along with I, II, and III John, and the Book of Revelation. As well, it includes all the writings of the Apostle Paul, which, counting the others, make up the entirety of the New Testament.

Even though Paul was not one of the Disciples of Christ during His earthly Ministry, still, concerning the visible appearance of Christ, he said, *"And last of all He was seen of me also, as of one born out of due time"* (I Cor. 15:8).

Consequently, all the writers of the New Testament had either been with Christ or at least had seen Him, as Paul. (Paul is speaking of the time that Christ appeared to him on the road to Damascus, which resulted in his conversion [Acts, Chpt. 9]).

B. The Holy Spirit was promised to them, as to us, Who would lead them into all Truth (Jn. 15:26-27; 16:13).

This combination of eyewitness testimony and Spirit-guided witness produced a *"tradition"* that was a true and valid complement to the Old Testament. So, I Timothy 5:18 and II Peter 3:16 place apostolic tradition alongside Scripture and describe it as such.

DIRECT REVELATION OF THE HOLY SPIRIT

That which was passed down by the Apostles, and which was called *"tradition,"* was not their own thoughts and ideas, as the tradition of the Scribes which Jesus rebuked, but rather the Words and Actions of Christ, or direct Revelation of the Holy Spirit. That which transpired in Jesus' day, i.e., the Scribes and Elders proclaiming their own thoughts and ideas, which did not measure up to the Word, happens no less today! From behind most pulpits in America, the Word of God is either totally ignored or twisted and perverted to mean something it did not originally proclaim. Paul called it *"another Gospel"* (II Cor. 11:4).

In fact, if what is being preached is not *"Jesus Christ and Him Crucified"* (I Cor. 1:23), which related to the fact that Christ is the Source of all things, while the Cross is the Means by which all things are given to us, then, pure and simple, what is being preached is not the Gospel. As the true Word of God, as proclaimed by Christ, was very scarce during those days of long ago, likewise, it is very scarce presently! The greatest barometer of this is the condition of the nation as a whole.

AUTHORITY

The phrase, *"For He taught them as One Who had authority, and not as the Scribes,"* refers to the Scribes teaching their own thoughts and ideas, which were not the Word of God, and consequently not anointed by the Holy Spirit, relative to what Christ taught, which definitely was anointed by the Holy Spirit.

The word *"authority,"* as it is normally used, refers to the power a person has that is delegated to him from someone else. In the case of the Preacher of the Gospel, or any Believer for that matter, it refers to the Lord giving that authority, which means *"delegated authority."* However, the word *"authority,"* as used here of Christ, is different in that His authority was in Himself, and not derived from others. (The Believer has authority within himself only in the sense that the Holy Spirit resides in him. While it is true that the Holy Spirit abided in Christ, on Whom He depended constantly, still, Christ was the *"Living Word"* as no Believer can ever be, except to the degree that Christ abides in Him.)

The *"Scribes"* were those learned in Mosaic Law and in the Sacred Writings; consequently, they were supposed to be interpreters and teachers.

(23) "AND THERE WAS IN THEIR SYNAGOGUE A MAN WITH AN UNCLEAN SPIRIT; AND HE CRIED OUT."

The structure is:

We find from this account that the Ministry of the Lord Jesus Christ, which was the only perfect Ministry that has ever been, always, and without fail, exposed demon spirits, and was always victorious over them.

THE UNCLEAN SPIRIT

The phrase, *"And there was in their Synagogue a man with an unclean spirit,"* is indicative of a spirit which resides in and controls the people which are inhabited by them, whoever they might be. The term, *"unclean spirit,"* is used some 22 times of demons, 10 times in Mark alone. The word *"unclean"* runs the gamut of all the activity of Satan, from immorality to deceptive, lying, religious spirits (Rev. 16:13-16).

Concerning this man and the *"unclean spirit,"* the Greek is literally *"in a spirit, an unclean one."* On the other side of the spectrum, it is the same as the idioms, *"in Christ"* and *"in the Lord,"* which are so common with Paul. The unclean spirit was in the man in the sense that he, an incorporeal being, entered the man's body, and took up his residence in it, and controlled the person in whose body he dwelt. The man was in the demon, in that he lived within the sphere of the demon's control.

Satan is different than a demon. There is

one Devil (Satan) and many demons. The Devil is a fallen angel. Demons constitute a different category of beings. From the fact that the demons have no rest unless they are living in some physical body, it seems clear that, at one time, they did have physical bodies and they were deprived of them by some judgment of God. Some, including this Evangelist, think that they are the disembodied beings of a pre-Adamite race, who inhabited the first perfect Earth (Gen. 1:1), and that they followed their leader Lucifer (who became Satan) into sin and were disembodied and deprived of residence upon the Earth by the cataclysm of Genesis 1:2, which was coincident with the Fall of Lucifer (Isa. 14:12-17).

DEMON POSSESSION

Demon possession speaks of spirits of darkness which enter into a person's body, taking up residence in it, and controlling the mind of the person in whose body they dwell. These spirits exercise control over the individual they possess at all times, but more so at some times than others, as here illustrated. After Jesus finished His Message, the demon spirits screamed out, using the man's vocal cords. In other words, the man was the instrument, but the demon spirit was the actual control.

The torture of one afflicted by such knows no bounds; consequently, the torture of Mary Magdalene, from whom Jesus cast out seven demons, must have been awful indeed! (Lk. 8:2).

CAN CHRISTIANS BE DEMON POSSESSED?

No!

Christians can very definitely be demon-oppressed, and even demon-suppressed, but not demon-possessed.

The reason that some think that Christians can be possessed by demon spirits is because they do not have a proper understanding of the sin nature and the Cross of Christ.

THE SIN NATURE

Concerning the believing sinner coming to Christ, Paul said, *"Knowing this, that our old man is crucified with Him, that the body of sin be destroyed, that henceforth we should not serve sin"* (Rom. 6:6). The word translated *"destroyed"* should have been translated *"made ineffective,"* because the Greek word does not mean annihilation or obliteration, concerning the sin nature. At conversion, it is simply made ineffective.

But then, and all too often, new converts, little knowing and understanding God's Prescribed Order of Victory, and not hearing it from behind the pulpit, make things other than Christ and the Cross the object of their faith. When they do this, which we all have done, they, in essence, according to Paul, are committing *"spiritual adultery"* (Rom. 7:1-4). The Believer is married to Christ, and, as such, Christ meets our every need, and does so by the means of the Cross, i.e., *"its benefits."* But when the Believer begins to look elsewhere, through ignorance or otherwise, in a sense, such a Believer is being unfaithful to Christ, which constitutes, as stated, *"spiritual adultery."*

When this happens, the Holy Spirit, while He doesn't leave us, will draw back, because He certainly will not help someone commit spiritual adultery. When this happens, the Believer, because of what I have stated, is now functioning with not much help from the Holy Spirit, and he will then fail the Lord. When this happens, the sin nature, which has been dormant, i.e., made ineffective, now roars to life, and with a vengeance. In fact, in some manner, it begins to control the Believer, with the Believer now beginning to do things he never dreamed he would do.

That's why Paul told the Galatians, *"Stand fast therefore in the liberty wherewith Christ has made us free, and be not entangled again with the yoke of bondage."* He went on to say, *"Behold, I Paul say unto you, that if you be circumcised* (make anything other than the Cross of Christ the object of your faith), *Christ shall profit you nothing."* In other words, all that Christ did at the Cross will be of no benefit (Gal. 5:1-2).

THE BELIEVER IN TROUBLE

Now the Believer is in trouble! The sin nature has roared to life, and is actually controlling such a Believer, with him doing things, as stated, he never dreamed he would do, and I'm speaking of things which are wicked and ungodly. He then begins to make every effort to stop this sinful action, whatever it is, but to no avail. In other words, the harder he tries, the worse the situation becomes. His willpower is not enough, meaning that he simply cannot stop what he is doing. He is being controlled by the sin nature.

Not understanding the Cross, he listens to certain Preachers, who tell him that his problem is that he is possessed with a particular demon. In other words, if he's having trouble with uncontrollable temper, well, he's got a temper demon, they say! If it's a problem with alcohol, he's got an alcohol demon. If it's lust, he has a lust demon. In fact, the list is long.

Trying so hard not to yield to the sin which he is committing, whatever it might be, he begins to believe these Preachers, thinking that he just might be demon-possessed. He is then encouraged to go to these Preachers, whoever they might be, and for them to lay hands on him and rebuke this demon spirit. From then on he will be free.

THE BIBLE

First of all, there is no precedent found in the Word of God for Christians being demon-possessed. You won't find Paul, or Peter, or others, laying hands on Christians and casting demons out of them. So, if there is no precedent for it in the Word of God, then it's unscriptural, meaning that such efforts will not help.

So, what is the problem and what is the solution?

The problem, as stated, is the sin nature that has, once again, become very active, which will become worse and worse, irrespective as to what the individual may try to do. In fact, the entirety of the Seventh Chapter of Romans proclaims Paul, before the Lord gave him the meaning of the Cross, attempting to live for God, but failing miserably, just the same.

Now, let's look at the answer.

THE CROSS

There is only one answer for sin, and that is the Cross of Christ (Heb. 10:12). When the Believer exercises his faith totally in Christ and what Christ did at the Cross, the Holy Spirit, Who works entirely within the parameters of the Finished Work of Christ, will then go to work in the heart and life of the Believer, bringing about the victory so long desired.

The Holy Spirit doesn't demand much of us; however, He does demand, and vigorously, that our faith ever be in Christ and what Christ has done for us at the Cross (Rom. 6:11). As stated, whenever the Holy Spirit through Paul proceeds to tell us how to live a victorious life, He takes us directly to the Cross (Rom. 6:3-5). In fact, we are to never leave the Cross. That's the reason that Paul also referred to the Finished Work of Christ as *"The Everlasting Covenant"* (Heb. 13:20). In other words, what Jesus did at the Cross is so right, so absolute, so perfect, that it will never have to be amended, will never fade away for something else to take its place, but will always stand as the triumph of victory, which, in effect, broke Satan's back. The actual statement is: at the Cross, Jesus bruised Satan's head, meaning that He bruised (destroyed) his headship, i.e., *"dominion,"* and did so by removing Satan's legal right, i.e., sin, to hold man in bondage. Once all sin was atoned, Satan lost that right, and is, therefore, rendered helpless (Col. 2:14-15).

So, the Cross of Christ is the answer to man's dilemma, whether it's the sinner being saved or the Christian being sanctified.

THE CRY OF DOOM

The phrase, *"And he cried out,"* refers to a terrible cry of impending doom. It was a member of one race of beings speaking through and by means of a member of the human race. This spirit saw in Christ Power far greater than his power of darkness; consequently, he knew it spelled his doom, at least regarding his habitation in this man. At the Name of Jesus, every power of darkness, irrespective as to what it might be, trembles, and for valid reason.

(24) "SAYING, LET US ALONE; WHAT HAVE WE TO DO WITH YOU, YOU JESUS OF NAZARETH? ARE YOU COME TO DESTROY US? I KNOW YOU WHO YOU ARE, THE HOLY ONE OF GOD."

The exposition is:

Demon spirits respond only to the Lord Jesus Christ. They immediately recognized His Power, His Supremacy, and His Victory.

A DEMONIC REQUEST

The phrase, *"Saying, Let us alone,"* represents the teaching and preaching of Jesus as having thrown the whole world of evil spirits into a state of alarm. Likewise, the True Proclamation of the Gospel will do the same presently.

In 1987, we were conducting a crusade in Monrovia, Liberia, in West Africa. The meeting was held in the Stadium, which seated approximately 50,000 people. That Sunday afternoon, the newspapers reported that well over 100,000 were present, although possibly they exaggerated. At any rate, the Stadium was completely filled, even with thousands standing in the infield.

As I began to minister, something took place which I had never encountered in all of my many years of Ministry. Two or three individuals began to bark like dogs in this vast Stadium, with thousands of others immediately beginning to take it up. Soon the Stadium was filled with a roar of what seemed like thousands of dogs barking, but which, in reality, were demon spirits.

Of course, it was impossible to continue to preach under such circumstances; consequently, I stopped, and addressed these spirits by saying, *"In the Name of Jesus, I command you to shut up!"* The results were astounding!

The barking stopped in an instant. It was as if a faucet was running water, and then someone turned it off instantly. Whereas the noise of the barking had filled the stadium, now there was nothing but silence. To be sure, it was not necessarily to me that this vast number of demon spirits responded, but, instead, to the Name of Jesus proclaimed by me.

That afternoon, thousands responded to the invitation to come to Christ. No doubt, as Christ came into these many lives, evil spirits also departed!

THE INTRUSION OF CHRIST

The question, *"What have we to do with You, Thou Jesus of Nazareth?"* means they resented the intrusion by Christ into their domain. As well, the question means that there was no association whatsoever between the world of Light, as represented by Jesus, and the world of darkness, as represented by these evil spirits. Incidentally, the pronoun *"we"* is used, denoting many demons in this man, headed up by a head or chief demon.

As well, *"Jesus of Nazareth"* is specified respecting this particular *"Jesus"*!

Actually, the demon would have said, *"Joshua of Nazareth,"* for Jesus is the Greek derivative of the Hebrew Joshua. As Joshua was a common name in Israel, Nazareth was specified, consequently denoting a specific *"Joshua,"* i.e., Jesus.

DESTROY THE WORKS OF THE DEVIL

The question, *"Are You come to destroy us? I know You Who You are, the Holy One of God,"* has reference to the fact that they possibly thought they were at once to be judged. They knew He had Power to do whatever He desired. These evil spirits knew Who He was, but the religious leaders of Israel did not know. Or, if the religious leaders of Israel did recognize Him as the Messiah, the Son of God, with there being some evidence that they did, yet in their apostasy, they rejected Him (Mat. 21:37-39).

(25) "AND JESUS REBUKED HIM, SAYING, HOLD YOUR PEACE, AND COME OUT OF HIM."

The overview is:

The Lord Jesus Christ has Power over all powers of darkness, meaning that they must obey Him.

THE REBUKE

The phrase, *"And Jesus rebuked Him,"* is interesting indeed! First of all, Jesus desired no acknowledgment from the Devil whatsoever; He, therefore, told him to *"shut up!"* As well, the word *"rebuked"* in the Greek is *"epitimao,"* which means a rebuke with no effort to bring the offender to the acknowledgment of his sin. In other words, Satan, fallen angels, and demons are incorrigible. They refuse to be convicted of their sin, and they will neither acknowledge it nor repent.

So, this one statement by Christ completely refutes the erroneous doctrine of

"Ultimate Reconciliation," which means that ultimately everything will be reconciled unto God, even demon spirits and Satan himself. The Bible in no way teaches such gross, blatant error, but actually the very opposite (Rev. 20:10).

Inasmuch as the Bible is the story of the Fall of man and his Redemption by Christ, only a little information is given concerning the Fall of Satan, along with his angels and spirits. Consequently, regarding their past opportunity to repent, we have no knowledge. And as here recorded, the die is cast, signifying that no reconciliation will ever be possible between God and Satan and the works of darkness.

HOLD YOUR PEACE

The phrase, *"Saying, Hold your peace,"* is glossed somewhat in the English translation. It should have been translated, *"Saying, Shut up!"* As we have stated, we can here gather something of the attitude of God towards Satan, fallen angels, demons, and the enormity of their sin.

DEMON SPIRITS OBEY CHRIST

The phrase, *"And come out of him,"* should have been translated, *"Shut up, and come out of him."* Both commands, *"Shut up,"* and *"Come out of him,"* are military in their usage. It would be the same as a General giving orders to a Private, which would instantly be obeyed. However, it is much greater than that, although there is no idiom in any language to properly convey the authority here used by Christ, and heard by the demon spirit. This demon spirit knows that Christ has absolute Power and can use it absolutely!

Consequently, the *"Name of Jesus,"* used according to the Word of God, and exclaimed by Mark, *"In My Name shall they cast out devils,"* expresses the same type of Power (Mk. 16:17).

(26) "AND WHEN THE UNCLEAN SPIRIT HAD TORN HIM, AND CRIED WITH A LOUD VOICE, HE CAME OUT OF HIM."

The synopsis is:

Demon spirits must obey the Lord, and in every respect. Only the Lord knows the number of unsaved people who are demon-possessed, exactly as this man here. As a result, they are controlled by these spirits, which have but one goal in mind, to *"steal, kill, and destroy"* (Jn. 10:10). So one can well imagine the convulsed state of such a person. And only the Lord can set them free. Humanistic psychology holds no answer, nor anything else the world might have, only Christ.

THE UNCLEAN SPIRIT

The phrase, *"And when the unclean spirit had torn him,"* means that the exit of this spirit was of a violent nature. It can be looked at in two ways:

1. The spirit was angry at having to leave out of the man, and consequently showed his displeasure, even when he was leaving, by his action against the man.

2. At the command of Christ, this spirit was so overcome by fear that he hastened to remove himself from this man with such speed that it caused convulsions. Luke, in his description, says, *"he came out of him, and hurt him not,"* emphasizing that the spirit was hastily trying to make his exit upon the command of Christ (Lk. 4:35). This, I think, is the correct interpretation.

FEAR OF CHRIST

The phrase, *"And cried with a loud voice, he came out of him,"* represents a screech of fear — fear of Christ, and fear not to obey Christ immediately! The spirit came out immediately.

HUMANISTIC PSYCHOLOGY

When the Church recommends humanistic psychology, do they actually believe that the prattle of man, and unredeemed man at that, is going to have any effect against spirits of darkness such as this? As a case in point, the world has witnessed the terrible problems of the Catholic Church, i.e., of homosexual Priests molesting little boys. Unfortunately, this problem is not confined to the Catholic Church, but is pandemic in other religious Denominations as well; however, due to the fact that the Catholic Priesthood is a haven for homosexuals, the problem there is much more acute, and for the obvious reasons.

To prove my point, the Catholic Church has the most qualified psychologists in the world in their ranks. Not believing at all in the Power of God, at least from a Scriptural basis, they have specialized in the psychological way. So, if humanistic psychology holds any answer whatsoever, why doesn't it prove effective in the Catholic Church, as it regards the problem at hand?

Well, of course, the answer is obvious in this, as well. Humanistic psychology holds no answer whatsoever. Only the Power of God can set the captive free. Paul said: *"The Preaching of the Cross is to them who perish foolishness, but unto us who are saved it is the Power of God"* (I Cor. 1:18).

HOW IS THE PREACHING OF THE CROSS THE POWER OF GOD?

Jesus Christ is the Source of all things that we receive from God, while the Cross is the means by which those things are given unto us. The Cross made it possible for the Holy Spirit to work mightily within our hearts and lives. This refers to the fact that what Jesus did there completely settled the sin debt, which makes it possible for the Spirit of God permanently to make His Habitation within the hearts and lives of Believers (Jn. 14:17).

The Power is registered in the Holy Spirit (Acts 1:8). When the Believer is baptized with the Holy Spirit and understands that all of this is made possible by the Cross, which means that the Cross of Christ is ever the Object of the Faith of such a Believer, the Holy Spirit can work mightily in such a one. The Lord has given the right and authority to any Spirit-filled Believer whose Faith is properly placed, and we continue to speak of the Cross, to cast out demons in the Name of Jesus (Mk. 16:17). This refers, as well, to driving away oppressive spirits which cause great problems with Christians.

PREACH DELIVERANCE

Jesus said: *"The Spirit of the Lord is upon Me, because He has anointed Me to preach the Gospel to the poor; He has sent Me to heal the brokenhearted, to preach deliverance to the captives, and recovering of sight to the blind, to set at liberty them who are bruised, to preach the acceptable Year of the Lord"* (Lk. 4:18-19). If it is to be noticed, the Lord said, *"Preach deliverance to the captives,"* which is a little different than to simply say, *"Deliver the captives."* While the former will definitely carry out the latter, if the former is not properly understood, the latter will not come to pass, either.

The trouble is, we have Preachers and others attempting to deliver people, when that's not what the Scripture says. We rather are to *"preach deliverance to the captives."* Now what does that mean? It means exactly what we are doing here, explaining how deliverance comes, which is always, and without exception, through Christ and the Cross. Jesus also said, *"And you shall know the Truth, and the Truth shall make you free"* (Jn. 8:32).

The Lord didn't say that people would be delivered by the means of manifestations, or anything of that nature. But that's exactly what the modern Church has by and large attempted to do. Preachers have insinuated that if they can lay hands on people, with them falling out under the power, they will then be delivered. While the laying on of hands is definitely Scriptural, and while, at times, the Lord definitely does strike someone down by His Power, still, if the man or woman doesn't know and understand the truth about their deliverance, which is Christ and the Cross, then the problem will very shortly be back, leaving such a Believer more confused than ever.

The reason is simple! Such people are making these manifestations the object of their faith, which is not Scriptural. While the manifestation itself definitely may be Scriptural, that is not the means by which the Lord delivers people. He wants Preachers to *"preach deliverance to the captives,"* which refers to the fact of them being told the truth as to why the problem, whatever it is, is there to begin with.

To be sure, Satan most definitely responds to the use of the Name of Jesus, but it must be understood by the Believer that this Name is not a magic wand that works its magic.

THE NAME OF JESUS

The very Name *"Jesus"* means *"Saviour."* And, of course, Jesus is Saviour by and through what He did at the Cross. The Cross is what effects Salvation, which makes it possible, because it was there that all sin was atoned, past, present, and future, at least for all who will believe (Jn. 3:16). It was at the Cross that all Satanic powers, including Satan himself, were defeated.

Listen to Paul: *"Blotting out the handwriting of ordinances that was against us* (the Law of Moses), *which was contrary to us* (the Law is like a mirror that shows man what he is, but gives him no power to change), *and took it out of the way* (satisfied its righteous demands), *nailing it to His Cross* (meaning that it was at the Cross where the victory was won);

"And having spoiled principalities and powers (every power of darkness, including Satan), *He* (Jesus) *made a show of them openly* (the entirety of the spirit world knows that Satan and his cohorts were totally defeated at Calvary), *triumphing over them in it* (His triumph was that He removed all sin by atoning for it, which removed Satan's legal right to hold man in captivity)" (Col. 2:14-15).

So it was at the Cross where every victory was won. When the Believer understands that, he will then know what the Name of Jesus actually means, and also understand the use of its power. Understanding that truth, then Deliverance is understood.

In these paragraphs, I am literally *"preaching deliverance to the captives."* Any and every Believer who reads these words, believes them, and acts upon them with his faith, meaning that his faith is exclusively in Christ and the Cross, such a Believer will begin to walk in Truth and will know Deliverance in every respect.

DELIVERANCE

It's a tragedy that most Christians actually need Deliverance. I speak of deliverance from works of the flesh of any and every capacity (Gal. 5:19-21). Instead of the Fruit of the Spirit being manifested in their lives (Gal. 5:22-23), conversely *"works of the flesh"* are manifested, which, to be sure, makes for a miserable Christian.

It would be bad enough were this the case with only a few, but when we realize that virtually the entirety of the modern Church has little understanding as it regards the Cross of Christ, then we know that most of modern Christendom is *"entangled again with the yoke of bondage"* (Gal. 5:1). As we have repeatedly stated in these paragraphs, their answer is not getting in a prayer line somewhere, with hands laid on them, as Scriptural as that might be in its own right. Their answer is in knowing the Truth of Christ and the Cross, exactly as we have given here, thereby, ever making that the Object of their Faith, which will guarantee their Victory. The Word of God says so!

"For sin (the sin nature) *shall not have dominion over you: for you are not under the Law, but under Grace"* (Rom. 6:14). The idea is, to be *"under Grace,"* the Believer must understand the Cross of Christ (Gal. 6:14). Otherwise, such a Believer will be under *"Law,"* whether he realizes it or not, which means that he is actually functioning in the realm of *"spiritual adultery,"* which the Lord can never bless (Rom. 7:1-4).

John said: *"And this is the victory that overcomes the world, even our Faith"* (I Jn. 5:4).

(27) "AND THEY WERE ALL AMAZED, INSOMUCH THAT THEY QUESTIONED AMONG THEMSELVES, SAYING, WHAT THING IS THIS? WHAT NEW DOCTRINE IS THIS? FOR WITH AUTHORITY COMMANDS HE EVEN THE UNCLEAN SPIRITS, AND THEY DO OBEY HIM."

The synopsis is:

Because of Jesus' revealed Power over the spirit world of darkness, it should have been obvious to the religious leaders of Israel that He was the Messiah; however, later they would accuse Him of casting out demons by the power of Satan, which, in effect, blasphemed the Holy Spirit. Such is the wicked heart of man, especially religious man.

AMAZED

The phrase, *"And they were all amazed,"* means that the onlookers were frightened, even terrified. The short, simple Command of Christ to this demon spirit, which had caused his immediate exit, and which was obvious to all, left the onlookers speechless at what they had seen, and even terrified at the Power exhibited. Let us emphasize again that the change which instantly came about in this man's life is indicative of what Jesus can do for any and all who dare to believe Him. His Power is instant and can effect the New Birth and the resultant instant change which man so desperately needs.

NEW DOCTRINE?

The phrase, *"Insomuch that they questioned among themselves, saying, What thing is this?"* means that they had begun to reason that anyone who could bring about such instant miracles must be the Promised Messiah, the True God; for He Alone by His Power could rule evil spirits in such a fashion. This was an animated, prolonged discussion about what they had just observed.

The *"new"* regarding *"doctrine"* doesn't refer to *"new"* in respect to time, but instead in comparison to the dry-as-dust droning of the Rabbis and Scribes. Someone has said, *"Compared to that droning, the teaching of Jesus was like the fragrance of a field of clover in the springtime; it was fresh with the dew of Heaven upon it."*

AUTHORITY

The phrase, *"For with authority commands He even the unclean spirits, and they do obey Him,"* reflects the Lord as having the hosts of Satan under His absolute Power at all times. Irrespective of their wickedness and evil, He can command them at will and they instantly obey Him.

Notice that the military word, *"commands,"* is used, once again speaking of an *"authority"* that is all-powerful, as well as all-knowing.

The words, *"They do obey Him,"* referring to the demon spirits, mean they do so forthwith, and without argument. While it is true that these spirits may, at certain times, seek a particular disposition, such as the account of them requesting that they be allowed to go into the swine, still, there was no doubt as to their obedience (Mk. 5:10-13). With this one exhibition of Power, and especially the manner in which it was used, all present had absolutely no doubt as to Who Jesus was, the Messiah of Israel!

AUTHORITY OF THE BELIEVER

In the last few years, the Church has heard much about *"the authority of the Believer,"* with, I'm afraid, most of what they've heard being wrong. To make it very simple, Believers, and we speak of Spirit-filled Believers, definitely do have spiritual authority.

Now what does that mean?

It refers exclusively to authority over the spirit world of darkness (Mk. 16:17-18; Jn. 15:7; Mk. 11:23-24; Mat. 21:21-22). However, two things must be considered:

1. First of all, this *"spiritual authority"* is to be registered only against the spirits of darkness regarding the spirit world, and never against other human beings. Some have the idea that since they have been elected to a particular office in a Denomination, this gives them spiritual authority over those in that Denomination. It doesn't! As stated, no human being on this Earth has any type of spiritual authority over another human being.

Jesus addressed this by saying, *"You know that the princes of the Gentiles exercise dominion over them, and they who are great exercise authority upon them.*

"But it shall not be so among you: but whosoever will be great among you, let him be your minister (servant)*"* (Mat. 20:25-26).

Also concerning this, Paul said, *"Owe no man anything, but to love one another"* (Rom. 13:8). The first seven Verses of this Chapter in Romans speak to civil authority, to which the Believer must acquiesce, providing it is not a violation of his conscience. But when it comes to Brothers and Sisters in the Lord, Paul here plainly says that we do not owe them such submission, but only love. To be sure, if we properly love our Brother and Sister in the Lord, we will never do anything to hurt them.

2. The Will of God: spiritual authority by the Believer can never be used to circumvent the Will of God. It is always subservient to the Will of God. It is *"His Will be done,"* not *"my will be done"* (Mat. 6:10).

(28) "AND IMMEDIATELY HIS FAME SPREAD ABROAD THROUGHOUT ALL THE REGION ROUND ABOUT GALILEE."

The composition is:

As we have stated, there was absolutely no reason as to why the religious leaders of Israel did not know that Jesus was the Messiah.

Why didn't they know?

In the first place, He didn't fit their stereotype. And that's the reason most people do not receive from the Lord. As the Jews didn't like Christ, likewise, most modern Believers simply do not approve of the one the Lord uses. So, tragically, they miss what God is doing.

FAME

The phrase, *"And immediately His fame spread abroad,"* refers to word-of-mouth, but with great haste. In other words, everybody was talking about what Jesus had done and was doing! In these conversations, no doubt, the question of His Messiahship was discussed constantly.

There has never been, even remotely, a Ministry like that of Christ. He healed all who came to Him, irrespective as to who they were or the degree of their malady. Likewise, He delivered all who came to Him, irrespective of the degree of their bondage. His life was impeccable, His Ministry was perfect, and He fulfilled all the Scriptures concerning His Person. So there was no excuse for the religious leaders of Israel not to know.

GALILEE

The phrase, *"Throughout all the region round about Galilee,"* mostly spoke, at least at this time, of lower Galilee. This would have included the western shore of the Sea of Galilee, to Nazareth and Cana in the east, and down to Nain in the South. This was the beginning of His Ministry, with His fame spreading to the entirety of Israel a short time later, which would infuriate the religious leaders of Israel.

The Prophet Isaiah had spoken nearly 800 years before of this moment by saying, *". . . beyond Jordan, in Galilee of the nations. The people who walked in darkness have seen a great light: they who dwell in the land of the shadow of death, upon them has the light shined"* (Isa. 9:1-2).

(29) "AND FORTHWITH, WHEN THEY (Jesus and those with Him) WERE COME OUT OF THE SYNAGOGUE, THEY ENTERED INTO THE HOUSE OF SIMON AND ANDREW, WITH JAMES AND JOHN."

The diagram is:

This Synagogue was in Capernaum and, more than likely, the home of Peter became His Headquarters.

THE HOME OF SIMON PETER

The indication is that Jesus, at this time, only had four Disciples, or else these were the only Disciples which were involved in this particular incident concerning Peter's wife's mother.

I have personally been, several times, at the ruins of Capernaum. Due to the excavations, they know where the Synagogue sat. It is believed that Peter's house was very near, actually hard by the Sea of Galilee. Even though He was raised in Nazareth, it is obvious here that Jesus made His Headquarters in Capernaum, which was about 30 miles northeast of Nazareth. He didn't make His Headquarters in Nazareth for several reasons, the least not being, as He said, *"A Prophet is not without honor, but in his own country, and among his own kin, and his own house"* (Mk. 6:4).

(30) "BUT SIMON'S WIFE'S MOTHER LAY SICK OF A FEVER, AND ANON THEY TELL HIM OF HER."

The overview is:

This was to prove to be a great day in the home of Simon Peter, in that his mother-in-law would be instantly and completely healed by the Power of God. Jesus never enters a home but that He makes it far, far better! In fact, no home is truly a home without Christ.

SICKNESS

The phrase, *"But Simon's wife's mother lay sick of a fever,"* means that she had been sick for some time, was actually burning up with fever, and had taken to her bed, unable to rise.

Sickness is a result of the Fall, which means that it was never intended or meant to be by God. In fact, by virtue of the eating of the fruit of the *"Tree of Life,"* which was in the Garden, man was destined to *"live forever"* (Gen. 3:22). This means that man would not grow old, but would remain vigorous and healthy forever. But that was destroyed by the entrance of death, which was a result of the Fall (Gen. 2:17). The *"death"* spoken of here by the Lord had to do with spiritual death, which is separation from God; however, spiritual death also opened the door for *"physical death."*

Medical Science claims that the organs of the physical body should last forever. They claim that approximately every seven years the physical body rejuvenates itself, which should stop the aging process, but doesn't. No doubt this is what the Lord intended for the original human body to be and do; however, as stated, the Fall stopped this. Medical Science really doesn't really understand why the human body ages, which is what brings on death. The reason they don't understand it is because the problem is not physical, but rather spiritual.

Concerning all of this, the Scripture says, *"Wherefore, as by one man sin entered into the world* (by Adam), *and death by sin* (both spiritual and physical death); *and so death passed upon all men* (for all were in Adam), *for that all have sinned* (all are born in sin, because of Adam's transgression)" (Rom. 5:12).

However, there is coming a day when sickness will be no more. Every Saint of God will have a Glorified Body, which will be similar to the Body had by Christ when He was raised from the Dead. As well, in the coming Kingdom Age, those with natural bodies will stay youthful and healthy by partaking of the fruit and the leaves growing on the trees beside the river flowing from under the Sanctuary (I Cor. 15:28; Ezek. 47:1, 12).

THE REQUEST

The phrase, *"And anon* (immediately) *they tell Him of her,"* means that they immediately made Jesus aware of her serious condition. Luke speaks of Jesus standing over her like a doctor, which is exactly what He was — the Great Physician!

In all of this, Peter's wife is not mentioned, although Paul intimates that Peter was a married man and that his wife accompanied him on his missionary tours (I Cor. 9:5). According to the testimony of Clement of Alexandria and of Eusebius, Peter's wife suffered martyrdom, and was led away to death in the sight of her husband, whose last words to her were: *"Remember thou the Lord."*

(31) "AND HE CAME AND TOOK HER BY THE HAND, AND LIFTED HER UP; AND IMMEDIATELY THE FEVER LEFT HER, AND SHE MINISTERED UNTO THEM."

The overview is:

We will learn some things about sickness from this particular Verse of Scripture.

HE REBUKED THE FEVER

The phrase, *"And He came and took her by the hand, and lifted her up,"* means that He stood over her, and, as Luke also said, *"He rebuked the fever"* (Lk. 4:39). The same word *"rebuked"* is used here as is used in Verse 25, when Jesus rebuked the unclean spirit. The indication is: this *"fever"* could very well have been, and no doubt was, caused by a demon spirit; however, this doesn't mean that Peter's mother-in-law was demon-possessed, as was the man, for she was not.

Even though all sickness is not directly caused by demon spirits, all sickness has, as its origin, demon spirits. This means that many sicknesses can be treated successfully by proper medicines (Ezek. 47:12; Rev. 22:2), but some, as here, will not respond to such treatment and must be *"rebuked,"* as Jesus did here. In fact, he rebuked the spirit causing the *"fever,"* which refers to *"oppression"* (Acts 10:38). In other words, Believers cannot be demon-possessed, but they definitely can be *"demon-oppressed,"* as here.

This spirit was no doubt trying to kill her with this *"fever,"* as evil spirits seek to kill many Believers. They, at times, may even succeed, especially considering that many Believers, even Preachers, do not properly understand the spirit world as they should.

MINISTRY

The phrase, *"She ministered unto them,"* means, most probably, that she began to prepare a meal for them, which also means that she was healed immediately. She did not improve by degrees, but instead was well instantly!

As stated, Jesus healed everyone instantly. In the four Gospels, there is no such thing as Him healing someone gradually. Every healing was instant, or else took no more than a few moments. But yet, presently, and due to human involvement, it is quite possible that healings from the Lord might be gradual.

A PERSONAL HEALING

If I remember correctly, I was about 10 years old. The doctors were never able to find out what was wrong with me, even though my parents took me to several doctors.

I stayed nauseous almost constantly, and, at times, I would simply go unconscious. In fact, this happened several times at school, which I can only vaguely remember. On the last occasion this happened, my parents were called. I remember the school principal telling them, *"Something is going to have to be done for Jimmy, or else, you're going to have to take him out of school."* His exact words then were: *"We don't want him dying on our hands."*

As stated, my Mother and Dad had already taken me to several doctors, and they were unable to find out what was wrong. It wasn't malaria, or anything else that was quite common in those days. In other words, they ruled those things out.

It is my personal belief that whatever it was, the Devil was trying to kill me, knowing that the Lord had called me to preach His Gospel, and that He would use me to touch many people in the world for Christ. At any rate, I had been prayed for many times by the Pastor and others, but to no avail. As to why the Lord didn't heal me at those particular times, and why the healing came in the manner it did, for that I have no answer.

THE DAY OF THE HEALING

It was Sunday. My Mother and Dad were taking the Pastor and his wife for lunch after Service. Of course, my younger sister, Jeanette, and I were along. But before lunch, they went by the home of a particular parishioner, to pray for the person in question. We all went back into the bedroom where the individual was, with prayer being offered up. Then we came back to the living room. All of us were standing in the living room, and I was near the door. We were preparing to leave, as stated, to go have lunch.

My Dad requested of our Pastor, Brother Culbreth, that he should pray for me. Then my Dad stated, *"If the Lord doesn't do something, we're going to have to take Jimmy out of school."* The same Pastor, as stated, had prayed for me any number of times before this moment. Why this moment had special validity, I cannot honestly say.

Brother Culbreth had a bottle of oil in his hands, which he had just used to pray for the brother in question. He smiled, walked across the room, and touched my forehead with his finger, which had a little oil from the bottle, and began to pray. So did everyone else in the room.

I felt it instantly! It was like a ball of flame about the size of my fist, going down my back all the way from my head, slowly going through my physical body, down even to my feet. I felt it every inch of the way, and I knew, beyond the shadow of a doubt, that I was healed. And so I was!

I never had another problem with that situation, and still have not unto this hour. As I write these notes, in October of 2004, I will be 70 years old on March 15, 2005. In all of these years, I very rarely have been sick. I had what is referred to as *"walking pneumonia,"* some years ago, but it quickly passed. Also, I had a heart stint placed in one of my arteries in February of 2001. As I dictate these notes, I feel excellent, I am in excellent health, and I give the Lord all the praise and glory.

THE BALL OF FIRE

As I've stated, I don't know why the Lord didn't heal me the first time our Pastor prayed, which was some months before the Lord actually healed me. But of this much I am glad:

Thank God that we attended a Church which had a Godly Pastor, who believed in Divine Healing, and who also believed that if the answer didn't come immediately, we were to keep asking, which we did. Had it not been for those simple things, I might not be here today.

Furthermore, why the Lord chose to use a manifestation as He did, and I speak of the *"ball of fire"* which went down through my body, which is the best I can describe it, of that I have no explanation. To receive healing, such doesn't have to be; however, that's what happened to me. As stated, I was instantly healed. When I went with my parents to lunch that day, I knew that I would never have that problem again, and so I haven't!

Let me say it again: I give the Lord all the praise and glory, for that which He did so long ago!

(32) "AND AT EVENING, WHEN THE SUN DID SET, THEY BROUGHT UNTO HIM ALL WHO WERE DISEASED, AND THEM WHO WERE POSSESSED WITH DEVILS (demons)."

The synopsis is:

When the news spread, as it did regarding the Deliverance of the man in the Synagogue, and also of the healing of Peter's wife's mother, all the sick began to come to Him, and rightly so!

THE DISEASED

The phrase, *"And at evening, when the sun did set, they brought unto Him all who were diseased,"* has reference to the fact that it was Saturday, and, therefore, the Sabbath, which ended at sunset.

The Jewish reckoning of the 24-hour day, in fact, was somewhat different than ours presently. The new day begins for us at 12 o'clock midnight, whereas the new day then began at sunset. So, in their reckoning, their Sunday began at approximately 6 p.m. on what we refer to as Saturday evening.

The phrase, *"They brought unto Him all who were diseased,"* means that the people could now go about and bring the sick and diseased to Jesus, inasmuch as the Sabbath was now past. (The people were very limited as to what they could do on the Sabbath, due to the many rules made up by the Scribes and Pharisees, with which Jesus was constantly coming into conflict, because of His healing on this day.)

The *"diseased"* consisted of any and all types of sicknesses, ailments, afflictions, and diseases. The words, *"they brought,"* mean that the people were carrying the sick in a steady stream to Jesus. As stated, they no doubt had heard of the Deliverance of the man in the Synagogue and the healing of Peter's mother-in-law.

Moreover, it is said that Tiberias, which was about 10 miles south of Capernaum, contained hot mineral baths, which were claimed to have certain curative properties; consequently, the sick came from all over Israel to this place. No doubt, therefore, quite a few of these people made their way to Jesus, with every need being met.

How much good the health spa did is anyone's guess; however, for those who came to Jesus, which no doubt were many, they were not merely *"helped,"* but totally healed.

DEMON POSSESSION

The phrase, *"And them who were possessed with devils,"* should have been translated *"demons."* This was probably the result of the man who had been delivered hours earlier in the Synagogue. All through the Gospels, attention is given repeatedly to the extremely high number of individuals who were demon-possessed, and who then were delivered by Christ.

The Book of Acts and the Epistles do not record such activity with nearly the frequency as the Gospels.

Why?

There are possibly several reasons for this:

1. Some have suggested that due to the Advent of Christ, demon spirits congregated in Israel to oppose Him. While this is possible, it is doubtful that they would have done such a thing, due to His Mighty Power, over which they would have had no defense.

2. Israel had opened herself up to a tremendous influx of demon spirits, due to her heavy religious activity, which was a departure from the Word of God. Religion is man-made and man-devised; consequently, it is not of God. As such, it is fostered and nurtured by demon spirits.

Wherever false religions are predominant, as Judaism had become, there is, therefore, a heavy activity of demon spirits. Such is the case in Central and South America, with its heavy domination by Catholicism. The same could be said for Mexico, or anywhere in the world for that matter, where Catholicism is predominant.

The same can be said for the areas where Islam, Hinduism, Shintoism, or Buddhism dominate. These areas are rife with demon activity. The same can be said for Africa, Haiti, and other such countries, where demon spirits openly are worshipped.

In America, Canada, and other countries where true Bible Christianity has at least some influence, the activity is less, although increasing because the Word of God in these countries is being preached less and less!

(33) "AND ALL THE CITY WAS GATHERED TOGETHER AT THE DOOR."

The structure is:

This is but a small example of what will take place in the coming Kingdom Age, when the entirety of the world, in one way or the other, will come to Jesus. The results then will be the same as that occasioned in the Scripture of our study.

THE GATHERING

The word *"all"* doesn't literally mean everybody, but does refer to *"all"* who needed the touch of Christ. Their being *"gathered together at the door"* means that they came to the door of Peter's home, with the determination to remain there until Jesus healed and delivered them. It must have been quite a sight!

Let it ever be said: all who truly come to Christ, and who truly believe, will most definitely be healed spiritually, and many times physically, as well.

I grieve, as any True Believer does, realizing that most of mankind simply will not come to Him that they might have life. Just this morning, I heard a speaker for the United Nations stating that if they were given more money, they could solve the problems of the world. How foolish! All of humanity keeps attempting man-devised solutions, which, in reality, are no solutions at all, and which, upon implementation, automatically reveal their inherent uselessness.

Regrettably, and as stated, the modern Church holds up humanistic psychology as a solution for the behavior problems of man. It is tragic when most of the Church will not recognize Jesus as the Answer to the problems of humanity; however, the so-called Church in Jesus' day did the same thing, rejecting Him and holding up their religion as the answer for man's dilemma! Consequently, the more things change, the more they stay the same!

(34) "AND HE HEALED MANY WHO WERE SICK OF DIVERS DISEASES, AND CAST OUT MANY DEVILS (demons); AND SUFFERED NOT THE DEVILS (demons) TO SPEAK, BECAUSE THEY KNEW HIM."

The exegesis is:

What a day of blessing this was for the city of Capernaum, and what a day of blessing it is for any city where Jesus Christ is proclaimed. When this great Gospel was brought to our little town of Ferriday, Louisiana, my whole family would find Christ, which, without a doubt, would be the greatest thing that every happened to us.

HEALINGS AND DELIVERANCES

The phrase, *"And He healed many who were sick of divers diseases, and cast out many demons,"* does not mean, respecting numbers, what it seems to mean on the surface. He actually healed all, which were *"many"*! *"Divers diseases"* spoke of many and varied types of diseases, and of every kind. In other words, it didn't matter what type of disease it was, or how serious it was, all were healed!

Moreover, every single person who was demon-possessed and who came to Him was delivered. He cast out all, which were *"many"*! Not one person who came sick, went away sick. Likewise, not one person who came demon-possessed, went away in that condition. All were healed and delivered!

As we've already stated, this is the way it will be in the coming Kingdom Age.

THE WITNESS OF DEMONS NOT ACCEPTED

The phrase, *"And suffered not the devils (demons) to speak,"* means the demons clamored to be heard. To be sure, as the evil spirit of Verse 24 said positive things, no doubt these would have, as well! However, the Lord, as is here obvious, had no interest in whatever they said, irrespective as to what it was.

The phrase, *"Because they knew Him,"* means they knew Him to be the Messiah; nevertheless, to have them screaming such information, irrespective of its Truth, was not something desired. Truth in the mouth of a liar becomes, at least in some form, a lie!

(35) "AND IN THE MORNING, RISING UP A GREAT WHILE BEFORE DAY, HE WENT OUT, AND DEPARTED INTO A SOLITARY PLACE, AND THERE PRAYED."

The composition is:

Mark, as possibly no other of the Gospels,

gives us insight into the Master's personal habits, along with His occupation. It's a lesson we should take to heart, and avidly learn.

PRAYER

The phrase, *"And in the morning, rising up a great while before day,"* concerns the last watch of the night, which was between 3 a.m. and 6 a.m. So, this was probably about 4 a.m. This was done after a very heavy evening of healing the sick and casting out demons, which could have lasted well until near midnight, or even later.

The phrase, *"He went out, and departed into a solitary place, and there prayed,"* portrays an example for all, and in many ways.

1. He set the example of a strong prayer life, which was a habit with Him (Mat. 14:23; Mk. 1:35; 6;46; Lk. 6:12; 9:28; 11:1). It is absolutely impossible for any Believer, and especially Preachers, to know the Mind of God without having a strong prayer life. This is, to say the least, imperative!

Unfortunately, in the last few years, the *"Confession Message"* has pretty much eliminated intercessory prayer. People have been led to believe they can confess their loved ones to Christ, or confess their consecration into being, etc. However, we should stop to think that if Jesus or the Apostles did not employ such theology, then quite possibly it just might not be Scriptural, at least in this manner.

In fact, even though a proper confession is important, and should be diligently practiced, still, absolutely nothing can take the place of intercessory prayer. If Jesus practiced such, and had to do so, as is here obvious, where does that leave those of us who are supposed to *"follow Him"*?

2. He set the example of looking entirely to His Heavenly Father, giving little thought to the accolades of the crowd. In no way did man make His decisions, or even influence them. He was led strictly by His Heavenly Father.

3. He set the example of finding the Will of God and following it, which, in this instance, pertained to His first preaching mission respecting an Evangelistic tour, as the next Verses proclaim.

A PERSONAL PRAYER LIFE

When I was eight years old, the Lord saved me. A few weeks after my Salvation experience, I was baptized with the Holy Spirit, with the evidence of speaking with other tongues, as the Spirit of God gives the utterance (Acts 2:4). During those formative years, I was in a prayer meeting almost every day of my life, at least during the summer months, when I wasn't in school. My Grandmother taught me to pray, taught me to believe God, and taught me that God answers prayer. One of her great statements to me, which she made any number of times, was: *"Jimmy, God is a big God, so ask big!"*

Concerning some of the things I've had to face, had it not been for my prayer life, I don't think I would have made it.

In October of 1991, at a crisis time in the Ministry, the Lord instructed me to begin two prayer meetings a day. He told me that I should seek Him, not so much for what He could do, but rather for Who He is. Thankfully, I was faithful to the admonition of the Lord. For approximately 10 years, a small group of us met every morning at 10 a.m. and every evening at 6:30 p.m., with the exception of Saturday morning and Sunday. In fact, I personally continue to hold to this regimen, even unto this hour. I will continue until the Lord comes or until He calls me home.

It is impossible to have a proper relationship with the Lord without a proper prayer life. If every Believer would dedicate a few minutes each day, seeking the Face of the Lord, telling Him our needs, and asking His Leading and Guidance, and would be faithful with that quest, everything would run much smoother. Tragically, the modern Church is not a praying Church.

In fact, at the great Azuza Street outpouring of the early 1900's, a prophecy was given, which stated, *"The Church will come to the place that it praises Me, but no longer prays to Me."* Let's say it in this way. Considering that Jesus had to pray, Who was Perfect, and Who had a Perfect Relationship with His Father in Heaven, where does that leave us?

(36) "AND SIMON AND THEY WHO WERE WITH HIM FOLLOWED AFTER HIM."

The diagram is:

To follow Jesus is the greatest privilege that anyone could ever have. I have followed

Him now for some 61 years. He is truly a Friend Who sticks closer than a Brother.

FOLLOWING JESUS

At some point after Jesus had left Peter's house, having gone out that early morning hour to pray, He was missed. Their *"following after Him"* meant that they sought Him out. Exactly how they were able to find Him is anyone's guess. Maybe they had an idea where He had gone, possibly having overheard Him speak of this *"solitary place."* It was probably on the outskirts of this small town, perhaps even close to the Lake.

The group seeking Him would have been Peter, Andrew, James, John, and possibly others.

(37) "AND WHEN THEY HAD FOUND HIM, THEY SAID UNTO HIM, ALL MEN SEEK FOR YOU."

The overview is:

The pronoun *"You"* is emphatic, meaning that those who sought Jesus would not be satisfied with only seeing His Disciples.

SEEKING JESUS

The phrase, *"And when they had found Him,"* implies that they had to look for a period of time. The phrase, *"They said unto Him, All men seek for You,"* means that individuals were seeking for Him at that very moment. Even at that early morning hour close to daylight, the sick were at Peter's door to be healed.

Inasmuch as scores had been healed a few hours earlier, they had no doubt told many others about their joyful experience. This would have precipitated many who were sick in going to the home of Peter, even at daylight. It was not a question that maybe they would be healed or delivered, but of a certainty, at least if they could be in His Presence.

However, it seems that Jesus, as important as this was, knew that it was more important for Him to be Alone with the Father for a period of time in prayer. Consequently, He would leave Peter's home at a very early hour for this all-important task.

(38) "AND HE SAID UNTO THEM, LET US GO INTO THE NEXT TOWNS, THAT I MAY PREACH THERE ALSO: FOR THEREFORE CAME I FORTH."

The composition is:

This Servant made healing subordinate to preaching. He left Capernaum. Had He stayed there, He would have established Himself as a Healer of diseases. But He came to Earth to preach and to die; and He allowed nothing to hinder Him in this double purpose.

THE SPREAD OF THE GOSPEL

The phrase, *"And He said unto them, Let us go into the next towns,"* implies that He had heard from Heaven and had been given direction respecting what to do and where to go. This is beautiful, and, as we have stated, sets an example for all who follow Christ to be minutely directed by the Lord, which can come about only by intercessory prayer.

According to Josephus, Galilee was a densely populated district, with upwards of 200 villages and towns, each containing from several hundreds to several thousands of inhabitants.

This is the reason that we plead for help regarding our Radio and Television Ministry, actually that which the Lord has called us to do. The *"next towns"* must have the opportunity to know, as well.

THE TRUE GOSPEL

I realize that both American Television and Radio are basically glutted with Gospel Programming, so-called; however, the extent of Programming which is true and Biblical is very little. In other words, the percentage of Programming which is truly Biblical is so small as to be almost nonexistent.

Many of the Programmers repudiate the Baptism with the Holy Spirit, with the evidence of speaking with other tongues, which means they are powerless. The best they can do, even if they do preach some truth, is to appeal to the intellect of the individuals who listen to them. In such Ministries, the Holy Spirit is given very little opportunity to function; consequently, many of the adherents of these Ministries, whoever they might be, are religious only, which means they aren't actually Born-Again.

And then we have the *"shyster"* element, which is there for money, irrespective as to what type of face they may try to put on their programming.

In the midst of all of this, false doctrine is rampant. The truth is, if Preachers aren't preaching the Cross, pure and simple, while they may be, more or less, preaching *about* the Gospel, they simply aren't preaching the Gospel.

Jesus said: *"And I, if I be lifted up from the Earth, will draw all men unto Me. This He said, signifying what death He should die"* (Jn. 12:32-33). Jesus being *"lifted up"* refers to His Death at Calvary; He was *"lifted up"* on the Cross, which means that the Cross is the foundation of all victory.

Concerning the Scripture, *"This He said, signifying what death He should die,"* Reynolds says, *"In these Words, we learn that the attraction of the Cross of Christ will prove to be the mightiest and most sovereign motive ever brought to bear on the human will, and, when wielded by the Holy Spirit as a Revelation of the matchless Love of God, will involve the most sweeping judicial sentence that can be pronounced upon the world and its prince, who is Satan."*

While we certainly aren't the only ones preaching the True Gospel, the fact remains, as stated, that the actual number of true Preachers is abysmally small. That's the reason I plead for funds to help us take this Message of the Cross to others. I know this is their only hope; there is no other!

PREACHING

The phrase, *"That I may preach there also: for therefore came I forth,"* proclaims healing and Deliverance as being very important, but secondary to the *"preaching"* of the Word. All of this refers to Him coming from Heaven, carrying out the Plan of God in order to redeem fallen humanity. His every step was governed by the Holy Spirit, with the Spirit of God even directing the thrust of His Message (Lk. 4:18-19).

(39) "AND HE PREACHED IN THEIR SYNAGOGUES THROUGHOUT ALL GALILEE, AND CAST OUT DEVILS."

The diagram is:

The order of the Ministry of Christ was to proclaim the *"Good News"* of the Gospel, which would set captives free from the domain of darkness. Satan holds humanity in bondage, and there is only one thing that will set them free, and that is the *"Truth"* of the Gospel (Jn. 8:32).

PREACHING AND DELIVERANCE

The phrase, *"And He preached in their Synagogues throughout all Galilee,"* does not mean that He preached in every Synagogue, but rather in a different Synagogue every Sabbath. How so much these towns and villages must have buzzed with excitement, as Jesus began to heal the sick and cast out devils, as well as proclaiming the Gospel in a manner they had never heard before.

The phrase, *"And cast out devils,"* actually refers to demons. That does not mean that's all He did, but that along with *"preaching"* and *"healing,"* he continued to perform this work. Mark is letting us know that the *"casting out of demons"* was a constant part of the Ministry of Christ. This signals the fact that Israel was in a terrible spiritual condition at this time, which, as well, affected them in every other way!

What joy must have filled the hearts of those who were delivered! The torment they had experienced was now gone! And all because of Jesus.

(40) "AND THERE CAME A LEPER TO HIM, BESEECHING HIM, AND KNEELING DOWN TO HIM, AND SAYING UNTO HIM, IF YOU WILL, YOU CAN MAKE ME CLEAN."

The overview is:

The leper kneeling down before Christ was not merely a rendering of honor to an Earthly being; it was a rendering of reverence to a Divine Being. Leprosy was so loathsome that the leper didn't know if Jesus would heal him or not, even though he knew that Jesus had the Power.

THE LEPER

The phrase, *"And there came a leper to Him, beseeching Him, and kneeling down to Him,"* proclaims an extremely important episode in the Ministry of Christ. This healing would deal with the particular man; however, even more importantly, it would serve as a symbol of Christ dealing with the even more horrible effect of sin, of which leprosy was a type.

This *"leper,"* as Luke describes him, was *"full of leprosy"* (Lk. 5:12), which meant it had spread over his entire body. He was leprous from head to foot. This also meant that he was in the last stages, even near death. Quite possibly, and even likely, body parts, such as fingers, toes, or even his nose or lips, had been eaten away. This happened often regarding lepers who were in the last stage of this disease. It is also stated that most of these were filled with an odor that was unbearable!

This awful thing, for which there was no human cure, was meant as a type of sin, as proclaimed in the Old Testament. The revolting appearance of this disease was meant to serve as a symbol of what it represented, the terrible spiritual death of sin. It was cured, as sin is cured, only by the Mercy and Favor of God. No wonder, then, that our Lord especially displayed His Power over this terrible malady, that He might thus prove His Power over the still worse malady of sin.

The phrase, *"Beseeching Him,"* means to plead. The Mosaic Law stated that the leper must remain about 100 feet away from any and all contact with fellow human beings. If he approached any closer, he could be stoned! Therefore, his approaching Christ proclaimed his absolute desperation.

No doubt it had come to his ears concerning the miracle-working Power of Jesus. Consequently, he was determined to approach Christ, even if it meant his life. He felt he had nothing to lose!

There is no way that one can comprehend the pain and suffering this poor wretch had endured. He was dying and he knew it; however, his death would not be pleasant or easy. In fact, it would be one of the most horrible deaths that one could ever die. He was actually dying by degrees and by the hour.

This incident is so important that it is recorded by Matthew, Mark, and Luke. His kneeling down before Christ is expressed by Matthew with the phrase, *"he worshipped Him"* (Mat. 8:2). Luke said, *". . . who seeing Jesus fell on his face"* (Lk. 5:12), which probably was after he had knelt, as recorded by Mark.

THE CLEANSING OF THE LEPER

The phrase, *"And saying unto Him, If You will, You can make me clean,"* refers to the fact that he knew Jesus was able to do this thing. He had probably heard others who had had terrible diseases, but who had been instantly healed by Christ. How this information came to his ears, considering he was a leper and not allowed to mix with people, is not known. At any rate, the indication is that he knew Who Jesus was, and what Jesus could do! So, he does not question His Power, only His Will!

This was done for the following reason:

His disease was so awful, with him actually being in the final stages, even near death! As well, and which he well knew, leprosy was looked at as a curse of God, and, as such, most of Israel did not even believe a leper could be saved. There was nothing more horrible, therefore, than for a person to be told by a Priest: *"you have leprosy."* It meant his death warrant and a horrible death, at that, as well as being spiritually cursed.

THE CONDITION OF THE LEPER

The leper was not doomed so much for what he did, as for what he was. That presents man's basic problem. While he might try to address what he does, he little addresses what he is, because he doesn't really believe he is what God actually says he is.

And what does the Bible actually say?

"There is none righteous, no, not one:

"There is none who understands, there is none who seeks after God.

"They are all gone out of the way, they are together become unprofitable; there is none who does good, no, not one.

"Their throat is an open sepulcher; with their tongues they have used deceit; the poison of asps is under their lips:

"Whose mouth is full of cursing and bitterness:

"Their feet are swift to shed blood:

"Destruction and misery are in their ways:

"And the way of peace have they not known:

"There is no fear of God before their eyes" (Rom. 3:10-18).

What you've just read is what man actually is, and is typified by the leper.

THE CROSS IS THE ONLY ANSWER FOR SIN

If men do not preach the Cross, then they

offer no cure for sin; because sin is not merely a surface condition, but rather is a product of the very vitals of the human being, his soul and his spirit. Unless the Preacher proclaims the Cross, which alone is the answer, then the following illustration pretty well describes what he is doing.

THE SOURCE

If a pump is pumping poisoned water, it won't do any good to dress up the pump. You can paint the pump, even change out the pump with a more decorative design, or even make one of precious metal. You can plant a garden around the pump, with all types of beautiful flowers growing, which is very pleasant to the eyes. However, none of that will have any effect on the water that comes from the depths, and for all the obvious reasons. To cure the poisoned water, one has to go to the source. Calvary alone went to the source of sin, which is Satan himself (Col. 2:14-15).

But what do we have presently?! We have all types of pump-decorators, seemingly oblivious to the fact that the water is still poisoned. In fact, man, within himself, has absolutely nothing that can solve this problem. There is only one solution, and that is *"Jesus Christ and Him Crucified"* (I Cor. 1:23).

At the time of this writing (2004), the Church world has embraced completely the *"Purpose Driven Life"* scheme. To date, the book has sold over 15 million copies, with Churches of every stripe attempting to put into practice this false doctrine — and false doctrine it is!

The other scheme which seems to get a hearing among many Churches is the *"Government of Twelve"* theory. These two, along with the *"Word of Faith"* doctrine, pretty well dominate the Church scene. All three, as stated, are false.

And how can I be so sure that these things are false?

THE ELIMINATION OF THE CROSS OF CHRIST

The *"Word of Faith"* doctrine openly repudiates the Cross. It refers to it as *"past miseries"* and *"the worst defeat in human history."* It claims that redemption is brought

NOTES

about by Jesus dying as a sinner, even demon-possessed, on the Cross and going down into the burning side of Hell, even as all sinners go to Hell. There He was tormented for three days and nights, they say, when God then said, *"It is enough,"* with Jesus then being *"born again,"* as any sinner is born again, etc. He was then raised from the dead, which means, according to their teaching, that the great Redemption Plan was completed in, of all places, Hell.

No matter how hard you look, you won't find a shred of this in the Word of God. In other words, it is made up of out of whole cloth. That being the case, how is it that this doctrine has such an appeal?

Its great appeal is its claim of Faith, which will make people rich. In other words, it appeals to greed. Unfortunately, there seems to be a modicum of greed in all of us. Of course, the only ones getting rich are the Preachers.

The *"Purpose Driven Life/Church"* teaching is, pure and simple, a moral essay. It tells the person that they can better themselves by following the teaching outlined in these particular books. Never mind that there is no such thing as moral evolution, man seems to keep trying, especially religious man. This *"angel of light"* completely ignores the Cross (II Cor. 11:13-15).

The *"Government of Twelve"* claims to preach the Cross, as it regards Salvation; but then they revert strictly to Law, as it regards Sanctification, which guarantees the defeat of those who associate themselves with this false way. Once again, if the Message is not *"Jesus Christ and Him Crucified,"* and that alone (because it needs nothing added), then, pure and simple, it is not the Gospel.

No matter what type of face that Satan may place upon these false directions, when that face is pulled off, irrespective of the direction it takes, it is not the Gospel, simply because it repudiates or ignores the Cross.

Paul said, *"Behold, I Paul say unto you, that if you be circumcised* (resort to Law in any manner, whether the Law of Moses or laws made up by men), *Christ shall profit you nothing"* (Gal. 5:2). This means that all that Christ did at the Cross is of no consequence to those who make other things the object of their faith.

THE LEPER AND HIS CONDITION

The Old Testament type of leprosy and its cleansing is found in Leviticus, Chapters 13 and 14. It is an apt description in the physical of that which is actually spiritual. The following is what the leper had to do:

1. HIS CLOTHES SHALL BE RENT: This meant that his garment or robe had to be split up the back to the hem at the neck, in order to portray him being undone before God. The torn garment signified his utter lack of Righteousness.

2. HIS HEAD BARE: This signified that the Judgment of God was upon him as a result of the Covenant being broken. The men of Israel were to wear a little cap, signifying that the Lord was their protection. The leper could wear nothing on his head, signifying that he had no protection from the Judgment of God.

3. HE SHALL PUT A COVERING UPON HIS UPPER LIP, AND SHALL CRY, UNCLEAN, UNCLEAN: Any time anyone came within approximately 100 feet of him, he must shout these words. Whenever anyone attributes his supposed Salvation to anything other than Christ and Him Crucified, whether they realize it or not, they are, in effect, crying, *"Unclean, unclean"*!

4. HE SHALL DWELL ALONE: Even though he could be with other lepers, he could not be with anyone else. Such signified the terrible loneliness of sin, and of being cut off from God (Lev. 13:45-46).

THE LAW OF CLEANSING

As the Law was for leprosy, likewise, the Law was for cleansing (Lev., Chpt. 14). It is as follows:

1. HE SHALL BE BROUGHT UNTO THE PRIEST: Being brought to the Priest showed that the problem was spiritual rather than physical, but had manifested itself in a physical way, as well as every manner. Here the Priest is a Type of Christ; consequently, the leper (sinner) is to be brought to Jesus, since Jesus is the only hope.

2. AND THE PRIEST SHALL LOOK: This spoke of minute inspection, which determined if the disease was gone. Even though men constantly pronounce that the sinner is clean as a result of joining certain Churches or participating in certain religious ceremonies, rituals, or schemes, still, such holds no validity with the Lord whatsoever. Only the Lord can pronounce one *"clean"*!

3. TWO BIRDS ALIVE: This ceremony of old was meant to portray, when the act was completed, the dead and risen Christ.

4. AND CLEAN: This spoke of two pigeons or turtledoves, which were often mentioned as Sacrifices. They typified Jesus as being absolutely Perfect in His Body and Life.

5. AND CEDAR WOOD: This spoke of the Cross, on which Jesus would die.

6. AND SCARLET: This spoke of the shedding of His Blood.

7. AND HYSSOP: This was a type of branch, which was used to dip into the blood. It referred to the vinegar which was offered to Christ while He was on the Cross, which was on a sop made from the leaves of hyssop.

8. ONE OF THE BIRDS BE KILLED: This typified the coming death of Christ.

9. IN AN EARTHEN VESSEL: This spoke of Christ's human Body.

10. OVER RUNNING WATER: This spoke of the Word of God, which dictated the actions of Christ at Calvary, energized by the Holy Spirit.

11. THE LIVING BIRD: This symbolized the Resurrected Christ.

12. THE PROCESS: The Scripture says, *"He shall take it* (the living bird) *and the cedar wood, and the scarlet, and the hyssop, and shall dip them and the living bird in the blood of the bird that was killed over the running water"*: this spoke of the Resurrected Christ, Who had purchased our Redemption by His Death at Calvary.

13. SEVEN TIMES: The Scripture says, *"And he shall sprinkle upon him who is to be cleansed from the leprosy seven times." "Seven"* is God's number, symbolizing perfection, and, consequently, the completeness and perfection of the remedy, which foreshadowed the removal through Jesus Christ of all sin, sickness, pain, and suffering (Isa., Chpt. 53; Mat. 8:17; 11:1-6; 13:15; Jn. 10:10; Acts 10:38; I Pet. 2:24).

14. AND SHALL PRONOUNCE HIM CLEAN: This refers to God's Word proclaiming Salvation to the believing sinner.

15. AND LET THE LIVING BIRD LOOSE INTO THE OPEN FIELD: As this living bird represented the Resurrected Christ, likewise, it also represents the believing sinner who has been cleansed, washed, and set free by the Power of God.

ONLY JESUS!

There were many other things that the cleansed leper was to do; however, that which we have given in brief proclaims the Law of Cleansing. The Believer, however, would be blessed greatly by doing an entire study on Leviticus, Chapter 14, in order to investigate the entirety of this ceremony, and, more importantly, what is represented and symbolized respecting one's Salvation in Christ.

(I would recommend our Commentary on Leviticus for this study.)

So, even though the Law of Moses did not say that a leper could not be cleansed and thereby saved, still, the paucity of such cleansings, before Jesus, spoke of its improbability. Actually, there is record of only three being cleansed from this terrible malady.

One was Naaman, the Syrian General (II Ki. 5:10, 14); Miriam, the sister of Moses, who became leprous as a result of criticizing her brother Moses, was healed as a result of Moses' intercession (Num. 12:13-15); and Moses himself, who the Lord used as an example by causing his hand to become leprous and then healing him (Ex. 4:6-7).

Considering this dismal record, one can well understand the absolute hopelessness, at least until Jesus came!

So, in light of all of this, the leper felt that his disease was so loathsome that maybe Jesus simply would not heal him, even though He had the Power! Consequently, when he uttered these words, *"If You will,"* he was either uttering his death warrant or his Resurrection! One can well imagine his thoughts as he awaited the answer of Jesus. He would know in just a moment, and so would the whole world.

(41) "AND JESUS, MOVED WITH COMPASSION, PUT FORTH HIS HAND, AND TOUCHED HIM, AND SAID UNTO HIM, I WILL; BE THOU CLEAN."

The exposition is:

According to the Greek, our Lord's Word, and not His touch, healed the man. When He touched him, the healing had already been effected, and the man was *"clean."* The words, *"I will,"* forever settle the question of the Will of God to heal the sick.

COMPASSION

The phrase, *"And Jesus, moved with compassion,"* presents a portrayal of the Heart of God. Salvation in Christ is not a cold, calculating formula, neither is it a philosophic superiority. It is a warm, moving, touching, heart-feeling sympathy and compassion for the plight of humanity. Such is instigated by love; in fact, such can only be instigated by love.

The religions of the world have no concern or compassion for the hurts of people. Whatever they do is from a motivation of selfishness. In other words, *"If there is nothing in it for me, I have no concern or regard."* Consequently, life is cheap in such a spiritual climate.

The idea of hospitals, nursing homes, orphan homes, and a government which cares has its roots in Christianity. Regarding a caring government, it may very well be true that political motivation is the guiding force; however, it was the rudiments of Christianity which charted the course in the first place.

Consequently, when the Church begins to leave the True Principles of Bible Christianity, rather instituting its own, compassion and love are the first casualties. Then, the Church becomes hard, cold, unfeeling, and unmoved at the plight of others. It becomes more concerned about self-preservation and its rules and regulations.

The compassion shown by Christ in this example was not directed toward a multi-millionaire who could swell the coffers of this evangelistic party, but rather toward a pitiful leper, who, at best, could only say, *"Thank You,"* for the great miracle he was about to receive.

LOVE

There are basically three types of love in

the world. They are as follows:

1. AGAPE: This is the God-kind of love, shown here by Christ, which is imparted to all True Believers. It is type of love that the world does not have, and, in fact, cannot have without making Christ the Lord of one's life. It is the type of love that is here evidenced toward the leper (I Jn. 4:7).

2. PHILEO: This is the Greek word expressed in the Bible as another type of love. It could be better described as fondness or affection. For example, when Jesus asked Peter, *"Lovest thou Me more than these?"* He was speaking of *"agape"* love; however, when Peter answered Him, saying, *"I love You,"* the word *"love"* used by the Apostle was *"phileo,"* which means, as stated, fondness or affection (Jn. 21:15).

Peter is not to be chided for this, because his answer was not predicated on what he really felt toward the Lord, which was a deep, abiding *agape* love, but rather on his recent denial. Peter was fearful of claiming too much, as he had once done, and he was greatly humbled.

The *"phileo"* type of love is the highest form of love the world can have; consequently, it can turn or change almost overnight, hence, the great *"love affairs"* promoted by Hollywood and country/western songs suddenly turning sour.

3. EROS: This type of love so prominent in the world, and even in the Church, is not mentioned even once in the Bible. From that omission we learn exactly what the Lord thinks of such. *Eros* is a Greek word which actually means *"the sum of all instincts for self-preservation."* In other words, *"I love you, if you, in turn, can help me in some way."* It is the epitome of selfishness, hence, self-preservation.

THE FUNCTIONING OF THE EROS-TYPE OF LOVE

This type of love is understandable in the world, but should have no place in the Church. Sadly, however, the Church is full of it! Consequently, scores of Churches either subtly (or not so subtly) suggest (or blatantly state) that they desire only a certain type of *"clientele."* In other words, they want people who make their Church look good. This would speak of people with money, education, talent, or some type of ability that is useful. Anyone who does not fit that mold in some way is made to feel somewhat less than welcome.

This is the type of love that uses up someone; then, when they have nothing left to give, they are discarded. Sadly and tragically, this type of love permeates and fills society. As stated, it is, as well, all too prominent in the modern Church.

As is obvious, this was not the type evidenced by Christ toward the leper. Everything Jesus did, not only with this man, but with everyone, was done with no idea or thought of any type of financial, physical, material, or even spiritual return. It was done simply because He loved the person, not because the person necessarily loved Him. In fact, most did not!

THE TOUCH

The phrase, *"Put forth His hand, and touched him,"* presents itself as symbolic of what Christ had to do to save lost humanity. God was able, so to speak, to speak the worlds into existence; however, due to the fundamentals of sin and the subtle way that Satan had woven his web of destruction, God could not speak Salvation into existence. Of course, He had the Power to do so, but His Nature, which is Holiness Personified, would not allow such. He had to come down here and die, actually taking upon Himself the penalty for the sin of man, in essence, *"putting forth His hand"*!

When Jesus touched the leper, this was symbolic of Paul's word, *"For He* (God the Father) *has made Him* (God the Son) *to be sin for us* (to be made a Sin Offering; Isa. 53:10), *Who* (Jesus) *knew no sin* (had never sinned); *that we might be made the Righteousness of God in Him"* (II Cor. 5:21).

The Scripture further says: *"For what the Law could not do, in that it was weak through the flesh* (those under Law had only their willpower, which is woefully insufficient; so despite how hard they tried, they were unable to keep the Law then, and the same inability persists presently; any person who tries to live for God by a system of laws is doomed to failure, because the Holy Spirit will not function in that capacity), *God sending His*

Own Son (refers to man's helpless condition, unable to save himself and unable to keep even a simple law, and, therefore, in dire need of a Saviour) *in the likeness of sinful flesh* (this means that Christ was really human, conformed in appearance to flesh which is characterized by sin, but yet sinless), *and for sin* (to atone for sin, to destroy its power, and to save and sanctify its victims), *condemned sin in the flesh* (destroyed the power of sin by giving His Perfect Body as a Sacrifice for sin, which made it possible for sin to be defeated in our flesh; it was all through the Cross [Rom. 8:3]).

The Levitical Law forbade a Jew to touch a leper. Our Lord lived under the Law, exactly as we have just quoted, and obeyed it, because He, in effect, was the One Who gave it originally.

So, what actually happened here?

The first kind touch of a human hand this leper ever experienced was the gentle touch of the Son of God.

CLEANSING POWER

The phrase, *"And said unto him, I will; be thou clean,"* tells us exactly what happened! The rule of Greek grammar that governs this sentence construction, we are told, is that the action of the proclamation, *"I will,"* is going on at the same time, or immediately preceding, the action of the touch. That is, Jesus was saying, *"I will,"* at the time He was touching the leper; however, the thought in His Mind, *"I will,"* actually preceded the act of touching him. In other words, when Jesus touched the leper, he actually had already been healed.

All of this means that our Lord did not touch the leper in order to cleanse him, but to show him and others present that he was already cleansed of his leprosy. This means that Jesus did not break the Mosaic Law, which forbade one to touch a leper. As stated, it was the Word of Christ which healed the leper, which means that when Christ subsequently touched him, there was no leprosy present. So, He didn't break the Law in any capacity.

A SYMBOL OF THE FORGIVEN, CLEANSED SINNER

So, as this symbol bears out, when the Lord touches the forgiven sinner, which speaks of fellowship, it is not in order to save him, for that has already been accomplished by God's favorable response to Faith. When the believing sinner cries to the Lord, as did the leper, love is already big in the Heart of God for the sinner, and the answer is an immediate *"I will,"* which is followed by the touch. Jesus does not touch the sin, but the forgiven sinner. When He died on Calvary for humanity, He in no way sinned, or even touched our sin. What He actually did was according to the following:

First of all, He provided the Perfect Sacrifice in the giving of His Perfect Human Body, which had never been tainted by the terrible ruin of sin; it was, consequently, a Sacrifice that God could and would accept (Heb. 10:5).

Jesus, on the Cross, did not become adultery, theft, lying, stealing, rape, murder, hate, etc., in other words, *"sin,"* as we think of such, but, as stated, a *"Sin Offering,"* which means He paid the penalty, thereby suffering the Judgment (II Cor. 5:21).

So, this beautiful example of Christ cleansing the leper typifies in brief that which He does for the believing sinner.

No doubt, the Priests would have gladly censured Christ for touching this leper, if there had been any evidence; however, he was no longer a leper, which was obvious to all. There was, therefore, no evidence with which to charge Christ. Moreover, Satan would definitely charge Christ with touching unclean sinners, if there was any evidence; however, the evidence, i.e., *"sin,"* is gone, with the person in Christ becoming *"a new creation: old things are passed away; behold, all things are become new"* (II Cor. 5:17).

In John 1:12, Justification precedes Regeneration in the Divine economy. Mercy is only given on the basis of justice satisfied. So, as the sinner recognizes the Lord Jesus as the One Who, through His outpoured Blood on the Cross, procured for sinful man a legal right to the Mercy of God, he becomes the recipient of Regeneration and of all other blessings of Salvation.

The words, *"Be thou clean,"* mean that the leper was cleansed at once. It was an immediate cure; likewise, all who come to Christ are instantly saved upon Faith (Eph. 2:8-9).

(42) "AND AS SOON AS HE HAD SPOKEN, IMMEDIATELY THE LEPROSY DEPARTED FROM HIM, AND HE WAS CLEANSED."

The exegesis is:

This proclaims the fact that the spoken Word is enough, especially when coming from Christ Personally.

THE SPOKEN WORD

The phrase, *"And as soon as He had spoken,"* proclaims, as we have stated, that it was not the touch that cleansed him, but rather the Will of God evidenced in the spoken Word. If God says it, we should believe it!

The phrase, *"Immediately the leprosy departed from him,"* must have been a sight to behold. Leprosy leaves terrible marks on the human body. As stated, fingers, toes, and other body members are, at times, literally eaten away and fall off. So, the meaning is that immediately every sore was healed on this man's body.

Furthermore, as quickly as this leprosy departed at the Word of Christ, likewise, sin departs upon Faith in the Glorious Name of Jesus.

CLEANSED

The phrase, *"And he was cleansed,"* means that he would never again have to cry, *"Unclean, unclean"*! The evidence was so obvious that no one could deny what had happened to him. Now he could say, *"Clean, clean"*!

Equally, the new person in Christ Jesus can say:

"Saved by His Pow'r Divine,
"Saved to new life sublime!
"Life now is sweet and my joy is complete,
"For I'm saved, saved, saved!"

(43) "AND HE (Jesus) STRAITLY CHARGED HIM, AND FORTHWITH SENT HIM AWAY."

The diagram is:

He is sent to the Priests, in accordance with that demanded by the Word of God (Lev. 14:2).

THE CHARGE

The phrase, *"And He straitly charged him,"* refers to what was said in Verse 44. The word *"straitly"* means *"to forcibly charge."* In other words, Christ was stern in His admonition. The reason was this: one can well imagine the joy that filled the leper's heart upon his instant cleansing. As a result, he was desiring to show everyone exactly what had happened to him; consequently, the idea of going to the Priests, as the Law demanded, was the furthest thing from his mind, as would be obvious!

By not obeying this injunction and instead going out among the people, the religious leaders would have occasion to accuse Christ of disobeying the Law of Moses, or they may have even denied that the man had ever been a leper. At any rate, Jesus, knowing the man's intense joy and his desire to proclaim to others of his great Miracle, charges him to go first to the Priests, as the Law demanded (Lev. 14:2).

The phrase, *"And forthwith sent him away,"* refers to sending him away for this purpose, and this purpose alone!

(44) "AND SAID UNTO HIM, SEE YOU SAY NOTHING TO ANY MAN: BUT GO YOUR WAY, SHOW YOURSELF TO THE PRIEST, AND OFFER FOR YOUR CLEANSING THOSE THINGS WHICH MOSES COMMANDED, FOR A TESTIMONY UNTO THEM."

The composition is:

This pertained to the Law of the cleansing of the leper, to which we have alluded, which was a complicated affair, as is recorded in Leviticus, Chapter 14.

THE PRIEST

The phrase, *"And said unto him, See you say nothing to any man: but go your way, show yourself to the Priest,"* was meant to fulfill Leviticus 14:1-32, respecting the Law of the cleansed leper.

The phrase, *"And offer for your cleansing those things which Moses commanded,"* pertained to all the things listed regarding Leviticus, Chapter 14. The Law of the cleansing of the leper was complicated indeed! All the ceremony, as outlined, was meant to portray the Sacrifice of Christ in His expiatory Work; however, there is little, if any, record that it was ever done, because no lepers were cleansed other than Naaman, a Gentile, who would not have been subject to the Law of Moses.

As well, Moses was healed of his leprosy before the Law was given (Ex. 4:6).

Concerning Miriam, Moses' sister, the Scripture doesn't exactly say what she did, only that she was *"shut out from the camp seven days"* (Num. 12:15).

So, if this man had obeyed Christ, which he did not, and the Priests then had faithfully followed the Law, this would have been, most probably, the first time for such action, at least which is recorded. As such, it would have beautifully fulfilled the type.

THE TESTIMONY

The phrase, *"For a testimony unto them,"* refers to the testimony of the Priests to the people to the effect that the leper was officially pronounced clean.

Even though the Priests no doubt heard about this tremendous Miracle, inasmuch as it was noised abroad everywhere, there is no record of what actually did occur, as it regards the ritual cleansing. As stated, due to the fact that this rarely had been done, or possibly never had been done, the Priests were probably little inclined to take action.

(45) "BUT HE (the former leper) WENT OUT, AND BEGAN TO PUBLISH IT MUCH, AND TO BLAZE ABROAD THE MATTER, INSOMUCH THAT JESUS COULD NO MORE OPENLY ENTER INTO THE CITY, BUT WAS WITHOUT IN DESERT PLACES: AND THEY CAME TO HIM FROM EVERY QUARTER."

The diagram is:

The man not obeying what Jesus told him to do gave occasion for the enemies of Christ to accuse Him; in other words, they would say that He had ignored the Law, which, of course, He hadn't. But the man did, despite the admonition.

DISOBEDIENCE

The phrase, *"But he went out, and began to publish it much, and to blaze abroad the matter,"* spoke of him blatantly disobeying the Lord. It is hard to understand how that he could be so sternly charged by Christ and then not obey, especially considering what Jesus had done for him! However, his example, I'm afraid, is all too often our example.

How often does the Lord do great things for us, which make us so gloriously joyful, and yet we turn around and disobey Him? Such is Christ and such is man!

CAPERNAUM

The phrase, *"Insomuch that Jesus could no more openly enter into the city,"* means that He could not minister any more in Capernaum, at least at this time. Upon seeing the healings which Christ had previously performed, the entirety of the city was no doubt greatly overjoyed; however, now, upon hearing the testimony of the leper, no doubt knowing him and realizing this was the first leper cleansed since Naaman, the Syrian, their joy knew no bounds. Everyone was wanting to see Jesus, irrespective of the need! So, if He attempted to enter the city, He would be mobbed!

The word *"openly"* means that He did go into Capernaum at times during this particular period, probably very late at night or disguised in some way.

DESERT PLACES

The phrase, *"But was without in desert places, and they came to Him from every quarter,"* not only meant that Jesus could not openly enter Capernaum, but could not openly enter any city. If He did so, He had to be as discreet as possible! Even then, He would be mobbed! Consequently, at least at this time, much of His Ministry was carried out in the countryside. They kept coming to Him for healing and Deliverance, irrespective as to where He was!

The First Chapter of Mark is thought to encompass approximately the first twelve months of the Ministry of Jesus. At this time, the animosity and hatred of the Pharisees and Scribes had not yet risen to the fore, which this adulation actually helped arouse. Due to this hatred and opposition by the religious leaders of Israel and their threat to excommunicate anyone who showed love for Christ or followed Him, the coming last year of His public Ministry showed the crowds thinning out considerably (Jn. 9:22).

CHAPTER 2

(1) "AND AGAIN HE ENTERED INTO CAPERNAUM AFTER SOME DAYS; AND IT WAS NOISED THAT HE WAS IN THE HOUSE."

The overview is:

This was Peter's home!

THE PRESENCE OF CHRIST

The phrase, *"And again He entered into Capernaum after some days,"* probably referred to several weeks, maybe even months. He had been on a preaching tour to other parts of Galilee, which would have taken some time. At any rate, He probably slipped into the city during the night, or was spirited into Peter's home by the back streets, etc.

The phrase, *"And it was noised that He was in the house,"* referred to Peter's house, where He had made His Headquarters. Somehow the news got out that Jesus was there. And I don't wonder! He Alone was, and is, the Answer to every problem that faces mankind; consequently, they would mob the house, because only He could heal, could deliver, could save! And yet, too oftentimes men desire Him, not because of Who He is, but instead for what He can do.

(2) "AND STRAIGHTWAY MANY WERE GATHERED TOGETHER, INSOMUCH THAT THERE WAS NO ROOM TO RECEIVE THEM, NO, NOT SO MUCH AS ABOUT THE DOOR: AND HE PREACHED THE WORD UNTO THEM."

The synopsis is:

Preaching and teaching always came first.

THE CROWD

The phrase, *"And straightway many were gathered together,"* concerned those who were sick, demon-possessed, or were there as onlookers. The phrase, *"Insomuch that there was no room to receive them, no, not so much as about the door,"* means that the house was filled, along with the courtyard, and even all around the outside of the house.

People were no doubt all around, even on the shore of the Lake, attempting to catch a glimpse of Jesus. I hope the Reader can understand the majesty of this moment. The terrible opposition of the Scribes and Pharisees had not yet begun, and consequently the people did not fear their wrath and felt free to seek the help of Christ. Some were hungry; some were hurting; some were curious; however, all were in need of what He had to give.

PREACH THE WORD

The phrase, *"And He preached the Word unto them,"* proclaims to all that this was the Object of His Ministry. The exercise of miraculous Power was subordinated to this; the Miracles were simply designed to meet the need of the person in question and to fix the attention upon the Teacher as One sent from God.

The manner in which the word *"preached"* is used is not the normal word for preaching. This word *"preached,"* in this instance, means to speak to the people in a conversational tone, because He was in the house, but yet loud enough for all to hear.

The emphasis concerns not only what He said, but also His Person. His kindness, exhibited in the beauty of His Voice, especially considering what He said, must have been like rain on dry ground. It must have been like a fragrance that came from a newly-opened flower. Moreover, what made His Message so powerful was because He preached *"the Word."* This consisted, at that time, of Genesis through Malachi. To be sure, the people had heard it expounded many times before, but never in this fashion.

So, the meaning is that He *"preached the Word,"* but His Person made the Word alive.

Even though my statement will be rejected by some, still, this very Passage bears out that the mere preaching of the Letter is not enough, as truthful as it may be, but that it also must be anointed by the Holy Spirit for it to accomplish its intended purpose.

Paul said, *"For our Gospel came not unto you in word only, but also in power, and in the Holy Spirit"* (I Thess. 1:5).

(3) "AND THEY COME UNTO HIM, BRINGING ONE SICK OF THE PALSY, WHICH WAS BORNE OF FOUR."

The exegesis is:

Everything that Jesus did was designed not

only to help the person or persons in need, but also to serve as a lesson for all time. The lessons learned here are that this *"palsy"* is a type of sin, which incapacitates the individual; and that help is needed, as here, to come to Christ.

PARALYSIS

The phrase, *"And they come unto Him,"* is said by Mark in such a way that it places the Reader in the very presence of the desperate ones. They were coming to *"Him,"* not someone else, for Jesus Alone would do. Tragically, most of the world, at least as it relates to Christianity, come to Churches, religious Denominations, men, or even particular doctrines. Few actually come to Christ; but those who do, receive the help this man received so long ago.

The phrase, *"Bringing one sick of the palsy,"* actually refers to *"paralysis,"* and not *"palsy,"* as we presently know it. Being paralyzed, the man could not walk; he was consequently placed on some type of cot, which was then borne on the shoulders of four men.

THE HELP

The phrase, *"Which was borne of four,"* means that these men were not just doing a duty as servants; they were expressly bringing him to Jesus. As well, and as the following Verses show, their faith was joined with that of the sick man, which helped bring about his healing. This is a perfect example of Believers showing care and concern in bringing one to Christ.

The paralyzed man represents the unsaved, who, on their own, cannot come to Christ. They must have help, which is described by these *"four."* These *"four"* represent not only those who personally bring someone to Christ, but also those who earnestly seek the Lord for the Salvation of others, or even Revival in particular places. It, as well, refers to those who give of their financial resources in order that others may have opportunity to hear the Gospel and be saved. All of us were once in the place of the *"paralytic,"* and all of us now, after we have come to Christ, should be in the place of the *"four"*!

These *"four"* did not beg off, claiming that they did not have the time. Neither did they complain about the difficulty of their task. They were determined to get to Jesus; irrespective of the cost, this they would do. They would not be disappointed!

(4) "AND WHEN THEY COULD NOT COME NEAR UNTO HIM FOR THE PRESS, THEY UNCOVERED THE ROOF WHERE HE WAS: AND WHEN THEY HAD BROKEN IT UP, THEY LET DOWN THE BED WHEREIN THE SICK OF THE PALSY LAY."

The overview is:

Houses have flat roofs in that part of the world, usually with steps on the outside leading to the top. There were usually one or more trap doors in the roof, and it was one of these which they probably enlarged.

DRASTIC MEASURES

The phrase, *"And when they could not come near unto Him for the press,"* concerns them coming to the front of the house, but, with the crowd surrounding the place, there was no way they could gain entrance. Faith in Christ is never presented as an easy path, but Faith in Christ, being Faith, always finds a way. For those who have no faith, the *"press"* will always serve as a sufficient obstacle. As the *"press"* hindered then, the *"press,"* i.e., the media, seeks to hinder now!

The phrase, *"They uncovered the roof where He was,"* concerned drastic measures, to say the least! On the roof was normally a trap door, which led down into the house, and where people could come and go; for the roof was used for many and varied things, even as now. Some even slept there during the summer, obtaining the benefit of night breezes.

The phrase, *"And when they had broken it up,"* probably refers to them enlarging the opening where the trap door was located, it being too small to accommodate the prostrate man on the cot.

I wonder what were the thoughts of Peter at seeing his roof being torn up in this manner? Considering the Miracle performed on this man, however, I am certain that the matter was favorably resolved.

The phrase, *"They let down the bed wherein the sick of the palsy lay,"* means they made an opening large enough for the entrance of the man on the cot. There is every evidence that he was paralyzed and unable to help in any way, or even to move; therefore, he would have been dead weight. Either they had ropes or else the people in the room, upon seeing what was being done, may have joined in to help from inside the room, as the man was being lowered down by the *"four."*

At any rate, it must have been quite a sight, and it no doubt interrupted the Message Christ was preaching. However, it must always be remembered that the Message is for people, not people for the Message! So, the interruption, which represented the need, would be, in effect, no interruption at all, because this is that for which Jesus came.

(5) "WHEN JESUS SAW THEIR FAITH, HE SAID UNTO THE SICK OF THE PALSY, SON, YOUR SINS BE FORGIVEN YOU."

The exposition is:

The wretched physical condition of the sick man was due to his sinful life; therefore, Jesus first of all addressed the real cause, but with no condemnation, just forgiveness and healing.

FAITH

The phrase, *"When Jesus saw their faith,"* presents a startling revelation concerning this great subject. Several things are here said:

1. Faith can be seen. This means the action of Faith is never passive. This is what James was speaking of when he said, *"What does it profit, my brethren, though a man say he has Faith, and have not works?"* He then said, *"Even so Faith, if it has not works, is dead, being alone"* (James 2:14, 17). He is saying that Biblical Faith will always show itself in works, as here by the *"four."*

2. Faith in God never says anything is impossible, because with God all things are possible; consequently, these men did not allow the hindrances to stop them (Mk. 9:23).

3. The very ingredient of Faith demands that, irrespective of the obstacles, it be pushed through to its intended purpose and successful conclusion. In other words, it will not stop until the goal is reached (James 1:6-8).

4. All faith is tested; consequently, great faith is tested greatly! However, the test is not meant to stop Faith, because True Faith cannot be stopped, but only to guarantee that it is Faith (I Pet. 1:6-7).

So Jesus *"saw their faith."* Inasmuch as it is recorded here, it means that it gladdened His heart.

FORGIVEN SINS

The phrase, *"He said unto the sick of the palsy, Son, your sins be forgiven you,"* tells us several things:

1. The wretched physical condition of the sick man was due to his sinful life. Jesus, therefore, first of all addressed the real cause.

2. He uses the word *"son,"* intimating kindness, irrespective of his wretched spiritual and physical condition. There is not even a hint of condemnation. What a lesson we should learn from this encounter.

3. The Greek word for *"forgiveness"* is *"aphiema,"* which means *"to send away"* or *"to remit, forgive."* It is altogether different than the word *"forgive"* used by men in relationship to each other.

When we forgive someone who has wronged us, it means we no longer hold any animosity against them, and the situation has changed to one of renewed friendliness and affection, providing, that is, that the other party acts accordingly! However, even though such an act of *"forgiveness"* does not hold the wrong against the person anymore, still, as far as the act itself is concerned, it is still there, and there is nothing anyone can do about it.

But the word used by Christ has a double meaning:

A. The sin is put away on a judicial basis by the poured-out Blood of Christ. He paid the penalty required by the broken Law, and thus, satisfied Divine Justice.

B. The Lord not only forgives the sin, but removes the guilt of that sin in such a way that the believing sinner is looked at by God as if the sin had never been committed. It is called *"Justification by Faith,"* and is what is meant by Bible forgiveness in the case of God and a believing sinner.

This can legally be done because Jesus Christ not only paid the price for our forgiveness of sin by the shedding of His Blood, but He also, by giving His Life, took upon Himself the Judgment of God, which we should have taken. As a result, not only are we forgiven, but we are also justified, meaning that the act is not only forgiven, but its very existence is removed from the Books.

That's the reason *"there is therefore now no condemnation to them which are in Christ Jesus, who walk not after the flesh, but after the Spirit"* (Rom. 8:1). As Jesus said, *"Son, your sins be forgiven you,"* He, as well, has said the same thing to untold millions of others.

(6) "BUT THERE WAS CERTAIN OF THE SCRIBES SITTING THERE, AND REASONING IN THEIR HEARTS."

The diagram is:

There were hostile spirits there, which were in the hearts of these Scribes, and which could be felt by Christ.

THE SCRIBES

The phrase, *"But there was certain of the Scribes sitting there,"* pertains to individuals who were opposed to Christ, and who either had come early or else had pushed their way to the front so they could stand near Him, with the purpose in mind of finding fault. These were some of the religious leaders of Israel!

Scribes were experts in the study of the Law of Moses. At first this occupation belonged to the Priests. Ezra, as an example, was both a Priest and a Scribe (Neh. 8:9); the offices were not necessarily separate. The chief activity of the Scribe was undistracted study. The rise of the Scribes may be dated after the Babylonian Exile.

Scribes were the originators of the Synagogue service. Some of them sat as members of the Sanhedrin (Mat. 16:21; 26:3). After A.D. 70, the importance of the Scribes was enhanced. They preserved in written form the oral law and faithfully handed down the Hebrew Scriptures. They expected of their pupils a reverence beyond that given to parents.

Their task was to preserve the Law. They were the professional students of the Law and its defenders, especially after the Priesthood had become corrupt. They transmitted unwritten legal decisions which had come into existence in their efforts to apply the Mosaic Law to daily life. They claimed this oral law was more important than the written law (Mk. 7:5). By their efforts, religion was liable to be reduced to heartless formalism.

They were also referred to as *"lawyers"* and *"teachers of the Law,"* because they were entrusted with the administration as judges in the Sanhedrin (Mat. 22:35; Mk. 14:43, 53; Lk. 22:26; Acts 4:5). In fact, *"lawyer"* and *"Scribe"* are synonymous, and thus, the two words are never joined in the New Testament.

By and large, the Scribes clashed with Christ, for He taught with authority (Mat. 7:28-29), and He condemned the external formalism which they fostered. They persecuted Peter and John also (Acts 4:5), and had a part in Stephen's martyrdom (Acts 6:12). However, although the majority greatly opposed Christ (Mat. 21:15), some few believed (Mat. 8:19).

THE HEART

The phrase, *"And reasoning in their hearts,"* represents a hostile spirit on their part, which could be felt by Christ. It did not stop anything He did, but it did sully the atmosphere. There is no record in the Ministry of Christ of any such attitude or spirit on the part of the common people. All the opposition came from the religious leaders of Israel. Sadly, it is no different today!

What were they reasoning?

They were jealous of His popularity, and even more so of His Power with God. As a result of their evil hearts, they did not for a moment believe that He was the Messiah, and, as such, qualified to forgive sins. So, we are looking here at a denial of His Messianic claims.

THE ACTIVITY OF THE HEART

The word *"heart"* (including *"hearts"* and *"hearted"*) is used extensively in the Bible. The word *"heart"* occurs some 730 times in the Old Testament and 105 times in the New Testament. *"Hearts"* occurs 112 times in both Testaments combined. In fact, the total occurrences of the several forms of the word are found some 955 or more times throughout the Bible, as listed in Strong's Concordance.

When the Bible mentions the word *"heart,"* it is not speaking of the physical organ that we know of as such. It is speaking of the *"inner man," "the hidden person of the heart"* (I Pet. 3:4), that central essence of man with which God is primarily concerned. It is that portion or essence of man, which includes the soul and the spirit, which God the Lord looks on, searches, and tries (I Sam. 16:7; Prov. 10:8; Jer. 11:20; 17:10; 20: 12). It is the center and source of belief and Faith (Lk. 24:25; Rom. 10:10).

(7) "WHY DOES THIS MAN THUS SPEAK BLASPHEMIES? WHO CAN FORGIVE SINS BUT GOD ONLY?"

The composition is:

If Christ had been merely a man, then the reasoning of these Scribes would have been correct; however, inasmuch as He was God manifested in the flesh, they were totally incorrect. They will now come face-to-face with the Deity of Christ.

BLASPHEMIES?

The question, *"Why does this man thus speak blasphemies?"* registers their unbelief. First of all, the word *"man"* was inserted by the translators, but was not in the original Text. Consequently, they referred to Jesus as merely *"this,"* thereby showing their contempt! In fact, there is no record in the four Gospels that they ever referred to Him by the Name given to Him by the Angel Gabriel, *"Jesus"* (Lk. 1:26-31).

The Scribes were fond of throwing around the word *"blasphemies,"* tacking the label on anyone who disagreed with them. Actually, the *"blasphemies"* were on their part, because of their rejection of Christ. He will now prove to them the fact of His Deity.

GOD ALONE CAN FORGIVE SINS!

The question, *"Who can forgive sins but God only?"* proclaims a Truth, but yet Jesus was God! Even though this question was posed in unbelief by the Scribes, still, the question is valid and demands only one answer, *"God"*! Consequently, the Catholic confessional, where the Priests forgive sins, is not only unscriptural, but, as the Scribes said, *"blasphemous."*

As well, Jesus forgives sins on the basis of justice satisfied on the Cross of Calvary. At Calvary, all sin was atoned, past, present, and future, at least for all who will believe (Jn. 3:16). In fact, all sins have been forgiven, even from the very beginning, by virtue of the Cross (Eph. 2:13-18). Even before the Cross, all sins were forgiven on the premise that the Cross would ultimately be realized.

NOTES

One might say that before the Cross, God forgave sins *"on credit."* And yet the *"credit"* was backed up by the Sacrificial System, which had its beginnings almost immediately after the Fall of man (Gen., Chpt. 4).

Paul clearly said, *"And without shedding of blood is no remission"* of sins (Heb. 9:22). As well, John the Baptist said of Jesus, *"Behold the Lamb of God, Who takes away the sin of the world"* (Jn. 1:29). He *"took away"* the sin of the world by virtue of the Cross, which means He satisfied the claims of Heavenly Justice, thereby meeting all conditions of the broken Law (Col. 2:14-15).

As we keep saying, Christ is the Source and the Cross is the Means.

(8) "AND IMMEDIATELY WHEN JESUS PERCEIVED IN HIS SPIRIT THAT THEY SO REASONED WITHIN THEMSELVES, HE SAID UNTO THEM, WHY REASON YE THESE THINGS IN YOUR HEARTS?"

The overview is:

Jesus speaking to them in this fashion must have been startling. They had not spoken these things aloud, only thinking them in their hearts.

THE SPIRIT OF MAN

The phrase, *"And immediately when Jesus perceived in His Spirit that they so reasoned within themselves,"* means that He knew fully what they were thinking. It was not guesswork on His Part. The manner in which this was done was through the agency of the Holy Spirit, Who spoke to His Spirit, revealing this knowledge unto Him. This was not by any Divine attributes on His Part. Even though He was God, never ceased to be God, and, as such, could forgive sins, as illustrated here, still, every Miracle He performed was by the Power of the Holy Spirit and not His Own. The same could be said for all Revelation Knowledge, as well!

It was the same as, and in fact was, the twin Gifts in Operation of:

1. *"The Word of Knowledge"*;
2. *"Discerning of spirits"* (I Cor. 12:8-10).

Man is a *"living soul"* and *"has a spirit."*

The human spirit is the part of man which *"knows."* Paul said: *"For what man knows the things of a man, save the spirit of man which is in him?"* (The spirit of a man can know some things about another man, but, within itself, cannot know anything about God.) *Even so the things of God knows no man, but the Spirit of God.* (Men cannot learn about God through scientific investigation or human reasoning, but only as the Spirit of God reveals such to the Believer, and does so by the Word [I Cor. 2:11].)

This means that all knowledge, all perception, and all reasoning are done through the spirit of man. Through the soul, one deals with one's self. Through the human body, one deals with other members of the human race. Through one's spirit, one deals with the spirit world, whether good or evil.

The soul and the spirit of man are indivisible, meaning that they cannot be separated. They leave the body only at death; if unredeemed, they go to the underworld, i.e., "Hell" (Lk. 16:22-31); to Heaven, if redeemed (Phil. 1:21-23).

At the First Resurrection of Life, the soul and the spirit of the redeemed will be re-united with a Glorified Body (I Jn. 3:2). The Resurrection of the Unjust will not take place until 1,000 years later, when then the soul and the spirit of the unredeemed will be given an indestructible body, and will spend eternity in Hell (Rev. 20:11-15).

WHY THE FAULTY REASONING?

The question, *"He said unto them, Why reason ye these things in your hearts?"* must have been somewhat startling to them? What were their thoughts when He posed this question to them? Did not this, within itself, lend even more credence to His Deity?

Faith *"sees"* when there is nothing visible to see, but unbelief will not *"see"* even though the proof, as here, is obvious!

(9) "WHETHER IS IT EASIER TO SAY TO THE SICK OF THE PALSY, YOUR SINS BE FORGIVEN YOU; OR TO SAY, ARISE, AND TAKE UP YOUR BED, AND WALK?"

The exposition is:

God Alone can forgive sins, and God Alone can heal; therefore, to heal validates the power to forgive sins. As stated, they were now coming face-to-face with His Deity.

THE ANSWER TO UNBELIEF!

The question that Christ here poses will answer the *"reasonings"* of unbelief in their hearts. His proof will be irrefutable; however, proof is not what they were looking for.

(The following is derived from an exposition of Spence and Trench, and proclaims, in essence, what Jesus may have said.)

"You accuse Me of blasphemy. You say that I am usurping the attributes of God when I claim the power of forgiving sin. You ask for the evidence that I really possess this power; and you say it is an easy thing to lay claim to a power which penetrates the spiritual world, and which is therefore beyond the reach of material proof. Be it so.

"I will now furnish that evidence. I will prove, by what I am now about to work upon the body of this man, that what I have just said is effective upon the spirit. I have just said to this paralytic, 'Your sins are forgiven.' You challenge this power; you question My authority. I will now give you outward and sensible evidence that this is no fictitious or imaginary claim.

"You see this poor helpless, palsied man. I will say to him in the presence of you all, 'Arise, and take up your bed and go unto your house.' And if, simply at My bidding, his nerves are braced, and his limbs gather strength, and he rises and walks, which you know, within himself, he is unable to do, then judge ye whether I have a right to say to him, 'Your sins are forgiven.'

"Thus, by doing that which is capable of proof, I will vindicate My power to do that which is beyond the reach of sensible evidence; and I will make manifest to you, by these visible tides of My Grace, in what direction the deep undercurrent of My Love is moving."

(10) "BUT THAT YE MAY KNOW THAT THE SON OF MAN HAS POWER ON EARTH TO FORGIVE SINS, (HE SAYS TO THE SICK OF THE PALSY.)"

The synopsis is:

He did all of this in full view of everyone, even skeptics, and especially the skeptics!

POWER

The phrase, *"But that ye may know that the Son of man has power on Earth to forgive sins,"* proclaims the irrefutable proof, which will be evidenced by this healing; however, even though they would *"know"* by the actions of Christ, still, they would not admit it. For to have done so would have been admitting that He is the Messiah, the Eternal One, the Lord of Glory, the Son of God.

Their pride and religious jealousy would not allow them to do that, so, in the face of irrefutable proof, they would continue in unbelief. Actually, the entirety of the world travels the same course. The proof that there is a God, and, furthermore, Who He is, and that He sent His Son, Jesus Christ, to die for lost humanity, and that He rose from the dead, is irrefutable, as well! And yet, most, by far, will not believe.

Why?

Men love their sins, and in their sins is deception. In this deception, right seems to be wrong, and wrong seems to be right! (Mat. 13:13-15).

HIS WORD

The phrase, *"He said to the sick of the palsy,"* proclaims Him doing this in full view of all who were present, which would constitute a Miracle of astounding proportions.

When we hold the Bible in our hands, we are holding the written Word. In Jesus, we have the *"Living Word"* (Jn. 1:1). As powerful as His Name is, His Word carries even more authority. The Scripture says, *"For You have magnified Your Word above all Your Name"* (Ps. 138:2).

(11) "I SAY UNTO YOU, ARISE, AND TAKE UP YOUR BED, AND GO YOUR WAY INTO YOUR HOUSE."

The diagram is:

All there knew, including the skeptics, that this man could not take up his bed and carry it, unless he was truly healed; whether they admitted it or not, they also knew that only the Power of God could accomplish this.

THE WORD GIVEN

The phrase, *"I say unto you, Arise,"* is an order, not only to the man, but to the spirit world, as well!

It must be kept in mind that this is the same One Who *"said: Let there be light: and there was light"* (Gen. 1:3). Upon His Word, the light which had been withheld from the sun is now given admittance to planet Earth.

NOTES

Likewise, at the moment of His Word, strength began to flood this man's physical body, and instantly he does something that he had not heretofore been able to do. He instantly arises, and in perfect health!

The phrase, *"And take up your bed,"* was the proof of his immediate healing. That which had been his support, now becomes supported by him. The phrase, *"And go your way into your house,"* means that he can now go back under his own power, and, in any way he chooses, not being dependent on the *"four"* who brought him. Such not only proclaims healing, but also epitomizes the Salvation experience.

All unsaved are spiritual cripples, consequently unable to walk, at least in a spiritual sense; however, at the Word of Jesus, this situation is instantly changed, with spiritual strength given and the individual now able to spiritually walk upright. The *"bed"* spiritually symbolizes dependence on things of the world. The taking up of the *"bed"* symbolizes that dependence broken, with whatever it was becoming the servant instead of the master.

Before, the bed mastered him; now, he masters the bed!

(12) "AND IMMEDIATELY HE AROSE, TOOK UP THE BED, AND WENT FORTH BEFORE THEM ALL; INSOMUCH THAT THEY WERE ALL AMAZED, AND GLORIFIED GOD, SAYING, WE NEVER SAW IT ON THIS FASHION."

The overview is:

This Miracle was performed in such a fashion that it could not be denied, not even by the skeptics. They simply *"were all amazed."*

THE MIRACLE

The phrase, *"And immediately he arose,"* portrays no hesitancy whatsoever in his actions. He can do so because he is healed! The phrase, *"Took up the bed,"* portrays him bending down and picking up this which had once carried him, but now he is carrying it. All of this is in full view of everyone, with none being able to deny what has happened, and in front of their very eyes.

AMAZEMENT

The phrase, *"Insomuch that they were all*

amazed," refers to the fact that they evidently all knew the man who had been healed, and that he had not been able to walk, which had been obvious to all! Consequently, there was no doubt or argument concerning the miracle which had been performed upon his physical body.

What the Lord does for mankind, that is, for those who will believe Him, can only be construed as *"amazing"*! The word *"amazed,"* as used here, is very strong. In the Greek, it is *"existemi,"* which means *"out of wits, astounded, astonished."*

TO GLORIFY GOD

The phrase, *"And glorified God, saying, We never saw it on this fashion,"* means they glorified the Lord for the healing and not for the sickness. There is no record in the four Gospels, which record the Life and Ministry of Christ, that Jesus ever refused to heal anyone, claiming it was the Will of God for them to be sick. If such were the case, even remotely so, considering the thousands healed, one or two such examples surely would have shown up. Nothing of this nature surfaced, because it is absurd to think that it is the Will of God for Believers to be sick.

No! Jesus healed all who came to Him, no matter who they were or what their physical problem was.

Some would argue that if it's the Will of God for Believers never to be sick, then they would never be sick. But all would have to agree that it is always the Will of God for Believers never to sin; however, as we all know, Believers, at times, sin.

Unbelief has many arguments, but only Faith in Christ has positive results.

IF IT'S THE WILL OF GOD FOR ALL BELIEVERS TO ENJOY HEALING, WHY AREN'T ALL HEALED AT THE MOMENT OF PRAYER?

The truth is, the Will of God never changes; however, mitigating factors may be involved, which will not allow the Will of God to be realized at all times. Of course, God has the Power to do anything He desires; however, He has perfected laws which He will not abrogate.

For instance, the *"Law of Sin and Death"* was instituted by the Lord in the event of man disobeying God, which man did. This Law of Sin and Death carries with it all types of problems, not the least being sickness. Inasmuch as the human body has not yet been redeemed (Rom. 8:23), due to the Law of Sin and Death now reigning in this world, such has brought *"suffering,"* even in the lives of Believers (Rom. 8:18).

This will not be rectified until the Trump of God sounds, and then the Scripture says, *"We shall all be changed"* (I Cor. 15:51). Then, all sickness and death will be things of the past. Until then, the Lord, at times, heals in answer to believing prayer, and, at times, He doesn't choose to do so.

IS A LACK OF HEALING ALWAYS CAUSED BY A LACK OF FAITH?

No, it isn't! Were that the case, then God would be subservient to the whims of man, which He never is, and never shall be. While it is certainly true that some Christians do not experience healing because of a lack of faith, it is certainly not true in all cases.

A case in point is Paul's *"thorn in the flesh"* (II Cor. 12:7). Whether this *"thorn"* was a physical problem, or something else altogether, actually is immaterial. Paul knew that the Lord could remove it, if He so desired. That holds true with sickness, as well; however, as the Lord chose not to remove Paul's thorn, He chooses, at times, not to heal the Believer, even though such a Believer might have faith for healing. He simply tells the Believer, as He told Paul, *"My Grace is sufficient for you: for My strength is made perfect in weakness"* (II Cor. 12:9).

Now, this is not meant to serve as an excuse why Christians don't receive their healing. The truth is, every Christian, in the time of sickness or infirmity, should always go before the Lord in prayer, asking for healing and believing for such (James 5:14). But, as stated, the Lord doesn't always heal. But if He doesn't, He has promised to give us *"Grace"* to rise above the affliction, whatever it might be (II Cor. 12:10).

WHAT IS FAITH?

The Scripture says, *"Now Faith is the substance of things hoped for, the evidence of things not seen"* (Heb. 11:1). In more elementary terms, Faith is simply believing God, which means to believe His Word. It's not something mysterious, difficult, or hard. In fact, it is very simple and easy. As well, the Scripture also tells us: *"So then Faith comes by hearing, and hearing by the Word of God"* (Rom. 10:17).

In other words, it is impossible for a Believer to increase in Faith unless there is a steady diet of the Word of God properly given to such a Believer.

Paul dealt with Faith more than any of the Apostles, because it was to Paul that the meaning of the New Covenant was given. However, we should understand that when Paul speaks of Faith, always, and without exception, he is speaking of Faith in Christ and what Christ has done for us at the Cross (I Cor. 1:17-18, 23; 2:2; Gal. 3:7-9; 6:14).

To be frank, every human being in the world has faith. While it's not faith in God, nevertheless, it is faith. They have faith in themselves, in their government, in their relatives, etc. Even the scientist who brags that he will accept nothing on faith does, in fact, function according to faith. He has faith that his experiments will bring about the desired results, etc.

In addition, the nations of the world which operate on the free market principle enjoy a greater prosperity, simply because they are operating by faith. But though these all may be examples of faith, it is not faith that God will recognize.

Furthermore, Christians do exhibit faith in God and, in a sense, in His Word, but most of the time, their faith is an incomplete faith.

INCOMPLETE FAITH?

What do we mean by the term *"incomplete faith"*?

It means that the faith of such a person is in the Word of God, but they have an improper understanding of the Word. As well, it is faith in God, but they have an improper understanding of God. The same can be said for Christ. Millions of Christians talk about their faith in Christ, but they have an incomplete knowledge of Christ.

What do we mean by all of this?

If the Believer doesn't understand the Word of God relative to the Cross, in other words, that the story of the Bible in its totality is the story of Jesus Christ and Him Crucified, then one's understanding of the Bible will be incomplete.

In capsule form, John the Beloved gave us the entire meaning of the Word of God in just three Scriptures.

John said, *"In the beginning was the Word, and the Word was with God, and the Word was God"* (Jn. 1:1).

In this one Verse, we are told exactly Who Jesus is. He is the *"Living Word,"* which means, in effect, that the entirety of the Word of God points exclusively to Christ, and in every capacity.

Then John said, *"And the Word was made flesh, and dwelt among us, and we beheld His Glory, the Glory of the Only Begotten of the Father, full of Grace and Truth"* (Jn. 1:14).

Now we learn that this *"Word"* became a Man, toward which the Bible also exclusively pointed (Gen. 3:15; 49:10; Isa. 7:14).

Why did He become a Man?

John gives us the answer to that, as well. He said, as he quoted John the Baptist: *"The next day John sees Jesus coming unto him, and said, Behold the Lamb of God, Who takes away the sin of the world"* (Jn. 1:29).

All of this tells us that the *"Living Word"* became a *"Man"* in order to go to the Cross, so that all *"sin would be taken away."*

So, if we do not understand the Word relative to Christ, then our understanding is incomplete. Also, if we do not understand Christ relative to the Cross, then our understanding of Christ is incomplete. And, regrettably, most Christians do not understand the Cross, so their Faith is incomplete.

Let us say it in this fashion:

GOD'S WAY

There is no way a person can come to God, except through the Lord Jesus Christ (Jn. 14:6).

There is no way that one can come to Christ, unless one comes by the way of the Cross (Lk. 9:23).

There is no way one can come to the Cross, without a denial of self (Lk. 9:23).

THE FASHION OF THE LORD

The phrase, *"Saying, We never saw it on*

this fashion," referred to several things:

1. They had never seen anyone whose sins had been instantly forgiven, along with his physical body being instantly healed.

2. As only Jesus could do this, truly they had never seen it *"on this fashion."*

3. They had never in their lives seen a healing so total and quick, especially considering the former helplessness of the man.

4. They had never seen such power demonstrated.

5. They had never seen such proof given in the answering of an argument, and given so irrefutably! They were seeing the Lord in action doing what only He could do.

This is the difference between Christ and man. Man can only register unbelief, as these Scribes, or marvel. Man cannot, at least by his own power and strength, carry forth the work, and it is foolish to think he can do so. Consequently, modern psychologists could have counseled this man until the sun rose in the west, and no forgiveness of sin or healing of the body would have taken place. Only Jesus could do such a thing.

One grieves, therefore, when one looks at the modern Church, knowing that she has traded the miracle-working Power of God for the prattle of poor helpless man! What a sorry trade!

We are not informed of the effect of this Miracle upon the Scribes and Pharisees, but it is all too evident that, though they could not deny the fact, they would not acknowledge the power. The multitude gave Praise and Glory to God, as they should have, while unbelief was working its deadly result of envy and malice among those who ought to have been their guides and instructors.

But yet, at least one question remains, as it regards Divine Healing!

DID NOT JESUS, IN HIS EARTHLY MINISTRY, HEAL EVERYONE WHO CAME TO HIM?

Yes, He did, and without exception!

The Truth is, He never turned one single person down, as it regards healing, irrespective as to what their life had been previously. It stands to reason that He healed many who really were not serving God, which means that many had sin in their lives. But He never condemned anyone, never chided anyone, but simply gave them that for which they asked and desperately needed.

So, if He healed everyone during the time of His Earthly Ministry, why doesn't He presently heal all who come to Him?

The manner of His Ministry at His First Advent was for a specific purpose and reason. He introduced the Kingdom to Israel, and, in effect, told them they could have the Kingdom, that is, if they did certain things. Those certain things were that they repent of their sin and wickedness and accept Him as their Messiah. They would not do either!

Irrespective of the attitude of Israel, Jesus continued to proclaim the Kingdom, showing them, in effect, how it could be, if Israel would only accept Him. When they do, in fact, accept Him, which will be at the Second Coming, which will begin the Kingdom Age, He will heal, at that time, every sick person on the face of the Earth.

Regarding that time, Isaiah says, *"And the inhabitant shall not say, I am sick: the people who dwell therein shall be forgiven their iniquity"* (Isa. 33:24). He also says, *"Then the eyes of the blind shall be opened, and the ears of the deaf shall be unstopped. Then shall the lame man leap as an hart, and the tongue of the dumb sing: for in the wilderness shall waters break out, and streams in the desert"* (Isa. 35:5-6).

So, Jesus was introducing the Kingdom, at least telling what it would be like. But, as is obvious, Israel rejected Him.

But this is the great reason why He healed all during His Earthly Ministry. At the Second Advent, Divine Healing will be carried out over the entirety of the Earth. As well, the aging process will be halted, because the entirety of the world will partake of the *"fruit"* and the *"leaves,"* which will grow on the trees lining the River which will come out from under the Sanctuary, which will have, as is obvious, miraculous properties (Ezek. 47:12).

The world could have had that upon the First Advent of Christ, if only Israel had accepted Christ. But she would have none of Him, thereby subjecting the world to a continued glut of sickness, sorrow, heartache, war, and man's inhumanity to man, which has lasted now for nearly 2,000 years. However, we are very, very close to the end of the Church Age and the Restoration of Israel, which will occasion the Second Coming.

(13) "AND HE WENT FORTH AGAIN BY THE SEA SIDE; AND ALL THE MULTITUDE RESORTED UNTO HIM, AND HE TAUGHT THEM."

The construction is:

Jesus constantly preached and constantly taught, actually giving preeminence to these twin attributes.

THE TEACHING OF CHRIST

The phrase, *"And He went forth again by the sea side,"* has reference to the fact that Christ did not walk this way by necessity, but by choice. It suggests the idea that He loved to walk along the shore in order to be alone with His Heavenly Father, as well as to enjoy the beauty of His Creation.

This area, and we speak primarily of the Sea of Galilee, which the Holy Spirit chose from eternity to be the site of the Ministry and Miracles of Christ, is beautiful, to say the least! However, even though the topography has not changed from that day until now, still, its appearance probably has changed. Then it would have had quite a heavy growth of trees on the hills, which now, for the most part, are denuded, except for those planted by modern Israel.

The Lower Galilee was then very densely populated, with hundreds of fishing boats plying the waters of the Lake. As a result, there probably wasn't much solitude along the western shore of the Sea of Galilee, but yet which Christ would have enjoyed immensely, even despite the activity.

The phrase, *"And all the multitude resorted unto Him,"* proclaims Him being eagerly sought out. No wonder!

The phrase, *"And He taught them,"* means that as the crowd kept coming to Him, which they did, He kept on teaching them. What a wonder and joy it must have been to have sat at the feet of Jesus!

(14) "AND AS HE PASSED BY, HE SAW LEVI THE SON OF ALPHAEUS SITTING AT THE RECEIPT OF CUSTOM, AND SAID UNTO HIM, FOLLOW ME. AND HE AROSE AND FOLLOWED HIM."

The exposition is:

Matthew was a tax-collector, which was an abomination in the eyes of Israel, but not in the eyes of our Lord.

MATTHEW

The phrase, *"And as He passed by, He saw Levi the son of Alphaeus sitting at the receipt of custom,"* speaks of Matthew. This was not the first time the Lord had seen Levi. His choice of this man as one of the Twelve was based on long observation of him, as he sat at his tax-collector's desk. Moreover, this is not the first time that Levi had seen the Lord. The whole city of Capernaum, of which Matthew was a citizen, was flooded with the fame and reputation of the Lord; consequently, this was no chance meeting or sudden calling. It was designed by the Holy Spirit.

THE RECEIPT OF CUSTOM

Most Jews who were tax-collectors, who consequently were considered to be traitors by their fellow countrymen, usually hired others to actually collect the taxes. Matthew, however, seems to show his defiance by his actions of performing this chore himself, seemingly not caring what others thought.

His tollgate would have been on the Great West Road from Damascus to the Mediterranean. It was also the Customs Office of Capernaum and the landing place for many ships that sailed the Lake or coasted from town to town. He was a tax-collector who collected toll for Herod Antipas. In a sense, he was in the employ of the Roman Government, which meant the Jews hated and despised him, classed him with sinners, and believed him to be a lost soul, i.e., one who could not be saved.

At his tollgate, there would have been an elevated platform or bench on which he sat, which would have been obvious to all. Here he collected the taxes and had power to stop anyone, as well as rummage through their belongings at his pleasure. He could assign and collect taxes on the spot, or confiscate goods, and was backed by the mighty Roman Government.

The manner in which one became a tax-collector varied from district to district. One of the principal ways employed by Rome was to auction off particular districts to the highest bidder. In this manner, Rome would collect a lump sum, with the tax-collector free to collect as much as the traffic would bear.

If, indeed, he had bid high, it was up to him to levy enough taxes to get back his investment, plus a good return. To be sure, inasmuch as he was free to tax within reason, most tax-collectors became very wealthy, and were, in turn, hated and despised by their countrymen.

First of all, the idea of an Israelite having to pay taxes to a Gentile power was unthinkable! And then to have to pay those taxes to a renegade Jew was adding insult to injury. Such a person, consequently, was thought to be not only a traitor, but a sinner of the worst kind.

THE GREAT COMMAND

The phrase, *"And said unto him, Follow Me,"* is the same Command given to Peter, Andrew, James, and John. It also had the same meaning with respect to Matthew as it did for the others.

This was, however, more than an invitation, it was a Command! It is not, as Wuest, the Greek Scholar, says, *"Would you like to follow Me? I extend this invitation to you?"* Here was a King, sovereign in His demands. Levi would have recognized the imperative tone of our Lord's Voice. This was an effectual call, like the call to Salvation.

This call of Christ was anointed heavily by the Holy Spirit and would have had its intended effect upon Matthew, just as the Holy Spirit convicts sinners to come to Christ. It is a power that one, if he so wills, can resist, but which, at the same time, is strong enough to overcome all obstacles and hindrances.

OBEDIENCE

The phrase, *"And he arose and followed Him,"* proclaims Levi leaving his tollbooth, instantly responding to the Master's Command. The statement actually meant *"start following Me, and continue as a habit of life to follow Me."* This meant that Levi was henceforth to walk the same road that Jesus walked, a road of self-sacrifice, a road of separation, a road of suffering, if you please!

NOTES

It was, however, more than just *"Follow Me,"* but instead *"Follow with Me."* As such, it did not mean one following after another, but rather walking side-by-side down the same road. As Wuest also brings out, *"This blessed fellowship is for every Believer in the Lord Jesus."*

What an honor!

What a joy!

As far as the world was concerned, to do this thing meant poverty for Levi instead of the affluence and luxury to which he had been accustomed.

Sadly, the modern Church, at least a large segment of it, has attempted to materialize this Call. Matthew, if transported into today's setting, would be urged to continue his tax-collecting business, while he follows Jesus on the side. Or he is promised that his material riches will not only not be left behind, but, in fact, will be increased. It is a heady doctrine for modern Matthews, but totally unscriptural, and thereby heresy!

PROSPERITY!

While it is certainly true that the Lord does bless His Children financially, still, it is a woeful perversion of the Gospel of Christ to lower the *"Blessing of Abraham"* to the level of money, as I heard one Preacher do. Actually, I'm grossly understating the case.

Salvation has Christ as its Object, and not money. Jesus did not say, *"Follow Me for the things I will give you,"* but instead *"Follow Me,"* which is something else entirely!

The Believer must never misunderstand this Call by reducing it to *"things."* Christ and the Cross must always be the Object, and must never cease to be the Object. The idea is, and as stated, that Matthew left his tollhouse immediately. It is not known whether others were there or not, although probably there were. The moment that this tax-collector said, *"Yes,"* was the greatest moment of his life. Thank God he did not hesitate!

(15) "AND IT CAME TO PASS, THAT, AS JESUS SAT AT MEAT IN HIS HOUSE, MANY PUBLICANS AND SINNERS SAT ALSO TOGETHER WITH JESUS AND HIS DISCIPLES: FOR THERE WERE MANY, AND THEY FOLLOWED HIM."

The composition is:

This Verse expresses a gathering called by Matthew, evidently to celebrate him being called by Christ; he was giving up the tax-collecting business.

There is indication in this Verse that many on that day at that gathering accepted the Lord as the Master of their lives.

THE GATHERING

The phrase, *"And it came to pass, that, as Jesus sat at meat in his house,"* refers to Matthew's house. Luke 5:29 makes it clear that it was the home of this Disciple.

The phrase, *"Many publicans and sinners sat also together with Jesus and His Disciples,"* expresses a gathering called by Matthew, evidently to celebrate him being called by Christ. No doubt, and quickly, the news of Matthew's decision had spread all over Capernaum. As well, there is some evidence that he was held in high regard by fellow tax-collectors; quite possibly, he was a man of some wealth.

In effect, *"Publicans"* were tax-collectors, and, as stated, were considered to be traitors by those in Israel. The term *"sinners"* refers to those who make no pretense whatsoever at living for God, but did what they wanted to do, irrespective as to what others thought. To be sure, these two groups, *"Publicans"* and *"sinners,"* were somewhat classified as outcasts, as it regards the nation of Israel as a whole.

They would have been attracted to Christ, because they saw in Him a reality with no pretense. In other words, He was the genuine article.

FOLLOWING HIM

The phrase, *"For there were many, and they followed Him,"* does not necessarily mean that all who were there wholeheartedly gave their hearts to Christ, but rather that they were very interested in what was being done, and especially that the influence of Christ had been so powerful on one of their fellow Publicans. But it also means, as Matthew, some did wholeheartedly follow Christ! It seems, also, that some had not received a formal invitation to this gathering, but, upon hearing the news, came anyway!

NOTES

THE RELIGION OF JUDAISM

It is evident that these *"Publicans"* felt totally cut off from the mainstream of Jewish life, and the evidence seems clear that they were also excluded from the Synagogue. In other words, they were not wanted there, and would have been told to leave, had they attended. But yet, they felt comfortable with Jesus, as this Text graphically proclaims.

Why?

The religious leaders had long since left the Precepts of the Word of God, introducing their own concepts, which obviously were man-instituted and, therefore, not of God. As such, it had become a religion of the Jews. To become a part of this religion, one had to subscribe to a plethora of rules and regulations in which the Word of God had been twisted from its original context.

It little offered God any more to the people, but rather man-made philosophies and traditions; consequently, these Publicans and others, seeing a way to make a great amount of money by becoming tax-collectors for the Romans, opted for the money. They knew they would become castoffs from Jewish tradition, but felt they were losing nothing in the process! Some, like Matthew, brazenly flaunted their defiance by openly collecting the taxes themselves, instead of hiring others to do it.

When Jesus came preaching, teaching, healing, and performing miracles, He seemed to be totally different than this mishmash of Judiastic religion. His Words were not endless arguments generating continued debates over trifles, but rather exploded with life. As well, His demeanor was one of friendliness and kindness, which was totally unlike the Pharisees and Scribes, with their long religious faces. Moreover, it was obvious that the Power of God was with Him, considering the tremendous miracles being wrought on a daily basis.

And then, miracle of miracles, He made no harsh statements about their tax-collecting business. Now, He had even called one of their own to be His close Disciple. As a result, they wanted to know more about Him.

Why did He not condemn the tax-collecting business?

The next two Verses will tell us!

(16) "AND WHEN THE SCRIBES AND PHARISEES SAW HIM EAT WITH PUBLICANS AND SINNERS, THEY SAID UNTO HIS DISCIPLES, HOW IS IT THAT HE EATS AND DRINKS WITH PUBLICANS AND SINNERS?"

The composition is:

It seems that many of the Scribes and Pharisees had heard of the Call of Matthew; this also resulted in their gathering and coming, although uninvited, to see what was taking place.

This Verse proclaims the fact that they thought that Jesus was committing a great sin by associating with these people. This was their self-righteousness in action.

SCRIBES AND PHARISEES

The phrase, *"And when the Scribes and Pharisees saw Him eat with Publicans and sinners,"* means that they, upon hearing about the Call of Matthew, came to see for themselves.

As we have explained, the Scribes were supposed to be those who were Scholars in the Law of Moses, and consequently instructors of the people in these fundamentals. The Pharisees were a sect in Israel, numbering approximately 7,000 at this time, who would have been called the fundamentalists of that day; in other words, those who claim to believe all the Bible. They by and large controlled the religious life of Israel. Some few accepted Christ, but the majority of them hated Him with a passion, which meant that they really did not know God, despite their profession. Jesus denounced them with scathing rebukes (Mat., Chpt. 23).

What we are seeing here is the beginning of the terrible animosity that would result in them crucifying Christ. Because of many and varied reasons, they hated Him with a passion. In effect, they were the apostate Church, while He was the True Church.

According to students of the customs of that day, the banquet hall in houses of the well-to-do, which was the type of house Matthew seemed to have, and which was where this gathering was being held, was approximately 50 feet long, 20 feet wide, and 20 feet in height. The walls were covered with a type of stucco, either washed brown or white. The roof was of timber and flax; the floor, it is said, was strewn with fine, clean sand and garnished with strips of carpet upon which cushions had been placed.

THE MANNER OF CHRIST

The question, *"They said unto His Disciples, How is it that He eats and drinks with Publicans and sinners?"* posed the idea that they thought He was committing a great sin by associating with these people. In their minds, they were too holy and righteous to associate with such people. To have done so would have greatly degraded their lofty claims of great piousness.

To be sure, it was this attitude that the Publicans hated, and which Christ also hated!

The Scribe's and Pharisee's hatred of the tax-collectors went much further than detestation of the mere practice of collecting taxes. Israel was now subject to Rome; they greatly chaffed at this, thinking themselves to be greatly superior. They maintained that they were Abraham's seed, and protested that as a people dedicated to God, they ought not to be subject to the Romans, who were Gentiles and idolaters. They considered that it was contrary to the liberty and dignity of the Children of God that they should pay tribute to them, a view which increased their prejudice against these tax-gatherers.

They felt that Israel's destiny was to be the premier nation in the world, which, in fact, they had been many years before, under David and Solomon.

ISRAEL AND ROME

In Truth, it was the Plan of God for Israel to be the leading nation; however, by their own sin, wickedness, and rebellion, they had abrogated this position. The Lord had repeatedly sent Prophets, such as Jeremiah, who made every effort to turn them away from their sin and rebellion, but without success. Consequently, Israel, first of all, fell to the Babylonians, and had remained under the Gentile yoke for these many years, and that despite the fact that they had fought continuously to regain their place of superiority.

Even at this time, there were constant insurrections against Rome, attempting to throw off this yoke, which would ultimately result in their destruction by the Roman General, Vespasian, and his son, Titus, in A.D. 70.

What they little knew or realized in their self-righteousness was that Jesus actually was the Son of God, and, in reality, the Messiah. Had they accepted Him, doing so sincerely from a broken and contrite spirit, their nation could have been vaulted once again to prominence. But this they did not do and, in fact, would not do!

So, they hated these *"Publicans,"* which were symbolic of their domination by the Romans.

SINNERS

The word *"sinners"* is interesting here! In the Fifteenth Verse and following, they are separated from the Publicans; however, inasmuch as the word *"Publicans"* is listed first, their sin would have been looked at by the Jews as greater even than the *"sinners,"* whoever they may have been, and whatever they may have done and were doing! And yet, Jesus was *"eating and drinking"* with them, seemingly without censure.

To the Scribes and Pharisees, this entire scene would have been, as stated, unthinkable! First of all, for Jesus to mix with these people was bad enough, but to do so with the enjoyment that seemed to permeate the gathering was not only unthinkable, but, in their minds, blasphemous!

(17) "WHEN JESUS HEARD IT, HE SAID UNTO THEM, THEY WHO ARE WHOLE HAVE NO NEED OF THE PHYSICIAN, BUT THEY WHO ARE SICK: I CAME NOT TO CALL THE RIGHTEOUS, BUT SINNERS TO REPENTANCE."

The overview is:

Christ was, and is, the Physician of sinners, not their companion.

THE GREAT PHYSICIAN

The phrase, *"When Jesus heard it, He said unto them, they who are whole have no need of the physician, but they who are sick,"* explains fully as to the *"Why?"* of His Presence. As someone has said, *"The physician is not infected by the disease of the patient, but rather overcomes it and drives it from him; and so it is no disgrace, but rather an honor, to the physician to associate himself with the sick, and so much more the greater the sickness."*

Jesus was in this place, not because He especially enjoyed this type of company, for He did not. There was sin all about Him, because there were sinners, and His righteous, sensitive soul shrank back from it. But He was there to reach their souls for Salvation.

Bickersteth, a Greek expositor of the Nineteenth Century, said the following may have been the thoughts of Christ regarding the question of the Scribes and Pharisees:

"I, Who am sent from Heaven by the Father, that I might be the Physician of the souls of sinners, am not defiled by their sins and spiritual diseases when I converse with them; but rather I cure and heal them, which is alike for My Glory and for their good, so much the more the greater their sins.

"For I am the Physician of sinners, not their companion. But you, O Scribes and Pharisees, are not the physicians, but the companions of sinners, and so you are contaminated.

"Nevertheless, you desire to be thought righteous and holy; and therefore, I do not associate with you:

1. Because you think you are righteous, when in Truth you are not, actually not even as good as these Publicans and sinners; and,

2. Because your insincerity and hypocrisy are an offense to Me."

THE MANNER OF CHRIST

Many in the modern Church mistake and misunderstand the actions of Christ, thinking, by His association with sinners, that He condoned their activity; consequently, too many in the modern Church think very little is wrong or sinful. As a result, any and all are embraced as fellow Believers, and irrespective of their erroneous doctrine, such as Catholicism, etc. The world is thus brought into the Church under the guise of winning them to Christ. Regrettably, such does not win the world, but rather destroys the Church.

Christ was no companion of the sinful activities of these *"sinners,"* whatever they may have been, but He was a companion in the sense of loving these people, and irrespective of what they had done. He was not there to criticize or to condemn them, but rather to show them a better way. In effect, they were on His territory, instead of Him being on theirs.

Not for a moment did He condone their sinful activities, nor did He show any inclination to such by His attitude toward them. To love them did not mean to accept them, neither did it mean to condemn them. He was there to bring them out of their sin, instead of accepting them in their sin. A holier-than-thou attitude would in no way have accomplished this purpose. He was *in* their company, but not *of* their company! As such, we, as well, are to be *in* the world, but not *of* it! This we must never forget, conducting ourselves as Christ conducted Himself.

One does not win the drunk or the thief, etc., to Christ by condemning him, but by loving him. At the same time, however, condemning the act is not condemning the person. Jesus, by His lifestyle, Messages, conduct, and actions constantly condemned the acts of sin; however, He never condemned sinners. There is a vast difference!

So, Jesus did not use this occasion to condemn the sinners who were present, but rather to show them, by His Love for them, a better way.

SINNERS

In effect, sinners, and especially these kind, know they are sinners. They don't really have to be reminded of it. They actually live under constant condemnation, and heaping more condemnation upon them does not tend to pull them out of their sin, but actually drives them further into it. That is the reason a parent seldom does any good by constantly haranguing a son or daughter over their waywardness. Certainly the waywardness cannot be condoned, but, at the same time, it is only love which will bring them back.

Taking the example of Christ, this is the only method which will work. No, it doesn't work with all, but it worked with Matthew, and it has worked with a host of others!

REPENTANCE

The phrase, *"I came not to call the righteous, but sinners to Repentance,"* tells us the very reason why He came. Thank God He did, because His Call reached me, and prayerfully

NOTES

you. The truth was, and still is: only *"sinners"* populate the Earth. Paul said, *"There is none righteous, no not one,"* referring to righteousness within ourselves (Rom. 3:9-18).

For a period of time, we placed our Telecast on *"Public Access"* channels in various cities across America. These are Cable Channels set aside by Congress, with supposedly one in each city, to be used for whatever the public desires to air over it, within bounds of certain decency, which, at times, seems not to exist very much at all. In other words, about anything, as inane as it may be, and sometimes as vulgar as it might be, can be aired over these Channels.

While there is no charge for the airtime, still, no appeal for financial help can be made to offset production costs, etc. At any rate, we were airing on approximately 200 Public Access Channels in as many cities in America. It has been implied by some that it might not be proper to air a Gospel Program on such a Channel, especially considering the type of programming which surrounds it, and that only hard-core *"sinners"* watch it.

Of course, the answer is simple. That is the very reason for airing it on these Channels. If you want to catch fish, you go where the fish are, exactly as Jesus did at this gathering. To think any other way is to place oneself in the same position as the Scribes and Pharisees!

Beautifully enough, some of the greatest testimonies we have ever received came from these *"Public Access"* Channels. These are testimonies of Deliverance and Victory. And beautifully enough, most of them are from young people caught so terribly in such a bondage of sin and iniquity that it defies description. And yet, by the Power of God, they are being set free. I will give one brief example.

A PERSONAL TESTIMONY

A 17-year-old girl wrote and told of what Jesus had done for her. She related how she had been an alcoholic at 13 years old, which is unthinkable to a rational mind. Yet she found herself in this terrible bondage.

She related how her stepfather had sexually abused her over and over again, but her mother would not do anything about the situation, causing her to be driven further into this prison of darkness. As a result of the abuse and alcoholism, and seeking companionship and acceptance from almost anyone, she became pregnant at 16 years old. She was, as a result, driven out of the house and forced to live on her own.

She related how she sought employment at a service station, and rented a small mobile home for $60 a week in order to have a place to live. There was nothing in this small mobile home but a couch, a table, a bed, and a small black-and-white TV.

Not knowing what to do about her situation of pregnancy, she had scheduled an abortion. The day before she was to have the abortion, having taken two or three days off work for this purpose, she came home that afternoon. Her shift had ended. It was 4 p.m. She related how she lay down on the couch, after turning on the small TV set. It was on the Public Access Channel.

Having no idea what was coming on, all of a sudden she was surprised to see our Program beginning to air. She really did not know who we were, and really had little interest; however, she enjoyed the music and remained to listen to the Message.

THE WAYS OF THE LORD

During the course of the Message, I mentioned something about abortion. I stated, *"The answer to abortion is not killing doctors or bombing abortion clinics, but instead bringing the precious soul to Jesus Christ."* As she heard these words, she came under great conviction by the Holy Spirit. She went on to say that when the Message ended, and I began to pray, she slipped onto her knees beside the couch and began to pray with me.

"Brother Swaggart," she said, *"even though I knew nothing about the Lord, not having been raised in a Christian family, when I began to pray with you, something happened to me such as I had never experienced before. For the first time I knew that Someone loved me and I knew it was Jesus."*

She related how she did not really know too much about what had happened to her; but she did know something had changed within her. In the first place, she almost instantly went to sleep, without drinking two or three glasses of Vodka, which she normally consumed before going to bed. She related how she slept all night, waking the next morning with no desire for alcohol.

In her mind, she had already canceled the abortion, but yet she did not know what she was going to do. She only had $3 to her name. With that, she walked over to a nearby Denny's Restaurant and ordered some breakfast, which she seldom ever did. She had just turned in her order when a lady with a Bible under her arm walked up to her table.

The lady, without introducing herself, looked down at her and said: *"I come into this restaurant every morning, and the Lord generally gives me someone to witness to. But yesterday, something happened to me that was special."* She continued by saying, *"I was watching Brother Swaggart on the Public Access Channel, when he mentioned something about abortion. The Lord spoke to my heart and told me that I was, without fail, to be in this Restaurant this morning, and there would be a young lady present who was pregnant and needed help!"*

The lady then looked straight at the girl and said, *"You are that person, aren't you?"*

Startled, the girl began to weep, actually sobbing! The lady sat down across from her and began to console her and pray with her.

As the lady continued to speak with her, she again mentioned my name and the Message I had brought the day before. *"But you probably don't know who or what I'm talking about,"* remarked the lady. Once more, the young girl began to weep, saying, *"Oh yes, I do! Yesterday afternoon, I saw that same Program, and gave my heart to Jesus Christ."*

The young girl wrote us about how this Christian lady immediately took her into her home, buying her some clothes, and helping her to find a better job. A few weeks later, while watching our Telecast, she was Baptized with the Holy Spirit, with the evidence of speaking with other tongues.

"Brother Swaggart," she wrote, *"my little son was born just a few days ago. He was two or three weeks early, but in perfect health."*

This testimony that I have related to you could be construed as nothing other than a miracle. Not only was this girl's soul and life saved, but her baby also was saved. To be sure, this is why Jesus came. This is His very purpose.

The word *"Repentance"* is the seed of Salvation. Men had sinned against God, and they must repent to Him, admitting they are a sinner and in desperate need of His help. The words may vary and the sinner may not even know what Repentance is; nevertheless, their heart action toward God must be in that spirit. Moreover, they must have Faith in Jesus Christ, even though they may know very little about Him or what He has done respecting His Death at Calvary, which was for lost sinners.

Repentance toward God and Faith in Christ guarantee Redemption for any and all! (Acts 20:21).

YOU FURNISH THE SINNER, AND GOD FURNISHES THE SAVIOUR

It happened in West Texas. A little boy had died. He was only three or four years old. When the funeral was over, the people gradually began to leave.

The Pastor who had preached the funeral lingered behind to console the people. Finally, all were gone except one elderly gentleman standing beside the open grave. The Pastor walked up to him and asked, *"Sir, was the little boy kin to you?"*

The man slowly nodded his head in the affirmative, saying, *"He was my grandson."*

The Pastor then expounded as to how the little fellow was now in Heaven, and concluded by asking, *"Sir, are you ready to meet your grandson?" Have you accepted Christ as your Saviour?"*

The elderly gentleman slowly turned around, looking at the Pastor, saying, *"I really don't understand how to be saved!"*

The Pastor stood there for a moment. Finally, he said, *"Sir, it's very simple. All you have to do is furnish the sinner. He furnishes the Saviour."*

Even though it's almost impossible that an unsaved person would be reading this Commentary, still, I feel led of the Lord to include the following. I am speaking of the Sinner's Prayer. I would ask you, if you need to pray this prayer, please pray it slowly now and believe it with all of your heart. That being done, you definitely will be saved (Rom. 10:9-10, 13).

THE SINNER'S PRAYER

"Dear Heavenly Father, I come to You in the Name of Jesus.

"I'm sorry for my sins, the way I've lived, the things I've done.

"Please forgive me, and cleanse me, with Your Precious Blood, from all unrighteousness.

"With my mouth, I confess the Lord Jesus,

"And with my heart, I believe that God has raised Him from the dead.

"This very moment, I accept Jesus Christ as my Saviour and as my Lord.

"According to His Word, I have called on Him, and according to His Word, I am saved" (Rom. 10:13).

(18) "AND THE DISCIPLES OF JOHN AND OF THE PHARISEES USED TO FAST: AND THEY COME AND SAY UNTO HIM, WHY DO THE DISCIPLES OF JOHN AND OF THE PHARISEES FAST, BUT YOUR DISCIPLES FAST NOT?"

The diagram is:

Any ordinance or ritual given in the Bible, such as fasting, must never be looked at as holy within itself, but rather as to what it represents.

These following Passages will prove to be a tremendous insight into the world of religion versus the following of Christ, i.e., a relationship with Christ.

THE DISCIPLES OF JOHN

The phrase, *"And the Disciples of John and of the Pharisees used to fast,"* concerns the joining of the Pharisees with the Disciples of John the Baptist, who was now in prison. Why would the Disciples of John have joined with the Pharisees, especially considering that John had called the Pharisees *"a brood of vipers"*? Here they joined with these vipers in criticizing Jesus.

Quite possibly, they were hurt and jealous respecting the incarceration of their leader, and the gaining influence of Christ. They may have reasoned within their hearts that if Jesus were actually the Messiah, He would effect the release of John. If, in fact, these thoughts were in their minds, it shows they did not properly understand the mission of John, which was to introduce Christ, which he capably did.

Christ, in fact, definitely could have delivered John from prison. But that was not the Will of God. John had finished his mission, and had done it well. Even though he would die an early and violent death, still, he would do so knowing that he had carried out in totality that which he was called to do. There is no greater accomplishment than that.

Furthermore, each of these Disciples whom Jesus called, with the exception of the John the Beloved, the brother of James, ultimately would die a martyr's death, and would not be delivered by the Lord. But, at the time of their deaths, their work would be finished as well!

It seems that John's Disciples allowed personal ambition to crowd out the Will of God, with them, in effect, joining the enemies of God. The modern Believer must be very careful in respect to this temptation. Self-interest must be laid aside in favor of the Will of God. To side with the enemies of God is a position that cannot be blessed, irrespective of its seeming present prosperity.

FASTING

"Fasting" was a ritual practiced two days a week by the Pharisees, and possibly also by the Disciples of John. More than likely, the Feast held in the home of Matthew was being held on one of these fast days. This was not one of the fasts prescribed by the Law; had it been so, it would have been observed by our Lord. Actually, in the Law of Moses, only one day a year was to be set aside for fasting, and that was on the *"Great Day of Atonement"* (Lev. 16:29-31). However, fasting was also undertaken in times of deep trouble and underlined the seriousness of personal and national appeals to God (II Sam. 12:16-22; II Chron. 20:1-29; Neh. 1:4; Jer. 36:1-20; Dan. 9:3-19).

Fasting, at times, was carried out as a sign of honest Repentance (I Ki. 21:27; Joel 2:12-15; Jonah 3:5-10). However, the Pharisees, evidently thinking that more is better, now fasted 104 days a year. This was a part of their self-righteousness, which they, as here, loudly trumpeted. To be sure, this type of fasting may have been of some benefit to them physically, but it held absolutely no spiritual significance.

NOTES

The sight of Jesus, all his Disciples, and all these *"Publicans"* and *"sinners,"* with their feasting, laughing, and talking, was an offense to the Pharisees and the Disciples of John. Therefore, they asked the following: *"Why do the Disciples of John and of the Pharisees fast, but Your Disciples fast not?"* Actually, there is no record that Jesus or His Disciples fasted at all, even on the *"Great Day of Atonement."*

(The Great Day of Atonement could not now be carried out, because there was no Ark of the Covenant in the Holy of Holies in the Temple at Jerusalem. On this special day, which came once a year, the High Priest, who was a Type of Christ, was to kill a goat and offer its blood upon the Mercy Seat of the Ark of the Covenant. This was to atone nationally for the sins of the people. Due to the Ark of the Covenant being missing since the Babylonian invasion of some 600 years earlier, this ritual could not now be carried out.)

(19) "AND JESUS SAID UNTO THEM, CAN THE CHILDREN OF THE BRIDECHAMBER FAST, WHILE THE BRIDEGROOM IS WITH THEM? AS LONG AS THEY HAVE THE BRIDEGROOM WITH THEM, THEY CANNOT FAST."

The exposition is:
Jesus is the Bridegroom!

THE BRIDEGROOM

The question, *"And Jesus said unto them, Can the children of the bridechamber fast, while the Bridegroom is with them?"* tells us several things:

1. Jesus was alluding to Himself as the Bridegroom. John the Baptist had even called himself the friend of the Bridegroom, that is, of Christ.

2. People do not fast, as would be obvious, in the midst of a wedding feast.

3. By using this type of illustration, Jesus is actually referring to Himself as the Messiah, the One for Whom Israel had been waiting!

FASTING NOW AND THEN

The phrase, *"As long as they have the Bridegroom with them, they cannot fast,"* gives us some idea as to what fasting is all about. Even though fasting, as we have already stated, should be done for many reasons, still, the primary reason for fasting is that Jesus is not here visibly present; and, without the Lord's presence, the Will of God is not being done on Earth as it is in Heaven. Consequently, people fasted before Jesus came, and we now fast because He has been rejected. When He comes back, however, as He shall, and the Kingdom Age begins, there is no record in the Bible of people fasting at that time.

Fasting speaks of the Believer being in a hostile environment, which this world is, with the flesh subject to the pull of the world. This is because Jesus is not reigning Personally in this world, even though reigning in our lives.

"Fasting" presently will help in any and all situations as it regards our living for God; however, it only *helps*, which means its not the solution.

The other day, a Brother said to me that *"fasting"* was the answer to the sin question. No, it isn't!

There is no place in the Bible that speaks of such. The Bible does tell us that the Cross, and the Cross alone, is the answer for sin.

Paul said: *"But this Man* (Christ Jesus), *after He had offered One Sacrifice for sins forever* (speaks of the Cross), *sat down on the Right Hand of God* (refers to the great contrast with the Priests under the Levitical system, who never sat down, because their work was never completed; the Work of Christ was a *'Finished Work,'* and needed no repetition") (Heb. 10:12).

(20) "BUT THE DAYS WILL COME, WHEN THE BRIDEGROOM SHALL BE TAKEN AWAY FROM THEM, AND THEN SHALL THEY FAST IN THE THOSE DAYS."

The composition is:

While fasting helps the Believer in many ways, the greatest way of all is what it symbolizes; in essence, fasting states that things aren't right and will not be right until Jesus comes back. So fasting, at least in part, is a plea for Him to come quickly.

THE BRIDEGROOM TAKEN AWAY

The phrase, *"But the days will come, when the bridegroom shall be taken away from them,"* is a statement, whether understood at that time or not, that Jesus would be rejected as the Messiah of Israel, and would be *"taken away,"* which He was at the Ascension.

The phrase, *"And then shall they fast in those days,"* refers to the time after His Ascension on through to the present, and on through to His Coming.

After the Lord's Ascension, His Disciples frequently fasted as of necessity, because they went through much privation and trial. As stated, such continues unto this moment, and will be the part and parcel of those who live Godly in Christ Jesus, until He returns to take to Himself His Kingdom, when there will then be a constant Campmeeting and everlasting Festival filled with joy, which will then require no fasting.

(21) "NO MAN ALSO SEWS A PIECE OF NEW CLOTH ON AN OLD GARMENT: ELSE THE NEW PIECE THAT FILLED IT UP TAKES AWAY FROM THE OLD, AND THE RENT IS MADE WORSE."

The diagram is:

The *"new cloth"* symbolizes the New Covenant which Christ would bring in; it would not be a part of the Old Covenant, that being done away, but would be completely new. To try to mix the two, as He states, will not work; regrettably, most modern Christians, whether they realize it or not, are actually attempting to mix the two.

THE NEW COVENANT

The phrase, *"No man also sews a piece of new cloth on an old garment,"* once again portrays Christ using something familiar to all to explain a great Truth. The idea is this:

The *"new cloth"* spoken of here refers to cloth which had not been made usable by the process of cleansing, shrinking, and thickening, through the use of moisture, heat, and pressure. If such cloth was used as a patch on an *"old garment,"* the *"new cloth"* would tend to shrink, thereby tearing away from the *"old garment."*

The phrase, *"Else the new piece that filled it up takes away from the old, and the rent is made worse,"* was easily understood by all, and by which they also should have understood the spiritual implication. The patch refers to the Messiah's new type of Ministry, which was Grace, which is, in fact, the *"New Covenant,"* as compared to the Mosaic Law, the old worn-out garment, which was ready to be satisfied.

It speaks of those today who attempt to retain the Mosaic Law, or law of any nature, which God set aside at the Cross, and put upon it the patch of Grace. It happens as our Lord said, *"The new piece . . . will take away from the old, and the rent is made worse."* When the attempt is made to mix Law and Grace, both lose their true identity, and one is left with the doctrine of the Judaizers, as in the Galatian heresy.

THE TRUTH OF LAW AND GRACE

Every single Believer in the world is either under the administration of *"Law"* or the administration of *"Grace."* Most think, erroneously enough, I might quickly add, that because this is the Dispensation of Grace, we are automatically under that government.

However, Paul said: *"I do not frustrate the Grace of God: for if righteousness come by the Law, then Christ is dead in vain"* (Gal. 2:21). The Apostle also said: *"Christ is become of no effect unto you, whosoever of you are justified by the Law; you are fallen from Grace"* (Gal. 5:4).

So, Paul here tells us that we can *"frustrate the Grace of God"* or even *"fall from Grace,"* which means that such a Believer is then resorting to Law. As stated, every Believer is either under Grace or Law.

No! Just because we are living in the Dispensation of Grace doesn't mean that we automatically are under Grace. The truth is this:

If the Believer doesn't properly understand the Cross of Christ, by default, they will simply place themselves, whether they realize it or not, under Law. And then you've got a problem. As we have stated, when the attempt is made to mix Law and Grace, whether the individual understands that this is being done or not, both lose their true identity, and one is left with the Galatian heresy.

THE GALATIAN HERESY

The reason that Paul wrote the Epistle to the Galatians is because Judaizers had come in from Jerusalem and were attempting to get the Galatians to add Law to the Grace which Paul had originally taught them. These Galatians had accepted Christ, and had done so by Grace through Faith, which is the only way one can truly be saved. However, after hearing the Judaizers, and trying to embrace Law, they were then trying to sanctify themselves by their own machinations. In other words, it was Salvation by Grace, and Sanctification by Self.

That's why Paul asked the question, *"Are you so foolish? Having begun in the Spirit, are you now made perfect by the flesh?"* (Gal. 3:3). But yet, that's where many modern Christians are presently. Christians are attempting to do what only the Holy Spirit can do. And to be sure, He will do what needs to be done, if we will simply place our Faith in Christ and what Christ did at the Cross, understanding at all times that Christ is the Source, while the Cross is the Means. We must never forget that!

(22) "AND NO MAN PUTS NEW WINE INTO OLD BOTTLES: ELSE THE NEW WINE DOES BURST THE BOTTLES, AND THE WINE IS SPILLED, AND THE BOTTLES WILL BE MARRED: BUT NEW WINE MUST BE PUT INTO NEW BOTTLES."

The overview is:

This is the same principle as the *"new cloth,"* but given in a different way, in order to emphasize this Truth.

NEW WINE AND OLD BOTTLES

The phrase, *"And no man puts new wine into old bottles,"* has nothing to do with glass bottles, as we think of such presently. The Greek word refers to *"wineskins."* The Gospel of Jesus Christ is here referred to as *"new wine,"* with the *"old bottles"* or *"old wineskins"* referring to the Law.

The phrase, *"Else the new wine does burst the bottles, and the wine is spilled, and the bottles will be marred,"* refers to unfermented wine placed in *"old bottles,"* which, upon beginning to ferment, would expand and consequently *"burst the bottles,"* i.e., *"wineskins."*

The phrase, *"But new wine must be put into new bottles,"* was something that everyone understood.

Once again, Jesus uses an illustration of material things familiar to all. He is actually saying the same thing that He said in the previous Verse, except in a different way.

To attempt to attach the Gospel of Grace

to the Law of Moses would only destroy both! Consequently, the *"new wine"* of the Gospel must likewise have *"new bottles,"* i.e., a new presentation, which would actually be a *"New Covenant."*

Jesus is actually referring back to the statement in Verse 20, *"The Bridegroom* (speaking of Himself) *shall be taken away from them."* The Church would then be ushered in, founded not upon the old Mosaic System, but instead upon the foundation of Grace, which was an entirely new presentation. In this new presentation, i.e., *"new bottles,"* both Gentiles and Jews would come the same way. All would be by Faith, with the Sacrifices coming to an end, because Jesus, as the Perfect Sacrifice, would fulfill that type.

In fact, the Disciples, as well as all who were hearing Him that day, probably little understood what He was speaking of at that time, but which the Disciples would graphically understand after the Day of Pentecost.

THE GREAT STRUGGLE

It is easy to understand from Paul's writings, and to Paul was given the meaning of the New Covenant, that the great problem in his day was actually the same problem we are having now, i.e., the struggle between Law and Grace. There is something in the human being, even consecrated Christians, which wants to try to adhere to Law.

Think about this for a moment:

Paul founded the Churches in Galatia. Consequently, those people who came in under his Ministry had the benefit of the greatest teaching on the face of the Earth. In fact, they were hearing this Message of Grace from the very man to whom the Revelation had been given by the Lord Jesus (Gal. 1:11-12). And yet, when the Judaizers came into these Churches (after Paul had gone on to other fields of endeavor), they were able to turn the heads and hearts of some of the Galatians toward Law, despite the fact that the Galatians had come in under the greatest teaching ever. In other words, their foundation was right, but there is such a propensity in man to depend upon his own ability, or the ability of others, that it's easy to turn in that direction.

It is the easiest thing in the world to have simple faith in Christ and the Cross, but yet the hardest thing to do. We keep desiring to add our own efforts into the mix, and, as we've already stated, when this is done, both Law and Grace lose their true identity, and one is left with neither.

It's very hard for the unsaved to admit they cannot save themselves; likewise, it's very hard for the Believer to admit that he cannot sanctify himself. The Gospel is simple. By simple faith, one is saved (Eph. 2:8-9); and by simple faith, one is sanctified (Rom. 6:3-14).

(23) "AND IT CAME TO PASS, THAT HE WENT THROUGH THE CORN FIELDS ON THE SABBATH DAY; AND HIS DISCIPLES BEGAN, AS THEY WENT, TO PLUCK THE EARS OF CORN."

The exposition is:

The word *"corn"* should have been translated *"barley"* or *"wheat,"* because there was no corn, as we think of such, in the Middle East or Europe, at that time.

THE SABBATH DAY

The phrase, *"And it came to pass, that He went through the corn* (wheat or barley) *fields on the Sabbath Day,"* will occasion a confrontation with the Pharisees.

The phrase, *"And His Disciples began, as they went, to pluck the ears of corn,"* spoke of their doing this in order to eat the grain. This was a common practice, with the individual taking the ripened grain, rubbing it briskly in his hands to remove the chaff, and then eating it raw. It was, incidentally, very nutritious.

This was being done on the *"Sabbath Day,"* and, as usual, the Pharisees were watching everything He did, in order that they might someway find fault.

(24) "AND THE PHARISEES SAID UNTO HIM, BEHOLD, WHY DO THEY ON THE SABBATH DAY THAT WHICH IS NOT LAWFUL?"

The synopsis is:

They claimed the Disciples were breaking the Law of Moses by plucking and eating the grain on the Sabbath; Deuteronomy 23:24-25 says otherwise.

THE PHARISEES

The phrase, *"And the Pharisees said unto*

Him," actually means in the Greek that they kept on speaking to Him about this matter, refusing to let the matter rest, in other words, badgering Him!

The question, *"Behold, why do they on the Sabbath Day that which is not lawful?"* proclaims them taking issue with Him on the legality of gathering the grain on the Sabbath, which, to them, was reaping on a small scale. In fact, they did the same with the dragging of a chair across the floor on the Sabbath, or even a woman combing her hair. They claimed these things should not be done because a speck of dust might be moved and could be construed as *"plowing,"* which was forbidden on the Sabbath.

The Law of Moses actually stated that anyone walking through a vineyard or field of grain could feel free to pluck some grapes or grain to eat, although they must not pluck enough to put into a vessel (Deut. 23:24-25). Consequently, Jesus and His Disciples were not doing anything wrong by taking a small amount of grain from someone else's field, and, as stated, it was a very common practice. Furthermore, the idea in Deuteronomy is that it was to be eaten immediately, and not taken home, etc. Moreover, no stipulation in the Law prevented such being done on the Sabbath. This was strictly an addition by the Pharisees.

Actually, most criticism by the Pharisees concerned outward religion, the things they held as proof of religion, which anyone could do, even the ungodly. This was the cause of the constant conflict between these hypocrites and Christ.

(25) "AND HE SAID UNTO THEM, HAVE YOU NEVER READ WHAT DAVID DID, WHEN HE HAD NEED, AND WAS HUNGRY, HE, AND THEY WHO WERE WITH HIM?"

The exegesis is:

He could have taken them to Deuteronomy, but instead He took them to I Samuel, Chapter 21; He would take them at their own game.

He was showing them the futility of religion and ceremony, when there was no change in the heart.

DAVID

The phrase, *"And He said unto them,"* portrays Him taking them to I Samuel, Chapter 21, which, of course, they knew very well. He could have argued the point that there was nothing in the Law that forbade them eating this grain on the Sabbath Day, but instead He would take them at their own game.

The Pharisees, Scribes, and Sadducees did everything they knew to do to snare Christ in His words, but all to no avail. It should be understood that He knew the Word as no one else knew the Word. In fact, He was the Living Word, which means that every single thing in the Word of God, in some way, pointed to Christ. So the idea that they could best Him in their use of the Scriptures was foolish.

The question, as asked by Christ, *"Have you never read what David did, when he had need, and was hungry, he, and they who were with him?"* took them back to an incident which would embrace His position in total. However, it didn't matter that He proved His point again and again from the Word of God. They had no desire for Truth. They simply hated Him, as all religion hates Jesus!

(26) "HOW HE WENT INTO THE HOUSE OF GOD IN THE DAYS OF ABIATHAR THE HIGH PRIEST, AND DID EAT THE SHEWBREAD, WHICH IS NOT LAWFUL TO EAT BUT FOR THE PRIESTS, AND GAVE ALSO TO THEM WHICH WERE WITH HIM?"

The structure is:

David was not a Priest, so by the Law could not eat one of these special loaves in the Tabernacle; however, he wisely judged that a positive law forbidding the laity to eat this bread, which it did, ought to yield to a law of necessity and or nature, which it did!

THE HIGH PRIEST

The beginning of the question, *"How he went into the House of God in the days of Abiathar the High Priest . . ."* seems to be a discrepancy, for Ahimelech was High Priest at that time (I Sam. 21:1; 22:9); consequently, it can be explained in one of two ways:

1. It seems that Ahimelech was Abiathar's father; however, both the father and the son could have had both names, which was sometimes the case.

2. It is said that both Ahimelech the father and Abiathar the son were present when David came in his distress and obtained the shewbread; however, shortly after, Ahimelech

was killed by Saul, with Abiathar fleeing to David and becoming his companion in exile. A short time later he succeeded to the High Priesthood, taking the place of his father, and doing far more good than this father had done. In view of this, the possibility is that he was given this special commendation at this time as though he actually was the High Priest, even though his father was then living.

Consequently, the words may be properly translated, *"In the days when Abiathar was living, who became High Priest."*

THE SHEWBREAD

The conclusion of the question, *"And did eat the Shewbread, which is not lawful to eat but for the Priests, and gave also to them which were with him?"* concerned the bread which was called the *"bread of the face,"* or the Divine Presence, symbolizing the Divine Being Who is the Bread of Life.

It was directed by the Law that within the Sanctuary there should be a table of shittim (acacia) wood; and every Sabbath twelve newly-baked loaves were placed upon the table in two rows. These loaves were sprinkled with incense, and then remained there until the following Sabbath. They were then replaced by twelve newly-baked loaves and the old loaves were eaten entirely by the Priests in the Holy Place, from which it was unlawful to remove them. These twelve loaves corresponded to the Twelve Tribes of Israel, but more particularly they referred to Christ, Who is the Bread of Life, and His Government, symbolized by the number *"Twelve."*

When David came, even though he was not a Priest, still, he ate the loaves, which, under ordinary circumstances, were not lawful for lay people to eat; however, he wisely judged that a positive law forbidding the laity to eat this bread ought to yield to a law of necessity and of nature, which it did!

As well, David divided these loaves with those who were with him, it seems, at a later time.

(27) "AND HE SAID UNTO THEM, THE SABBATH WAS MADE FOR MAN, AND NOT MAN FOR THE SABBATH."

The composition is:

The original construction contains the idea that Jesus said these things over and over. It took some talking to get the idea across to their minds, which were warped with a warped theology.

The force of the argument is this: the Sabbath was made on account of man, not man on account of the Sabbath; the Sabbath was a day of rest; it was meant to point to the *"spiritual rest"* which would come in Christ.

THE SABBATH

The phrase, *"And He said unto them,"* proclaims Jesus as Lord of the Sabbath, and that He could not submit to the authority of men, who, in their spiritual ignorance, opposed the true meaning of the Sabbath. The Scribes, being unspiritual men, did not understand the Sabbath or its purpose. They limited God's goodness and refused the New Wine of the Kingdom.

The idea of the phrase, *"And He said unto them,"* is that He said these things to them, and kept on saying them. It took some time and some talking to get the idea across to their minds, which were warped, to say the least.

One can hear Christ making these statements of Verses 27 and 28 over and over again, until they finally heard what He was saying. And yet, after they finally heard it, knowing what He was saying, and that it was correct, still, there is no evidence that they believed. Why?

To have done so would have meant unraveling all of their man-made rules and regulations. Doing such would be admitting that they were wrong in their theology. Self-righteousness, even when coming face-to-face with its error, as here, is loath to do that which is demanded of the humble, penitent heart.

WHAT THE SABBATH IS ALL ABOUT

The phrase, *"The Sabbath was made for man and not man for the Sabbath,"* proclaimed in a few words what the Sabbath was all about!

The principle is that the Sabbath is only a means to an end, the good of man. The Rabbis, with all their petty rules, seemed to think that man was made for it. The force of the argument is this: the Sabbath was made on account of man, not man on account of the Sabbath.

In fact, the Sabbath was a day of rest, and was meant to portray Christ, Who would give *"spiritual rest."* In fact, Jesus said, *"Come unto Me, all you who labor and are heavy laden, and I will give you rest. Take My yoke upon you and learn of Me; for I am meek and lowly in heart: and you shall find rest unto your souls. For My yoke is easy, and My burden is light"* (Mat. 11:28-30).

Even though the Sabbath was a day of rest, and was meant to point to Christ, Who Alone could bring spiritual rest, still, our Lord showed these religious leaders that as great as the Sabbath is, it must be subordinate to man. If something needed to be done on the Sabbath that would benefit man, such as His Disciples gathering a little grain to eat, then the Sabbath must be subordinate to that.

The Sabbath, as all Bible Students understand, was a part of the Law of Moses. This Law, which was instituted in totality by God, was meant to serve as a way of life for Israel, God's people. It covered every aspect of the human endeavor from the minute to the mighty. It was meant to show man how to live, what to do, and how to conduct himself toward his fellowman and God.

To be sure, there were other laws in the world, which had been devised by man; but God's Law, as given to Moses, was so superior, as should be obvious, that there was no comparison. In fact, the entirety of the Mosaic Law, and in its every capacity, pointed to Christ, in either His Mediatorial, Atoning, or Intercessory Work (Heb. 4:1-6).

(28) "THEREFORE THE SON OF MAN IS LORD ALSO OF THE SABBATH."

The composition is:

In this statement, Christ was saying, *"I am the Messiah."* And these religious leaders knew what He was saying!

LORD OF THE SABBATH

This Scripture, although short, encompassing only one sentence, is nevertheless freighted with meaning.

The phrase, *"Therefore the Son of Man,"* referring to Himself, in effect, proclaims God the Son, manifest in human flesh, identifying Himself in Incarnation with mankind.

He was saying, *"I am the Messiah,"* and these religious leaders knew what He was saying!

The phrase, *"Is Lord also of the Sabbath,"* means that He is the Owner of the Sabbath, because He is the Creator of it, as well as all things! The Creator is Lord of creation, and thus the Lord of the Sabbath, which He brought into being for the sake of mankind, and to serve, as stated, as a symbol of the *"rest"* that one would find in Christ.

The title *"Lord"* is the august title of God, which we know as Jehovah, and thus proclaims Deity. To be sure, Jesus, even as Lord of the Sabbath, was no Sabbath breaker; however, He set Himself against an attitude towards the Sabbath that would not permit the doing of good to a fellow human because it involved what the Pharisees called *"work,"* such as His healing of the sick on the Sabbath.

Robertson says that Jesus completely upset the ritualistic and ceremonial, which was a total shock to the religious leaders, insisting rather that emphasis be placed on the spiritual — in other words, the true meaning of the Word of God!

Men love to make rules, and religious men most of all, and they rather enjoy forcing other men to obey them. But not only is the Letter of the Word important, we must also take into account the spiritual emphasis, exactly as Christ did in these circumstances, thereby setting an example for us in our interpretation of the Word.

CHAPTER 3

(1) "AND HE ENTERED AGAIN INTO THE SYNAGOGUE; AND THERE WAS A MAN THERE WHICH HAD A WITHERED HAND."

The composition is:

This is a symbol of withered, undone humanity, all as a result of the Fall.

THE WITHERED HAND

The phrase, *"And He entered again into the Synagogue,"* spoke of the Sabbath, because this is when Synagogue services were conducted. Which Synagogue it was, is not stated, but most likely it was in Capernaum.

The phrase, *"And there was a man there which had a withered hand,"* sets the stage for the next confrontation with the Pharisees, although this was not the intention in the healing of this man. The implication in the language is that the man's hand had not always been this way, but had withered due to an accident or disease. Luke tells us it was his right hand. Certain things will happen in this scenario:

1. This man's *"withered hand"* is a symbol of withered, undone humanity, all as a result of the Fall. As the hand could little function in its present capacity, similarly, man little functions properly.

2. Only Jesus could straighten this hand, as only Jesus can straighten the withered hand, spiritually speaking, of mankind. This means that He is the only Remedy, and not the Synagogue itself.

Many mistake the Church for the Saviour. Emphatically, it is not! It took Jesus' Presence in the Church (Synagogue) to bring about this miraculous result; consequently, Church without Jesus is no more than any other gathering. But with Jesus, it becomes a powerful conduit to bring about change for the better.

3. The religious leaders, as religious leaders everywhere, had absolutely no concern about this man being healed. They were only concerned that their petty rules be obeyed. The man meant nothing to them, as humanity means nothing to any religion. They did not care that his hand was withered; they consequently had no regard or concern that he be healed. In effect, he was nothing to them, and probably they wished he had not come to the Synagogue, because the *"withered hand"* was unsightly, therefore, making their gathering a little less than they desired.

So, in this scenario, the entire aspect of the God-man relationship becomes obvious, as well as the great hindering force of religion, which is inspired by Satan.

(2) "AND THEY WATCHED HIM, WHETHER HE WOULD HEAL HIM ON THE SABBATH DAY; THAT THEY MIGHT ACCUSE HIM.

The construction is:

Religion really doesn't care for people, only its rules and regulations.

THE ACCUSATION

The phrase, *"And they watched Him,"* spoke of the Pharisees, and means that they dogged his footsteps, which spoke not only of this occasion, but continuously.

In the situation regarding His Disciples plucking the grain on the Sabbath, they had not been able to lay much to His charge, due to the fact that He did not do it Himself; however, knowing His propensity to heal, they suspected that an occasion would arise on the Sabbath which would call for His healing Power, which it did!

The evil of these Pharisees knew no bounds! Even though they talked constantly of God, they did not, in fact, know God. This is the reason that Church without Christ is so damning. It is the reason that any form of religious activity without Christ is anathema to the human soul.

RELIGION

Religion is a program, scheme, or effort of some kind, devised by men, with an effort to reach God, or to better oneself in some way. It is not of God, because anything spiritually devised by man is not of God. Salvation in its entirety is all of the Lord, and for man to receive its benefits, all man has to do is simply place his faith and trust in Christ and what Christ has done at the Cross, and Salvation will instantly be imputed to him (Jn. 3:3, 16; Eph. 2:8-9; Rom. 10:9-10, 13; Rev. 22:17).

As well, even though Christ be lauded, if Denominational structure, doctrine, or religious activity take precedent over Christ in any way, therefore, ceasing to be subordinate to Him, then it becomes Christ *"plus,"* whether it is realized or not, and consequently of no effect!

These religious leaders knew full well that Jesus claimed to be the Messiah, even though, at this time, He had not said it outright; nevertheless, they understood His implications. But, they did not at all believe, even though His proof was irrefutable.

Why?

To have done so would have meant subordination to Him, and this, religion refused to do. The entirety of religion is wrapped up in its man-devised ways, which place these religious leaders in a position of authority, consequently lauding it over others, which religious man loves to do. In a nutshell, it comes down to Christ being Lord, or man being lord!

In fact, the far greater majority of that which calls itself *"Christianity"* is ruled and guided by men and, therefore, not by God. In other words, even though Jesus may be spoken of, He is not Lord, because man and Lord cannot reign at the same time.

This would include all organized religion, and of every stripe. It would also include most of that which calls itself *"independent."* Too often, even in these circles, man is still Lord. Tragically, now as then, Jesus is Lord in only a few lives. Consequently, all Believers should resolutely investigate that which they are associated with regarding Church and that which they are supporting. If it is ruled, regulated, and devised by man, it cannot be ruled by the Lord, and, consequently, association will be the same as those who sided with the religious leaders of Jesus' day.

HEALING

The phrase, *"Whether He would heal him on the Sabbath Day,"* brings us to the crux of the situation. St. Jerome informs us that the man whose hand was withered is described as a Mason, and is said to have asked for help in the following terms: *"I was a Mason, seeking my living by manual labor. I beseech You, Jesus, to restore to me the use of my hand, that I may not be compelled to beg bread."*

The phrase, *"That they might accuse Him,"* refers to the Pharisees, who, as the watchdogs of Israel's religion, attempted to discredit the claims of Christ as Messiah by finding Him violating its regulations. These religious leaders would have nothing to do with the Lord, and kept themselves away from any fellowship with Him, lest they be understood to be in sympathy with Him. They maintained an attitude of aloofness. They had only one thing in mind:

There was no desire to see if He really was the Messiah. Their minds were closed on the subject; consequently, the entire framework of their thoughts and actions was one thing only, and that was to see how they could take anything He did and twist it to their own satisfaction in order that they might *"accuse Him"*!

In effect, and as stated, they were watchdogs and spies.

A PERSONAL EXPERIENCE

This somewhat hits home, as individuals designated by a particular religious Denomination have stood in front of auditoriums where we were conducting meetings, in order that they may note anyone going to our meetings who they thought may be a member of the Denomination in question.

Why did they object to their people coming to our meetings?

I suppose my question answers itself. They would like to have objected to what we preach, but this they could not do, at least not Scripturally, because its Truth was undeniable. Did they object to souls being saved or people being baptized with the Holy Spirit, of which there were many?

Actually, their actions proved that they had little regard or concern about people being saved. As the Pharisees of old, the people meant little to them, except as to how they could be used. Precious lives being totally changed by the Power of God were of no consequence! Alcoholics being made sober or drug addicts being delivered meant little to them! Broken homes being put back together by the Power of God were not worthy of mention. Actually, all the things that pertained to the True Gospel of Jesus Christ were of no consequence whatsoever. There was only one thing in which they were interested — control!

As the religious leaders of Israel, the Denomination was supreme, therefore, its rules and regulations, no matter how unscriptural, were sacrosanct. To be frank, there is little difference in the two. Both, the Pharisees and those of whom I speak, talk much about God, but little knew Him. As the Pharisees, had they known Him, they would not have fought Him or those who were His. It is impossible to be of God and to oppose God at the same time! One cannot love God and fight God. So, to oppose His (that which belongs to Him) is to oppose Him.

(3) "AND HE SAID UNTO THE MAN WHICH HAD THE WITHERED HAND,

STAND FORTH."

The diagram is:

Whatever He did was done openly. In other words, He threw this challenge to the Pharisees and into their teeth.

THE WITHERED HAND

The phrase, *"And He said unto the man,"* is meant to bring the entirety of this situation out into the open. Whatever Christ would do, it would be in full view of everyone, leaving no doubt regarding His action or purpose. In other words, He threw this challenge to the Pharisees and into their teeth.

I suppose if He had conducted Himself as many today, He would have told the man to wait until after the service, where we would have subtly taken him out back and there performed the healing, telling him it was being done in this manner so as not to arouse animosity; however, in this scenario, we see the very opposite!

To give one inch to ungodliness is, in effect, to be ungodly! To compromise the standards of the Word of God, even in the slightest, is to compromise all! There is only one way to do a thing, and that is the right way. One cannot be in union with both the Pharisees and Christ. One or the other must go. It is identical presently. One either follows the Lord, or one follows man. One cannot follow both!

THE SYMBOL OF MAN'S HELPLESSNESS

The phrase, *"Which had a withered hand,"* proclaims this man as the object. The religion of that time did not want him to be healed and, in fact, had no regard for him. By contrast, Jesus wanted him to be healed, because that's the very reason that Christ came. The Lord did not come to this Earth to perpetuate religious Denominations. He did not come to build the *"Baptists,"* or the *"Assemblies of God,"* or the *"Catholics,"* etc., but rather to liberate fallen humanity.

What I am about to say is strong, but I feel it needs to be said.

THE GREATEST HINDRANCE TO THE WORK OF GOD

Those which I have mentioned, plus many I have not mentioned, are probably the greatest hindrance, as were the Pharisees of old, to this all-important work being carried out.

Let's say it again:

The greatest hindrance to the Work of God on Earth is not the liquor business, or the drug business, or vice, as wicked and evil as these things are, but rather, institutionalized religion. There is no wickedness on the face of the Earth that is even as remotely wicked as institutionalized religion.

To explain, it is not wicked because it is institutionalized. That is not the cause of the wickedness. The cause pertains to the fact of men putting religion before God, and doing anything to preserve that religion, and I mean anything! In fact, one could probably say that institutionalized religion has been one of the worst causes of the shedding of innocent blood down through the centuries.

While the law of the land stops such presently, still, institutionalized religion seeks to hinder the Work of God, and does so by trying to hinder those who are truly called of God. The Life and Ministry of Christ is a perfect example of this. It was not the gamblers, harlots, thieves, etc., who crucified Christ, but rather the *"Church"* of that day! This means that the greatest opposition to Christ during His Ministry was not the Roman Government, or even the known vices of that day, such as alcohol, immorality, gambling, etc., as bad as they may have been, but rather those who claimed to know the Lord.

It is the same now!

The Work of God on Earth is not the perpetuation of religious Denominations, or even particular religious doctrines, but rather the healing of the *"man with the withered hand,"* i.e., Salvation of withered souls.

STAND FORTH

The phrase, *"Stand forth,"* is, in the literal Greek, *"Be arising into the midst."* That is, according to Wuest, *"Step into the midst of all the people so that all can see you."* Consequently, Jesus answered the attitude of these Pharisees by this daring act. He brought things out into the open at once, so that all may know exactly why and what He was doing. He demands no less presently of His followers!

Any yielding, and to any degree, to that which is wrong, is to yield totally to the wrong. There are many excuses one may use to do wrong, while there is only one reason to do right.

"If I do this, which I know in my heart to be right, I will lose my Church," is the answer of many Preachers. Consequently, the question must be asked as to whose Church it is? Or who gave it to you in the first place? Which brings up the greatest question of all!

Who are you following, God or man? The declaration of man is, *"If I do what I know to be right, they will crucify me!"*

Yes, they will, exactly as they did Christ! Consequently, many opt to follow man instead of the Lord.

(4) "AND HE SAID UNTO THEM, IS IT LAWFUL TO DO GOOD ON THE SABBATH DAYS, OR TO DO EVIL? TO SAVE LIFE, OR TO KILL? BUT THEY HELD THEIR PEACE."

The composition is:

Jesus was telling them that living for God was not a question of keeping rules and regulations, but a question of *"doing good or evil"*! To have the power to set this man free and not do so was *"evil."*

GOOD AND EVIL

The question, *"And He said unto them, Is it lawful to do good on the Sabbath Days, or to do evil?" to save life, or to kill?"* points its intent directly to these Pharisees. He didn't want anyone to misunderstand as to whom He was speaking and consequently pointed them out for all to see and hear.

To have the power to set this man free and not do so was *"evil."* Likewise, to have the power to save his life and not do so was, in effect, to *"kill him."* Consequently, the Pharisees opted for *"evil,"* and desired to *"kill,"* which was actually the intent of their murderous hearts.

Please allow me to state it in this way, and, once again, to be personal.

TO OPPOSE THAT WHICH BELONGS TO GOD IS TO OPPOSE GOD!

It is very easy to see here the open hostility of the Pharisees toward Christ. And one must remember that the Pharisees were, in fact, what one might call the fundamentalists of that day. They were, in essence, the religious leaders of Israel. It would have been very difficult at that time to have gotten anyone to see and properly discern what the Pharisees actually were. As the near future proved out, they were murderers at heart.

True Righteousness will always expose self-righteousness. When something is truly of God, even as Christ most assuredly was, everything He did exposed their ungodliness. In other words, it pulled out of the deep of their hearts the murderous intent which was there.

Someone asked me the other day as to how a particular Church Denomination was getting along. My answer to them was short, crisp, and to the point. *"They are doing everything within their power to stop the Gospel,"* was my answer!

As so many religious Denominations, their business is not the spread of the Gospel, but rather the perpetuation of that Denomination. To be sure, they will go to any lengths, and I mean any lengths, to preserve that Denomination. In fact, it is the Denomination they serve, and not God. While they constantly use the Name of the Lord, exactly as did the Pharisees, still, neither group serves the Lord, and both groups were, and are, propelled by the same spirit.

CHRIST AND THE PHARISEES

In all of this, Christ placed the Pharisees in a juxtaposition with Himself. The two doctrines, that of the Pharisees and that of Christ, were placed, in effect, side-by-side, and done so by the questions and actions of Jesus. One was shown to be good, while the other was shown to be evil, and by its actions. One was shown to give life, while the other was shown to give death, and by its actions.

Therein essentially lay the difference between Him and the Pharisees, in whose theory and practice, duty and benevolence, the Divine and the human, were divorced. To do good or to do evil, these were the only alternatives, not some rule about the Sabbath. To omit to do good which is in one's power is evil; not to save life when one can is to destroy it.

So, what are we going to do, save souls or

keep our silly man-made rules?

THE EMBARRASSING SILENCE

The phrase, *"But they held their peace,"* means that the Pharisees had no answer to the questions posed by Christ. Not only were they quiet, but they kept on being quiet. Wuest says, *"Theirs was a painful, embarrassing silence."*

Someone else said, *"What could they have replied to a question which looked at the subject from a wholly different point of view, the ethical from the legal one they were accustomed to?"* There was nothing in common between them and Jesus, and that was the crux of the whole matter.

They were obstinate in their infidelity; when they could say nothing against the Truth, they refused to say anything for it.

(5) "AND WHEN HE HAD LOOKED ROUND ABOUT ON THEM WITH ANGER, BEING GRIEVED FOR THE HARDNESS OF THEIR HEARTS, HE SAID UNTO THE MAN, STRETCH FORTH YOUR HAND. AND HE STRETCHED IT OUT: AND HIS HAND WAS RESTORED WHOLE AS THE OTHER."

The diagram is:

There is no hardness of the heart like religious hardness; Jesus knew that this would lead the Pharisees and Israel to destruction.

ANGER

The phrase, *"And when He had looked round about on them with anger,"* presents a righteous indignation, and for all the obvious reasons. With the man standing in the midst of all the onlookers, and the Pharisees standing or sitting nearby, Jesus, with a sweep of His Eyes, stares at them for a few moments with anger registered on His countenance. In other words, the anger is obvious to all.

Here is the difference between the anger of fallen man and the anger of the Sinless One. With fallen man, anger is the desire of retaliation, punishing those by whom you consider yourself unjustly treated. Hence, in men, unrighteous anger springs from self-love; in Christ, it sprang from the Love of God, which must always be opposed to sin, and especially this type of sin.

Jesus loved God above all things; hence, He was distressed and irritated on account of the wrongs done to God by sin and sinners. Consequently, His Anger was a righteous zeal for the honor of God; and hence, it was mingled with grief because, in their blindness and obstinacy, they would not acknowledge Him to be the Messiah, but misrepresented His kindnesses wrought on the sick on the Sabbath Day and found fault with them as evil.

THREE TYPES OF ANGER

There are three Greek words in the New Testament which speak of anger:

1. PARORGISMOS: This speaks of anger in the sense of exasperation, and is forbidden in Scripture. Paul said, *"Let not the sun go down upon your wrath,"* (Eph. 4:26). Actually, this type of anger is that which is most often exhibited.

2. THUMOS: This speaks of a sudden outburst of anger that quickly cools off, and which is the cause of much sin, including murder. By its very definition, it is prohibited in Scripture. Actually, the curtailing of this *"anger"* is one of the great changes brought about in the lives of those who are *"born again."* The explosive nature is changed to one of gentleness (Gal. 5:19-26).

A lady once said to the great Evangelist, Billy Sunday, *"I'll admit I have a temper, but it's over in just a minute!"* Sunday answer her by saying, *"Yes, Ma'am, and so is the blast of a shotgun, but it destroys everything it hits."*

3. ORGE: This is an abiding and subtle habit of mind, not operative at all times, but exhibiting itself in the same way when the occasion demands it. This is the word and type of anger used in relationship to Christ. As would be obvious, under certain conditions, the *"orge"* type of anger is a righteous passion to entertain. The Scripture has nothing in common with the Stoic's absolute condemnation of anger. So, as is here obvious, the Scripture not only permits it, but, on fit occasions, demands it. There is a Wrath of God (Mat. 3:7), Who would not love good, unless He hated evil, the two being so inseparable, that either He must do both or neither.

Gourd says, *"Anger against wrong as*

wrong is a sign of moral health." Consequently, Godly men and women must rise up in moral indignation at the sin and iniquity which destroy this generation. To not do so portrays an apathy or else ignorance of the true condition of mankind. However, this righteous anger does not exhibit itself in the killing of doctors who perform abortions, as sinful and wicked as the abortions may be. In other words, it does not become evil in order to oppose evil.

RIGHTEOUS ANGER

Such righteous anger is expressed in the utterances of the Prophets of the Old Testament and the Apostles of the New. Stephen said, speaking to the religious leaders of his day, *"You stiffnecked and uncircumcised in heart and ears, you do always resist the Holy Spirit: as your fathers did, so do you."* He then called them *"betrayers and murderers"* (Acts 7:51-52).

If that is not righteous anger, I don't know what it is, and, as well, approved by the Holy Spirit! To be sure, his hearers did not take his words kindly. The Scripture says, *"When they heard these things, they were cut to the heart, and they gnashed on him with their teeth"* (Acts 7:54).

Most preaching presently little registers any anger, because it mostly consists of motivation, and actually little of the True Word of God. Such is the sign that the Prophetic and Apostolic voice is silenced.

HARDENED HEARTS

The phrase, *"Being grieved for the hardness of their hearts,"* means that His Anger was tempered by grief. He knew to where this hardness would lead, which was total destruction. They were trying to defend their self-will, never dreaming that their nation, in about 38 years, would be so totally destroyed that it would actually cease to exist.

What causes *"hardness of heart"*?

Almost without exception, hardness is caused by rejection of the Gospel. This can refer to the unsaved who consistently say *"No"* to the appeal of Christ, or to Believers, so-called, who reject the True Gospel, i.e., *"the Message of the Cross,"* turning more and more, as these Pharisees, to the false.

Such creates a *"hardness of the heart,"* spiritually speaking, because of self-will and self-righteousness.

The *"hardness"* represents itself in their attitude toward the *"man with the withered hand,"* which is a perfect example. They had no regard for him or his needs. They were *"hard"* to true feeling and passion, as are all of this nature. They would rather see the man's hand remain withered than for it to be healed by Christ.

Likewise, most who follow in their train would prefer to see people die lost and go to an eternal Hell rather than they be saved watching our Telecast. It is the result of a *"hardened heart."*

To accept the Gospel of Jesus Christ and to walk in all the light that one is given results in every facet of one's being becoming more and more tender and soft toward God. To reject the Gospel, and thereby to reject the light shown, is to have the opposite effect regarding one's being. Every faculty and passion of such a person becomes steadily harder and harder, until they finally come to the place, that is if they do not allow the Holy Spirit to turn them around, that they are *"past feeling."*

Paul said, *"Who being past feeling* (moral insensibility, which brings about man's inhumanity to man) *have given themselves over to lasciviousness* (a complete surrender of self unto evil), *to work all uncleanness with greediness* (such a person is greedy for such a lifestyle)*"* (Eph. 4:19).

THE MIRACLE

The phrase, *"He said unto the man, Stretch forth your hand,"* proclaims this being done in full view of all; consequently, there would be absolutely no doubt as to the Miracle which was about to take place.

What were the thoughts in this man's mind, as he stretched forth that withered, shrunken hand and arm, in obedience to the command of Christ? (The disease probably extended through the whole arm, according to the meaning of the Greek word here used. It seems to have been a kind of atrophy, causing a gradual drying up of the limb.)

The phrase, *"And he stretched it out: and his hand was restored as the other,"* portrays a Miracle instantly taking place, without Christ even saying a word! The stretching out of the hand and arm was an act of Faith on the part of the man, with the Power of Christ instantly making it whole in front of the eyes of all onlookers.

What must their thoughts have been? One moment they are staring at a withered hand and arm, and the next moment, even in front of their very eyes, they watch it become whole as the other. This is so astounding that it beggars description! Only God can do such a thing.

This is also a perfect picture of the immediate transformation of the believing sinner upon Faith in Christ. That which is spiritually withered and shrunken is instantly made *"whole."* The willingness of Jesus to perform this gracious act is equaled only by His ability to do so. Now this man can lay brick or stone, or do any other type of manual labor that is required. He is now made whole!

(6) "AND THE PHARISEES WENT FORTH, AND STRAIGHTWAY TOOK COUNSEL WITH THE HERODIANS AGAINST HIM, HOW THEY MIGHT DESTROY HIM.

The overview is:

As we read these words, we are reading the condition of the religious leaders of Israel. I wonder, is it much different presently?

THE HERODIANS

The phrase, *"And the Pharisees went forth, and straightway took counsel with the Herodians against Him,"* means that they have now fully made their decision to oppose Him, and in every way! This action indicates that they (the Pharisees) had come to the place that they must either accept His teaching, or they must take steps against Him.

What, however, had He done?

The Miracle had been wrought by no action on His part whatsoever. He had not even said anything, much less performed some type of labor, etc. Therefore, to get a judgment against Him, claiming He had broken the Sabbath, would be difficult, to say the least! Consequently, they seek a meeting with the Herodians, who were their enemies. These individuals were the natural opponents of the Pharisees, and they of them!

So, what common ground would they have for such a meeting?

Jesus!

The enemy of my enemy becomes my friend, or so goes the idea.

HEROD

Herod the Tetrarch (Lk. 3:19), who also bore the distinctive name of Antipas, had inherited the Galilean and Peraean portions of his father's kingdom. He is the man who imprisoned and executed John the Baptist (Mk. 6:14-28), and was the Herod to whom Jesus was sent by Pilate for judgment (Lk. 23:7). Jesus is recorded as having once described him as *"that fox"* (Lk. 13:32).

The Herods were not of proper Jewish descent, and were able to stay in power only because of the support of Rome; consequently, they catered to their Roman patrons by doing everything they could to please them. In this atmosphere sprang up the party known as the *"Herodians,"* which is mentioned in this Verse. They were a Jewish party who favored the Herodian dynasty. As such, they were willing to compromise any belief in order to appease Rome. They really had few religious leanings, and were more secular and political than anything else; consequently, and as would be obvious, they had great influence at court.

The entirety of the lifestyle and belief system of the Herodians threw them into direct antagonism with the Pharisees; consequently, they hated each other! But in the case of Jesus, they would unite in order to stop Him. The Pharisees no doubt felt that they would need the political assistance of this party to carry out their devious intent.

TO KILL CHRIST

The phrase, *"How they might destroy Him,"* meant they were planning to kill Him. It is difficult to imagine those who claimed to be of God, and we speak of the Pharisees, and especially that they wore their religion so outwardly, who could be so evil as to plot the murder of a fellow human being, especially the Christ of Glory. But they did!

Wickedness in any form or variety is awful; however, religious wickedness is the most wicked of all!

(7) "BUT JESUS WITHDREW HIMSELF WITH HIS DISCIPLES TO THE SEA: AND

A GREAT MULTITUDE FROM GALILEE FOLLOWED HIM, AND FROM JUDAEA."

The overview is:

In essence, Jesus is withdrawing from the controversy.

THE MULTITUDES

The phrase, *"But Jesus withdrew Himself with His Disciples to the Sea,"* concerns itself somewhat with the hostility of the Pharisees and Herodians, but especially the Pharisees. To be sure, He did not retire because of fear, but that He may continue the Work of God without further confrontation. His purpose was not to confront the Pharisees, even though He was forced to do it repeatedly, but rather to preach, heal, and deliver!

Some have suggested that Jesus was not in Capernaum when the Miracle of the withered hand occurred, but elsewhere, due to His now retiring to the Sea; however, while that may be true, still, Mark could well have spoken of Jesus and His Disciples leaving the Synagogue and going out beside the Lake, which He often did.

The phrase, *"And a great multitude from Galilee followed Him, and from Judaea,"* concerns the tremendous number of people who were now being attracted to Jesus because of what He preached, but mostly because of the healings and miracles. It said they *"followed Him."* No wonder!

(8) "AND FROM JERUSALEM, AND FROM IDUMAEA, AND FROM BEYOND JORDAN; AND THEY ABOUT TYRE AND SIDON, A GREAT MULTITUDE, WHEN THEY HAD HEARD WHAT GREAT THINGS HE DID, CAME UNTO HIM."

The great crowds will be repeated in the coming Kingdom Age, but on a far grander scale.

COMING TO JESUS

The phrase, *"And from Jerusalem,"* is interesting. The religious leadership of Israel resided in this city. That the Name of Jesus was, no doubt, the topic of every conversation must have been galling to them. The phrase, *"And from Idumaea,"* concerned the area south of the Dead Sea, and would have been over 100 miles from the Sea of Galilee, the area of the Ministry of Christ. Inasmuch as most people in those days had to walk, the journey could have taken upwards of a week. Consequently, they were strongly desirous of seeing Jesus.

The phrase, *"And from beyond Jordan,"* spoke of east of the Jordan River, which would have included Paneas and Decapolis. The phrase, *"And they about Tyre and Sidon,"* spoke of the twin cities on the Mediterranean, basically occupied by Gentiles. The phrase, *"A great multitude,"* refers to an exceptionally large crowd. They did not gather in a short time, but over a period of several days. It took some time for this vast assemblage of thousands to gather.

THE GREAT THINGS HE DID

The phrase, *"When they had heard what great things He did, came unto Him,"* concerned what the entirety of Israel was speaking of, i.e., His healings and miracles. John the Beloved said, *"And there are also many other things which Jesus did, the which, if they should be written every one, I suppose that even the world itself could not contain the books that should be written"* (Jn. 21:25).

Consequently, all the Miracles He performed are not recorded in the four Gospels, probably only a few. As well, the things He did were so absolutely outstanding, they beggar description. Not only was every type of loathsome disease healed, with even the dead being raised, but the indication from the Text is that missing limbs were replaced, such as arms, fingers, etc. But of course, even that does not compare with one being raised from the dead!

This is what Israel could have had, and the entirety of the world for that matter, but they did not want Him.

Why?

Their deeds were evil; consequently, His Righteousness offended them, and greatly!

They would rather have sickness and disease than healing and health! They would rather have poverty than prosperity and plenty! They would rather have hate than love! They would rather have war than peace! They would rather have death than life!

We look back and marvel, and yet, is it any different now?

The peace that passes all understanding,

and which can only be given by Christ, is available to all, but with few takers. More abundant life is free for the asking, but again, few takers! (Jn. 10:10).

THE MESSAGE OF THE CROSS

When the Message of the Cross first began to be revealed to me in 1997, the elation and joy which I experienced knew no bounds. I realized that the Lord was showing me the secret of victorious, overcoming Christian living. He was showing me victory over the world, the flesh, and the Devil. My immediate thoughts concerning the Church was, *"They do not know this. But if it is presented to them, they will be as happy as I am to receive it."* But to my dismay, I found that they were not happy at all to receive it.

In those days, I thought the problem was ignorance; however, even though ignorance definitely is a problem, it's not the greatest problem of all, by far! The greatest problem is *"unbelief,"* the same problem that characterized the Pharisees of Jesus' day.

We believe that the Bible teaches that the Message of the Cross is, in effect, the Message of the entirety of the Bible. In fact, if the entirety of the Word of God, from Genesis 1:1 through Revelation 22:21, could be digested into one phrase, it would be *"Jesus Christ and Him Crucified"* (I Cor. 1:23).

We believe the Bible teaches that what Jesus did at the Cross atoned for all sin, past, present, and future, and thereby defeated Satan, and every Power of Darkness (Col. 2:14-15). With simple faith registered in Christ and what He did at the Cross, the Holy Spirit will then work within our lives, giving us victory over the flesh, and in every capacity (Rom. 8:1-2, 11). This means that every single Believer can be free from every type of bondage, every type of sin, etc. (Jn. 8:32). In fact, the Holy Spirit through Paul plainly said, *"sin shall not have dominion over you"* (Rom. 6:14).

Now, the upshot is, the far, far greater majority of the modern Church, even including those who claim to be Spirit-filled, simply do not believe what I've just said. They might pay lip-service to what I've said, simply because it looks very bad for them to disavow the Cross; however, their actions speak louder than their words.

As it regards bondages of darkness, the greatest counsel of the modern Ministry is, *"You need professional help,"* speaking of humanistic psychology. Never mind that there is no help in that capacity whatsoever. Not only is there no help in that sector, there is great harm in that sector. These religious leaders, whoever they may be, simply do not believe that what Jesus did at the Cross is sufficient for every need that we might have, whatever it might be. But irrespective of their unbelief, *"Let God be true, and every man a liar"* (Rom. 3:4).

(9) "AND HE SPOKE TO HIS DISCIPLES, THAT A SMALL SHIP SHOULD WAIT ON HIM BECAUSE OF THE MULTITUDE, LEST THEY SHOULD THRONG HIM."

The synopsis is:

This would have been a small boat, pushed out a little distance from the shore, with Him teaching the people from this particular platform.

A PREACHING PLATFORM

The phrase, *"And He spoke to His Disciples, that a small ship should wait on Him because of the multitude,"* pertains to the fact that the crowds were pushing Him so close that He was actually being pushed into the water; consequently, He would get a little boat, push out a little ways, and then address the people.

There were, no doubt, thousands of people around Him at this time, trying to touch Him, trying to get close to Him, with all of this being understandable. Never before in human history had there ever been One like this on the face of the Earth. Irrespective of the disease, irrespective of the demon possession, no matter how bad the situation was, when they came to Jesus, they were all healed and delivered, and without exception.

Therefore, it is easy to understand how they came to Him, irrespective of the distance, and no matter what the hardship was to get there. As the little chorus says,

*"You won't leave here like you came,
   in Jesus' Name,
"You won't be bound, oppressed, tormented, sick, or lame,*

"The Holy Ghost of Acts is still the
 same,
"You won't leave here like you came,
 in Jesus' Name."

The phrase, *"Lest they should throng Him,"* speaks of the crush of people attempting to get to Him for healing, etc.

No doubt, His Disciples did the best they could to keep order in the crowd, but at times it would get out of hand, hence, the small boat.

(10) "FOR HE HAD HEALED MANY; INSOMUCH THAT THEY PRESSED UPON HIM FOR TO TOUCH HIM, AS MANY AS HAD PLAGUES."

The exposition is:

All were healed; He never turned one away.

HEALING

The phrase, *"For He had healed many,"* actually means that He healed all who came to Him, which were *"many."* There is no record of anyone who came for healing who left unhealed! As we've already stated, it didn't matter how bad the disease, how awful the bondage, irrespective, immediately they were healed and set free.

As we've also stated, this is but a sample of what will take place in the coming Kingdom Age, when the entirety of the world, in one way or the other, will come to Christ. Of course, then there will be different ways of handling the vast number of people than at His First Advent; still, that Coming Day will be a day to behold. And to be sure, that Day is definitely coming!

TOUCHING JESUS

The phrase, *"Insomuch that they pressed upon Him for to touch Him,"* now tells, at least somewhat, how the healings were brought about. There was so much power that emanated from His Person that anyone who touched Him was instantly made whole, irrespective of whatsoever type of disease or plague they had. What this cost Him, no one will ever really know.

This much we do know: when the woman with the *"issue of blood"* touched the hem of His garment and was immediately healed, He said, *"Who touched Me?"* Peter remonstrated that many were touching Him. But Jesus replied, *"Somebody has touched Me: for I perceive that virtue* (power) *is gone out of Me"* (Lk. 8:43-46).

Why Jesus spoke of this one woman, as Luke records, even though many others were touching Him, is not fully known. No doubt, it had something to do with her Faith, as becomes quickly obvious! However, the point is that He felt power leave His Body and go into her. As Mark records the incident of many touching Him, even throwing themselves against Him, the implication is that all were healed, which must have drained Him physically, which is the point we are attempting to make.

There were, no doubt, many sick ones in this huge crowd of thousands, with them quickly getting the idea that if they could only touch Him, they would be made whole. The phrase, *"Pressed upon him,"* speaks of them literally throwing themselves against Him, to the extent that all decorum was thrown aside.

Sickness is a terrible thing, and a result of the Fall, with the advent of sin as the cause, and instituted by demon spirits. The Giver of Life was now in the midst of men, and, as such, the results of the Fall had to give way, at least for those who would believe. The scene must have been pathetic and glorious at the same time.

THE DISCIPLES

The Disciples were frantically attempting to keep some type of order in the crowd, with the sick becoming fearful that they might not have their turn, and then clamoring to get to Him. On top of that, those healed would have known a joy with no bounds, expressing themselves with loud shouts of praises to God, especially considering that blinded eyes were opened, deaf ears unstopped, paralyzed limbs instantly healed, as well as every other disease and scourge that one might imagine.

What a time that was for Israel! What a time it was for the world! And yet, they rejected Him and crucified Him; such is the wickedness of man.

PLAGUES

The phrase, *"As many as had plagues,"*

actually means *"scourges,"* which were destroying the people. The word *"scourges"* reminds us that these things were caused by their sins. In other words, some of the people, even more than others, were physically ill because of their great sin. Satan had been allowed to scourge them greatly and had taken advantage of the opportunity to do so. But yet, Jesus healed them all, irrespective of their spiritual condition, and without a word of condemnation.

DIVINE HEALING

Even though we have addressed ourselves to these questions elsewhere in this Volume, due to their significance, perhaps we should briefly allude to them again!

If we take Jesus as the example, and as the only example, then most questions are cleared up immediately.

1. First of all, Jesus healed all who came to Him, without excluding anyone, irrespective of whatever spiritual condition they may have had. In this great crowd, I am positive that many of the people were not living as righteously as they should have, even as the Text brings out! But still, all were treated impartially. Not one time did Jesus say, *"I'm sorry, but your life does not measure up, so I cannot heal you."*

Not only was nothing like that ever said, but actually the opposite was said, at least if we take His actions as any indication, which we certainly should!

2. Jesus never said to a single soul, *"You need to remain sick, because you will live closer to Me if you do so"* or *"your sickness brings Glory to God"*! All of these excuses, and many more, are constantly used by Preachers, etc. But there is nothing in the Word of God that lends credence to such a thing. Moreover, it would certainly seem that if such had Scriptural validity, Jesus would have alluded to such, at least a few times. But He never did!

We gather from these things that it is always God's Will to heal the sick, and irrespective as to whom they may be.

3. Many Preachers claim that it's a lack of faith on the part of the sick person that keeps many from being healed. At times, Jesus did allude to such, by making statements such as, *"If you can believe, all things are possible to him who believes"* (Mk. 9:23); however, every indication is that even if they did not have the Faith, He instantly gave it to them, with none being turned away. In other words, he never one time said, *"I'm sorry, you do not have Faith, so I cannot heal you,"* or words to that effect!

So, even though there may be a lack of Faith on the part of the person who needs help, still, even that should not stop the healing.

4. It seems that the only requirement respecting healing, at least as far as Christ was concerned, was that they come to Him. Someone has said concerning Salvation, *"All the person has to do to be saved is to furnish the sinner, and Jesus will furnish the Saviour."* Likewise, it seems that the only requirement for healing was for the person simply to furnish the need, and it was instantly met!

Sometimes the person who was sick didn't even have to show up, with someone else coming in his place. The Bible records this happening several times (Mat. 8:5-10; Mk. 7:24-30).

5. The introduction of the Kingdom, to which we have already alluded, had a lot to do with this. Jesus was showing Israel what it could be like and what it was, in fact, meant to be like. It is not God's Will for some ten thousand people a day around this world to die of starvation, many of them little children. It's not God's Will for sickness and disease to ravage the planet. It's not God's Will for war to rage, with hundreds of thousands being killed, and even millions.

No! All of those things are because of sin.

But one day soon, the Lord Jesus Christ is coming back to this planet. When He comes back the second time, it will not be to be beaten, spit upon, and scourged. He will, rather, come back *"King of kings, and Lord of lords"* (Rev., Chpt. 19). The world will then know healing, prosperity, Deliverance, Victory, and *"more abundant life,"* as it has never known in all of its history. In fact, Jesus will reign Personally from Jerusalem and Israel will finally come to the place that God originally intended for her to be, the premier nation in the world.

During that Coming Day, Jerusalem will be the greatest city on the face of the Earth.

It will be great, simply because this is where Jesus will reign supreme (Zech., Chpt. 14).

(11) "AND UNCLEAN SPIRITS, WHEN THEY SAW HIM, FELL DOWN BEFORE HIM, AND CRIED, SAYING, YOU ARE THE SON OF GOD."

The synopsis is:

Demon spirits kept falling down before Him and kept constantly crying; they knew He was the Son of God, even though the religious leaders of Israel did not.

UNCLEAN SPIRITS

The phrase, *"And unclean spirits,"* in the Greek says, *"the spirits, the unclean ones."* Some think, and it is probably correct, that demon spirits are the disembodied spirits of a pre-Adamic race which inhabited the perfect Earth of Genesis 1:1. At that time, they were not demons, but created beings serving and worshipping God. However, when Lucifer fell, becoming Satan, the archenemy of God, along with one-third, it seems, of the Angels, these beings threw in their lot with the Evil One. In some manner, they then became disembodied, consequently, seeking a person or animal to possess.

These *"unclean spirits,"* although unseen by the natural eye, are the contributors of much of the destruction in the world (Jn. 10:10). Actually, demon spirits rule and control, in the background, entire nations. Hence, the starvation, witchcraft, religion, poverty, hatred, and war! If one could see into the spirit world, one would see evil spirits causing every single war that's ever been fought, with either one or both sides heavily controlled by these spirits of destruction. The same can be said for most every other disorder in the world (Rev. 16:12-16).

THE SON OF GOD

The phrase, *"When they saw Him, fell down before Him, and cried, saying, You are the Son of God,"* means they instantly knew Who He was, the Son of God! Consequently, they were terrified, and acted accordingly. However, there is no indication that they had any knowledge of what He would do respecting the Redemption of mankind, which would entail dying on the Cross, etc.

In their ignorance of the Plan of God, they would foment hatred against Him, using the hearts of the religious leaders of Israel, not realizing that this action would ultimately spell their own doom! His Death at Calvary would defeat every power of darkness, as well as satisfy the claims of Heaven (Col. 2:14-15).

Them falling down before Him means they kept on falling down before Him and kept on constantly crying. They were using the bodies of those they possessed to do and say these things. By them referring to Him as *"The Son of God,"* they were also saying, in essence, that God the Father was His Own unique, private Father, in a sense in which He was not the Father of anyone else (Jn. 5:18). This indicates some knowledge by the demons of the Trinity.

(12) "AND HE STRAITLY CHARGED THEM THAT THEY SHOULD NOT MAKE HIM KNOWN."

The structure is:

Jesus wanted no advertisement from this sort.

CHARGE

The phrase, *"And He straitly charged them,"* refers to a command such as would be given in the military. This indicates rank. As a result, in the ranks of spirit beings, these *"unclean spirits,"* relative to Jesus, the *"Son of God,"* were about the same as an Army Private compared to the President of the United States. Actually, even though that is the greatest comparison that one could give in the natural, in the spiritual, to which this relates, it would be far beyond even that! So, whenever He *"charged them,"* they fell over themselves in order to obey, and instantly!

OUR LORD WANTED NO ADVERTISEMENT FROM DEMON SPIRITS

The phrase, *"That they should not make Him known,"* did not imply that they were wrong in their statement about Him being the *"Son of God,"* but that He wanted no advertisement from this sort. Actually, His attitude toward these spirits was one of total opposition and ultimate subjugation. He would spoil their goods and their house (Mk. 3:27).

The Lord wants all to *"make Him known,"* but not, under any circumstances, these spirits of darkness! He had come to destroy these works of the Devil, and this He would do (I Jn. 3:8).

(13) "AND HE WENT UP INTO A MOUNTAIN, AND CALLED UNTO HIM WHOM HE WOULD: AND THEY CAME UNTO HIM."

The exegesis is:

There could have been as many as 40 or 50 people personally selected, maybe even near 100.

THE MOUNTAIN

The phrase, *"And He went up into a mountain,"* has Luke saying that He went up into a mountain to pray (Lk. 6:12). Inasmuch as the mountain is not stipulated, it is useless to speculate. However, it must have been one not far from the Sea of Galilee, possibly the one on which the Transfiguration would later take place. He actually spent the entirety of the night in prayer. This is an especially interesting time, the lesson of which must not be lost upon the Reader.

Due to the many healings and miracles, great fame had attached itself at this time to Christ. There were, consequently, no lack of followers. Even though it would change a little later, at this time, many wanted to be His Disciples.

As He went to this mountain to seek God concerning the all-important selection of the Twelve, there was, no doubt, a larger number than that traveling and associating with Him. Some months later, He *"appointed other seventy also, and sent them two and two before His face into every city and place, where He Himself would come"* (Lk. 10:1). At this time, however, He would concern Himself only with the Twelve.

PRAYER

Considering that He had spent the entirety of the night in prayer regarding this all-important selection, this should also be, as stated, a lesson to all of us. Several things unfold before us:

1. Jesus sought the Heavenly Father incessantly concerning leading and direction, which would then be given to Him by the Holy Spirit. It is very obvious that He had a strong prayer life. As He was our example, likewise, we should follow suit respecting prayer.

NOTES

2. Inasmuch as He sought His Father all night long about this matter, this should also tell us that some things require more intercession than others. Regrettably, we are living in an age when intercessory prayer of this nature is almost unheard of. Actually, most, greatly influenced by the *"confession message,"* do not even believe in prayer, much less practice it! The members of this group, which is large, claim they can confess whatever they need into existence.

First of all, and irrespective of their boasts, they cannot do any such thing. If they could, it would prove to be disastrous, because of not having the Will of God. Many of the modern confession principle claim they automatically know the Will of God in any and all matters. If this is true, one might quickly add, then they must be far ahead of Christ, which is a preposterous idea, to say the least!

No! There may be such a thing as a *"McBurger,"* in the matter of fast food, but there is no such thing as a *"McFaith"* or *"McPrayer"*! Sometimes it takes more, much more, than a hurried petition.

3. The Twelve were not chosen respecting their personalities, abilities, talents, wealth, or eagerness. Each individual was selected by the Holy Spirit, with no man, even Christ, having a say in that selection. This was one of the reasons a night of prayer was needed.

Much of the modern Church world is man-directed, man-guided, and man-instituted. However, that which is man-ordered is not God-ordered; hence, most of that which calls itself *"Church"* is little more than a meeting of the local Chamber of Commerce, at least as far as the Lord is concerned!

Tragically, the modern Church knows almost nothing about prayer; as stated, the modern Church is, consequently, little led by the Holy Spirit. If the Believer could only realize the tremendous blessings from the Lord which are part of prayer, this all-important privilege would be far more heavily engaged. In the act of prayer, far more is engaged than merely a request for help, as all-important as that is.

The manner in which Jesus prayed, which, as stated, is our example, proclaims that He had total trust in the Heavenly Father, and sought Him accordingly. If the modern Church little seeks the Lord, it shows that it little trusts the Lord.

THE CALL

The phrase, *"And called unto Him whom He would,"* means those who were called did not have a say in the matter, being selected entirely by Christ, as He was given direction by the Heavenly Father. Once again, this emphasizes that man had absolutely nothing to do with this calling, all being strictly a Work of the Holy Spirit.

The phrase, *"And they came unto Him,"* means that He called out to them, and they stepped out from the larger group. The idea that they would judge the Twelve Tribes of Israel forever and have their names inscribed on the foundations of the New Jerusalem was something, at least at that time, that they could not even remotely have comprehended (Mat. 19:28; Rev. 21:14).

Above that, they would be privileged to stand side by side with Christ for the entirety of His earthly Ministry, which would culminate at Calvary and the Resurrection, where He would redeem mankind.

(14) "AND HE ORDAINED TWELVE, THAT THEY SHOULD BE WITH HIM, AND THAT HE MIGHT SEND THEM FORTH TO PREACH,

(15) "AND TO HAVE POWER TO HEAL SICKNESSES, AND TO CAST OUT DEVILS."

The structure is:

Now the training begins for the chosen Twelve!

THE CHOOSING OF THE TWELVE

The phrase, *"And He ordained Twelve,"* was for a purpose. *"Twelve"* symbolizes Government, and, more perfectly, the Government of God. It is God's Government versus man's Government, which is symbolized by the choice of the Twelve Tribes of Israel. There were *twelve gates"* in the wall of the New Jerusalem, with *"twelve angels"* at those gates, and the names of the *"Twelve Tribes of the Children of Israel"* written on the gates.

The wall of the city had *"twelve foundations,"* and in them the *"names of the Twelve Apostles of the Lamb."* The city is *"twelve thousand furlongs"* in measurement, which is about 1,500 miles, on each side. The foundations were garnished by *"twelve types of precious stones,"* and the *"twelve gates"* were made of *"twelve pearls"* (Rev. 21:12-21).

All of this is meant, as stated, to express God's Government. Unlike man's Government, it is a Perfect Government. From this we should learn that the government of the world must never be allowed to enter into the government of the Church. And yet, most Church government is plagued by man's government, with little or none of the Government of the Lord. The Holy Spirit-filled Church does not take its cue from the world, does not get its advice from the world, and does not conduct itself according to the world. If the world accepts the Church, then it becomes very obvious that the Government of God is not ruling in that particular Church or Denomination.

GOD'S GOVERNMENT

First of all, God's Government is His Word. This means that everything we do must be according to the Word. It also means that the Word must not be pulled out of context and must not be perverted in any way.

Peter said: *"Which they who are unlearned and unstable wrest, as they do also the other Scriptures, unto their own destruction"* (II Pet. 3:16).

Paul said: *"Now the Spirit speaks expressly, that in the latter times* (the times in which we now live) *some shall depart from the faith* (refers to departing from the Cross), *giving heed to seducing spirits* (religious spirits), *and doctrines of Devils"* (I Tim. 4:1).

Whenever the Church goes wrong, it is always in the realm of *"government."* It is the Church leaving the Word of God, which is God's True Government, and thereby inserting their own government, and declaring it to be Scriptural, or whatever! This is where entire Denominations go wrong. They leave the Government of the Word of God, most of the time doing so gradually, and then, little by little, insert their own government which is not Scriptural, exactly as Israel did, or had done, at the time of Christ.

THE GOVERNMENT OF TWELVE

Another fad, called *"the Government of*

Twelve," is being accepted by quite a few Churches. A particular brother in South America claims that he had a revelation from the Lord concerning this particular Church Growth program, etc. As the *"Purpose Driven Life"* scheme functions on the number *"forty,"* this scheme functions on the number *"twelve."* Of course, there is always a little truth in every lie.

Pure and simple, the *"Government of Twelve"* scheme is a system of *"law,"* which means that it's not Scriptural. While they talk about the Cross, what they actually talk about has little relationship to the Word of God. And you can mark down as unscriptural anything that is not purely and simply the Cross. This means that all of these Church Growth schemes have no Scriptural validity, and they will not fall out to bettering the lives of their adherents.

For something to be Scriptural, it must be totally and completely the Cross of Christ. Please understand, the Message of the Cross needs no help (I Cor. 1:18). It is a *"Finished Work"* and is the theme of the Word of God.

The Message of the Cross, as we've already stated, is the Message of the Bible. It's the same as it always has been, and it's the same as it always will be. It doesn't need to change, because it is a perfect Covenant and, therefore, *"The Everlasting Covenant"* (Heb. 13:20).

ORDAINED

The word *"ordained"* means *"to appoint"* or *"to choose."* It is a calling to a specific work and is done by the Lord and not man. Whenever God calls a man or woman to preach the Gospel, and for a specific work, as here designated, that is actually the only Ordination that counts. Man cannot give this *"ordination"* and man cannot take it away. All man can do is recognize that which God has already done, which, sadly, is not too often the case! Man generally only recognizes what he has *"ordained,"* which, in turn, will not be recognized by God.

This system of man-control was already rearing its ugly head in the Early Church. Some were demanding of the Apostle Paul that he produce his letter of *"commendation"* or *"ordination."* His answer to them was revealing:

"Do we begin again to commend ourselves? or need we, as some others, Epistles of commendation to you, or letters of commendation from you?

"You are our Epistle written in our hearts, known and read of all men:

"Forasmuch as you are manifestly declared to be the Epistle of Christ ministered by us, written not with ink, but with the Spirit of the Living God; not in tables of stone, but in fleshly tables of the heart . . . but our sufficiency (Ordination) *is of God"* (II Cor. 3:1-5).

In other words, Paul was saying that the proof of his credentials or *"ordination"* was not in a piece of paper that some man had given him, but rather the fruit of his calling, which translated into souls.

Sadly and regrettably, most of the modern Ministry can only produce a card from a particular religious Denomination to prove their Ordination. The true proof, and the only proof that God will accept, is the fruit of souls won to Christ, which will always accompany a true Ordination.

The phrase, *"That they should be with Him,"* was the secret of all that the Disciples would ever do for the Kingdom of God. It is the secret no less presently. Actually, the Disciples were not only to be with Christ, they were to be with Him constantly! If the following is to be proclaimed in the life and ministry of the Preacher, being with Christ Alone will bring it about.

Most Preachers are with religious Denominations, family, or personal interests, but few are with Christ.

PREACHING

The phrase, *"And that He might send them forth to preach,"* presented their actual mission, even though the power to heal the sick and cast out devils was also given. The healing and delivering must, however, not overpower the preaching, because it is from the *"preaching"* that the other is derived.

Please notice that He was to send them, and not some religious Denomination, etc. In fact, if the Church of that day, which obviously was comprised of the religious leaders of Israel, had had their way, they would have stopped them immediately. Similarly, the God-called Preacher will, for most of his life, fight the battle of whether he is to be controlled by God or man. That struggle is by and large an unending struggle.

I am not saying that one who is associated with a religious Denomination cannot, at the same time, be led of the Lord. In fact, some are led exclusively by the Lord in these situations. However, almost invariably, religious Denominations seek to control men. Quite possibly, many of them do not begin that way, but almost, if not all, conclude in that manner. So the Preacher affiliated with a religious Denomination must ever be cognizant of the fact that the Word of God must be obeyed at all times, irrespective of how small the matter may seem to be. God must ever take precedence over man.

This does not mean that one should not solicit the advise and counsel of others of like Faith, but it does mean that the Holy Spirit, and irrespective of the advice and counsel of others, has the final say.

A CONTROLLING SPIRIT

Any time a controlling spirit comes into men (a desire to control others), one can be sure that it's not of God; it should, consequently, be strongly resisted. And yet, at the same time, every action must be judged by all respecting its Scriptural validity. It is the responsibility of every Minister of the Gospel, as well as every Believer, to apply Scripture to any and all situations. If it is not Scriptural, it is not of God (I Cor. 14:24, 32-33).

We emphasize, again, that Jesus sent these individuals, and not man. The indication is that wherever they went, He designated such places. The Preacher of the Gospel is to seek the face of the Lord incessantly concerning direction. He is not to be sent anywhere by any man unless he first has the direction of the Holy Spirit that this is the place the Lord desires that he go. Regrettably, most Preachers are occupying pulpits because they were sent there by man; however, unless the Lord sends one, the Lord will not bless one!

This is where religious denominations too often, little by little, take on an authority which is not theirs. In their desire to control, they want to tell the Preacher where he can preach. They also want to tell him who can preach for him. Little by little, they also desire to tell Preachers what to preach. Such action, therefore, must be resisted at all times, which means that if a Preacher of the Gospel is truly called of God, he will find it very difficult, if not impossible, to remain in some religious Denominations or Churches.

The battle for control, as stated, goes on constantly. Either the Lord controls the man, or man controls the man. Both cannot! If man controls, God will not; if God controls, man cannot!

HOLY SPIRIT CONTROL

Control exercised by the Holy Spirit will always be that which is freely given to Him by the Believer. He will never coerce, threaten, or force His Way into the life of anyone. The Believer is exhorted, *"Be filled with the Spirit"* (Eph. 5:18), which could well be translated, *"Be controlled by the Spirit."* However, the Believer is not automatically controlled by the Spirit just because the Spirit indwells him. The control which the Spirit exerts over the Believer is dependent upon the Believer's active and corrective adjustment to the Spirit.

The Lord Jesus did not save us until we recognized Him as the Saviour and put our trust in Him for Salvation; consequently, the Holy Spirit does not control us, in the sense of permeating our will, reason, and emotions, until we recognize Him as the One Who has been sent by the Father to sanctify our lives and trust Him to perform His Ministry in and through us (Jn. 16:7-15).

There must be an ever-present conscious dependence upon, and definite subjection to, the Holy Spirit, a constant yielding to His Ministry and leaning upon Him for guidance and power, if He is to control the Believer in the most efficient manner and with the largest and best results.

Even though the Lord is the One Who sends, nevertheless, He does this by and through the Agency and Person of the Holy Spirit. So, the more fullness of the Spirit in a person's life, the greater control and the greater leading.

THE HOLY SPIRIT AND THE CROSS OF CHRIST

The Believer must understand that the

Holy Spirit works exclusively within the parameters of the Finished Work of Christ.

Paul said: *"For the Law of the Spirit of Life in Christ Jesus has made me free from the law of sin and death"* (Rom. 8:2).

That which is being discussed here is a *"Law,"* a Law, incidentally, devised by the Godhead, and that which will function at all times. The Holy Spirit functions within this Law, and it is *"in Christ Jesus."*

Any time that Paul uses the term, *"in Christ Jesus,"* or one of its derivatives, such as *"in Him,"* or *"in Whom,"* always, and without exception, he is speaking of Christ and what Christ did at the Cross. So, this tells us that the Holy Spirit works strictly within the legal confines of the Cross of Christ.

As a Believer, we are to place our faith exclusively in Christ and what Christ did at the Cross. Jesus said of the Holy Spirit, *"He shall glorify Me: for He shall receive of Mine, and shall show it unto you"* (Jn. 16:14).

So, the Believer, as stated, must at all times evidence Faith in Christ and what Christ did at the Cross. This is the premise on which the Holy Spirit works, and that premise alone. If our faith is properly placed, and we are speaking of ever making the Cross of Christ the Object of our Faith, to be sure, the Holy Spirit will then lead us and guide us, and do so to His full potential.

Even without the Believer understanding the Cross, the Holy Spirit will always do all that He can do. Without proper faith, He is, however, greatly limited, which always causes problems.

I have noticed, and extensively so, since the Lord has begun to open up to me the Revelation of the Cross, that I have sensed, more and more, a stronger leading and guidance by the Holy Spirit — far more than it once was.

With the Believer properly placing his Faith in Christ and the Cross, then the following admonition from our Lord will be realized to a greater degree within our lives.

In John 7:37-38, Jesus lays down two simple requirements, as it regards the Operation of the Holy Spirit within our lives:

1. Thirst for His control.
2. Trust in the Lord Jesus for the Spirit's control.

THIRST

Jesus said, *"If any man thirst."* This refers to a desire on the part of the Believer that the Holy Spirit be the One to control one's every thought, word, and deed. We do not take a drink of water unless we are thirsty. We do not appropriate the control of the Spirit unless we desire Him to control us.

A desire for His control will include, among other things: a desire that He call us to judge sin in our lives, a desire that He put sin out of our lives and keep it out, a desire that He separate us from all the ties we might have with that system of evil called the world, a desire that He dethrone our self-life and enthrone the Lord Jesus as absolute Lord and Master, a desire that He produce in us His Own fruit, a desire than He make us Christlike, a desire that He lead us and teach us. Such a desire is a serious thing. It involves the crucifixion of self, and self dies hard. The Spirit-controlled life is a crucified life, and that comes about by the Believer denying himself, taking up his cross daily, and following Jesus (Lk. 9:23).

TRUST

Our Lord also said, *"He who believes on Me, out from his innermost being shall flow rivers of living water."* The trust here in this context is not only trust in Him as Saviour, but trust in Him as the One Who fills with the Spirit. The Spirit-controlled life is, therefore, a matter of trust. Salvation is by Faith (Eph. 2:8-9). We receive our Justification by Faith. We are also to receive our Sanctification by Faith, which refers to Faith in Christ and the Cross, which then gives the Holy Spirit latitude to work within our lives, Who Alone can bring about the Sanctification process.

It is this constant desire for the Spirit's control and a trust in the Lord Jesus for the Spirit's control that results in the Spirit-controlled life. When one faces a new day, it is well to include in our prayers thanksgiving for the Presence of the Holy Spirit in our hearts, the expression of our desire for His control, and a definite assertion of our trust in the Lord Jesus for the Spirit's control during that day.

We must remember, however, that the key to all of this is our constant faith in Christ and the Cross. The Holy Spirit doesn't require very much of us, but He does require that of which I have just stated.

MECHANICS AND DYNAMICS OF THE SPIRIT

Someone has said that the Sixth Chapter of Romans proclaims to us the *"mechanics of the Holy Spirit,"* which tells us *"how"* the Holy Spirit does what He does in our hearts and lives. They have also stated, and rightly so, that the Eighth Chapter of Romans proclaims to us the *"dynamics of the Holy Spirit,"* which tells us *"what"* the Holy Spirit does, once we understand *"how"* He does it.

Whenever the Holy Spirit through Paul told us how to successfully live for the Lord, which is given to us in the Sixth Chapter of Romans, the first place He takes us is the Cross (Rom. 6:3-5). From those three Scriptures, we learn that we are *"baptized into His Death,"* then *"buried with Him by baptism into death,"* and then *"raised with Him in Newness of Life."* He, as our Substitute, did for us what we could not do for ourselves, and our faith in Him and what He did at the Cross places us in the very action of the Sacrifice He performed on our behalf.

HOW THE HOLY SPIRIT WORKS

The greatest problem with Christians, even those who claim to be Spirit-filled, is a lack of understanding as to how the Holy Spirit works within our lives. As I've already stated in this Volume, we too often take Him for granted, mostly because we understand very little about Him.

Of course, since the Holy Spirit is God, He is far beyond our grasp, as should be overly obvious. The Word does tell us, however, even as we've already given you the information from Romans 8:2, as to how the Holy Spirit works. To understand that is to understand the key to victory. To fail to understand that is to fail.

POWER TO HEAL THE SICK

The phrase, *"And to have power to heal sicknesses,"* presents that which was given by Christ to the Twelve, and to many others since, for that matter.

The word here translated *"power"* is the Greek word *"exousia,"* which means *"delegated authority."* It does not mean, consequently, that God put His supernatural Power into the hands of the Twelve to be exercised by them. What He did do was delegate to them the authority to heal sicknesses, meaning that they would speak the word declaring healing and God's Power would effect the Work.

Regrettably, this is where some Pentecostals and Charismatics miss it. We tend to have it in our minds that the *"power"* is ours, to do with it as we like. Nothing could be further from the truth! Too often such thinking results in Preachers, who once may have had this power but no longer do, continuing to exercise it within their own abilities, or rather trying to do so. The power of suggestion and psychological manipulation, which even skirt the edge of witchcraft, now become the *"gimmick."*

To run this charade out to its conclusion, Believers are frequently told they are healed of diseases they never even knew they had or told to confess their healing to all and sundry, even though there is no evidence of it. Thank God all who pray for the sick do not function in that capacity, but some do! I might quickly add that far too many Believers have such little Biblical foundation that they hardly know the false from the real. Nevertheless, Jesus Christ continues to heal the sick for those who will dare to believe Him — at least at times.

The *"power"* granted is strictly a work of Grace on the part of the Lord, delegating such to the humble heart and life. The continued understanding of this Truth is absolutely imperative if He is to continue to use us.

THE CASTING OUT OF DEMONS

The phrase, *"And to cast out devils,"* should have been translated *"demons,"* because there actually is only one Devil, but many demons. Moreover, Satan and demons are actually two different categories of beings. Satan is a fallen angel, whereas demon spirits are not in the angelic category. As previously stated, many believe, as this writer, that these spirits of darkness come from a pre-Adamic creation which fell with Lucifer in his revolution against God (Isa. 14:12-15; Ezek. 28:11-19).

The Disciples were given power to cast out demons. The Lord is still giving that power (Mk. 16:17).

(16) "AND SIMON HE SURNAMED PETER;

(17) "AND JAMES THE SON OF ZEBEDEE, AND JOHN THE BROTHER OF JAMES; AND HE SURNAMED THEM BOANERGES, WHICH IS, THE SONS OF THUNDER:

(18) "AND ANDREW, AND PHILIP, AND BARTHOLOMEW, AND MATTHEW, AND THOMAS, AND JAMES THE SON OF ALPHAEUS, AND THADDAEUS, AND SIMON THE CANAANITE,

(19) "AND JUDAS ISCARIOT, WHICH ALSO BETRAYED HIM: AND THEY WENT INTO AN HOUSE."

The exegesis is:

Judas Iscariot was the only one of the Disciples who was of the Tribe of Judah; Christ was from that Tribe, as well!

SIMON

The phrase, *"And Simon He surnamed Peter,"* which means *"a stone."* In fact, this was not the character and nature of Peter, but it was that which the Lord would make of him. What a blessing it is to read this, knowing that the Lord can change one in such a manner — to the total opposite of what one once was. This is what Jesus was speaking of when He said in Matthew 16:18, *"As for you, you are Petros* (a fragment of rock), *and upon this Petra* (Jesus, a massive Living Rock), *I will build My Church."*

So, Jesus, by giving Simon the name of *"Peter,"* was actually saying to him, *"I will make of you a rock-like man, dependable, immovable, and equal to the emergencies and crises that confront you."*

JAMES AND JOHN

James and John, as Peter, were surnamed *"Boanerges,"* which means *"sons of thunder."* It was intended, as Peter, to be a title of honor, although it was not perpetuated like the surname *"Peter."* The name suggested their impetuosity and zeal, which characterized both the brothers. Christ would take the natural dispositions of these men and elevate them by His Grace, which would channel this fiery zeal into the proclamation of the Gospel.

Actually, John the Beloved was called *"the thunder-voice."* This may have been after his death and due to the Visions he saw, including the *"thunders,"* which resulted in the Book of Revelation. However, it could also have had an earlier meaning, referring to his manner of Preaching, which well could have been with power and authority, and no doubt was.

It is interesting that Jesus selected the three, Peter, James, and John, as recipients of these surnames, who alone would share great intimate experiences with Christ, even apart from the remainder of the Twelve.

ANDREW

This name means *"manly."*

PHILIP

This name means *"fond of horses."* In Ecclesiastical legend, he is said to have been a *"chariot-driver."*

BARTHOLOMEW

This is Nathanael, of whom we first read in John 1:46 as having been found by Philip and brought to Christ.

MATTHEW

This name means *"a gift of God."* The meaning of his name was truly brought to pass in that he was selected to this all-important Twelve.

THOMAS

This name means *"twin."*

JAMES, THE SON OF ALPHAEUS

He is not the same as the other *"James"* listed above, which should be obvious, and neither is he the half-brother of Jesus. His name, as the other James, in the Hebrew means *"Jacob."* He is thought to have been a brother to Judas (not Iscariot), Matthew, and Simon Zelotes. If that, in fact, is correct, he would have been a member of four brothers selected by Christ as His chosen Disciples, as well as the two sets of two brothers — James and John, and Peter and Andrew.

THADDAEUS

He is the same as Judas of John 14:20 (not Iscariot). Martin Luther called him the *"good Judas."*

SIMON THE CANAANITE

His name is properly called *"Simon, the Canaanaean."* As well, he was called *"Simon the Zealot,"* which meant that he had formerly been connected with one of the fierce war-parties of that day, dedicated to the overthrow of Rome, respecting the occupation of Israel. His life also would be gloriously changed.

JUDAS ISCARIOT

This man was born in Kerioth, which is a small town mentioned in Joshua 15:25, and which was one of the uttermost cities of Judah toward the coast of Edom southward. In this town was born the betrayer of the Saviour. He was the only one of the group who was of the Tribe of Judah, as was Christ.

(20) "AND THE MULTITUDE COMES TOGETHER AGAIN, SO THAT THEY COULD NOT SO MUCH AS EAT BREAD."

The composition is:

Because of the need, wherever Jesus was, multitudes came.

THE MULTITUDE

The phrase, *"And the multitude comes together again,"* refers to the people in Capernaum hearing that Jesus was here once again, which would result in scores coming for healing or for whatever purpose. The phrase, *"So that they could not so much as eat bread,"* proclaims the impossibility of even carrying on the necessary affairs of life. They could not even find the time to eat!

There were many reasons for the gathering of these tremendous crowds, but probably the greatest reason was that every single person who came to Christ for healing or Deliverance received exactly that for which they came. Some 23 times it is stated that He healed them all. So mighty were His Works that Christ drew vast multitudes even out in the desert places where men would go willingly for days without food to hear Him and to be healed by Him (Mat. 14:13-21; 15:29-39).

(21) "AND WHEN HIS FRIENDS HEARD OF IT, THEY WENT OUT TO LAY HOLD ON HIM: FOR THEY SAID, HE IS BESIDE HIMSELF."

The diagram is:

NOTES

These were His immediate relatives, even as Verse 31 proclaims. They intended to stop Him, even by using force and against His Will, if necessary. They actually believed He was insane. His open opposition to the Pharisees and the religious leaders of Israel would have occasioned this, with them knowing that it was ultimately going to bring severe trouble. His brothers, however, at that time, did not actually believe He was the Son of God (Jn. 7:5).

HIS FRIENDS

The phrase, *"And when His friends heard of it,"* spoke of His immediate relatives, such as His Mother and brothers. Of course, His family had heard of the massive crowds, the healings, the Miracles, and the great Deliverances. It was the talk of all of Israel. However, what prompted them to make this journey from Nazareth to Capernaum, a distance of approximately 30 miles, and by foot at that, was no doubt the tremendous animosity being stirred up against Christ by the religious leaders.

As the next Verse proclaims, they were accusing Him of performing these mighty Miracles and casting out demon spirits by the power of Satan. Fearful of what this animosity would lead to, His relatives came, apparently, to talk Him into returning to Nazareth with them, and ceasing His Ministry.

INSANE?

The phrase, *"They went out to lay hold on Him, for they said, He is beside Himself,"* means that they actually felt He was insane, and that they would stop Him, which refers to stopping His Ministry, even by using force and against His Will, if necessary!

First of all, John said: *"Even His brethren did not believe in Him"* (Jn. 7:5). In other words, they did not believe, at least at this stage, that He was the Messiah, and really had little explanation as to the source of His great power. It was all an enigma to them and they were not able to put it together. They could not equate the older brother they once knew with what was now happening!

Such is not meant to impugn His life before His Ministry, because it was perfect before man and God. Still, He exhibited no miraculous powers during this time of some 30 years. How was it that He was now able to do all of these miraculous things? There is no hint that Mary, His Mother, joined in with the unbelief registered by His brothers. She was here on this day because she was truly concerned about His welfare.

And yet, it is doubtful that she fully understood all the things which were happening. Of course, His miraculous conception was undoubtedly in her mind constantly. And what the great Angel Gabriel had said to her was ever before her:

"He shall be great, and shall be called the Son of the Highest: and the Lord God shall give unto Him the Throne of His father David:

"And He shall reign over the house of Jacob forever; and of His Kingdom there shall be no end" (Lk. 1:32-33).

MARY

Mary, no doubt, had written down these words and had, beyond doubt, memorized them, quoting them to herself over and over again. Also, she no doubt very well remembered the words given to her by the Holy Spirit when she came to Elizabeth, the soon-to-be mother of John the Baptist. These words extolled what God had done and would do, which all pertained to this Miracle Child which she carried in her womb (Lk. 1:46-55).

I think, without a doubt, she knew Who He was and that He was the Messiah. And yet, as a Mother, and especially His Mother, she grieved in her heart at the anger and animosity that were building, rapidly and certainly, in Israel against Him, especially by the religious leaders. Surely she remembered the words uttered by Simeon in the Temple concerning the child and her, as well: *"Yea, a sword shall pierce through your own soul also!"* (Lk. 2:35).

Fearful of what might come, and which, in fact, did come, she was here this day because she hoped that somehow something could be done that would cool the burning hatred toward her Son, who was, above all, God's Son! As stated, there is almost no evidence that she thought He was *"beside Himself,"* as his half-brothers thought!

(22) "AND THE SCRIBES WHICH CAME DOWN FROM JERUSALEM SAID, HE HAS BEELZEBUB, AND BY THE PRINCE OF THE DEVILS CASTS HE OUT DEVILS."

The overview is:

These men were evidently sent by the Sanhedrin in order to find something with which they could undermine the influence of Christ. They blasphemed the Holy Spirit when they accused Christ of casting out demons by the power of Satan.

JESUS OF NAZARETH

The phrase, *"And the Scribes which came down from Jerusalem,"* proclaims these individuals as evidently being sent by the Sanhedrin, the governing body of Israel, in order to watch Him, and thereby to find something with which they could undermine His influence.

The evidence as to Who He is presents an overwhelming case, not only to the religious leaders of Israel, but to the entirety of the world, for that matter! As to the fact that such a person as Jesus of Nazareth lived and flourished in the First Century A.D., there is hardly any dispute today. Actually, there is far more proof that Jesus lived than even Julius Caesar. And yet, concerning the writings of the First Century, there isn't much said about Him by the secular historians.

There is a reason for that:

He was born in an obscure part of the Roman Empire. Israel was far removed from Rome, with few secular historians noting anything of this region. Further, He was not a person of high birth, at least as far as the world was concerned, although His lineage was in the royal line of David. However, that dynasty was not in power then, nor had it been in power for about 600 years. It's not hard to understand that historians did not take note of a Peasant (for that's what Jesus was) of a province far removed from Rome.

Even though today we think of His Crucifixion marking Him as the subject of an outstanding event, still, from the standpoint of the First Century, it was a common event. The Roman roads were literally lined with crosses upon which victims writhed in agony until death put an end to their struggles.

THE DEITY OF CHRIST

His claiming Deity for Himself, which He

did, was anything but uncommon. The Roman Emperors claimed to be divine and they required their subjects to worship them. Other officials (Herod, for example) deified themselves. Thus, the secular historians of the First Century took little notice of Jesus of Nazareth, and for the obvious reasons. He was not, however, totally ignored, as we shall see.

THE HISTORICAL ACCOUNT OF CHRIST

Josephus, the Jewish historian, was born in A.D. 37. His works were accepted by the Imperial Library of Rome, and he had this to say about Jesus:

"Now there was about this time, Jesus, a wise man, if it be lawful to call Him a man, for He was a doer of wonderful works, a teacher of such men as received the Truth with pleasure. He drew over to Him both many of the Jews and many of the Gentiles. He was (the) *Christ; and when Pilate, at the suggestion of the principal men among us, had condemned Him to the Cross, those who loved Him at the first did not forsake Him, for He appeared to them alive again the third day, as the Divine Prophets had foretold these and ten thousand other wonderful things concerning Him; and the tribe of Christians so named after Him is not extinct at this day"* (Antiquities of the Jews, by Josephus, Book 18, Chapter 3, Paragraph 3).

Tacitus, a Roman historian, lived in the First Century. His high character as an historian is generally conceded. He wrote about Jesus of Nazareth in the following words, which are most informative, especially considering the attitude of the Roman Empire towards Jesus and Christianity. He spoke of Nero, who burned Rome, and then attempted to place the blame on the Christians.

Tacitus said:

"Nero caused others to be accused, on whom he inflicted exquisite torments, who were already hated by the people for their crimes, and who were commonly called Christians. This name they derived from Christ their leader, Who, in the reign of Tiberius, was put to death as a criminal, while Pontius Pilate was Procurator."

Suetonius, another Roman historian who lived in the First Century, said:

NOTES

"He (Claudius) *banished the Jews from Rome, who were continually raising disturbances, Christ* (Chrestus) *being their leader."*

Even though the statements given by these Roman historians, and other we could name, were not positive, still, they admitted to His existence.

PROOFS OF DEITY

Among all the other proofs of His Deity, it must be understood that Jesus of Nazareth was much more than just a man, for His followers must have been convinced of that fact, for many willingly suffered a horrible martyrdom for their testimony to His Deity. Thousands upon thousands of people do not go to a violent death for something they know or suspect is a fraud.

One cannot explain the willing acceptance of Jesus of Nazareth as Saviour by a sin-loving pagan, who accepted with Him that which he formerly hated, namely Righteousness, and by that forsook his sin, which he loved, knowing that by so doing, he would be liable to capital punishment for his act, except upon the basis of a supernatural working in his heart, providing for the willing acceptance of that which he formerly hated, Righteousness.

Jesus of Nazareth, therefore, stands as history's outstanding enigma, unless He is accorded the place which the Bible gives Him, Very God of Very God. One cannot explain Him without this fact of His Deity. One can dismiss Him with an *"I do not believe that,"* but that does not solve the problem nor blot Him from the pages of history. He stands there, astride the world of mankind, a unique individual, God and Man in One Person.

As well, it must be considered that of all the founders of religions of this world, including Islam, Buddhism, Confucianism, etc., Jesus of Nazareth stands alone in asserting that He was God, and in accepting the worship of individuals.

BEELZEBUB

The phrase, *"Said, He has Beelzebub,"* actually meant that Beelzebub had Him, and was using Him as his agent. Wuest says, *"The expression points to something more than an alliance, as in Matthew, to possession,* and that on a grand scale: *a divine possession by a based deity, doubtless, god of flies* (Beelzebub) *or god of dung* (Beelzebul), *still a god, a sort of Satanic incarnation."*

The accusation of these religious leaders was, therefore, serious indeed, so serious, in fact, that they blasphemed the Holy Spirit, thus dooming themselves for time and eternity.

SATAN

The phrase, *"And by the prince of the devils casts He out devils,"* presented these religious leaders accusing Jesus of casting out demons by the help of Satan, i.e., *"prince of Devils."* They were trying to break the force of the attesting power of the Miracles performed by Jesus, and done in the energy of the Holy Spirit. If, of course, this could be done, it would disprove His claims to Messiahship; consequently, they attributed the Works of God to the Devil, which Jesus labeled as *"blasphemy against the Holy Spirit"* (Vs. 29).

Why did they do this?

They rejected Him and His claims because of sin in their lives, sin, incidentally, of which they would not repent, by reason of their entrenched ecclesiasticism, which would allow no interference with its position. It would be well to remember that here the testimony to the effect that Jesus claimed Deity in these exchanges did not come from His followers, but from the ranks of the opposition (Jn. 10:20-30).

His family pronounced Him a lunatic (Vs. 21), and the Scribes declared Him a demoniac. Thus, the natural heart judged the Lord of Glory!

(23) "AND HE CALLED THEM UNTO HIM, AND SAID UNTO THEM IN PARABLES, HOW CAN SATAN CAST OUT SATAN?"

The exposition is:

Why would Satan desire to undo what he had done?

SCRIBES

The phrase, *"And He called them unto Him,"* means that He called these *"Scribes"* close to Him, in order that He might answer their accusation. The manner in which the language is constructed tells us that He was not in the least bit awed by their alleged

NOTES

scholarly claims. In fact, there is a slight note of contempt in that which He did!

The phrase, *"And said unto them in parables,"* refers to Him using illustrations which would not only be easily understood by them, but also by all who stood nearby. This was done for a purpose. The Scribes generally taught with an air of superiority, talking down to the people, and in terminology that was little understood. Jesus did the very opposite!

The question, *"How can Satan cast out Satan?"* declares the impossibility of such stupidity. Wuest said, *"Our Lord's argument is, briefly: Grant it for the moment that spirits may be cast out by the aid of other spirits, which they cannot! More is needed in the latter than superior strength. There must be a motive, and Satan would have no desire to operate against himself."*

(24) "AND IF A KINGDOM BE DIVIDED AGAINST ITSELF, THAT KINGDOM CANNOT STAND."

The overview is:

His argument is irrefutable!

A KINGDOM

This is the first of three illustrations which will be given by Christ respecting the absurdity proposed by the Scribes. In essence, Jesus is saying that it should be obvious to all that a kingdom warring within itself will ultimately destroy itself; consequently, if Satan is busily engaged in placing spirits of darkness into people, then for him, at the same time, to cast those spirits out would be absurd! He would destroy himself, and, to be sure, he will not do that!

(25) "AND IF A HOUSE BE DIVIDED AGAINST ITSELF, THAT HOUSE CANNOT STAND."

Internal fighting respecting a family will ultimately lead to the destruction of that family, as was obvious to all who stood nearby, including the Scribes. So, the family of Satan is not warring against itself, as the Scribes should know!

(26) "AND IF SATAN RISE UP AGAINST HIMSELF, AND BE DIVIDED, HE CANNOT STAND, BUT HAS AN END."

So, as Jesus continues, the third illustration proposes that if the *"kingdom"* and "house" work to war internally against themselves, as they would be obviously destroyed, likewise, Satan would come to the same "end." So their accusation and claim are preposterous!

(27) "NO MAN CAN ENTER INTO A STRONG MAN'S HOUSE, AND SPOIL HIS GOODS, EXCEPT HE WILL FIRST BIND THE STRONG MAN; AND THEN HE WILL SPOIL HIS HOUSE."

The synopsis is:

Christ defeated Satan at the Cross by atoning for all sin (Col. 2:14-15).

THE STRONG MAN

The phrase, *"No man can enter into a strong man's house,"* refers to Satan as a *"strong man."* However, even though he is *"strong,"* nevertheless, Jesus is much *"stronger,"* because He is able to enter into this house of evil, and there is nothing that can be done about it. This is proved by Jesus casting out demons. If Satan could have stopped Him, he would have done so; however, by his not doing so, this proves that he simply does not have the power.

SPOIL SATAN'S GOODS

The phrase, *"And spoil his goods,"* means that not only will He enter Satan's domain of darkness, but He also will destroy his kingdom, i.e., *"spoil his goods."* Satan's *"goods"* are sin, bondage, poverty, sickness, ignorance, superstition, error, and the lie. Jesus has spoiled all of this, as the Scripture says, *"For this purpose the Son of God was manifested, that He might destroy the works of the Devil"* (I Jn. 3:8).

BINDING THE STRONG MAN

The phrase, *"Except He will first bind the strong man,"* means that Satan is rendered defenseless in the face of Christ, and is unable to protect his kingdom of darkness. In effect, Satan and all of his cohorts of darkness were defeated at the Cross of Calvary. As should be understood, there has never been any physical contact, as it regards Satan or demon spirits and Christ. Satan, who is a created being, obviously is no match for Christ, Who is the Creator.

So how did Jesus render Satan helpless?

NOTES

Colossians 2:14-15 tells us how.

Jesus satisfied the demands of the broken Law, and did so by atoning for all sin, past, present, and future, which necessitated Him giving His Life, which was the very reason He came to this world (Jn. 3:16). When He atoned for all sin, that took away Satan's legal right to hold mankind in captivity. That was the way Satan was defeated, and his house spoiled.

When Jesus cried on the Cross, *"It is finished,"* He, in effect, was saying, *"Sin is finished!"* and *"Bondage is finished!"* and *"Poverty is finished!"* and *"Ignorance is finished!"* and *"Satan is finished!"*

PREACHING THE CROSS

Paul said, *"For the preaching* (Word) *of the Cross is to them who perish foolishness; but unto us which are saved it is the Power of God"* (I Cor. 1:18).

How is the preaching of the Cross the *"Power of God"*?

The *"Power"* is registered in the Holy Spirit (Acts 1:8). However, and as we have said repeatedly, the Holy Spirit works entirely within the parameters of the Finished Work of Christ, meaning that He does not work apart from the legal Work of Christ on the Cross, which is a Finished Work. Once again, as we've already said, this particular doctrine is so strong that it is referred to as a *"Law,"* i.e., *"the Law of the Spirit of Life in Christ Jesus"* (Rom. 8:2).

THE SLAIN LAMB AND THE HOLY SPIRIT

In the great Vision of John the Beloved on the Isle of Patmos, which was given to him of the Throne of God, he portrays to us the *"Book"* that had to be opened with no one in Heaven or Earth *"able to open the Book, neither to look thereon"* (Rev. 5:3). He went on to say how he *"wept much, because no man was found worthy to open and to read the Book, neither to look thereon"* (Rev. 5:4).

The Scripture then says, *"And one of the Elders said unto me, Weep not: behold, the Lion of the Tribe of Judah, the Root of David, has prevailed to open the Book, and to loose the Seven Seals thereof"* (Rev. 5:5). Of course, the *"Lion of the Tribe of Judah"* and the *"Root of David"* portray Jesus Christ, Who Alone is worthy!

But then when John was shown the Son of God, i.e., *"the Lamb of God,"* strangely enough, he saw *"a Lamb as it had been slain, having seven horns and seven eyes, which are the Seven Spirits of God sent forth into all the Earth"* (Rev. 5:6). In this portrayal, Jesus is portrayed as the Crucified Lamb, telling us, in effect, that the only way one can reach the Throne of God is through the Crucified Lamb. We also see the *"Lamb as it had been slain"* and the Holy Spirit so closely intertwined that it's not really possible to distinguish between the two. The idea is:

What Christ did at the Cross is what makes it possible for the Holy Spirit to do what He does for humanity. Before Jesus died on the Cross, even though animal blood was offered up, it was not sufficient to take away sins; therefore, the Holy Spirit was greatly limited in what He could do, as it regards help for Believers. But when Jesus died on the Cross, He atoned for all sin, which then made it possible for the Holy Spirit to come into the heart and life of each Believer, and to abide there forever (Jn. 14:16-17; 16:7).

SEVEN HORNS AND SEVEN EYES

The seven horns on the *"Lamb"* stand for dominion. The number *"seven"* stands for total dominion. In other words, the *"seven horns"* stand for total victory by the Child of God, providing one's faith is anchored firmly in Christ and Him Crucified. It means that there is no way that any Believer can walk in perpetual victory (Rom. 6:14), unless their faith is anchored squarely in Christ and Him Crucified, typified by what John saw in his Vision.

The *"seven eyes"* stand for total illumination, which means that the Believer cannot truly know the way to go, unless he understands Christ and the Cross. If one's faith is anchored firmly in Christ and the Cross, ever making that the Object of his Faith, he will very easily be able to spot false doctrine and he will not be deceived, hence, the *"seven eyes"* portraying perfect illumination, all made possible by the Cross.

(28) "VERILY I SAY UNTO YOU, ALL SINS SHALL BE FORGIVEN UNTO THE SONS OF MEN, AND BLASPHEMIES WHEREWITH SOEVER THEY SHALL BLASPHEME:

(29) "BUT HE THAT SHALL BLASPHEME AGAINST THE HOLY SPIRIT HAS NEVER FORGIVENESS, BUT IS IN DANGER OF ETERNAL DAMNATION."

The structure is:

Only a Believer who has ceased to believe, i.e., ceases to evidence Faith in Christ, as well as a professor of religion, such as these Pharisees, etc., can blaspheme the Holy Spirit. An unsaved person, who has no profession of faith, cannot blaspheme the Spirit. And when one does blaspheme the Holy Spirit, there will not be any desire to serve Christ, as there was no desire by the Pharisees, etc., to serve Christ.

THE GLORIOUS PROMISE

Verse 28 presents a glorious and wonderful promise. These *"sins"* and *"blasphemies"* include every vile thing that can be thought of, such as murder, rape, treason, incest, homosexuality, adultery, hate, pride, etc. That the Lord will forgive any and all sin, upon proper Repentance and confession of sin, is a promise of unprecedented proportions. Every human being should thank God day and night for this great provision by the Lord (I Jn. 1:9).

When Jesus died on the Cross, He addressed every single sin, with the exception of one, which we will study next.

BLASPHEMING THE HOLY SPIRIT

The phrase, *"But he that shall blaspheme against the Holy Spirit has never forgiveness,"* constitutes a chilling thought, to say the least! It means that the sin is an eternal sin, which cannot be forgiven, which means the sinner is bound by a chain of sin from which he can never be loosed. Consequently, Jesus said to some of the Pharisees, *"Therefore your sin remains,"* i.e., meaning these Pharisees could not be forgiven, because they would not be forgiven (Jn. 9:41).

The word *"blaspheme,"* as used here, concerns the Holy Spirit. Actually, any and all sin, irrespective of its nature, is, in effect, a sin against God the Holy Spirit, as it is against God the Son or God the Father. However, the word *"blaspheme,"* as it applies to the Holy Spirit means *"to speak reproachfully, to rail at, revile, calumniate."* It means, in its simple sense, *"malicious misrepresentation."*

Wuest says: *"It is used specifically of those who by contemptuous speech intentionally come short of the reverence due to God or to sacred things. Here the words speak of the action of the Scribes, who, knowing that our Lord was performing miracles in the Power of the Holy Spirit, deliberately and knowingly attribute them to Satan, and do this in an attempt to break the attesting power of the miracles our Lord was performing. This is the unpardonable sin."*

It is possible to blaspheme the Son or the Father without committing the unpardonable sin. Jesus said, *"Whosoever speaks a word against the Son of Man, it shall be forgiven him"* (Mat. 12:32). However, if one speaks against the Holy Spirit in such a malicious tone as these Scribes, it is a sin which cannot be forgiven and, in fact, will not be forgiven!

THE ETERNAL SIN

The phrase, *"But is in danger of eternal damnation,"* according to Greek Scholars should have been translated, *"but is in danger of eternal sin."* The idea is this: as the Text presently reads, it seems that Jesus is saying that upon the committing of such a sin, the person is merely in *"danger"* of damnation instead of such being guaranteed, which is not the case. As we have stated, and as the original Greek of this Text proves, this sin committed is an eternal sin. As a result, it carries with it an eternal damnation.

Jesus is impressing upon all that when one begins to speak in any manner disparaging of the Holy Spirit, the *"danger"* of committing this unpardonable sin becomes acute! Consequently, and in view of that, nothing must be said that could even remotely be construed as opposition to the Holy Spirit.

(30) "BECAUSE THEY SAID, HE HAS AN UNCLEAN SPIRIT."

The exegesis is:

When the Scribes and Pharisees attributed the Miracles of Christ to the operation of demon spirits, they blasphemed the Holy Spirit.

NOTES

THE OCCASION OF BLASPHEMING THE HOLY SPIRIT

The phrase, *"Because they said,"* means that these Scribes knew full well that Jesus was casting out these demons by the Spirit of God. There was no doubt about that, by its disposition, or in their minds. The phrase, *"He has an unclean spirit,"* proclaims them hatching up this idea that Jesus cast out demons by the power of the Devil. In effect, they were saying that Jesus was an *"incarnate Devil,"* i.e., a Devil in human form!

They knew this wasn't true; however, they hatched up this scheme among themselves in order to attempt to discredit Him in the eyes of the people. Thus, their sin was willful, malicious, knowing, arbitrary, and deliberate. The lie they were projecting was bad enough! But to attribute the Works of God, which were overwhelmingly obvious, to the Devil was blaspheming the Holy Spirit. Thus, at that moment, they were condemned to an eternal Hell, which is where they are presently and ever shall be, because from this place there is no escape, which means that they doomed themselves eternally.

Inasmuch as we have given extended coverage to this important subject in our Commentary on Matthew (Chpt. 12), we will address it here in a more abbreviated form. But yet, we trust, we will answer the questions posed by some Readers.

WHO CAN COMMIT THE SIN OF BLASPHEMING THE HOLY SPIRIT?

The only record in the Word of God of anyone blaspheming the Holy Spirit is found among these professors of religion called *"Scribes and Pharisees."* There is no record of unsaved people committing this sin, only professors of religion, only those, we might quickly add, who claim to be involved in that which we presently call *"Christianity."*

ARE THERE PEOPLE WHO DESIRE TO GIVE THEIR HEART TO GOD, BUT CANNOT, BECAUSE THEY HAVE BLASPHEMED THE HOLY SPIRIT?

No! Any person who wants to be Saved can be Saved (Rev. 22:17).

Some Preachers have claimed such,

stating that some people have refused the Lord so many times that when they finally desire to be Saved, the Lord refuses to save them, because they have committed this sin. That is totally incorrect! There is no record in the Word of God, which must be our criteria, that anyone who came to Christ was turned away. They were not then, and they are not now!

Anyone who desires in their heart to be Saved, and who turns to the Lord, will always, without exception, find Him a willing recipient of their lost soul. Actually, Jesus is actively seeking those who are lost (Mk. 2:17). One of the greatest signs that one has not blasphemed the Holy Spirit is the desire for God and His Ways.

WHAT IS BLASPHEMING THE HOLY SPIRIT?

It is, as stated, the willful ascribing of the Works of God to Satan. It is done so when all the evidence is contrary to the accusation. Since the Day of Pentecost (Acts 2:1-4), the Holy Spirit has been poured out on all who will believe. As a result, multiple millions have been Baptized with the Spirit, with the evidence of speaking with other tongues (Acts 2:4; 10:46; 19:1-7).

This Gift of God has been multiplied since the turn of the Twentieth Century, with more receiving the Holy Spirit than probably all the previous centuries combined. This is in direct fulfillment of Bible Prophecy, where Peter said, *"And it shall come to pass in the last days, saith God, I will pour out of My Spirit upon all flesh"* (Acts 2:17).

Even though the *"last days"* actually began on the *"Day of Pentecost,"* still, Acts 2:19-20 tells us that this *"pouring out of the Spirit"* will intensify in the last of the last days. And yet, even though many have received, many have also opposed this which the Lord is doing. The opposition has almost entirely come from the religious sector, exactly as it did in the days of Christ.

In this opposition, I am concerned that some have blasphemed the Holy Spirit. Most of the opposition has centered up against *"speaking with tongues."* For one to say, *"I do not believe in it,"* or *"I do not see this Doctrine in this manner,"* or some other such term, is one thing! However, to say that speaking in tongues is *"of the Devil"* or *"inspired by demon spirits"* puts one in the very position that Jesus spoke of when He said, *"is in danger of eternal damnation."*

Only the Lord can make the final determination that one has blasphemed the Holy Spirit. But if *"speaking with other tongues, as the Spirit gives the utterance"* is truly of God, as should be obvious by its Biblical terminology (Acts 2:4), then attributing such to Satan is dangerous indeed! And yet some, if not many, have done this!

If these who have committed such acts are unsaved people rather than professors of religion, that would be another thing altogether; however, to be as the Scribes and Pharisees of old, the proof is irrefutable and Scriptural. There is no excuse for modern Pharisees to make such statements. Consequently, such are done willfully, deliberately, and intentionally.

WILL ONE KNOW HE HAS BLASPHEMED THE HOLY SPIRIT?

No, they will not know such a thing, and neither will they have any desire to follow God's Way. In fact, they will continue on with their own religious way, as the Scribes and Pharisees of old! These individuals did not even remotely agree with Christ as to what they had done, neither did they turn their way at all toward God. They continued to think they were right with God and that all was well. In other words, there was no desire for Repentance, because such desire can only be generated by the Holy Spirit, Whom they had denied.

So, a person who has blasphemed the Holy Spirit will not know they have done so, will not think they have done so, and will have no desire to change their way. In fact, if there is a fear which arises in the heart of a person over something they may have said in this respect, such is a sign that they have not blasphemed the Holy Spirit. Any attitude toward God in the hearts of people must be generated by the Holy Spirit. He works or acts upon the Word of God being presented to individuals. Without that, i.e., the drawing of the Holy Spirit, it is impossible for the individual to come to God (I Jn. 5:6; Rev. 22:17).

If the Spirit of God is not present to draw the person or to perform His Office Work in any way, because He has been rejected by attributing to Him works of Satan, there is no way for that person to be drawn to the Truth. Consequently, they are lost, and hopelessly so!

I am persuaded, and sadly so, that some, if not many, Preachers in modern pulpits have committed this grave sin. As such, and as would be obvious, there is absolutely no moving or Operation of the Holy Spirit whatsoever in their Ministries or Churches. If it were so in Jesus' day, and it definitely was, it very likely could be so at present!

(31) "THERE CAME THEN HIS BRETHREN AND HIS MOTHER, AND, STANDING WITHOUT, SENT UNTO HIM, CALLING HIM."

The composition is:

Jesus had four brothers (Mat. 13:55), and several sisters.

THE RELATIVES OF CHRIST

The phrase, *"There came then His brethren and His mother,"* proclaims Mark resuming this account, which had been interrupted by the encounter with the Scribes. The phrase, *"And standing without,"* refers to them standing outside the house at the edge of the crowd. To be sure, this is sad! Did He know they were out there, and yet failed to invite them in? There is evidence according to His answer that He did. So why did He not invite them in, if, in fact, He knew they were there, paying them proper respect as His close relatives?

Sadly and regrettably, He knew their intentions were not right or Scriptural. They had not come to rejoice with Him at the great Work for God that was being carried out, but rather to attempt to stop that Work. Whether their motives were right or wrong is not really called into question; however, their actions are perfectly clear, in that they thought He was *"beside Himself,"* i.e., *"out of His mind"* (Vs. 21). As much as He loved His Mother and His brethren, He must not and, in fact, could not, allow them to hinder His Work. God must come first in all things.

Inasmuch as their attitude was antagonistic, there was really very little He could do, with them leaving without ever really having seen Him. (As we have stated, His Mother probably did not have the same attitude and thoughts as her other sons, the half-brothers of Christ. Nevertheless, the very fact that she was with them would, of necessity, place her, at least in some respect, in a negative position.) Consequently, all who do not line up exactly with the Ways of the Lord, promoting, in effect, their own ways, will be, as these, *"standing without."*

The phrase, *"Sent unto Him, calling Him,"* means that they sent Him word by way of the crowd that they desired to see Him. According to Verse 21, the possibility definitely existed that they made it known to the crowd that He was *"beside Himself."* If so, how much this must have hurt the Son of God, Who loved them more than they would ever know!

(32) "AND THE MULTITUDE SAT ABOUT HIM, AND THEY SAID UNTO HIM, BEHOLD, YOUR MOTHER AND YOUR BRETHREN WITHOUT SEEK FOR YOU."

The diagram is:

While they were seeking for Him, still, they were not seeking for Him for the right reasons.

SEEKING

The phrase, *"And the multitude sat about Him,"* referred to as many as possible coming as close as they could to Him. Evidently, He was seated while He taught and healed, and the multitude were seated around Him, whether on the floor or wherever. The phrase, *"And they said unto Him, Behold,"* refers to the information that filtered to them from the outside respecting the desire of His relatives to see Him. The phrase, *"Your Mother and Your brethren without seek for You,"* will serve as the occasion for a tremendous Truth to now be presented.

(33) "AND HE ANSWERED THEM, SAYING, WHO IS MY MOTHER, OR MY BRETHREN?"

The overview is:

He meant to place this relationship in its proper setting.

THE ANSWER OF CHRIST

The phrase, *"And He answered them,"* concerns what He will say, but also probably means that His teaching and healing were interrupted. The question, *"Saying, Who is My Mother, or My brethren?"* seems, on the surface, to be harsh! However, He knew the reason for which they had come. In this question and its answer, He in no way meant to disavow or even to demean human relationships. However, He did mean to place this relationship, as stated, in its proper setting.

(34) "AND HE LOOKED ROUND ABOUT ON THEM WHICH SAT ABOUT HIM, AND SAID, BEHOLD MY MOTHER AND MY BRETHREN!"

The overview is:

He gestures toward those who hungrily desired to hear His Words and answered His Own question.

THE ANSWER

The phrase, *"And He looked round about on them which sat about Him,"* presents a look that is serious, but yet not critical. When He asked the question, it is positive that it occasioned a deep contemplation in the hearts of those who heard it. In the silence that followed, He looked at them closely, which they also probably observed. Those who were closest to Him would have been the Twelve.

And yet, some of the Twelve may have been with the crowd, helping them respecting their coming to Jesus. At any rate, those who hungered greatly for Him, not only for His healings, but for His teaching, would have lingered close. They were there because they wanted and desired Him. They saw in Him the answer to their heart's cry. As a result, they lingered close!

HIS MOTHER AND HIS BRETHREN

The phrase, *"And said, Behold My Mother and My brethren,"* may have been spoken as His outstretched hand swept those assembled. He answers His Own question by pointing out those whom He considered as His *"Mother"* and *"brethren"*! At the same time, He was not demeaning His personal relationship with Mary or His half-brothers. He was rather showing that spiritual relationship with Christ is on a higher level even than earthly family relationships. Consequently, the spiritual relationship with Christ always takes precedence over any other relationship, as dear as they may be. This relationship refers to the great Family of God.

If one is to notice, Jesus never mentioned the word *"father"* in His statement.

Why?

He had no earthly father, since Joseph was only His foster father. God was His Father, and in a unique way in which He is *"Father"* to no other.

At the same time, Jesus is addressing Himself to the cult of Mary worship, which would later come, and which now characterizes the Catholic Church.

THE CULT OF MARY WORSHIP

While the Catholics claim they do not worship Mary, their actions prove differently. Just last evening over a Catholic program, while the Pope was being taken through a large crowd in his *"Popemobile,"* a song was playing in the background, *"You are the light of my life,"* or words to that effect, with further lines stating such to be *"Mary"*!

Any time anyone proclaims that something or someone is the *"light of their life,"* that is worship, pure and simple!

In their elevating of Mary, she is called *"the Mother of God."*

Is this true?

Infallibly, no!

Mary is not the Mother of God. Mary was the Mother of the human being, Jesus. Mary served a biological function that was necessary to bring about a unique situation. The preexistent Son of God was to take on human form. As He walked the Earth (in human form), He was Very God and Very Man. As God, He had always been. As Man, He came into being in His Mother's womb. While Mary had something to do with the Incarnation in that she provided a harbor (her womb) for His developing human form (for 9 months), she had absolutely nothing whatsoever to do with His Godhead! Mary was, therefore, the Mother of Jesus, the Man. She was not, by any stretch of the imagination, the Mother of God.

God has no mother. If one understands the Incarnation, one understands that God, while never ceasing to be God, became completely Man.

"Wherefore when He comes into the world, He said, Sacrifice and Offering You

would not, but a Body have You prepared Me" (Heb. 10:5).

It was this Body that God prepared for His Son — Jesus Christ — Who would become Man. Of necessity, He would be born into the world as are all other human beings, but with one tremendous difference:

"Therefore the Lord Himself shall give you a sign; Behold, a virgin shall conceive, and bear a Son, and shall call His Name Immanuel" (Isa. 7:14).

This Virgin was the little maiden Mary, who was probably in her late teens, who was to bring the Son of God into the world. But it was not God Who would be born, it was *"The Man Christ Jesus"* (I Tim. 2:5).

THE IMMACULATE CONCEPTION

Even though we have dealt with *"Mary worship"* in our Commentary on Matthew (Chpt. 12), still, due to the significance of the subject, please allow us to make a few more statements.

The Catholic Doctrine of *"The Immaculate Conception"* is another case in point. This erroneous (and confusing) term does not refer to the conception of Jesus Christ (as most non-Catholics and many Catholics believe). It refers to the conception of Mary in her mother's womb. The Catholic Catechism says, *"The Blessed Virgin alone, from the first instant of her conception, through the foreseen merits of Jesus Christ, by a unique privilege granted her by God, was kept free from the stain of original sin . . . from the first moment of her conception (she) possessed justice and holiness, even the fullness of Grace, with the infused virtues and gifts of the Holy Spirit."*

This Doctrine, a total fiction, with no Scriptural support, was infallibly defined by Pope Pius IX as part of the *"Revealed Deposit of Catholic Faith"* in 1854. There was great opposition to this pronouncement, at the time, within the Catholic Church.

The Doctrine of the Immaculate Conception implies that for Mary to be born without original sin, her mother also had to be a sinless Virgin. The only other alternative is that God granted a unique immunity to the all-persuasive original sin that is an inescapable element of the human condition.

NOTES

To be frank, Roman Catholic theologians lamely defend their assertion of the Immaculate Conception by saying that *"God could have done it"* or *"It was fitting that He should do so — and therefore He did it."* However, if God had decided on such a course, it would have meant that He was replacing the Plan of Salvation described in the Bible with a totally new concept. If this had happened, it is conceivable that we would have a *"quadrinity"* instead of the Trinity. God's Word then would have stated that the Godhead consists of God the Father, God the Son, God the Holy Spirit, and Mary, the Mother of God. Or, as Catholics now put it, Mary would have come first!

In the 1990's, Pope John Paul II actually did float the idea of a *"quadrinity."* Wiser heads in the Catholic hierarchy persuaded him to drop the idea, feeling that it might be difficult to get it accepted. This Pope claims, in fact, that he owes his position as Pope to a vision he had of Mary, who told him, many years ago, that he would be Pope. *"Mary worship"* has consequently increased dramatically upon the advent of Pope John Paul II.

The Bible does not so state, so we can conclude that this aberrant Doctrine of the *"quadrinity"* is not of God.

A MEDIATOR

Mary is looked at by the Catholic Church as an intercessor and a mediatrix. Is this Biblical?

No, it is not Biblical! Jesus Christ is our only Intercessor. The Scripture says, *"Wherefore He is able also to save them to the uttermost who come unto God by Him, seeing He ever lives to make intercession for them"* (Heb. 7:25). There is no hint or suggestion in the Word of God that Mary should or would occupy such a role. Whenever Mary is inserted into the role of intercessor (as she is by the Catholic Church, to intercede with her Son, Jesus Christ, on behalf of individuals on Earth), this robs Christ of the rightful position He earned through His tremendous Sacrifice on Calvary. He paid the full price on the Cross with the shedding of His Precious Blood.

Christ Alone is worthy to make intercession for us. Christ Alone paid the price. Mary did not suffer and die on the Cross. She did not shed her blood. And neither does Christ need an assistant to motivate Him to intercede for the Saints. He is perfectly capable of performing this duty Himself. This duty, in fact, is automatically performed by Him sitting at the Right Hand of the Father.

"It is Christ Who died, yea rather, Who is risen again, Who is even at the Right Hand of God, Who also makes intercession for us" (Rom. 8:34).

We blaspheme when we imply that Jesus Christ would not satisfactorily accomplish His Eternal Work of Intercession without persuasion from His earthly Mother.

IT IS BLASPHEMY TO ADD TO THE WORD OF GOD

"For there is one God, and one Mediator between God and men, The Man Christ Jesus; Who gave Himself a ransom for all" (I Tim. 2:5-6).

Please note, there are not two mediators, not three or four, just One! And then, if there is any confusion, the identity of the One Mediator is revealed: Jesus Christ (I Tim. 2:5).

The Roman Catholic position is that God the Father and His Son, Jesus Christ, are, through normal human efforts, unreachable. By extension, they then propose that since Christ's Mother is available, petitions delivered by her will not be ignored. Who would turn away his own mother, they reason, if she came seeking a minor favor?

In Catholic tradition, therefore, when a person goes through the Mother, he gets through more quickly and more surely. No doubt, Jesus will look with more favor on her requests than on any delivered directly. Hence, the bumper stickers: *"Can't find Jesus? Look for His Mother."*

Such statements totally misinterpret the Person of God, the Incarnation, Redemption, and the Plan of God for the human family.

Paul said it well: *"Now the Spirit speaks expressly, that in the latter times some shall depart from the Faith, giving heed to seducing spirits, and doctrines of Devils,*

"Speaking lies in hypocrisy; having their conscience seared with a hot iron;

"Forbidding to marry, and commanding to abstain from meats, which God has created to be received with thanksgiving of them which believe and know the Truth" (I Tim. 4:1-3).

Obviously, Catholics do not know the Truth!

In all of Early Church history, no statement is reported of an Apostle referring to Mary as the *"Mother of God."* There is no hint of prayers being offered to her, nor admonitions given to the Saints to honor her beyond what the Bible suggests as normal deference. Surely if this great fabrication were valid, we would at least have a word from the Early Church concerning Mary. The silence is deafening!

(35) "FOR WHOSOEVER SHALL DO THE WILL OF GOD, THE SAME IS MY BROTHER, AND MY SISTER, AND MOTHER."

The exposition is:

The statement of Christ proclaims the qualifications for the high and lofty position of being in His Family. All Born-Again Believers are placed in a status even greater than flesh-and-blood relationships, while never for a moment demeaning those relationships.

THE FAMILY OF GOD

The phrase, *"For whosoever shall do the Will of God,"* proclaims the qualifications for the high and lofty position of being His relative. What is the *"Will of God"*? The *"Will of God"* is the *"Word of God."* It alone is the criteria, and not the statements of a Pope, be he Catholic or otherwise! Neither is it a Church or religious Denomination. It is also not Harvard, Yale, Oxford, or any other institution of higher learning. Neither is it Congress, the Supreme Court, Government, or the Law of the Land.

These things may all have their place, but the criteria for life, conduct, and, above all, the Plan of Salvation is the Bible. It is not enough to just believe the *"Word of God,"* i.e., *"Will of God,"* but rather to *"Do the Will of God."* This means for one to *"Love the Lord your God with all your heart, with all your soul, and with all your mind . . . and . . . you shall love your neighbor as yourself"* (Mat. 22:37-39).

The phrase, *"The same is My brother, and My sister, and Mother,"* places all Born-Again Believers in a status even greater than flesh-and-blood relationships, which should be obvious. In all of these statements, however, not one time did the Lord demean flesh-and-blood relationships.

CHAPTER 4

(1) "AND HE BEGAN AGAIN TO TEACH BY THE SEA SIDE: AND THERE WAS GATHERED UNTO HIM A GREAT MULTITUDE, SO THAT HE ENTERED INTO A SHIP, AND SAT IN THE SEA; AND THE WHOLE MULTITUDE WAS BY THE SEA ON THE LAND."

The exposition is:

As is here obvious, the Lord was constantly teaching and preaching.

TEACHING

The phrase, *"And He began again to teach by the sea side,"* reflects that teaching and preaching are more important than healing, as important as that may be! Had He stayed on the shore, the diseased could have touched Him and been healed. But His business as a Servant was to deal with sin rather than its effects.

The words, *"to teach,"* do not address themselves in the Greek to the fact of teaching, but rather to the process; consequently, the teaching was simplicity itself, and probably was repeated over and over, at least in a sense, in order that the people may understand. At this stage, He was standing next to the water, while the people stood in a group around Him.

THE MULTITUDE

The phrase, *"And there was gathered unto Him a great multitude,"* probably refers to several thousand people. It had been a *"multitude"* and now it is a *"great multitude"*! The action of the words proclaims the fact that not only were they there for the healing and Miracles, but also to hear what He had to say. His subject was always the Word of God, but two things were in focus:

A KNOWLEDGE OF THE WORD

First of all, He had a knowledge of the Word which no one else had, as would be overly obvious. It must also be quickly added,

NOTES

this knowledge did not come automatically, but was acquired. It is said of Him, *"O how I love Your Law! It is My meditation all the day"* (Ps. 119:97). Actually, all of the Psalms speak of Christ, whether in His Atoning, Mediatorial, or Intercessory role.

The little town of Nazareth, in which He was raised and lived even until His thirtieth year, is still interesting today. On one of our trips there, I asked to be taken, along with our Television people, to the brow of the hill, from which the good city fathers were determined to cast Him down (Lk. 4:29). As it was a place of solitude now, more than likely it was the same then. Probably He had stood on this very hill countless times as He meditated on the Word of God.

There is also every evidence that He began this prayerful study and meditation of the Word at a very young age. Even at twelve years old, He would ask the question, *"Wist ye not that I must be about My Father's business?"* (Lk. 2:49). So His Life was spent in the Word of God.

THE ANOINTING OF THE HOLY SPIRIT

He was anointed to teach and preach the Word, as no man had ever been (Lk. 4:18-19). As a result, this combination produced not only an understanding of the Word as no other, but also a presentation as no other! What a privilege for those people to hear Him teach and preach! Likewise, what a privilege we have today to study and learn His Word!

THE SHIP

The phrase, *"So that He entered into a ship, and sat in the sea,"* refers to a vessel that was somewhat larger than the small rowboat of Mark 3:9. This larger vessel was brought as close to the shore as possible, with only a narrow strip of water between Jesus and the crowd. There He sat on the deck of the boat, encircled by the water, and taught the people. This was done, as would be obvious, because of the press of the crowd.

The phrase, *"And the whole multitude was by the sea on the land,"* referred to their listening to Him attentively as He taught!

(2) "AND HE TAUGHT THEM MANY THINGS BY PARABLES, AND SAID UNTO

THEM IN HIS DOCTRINE."

The exposition is:

His Doctrine refers to what He taught and the manner in which it was taught.

PARABLES

The phrase, *"And He taught them many things,"* means that He kept on teaching them and, in fact, was constantly teaching them. His form of address was of two kinds:

1. He preached: this means *"to make a proclamation"* or *"to call attention to Truth."*

2. He taught: this refers to imparting information, or rather to explain Truth.

The phrase, *"By Parables,"* proclaims a new system of teaching. Previously, He had spoken directly concerning particular Truths. However, inasmuch as this was met too often by ridicule and scorn, He now resorted to *"Parables."* This method used illustrations taken from everyday life, thrown alongside of Truth, in order to explain it. It could be used to make the subject easier to understand, or, if so desired, to shade its meaning, which He sometimes did.

It would seem somewhat inconceivable that He would purposely attempt to conceal what He was giving to the people, but yet, this is exactly what happened. Possibly, there were several reasons why He did this; however, the major reason was to draw closer those who were sincere, while at the same time repelling those who were there merely out of idle curiosity. Verses 10 through 13 proclaim this.

DOCTRINE

In the New Testament, two words are used regarding Doctrine. *"Didaskalia"* means both the act and the content of teaching. It is used of Pharisees' teaching (Mat. 15:9; Mk. 7:7). Apart from one instance in Colossians and one in Ephesians, it is otherwise confined to the Pastoral Epistles (and seems to refer often to some body of teaching used as a standard of orthodoxy).

"Didache" is used in more parts of the New Testament. It too can mean either the act or the content of teaching. It occurs of the teaching of Jesus (Mat. 7:28, etc.), which He claimed to be Divine (Jn. 7:16). After Pentecost, Christian Doctrine began to be formulated as the instruction given to those who had responded to the Word (Acts 2:42; Rom. 6:17). In fact, there were some in the Church whose official function was to teach these converts (I Cor. 12:28-29).

(3) "HEARKEN; BEHOLD, THERE WENT OUT A SOWER TO SOW."

The synopsis is:

This Parable is given in Matthew, Chapter 13, and is repeated, but worded somewhat differently, in Luke, Chapter 8. These illustrations, which the people understood, were taken from everyday life and living, but yet they seldom understood His Parables.

THE SOWER

The word *"Hearken"* begins this Parable, and does so intentionally. It means *"Be listening."* The crowd, as usual, even though interested in what He had to say, still, was more interested in the healings and the miracles; consequently, He would proclaim to them that the Salvation of their souls was far more important than the healing of their sick bodies, as important as that was! To proclaim the significance of what is about to be said, in addition to the word *"Hearken,"* Jesus follows with the word *"Behold,"* which gives added strength to the first word, and means *"Give attention to this!"*

The phrase, *"There went out a sower to sow,"* presents the first Parable and the key to understanding all other Parables. The illustration of the *"sowing of seed"* was something understood by all. And yet, even though the Parable was given, what it represented and meant regarding its explanation was not given to the people, but only to the Disciples.

Why?

Knowing that Israel would not accept the Gospel, Jesus shaded its presentation and meaning to a certain extent in order that the merely curious would not know, but the truly hungry would press in for the true meaning. The merely inquisitive and curious would find little solace, but those who truly *"hunger and thirst after Righteousness shall be filled"* (Mat. 5:6). Jesus outlined this in Verses 11 through 13.

The method in those days for sowing, which still is the method in some places, was for plows to be run over the ground, which actually only scratched the surface a few inches deep. In the doing of this, stones which were meant to be cleared were upturned, as well as all other obstacles. For the ground to produce a good harvest, the proper preparation had to be made, which is emphasized in this Parable.

The time of plowing for some crops began with the early rains in September and October, and continued until March. After the ground was properly prepared, the farmer would walk over it, scattering the seed around Him, which he took from a bag or bushel measure. After the grain was sowed, sometimes a harrow was dragged across it, or a flock of sheep or goats driven over it, to tread the seed into the soil and give it enough depth of earth to grow and produce properly.

All of this, as we shall see, is an illustration of the presentation of the Gospel, and its resultant fruit. We will see what happens when the ground is improperly prepared, somewhat prepared, and well prepared.

(4) "AND IT CAME TO PASS, AS HE SOWED, SOME FELL BY THE WAY SIDE, AND THE FOWLS OF THE AIR CAME AND DEVOURED IT UP."

The diagram is:

The *"seed sowed"* is the Gospel; the *"fowls of the air"* represent Satan and his demon powers.

THE WAYSIDE

Inasmuch as the explanation is given in Verses 14 through 20, we will not attempt to cover the ground with the presentation of the Parable, but only to provide foundation. The farmer sowing seed and the birds of the air swooping down to retrieve it off the ground, before it had any opportunity to germinate, was a familiar sight to all who were listening to Christ.

(5) "AND SOME FELL ON STONY GROUND, WHERE IT HAD NOT MUCH EARTH; AND IMMEDIATELY IT SPRANG UP, BECAUSE IT HAD NO DEPTH OF EARTH."

The overview is:

Proper preparation was lacking here.

STONY GROUND

This was ground which had not been properly broken up by the plow; the layer of topsoil immediately above the stone was too thin to nurture the plants, even though it would germinate and flower. The farmer knew there was little hope of any grain being produced in this type of soil, but would sow the seed anyway in hope that there would be at least some harvest.

(6) "BUT WHEN THE SUN WAS UP, IT WAS SCORCHED; AND BECAUSE IT HAD NO ROOT, IT WITHERED AWAY."

The exposition is:

Many start out for Christ, but don't last long; all of this completely refutes the unscriptural doctrine of Unconditional Eternal Security.

SCORCHED EARTH

Actually, all the seed was identical, as is here illustrated, so the fault was not in the seed, but rather in the type of ground on which it fell, which determined the amount and kind of fruit that would result. On this particular ground, because the sun was hot and there were no roots to speak of, the plant soon withered away. All of this is meant to describe the hearts of men in receiving the Gospel, whether receptive or unreceptive, and the reasons why!

(7) "AND SOME FELL AMONG THORNS, AND THE THORNS GREW UP, AND CHOKED IT, AND IT YIELDED NO FRUIT."

The exegesis is:

More hindrances to the Gospel.

THORNS

This particular ground seemed to be sufficient, with the plant developing a suitable root system, but the seed was sown in the midst of *"thorns."* Consequently, the bramble-bush or briars wrapped themselves around the plant and choked it to death.

Those who stood before Christ fully understood what the Parable said, even though they would have had little knowledge as to what it represented. However, it was something they would easily remember, and no doubt mull over in their minds long after it had been uttered. Without a doubt, some few later asked the Disciples about the meaning, and, if so, it was readily given to them, with their *"spiritual hunger and thirst"* then satisfied.

(8) "AND OTHER FELL ON GOOD GROUND, AND DID YIELD FRUIT THAT SPRANG UP AND INCREASED; AND BROUGHT FORTH, SOME THIRTY, AND SOME SIXTY, AND SOME AN HUNDRED."

The exegesis is:

Now comes the proper yield, which should be the state of all who hear the Gospel, but sadly isn't.

GOOD GROUND

The *"good ground"* producing different amounts in different places was, as well, very familiar to those who heard Jesus speak. Consequently, the entirety of the Parable presented four different stages:

1. In the first case, the seed produced nothing.
2. In the second, it produced only the blade and then it quickly withered.
3. The third case was near the point of producing fruit, and even looked like it would, but was choked by briars and brambles, therefore, producing nothing.
4. This ground produces fruit, but in different measures.

All, as stated, represent the hearts of men in hearing the Gospel.

(9) "AND HE SAID UNTO THEM, HE WHO HAS EARS TO HEAR, LET HIM HEAR."

The overview is:

Those who would properly *"hear"* would attend to these words of Christ, pondering them until somehow the Truth was eventually revealed; the Gospel is designed this way purposely by the Holy Spirit in order to ferret out the insincere.

EARS TO HEAR

The phrase, *"And He said,"* is proclaimed in Luke 8:8 as *"He cried,"* proclaiming the significance of what He has said and of what He is now saying. The phrase, *"He who has ears to hear, let him hear,"* gives us the explanation as to the reason Jesus proclaimed the Parable and did not explain it, at least to the people. These *"ears,"* i.e., those which would properly hear, would attend to these Words of Christ, pondering them until somehow the Truth was eventually revealed.

As stated, it was designed this way by the Holy Spirit in order that the preciousness of the Gospel not be lost on mere curiosity-seekers. It is a principle that holds even unto this moment. Several people can hear the Gospel, and even though it is the same in all cases, it will be received differently by most. Some have ears for it, and some don't.

PREDESTINATION

From this, some have arrived at an improper explanation of predestination or election. They erroneously conclude that all are born predestined to be either saved or lost, of which the individual has no say! However, the very tenor of these Passages proclaim the very opposite. While it is true that God in His Omniscience, which means that He knows all things, past, present, and future, can very well know the eternal destiny of all, still, the choice is always left up to the individual, with *"whosoever will"* eternally stamped upon the Gospel (Rev. 22:17).

While predestination is a viable Bible Doctrine, still, it must be properly understood, i.e., *"rightly dividing the Word of Truth"* (II Tim. 2:15). Predestination in its most simple form means that the Plan of God is predestined, and consequently cannot be changed. In this Plan, it is predestined that God will have a people who will serve Him, thereby bringing Him glory; however, who those individual people will be is not predetermined. That is decided by the individual and their reception or rejection of the Gospel, in respect to, and as stated, *"whosoever will,"* exactly as this Parable of the Sower presents.

While it is true that the Lord, through foreknowledge, will proclaim something in detail which will happen hundreds of years in the future, such as Judas betraying Christ, still, it was not predestined that Judas would do this, but that the Lord would simply look into the future and see what Judas would do of his own free will (Ps. 41:9; 55:12-14; 109: 6-20). Actually, every human being begins life on a level playing field respecting their personal heart toward God, even though the occasion of the Gospel may be and, in fact, is, totally different, with some having great opportunity, others little opportunity, and others no opportunity at all.

Concerning the level playing field, in other words, none are born with a predisposition more or less toward the Lord. The Scripture says, *"He fashions their hearts alike"* (Ps. 33:15). This means that in the original Creation the Lord designed and molded identically every heart respecting the all-important aspect of predisposition toward God.

So, if all begin alike, as they do, why do some accept the Gospel and some reject?

WHOSOEVER WILL

The answer is found in the *"will"* of the individual. They either want the Lord, or they don't; or they want Him, but are not willing to forsake all and follow Him. At any rate, whatever the person does, be it toward the Lord or in opposition to the Lord, the disposition is found strictly in the person, even though both the Lord and Satan deal with the individual attempting to pull them accordingly. However, even though dealt with by both, the final decision is strictly up to the individual. Satan cannot force a person against his will, although greatly persuading Him, while the Lord will not force a person against his will, while, at the same time, persuading him.

So, the *"ears to hear"* are strictly up to the individual!

Sadly, many, as stated, have no opportunity to *"hear"*! Paul said, *"And how shall they hear without a Preacher? And how shall they preach, except they be sent?"* (Rom. 10:14-15).

If one properly understands the Word of God, he will understand that the entire complexion of all that it teaches is that all of mankind, no matter who they are or where they may be, must have the opportunity to *"hear"* the Gospel. For those who do not have that opportunity, Jesus, as far as they are concerned, died in vain! If we properly understand that, then we properly understand how serious this situation is.

THE SPREAD OF THE GOSPEL

For God to do what He did in the sending of His Son, considering the price paid by the Lord of Glory in dying on Calvary's Cross, and then for a high percentage of the world's population to know little or nothing about it, constitutes a crime of the highest order. No wonder the Lord told Ezekiel that if he did not warn the wicked, *"his blood will I require at your hand"* (Ezek. 3:18). It is a sobering thought that the entirety of the Church must consider constantly.

I do not have to answer, and neither can I answer, for the generations of human beings which preceded me, and had no opportunity to hear and know; however, I am responsible, as you are, for this generation. That is the reason that we at Jimmy Swaggart Ministries struggle daily, even against impossible odds, to place the Telecast in any and every country of the world where possible. This is also the reason we are attempting to fill the United States with Radio Stations, all for the purpose of the Gospel. This is what God has called me to do, and I must be able to say, as Paul said, *"I was not disobedient unto the Heavenly Vision"* (Acts 26:19).

And yet, I cannot carry out this task without your help, for as Paul also intimated, the one who does the sending is just as important as the one who is sent (Rom. 10:14-15).

(10) "AND WHEN HE WAS ALONE, THEY WHO WERE ABOUT HIM WITH THE TWELVE ASKED OF HIM THE PARABLE."

The synopsis is:

They were anxious to know exactly what the parable meant!

THE PARABLE

The phrase, *"And when He was alone,"* proves according to the following that Jesus did not explain this Parable to the multitude, and for the reason that will be given. The phrase, *"They who were about Him with the Twelve,"* refers not only to the chosen Disciples, but also another group from which the Twelve were chosen, which could have numbered as many as 100 or more. We know a little later the Lord *"appointed other seventy also, and sent them two and two before His Face into every city and place, where He Himself would come"* (Lk. 10:1).

The phrase, *"Asked of Him the Parable,"* presents all of them wanting to know the meaning of the simple little illustration He had just given to the people. Thank the Lord, they had *"ears to hear,"* and, no doubt, others did, as well!

(11) "AND HE SAID UNTO THEM, UNTO YOU IT IS GIVEN TO KNOW THE MYSTERY

OF THE KINGDOM OF GOD: BUT UNTO THEM WHO ARE WITHOUT, ALL THESE THINGS ARE DONE IN PARABLES."

The structure is:

Parables, as stated, were used to reject the merely curious, and to pull in the sincerely desirous.

THE MYSTERY OF THE KINGDOM OF GOD

The phrase, *"And He said unto them,"* will proclaim the patient explanation which He will give to any and all who earnestly seek Him. He is no respecter of persons. The phrase, *"Unto you it is given to know,"* refers to all honest, earnest, sincere hearts who seek after God, humbly inquiring into the full meaning of the Gospel, in order that they may *"know."*

The word *"given"* shows that this efficiency cannot be attained by our own strength or ability, but must be humbly sought from God. It is His Own Gift, which He bestows on all who earnestly seek His Face, while denying it to those who are not sincere. Hence, Paul would say, *"Be not conformed to this world: but be ye transformed by the renewing of your mind, that you may prove what is that good, and acceptable, and perfect, Will of God"* (Rom. 12:2).

The phrase, *"The mystery of the Kingdom of God,"* refers to the secret counsels of God, which are hidden from the ungodly, but, when revealed to the Godly, are understood by them. The Mystery is not in the fact that they are difficult of interpretation, but that they are actually impossible of interpretation until their meaning is revealed by the Holy Spirit, when they become plain. There is another type of *"Mystery,"* such as the *"Mystery of iniquity,"* which the Lord is not addressing here.

The first Mystery is what Paul was speaking of when he said, *"But the natural man receives not the things of the Spirit of God: for they are foolishness unto him: neither can he know them, because they are spiritually discerned"* (I Cor. 2:14). Regarding the overall picture, the meaning of the *"Mystery of the Kingdom of God,"* as Jesus uses it here, refers to the New Covenant, which was shaded in the Old Covenant, but now

NOTES

revealed, at least to earnest, seeking hearts.

The phrase, *"But unto them who are without,"* means those outside this circle, referring to the Pharisees, with their hostile minds, and all who follow in their train. The phrase, *"All these things are done in Parables,"* records the reason for this type of teaching, which will be given in the next Verse.

(12) "THAT SEEING THEY MAY SEE, AND NOT PERCEIVE; AND HEARING THEY MAY HEAR, AND NOT UNDERSTAND; LEST AT ANY TIME THEY SHOULD BE CONVERTED, AND THEIR SINS SHOULD BE FORGIVEN THEM."

The diagram is:

Judicial blindness and deafness justly befall those who do not wish to see and hear; the emphasis is on the person and not on God. He desires that all see and hear.

THOSE WHO REFUSE TO SEE AND HEAR

The intent of this Verse is that judicial blindness and deafness justly befall those who do not wish to see and hear. It doesn't mean they cannot, but that they will not!

The phrase, *"That seeing they may see, and not perceive; and hearing they may hear, and not understand,"* has to do with what is presented and the manner in which it is received. As stated, these Parables and thus, this manner of teaching, which actually constitute much of the Word of God, are designed to blind further or to give light, to deafen or to give greater hearing, according to the disposition of the heart of the listener. The Word or Parable is the same to all. It is similar to the Sun, which either hardens clay or softens wax. The change brought about is not in the Sun, but rather in the material which is exposed to the Sun.

Upon reading this Verse, many may erroneously think, and according to the English translation, that the Parable was supposedly designed to blind and deafen; however, that is totally incorrect! The same Parable which definitely does blind and deafen some, at the same time, enlightens others. The Parables are thus a condemnation on the willfully blind and hostile, while a guide and blessing to the earnest seeker.

This is what Jesus was speaking of when

He said, *"For whosoever has, to him shall be given, and he shall have more abundance: but whosoever has not, from him shall be taken away even that he has"* (Mat. 13:12).

THE MANNER OF THE GOSPEL

From the Scribes and Pharisees who would not believe Jesus, as well as all who had the same spirit, God took away even that small knowledge which they had of Him and His Kingdom. This is on the same principle that God hardened Pharaoh's heart by forcing him to an issue which he did not want to meet (Rom. 9:14-18). Light resisted, blinds. The Pharisees attempted to show that the Lord was in league with Satan. They did not want the Truth. Thus, rejecting the Truth, they, in a sense, blinded themselves. As we have repeatedly stated, the Parables are so adjusted that they blind the one who wickedly rejects the Truth, and enlighten the one who desires it.

The phrase, *"Lest at any time they should be converted, and their sins should be forgiven them,"* means they have willfully rejected the Truth, and consequently cannot have their sins forgiven and, therefore, *"be converted."*

(13) "AND HE SAID UNTO THEM, KNOW YE NOT THIS PARABLE? AND HOW THEN WILL YE KNOW ALL PARABLES?"

The exposition is:

The Parable of the Sower lays down the principle of all Parables concerning the understanding thereof.

UNDERSTANDING THE PARABLES

The question, *"And He said unto them, Know ye not this Parable?"* actually contains a gentle reproof. They wanted to know, but they did not know! Actually, the question indicates that they should have known!

Could not the same be said to us?

Too often the Believer is so taken up with the things of the world, even though innocent within themselves, that little time and attention are given to the things of God; consequently, there is a dullness of *"hearing"* and a blindness of *"seeing,"* sometimes even with the best of us.

The question, *"And how then will you know all Parables?"* signifies two things:

NOTES

1. The Parable of the Sower lays down the principle of all Parables, and the understanding thereof.
2. Consequently, the Disciples, as well as every Believer, must learn the full meaning of this particular Parable.
3. More information will be given in Commentary on the next Verse, telling us how this Parable provides understanding for all Parables.

(14) "THE SOWER SOWS THE WORD."

The structure is:

This *"Seed"* is the Word of God, and must be sowed to the entirety of the world (Mk. 16:15).

SOWING THE WORD

The phrase, *"The Sower,"* refers to the Lord Jesus Christ, and all He calls to minister His Word (Mk. 16:15-20; I Cor. 1:18-21); however, it should be clearly understood that all Believers are called in some respect to minister the Word. It may not necessarily be one of the fivefold callings (Eph. 4:11), but it definitely is a calling, which includes all! Some are called to be *"sent,"* while some are called to *"send"* (Rom. 10:14-15).

The phrase, *"Sows the Word,"* means that the Seed is the Word of God, exactly as the sower sowed natural seed (Mat. 13:19; Lk. 8:11; Rom. 1:16). So, by its very application, this Parable, which is the key to all Parables, begins with the admonition that the *"sowing"* of the Gospel is the foundation of the *"Kingdom of God."* If this is priority with God, and it is, then it should be priority with the Church.

Regrettably, it is of little priority with much of the Church, with other things taking its place. Priority in too many Church circles is beautiful buildings, education, manifestations of what purports to be the Spirit, getting rich, etc. Sadly, very few are properly sowing the Seed.

As Mark relates at the conclusion of his Book, this *"Seed"* must be sowed to the entirety of the world (Mk. 16:15). The Early Church understood this perfectly, inasmuch as they evangelized in the First Century almost all of the civilized world of that day. Remarkably, they did it without the aid of modern transportation, communications, or assimilation, which made their task more difficult! However, they did have the one thing that truly mattered, and that was the Holy Spirit in all His Power and Glory, Who aided and abetted them in all they did, which made the impossible possible. If there is any one thing the modern Church truly lacks, it is the Holy Spirit. To have all the other and not have Him is to have nothing.

(15) "AND THESE ARE THEY BY THE WAY SIDE, WHERE THE WORD IS SOWN; BUT WHEN THEY HAVE HEARD, SATAN COMES IMMEDIATELY, AND TAKES AWAY THE WORD THAT WAS SOWN IN THEIR HEARTS."

The exposition is:

The structure of the sentence is that these individuals do not have to allow Satan to take away the Word.

THE WAYSIDE

The phrase, *"And these are they by the way side, where the Word is sown,"* refers to the first group, who hear the Word, even with it properly given unto them, but really go no further, with the next phrase explaining why!

The phrase, *"But when they have heard, Satan comes immediately, and takes away the Word that was sown in their hearts,"* proclaims the adversarial position of the Evil One against the Word of God, and especially against it being received by the unbeliever. Several things are here said:

1. *"But when they have heard"*: such refers to the grand time the Gospel is given to this particular individual. It is the single most important day of his or her life. Once again, we state, the Holy Spirit is insistent that they have the opportunity, whether they accept or reject.

2. *"Satan"*: the Greek says, *"The Satan,"* meaning a concentrated plan engineered and devised by Satan himself, in his attempt to keep men from accepting the Gospel. In other words, this is not a haphazard, last-minute effort, but instead a carefully designed plan. It includes all the minions of darkness, such as demon spirits and fallen angels, which carry out the directives issued by the Prince of Darkness himself, Satan (Eph. 6:10-12).

3. *"Comes immediately"*: the plan is designed that the moment the Gospel is presented, it is also attacked within the heart of the recipient. I would pray that God's people would be as diligent in getting the Gospel to others as Satan is diligent in attempting to stop it.

4. *"And takes away the Word that was sown in their hearts"*: this refers to the plan being carried out to its intended conclusion, but with the permission of the one who has heard the Gospel. This is what Jesus meant by the fowls of the air devouring the Seed (Vs. 4). However, there is a difference! The ground on which the Seed fell in the illustration had no will of its own, and consequently could do nothing to stop the devouring; however, the human heart does have the power of choice and can, therefore, say *"Yes"* or *"No"* to Satan.

As outlined by Christ, this group illustrates the Seed of the Gospel coming to their hearts, with them entertaining it for some time, but then, of their own volition, allowing Satan to pull the Seed out.

(16) "AND THESE ARE THEY LIKEWISE WHICH ARE SOWN ON STONY GROUND; WHO, WHEN THEY HAVE HEARD THE WORD, IMMEDIATELY RECEIVE IT WITH GLADNESS;

(17) "AND HAVE NO ROOT IN THEMSELVES, AND SO ENDURE BUT FOR A TIME: AFTERWARD, WHEN AFFLICTION OR PERSECUTION ARISES FOR THE WORD'S SAKE, IMMEDIATELY THEY ARE OFFENDED."

The overview is:

This group cannot stand the opposition, because they have no root, meaning that the ground was not sufficiently prepared.

INSUFFICIENT PREPARATION

This is the second group to which Jesus refers. It falls out as follows:

1. *"And these are they likewise which are sown on stony ground"*: this pertains to the Word of God presented and received, actually with a better reception than the previous group. In other words, the heart is more receptive, and Satan is not able to snatch it away, as before.

2. *"Who, when they have heard the Word, immediately receive it with gladness"*: these actually make a start, and with great joy,

giving every appearance of a true *"born again"* experience, which it actually is! Such characterizes so many. They show such promise, but, after a while, they fall by the wayside. The next phrase tells us why.

3. *"And have no root in themselves, and so endure but for a time"*: these are like the Seed sown on the ground which looked fine on the surface, but almost immediately beneath was rock. Consequently, as the *"root"* could not extend down because of the rocks, likewise, the Seed of the Gospel is hindered. Until the root hits the rock, everything looks and seems well. However, Satan, being unsuccessful in snatching the Seed away, will now try another tactic.

4. *"Afterward, when affliction or persecution arises for the Word's sake, immediately they are offended"*: Satan's next step is to bring *"affliction"* and *"persecution."* Likewise, it is clear from the Text that this *"affliction"* and *"persecution"* come strictly because of the *"Word of God"* being received into the heart.

SATAN'S METHODS

I remember years ago working with a particular individual, who made the remark several times that when he was unsaved, it seemed as if he had few if any problems. Now that he had come to the Lord, he remonstrated, it seemed there were problems galore. He was right!

Satan was attempting to discourage him, as he attempts to do so with all, hoping the individual will give up and quit. Regrettably, many do! Many in the modern Church have erroneously attempted to do away with all *"affliction"* and *"persecution,"* claiming that proper confession, based on great faith, will eliminate these things. If that is true, then Jesus did not know what He was talking about!

Realizing that He did know very much as to what He was talking about, we must conclude that this modern Gospel is, in effect, *"another gospel"* and, therefore, has no Scriptural validity (II Cor. 11:4). This group is *"offended"* when the affliction or persecution comes, as come it shall. Even though making an excellent start, they fall by the wayside.

(18) "AND THESE ARE THEY WHICH ARE SOWN AMONG THORNS; SUCH AS HEAR THE WORD.

(19) "AND THE CARES OF THIS WORLD, AND THE DECEITFULNESS OF RICHES, AND THE LUSTS OF OTHER THINGS ENTERING IN, CHOKE THE WORD, AND IT BECOMES UNFRUITFUL."

The diagram is:

This group actually did bear fruit for a while, but allowed the things of the world to choke it off until they became totally unfruitful and lost their way. The Parable of the Sower completely refutes the unscriptural doctrine of Unconditional Eternal Security, as should here be obvious.

CARES OF THIS WORLD

Jesus now explains the third group, who, likewise, heard the Word, made an excellent start, even with some progress, but who ultimately lost their way, as well!

1. *"And these are they which are sown among thorns; such as hear the Word"*: this ground was far better prepared than the other two. Satan was not allowed to come and snatch away the Word when it was presented. Likewise, the soil had proper depth and was not hindered by the hardness of the rocks. As a result, the roots could reach down as they desired. So, this shows and portrays spiritual depth, with every indication that the Word will have its desired effect, and the individual will bring forth *"much fruit."* As we shall see, however, the one who sows the Word will be disappointed.

2. *"And the cares of this world"*: this really speaks of the *"worries"* of this world. In other words, this person allows, at least after a period of time, the disturbances of the world to affect him adversely. He is not properly tuned to Christ, with one hand actually holding to the world, and the other to the Lord. After a while, one or the other must go, because no man can serve two masters. Consequently, at least in this case, the world is embraced, with Christ ultimately being spurned. It is not so much the things of the world serving as an enticement as it is the individual allowing the adverse things of the world to distract. Luke called it the *"cares of this life"* (Lk. 21:34).

In mundane terms, it refers to someone else getting the promotion, or the job being lost, and the house-note unpaid, etc.

3. *"The deceitfulness of riches"*: two things are here said:

A. The Believer is not to seek riches. Such may come to some and, in fact, have and it is not wrong if the Lord and His Work have priority. Many times, however, the priority is the seeking of riches, with right and wrong becoming blurred, and the person being consumed with this quest. This is what the Lord condemns.

B. Riches are *"deceitful"* in the sense that oftentimes the rich feel superior. Others feel their riches constitute the Blessings of God; others who are not so materially blessed evidently and obviously, as it is thought, do not have as much faith. Consequently, the individual is deceived.

Sometimes riches are the Blessings of God and sometimes they are the curse of Satan. Furthermore, others at times who have little of this world's goods have great faith. So the acquisition of great wealth does not necessarily mean that one has Faith at all, at least in God.

MONEY

If money is used for the Glory of God, it can be a tremendous blessing; however, it is seldom used accordingly. Too often those who claim the Lord as their Saviour and who have acquired great wealth, much of the time, give little of it for the furtherance of the Gospel. Thankfully, there are some exceptions, but precious few!

What a blessing it is to see someone whom the Lord has greatly blessed in material things, who will keep enough for himself and his family, but give the rest to the taking of the Gospel around the world. These are few and far between, but they have made a tremendous impact for the Cause of Christ.

4. *"The lusts of other things"*: the word *"lust,"* as it is used here, does not necessarily mean things which are wrong or bad, but actually could be something good, but yet not *"things"* which pertain to the Work of the Lord. The sense of this statement is that the Believer, no matter who he is, must not become engrossed in anything, regardless of how innocent it may be, unless it pertains to the Lord and His Work. This would mean that some Christians are far too involved in sports, business, hobbies, etc.

While it certainly is not wrong to be involved in business, still, the overlording passion, drive, concern, and interest must be the Work of the Lord. He has promised us that if we will seek first the Kingdom of God and His Righteousness, He will add all of these other things to us (Mat. 6:33).

Probably this one thing, the *"lust of other things,"* is the greatest hindrance to the Child of God, because it covers both the legitimate and the illegitimate.

UNFRUITFUL

The phrase, *"Choke the Word, and it becomes unfruitful,"* proclaims that which Satan attempts to do. We are told here that it is the resident Word of God in the life of the individual, which, when properly acted upon, brings forth Fruit. Consequently, as there is no Word, there is no Fruit. Tragically, this would be the case in most who call themselves *"Christian,"* simply because they attend a Church where the Word of God is not preached, or else it is preached, but it finds no favorable lodging in their hearts.

The Bible, sadly enough, is an unread Book in many, if not most, Christian circles. Probably one could say, without any fear of contradiction, that most Christians have never even read the Bible completely through one time, much less made it an habitual part of their daily spiritual exercise. Actually, Jesus placed the daily necessity of the Word of God alongside the daily necessity of food (Mat. 4:4). We would greatly benefit ourselves if we heeded His Words.

THE BIBLE

Inasmuch as the Bible is the Word of God, it is, in effect, a Living Organism. The more it is studied, the more one wants to study it, and the more one derives from it. It is inexhaustible! Consequently, Satan will do everything within his power to steer the Believer away from the Word.

Tragically, he has been very successful respecting many Preachers in modern Churches. All one had to do is to look at that which is offered in most Christian bookstores. You will find that much, if not most, is based on psychology instead of the Word of God. In fact, one of Satan's greatest ploys is to commingle his false teaching in with the Word of God. To be sure, the *"little leaven"* is not purified by the pure, but rather the opposite takes place, with the pure being totally leavened (I Cor. 5:6).

THE GREATEST ATTACK ON THE BIBLE

A flood of so-called translations is presently reaching the market concerning what purports to be the Word of God. They actually aren't translations or anything close. They are interpretations and, in many cases, they aren't even that. I speak of the *"Message Bible"* and those similar. These things cannot, even with the greatest imagination, be referred to as the Word of God. They are designed by Satan, irrespective of the name on the cover, and done so with the purpose of leading people away from the True Word of God.

I personally prefer the King James Version, feeling that it is closer to the original Text than anything else. In fact, I have never used anything but the King James Version, with one exception, several years ago, of using another similar Version, which, in some cases, seemed to fit the proposed Text a little better. However, as stated, that's been years ago.

I would strongly advise the Reader to secure for yourself THE EXPOSITOR'S STUDY BIBLE. It is, as stated, the King James Version, but its presentation is unique. It is designed with one purpose in mind and that is to help the Believer more fully understand the Word of God. The expository notes immediately follow the Text, making it extremely easy to understand what is being said and, thereby, to more properly understand the Text.

When Jesus spoke of *"Fruit,"* exactly what did He mean?

It is in the Gospel of John and the Epistles of Paul that the concept of Fruitfulness shifts from that of the product of character to the product of God's Work within us.

THE IMAGE OF THE VINE

In John 15:1-16, Jesus takes the image of the Vine, with God as Gardener, from Isaiah. We Believers are carefully tended by the Father, pruned and cared for, that we may *"bear much Fruit."* Fruitfulness is possible, He said, if we remain in Him and His Words remain in us. The point Jesus makes is that Fruitfulness is rooted in our personal relationship with Him, and our personal relationship with Him is maintained by living His Words: *"If you keep My Commandments, you shall abide in My Love"* (Jn. 15:10).

God has chosen us. It is His intention that we be Fruitful. It is for this reason that He has given us the most intimate of relationships and Jesus' Own Words to guide us. It is our responsibility to walk in close fellowship with our Lord. Consequently, we learn from these Passages in John that relationship with Christ is the key to successful Fruit-bearing.

THE LESSON GIVEN BY THE APOSTLE PAUL

In Romans 7:4-6, it is explained that human actions are energized from one of two sources. We can, on the one hand, be energized by our sinful nature; but, when we are, we produce *"fruit for death."* Or we can be energized by the Holy Spirit. When we are controlled by the Spirit, we bear *"Fruit to God."*

The Believer is to ever look to Christ and the Cross, which will guarantee the help of the Holy Spirit. If other things are made the object of our faith, this constitutes *"spiritual adultery,"* which means that the Holy Spirit will not then help us, which guarantees failure (Rom. 7:1-4).

In Galatians 5:16-26, Paul defines the fruit of sinful human nature and the Fruit that the Spirit-energized nature produces. It is striking that the Fruit God seeks, as defined here, is exactly as the Fruit sought in His Old Testament people!

Bad fruit, the acts of the sinful nature, are *"sexual immorality, impurity and debauchery; idolatry and witchcraft; hatred, discord, jealousy, fits of rage, selfish ambition, dissensions, factions and envy; drunkenness, orgies, and the like."*

The Fruit of the Spirit, which is the opposite of the fruit of the flesh, is both inner (in the quality of our personal experience) and external (in the quality of our relationship with Christ); because *"the Fruit of the*

Spirit is love, joy, peace, patience, kindness, goodness, faithfulness, gentleness, and temperance"* (Gal. 5:22-23).

A CONSISTENT CONCEPT

Fruitfulness is a consistent concept in the Old Testament and the New Testament. The Fruit God seeks in human beings is expressed in righteous and loving acts that bring peace and harmony to the individual and to society. But that Fruit is foreign to sinful human nature. Energized by sinful passions, fallen humanity acts in ways that harm and bring dissension.

God's solution is found in a personal relationship with Jesus and in the supernatural working of God's Spirit within the Believer. As we live in intimate, obedient relationship with Jesus, God's Spirit energizes us as we produce the peaceable Fruits of a Righteousness that can come only from the Lord.

(The summary on Fruitfulness was derived, in part, from the teaching of Lawrence Richards.)

(20) "AND THESE ARE THEY WHICH ARE SOWN ON GOOD GROUND; SUCH AS HEAR THE WORD, AND RECEIVE IT, AND BRING FORTH FRUIT, SOME THIRTYFOLD, SOME SIXTY, AND SOME AN HUNDRED."

The overview is:

The individual determines whether the ground is good or not.

THE GOOD GROUND AND MUCH FRUIT

The phrase, *"And these are they which are sown on good ground; such as hear the Word, and receive it, and bring forth fruit,"* presents that which the Holy Spirit strives for in the life of the Believer. The *"good ground"* refers to the heart of the individual, which is prepared and cultivated in order that the Seed of the Word will have a proper lodging place. They *"hear the Word"* and then they *"receive the Word,"* which means they *"act upon the Word,"* allowing it to *"bring forth Fruit,"* even *"much Fruit"* (Jn. 15:5).

If one properly understands this Parable, one will properly understand the Ways of God in this world.

THE FRUIT

For instance, the *"Fruit"* here spoken of by Christ, and outlined by the Apostle Paul in Galatians 5:22-23, can only be brought about by a proper relationship with Christ, which is the only way the Holy Spirit can work. As well, the only way the Believer can actually have a proper relationship with Christ is by constantly exhibiting Faith in Christ and the Cross (I Cor. 1:17-18, 23; 2:2; Gal. 6:14).

Every single thing, as it relates to the Lord, must, and without exception, be based on the principle of Faith. The Lord accepts no works, merit, or anything such like. However, and as previously stated, when we say *"faith,"* without fail, we are speaking of Faith in Christ and what Christ did for us at the Cross (Eph. 2:13-18).

The Holy Spirit, Who Alone can carry out this work within our lives, and we continue to speak of relationship with Christ, works strictly within the parameters of the Finished Work of Christ, which requires that we ever evidence Faith in that Finished Work, which guarantees Spiritual Growth.

WORLDLY WISDOM

It is sad, when one realizes that the Church, for all practical purposes, has departed from Christ and His Word, gravitating toward worldly wisdom. Paul addressed this about every way it could be addressed in the First Chapter of I Corinthians. In that Chapter, he portrays the wisdom of this world as completely lacking in capability, and projects the Cross as the answer, and the only answer, to the hurting ills and perversions of man (I Cor. 1:17-18).

AN HUNDREDFOLD

The phrase, *"Some thirtyfold, some sixty, and some an hundred,"* presents, as is obvious, various stages; however, the goal of the Holy Spirit in the life of the Believer is always *"an hundredfold."* This is what Jesus meant when He said, *"He purges it, that it may bring forth more fruit"* (Jn. 15:2). He then said, *"He who abides in Me, and I in him, the same brings forth much Fruit"* (Jn. 15:5). He further said, *"For without Me you can do nothing,"* which should settle, once and for all, that all the efforts of man are fruitless, regarding changing men by any other means.

The Believer is to never be satisfied with merely bearing *"thirtyfold,"* or even *"sixtyfold"*; the goal must always be *"an hundredfold."* This the Spirit of God will do, if allowed to have His Way. As stated, it only requires of us that we ever understand that Jesus is the Source, and the Cross is the Means, with our faith ever anchored in that Finished Work (Rom. 8:1-2, 11).

Even though Jesus does not mention it here, but does elaborate on it more fully in John, Chapter 15, this process of *"an hundredfold"* is not easily arrived at. It takes *"purging,"* and the purging process is not pleasant, easy, or of short duration.

The flesh has to die, which refers to all dependence on self, self-ability, self-power, self-education, etc. This is the reason that Paul said, *"But what things were gain to me, those I counted loss for Christ.*

"Yea doubtless, and I count all things but loss for the excellency of the knowledge of Christ Jesus my Lord: for Whom I have suffered the loss of all things, and do count them but dung, that I may win Christ,

"And be found in Him, not having my own righteousness, which is of the Law, but that which is through the Faith of Christ, the Righteousness which is of God by Faith" (Phil. 3:7-9).

Then Jesus said, *"Verily, verily, I say unto you, Except a corn of wheat fall into the ground and die, it abides alone: but if it die, it brings forth much fruit"* (Jn. 12:24).

(21) "AND HE SAID UNTO THEM, IS A CANDLE BROUGHT TO BE PUT UNDER A BUSHEL, OR UNDER A BED? AND NOT TO BE SET ON A CANDLESTICK?"

The exposition is:

The Gospel is not to be merely enjoyed privately, but rather imparted as a lamp imparts its light.

A CANDLE

It may seem as if Jesus is changing the subject; however, He is merely proclaiming the result of those who *"bring forth Fruit."* The phrase, *"And He said unto them,"* is meant to explain what the Work of God is all about as it is carried forth in the life of a Believer.

The question, *"Is a candle brought to be put under a bushel, or under a bed?"* is meant to proclaim the lamp or *"candle"* as Divine Truth, shining in the Person of Christ, and evidenced in the life of the Believer. In other words, all of this work carried out by Christ in the life of the Believer is meant to do two things:

1. To change the Believer from the *"works of the flesh,"* which are listed in Galatians 5:19-21, to the *"Fruit of the Spirit"* listed in Galatians 5:22-23.

2. The changed life of the Believer made possible by Christ is to be a *"Light"* to the world.

In reality, Christ is the Light, but we are to be a reflection of that light. The world is covered by spiritual darkness, which can only be penetrated by the Light of Christ, as it is presented in the Gospel; consequently, it is imperative that this *"Light"* not be hid, as should be obvious!

THE MANNER OF THE LIGHT

Not too long after the turn of the Twentieth Century, efforts were made by a group of Christians to establish a Christian community in the United States, and incorporate a town, if you please! The result was Zion, Illinois. This was to be the perfect community, with the perfect environment, etc. To live in this town, one must be Born-Again, plus subscribe to a host of rules and regulations, etc.

In short, it did not work, even though the town was established, and thrives even unto today, but in a different manner.

It is not God's Will, as is evidenced in these very Passages, for Believers to be bunched up in this manner. The Lord desires that we be *"in"* the world, but never *"of"* it, and that we let our light shine. Actually, this is the only Saving Grace in the world today, this Light brought out in the life of the Believer, as given by Jesus Christ.

Consequently, this Light must not be hidden, but rather *"set on a candlestick"* that it may given illumination, which is what light is all about.

(22) "FOR THERE IS NOTHING HID, WHICH SHALL NOT BE MANIFESTED; NEITHER WAS ANY THING KEPT SECRET, BUT THAT IT SHOULD COME ABROAD."

The overview is:

The Gospel is not meant to be hidden or kept secret, but is to be spread abroad throughout the world. The Gospel of Jesus Christ being the only Light in the world, it is absolutely imperative that this Light be given to the world, and the entirety of the world.

NOTHING HID

The phrase, *"For there is nothing hid, which shall not be manifested,"* could be better translated, *"There is nothing hid save that it should be manifested."* In other words, the Lord is saying that the New Covenant of Grace, which was hidden in the Old, is to now be manifested, and to the entirety of the world. These great Truths will no longer be *"hidden,"* but will be manifested to all! A tremendous Truth is here given:

Inasmuch as the Light is given to any and all who will believe, with Fruit being realized in their lives, accordingly it must be given to others. To not *"manifest"* this Light is to deny Christ. That's the reason we plead for funds, that we may air more Television programming, that we may purchase another Radio Station. It is all because of what Jesus is here saying — the Light must be shone.

As well, and even more so, that's the reason we cry to the Lord constantly that the Holy Spirit would manifest Himself in our hearts and lives and in our Ministry. In fact, this is the most important aspect of everything, as it regards Ministry. We must be led by the Spirit, guided by the Spirit, empowered by the Spirit, for nothing will be done for the Lord unless the Spirit of God does the doing. We are to be vessels which He can use.

NO LONGER A SECRET!

The phrase, *"Neither was any thing kept secret, but that it should come abroad,"* means that even though this great Gospel of Grace was kept secret for a period of time, and for a reason, due to what Christ has done at the Cross, now this *"secret"* is to be manifested to all.

And what is that secret?

"And the Spirit and the Bride say, Come. And let him who hears say, Come. And let him who is athirst come. And whosoever will, let him take the Water of Life freely" (Rev. 22:17).

(23) "IF ANY MAN HAVE EARS TO HEAR, LET HIM HEAR."

The composition is:

NOTES

The Lord will make the Gospel known to all nations and all will be held responsible who hear it.

EARS TO HEAR

In the Greek, the *"If"* does not mean that some did have ears to hear and some did not, but in fact that all had ears to hear, and therefore they ought to use them. In effect, Jesus is saying, *"Since a person has ears to hear, let him be hearing."* Two things are said:

1. We are meant to *"hear"* what He is saying about bearing Fruit, and taking the Gospel to the world, i.e., letting our Light shine.

2. The world must have the opportunity to *"hear,"* whether they accept Christ or not! Paul said, *"How shall they hear without a Preacher?"* (Rom. 10:14). All Believers are held responsible to hear what Christ is saying regarding this all-important subject, even as all unbelievers will be held responsible for their actions upon hearing the Gospel.

OPPORTUNITY

Never before in history has the opportunity presented itself as it does presently regarding the opportunity to take the Gospel to the world. I speak of many ways this can be carried out, but primarily through Radio and Television. While there is a plethora of that which claims to be the Gospel being aired over Radio and Television constantly, the truth is, only a very small portion of that which goes under the claim of Gospel can really be said to actually be *"Gospel."*

It is incumbent upon every Believer to properly discern that which is of God, and that which isn't. One of Satan's greatest efforts is to make Christians think that this which really is of God, isn't; and that which isn't of God, is. He is a past master at such deception.

So, the Believer must avidly seek the Lord, asking Him what Ministry is truly of the Lord. We must not make that decision on our own. And to be sure, if we ask the Lord, and do so sincerely, He will most definitely let us know what is right and what isn't right.

It is tragic that most Christians support that which is really not of God. Let all understand that when we stand at the Judgment Seat of Christ, we will have to give account for our life lived on this Earth, and what we did with that which the Lord put into our hands. It's not going to be very pleasant to hear Christ say to many, *"What you supported was wood, hay, and stubble, which is fit for nothing but to be burned."*

Paul said, *"For other foundation can no man lay than that is laid* (anything other than the Cross is another foundation and, therefore, unacceptable to the Lord), *which is Jesus Christ* (Who He is, God manifest in the flesh, and what He did, Redemption through the Cross).

"Now if any man build upon this foundation gold, silver, precious stones (presents Paul using symbols; the first three are materials which will stand the test of fire, symbolic of the Word of God, which is the Standard), *wood, hay, stubble* (will not stand the test of fire);

"Every man's work shall be made manifest (at the Judgment Seat of Christ): *for the day shall declare it* (the time of the Judgment Seat of Christ), *because it shall be revealed by fire* (the fire of God's Word); *and the fire shall try every man's work of what sort it is* (*'fire'* in the Greek is *'puri,'* and speaks of the ability of Christ, Who will be the Judge and Who sees through everything we do [Rev. 2:18]. He Alone knows our very motives!).

"If any man's work abide which he has built thereupon (assuming it to be true), *he shall receive a reward* (pertains to that which will be eternal, although we aren't told what it will be).

"If any man's work shall be burned, he shall suffer loss (refers to the loss of reward, but not the loss of Salvation): *but he himself shall be saved; yet so as by fire* (actually, this means the person is saved *'despite the fire.'* While the fire of the Word of God will definitely burn up improper works, it will not touch our Salvation, that being in Christ and the Cross)" (I Cor. 3:11-15).

(24) "AND HE SAID UNTO THEM, TAKE HEED WHAT YOU HEAR: WITH WHAT MEASURE YOU METE, IT SHALL BE MEASURED TO YOU: AND UNTO YOU THAT HEAR SHALL MORE BE GIVEN."

The exegesis is:

In proportion to the diligence given to Bible Study, so will spiritual intelligence be measured to the student.

TAKE HEED WHAT YOU HEAR

The phrase, *"And He said unto them, Take heed what you hear,"* is a solemn statement indeed!

First of all, He means for us to hear correctly what He is saying, and that there is no excuse for us not to hear correctly.

Second, the implication given here is that tares (false doctrine) will be sown among the wheat (the True Gospel), and we must know and understand the Word well enough to be able to recognize what is false.

The reason that false prophets and false gospels make such inroads into the Church is because the people do not *"take heed what they hear."* Everything we *"hear"* must be judged by the Word of God. Is it Scriptural? And please understand, it is not Scriptural merely because Scriptures are quoted. It is Scriptural only if it agrees with the Word in every respect.

Unfortunately, far too many Believers little know the Word, meaning they have not studied it for themselves, but have allowed others to think for them. Please understand, untold millions are in Hell today, and will be there forever, because of this one problem — they allowed somebody else to think for them.

That's the reason I plead with people to get THE EXPOSITOR'S NEW TESTAMENT and THE EXPOSITOR'S STUDY BIBLE. That's the reason I also plead with them to check everything we say according to the Word of God. The Word of God must always be the criteria for all things. That means that Denominations aren't the criteria, nor particular Churches, nor particular Preachers, but the Word Alone!

When we all stand before Christ and, of course, I speak of the Believer, our Denomination won't be mentioned, or our Church, or Preachers, or anything else for that matter, only the Word of God and our having abided in, through, and of the Word.

THE MEASURE YOU METE

The phrase, *"With what measure you mete, it shall be measured to you,"* explains the increase from *"thirtyfold"* to *"an hundredfold,"* or conversely the opposite! The idea, as given here by Christ, pertains to the diligence that we put forth, as it regards our understanding of the Word, for this is what all of this Message is about. I constantly tell the following to people:

If we will ask the Lord to help us understand His Word, to properly and rightly divide His Word, to be sure, this is a prayer the Lord will most definitely answer. While the *"measure we mete"* is to be applied to every aspect of our life and living, still, the greater thrust, as given here by Christ, is our diligence, as stated, to study, learn, and understand the Word. It is tragic when far too many Believers know more about sports figures than they do the Word of God. It is tragic when the only revealed Truth in the world today is given lackadaisical attention by most Believers! It is tragic when Believers spend their time learning anything and everything except that which really matters, the Word of God!

MORE GIVEN

The phrase, *"And unto you that hear shall more be given,"* means not only to *"hear,"* but to act upon that which is heard, i.e., take the Light to the world. If this is done, the fruit-bearing increases accordingly! In other words, as the street term says, *"The ball is in our court."* So the matter is up to us!

(25) "FOR HE WHO HAS, TO HIM SHALL BE GIVEN: AND HE WHO HAS NOT, FROM HIM SHALL BE TAKEN EVEN THAT WHICH HE HAS."

The exposition is:

Spiritual gifts, if exercised, will be developed; if not, they will be lost.

MORE WILL BE GIVEN

In proportion to the diligence given to this of which Christ speaks, so will spiritual intelligence be measured to the student. Spiritual gifts, if exercised, will be developed; otherwise, they will be lost. The action of this True Servant and of the under-servants and the fortunes of the Gospel Kingdom between the First and Second Advents are set out in this Chapter. This history of that service, the responsibility of its agents, their quietness and Faith in danger, and the storms which must exercise that Faith are here foreshadowed.

The phrase, *"For he who has, to him shall be given,"* means that he is properly using that which is given him, therefore, more can be entrusted.

THE RESPONSIBILITY OF EVERY BELIEVER

Satan doesn't want us living for God at all, but if he cannot stop our Salvation experience, then he will try to get us to waste our time, talents, ability, and efforts on that which is nonproductive. Even as Jesus has born out in this Chapter, the *"Light"* which He has given us is not be *"put under a bushel, or under a bed"*; in other words, it must not be hidden. We must instead *"set it on a candlestick"* that it may give illumination to a darkened world.

Now, how are we to do that?

Every single Believer must seek the Lord earnestly about this matter, because it is the single most important thing there is, as it regards our life and living for the Lord. As we've already stated, one day every Single Believer will stand at the Judgment Seat of Christ (I Cor. 3:11-15). We will there give account for the life that we've lived. Please understand, we're not speaking of our Salvation, for that has already been decided at Calvary. We are discussing what we have done with this Salvation which God has given us.

Even though I'm repeating myself, having addressed this very subject some paragraphs back, it is so important that I must make certain that you the Reader understand perfectly what is being said. Every single Believer is building on the foundation which was at first laid down by the Apostle Paul (I Cor. 3:10).

The Apostle symbolically uses *"gold, silver, precious stones, wood, hay, and stubble"* as examples of our *"works"* (I Cor. 3:12-13). The first three, *"gold, silver, and precious stones,"* will not only not be hurt by the fire (fire of the Word of God), but will actually become more pure. The other three, *"wood, hay, and stubble,"* obviously, will burn quickly. In other words, what we're doing for the Lord can be likened either to *"gold, silver, and precious stones"* or *"wood, hay, and stubble."* The latter three simply won't stand the test.

What is the test?

Of course, the test is the Word of God. However, as Jesus laid down in this Fourth Chapter of Mark, it is our responsibility to help take this Gospel to others.

Let me elaborate on that:

THE RESPONSIBILITY OF THE GOSPEL

Satan, to which we have already alluded, is perfectly satisfied to get us to expend our energy on humanitarian causes and things which, in the final analysis, really will not amount to anything. In other words, they are *"wood, hay, and stubble."* The great responsibility of every Believer, and I mean every Believer, is to do everything within our power to take this *"Light"* to others.

And here is how it is done:

As a Believer, you should avidly seek the Lord as to what you should support. You should select a Ministry that's truly doing the Work of God, truly preaching the Gospel, and truly seeing the results of the Gospel. You should get behind that Ministry and support it grandly, both prayerfully and financially. Paul also said that the entirety of this effort is a twofold process.

The Lord calls someone to take the Gospel, and then He calls others to send that one whom He has called (Rom. 10:14-15). The truth is, millions of Christians are supporting Churches which aren't supporting the Gospel, Evangelists who aren't preaching the Gospel, etc. That being the case, and it definitely is in the far greater majority of the cases, the Lord will liken such to *"wood, hay, and stubble."* We better consider these things very carefully, because each one of us is going to stand at the Judgment Seat of Christ and give account. Then, what will it be?

TAKEN AWAY

The phrase, *"And he who has not, from him shall be taken even that which he has,"* is the very opposite of the previous phrase, and presents a startling concept. In other words, and according to Christ, we bear Fruit or else we die (Jn. 15:6). This one Verse epitomizes the Parable of the *"Talents,"* as given

NOTES

by Christ (Mat. 25:14-30). The ones who used their talents and gained others were rewarded accordingly, while the one who did not use his talent, but rather hid it, had *"taken away even that which he has"* (Mat. 25:29).

If the Believer does not walk in the Light as it is given to him, he will, of necessity, regress into darkness. That is one of the reasons that particular religious Denominations, which were given the Light of the Baptism with the Holy Spirit, but little by little are rejecting it, are now void of any spiritual move whatsoever. In other words, all their activity (at least those who fall into this category) is man-inspired; consequently, man-led; and, of necessity, of no spiritual consequence.

As someone has well said, *"Use it, or lose it."*

(26) "AND HE SAID, SO IS THE KINGDOM OF GOD, AS IF A MAN SHOULD CAST SEED INTO THE GROUND."

The synopsis is:

It is the responsibility of all Believers to spread the Gospel of Jesus Christ.

THE KINGDOM OF GOD

This has been called the *"Parable of the Wheat."* It speaks of the consciousness of Jesus as to the success and nonsuccess of His preaching as it appears in the Parable of the Sower; but only success is predicted in this beauteous Parable of the Man and Seed. Christ sows, He reaps, and between these actions He waits. This is His present attitude. He is absent; He does not outwardly interpose. The Seed (Gospel) is left to itself to accomplish its purpose, which it definitely shall! During His absence, the laborers are responsible to work in the field (Williams).

The phrase, *"And He said, So is the Kingdom of God,"* is meant to express the manner in which the Gospel will take its course.

THE CASTING OF THE SEED

The phrase, *"As if a man should cast seed into the ground,"* is meant to explain how this will be done. As we shall see, the Lord will use the germination of the Seed to explain how the Gospel works. Even though the explanation is given, the far greater responsibility of the Believer is to *"cast the Seed."* If we don't *"cast the Seed,"* nothing can be done, as would be obvious.

So, once again, the great questions must be asked, *"What kind of seed are we casting?"* or *"Are we casting any at all?"*

(27) "AND SHOULD SLEEP, AND RISE NIGHT AND DAY, AND THE SEED SHOULD SPRING AND GROW UP, HE KNOWS NOT HOW."

The exposition is:

The Word properly sown will, without fail, have its proper effect.

THE PLANTING OF THE SEED

The phrase, *"And should sleep, and rise night and day,"* means that after planting the Seed (Gospel), there is nothing more the individual can do. But, as we've already stated, if someone doesn't plant the Seed, nothing can happen. As well, if we plant seed that we think is the true and right seed, but actually it isn't, then, as should be obvious, we're not going to get the proper fruit.

Even though my words sound negative, the truth is, the far, far greater majority of the *"seed"* being planted is not the True Seed of the Gospel, but something else entirely. We only have one life to live for the Lord. If we throw it away by supporting that which is actually not of God, then the loss will have been staggering.

THE GROWTH OF THE SEED

The phrase, *"And the seed should spring and grow up,"* refers to the germination of the Seed, which is brought about if the Seed is properly planted. The phrase, *"He knows not how,"* means that the individual has no understanding how the Seed germinates after it is properly planted in the soil. This Verse is meant to proclaim the Power of the Gospel. It is up to the laborers (Christian workers) to sow the Seed, but how it is received is according to the hearts of the individuals, which was epitomized in the Parable of the Sower.

As well, after sowing the Seed, and as stated, there is nothing more a person can do, but rather must depend on the Power of God for the Seed to bring forth Fruit in the life of the hearer. Being finite, the Believer who has cast the Seed does not know or understand how this is carried out, and is not responsible for that part of the process. It is our responsibility to plant the Seed (Gospel) and God's responsibility to make it germinate, at least in the hearts of those who will believe.

Again, let us make the statement:

The Seed cannot *"spring and grow up"* unless it is first *"cast into the ground,"* i.e., presented to the world.

(28) "FOR THE EARTH BRINGS FORTH FRUIT OF HERSELF; FIRST THE BLADE, THEN THE EAR, AFTER THAT THE FULL CORN IN THE EAR."

The overview is:

This is the Law of the Gospel in *"sowing and reaping."*

FRUIT

The phrase, *"For the Earth brings forth fruit of herself,"* is meant to explain that sowing Seed and the Gospel are very similar. If the Seed is planted, it will ultimately *"bring forth Fruit of herself."* While the sowing of the Seed is the responsibility of the Christian Worker, the bringing forth of the *"Fruit"* is the responsibility of the Holy Spirit.

Let it be understood, however, that the Work of the Holy Spirit cannot progress forward until the Seed is first planted.

During the time of Christ, Israel had never been more religious. But yet, there was precious little true seed being planted. Presently, the same thing is happening! The Church has never been more religious, more filled with religious activity. But the truth is, precious little True Gospel Seed is actually being sowed.

THE BLADE, THE EAR, THE FULL CORN IN THE EAR

The phrase, *"First the blade, then the ear, after that the full corn in the ear,"* is meant to express a Law, not only of seed in the Earth, which is obvious to all, but, as well, the Law of the Gospel in *"sowing and reaping."* The Work of the Holy Spirit is developed in three stages:

1. *"First the blade"*: after the Seed is planted, the first little shoot comes above the soil, which represents the germination of the Seed. This is the acceptance of the Gospel by the hearer after it is presented.

2. *"Then the ear"*: this speaks of what surrounds that which will ultimately be brought

forth. In other words, it is a sort of protective shield for the *"full corn"* which will ultimately spring forth. Were this not done, Satan would be able to destroy it!

3. *"After that the full corn in the ear"*: this presents the finished product and is the result of the labor of sowing the Seed.

Consequently, the Lord is telling us that our part of the task is simple, to say the least. We are to just present the Gospel, with the Holy Spirit doing all the work in the hearts and lives of those who believe. As we have repeatedly stated, the Worker is not responsible for the developed Fruit, for it is God Who gives the increase, but is definitely responsible for the sowing of the Seed, without which no Fruit is possible (I Cor. 3:6).

(29) "BUT WHEN THE FRUIT IS BROUGHT FORTH, IMMEDIATELY HE PUTS IN THE SICKLE, BECAUSE THE HARVEST IS COME."

The overview is:

This has reference to the end of the age, when the Church will be called to account.

THE HARVEST

While the *"harvest"* of souls has gone on from the very beginning, in effect, this particular Scripture refers to the very end of the age, actually to the time of the First Resurrection. What Jesus did at Calvary will bring forth that which He intended and, in effect, has brought forth that which He intended!

He said, *"And I, if I be lifted up from the Earth, will draw all men unto Me.*

"This He said, signifying what Death He should die" (Jn. 12:32-33).

Concerning this, Reynolds says, *"In these Words, we learn the attraction of the Cross of Christ will prove to be the mightiest and most sovereign motive ever brought to bear on the human will, and, when wielded by the Holy Spirit as a revelation of the matchless Love of God, will involve the most sweeping judicial sentence that can be pronounced upon the world and its prince."*

THE DOUBLE MEANING OF THIS PARABLE

1. It pertains to each individual who sows the Seed of the Gospel, as well as those who hear it. It promises that some will receive and will bring forth Fruit. God's Word will not return void.

2. The meaning of the Parable concerns the entirety of the Plan of God regarding the Church. It speaks of all the efforts which have been made for all time, and for the time that remains. Soon it will be over, and the *"harvest is come."* As stated, this will be at the end of the age, at the First Resurrection of Life.

(30) "AND HE SAID, WHEREUNTO SHALL WE LIKEN THE KINGDOM OF GOD? OR WITH WHAT COMPARISON SHALL WE COMPARE IT?"

The structure is:

It is meant to proclaim the manner in which Satan will endeavor to corrupt the Word of God.

WHAT IS LIKE THE KINGDOM OF GOD?

The question, *"And He said, Whereunto shall we liken the Kingdom of God?"* is meant, by the Master, to forearm all those who follow Him against disappointment and confusion. While the inner Kingdom of God (Vss. 26-29) would be pure, and continue pure, the outward professing Kingdom (Vss. 30-32) will become a great Earthly institution having great branches, and will become the home of Satan and his angels. And so it has come to pass (Williams).

A COMPARISON?

The question, *"Or with what comparison shall we compare it?"* is meant to proclaim the manner in which Satan will endeavor to corrupt the Work of God.

I think that one can say, and without fear of contradiction, that always Satan works from within. He uses Preachers who will not preach all the Gospel, but only part, and then he uses those who are into gross error, and then he uses those who are *"shysters."* The number of True Preachers of the Gospel at the present time, if the truth be known, is abysmally small, in fact, shockingly so!

Paul said, *"Now the Spirit* (Holy Spirit) *speaks expressly* (pointedly), *that in the latter times* (the times in which we now live, the last of the last days, which begin the fulfillment of Endtime Prophecies) *some shall depart from the faith* (anytime Paul uses the term *'the faith,'* in short, he is referring to the Cross; so, we are told here that some will depart from the Cross as the means of Salvation and Victory), *giving heed to seducing spirits* (evil spirits, i.e., *'religious spirits,'* making something seem like what it isn't), *and doctrines of devils* (should have been translated *'doctrines of demons'*; *'seducing spirits'* entice Believers away from the True Faith, causing them to believe *'doctrines inspired by demon spirits'*)" (I Tim. 4:1).

(31) "IT IS LIKE A GRAIN OF MUSTARD SEED, WHICH, WHEN IT IS SOWN IN THE EARTH, IS LESS THAN ALL THE SEEDS THAT BE IN THE EARTH."

The diagram is:

The Church began very small.

A GRAIN OF MUSTARD SEED

The phrase, *"It is like a grain of mustard seed,"* is the illustration that Jesus will use as a comparison to the Kingdom of God. The phrase, *"Which, when it is sown in the Earth, is less than all the seeds that be in the Earth,"* has reference to the size of the plant that can come from this particular type of seed. It does not mean that it is actually the smallest seed, for there are actually other seeds which are smaller, but rather the smallest seed which produces such a large plant.

The Lord is here referencing the beginning of the Church as being small and insignificant, but rapidly expanding until it covers the entirety of the Earth.

(32) "BUT WHEN IT IS SOWN, IT GROWS UP, AND BECOMES GREATER THAN ALL HERBS, AND SHOOTS OUT GREAT BRANCHES; SO THAT THE FOWLS OF THE AIR MAY LODGE UNDER THE SHADOW OF IT."

The composition is:

Christianity is presently the largest religion on Earth, claiming nearly two billion adherents, in one form or the other. The latter phrase of this Verse refers to most of Christianity being corrupted by Satanic Powers, as explained in Matthew 13:19 and Luke 8:12.

CHRISTIANITY, THE GREATEST RELIGION

The phrase, *"But when it is sown, it grows up, and becomes greater than all herbs,"* refers to Christianity being larger than all the other efforts of religion in the world. In truth, Bible Christianity is not a religion, but rather a relationship and, more particularly, a relationship with a Man, The Man, Christ Jesus. If both the Protestant sector and Catholicism are joined together, the adherents number approximately 2 billion souls. Of course, the true number of that inflated figure who are truly Born-Again, only the Lord knows; however, by comparison, the true number probably would be abysmally small (Mat. 7:14).

GREAT BRANCHES

The phrase, *"And shoots out great branches,"* refers to all the various divisions of Christianity, such as Catholicism, Baptists, Methodists, Pentecostals, Charismatics, etc. In fact, there are probably several hundreds of Church Denominations in the United States alone. Some few are Biblical, most aren't!

FOWLS OF THE AIR

The phrase, *"So that the fowls of the air may lodge under the shadow of it,"* refers to Satanic powers, as explained, and as stated, in Matthew 13:19 and Luke 8:12. This is another way of Jesus saying what He said in the Parable of the Leaven: *"The Kingdom of Heaven is like unto leaven, which a woman took and hid in three measures of meal, till the whole was leavened"* (Mat. 13:33).

This is what I have repeatedly warned the Reader about in all of our Commentaries, respecting the True Church and the apostate church. In everything which is referred to as *"Christianity,"* the True Church, although present, is far, far smaller than the apostate church. In fact, the apostasy is so great and widespread that it looks as if the *"whole"* is leavened, but, in fact, the True Church is present, but not so easily discerned or observed.

It is somewhat as ancient Israel when Elijah complained, *"And I, even I only, am left; and they seek my life, to take it away"* (I Ki. 19:10). However, the Lord told him, *"Yet I have left Me seven thousand in Israel, all the knees which have not bowed unto Baal, and every mouth which has not kissed him"* (I Ki. 19:18).

THE APOSTATE CHURCH

Satan has sought to infiltrate the Church and he has succeeded admirably so! Consequently, every Believer must be diligent that he follow the Word of God only and not man.

I have preached much in the great country of Brazil. In fact, there are two branches in this particular country of a particular Pentecostal Denomination. One has about 12 million adherents, with the other approximately 3 million. As far as I can tell, at least in this case, the larger (which is unusual) follows the Lord, while the smaller, at least its leadership, follows man.

As an example, a particular Evangelist recently joined this Pentecostal Denomination, which has its headquarters in the U.S.A. Before he joined it, he was blackballed, blacklisted, and roundly rejected by the smaller Pentecostal organization in Brazil, who had some occasion to come in contact with his Ministry. However, the moment he joined this Denomination, which was the same as the smaller Denomination in Brazil, their statements concerning him changed 180 degrees. Now he is a Godly Evangelist, according to them!

Why did they change so quickly?

One day they were saying he was of the Devil (before he joined their Denomination), and the next day they were saying how Godly he was (this was the day after he joined their Denomination).

Again, I ask the question, *"Why did they change so quickly?"*

They changed because they were parroting the party line. Whatever the Denominational leaders said, they said the same. Before this Brother became a part of their Denomination, he was spoken of very negatively by its Leadership. But when he joined the Denomination, all of a sudden, he becomes pure and holy.

All of this tells us several things:

1. They had equated belonging to their Denomination as belonging to the Kingdom of God. They may deny that, but their actions prove otherwise.

2. It is obvious that this group in Brazil was following man instead of the Lord. It did not really matter what the true spiritual condition was, but only what the religious leadership said about him. The day before he joined, he was a *"false apostle,"* but the day after he joined, he was a *"true apostle"*! Such is man-directed and not God-directed!

3. Anyone who is not led by the Holy Spirit is apostate. This does not mean that everyone associated with that Denomination of which we have spoken is apostate, but definitely does mean that a part or all of its leadership is apostate. If one is led by the Holy Spirit, one is led by the Word of God. If one is not led by the Holy Spirit, one is led by the word of man.

Actually, whatever the man was before he joined this Denomination, he was the same after he joined it. His spiritual status did not change, but yet, in the eyes of these individuals, whoever they may have been, his status did change, and because he had associated himself with this earthly organization.

DENOMINATIONALISM

In truth, many religious Denominations feel and do the same about their own particular group. Actually, this even occurs in local Churches. In other words, if you're not a member of our group, you are not accepted by the Lord, etc. In fact, racism and Denominationalism are very similar. Racism claims that one particular race is more intelligent, greater, etc., than the other races. Denominationalism does the same thing.

This doesn't mean that it's wrong to belong to a Denomination, for it isn't. Ideally, a Denomination is supposed to be a tool to help spread the Gospel. If it functions in that capacity, it can provide a great service for the Work of God. However, when it begins to believe that association with that particular Denomination affords some type of spirituality, then it has gone into Denominationalism, and those who truly love the Lord would be wise to seek greener pastures.

DEMON SPIRITS

Considering that these *"fowls of the air,"* i.e., religious demon spirits, are *"lodged under the shadow of the Church,"* millions think they are legitimate, and consequently accept their teachings, which lead to destruction.

Paul called them, *"false apostles, deceitful workers, transforming themselves into the Apostles of Christ."*

He then said, *"And no marvel; for Satan himself is transformed into an angel of light."*

And lastly, *"Therefore it is no great thing if his ministers also be transformed as the ministers of righteousness; whose end shall be according to their works"* (II Cor. 11:13-15).

He likened it all to *"another Jesus,"* *"another spirit,"* and *"another gospel"* (II Cor. 11:4).

The tragedy is, *"another Jesus, by another spirit, presenting another gospel"* is being given to the American public, and most Christians do not even have enough spiritual discernment to know the true from the false.

Why can't they tell?

The can't tell because they do not know the Word of God. The Psalmist said, *"Your Word is a Lamp unto my feet, and a Light unto my path"* (Ps. 119:105). They have no *"Lamp"* or *"Light"* because they do not know the *"Word."*

(33) "AND WITH MANY SUCH PARABLES SPOKE HE THE WORD UNTO THEM, AS THEY WERE ABLE TO HEAR IT."

The synopsis is:

Being *"able to hear it"* means they were able to understand.

(34) "BUT WITHOUT A PARABLE SPOKE HE NOT UNTO THEM: AND WHEN THEY WERE ALONE, HE EXPOUNDED ALL THINGS TO HIS DISCIPLES."

The phrase, *"But without a Parable spoke He not unto them,"* means this was the method He used to impart teaching unto the hearers. The Greek word for *"Parable"* means *"something set alongside."* Sometimes Scripture records people illustrating what they are saying by setting a concrete situation alongside an abstract concept (Judg. 9:8-15; II Sam. 12:1-7; Isa. 5:1-7).

However, and as is obvious, the most well-known Parables in the Bible are those of Jesus. Many of these have an illustrative thrust, and a true-to-life experience, such as those of the Good Samaritan (Lk. 10:27-37), the Prodigal Son (Lk. 15:11-32), and the Talents (Lk. 19:11-27). But some Parables, related to a yet hidden form of the Kingdom, were told in such a way (as we have stated)

NOTES

that they concealed rather than illustrated Jesus' meaning.

DISCIPLES

The phrase, *"And when they were alone, He expounded all things to His Disciples,"* means that He explained it plainer and clearer. The idea is that He took the time to explain fully what He was speaking of, which actually amounted to fresh revelations concerning the mysteries of the Kingdom of God. The word *"Disciples"* refers to the *"Twelve,"* even though Jesus had other Disciples, as well!

I wonder how it must have been to sit at the feet of Jesus and to hear Him expound more fully the Word of God! Considering that He was the Living Word, if you please, the Incarnate Word, how wonderful these times must have been for the Disciples!

And yet, He does the same identical thing with us, if we will only wait on Him.

(35) "AND THE SAME DAY, WHEN THE EVENING WAS COME, HE SAID UNTO THEM, LET US PASS OVER UNTO THE OTHER SIDE."

The composition is:

This incident presents itself as a microcosm of this present life; the storms come, and it is only with Christ that we can make it to the other shore.

THE OTHER SIDE

The phrase, *"And the same day, when the evening was come,"* refers to the same day that He had been teaching the people through Parables. The phrase, *"He said unto them, let us pass over unto the other side,"* is freighted with meaning.

First of all, the *"other side"* represents that to which Christ came. He left the portals of Glory in order to come down to a world infested by demon spirits, and for the purpose of redeeming mankind, represented by the maniac of Gadara. The storm He calmed on the Sea of Galilee was representative of the storm in this man's soul, as the next Chapter reveals.

Last of all, he would be opposed greatly by the powers of darkness in the realm of the storm, but as long as Jesus is in the boat, it cannot sink.

(36) "AND WHEN THEY HAD SENT

AWAY THE MULTITUDE, THEY TOOK HIM EVEN AS HE WAS IN THE SHIP. AND THERE WERE ALSO WITH HIM OTHER LITTLE SHIPS."

The diagram is:

Jesus was very tired, even to the point of physical exhaustion; as a man, He grew tired, just as we do.

PHYSICAL EXHAUSTION

The phrase, *"And when they had sent away the multitude,"* means such was done only after they had been amply fed by the Word of God, with, as well, many, no doubt, being healed. The phrase, *"They took Him even as He was in the ship,"* refers more than likely to one of the vessels owned by Zebedee, which Jesus often used as a platform from which to preach and teach. The idea of the phrase is that Jesus was so exhausted from the full day of teaching, preaching, and healing, they almost had to carry Him to the ship. In His Incarnation, He grew tired exactly as any other man.

The phrase, *"And there were also with Him other little ships,"* refers, no doubt, to those who wanted to be near Him wherever He went. Consequently, they also would experience the stilling of the storm.

(37) "AND THERE AROSE A GREAT STORM OF WIND, AND THE WAVES BEAT INTO THE SHIP, SO THAT IT WAS NOW FULL."

The diagram is:

This represents in the spiritual sense the storms of life which come to every person.

A GREAT STORM

The phrase, *"And there arose a great storm of wind,"* refers to a furious storm or hurricane. Wuest says, *"A storm breaking forth from black thunderclouds in furious gusts, with floods of rain, and throwing everything topsy-turvy."* The phrase, *"And the waves beat into the ship, so that it was now full,"* meant that it was full of water. The phrase has reference to the waves beating into the ship, and repeatedly doing so.

As well, the inference is that the storm came up suddenly, and consequently without warning. This account is given that the lesson not be lost upon the Reader.

NOTES

1. In this Christian Life, there will be opposition, as is evidenced by the storm. Some foolishly and erroneously claim that they can confess such away, claiming an idealistic life free from such disturbances. However, such is not Scriptural. It is not a question of *if* the storm may come, but rather *when* it comes!

2. Some claim they can have faith enough that they can ward off all such things. Are they accusing Christ of not having enough faith? I seriously doubt anyone would want to be guilty of such an accusation. No! The storm did not come up because of a lack of faith, but rather that their faith (the Disciples) might be tested. Great faith must be tested greatly!

3. Even though Satan sent the storm, he had to have permission from God to do such. Satan cannot do anything to a Believer unless the Lord permits or allows it; consequently, the Lord allowed this storm to come up, and for a reason (Rom. 8:28).

(38) "AND HE WAS IN THE HINDER PART OF THE SHIP, ASLEEP ON A PILLOW: AND THEY AWOKE HIM, AND SAY UNTO HIM, MASTER, CAREST THOU NOT THAT WE PERISH?"

The overview is:

The Lord had said, *"Let us pass over unto the other side."* This means that, despite the storm, or anything else for that matter, they would reach the other shore.

The people of God are in the same boat with Christ, and we cannot perish because He cannot perish. But we must expect storms of opposition, for they are sure to come (Ps. 93).

DOES HE CARE THAT WE PERISH?

The phrase, *"And He was in the hinder part of the ship, asleep on a pillow,"* referred to His exhaustion from the long day of teaching, preaching, and healing. As well, the *"pillow"* here in question was not a soft pillow, but rather the leather cushion of the steersman, or the low bench on which the steersman sometimes sits.

The phrase, *"And they awoke Him, and say unto Him,"* concerns their desperation! Inasmuch as the boat was filling up with water, and even was now *"full,"* and due to the ferocity of the storm, their efforts to keep the ship afloat were in vain; consequently, they resort to Christ, but only after all their efforts had failed.

No doubt, knowing of His physical exhaustion, they did not want to disturb Him; nevertheless, they soon arrive at a place where they have no choice. It is amazing that He was able to continue sleeping, especially considering that the ship was violently rocking from side to side, being beaten violently by the waves. As well, the water had to be pouring over Him, even as it did the Disciples. And yet, there is a possibility that the ship was large enough that the waves did not reach Him, which is probably the case.

IMPERTINENCE?

The question, *"Master, carest Thou not that we perish?"* is claimed by some to have been impertinence on the part of the speaker. Some have attributed the question to Peter. However, those who would accuse the Disciples of impertinence obviously have not been where the Disciples were. Oftentimes, the Lord allows things to come very close to destruction before He steps in and takes a hand. Personally, I know what it is to cry, *"Master, carest Thou not that I perish?"*

The powers of darkness can be so strong, as evidenced by this storm, that it looks like there is no way out. But yet, we hear the Words of Christ, *"Let us pass over unto the other side."* He did not say, *"Let us go out into the sea and perish!"*

So, He does care, enough, I might quickly add, to go with us through the storm, and then to calm it when it looks like we will surely perish. I might quickly add that even though the storms have beaten furiously upon this old ship of the Church, still, not a single ship or passenger has ever been lost, at least for those who trust Him.

(39) "AND HE AROSE, AND REBUKED THE WIND, AND SAID UNTO THE SEA, PEACE, BE STILL. AND THE WIND CEASED, AND THERE WAS A GREAT CALM."

The exposition is:

The Greek intimates *"Silence! Hush!"*

PEACE BE STILL

The phrase, *"And He arose,"* literally means

NOTES

"He awakened!" The phrase, *"And rebuked the wind, and said unto the sea,"* implies in the original Greek that before the Word was uttered, the thing was done, and by the simple power of His Will, which preceded His Word. So, what He said to the sea was, more than anything, a calming of the Disciples.

The phrase, *"Peace, be still,"* is a beautiful Word. Wuest says it probably meant *"Silence! Hush!"* The phrase, *"And the wind ceased, and there was a great calm,"* means that the wind instantly ceased, and the sea instantly calmed.

This Miracle invaded the laws of nature, interposing a greater Law, which was the Word of God. Consequently, Jesus proved Himself as the Creator of all things and, therefore, God, although manifest in the flesh. In other words, only God could do such a thing!

To emphasize the point, there was no gradual subsiding of the storm, as in the ordinary operations of nature; but, almost before the Word had escaped His lips, there was a perfect calm, which had to be the most amazing thing these Disciples had seen to date.

(40) "AND HE SAID UNTO THEM, WHY ARE YOU SO FEARFUL? HOW IS IT THAT YOU HAVE NO FAITH?"

The synopsis is:

The Disciples had accepted His Messiahship, but had a most inadequate view of what that Office carried with it.

FEAR

The phrase, *"And He said unto them,"* refers to Him speaking to men who were transfixed with amazement at that which had happened before their very eyes — the instant stilling of the storm. Even though He would give them the lesson intended by the Holy Spirit, nevertheless, at least at this moment, their minds were totally on Him and what He had done, rather than learning the lesson He taught. However, as is here recorded, the lesson would ultimately become unmistakably clear to them.

The question, as asked by Christ, *"Why are you so fearful?"* refers to an imperfect love on the part of the Disciples for the Lord (I Jn. 4:18). This question, as it was asked of them so long ago, is also asked of each and every Believer. As the Disciples, there has not been a single Believer, at one time or the other, who has not *"feared."* Nevertheless, the *"fear"* shows an imperfect love and an imperfect Faith. Perfect Love trusts, while Perfect Faith believes!

The storms are allowed to teach us trust, and also that we may learn how to use our Faith. No! No one enjoys such and admittedly, many storms come upon us because of our own foolishness, etc. However, some are allowed, as here, and as stated, for a purpose. As we've also stated, great faith must be tested greatly!

FAITH

The question, *"How is it that you have no Faith?"* is actually saying, *"Do you think any harm could come to you, while I am in the ship?"* The question is not meant to imply that the Disciples have no faith at all, but that they did not have enough faith for this particular situation. According to what the Lord asks of us, accordingly is the Faith we must have. Oftentimes, such Faith is not readily available. Nevertheless, whatever the Lord asks us to do will always be accompanied by the necessary Faith, that is, if we will dare to believe Him.

By these questions, was He meaning that they should have calmed the storm themselves without awakening Him?

No! That is not the idea at all. These questions cover the entirety of the scenario, meaning they were afraid they were going to die. So, He is asking them, *"How could such happen with Me in the ship?"*

In truth, it could not happen! The Creator and Sustainer of the Universe was with them in the boat. Wuest said that the Disciples had accepted His Messiahship, but had a most inadequate view of what that Office carried with it.

(41) "AND THEY FEARED EXCEEDINGLY, AND SAID ONE TO ANOTHER. WHAT MANNER OF MAN IS THIS, THAT EVEN THE WIND AND THE SEA OBEY HIM?"

The structure is:

This means that their fear of Him was greater even than their fear had been of the storm.

NOTES

FEAR OF CHRIST

The phrase, *"And they feared exceedingly,"* means that they were beginning to realize exactly Who He was, in other words, God manifested in the flesh. As such, they feared Him actually more than their fear had been of the storm. To see the storm raging one moment, and then to see utter calm the next, was beyond their power of comprehension.

However, the type of fear they had of Christ was not a slavelike fear, but rather, as stated, a recognition, and for the first time, as to exactly Who He was. They had seen great things, but they had seen nothing like this instant calming of the storm.

In effect, the storm calming instantly is what happens to demon spirits at the Name of Jesus. Every demon spirit and every fallen angel know the Power of Christ, and they literally tremble in the presence of that Power. The trouble with the modern Church is that it has opted so heavily for the wisdom of the world that it has lost sight of the Power of Christ, seldom even referring to such. What a waste!

WHAT MANNER OF MAN IS THIS?

The question, *"And said one to another, What manner of Man is this, that even the wind and the sea obey Him?"* actually says, *"What manner of is this?"* with the word *"Man"* not found in the Greek. According to Wuest, Mark has it, *"Who then is this Person?"*

We know that Satan was the cause of this storm, even though permitted by God. So, how could Satan think that he could do damage to someone as powerful as Christ? I am certain he knew that he could not do anything to Christ, but perhaps, with Christ being asleep, he thought he might be able to swamp the boat and possibly even kill one or more of the Disciples. But, of course, that was futile, as well, inasmuch as Christ had said at the beginning of the journey, *"Let us pass over unto the other side."*

But still, the Evil One would try to wreak havoc, even though he had little or no chance of succeeding! The Disciples were right! The *"wind and sea do obey Him,"* as well as everything else, other than, regrettably and sadly, most people.

CHAPTER 5

(1) "AND THEY CAME OVER UNTO THE OTHER SIDE OF THE SEA, INTO THE COUNTRY OF THE GADARENES."

The composition is:

This was the eastern shore of Galilee. The area of the town of Gadara was about 3 miles from the Sea of Galilee.

A MISSION OF MERCY

The phrase, *"And they came over unto the other side of the Sea,"* refers to the shore opposite of Capernaum. It was the eastern shore. The phrase, *"Into the country of the Gadarenes,"* is the only reference to this area in the Bible, and concerns the Deliverance of the man called *"Legion."*

Jesus had just calmed a storm on the Sea, and now he would calm the storm in a man's soul. Again, it would be one of the most outstanding Miracles ever. It portrays a picture of humanity completely taken over by Satan.

(2) "AND WHEN HE WAS COME OUT OF THE SHIP, IMMEDIATELY THERE MET HIM OUT OF THE TOMBS A MAN WITH AN UNCLEAN SPIRIT."

The composition is:

This symbolizes the great mission for which Christ came to the world; He had calmed the storm on the Sea, but the storm He would now calm would be even greater. Dealing with the elements is one thing. Dealing with man is something else.

THE TOMBS

The phrase, *"And when He was come out of the ship,"* concerns the very reason for which He came, which was to deliver the maniac of Gadara. As we have stated, this, in a way, symbolizes the great mission for which Christ came to the world.

Many may object, claiming that man is not nearly in the condition of the maniac of Gadara and, hence, such would not provide a suitable example. To be sure, only those who hide their heads in the sand would think such a thing. Even at the present time, and despite the thousands of years of intellectual pursuit and education, the fallen nature of man has never been more obvious.

As I dictate these words, just a few days ago, a mass grave was found in former Yugoslavia, containing the bodies of approximately 5,000 people. They had been recently shot, in what was referred to as *"ethnic cleansing."*

Lest the Reader think that such is indigenous only to the guilty ones, if the ones shot had had the opportunity, they would, more than likely, have visited the same on their assailants.

Some time ago, Frances and I, along with friends, were in Munich, Germany. A few miles from this beautiful city is the concentration camp called *"Dachau,"* actually, the first such camp built by Hitler. I personally looked at the ovens where the thousands of Jews were gassed to death, with their bodies then burned. It is said that when the wind was blowing toward Munich, the smell of burning bodies filled the air.

How could educated, civilized, so-called, human beings engage themselves in such horror?

Man should learn from that horrid debacle of World War II that education, as helpful as it is in many respects, is not the answer to the evil hearts of men. The men who murdered 6,000,000 Jews, plus many millions of others, were educated men. However, an evil heart which undergoes education is, when it's all over, only an educated evil heart!

No! The example of the maniac of Gadara is not an overemphasis of the state of man. Actually, it perfectly symbolizes the unregenerate heart.

THE UNCLEAN SPIRIT

The phrase, *"Immediately there met Him out of the tombs a man with an unclean spirit,"* instantly proclaims the one Jesus had come to deliver. Matthew says there were two, while Mark and Luke only mention one. Actually, there were two, but the one mentioned by Mark and Luke was, no doubt, the more prominent and fierce of the two.

More than likely, there were others in the general area, as well! However, only two were delivered, because the others (if, in fact, there were others) would not come to Christ.

The Jews did not have their burial places in their cities, lest they should be defiled;

consequently, they buried their dead without the gates in the fields or mountains, etc. Their sepulchers were frequently hewn out of the rock in the sides of limestone hills, etc.

The demon spirits that possessed this man guarded their territory with diligence; consequently, when the ship carrying Jesus and His Disciples came close to the shore, with them disembarking, their response was immediate! Matthew, speaking of the two, says they were *"exceeding fierce, so that no man might pass by that way"* (Mat. 8:28). However, they did not know Who this *"Man"* was!

The phrase, *"Unclean spirit,"* seems to be a designation applied to any and all spirits, irrespective of their activity. However, some were given such designations as a *"dumb and deaf spirit"* (Mk. 9:25), *"a spirit of infirmity"* (Lk. 13:11), and *"a spirit of divination"* (Acts 16:16). However, and as stated, the catch-all phrase seems to be *"unclean spirit."*

DEMON POSSESSION

To be demon possessed is an awful thing, and from what description we have, it seems to always include at least some form of insanity. To be sure, everyone, even consecrated Believers, as we've previously stated, are at times oppressed by demon spirits, or even influenced. However, oppression or influence are not possession.

Despite the teaching of some, a Believer cannot be demon possessed — influenced and oppressed, yes!

Why was this man demon possessed? In fact, why is any person demon possessed?

The answer to that would not be simple, but would probably come under the category of one of several things:

Environment may well be one of the principal causes of demon possession. In areas where demons are actually worshipped, as in some places in Africa and elsewhere, possession, as should be obvious, is rife.

Association is another cause. This is the cause, I believe, of homosexuality and such perversions. A child is molested, and then at times (but not always) takes upon himself (or herself) the spirit of the molester. As well, association with any perverted activity will, sooner or later, wreak its terrible toll, and can result in demon possession.

NOTES

Lastly, territorial possession may be more extended than one realizes. I speak of families. I feel it is improper to take this too far; however, I think there is some evidence that demon possession can literally be handed down from father to son, etc. However, the terrible chain is broken upon any member of the family coming to Christ.

The truth is, the Salvation of any member of a family, and especially an entire family coming to Christ, is of far greater consequence than even the immediate Salvation of the principals involved, as wonderful as that may be. This horrible chain of demon influence, oppression, and even possession, is now broken. It does not mean that demon powers cannot have some access, even to Believers, but it does mean that their authority to steal, kill, and destroy is broken — that is, if the Believers involved will ever make Christ and the Cross the Object of their Faith. This is absolutely imperative!

THE FAMILY CURSE

There has been a teaching in the last few years, which has become quite prominent, called *"the family curse."* Basically, this teaching is taken from an erroneous understanding of Exodus 20:5.

The Scripture says: *"You shall have no other gods before Me.*

"You shall not make unto you any graven image, or any likeness of anything that is in Heaven above, or that is in the Earth beneath, or that is in the water under the Earth.

"You shall not bow down yourself to them, nor serve them: for I the LORD your God am a jealous God, visiting the iniquity of the fathers upon the children unto the third and fourth generation of them who hate Me;

"And showing mercy unto the thousands of them who love Me, and keep My Commandments" (Ex. 20:3-6).

This teaching claims that a man committing a grievous sin can have the curse of that sin pass down through his family *"unto the third and fourth generation."* They claim this is the problem with many Christians. Because of something someone did many years before, this curse is passed down to them, causing terrible problems in their lives, etc.

They are then admonished to seek out a

Preacher who understands these things, who will lay hands on them, rebuking this *"family curse,"* and then they will be free. Such teaching is totally unscriptural!

There truly are all kinds of curses on people who do not know God. But the moment a person accepts Christ, the Scripture plainly tells us, *"Christ has redeemed us from the curse of the Law, being made a curse for us"* (Gal. 3:13). It also says, *"Therefore if any man be in Christ, he is a new creation: old things are passed away; behold, all things are become new"* (II Cor. 5:17).

Now, either the Word of God tells the Truth, or it doesn't! I happen to believe that it does.

What the purveyors of this false doctrine called the *"family curse"* fail to see are the words, *"of them who hate Me."* In other words, the Scripture is speaking of generations of people who continue to hate the Lord, which means they don't serve Him. In that case, family curses can definitely pass down. But when even one member of the family comes to Christ, the deadly chain is broken.

THE CAUSE OF TROUBLE

So, why are these particular people having trouble, whatever type of trouble they might be having?

That problem is not a family curse. Their problem is that they have made something the object of their faith other than Christ and the Cross. Jesus said, *"You will know the Truth, and the Truth will make you free"* (Jn. 8:32).

Not understanding Christ and the Cross, the sin nature begins to rule such an individual, with the poor person thinking they are *"demon possessed,"* or some such like problem. So when they hear this false doctrine about the *"family curse,"* they readily and eagerly buy into such, because of the problems they constantly are having. However, even though the Preacher may be sincere who prays for them, still, believing something erroneous, and engaging in something erroneous, is not going to turn out to a successful conclusion.

Once again, let me state that which must be brought about for such a person to walk in victory. Even though the following is

NOTES

given elsewhere in this Volume, simply because of the seriousness of the situation, please allow us to give it again:

FOCUS: The focus must always be Christ as the Source.

OBJECT OF FAITH: The Cross of Christ must always be the Object of one's Faith. As Christ is the Source, the Cross is the Means by which He gives us all things (Rom. 6:3-14).

POWER SOURCE: With Christ as the Source and the Cross as the Means, the Holy Spirit will then help us mightily, bringing about all the things which only He can do (Rom. 8:1-2, 11).

RESULTS: Victory!

If every Believer in the world would adhere to this little simple formula that we've just given, their whole world would turn around, and most definitely for the better.

(3) "WHO HAD HIS DWELLING AMONG THE TOMBS; AND NO MAN COULD BIND HIM, NO, NOT WITH CHAINS."

The diagram is:

Sin and the powers of darkness will yield only to Christ and what He did at the Cross on our behalf. This rules out humanistic psychology, and anything else instituted by man in order to address this problem.

BONDAGE

The phrase, *"Who had his dwelling among the tombs,"* is meant to insinuate more than a place of abode. There was a spiritual attraction to the death represented by the *"tombs."* The man was possessed by an *"unclean spirit,"* which was the epitome of death, even while he lived. The further away from God, Who is Life, the closer to death. If one does not have Light, one has darkness! There is no in-between. The Scripture says, *"He who has the Son has life"* (I Jn. 5:12). It can also be said, *"He who has not the Son has death"*

So, this man dwelt among the tombs because every fiber of his being spoke of death! Death is the ultimate conclusion of sin!

HOW POWERFUL IS SIN?

Paul said, *"For the wages of sin is death; but the Gift of God is Eternal Life through Jesus Christ our Lord"* (Rom. 6:23).

"Death," as used here, represents eternal separation from God, Who Alone is the Source

of all Life, which results in physical death, which results in eternal death. Separation from God can be stopped and, in fact, is stopped, by the Born-Again experience (Jn. 3:3). Physical death will be stopped at the First Resurrection of Life, when every Saint of God, dead and alive, will receive a Glorified Body.

There is only one way out of this dilemma, and that is by one accepting the Lord Jesus Christ as one's Saviour, which then stops the process of death. Other than that, the spiritual death which causes separation from God, and ultimately physical death, will result in eternal death. The only hope is Jesus Christ and what He did for us at the Cross (Jn. 3:16; Rom. 6:10).

Paul also said: *"Who* (Christ) *gave Himself for our sins* (which He did on the Cross), *that He might deliver us from this present evil world* (the Cross alone can set the captive free), *according to the Will of God and our Father"* (Gal. 1:4). This is the standard of the entire process of Redemption.

When we consider that sin is so powerful that it has killed every human being that has ever been born, with the exception of Enoch and Elijah, both being translated that they should not see death, then we should understand just how powerful that sin is. It is so powerful that God had to become Man (Isa. 7:14), and go to a cruel Cross in order that the terrible sin debt be paid, and man may be loosed from these clutches of sin and death (Col. 2:14-15).

That's the reason that Paul said, *"We preach Christ crucified"* (I Cor. 1:23). Concerning a Preacher who preaches anything else, Paul said, *"Let him be accursed"* (Gal. 1:8).

HUMANITY HAS NO SOLUTION FOR SIN

The phrase, *"And no man could bind him, no, not with chains,"* speaks of the superhuman strength given to him by these demon spirits. As well, the words, *"no man,"* proclaim the fact that there was no Earthly remedy for his terrible condition. Let those words, *"no man,"* ring out in your soul! The only hope for the sinner is *"Jesus Christ and Him Crucified."*

NOTES

(4) "BECAUSE THAT HE HAD BEEN OFTEN BOUND WITH FETTERS AND CHAINS, AND THE CHAINS HAD BEEN PLUCKED ASUNDER BY HIM, AND THE FETTERS BROKEN IN PIECES: NEITHER COULD ANY MAN TAME HIM."

The composition is:

All of this enforces the great Truth that Christ and the Cross Alone are the only answer.

FETTERS AND CHAINS

The phrase, *"Because that he had been often bound with fetters and chains,"* proclaims the efforts of men to restrain him. These bindings were probably made of ropes, etc. The word *"often"* proclaims the fact that they had done this many times, but all to no avail.

To be frank, we are looking here at the extent of man's ability and effort to deliver individuals from the bondages of darkness. Concerning sin, the only answer that mankind has is to lock up the individuals (prison), if the situation becomes too bad. *"Fetters and chains"* are the only answer that man has.

Back in the early 1900's, the psychologists came up with a proposed answer to the rehabilitation of criminals. Incidentally, there is no such thing in the Bible as rehabilitation. This means there is no such thing as moral evolution. The truth is, along with the fact that it's not possible to rehabilitate anyone, so-called rehabilitation is not what one needs. One must be *"born again,"* if the cycle of sin is to be stopped (Jn. 3:3).

They claimed that if the prisoner could be put in total isolation for a period of several months, actually allowed to go outside about 30 minutes a day, and then not to mingle with other people, that the solitude would cleanse him from his desire to do wrong, whatever the wrong might be. Of course, they found out it didn't work, because, as stated, man has no answer.

THE MUZZLE

A dog that is a biter really cannot be stopped from this situation. So the only answer is to put a muzzle over the dog's mouth. While he no longer can bite, the truth is, the desire to bite is still there. That's why the alcoholic is encouraged by AA to say, *"I am a recovering alcoholic."* No! That's not the answer.

BROKEN CHAINS AND FETTERS

The phrase, *"And the chains had been plucked asunder by him, and the fetters broken in pieces,"* represents, as stated, the superhuman strength of this individual, given to him by demon spirits. In the spiritual sense, the idea is, every remedy tried by man is *"broken in pieces"* by the individuals on whom the remedy is practiced.

DRUG ADDICTION

Some years back, I happened to see a Television program regarding drug addiction and its cure. Barbara Walters hosted the program. On the program that day, the panelists consisted of: a representative from the Governor's office of the State of New York, the head of one of the largest rehabilitation centers in the nation, a psychologist, and a representative from one of the nation's youth groups which depended on the Lord.

The representative from the Governor's office claimed that the answer was more money and proper legislation. I really don't know what he meant by that.

The psychologist claimed that education was the answer. The representative from the rehab center at least was honest. He basically stated that he really didn't know what the answer was.

Ms. Walters asked the head of the rehab center about their cure-rate. His answer again was very candid, *"About one half of one percent."* And then he quickly added, *"We're not really even sure of that!"*

Ms. Walters turned to the young lady who represented the group which depended on the Lord and asked her what her *"cure-rate"* was.

The young lady said, *"Of all who come through our center, about 75 percent never return to drugs."*

Ms. Walters looked at her incredulously for a moment, and then asked, *"Do you have documentation for that?"*

"Yes, we do," the young lady quickly replied, *"and you are welcome to check it for yourself, if you so desire."*

Ms. Walters then spoke up and said, *"You mean that these people who are cured have some type of religious experience?"*

The young lady said, *"Yes, they have an experience with Jesus Christ, Who Alone can set the captive free."*

Everyone on the program sat there for a few moments and stared at the young lady. No one asked her any more questions. Here was the answer to the drug problem set before them, and they totally ignored it. For the rest of the program, Ms. Walters discussed the problem with the three men who were there, completely ignoring the young lady, even though she had the answer. If the answer had been anything other than Jesus Christ, all the air time in the world would have been given to that particular solution. But inasmuch as it was Christ, there was no interest!

God help us!

IS HUMANISTIC PSYCHOLOGY THE ANSWER?

The phrase, *"Neither could any man tame him,"* presents the conclusion then, which is also the conclusion now. In other words, this is beyond the pale of human endeavor, irrespective of its intellectual knowledge. Despite this plain statement as written by Mark, which was inspired by the Holy Spirit, man now feels he is able to do what his ancient counterparts could not do. I speak of the field of humanistic psychology.

Of course, the advocates of this philosophy would disavow their abilities in such desperate situations; however, my question would be, *"To what degree can psychology be of service?"* *"If, in his demon possession, he can break ropes which are 1/8 inch in diameter, could psychology help him then, but not if he can break ropes up to 1/4 inch in diameter?"*

I do not mean to be sarcastic, but the truth is, psychology holds no answer whatsoever, despite the fact that the modern Church has bought this humanistic line, proverbially speaking, hook, line, and sinker. Even though the following has been given elsewhere in other of our Commentaries, I personally feel that the significance of this subject demands that we repeat the information.

THE REPLACEMENT OF BIBLICAL COUNSELING

I am absolutely convinced that psychotherapy (psychological counseling) is rapidly replacing Biblical Truth, and that the whole Christian structure is being, to a great extent, subverted by this *"false religion,"* and a *"false religion"* it is!

If the Preacher knows the Bible, thereby understanding the Cross, and he Preaches the Cross as he should, that is all the Biblical counseling that is needed. Counselors, who sit in offices in Churches for hours on end, and listen to one tale of filth after the other, are not helping anyone. It might be referred to as *"Biblical counseling,"* but actually it isn't. While, at times, one-on-one counseling definitely may be needed, still, the greater thrust should come from behind the Pulpit.

This is the problem: either the Preacher is ignorant as it regards the Cross of Christ, or else, it is a matter of unbelief. In other words, he simply doesn't believe that Jesus answered every question, solved every problem, and overcame every demon spirit at the Cross (Col. 2:14-15).

Irrespective of the perversion, the aberration of the human spirit, or how bad the situation is, Jesus Christ truly answered it all at the Cross. In other words, He totally and completely atoned for all sin, which then removed Satan's right to hold man in bondage. The Scripture plainly says, *"And having spoiled principalities and powers"* (Satan and all of his henchmen were defeated at the Cross by Christ atoning for all sin; sin was the legal right Satan had to hold man in captivity; with all sin atoned, he has no more legal right to hold anyone in bondage), *He* (Christ) *made a show of them openly* (what Jesus did at the Cross was in the face of the whole universe), *triumphing over them in it"* (Col. 2:15). The triumph is complete; it was all done for us, meaning that we can walk in power and perpetual victory due to the Cross.

If the Preacher preaches the Cross, and the individual makes Christ his Saviour and His Lord, thereby placing his faith 100 percent in Christ and what Christ did at the Cross, and if what he is doing is continually reinforced by the Preacher from behind the pulpit, such a person will know total and complete victory, irrespective as to what the problem might be.

However, there are a couple of hitches in this solution. The first hitch is the Preacher who doesn't believe in the Cross, and the second hitch is the individual who desires victory over the problem, whatever the problem might be, but doesn't want to fully and wholly give their heart and life to the Lord Jesus Christ. In other words, they want to continue to sin, but just not be bothered by the bondage of sin.

PSYCHOTHERAPY AND THE PREACHING OF THE CROSS

In a recent book review in a major Pentecostal publication, a book entitled *"The Holy Spirit in Counseling"* was lauded. Here is what was said:

The authors, whom I will leave nameless, Ministers in this particular Pentecostal Denomination, examined (according to the book report) the Biblical foundations of the Holy Spirit's dynamics as Comforter in the counseling process. Both authors, during the time of writing, were professors in one of the schools in this Pentecostal Denomination. The following is a statement they made in their book:

"It is impossible to separate psychology and theology — as they relate to the counseling process. The object of counseling is a human being created in God's Image. Wholeness is achieved only when life is lived in the manner in which He intended. Therefore, it is not a question of whether therapists rely upon the Holy Spirit or upon their counseling skills. We must equip ourselves with the best tools available, while being certain that the Presence and Power of the Holy Spirit permeates our personalities."

If one is to notice, even though cleverly stated, they are saying that it doesn't really matter what one uses, the Holy Spirit or their counseling skills (psychology).

They went on to say, *"We must equip ourselves with the best tools available,"* which actually says that at times psychology is a better tool than the Holy Spirit.

Then, they tried to gloss it over by saying that while they are using the psychological tools, they must make certain *"that the Presence and Power of the Holy Spirit permeates our personalities."*

First of all, to conclude that poor, failing, perverted man has developed greater means for dealing with the human problem than the Holy Spirit is ignorance at its best, and blasphemy at its worst. How can the Holy Spirit permeate personalities who are using false methods of humanistic psychology devised mostly by agnostics and atheists? Actually, these two men do not believe that what Jesus did at the Cross is sufficient. They believe that it has to have help, and the help they are suggesting is humanistic psychology.

What did the Holy Spirit through Peter say:

"According as His Divine Power has given unto us all things (the Lord, with large-handed generosity, has given us all things) *that pertain unto Life and Godliness* (pertains to the fact that the Lord Jesus has given us everything we need regarding life and living), *through the knowledge of Him Who has called us to Glory and Virtue* (the *'knowledge'* addressed here speaks of what Christ did at the Cross, which alone can provide *'Glory and Virtue'*):

"Whereby are given unto us exceeding great and Precious Promises (pertains to the Word of God, which alone holds the answer to every one of life's problems): *that by these* (Promises) *you might be partakers of the Divine Nature* (the Divine Nature implanted in the inner being of the believing sinner becomes the source of our new life and action; it comes to everyone at the moment of being *'born again'*), *having escaped the corruption that is in the world through lust* (this presents the Salvation experience of the sinner, and the Sanctification experience of the Saint)" (II Pet. 1:3-4).

Now, either what Peter said is the Truth and we should abide by that Truth, thereby receiving its glorious benefits, or else it isn't the truth and we should buy the book written by these two individuals, whoever they might be.

WHAT IS PSYCHOLOGY?

The primary Greek word, *"psyche,"* is the root from which we derive the English terms, *"psychology"* and *"psychologist."* Interestingly, the word *"psyche"* is utilized in the New Testament for *"soul."* Hence, a psychologist is a *"worker with souls,"* that is, if the true meaning of the word is maintained. However, the foundation of psychological teaching does

NOTES

not even believe that man has a soul.

Consequently, a specific distinction should be made. The secular psychotherapist considers himself a worker with *"minds,"* while the (so-called) *"Christian"* psychologist considers himself a worker with *"souls."* Most Bible Colleges and Seminaries offer at least some basic introduction to psychology for their would-be Preachers of the Gospel. Thus, a foundation is laid for a subtle deflection away from the Bible and toward psychotherapy.

Actually, I suspect that the psychology offerings in most Bible Colleges and Seminaries do far more than offer a basic introduction to psychology. A short time ago, I happened to pick up a catalog advertising the course offerings of a long list of Bible Colleges and Seminaries. Almost all of the subjects were in the field of psychology, or at least leaned in that direction. So, I feel that the subtle deflection away from the Bible and toward psychotherapy has turned into something that is not so subtle after all. It could be better described as a wholesale rout.

Consequently, the Preachers graduating from these schools come away with little knowledge of the Bible, if any, but steeped in the new *"psychological way"*; therefore, those who sit under their charge have the terrible misfortune of being led astray. It has even today been suggested that if a person has only Bible knowledge (and this comes from Bible Colleges and Seminaries), he is ill-equipped to handle the pressing problems of humanity. He must (they say) be grounded also in psychology to meet *"human needs."* This is implanted early, with the unspoken implication that the Bible in itself is insufficient to solve human problems.

PROFESSIONAL HELP

As well, it is constantly being suggested that Ministers are ill-prepared and ill-equipped to meet the needs of modern man. If the Preacher is to be truly effective and proficient in his role, they say, he should be referring a large percentage of those who seek his help to *"professionals."* *"Professionals"* or *"therapy"* used within this context means, of course, psychologists or psychotherapy.

Sometime back, I received a letter from a *"Christian psychologist"* telling about his wife, who once had serious problems. He said, *"We needed competent Christian mental health care. We couldn't find it in the Church; people didn't understand her emotional problems. We couldn't find it in the world; mental health professionals didn't understand our Faith."*

He went on to say that psychotherapy combined with the Holy Spirit gave her the victory. But regrettably, time was to prove that was not the case.

Now, I don't know exactly what he meant when he said, *"We couldn't find it in the Church."* Perhaps he was speaking of a specific Church they attended or a particular Pastor — which is certainly understandable. But if he was speaking of *"The Church,"* meaning the Body of Christ and the Work of the Holy Spirit within the Church, he was, in effect, saying that the Bible does not hold the answer to human problems, and that we must look outside of the Word of God for help.

At the very least, it would seem that his statement (as the two authors' statements) suggests that we must combine the Work of the Holy Spirit with secular psychotherapy. The end-product of this growing dependence on *"scientific"* compromises is that:

• Psychotherapy has been widely accepted as *"scientific"* and, therefore, must be a useful tool. As a consequence, it has become accepted within Pentecostal and Charismatic fellowships and, in fact, most all Church Denominations.

• Most Pentecostal Bible Colleges and Seminaries now promote psychotherapy as a legitimate tool for meeting *"the human need."*

• As a result, most of our younger Preachers are now convinced that psychotherapy is *"spiritually neutral."* It is, therefore, a legitimate tool to be employed with a clear conscience when trying to help humanity.

• The old-fashioned, tried-and-true Word of Almighty God is given lesser and lesser place when considering methods for solving man's problems, if any place at all!

COUNSELING?

The other day I spoke with a professor who has many years of experience teaching in Pentecostal Bible Colleges. I asked him why homiletics (the preparation of sermons) is seldom taught any more in Bible Colleges. His answer shocked me! He said, *"Most are no longer looking to preaching as a means of meeting humanity's needs. Counseling has now become the express way for help in this area."*

Once again, the truth is, in the last several decades the Church has been pushed so far away from the Cross, that anymore it is left with no power to address these problems of life.

Paul said, *"For the Preaching of the Cross is to them who perish foolishness; but unto us who are saved it is the Power of God"* (I Cor. 1:18).

If the Preacher is not preaching the Cross, then he's preaching a gospel which has no power. That's what Paul referred to as *"another Jesus, another spirit, and another gospel"* (II Cor. 11:4). So, that particular type of preaching is not really going to help very much at all. However, if the Preacher will preach the Cross, understanding that Jesus met every need at the Cross, answered every question, atoned for all sin, and provided every solution, the people's needs, irrespective as to how bad they might be, can be met (Rom. 6:3-14).

IS PSYCHOTHERAPY TRULY SCIENTIFIC AND, THEREFORE, NEUTRAL?

Proponents of psychotherapy call it scientific and camouflage its discrepancies with scientific jargon and medical terminology; however, the questions must be asked: Is psychotherapy a science or a superstition? Is it fact or fabrication?

These questions must be asked, because we have come to venerate almost anything labeled as *"science."* If, indeed, psychology and psychotherapy are scientific, they should command our respect and be used within every community. However, if they are not, we have valid grounds for questioning the propriety of intruding them into the Preachers' methodology.

In Martin and Deidre Bobgan's book, *"The Psychological Way/The Spiritual Way,"* they state, on page 44:

"In attempting to evaluate the status of psychology, the American Psychological

Association appointed Sigmund Koch to plan and direct a study which was subsidized by the National Science Foundation. This study involved 80 eminent scholars in assessing the facts, theories, and methods of psychology. The results of this extensive endeavor were then published in a seven-volume series entitled 'Psychology: A Study Of A Science.'

"After examining the results, Koch concluded, 'I think it is, by this time, utterly and finally clear, that psychology cannot be a coherent science.' He further declares that 'such activities as perception, motivation, social psychology, psycho-pathology, and creativity cannot be properly labeled science.'

"E. Fuller Torrey says, 'The medical model of human behavior, when carried to its logical conclusion, is both nonsensical and nonfunctional. It doesn't answer the questions asked. It doesn't provide good service, and it leads to a stream of absurdities worthy of a Roman Circus.'"

A PERSONAL EXPERIENCE

Picking up on the statement made by Dr. Torrey, *"It leads to a stream of absurdities worthy of a Roman Circus,"* I was interviewed once (quite extensively, lasting several days) by a writer for Life Magazine. During the course of the interviews, I happened to ask the interviewer what her next assignment was. She laughed and said, *"I'm going to California, and I'm going to write a story on the latest psychological method."*

So, I asked her what the latest psychological method was, and she laughed again, stating, *"All the people in the group pull off all their clothes, and they sit around in a circle, and close their eyes."* She then said, *"They then begin to gently pinch the one sitting beside them, feeling of them, all the while with their eyes closed."*

"How is this supposed to help anyone?" I asked.

She laughed again, and said, *"I don't know, but they say this is the newest psychological craze, and it's helping people in a grand way."*

Yes, *"It leads to a stream of absurdities worthy of a Roman Circus."*

It helps no one, as should be obvious, but, without God, people come up with stupid conclusions.

While that's bad enough, it's worse yet when the Church buys into this stupidity. The Church may claim that they do not indulge in such absurdities, but I remind the Church, and I speak of the Church as a whole, that this *"absurdity"* we've just mentioned comes from the same minds, producing the same stuff, that the Church is, in fact, accepting.

The Lord through Jeremiah said, *"For My people have committed two evils; they have forsaken Me, the Fountain of Living Waters, and hewed them out cisterns, broken cisterns, that can hold no water"* (Jer. 2:13).

William Kirk Kilpatrick says, *"True Christianity does not mix well with psychology. When you try to mix them, you end up with a watered-down Christianity instead of a Christianized psychology."*

"But the process is subtle," he went on to say, *"and is rarely noticed. It is not a frontal attack on Christianity. It is not even a case of the wolf at the door. Actually, the wolf is already in the fold, dressed in sheep's clothing. From the way it was petted and fed by some of the shepherds, one would think it was a prized sheep."*

Jacob Needleman says, *"Modern psychiatry arose out of the vision that man must change himself and not depend for help on an imaginary God. Over half a century ago (mainly through the insights of Freud and through the energies of those he influenced), the human psyche was wrested from the faltering hands of organized religion and was situated in the world of nature as a subject for scientific study."*

Incidentally, Freud opened his office in Vienna, the first devoted to psychotherapy, at about the turn of the Twentieth Century. Martin Gross, in his book, *"The Psychological Society,"* says:

"When educated man lost faith in formal religion, he required a substitute belief that would be as reputable in the last half of the twentieth century as Christianity was in the first. Psychology and psychiatry have now assumed that special role."

WHAT IS THE ORIGINATION OF PSYCHOLOGY?

Modern-day psychotherapy has its roots

in atheism, evolution, and humanism. Psychology pretends to have a cure for troubled souls. It is taught in atheistic universities, oftentimes by atheistic professors. And this same subject, with the same foundations and influences, is accepted today as an integral part of Christian curriculum in most Bible Colleges and Seminaries. There aren't two kinds of psychotherapy. There is only one. And as Paul Witz says, *"It is deeply anti-Christian."*

Someone else said, *"America's problem is not ignorance; America's problem is that she accepts a lie."*

One might say that the Church has done the same!

The problems with our Preachers once may have been ignorance, but this is no longer the case. The Lord has raised up this Ministry (Jimmy Swaggart Ministries), as well as others, I'm sure, to preach the Gospel of Jesus Christ, in effect, to *"preach the Cross"* (I Cor. 1:17-18, 21, 23; 2:2).

As I've already mentioned, when the Lord first began to open up to me the great Revelation of the Cross, which by no means is new, but actually is that which was originally given to the Apostle Paul (Gal, Chpt. 1), knowing how far the Church has drifted from this all-important teaching, I at first thought the reason for the delving into psychology was because of Scriptural ignorance.

While, of course, due to the Cross being so little preached, ignorance was, and is, rampant; however, after preaching this great subject for a number of years over our Radio Network and over Television, I've had to come to the conclusion that the problem is more *"unbelief"* than anything else. In other words, the same problem that plagued Judah when Jeremiah was prophesying to this beleaguered people is the same problem that plagues the modern Church. As Judah wouldn't believe the preaching and prophesying of Jeremiah, likewise, the modern Church little believes the Message of the Cross presently.

I know, beyond the shadow of a doubt, that what Jesus did at the Cross is the answer and, in fact, the only answer, to the human problem. I know that if the Cross is preached, not only as Salvation for the soul,

NOTES

but also Sanctification for the Saint, the need will be met, that is, if the individual in question, whoever that might be, desires to truly follow Christ.

I maintain that psychotherapy is not scientific, that it is not even an *"art,"* as claimed. It is a lie, pure and simple, and has no basis in scientific or Biblical fact. Actually, psychology is a past master at cataloging symptoms, and because it is so very good at this particular aspect, many believe it knows the cause and the cure. However, it doesn't.

Let me say it again:

Psychology has no clue as to the cause of man's problem, and it certainly has no clue as to the cure. While it can tell you readily as to why Pavlov's dog does what he does, that's as far as it can go. In one way or the other, the cause is sin, whether directly or indirectly. The cure is Jesus Christ and Him Crucified.

Consequently, when Seminaries teach psychology, they are teaching a lie. When would-be preachers immerse themselves in psychology, they immerse themselves in falsehood. When individuals accept a doctorate in this nefarious shamanism, they are receiving a certificate without any scientific validity.

I say that Preachers of the Gospel attempting to meld psychotherapy with the Word of God will help no one. They will deliver only confusion. People will be led away from the true aid available through the Word of God.

The two, psychology and the Gospel of Jesus Christ, are as different and antagonistic as oil and water.

WHAT IS THE BIBLICAL SYSTEM FOR HELP?

Our Lord said:

"Come unto Me, all ye who labor and are heavy laden, and I will give you rest.

"Take My yoke upon you, and learn of Me; for I am meek and lowly in heart: and you shall find rest unto your souls.

"For My yoke is easy, and My burden is light" (Mat. 11:28-30).

When it was suggested that modern-day psychology is not found in the Bible, one Preacher, evidently trying to defend psychology, stated that neither is the automobile, the airplane, or the computer. *"We do not,"* he reasoned, *"resist utilization of these tools in our lives, so why should we resist the tool of psychology, or any other self-help method or technique?"*

My answer is this:

Admittedly, the Bible has nothing to say about the automobile, computer, airplane, or a host of other crafts developed since it was written. However, the Bible does not claim to be a handbook on engineering, science, or whatever, because these extraneous subjects are not man's problems. Man can be an expert scientist, a qualified engineer, or a host of other things, and still be a moral and spiritual wreck. (Let it quickly be said, however, that whatever the Bible does say regarding science, etc., is right in every respect.)

But the Bible does claim to be a handbook on *"the human condition"* — and does come right out and claim to hold all the answers to this particular human area (II Pet. 1:3-4).

Let me say it again:

The Biblical method for help is for the individual in need to be pointed strictly to Christ and what Christ did at the Cross. Such a Believer is enjoined to have Faith in Christ and what Christ has done for us, and that *"Jesus Christ and Him Crucified"* ever be made the Object of his Faith. Jesus said that one's Faith in the Cross must be renewed even on a daily basis (Lk. 9:23).

If the Believer will simply believe that what Christ did at the Cross guarantees victory over the world, the flesh, and the Devil, and continues to believe such, never allowing his Faith to be moved from the Cross to other things, the Bible emphatically states, *"Sin shall not have dominion over you"* (Rom. 6:14).

IS SUCH VICTORY INSTANT OR GRADUAL?

It is both!

In fact, every single Believer has already been delivered and in totality, as it regards any and every problem of the flesh. In other words, total victory over the sin nature is ours, and in every capacity, due to what Christ has already done at the Cross. I remind the Reader that this great victory is a *"Finished Work"* (Jn. 19:30). This great *"Finished Work"* is not partially done, but is totally done. Nothing has to be added, because nothing can be added. That's why Paul referred to this as *"The Everlasting Covenant"* (Heb. 13:20).

And yet, I think one can say, and not be contradicted, that this great Victory is also a gradual process. Let me give you the perfect example from the Word of God.

THE DELIVERANCE OF THE CHILDREN OF ISRAEL

When the Lord called Moses to deliver the Children of Israel out of Egyptian bondage, it was a task, as would be obvious, so far beyond the capabilities of a mere human being, that it beggared description. How in the world could one man deliver nearly three million Israelites out of the clutches of the most powerful nation on Earth? Well, of course, no human being, or any number of human beings, could have accomplished this task. But it was God Who would provide the Power (Ex., Chpt. 3).

When Moses and Aaron went into Egypt, the Lord told Moses exactly as to what was to be said to Pharaoh, who, incidentally, was a type of Satan. The words were: *"Thus saith the LORD God of Israel, Let My people go, that they may hold a feast unto Me in the wilderness"* (Ex. 5:1).

Even though the Lord spoke through Moses and would back it up with great power, even as the Book of Exodus proclaims, still, Pharaoh did not buckle quickly. In fact, some seven times Moses stood before Pharaoh, with Aaron delivering the message, *"Let My people go."*

LET MY PEOPLE GO

This tells us that Satan doesn't give up easily or quickly.

This means that he probably will not give up on you very quickly either. Irrespective that the Lord has proclaimed your spiritual freedom, exactly as He did for the Children of Israel, still, Moses and Aaron had to keep believing and had to keep demanding. You and I will find that the same order is upon us as well.

Don't think that just because you've read the Message of the Cross and you have embraced it, knowing in your heart it is right, that Satan is suddenly going to fold his tent and leave. He's not going to do that! He's going to test your metal, so to speak, and the Lord is going to allow him to have a certain degree of latitude, all to see whether you mean business or not!

INCREASED PRESSURE

Instead of letting the Children of Israel go, Pharaoh instead doubled their work load. Whereas heretofore they were commanded to make so many bricks, with the ingredients provided, now they will have to provide the ingredients (the straw) themselves, but the number of bricks must not be diminished. This tells us that once you as a Believer embrace Christ and the Cross, and do so without reservation, Satan may very well intensity his efforts. Your thoughts will be, *"If the Cross is the right way, why has my situation become worse instead of better?"*

As it happened to the Children of Israel, it probably also will happen to you. Instead of the temptation becoming less and even going away entirely, it will increase in intensity.

But let us say it again:

The Lord allows this, all in order to test our Faith.

FAITH

Never forget, the entire scenario of living for God is all wrapped up in the one word *"Faith"* (Rom. 4:5, 12-14, 16; 5:1-2). Faith must be tested, and great Faith must be tested greatly.

FRIENDS TURNED AGAINST MOSES AND AARON

When the task of the Children of Israel became even harder, they then began to blame Moses and Aaron for their predicament (Ex. 5:19-23). Whenever you, as a Believer, begin to embrace the Cross, and to do so unabashedly, unreservedly, and unequivocally, don't be surprised if some of your close friends, and even your family, turn against you.

Concerning this, Paul said, *"And I, Brethren, if I yet preached circumcision, why do I yet suffer persecution?"* (any message other than the Cross draws little opposition) *then is the offense of the Cross ceased* (the Cross offends the world and most of the Church. So if the Preacher ceases to preach the Cross as the only way of Salvation and Victory, then opposition and persecution will, by and large, cease. But so will Salvation and Victory!)" (Gal. 5:11).

So here we have the triple efforts of Satan:

1. Pharaoh didn't obey instantly, and neither will Satan, of which Pharaoh was a type.

2. As Pharaoh increased the pressure when the demand was made that Israel be released, likewise, Satan is going to increase the pressure on you.

3. As Moses' own people began to turn against him, likewise, your own family and friends may do the same with you.

As a Believer, you must expect all three things to happen, once you embark upon this great road of Faith, as it respects Jesus Christ and what He has done for us at the Cross.

So, victory is instantaneous and, at the same time, as stated, it is a gradual process. However, if you do not allow Satan to push you off this path of the Cross, the day will come when victory will be yours as you've never previously known, and a victory which will be so much broader than you now can comprehend.

IS THERE SUCH A THING AS A CHRISTIAN PSYCHOLOGIST?

No! The term is misleading. It insinuates that the type of psychology offered by these who called themselves *"Christian psychologists"* is different than that offered by their worldly counterparts. However, there is only one type of psychology, which is taught by all, Christian or non-Christian. There may be Christians who are psychologists, but, in the true sense of the word, there is no such thing as a *"Christian psychologist."*

If we have Christian psychology, why not have Christian medicine, Christian physics, or Christian biochemistry? Of course, the reason we don't have these things is that such things don't exist in real-life terms. Medicine is the same for Christians as for non-Christians. Chemistry is the same for the Christian or the non-Christian, etc.

However, some educators who are Christians have attempted to take an ungodly, atheistic, anti-Christian, immoral, unbiblical, worldly system called psychology and integrate it into Biblical counseling. It cannot be done!

CAN A PSYCHOLOGIST HELP PEOPLE IF HE LOVES GOD AND HAS A TRUE DESIRE TO BE OF SERVICE?

While we do not demean the motivation of anyone, still, we must say, and do so as strongly as possible, there is no help for anyone in this capacity outside of the Bible. And as we've already stated, you cannot mix the Bible and psychology. The two are totally antagonistic to each other. The only way that individuals can be helped is for those trying to help them to renounce all psychological training and turn instead to the Word of God as the sole source and guide. To do otherwise is to try to mix light with darkness. It cannot be done.

The Scripture asks us this question, *"And what concord has Christ with Belial? Or what part has he who believes with an infidel?"* (II Cor. 6:15).

IS THE PREACHER OF THE GOSPEL QUALIFIED TO DEAL WITH THE PROBLEMS OF MANKIND?

If the Preacher of the Gospel is thoroughly grounded in the Word of God, which means that he understands that Christ is the Source of all things and that the Cross is the means, and preaches that accordingly, in fact, he is the only one who is capable of meeting these particular needs. Perhaps it would be better said that we point to the One Who Alone can meet the needs, and we speak of the Lord Jesus Christ and what He did for us at the Cross.

In fact, the true Preacher, or any Believer for that matter, is a *"way-shower."* That's about the best that can be said for true Preachers. There is only one *"Way,"* and that is the Lord Jesus Christ. He said, *"I am the Way, the Truth, and the Life, and no man comes to the Father, but by Me"* (Jn. 14:6). I realize it is being grandly suggested today that the Preacher of the Gospel is not qualified to address the *"human condition."* He has not, they say, been specifically educated and trained in these areas. But the fact is, the so-called professionals in the field of *"the cure of the soul"* are actually the ones who are unqualified to help the individual in need.

Now, of course, this would be ludicrous to the world, and, sadly, it is ludicrous to much of the modern Church. *"Don't they have a Master's or a Doctor's degree in Counseling or Psychotherapy?"* Still, I am stating that these individuals who are trained in the wisdom of the world are not qualified to help the individual. They hold certificates in a system that is grounded in atheism and humanism. As such, the whole system has no basis in truth and has no inherent qualification for addressing itself to *"the cure of the soul."*

Again, Paul said, *"For after that in the wisdom of God the world by wisdom knew not God, it pleased God by the foolishness of preaching* (preaching the Cross) *to save them who believe."* Paul is not dealing here with the art of preaching, but with what is preached.

He then said, *"But unto them which are called, both Jews and Greeks, Christ the Power of God, and the wisdom of God"* (this Wisdom devised a Plan of Salvation which pardoned guilty men and, at the same time, vindicated and glorified the Justice of God, which stands out as the wisest and most remarkable Plan of all time [I Cor. 1:21, 24]).

He then said, *"That no flesh* (human effort) *should glory in His Presence"* (I Cor. 1:29). In fact, the entirety of the First Chapter of I Corinthians proclaims the fact that all the wisdom of this world cannot address the problems of mankind. Instead, the Holy Spirit through Paul very succinctly claims that the Cross of Christ has met every need (I Cor. 1:17-18, 23).

In closing this statement on humanistic psychology, Paul also said, *"Beware lest any man spoil you through philosophy and vain deceit, after the tradition of men, after the rudiments of the world, and not after Christ.*

"For in Him dwells all the fullness of the Godhead bodily.

"And you are complete in Him, which is the Head of all principality and power" (Col. 2:8-10).

Consequently, the words given by the Holy Spirit to Mark, *"neither could any man tame him,"* still hold true today. However, Jesus Christ, as exampled here, can tame this individual, as well as all who are brought to Him.

(5) "AND ALWAYS, NIGHT AND DAY, HE WAS IN THE MOUNTAINS, AND IN THE TOMBS, CRYING, AND CUTTING HIMSELF

WITH STONES."

The diagram is:

This is a symbolic picture, which takes place in the spiritual, in one way or the other, to one degree or the other, with all unredeemed. There is no peace for those who do not know the Lord.

CONSTANT MISERY

The phrase, *"And always, night and day,"* proclaims the constant misery which never ends, as a result of the demon possession. This is one of the reasons for the some twenty million alcoholics in the United States, as well as approximately thirty million drug addicts. There are about twenty million who are hooked on prescription drugs, and about ten million on street drugs. However, the bondage is the same in either case. During the day or during the night, the misery never stops.

Of course, every unredeemed person doesn't fall into the category of the maniac of Gadara; however, in some way, all of the symptoms of this extreme case are prevalent in all who are unredeemed. The word *"always"* is an apt description.

THE DILEMMA OF THE UNREDEEMED

The phrase, *"He was in the mountains, and in the tombs, crying and cutting himself with stones,"* referred to the shrieks that must have pierced the air, especially at night. Jesus said, *"The thief comes not, but for to steal, to kill, and to destroy"* (Jn. 10:10). Whatever Satan promises, the *"stealing, killing, and destroying"* is what he actually gives, and all that he gives. While this madman of Gadara is, as is obvious, the extreme, still, this is the end result of Satan's handiwork.

Let every person read this account: All who do not know Jesus are, without exception, bending toward the terrible condition of the maniac of Gadara. While most who are unsaved would violently disagree with my statement, still, there are traits in the unsaved, and in all of them, that more or less bend toward this horrid situation. As well, as each day passes, all unredeemed get a little closer to total destruction.

There is only one answer for this terrible dilemma, and that is Jesus Christ and Him Crucified. If there is any reason that this Ministry (Jimmy Swaggart Ministries) is so important, it's certainly not because of me or any of my associates. It is the Message that we preach, the Message of the Cross. It alone will set the captive free.

(6) "BUT WHEN HE SAW JESUS AFAR OFF, HE RAN AND WORSHIPPED HIM."

The composition is:

The demon spirit worshipped Him; all demon spirits and Satan himself are made to pay homage to God the Son; Satan and all of his minions were defeated at the Cross (Col. 2:14-15).

JESUS

The phrase, *"But when he saw Jesus afar off,"* is not meant to insinuate that he recognized Christ at that distance, but that the demons within the man thought he was another intruder; therefore, they would take action! Little did they realize that they were about to meet One Who was totally unlike any other they had ever seen. They were about to come into the presence of the Creator of the ages.

Due to the fact that this was an isolated region, they thought they were safe. They were to find out differently, for Jesus would come all the way across the lake, would come to this deserted place, just to deliver one man. This is symbolic of what Christ did in coming down here from Heaven to this soiled, polluted, demon-possessed planet. But thank God He came!

Never before in history has it been made possible for the Gospel to go to the isolated regions of the world, as it is now. I speak of Television. Knowing this, Satan has taken full advantage of the opportunity to fill the airways with that which looks like the Gospel, and which, in some cases, sounds like the Gospel, but, in reality, is not the Gospel. Therefore, despite the bluster and blow, those particular gospels, whatever they might be, will deliver no one. There is only one Message that will set the captive free, and that is, even as we have repeatedly stated, *"Jesus Christ and Him Crucified"* (I Cor. 1:23).

This is the very reason that Paul, to those who preached *"another gospel,"* said, *"But though we, or an Angel from Heaven, preach any other gospel unto you than that which we have preached unto you, let him be accursed"* (Gal. 1:8). Unfortunately, the far greater majority of that which goes under the guise of the Gospel, and I continue to speak of Television, is, in fact, not the Gospel, but something else entirely.

HOW CAN I BE SO CERTAIN THAT IT IS NOT THE GOSPEL?

The recognition is very simple! If they aren't preaching the Cross, then it's not the Gospel. As stated, it may contain some things that are true, but if the Cross is not preached, then it's not the Gospel. That's why Paul said *"that if you be Circumcised* (rely on anything other than Christ and the Cross), *Christ shall profit you nothing"* (Gal. 5:2).

Please understand: To *"preach the Cross"* means more than a casual mention once in a while. In fact, if one properly understands the Cross, and properly preaches the Cross, it will be the whole of all of the doctrine that one espouses. That means they won't be subscribing to the *"Purpose Driven Life,"* the *"Government of Twelve,"* or the *"Word of Faith,"* etc. It means they won't be looking to their Denomination either, nor to their own good works, etc. Their faith must be 100 percent in Christ and what Christ did at the Cross, adding nothing to that Message, nor taking anything from it.

As we've already said in this Volume, the Preacher mentioning the Cross once in a while doesn't mean that he is preaching the Cross. Millions admit that Jesus died for them, and I'm speaking of Christians, even Preachers, but they relegate the Cross to their Salvation experience only, and then place their faith in something else, as it regards our everyday living for God. In other words, they don't understand at all what it means to live a sanctified life by virtue of Faith in Christ and the Cross, which then gives the Holy Spirit latitude to work within our lives. Satan, therefore, has filled the Television airways with a message, as stated, which looks right, and which, in many cases, sounds right, but which, in reality, isn't right.

Let me give you another example:

Despite more gospel television, so-called, being aired than ever before, and all over the world, there are fewer people presently being saved than at any time since the Reformation, and also fewer Believers being baptized with the Holy Spirit. Oh, yes, gigantic numbers are thrown around, about hundreds of thousands and millions being saved, but precious few are truly being saved presently. Most Preachers have learned the art of *"hype,"* especially those on Television, a system which is borrowed from the world.

A PERSONAL EXAMPLE

There was a Preacher in my office, just the other day. He was a man I really did not know, but he was from a particular country where our Ministry was somewhat known. While talking to me, he made mention of a particular Preacher, who was then in Africa conducting meetings. He went on to say that this man had had over a million people saved in the last 30 days.

I did not take issue with him, inasmuch as he was a guest. However, I knew the Preacher of whom he spoke. There may have been a few people saved in his meetings, and, if so, I thank God for that; however, I also knew that the gigantic figures being given out were *"hype."* In other words, they were not true.

The man in question doesn't preach the Cross and, in fact, knows very little about the Cross. So the gospel he preaches says some good things and is partially Biblical, but that's the problem. It is only partially Biblical. And so is the gospel of most Preachers. The only Message that will truly set the captive free is the Message of Jesus Christ and what He did for us at the Cross. In total, that is the Gospel (Rom. 6:3-14; 8:1-2, 11; Gal. 6:14; I Cor. 1:17-18, 21, 23; 2:2; Eph. 2:13-18; Col. 2:14-15).

WORSHIP

The phrase, *"He ran and worshipped Him,"* refers to the man drawing closer, with Jesus evidencing the Spiritual Power and Grace that always pervaded the personality of the Son of God, which quieted the man's spirit and caused him to fall on his knees in reverence.

The word *"worship"* is here used of homage shown to men of superior rank or of homage shown to God. Here it speaks of homage to God, the act of worship, for the demon recognizes our Lord as the Son of God. Here we have a being, incorrigible in his nature, destined to be damned for all eternity, one of the cohorts of Satan, bending the knee to God the Son.

This is what Paul was speaking of when he referred to the universal adoration of the Lord Jesus, even by beings *"under the Earth"* (Phil. 2:10). They are even now bending the knee to the Son of God. Actually, it was not just the man who was prostrating himself before the Lord Jesus. He was under the control of the demon, and the latter was the source of the homage paid to the Son of God (Wuest).

It should be quickly added that even though demon spirits worship the Lord, most of the human family does not have sense enough to do so. Even most of the Church little worships Him! However, as we have stated, the type of worship here enjoined was not *"in Spirit and Truth,"* but rather a worship of deference or homage, as one would pay to a superior being.

(7) "AND CRIED WITH A LOUD VOICE, AND SAID, WHAT HAVE I TO DO WITH YOU, JESUS, THOU SON OF THE MOST HIGH GOD? I ADJURE YOU BY GOD, THAT YOU TORMENT ME NOT."

The diagram is:

This refers to the evil spirit knowing exactly Who Jesus was! A certain time has been appointed by God to which these spirits will be confined to the pit (Rev. 20:1-3).

JESUS, THE SON OF THE MOST HIGH GOD

The question, *"And cried with a loud voice, and said, What have I to do with You, Jesus, Thou Son of the Most High God?"* refers to the demon spirit using the vocal cords of the man, thus speaking to Christ. This evil spirit knew exactly Who Jesus was! Some have suggested that Satan in the wilderness temptation used the exclamation, *"If You are the Son of God . . ."* meaning that he was not quite sure respecting the status of Christ; however, that is incorrect. The translation should read, *"Since You are the Son of God. . . ."* Satan knew, at that time, exactly Who Jesus actually was, and addressed Him accordingly.

NOTES

To be sure, Satan, every fallen angel, and every demon spirit all know exactly Who and What Jesus is. There is absolutely no doubt about that. So, if Satan and all of his cohorts know Who Jesus is, why is it that the majority of the human race doesn't know? The answer is unbelief!

UNBELIEF

Unbelief, as it refers to the Lord, always carries with it the spirit of deception. Paul said: *"Now the Spirit speaks expressly, that in the latter times some shall depart from the Faith, giving heed to seducing spirits, and doctrines of Devils"* (I Tim. 4:1). *"Seducing spirits"* have been on the Earth from the very beginning, all due to the Fall in the Garden of Eden. However, at this particular time, and we speak of the last of the last days, the time which Paul addressed, the activity of these *"seducing spirits"* is predicted to be far more involved. They are promoting *"doctrines of devils,"* but yet doctrines which seem to be right and, in fact, which may even contain some truth.

Spirits of seduction do not stop a person from thinking, but rather cause them to think incorrectly. In other words, there is a power behind what is taking place, i.e., in this case, spiritual seduction. That power is demon spirits. An individual can be delivered from this terrible spirit of unbelief, but it's not easy.

Very few are delivered, because very few will push past the erroneous thinking, thereby giving the Holy Spirit an opportunity to work in their lives. To be frank, there is only one Power on the face of the Earth that is stronger than these spirits of seduction, i.e., *"the Law of Sin and Death,"* and that is *"the Law of the Spirit of Life in Christ Jesus"* (Rom. 8:2).

This particular *"Law"* has to do with the Cross of Christ, and actually demands that the person anchor their faith in Christ and the Cross. Only then can the Holy Spirit set that person free. Considering the paucity of teaching and preaching as it regards the Cross of Christ, it quickly becomes obvious as to the reason that not many people are delivered from the terrible position of unbelief.

TORMENTING SATAN

The phrase, *"I adjure Thee by God, that*

You torment me not," presents this demon spirit as attempting to put Jesus under oath. Matthew uses the phrase, *"To torment us before the time,"* meaning that a certain time has been appointed by God to which these spirits will be confined to the pit, which is without doubt described in Revelation 20:1-3 (Mat. 8:29).

As severe as the misery may be at present for these spirits of darkness, still, it is nothing compared to what they will yet suffer. At the present, they are allowed to wander about and find their depraved pleasure in tempting men. If possible, they may at last drag them with them into the abyss. For they are full of hatred of God and envy of man; and they find a miserable satisfaction in endeavoring to keep men out of those Heavenly mansions from which they are themselves, through pride, forever excluded.

(8) "FOR HE SAID UNTO HIM, COME OUT OF THE MAN, THOU UNCLEAN SPIRIT."

The overview is:

This constitutes a direct order, which the unclean spirit must obey.

THE UNCLEAN SPIRIT

The phrase, *"For He said unto him,"* could have been translated, *"For He had been saying...."* The phrase, *"Come out of the man, thou unclean spirit,"* constituted a direct order which the spirit knew he must obey! If there is sin involved, demon spirits are involved somewhere along the way, or else will ultimately become involved.

This is one of the reasons that humanistic psychology cannot even begin to hope to address these problems. In fact, as we have previously stated, man has no solution, at least within himself. It takes the Power of God to set the captive free, and only the Power of God can set the captive free. Tragically, most of the modern Church doesn't even believe in the Power of God.

Satan hates the Cross, because it was at the Cross where he and all his minions of darkness were totally and completely defeated (Col. 2:14-15; Rom. 6:3-14).

WALKING AFTER THE FLESH

If the Christian doesn't understand the Cross as it regards Sanctification, such a Christian, without fail, is going to *"walk after the flesh"* (Rom. 8:1). And what does it mean to walk after the flesh? As Paul uses the word *"flesh,"* the Holy Spirit through him is speaking of the power, strength, and ability of the human being. It is referred to as *"the flesh."*

Whatever type of power and ability that a man or woman may have, it is not strong enough, not even nearly strong enough, to defeat the powers of darkness. So, *"walking after the flesh"* constitutes the Believer placing his faith in something other than the Cross of Christ. It really doesn't make much difference what the other is. In fact, most of the time the things in which one places one's faith are very spiritual in their own right. And that's what confuses the Christian. Most of the things he does are *"good,"* so he cannot understand why that does not give him victory.

Let's say it another way:

Suppose the Believer is fasting one day each week, praying 30 minutes a day, and reading three chapters a day in his Bible, which, within themselves are very, very good for any and all Believers to do. However, if he does those things, but he doesn't understand the Cross, his faith will be placed in the doing of these things. Even though he will be blessed, the Holy Spirit, because of his misplaced faith, won't help such a person in the realm of sin; such an individual, despite his diligence and consecration, will find himself failing and not understanding why.

This is what Paul was talking about when he said, *"For that which I do* (the failure) *I allow not* (should have been translated, *"I understand not"*): *for what I would, that do I not* (refers to the obedience he wants to render to Christ, but rather fails. Why? As Paul explained, the Believer is married to Christ, but is being unfaithful to Christ by spiritually cohabiting with the Law, which frustrates the Grace of God; that means the Holy Spirit, as stated, will not help such a person, which guarantees failure [Gal. 2:21]); *but what I hate, that do I* (refers to sin in his life, which he doesn't want to do and, in fact, hates, but finds himself unable to stop; unfortunately, due to the fact of not understanding the Cross as it refers to Sanctification, this is the plight of most modern Christians [Rom. 7:15]).

If most Christians were asked as to the meaning of *"walking after the flesh,"* they would think that it meant watching too much Television, or going fishing too often, etc. No! That's not walking after the flesh. *"Walking after the flesh"* is one placing one's faith in something other than the Cross, which means they are depending on their own strength, ability, and power, i.e., *"the flesh,"* which the Holy Spirit cannot sanction.

WALKING AFTER THE SPIRIT

Most people think that *"walking after the Spirit"* is doing spiritual things, such as reading one's Bible, witnessing to souls, praying, etc. Again, those things are very, very good, in fact, something which every dedicated Christian will do. However, that's not *"walking after the Spirit."*

As would be obvious, Paul is here speaking of the Holy Spirit. One walks after the Spirit simply by placing one's faith in Christ and the Cross, and doing so exclusively (Rom. 8:2). In other words, it is by and through the Cross of Christ in which the Holy Spirit operates; consequently, we must ever know and understand that everything we receive from God comes through Christ as the Source, with the Cross as the Means. In a sense, that's why the Sixth Chapter of Romans is referred to as the *"mechanics of the Holy Spirit,"* which tells us *"how"* He works; and the Eighth Chapter of Romans, the *"dynamics"* of the Spirit, which tells us *"what"* He does, after we understand *"how"* He does it.

(9) "AND HE ASKED HIM, WHAT IS YOUR NAME? AND HE ANSWERED, SAYING, MY NAME IS LEGION: FOR WE ARE MANY."

The exposition is:

Why did Jesus ask this question? He did so, because He knew that other spirits inhabited this man also.

LEGION

The question, *"And He asked him, What is your name?"* actually meant, *"He kept on asking him."* It seems at first the demon would not respond, but finally did after repeated questioning.

NOTES

The phrase, *"And he answered, saying, My name is Legion: for we are many,"* finally proclaims the answer as elicited by Christ. A *"legion"* was a designation for a company of Roman soldiers numbering about 6,800 men, although at times it could refer to an undetermined number. Quite possibly this latter is the meaning respecting the *"many"* which possessed this unfortunate man.

Why did Jesus ask this question concerning the name of the demon? No doubt, Jesus knew that there were other demons there, and wanted this head demon to admit it. Possibly the demons were conspiring among themselves that one or more would depart, with the others remaining. The question asked by Christ would forestall these darkened plans. Even though these spirits were liars, still, they knew it was pointless to lie to Christ; therefore, the head demon related the truth as to their infestation.

(10) "AND HE BESOUGHT HIM MUCH THAT HE WOULD NOT SEND THEM AWAY OUT OF THE COUNTRY."

The synopsis is:

This area was full of Hellenistic apostate Jews, and evidently was loved by demon spirits; we learn here that demon spirits enjoy places that have little or no mention of Christ.

THE COUNTRY

The phrase, *"And he besought Him much,"* means that the demon kept on pleading with Christ. This one who called himself *"Legion"* was asking on behalf of all the other demons, as well. The phrase, *"That He would not send them away out of the country,"* seems to insinuate that they enjoyed this particular area better than others. It is said that Decapolis, of which Gadara was a part, was full of Hellenistic apostate Jews, and, therefore, was loved by demon spirits.

From this statement, we learn that demon spirits enjoy certain places which have little or no mention of Christ; consequently, in some countries of the world, such as those ruled by Islam, Buddhism, or Hinduism, etc., demon activity is rampant. The same can be said for those ruled by Catholicism. All of these are false religions, actually instigated and energized by Satan. Therefore, demon activity is plentiful and abundant.

Only Bible Christianity is a ward against these spirits of darkness. They fear only the Name of Jesus, and that only when wielded by Faith-filled hearts and lives.

THE ANSWER TO POVERTY, SICKNESS, AND SUFFERING

In this one Verse, we find the answer to poverty, sickness, suffering, murder, slavery, bondage, filth, disease, man's inhumanity to man, and every other vice imaginable! Sadly and regrettably, most countries of the world fall into this category, because there is little or no light of the Gospel which penetrates this darkness; consequently, demon spirits are rampant in their stealing, killing, and destroying (Jn. 10:10).

Actually, the terrible increase of crime in America is a direct result of improper Bible preaching of the Gospel. As the spiritual temperature of this or any nation rises, the crime rate falls; conversely, as the spiritual temperature falls, so to speak, as it is now doing, the crime rate rises, plus every other type of problem imaginable.

When Jesus comes back, as He certainly shall, the world will be rid of these spirits of darkness, which are now the cause of so much suffering and pain. Then the Earth will be *"filled with the knowledge of the Glory of the LORD, as the waters cover the sea"* (Hab. 2:14).

(11) "NOW THERE WAS THERE NIGH UNTO THE MOUNTAINS A GREAT HERD OF SWINE FEEDING."

The structure is:

These swine were, no doubt, owned by Jews, even though Jews were forbidden by the Law to eat pork.

THE SWINE

This *"herd of swine,"* which Mark said numbered *"about 2,000,"* was, no doubt, owned by the Jews. Even though Jews were forbidden by the Law of Moses to eat pork, yet they were not forbidden to breed swine for other uses, such as provisions for the Roman Army. Jesus was on the seashore when this confrontation with the maniac of Gadara took place, while the hogs were at some distance, feeding on the slopes of the mountain.

As stated, this was the Decapolis area, which actually referred to ten cities, mostly occupied by the Romans, with some Jews.

(12) "AND ALL THE DEVILS BESOUGHT HIM, SAYING, SEND US INTO THE SWINE, THAT WE MAY ENTER INTO THEM."

The exegesis is:

These demons could not enter into the hogs without the express permission of Christ, so how much less could they enter into *"the sheep of His pasture"*!

DEMONS

The phrase, *"And all the devils* (demons) *besought Him,"* proclaims these spirits as frantic, with many of them using the man's vocal chords to express their desire to enter into the swine. As well, we learn from this request made by the demons that they could not even enter into the hogs without the express permission of Christ, so how much less could they enter into Believers! This means that a Child of God cannot be demon-possessed, as some Preachers claim!

The phrase, *"Send us into the swine, that we may enter into them,"* shows that demons at one time had physical bodies, for they have no rest unless they inhabit a physical body, either that of a human being or an animal.

(13) "AND FORTHWITH JESUS GAVE THEM LEAVE. AND THE UNCLEAN SPIRITS WENT OUT, AND ENTERED INTO THE SWINE: AND THE HERD RAN VIOLENTLY DOWN A STEEP PLACE INTO THE SEA, (THEY WERE ABOUT TWO THOUSAND;) AND WERE CHOKED IN THE SEA."

The composition is:

This means that Christ did not command the demons to do this, but instead gave them permission. Many have questioned the right of Christ to allow these spirits to enter into these hogs, which thereby destroyed other people's property. However, even though the Holy Spirit through Mark didn't explain it, we know everything the Lord does is right. It's not merely right because He does it, but because it actually is right.

DELIVERANCE

The phrase, *"And forthwith Jesus gave them leave,"* means that He did not command them to do this, but instead, as stated, gave them permission. The phrase, *"And the unclean spirits went out, and entered into the swine,"* reflects, as is obvious, the demons doing what Jesus had given them permission to do. The functional abilities of these spirits seem to be very limited unless they can inhabit a physical body, be it human or animal; however, the reaction of the animals, as the next phrase portrays, would result in their deaths. Consequently, these spirits would not help themselves that much!

THE VIOLENT REACTION OF THE ANIMALS

The phrase, *"And the herd rain violently down a steep place into the sea, (they were about two thousand;) and were choked in the sea,"* represents a loss of approximately $250,000, or more.

WAS OUR LORD CORRECT IN DOING THIS, CONSIDERING IT CAUSED THE LOSS OF MUCH PROPERTY?

The question has been asked repeatedly as to the right or wrong of Jesus allowing these spirits to go into these swine, which resulted in this tremendous loss for the owners. First of all, we know that Jesus did not do wrong, because everything He did was in the Will of the Heavenly Father (Jn. 8:28). Everything done by the Lord, whether constructive or destructive, is meant for one purpose — to draw the individual(s) to Christ.

Even if it is extended judgment on a person or nation, such as Egypt of old, and after much pleading and mercy, still, the act itself is meant to serve as an example to hopefully draw others to Christ. Consequently, this act of allowing the spirits to enter the swine, with their resultant loss, was an act of Mercy on the part of God. It was designed to bring their owners to Christ, which it did, but with them rejecting Him. They did not allow the transformation enacted on the former maniac to extend to them.

Oftentimes, the Lord allows inclement weather, such as hurricanes, earthquakes, etc., to wreak a deadly toll, destroying property and even lives. Even though some may question His right to do this, that is, if they confess His existence at all, still, He is the Creator, and He, therefore, has all knowledge, all power, and always does what is best for man; the wise individual will therefore say, as Job of old, *"The LORD gives, and the LORD takes away; blessed be the Name of the LORD"* (Job 1:21).

Many erroneously claim that it was not the Lord Who took away Job's possessions, but Satan. They also attribute all natural disasters to Satan! However, the Holy Spirit said, concerning Job, *"In all this Job sinned not, nor charged God foolishly"* (Job 1:22). While it certainly may be true that Satan is, at times, the instrument, nevertheless, he can only do what God allows him to do. To think he has unlimited latitude in any given area is to limit God's Power, which no right-thinking person desires to do. God controls all, even Satan and his minions of darkness. To attribute less to Him denies Who He is!

(14) "AND THEY WHO FED THE SWINE FLED, AND TOLD IT IN THE CITY, AND IN THE COUNTRY. AND THEY WENT OUT TO SEE WHAT IT WAS THAT WAS DONE."

The composition is:

A great multitude came out to see what had happened.

THE MESSAGE WAS DELIVERED

The phrase, *"And they who fed the swine fled, and told it in the city, and in the country,"* represents the scenario that must have been played out in this fashion.

Evidently, those who tended the hogs were nearby, or even observing, when Jesus cast the spirits out of the maniac. They may have even heard the unclean spirits asking permission for all the demons to go into the swine, or else the Disciples told them what had happened. At any rate, they knew what had taken place, and made certain the owners of the swine knew they were not responsible for this large loss. The implication is that they also related the story of Jesus delivering the maniac, who was probably well known in the area.

The phrase, *"And they went out to see what it was that was done,"* concerned a large group of people, who, upon hearing the story of the swine-herders, immediately came to see for themselves. This presented the greatest opportunity they would ever have, i.e., meeting Jesus. Every sick person among them could have been healed. And, above all, their souls could have been saved; however, they threw away the greatest opportunity a human being would ever have.

How many more do the same thing, and I speak of present times?

It is bad enough for people living in countries where Jesus is little preached, if preached at all, to fail to accept Him; however, for those living in the United States, and certain other countries of the world, who have opportunity after opportunity, but still refuse to accept Christ, the torment of Hell will be all the greater still, for these particular millions upon millions of individuals.

(15) "AND THEY COME TO JESUS, AND SEE HIM WHO WAS POSSESSED WITH THE DEVIL, AND HAD THE LEGION, SITTING, AND CLOTHED, AND IN HIS RIGHT MIND: AND THEY WERE AFRAID."

The overview is:

The loss of the animals would have been nothing in comparison to what they would have received upon their acceptance of Christ, at least had they done so, which they didn't.

HIS RIGHT MIND

The phrase, *"And they come to Jesus,"* actually gives us the reason, as we have stated, that the Lord allowed the loss of the large herd of swine. It was done, at least in part, by the Holy Spirit in order to bring this crowd to Jesus, which, if they had taken advantage of it, would have been the greatest day of their lives. The loss of the animals would have been nothing in comparison to what they would have received upon their acceptance of Christ, i.e., eternal life.

The phrase, *"And see him who was possessed with the devil,"* means that they minutely inspected him, evidently because they had known him in his previous state. They were flabbergasted at what they saw! The phrase, *"And had the Legion, sitting, and clothed, and in his right mind,"* gives a compendium of what spiritually happens in the Salvation of a soul.

1. SITTING: This speaks of the *"rest"* that is given to those who put their trust in Christ (Heb. 4:9). There is a terrible tumult in the hearts and lives of all unbelievers, which expresses itself in many and varied ways. As well, it is impossible for the unbeliever to know or understand the opposite of that, because he has never experienced it; however, upon coming to Christ, the unrest is quieted and settled, with a beautiful *"peace"* given to the recipient. It is, no doubt, the greatest attribute of Salvation, hence, given first.

2. AND CLOTHED: This speaks of being clothed in Righteousness, which can only be given by Christ. Isaiah called it *"the garment of praise for the spirit of heaviness"* (Isa. 61:3). The evil is taken away and the righteousness is given in turn. As the song says, *"I got the best of the trade."*

3. IN HIS RIGHT MIND: Irrespective of one's education, intellect, or genius, if one does not know Christ as one's personal Saviour, to one degree or the other, one is not in his right mind. Of course, the case illustrated in this Chapter would be in the extreme; however, the principle holds for all, irrespective of their state, position, status, race, or educational accomplishments.

In other words, a correct view of the world and mankind cannot be obtained outside of Christ. The illustrations are obvious! One need only recall the horrors of Nazi Germany to observe education and intellect without God. Unfortunately, that scene has been repeated tens of thousands of times, albeit to a lesser degree, before and since.

The world also has many, and always has had many, of those who are rich respecting money, but with no solutions for the ills of humanity. In other words, they hurt, sicken, and die, just like the most poverty-stricken. The only *"Light"* in the world is Jesus. To be sure, He does not merely contain light, but, in effect, is Light (Jn. 8:12). The only *"right-minded"* is that which knows Christ, and it is *"right"* only as it remains in Christ, and is led by Christ. Unfortunately, Christians, at times, do foolish things, but never because of Christ, but rather because of departing from Christ.

FEAR

The phrase, *"And they were afraid,"* means they were afraid of the Power of Christ. They had, no doubt, known the man in his previous condition, with some of them possibly even having attempted to restrain him. As well, his insanity had been such that he had been a raving maniac. And now they observe him sitting and clothed, with them possibly even questioning him. His answers, if, in fact, that did happen, were lucid and intelligent, as he related what Jesus had done for him.

In their minds, there was very little difference than someone being raised from the dead. And then, on top of that, these spirits of darkness, which had been the cause of this man's terrible condition, were allowed to go into the swine, with the hogs consequently destroying themselves. They realized they were in the presence of a Power far greater than anything they had ever known, experienced, or witnessed. And yet, this fear, which is proper, did not bring them to Christ, but rather the very opposite.

(16) "AND THEY WHO SAW IT TOLD THEM HOW IT BEFELL TO HIM WHO WAS POSSESSED WITH THE DEVIL, AND ALSO CONCERNING THE SWINE."

The overview is:

This lends credence to the thought that the swine-herders had witnessed the entire episode concerning the action of Christ in delivering the demoniac, and allowing the demons to go into the hogs.

THE TESTIMONY THAT WAS UNHEEDED

The phrase, *"And they who saw it,"* lends credence to the thought that the swine-herders had witnessed the entire episode concerning the action of Christ in delivering the maniac. The phrase, *"Told them how it befell to him who was possessed with the devil,"* relates the swine-herders giving a blow-by-blow account of what Jesus had done, with the owners and others now observing with their own eyes what they had been told. The phrase, *"And also concerning the swine,"* means that the swine-herders made certain that the owners knew that dereliction of duty had not been a part of this episode, but rather the demon spirits.

At the outset, every evidence is that the story was completely preposterous! The idea that this maniac was completely delivered was, no doubt, unbelievable whenever it was first told. And then, for the owners of this herd of swine to be told that all 2,000 of the hogs had run into the sea and drowned, and because of demon spirits, was even more preposterous. But to their amazement, they find it exactly as they have been told.

(17) "AND THEY BEGAN TO PRAY HIM TO DEPART OUT OF THEIR COASTS."

The exposition is:

It is remarkable! They thought more of the swine than they did of eternal life that Christ could have given them. And so it is with most of the world.

THE REJECTION OF CHRIST

This Verse has to be one of the saddest in the entirety of the Bible. Instead of accepting Him as their Lord and Saviour, they wanted Him to *"depart."* The evidence was irrefutable! What He had done for this maniac, He could do for them. Every need in their lives, whether physical, spiritual, mental, domestic, or financial, could easily be handled by Christ. The opportunity of the ages was before their eyes, and with irrefutable proof; but yet, they did not want it.

Why?

Sadly and regrettably, the decision of these people was not unique or isolated. Almost all the world follows in their train. The proof is irrefutable as to Who Christ is and what He can do! And yet, even despite the dire need, most of the world conducts themselves exactly as these cities of Decapolis.

The *"Why?"* is answered in the fact that they loved their sin more than they desired a change. In other words, they did not want to change!

A newsman mentioned to me once that most of the people who accept the Lord do so in dire circumstances. He was correct. As someone has said, *"Man's extremity is God's opportunity."* The maniac was thrilled to turn to Christ when given the opportunity, but his neighbors, not nearly in the condition he was in, did not see their need. Therefore, most of the world follows suit!

And yet, no doubt, some of these very people who urged Jesus to leave their locality would later come to dire straits in life. But now, they do not see themselves in that position. Some have ventured that they were more concerned about the loss of the swine than the Deliverance of the maniac. While that is certainly true, still, that, I think, was not their real reason for refusing Christ. They refused Him because they simply did not see their need of Him.

I have had the occasion on various news programs in Washington, New York, or elsewhere, to enter into discussion with various intellectuals. The attitude of most, if not all, was, and is, that accepting Christ may be proper for some people, but not for them. In other words, they think they are above the need. *"Those who are less educated or less knowledgeable in the ways of the world may need such,"* is, in effect, what they think, but not them!

There are a few exceptions, but not many. That is one of the reasons Jesus said, *"How hardly shall they who have riches enter into the Kingdom of God"* (Mk. 10:23).

I happened to be in the presence once of the Vice President of the United States, who became President shortly thereafter. He was asked the question, *"Mr. Vice President, are you born again?"* He was honest and forthright in his answer. He claimed that he did not understand the Born-Again experience. He related how he and his wife attempted to live a *"good, clean life,"* but still some things had happened which they did not understand; consequently, they had rejected the Lord.

Let it ever be understood that men never reject the Lord for good and noble purposes. Those reasons are always sinister, dark, foreboding, and ultimately destructive!

The implication in the Greek is that the moment they began to urge Christ to depart, He withdrew on the first hint of their wish; however, when He walked away, Eternal Life also walked away with Him! For such is in no other.

(18) "AND WHEN HE WAS COME INTO THE SHIP, HE WHO HAD BEEN POSSESSED WITH THE DEVIL PRAYED HIM THAT HE MIGHT BE WITH HIM."

The exegesis is:

He wanted to go with Jesus and the Disciples, and no wonder!

THE REQUEST

The phrase, *"And when He was come into the ship,"* refers to the departure of Christ. The phrase, *"He who had been possessed with the devil,"* is spoken of in the past tense, meaning that he was no longer possessed, and would never be possessed again. One can only shout, *"Hallelujah!"*

As I dictate these words, I think of the multiple millions of letters we have received over the years, with many of them containing some of the most wonderful stories of Redemption that could ever be related. Actually, they are little different than the story of the former maniac of Gadara. Lives which were totally ruined and wasted were suddenly changed by the glorious power of Jesus Christ. As He did it then, the evidence is glaringly obvious that He does it today.

The phrase, *"Prayed Him that He might be with Him,"* is certainly understandable in all its implications. What this man had been was horrible, and what he now is, is wonderful, to say the least, and all because of Jesus. Consequently, he wants to be with Jesus, even as His Disciple.

(19) "HOWBEIT JESUS SUFFERED HIM NOT, BUT SAID UNTO HIM, GO HOME TO YOUR FRIENDS, AND TELL THEM HOW GREAT THINGS THE LORD HAS DONE FOR YOU, AND HAS HAD COMPASSION ON YOU."

The overview is:

A. Go tell!

B. Tell the great things which the Lord has done for you.

C. Tell of His compassion.

GREAT THINGS

The phrase, *"Howbeit Jesus suffered him not,"* speaks of a gentle persuasion. The Lord spoke kindly to him, even giving him explicit directions, and the evidence is that he carried them out totally. The phrase, *"But said unto him, Go home to your friends,"* actually in the Greek says, *"Go into your home to your own."* He was directed by the Lord to first of all testify to his own flesh and blood, his own family.

I think one should not make more of this episode than one should, but yet the following may well have happened.

THE MIRACLE OF REDEMPTION, THE ONLY SOLUTION FOR THE HUMAN DILEMMA!

If the man had been married with children, the terrible horror of his past life had, no doubt, been woefully destructive on those he loved the most, and who loved him in return. No doubt, they had painfully observed his deterioration, until finally he could no longer remain at home, but was forced in his demon-possessed agony to leave.

What brought it on, the Bible does not say. But yet, we know that Satan is the one who *"steals, kills, and destroys"* (Jn. 10:10). Maybe the man was profligate in his lifestyle! Maybe he courted evil! And then again, maybe none of these things happened. But yet, through a series of events not exactly of his choosing, he finds himself in this awful condition.

The grief that must have followed his departure and him being driven to the tombs must have been awful, to say the least! The children and the wife would have grieved terribly. And yet, they were helpless! There was nothing they could do. Maybe at night they could hear his screams. Most assuredly, it was related to them how men had attempted to restrain him, but with no success.

DELIVERANCE

Whether the news of his Deliverance came to his wife (or mother, etc.) before he personally related such is anyone's guess. Upon hearing the swine-herder's story, the news, no doubt, quickly spread abroad of this man's Deliverance. And yet, there were others in this area in the same condition, so whatever his loved ones heard, if anything, the information would have been scant. And then it happened!

One can see him swiftly walking down the road, with others close to him, no doubt, desiring to hear his story. As he gets closer to his house, he can hardly believe what has happened to him. There is no explanation for it, at least that one could ever begin to understand. A Man called Jesus....

He draws closer to his house, almost running, with others, no doubt, running ahead to inform his wife (or loved ones) about him coming. Immediately upon receiving the news, the wife would have run out of the house with the children closely following (that is, if he had such a family), all running to meet him. The crowd, no doubt, stands with smiles on their faces, as they observe this meeting. It should have been private, but there is no way that such could have been. Despite the owners of the swine telling Jesus to depart,

NOTES

undoubtedly there were many who were thrilled at what had happened with this former maniac of Gadara.

After holding him close for a period of time, his wife (or mother, etc.) must have asked the all-important question, *"What happened?"* One can almost feel the words tumbling out of his mouth. He relates how Jesus came with His Disciples. To the best of his ability, he describes how he was set free by the Power of Jesus Christ. Undoubtedly, he proceeded to tell her about the Person of Christ. What He was like! How He sounded! How His eyes seemed to look into the very depths of one's soul!

He would have said, *"I have never seen anyone like Him! His very Presence seemed to permeate everything in the immediate vicinity. And it was a Presence that spoke of goodness, kindness, and love as I have never known before."*

Maybe this is not exactly the way it happened, but from the description given by Mark, it may have been similar.

The phrase, *"And tell them how great things the Lord has done for you,"* has reference to three things:

1. He was to testify to any and all what was done.

2. He was to tell that it was Jesus Who had done it.

3. He was to understand that the cure was permanent. The demons would never return!

COMPASSION

The phrase, *"And has had compassion on you,"* is a statement of depth! The culpability of humanity, such as this man, is not denied. But yet, in the word *"compassion,"* Christ proclaims the scheme of evil perpetuated by Satan, which wreaks havoc in the human family. Even though man is definitely responsible, still, the scope of this evil is so wide and deep as to be beyond the pale of comprehension. In other words, it is a dilemma from which the human family cannot even hope to extricate itself, at least according to its own ability and ingenuity. This is the reason for the *"compassion,"* and it is the reason for the coming of Christ. He Alone can lift man out of this terrible and horrible dilemma, even as He lifted the maniac from this demon possession.

As valuable as education is, man cannot be educated out of this pit of darkness. As necessary as right legislation is, laws can never set the captive free. Men use the word *"rehabilitation,"* but this is a word referring to results which cannot be realized in the domain of human ability. In effect, the Lord does not rehabilitate anyone! He instead makes of them a new creature (a new creation) in Christ Jesus (II Cor. 5:17). That new creation is made possible totally and entirely by and through what Jesus did at the Cross. This is the only answer — the Cross — for the human dilemma!

Because that is so very, very important, let us say it again:

There is no answer to the human dilemma, the human evil and wickedness, the terrible plight of man's inhumanity to man, the war, privation, poverty, and want — and yes, even demon possession — other than the Cross. This totally is the theme of the Word of God.

THE CROSS OF CHRIST

Other than what Jesus did at the Cross, man cannot be saved. Other than what Jesus did at the Cross, the Believer cannot live a sanctified, victorious life. In fact, there is *"one"* emblem of the Church of Christianity, of the New Covenant and, in fact, of the entirety of the Bible, and that emblem, so to speak, is *"the Cross of Christ."* There all sin was atoned, and Satan and every evil cohort were totally and completely defeated (Col. 2:14-15). This means that if the Preacher is not preaching the Cross, he's not preaching the Gospel (I Cor. 1:18).

Just last night, for a few moments, I watched a particular Charismatic Preacher, who ministers regularly over Television, offer particular tapes and videos which purported to deal with the human dilemma. In other words, she was telling Christians how to live right, how to be victorious, how to be prosperous, etc. The dear lady, as sincere as she might be, does not preach the Cross, but something else entirely. Oh yes, she, as untold thousands of other Preachers, mentions the Cross, and even speaks of Jesus dying on the Cross for our sins, etc., all of which is correct; however, the object of her faith is not the Cross of Christ, but something else entirely. So this means that whatever she's preaching, and the material that she was offering to the Christian public, will be, in effect, of no help whatsoever. Without the Preacher understanding that Christ is the Source and the Cross is the Means, no true Gospel can be preached. In fact, that which is preached coincides with the following:

ANOTHER JESUS, ANOTHER SPIRIT, ANOTHER GOSPEL

Paul said, *"For if he* (false apostles) *who comes preaching another Jesus* (a Jesus who is not of the Cross), *whom we have not preached* (Paul's Message was *'Jesus Christ and Him Crucified'*; anything else is *'another Jesus'*), *or if you receive another spirit* (which is produced by preaching another Jesus), *which you have not received* (that's not what you received when we preached the True Gospel to you), *or another gospel, which you have not accepted* (anything other than *'Jesus Christ and Him Crucified'* is *'another gospel'*), *you might well bear with him"* (II Cor. 11:4).

The Apostle is telling the Corinthians they have, in fact, sinned because they tolerated these false apostles who had come in bringing *"another gospel,"* which was something other than Christ and the Cross.

Let me say it again:

If the Preacher preaches Jesus without making the Cross the theme, i.e., the very reason why God became Man, then the Jesus he is preaching, pure and simple, is not the Jesus of the Bible, but rather a Jesus of his or someone else's fabrication. Moreover, the preaching of the *"other Jesus"* is always instituted by *"another spirit,"* which means it's not the Holy Spirit moving and working in such a Ministry, but something else entirely.

This *"other Jesus,"* nurtured by *"another spirit,"* results in *"another gospel."* And regrettably, that's what the majority of Preachers are proclaiming presently.

How do I know that?

I know it because they aren't preaching the Cross. If they aren't preaching the Cross, then, without fail, it's *"another Jesus, nurtured by another spirit, presenting another gospel."* Under such a gospel, there will be no lives changed, no bondages broken, no souls brought from darkness to light, no one baptized with the Holy Spirit, and no one healed by the Power of God. How can it be, whenever *"another spirit"* is operating in these particular Ministries!

Let us say it again:

Without fail, that is, if souls are to be saved and if lives are to be changed, the Preacher must preach the Cross. It is the only answer for the human problem. I mean the only answer! (I Cor. 1:17-18, 21, 23; 2:2).

(20) "AND HE DEPARTED, AND BEGAN TO PUBLISH IN DECAPOLIS HOW GREAT THINGS JESUS HAD DONE FOR HIM: AND ALL MEN DID MARVEL."

The exposition is:

Evidently, many had known him before; they now see what the Lord has done for him. This is the story of untold millions.

THE TESTIMONY

The phrase, *"And he departed,"* means that he determined to do that which Christ had instructed Him to do. The phrase, *"And began to publish in Decapolis,"* means *"to make a public proclamation."* In other words, he probably stood on the corner of busy intersections, and in all the ten cities of the region, giving his testimony about what Christ had done for him. In effect, he became an Evangelist.

The phrase, *"How great things Jesus had done for him,"* proclaims for a certainty that it was *"great"*!

The giving of one's testimony as to what Christ has brought about in one's life is the greatest, most compelling witness that can ever be given. The Apostle Paul, as the Book of Acts records, gave his testimony over and over (Acts, Chpts. 9, 22, 26). So, every Believer should follow this example of telling others what *"Jesus has done for him."*

The phrase, *"And all men did marvel,"* proclaims the fact that many, no doubt, had known him previously, and they now saw the astounding change. Consequently, they *"marveled"*! To be sure, what Christ does in the human heart is a *"marvel"*!

What a story of the miracle-working Power of Christ!

What a story of Redemption!

NOTES

(21) "AND WHEN JESUS WAS PASSED OVER AGAIN BY SHIP UNTO THE OTHER SIDE, MUCH PEOPLE GATHERED UNTO HIM: AND HE WAS NEAR UNTO THE SEA."

The exposition is:

This means that hundreds, if not thousands, were waiting on the shore for Him to come back to Capernaum.

MUCH PEOPLE

The phrase, *"And when Jesus was passed over again by ship unto the other side,"* refers to Him going back to Capernaum on the west side of the Sea of Galilee. The phrase, *"Much people gathered unto Him,"* speaks of a great crowd. Luke said, *"For they were all waiting for Him"* (Lk. 8:40). There were many who needed healing, and who had come perhaps from afar.

The phrase, *"And He was near unto the Sea,"* means that He had departed out of the ship and was on the shore.

(22) "AND, BEHOLD, THERE COMES ONE OF THE RULERS OF THE SYNAGOGUE, JAIRUS BY NAME; AND WHEN HE SAW HIM, HE FELL AT HIS FEET."

The structure is:

The petition of Jairus is great, because his need is great!

JAIRUS

The phrase, *"And, behold, there comes one of the rulers of the Synagogue,"* refers to a sudden appearance by this man. As well, the words, *"And, behold,"* exclaim a happening of great significance which is about to take place. There were several rulers in each Synagogue, of which Jairus was one. Their duties were to select the readers or teachers on the Sabbath, to examine their discourses, and to see that all things were done with decency and in accordance with ancestral usage.

The phrase, *"Jairus by name,"* was this man whose name meant *"whom Jehovah enlightens."* To be sure, he was to be enlightened more so than he could ever begin to realize. The phrase, *"And when he saw Him, he fell at His feet,"* means that he had heard that Jesus had arrived, and he rushes to seek His help. His request is preceded by his *"falling at Jesus' feet,"* in a posture of worship because the need is so great, i.e., the saving of his daughter from death.

(23) "AND BESOUGHT HIM GREATLY, SAYING, MY LITTLE DAUGHTER LIES AT THE POINT OF DEATH: I PRAY YOU, COME AND LAY YOUR HANDS ON HER, THAT SHE MAY BE HEALED; AND SHE SHALL LIVE."

The structure is:

The Greek actually says: *"to save her from death."*

A MIRACLE IS SOUGHT

The phrase, *"And besought Him greatly,"* proclaims an impassioned plea. The phrase, *"Saying, My little daughter lies at the point of death,"* means, as is obvious, that the child is about to die. Actually, in a few minutes, someone would come from the home of Jairus, telling him that his daughter, in fact, was dead. In other words, she probably died about the time that her father was imploring Christ to come and heal her.

The phrase, *"I pray You, come and lay Your hands on her, that she may be healed; and she shall live,"* proclaims the fact that the man had Faith in Jesus. Without a doubt, he had seen the Lord heal many in the preceding days; however, what he was about to see now would far eclipse what he had previously seen.

A point should be brought out. The Gentile Centurion had said to Jesus, *"Speak the Word only,"* referring to his servant, but the Faith of Jairus does not seem to have risen to such degree (Mat. 8:5-13).

(24) "AND JESUS WENT WITH HIM; AND MUCH PEOPLE FOLLOWED HIM, AND THRONGED HIM."

The exegesis is:

Many were there who, no doubt, desperately needed healing.

FAITH

The phrase, *"And Jesus went with him,"* proclaims a like response to the man's Faith. If Jairus had requested Christ *"to speak the Word,"* as the Centurion, Jesus would have undoubtedly done so, and the child would have been healed or even raised from the dead at that moment. Nevertheless, Jesus meets him on his own level and proceeds to go to his house.

NOTES

This tremendous lesson of Faith relative to comparing the Centurion with Jairus must not be lost upon the Reader. God responds to Faith, and at whatever level. He seldom seeks, however, to increase the Faith at the moment, but rather responds to its present level, whatever that level may be! The level of Faith receives the same level of response. Actually, Jesus, at times, would say, *"According to your Faith be it unto you"* (Mat. 9:29).

He also used terms such as, *"O thou of little faith, wherefore did you doubt?"* (Mat. 14:31). He also said, *"O woman, great is your Faith"* (Mat. 15:28). So, we are made to see in these responses by Christ that there are levels of Faith which receive the same level of response. Jairus seemed to need Jesus to come personally to his house, and even to physically *"lay His Hands on his daughter."* Consequently, that is what Jesus would do!

The phrase, *"And much people followed Him, and thronged Him,"* sets the stage for the next great Miracle and another lesson in Faith, which is astounding, to say the least! The crowd was so intense around Christ so as to almost suffocate Him. There were many people with many needs, and they knew that He Alone had the answer.

(25) "AND A CERTAIN WOMAN, WHICH HAD AN ISSUE OF BLOOD TWELVE YEARS."

The exegesis is:

The Verse speaks of a constant hemorrhage for that period of time. It was a female disorder.

A CERTAIN WOMAN

The phrase, *"And a certain woman,"* is said by tradition to have been named *"Veronica,"* a native of Caesarea Philippi. The phrase, *"Which had an issue of blood twelve years,"* spoke of a constant hemorrhage, which she had suffered for twelve years.

(26) "AND HAD SUFFERED MANY THINGS OF MANY PHYSICIANS, AND HAD SPENT ALL THAT SHE HAD, AND WAS NOTHING BETTERED, BUT RATHER GREW WORSE."

The composition is:

Many of these physicians had treated her merely for the money, knowing all the time they could not help her.

PHYSICIANS

The phrase, *"And had suffered many things of many physicians,"* means that she had suffered extreme pain at the hands of these doctors, but to no avail. Luke, himself a physician, added, *"which had spent all her living upon physicians, neither could be healed of any"* (Lk. 8:43). Their manner of treatment in those days, for sicknesses such as this, was primitive, to say the least. In effect, there was really nothing they could do, with whatever they did, as is here obvious, mostly exacerbating the problem instead of relieving it.

The phrase, *"And had spent all that she had,"* suggests that many of these doctors had attempted to treat her merely for the money they could receive out of it, knowing they could not help her. The implication is that she had once been quite wealthy and had spent basically all her worth on this effort to obtain relief.

The phrase, *"And was nothing bettered, but rather grew worse,"* means that the physicians had not helped her at all, but, if anything, had made the situation worse.

(27) "WHEN SHE HAD HEARD OF JESUS, CAME IN THE PRESS BEHIND, AND TOUCHED HIS GARMENT."

The composition is:

This probably referred to the touching of the hem of the shawl thrown over His shoulder, which contained a blue fringe, which the Jews were required to wear to remind them that they were God's people (Num. 15:38-41; Deut. 22:12).

WHEN SHE HEARD

The phrase, *"When she had heard of Jesus,"* is interesting indeed!

First of all, the idea is that she had not known of Jesus before her trip to Capernaum at this present time. Upon arriving in the city, she heard of the One Who was the topic of every conversation; upon inquiring, she learned of His great healing Power. She had tried all the doctors for twelve long years, and now she must try Him. However, this experience with the Great Physician will not be as with the other physicians.

NOTES

The Greek actually says, *"When she had heard of The Jesus,"* meaning that He had become so popular that even though this Name was commonly used, still, He was distinguished from all others, hence, *"The Jesus."* (Jesus, in the Hebrew, means Joshua, which He was actually called.)

The phrase, *"Came in the press behind,"* means that she made her way through the crowd which was at the back of our Lord. The phrase, *"And touched His garment,"* probably referred to touching the hem of the shawl thrown over His shoulder. Even though there were indications she may have been a Gentile, even with tradition saying so, this particular phrase seems to indicate she may have been Jewish, although living in a Gentile area. Otherwise, it seems she would have little knowledge or understanding respecting the touching of this part of His garment (Num. 15:38-41; Deut. 22:12). At any rate, this is the part of His garment she touched, and with reason!

(28) "FOR SHE SAID, IF I MAY TOUCH BUT HIS CLOTHES, I SHALL BE WHOLE."

The overview is:

It means she kept saying it over and over to herself, or even possibly to others nearby.

ONE TOUCH

The phrase, *"For she said,"* also proclaims the fact that something had transpired within her heart respecting a way to be healed. No doubt, she would have loved to have approached Him, with the opportunity to tell Him of her difficulties and problems. But such, as is now obvious, was not possible. The crowd is too great, with too many clamoring to get to Him. So, the Holy Spirit dropped a word within her heart which generated Faith and found a way. She would touch the hem of His garment (Lk. 8:44).

The phrase, *"If I may touch but His clothes, I shall be whole,"* concerns her level of Faith. Jairus wanted Jesus to touch his daughter, while this *"certain woman"* knows this, with her, is not possible; therefore, she will touch Him. The entire scenario tells us that Faith will find a way. It will not take *"No"* for an answer, neither will it be hindered by seemingly impossible circumstances.

So, if Jesus has not touched you, that

doesn't mean that all hope is gone. You can touch Him! And if you touch Him by Faith, and with Faith, you will receive just as much as if He had touched you. This opens up the possibility for the receiving of whatever is needed to any and all. No one is excluded, except those who will not believe.

THE POWER OF GOD

Sometimes the Power of God is so real that the Lord touches all in the place, or at least some. But sometimes there is no touch. But yet, and according to this woman, which is at least a part of the lesson the Holy Spirit desires that we learn, whatever is needed can still be obtained. Even though He may not touch you, you can touch Him!

What does it mean to touch the Lord?

Well, of course, regarding this *"certain woman"* realizing she would not be able to get Him to touch her, she reasoned in her mind and spirit, no doubt inspired by the Holy Spirit, that she could touch Him, and the effect would be the same. It was! It was just that simple.

However, the situation presently, because Jesus is not here physically as then, is a tiny bit different. The difference is that it only requires a slightly higher level of Faith. In effect, He is here, but just not physically. When individuals are in a Church Service, or wherever, and the Spirit and Power of God are moving greatly, with many being touched and healed, it doesn't really take near the Faith as this of which we speak. However, some, if not many, at these times, do not receive a touch from the Lord, and are led to believe, by the lack of obvious evidence, that they are not able to receive what others have received. This Passage tells us differently.

GOD'S WAY

First of all, there is no formula given in the Word of God concerning receiving from the Lord. The reason is obvious. Each individual and their situation is unique. Faith always requires different things of different people. Consequently, the formulas given by most Preachers simply do not work. Therefore, one must understand that no formula is available; the few steps I will give also must not be construed as a formula.

NOTES

THE WILL OF GOD

The individual, exactly as this woman, must settle it in his or her mind that it is the Will of God for them to receive from the Lord. If they vacillate on this point, it shows a lack of faith. We must believe that *"God is, and that He is a rewarder of them who diligently seek Him"* (Heb. 11:6).

James told us that Faith cannot work in a double minded atmosphere. He said, *"A double minded man is unstable in all his ways"* (James 1:8). He also said, *"But let him ask in Faith, nothing wavering"* (James 1:6).

GOD'S WORD

Touching the Lord, as this woman, must be anchored in God's Word, in other words, *"claiming His Promises."* In effect, this is exactly what she did. She must have had an inkling of knowledge as to what this blue tassel on Jesus' garment meant. Therefore, she touched it, and in Faith. So, claim the Word for your particular case, and believe it.

PERSEVERE

Persevere until the answer comes. This is where many Believers break down. They do the things mentioned, and no answer is forthcoming, at least at that particular time. They soon weary and quit. The Holy Spirit desires that we keep believing, even though circumstances may say the opposite, as they often do. The answer will come, even though at times it may be delayed. As stated, and as by now should be obvious, it is not nearly as simple to touch the Lord as Him touching us, and for the obvious reasons. However, it can be done, as evidenced by this dear lady. This Passage was given for this very purpose by the Holy Spirit.

(29) "AND STRAIGHTWAY THE FOUNTAIN OF HER BLOOD WAS DRIED UP; AND SHE FELT IN HER BODY THAT SHE WAS HEALED OF THAT PLAGUE."

The structure is:

She knew she was healed!

THE HEALING

The phrase, *"And straightway the fountain of her blood was dried up,"* contains a powerful meaning. It not only means that the bleeding stopped, and instantly, but that what was causing the bleeding, the fountain, if you please, was instantly dried up. In other words, she was totally and completely healed.

The phrase, *"And she felt in her body that she was healed of that plague,"* means that she had felt oftentimes the efforts of the doctors attempting to help her, but only hurting her. As she felt that, she feels this, but with a great difference. Then she felt pain; now she feels healing! Because of what she feels in her body, she knows, beyond the shadow of a doubt, that *"she was healed of that plague."* And so she was! The cure was instantaneous.

(30) "AND JESUS, IMMEDIATELY KNOWING IN HIMSELF THAT VIRTUE HAD GONE OUT OF HIM, TURNED HIM ABOUT IN THE PRESS, AND SAID, WHO TOUCHED MY CLOTHES?"

The exposition is:

The Holy Spirit had not seen fit to reveal to Him who had touched Him.

VIRTUE

The phrase, *"And Jesus, immediately knowing in Himself that virtue had gone out of Him,"* tells us several things:

First of all, that which was done by Christ for others had a price tag attached to it, as is obvious in this Verse, at least as it pertains to Him. *"Virtue* (power) *went out of Him."* This would have had some effect on Him physically, emotionally, and spiritually.

Second, we learn from this the tremendous power of Faith in God.

In mid-1995, Frances and I were in a series of Evangelistic meetings in Mexico, with a couple of services on the U.S. side of the border. This particular Monday night, we were to be in Harlingen, Texas. I was almost ready to leave for the Service that night, when I greatly sensed the Presence of the Lord. My mind was on the Message I would preach that evening, which was this very Text.

The Lord spoke to my heart, saying, *"I'm going to show you something about this illustration of the woman touching the hem of My garment that you have not previously seen."* Actually, as my memory comes back, even as I dictate these notes, some of it began to unfold even then; however, it was only during the Message that the Spirit of God greatly outlined that of which He had spoken. The auditorium was jammed to capacity that night, and, correspondingly, there was a mighty moving of the Holy Spirit in the entirety of the Service.

As I began to preach, greatly sensing the Presence of the Lord, with the congregation sensing it as well, when I came to the part of the woman touching the hem of Jesus' garment, the Holy Spirit fully brought out that which He had given me in part before the Service. It was as follows:

A MESSAGE OF FAITH

Jesus did not know this woman was in the crowd, did not know of her illness, did not know of her determination to receive her healing, and actually didn't even know she existed. As stated, the Holy Spirit did not see fit to reveal this to Him, perhaps for the very reason I'm about to give.

Her experience portrays to any and all that Faith in God is such a powerful force, even such a powerful commodity, if you please, that it would pull healing from Jesus, even though He did not even know this woman existed. As I began to expound this to the congregation, you could sense Faith building greatly in the audience. As well, it was so powerful on me all night long that I actually slept very little that night. On the way to the airport the next morning, if anything, it increased respecting that which the Lord had given me.

God loves Faith! Actually, one cannot even please God without Faith (Heb. 11:6). He wants His Children to believe Him! If something is so powerful, as this obviously is, that it would bring healing from Christ, even though He did not even know the woman existed, then we're talking about something that is powerful beyond our comprehension. Every Believer should diligently seek to increase his Faith in the Lord. Such is done by the diligent study of the Word of God, for *"Faith comes by hearing, and hearing by the Word of God"* (Rom. 10:17).

The question, *"Turned Him about in the press, and said, Who touched My clothes?"* actually says, in the Greek, *"Who touched Me on My clothes?"* Considering the great press of people around Him, and that many were attempting to touch Him, as the next Verse proclaims, but without any recorded results, the difference was that this woman had Faith. Consequently, He felt it.

(31) "AND HIS DISCIPLES SAID UNTO HIM, YOU SEE THE MULTITUDE THRONGING YOU, AND YOU SAY, WHO TOUCHED ME?"

The exegesis is:

The Disciples were not privileged to know what was going on, but the Lord knew something had happened — something wonderful!

HIS DISCIPLES

The phrase, *"And His Disciples said unto Him,"* proclaims their exclamation! They did not understand His question, especially considering that scores of people were pressing Him, even thronging Him, and consequently touching Him. What did He mean, *"Who touched My clothes?"*

Consequently, we see from this act of Faith performed by this dear woman that the only thing she actually needed was Faith in God. She didn't have to go through the Disciples, and, in fact, did not do so! So that shoots down the Roman Catholic appeal to dead Saints — or live ones, for that matter! She went personally to Jesus, without Him even knowing she was there. By her Faith, she was able to receive exactly what she needed.

WHO TOUCHED ME?

Peter's question, *"You see the multitude thronging You, and You say, Who touched Me?"* portrays that this was completely beyond his understanding, or any of the other Disciples, for that matter (Lk. 8:45).

Why would one touching Him mean more, or be different, than others touching Him?

The difference was Faith!

Why did this woman have Faith and the others did not?

There is no answer to that. Actually, they should have had more Faith than she did. They had already witnessed many of the Miracles of Christ, while she had only recently heard what Jesus could do. But yet, she had great Faith in Christ.

MUSICAL TALENT

When I was eight years old, I asked the Lord to give me the talent to play the piano. It happened in a particular Church Service with a visiting Evangelist, who played the piano fairly well. As a child, I became more and more enamored each night as the meetings progressed. On the night in question, I began to ask the Lord to give me this particular talent. I had never tried to play the piano before and, at eight years of age, had absolutely no musical expertise.

Immediately after the Evangelist concluded with his musical rendition and singing, I began to implore the Lord, very quietly under my breath, to give me this talent. If He would do so, I promised I would forever use it for His Glory. Just a few days earlier, I had been Baptized with the Holy Spirit, with the evidence of speaking with other tongues (Acts 2:4). Inasmuch as I was now filled with the Spirit, I felt and thought that I could ask the Lord for things and that He would give them to me. It was a beautiful demonstration of childlike Faith. So, when I prayed that night, I fully expected the Lord to hear me and to answer me.

MY PROMISE TO THE LORD

As I began to importune the Lord, I made a promise to Him about certain things. Being only eight years old, I did not know much about sin or the world, but I promised the Lord, if He would give me this talent, I would never use it in the world, and I would never play in a night club. Actually, I had never seen a night club, but somehow I knew this was a place where the Lord was not glorified.

At any rate, when the Service ended, I could hardly wait to go to the platform to see if I could play the piano. I was that serious with my request, and that expectant!

I remember the Service finally concluding, with the final *"Amen."* Very slowly and hesitantly I made my way to the small platform, walking up to the piano. I did not really even sit down on the piano stool, but just stood in front of the black and white keys, placing my hands on them. Instantly, I began to make chords. At that time, I actually did not know they were chords, but I did know they sounded right.

Some may argue that musical talent was in my family, which is true, and that would account for this ability, with my petition to the Lord having nothing to do with it. I don't believe that! I believe the Lord heard my prayer and answered me by giving me that for which I had asked.

Upon arriving home after Service, my Dad asked me, *"Where did you learn those chords I heard you play after the Service? Have you been practicing at Church? Or somewhere else?"*

I replied to him that I had never touched a piano before, but that I had asked the Lord that night to give me the talent. *"I suppose He has already started,"* I exclaimed.

Yes, it took many months, even years, of practice, and practice, and more practice, but eventually it came. By God's Grace, I have kept that promise I made to Him, and He certainly has blessed abundantly.

LOOK TO ME

I know beyond the shadow of a doubt that the Lord heard and answered that prayer because of my Faith in Him. He has helped us to bless untold millions with this talent, for which I will ever be thankful. However, I related that in order to emphasize the childlike Faith I had, which brought about the request in the first place, and the belief that He heard me, and that He would answer, which He did!

From the time the Lord spoke to my heart in Harlingen, Texas, respecting this small Truth that I have attempted to relate to you, I have sensed an urgency of the Holy Spirit respecting the increase of my Faith. It is as if He is telling me, *"Do not look at circumstances, or situations, but look to Me, and believe Me."* I have sensed and felt that as never before! As well, I believe it is Faith which will be used to touch untold millions for the cause of Christ. For God never does anything of this nature but that it is for an intended purpose.

(32) "AND HE LOOKED ROUND ABOUT TO SEE HER WHO HAD DONE THIS THING."

The composition is:

The Lord looks for those who evidence Faith in His Person and in His Name!

THE LORD LOOKS FOR THOSE WHO EXHIBIT FAITH IN HIM

Irrespective of the question Peter had asked, Jesus begins a scrutinizing gaze in search for the woman. It is amazing how the Holy Spirit works. Jesus knew someone had touched Him with great Faith, and that it was a woman, but that is as much as the Spirit gave to Him. He did not tell Him where the woman was in the crowd. All of this was for purpose. There is a possibility that she was very shy. Again, because of her disease, she had actually broken the Law of Moses by touching Him. In other words, she was unclean. Consequently, the Holy Spirit would give her time to compose herself before she would give her testimony.

She had only *"touched"* the garment, and had not, by any means, grabbed it. Therefore, His knowing of this touch was not because of its action, but because of what it represented, her Faith. While it was unlawful for her to touch the Lord, due to her particular physical malady, still, this was only a ceremonial law, and by no means a moral law; consequently, the Law of Faith, which she evidenced, overrode this ceremonial law, exactly as it did when David ate the Shewbread, thereby breaking a ceremonial law (I Sam., Chpt. 21).

(33) "BUT THE WOMAN FEARING AND TREMBLING, KNOWING WHAT WAS DONE IN HER, CAME AND FELL DOWN BEFORE HIM, AND TOLD HIM ALL THE TRUTH."

The diagram is:

This Passage proclaims her now seeking mercy, as she had previously sought healing; it would also be granted!

FEAR

The phrase, *"But the woman fearing and trembling,"* pictures something going on in her soul. Luke prefaced this statement by saying, *"And when the woman saw that she was not hid"* (Lk. 8:47). Perhaps the consternation was caused by the knowledge that, inasmuch as she was unclean, she had broken a ceremonial law by touching Him. She had not asked His permission, carrying out her act of Faith, so to speak, behind the scenes. Now He had stopped the entire procession, looking earnestly through the crowd, proclaiming that *"Virtue had gone out of Him!"* She was found out; however, the results would be not at all what she feared. This she did know, the disease was gone.

HER HEALING

The phrase, *"Knowing what was done in her,"* has a double meaning:

1. First of all, and as stated, she knew the disease was gone. Especially considering that she had spent all her living on doctors, and for some twelve years, and had grown no better at all, but rather worse, there was no doubt in her mind or body that she was whole of that plague. Actually, she could feel it deep within her that the problem was gone. Furthermore, she would never be troubled with it again. It was a complete and permanent cure.

2. And yet, she was fearful that she had done something wrong. She, no doubt, knew of the strict censure of the Pharisees. Not knowing Jesus before now, due to living a goodly distance away (according to tradition), she wondered if He might be angry.

MERCY

The phrase, *"Came and fell down before Him,"* proclaims her seeking Mercy, as she had previously sought healing. This much she did know. Anyone Who, as Jesus, had the type of power manifested was more than ordinary, and deserved worship, which she freely gave! She did not know what He might do, but she did know what had already been done. She had been gloriously and wondrously healed, and of that there was no doubt!

The phrase, *"And told Him all the truth,"* proclaims her giving exactly the thoughts of her heart concerning the touching of the hem of His garment. Luke, being a doctor, added the words, *"how she was healed immediately"* (Lk. 8:47).

The song says:

"Tell it to Jesus, Tell it to Jesus,
"He is a friend that's well-known;
"You've no other such a friend or brother,
"Tell it to Jesus alone."

She told everything exactly as it had happened. In her heart she knew that Anyone Who had such Power would also know it if she told otherwise.

(34) "AND HE SAID UNTO HER, DAUGHTER, YOUR FAITH HAS MADE YOU WHOLE; GO IN PEACE, AND BE WHOLE OF YOUR PLAGUE."

The overview is:

In the Twenty-fifth Verse, she was addressed merely as *"a certain woman."* Now she is called *"daughter,"* which signifies relationship. He, in effect, had made her a member of the Family of God.

DAUGHTER

The phrase, *"And He said unto her, Daughter,"* proclaims far more than meets the eye and ear.

First of all, the word *"Daughter"* was a word of endearment. In effect, He was claiming her as a member of the family, so to speak! Not only was she healed, but she is now saved, as well! She is now a member of the Family of God, the same family to which the Disciples belonged, as well as all who have prostrated themselves, as she did, before the lowly Galilean. Even though she was near His age, or possibly even older, His using the word *"Daughter"* proclaimed Him as the Messiah. Therefore, He spoke as a Father to a Daughter.

THE REMEDY ALONE IS CHRIST

Second, this entire episode has a far greater meaning than just the healing of an individual, as wonderful and gracious as that was. It is obvious here to remark that this malady represents to us the ever-flowing bitter fountain of sin for which no treatment can be found in human philosophy. The remedy is only to be found in Christ.

To touch Christ's garment is to believe in His Incarnation, whereby He has touched us and so has enabled us by Faith to touch Him and to receive His Salvation of Grace (Bickersteth). As stated, there is no Earthly remedy for sin, but there is a remedy! That remedy is Christ, and Christ Alone!

FAITH

The phrase, *"Your Faith has made you whole,"* carries a powerful statement. He said to her, *"your Faith,"* implying the ingredient that one must have in order to receive from God, be it physical, financial, domestic, or spiritual. The word *"Faith"* is central to the Christian experience and Message. And yet, at times, this word is corrupted by a misunderstanding of its true Biblical meaning.

Oftentimes, people use the word *"Faith"* to indicate what is possible but uncertain. This is what causes most people to not receive from the Lord. The Bible uses *"Faith"* in ways that link it with what is assuredly and certainly true. Consequently, this is the type of *"Faith"* this woman had and that all are demanded to have, that is, if we are to receive from the Lord. The object of our Faith must not be ourselves, or others, but rather Jesus Christ and Him Crucified, and that alone (Rom. 6:3-14; I Cor. 1:17-18, 21, 23; 2:2; Gal. 6:14).

There is no limit to what Faith in God can do! It holds out a promise to all of mankind that can, because of a personal relationship with God in Jesus Christ, literally transform any situation.

THE OBJECT OF FAITH MUST EVER BE JESUS CHRIST AND HIM CRUCIFIED

The Old Testament speaks of false sources of security. It holds each of them up and examines them in contrast to the security that is ours in the Lord, and in the Lord Alone. Over and over again, it proclaims the foolishness of man in turning from reliance on God in order to seek the security of other men (Ps. 118:8; 146:3; Jer. 17:5).

We are also warned not to have faith in riches (Ps. 49:6; 52:7), military power (Deut. 28:52; Ps. 44:6; Jer. 5:17), or in our own goodness (Ezek. 33:13; Hos. 10:13). True Faith fastens on God as One Who, by His Nature, is the sole certainty and sure reality. God is faithful and unchanging, established in eternity. Because He is Who He is, we can commit ourselves to Him.

We do this, and I continue to speak of having Faith in God, by understanding that His Son, our Saviour, the Lord Jesus Christ, is the Source of all Blessings, whatever those Blessings might be; however, the Means by which all of this comes to us is the Cross of Christ, and the Cross alone!

Let me say it again:

1. The only way to God the Father is through Jesus Christ (Jn. 14:6).

2. The only way to Jesus Christ is by the Cross (Lk. 9:23).

3. The only way to the Cross is a denial of self, i.e., denying our own strength, personal ability, etc. (Lk. 9:23).

As our Faith is anchored in Christ and what He has done for us at the Cross, God the Father commits Himself to us in Covenant relationship; the placing of our confidence in Him brings us true well-being and safety.

THE OLD TESTAMENT VIEW OF FAITH

In Old Testament times (which also carries over into the present), God demanded that those who followed Him do so because He is utterly faithful and trustworthy. In the great Faith worthies, the New Testament points to Abraham as Faith's primary example. Genesis, Chapter 15, describes Abraham, then a very old man, in dialogue with God. Abraham complained that God had given him no children of his own, despite an earlier Promise (Gen. 12:2). God responded by amplifying the Promise. Abraham looked to the sky, filled with its numberless stars, and heard God say, *"So shall your seed be"* (Gen. 15:5).

The next Verse tells us, *"And Abraham believed in the LORD; and He counted it to him for Righteousness"* (Gen. 15:6). The Apostle Paul says of this incident: *"Who against hope* (Abraham) *believed in hope, that he might become the father of many nations, according to that which was spoken, So shall your seed be.*

"And being not weak in faith, he considered not his own body now dead, when he was about an hundred years old, neither yet the deadness of Sarah's womb:

"He staggered not at the Promise of God through unbelief; but was strong in Faith, giving Glory to God;

"And being fully persuaded that, what He (the Lord) *had Promised, He was able also to perform"* (Rom. 4:18-21).

Abraham examined the circumstances, and, despite everything, decided that God was to be trusted. Abraham consciously chose to put his trust in God, and this act of Saving Faith was accepted by the Lord in place of a righteousness that Abraham, within himself, did not possess. Abraham was not perfect by any standard, as the Scriptures bear out, but his life, as recorded in the Old Testament, shows again and again that he trusted God and acted on God's Promises, certain the Lord could be counted on (Heb. 11:8-12).

THE EXAMPLE

The example of Abraham stands as the Biblical illustration of Faith as a believing response to God. God spoke in Promise and Command. Abraham trusted himself to God and Abraham's Faith was demonstrated as he subsequently acted on what God had said (Gen., Chpts. 12-22).

Concerning Abraham's Faith, Jesus said, *"Your father Abraham rejoiced to see My day: and he saw it, and was glad"* (Jn. 8:56). What did Jesus mean by Abraham *"seeing My day"*? He was speaking of the fact that everything which the Lord had showed Abraham, as it regards Justification by Faith, depended totally upon the coming of the Redeemer, Who was to come through the lineage of Isaac, the son of Abraham and Sarah. The Redeemer also would have to die in order to redeem fallen humanity. This great truth was given to Abraham, as it regards the command of the Lord for Abraham to offer up Isaac in Sacrifice, which, as is known, was stopped at the last moment (Gen., Chpt. 22).

However, even though the Lord showed Abraham that Redemption would come by and through the death of the Redeemer (Gen. 22:13-14), He didn't show the Patriarch how that death would come about. That Revelation was given to Moses, and we speak of the Cross. It concerned the serpent on the pole (Num. 21:4-9).

Jesus mentioned this, as well. He said, *"And as Moses lifted up the serpent in the wilderness, even so must the Son of Man be lifted up"* (which spoke of the Cross): *"That whosoever believes in Him should not perish, but have eternal life"* (Jn. 3:14-15).

So it has always been the Cross (Gen. 3:15).

AN EXAMPLE OF UNBELIEF, OR LACK OF FAITH

While a study of Abraham's life helps us to understand the nature of belief or Faith, by contrast, the history of the generation of Israelites who were redeemed from Egypt helps us to understand the nature of unbelief. Exodus 4:1-8 is the foundation, and Numbers, Chapter 14, the culmination of a theme.

Exodus, Chapter 4, reports a dialogue between the Lord and a hesitant Moses. Moses had been told to return to Egypt. He would become the instrument of Israel's deliverance. But Moses objected: *"But, behold, they will not believe me, nor hearken unto my voice: for they will say, the LORD has not appeared unto you"* (Ex. 4:1). God gave Moses the power to perform three Miracles and explained: *"And it shall come to pass, if they will not believe you, neither hearken to the voice of the first sign, that they will believe the voice of the latter sign"* (Ex. 4:8).

The Book of Hebrews warns New Testament Believers not to permit a hardened heart to drag them into error so that they would become like the evil generation that heard God's Word, but whose *"unbelieving heart"* was shown by their refusal to obey (Heb. 3:12). The stories of Abraham and of the Exodus generation show the meaning of Faith in positive and negative terms. Through them we see several basic aspects of Faith.

THE BASICS OF FAITH

First, faith is not some response to evidence, even when that evidence is clearly miraculous. Abraham believed God. His Faith was a response to God Himself, Who met Abraham directly in a Word of Promise. That Word from God is far more compelling for Faith than any miracles performed in the material universe.

Second, Faith in God engages the total person. It is expressed in presumption and action. Abraham was well aware of his and Sarah's advanced age. But Abraham also considered God's Power and Faithfulness. The fact of God so transformed Abraham's perspective that he easily accepted God's Promise, although fathering a son was humanly impossible for him. But Israel, poised on the borders of Canaan, could see only the military strength of that land's inhabitants. They treated God *"with contempt"* (Num. 14:11; 16:30) by refusing to consider His Power and reality.

Faith is also expressed in actions. When

Abraham was told to go to Canaan, he packed up and went (Gen., Chpt. 12). When the Exodus generation was told to conquer the land, they refused even to try. They were betrayed by their *"unbelieving heart."*

Third, the outcome of faith was demonstrated. When a person responds to God's self-disclosure, Faith-generated obedience leads to Blessing. Abraham believed God and knew God's protection during his lifetime. Conversely, the unbelieving generation of Israelites wandered back into the wilderness to die in its desolate wastes.

FAITH AS EXPRESSED IN THE NEW TESTAMENT

The Object of Faith in the New Testament continues to be God, as in the Old, but now, through Jesus, Who is a reality, whereas in the Old Testament, He was only a shadow; consequently, Faith, as expressed in the New Testament, and in Christ, is far more developed than in the Old. The reason is clearly expressed by Jesus Himself: *"I am the Way and the Truth and the Life. No man comes to the Father except by Me"* (Jn. 14:6). God the Father has revealed Himself in the Son. The Father has set Jesus before us as the One to Whom we must entrust ourselves for Salvation. It is Jesus Who must be the focus of Christian Faith and, more particularly, what He did for us at the Cross (Eph. 2:13-18).

In the context of our Faith and in our relationship with Jesus, which are inseparable, *"believing"* has come to mean:

A. The happy trust that a person places in the Person of Jesus and what He has done for us at the Cross; and

B. The allegiance to Him that grows out of that very personal commitment.

FAITH AS EXPRESSED IN THE GOSPELS

The Gospels report many signs (Miracles) that Jesus performed as He traveled and taught. Often, but not always, Jesus' healings were intimately associated with the faith of the sick person, exactly as is expressed in this woman, who touched the hem of His garment (Mat. 9:2, 22, 29; Mk. 2:5; 5:34; Lk. 17:19; 18:42).

However, a survey of the Gospels shows that for most of the people, Jesus' Miracles failed to produce True Faith. Even as Jesus hung on the Cross, the mocking promise of His watching enemies was alive. *"Come down now from the Cross,"* they pledged, *"and we will believe"* (Mat. 27:42; Mk. 15:32). And when Jesus was raised from the dead, what happened? These men were the first to attempt to hide the evidence (Mat. 28:11-15).

In this, we see the phenomenon we noted in the Old Testament report of ancient Israel's unbelief. The Exodus Miracles provided incontrovertible proof of God's Power and His Presence. Yet, the Exodus generation would not commit themselves to Him. The nation in Jesus' day saw His healings, watched Him cast out demons, and even saw Him raise Lazarus from the dead; yet they refused to believe.

But belief in the full flow of God's Power was difficult, even for the Disciples. They had trusted themselves to Jesus as the Son of God. But when the Lord was crucified, their hope and confidence drained away. They could not, on the day of the Resurrection, bring themselves to believe that the One they trusted had come to life again (Mat., Chpt. 28; Mk., Chpt. 16; Lk., Chpt. 24). But in the Gospels, one vital fact is made clear in Jesus' Words about Faith: a lack of trust in God in Whom we have Faith closes off life's possibilities. When we fail to believe, we do not experience the full range of God's activity (Mat. 21:22). But when we trust, we open up our future to a full experience of God's Power (Mat. 17:20; 21:21; Lk. 7:9-10). All things are possible to the one who believes.

For you and me, Faith in Jesus does not come through an observation of miracles, as wonderful as they may be. Faith is born as we learn about Jesus, find out what He said, and what He did for us, as it refers to the Cross, and then put our trust in Him. We then go on to deeper Faith, and active reliance on the Power and Presence of God. And as we trust, our life opens up to all sorts of possibilities. Miracles follow Faith. Believing, we experience God at work in our lives.

FAITH AS LOOKED AT BY JOHN THE BELOVED

John looks at the relationship between

believing and evidence. He examines superficial belief. And he connects True Faith with life and death. In addition, several Passages of John's Gospel called for careful study. In Christian Faith, knowing and believing are linked. We respond to testimony about Jesus with our intellect as well as with our heart. John's Gospel looks at two kinds of testimony. There is the testimony of Jesus' Miracles and the testimony of Jesus' Words.

At times, these two lines of testimony enhance each other. Thus, the Twelve, who were already committed to Jesus, saw the Miracle at Cana (Jn. 2:11) and found their belief in Jesus strengthened. It is not unusual to find that many of the observers of Jesus' Works were moved to some kind of belief. The testimony of His Miracles was compelling (Jn. 7:31; 11:45; 12:11). Yet others who saw the same signs chose not to believe, rejecting Jesus against the evidence of the Lord's Works (Jn. 10:38; 14:11).

In John, we see that the testimony provided by Miracles and signs forced observers to take Jesus seriously. But signs and Miracles alone do not bring about Saving Faith.

SUPERFICIAL BELIEF

John distinguishes between two types of *"believing."* His Gospel was written, he told his readers, *"that you might believe that Jesus is the Christ, the Son of God; and that believing you might have life through His Name"* (Jn. 20:31). Yet when John describes the response of the crowds to the testimony of Jesus' Miracles, it is clear that those who *"believed"* did so in a way that fell short of life-giving belief in Jesus as the Son of God.

John 2:22-23 tells us of many who saw His signs and *"believed in Him."* But later, after that same crowd of shallow Disciples heard Jesus speak about Himself as the Bread of Life (Jn., Chpt. 6), they complained: *"This is an hard saying; who can hear it?"* (Jn. 6:60). John observes that *"from that time many of His Disciples went back, and walked no more with Him"* (Jn. 6:66).

Superficial faith came in response to the miraculous, and it died when Jesus communicated the Divine content of His Message. Nicodemus, a religious leader, confessed, *"We know that You are a Teacher come from God: for no man can do these miracles that You do, except God be with Him"* (Jn. 3:2). Yet when other religious leaders heard the Message that Jesus spoke (Jn. 7:16-17), they refused to go on to the belief that involves commitment to Jesus as Lord (Jn. 7:45-47). Wonder at Jesus' powers, even agreement that God must have sent Him, falls short of Saving Faith.

Only when one recognizes Jesus as the Son of God and commits himself completely to Him does a person believe in the fullest, saving sense. This commitment involves accepting His Words and making them the framework of one's life.

FAITH AND LIFE

Over and over in his writings, John links Faith with Life, and unbelief with death. The one who believes in Jesus has Eternal Life. The one who does not believe is already condemned to eternal death. The intimate connection between life and believing is as marked in John's Gospel and Epistles as is the connection between Faith and Righteousness in the writings of Paul.

The Eighth Chapter of John's Gospel explores the link between the testimony of the miraculous and the testimony of the Message. Jesus teaches clearly that He and the Father are inseparably One. Thus, belief in Jesus is the critical issue for every hearer: *"For if you believe not that I am He, you shall die in your sins"* (Jn. 8:24).

The Miracles of Jesus, likewise, cannot be argued away. But when Jesus spoke the Truth, the religious leaders attacked Him. Unlike Abraham, who heard God speak and responded with belief in the Lord, this generation did not respond to the Word of Truth. When the physical descendants of Abraham rejected the fresh Word of God that came through Jesus, they proved themselves to be of a different spiritual family, for Abraham believed God, but these men refused to believe God's Son.

The Eleventh Chapter of John's Gospel tells the story of the raising of Lazarus. While many accepted the testimony of the Miracle and accepted Jesus' Word about Himself, the story itself looks at believing from a slightly different perspective. Mary and Martha, the sisters of Lazarus, did believe in Jesus. They believed that Jesus, as the Source of Life, would raise Lazarus *"at the last day"* (Jn. 11:24), for Jesus was the Christ and the Son of God (Jn. 11:27). But although Saving Faith was present, the women stilled failed to understand the life-giving Power of Jesus, Power that enabled Him to raise their brother then and there, recalling him to life, even though he had been dead for four days.

This proclaims to us that one may have Saving Faith in Jesus, as the sisters of Lazarus, and yet limit His Power. When we put our trust in Jesus, the Son of God, we enter a relationship with One Who is Lord, and Whose ability to act in our world is without limitations. Actually, this characterizes the greater majority of the modern Church. Saving Faith in Christ is believed and maintained. Yet many limit Him thereafter!

PAUL AND FAITH

To Paul fell not only the task of presenting the Gospel, but also of giving testimony and explanation. Consequently, he deals with Faith and Salvation, Faith and Righteousness, and Faith and Fellowship with God. In the first three Chapters of Romans, Paul demonstrated the fact that all humanity is lost, without a shred of righteousness that would permit God to accept any individual, at least on their own merit. He said, *"Therefore by the deeds of the Law there shall no flesh be justified in His sight"* (Rom. 3:20). Yet, God has determined to bring mankind a Salvation that necessarily involves sinners becoming Righteous in His Sight. This, Paul explains, is accomplished in the death of Christ, which was a Sacrifice of Atonement. Through *"Faith in His Blood,"* the individual who believes is declared Righteous. Thus, Salvation and Righteousness come through Faith in Jesus and what He did for us at the Cross; and, through Faith, Salvation and Righteousness are available to all.

THE NATURE OF FAITH

In the Fourth Chapter of Romans, Paul argues that Faith is the same today as it was when it was exercised by Old Testament Saints such as Abraham and David. Also, Faith has the same result. Abraham and David won forgiveness by Faith (Rom. 4:1-8); and for us today, forgiveness is also found by Faith. We see in Romans, Chapter 4, that to believe means simply to count on God's Promise. We accept the Word of God Who spoke; in doing so, we accept God Himself.

Paul shows that the God Who spoke with Promise to Abraham is the same God Who, in Jesus, speaks with Promise to us: the God *"in Whom he* (Abraham) *believed, even God, Who quickens the dead, and calls those things which be not as though they were"* (Rom. 4:17). In Romans 4:18-25, Paul further defines Faith. Here he analyzes Abraham's Faith. Abraham faced the fact of his and Sarah's advanced age. He knew this meant that conceiving a child was impossible. But Abraham *"staggered not at the Promise of God through unbelief; but was strong in Faith, giving Glory to God."* Instead he was *"fully persuaded that, what He had Promised, He was able also to perform."* And so Paul concludes, *"therefore it was imputed to him for Righteousness"* (Rom. 4:20-22).

Abraham heard the Promise. He looked beyond the impossibility of its fulfillment and considered God. Abraham, confident that God would keep His Promise, accepted that what God announced would come to pass. The Promise Abraham believed was the Promise that he would father a child.

The Promise held out today in the Gospel in which we are to believe is the Promise that God, Who has delivered Jesus up for our sins and raised Him to life again for our Justification, will save us because of Jesus and His Atoning Work at the Cross, and our Faith in that Finished Work. We look beyond the impossibility that the natural person sees. We consider God. And we too are convinced that what God has announced will come to pass. Believing, we receive the Gifts of Salvation and Righteousness.

MAINTAINING OUR SALVATION

In Galatians, Chapter 3, Paul not only proclaims the necessity of Faith in Christ for one's Salvation, but he argues that our relationship with the Lord is also maintained by Faith. We are not to attempt to live in fellowship with God by trying to keep the Law. Paul reminds us, *"The righteous shall live by Faith"* (Gal. 3:11), and that refers to Faith in Christ and His Atoning Work on Calvary's Cross.

Law is based on a contrary principle: reliance on human activity and performance. It is not based on Promise. Since we must relate to God through His Promise rather than through His Works, we must continue on in our relationship with the Lord by Faith. We must hear the Words of Scripture as Promise, and we must rely on them as Promise.

In his personal testimony, Paul says, *"I am Crucified with Christ* (as the foundation of all victory; Paul here takes us back to Romans 6:3-5): *nevertheless I live* (have new life); *yet not I* (not by my own strength and ability), *but Christ lives in me* (by virtue of my dying with Him on the Cross, and being raised with Him in newness of life): *and the life which I now live in the flesh* (my daily walk before God) *I live by the Faith of the Son of God* (the Cross is ever the Object of my Faith), *Who loved me and gave Himself for me* (which is the only way that I could be saved)" (Gal. 2:20).

The life of Faith is ours as we continue to count on God's Words to us. We hear them as Promise and believe that God will do in us all that He has spoken. As we live by Faith, the Righteousness of which the Bible speaks as being ours in God's sight gradually infuses our life and character, and we become righteous persons in fact and in deed. It is all by Faith in Christ.

However, we must ever understand that Faith in the Word of God, at least for it to be True Faith, must be with the understanding that the entirety of the Bible points to Christ and Him Crucified. So, when we speak of making the Bible the Object of our Faith, it must be with that in mind. That which says too much concludes by saying nothing. So, when we speak of having Faith in the Word of God, it must ever be with the understanding that the Word of God, as stated, points strictly to Christ and His Atoning Work. In a sense, this means that Christ and Him Crucified must ever be the Object of our Faith. Only in this manner can we maintain our Salvation.

In Romans, Chapters 4 and 5, Paul tells us, as we've already stated, that Salvation comes by Faith, and that speaks of Christ and His Atoning Work at the Cross. When we come to Chapter 6 of Romans, this Chapter explains to us how we can maintain our Salvation, and do so by ever understanding that it is the Cross of Christ and Faith in that Finished Work which give us power through the Holy Spirit to live the life we ought to live. Then, and only then, *"sin shall not have dominion over you"* (Rom. 6:14).

So, when the Holy Spirit through Paul tells us how to successfully live for the Lord, for this is what the Sixth Chapter of Romans is all about, He takes us straight to the Cross (Rom. 6:3-5). This means that the Cross of Christ must ever be the Object of our Faith.

LOOKING BACK AT FAITH

The Object of Faith, we find as we study the Word of God, has differed somewhat from age to age. For in different ages, God has spoken different Words of Promise; however, even though the direction at times would be slightly different, the actual Object of Faith was always Christ and the Cross.

At the very dawn of time, and at the Fall of man, God promised that a Redeemer would come (Gen. 3:15). This sets the stage for Christ and His Cross. To Abraham, in keeping with that Promise, He promised a son and multiplied descendants. To those under the Law, there was the Promise of Blessing to accompany obedience. To us, there is the Promise of cleansing and acceptance through Christ, to Whom all the other Promises pointed.

In each age, Faith is man's response to the Promise. In each age, Faith is trusting one's self to the God Who has spoken. In each age, Faith is accepted by God in place of a righteousness that no human being had, or could have, at least on his own.

In the New Testament, to which the entirety of the Old pointed, we see with unmistakable clarity that it is through Faith that God gives Salvation and Righteousness — Faith in Christ and His Finished Work. It is in the New Testament that we see with unmistakable clarity that Faith is a personal response to God and a complete commitment of ourselves to Him. There also we see that Faith calls for a continuing relationship of response to Jesus' Word.

It is in the New Testament that we see with unmistakable clarity that Faith transforms human beings, bringing us a life that is eternal, and which can be experienced now. Through Faith we come into a relationship with God in which He commits Himself not simply to declare us righteous, but also to make us truly good persons after the example of Christ, which is done solely by Faith in the Sacrifice of Christ. Only then can the Holy Spirit work satisfactorily within our lives, developing His Fruit. Trusting God is the heart and soul of the Faith that centers in our Lord Jesus Christ and His Atoning Work.

ONCE AGAIN, CHRIST AND THE
CROSS MUST EVER BE THE
OBJECT OF OUR FAITH

The Believer must be careful not to fall into the trap into which Abraham almost succumbed. Distraught and discouraged because the Promised Son had not yet appeared, and inasmuch as it seemed the obstacles were abundant, he began to gradually take his eyes off the Giver onto the Gift. This is a danger for many Believers.

In response to this, *"the Word of the LORD came unto Abram in a Vision, saying, Fear not, Abram: I am your shield, and your exceeding great reward"* (Gen. 15:1). In this Passage, the Lord brings Abraham back to the correct position of Faith. The Believer must never allow himself, for whatever reason, to be pulled away from the Giver to the Gift. While it is certainly important, and exceedingly so, that the Gift, the Promised Son, be brought into the world, still, the Lord would tell the Patriarch, *"It is not the Gift, but rather My Person Who is 'your exceeding great reward.'"*

The modern Faith Movement has fallen into the error in which Abraham found himself. Faith has become the object with many, instead of the Giver of Faith. In so doing, the danger is always prevalent that God's Word will in turn be used against Himself — or at least, there is an attempt to do so. In other words, with Faith solely as the object instead of Christ and the Cross, the Believer automatically concludes that he knows the Will of God in any and all situations, and thereby, sets about to use his faith to bring about that which he desires instead of what God desires.

Actually, this is what Satan attempted to get Christ to do respecting the temptations in the wilderness. Christ was hungry, so why not introduce His Power to His need? It was a logical conclusion, at least in the manner in which Satan proposed it. There was nothing sinful in bread, and neither was there anything sinful in the Lord using His Power accordingly, or so Satan suggested! And so reason millions!

However, if Jesus had done so, He would have been using His Power for His Own betterment, which would have been stepping outside the Will of God; consequently, He will say to Satan, *"It is written, Man shall not live by bread alone, but by every word that proceeds out of the Mouth of God"* (Mat. 4:4).

So, to use Faith as an object, i.e., in order to acquire things at random pleasure, is not the Will of God at all! The Object of Faith must ever be the Giver of Faith, Who is the Lord Jesus Christ, and His Atoning Work. While the Gift is always important, such as the Promised Son to Abraham, still, and as stated, the Giver of that Gift was the *"exceeding great reward,"* and not the Gift itself.

(Many of the thoughts on Faith were taken from the teaching of Lawrence O. Richards.)

PEACE

The phrase, *"Go in peace, and be whole of your plague,"* adds a new dimension to the entirety of this episode. This woman not only gained healing, but Salvation, as well! The word *"peace"* assures this. It spoke of the health of both body and soul. As such, the proclamation of Salvation, and in few words, is beautifully given. The *"peace"* spoken of refers to *"peace with God."* As a result of the Fall, man lost his peace with God. As a result of sin which entered, there was an enmity which intruded between God and man. Because of his disobedience which brought about this enmity, man was estranged from God (Rom. 8:7; Eph. 2:15-16).

This lack of *"peace"* presents a troubled soul to the individual, which expresses itself in many ways, all adverse, whether physical, mental, domestic, and, above all, spiritual. Such flows from a twisted human nature. It can only be assuaged by Christ, as Faith is evidenced in Him, as exampled by the woman who touched the hem of His garment.

THE OLD TESTAMENT CONCEPT OF PEACE

The Hebrew word for *"Peace"* is *"Shalom."* It is derived from a root that conveys the image of wholeness, unity, and harmony — something that is complete and sound. It also conveys the idea of prosperity, health, and fulfillment. In the Old Testament, Peace takes on its deepest significance when we move into the Psalms and the Prophets. Although the word is expressed in other ways, still, its greatest fulfillment comes to human beings when they experience God's Presence.

As an example, the Lord said that He would *"bless His people with Peace"* (Ps. 29:11). But more than national blessing is involved in the Peace that God gives. David, fleeing from Absalom during that son's rebellion, felt intense strife and pressure (Ps. 4:1-2). But David fixed his thoughts on God and remembered the joy that came with trust in Him. Comforted and at rest despite overwhelming danger, David concluded, *"I will both lay me down in peace, and sleep: for You, LORD, only make me dwell in safety"* (Ps. 4:8).

For us, as for David, Peace in difficult circumstances is a result of our relationship with the Lord. *"Great peace,"* David says, *"have they which love Your Law: and nothing shall offend them"* (Ps. 119:165). The one whose life is in harmony with God's revealed Will experiences inner harmony as well. It is not surprising, then, to find Psalm 37 contrasting the wicked and ruthless with *"the man of peace"* (Ps. 37:35-37). The man of peace lives in a right relationship with God, for God Alone is the Source of human rest and fulfillment.

For those who have missed the way of Faith and are struggling to find fulfillment apart from God, there is no such blessing. As Isaiah warns, *"But the wicked are like the troubled sea, when it cannot rest, whose waters cast up mire and dirt. There is no peace, saith my God, to the wicked"* (Isa. 57:20-21). Consequently, peace in the Old Testament speaks of the Blessing of inner and outer harmony that comes to a person or people who live in a close relationship with God.

Believers can, like David, experience peace despite dangerous circumstances by being conscious of God's Presence, or at least of His sure Promises. Ultimately the world also will know international and interpersonal peace, as the very Presence of God in the Person of Jesus halts strife and war. One day it will come!

THE PEACE OFFERING OF THE OLD TESTAMENT

One of the Old Testament Offerings was called *"the Peace Offering."* It is mentioned over 80 times. This Offering, which came after the Sacrifices for sin, was partially burned and partially eaten by the worshippers. Thus, it symbolized the *"Shalom,"* the overflowing joy and fulfillment that forgiveness brings us, causing us to be at peace with the Lord. This was fulfilled by Christ at Calvary, where He thereby became our peace (Col. 1:20).

THE PEACE THAT JESUS BRINGS

There are multiplied greetings and farewells in the Epistles proclaiming that believing readers will receive Grace, Mercy, and Peace. This Peace is *"from God our Father and from the Lord Jesus Christ"* (Rom. 1:7; I Cor. 1:3; II Cor. 1:2; Gal. 1:3; Eph. 1:2, etc.). First and foremost, the peace human beings need is peace with God. This is ours in Jesus, and Jesus Alone.

"Therefore being Justified by Faith, we have peace with God through our Lord Jesus Christ" (Rom. 5:1). Ephesians 2:14 adds that Jesus Himself *"is our Peace."* Among God's people, Peace means that hostility has been replaced by unity (Eph. 2:14-17; 4:3).

PEACE IN THE EPISTLES

Peace, in the Epistles, is most often that restored wholeness that Jesus brings to our relationship with God and others, although this cannot be separated from the inner sense of well-being that accompanies them; however, this does not necessarily mean the absence of all outward strife. Jesus warned His Disciples not to imagine that serving Him meant that they would be freed from all external pressures and strife *"on Earth"* (Mat. 10:34; Lk. 12:51). Instead, Jesus focuses on peace despite external pressures and even suffering.

John most clearly developed that theme. He reports Jesus' Words of peace: *"Peace I leave with you, My Peace, I give unto you: not as the world gives, give I unto you. Let not your heart be troubled, neither let it be afraid"* (Jn. 14:27). He then said, *"These things I have spoken unto you, that in Me you might have peace. In the world, you shall have tribulation: but be of good cheer; I have overcome the world"* (Jn. 16:33).

Jesus provides an inner peace that lets the Believer face danger and suffering without fear or a trembling heart. Through Jesus an inner peace is possible, no matter how turbulent the external situation may be.

PEACE AND THE CROSS

The great Word given by Christ to His Disciples, as recorded in John 14:27, is all made possible by the Cross. In fact, every single thing that the Lord gives us, irrespective as to what it might be, which Bearer is always the Holy Spirit (Jn. 16:14-15), all, and without exception, are made possible by the Cross (Eph. 2:13-18).

The Cross of Christ, which took away all sin, which means that it atoned for all sin, upon that being done, hostility, caused by sin, was forever removed. Now, the Believer can *"come boldly unto the Throne of Grace, that we may obtain Mercy, and find Grace to help in time of need"* (Heb. 4:16).

SANCTIFYING PEACE

There is a vast difference in *"Justifying Peace,"* which every single Believer in the world has, than *"Sanctifying Peace."* Justifying Peace is the peace that comes to the new Believer upon the Born-Again experience. As stated, at that moment, all hostility between God and the believing sinner is removed by virtue of what Christ did at the Cross and the Faith of the believing sinner expressed in that Finished Work (Jn. 3:16).

However, the peace which Jesus mentioned in John 14:27 and 16:33 is *"Sanctifying Peace."* This is the type of *"Peace"* which Paul addressed in almost all of his Salutations to his Epistles. For instance, he said to the Galatians, *"Grace be to you and Peace from God the Father, and from our Lord Jesus Christ."* This is *"Sanctifying Peace."*

He then tells us how this peace is made possible. He said, *"Who gave Himself for our sins* (the Cross), *that He might deliver us from this present evil world, according to the Will of God and our Father"* (Gal. 1:3-4). All Believers have Justifying Peace, and have such in the same capacity; however, the capacity of *"Sanctifying Peace"* is altogether different in different Believers. In other words, some will have *"Sanctifying Peace"* to a far greater degree than others.

As an example, when the Lord told Moses to tell the Children of Israel that He was going to pass through the land of Egypt that night, and that, in every home that didn't have the blood applied to the doorposts, the firstborn would die, it was, to say the least, a chilling announcement! More than likely, there were some Israelites who went to bed that night and slept soundly, totally trusting in what the Lord had said, because they had applied, as the Lord commanded, the blood to the doorposts. Therefore, they rested calmly and serenely. However, on the other hand, there undoubtedly were some of the Children of Israel who, even though the blood was applied to the doorposts, still, spent the night in anxiety and fear.

Irrespective, even though there was anxiety and fear in their hearts, which robbed them of peace that particular night, still, they were just as safe as the person who slept soundly. Moreover, the person who slept soundly was just as secure as the one who did not sleep soundly at all. One, as it might be said, had *"Sanctifying Peace,"* while the other didn't.

HOW CAN THE BELIEVER HAVE SANCTIFYING PEACE?

Going back to the deliverance of the Children of Israel from Egyptian bondage, the degree of peace on the fateful night all pertained to the degree of faith in the blood applied to the doorpost. The Lord had said, *"When I see the blood, I will pass over you"* (Ex. 12:13). It is the same presently!

You as a Believer are to place your Faith

exclusively in Christ and the Cross, trusting totally and completely in what He has done for you, and not allow your Faith to be moved from Christ and the Cross to something else. If you do that, and you continue to do that, the Holy Spirit will guarantee your Peace.

As we've stated, this *"Sanctifying Peace"* doesn't guarantee an absence of all problems, difficulties, and troubles; however, it does guarantee a *"Peace"* in the midst of all of those troubles.

WHOLENESS OF MIND, BODY, AND SPIRIT

Moreover, from the phrase, *"Go in peace and be whole of your plague,"* one can make an excellent Scriptural case that healing for the body, as well as Salvation of the soul, is a part of the Atonement, i.e., the price that Jesus paid at Calvary. Man cannot be *"whole"* unless he is whole in every capacity. To argue that the *"Atonement"* only included Salvation from sin is a failure not only to understand the total Fall of man, but also a failure to understand the total Redemption of man by Christ at Calvary. Man is either totally redeemed, made whole in every respect, or not redeemed at all! Of course, we know that Jesus redeemed the *"whole"* man.

To argue that, because Christians still get sick, healing was not included in the Atonement is to argue that Salvation from sin is not in the Atonement, because at times Christians still sin. In Truth, the total Redemption of man in the Atonement, including both spiritual and physical, is not affected by the fact of both continued sin and sickness. But, the entirety of the Salvation process, as provided at Calvary, is not yet completed as far as results are concerned, even though it is completed as far as the fact is concerned.

Concerning this very thing, Paul said, *"But ourselves also, which have the Firstfruits of the Spirit, even we ourselves groan within ourselves, waiting for the Adoption, to wit, the Redemption of our body"* (Rom. 8:23). As the Apostle said, we presently only have the *"Firstfruits of the Spirit,"* as it regards all that Jesus did in the Atonement. The balance will be received at the Resurrection, when this physical body will be redeemed —

NOTES

exchanged, in effect, for a Glorified Body. Then the totality of what Jesus paid for at the Cross will be completely realized.

The Believer has presently been Sanctified and Justified *"in the Name of the Lord Jesus, and by the Spirit of our God"* (I Cor. 6:11). However, the Believer has not yet been *"Glorified,"* which will take place at the First Resurrection of Life, which will then, and for all time, complete the Salvation process. Then sin and sickness will no longer be possible (Rom. 8:17-25; I Cor. 15:51-54).

(35) "WHILE HE YET SPOKE, THERE CAME FROM THE RULER OF THE SYNAGOGUE'S HOUSE CERTAIN WHICH SAID, YOUR DAUGHTER IS DEAD: WHY TROUBLE THOU THE MASTER ANY FURTHER?"

The synopsis is:

The faith of this certain person wasn't high enough to believe that Jesus could raise the dead.

THE APPALLING NEWS

The phrase, *"While He yet spoke,"* refers to someone coming from the home of Jairus, and bringing a message, even while the Lord was speaking to the woman who had just been healed. The message would not be good!

The phrase, *"There came from the ruler of the Synagogue's house certain which said, Your daughter is dead,"* constituted a terrible blow to Jairus. He was, no doubt, very pleased at the healing of this dear woman, but, at the same time, his heart was breaking for his little daughter. He must have been extremely concerned regarding the delay brought about by the healing of the woman. Jesus' searching for her after her healing, and the time it took for her to give her testimony, must have caused terrible anxiety in the heart of this man. And now, he receives the worst message of all, confirming his fears, *"Your daughter is dead!"*

The question, *"Why trouble thou the Master any further?"* proclaims the end of their Faith, at least those who had brought the disconcerting message. I think the next Verse proclaims that Jairus also felt that it was now too late!

(36) "AS SOON AS JESUS HEARD THE WORD THAT WAS SPOKEN, HE SAID

UNTO THE RULER OF THE SYNAGOGUE, BE NOT AFRAID, ONLY BELIEVE."

The composition is:

In effect, Jesus said, *"Stop fearing, and be believing."*

BE NOT AFRAID, ONLY BELIEVE

The phrase, *"As soon as Jesus heard the word that was spoken,"* means that Jesus overheard what was being said. The phrase, *"He said unto the ruler of the Synagogue,"* proclaims, according to the statement given by Christ, that Jairus, upon the news of the death of his daughter, had ceased to believe. The phrase, *"Be not afraid, only believe,"* constituted some of the greatest words that Jairus would ever hear, but yet completely beyond his comprehension. In effect, Jesus said, *"Stop fearing,"* and *"Be believing,"* meaning to continue believing, even in the presence of death. What a valuable lesson this should be to all!

To believe is one thing, but to continue to believe, even in the face of extremely adverse circumstances, as here proclaimed, is the key to receiving what we want from the Lord. At what level does our faith weaken and die? The Lord is ever seeking to strengthen our Faith, which is always done through the Word of God (Rom. 10:17). This simply means we are to believe the Word of God, and to believe it despite the circumstances.

I am convinced that the more mature one is in Christ, that the Lord allows circumstances to build, which, at times, make the situation even more impossible, in order that our Faith may be increased, by trusting solely in God's Word.

The idea is, that we walk by Faith, not by sight (II Cor. 5:7).

Consequently, the Lord will allow the *"sight"* to be increased by adverse circumstances, difficulties, and even impossibilities! Because of their loud clamor and obvious disabilities, it becomes very easy to look at these things. The secret is to keep one's eye and heart on the Word, despite the circumstances or difficulties.

I think the difficulties could not be any worse than here recorded, with the child actually having died. And yet Jesus says to him, *"Don't fear, keep believing!"* He says the same to us, as well!

(37) "AND HE SUFFERED NO MAN TO FOLLOW HIM, SAVE PETER, AND JAMES, AND JOHN THE BROTHER OF JAMES."

The synopsis is:

He took these three with Him to the home of Jairus.

PETER, JAMES, AND JOHN

Why these three, *"Peter, James, and John"*?

This is the first of three occasions when Jesus will single them out from the other Disciples.

1. On this occasion, the raising of the girl from the dead, Jesus would portray to these three His *"Power."*

2. At the transfiguration, only these three were allowed to witness this event (Mk. 9:1-2). Here, He showed them His *"Glory"*!

3. During His Passion in the Garden of Gethsemane, likewise, only the three were allowed (Mk. 14:32-35). Here, He showed them His *"Sufferings"*!

The only answer why these three were included, with the others excluded from these momentous occasions, is that the three showed, by their actions, that they desired a closer walk with Him. I am aware of no other explanation. Those who *"hunger and thirst after Righteousness are filled."* Consequently, it stands to reason that they who *"hunger and thirst"* the more are filled the more (Mat. 5:6).

(38) "AND HE COMES TO THE HOUSE OF THE RULER OF THE SYNAGOGUE, AND SEES THE TUMULT, AND THEM WHO WEPT AND WAILED GREATLY."

The overview is:

These were hired mourners, which was the custom in those days.

THE HOUSE

The phrase, *"And He comes to the house of the ruler of the Synagogue,"* spoke of the home of Jairus.

What was in the mind of Jairus all the time they were on the way to his house? Did he really realize what Jesus was about to do? It seems from Luke 7:11 that this was not the first occasion of Jesus raising one from the dead, although that chronology is not confirmed.

The phrase, *"And sees the tumult,"* referred to the activity of the paid mourners, and Jesus examining their actions with a critical and careful eye. The phrase, *"And them who wept and wailed greatly,"* had to do with the practice and custom of that time of hiring mourners to do this thing. Their mourning was not real, only fake, due to most of them probably not even knowing the child.

The actions of Christ, as the next Verse portrays, proclaim the fact that He was not in sympathy with such activity.

(39) "AND WHEN HE WAS COME IN, HE SAID UNTO THEM, WHY MAKE YOU THIS ADO, AND WEEP? THE DAMSEL IS NOT DEAD, BUT SLEEPS."

The exposition is:

This did not mean that she was actually not dead, but that the child was not dead to stay dead; as well, the word *"sleeps"* brings us to the fact of the Resurrection; in the Scriptures, the believing dead are constantly referred to as *"sleeping"*; however, it is only the body which sleeps, with the soul and the spirit at death instantly going to be with Christ, that is, if the person is saved.

SLEEP!

The phrase, *"And when He was come in,"* refers to Him entering into the midst of the paid mourners. Jairus, Peter, James, and John were with Him. The question, *"He said unto them, Why make you this ado, and weep?"* refers to all the uproar and constant wailing. As stated, Jesus was not in sympathy with this custom and practice.

The phrase, *"The damsel is not dead, but sleeps,"* did not mean that she was not actually dead, but, as stated, that the child was not dead to stay dead. Some false cults teach soul-sleep, meaning that at death the soul sleeps until the Resurrection, etc. Such is not taught in Scripture. All the Scriptures used by these cults clearly refer to the body, which does sleep in the dust of the Earth until the Resurrection of the Body (Dan. 12:2; Jn. 5:28-29).

The body is the only part of man that dies at physical death (James 2:26). The reason it dies is because the inner man, the soul and spirit, the life of the body, leaves the body. The body then goes back to dust and is spoken of as being asleep (Gen. 3:19; Eccl. 3:19-21; Mat. 9:24; Jn. 11:11; I Cor. 11:30; 15:6, 18-20, 51; I Thess. 4:13-17).

(40) "AND THEY LAUGHED HIM TO SCORN. BUT WHEN HE HAD PUT THEM ALL OUT. HE TAKES THE FATHER AND THE MOTHER OF THE DAMSEL, AND THEM WHO WERE WITH HIM, AND ENTERS IN WHERE THE DAMSEL WAS LYING."

The structure is:

The word *"enters"* actually refers to a person going on a journey, even though only a few feet, at least in this instance. It conveyed the idea of distance; in effect, it pointed forward to the coming Resurrection.

SCORN

The phrase, *"And they laughed Him to scorn,"* refers to their weeping suddenly turning to laughing. I think it now becomes obvious why Jesus was opposed to this custom. Moreover, their deriding and jeering were at Him! They were not content to merely disagree with Him about the child being dead, but they felt they must loudly proclaim their disagreement by jeering Him.

The phrase, *"But when He had put them all out,"* is a strong statement, meaning that He had to use pressure to make these individuals leave. It was somewhat akin to the forceful ejection when He cleansed the Temple. There is no evidence that it went quite that far, but very close to it!

THE FAMILY

The phrase, *"He takes the father and the mother of the damsel, and them who were with Him,"* referred to Jairus, his wife, Peter, James, and John. The phrase, *"And enters in where the damsel was lying,"* is an interesting statement. The word *"enters"* actually refers to a person going on a journey.

Wuest says that the word was chosen because it conveyed the idea of distance. Even though it was only a few feet from this room to where the child was lying dead, what would transpire, the raising of the child from the dead, would portray a journey of incomprehensible proportions. All would be taken to a dimension of Faith and Power that are impossible in the natural sense.

(41) "AND HE TOOK THE DAMSEL BY THE HAND, AND SAID UNTO HER, TALITHA CUMI; WHICH IS, BEING INTERPRETED, DAMSEL, I SAY UNTO YOU ARISE."

The exegesis is:

This was spoken in Aramaic, the same tongue used concerning our Lord's Words on the Cross, *"My God, My God, why have You forsaken Me?"* As the original language was reported in these two cases, quite possibly they relate to each other; as Jesus defeated death at the home of Jairus, likewise, and for the whole world, He defeated death at Calvary.

THE MIRACLE

The phrase, *"And He took the damsel by the hand,"* refers to a strong grip.

What were the thoughts of Jairus and the girl's mother when Jesus reached down and took her hand?

The phrase, *"And said unto her, Talitha cumi,"* is Aramaic, and means *"little girl, I say unto you, Arise."* Consequently, it means that Mark gave us the original language in which Jesus spoke this Word.

(42) "AND STRAIGHTWAY THE DAMSEL AROSE, AND WALKED; FOR SHE WAS OF THE AGE OF TWELVE YEARS. AND THEY WERE ASTONISHED WITH A GREAT ASTONISHMENT."

The overview is:

While the Scriptures only record three people being raised from the dead by Christ, Augustine says that He raised many more.

ASTONISHMENT

The phrase, *"And straightway the damsel arose, and walked,"* means that she immediately arose upon the Command of Christ, and began to walk about the room, possibly to her mother and father, and then maybe even to Christ.

The phrase, *"For she was of the age of twelve years,"* simply relates her age. What her sickness had been which had caused her death, we are not told; however, whatever it was, she no longer has it.

The phrase, *"And they were astonished with a great astonishment,"* means they were simply amazed beyond words. Peter, James, and John, along with the mother and father, simply stood there as if in a trance, knowing that what they had seen was true. Yet they were hardly able to believe it.

As someone has said, *"He raised the dead then to show that He will be able to raise the dead on that Resurrection Morn!"*

(43) "AND HE CHARGED THEM STRAITLY THAT NO MAN SHOULD KNOW IT; AND COMMANDED THAT SOMETHING SHOULD BE GIVEN HER TO EAT."

The exposition is:

They must not relate the account of this Miracle; there were reasons for this, the least not being the furor which religious leaders would cause; but it is certain that such news could not be kept.

THE CHARGE

The phrase, *"And He charged them straitly that no man should know it,"* was done in order that the religious leaders may not be further aroused. However, His Command was probably futile, inasmuch as the paid mourners knew what He had proposed to do, and certainly the very appearance of the child would prove beyond the shadow of a doubt that He had done it — raised her from the dead. So, even though they were *"charged straitly,"* i.e., with insistence, still, it is doubtful that the secret was kept for very long.

The phrase, *"And commanded that something should be given her to eat,"* probably was in reference to her past illness. Possibly food had exacerbated whatever problem she had. Nevertheless, if that was the problem, it no longer is, and she can now eat anything she desires.

This Chapter encompasses the former maniac of Gadara being commanded to go into the Gospel field (Vs. 19); the woman, to go into peace (Vs. 34); and the child, to go into dinner (Vs. 43). These three commands, in reverse order, apply to all who have experienced the Saving Grace and Power of Christ. The Bible must be their food; assurance of Salvation, their experience; and preaching the Gospel, their employment.

All Christians, honorably earning their bread, should regard preaching the Gospel, at least in some way, as their main business (Williams).

CHAPTER 6

(1) "AND HE WENT OUT FROM THENCE, AND CAME INTO HIS OWN COUNTRY; AND HIS DISCIPLES FOLLOW HIM."

The overview is:

This refers to Christ leaving Capernaum. Quite possibly, He left before the news got out concerning the raising of the daughter of Jairus from the dead.

NAZARETH

The phrase, *"And He went out from thence, and came into His Own country,"* refers to Nazareth. Even though He was born in Bethlehem, still, Nazareth had been His home from the time that Joseph, his foster father, had been warned by the Lord in a dream, concerning where He should live; consequently, the Scripture says, *"And He came and dwelt in a city called Nazareth"* (Mat. 2:23). Nazareth was about a day's journey from Capernaum.

There is debate over whether this is the same journey recorded in Luke 4 or another. Most think that Luke 4 was His first, with this being His second. And yet, the terminology is such that the possibility definitely exists that Luke 4 and Mark 6 are one and the same. Luke 4 could well be given out of chronological order, as some of the experiences often are.

The phrase, *"And His Disciples follow Him,"* speaks of the entirety of the Twelve.

(2) "AND WHEN THE SABBATH DAY WAS COME, HE BEGAN TO TEACH IN THE SYNAGOGUE: AND MANY HEARING HIM WERE ASTONISHED, SAYING, FROM WHENCE HAS THIS MAN THESE THINGS? AND WHAT WISDOM IS THIS WHICH IS GIVEN UNTO HIM, THAT EVEN SUCH MIGHTY WORKS ARE WROUGHT BY HIS HANDS?"

The synopsis is:

They did not question the wisdom or the works, but rather His right to do such things. In their thoughts, He wasn't worthy!

WHO IS THIS MAN?

The phrase, *"And when the Sabbath Day was come,"* lends credence to the thought that He arrived in Nazareth several days before the Sabbath. The phrase, *"He began to teach in the Synagogue,"* records the practice of most Synagogues. If a speaker of note came by, the ruler of the Synagogue, could, if he so desired, request that he speak. Having heard many wonderful things about Jesus, especially considering that He was a home-boy, they, no doubt, eagerly requested that He teach them. The method varied in different Synagogues. Sometimes a Text was appointed, and sometimes the speaker was allowed to chose that which He desired.

ASTONISHMENT

The phrase, *"And many hearing Him were astonished,"* actually proclaims two reasons why!

1. The tremendous insight He had in the Scriptures far eclipsed any and all they had ever heard. Little did they realize it, but the Psalms declare the attention He gave to the Word, even when He was growing up among them.

"O how I love Your Law! it is my meditation all the day.

"Thou through Your Commandments have made me wiser than my enemies: for they are ever with Me" (Ps. 119:97-98).

Consequently, on these very hills around Nazareth, in places of solitude and privacy, He had sought the Lord earnestly, and for all His Life. His knowledge of the Word was far greater than any had ever been.

"I have more understanding than all my teachers: for Your Testimonies are my meditation.

"I understand more than the ancients, because I keep Your Precepts" (Ps. 119:99-100).

2. He was but a peasant's Son, and, consequently, a peasant Himself. Therefore, how was it possible, at least in their thinking, that He would have such understanding?

CONTEMPT!

The question, *"Saying, From whence has this Man these things?"* is asked in contempt. The word, *"Man,"* was inserted by the translators, meaning it was not in the original, with them actually asking, *"From whence has 'this' these things?"* They were overly contemptuous in their question.

The question, *"And what wisdom is this which is given unto Him, that even such mighty works are wrought by His Hands?"* proclaims them addressing both that which He taught and the *"mighty works"* which He performed. They did not deny the *"wisdom"* or the *"mighty works,"* nor that they were *"wrought by His Hands"*; their complaint was actually that He had no right to do such things. This has ever been the criticism of those who do not desire God's choice. They could not attack what He said or did; consequently, they will attack Him.

He wasn't worthy! He wasn't qualified! He did not pass their test, whatever that test was! It has little changed unto the present. Those who pass God's test will not pass man's; those who pass man's, will not pass God's.

(3) "IS NOT THIS THE CARPENTER, THE SON OF MARY, THE BROTHER OF JAMES, AND JOSEPH, AND OF JUDA, AND SIMON? AND ARE NOT HIS SISTERS HERE WITH US? AND THEY WERE OFFENDED AT HIM."

The exposition is:

Chrysostom said that He made plows and yokes for oxen; in the minds of His critics, this disqualified Him as a great teacher.

The latter part of this Verse disproves the claims by the Catholic Church that Jesus had no brothers or sisters.

THE CARPENTER

The beginning of the question, *"Is not this the carpenter . . . ?* no doubt, actually meant that He worked at the trade of a carpenter, and continued to do so until He entered public Ministry. So, their complaint was that He was a carpenter, and consequently ill-prepared to be a great Teacher. For His townspeople, the contrast was too great between the Peasant of Galilee, Who had earned His daily bread by the sweat of His brow for the first 30 years of His Life, and the Person Who delivered those wonderful discourses and performed those Miracles. They could not see past His role and position as a carpenter. This was lowly in their estimation, and certainly offered no preparation for a position as one of the great Teachers of Israel. So, they were offended!

BROTHERS AND SISTERS

The continuation of the question, *"the Son of Mary, the Brother of James, and Joseph, and of Juda, and Simon?* concerns Jesus, as the Firstborn of Mary, and then His brothers. Some have contended that the word *"brother"* could refer to *"cousins,"* which they claim these were, with Mary remaining a perpetual virgin; however, that is incorrect. Had they been *"cousins,"* the term would have been *"sungenes,"* which is used of *"kin, kinsman, or kinsfolk."* The question, *"And are not His sisters here with us?"* probably means that He had more than two sisters, for if there had been only two, the word *"both"* probably would have been used.

OFFENSE

The phrase, *"And they were offended at Him,"* means that He did not meet with their approval; consequently, they were scandalized that He was able to do these great things. In some weird way, they felt He brought reproach on their town of Nazareth. They were fearful they would become a laughing-stock over Israel.

The very idea that this Peasant, or this *"oaf,"* as they would have put it, would aspire to be one of the great Teachers of Israel is what was beyond their comprehension. Never mind that His Words were given with more wisdom than any they had ever heard before, and that *"mighty works"* constantly were performed by His Hands, still, they could not, or, in truth, would not, accept Him, irrespective of the great things He did! As stated, they could not explain Him, so they rejected Him.

The saddest part of all was that His Own half-brothers and half-sisters, sons and daughters of Mary and Joseph, disbelieved His Messianic claims. They had lived in the same home with Jesus for many years, and had been the recipients of the financial support He brought into the family by His carpentry work. But, His singularly beautiful life had made no effective impression upon their dull, cold hearts (Wuest).

(4) "BUT JESUS SAID UNTO THEM, A PROPHET IS NOT WITHOUT HONOUR, BUT IN HIS OWN COUNTRY, AND AMONG

HIS OWN KIN, AND IN HIS OWN HOUSE."

The structure is:

I don't personally think that Mary was a part of this unbelief, but it definitely included the balance of the family; Joseph, by now, probably had passed on.

HONOUR

The phrase, *"But Jesus said unto them,"* represents His answer to their unbelief. The phrase, *"A Prophet is not without honour,"* is actually a catch-all phrase referring to any and all who hold this office. A *"Prophet"* is a *"forth-teller,"* which means *"one who speaks out God's Message."* It also included the predicting of future events, but such is only incidental to the chief work of proclaiming the Message.

Even though the phrase was a catch-all, still, in the phrase, Jesus makes a definite claim to being a Prophet. He had already claimed to be the Jewish Messiah (Lk. 4:21; Jn. 4:26); the Son of Man, with the Power of God (Mat. 9:6; Mk. 1:10; Lk. 5:24); and the Son of God (Jn. 5:22).

The word *"honour"* means to show respect, deference, and reverence (Wuest).

The phrase, *"But in His Own country, and among His Own kin, and in His Own house,"* not only speaks of all *"Prophets,"* but also, and more specifically, of Christ Himself.

There was no way that these people would even remotely consider that He was born of a Virgin and had God Alone for His Father.

As stated, the phrase also proclaims the disbelief of His *"kin"* and *"house."*

MARY

And yet, I cannot believe that Mary shared the unbelief of her other sons and daughters. From what little description we have, it seems that she was not a forceful woman; consequently, she said very little at these times, although she was hurting deeply in her heart. She knew what the Angel Gabriel had said unto her, and she also remembered the Spirit of Prophecy that came on her at this occasion (Lk. 1:26-38, 46-56). So, I think we must confine the unbelief to the half-brothers and half-sisters! (It seems, as stated, by this time, Joseph had passed on.)

The rejection suffered here by Christ had to be the *"unkindest"* cut of all. These people knew Him, and especially His Own loved ones. They knew of His impeccable Life and Perfect Character. They knew He was the personification of kindness. There was, therefore, no reason for their actions. It could only be summed up as the result of cold, calculating, hardened hearts, which were so removed from God that even though they constantly spoke of Him, they did not in reality know Him at all! Had they known God the Father, they would have known God the Son!

(5) "AND HE COULD THERE DO NO MIGHTY WORK, SAVE THAT HE LAID HIS HANDS UPON A FEW SICK FOLK, AND HEALED THEM."

The overview is:

It actually means that not even one mighty work could be performed; it was not that He couldn't, but that they wouldn't bring the sick and the diseased to Him. They would rather see their loved ones sick than to see Christ heal them!

UNBELIEF

The phrase, *"And He could there do no mighty work,"* doesn't mean that He attempted to bring deliverance to the worst cases and then failed, but instead that no one would bring their sick and afflicted to Him. These people of Nazareth were so consistently unbelieving that they would rather see their loved ones remain sick, and possibly even die, than to be healed by Christ.

Such is the hardened, religious heart!

The phrase, *"Save that He laid His Hands upon a few sick folk, and healed them,"* actually meant that a few sickly ones came to Him and did receive their healing. From the terminology, it seems that they would have been belittled greatly for their coming to Christ.

Unbelief shuts Heaven out of men and men out of Heaven; but where need was, His pity never chilled or tired, but continued to work. The few sick folk profited by a love that overleaps every obstacle because it never seeks *"self"* (Williams).

(6) "AND HE MARVELLED BECAUSE OF THEIR UNBELIEF. AND HE WENT ROUND ABOUT THE VILLAGES, TEACHING."

The diagram is:

The Holy Spirit mentions Christ marveling twice: once, at the Faith of the Gentile, and, again, at the unbelief of His Own (Mat. 8:10).

MARVELLED

The phrase, *"And He marvelled because of their unbelief,"* expresses the view of His humanity. As Deity, He, of course, would not have marvelled at anything. The idea is, He did not expect the negative reception that He received at Nazareth. Inasmuch as there was no cause or reason for their attitude and action, it surprised Him at their wholesale rejection.

A sincere, honest, pure heart, as the Heart of Christ, which has nothing but good for anyone, does not expect the hatred and opposition that was here evidenced. There was no reason for them to do this, inasmuch as He had lived among them for about 30 years. During all of that time He had conducted Himself in a manner that was Perfect. In Truth, their hatred of Him did not spring from anything He had done, but for Who He was! Their unrighteousness rebelled as His Righteousness.

The phrase, *"And He went round about the villages, teaching,"* means that He visited all the villages around Nazareth, teaching, more than likely, in their Synagogues. What a privilege it was to have Him in their midst! And yet, the far greater majority did not know Him, and actually never would know Him!

(7) "AND HE CALLED UNTO HIM THE TWELVE, AND BEGAN TO SEND THEM FORTH BY TWO AND TWO; AND GAVE THEM POWER OVER UNCLEAN SPIRITS."

The composition is:

This speaks of the first mission of the Twelve where they were sent without Him.

THE TWELVE

The phrase, *"And He called unto Him the Twelve,"* proclaims them being sent out to do the Work of the Lord. The phrase, *"And began to send them forth by two and two,"* records the manner in which they were sent.

UNCLEAN SPIRITS

The phrase, *"And gave them power over unclean spirits,"* presents a great Truth. Bickersteth says that Mark here fixes the attention upon the great central object of Christ's mission — to contend against evil in every form, and especially to grapple with Satan in his stronghold in the hearts of men.

If one is to notice, it is not mentioned here about praying for the sick, even though they did this. And the Thirteenth Verse says that many were healed. Neither were other problems mentioned, only the *"unclean spirits."* As we have stated, the designation, *"unclean spirits,"* covers all spirits of darkness. As well, the Holy Spirit mentions this alone because, either directly or indirectly, evil spirits are the cause of all problems that beset humanity, be it physical, domestic, material, or spiritual.

This does not mean that demons are the direct cause of any and all problems, but it does mean that if not directly, then indirectly! For instance, demon spirits are the instigators of all false doctrine (I Tim. 4:1). They are also the originators of all sicknesses and diseases, at least in their original form. That does not mean that the cause of every headache, etc., is a demon spirit, for it isn't. But it does mean that evil spirits are the cause of original sickness in man as a result of the Fall (Mk. 6:13).

Also, evil spirits are the cause of anarchy and war (Rev. 16:13-16).

WARFARE

Verse 7 proclaims to the Church the area of its warfare. Tragically, the greater majority of the Church has absolutely no idea what it means to oppose demon spirits in the Name of Jesus. About half of the so-called Church doesn't even believe in the Holy Spirit, at least as He is proclaimed in the Word of God; consequently, they do not believe in the Work of the Holy Spirit, which includes healing the sick and casting out devils. Therefore, it is by and large a man-led Church, which in no way engages Satan in spiritual warfare. It's pretty much a social club and little else!

Regrettably, great segments of the Pentecostal and Charismatic community, which claim to believe in the Power of God, still, for the most part, are promoting the *"political message"* and the *"prosperity message"*

— and both are false doctrines. While the Lord blesses people financially, and while Believers should take a hand in the political process, still, the culture is not going to be Christianized, nor is society going to be changed. There is nowhere in the Bible where men are called to change society, but rather to save men out of society.

Sadly, only a handful of Believers throughout the world are truly filled with the Holy Spirit, and are truly carrying out the Work of God in combating the forces of darkness by using the Biblical principles laid down by Christ. Jesus *"gave them power"* at that time, but now power automatically comes with the infilling of the Holy Spirit (Acts 1:8). Regrettably, it is little used by most Believers!

The *"power"* given here by Christ is little sought by most Preachers, or anyone for that matter. Most are seeking Doctorates or recognition by the world, etc. The desperate need, however, is *"Power from on High"*!

(8) "AND COMMANDED THEM THAT THEY SHOULD TAKE NOTHING FOR THEIR JOURNEY, SAVE A STAFF ONLY; NO SCRIP, NO BREAD, NO MONEY IN THEIR PURSE."

The synopsis is:

This means that they were not to store up these things before they went, but rather were to trust the Lord.

A COMMAND

The phrase, *"And commanded them that they should take nothing for their journey,"* does not present a suggestion, but, as stated, a *"Command."* The phrase, *"Save a staff only,"* referred to a wooden staff for walking. The phrase, *"No scrip, no bread, no money in their purse,"* refers to the obvious! There are actually two meanings in this phrase:

1. The idea is that they were not to make any special provisions for their journey, but to go forth just as they were, depending upon God. Some have been called by God, and then thought they would earn a goodly sum of money before answering the Call, in order that their needs may be met, etc. Such shows a lack of trust in God, and is forbidden by the Lord.

2. The idea of *"no money in their purse"* is that the emphasis be placed on the rightful priority, which is doing the Work of God, and not specializing in money. It did not mean they were to never take money, or bread, etc., but that they would trust God to meet their needs on these Evangelistic tours. Money is never to be an overriding object.

Tragically and sadly, many Preachers have sold out for money; consequently, they have lost their way and ceased to be effective for the Lord.

(9) "BUT BE SHOD WITH SANDALS; AND NOT PUT ON TWO COATS."

The structure is:

The simplest in terms of quality and quantity were sufficient.

THE REQUIREMENTS

Matthew says that shoes were forbidden, while Mark says, *"Be shod with sandals."* There is no contradiction. In that climate and culture, the *"sandals"* spoke of association with the common people, etc., but *"shoes,"* which covered the entirety of the foot, spoke of the aristocracy. Bickersteth says that it is worthy of notice that Peter, after the Lord's Ascension, used sandals; the Angel who delivered him out of prison said to him, *"Gird yourself, and bind on your sandals"* (Acts 12:8).

These commands applied only to those missions on which the Disciples were then sent. Later this was changed (Lk. 22:35-36); however, the fundamental principle of what was here taught, and which was actually intended, was not changed.

(10) "AND HE SAID UNTO THEM, IN WHAT PLACE SOEVER YOU ENTER INTO AN HOUSE, THERE ABIDE TILL YOU DEPART FROM THAT PLACE."

The exegesis is:

They were not to flit from place to place!

INSTRUCTIONS

Several things are said here:

1. They were not to stay too long anywhere, lest they should be burdensome to any.

2. They were not to go from house to house seeking better quarters. Wherever they were first invited, there they were to remain, irrespective of the circumstances, at least if hospitality was afforded them.

3. They were always to conduct themselves

in a manner that was befitting of their mission as Ambassadors for Christ; consequently, they were not to be a burden, but kind and hospitable at all times. If truly sent by the Lord, they would be a blessing to the house, which is here intended!

(11) "AND WHOSOEVER SHALL NOT RECEIVE YOU, NOR HEAR YOU, WHEN YOU DEPART THENCE, SHAKE OFF THE DUST UNDER YOUR FEET FOR A TESTIMONY AGAINST THEM. VERILY I SAY UNTO YOU, IT SHALL BE MORE TOLERABLE FOR SODOM AND GOMORRHA IN THE DAY OF JUDGMENT, THAN FOR THAT CITY."

The exposition is:

This has reference to the fact that Sodom and Gomorrha had no Gospel witness, while these places did.

A TESTIMONY AGAINST THEM

The phrase, *"And whosoever shall not receive you, nor hear you,"* basically refers to the area, even the city, and not the house in which they were invited. The phrase, *"When you depart thence,"* is meant to express the significance of the visit. The Lord had sent His emissary to this particular city; accordingly, this visit would be held against this place in the Judgment.

Maybe most in the city were not even aware of the visit, and even if they had been aware, they would have greeted it with skepticism and rejection. Still, in the eyes of God, the city had been visited with Mercy and Grace, irrespective of its rejection or lack of interest.

Inasmuch as the Lord has called me for Media Ministry, wherever we go on Television, or purchase a Radio Station, thereby airing Biblical programming, the Lord looks on such as a visitation to that area, with every person there being held responsible for either their acceptance or rejection. The same can be said for any God-called Preacher of the Gospel.

The phrase, *"Shake off the dust under your feet for a testimony against them,"* is not necessarily to be taken literally, but is actually a symbolic act. If the Message is rejected, there is no point in continuing to make the effort. However, the following should ever be noted:

Acceptance of the Gospel is the greatest thing that could ever happen to a person or community. The entire nature is changed for the better, and visibly so! However, if rejected, the person or area is not left as it was found, but measurably worse! I've had a number of discussions with Muslims about this very thing. They label the sin and debauchery in America as the failure of Christianity. What they fail to understand is that it's not the failure of Christianity, but the failure to accept what Christianity offers, namely Christ. This failure has left America the worse!

However, what little Gospel America has accepted has made it, without a doubt, the greatest nation of freedom in the world, the nation of which most people in the world would like to be a part. With Islam, or any other religion, for that matter, a person or nation is only made worse by accepting it, and is greatly bettered by rejecting it. All one has to do is look at the nations where these various religions are predominant. The proof speaks for itself!

SODOM AND GOMORRHA

The phrase, *"Verily I say unto you, It shall be more tolerable for Sodom and Gomorrha in the Day of Judgment than for that city,"* has reference to the fact that Sodom and Gomorrha had precious little Gospel Witness, while these places did! The same holds true presently! Every city in the world that has had the privilege of hearing the Gospel of Jesus Christ will be judged more severely even than the twin cities mentioned here, which were burned for their sin and iniquity (Gen. 19:24-25).

Despite the denial of many Preachers and the majority of the world, *"The Day of Judgment"* is coming, where all will have to answer!

JUDGMENT

Man, today, rejects out of hand the idea that he must one day render account for his life and its decisions. His loss of conviction concerning an after-life, combined with the erosion of the notion of moral responsibility on the basis of popular understanding of psychological and psychoanalytical theories, has contributed to the moral indifference and pragmatism of our times.

According to the basis of psychology, moral issues, insofar as they matter at all, relate only to the present moment and to considerations of personal happiness. The thought that they might relate to some Divine dimension, or that all men will one day be inescapably summoned to accept responsibility for these very moral decisions in the all-seeing presence of their Creator, is foreign to such thinking.

Unfortunately for modern man, it happens to be true. Judgment is inevitable and awaits us all. In face of this modern tendency to dismiss future Judgment, there is the greater and more urgent responsibility placed upon the Church to maintain tenaciously the Biblical perspective.

PRESENT ATTITUDES CONCERNING JUDGMENT

There are few points at which the teaching of the Bible is more sharply in conflict with the assumptions of our age than in its teaching concerning God's future Judgment of all men. It is correspondingly one of the most serious contemporary expressions of Christian intellectual and spiritual capitulations that this particular Truth should be so little reflected in modern Preaching and writing. Regrettably, the world has been permitted at this point, only too clearly, to squeeze the Church into its own mold (Rom. 12:1-2). Thus a theological commentator can complain with full justice that today the notion of final justice *"figures so little in the theology and preaching of the modern Church."*

This is even more inexcusable in that this century has witnessed an unprecedented recovery of the Biblical prophetic perspective; however, a future Divine Judgment has been largely set aside in favor of the more popular doctrines of the now and present.

THE OLD TESTAMENT TEACHING OF JUDGMENT

God appears in the Old Testament very commonly in the role of *"Judge of all the Earth"* (Gen. 18:25), or more generally as a *"God of Justice"* (Deut. 1:17; 32:4; Ps. 9:8; 94:2; 97:2; Isa. 30:18; 41:1; 61:8; Mal. 2:17). Judgment does not simply imply an impartial and detached weighing up of good and evil, but rather the thought of vigorous action against evil. It is on this understanding that the people of God are summoned to exercise Judgment in turn (Isa. 1:17; Mic. 6:8; Zech. 8:16).

The Judgment of God is not impersonal, the operation of some undeviating principle; it is a strongly personal notion. It is closely linked to the thought of God's Character of Mercy, Lovingkindness, Righteousness, and Truth (Ps. 36:5; Ezek. 39:21; Hos. 2:19). It is the working out of the Mercy and Wrath of God in history and in human life and experience. Thus, the Judgment of God can bring Deliverance for the righteous (Deut. 10:18; Ps. 25:9-10), as well as doom for the wicked (Ex. 6:6; Num. 33:4; Deut. 32:41; Isa. 4:4; Jer. 1:10; 4:12; Ezek. 5:10).

As the Old Testament draws toward its close, the thought of God's Judgment becomes increasingly bound up with the eschatological expectation of this coming Day of the Lord (Joel 2:1; Amos 5:18; 8:9; Obad. 15; Zeph. 1:7, 14; Mal. 4:1).

JUDGMENT IN THE NEW TESTAMENT

The New Testament, as we should expect, continues the Old Testament stress upon Judgment as belonging to the Nature of God, and as part of His essential activity (Rom. 1:18; Heb. 12:23; I Pet. 1:17; 2:23; Rev. 16:6). As in the Old Testament, God's Judgments are not confined to the future, but are already at work in man's life in the present age (Jn. 8:50; Rom. 1:18-22, 24, 26, 28; Rev. 18:8). Judgment is associated even now with Christ, Who exercises the Father's Judgment (Mat. 3:11-12; 10:34; Jn. 3:19; 5:30; 8:12, 16; 9:39).

The Light of God's Word is already shining into the world through His Self-revelation in man's moral experience, and supremely in the Incarnate Word, Jesus Christ. The Judgment of men is, therefore, already in operation, for they show by their evil deeds that they *"love darkness rather than light"* (Jn. 3:19). The spotlight in the New Testament, however, falls upon the *"Judgment to come,"* a future and final Judgment which will accompany the Return of Christ, and will mostly be confined to nations (Mat. 25:31-46; Jn. 5:22, 27; Rom. 3:5; I Cor. 4:3-5; Heb. 6:1).

The great culminating Judgment, which will take place at the conclusion of the Kingdom Age, will be that which is referred to as *"the Great White Throne Judgment"* (Rev. 20:11-15). Even though there have been, and are, many Judgments, still, the culminating Judgment of all will be this particular time. It will take place, as stated, at the conclusion of the thousand-year Millennial Reign. Satan will then be locked away in the Lake of Fire, along with all his minions of darkness, which will include all demon spirits and fallen angels (Rev. 20:10). At that time, all men who have rejected Christ, and from the beginning of time, will stand before Him. Today, He is the Saviour; then, He will be the Judge!

No Believer will be at this *"Great White Throne Judgment,"* for their sins have already been judged at Calvary. This Judgment will be strictly for unbelievers, and *"according to their works"* (Rev. 20:12). The eternal destiny of all who will appear at that Judgment will be *"the Lake of Fire"* (Rev. 20:15). Once again, we emphasize that it doesn't really matter what the world thinks concerning this coming Judgment, nor does it matter that the Church is lax in its presentation and proclamation of this coming Day. It will come about exactly as it is given in the Word of God.

It consequently behooves the God-called Preacher to proclaim that which is so prominent in Scripture, and so certain of fulfillment.

(12) "AND THEY WENT OUT, AND PREACHED THAT MEN SHOULD REPENT."

The overview is:

The Message didn't change, and it shouldn't change now. As the need then, so the need now!

REPENTANCE

The Message of *"Repentance"* was the Message that was needed during the time of Christ, and it is the Message that is needed presently. In fact, it has always been needed. Are men any different today than they were then? Is the spiritual need any different now than then?

The word *"preached"* means that they made a public proclamation with gravity, formality, and authority, which demanded it be heeded. In essence, it was *"Good News,"* even though it proclaimed Judgment to those who would not accept. Still, it proclaimed Eternal Life to those who would heed its clarion call. Consequently, it was Good News to the sinner. This Message of Repentance, which demanded a turnabout, was also accompanied with the announcement of Salvation from sin, as provided by the Lord.

If one is to notice, the preaching of the Gospel was their great work, to which the miracles were subordinate. If the order is reversed, it ceases to be the Gospel!

REPENTANCE AND FAITH

Salvation demands *"Repentance toward God, and Faith toward our Lord Jesus Christ"* (Acts 20:21).

Why is it in this order?

Repentance comes first because God has been offended by the sin in the lives of unbelievers; consequently, the sinner must repent of that sin. It is not so much the word said, but rather the attitude of the heart. Along with Repentance, there must be Faith evidenced in Jesus Christ relative to what He did at Calvary and the Resurrection in paying the price for man's sins. To be sure, the sinner may understand very little of what Jesus actually did, but there must be Faith extended in some manner, even though little understood, as to what Christ did at Calvary. In fact, as the Gospel is preached and heard, with the Holy Spirit then bringing about conviction, the Holy Spirit will also give Faith to the unbeliever, without which it would not be possible for such a one to be saved.

The Scripture teaches total depravity, meaning that unbelieving man cannot know God, cannot understand God, and cannot have any true leanings toward God. Any understanding he thinks he has of the Lord is twisted and perverted.

Concerning the unredeemed, the Scripture says, *"And you has He quickened, who were dead in trespasses and sins"* (Eph. 2:1). As should be understood, *"dead"* is *"dead."* Of course, it is speaking of spiritual death.

Inasmuch as such a person is dead to the Lord, this means they can have no understanding of the Lord. So whatever it is they must have in order to accept Christ as Saviour, the Holy Spirit has to supply such, which He does!

(13) "AND THEY CAST OUT MANY DEVILS, AND ANOINTED WITH OIL MANY WHO WERE SICK, AND HEALED THEM."

The exposition is:

Oil is symbolic of the Holy Spirit. It has nothing to do with medicine (Ex. 27:20; 30:25; Num. 6:15; I Sam. 16:1, 13; Ps. 45:7).

The Disciples were able to do these things only because Jesus *"gave them Power"* (Vs. 7). As Jesus sent out the Disciples *"two and two,"* likewise, He is still sending out Believers whom He has called to do His Work.

(14) "AND KING HEROD HEARD OF HIM; (FOR HIS NAME WAS SPREAD ABROAD:) AND HE SAID, THAT JOHN THE BAPTIST WAS RISEN FROM THE DEAD, AND THEREFORE MIGHTY WORKS DO SHOW FORTH THEMSELVES IN HIM."

The composition is:

This proclaims a troubled and guilty conscience for putting John the Baptist to death.

KING HEROD

The phrase, *"And King Herod heard of Him,"* refers to Herod Antipas, son of Herod the Great, who had appointed him *"Tetrarch"* of Galilee and Peraea. (The title *"Tetrarch"* means *"a rule by four,"* and consequently meant that King Herod was one of four men at that time ruling Israel. As well, Mark was correct in calling him a *"King,"* for this title was applied freely in the Roman world to all Eastern Rulers.) To only hear of Jesus now is, as one man said, *"A palace is late in hearing spiritual news."*

The phrase, *"For His Name was spread abroad,"* actually referred to the Miracles performed by Christ, and the fame that such had gained.

JOHN THE BAPTIST

The phrase, *"And he said, That John the Baptist was risen from the dead,"* proclaims a troubled and guilty conscience more than anything else, for Herod had put to death an innocent and holy man. As well, it is a high

NOTES

testimony to John the Baptist that Herod should have such a testimony of him.

The phrase, *"And therefore mighty works do show forth themselves in him,"* actually has reference to the idea that vengeance may be taken on Herod. A sinful conscience imagines all sorts of things, and consequently never knows peace. Chrysostom says, *"What a great thing is virtue, for Herod fears him, even though dead."* This is the same Herod who mocked Jesus when Pilate sent Jesus to him in the hope of relieving himself of the terrible responsibility of condemning One Whom he knew to be innocent.

(15) "OTHERS SAID, THAT IT IS ELIJAH. AND OTHERS SAID, THAT IT IS A PROPHET, OR AS ONE OF THE PROPHETS."

The overview is:

It seems that Israel would admit to anything, except the Truth that He was the Messiah, the Son of the Living God.

THE MESSIAH

The phrase, *"Others said,"* referred to the Court, as well as many in Israel. The idea is that Israel would admit to anything, except the Truth, which was that He was the Messiah, the Son of God. And then, again, there were other comments, with most of the religious leaders of Israel calling Him a *"deceiver"* (Mat. 27:63; Jn. 7:12).

(16) "BUT WHEN HEROD HEARD THEREOF, HE SAID, IT IS JOHN, WHOM I BEHEADED: HE IS RISEN FROM THE DEAD."

The structure is:

This means he kept saying it over and over, in response to the prediction of others as to Who Christ was!

THE GUILTY CONSCIENCE

The phrase, *"But when Herod heard thereof,"* proclaims his prediction, and because of his troubled conscience. The phrase, *"He said, It is John, whom I beheaded,"* means he kept saying it over and over, in response to the predictions of others as to Who Christ was! It was not just the Prophet John he remembered, but that he beheaded him. The sight of that head dripping blood would not leave his conscience, tormenting him day and night! So the expostulation of others concerning the identity of Christ was always met by Herod with his pronouncement that it was John.

The phrase, *"He is risen from the dead,"* is said with the thought in mind that this is done for one purpose, and he, Herod, is the target.

(17) "FOR HEROD HIMSELF HAD SENT FORTH AND LAID HOLD UPON JOHN, AND BOUND HIM IN PRISON FOR HERODIAS' SAKE, HIS BROTHER PHILIP'S WIFE: FOR HE HAD MARRIED HER."

The overview is:

John had been put in prison because Herod's wife, Herodias, had demanded it.

THE UNCOMPROMISED PREACHING OF JOHN THE BAPTIST

The phrase, *"For Herod himself had sent forth and laid hold upon John, and bound him in prison,"* is looking back in the past tense to what Herod had done. As well, it is as if the Holy Spirit is wanting to make certain that no one misunderstands that it was *"Herod"* who had done this dastardly thing. John had been imprisoned in the fortress of Machaerus, situated on the barren heights of Moab above the Dead Sea.

The phrase, *"For Herodias' sake, his brother Philip's wife,"* means that John had been imprisoned because Herod's wife, Herodias, had demanded it. The phrase, *"For he had married her,"* constituted the reason for John's pointed Message concerning Herod marrying Herodias, who had been his brother's wife.

Herod had originally married the daughter of the Nabataean King Aretas IV, but divorced her in order to marry Herodias, the wife of his half-brother Herod Philip. John denounced this second marriage as unlawful and consequently incurred the wrath of Herod. Josephus says that, along with the carping of Herodias, Herod was afraid that John's great public following might develop into a revolt; consequently, he imprisoned him in order to silence him.

Aretas, at this time, resented the insult offered to his daughter, and seized the opportunity a few years later to wage war against Herod. At this time, A.D. 36, the forces of Herod were heavily defeated, and Josephus says that many people regarded the defeat as Divine retribution for Herod killing John the Baptist.

In A.D. 39, Herod was denounced to the Emperor Gaius by his nephew Agrippa as a plotter; he was deposed from his Tetrarchy and ended his days in exile.

(18) "FOR JOHN HAD SAID UNTO HEROD, IT IS NOT LAWFUL FOR YOU TO HAVE YOUR BROTHER'S WIFE."

This means that he said it more than once, to both Herod and to the people.

STRAIGHTFORWARD PREACHING

The phrase, *"For John had said unto Herod,"* means that John said this, not only once, but many times, and pointedly so! The phrase, *"It is not lawful for you to have your brother's wife,"* pulls no punches and minces no words. Herod knew exactly what John was saying, and so did the people. No one could accuse this Preacher of compromise! And yet, Jesus had very little to say about Herod, with the exception of once describing him as *"that fox"* (Lk. 13:32).

(19) "THEREFORE HERODIAS HAD A QUARREL AGAINST HIM, AND WOULD HAVE KILLED HIM; BUT SHE COULD NOT."

The synopsis is:

She never let up on her fury toward the Baptist for daring to denounce her private relations with Herod. She waited her time for revenge.

HERODIAS

The phrase, *"Therefore Herodias had a quarrel against him,"* means that she *"had it in for him."* Wuest says that she never let up on this fury of hers toward the Baptist for daring to denounce her private relations with Herod. She hungered for revenge and would ultimately exact what she desired.

The phrase, *"And would have killed him; but she could not,"* means that she did not lack the will, only the way! Matthew had stated that Herod, as well, desired to kill John, but feared the people (Mat. 14:5). However, there is no contradiction in the accounts given by Matthew and Mark, because it seems that Herod at the first desired to put John to death;

but, little by little, as Herod observed the Prophet, the force of his character and holy life made an impression upon him, as the next Verse portrays.

(20) "FOR HEROD FEARED JOHN, KNOWING THAT HE WAS A JUST MAN AND AN HOLY, AND OBSERVED HIM; AND WHEN HE HEARD HIM, HE DID MANY THINGS, AND HEARD HIM GLADLY."

The exposition is:

Herod kept going back to the dank prison cell over and over again to speak with the Prophet; in other words, the Holy Spirit was dealing with Herod's soul.

THE GODLINESS OF JOHN THE BAPTIST

The phrase, *"For Herod feared John,"* means in the Greek that he was in a continual state of fear respecting the Prophet. There was a reason for the fear. He knew that John was right respecting his sin, and he knew that John was a Prophet sent from God. Considering that he had arrested him, he feared the Wrath of God.

The phrase, *"Knowing that he was a just man and a holy,"* proclaims John's character. What a compliment to John coming from a man who had been his bitter enemy!

The phrase, *"And observed him,"* means that he watched over John to keep him safe from the evil plots of Herodias, who was seeking to kill him. He kept a constant watch over the Prophet.

The phrase, *"And when he heard him, he did many things, and heard him gladly,"* means that John's Messages to him caused him consternation of soul, but yet he kept going back to this dank prison cell over and over again to speak with the Prophet. In other words, he was under great conviction, as the Holy Spirit made a plea for his soul.

What a sight this must have been! The King, dressed in his royal robes, came down to this dungeon and then went in to talk with the Prophet, sometimes for hours on end. He came so close, but yet not quite close enough. Herod fought the battle that most all have to fight. If he accepted the teaching of John the Baptist and, therefore, the Lord as his Saviour, the entirety of his lifestyle would change. He would probably have to give up everything, and he was not sure that he was willing to do that.

It was tragic, at it always is, but Herod lost his soul and his kingdom. That for which we sell the soul is lost, as well!

(21) "AND WHEN A CONVENIENT DAY WAS COME, THAT HEROD ON HIS BIRTHDAY MADE A SUPPER TO HIS LORDS, HIGH CAPTAINS, AND CHIEF ESTATES OF GALILEE."

The composition is:

Herodias would find her time for revenge at this gathering.

THE BIRTHDAY OF HEROD

The phrase, *"And when a convenient day was come,"* refers to a convenient time for Herodias to kill John the Baptist. She would now spring her trap!

Bede says, *"She feared lest Herod should at length repent, and yield to the exhortations of John, and dissolve this unreal marriage, and restore Herodias to her lawful husband."*

The phrase, *"That Herod on his birthday made a supper to his lords, high captains, and chief estates of Galilee,"* referred to a notable gathering, composed of men from governmental, military, and civil life. So, not only were Romans present, but also the chief Jews of Galilee. Regrettably, these Jews would raise no protest against the death of the Baptist.

(22) "AND WHEN THE DAUGHTER OF THE SAID HERODIAS CAME IN, AND DANCED, AND PLEASED HEROD AND THEM WHO SAT WITH HIM, THE KING SAID UNTO THE DAMSEL, ASK OF ME WHATSOEVER YOU WILL, AND I WILL GIVE IT YOU."

The overview is:

All of these that night were probably drunk, or nearly so. Herodias would now spring her trap.

THE LICENTIOUS DANCE

The phrase, *"And when the daughter of the said Herodias came in, and danced,"* refers to Herodias' own daughter, who degraded herself in a licentious dance, in which normally only professional actors of loose morals would engage. The phrase, *"And pleased*

Herod and them who sat with him," presents a scene of debauchery. No doubt, all were drunk, or nearly so!

The phrase, *"The king said unto the damsel, Ask of me whatsoever you will, and I will give it to you,"* presents the trap set by Herodias now ready to be sprung. No doubt, Herod was accustomed in his drunkenness and debauchery to offering such sweeping gifts. It made him look big in the eyes of all who were present!

Herodias, no doubt having observed this many times, sets the trap by having her daughter dance before the king and his gathering, even in a licentious manner, which elicited exactly what she thought it would.

(23) "AND HE SWORE UNTO HER, WHATSOEVER YOU SHALL ASK OF ME, I WILL GIVE IT TO YOU, UNTO THE HALF OF MY KINGDOM."

The diagram is:

Herod put himself under an oath!

THE OATH

The phrase, *"And he swore unto her,"* refers to the daughter of Herodias. Did he really mean what he said, concerning whatever she wanted? He assures her he does by putting himself under an oath.

The phrase, *"Whatsoever you shall ask of me, I will give it to you, unto the half of my kingdom,"* was not really to be taken literally, but was meant to add tremendous force to the answering of any reasonable request.

Now he is on the hook!

(24) "AND SHE WENT FORTH, AND SAID UNTO HER MOTHER, WHAT SHALL I ASK? AND SHE SAID, THE HEAD OF JOHN THE BAPTIST."

The composition is:

It is almost positive that the daughter of Herodias knew of the hatred of her mother for John the Baptist.

THE GRUESOME REQUEST

The phrase, *"And she went forth, and said unto her mother,"* implies her knowledge of at least a part of the plan. Whether her mother had related her full intentions to the girl is not known. At any rate, she knew to go to her mother when the trap was sprung. The question, *"What shall I ask?"* implies that she knew of a plan but not exactly its direction. She had done her part. She had enflamed the passions of the king and all who were with him, causing him to make this wild gesture! Everything had played into the hands of this wicked woman.

The phrase, *"And she said, The head of John the Baptist,"* meant that she wanted him to die by being beheaded!

(25) "AND SHE CAME IN STRAIGHTWAY WITH HASTE UNTO THE KING, AND ASKED, SAYING, I WILL THAT YOU GIVE ME BY AND BY (IMMEDIATELY) IN A CHARGER THE HEAD OF JOHN THE BAPTIST."

The exegesis is:

She immediately made her demand, so the king would have no opportunity to renege on his promise.

JOHN THE BAPTIST

The phrase, *"And she came in straightway with haste unto the king,"* presents her immediately making her demand. Little did Herod realize what she was about to ask.

The word, *"Saying,"* presents the evil of this moment about to unfold in all its horror. No doubt, the crowd is mostly drunk, including Herod! As well, prominent Jews were at this so-called celebration, but none would lift a hand or voice in defense of the great Prophet. So much for the world and so much for the Church!

The phrase, *"I will that you give me by and by in a charger the head of John the Baptist,"* actually meant immediately, with the words, *"by and by,"* having a different meaning then than now. The evil of this woman, in asking this, knew no bounds! She would not rest until she had silenced the voice of the greatest Prophet who ever lived; however, even though she would carry out this bloody scheme, still, John had finished the Work that God had called him and sent him to do.

(26) "AND THE KING WAS EXCEEDING SORRY; YET FOR HIS OATH'S SAKE, AND FOR THEIR SAKES WHICH SAT WITH HIM, HE WOULD NOT REJECT HER."

The diagram is:

The life of the greatest Prophet who ever lived had boiled down to the worth of a lewd dance, at least to these men.

THE TRAP

The phrase, *"And the king was exceeding sorry,"* means that Herod now realizes what he has done. He is now to become the murderer of the Prophet whom he feared and respected.

The phrase, *"Yet for his oath's sake,"* means that when he extended this offer, it really was not taken seriously to begin with, but then he restated it with force, which made it harder for him to back down.

The phrase, *"And for their sakes which sat with him,"* refers to him saving face. All had heard him make the oath, verify it, and now they eagerly awaited what she would request.

The phrase, *"He would not reject her,"* means that the life of John the Baptist, at least to these men, was worth nothing.

In all of this, we see the horror of the human heart. No wonder the great Prophet Jeremiah said: *"The heart is deceitful above all things, and desperately wicked: who can know it?"* (Jer. 17:9).

(27) "AND IMMEDIATELY THE KING SENT AN EXECUTIONER, AND COMMANDED HIS HEAD TO BE BROUGHT: AND HE WENT AND BEHEADED HIM IN THE PRISON."

The overview is:

The prison was actually connected to the palace where the celebration was being held.

THE EXECUTION OF JOHN THE BAPTIST

The phrase, *"And immediately the king sent an executioner,"* is the beginning of the horrible deed which will haunt Herod for the rest of his life.

The phrase, *"And his head to be brought,"* proclaims the manner in which he was executed.

As stated, John was incarcerated in the Fort of Machaerus. Within the Fort, Herod's father had built a magnificent palace, which is undoubtedly where this birthday celebration was conducted. It was only a short distance to the dungeon where John was being held.

The phrase, *"And he went and beheaded*

NOTES

him in the prison," concerns the dastardly deed being carried out!

(28) "AND BROUGHT HIS HEAD IN A CHARGER, AND GAVE IT TO THE DAMSEL: AND THE DAMSEL GAVE IT TO HER MOTHER."

The exposition is:

Jerome said that Herodias approached the charger containing John the Baptist's head, which had just been severed from his body, and opened his mouth, pulled out his tongue, and thrust the tongue through with a long pin. She could not bear to hear the truth; therefore, she would puncture the tongue that had spoken the truth. A short time later, both Herodias and Herod, by a decree of the Roman Senate, were banished to Lyons, where they both perished miserably. Salome, the daughter who danced, died shortly thereafter by having her head nearly cut off by the sharp edges of broken ice. *"Vengeance is Mine; I will repay, saith the Lord"* (Rom. 12:19).

THE TERRIBLE DEED DONE

The phrase, *"And brought his head in a charger,"* must have been a gruesome sight, with it dripping blood as it was brought into the banquet hall. The phrase, *"And gave it to the damsel,"* referred to the girl who had danced, the daughter of Herodias. The phrase, *"And the damsel gave it to her mother,"* proclaims that the terrible deed is now done.

Nicephorus relates that Salome, the daughter who danced, died by a remarkable incident. She fell through some treacherous ice over which she was passing in such a manner that her head was caught while the rest of her body sank into the water. Thus, it came to pass that, in her efforts to save herself, her head was nearly severed by the sharp edges of the broken ice.

Let us say it again:

"Vengeance is Mine; I will repay, saith the Lord."

(29) "AND WHEN HIS DISCIPLES HEARD OF IT, THEY CAME AND TOOK UP HIS CORPSE, AND LAID IT IN A TOMB."

The synopsis is:

Josephus says that after the beheading, the mutilated remains were cast out of the prison and left neglected.

THE DISCIPLES OF JOHN THE BAPTIST

The phrase, *"And when his disciples heard of it,"* proclaims that the corpse lay uncared for and unburied until the disciples of John showed their respect for it. The phrase, *"They came and took up his corpse, and laid it in a tomb,"* concludes the Life and Ministry of the greatest Prophet who ever lived.

(30) "AND THE APOSTLES GATHERED THEMSELVES TOGETHER UNTO JESUS, AND TOLD HIM ALL THINGS, BOTH WHAT THEY HAD DONE, AND WHAT THEY HAD TAUGHT."

The exposition is:

This relates back to Verse 7, where the Twelve had been sent forth *"two and two"*; they now come back to report to Christ.

THE APOSTLES

The phrase, *"And the Apostles gathered themselves together unto Jesus,"* relates back, as stated, to Verse 7. The phrase, *"And told Him all things, both what they had done, and what they had taught,"* represents a victorious mission. They had seen many healings and Miracles, and had taught the Word with Power.

The word *"Apostle"* simply means *"one sent."* The *"Message"* is what characterizes the Apostle. In other words, the Lord gives the Apostle a particular Message, which always coincides perfectly with the Word of God, which represents the way the Church needs to go. The Lord leads the Church through the Ministry of the Apostle. The Office of Apostle is still in the Church, i.e., the Lord is still placing Apostles in the Church, at least those Churches which are trying to follow the Word of God (Eph. 4:11-15).

Paul was what one might call *"The Apostle of Grace."* As well, those who came up under his Ministry were likewise Apostles, because of the special emphasis given to them by the Holy Spirit as it regards proclaiming the same Message.

During Old Testament times, Israel was led by Prophets; the Office of Apostle did not then exist. But with the Advent of Christ, the Office of the Apostle, beginning with the original Twelve, was brought into focus. In fact, along with the original Twelve, of which there will never again be any similar, and for the obvious reasons, there are some 24 Apostles recorded in the New Testament, that is, if one includes Christ (Heb. 3:1).

Now let us say it again, because it's so very important. The characterization of the Apostle is the Message given to him by the Lord and, more particularly, the emphasis placed on that Message. It is meant to serve as direction for the Church. Also, the Apostle can function in any of the fivefold callings: Apostle, Prophet, Evangelist, Pastor, and Teacher (Eph. 4:11). We ascertain this from the action of the Apostles in the Book of Acts and the Epistles. And from the Book of Acts and the Epistles, we also ascertain the manner in which the Church was led. It was always by Apostles, with the emphasis being on the Message they preached.

(31) "AND HE SAID UNTO THEM, COME YE YOURSELVES APART INTO A DESERT PLACE, AND REST A WHILE: FOR THERE WERE MANY COMING AND GOING, AND THEY HAD NO LEISURE SO MUCH AS TO EAT."

The composition is:

The crowds were desiring to see Christ; the sick and afflicted were most definitely desiring to see him, and for all the obvious reasons.

REST

The phrase, *"And He said unto them, Come ye yourselves apart into a desert place, and rest a while,"* concerns the tremendous activity which engaged Jesus and His Disciples regarding the preaching of the Word, healing the sick, and casting out demons. The needs among the people, as would be obvious, were abundant. As well, Jesus was the only One Who could meet these needs, as He is the only One today. Unceasing activity and dealing with the crowds would have taken its toll both physically and spiritually; consequently, and despite the needs, they must *"rest a while."*

While Jesus was definitely Very God, and He never ceased to be Very God, at the same time, He was Very Man. As such, He grew tired the same as any other man. In other words, while He laid aside the expression of

His Deity, He never laid aside the possession of His Deity.

BURN OUT?

The phrase, *"For there were many coming and going, and they had no leisure so much as to eat,"* gives one an idea as to the press of the crowds, the needs of the people, and the attention given to these needs.

It should quickly be added that some few Ministers of the Gospel work themselves into exhaustion respecting the same type of activity as Jesus and His Disciples; however, the far greater majority of physical and emotional breakdowns among Ministers are caused not necessarily from overwork, but rather from an improper understanding of the Cross. In other words, they are trying to do what only the Holy Spirit can do, and the result is *"burn out."* However, no Preacher ever need experience burn out and, in fact, will not experience such, if they properly understand Christ and the great Work of the Cross.

THE CROSS, THE ONLY ANSWER FOR BURN OUT

Some may ask, *"How is the Cross of Christ the solution for burnout?"* or *"How does the Cross keep the Preacher* (or anyone, for that matter) *from experiencing physical, emotional, or mental breakdown?"* The Cross of Christ is not only the answer for these things; in Truth, it is the only answer.

The answer is found in the Words of Christ, where He invited Israel, and the entirety of mankind, for that matter, to *"Come unto Me* (is meant by Jesus to reveal Himself as the Giver of Salvation), *all you who labor and are heavy laden* (trying to earn Salvation and Sanctification by works), *and I will give you rest* (this 'rest' can only be found by placing one's Faith in Christ and what He has done for us at the Cross [Gal. 5:1-6].)

"Take My yoke upon you (the 'yoke' of the 'Cross' [Lk. 9:23]), *and learn of Me* (learn of His Sacrifice [Rom. 6:3-5]); *for I am meek and lowly in heart* (the only thing that our Lord Personally said of Himself): *and you shall find rest unto your souls* (the soul can find rest only in the Cross).

"For My yoke is easy, and My burden is light (what He requires of us is very little, just to have Faith in Him, and His Sacrificial Atoning Work)" (Mat. 11:28-30).

At that particular time, Our Lord did not explain Himself as to what He meant by coming to Him, because the timing was premature. After the Cross, He then gave to the Apostle Paul the meaning of being *"in Christ."* Paul said, *"For the Preaching of the Cross is to them who perish foolishness, but to us who are saved it is the Power of God"* (I Cor. 1:18).

HOW IS THE CROSS THE POWER OF GOD?

In Truth, the Cross, within itself, contains no power; there also really was no power in the Death of Christ. The Scripture actually says, *"He was Crucified through weakness"* (II Cor. 13:4). Now that doesn't mean that He actually was weak, but rather that He did not use His Power, which was available at all times to Him. In other words, it was a contrived weakness. So, where does the Power come in?

The Power is in the Holy Spirit. It is the Cross of Christ which gives the Holy Spirit legal latitude to work within our hearts and lives, thereby bringing about the desired results (Rom. 8:2; I Cor. 2:12-14). For the Believer to avail himself of the Power of the Holy Spirit, all the Believer has to do is to constantly keep his Faith anchored in Christ and the Cross.

That's why Paul said, *"But God forbid that I should glory* (boast), *save in the Cross of our Lord Jesus Christ* (what the opponents of Paul sought to escape at the price of insincerity is the Apostle's only basis of exultation), *by Whom the world is Crucified unto me, and I unto the world* (the only way that one can overcome the world, and I mean the only way, is by placing our Faith exclusively in the Cross of Christ and keeping it there)" (Gal. 6:14).

When the Believer anchors his Faith exclusively in Christ and the Cross, keeps it there, and doesn't allow it to be moved to other things, the Holy Spirit, Who Alone can perfect our lives, will then work mightily on our behalf. A perfect example is the *"bush which burned with fire"* in front of Moses, and yet *"the bush was not consumed"* (Ex. 3:2). If the bush burns in the Spirit, it will not be consumed. But if it is a man-directed effort, in other words, the flesh, the bush will be consumed, i.e., *"emotional breakdowns, etc."*

Any effort made in the flesh, which refers to man leaning on his own strength and power, which regrettably constitutes much, if not most, of that done in the Name of the Lord, will exact a heavy toll and accomplish nothing for the Lord.

Let's say it this way:

WALKING AFTER THE FLESH
LEADS TO BURN OUT

"Walking after the flesh" (Rom. 8:1) is not watching too much TV, as some suppose, or spending too much time going fishing, or being too interested in sports, etc. Instead, *"walking after the flesh"* is the Believer trusting in his own ability and strength, or the ability and strength of someone else, instead of the Power of God.

But the catch to this situation is according to the following:

Almost every Believer who is *"walking after the flesh"* thinks they are *"walking after the Spirit."* However, if one doesn't have his Faith exclusively in Christ and the Cross, which then gives the Holy Spirit latitude to work, then, without fail, one is *"walking after the flesh."* And that's the problem!

When we *"walk after the flesh,"* which means that our faith is in ourselves, or someone else, which means it's not in Christ and the Cross, irrespective of our claims, the Holy Spirit simply won't help us. To be sure, every single thing that must be done in the Lord can only be carried out by the Holy Spirit. The only thing I am called to provide is faith, and this applies to any Believer. The Faith which I provide, however, must ever have as its Object the Cross of Christ (I Cor. 1:17-18, 21, 23; 2:2).

No matter the work load, no matter the pressure, if our Faith is properly placed in Christ and the Cross, we need not fear any type of burn out.

(32) "AND THEY DEPARTED INTO A DESERT PLACE BY SHIP PRIVATELY."

The diagram is:

This was probably one of the vessels belonging to Zebedee.

NOTES

PRIVATELY

From the frequent mention of such vessels, it seems that Zebedee may have kept one of these ships ready at all times for the Master's use. Quite possibly, he donated the use of it. We learn from Luke that the *"desert place"* was near to *"a city called Bethsaida,"* the one to the northeast of the Sea of Galilee. The word *"privately"* means that other ships, at least at this time, did not go with them. And yet, as the following Verses proclaim, it seems that their efforts to get a little rest will be in vain.

(33) "AND THE PEOPLE SAW THEM DEPARTING, AND MANY KNEW HIM, AND RAN AFOOT THITHER OUT OF ALL CITIES, AND OUTWENT THEM, AND CAME TOGETHER UNTO HIM."

The overview is:

This presents them waiting for Him whenever the boat docked in this desert place.

THEY CAME TO JESUS

The phrase, *"And the people saw them departing, and many knew Him,"* refers to the action which will follow. The phrase, *"And ran afoot thither out of all cities,"* means that some ran from village to village, telling them that Jesus was coming their way. Quite possibly, they did not know exactly where He was going; but yet, since they were visibly able to follow the ship, it quickly became obvious as to His destination. When the boat would land, Jesus would be met by about 5,000 men, in addition to the women and children.

The needs were obvious: many, no doubt, were very ill; others desperately needed Miracles; scores needed Deliverance from demon spirits, etc. When the day would end, it would result in many Miracles being performed, not the least of which was the feeding of this tremendous crowd with five loaves of bread and two fish.

According to John, Chapter 6, however, this would prove to be the height of His popularity. After this, the crowds, at least for the most part, would begin to thin out, and for varied reasons. What He taught seemed to be more than many could bear, and then the Pharisees were beginning to threaten excommunication to anyone who followed the Lord (Jn. 6:66).

The phrase, *"And outwent them, and came together unto Him,"* presents them waiting for Him whenever the boat docks in this desert place.

(34) "AND JESUS, WHEN HE CAME OUT, SAW MUCH PEOPLE, AND WAS MOVED WITH COMPASSION TOWARD THEM, BECAUSE THEY WERE AS SHEEP NOT HAVING A SHEPHERD: AND HE BEGAN TO TEACH THEM MANY THINGS."

The exposition is:

Israel was more religious than ever, but with few true shepherds.

COMPASSION

The phrase, *"And Jesus,"* presents the Master as being the principal One Who was concerned about the people. His great heart went out to them, as would be obvious!

The phrase, *"When He came out, saw much people, and was moved with compassion toward them,"* presents the heart of God for the human family.

WHAT IS COMPASSION?

The word means *"to love deeply"*, *"to be compassionate,"* or *"to have mercy."* It, or one of its derivatives, is found 133 times in the Old Testament, and nearly that many times in the New, as it is coupled with the word *"Mercy."* In the Old Testament, God is looked at somewhat more in the sense of Judgment than in the New; however, even then His Compassion is presented as a strong earmark of His Nature and Character. Even when His people are being disciplined, Malachi records promise and Restoration, which, of necessity, must be linked with compassion.

"And they shall be Mine, saith the LORD of Hosts, in that day when I make up My jewels; and I will spare them, as a man spares his own son who serves him" (Mal. 3:17).

GOD TRULY CARES

The entire theme of the Bible is that God compassionately and truly cares about what happens to us (Rom. 12:1; II Cor. 1:3). Consequently, we are to imitate our Heavenly Father (Lk. 6:36) and let His kind of caring

NOTES

bind Believers to each other in unity (Phil. 2:1; Col. 3:12).

When the Scripture mentions Jesus being moved with compassion, it is usually the occasion of a turning point in someone's life. A leper came to Jesus and begged for healing. Jesus, *"filled with compassion,"* reached out to touch and heal (Mk. 1:40-42). Traveling in the towns and villages of Judaea and Galilee, Jesus saw the confused crowds and *"had compassion on them,"* as we are studying here.

From these incidents, we learn that it is compassion which moves Jesus to take action that affects the lives of those whose needs moved Him.

THE ROOT OF COMPASSION

We see the same active aspect of compassion in two Parables Jesus told. In Matthew 18 there is the story of a servant who owed an unpayable debt. He begged the king, to whom he owed the money, to give him time to pay it. But the king was so *"moved by compassion"* that he canceled the debt. Luke 15 tells the story of the Prodigal Son. The wayward youth returned home to confess his sins and beg for a job as a hired man. But the father was *"filled with compassion for him,"* and welcomed him back as a son.

The loving compassion of one person literally changed the life of another, for the person who cared was moved to act and so set the needy person on a new course in life. God called you and me to have compassion on others. That call is more than an appeal for us to feel with and for the needy. It is a call to care enough to become involved and to help by taking some action that will set others' lives on a fresh new course.

COMPASSION AS A WORD

As a word, compassion indicates the inner parts of the body, and came to suggest the seat of the emotions — particularly emotions of pity, compassion, and love. This is the word used in the Gospels to speak of Jesus having compassion on someone in need. The word originated, it is believed, from the Greek language, and, more specifically, from the offering up of heathen sacrifices.

When the animal slated for the Sacrifice

was killed, it was dissected with its intestines removed. This entire mass was held up toward the heavens in the hands of the priests and called *"the compassion."* As is obvious, it pertained to the very inward parts of the animal, hence, an apt description of one's own emotions, etc.

So, when it is said that Jesus was *"moved with compassion,"* it meant that every fiber of His Being was involved.

WHO CAN HAVE COMPASSION?

While the word may be used regarding any and all, still, true *"compassion"* can only be had by those who truly follow Christ. It has to do with *agape* love, which is the God kind of love, and is the kind that caused God to send Jesus to this world to die for lost humanity. The word really comes into play in doing for those who cannot return such kindness; this is the deepest root and, in fact, the only root, of the word. It is perhaps explained in its totality by Jesus dying for those who did not love Him. *"But God commendeth His love toward us, in that, while we were yet sinners, Christ died for us"* (Rom. 5:8).

Consequently, the only true *"compassion"* shown in the world is that evidenced by Christ through His people. Islam, Buddhism, Hinduism, etc., have no compassion, because they do not have the God-kind of love. Regrettably, many alleged Christians also have little compassion. However, the closer to Christ, the more compassion.

Actually, *"compassion"* is the greatest cause of the spread of the Gospel. The closer to the Lord men are, the more they desire to get the Gospel to others, because they feel exactly as Christ — *"moved with compassion toward them."* If there is little nearness to Christ, there is also little compassion.

COMPASSION AND THE MINISTRY

The phrase, *"Because they were as sheep not having a shepherd,"* presents Israel at that particular time. The nation was perhaps more religious than ever before, but with few true shepherds. Chrysostom observes that the Scribes, who were supposed to serve as the Pastors of the people, were not so much Pastors as wolves, because, by teaching errors both by word and by example, they perverted the minds of the simple.

As well, the description of the *"sheep"* is appropriate, in that no animal is more helpless, more in need of a shepherd, than sheep. This is the reason the Lord has given *"some, Apostles; some, Prophets; and some, Evangelists; and some, Pastors and Teachers."* He then said, *"For the perfecting of the Saints, for the work of the Ministry, for the edifying of the Body of Christ"* (Eph. 4:11-12). But sadly, there are many *"false apostles"* now, as then, and if the sheep follow these *"false prophets, which come to you in sheep's clothing, but inwardly they are ravening wolves,"* the results are obvious (Mat. 7:15).

This is perhaps Satan's greatest and most effective weapon, *"wolves in sheep's clothing."* If we are to take an example from the time of Christ, such example is shocking!

WOLVES IN SHEEP'S CLOTHING

There were almost no true shepherds in Christ's day. Hopefully, there are a few more at present; but, if the Truth be known, the actual number would be shockingly small. In fact, the most dangerous place in town for the Christian, or anyone for that matter, is, most of the time, *"the Church."* There, too often, people are led astray by *"wolves in sheep's clothing."* They are taught false doctrine, used and abused, with no true Salvation of Christ offered. Tragically, many who claim to be Believers, but who really aren't, desire this religious facade.

Religion is the biggest business in the world, far eclipsing any and all giant corporations. However, all religion is of man, and, ultimately, of Satan. It is a way devised, instigated, instituted, and developed by man and, therefore, not of God. True Salvation is all of God and none of man. That is the reason Bible Christianity is not a religion, but rather a relationship — a relationship with a Man, the Lord Jesus Christ (Mat. 11:28-30).

THE TEACHING MINISTRY OF THE MASTER

The phrase, *"And He began to teach them many things,"* presents the only True Gospel that many of them had ever heard. Wuest says, *"The crowd, tired of the powerless preaching of the Rabbis, and sensing a new type of teaching, was eager to hear the new Teacher. What they were hearing was 'Truth!'"* If those who follow in the train of Christ do not teach exactly as He taught, which is the Word of God, and the Word of God exclusively, the people will not be helped. Only the Word of God is Truth. It must not be added to or taken from.

(35) "AND WHEN THE DAY WAS NOW FAR SPENT, HIS DISCIPLES CAME UNTO HIM, AND SAID, THIS IS A DESERT PLACE, AND NOW THE TIME IS FAR PASSED."

The exposition is:

It was growing late in the day.

THE DESERT PLACE

The phrase, *"And when the day was now far spent,"* means it was almost sunset. The phrase, *"His Disciples came unto Him, and said,"* represents human thinking, which did not bring Jesus into the equation. The phrase, *"This is a desert place, and now the time is far passed,"* means that no accommodations were nearby, and the time for finding such accommodations in nearby villages was rapidly slipping away.

The term *"desert place,"* however, has a far greater connotation than that immediately locality. In effect, it speaks of the entirety of the world as a *"desert place,"* because the world doesn't know God. As a result, the world has no spiritual sustenance, other than what it receives through Christ. Despite the world being filled with religions of every kind, these religions do not in any way alleviate the *"desert place,"* but rather add to it. In other words, they make it worse!

Look at the nations of the world where Islam prevails. They are the most backward, uneducated, superstitious, poverty-stricken people on the face of the Earth. Then there is Japan, which is materially prosperous, but which, due to the influence of Buddhism and Shintoism, is like a country without a soul.

The only True Way which makes a dent in this *"desert place"* called the world, and which is made so by sin, is Bible Christianity, i.e., *"Christ."* Outside of Christ, the desert remains, whether materially or spiritually, and, in most cases, both materially and spiritually.

NOTES

(36) "SEND THEM AWAY, THAT THEY MAY GO INTO THE COUNTRY ROUND ABOUT, AND INTO THE VILLAGES, AND BUY THEMSELVES BREAD: FOR THEY HAVE NOTHING TO EAT."

The synopsis is:

Outside of Christ there is no answer for the human dilemma!

SEND THEM AWAY?

The phrase, *"Send them away,"* is about all that one person can do for another, that is, if they are not depending on Christ. It is tragic that the world claims to be able to help mankind, with all of the attendant problems, but despite the great claims and the large sums of money charged, the end result is to *"send them away,"* without any help whatsoever. It is sad and tragic, but the Church has also bought into this ungodly, humanistic concept of psychology. But let it be known, there is no answer other than Christ, and the Church, of all people and places, should be the first one to say so!

As an example, the modern Church has, by and large, embraced humanistic psychology as the answer to the emotional and even spiritual needs of man. It has done so even though the roots of psychology are in humanism, atheism, and evolution. The Church has taken this direction because it no longer believes the Bible. As well, there is no way the two can be mixed. The little leaven ultimately leavens the entirety of the lump; consequently, at present, precious few Preachers claim Christ and the Cross as the answer to the problems of man, with almost all recommending humanistic psychology.

The Church must come back to the correct position that man is a *"troubled soul,"* and not a *"damaged self."* Psychology addresses the *"self,"* or *"mind,"* while the Word of God addresses the *"soul"* and the *"spirit."* This is proper terminology, because of the way man is created.

PSYCHOLOGY

The problem is that psychology, at its roots, and despite the smearing of Christianity, does not even believe that man has a soul and spirit. Or if it does, its explanation steers it away from its Creator, which, in reality, actually denies its existence. Most of the world, including the Church, is preoccupied with *"self."* However, while man is certainly a person, or *"self,"* still, such is only the result of the soul and spirit; consequently, to treat *"self"* is to treat only the symptoms instead of the cause. The Word of God goes to the cause.

In one basic sentence, Jesus addressed the entire structure. He said, *"If any man will come after Me* (the criteria for Discipleship), *let him deny himself* (not asceticism, as many think, but rather that one denies one's own willpower, self-will, strength, and ability, thereby depending totally on Christ), *and take up his cross* (the benefits of the Cross, looking exclusively to what Jesus did there to meet our every need) *daily* (this is so important, our looking to the Cross, that we must renew our Faith in what Christ has done for us, even on a daily basis, for Satan will ever try to move us away from the Cross as the Object of our Faith, which always spells disaster), *and follow Me* (Christ can be followed only by the Believer looking to the Cross, understanding what it accomplished, and by that means alone [Rom. 6:3-5, 11, 14; 8:1-2, 11; I Cor. 1:17-18, 21, 23; 2:2; Gal. 6:14; Eph. 2:13-18; Col. 2:14-15; Lk. 9:23]).

SELF

Self is to be hidden in Christ, which can be done only by the Believer evidencing Faith in Christ and what Christ did at the Cross. *"Self"* addressed any other way will always lead to personal problems. As someone has well said, *"When Jesus died on the Cross, He there died not only to save us from sin, but also to save us from self."*

Self-improvement is one of the great pasttimes of this nation; however, in Truth, self, through and by itself, cannot be improved. In other words, there is no such thing as *"moral evolution."* Self must be denied, which speaks of denying our own ability, strength, prowess, efforts, etc. Self must then be placed entirely in Christ, which Paul explains to us in Romans 6:3-5.

Paul, incidentally, in Romans 6:3-5, is not talking about Water Baptism, as many believe, but rather of our Baptism into Christ, which speaks of His Crucifixion, which paid the price that we could not pay.

NOTES

LOW SELF-ESTEEM

Many modern Christians are fond of claiming that man's problem is *"low self-esteem."* They claim that if one can gain a high self-esteem, then one's problems will be solved.

But let the Reader understand:

Whether it's low or high, *"self"* is the problem.

No! The answer is not a *"high self-esteem,"* but rather *"self"* being hidden completely in Christ, which is done only by us looking to Christ as our Substitute, which He was, and identifying with Him, and I speak of identification with His Cross.

THE BREAD

The phrase, *"That they may go into the country round about, and into the villages, and buy themselves bread,"* is certainly understandable in the literal sense; however, the *"bread"* which Jesus Alone gives cannot be obtained in the places of the world. *"Bread"* of the world will not satisfy. Only He is the True Bread of Life. Actually, this is what Jesus was teaching His Disciples.

The phrase, *"For they have nothing to eat,"* was true in the literal sense, and is also true in the spiritual sense. This is the great error of the modern Church. It tries to exist on *"bread alone,"* or else it substitutes another type of religious bread for Jesus Christ, which, in reality, is no bread at all; hence, *"they have nothing to eat."*

One must always remember:

The Church is not the *"bread"*; it only is supposed to show people where the *"Bread,"* i.e., Jesus Christ, actually is, i.e., the Bible.

(37) "HE ANSWERED AND SAID UNTO THEM, GIVE YE THEM TO EAT. AND THEY SAY UNTO HIM, SHALL WE GO AND BUY TWO HUNDRED PENNYWORTH OF BREAD, AND GIVE THEM TO EAT?"

The synopsis is:

Jesus was speaking in both the physical and spiritual sense.

GIVE YE THEM TO EAT

The phrase, *"He answered and said unto them, Give ye them to eat,"* is meant to address the subject on a spiritual level, which they, at that time, could not begin to grasp.

Even though Jesus definitely was speaking of the physical, even more so was He speaking of the spiritual. This, which they would understand later, referred to the Word of God. This corresponds with what Jesus answered Satan, *"Man shall not live by bread alone, but by every Word that proceeds out of the Mouth of God"* (Mat. 4:4).

The tragedy is, as stated, that the majority of Preachers are not giving the Word for their listeners to eat, but rather something else! The question, *"And they say unto Him, Shall we go and buy two hundred pennyworth of bread, and give them to eat?"* pertains to the problem at hand, and the Disciples trying to solve it. The people had been without physical food for some time, although having received the greatest spiritual food they would ever have. But still, their physical bodies demanded nourishment. The Disciples had one of two solutions. They could either send the people away so they could obtain food on their own, or else they could buy enough food to feed this massive crowd, which actually was impossible, at least in this *"desert place."*

Even though numbers are readily given in some Commentaries, still, the consensus is that there is actually no way presently to know, at least according to inflated dollars, exactly how much bread *"two hundred pennyworth"* would buy. The consensus is that it was a sizable amount of money, probably equivalent to $7,000 to $8,000 presently.

(38) "HE SAID UNTO THEM, HOW MANY LOAVES HAVE YOU? GO AND SEE. AND WHEN THEY KNEW, THEY SAY, FIVE, AND TWO FISHES."

The structure is:

According to Andrew, this small collection belonged to a boy (Jn. 6:8-9); little is much if God be in it.

THE FOOD IN HAND

Jesus does not at all comment on their question. He ignores it, as if it is of no consequence, which it wasn't. The phrase, *"He said unto them,"* shows them what He will now do. It's very easy to criticize the Disciples, but most of us, as they, do not think in spiritual terms nearly as much as we should. Too often, we try to figure the thing out from a natural basis, when those things certainly should be considered, but, at the same time, realizing that God is able to do all things.

Actually, Jesus will take the Disciples to a dimension they had never dreamed possible. He would take them from the natural to the supernatural! He would take them from the impossible to the possible! He would take them to the miraculous! Among all the lessons He is now teaching, this is perhaps the greatest lesson of all.

The Believer must look at every situation, whether little or large, in the context of what God is able to do, instead of what man is able to do. If Jesus would go to this length to teach this lesson, surely it must be learned. This is the reason He made such statements as, *"If you abide in Me, and My Words abide in you, you shall ask what you will, and it shall be done unto you"* (Jn. 15:7). Or, *"If you shall ask anything in My Name, I will do it"* (Jn. 14:14).

Actually, the four Gospels are replete with such glorious and miraculous Promises. To be sure, He meant what He said, and said what He meant!

THE MIRACLE

The question, *"How many loaves have you?"* pertains to literal loaves of bread. In fact, most everything the Lord does addressed itself to literal things; however, He turns it into a Miracle. They were thinking of thousands of loaves to feed this massive crowd, while He addressed Himself to whatever they had, as little as it might have been. In fact, He is asking the same question to every Believer, *"How many loaves do you have?"*

It is meant to tell each and all that whatever we do have, as little as it may be, it can be miraculously touched by Him and made to serve in great capacities. In fact, the *"five loaves and two fishes"* which were here supplied were about as nothing as could ever be, respecting the size of this massive crowd. So, the Lord is trying to pull us away from what little we have to how big He is, and what He can do!

GO AND SEE

The phrase, *"Go and see,"* directed to them,

is directed to us, as well! We may think we have nothing, especially considering the tremendous task ahead, but all of us have at least something. The problem is, we have considered it without Him, instead of with Him. We keep looking at the smallness of our assets instead of the bigness of His Abilities.

Many people refuse to give to God for this very reason. They reason within themselves that it is so little that it is of no consequence. The lesson here taught, as stated, is not the smallness of our gift, especially if, as here, that is all we have, but the miracle-manner in which He is able to enlarge it.

What a lesson, that is, if we can only learn it!

The phrase, *"And when they knew, they say, five, and two fishes,"* means that at first they did not even really know they had that. Actually, according to Andrew, this small collection belonged to a boy (Jn. 6:8-9). He had sent them to find whatever bread they could find, and this is what they came back with, *"five loaves and two fishes."*

(39) "AND HE COMMANDED THEM TO MAKE ALL SIT DOWN BY COMPANIES UPON THE GREEN GRASS."

The composition is:

Considering that the grass was green, it was probably about April.

THE COMMAND

The phrase, *"And He commanded them,"* proclaims them taking charge, as He will do, if we will only allow Him. When He is given that latitude, He will begin to give instructions, and things will begin to fall into place. We do not really know how He does it, but we just know things start to happen!

The phrase, *"To make all sit down by companies by the green grass,"* tells us that it was Passover time; therefore, it was the month of April (Jn. 6:4). The *"companies"* spoke of order, which always characterizes that which the Lord does. He is not a God of confusion!

(40) "AND THEY SAT DOWN IN RANKS, BY HUNDREDS, AND BY FIFTIES."

The exposition is:

Once again, this proclaims God's Order, which is always systematic.

NOTES

GOD'S ORDER

The word *"ranks"* probably best describes this which was done. In other words, the entirety of the gathering of at least 10,000 people, and possibly more, was organized that all may be properly cared for. There is even some slight evidence that the men were separated from the women and children (Mat. 14:21).

Other than *"order,"* which is always characteristic of the Work of the Lord, perhaps this suggests to us all the nations of the world, which must be equally fed. The organization was such that those in the very back ranks were given just as much as those in the forward ranks. This is the intention of the Lord respecting the dissemination of the Gospel. Unfortunately, it has not worked that way, at least at the present time. Some nations seem to be given far more than others.

(41) "AND WHEN HE HAD TAKEN THE FIVE LOAVES AND THE TWO FISHES, HE LOOKED UP TO HEAVEN, AND BLESSED, AND BROKE THE LOAVES, AND GAVE THEM TO HIS DISCIPLES TO SET BEFORE THEM; AND THE TWO FISHES DIVIDED HE AMONG THEM ALL."

The composition is:

The Miracle took place between the breaking and the giving; each Disciple soon exhausted his supply and so had to return to Jesus for more, and was never disappointed.

ALL BLESSINGS ARE FROM HEAVEN

The phrase, *"And when He had taken the five loaves and the two fishes,"* signifies the beginning of the Miracle, because it was in His Hands. That is the secret! In our hands, it is nothing; in His Hands, it is everything! Sadly, mankind is reluctant to place it in His Hands, even though it is insignificant to begin with.

The phrase, *"He looked up to Heaven,"* proclaims that it is from God from whence the Blessings come. Man keeps thinking it is his ability, when the opposite is true. Even regarding those who do not live for God, or even recognize Him, it is the Lord Who gives the breath that man breathes and the strength to do what is done both mentally and physically. However, precious few give Him the praise and the glory.

GOD IS THE SOURCE

The phrase, *"And blessed,"* signifies thanksgiving, and God as the Source of all Blessing.

"LORD, You bless the Righteous," says the Psalmist (Ps. 5:12). God not only gives life, but also enriches life. Even the power to give wealth (Deut. 8:18) comes from the Lord. We are totally dependent on Him. Jesus' action consequently portrays this.

COVENANT BLESSINGS

Basically, the beginning of Blessings, at least as far as Covenant was concerned, began with Abraham and followed through to his descendants. The Lord committed Himself to bless them (Gen., Chpts. 12, 17). But the Covenant had to be accepted by Faith by each succeeding generation, and blessing was found in obedience to a way of life that God later laid down.

"Behold, I set before you this day a blessing and a curse;

"A blessing, if you obey the Commandments of the LORD your God, which I command you this day:

"And a curse, if you will not obey the Commandments of the LORD your God, but turn aside out of the way which I command you this day, to go after other gods, which you have not known" (Deut. 11:26-28).

Actually, this Truth, restated often in Deuteronomy (Deut., Chpts. 12, 15, 28), is basic to the Old Testament concept of Blessing. The abundant life is to be found in the Lord and experienced as we live His Way. The Old Testament rightly assumed from God's Covenant Promises that the enriched life included material blessings. These follow consecration as the individual lives by Faith and in obedience to God; however, Jesus moved beyond the Old Testament regarding Blessing.

JESUS AND BLESSINGS

The Lord makes the startling statement that God's Kingdom is a present Kingdom and that His blessed ones already know (are happy with) a unique joy which comes from living in that Kingdom. The Old Testament describes the path that leads to God's Blessing. Jesus describes that Blessing itself. God's Blessing comes to us in all our circumstances and makes us fortunate no matter how others may view our lives.

The New Covenant takes us even further into God's Blessings, as Paul announced it in Ephesians 1:3, i.e., *"blessed with all spiritual blessings."* All of this is in Christ. Because our Blessing is found in personal relationship with Jesus and because that relationship is so intimate and real, we have in Jesus Himself the abundant life for which we yearn and which God has ever yearned to give straying mankind.

However, and as stated, the main thrust of the action of Christ in blessing the food is the reminder that God is the Source of all Blessings.

The phrase, *"And broke the loaves,"* signifies the act of the Miracle. In other words, the Greek structure of the language tells us that the Miracle of the multiplication took place between the breaking and the giving. There is a tremendous lesson in this, which we will discuss in greater detail momentarily!

The phrase, *"And gave them to His Disciples to set before them,"* means that the provision was not to be kept by the Disciples, but instead to be given to the hungry. The phrase, *"And the two fishes divided He among them all,"* proclaims that they also were multiplied as the bread.

There is a tremendous pattern outlined in the action of Christ, which addresses itself to every Believer, and which also proclaims the manner in which God carries out His Work in our lives.

HE TAKES

"When He had taken": Of course, this is speaking of the bread and fish; still, it also pertains to our lives. Whenever we, as individuals, come to Christ, the Lord is kind and generous to take us, even though we have nothing to offer Him.

BLESSING

"And blessed": Almost immediately after Salvation, the Lord blesses the individual

greatly. These Blessings come in all shapes and sizes and come from every direction. It is somewhat like an initiation into Christianity, which is the opposite of most initiations of the world.

THE BREAKING

"And broke": Then comes the *"breaking,"* which is a very painful experience for any and all Believers; however, if we are to be used by the Lord, this process must be engaged. It is the struggle between the flesh and the Spirit.

For a while, it seems as if all Blessings stop, with everything we hold dear being stripped away. Actually, and in some manner, this *"breaking"* never ends. This is done that the flesh may be subdued and Christ may be all-in-all. As stated, it is a debilitating process, and it is meant to be so. Unfortunately, many of our Faith friends have endeavored to confess away this part of the Christian experience, entertaining only the Blessing; however, such cannot be done and, in fact, is not meant to be done.

David is a perfect example! He was anointed by the Lord, which constituted tremendous blessing. Very shortly thereafter, he killed the giant, with all the attendant blessings that followed; however, the time soon came that it seemed like all blessing left, with David being persecuted by Saul, even to the place he thought he would lose his life. It was the *"breaking process,"* and was necessary before he could take the Throne.

THE GIVING

"And gave": The breaking, as stated, is absolutely necessary. It is totally of Christ. Without the *"breaking,"* it is the flesh which is given to the world, i.e., man-devised efforts, which will bless or help no one. After the *"breaking,"* the flesh is subdued, with Christ being supreme and *"given"* to lost humanity. Consequently, Miracles result in changed lives, because Christ is properly presented.

If one is to notice, and to which we have alluded, the Disciples did not hoard the food for themselves, but instead gave it to the multitudes as intended! Regrettably, the modern Church, especially the segment in the Pentecostal and Charismatic community, has attempted to do the opposite of what is proclaimed here. Most of the so-called faith is used to confess personal riches, etc. Very little of the Gospel is given to a hurting world, at least from this part of the Church.

Even though my statement may offend some, I must say it because it is true: *"The Modern Faith Message is a selfish Message, which is the opposite of the Bible Message."* Even though it talks about *"giving,"* still, its action is the very opposite. Even if it does give, it is not without great strings attached, demanding much more in return than was given. Such is not giving, but rather covetousness.

If *"self"* is properly hidden in Christ, as it must be, it will do exactly as Christ said, *"Take no thought for your life, what you shall eat, or what you shall drink; nor yet for your body, what you shall put on"* (Mat. 6:25). While the Lord certainly does bless materially, as we have already stated, still that is a by-product of His Great Salvation, and certainly not the main thrust, which is Salvation from sin.

(42) "AND THEY DID ALL EAT, AND WERE FILLED."

The diagram is:

Jehovah of Psalm 132 here revealed Himself.

THE SATISFACTION OF CHRIST

Eating and being *"filled"* is always the case with Christ. When men eat that which is offered by the world, at least in the spiritual sense, it never satisfies; consequently, they are never *"filled."* That which Christ gives is filling, i.e., satisfying. As well, that which was given satisfied *"all,"* and not just a few. In other words, what Christ has to offer is meant for all; and all need what Christ has to offer.

I have had the opportunity to appear on nationally televised news and interview programs with some of America's most noted political pundits. Of course, many of these individuals consider themselves to be the cream of the intelligentsia of the nation. Almost entirely, they place themselves beyond the need for Christ and what He offers. Their attitude is that the ignorant and unlearned may need this *"crutch,"* but not them. They have it all together, at least in their thinking.

But truthfully, the only difference in these individuals and the ignorant and unlearned, as they put it, is a little education, which, for the most part, is no education at all, simply because it is error. The truly ignorant are these pseudo-intellectuals. To be uneducated is simply not to know. To be ignorant is to not know that you don't know! Such describes those who think they know so much, but who, in reality, know so little.

Solomon said, *"The fear of the LORD is the beginning of wisdom"* (Prov. 9:10).

The Truth is: Whether rich or poor, great or small, educated or uneducated, young or old; all need the Lord Jesus Christ. As well, and as stated, He Alone can provide what the soul of man desperately needs.

(43) "AND THEY TOOK UP TWELVE BASKETS FULL OF THE FRAGMENTS, AND OF THE FISHES."

The overview is:

With the Lord, there is always enough, even with some left over.

TWELVE BASKETS

The number *"twelve"* speaks of Government, and God's Government, at that! The idea is that if God's Government was paramount in the world, the entirety of the world would be fed and prosperous. One day it shall!

They began with *"five loaves and two fishes"*; they fed 10,000 or more people; and they ended up with *"twelve baskets full of the fragments, and of the fishes."* What a Miracle! As is obvious, Christ does not carry out His Work according to the particular laws of this Earth, laws He in fact originally created, but which, no doubt, were twisted by the Fall of man. Christ brings Heaven down to Earth, which introduces a completely new way of doing things.

That is the reason He prayed, *"Your Kingdom come, Your Will be done in Earth, as it is in Heaven."* Then He said, *"Give us this day our daily bread"* (Mat. 6:10-11). To be sure, and as is obvious, He can give bread in a manner in which the world cannot, and which the world does not even understand.

HAMILTON'S LAW

There is a law called *"Hamilton's Law."* It basically states that for everything built, something must be destroyed. In other words, if a house is built, trees must be cut down to provide the lumber; and rock and sand of the Earth must also be depleted in order for the bricks to be made, etc. However, with Christ, no such law exists. Even though the original five loaves and two fish caused depletion, at least to a small degree, still, the multiplication caused no depletion whatsoever.

Where did the extra bread and fish come from?

Of course, what the Lord carried out was a Miracle. Such sets aside natural law and can only be done by the supernatural Power of God. Actually, the Power was in Jesus, not in a formula or some type of magical control of the supernatural.

MIRACLES

The Message of Miracles is that God has shown us His Power and has proven that His Power will be used for our benefit. We can trust Jesus fully. He is able, and He wills only our good. To be sure, if how the Lord performed the Miracle can be explained, then, in actuality, it was not a miracle. A Miracle simply cannot be explained by natural means or according to phenomenon.

AN OBSERVATION

Sometime back, I had the occasion to see a program over Television, which addressed itself to this very subject — the subject of miracles. One group did not believe at all. The other group claimed to believe, but was, is reality, also faithless!

The ones who claimed to believe attempted to explain, as the result of natural means, the Miracles of the opening of the Red Sea and the Hebrew Children in the fiery furnace. In other words, they said the opening of the Red Sea was caused by an earthquake. While it certainly may have been possible that the Lord used an earthquake to carry out this grand Miracle, still, for it to happen at the exact time the Children of Israel were standing on the banks of the Red Sea, and then for it to conclude at the very time the last Israelite gained the opposite shore, is more, much more, than just a mere earthquake. It cannot be explained according to natural phenomenon, earthquake or no earthquake!

They also attempted to explain the Hebrew Children in the fiery furnace as finding a *"cool spot"* in the midst of the furnace. They claimed that *"cool spots"* are found in all furnaces, etc. In all honesty, the unbelief of the Believers was worse even than that of the unbelievers. If they were saved by this *"cool spot,"* how did they get to the cool spot in the first place? The fire was already raging when they were thrown in, so much in fact that it killed those who threw them into the furnace (Dan. 3:22).

No! The Lord performed a Miracle by suspending the heat and its effect on the Hebrew Children. In truth, it cannot be explained by any natural law or phenomenon, only by the Power of God.

So, how the Lord performed the Miracle of multiplying the loaves and the fish is not known. But that He did it is obvious! He is a God of Miracles; He is the same today as He was yesterday (Heb. 13:8).

(44) "AND THEY WHO DID EAT OF THE LOAVES WERE ABOUT FIVE THOUSAND MEN."

The exposition is:

There were possibly as many as 10,000 to 15,000 total, including women and children.

AN ASTOUNDING MIRACLE

Wuest says that the word for *"men"* is not *"anthropos,"* the generic term, which could include men and women, but *"aner,"* the word for a male individual. Matthew added that there were women and children; consequently, there must have been at least 10,000, or more, who were fed that day.

I have to believe that the *"bread and fish"* multiplied by Jesus and given to the multitude were the finest *"bread and fish"* that these people had ever eaten. I can imagine that thousands exclaimed as to how delicious the food was. While we must not be carried away, still, everything the Lord does is perfect; consequently, this must have been a perfect meal! Likewise, the Salvation afforded by Christ is a Perfect Salvation!

NOTES

(45) "AND STRAIGHTWAY HE CONSTRAINED HIS DISCIPLES TO GET INTO THE SHIP, AND TO GO TO THE OTHER SIDE BEFORE UNTO BETHSAIDA, WHILE HE SENT AWAY THE PEOPLE."

The structure is:

Even though He sent them away, they were sent away healed, fed, and filled.

A LESSON FOR THE DISCIPLES

The phrase, *"And straightway He constrained His Disciples to get into the ship,"* proclaims their reluctance to do so, with Jesus having to sternly command them to obey. They had witnessed a tremendous Miracle, and did not desire to leave Him; they also were perplexed at His action.

Why would He want to stay there alone?

He offered no explanation, but rather demanded their obedience.

The phrase, *"And to go to the other side before unto Bethsaida,"* probably referred to the Bethsaida near Capernaum. Actually, there were two Bethsaidas. One was at the northeast end of the lake, near to where they probably were at the moment, but the other, as stated, was across the lake near Capernaum. The one at the northeast was called *"Bethsaida Julias."*

The phrase, *"While He sent away the people,"* proclaims Him doing so only after they were fed and filled. Also, it seems as if the people, as the Disciples, did not desire to leave Him, with Him having to ask them to go their respective ways. Nevertheless, the admonition to the Disciples was far stronger than to the crowd.

(46) "AND WHEN HE HAD SENT THEM AWAY, HE DEPARTED INTO A MOUNTAIN TO PRAY."

The overview is:

Prayer establishes relationship.

PRAYER

The phrase, *"And when He had sent them away,"* proclaims the beginning of a lesson they will soon be taught. The phrase, *"He departed into a mountain to pray,"* gives the reason for His desiring to be alone.

The word *"pray,"* as used in this sentence, speaks of the consciousness on the part of the one who prays of the fact of God's Presence and His listening ear (Wuest).

Prayer is not understood too well by most Christians. Actually, it remains one of the mysteries of our Faith.

The questions are asked, *"How can prayer change the Mind of God, or modify events?"* or *"How does prayer relate to Divine Sovereignty?"*

Actually, prayer does not change the Mind of God, though it does modify events. Respecting Divine Sovereignty, the Lord has so designed His Work and Word, that He allows the Believer to enter into the carrying out of God's Will by using our Faith in seeking His Face.

Believers are commanded to pray about everything, confident that God hears prayer, cares, and is able to act (I Thess. 5:17).

PRAYER IN THE OLD TESTAMENT

The Old Testament is filled with references to prayer. God's people pray to Him, call on Him, and cry out to Him. Using David as an example, the Passages of Scripture which deal with David's life portray the shepherd-king consistently inquiring of the Lord (Ps. 4:1; 69:16-17). Prayer indicates an humbling of one's self before the Lord, i.e., a submission to God.

THE FOUNDATIONS OF OLD TESTAMENT PRAYER

Prayer in the Old Testament is an expression of personal relationship. This relationship was initiated by God, Who is recognized as Creator and Redeemer. As Creator, God is recognized as the Source of each life, as well as of the Universe. His limitless Power is expressed in the material world and in history itself, which unfolds according to His purposes. As Redeemer, God acted in history to deliver His people in their need. While the Exodus is the prime example of Redemption, God continued to act on Israel's behalf. He is a God Who saves, and His people can depend on His intervention.

PERSONAL PRAYER LIFE

The Lord saved me when I was but eight years old, and Baptized me with the Holy Spirit, with the evidence of speaking with other tongues, a short time later (Acts 2:4).

NOTES

At this particular time, in that year of 1943, which, if I remember correctly, was the month of June, I was in a prayer meeting every single day of my life, and sometimes even twice a day. We would meet for prayer at either my Grandmother's home, or else my Aunt's home, actually the Mother of Mickey Gilley. Both of these women were some of the Godliest I ever knew.

In those formative years, my Grandmother taught me to pray. She taught me to believe God. She taught me that God answered prayer today, just as He did in Bible times. So, I was raised on that type of Faith, that type of foundation, that type of expectation. To be frank, had I not had those early years of training, I don't think I would have survived, considering some of the things that we've faced.

It was in October of 1991. For all practical purposes, it looked as if the Ministry was totally destroyed. It had been the largest Evangelistic effort on the face of the Earth, but it was now reduced considerably. I didn't know what to do!

I UNDERSTAND NOT

I full well know what the Apostle Paul was talking about when he said, *"For that which I do* (the failure) *I allow not* (should have been translated *"I understand not"*; these are not the words of an unsaved man, as some claim, but the words of a Believer who is trying and failing): *for what I would, that do I not* (refers to the obedience he wants to render to Christ, but rather fails. Why? As Paul explained, the Believer is married to Christ, but is being unfaithful to Christ by spiritually cohabiting with the Law, which frustrates the Grace of God; that means the Holy Spirit will not help such a person, which guarantees failure [Gal. 2:21]); *but what I hate, that do I* (refers to sin in his life, which he doesn't want to do, which, in fact, he hates; but he finds himself unable to stop; unfortunately, due to the fact of not understanding the Cross as it refers to Sanctification, this is the plight of most modern Christians)" (Rom. 7:15).

Paul was doing everything he knew to do to live a Godly life; but, nevertheless, he was failing, and despite all of his efforts to do otherwise. Of course, as he writes these words, he is writing of the time before the Lord gave him the Revelation of the Cross. Until that Revelation came, it was impossible, no matter how hard he tried, for him to live the victorious life that he must live.

In fact, during those days, ever how long they lasted, the sin nature ruled in Paul's life. However, at that time, he didn't understand anything about the sin nature, or about the Cross, which is the only answer to the sin nature. Therefore, even as the Seventh Chapter of Romans proclaims, he lived a life of spiritual failure during that time, a time which possibly lasted for several years.

As stated, I empathize greatly with the great Apostle, simply because during that time (1991), I didn't understand the sin nature, nor did I understand the Cross, as it refers to Sanctification. I understood the Cross relative to Salvation, and preached it strongly as the answer to a lost world, in fact, the only answer. However, I knew nothing of the Cross as it refers to Sanctification. That being the case, as it is presently with the far, far greater majority of the modern Church world, it was impossible to live a victorious life, irrespective as to how hard I tried.

Thank God in 1997 the Lord gave me the same Revelation that He gave to the Apostle Paul. In other words, he opened up to me what the great Apostle was talking about in Romans, Chapters 6, 7, and 8. In fact, and as I've already stated any number of times, the Revelation, i.e., the meaning of the Cross, is actually the meaning of the New Covenant. It is that to which the Old Covenant pointed, and did so exclusively. Once the Lord portrayed to me that Revelation, which, in fact, continues to unfold even unto this hour, and I suspect ever will, only then did I begin to walk in victory.

WHAT IS VICTORY!

The Apostle John said, *"For whatsoever is born of God overcomes the world* (if we follow God's Prescribed Order, we will overcome the world): *and this is the victory that overcomes the world, even our Faith.* (John is speaking here of Faith in Christ and the Cross, which then gives the Holy Spirit latitude to work within our lives, Who Alone can bring about the victory which all of us must have)" (I Jn. 5:4).

First, let's see what victory is not!

Victory is not the absence of all bad things in our lives, and the presence of all good things. That rather is the *"result"* of victory, not the actual fact of victory. Victory is, exactly as John said it was, our Faith, and, we might quickly add, Faith which is in Christ Jesus and what He did for us at the Cross. Any time faith is mentioned, it is always, and without exception, meant in that capacity. This is what Paul was talking about when he said, *"I am crucified with Christ* (as the foundation of all victory; Paul here takes us back to Rom. 6:3-5): *nevertheless I live* (have new life); *yet not I* (not by my own strength and ability), *but Christ lives in me* (by virtue of me dying with Him on the Cross and being raised with Him in newness of life): *and the life which I now live in the flesh* (my daily walk before God) *I live by the Faith of the Son of God* (the Cross is ever the Object of my Faith), *Who loved me, and gave Himself for me* (which is the only way I could be saved)" (Gal. 2:20).

THE FAITH

If one is to notice, Paul used the term *"the Faith of the Son of God."* He didn't say, *"I live by evidencing faith in the Son of God,"* etc., but rather *"by the Faith of the Son of God."* He is meaning that any time the word *"Faith"* is used, it is always, and without exception, Faith in Christ and what Christ did for us at the Cross. If it's not that type of faith, in other words, if Christ and the Cross are not the Object of one's Faith, then really it's not faith that God will recognize.

So, victory is the Believer placing his Faith exclusively in Christ and the Cross, understanding that Christ is always the Source, while the Cross is always the Means. That is *"the Faith."* And that is *"victory."*

Victory doesn't necessarily mean that there will never be another problem, or that we will never again fail the Lord in any manner. It does mean that whatever it is that's causing the failure can be completely overcome, and ultimately will be overcome. Paul said, *"For sin shall not have dominion over you"* (the sin nature will not have dominion over us if we, as Believers, continue to exercise Faith in the Cross of Christ; otherwise, the sin nature most definitely will have dominion over the Believer): *for you are not under the Law* (means that if we try to live this life by any type of Law, no matter how good that Law might be in its own right, we will conclude by the sin nature having dominion over us), *but under Grace* (the Grace of God flows to the Believer on an unending basis only as long as the Believer exercises Faith in Christ and what He did at the Cross; Grace is merely the Goodness of God exercised by and through the Holy Spirit, given to undeserving Saints)" (Rom. 6:14).

Therefore, anyone who evidences Faith in Christ and what Christ did at the Cross, irrespective of their present circumstances, can claim the Victory, and I'm speaking of a present Victory, knowing that we now have Victory by Faith, and the concluding factor will be one of Victory, and all because of Christ and the Cross. Any victory claimed by any other means or method is not Victory based on *"the Faith,"* but is rather victory based on *"the flesh,"* which, in fact, is no victory at all.

PRAYER MEETING

At any rate, on that October morning in 1991, I did not know and understand these things that I am now teaching you; however, I did understand one thing, and that was the value and Power of prayer. In fact, the Lord, as I've already stated in this Volume, told me to begin two prayer meetings a day, morning and night.

I've always had a very strong prayer life, because my Grandmother taught me that; however, before this particular October morning, had you told me that the Lord desired two prayer meetings a day (and I speak only of that which is relative to myself), I would have thought that was a bit much. But, as someone has well said, *"Desperation always precedes revelation."* In other words, when a person is desperate, even as I was, this is the time that the Lord can speak to such a person, and do so without argument.

Concerning the Ministry, I did not know what to do. Should I try to stay on Television? Or should I cancel all Television? Of course, the Church world was demanding that I get off Television. In fact, I don't know of one single Preacher who encouraged me otherwise. They all, and almost to a man, wanted this Ministry stopped. Most would do anything within their power to see to it that it was stopped. However, man doesn't have the last say. It is the Lord Who has the last say.

A MOVE OF THE HOLY SPIRIT

That October morning, after arriving at the office, I called our principal people together. I spoke to them for a few moments, telling them that we must have an answer from the Lord as to what we should do. And, to be sure, the Lord didn't fail us.

I suppose there were 12 to 15 in the room that morning, when the Spirit of God fell like rain. I had taken my petition to the Lord: *"What do You want us to do?"* As it regards Television, He emphatically told me that I was to stay on Television. I remember protesting to Him: *"How can this be done?"*

An Evangelist such as myself is able to carry out what God has called him to do, only with the help of the people. As Paul said, the Lord sends some, and He calls others to do the sending (Rom. 10:14-15). With all confidence in this Evangelist destroyed, how could we pay for the Telecast?

Then the Lord spoke to my heart, and did so by taking me to His Word, as He always did. He took me to one of the experiences with Simon Peter, which is recorded only by Matthew. The great Apostle had come to Jesus about the matter of paying taxes. Did they owe taxes or not?

Jesus said, *"No, we don't owe them, but to keep from offending them, we will pay the taxes."* Jesus then told Peter, *"Go to the Sea* (Galilee), *and cast an hook, and take up the fish that first comes up; when you have opened his mouth, you shall find a piece of money: that take, and give unto them from Me and you"* (Mat. 17:24-27).

The Lord then spoke to my heart, saying, *"As I met the need that day, I will meet your needs, as well."* I knew it was the Lord! I had no doubt about it! However, I also knew that this was about the most unorthodox way that one could even begin to imagine for funds to be raised, as it regards the Work of God.

I dictate these notes on November 7, 2004, a little over 13 years after the Lord gave me that Promise. In looking back, He has found fish after fish, and has done so in the most unorthodox ways. In these last 13 years, time and time again, we have come to a financial standstill, not knowing what to do, with $1,000,000-plus worth of bills in the office, and no way to pay. But every time, even at the exact deadline of desperation, the Lord would find another fish, and pull us through.

In fact, He did that very thing this past week. It was, at least as I see it, a Miracle of unprecedented proportions. I will not go into any detail, perhaps addressing it at another time; however, I feel like the Psalmist, who was probably Hezekiah, who said, *"When the Lord turned again the captivity of Zion, we were like them who dream.*

"Then was our mouth filled with laughter, and our tongue with singing: then said they among the heathen, the LORD has done great things for them."

"The LORD has done great things for us; whereof we are glad.

"Turn again our captivity, O LORD, as the streams in the south.

"They who sow in tears shall reap in joy.

"He who goes forth and weeps, bearing precious seed, shall doubtless come again with rejoicing, bringing his sheaves with him" (Ps. 126).

LOOK WHAT THE LORD HAS DONE!

That Psalm was occasioned by Sennacherib, the king of Assyria, attacking Judah and Jerusalem. Against the mightiest army in the world, how could Judah defend herself? Well, truthfully, Judah didn't defend herself. The Lord did! He sent one Angel, which killed 185,000 Assyrian soldiers in one night, thereby completely destroying the plans of Sennacherib. To be sure, he would turn back from Jerusalem without shooting an arrow at the city, and would never look that way again (Isa. 37:36-38).

In effect, the inhabitants of Jerusalem went to bed one night with the sword of Sennacherib hanging over their heads; but when they awakened the next morning, that sword was gone, without them having to lift a hand. That's why Hezekiah said, *"When the Lord turned again the captivity of Zion, we were like them who dream"* (Ps. 126:1).

But it wasn't a dream. It was real.

As I watched the Lord work on our behalf this last week, this 126th Psalm has come to me again and again.

In the approximate 2 months preceding this time, I sought the Lord again and again, as it regards His help, which I knew we must have, or we simply wouldn't make it. In fact, about two months before the Miracle, I was earnestly seeking the Lord about this financial problem. It was a Saturday afternoon. I had been praying only a few minutes, when, all of a sudden, the Spirit of the Lord covered me, and the Lord brought to my mind a little chorus we used to sing a long time ago, which says:

"The answer's on the way, this I know,
"Jesus said it, I believe it, and it's so,
"Our Heavenly Father knows the need,
*   even before we pray,*
"And you can rest assured the answer
*   is already on the way."*

That Saturday afternoon, I knew beyond the shadow of a doubt that the Lord had spoken to my heart. However, I will admit that during the following approximate two months, I would wonder, time and time again, when the answer would come. In fact, I reminded the Lord again and again of that Promise, even as I saw the financial picture worsen with each passing day.

PLEAD WITH ME

Bringing this Promise which the Lord had given me to the Lord over and over again, I also quoted the Word of the Lord, as given to the Prophet Isaiah. The Lord said:

"Put Me in remembrance: let us plead together: declare thou that you may be justified" (Isa. 43:26).

The phrase, *"Put Me in remembrance,"* doesn't mean that the Lord forgets, but that He desires that we bring these Promises before Him again and again. This builds our faith and our trust in His Word.

Then, at the last moment, as stated, the Lord answered, and did so miraculously. I'll go back to the 126th Psalm:

"Then was our mouth filled with laughter,

and our tongue with singing." Moreover, I also firmly believe that shortly *"they will say among the heathen, the LORD has done great things for them"* (Ps. 126:2).

Most every one of you reading the words of these statements has had the Lord to promise you something which has not yet come to pass. Call it to His remembrance, and do so constantly. Plead with Him as it regards the answer, and you will find that your faith will begin to grow, even as His Word becomes more real in your heart and your life. Then the answer will come.

GOD'S COMMITMENT

God's basic commitment to the descendants of Abraham was given formal expression in the Covenant. God had chosen this people and blessed them. When Israel turned to God, they turned to the One Who had made Himself their God.

All this — knowing God as Creator, Redeemer, and Covenant-Giver — was the basis of the relationship within which God's Old Testament people approached Him in prayer. Knowing God also taught the Israelites their own place. Compared to God, the most exalted individual is but a humble supplicant. Matched against God's unlimited power, the greatest human force is wholly insignificant.

And please believe me, if there is anything I have experienced, it is that statement just made. Having the entirety of the Media attempting to destroy you, and then, sadly and regrettably, having the Church follow suit, puts one in a position that if the Lord doesn't save them, they cannot be saved. But I have learned that against God's unlimited Power, the greatest human force is wholly insignificant.

This means it is appropriate, then, for God's people to depend completely on Him. In the final analysis, His favor is all that matters. Every issue of life hinges on His Grace Alone. The Old Testament Believer was dependent on God in everything, just as a little child is completely dependent on his or her parents.

DEPENDENCE

Prayer, then, is the appeal of a child who

NOTES

recognizes his dependence. It is made to an all-powerful Person Who cares. It is not surprising that Old Testament prayers are personal, often motivated by need, and beautiful in their child-like simplicity.

This is, in fact, why *"Jesus called a little child unto Him, and set him in the midst of them,*

"And He said, Verily I say unto you, Except you be converted, and become as little children, you shall not enter into the Kingdom of Heaven.

"Whosoever therefore shall humble himself as this little child, the same is greatest in the Kingdom of Heaven" (Mat. 18:2-4).

Why did Jesus use a little child as an example?

He did so in order to teach the quality of dependence. As a little child has to depend on its parents for everything, and for the obvious reasons, we also must depend on our Lord for everything — and I mean everything.

We find in the Old Testament that prayer is a spontaneous expression. God can be approached at any time and in any place. It is significant, consequently, that the Old Testament presents no prayer liturgy. Prayer is not a matter of ritual religion. Prayer is a living, vital expression of relationship. Thus, true prayer is always a matter of the heart (Jer. 29:12-14), while false or meaningless prayers are only a matter of the lips (Isa. 29:13; Amos 5:23-24).

PRAYER IN THE NEW TESTAMENT

It is obvious in the New Testament that the view of prayer established in the Old Testament permeates the New; this is also true of the approach to God in prayer. As in the Old Testament, prayer is an expression of relationship, and must always be understood as an expression of fellowship between God and human beings, made possible by Jesus.

In the New Testament, prayer is related to the intimate relationship that the Believer sustains with the Father, the Son, and the Holy Spirit. Jesus condemns a ritualistic, hypocritical approach to prayer; He presents true prayer as an intimate expression of relationship with a God Who is one's Father (Mat. 6:5-8).

Jesus' model prayer, known to us as the

"Lord's Prayer," sums up the beautiful relationship we have with God. We approach Him as we would a Father. We acknowledge and praise Him as the Hallowed One in Heaven. We express our joyful submission to His Will. We acknowledge our dependence on the Lord for material and spiritual sustenance, and we ask for forgiveness as well! We acknowledge His right to direct our lives (Mat. 6:9-13).

Actually, Jesus taught His Disciples, assuring them by explaining the freedom from worry that Believers have: *". . . your Heavenly Father knows that you have need of all these things"* (Mat. 6:32). Coming in prayer to a God Who is Father, and resting in all that this means, we are free to *"seek first the Kingdom of God, and His Righteousness"* (Mat. 6:33).

JESUS

In the New Testament, Jesus is seen as the key to that Personal Relationship with God that is central to prayer. Only through Jesus and what He has done for us at the Cross can we *"approach the Throne of Grace with confidence,"* sure that we will *"receive Mercy and find Grace to help in our time of need"* (Heb. 4:16).

However, a continuing intimate walk with Jesus is vital to prayer. Jesus, using the image of the Vine and Branches (Jn., Chpt. 15), told the Apostles, *"If you abide in Me* (keep your Faith anchored in Christ and the Cross), *and My Words abide in you* (in fact, the entirety of the Word of God is the story of *"Christ and the Cross* [Jn. 1:1]), *you shall ask what you will, and it shall be done unto you"* (proper Faith in Christ and the Cross desires only the Will of God; this Will is now guaranteed to be carried forth)" (Jn. 15:7).

Enhanced by His Words, that intimate relationship with Jesus reshapes our personalities to fit with His Values and Character and then brings us into so rich a harmony with the Lord that what we wish is what God desires us to ask.

PRAYER AND THE HOLY SPIRIT

The Holy Spirit lives within Believers (I Cor. 3:16). He has a unique role in this intimate exchange known as prayer. *"Likewise the Spirit* (Holy Spirit) *also helps our infirmities* (the help given to us by the Holy Spirit is made possible in its entirety by and through what Jesus did at the Cross)*: for we know not what we should pray for as we ought* (signals the significance of prayer, but also that without the Holy Spirit, all is to no avail)*: but the Spirit Itself* (Himself) *makes intercession for us* (He petitions or intercedes on our behalf) *with groanings which cannot be uttered* (not groanings on the part of the Holy Spirit, but rather on our part, which pertain to that which comes from the heart and cannot properly be put into words)" (Rom. 8:26).

"And He Who searches the hearts (God the Father) *knows what is the mind of the Spirit* (what the Spirit wants to be done, not what we want to be done), *because He* (the Holy Spirit) *makes intercession for the Saints according to the Will of God* (the overriding goal of the Spirit is to carry out the Will of God in our lives, not our personal will; in other words, the Spirit is not a glorified bellhop)" (Rom. 8:27).

While the Spirit may assist us in prayer without our conscious awareness, our understanding clearly must be involved (I Cor. 14:13-15). Jesus told the Apostles that the Spirit would take from what belonged to Jesus and make it known to us (Jn. 16:15). Prayer is a continuous expression of relationship. The New Testament speaks of prayer as a continuous, constant experience for Christians (Acts 1:14; I Cor. 7:5; I Thess. 5:17; II Thess. 1:11; I Tim. 5:5). Just as we naturally and spontaneously talk with members of our family, so we converse with God, Who also shares our lives.

INTERCESSORY PRAYER

One of the most striking features of New Testament prayer, as it is portrayed in the Epistles, is its *"intercessory nature."* We read again and again of prayer being offered by Believers for one another. In this, we learn that prayer is an expression of relationship within the Body of Christ, as well as an expression of relationship with God. Out of the intimacy of shared lives grows a deep concern for others and their needs, and this provides the primary content for prayer in the Epistles.

CONDITIONS FOR ANSWERED PRAYER

Too often prayer is placed in the position of an obstacle course. Erroneous conditions for answered prayer are laid down. Often the treatment suggests that prayer will only be answered if certain obstacles are overcome. In other words, according to these false teachers, if we do not successfully negotiate the obstacle course, God will not hear us. Too often the Reader is given the impression that God stands watching like a tennis judge, ready to disqualify us if we are even slightly out of bounds. Consequently, the relational nature of prayer is missed, and prayer is recast as a spiritual exercise, with answers depending on our efforts rather than on God's Grace and Goodwill.

Everyone knows that if a child asks something of his parent, that even though the grammar may be wrong, or even the request somewhat out of order, still, the parent will do all he can to grant the request for the child, because he loves him. Jesus said, *"If you then, being evil, know how to give good gifts unto your children* (means that an earthly parent certainly would not give a stone to a child who had asked for bread, etc.): *how much more shall your Heavenly Father give the Holy Spirit to them who ask Him?* (which refers to God's Goodness, and the fact that everything from the Godhead comes to us through the Person and Agency of the Holy Spirit; and all that He does for us is based upon the Cross of Christ, and our Faith in that Finished Work)" (Lk. 11:13).

DISOBEDIENCE

In truth, disobedience is about the only thing which will prevent God from hearing and answering prayer (Deut. 1:43-45). It should be obvious that disobedience means that people are not living in fellowship with God, for the people who are close to Him are obedient and loving, and seek to do justice. It is in the context of a growing relationship with the Lord that prayer finds its place. Outside of such a relationship, prayer is a meaningless exercise.

The New Testament offers us encouragement that our request will surely be answered. This encouragement comes as a listing of indicators that reassure us that our relationship with God is vital and real. Those who *"ask, seek, and knock"* receive what they request (Lk. 11:5-13). Unfortunately, we quit asking, stop seeking, and discontinue knocking.

This Passage in Luke is very real to me personally.

ASK, SEEK, KNOCK

Once again, I take the Reader back to the late Fall of 1991, or the Spring of 1992. I don't remember which, but I most definitely remember the occasion. It was in one of our night prayer meetings. There were probably 10 to 15 people present. I also do not remember what was the occasion of my petition that night, whatever it might have been; however, I most definitely remember the answer the Lord gave me. He took me to this Passage in Luke, which I refer to as the *"Parable of the Three Loaves."*

That night, He made it very real to me how a man went to a friend at midnight and asked him, *"Friend, lend me three loaves."* He then went on to say, *"For a friend of mine in his journey has come to me, and I have nothing to set before him."* The man, from within the house, answered that he could not arise at the time, because the door was shut, and the children had been put to bed; besides that, it was midnight. In fact, he emphatically stated, *"I cannot rise and give to you."*

Jesus then said, *"Though he will not rise and give him, because he is his friend, yet because of his importunity he will rise and give him as many as he needs* (the argument of this Parable is that if a sufficiency for daily need can, by importunity, i.e., *'persistence,'* be obtained from an unwilling source, how much more from a willing Giver, Which and Who is the Lord.)" Then the Lord said, *"Ask, and it shall be given you; seek, and you shall find; knock, and it shall be opened unto you"* (Lk. 11:5-9).

Jesus then concluded the Parable by saying, which we have already related to you, that if we know how to give good gifts to our children, *"how much more shall your Heavenly Father give the Holy Spirit to them who ask Him?"* (Lk. 11:13).

At that time, the Lord was telling me

that no matter what the circumstances, no matter that it was midnight, spiritually speaking, no matter that it seemed that the answer was *"No,"* I was to keep asking, keep seeking, and keep knocking. Time and time again, the Lord would bring this back to me, refreshing it to my heart, which told me, in effect, that the answer was on the way. I simply must not stop asking, seeking, and knocking.

As stated, that was in the last days of 1991, or the first days of 1992. At any rate, approximately 6 years passed, with the Lord bringing this Promise back to me over and over again. And then in 1997, the Lord began to open that door, and please believe me, it has been worth all the asking, all the seeking, and all the knocking. The Revelation of the Cross, which is, in effect, a Revelation of Christ, of which the *"bread"* is a type, has been given to me in a fullness that is beyond anything I ever, at first, began to contemplate.

And that's the wonder of all of this. The Lord always gives us so much more than we request.

IN JESUS' NAME

Jesus told the Apostles that when two agreed regarding a matter, it would be done by the Lord, of course, providing it is God's Will (Mat. 18:19). To pray *"In Jesus' Name"* means to identify with His Character and Purposes (Jn. 14:13-14; 15:16; 16:23). The Believer must understand that the use of the Name of Jesus does not present some type of magic talisman. For the use of this Name to become effective and, of course, we are speaking of becoming effective in the spirit world, we must understand what the very Name Jesus actually means.

The Name Jesus means *"Saviour."* And, of course, Jesus is Saviour by virtue of what He has done for us at the Cross. Going to the Cross is the very purpose and reason for which He came (Gal. 1:4). When the Angel Gabriel appeared to Mary to tell her what was about to happen concerning the conception of our Lord, he said to her, *"And, behold, you shall conceive in your womb* (should have been translated, *'you shall forthwith conceive in your womb,'* meaning immediately), *and bring forth a Son* (proclaims the Incarnation, *'God manifest in the flesh, God with us, Immanuel'* [Isa. 9:6]), *and shall call His Name JESUS* (the Greek version of the Hebrew *'Joshua'*; it means *'Saviour,'* or *'the Salvation of Jehovah')"* (Lk. 1:31).

So, when any Believer uses the Name of Jesus, it must be understood that the use of this Name (and its veracity) has to do with the Believer understanding the Cross as the Means by which the Name can be used (I Cor. 1:17-18; 2:2; Gal. 6:14).

THE MANNER IN WHICH THE NAME OF JESUS MUST BE USED

The use of this mighty Name, which makes the spirit world of darkness tremble, can, in fact, only be used in that fashion — against powers, principalities, spiritual wickedness in high places, and the rulers of the darkness of this world, i.e., Satan, fallen angels, and demon spirits (Eph. 6:12). The *"Name"* cannot be used against people. It is effective only against the powers of darkness (Mk. 16:17).

PRAYER IN JESUS' NAME

Believers are guaranteed access to the very Throne of God by virtue of the Lord Jesus and what He did for us at the Cross. As we keep saying: Christ is the Source, while the Cross is the means. If we try to gain access by any other method than by what Christ has done for us at the Cross, the Holy Spirit, we are told, will bar all access (Eph. 2:18).

In fact, Jesus Himself told us exactly the manner in which we should pray. He said, *"And in that day* (after the Day of Pentecost) *you shall ask Me nothing* (will not ask Me Personally, as you now do, speaking to the Disciples). *Verily, verily, I say unto you, Whatsoever you shall ask the Father in My Name* (according to what He did at the Cross, and our Faith in that Finished Work), *He will give it you* (He places us in direct relationship with the Father, enjoying the same access as He Himself enjoys).

"Hitherto have you asked nothing in My Name (while He was with them, the work on the Cross had not been accomplished, so His Name could not be used as it can be used now)*: ask, and you shall receive* (ask in His Name, which refers to the fact that

we understand that all things are given unto us through and by what Christ did at the Cross), *that your joy may be full* (it can only be full when we properly understand the Cross)" (Jn. 16:23-24).

In other words, every Believer is to pray to the Father, and do so *"in the Name of Jesus."* But we must do so understanding that it is the Crucified Christ which gives us access (I Cor. 1:23). When we properly understand what the Name of Jesus is, what it represents, and how it is to be used, such will develop a trust in the Lord, which will calm our doubts and uncertainties, and which will also testify to us that God's Answer will come. Only those who show contempt for God by questioning His ability or willingness to act in human affairs and, thus, violate the relationship, will not be answered when they call (James 1:5-8).

OBEDIENCE

As we obey the Lord, we are assured that we live in a relationship with Him in which our prayers are heard and answered (I Jn. 3:22). As the Scripture and the Holy Spirit testify to us that what we ask is in the framework of God's Will, we can have confidence that this for which we ask will be granted (I Jn. 5:14-15).

Actually, disobedience, and in whatever form, is the reason that many, if not most, Christians do not pray. Automatically, the Holy Spirit makes us very much aware of such disobedience. Unless it is properly handled, continued prayer is a fruitless exercise. So, disobedient Christians seldom pray.

Other than being obedient, there really are no conditions that a person must meet before God will hear and answer prayer. The Bible provides indicators that force our attention back to the quality of our personal relationship with the Lord. In fact, those whose lives demonstrate that they have no significant relationship with God also have no basis on which to expect prayer to be heard.

But those who experience a growing relationship with the Lord, marked by trust, obedience, love, harmony with other Believers, at least as far as such harmony is possible, and a growing commitment to the revealed Will of God, can rest assured that the Lord will hear and answer prayer in His time.

NOTES

Verse 46 indicates that Jesus prayed. As someone has said, *"If He had to pray, what about us?"*

Truthfully, most Christians do not pray simply because they have little or no relationship with Christ. As a result, they little believe Him; consequently, they little resort to Him. In other words, they simply do not know Him.

(Some of the thoughts on prayer were supplied by Lawrence O. Richards.)

(47) "AND WHEN EVENING WAS COME, THE SHIP WAS IN THE MIDST OF THE SEA, AND HE ALONE ON THE LAND."

The composition is:

The Lord is about to teach His Disciples a most valuable lesson.

THE STAGE IS SET

The phrase, *"And when evening was come,"* represents the early evening after nightfall. The phrase, *"The ship was in the midst of the sea,"* refers to the problem the ship was now encountering. They could make little headway, due to the adverse wind. The phrase, *"And He alone on the land,"* represents Him coming down to the beach from the mountain where He had been praying. He did so on their behalf.

It must be understood that Jesus sent the Disciples away knowing they would have difficulties. He did it purposely! He wanted to teach them a most valuable lesson, which could only be taught in this manner.

The modern *"Word of Faith"* movement has tried to do away with all difficulties and problems; they claim that one can confess such things out of existence, and do so by confessing the Promises of God. While every Believer most certainly should daily confess the Promises of God, and do so on a consistent basis, still, adversity coming our way, as here, is not always the result of a lack of faith, as is claimed by some. Sometimes the Lord purposely puts us into precarious situations in order that our Faith may be strengthened.

While it wasn't the Will of the Lord for Israel to remain in the wilderness for some 40 years, it definitely was His Will that they take about 2 years to go through that howling waste. He could have led them another way, but He purposely led them by the way of the wilderness, because in that place there was no sustenance whatsoever for this tremendous number of people. The lesson they were to learn was to trust Him for all things. It was His Will for approximately 2 years, but it was unbelief that caused them to remain there for approximately 40 years (Ex., Chpts. 15-17).

Peter addressed this by saying, *"Wherein you greatly rejoice* (refers to the time when this earthly sojourn will be finished, the Trump of God sounds, and *'we shall be changed'* [I Cor. 15:51-54]), *though now for a season, if need be, you are in heaviness through manifold temptations* (this life is the dress rehearsal for Eternity):

"That the trial of your Faith (all Faith is tested, and great Faith must be tested greatly), *being much more precious than of gold that perishes* (the emphasis is the testing of our Faith to show whether or not it is genuine; the Holy Spirit says such is more precious than the testing of gold, which is the most precious commodity in the world. Is our faith really in the Cross or not?), *though it be tried with fire* (the fire of temptation, trouble, etc.; such are meant to show the weakness), *might be found unto Praise and Honor and Glory* (which can only be done if the Cross of Christ is the sole Object of our Faith) *at the appearing of Jesus Christ* (we are being prepared by the Holy Spirit as fit subjects for the appearing of our Lord, as it regards the Rapture [I Pet. 1:6-7]).

The Holy Spirit through Peter also said, *"Beloved, think it not strange concerning the fiery trial which is to try you* (trials do not merely happen; they are designed by wisdom and operated by love; Job proved this), *as though some strange thing happened unto you* (your trial, whatever it is, is not unique; many others are experiencing the same thing!)" (I Pet. 4:12).

(48) "AND HE SAW THEM TOILING IN ROWING; FOR THE WIND WAS CONTRARY UNTO THEM: AND ABOUT THE FOURTH WATCH OF THE NIGHT HE COMES UNTO THEM, WALKING UPON THE SEA, AND WOULD HAVE PASSED BY THEM."

The diagram is:

NOTES

Inasmuch as it was night, He could not have seen them physically, so the Holy Spirit must have revealed this to Him. As well, we may infer that the sandals of our Lord actually had contact with the water; He walked on the surface of the sea as we walk on a hard pavement.

THE LORD SEES OUR EVERY ACTION

The phrase, *"And He saw them toiling in rowing,"* uses the Greek word *"eidon,"* which means the actual perception of the object, and not the mere seeing with the eyes. The Sea of Galilee is about 7 miles wide; especially considering that it was night, He, as stated, could not have seen them physically. So, He saw them as the Holy Spirit revealed the situation to Him.

In His human form, He never used the Power of His Deity, although He never ceased to be God, not even for a moment; rather, He was led and empowered by the Holy Spirit in all that He did.

The short phrase, *"He saw them . . ."* should be a source of tremendous comfort and strength to every Believer. The Scripture plainly tells us that the Lord *"notes every sparrow's fall,"* and even *"numbers the very hairs of our heads"* (Mat. 10:29-31). In fact, absolutely nothing happens to a Child of God unless the Lord causes it or allows it. To be sure, He most definitely does not cause us to sin, but He will allow such if we are so foolish to go in such a direction. And, we will surely have to reap the consequences. Moreover, He allows those consequences.

However, there are many things that He causes to happen, exactly as the situation we are now studying in this Forty-seventh Verse. He caused the wind to be contrary, thereby impeding His Disciples' progress, and did it all for a purpose. We are truly under His watchful care at all times. He has paid a great price for us, a price so great that He would not think of allowing us to exist even one moment without His watchful care.

CONTRARY WIND

The phrase, *"For the wind was contrary unto them,"* pertains to considerably more than an adverse wind, and somewhat less than an outright storm. John called it *"a great wind that blew"* (Jn. 6:18). As we've already stated, the Lord caused this wind to be adverse, or at least allowed it to be such. There are some lessons in Faith which cannot be taught without the *"contrary wind."* To be sure, no one likes the contrary wind, but yet, if we learn to look at these situations as they really are, they will become much less fearful.

Paul said: *"And He* (the Lord) *said unto me, My Grace is sufficient for you* (speaks of enabling Grace, which is really the Goodness of God carried out by the Holy Spirit)*: for My strength is made perfect in weakness* (all Believers are weak, but the Lord tends to make us weaker, with the intention being that we then depend solely upon Him, thereby obtaining His Strength). *Most gladly therefore will I rather glory in my infirmities* (because of the end result)*, that the Power of Christ may rest upon me.* (If Paul needed so humbling and painful an experience of what the carnal nature is, it is evidence that all Christians also need it. Whatever weakens, belittles, and humiliates that proud and willful nature should be regarded by the Believer as most worthwhile.)

"Therefore I take pleasure in infirmities, in reproaches, in necessities, in persecutions, in distresses for Christ's sake: for when I am weak, then am I strong (then the strength of Christ can be exhibited through me, but only when I know I am weak)" (II Cor. 12:9-10).

THE FOURTH WATCH OF THE NIGHT

The phrase, *"And about the fourth watch of the night, He comes unto them, walking upon the Sea,"* referred to somewhere between 3 a.m. and 6 a.m. The *"fourth watch of the night"* can probably be said to be the most disconcerting time, with Satan taking advantage of such by endeavoring to fill the heart and mind of the Believer with doubt. It has happened, and does happen, to all of us, even the strongest in the Lord.

First of all, the Disciples were totally exhausted, having tried to row the heavy boat all night long against the adverse wind, a condition of which Satan took great advantage. However, the *"fourth watch,"* spiritually speaking, can take place at any time. It's

NOTES

when we, proverbially speaking, are at wit's end corner, not knowing what to do, having no answer for the situation, whatever the situation might be. In other words, if the Lord doesn't help us, the situation will only get worse, and it could become disastrous.

All of this was to show the Disciples that they could not get by without Him. Without Him, the adverse wind causes tremendous problems, many times stopping all forward progress. But with Him in the boat, the adverse wind only becomes an occasion for the Miracle-working Power of God.

Even as Jesus said: *"I am the Vine* (not the Church, not a particular Preacher, not even a particular Doctrine, but Christ Alone)*, you are the branches* (Believers)*: He who abides in Me, and I in him, the same brings forth much fruit* (let us say it again: the Believer must understand that everything we receive from God comes to us exclusively through Christ and the Cross; that being the case, the Cross must ever be the object of our Faith; then the Holy Spirit can develop fruit within our lives; it can be done no other way!)*: for without Me* (what He did for us at the Cross) *you can do nothing* (the Believer should read that phrase over and over)" (Jn. 15:5).

Sometimes, we have to have several occasions of the *"adverse wind"* before we will finally realize our constant need of Him.

CHRIST DRAWS NEAR

The phrase, *"And would have passed by them,"* is an unfortunate translation. The Greek word here used is *"parerchomai,"* which has the meaning *"passing by,"* but it also means *"to come near."* Consequently, the entirety of the Text tells us that Jesus had come near to help them, rather than passing them by.

In times of trouble, every Believer, from this experience alone, can rest in the confidence that Jesus will always come near. As stated, He has too much invested in us to leave us on our own. However, it's very difficult for the Believer to take his eyes off of circumstances and to place them exclusively on Christ. We see the difficulties, the problems, the hindrances, and even things which, within themselves, are definite impossibilities. We cannot see how the Lord can assuage the situation, whatever it might be. But we must believe that He can, and He will. He will come near, and it's not merely to console, but rather to meet our need, whatever that need might be.

(49) "BUT WHEN THEY SAW HIM WALKING UPON THE SEA, THEY SUPPOSED IT HAD BEEN A SPIRIT, AND CRIED OUT."

The overview is:

They couldn't believe their eyes, so they thought it was an apparition.

THE MIRACLE

The phrase, *"But when they saw Him walking upon the Sea,"* refers to something they in no way understood, and consequently did not believe — His appearance! In other words, they could not believe their eyes. Our Lord carried out this appearance for a distinct purpose. He *"walked upon the sea,"* which constituted a Miracle of unprecedented proportions, in order to tell us that whatever it takes, He will come to us, so to speak.

Even as this entire scenario bears out, *"He will never leave us or forsake us"* (Heb. 13:5).

AN APPARITION?

The phrase, *"They supposed it had been a spirit, and cried out,"* means they did not believe it really was Jesus, but rather a phantom or apparition. Under the circumstances, it is not difficult at all to understand their dilemma and response. Inasmuch as they had left late in the afternoon, they had probably been rowing for 8 or 9 hours; they had only covered about 3 miles. The Scripture says they were *"in the midst of the sea"*; since the lake was about 7 miles wide, they were making very little headway.

They knew that Jesus had pointedly told them to go to the other side, but, still, they seemingly were unable to carry out His Command. The wind was contrary, and despite their efforts, little headway was being made; consequently, they were confused, as well as physically exhausted. And now they see Jesus, or at least something that looks like Jesus, walking these choppy waves, and coming toward them.

Someone has suggested that the first watch of the night represented the age of the Law; the second, of the Prophets; the third, of the Gospel; with the fourth representing His Glorious Second Advent, when He will find Israel buffeted by the spirit of the Antichrist and by the storms of the world. His reception into the ship and the consequent calm prefigures the eternal peace of the Church and the world after His Second Coming.

(50) "FOR THEY ALL SAW HIM, AND WERE TROUBLED. AND IMMEDIATELY HE TALKED WITH THEM, AND SAID UNTO THEM, BE OF GOOD CHEER: IT IS I; BE NOT AFRAID."

The exposition is:

All Twelve saw Him, meaning that He evidently was very near when He spoke to them.

THE APPEARANCE OF OUR LORD

The phrase, *"For they all saw Him,"* means that this was not merely the hallucination of one member of the group, but instead that all Twelve *"saw Him."* Consequently, there was no doubt about what they were seeing, even though they did not understand it, at least at the time.

The phrase, *"And were troubled,"* pertains to all the difficulties which had accrued that night.

BE OF GOOD CHEER

The phrase, *"And immediately He talked with them, and said unto them, Be of good cheer: it is I; be not afraid,"* presents His Message. It is one of comfort, strength, and encouragement. It has not changed at all today!

Several things are here said:

1. *"Be of good cheer"*: It means *"to be of good courage,"* and consequently, not to be discouraged. It is very easy for one to get one's eyes on circumstances, such as the contrary wind, and the difficulties of the night. Despite His Command for them to go to the other side, their journey had been fraught with peril. As well, they were physically and mentally exhausted.

To be sure, in one's labor for the Lord, and even in the midst of His Will, doing exactly as He has said, difficulties, as here, will arise. Irrespective, at least part of the lesson of this episode is that we are not to be discouraged by adverse events. What Jesus said to them then, He says to us now!

As well, He is telling us that these times will come and, to be sure, cannot be confessed away. Unfortunately, and as stated, a large segment of the modern Church thinks that such things happen only because of a lack of faith on the part of the Believer. While that certainly may be true in some cases, still, in most, it is not true at all.

Why did the Lord allow such?

When Jesus sent the Disciples away, He knew He was sending them into difficult circumstances. He did it purposely! The only way some lessons can be learned is for the actual difficulty to be experienced. He could tell them all day long and, in fact, did tell them, but until they were in such circumstances, they really did not fully understand His meaning.

Some people erroneously think that if one is in the Will of God, there will not be any difficulties. I think one can say, without fear of contradiction, that the opposite is generally the case. The Will of God, as here, will be contested mightily, and for the obvious reasons. Satan hates the Will of God, and will do all within his power to get the Child of God to go into an opposite direction, either by disobedience or by discouragement. In this case, it would have been discouragement.

So, Jesus says, and right in the midst of their difficulties, *"Be of good cheer,"* which shows Faith, Trust, and Dependence on the Lord.

2. *"It is I"*: Wuest says that the pronoun *"I"* is used here for emphasis; literally, *"It is I and nobody else."* It is said in this manner in order that the Child of God will know and understand that whatever the Lord requires that we do, He will see to it that we are able to carry it out, even if He has to perform a Miracle, as here, to bring it about. If He tells us to do something, He, to be sure, will help us do it, and irrespective of what it takes. The emphatic *"I"* guarantees His Presence, and, therefore, our success.

3. *"Be not afraid"*: In other words, *"Stop being afraid."* Fear is that which is brought on by circumstances, our reaction to them, and a failure to trust God. *"There is no reason for any Believer to ever be afraid,"* is actually what the Lord is telling us. In fact, if our love for the Lord is as it should be, there will be no reason for fear, because *"Perfect Love casts out fear"* (I Jn. 4:18). He then went on to say, *"He who fears is not made perfect in love."*

(51) "AND HE WENT UP UNTO THEM INTO THE SHIP; AND THE WIND CEASED: AND THEY WERE SORE AMAZED IN THEMSELVES BEYOND MEASURE, AND WONDERED."

The synopsis is:

This emphasizes the fact that such was done solely because He was now in the ship.

THE PRESENCE OF CHRIST

The phrase, *"And He went up unto them into the ship,"* presents Mark not mentioning Peter walking on the water to go to Jesus, as recorded by Matthew (Mat. 14:28).

Why?

Inasmuch as the Holy Spirit superintended and guided all that was said and done respecting the recording of these events, the account of Peter in this instance was left out by design. Among other reasons, the Holy Spirit desired that the Reader's attention not be diverted to Peter, as important as that incident was. Matthew's account concerning Peter was enough, with this account focused more directly on the entirety of the Disciples, and consequently on all Believers.

Moreover, Peter probably divulged this account to Mark, as he did most of the accounts in Mark's writings, purposely leaving out his own experiences. Many scholars feel that Mark wrote his Book in collaboration with Simon Peter. There are homey and personal touches in it, which lend themselves to Peter's involvement.

Even as I dictate these words, I sense the Presence of the Lord! That the Lord would chose humble fishermen, as Peter, and others, such as Mark, giving them the privilege of associating with Him, and then allow them to give account of the greatest events in the history of mankind, leaves one utterly astonished! But such is the Grace of God!

During the earthly Ministry of Christ, Peter was a boastful man. And then came his terrible difficulty, with him denying Christ. Ever after, this boastful nature was completely gone, replaced by a quiet humility, which always sought to demote self and, as here, promote Christ.

THE ADVERSITY CEASES

The phrase, *"And He went up unto them into the ship,"* proves, beyond the shadow of a doubt, that it really was Jesus, and not an apparition. The phrase, *"And the wind ceased,"* emphasizes the fact that such was done solely because He was now in the ship. To be sure, He will come, although at times it seems like He waits forever; however, as the spiritual says, *"He's an on-time God."* He may not be early, but He's never late.

The phrase, *"And they were sore amazed in themselves beyond measure, and wondered,"* registers their response to His Action. He never ceased to amaze them, and *"beyond measure,"* which means that they had witnessed something beyond their power of comprehension.

(52) "FOR THEY CONSIDERED NOT THE MIRACLE OF THE LOAVES: FOR THEIR HEART WAS HARDENED."

The structure is:

The desire to make Jesus King, as John mentioned, was paramount in the minds of His Disciples; consequently, the true mission of Christ was lost on them, at least at this time. Deviation from the True Will of God always *"hardens the heart"*; nothing dulls spiritually like the religious enthusiasm of the carnal nature acting in fellowship with the religious world.

THE MIRACLE OF THE LOAVES

The phrase, *"For they considered not the Miracle of the loaves,"* has the implication that they did not understand the true meaning of this Miracle.

Williams says that the spiritual blindness occasioned in this Verse was most probably caused by their political unity with the world in its carnal enthusiasm and purpose (Jn. 6:15).

Jesus said, *"You seek Me, not because you saw the Miracles, but because you did eat of the loaves, and were filled"* (Jn. 6:26). The people saw Him using His Miracle-working Power to bring about an earthly government of prosperity, which would make Israel once again the leading nation in the world. As stated, the Disciples also were tainted with this thought.

The True Bread of Life, which He was, and which the Miracle of the loaves and the fish was meant to symbolize, was lost upon them. Consequently, *"their heart was hardened"* to the True Purpose of God.

THE HARDENED HEART

The phrase, *"For their heart was hardened,"* proclaimed the present condition even of the hearts of the Disciples.

Let us say it again:

When our desires are not the Will of God, but rather that of our own concoction, such always hardens the spiritual heart. In the case of the Disciples, they did not at all understand the mission of Christ, in that He came to this world in order to go to the Cross, which was an absolute necessity. They didn't see any such thing on the horizon. Instead, they saw Israel once again becoming the greatest nation in the world, exactly as it had been under David and Solomon, with themselves holding high positions in this government.

In this, they did not see Israel's real need, or the need of the entirety of the world, for that matter, which was Redemption from sin. Their thinking was in an entirely different direction altogether. And that's the problem of the modern Church, and it's the problem of each of us, as well.

To have the Mind of God in all things requires several things:

1. First and foremost, the Believer must understand that everything he receives from God comes, and without exception, from Christ as the Source, and the Cross as the Means. It is absolutely imperative that the Believer know this and understand this.

2. The Believer also must have an excellent relationship with Christ, which any Believer can have, providing such a Believer has a qualified prayer life. Without a proper prayer life, it's impossible to have any type of relationship with the Lord.

3. The Believer must avidly seek the Will of the Lord in all things. Our will truly must become His Will. Regrettably, this position

is not arrived at easily or quickly. In fact, it takes the Holy Spirit to do all of these things. That's the reason that Paul said:

"I beseech you therefore, Brethren (I beg of you, please), *by the Mercies of God* (all is given to the Believer, not because of merit on the Believer's part, but strictly because of the *'Mercy of God'*), *that you present your bodies a Living Sacrifice* (the word *'Sacrifice'* speaks of the Sacrifice of Christ, and means that we cannot do this which the Holy Spirit demands unless our Faith is placed strictly in Christ and the Cross, which then gives the Holy Spirit latitude to carry out this great work within our lives), *holy* (that which the Holy Spirit Alone can do), *acceptable unto God* (actually means that a holy physical body, i.e., *'temple,'* is all that He will accept), *which is your reasonable service* (reasonable if we look to Christ and the Cross; otherwise, impossible!).

"And be not conformed to this world (the ways of the world)*: but be transformed by the renewing of your mind* (we must start thinking spiritually, which refers to the fact that everything is furnished to us through the Cross, and is obtained by Faith and not Works), *that you may prove what is that good* (is put to the test and finds that the thing tested meets the specifications laid down), *and acceptable, and perfect, Will of God* (presents that which the Holy Spirit is attempting to bring about within our lives, and which can only be obtained by ever making the Cross the Object of our Faith)" (Rom. 12:1-2).

If the Believer doesn't have a *"renewed mind,"* then the Believer is going to have a hardened heart, which is a heart that is opposed to the Will of God.

(53) "AND WHEN THEY HAD PASSED OVER, THEY CAME INTO THE LAND OF GENNESARET, AND DREW TO THE SHORE."

The exegesis is:

The ship had begun without Jesus, but concludes with Him. What a Miracle!

THEY PASSED OVER

The phrase, *"And when they had passed over,"* refers to them coming, as is obvious, to the other side. Jesus had told them to go to the other side, but they were to find out that they could not accomplish this task without His Presence, and neither can we! Christ lives in the hearts and lives of all Believers by virtue of the Person, Office, and Work of the Holy Spirit. But all too often we ignore Him, or treat Him as a Stranger, all because of a lack of relationship.

The phrase, *"They came into the land of Gennesaret, and drew to the shore,"* presents a fertile plain on the north shore of Galilee, west of Jordan, about four miles long and two miles wide. This was an area where fruit trees of several different types abounded.

(54) "AND WHEN THEY WERE COME OUT OF THE SHIP, STRAIGHTWAY THEY KNEW HIM."

The composition is:

This insinuates they were in a ship of some size; probably one of the larger fishing vessels of Zebedee.

THE ARRIVAL OF JESUS

The phrase, *"And when they were come out of the ship,"* constitutes something that they had done, no doubt, many times, but yet this time was different that anything they had ever previously seen. They had been taught a great lesson, but yet a lesson they wouldn't fully understand until the advent of the Holy Spirit on the Day of Pentecost.

The phrase, *"Straightway they knew Him,"* refers to the people in the area. As well as knowing Him, they, above all, knew that He was present. So, as the next Verse proclaims, the entire region would be alerted, and for the obvious reasons.

(55) "AND RAN THROUGH THAT WHOLE REGION ROUND ABOUT, AND BEGAN TO CARRY ABOUT IN BEDS THOSE WHO WERE SICK, WHERE THEY HEARD HE WAS."

The diagram is:

This Verse proclaims runners going from village to village announcing that Jesus was in the vicinity.

THE PUBLISHING OF THE NEWS

The phrase, *"And ran through that whole region round about,"* proclaims the news being spread abroad through the entire region, proclaiming the fact that Jesus was here. It was to be a great day for this area. No wonder!

In fact, when Jesus comes into a heart, home, or life, everything changes, and a thousand times for the better. For the problems of life, there is no other answer. Christ Alone holds the solution!

A FOREGLIMPSE OF THE COMING KINGDOM AGE

The phrase, *"And began to carry about in beds those who were sick, where they heard He was,"* proclaims the sick being carried any place they thought Jesus might be. It was a pathetic, yet understandable, sight! This was the very height of His popularity, with the entirety of the countryside clamoring after Him. To be sure, this fame would arouse the ire of the Pharisees until they literally hated Him. Hence, at the time of the Crucifixion, it is said of Pilate, *"For he knew that for envy they had delivered Him"* (Mat. 27:18).

This which we see here, as stated, is a foreglimpse of the coming Kingdom Age, when the healing Power of the Christ will touch the entirety of the world. In fact, upon the First Advent of Christ, had Israel only accepted Him, this could have been the lot of the entirety of the world; however, Israel's rejection of Him sentenced the entirety of the balance of the world to a period of troubled time which has now lasted for approximately 2,000 years — a time, incidentally, filled with war, bloodshed, poverty, starvation, sickness, dying, and death. It will be remedied only upon His Second Advent.

(56) "AND WHITHERSOEVER HE ENTERED, INTO VILLAGES, OR CITIES, OR COUNTRY, THEY LAID THE SICK IN THE STREETS, AND BESOUGHT HIM THAT THEY MIGHT TOUCH IF IT WERE BUT THE BORDER OF HIS GARMENT: AND AS MANY AS TOUCHED HIM WERE MADE WHOLE."

The diagram is:

This had to have been a situation astounding to behold! What a sight it must have been! It will be this way when He comes back the second time, and even greater.

JESUS

The phrase, *"And whithersoever He entered, into villages, or cities, or country,"* refers to the entirety of the countryside, which was looking to Him for healing and deliverance. The situation was the same whether it was a *"village," "city,"* or *"countryside."* The need was the same in all places, as the need is the same presently! If it is truly the Lord, it will be the same, irrespective of the place or people.

THE NEWS MEDIA

The news media once questioned me as to which city was our largest Television audience. At that time, it happened to be New York City. Upon relating that to them, it was met with derision. In their thinking, how in the world could someone from the South garner that type of audience in New York City? This was the *"Big Apple,"* and they did not fall for such foolishness, etc.

However, my information was correct, which they found out when they checked the various ratings systems. While it may have been a mystery to them, it was no mystery to me, simply because the need is the same wherever it might be, and the True Gospel of Jesus Christ, and that True Gospel alone, meets that need.

THE SICK

The phrase, *"They laid the sick in the streets,"* referred to the tremendous number, and also the logical place to meet Him, that is, if He came down that particular street. This would have been a situation astounding to behold! No doubt, there were thousands of people who had come in from villages, cities, and the countryside, who desperately needed His healing Power. They were not to be disappointed!

The Power of God must have been so strong at these particular times that it could be sensed and felt by all. It was the greatest visitation by the Holy Spirit the world had ever known, because it was through the Incarnate Son of God.

TOUCHING JESUS

The phrase, *"And besought Him that they might touch if it were but the border of His garment,"* may well have been derived from the woman who touched the hem of His garment and was healed (Lk. 8:44).

She had undoubtedly told many of her healing, and the manner in which it was derived, which will now be copied by many, possibly thousands.

The *"border of His garment"* consisted of a *"hem"* or *"tassel,"* which was attached to the garment and was normally blue; it was meant to be a constant reminder of the Law of Moses, and that Israel's help came from the Lord. This *"hem"* or *"tassel"* was not at the border of His robe, but rather at the border of this *"tassel,"* which hung over His shoulder, probably down to about His waist.

The phrase, *"And as many as touched Him were made whole,"* must have spoke of many hundreds, and possibly even thousands.

One can well see the thousands which gathered wherever Jesus was, with these thousands all attempting to touch Him. What a sight that must have been! The moment they *"touched"* they were made perfectly *"whole,"* because of the Power of the Holy Spirit which emanated from Jesus. The moment they were healed, which was instantly, tremendous joy must have flooded the hearts and lives of those who experienced this Move of God, with shouts and acclamations of Praises to God literally filling the air. In effect, this could have happened to the entirety of Israel, and even the entirety of the world, had Israel accepted Christ instead of rejecting Him.

In Truth, it was the religious hierarchy which rejected Him, with the ordinary people having very little to say in the matter. Actually, the Scripture says, *"The common people heard Him gladly"* (Mk. 12:37). The world had never seen such before, and it will not see such again until Jesus comes back.

"Hear the Blessed Saviour calling the oppressed,
"O ye heavy laden, come to Me and rest,
"Come, no longer tarry, I your load will bear,
"Bring Me every burden, bring me every care."

"Have you by temptation often conquered been,
"Has a sense of weakness brought distress within?
"Christ will sanctify you, if you'll claim His best,
"In the Holy Spirit, He will give you rest."

"Come unto Me; I will give you rest;
"Take My yoke upon you, hear Me and be blest;
"I am meek and lowly, Come and trust My might;
"Come, My yoke is easy, and My burden's light."

───■───

CHAPTER 7

(1) "THEN CAME TOGETHER UNTO HIM THE PHARISEES, AND CERTAIN OF THE SCRIBES, WHICH CAME FROM JERUSALEM."

The overview is:

It seems that the religious leaders were becoming alarmed at the tremendous popularity of Jesus.

THE PHARISEES AND THE SCRIBES

The phrase, *"Then came together unto Him the Pharisees, and certain of the Scribes,"* should have been translated, *"And then...."* Mark used the Greek word *"kai,"* which means *"and."* This means that what is now given follows very closely that which went before. In other words, and as stated, the religious leaders were becoming alarmed at the tremendous popularity of our Lord.

Ironically enough, the Pharisees and the Scribes were the religious leaders, so to speak, of Israel. They were also the greatest enemies of Christ! This means that they were such enemies they ultimately would kill the Lord. Amazingly enough, they would kill the Lord in the Name of the Lord. It hasn't changed from then until now. The greatest enemy to the Work of God is institutionalized religion.

Let it ever be remembered:

It was not the bartenders, alcoholics, drug addicts, and harlots, etc. who crucified Christ, as evil and wicked as their sins were. It was the religious leaders of Israel who crucified Christ, which means that their sin was far greater.

Jesus had addressed this once by saying,

"Verily I say unto you, That the publicans and the harlots go into the Kingdom of God before you." (He said this to their faces, and before the people; He could not have insulted them more, putting them beneath harlots and publicans, whom the latter they considered to be traitors [Mat. 21:31].)

No! Jesus wasn't condoning harlotry or such like. God forbid! But He most definitely was saying that the sin of the Pharisees and Scribes was far worse. Some of the publicans and harlots repented, but there is very little evidence that very many Scribes and Pharisees repented!

It is the same presently! Institutionalized religion hates Christ now just as much as it did then!

JERUSALEM

The phrase, *"Which came from Jerusalem,"* concerns the religious hierarchy, or at least those sent by such. As stated, the greatest hindrance to the Work of God has always been that which calls itself *"the Church."* It is Satan's masterstroke. As such, it has taken more people to eternal Hell than all the vice in the world.

If Satan can make people think they are saved, when, in reality, they aren't, he, in effect, does two things:

First, the deceived soul will be eternally lost.

Second, the deceived soul will deceive others. That is why it was said of Jesus, that He *"was moved with compassion toward them, because they were as sheep not having a shepherd"* (Mk. 6:34).

Jerusalem was supposed to be the city of the King, i.e., Jesus Christ, but it was the city that rejected and murdered its King. Hence, Jesus would say, *"O Jerusalem, Jerusalem . . ."* (Mat. 23:37).

(2) "AND WHEN THEY SAW SOME OF HIS DISCIPLES EAT BREAD WITH DEFILED, THAT IS TO SAY, WITH UNWASHEN, HANDS, THEY FOUND FAULT."

The overview is:

This had nothing to do with sanitary cleanliness; the Pharisees taught that demons, unseen, could sit on the hands of anyone; consequently, if the hands were not washed, the demons could be ingested.

FOOLISH DOCTRINES

The phrase, *"And when they saw some of His Disciples eat bread with defiled, that is to say, with unwashen, hands,"* means they were earnestly seeking something for which they might accuse Him.

How sad!

They did not see the healings, the Miracles, or the people delivered from demon spirits. Neither did they hear the gracious words which proceeded out of His Mouth. They did not see that He fulfilled all the Prophecies concerning Himself as the Messiah.

Why could not they see the obvious?

As the Disciples were momentarily afflicted with the *"hardened heart,"* the Pharisees and Scribes were permanently afflicted. What they would *"see"* would be nothing, but yet they would attempt to make a case of it. It is sad that they were so close and yet so far away!

Tragically and sadly, millions today fall into the same category. They are in the Church, but not in Christ. They talk about the Lord, but they do not know the Lord!

This of which they accused Christ, eating with unwashed hands, concerned a concocted law. It had nothing to do with sanitary cleanliness. The Pharisees taught — erroneously, we might quickly add — that demons (unseen) could sit on the hands of anyone; if the hands were not washed, and washed in a certain way, the demons could be ingested, with the person then becoming demon possessed. In effect, they were saying that the Disciples, by eating with unwashed hands, could now be looked at as *"demon possessed."*

To be sure, there was absolutely no Scriptural foundation for this foolishness; however, as most who follow in that train, a little thing, such as the lack of Scriptural foundation, has never stopped them. In fact, the modern Church, especially the Full Gospel and Charismatic variety, is rife with foolishness which has no Scriptural foundation. It is simply rules and regulations made up by men, which they feel free to change if they so desire.

It should be understood that if such rules and regulations, whatever they might be, are Scriptural, they can't be changed. The very fact of them being changed, and changed constantly, portrays such absurdity.

FAULT!

The phrase, *"They found fault,"* means they were earnestly looking for something, as stated, with which Jesus and His Disciples could be accused. To be sure, they could find fault with neither His Life nor His Ministry. So they had to claim that what He was doing was, in fact, being done by and through the powers of demon spirits. When they did this, they blasphemed the Holy Spirit (Mk. 3:22-30).

(3) "FOR THE PHARISEES, AND ALL THE JEWS, EXCEPT THEY WASH THEIR HANDS OFT, EAT NOT, HOLDING THE TRADITION OF THE ELDERS."

The overview is:

This tradition was only of man, and not at all of God, as are many traditions in the modern Church.

RULES MADE UP BY MEN

The phrase, *"For the Pharisees, and all the Jews, except they wash their hands oft, eat not,"* presents the schism between Christ and the religious leaders of Israel. They constantly carried out this type of ceremonial religion. The placing of *"Pharisees"* ahead of *"all the Jews"* insinuates that the Pharisees were the promoters of these things, demanding that all of Israel follow.

Not only did they wash their hands, but they had to do it in a certain prescribed way. The washing was done with a clenched fist, the individual rubbing one hand and the arm up to the elbow with the other hand clenched. He then rubbed the palm of one hand with the other closed, so as to make sure that the part that touched the food would be clean. As stated, this was done because it was thought that an evil spirit by the name of Shibta sat upon the hands at night; consequently, he must be washed off or he might be eaten, etc.

The Pharisees had also linked Salvation with the keeping of these ceremonial rulings.

TRADITION

The phrase, *"Holding the tradition of the Elders,"* presented the Pharisees claiming that God had orally delivered this tradition to Moses on Mount Sinai, with it then being transmitted orally down to their time. Of course, it was totally untrue, and Jesus was quick to say so! The problem of men adding to the Word of God, or taking from it, has always been one of Satan's chief ploys.

The *"Elders"* were a group of men who held rank and position in Israel as members of the Great Council or Sanhedrin; consequently, the entire weight to these religious leaders was ensconced behind these ceremonies, which Jesus bitterly opposed, and which placed Him, therefore, in direct confrontation.

It is basically the same as a Preacher of the Gospel today publicly stating that the ceremonies of Roman Catholicism, or the Denominationalism of many Church organizations, are unscriptural. As the position of Christ was not met with grace and kindness, likewise, it is not met with much grace and kindness presently! However, if Jesus stood firmly for the True Gospel, which He certainly did, should not His Ministers follow suit? While it should be done with wisdom, still, it should be done, and must be done!

Jude said, *"That you should earnestly contend for the Faith which was once delivered unto the Saints"* (Jude, Vs. 3). Regrettably, there aren't many true *"watchmen"* gracing modern pulpits.

(4) "AND WHEN THEY COME FROM THE MARKET, EXCEPT THEY WASH, THEY EAT NOT. AND MANY OTHER THINGS THERE BE, WHICH THEY HAVE RECEIVED TO HOLD, AS THE WASHING OF CUPS, AND POTS, BRASEN VESSELS, AND OF TABLES."

The exposition is:

They spent an inordinate amount of time engaging in this foolishness.

TRUST IN RULES AND REGULATIONS

The phrase, *"And when they come from the market, except they wash, they eat not,"* presented these religious leaders and their followers basing their Salvation on the keeping of certain rules and regulations, all of it man-conceived and man-devised. Regrettably, it hasn't changed from then until now.

Coming up to the present time, if the Cross of Christ is not the total and complete Object of Faith for the Believer, then for certain such a Believer is depending upon *"works"* to save him, exactly as these Pharisees of old! I realize that many may take issue with what I've said; however, what I've said is correct (Gal., Chpt. 5).

And since it is so serious, please allow me to repeat myself:

The only thing that God presently recognizes, and the only thing He, in fact, has ever recognized (Gen., Chpt. 4), is Christ and Him Crucified. It is Faith in that Finished Work which gives us the Righteousness of God.

Paul said: *"For He* (God the Father) *has made Him* (Christ) *to be sin for us* (the Sin Offering [Isa. 53:6, 10; I Pet. 2:24]), *Who knew no sin* (He was not guilty; He was perfectly Holy and Pure); *that we might be made the Righteousness of God in Him* (made so by accepting what He did for us at the Cross)" (II Cor. 5:21).

MANY MORE RULES AND REGULATIONS

The phrase, *"And many other things there be, which they have received to hold, as the washing of cups, and pots, brasen vessels, and of tables,"* presents the fact that there were many other ceremonies of similar nature, as well. Actually, they were to even wash their *"cups"* and *"pots,"* etc., in a certain way. In fact, the entirety of the Law of Moses had been reduced by these individuals to mere ceremony.

These people were meticulous in holding to these outward ceremonies; and they roundly condemned all who did not follow suit, but registered hate toward their fellowman, as well as all other types of heart impurities. Regrettably, many foolish things, such as these *"washings"* of old, have made their way into modern Churches, making some Christian groups as ridiculous as the Pharisees (Mat. 15:1-3; 16:12; 23:1-33).

Believers need to be careful that their Salvation does not consist merely of rules and regulations. And yet, there are things a Christian should do or not do! To be sure, the Holy Spirit will most definitely point these things out. But yet, He cannot do so if we have made something other than the Cross the object of our Faith (Gal. 2:21; 5:4).

NOTES

CULTURE

Christians live on this Earth, scattered in every society. As such, the Believer must be careful that the culture of the society in which he lives does not impact him in a negative way. Actually, upon accepting Christ, the Bible becomes the yardstick for life and conduct, thereby presenting its own culture.

The Bible teaches that every human culture is warped and twisted by the impact of sin. The perceptions of each generation, the basic desires that move human beings, and the injustices institutionalized in every society testify to sin's warping power (Rom., Chpts. 1, 3).

Believers, constituting the Church, are gatherings called to display on Earth a completely different set of values, not based on the cravings, lusts, or the boastings of sinful humanity. Rather than being squeezed into the world's mold, we are to be *"transformed by the renewing of our minds"* (Rom. 12:2).

Bluntly put, the Believer is one who *"does not live his earthly life for human desires, but rather for the Will of God"* (I Pet. 4:2). If we remember that the world represents the systematic expression of human sin in human cultures, we understand why the Believer is not to be *"of"* of the world, though he is *"in"* it (Jn. 17:14-18). We are members of our society, yet the values we display and the structures we create in Church, home, and occupation are to be distinctively Christian, i.e., of the Bible.

WORLDLINESS

This understanding helps us sense the deadliness of worldliness. Worldliness is not a matter of engaging in those practices that some question. It is unthinkingly adopting the perspectives, values, and attitudes of our culture without bringing them under the Judgment of God's Word. It is carrying on our lives as if we did not know Jesus (Mat. 16:26; Mk. 8:36; Lk. 9:25; I Cor. 5:10; 7:31, 33-34; II Cor. 7:10; I Jn. 2:15-16; 4:17 — Richards.)

(5) "THEN THE PHARISEES AND SCRIBES ASKED HIM, WHY WALK NOT YOUR DISCIPLES ACCORDING TO THE TRADITION OF THE ELDERS, BUT EAT

BREAD WITH UNWASHEN HANDS?"

The synopsis is:

All of this was outward show only, and brought Christ into direct conflict with these religious leaders.

WHY DON'T YOU KEEP THESE RULES?

The phrase, *"Then the Pharisees and Scribes asked Him,"* means, in the Greek, that they kept on asking Him, but with Him not answering at first. However, with them continuing to ask, He would, as we shall see, ultimately answer.

The question, *"Why walk not Your Disciples according to the tradition of the Elders, but eat bread with unwashen hands?"* hits at the very heart of what was then taking place in Israel, which was outward show only, which means that it constituted no Salvation whatsoever. At this time, Israel was eaten up with all of these ceremonies, which made the people very religious; they consequently thought they were very saved, but, in reality, they were very lost!

When the *"six water pots of stone"* were mentioned at the Marriage Feast in Cana (Jn. 2:6), these contained water, and were there for these ceremonial cleansings in which the Jews constantly engaged. Even though there was some water in these pots, Jesus gave instructions for them to be filled to the brim, and then He proceeded to change it to wine. Consequently, His Miracle was a proclamation that He was going to bring men out of ceremonial religion, which, in effect, afforded no Salvation at all, into the Glory and Grace of God, which gave all Salvation. However, it is doubtful that anyone understood what He was doing, at least at that particular time.

Sadly, many, if not most, still cling to religious ceremonies. In Truth, they really do not know the Saviour. As then, so now!

(6) "HE ANSWERED AND SAID UNTO THEM, WELL HAS ISAIAH PROPHESIED OF YOU HYPOCRITES, AS IT IS WRITTEN, THIS PEOPLE HONOR ME WITH THEIR LIPS, BUT THEIR HEART IS FAR FROM ME."

The synopsis is:

The answer, as given by Christ, runs through Verse 13, and constitutes a startling answer, which pulls no punches and minces no words.

HYPOCRITES!

The phrase, *"He answered and said unto them, Well has Isaiah prophesied of you hypocrites,"* did not mean that the Prophet had these people in mind when he prophesied these words, but that they (the Pharisees) definitely fit what Isaiah said. As well, the definition doesn't end with the Pharisees, either! Actually, all should seriously ponder the answer given by Christ by checking our own hearts.

The words, *"You hypocrites,"* actually say in the Greek, *"You, The Hypocrites,"* which means the outstanding ones. The word *"hypocrites"* means that these people pretended to be something on the outside, which they were not on the inside.

AN EVIL HEART

The phrase, *"As it is written, This people honors Me with their lips, but their heart is far from Me,"* hits at the very heart of what True Salvation is, and isn't (Isa. 29:13). The Jews talked about God continuously, but, in reality, most did not know Him.

What did Jesus mean by the statement, *"but their heart is far from Me"*?

Wuest says that the picture is of one holding himself a great distance from someone else. He goes on to say that the person is far off because he wants to be. In other words, they wanted their sin, while all the time professing their great closeness to God.

Jesus called the religious leadership of Israel *"hypocrites."* I wonder what His statement would be today concerning religious leaders.

If one is to look at the condition of the Church, especially in America and Canada, one would have to come to the conclusion that the assessment given by Christ would be little different concerning the modern Church than concerning Israel of old! Most of the old-line Churches, such as Baptists, Methodists, etc., *"have a form of Godliness, but deny the power thereof."* Paul then went on to say, *"from such turn away"* (II Tim. 3:5).

Then the Pentecostal and Charismatic

varieties are chasing every fad and foolishness with enthusiastic vigor. We are laughing, when we ought to be mourning; praising (by rote), when we ought to be praying; and proclaiming fakery as revival, when we ought to be repenting. The Pentecostal and Charismatic communities have come to the place that most little know anymore what is God or not God! The spirit of discernment is gone, because the *"Spirit"* is gone!

(7) "HOWBEIT IN VAIN DO THEY WORSHIP ME, TEACHING FOR DOCTRINES THE COMMANDMENTS OF MEN."

The synopsis is:

The state (Herod) put to death the Preacher of Righteousness (Mat. 14:10), and the Church (the Scribes) corrupted the Word of Righteousness.

VAIN WORSHIP

The phrase, *"Howbeit in vain do they worship Me,"* presents a powerful statement indeed! The word *"vain"* means *"without profit"* or *"empty nothings."* In other words, it was *"worship"* that the Lord would not accept. Jesus had recently said to the woman at the well, *"The True worshipper shall worship the Father in spirit and in truth"* (Jn. 4:23).

A Prophecy was given a little after the turn of the Twentieth Century in the great Azusa outpourings, which said: *"In the last days, My people will worship Me, to Whom they no longer pray!"*

I think it can properly be said that there has never been more worship than that presently offered in Pentecostal and Charismatic Churches. Worship can been carefully honed into a fine art. But yet, is it worship that God will accept?

Worship which He accepts must be *"Truth"* first of all, thereby accounting to the Word of God, and will always be inspired and attended by the Holy Spirit. As someone has said, *"The Lord is not looking for holy worship, but instead for holy worshippers."* One should carefully analyze that statement, because it hits at the very heart of what Jesus was speaking of, and what the Spirit continues to speak of presently. In fact, there can be no holy worship without there first being *"holy worshippers"*!

Paul said, *"Though I speak with the tongues of men and of Angels, and have not charity* (love), *I am become as sounding brass, or a tinkling cymbal"* (I Cor. 13:1). In other words, the Holy Spirit is saying through the Apostle that the worship will sound in God's ears *"as sounding brass, or a tinkling cymbal."*

THE ALTAR OF INCENSE

The Altar of Incense in the Tabernacle of old symbolized the Intercession of Christ, which makes it possible for the Lord to receive our worship and hear our prayers (Ex. 30:1-10). Every morning at the time of the morning Sacrifice (9 a.m.), and every evening at the time of the evening Sacrifice (3 p.m.), the Priest would come into the Holy Place, with coals of fire from the Brazen Altar, which was a type of the Cross of Christ, and the price paid there, placing those coals on the Altar of Incense. At that time, Incense would be poured over the coals, with a cloud of fragrance filling the entire Holy Place, signifying the Intercession of Christ, all on our behalf.

If coals of fire were brought from some other ignition, i.e., other than the Brazen Altar, which alone God would accept, the results would be disastrous. In fact, Nadab and Abihu, sons of Aaron, both Priests, were instantly executed because they *"offered strange fire before the LORD, which He commanded them not."* The Scripture then says, *"And there went out fire from the LORD, and devoured them, and they died before the LORD"* (Lev. 10:1-2). All of this means that worship will never be accepted by the Lord unless the Faith of the Believer is anchored firmly in Christ and the Cross. Any other type of worship will ultimately bring about spiritual death.

We are saved only because of what Jesus did at the Cross. It is possible to be Baptized with the Holy Spirit only by and through what Jesus did at the Cross (Jn. 14:17). All of our victory in totality, as it regards living a sanctified life, is made possible solely by what Christ did at the Cross, and our Faith in that Finished Work (Rom. 6:3-14). As well, and as we are now studying, if worship is not anchored firmly on the foundation of Christ and the Cross, and that alone, it is not worship that God will accept.

Paul said, *"For through Him* (through Christ) *we both* (Jews and Gentiles) *have access by One Spirit unto the Father.* (If the person comes by the Cross, the Holy Spirit opens the door; otherwise, it is barred [Jn. 10:1])" (Eph. 2:18). This means that the Holy Spirit, Who works entirely within the framework of the Finished Work of Christ, which gives Him the legal means to do what He does, will not allow anything that isn't anchored firmly in the Cross.

COMMANDMENTS OF MEN

The phrase, *"Teaching for doctrines the commandments of men,"* presented the problem then, and presents the problem now!

What are *"commandments of men"*?

Anything that is not Bible, or with the Word not rightly divided, is a *"commandment of men,"* and must be rejected out of hand (II Tim. 2:15). This would have included much, if not most, of the religious doctrine of Israel of that day. Presently, it would include most, if not all, of Catholicism, and much of that taught in Protestant Churches.

For instance, the modern *"Government of Twelve"* teaching and the *"Purpose Driven Church"* teaching both constitute *"commandments of men."*

How do I know that?

I know that simply because these particular theories or teachings do not, by any stretch of the imagination, preach the Cross. Irrespective as to what else they say or claim, if the Cross is not preached, pure and simple, it is *"another Jesus, produced by another spirit, which presents another gospel"* (II Cor. 11:4). Of course, in all of these presentations, some Scripture is used; however, the use of Scripture does not make the teaching Scriptural. In fact, this is one of Satan's greatest ploys. If a Scripture is thrown in here and there, a Bible-illiterate Church automatically thinks that what is being promoted is Scriptural. It isn't!

If it is to be noticed, many of these false ways, presented by false apostles, use off-brand versions of the Bible, such as the *"Message Bible,"* which, by no stretch of the imagination, can be called the Word of God. But yet, because it claims to be *"a Bible,"* it is accepted by most modern Christians without a word of protest. And especially if it's used by these modern gurus, it is, by and large, accepted without question.

A FALSE MESSAGE

All the modern things we are now seeing, and I've just named a couple, are really nothing new. It's the same old attack by Satan, with a different face. In a few years, these things will fall by the wayside, and Satan will introduce something else. He doesn't really care too much what people believe, just so they don't believe, preach, and practice *"Jesus Christ and Him Crucified"* (I Cor. 1:23; 2:2). If it is to be noticed, the Message of the Cross is not new. It is the Message first presented in the Bible (Gen. 3:15; Chpt. 4), and it runs through the entirety of the Word of God, with the completed Message and meaning being given to the Apostle Paul (Gal. 1:11-12). The Message of the Cross is so much the Gospel and, in fact, is alone the Gospel, that Paul also said, *"But though we* (Paul and his associates), *or an Angel from Heaven, preach any other gospel unto you than that which we have preached unto you* (Jesus Christ and Him Crucified), *let him be accursed* (eternally condemned; the Holy Spirit speaks this through Paul, making this very serious)."

It is so serious that the Holy Spirit through the Apostle turned around and said it all over again: *"As we said before, so say I now again* (at some time past, He had said the same thing to them, making their defection even more serious), *If any man preach any other gospel unto you* (anything other than the Cross) *than that you have received* (which saved your souls), *let him be accursed* ('eternally condemned,' which means the loss of the soul)" (Gal. 1:8-9).

When it comes to false messages, *"Baptismal Regeneration"* is another *"commandment of men,"* as is *"Sacrament Salvation"* (the Lord's Supper). *"Unconditional Eternal Security," "Ultimate Reconciliation"* (the teaching that all will ultimately accept Christ, even the Devil, etc.), *"Denominationalism"* (the Church saves), and *"Law-keeping"* (Seventh Day Adventism, as well as many other Churches), are but to name a few!

Millions have lost their souls, simply because they did not know the Bible, and accepted for Gospel Doctrines which were, in effect, *"commandments of men,"* and thereby, not of God. That is the reason it is incumbent upon every single Believer to know and understand the Word of God, and not to depend on others to interpret it for them.

(8) "FOR LAYING ASIDE THE COMMANDMENT OF GOD, YOU HOLD THE TRADITION OF MEN, AS THE WASHING OF POTS AND CUPS: AND MANY OTHER SUCH LIKE THINGS YOU DO."

The structure is:

Jesus said this with sarcasm; they washed cups and pots, but not their hearts. The ceremonial washing of their hands could not remove the guilt that stained them, and neither can modern practices of *"works."*

THE COMMANDMENT OF GOD

The phrase, *"For laying aside the Commandment of God,"* refers to the Word of God laid side by side with traditions. The religious leaders purposely and with forethought made the decision to accept the *"tradition"* instead of the *"Word."*

(The Bible in that day consisted of the entirety of the Old Testament.)

It was not that the religious leaders did not have the Word of God; for, in fact, they did! It was that they did not want or desire the Word of God. Presently, there is an attack (2004) against the Bible, which is probably more sinister than any attack that's ever been leveled at the Word of God. Instead of denying the veracity of the Word, a flood of versions, paraphrases, etc., are currently on the market. These are not word-for-word translations, but rather constitute the thoughts of men.

While it's perfectly proper for Preachers of the Gospel to comment on the Word of God, it is not at all proper to change the meaning of the Word of God, which is exactly what is being done. There are a couple of versions which are word-for-word translations, which are very good. Still, to be on the safe side, I recommend nothing but the King James Version. But yet, this Version is little accepted any more.

Oh, it is not that Scholars are finding fault with that Version, not at all! It's that many claim that they cannot understand it. My answer to that is:

It is far better to labor a little in attempting to understanding something that is correct, rather than to understand completely something that is incorrect. And, to be sure, 99 percent of these modern versions are basely incorrect. In other words, when you study such, for example, *"The Message Bible,"* and scores of others similar, you aren't studying the Word of God, but something else entirely.

Jesus said, *"Man shall not live by bread alone, but by every Word that proceeds out of the Mouth of God"* (Deut. 8:3). Man is a spiritual being, as well as a physical being; therefore, he is dependent on God.

As stated, there are several qualified translations of the Word of God; however, the paraphrased versions can be construed not at all as the Word of God, but something else entirely. As such, those who subscribe to such will more than likely lose their soul.

THE TRADITION OF MEN

The phrase, *"You hold the tradition of men, as the washing of pots and cups,"* is said with some sarcasm. In other words, Jesus is saying that they have purposely selected these *"traditions,"* which were not *"Commandments of God,"* and have purposely accepted these silly ceremonies relating to *"pots and cups."* Tragically, the *"pots and cups"* would describe many modern Churches. In other words, they have a *"pot and cup"* religion!

As stated, these *"pots and cups"* were washed in particular ways, holding them in a certain manner, allowing the water to run in and on them in a certain fashion, with even the drying done in a certain way. Great care was taken that all of this was done properly. Jesus bitterly opposed this foolishness, while stating that true Salvation pertained to one's love of God and his fellowman, which had nothing to do with *"pots and cups."* Consequently, the contrast was succinctly drawn and made glaringly obvious to all, as it was intended to do!

The phrase, *"And many other such like things you do,"* spoke of reams of other ceremonial laws, which the religious leaders demanded that the people keep.

(9) "AND HE SAID UNTO THEM, FULL WELL YOU REJECT THE COMMANDMENT OF GOD, THAT YOU MAY KEEP YOUR OWN TRADITION."

The exegesis is:

Their rejection was a studied and deliberate rejection.

THE REJECTION OF THE WORD OF GOD

The phrase, *"And He said unto them, Full well you reject the Commandment of God,"* speaks of biting sarcasm, as it was delivered by Christ, and said to their very faces, and in front of scores of onlookers. The word *"reject"* means they studied the Word of God minutely, and then purposely made the decision that it was not sufficient, and needed additional laws and commandments, etc. It was, as stated, a studied and deliberate rejection.

Actually, this describes most all of mankind. The Holy Spirit so deliberately convicts men of sin that there is no doubt as to Who and What He is, even though further knowledge may be limited; consequently, any and all rejection is deliberate and studied.

YOUR OWN TRADITION

The phrase, *"That you may keep your own tradition,"* means these religious leaders purposely chose their own *"tradition"* over the Word of God. This is not surprising at all, considering that man has by and large ever followed this course. This is, consequently, the choice that men the world over must make. It is either the Word of God or Islam, Buddhism, Shintoism, Hinduism, Catholicism, Mormonism, or other corrupt forms of Christianity.

The world now, as then, has two choices. It can accept God's Word or man's word, which includes all these things we have named, plus others. Despite what the Mormons say, the Book of Mormon is not another *"Word of God,"* and neither is the *"Koran."* Furthermore, Churches, in their constitution and by-laws, must be very careful that the Word of God is strictly adhered to, and not their own fabrications.

THE WORD OF GOD

The Believer must set himself to keep only the Word of God, and not the commandments or silly traditions of men. If one keeps these silly traditions, even though he does not believe them in his heart, he is, whether he realizes it or not, abrogating the Word of God. In fact, millions keep silly rules of religious Denominations, even though they do not believe them, but do so in order to curry favor, or else to get along. Such is wrong!

If it's not the Word of God, and plainly so, it should be rejected out of hand. We must simply refuse to keep it. This is the position that Jesus took, as well as the Apostle Paul, even though they knew that this would evoke the hostility of the religious establishment. The True Gospel of Jesus Christ would not be lost if more Preachers took the position we have just addressed.

How many times have Preachers said, *"I don't believe it that way, and I know it's not Bible, but it's what my Denomination wants, and I suppose I have to do it."* No! They don't have to do it! They can get out of that religious Denomination. In fact, they should do so! *"For whatsoever is not of faith is sin"* (Rom. 14:23).

The phrase, *"That you may keep your own tradition,"* means that to keep this *"tradition"* is to reject the Word of God.

(Some traditions may be right and Biblical; these should be kept, but not those which violate the Word — II Thessalonians 2:15.)

(10) "FOR MOSES SAID, HONOR YOUR FATHER AND YOUR MOTHER; AND, WHOSO CURSES FATHER OR MOTHER, LET HIM DIE THE DEATH."

The synopsis is:

Jesus draws their attention back to the Word of God.

MOSES

The phrase, *"For Moses said,"* is meant to draw the people back to the Bible in relationship to their own tradition which is given in Verse 11. In Verses 6 through 10 and 13, the Lord declares the Bible, as written by Moses and Isaiah, to be *"the Word of God."* This is why it *"cannot be broken,"* namely, because it is the Word of God; man's word can be broken, whether written or spoken, and often is, but not God's Word (Jn. 10:35).

HONORING PARENTS

The phrase, *"Honor your father and your mother,"* concerns honor that is due and not honor that is given out of the kindness of one's heart. It is in view of who and what they are and their worth, which is their due. It is linked to reverence for the Heavenly Father. If there is no reverence for earthly parents, irrespective as to what they may be, there will be little reverence for our Heavenly Parent.

Ideally, parents are to be as God until the child reaches the age of accountability. During this formative time, and even thereafter, if the *"child is trained in the way he should go, when he is old, he will not depart from it"* (Prov. 22:6). Regrettably, most parents do not do this, and suffer the bitter results; however, the attitude of sons and daughters must always be of reverence and respect toward their parents, because of the symbolism of earthly parents in relationship to the Heavenly Parent.

THE CURSE

The phrase, *"And, Whoso curses Father or Mother, let him die the death,"* means *"to speak ill of, to revile or abuse."* According to Wuest, it does not mean *"to curse"* in the sense of Galatians 1:9, where *"accursed"* in that instance is a Divine curse, and speaks of one eternally losing his soul. The type of *"curse"* spoken of by Jesus is of far less severity, but yet carries with it a dire sentence.

The idea is this:

If he, who, by words, only speaks evil of his Father or his Mother, is, by law, deserving of death, how much more is he deserving of death who wrongs them by deeds, and deprives them of that support which he owes them by the law of nature; and not only so, but teaches others so from Moses' seat, as you Scribes and Pharisees do when you say, *"It is Corban,"* i.e., *"given to God"* (Bickersteth).

The sin of ill-treatment of parents, as spoken here by Christ, is one of the crowning sins presently of America; consequently, this is one of the reasons for the terrible mayhem now prevalent among the youth. Death, and even violent death, ultimately follows in the train of those who disregard this Commandment.

NOTES

The honoring of the Father and the Mother is the Fifth Commandment, which concludes with a Promise, *"That your days may be long upon the land which the LORD your God gives you"* (Ex. 20:12). Consequently, the young in America, even down to sub-teens, are dying violent deaths by the tens of thousands. I speak of suicide, drugs, alcohol, crime, etc.. If the root cause could be traced, it would be the disregard of the Fifth Commandment. To honor one's parents brings long life, while dishonor brings the opposite!

(11) "BUT YOU SAY, IF A MAN SHALL SAY TO HIS FATHER OR MOTHER, IT IS CORBAN, THAT IS TO SAY, A GIFT, BY WHATSOEVER YOU MIGHT BE PROFITED BY ME; HE SHALL BE FREE."

The composition is:

The Pharisees made it a practice of claiming they were giving their material possessions to the Temple, which absolved them of responsibility toward their parents, with a crooked Priest then giving it back to them for a small percentage. This is what Jesus was addressing.

CORBAN

The phrase, *"But you say,"* presents a stark contrast to the Word of God. In essence, the entirety of the Church falls into this choice. It is either *"The Word says,"* or *"you say"*! Regrettably, *"you say"* has replaced *"The Word says"* in too many religious circles.

The phrase, *"If a man shall say to his Father or Mother, it is Corban, that is to say, a gift,"* gives the explanation of the word *"Corban."* In other words, the erring son could absolve himself of responsibility to his parents respecting their support and upkeep during their old age by simply declaring that his material possessions were dedicated to God and he consequently could not help his parents.

THE TWISTING OF THE WORD OF GOD

The phrase, *"By whatsoever you might be profited by Me; he shall be free,"* presents a serious spectacle indeed!

The idea is this:

The Pharisees were teaching these people

to twist the Word of God for their own pecuniary gain. By claiming their material possessions had been given to God and, therefore, could not be used for support of their parents, they made God a part of their lie. Consequently, their sin was compounded. They were making *"profit"* by the recitation of God's Word, hence, the phrase, *"Profited by Me."*

All sin is evil, but this sin is even worse, because it makes God a part of these nefarious activities. Actually, the *"greed gospel"* is very similar, at least as far as making God a part of the sin.

MODERN PREACHERS

As an example, a Preacher addresses his Television audience; he suddenly acts as if the Spirit of the Lord is upon him; and then he tells his audience if they will call in the next five minutes (or some other amount of time), then whatever they give to the Work of God will be given back to them a hundredfold (or some other multiple). Others claim that the Lord has told them that if so much money will be given, then at the end of the year (or another period of time), every debt will be paid, with even their house being free and clear.

In Truth, the Lord has not told such Preachers, so-called, any such thing. In other words, pure and simple, they are lying! Consequently, by claiming the Lord has given them such instructions, they have made the Lord a part of their sin. To be frank, it would be a far less sin to put a gun to the head of a bank teller and demand money. At least, the bank robber does not include God in his nefarious activity. To be sure, the *"greed gospel"* is made up mostly of these types of sins.

THE BLESSINGS OF GOD

It is certainly true that God definitely does bless those who give to Him. Still, if that is the only motivation, then the entirety of what the Holy Spirit is teaching is lost. The Believer is to give to God to *"prove the sincerity of his love,"* and not because God is some type of Las Vegas slot machine (II Cor. 8:8).

Furthermore, any time a person says, *"The Lord told me,"* when, in reality, the Lord has said nothing, the lie of this person is compounded by the effort to make God a part of it. Among other things, this is *"taking the Name of the Lord in vain,"* with the penalty stated, *"For the LORD will not hold him guiltless who takes His Name in vain"* (Ex. 20:7).

Even though no set penalty is stated in the Third Commandment, death is specified in Leviticus 24:10-16, 23 and Numbers 15:30-31. While we are no longer living under Law, but rather under Grace, the penalty of these Commandments is still in force. While it is true that people are not presently stoned to death for breaking these Laws, still, God continues to exact the toll, and rightly so!

Even though the Pharisees told their followers, *"you shall be free,"* by following their nefarious counsel, thereby not having to care for their aged parents, still, Jesus, in effect, is saying, *"you will not go free."* God will collect!

(12) "AND YOU SUFFER HIM NO MORE TO DO OUGHT FOR HIS FATHER OR HIS MOTHER."

The diagram is:

To such extremities did these covetous Scribes and Pharisees drive their victims, i.e., their aged parents, who had no way to care for themselves.

THE SACRED DUTY

The word *"Corban"* came from the area in the Temple where the Offerings were deposited, which were called the *"Corbanas,"* or *"Sacred Treasury."* Hence, to say of anything, *"It is Corban,"* was to say that it had a prior and more sacred destination. Consequently, when the son or daughter said to the parent, *"It is Corban,"* it meant it was already appropriated for another purpose, a purpose of God, and could not be given to them. Thus, the parents would be silenced and alarmed, choosing rather to perish of hunger than to rob God.

To such extremities, as stated, did these covetous Scribes and Pharisees drive their victims, i.e., the aged parents, who had no way to care for themselves. In actuality, what was happening was grievous indeed! The Scribe would make a deal with an individual who did not want to care for his parents.

For a percentage, the son could claim that his material possessions were dedicated to God, with the Scribe verifying his actions; consequently, the Scribe was enriched, with the son sidestepping his responsibilities, and the helpless parents suffering greatly.

There was no separation of Church and State in those days, with the Church, in effect, being the State. Consequently, the actions of these individuals were legalized, because of the crookedness of both, the Scribe and the son (or the daughter).

(13) "MAKING THE WORD OF GOD OF NONE EFFECT THROUGH YOUR TRADITION, WHICH YOU HAVE DELIVERED: AND MANY SUCH LIKE THINGS DO YOU."

The overview is:

Jesus had just nailed them with the Fifth Commandment.

MAKING THE WORD OF GOD OF NONE EFFECT

The phrase, *"Making the Word of God of none effect through your tradition,"* constitutes a serious sin indeed, which is also the crowning sin of the our current day! It means *"to render void, deprive of force and authority, to invalidate."* In other words, they figured out a way to get around the Word of God, thereby absolving themselves of responsibilities; at the same time, they made themselves believe they righteously were keeping the Laws of God. This is one of the greatest ploys of Satan, i.e., attempting to get people to twist the Word, making it seem to justify their sinful actions.

Primarily, this is what Paul was speaking of when he asked the question, *"Shall we continue in sin, that Grace may abound?"* (Rom. 6:1). He answered, *"God forbid."* Individuals were taking the great Doctrine of Grace to mean that it really didn't matter what type of sin they committed, or how much sin they committed, Grace would cover it. In other words, they were using Grace as a license to sin. In doing so, they were subtly twisting the Word of God in order to make it justify their sinful actions. As stated, this sin abounds even now, and maybe more than ever!

ORAL LAWS

The phrase, *"Which you have delivered,"* referred to the oral laws of the Pharisees, which were handed down from generation to generation. The Pharisees, to whom our Lord was speaking, were adding weight to these laws by themselves transmitting them to their posterity (Wuest). The phrase, *"And many such like things do you,"* means that this of which Christ has spoken was only a sample of the many ways in which the Commandments of God were twisted, distorted, and annulled by these rabbinical traditions of men.

No doubt, there were many cases of parents who lived profligate lives, squandering their income, thereby making no provisions for their old age, thereby putting a hardship on their sons and daughters. In these cases, which, no doubt, were many, some offspring, at times in dire straits themselves, balked at caring for such parents.

However, the Commandment of the Lord to honor parents was not predicated on their conduct, but instead on the symbolism of the Heavenly Father. In other words, irrespective of the conduct of the parents, the obligation of the offspring did not change. Showing *"honor"* despite conduct showed a respect and understanding of the Word of God. As stated, the parents were, in a sense, a symbol of the Heavenly Father, and should be treated accordingly, at least as far as possible, and irrespective of their actions.

(14) "AND WHEN HE HAD CALLED ALL THE PEOPLE UNTO HIM, HE SAID UNTO THEM, HEARKEN UNTO ME EVERY ONE OF YOU, AND UNDERSTAND."

The exposition is:

The people have a choice. They can hear Him or these hypocritical Pharisees and Scribes. It is the same presently.

THE CALL OF GOD

The phrase, *"And when He had called all the people unto Him, He said unto them,"* constitutes a serious clash between Christ and the *"Pharisees, and certain of the Scribes, which came from Jerusalem"* (Vs. 1). Inasmuch as these dignitaries, fault-finders, we might quickly add, had come on the scene, quite possibly the crowd of people had retired into the background. Now Jesus calls them forth, because what He has to say primarily is to them.

THE CHOICE

The phrase, *"Hearken unto Me every one of you, and understand,"* will contain the most serious and important words they had ever heard. The people have a choice. They can hear Him or the Pharisees. They cannot hear both, because the teaching of each is diametrically opposed to the other. Several things of immeasurable significance are presented here. They are:

1. Jesus would not go over too well with present-day unity Preachers. As a result of His bold statements, He would, as then, not at all be appreciated today!

2. Inasmuch as what He was saying concerned the very Salvation of the souls of these people, and all others, for that matter, He would be bold in His assertions, leaving absolutely no room for doubt respecting what He was talking about.

3. In His delivery, and publicly, He did not mince words, plainly pointing out the error of the Pharisees and Scribes, and doing so in no uncertain terms, in fact, while they were standing there listening. As stated, His manner of approach would not have been too very much appreciated today.

4. Any modern Preacher of the Gospel should desire to follow Christ in this respect. While we should not go out of our way to antagonize, and we certainly must use wisdom and diplomacy, still, the Truth must be presented, and in a way that leaves no room for misunderstanding. To do this, error must be pointed out, as well as Truth. If Jesus set the example, and He did, then we must follow!

Let us never forget: We are dealing with eternal souls. As the Lord told Ezekiel, *"When a righteous man does turn from his righteousness, and commits iniquity, and I lay a stumblingblock before him, he shall die: because you have not given him warning, he shall die in his sin, and his righteousness which he has done shall not be remembered; but his blood will I require at your hand"* (Ezek. 3:20).

(15) "THERE IS NOTHING FROM WITHOUT A MAN, THAT ENTERING INTO HIM CAN DEFILE HIM: BUT THE THINGS WHICH COME OUT OF HIM, THOSE ARE THEY THAT DEFILE THE MAN."

The exposition is:

This refers to food, not intoxicating drinks, narcotics, poisons, or tobacco, etc.

It is evident that what comes out of the heart must exist in the heart.

DEFILEMENT

The phrase, *"There is nothing from without a man, that entering into him can defile him,"* is referring to food, not, as stated, to intoxicating drinks, etc. Actually, Paul dealt with this extensively, quite possibly from these very Words of Christ (I Cor. 8:7-8; II Cor. 7:1).

The Pharisees and Scribes dealt exclusively with that which is outward, even to the washing of cups and pots in a certain way, but not their hearts. The ceremonial washing of their hands could not remove the guilt that stained them, as Jesus declares here.

Far too much of the modern Church world is also made up of rules and regulations that have little to do with one's spirituality. It is all of religion and not at all of God; however, religious men love to make rules, which only engender more strife. Somehow it makes them feel religious and, therefore, acceptable to God. In Truth, these things pull people away from the Lord instead of closer to Him.

The phrase, *"But the things which come out of him, those are they that defile the man,"* presents the very heart of the problem of humanity.

Concerning this statement, Bickersteth translated the words of Christ in this fashion:

"The Scribes teach you that it is not lawful to eat with unwashed hands, because unwashed hands make the food unclean, and unclean food defiles the soul. But in this they err; because it is not that which enters from without into the mouth, but that which proceeds from within through the mouth, and so from the heart, if it be impure — this defiles the man."

It is the same presently.

Paul said, *"I do not frustrate the Grace of God (if we make anything other than the Cross of Christ the object of our Faith, we frustrate the Grace of God, which means we stop its action, meaning that the Holy Spirit will no longer help us): for if Righteousness* come by the Law (any type of Law), *then Christ is dead in vain.* (If I can successfully live for the Lord by any means other than Faith in Christ and the Cross, then the death of Christ was a waste)" (Gal. 2:21).

FRUSTRATING THE GRACE OF GOD

When Believers attempt to live for the Lord by any means, as stated, other than Faith in Christ and what He has done for us at the Cross, we *"frustrate the Grace of God."* This means that we actually stop the Grace of God from coming to us, which guarantees failure on our part.

Grace is simply the Goodness of God extended to undeserving Saints. We are guaranteed this supply as long as our Faith is properly placed. But when we try to earn our Salvation through works, which will most definitely be the case if the Believer doesn't understand the Cross as it relates to Sanctification, then we frustrate the Grace of God, which is most serious indeed!

Many Believers have the idea that because we are living in the Dispensation of Grace, that Grace comes automatically to the Saint. It is true that we are living in the Dispensation of Grace, but it is not true that Grace automatically comes. The Lord doesn't require very much of us, but He most definitely does require that our Faith be properly placed. The entire ingredient is Faith! The entire emphasis is Faith!

Paul is always, and without exception, referring to Faith in the correct object, which always is Christ and the Cross. To separate Christ from the Cross, and we speak of the benefits of what He there did, produces *"another Jesus, another spirit, and another gospel"* (II Cor. 11:4). Such a Believer will live a most miserable Christian experience, having *"more abundant life,"* but not at all enjoying more abundant life (Jn. 10:10).

That's why Paul also said, *"But God forbid that I should glory* (boast), *save in the Cross of our Lord Jesus Christ, by Whom the world is crucified unto me, and I unto the world"* (Gal. 6:14).

(16) "IF ANY MAN HAVE EARS TO HEAR, LET HIM HEAR."

The synopsis is:

The Lord is telling the people that they

NOTES

have a choice; they can hear Him or the Pharisees, but not both!

EARS TO HEAR

The statement of this Verse is used some fifteen times by Christ, seven times in the Gospels, and eight times in the Book of Revelation (Mat. 11:15; 13:9, 43; Mk. 4:9; 7:16; Lk. 8:8; 14:35; Rev. 2:7, 11, 17, 29; 3:6, 13, 22; 13:9).

In effect, the Lord is telling the people that they have a choice. They now know the Truth, and will have to make a decision as to Whom they will hear, the Pharisees or Jesus. Of course, it will cost something to side with Christ, as it always does. This is what Jesus was speaking of in the Beatitudes, when He said, *"Blessed are they which are persecuted for Righteousness' sake"* (Mat. 5:10).

Of course, it should be obvious to all how important it is for the True Gospel of Jesus Christ to be preached. Tragically, most people only hear error, or a mixture of Truth and error. As a result, it reaps its deadly harvest.

It should be obvious that very little True Gospel was preached and taught in the Israel of Jesus' day. It is the same presently and, in fact, always has been. Sadly, few Believers are truly led by the Spirit, resulting in most not really even knowing what is right and what is wrong. They rather are led by the flesh (self), which leads to corruption.

THE ANOINTING

John said, *"But the anointing which you have received of Him abides in you, and you need not that any man teach you: but as the same anointing teaches you of all things, and is Truth, and is no lie, and even as it has taught you, you shall abide in Him"* (I Jn. 2:27).

John wasn't meaning by this statement that Spirit-led Teachers aren't needed. Instead he is saying that if one is truly filled with the Spirit, and correspondingly led by the Spirit, a part of the Spirit's Office Work will be to anoint the Believer to discern between right and wrong teaching.

To be saved or even Spirit-filled does not necessarily mean that one is Spirit-led. To be Spirit-led, one has to walk close to God, which necessitates a strong prayer life and deep consecration. As well, the Holy Spirit will always draw one close to the Word, that He may *"hear and understand."* To be led other than by the Spirit is to be led by the flesh and, therefore, to fall into the trap of Romans 7:15, *"for that which I do I allow not* (understand not)*: for what I would* (desire to do)*, that do I not; but what I hate* (fail the Lord)*, that do I."*

To be led by the Spirit is to *"walk not after the flesh, but after the Spirit,"* which means that the Believer has his faith anchored solidly in Christ and the Cross (Rom. 8:1-2).

(17) "AND WHEN HE WAS ENTERED INTO THE HOUSE FROM THE PEOPLE, HIS DISCIPLES ASKED HIM CONCERNING THE PARABLE."

The synopsis is:

This Passage regards that which enters into a man, and that which comes from his heart.

THE PARABLE

The phrase, *"And when He was entered into the house from the people,"* probably referred to Peter's house. It seems that He made the statement, as outlined in Mark 7:14-16, and then went into the house, which may have been immediate, or perhaps even some hours later.

The phrase, *"His Disciples asked Him concerning the Parable,"* proclaims their curiosity concerning what He was talking about. Matthew said that Peter is the one who posed the question, with the others joining in (Mat. 15:15).

(18) "AND HE SAID UNTO THEM, ARE YOU SO WITHOUT UNDERSTANDING ALSO? DO YOU NOT PERCEIVE, THAT WHATSOEVER THING FROM WITHOUT ENTERS INTO THE MAN; IT CANNOT DEFILE HIM."

The composition is:

The Master now presents the exact opposite of what the Pharisees and Scribes taught.

UNDERSTANDING

The question, *"And He said unto them, Are you so without understanding also?"* shows some disappointment on the part of Christ respecting His Disciples. The teaching of the Pharisees and Scribes was so ingrained in them, as well as all of Israel, that most all had bought into this theology. Their Salvation had become a series of *"do's"* and *"don'ts."* Moreover, it was almost, if not altogether, pertaining to the externals. The Law of Moses had been so twisted and perverted that its true meaning had long since been lost on the people.

In this, we find the terrible sin of man in trying to make a religion out of anything, even the very Word of God. Man is not content to accept the Word at face value, but must put his own gloss onto it, thereby perverting its true meaning, which is Satan's intention! That is the reason Paul said, *"Study to show yourself approved unto God, a workman that needs not to be ashamed, rightly dividing the Word of Truth"* (II Tim. 2:15).

Regrettably, most Preachers do not *"rightly divide the Word of Truth"*! So, the Words of Jesus, as straight to the point as they were, came as a shock to His listeners, with even His Disciples little understanding what He said.

THE TEACHING OF THE CROSS

When the Lord first began to open up to me the Message of the Cross, which was in 1997, I set out immediately to teach this all-important subject over our Network of Radio Stations (SonLife Radio). I stayed on the subject for perhaps several weeks, and then I attempted to go to something else, as was my usual procedure regarding teaching. However, the Spirit of the Lord moved upon me greatly that I must continue teaching the Cross and not go to other subjects, at least at that time. Consequently, I continued for another period of several months.

Then, thinking surely I must go to something else, I attempted to do so. Right in the middle of our teaching, whatever the subject may have been, the Holy Spirit pulled me back to the Cross.

I usually get to my office an hour or so before it's time to go on the air with *"A Study In The Word,"* which begins at 7 a.m., seven days a week (Saturday, Sunday, and Monday are re-airings of Wednesday, Thursday, and Friday). At any rate, as I was walking out the door, the Spirit of the Lord came upon me, stating, in essence, *"Are you going to obey Me, as it regards what you are teaching?"*

I won't forget that moment, not ever! At that moment, I said to the Lord, *"I hear what You are saying, and, to be sure, I will do my best to carry out that which You are demanding. I will teach and preach the Cross over the SonLife Radio Network until You tell me otherwise."*

It wasn't that I didn't want to obey the Lord, I just wanted to make sure that what I was doing was the Lord. The reason should be obvious! It's one thing to teach one subject for several weeks, or even months, but to teach one subject for several years, with no end in sight, is something else altogether.

Since that day several years ago, I have more and more learned why the Lord demanded this. As the Disciples of old, who had been so inundated with the doctrine of the Pharisees that it was difficult for them to understand the Truth, even as is outlined in this Text, it is the same way with modern Christians presently.

The Church has been inundated with false doctrine for so long that layer after layer has to be pulled aside before the Truth can finally penetrate the heart of the individual. And this pertains to those who truly want the Ways of the Lord. That's the reason the Lord has had me to preach this Message unendingly, so to speak, and rightly so!

DEFILEMENT

The question, *"Do you not perceive, that whatsoever thing from without enters into the man; it cannot defile him,"* presents that which is the exact opposite of what the Pharisees and Scribes taught. As stated, almost all, if not entirely all, which they taught and believed pertained to the externals.

By this statement, Jesus shoots down the moralists, as well as every other religion in the world, for all religions work from the same principle, i.e., the externals. He also shows, and in no uncertain terms, that man's problem cannot be solved by whatever is addressed externally, but only by a change of the heart, which is the cause of man's difficulties. Consequently, this means that all psychology, at least as it attempts to adjust man's behavior patterns, is doomed to failure. This would also go for all self-help programs. All are a waste of time, which should be obvious, considering the 100 percent failure rate.

This means that all the rehab centers in America and around the world are of no use whatsoever to the poor individual who desperately needs help. This means that Alcoholics Anonymous is to no avail, even though in some few cases it may help the person to quit drinking. While that is certainly commendable, still, the individual, at least as far as his heart is concerned, is unchanged; consequently, he (or she) continues to be what he says he is, *"a recovering alcoholic"*!

However, when Jesus changes the heart, He also changes the life. He does not try to patch up the old man, but makes the person *"a new creation,"* and does so *"in Himself, Christ Jesus"* (II Cor. 5:17).

SELF-CONSCIOUSNESS

When man fell in the Garden of Eden, he fell from a position of total God-consciousness to a position of total self-consciousness, which resulted in a constant preoccupation with *"self."* He also changed lords, in that Satan is now man's lord; consequently, *"the lusts of man's father* (the Devil) *man will do"* (Jn. 8:44). This is the reason for all the hate, evil, murder, violence, and mayhem in the world today! Regrettably, the so-called intelligentsia of America and the world continues to looks elsewhere for the cause of evil! However, it is found in man's own heart (Jer. 17:9).

So, man's defilement is not his surroundings, and neither are the surroundings his cure. The Federal Government has spent, and is continuing to spend, hundreds of billions of dollars on housing, environment, and education, thinking that such will stem the crime rate among certain segments of society, but to no avail! Almost every day a new program is announced, which the social planners believe will solve the problem; however, with the passing of time and the spending of more billions of dollars, the situation is no better, but instead worse. As someone has said, *"It is about like putting lipstick on a hog!"*

To these ills of humanity, which cause all the heartache in the world, Jesus and what He did for us at the Cross is the only

Answer! To be sure, He and what He did is not a part of the answer, but is, in Truth, the only Answer!

(19) "BECAUSE IT ENTERS NOT INTO HIS HEART, BUT INTO THE BELLY, AND GOES OUT INTO THE DRAUGHT, PURGING ALL MEATS?"

The composition is:

The statement, as given by Christ, refers to the digestive and elimination system of the human body.

THE HEART

The phrase, *"Because it enters not into his heart,"* proclaims every effort by man to change human behavior to be, as stated, futile. How can it change man, when it does not go to the source of the problem, i.e., the heart, the seat of all intellect and will, i.e., *"the soul and the spirit"*?

The phrase, *"But into the belly, and goes out into the draught, purging all meats,"* refers, as stated, to the digestive and elimination system of the human body. As an aside, this also destroys the teaching of the Seventh Day Adventists that it is sinful to eat pork. The teaching of Jesus is so simple, simple enough that no one, in fact, need have any problem understanding. And yet, most of the world does not understand it. It keeps trying to change man by dealing with the externals.

That's really all that religion can do: deal with the externals. Religion is a system devised by man, which attempts to reach God or to better oneself in some way. Man cannot reach God by his own machinations. In actuality, God has to reach man, which He has done by and through His Son, our Saviour, the Lord Jesus Christ (Jn. 3:16).

In order that man might come to God, his fallen condition had to be dealt with. Man was contaminated with the disease of sin, so to speak; and for that disease, man has no cure. So God dealt with the problem by becoming Man and dying on a Cross, which was His destination, even from before the foundation of the world (I Pet. 1:18-20), which addressed man's problem, which is sin. Simple Faith in Christ and what Christ did at the Cross instantly brings a person from death to life, so to speak (Jn. 3:16; Rom. 10:9-10, 13; Rev. 22:17).

NOTES

(20) "AND HE SAID, THAT WHICH COMES OUT OF THE MAN, THAT DEFILES THE MAN."

The diagram is:

An evil heart produces evil actions.

THE CONDITION OF THE HEART

The phrase, *"And He said,"* refers to the Words of Jesus, and that which is Law and Gospel. As such, it is said in contradistinction to the Pharisees and Scribes. In other words, He totally contradicted them.

The phrase, *"That which comes out of the man, that defiles the man,"* gives the cause of all of man's inhumanity to man, and is listed in the following Verses. It means, as we have said, that man's problem comes from within him, and not from without; consequently, a change of environment will not solve the problem; education will not solve the problem; psychology will not solve the problem. Actually, other than Christ, the problem, whatever it is, is unsolvable.

(21) "FOR FROM WITHIN, OUT OF THE HEART OF MEN, PROCEED EVIL THOUGHTS, ADULTERIES, FORNICATIONS, MURDERS,

(22) "THEFTS, COVETOUSNESS, WICKEDNESS, DECEIT, LASCIVIOUSNESS, AN EVIL EYE, BLASPHEMY, PRIDE, FOOLISHNESS."

The overview is:

This statement by Christ destroys the belief that the natural heart is good; it makes foolish modern efforts to improve human nature.

THE SOURCE OF EVIL

The phrase, *"For from within,"* now, and in no uncertain terms, gives the cause of man's inhumanity to man — the heart, i.e., *"the soul and the spirit,"* and what proceeds from it. The phrase, *"Out of the heart of men,"* proclaims the evil things that come from within and defile the man. This statement by Christ, Who is the Truth, destroys the belief, as stated, that the natural heart is good; it also makes foolish modern efforts to improve human nature.

The assumption is here denied that only what goes into the heart defiles it; the necessity of the creation of a new heart is declared.

It is evident that what comes out of the heart must exist in the heart (Williams). Furthermore, the word *"proceed"* means that it is a fountain constantly producing that which is evil; consequently, it is a sobering thought. The action which proceeds from the evil heart is as follows:

1. *"Evil thoughts"*: Wuest says that the word *"thoughts"* carries the idea of discussion or debate, with an under-thought of suspicion or doubt, either in one's own mind, or with another. In the unconverted heart and mind, all the thoughts which proceed are *"evil,"* irrespective as to how they may appear otherwise. The unregenerate man is not capable of any other type of *"thoughts,"* whether these thoughts are *"good"* or *"evil."* They all come from the same *"tree of the knowledge of good and evil,"* and are consequently wrong (Gen. 2:17).

The *"good"* side of this tree greatly deceives men, because they think it is the opposite of the *"evil,"* not realizing that it all comes from the same tree, i.e., *"source."*

2. *"Adulteries"*: Adultery is sexual intercourse outside of the bonds of marriage, whether the person is single or married.

3. *"Fornications"*: This covers a wide range of illicit activity, including homosexuality, lesbianism, bestiality, promiscuity, etc. For instance, Esau was a fornicator (Heb. 12:16). In one way or the other, all fornication is adultery, but all adultery is not fornication.

4. *"Murders"*: The Greek word is *"phonoi,"* which not only means to take a person's life, but also to destroy their reputation, their influence, etc. It refers also to *"hatred"* (I Jn. 3:15). Consequently, the sin of *"murder"* refers to a lot more than the malicious taking of another human life.

5. *"Thefts"*: This is the stealing of property that belongs to another, and also refers to the destruction of one's name by slander or whispering, etc.

6. *"Covetousness"*: This is a greedy desire to have more. One American industrialist was asked how much more property he wanted; his answer was revealing: *"Only that which borders mine!"* However, the word *"covetousness"* speaks of far more than just the desire, but speaks of the action of the individual in eagerly attempting to obtain it, if at all possible, and sometimes by hook or crook.

This is what Paul was speaking of when he spoke of his efforts to keep the Law. He found that not committing the act was not enough. He also must not desire to do it, which came under the last Commandment, *"You shall not covet."* In other words, when he was about to congratulate himself, *"the Commandment came, sin revived, and I* (Paul) *died,"* i.e., failed spiritually, because the desire was still there (Rom. 7:7, 9).

All religion is made up more or less of rules and regulations, which automatically throw the adherent into *"covetousness."* In other words, he may not do what his rules say he cannot do, but that rule cannot keep him from desiring to do it; consequently, the evil heart is shown to be what it is and what it produces.

7. *"Wickedness"*: This speaks of depravity, and not merely in the abstract, but, in effect, active wickedness. It has the idea of *"being dangerous and destructive."* In other words, this type of wickedness is an active opposition to the good.

Some types of the wicked are content to perish in their own corruption. That is bad enough! However, the type of wickedness here spoken of by Jesus speaks of the individual who is not content unless he pulls everything down with him in his own destruction.

An excellent example is Adolf Hitler, who gave instructions that everything in Germany was to be destroyed when it became obvious that the war was lost. Even though that is an extreme example, millions follow in his train, because they have the same evil heart.

8. *"Deceit"*: Deceit is more than a *"lie."* In its most simplistic definition, it is a complex web of ideas which lead one astray. The word suggests undependable behavior in a given relationship. The person who thus deals falsely ultimately causes harm to others. The word refers to the violation of the basic relationship of truth and honesty that ought to exist between human beings, incorporating the idea of intending to mislead and harm another person.

The word *"deceit"* has to do with error urged by external evil powers and by things locked into the world's way of thinking. Satan is the epitome of deception, having used this method to ensnare Adam and Eve. Consequently, man is very easily deceived, because his entire premise operates, as a result of the Fall, on a foundation of deception. *"Deceit"* is still Satan's greatest weapon.

The world is fond of what it refers to as *"subjective truth,"* which means it may not be true for all, but it is *"true for you."* In contrast, the Lord and His Word operate on absolute (objective) Truth. The Bible clearly affirms objective Truth, and it grounds that belief in the Biblical concept of God. God is Truth. All that He says is in strict accord with reality. His Words are, therefore, firm and trustworthy.

By contrast, we human beings are trapped in illusion. We struggle to understand the meaning of the world around us and of our experiences. Unaided, we cannot distinguish between the real and the counterfeit, the Truth and the lie; consequently, all who do not know Christ, and all who do know Him but do not rely solely on Him, are perfect targets for Satan, as it regards Deceit.

Only reliance on God's Word, which is true, enables us to build our lives on a firm foundation. That is the reason that if something is not grounded firmly in the Word of God, it must be firmly denied.

9. *"Lasciviousness"*: This is unrestrained sexual instinct. Regrettably, it is the sin of the age!

10. *"An evil eye"*: This speaks of those who look at other people and things with the idea of positive, injurious activity in order to secure what is desired. It also speaks of one who sees *"evil"* wherever he looks, because his own eye is *"evil."* To this *"eye,"* Godliness is looked at as a scheme, etc. This is one of the reasons the News Media cannot write anything good about the Work of the Lord. They see it through *"an evil eye,"*; consequently attributing to it every devious practice.

A PERSONAL EXPERIENCE

Years ago, when our Television audience became quite large, we attracted Media attention. I had the erroneous idea that if I was totally open with reporters, they would not write or say that which was error; however, I was soon to find out differently.

I found that most of them had little interest in the Truth, at least as it regards the Lord and His Work. They had already made up their minds before the investigation started; consequently, the situation was whatever they wanted it to be, because their eye was *"evil."* They saw falsehood, chicanery, dishonesty, and deception in every act.

One investigative reporter went with us to a particular Crusade. On the return trip, he hit me with this bombshell: *"I believe you are stealing money!"* he said. I looked at him for a moment, somewhat taken aback by his accusation, and then I patiently attempted to explain to him how difficult such would be, even if I wanted to. After my explanation, I asked him why I would want to do such a thing, especially considering that I sold more Gospel records (at that time) than anyone else in the world.

"All I have to do," I explained to him, *"is to take a royalty on all these records, which is legal and moral. However, I don't even do that!"*

Completely discounting all I had said, he replied, *"I still believe you're stealing money!"*

I then looked at him and said, *"I know why you think that!"*

"Why?" he asked.

"If you were in my shoes, you would steal money!"

I will never forget his answer. He turned to me and stared at me for a while without saying anything. Then he said, *"Yes, if I could do it and get by with it, I would steal every dollar I could lay my hands on."*

Consequently, he was judging me according to his own evil heart. He had, as stated, *"an evil eye"*!

I learned the hard way that Truth meant nothing to these people, because of this very Word spoken here by Christ.

11. *"Blasphemy"*: Wuest said this word does not necessarily speak of blasphemy against God, but can be used of malicious misrepresentation of another person or thing.

12. *"Pride"*: This is the sin of an uplifted heart against God and man, and is the foundation sin of all sin.

13. *"Foolishness"*: This proclaims the fact that all evil terminates in the loss of all

moral and intellectual illumination; consequently, it becomes easier to understand the foolish ideas presented by those who call themselves *"intellectuals,"* respecting the solving of human problems.

It also speaks of the Church, and, above all, the Church which has left the tried and true Ways of the Lord, resorting rather to the *"foolishness"* of the ways of the world.

(23) "ALL THESE EVIL THINGS COME FROM WITHIN, AND DEFILE THE MAN."

The exposition is:

All of this proclaims the result of the Fall, and the absolute necessity of the New Birth.

EVIL THINGS

Men, that is to say, unredeemed men, are the efficient causes of their own choices. But yet, that is only half right. Because, without God in the soul, man's choices are heavily influenced and weighted by Satanic influence. Jesus ended this statement in Matthew 15:20 by saying, *"But to eat with unwashed hands defiles not the man."*

Once again, He is not speaking of proper sanitary necessity, but instead the religious practice of washing demons off before eating, etc. With His short statements, He succinctly addresses the real cause of man's problems, and the real cure. Men are ever treating symptoms, while ignoring the cause. Jesus addresses the cause, but instead of responding to it with treatment, He responds with Deliverance (Lk. 4:18).

That, Deliverance, in a nutshell, is the basic difference between the gospel of psychology and the Gospel of Jesus Christ. The first treats the problem, which, in reality, only treats the symptom, while Jesus delivers man from the problem.

DELIVERANCE

Men are delivered by knowing and obeying the Truth (Jn. 8:32). Jesus said, *"The Spirit of the Lord is upon Me* (we learn here of the absolute necessity of the Person and Work of the Holy Spirit within our lives), *because He has anointed Me* (Jesus is the ultimate Anointed One; consequently, the Anointing of the Holy Spirit actually belongs to Christ, and the Anointing we have actually comes by His Authority [Jn. 16:14]) *. . . to preach Deliverance to the captives* (if it is to be noticed, He didn't say 'to deliver the captives,' but rather 'to preach Deliverance,' which refers to the Cross) . . ." (Lk. 4:18; I Cor. 1:23; 2:2).

Preachers have tried to deliver people by laying hands on them, etc. While the *"laying on of hands"* is certainly Scriptural, and should be practiced, still, if the person on whom the hands are laid doesn't know the Truth, and I speak of the Truth of the Cross, then whatever happens will not result in Deliverance. By explaining the Cross in this Commentary, which we have tried to do, we are, in effect, *"preaching Deliverance."* For Believers to know the Truth is the only way that Deliverance can be effected.

WHY WOULD A CHRISTIAN NEED DELIVERANCE?

If the Christian doesn't understand the activity of the sin nature, and how it is brought under total control, even as Paul explains in Romans, Chapter 6, the sin nature will begin to rule such a Christian, with such a person being put in bondage (Gal. 5:1). The Christian will then be in real trouble, and will find that the problem steadily gets worse instead of better, despite all of his efforts otherwise. Sad to say, virtually all of modern Christians are in bondage to one degree or the other, because they do not understand the Cross as it refers to Sanctification.

In the Fifth Chapter of Galatians, Paul lists the *"works of the flesh,"* which he tells us will definitely manifest themselves, if the Christian doesn't avail himself of God's Prescribed Order of Victory, which is what Paul taught us in Romans, Chapter 6. As stated, virtually the entirety of the modern Church falls into the category of bondage, and I speak of those who are truly Born-Again, because they do not understand the Cross. Consequently, they need Deliverance, which can only be effected by learning and knowing the Truth, and applying it to their hearts and lives.

That *"Truth"* is *"Jesus Christ and Him Crucified,"* which means that the Cross is the only answer for the ills and aberrations of man. All it requires is the Believer ever making Christ and the Cross the Object of his Faith. That being done, victory will ultimately come! (Rom. 6:3-14).

(24) "AND FROM THENCE HE AROSE, AND WENT INTO THE BORDERS OF TYRE AND SIDON, AND ENTERED INTO AN HOUSE, AND WOULD HAVE NO MAN KNOW IT: BUT HE COULD NOT BE HID."

The synopsis is:

This Passage carries the idea from the Greek Text that Christ did not merely cross over the border into Gentile territory; he actually went deep into the heart of that country.

THE FAME OF CHRIST

The phrase, *"And from thence He arose,"* speaks of the clash between Himself and the Pharisees and Scribes. Accordingly, He takes leave of this area. The phrase, *"And went into the borders of Tyre and Sidon,"* has the idea, from the Greek Text, that our Lord did not merely cross over the border into Phoenician territory, but He actually went deep into the heart of that country.

The phrase, *"And entered into an house, and would have no man know it,"* seemingly refers to His desire to seek rest, as He had admonished His Disciples in Mark 6:31. The phrase, *"But He could not be hid,"* referred to His fame, which had preceded Him. Consequently, the stage is set for the Deliverance of a Gentile girl.

To whom the house belonged is not stated. What a privilege it was for them to have Jesus enter under their roof! He stands ready to come into any house, which is the only way it can become a home.

THE HOME

When I was a child, my parents did not have much, as far as worldly goods were concerned; however, the day my Mother and Dad said *"Yes"* to Christ was the greatest day of my life. Everything changed, and for the better! Before, we had only a *"house"*; now we had a *"home"*! To be sure, nothing really had changed, as far as the furnishings or the house itself were concerned; however, the hearts of my parents had changed, with love replacing hate. Now this *"home"* became the most wonderful place on Earth!

Had my parents come into millions of dollars, and consequently been able to construct a mansion, at least as far as externals are concerned, it still would have been a place of misery, if they had not found Jesus. Millions think that by building a new house, they have found the secret to life. They soon find that life really has not changed. In fact, and in Truth, it can only change when Jesus comes into the heart.

So, a *"home"* does not consist of finery, but rather who lives in it. And who lives in it determines what it will be, according to who lives in them, whether Christ or Satan.

(25) "FOR A CERTAIN WOMAN, WHOSE YOUNG DAUGHTER HAD AN UNCLEAN SPIRIT, HEARD OF HIM, AND CAME AND FELL AT HIS FEET."

The exposition is:

The need of humanity knows no bounds. Only Christ can meet that need!

AN UNCLEAN SPIRIT

The phrase, *"For a certain woman,"* refers to a Gentile. As Mark will say, she is a *"Syrophenician."* The phrase, *"Whose young daughter had an unclean spirit,"* is verified by the Holy Spirit in the giving of this account, i.e., the woman's summation of her daughter's condition was correct. It is ironical that this heathen woman, some 2,000 years ago, knew the problem of her daughter, but modern intellectuals, with all their vaunted knowledge, do not know!

As we have previously stated, the designation, *"unclean spirit,"* covers all evil spirits, and of whatever kind. That an evil spirit would possess a young girl would come as a shock to most. How could such happen?

DEMON SPIRITS AND CHILDREN

First of all, since this woman was a Gentile, this means she was an idol-worshipper, or at least the citizen of a nation of idol-worshippers. At any rate, demon spirits ruled this country of Tyre and Sidon, as evil spirits rule most countries today. As such, many were demon possessed, with many more demon oppressed.

Any parents who do not know Jesus are open to demon possession and oppression, whether in themselves or in their children. That holds true now, as then! The only protection against the powers of darkness is the Lord Jesus Christ. Education, money, and environment are no protection whatsoever!

Consequently, when unsaved parents bring a child into the world, due to its exposure to the powers of darkness, a few years after birth, it is possible for it to become demon possessed.

If one could pull back the cover and find the cause of all gang violence, teen murders, immorality among teenagers and subteens, etc., one would find demon possession as the cause, or, at the least, extreme demon influence. Even if only one parent is a Believer, *"the unbelieving husband is Sanctified by the wife, and the unbelieving wife is Sanctified by the husband: else were your children unclean; but now are they holy"* (I Cor. 7:14). This means that one believing parent can sanctify the family.

If the parents, or at least one parent, come to Christ after the birth of their child or children, Satan's power is broken in that family. It does not necessarily mean that he will discontinue all efforts of corruption and destruction, but it does mean that the believing parent(s) has powerful weapons at his or her disposal, which, upon proper Faith, will subdue the powers of darkness, and without fail (Jn. 15:7).

The phrase, *"And came and fell at His feet,"* concerns her desperation. Whatever she knew about Him, the results will show that she believed that He was the Answer to her dilemma. It was at this moment, more than likely, as Matthew records, that she addressed Jesus as *"Lord, Thou Son of David"* (Mat. 15:22). Mark omits this, and for purpose and reason.

Matthew proclaims Christ as King, and of the entire world; consequently, the woman's acclamation in his account would be included. Mark proclaims Jesus as a Servant; thus, such titles would not be given by Gentiles, although recorded if spoken by a Jew (Mk. 10:48).

(26) "THE WOMAN WAS A GREEK, A SYROPHENICIAN BY NATION; AND SHE BESOUGHT HIM THAT HE WOULD CAST FORTH THE DEVIL OUT OF HER DAUGHTER."

The exposition is:

We will find that Jesus never turned anyone away, irrespective as to who they were or what they were.

NOTES

A GENTILE

The phrase, *"The woman was a Greek, a Syrophenician by nation,"* means she was Greek by religion, spoke the Syrian language, and was Phoenician by race. Wuest says she was a Phoenician of Syria, as distinguished from a Phoenician of North Africa.

Matthew was a little more specific, calling her *"a woman of Canaan,"* meaning that she was a descendant from those seven nations of Canaan which had been driven out on God's Command by Joshua. In the context of this explanation as to who the woman was, one finds all the attendant horror of a life without God. She was an *"alien from the Commonwealth of Israel, a stranger from the Covenants of Promise, having no hope, and without God in the world"* (Eph. 2:12).

In these very words given by Paul, one can literally feel the lost condition of such a person! Everything that truly makes life worth living is denied to such an individual. And yet, sadder still, most of this present world is in that condition still. They do not know the Lord.

DEBTOR

I will ever thank God for that day so long ago when the Gospel of Jesus Christ was brought to my community. As the songwriter said:

*"Oh happy day,
"Oh happy day,
"When Jesus washed,
"My sins away."*

That is one of the reasons I have a burning burden to take this glorious Message of Redemption, this Message of the Cross, this Message of Christ, to a lost and dying world. In Truth, every Believer feels the same way, at least if they truly understand what Jesus has actually done for them! That is the reason Paul said, *"I am debtor"* (Rom. 1:14). He meant that he was under an obligation and bound by duty to take the Gospel to others, because the Lord had been gracious and kind to bring the Gospel to him.

THE REQUEST FOR HELP

The phrase, *"And she besought Him that*

He would cast forth the devil out of her daughter," actually means that she kept asking the Lord over and over again to do this thing, which was the cry of her heart. Someone has said that parents love their children more than their children love them, because love descends. Quite possibly, that is correct, inasmuch as God loves us more than we love Him.

At any rate, this woman has come to Christ; the results will proclaim that she means to receive what she came for — Deliverance for her daughter. The suffering and pain which her daughter's condition had caused must have been extremely debilitating. As it is, she sees no future for the girl. Actually, there is no future for anyone outside of Christ.

There was absolutely no way this girl could be delivered except by Christ. Even though the long span of years has crossed the bridge of time, and irrespective of vaunted science and the increase of medical knowledge, there is no Deliverer even today except Christ. He Alone can set the captive free. As we have repeatedly stated, this is the reason that the Gospel is so very important. It is not one of several solutions; it is, in fact, the only solution.

(27) "BUT JESUS SAID UNTO HER, LET THE CHILDREN FIRST BE FILLED: FOR IT IS NOT MEET TO TAKE THE CHILDREN'S BREAD, AND TO CAST IT UNTO THE DOGS."

The synopsis is:

Thus begins the odyssey which will proclaim a great display of Faith.

ISRAEL

The phrase, *"But Jesus said unto her,"* begins the odyssey which will proclaim a great display of Faith. The phrase, *"Let the children first be filled,"* has reference to Israel.

This order of procedure was not favoritism, but only the method of reaching the larger number through a selected smaller group — in this case, Israel. The Jew was the chosen channel through which God had elected to reach the Gentiles; consequently, it was proper that the *"children"* (Israel) receive first, in order that they may be able to give it to others.

This was, as stated, God's Plan. But, sorrow of sorrows, Israel would not receive it!

Nevertheless, Jesus would offer it to them first, as it should be.

DOGS

The phrase, *"For it is not meet to take the children's bread, and cast it unto the dogs,"* is not nearly as harsh as it seems on the surface. Jews actually did, in fact, look on all Gentiles as dogs. It was a term of reproach. Paul even called Judaizers *"dogs"* when he said, *"Beware of dogs"* (Phil. 3:2). However, the word used by Christ was not the word for *"dog"* as it is commonly used, but the word for *"a little dog,"* actually referring to *"pets."*

Wuest suggests that Jesus may have spoken Greek to this woman, for she possibly would not have known the Aramaic of the Jews. Greek, moreover, was the international language of the day.

WHY DID THE LORD ADDRESS THIS WOMAN IN THIS MANNER?

1. As we have repeatedly stated, everything He did had a far larger scope than the immediate need, although it certainly included that. His Miracles basically pertained to three directions:

A. To meet, as stated, the present need!

B. To serve as a lesson for the entirety of the Church, and for all time!

C. To serve as a lesson for each individual, and for all time!

2. He was testing her faith. As Satan's every effort is meant to weaken, or even destroy, our Faith, likewise, everything done by the Lord is meant to increase our Faith. Faith is the currency — in fact, the only currency — which spends in Heaven. Without fail, however, it must, be Faith in Christ and what Christ has done for us at the Cross.

Some may wonder how this woman could have Faith, inasmuch as she was a heathen, consequently a stranger to the Promises of God. Actually her condition was no different than anyone else. The moment an individual comes in contact with God and His Word, a *"measure of Faith is dealt to them"* (Rom. 12:3).

She had come to Christ; therefore, her faith is automatically increased, strictly by association with Him, even though it was an incomplete faith. Nevertheless, the Lord would meet her need at her level, whatever that level might be. If He didn't do that, none of us would be here today. In fact, His very Words were intended to increase her Faith, which they did!

3. He would show her how to have what she wanted, even though, at least at this time, she, as a Gentile, was not included in the Mission of Christ. By Jesus' use of the word *"dog,"* He was not insulting her, but rather showing her how she could receive what she wanted.

First, she attempted to appeal to Christ by saying, *"O Lord, Thou Son of David."* However, she was not a Jew and, therefore, had no right on that basis, because she was not a part of the Covenant (Mat. 15:22). But as a *"dog"* she could appeal on the merit of Mercy and Grace. As such, she could receive what she wanted. Actually, she could receive far more, because Mercy and Grace always have a greater supply than Covenant.

This should be a tremendous lesson for us all, in that God will honor Faith wherever He finds it. Even as I dictate these words, I sense the Presence of God. It does not matter what the circumstances are! If a person believes God, He will honor their Faith in Him, and without fail! This is a part of the lesson He is teaching us by the experience of this woman.

(28) "AND SHE ANSWERED AND SAID UNTO HIM, YES, LORD: YET THE DOGS UNDER THE TABLE EAT OF THE CHILDREN'S CRUMBS."

The structure is:

The word *"Lord"* in the Greek Text, as used by the woman, does not refer to Deity, or of Jesus being the Jewish Messiah; she would have had scant knowledge of this. Instead, she uses the word *"Lord"* in the sense of Jesus being an important Person, etc.

CRUMBS FROM THE TABLE

The phrase, *"And she answered and said unto him,"* proclaims a level of Faith which should be a lesson to all Believers. What determination! Even what desperation! But yet, True Faith is always in this vein. She fully agrees with the Lord by using the word *"Yes"*! Actually, she did exactly what He was desiring her to do. She used His Own words, which seemed to be negative, and turned them to the positive. I have to shout *"Hallelujah"*!

The phrase, *"Yet the dogs under the table eat of the children's crumbs,"* places her in the position, by Faith, to receive what she wanted. She is saying that his table is so heavily laden that surely a crumb, which will meet her need, will not be missed.

Actually, this very illustration used by Christ, which seems harsh on the surface, rather appeals to this Gentile. Jews did not look kindly on dogs at all, and would not have thought of having one in their houses and around their persons. Most Gentiles, however, had them as pets, even allowing them, at times, to come and go in the house, actually eating the crumbs which fell from the table. In the Gentile culture of that day, it was common for children to throw crumbs to the dogs at mealtime. Christ's statement consequently would have been perfectly understandable to this Gentile.

Isn't our Lord wonderful!

(29) "AND HE SAID UNTO HER, FOR THIS SAYING GO YOUR WAY; THE DEVIL IS GONE OUT OF YOUR DAUGHTER."

The exegesis is:

It means that this demon has gone out, and will stay out; it is a permanent cure.

VICTORY

The phrase, *"And He said unto her,"* constitutes a Divine answer to a terrible need, and to great Faith, as well. Actually, Matthew proclaims Jesus saying, *"O woman, great is your Faith"* (Mat. 15:28).

The phrase, *"For this saying, go your way,"* concerns her Faith, and great Faith at that! There is something else evident, however, in this Text, which we must not overlook. The humility registered here goes hand in hand with great Faith.

HUMILITY

Humility, as a Grace, is something not easily brought about. Humility is generally, if not always, brought about by the humbling process. This comes about, oftentimes, by the advent of great troubles and difficulties. As stated, this woman was desperate! Her daughter was in serious condition, and possibly getting worse, with death shortly in the offing, if something was not done. This dear woman consequently was humbled in the face of this great need.

Much of that which is presently called *"faith"* is, in fact, precious little True Faith, if any at all, because of the almost total lack of humility. The modern brand is self-aggrandizing and self-boasting, even though glossed with Scripture. In the modern variety, it is almost as if the louder one can boast, the more faith he has.

Paul said, *"But God forbid that I should glory* (boast), *save in the Cross of our Lord Jesus Christ* (what the opponents of Paul sought to escape at the price of insincerity is the Apostle's only basis of exultation), *by Whom the world is Crucified unto me, and I unto the world."* (The only way we can overcome the world, and I mean the only way, is by placing our Faith exclusively in the Cross of Christ and keeping it there)" (Gal. 6:14).

In Truth, if it's not Faith in Christ and the Cross, it is no Faith at all, but rather mere presumption! I think one can say, without fear of Scriptural contradiction, that True Faith will always be humble, or at least will be humbled in the process.

Naaman is a perfect example! When he was given instructions by Elisha, regarding the cure of his leprosy, the Scripture says that he *"went away in a rage"* (II Ki. 5:12). He was greatly offended because Elisha had not even bothered to come out himself, but had rather sent his servant to deliver the message. He was Naaman, the great Captain of Syria; therefore, at least in his mind, he warranted more than this cavalier treatment.

However, he ultimately humbled himself, and did as the Prophet said, and was totally healed. Had he not been humbled, there would have been no Faith, and there would have been no healing (II Ki. 5:14).

The phrase, *"The devil is gone out of your daughter,"* means that it is out and will stay out. It is a permanent cure, with the Mother never again having to worry that this *"unclean spirit"* will have access to her daughter.

(30) "AND WHEN SHE WAS COME TO HER HOUSE, SHE FOUND THE DEVIL GONE OUT, AND HER DAUGHTER LAID UPON THE BED."

NOTES

The exposition is:

Regarding the girl, it refers to a restful repose, which indicated that previously she had not been easily restrained.

DELIVERANCE

The phrase, *"And when she was come to her house,"* presents a beautiful picture indeed! Previously, her house had been one of turmoil and suffering — *"Hell on Earth,"* as one might say. Such is the condition of most *"houses."* However, her *"house"* has now changed and, in fact, would be changed forever.

The phrase, *"She found the devil gone out,"* once again has, in the Greek Text, the idea that the cure is permanent. It is not a temporary thing, but rather an eternal Deliverance. Hallelujah!

What joy must have filled this woman's heart!

What praises to God must have filled that house!

As it happened then, it can happen now and, in fact, does happen countless times, but only when Jesus speaks the Word. He stands ready, waiting, and willing to do for any and all who will believe Him, exactly as He did for this woman of so long ago.

REST

The phrase, *"And her daughter laid upon the bed,"* refers to a restful repose. There is every indication that the girl previously had been insane, or at least partially so! But now she is perfectly whole, and sound of mind as any human being could ever be. All of this because of the *"Word of Christ."* And yet, most of the world turns Him away.

All the same, what Jesus did for that family, for that house, and for that girl has been repeated untold numbers of times, and stands ready to be repeated now, in one way or the other, for all who will believe.

(31) "AND AGAIN, DEPARTING FROM THE COASTS OF TYRE AND SIDON, HE CAME UNTO THE SEA OF GALILEE, THROUGH THE MIDST OF THE COASTS OF DECAPOLIS."

The synopsis is:

He was now on the eastern side of the Sea of Galilee.

DECAPOLIS

Leaving the Tyre and Sidon area, the Lord probably went east through Caesarea Philippi, then turned south by the eastern side of Galilee, and came to the border of Decapolis. It could well have been a journey of some 60 or 70 miles, taking several days. Actually, this was not far from the area where He had delivered the maniac of Gadara.

Inasmuch as the Holy Spirit had Mark to carefully delineate the route of our Lord, we know that Jesus came here by design. The opposition by the Pharisees and Scribes was not pleasant, to say the least; therefore, the trip to Phoenicia and back to Decapolis would have been a respite from the venomous hatred of these religious leaders.

(32) "AND THEY BRING UNTO HIM ONE WHO WAS DEAF, AND HAD AN IMPEDIMENT IN HIS SPEECH; AND THEY BESEECH HIM TO PUT HIS HAND UPON HIM."

The structure is:

Now He will heal one who is deaf.

DEAFNESS

The phrase, *"And they bring unto Him one who was deaf, and had an impediment in his speech,"* proclaims the usual difficulties of the *"deaf."* Due to being unable to hear, speech impediments are normal, with total speech loss resulting many times; however, there was an added problem with this man's tongue, as we shall see!

The phrase, *"And they beseech Him to put His Hand upon him,"* refers to their belief that the man would be healed upon this action by Christ. It seems that the fame of Jesus was just as prominent on the eastern side of the Sea of Galilee as on the other side. There will be a day, and soon, that His fame will be the same in the entirety of the Earth.

Concerning the coming Kingdom Age, Isaiah prophesied, *"I will send those ... afar off, who have not heard My fame, neither have seen My Glory; and they shall declare My Glory among the Gentiles"* (Isa. 66:19).

(33) "AND HE TOOK HIM ASIDE FROM THE MULTITUDE, AND PUT HIS FINGERS INTO HIS EARS, AND HE SPIT, AND TOUCHED HIS TONGUE."

The exegesis is:

He probably spat on His finger first, touched the man's tongue, and then put both index fingers in the man's ears; the *"spittle"* represented His Perfect Life.

AN AMAZING HEALING

The phrase, *"And He took him aside from the multitude,"* was done for purpose and reason. More than likely, the Disciples were very near, but the multitude would have been some yards away.

Why did He do this?

Many reasons have been given, but I suspect He did not want the crowd to observe the strange manner in which He would bring about this healing, i.e., by using His spittle. Everything He did always had a reason to it. It may not be understood readily by the onlookers, but it was certainly understood by Him!

The phrase, *"And put His fingers into his ears,"* probably refers to an index finger in each ear.

THE SPITTLE

The phrase, *"And He spit, and touched his tongue,"* is probably the most unusual means of healing recorded in the entirety of the Bible. The order of events seems to be the following:

Jesus first of all had the man to stick out his tongue. Inasmuch as he was deaf, quite possibly Jesus, or one of the Disciples, protruded their own tongue in order that the man may know what Jesus was talking about. Upon understanding and thereby extending his tongue, Jesus spat on His Own finger and touched the man's tongue with the saliva. He then put a finger in each ear.

Why the spittle? As stated, this was most unusual!

We know that whatever He did was never a matter of self-will, but instead the instructions of the Heavenly Father. So, He was directed to do as He did (Jn. 5:19).

LIFE

Everything about the Person of Christ was sacred, even the spittle! Being the Incarnate Son of God, He was the only Perfect Person Who ever lived. As such, there was no taint of corruption, disease, sickness, or that which was unsanitary about Him. So, the spittle that touched this man's tongue was absolutely germ-free. Not only that, it also contained *"Life."*

Shortly before His Crucifixion, He spat on the ground, made clay of the spittle, and then placed it on a blind man's eyes (Jn. 9:6); however, this is the first time, at least recorded, that He touched someone's tongue with His spittle. A little later, spittle would be applied to a man's eyes, which was a different case than that recorded by John (Mk. 8:23).

The incident in John was meant to serve as a symbol of His Incarnation, while this incident is meant to serve in the same manner, but with a difference. As the *"clay"* represented His Incarnation, the *"spittle"* represented His Life. As such, when His Life touched the deformity of this man's tongue, the deformity was instantly healed.

(34) "AND LOOKING UP TO HEAVEN, HE SIGHED, AND SAID UNTO HIM, EPHPHATHA, THAT IS, BE OPENED."

The composition is:

Christ's sighing speaks of the terrible dilemma, due to the Fall, in which man now finds himself.

SIGH

The phrase, *"And looking up to Heaven, He sighed,"* tells us two things:

1. Even though the power was resonant totally within Him, still, He was from Heaven, signifying this is the place of God's Throne and the solution to man's problems. Regrettably, most Preachers presently are not looking up, but rather down toward themselves or others. To be sure, there is no help from that source, only from Heaven.

2. His *"sigh"* spoke of His response to hurting humanity. The *"sigh"* expressed the terrible dilemma in which man now found himself, and also the fact of rebellion against God, incorporating most all of mankind. It further expressed the terrible price that would have to be paid in order to redeem mankind.

The phrase, *"And said unto him, Ephphatha, that is, Be opened,"* expresses the Command.

(35) "AND STRAIGHTWAY HIS EARS WERE OPENED, AND THE STRING OF HIS TONGUE WAS LOOSED, AND HE SPOKE PLAIN."

The diagram is:

The healing of the man symbolizes in the physical that which takes place in the spiritual, as it regards the Salvation of the soul.

THE MIRACLE

The phrase, *"And straightway his ears were opened,"* means they were opened immediately. In other words, his hearing did not come back by degrees, but was instant. One second he could not hear; the next second he could hear everything clearly and plainly. What a wonder this man immediately experienced!

The phrase, *"And the string of his tongue was loosed, and he spoke plain,"* means that at the same time his ears were opened, the deformity of his tongue was also healed! Previously, he had spoken with great difficulty and was very difficult to understand. But now he speaks clearly and plainly, which began instantly.

What a Miracle!

The healing of this man's hearing and speech symbolizes the Redemption of the soul. Undone without God, man cannot hear what God has to say. Moreover, when man speaks of the Lord, he has an *"impediment,"* which means that whatever he does say about the Lord is error, without understanding, and only breeds confusion. Within himself, this situation cannot be rectified.

As Jesus took the initiative with this man, likewise, there must be a revelation by the Spirit before man can be awakened to his need for God. Upon yielding to the petition of that revelation, the Miracle of the New Birth commences, with the individual then being able to *"hear"* when the Lord speaks. And whatever he says about Christ is now understandable and *"plain."*

(36) "AND HE CHARGED THEM THAT THEY SHOULD TELL NO MAN: BUT THE MORE HE CHARGED THEM, SO MUCH THE MORE A GREAT DEAL THEY PUBLISHED IT."

The overview is:

Unfortunately, this is a Commandment given by Christ which was not obeyed.

THE CHARGE

The phrase, *"And He charged them that they should tell no man,"* was done for purpose and reason. The man and those who had witnessed this Miracle were given clear and positive orders that they were not to tell others what had happened. There were possibly many reasons why He commanded this; as previously stated, it was done at the Father's instructions. Still, it probably had to do with the fame of His Ministry.

The crowds were already gargantuan, with the sick and afflicted being brought from every quarter; consequently, the major thrust of Preaching and Teaching the Gospel was becoming lost in the constant prayer for the sick. Also, He desired that no more attention be directed toward Him than could be helped, simply because the situation could get out of hand. In fact, on at least one occasion, they desired to make Him King then and there (Jn. 6:15).

Furthermore, His fame was becoming so widespread that the religious leaders of Jerusalem were becoming more and more incensed. This, I'm sure, also played a part in all of this. No doubt, it was all of these things together which prompted this Command.

THE COMMAND THAT WAS NOT OBEYED

The phrase, *"But the more He charged them, so much the more a great deal they published it,"* means that they did not heed Him the first time, with Him admonishing them again, but still to no avail!

Yes! They certainly should have obeyed Him; however, I suspect it was a Command that was very difficult to heed. No doubt, many people knew this man who had formerly been deaf and partially dumb. Seeing him now perfectly whole would have occasioned much curiosity. It would have been very difficult for him to explain what had happened without telling Who had done it.

So, despite the admonishment of the Lord, *"so much the more a great deal they published it."*

I don't know why I sense the Presence of God so strongly, as I dictate these words, but I do! Possibly, at least to a small degree, I can feel what this man and his friends must have felt after experiencing this Miracle. He had been touched by the Son of the Living God, actually, the same One Who appeared to Moses on Mount Sinai — in reality, the One Who made the world and everything therein. Consequently, what he experienced was far more than just a healing; he experienced a Deliverance. The doors of the prison of deafness in which he had been locked were thrown wide open, and he had gone free!

The touch of the saliva of Christ on his deformed tongue had given him the ability to express what he had experienced and what he was now feeling. How could he help but speak!

I suspect it was a Command the Lord knew would little be obeyed. Perhaps the man's actions were wrong, but I believe his heart was right. The way the Holy Spirit instructs Mark to write this seems to say, at least in some small way, that the Spirit took some delight, or at least was not offended, in the widespread proclamation of this man and his friends.

Perhaps I'm wrong, but I suspect not!

(37) "AND WERE BEYOND MEASURE ASTONISHED, SAYING, HE HAS DONE ALL THINGS WELL: HE MAKES BOTH THE DEAF TO HEAR, AND THE DUMB TO SPEAK."

The composition is:

The entire life of Christ on Earth was one connected, continued manifestation of His lovingkindness.

ASTONISHMENT

The phrase, *"And were beyond measure astonished,"* means they were struck with astonishment, with the words, *"beyond measure,"* adding to their astonishment a double measure, which meant what Jesus had done was beyond comprehension.

The phrase, *"Saying, He has done all things well,"* means they said this, and continued to say it over and over. The phrase, *"He makes both the deaf to hear, and the dumb to speak,"* spoke of the great Miracle which had been performed on this man, and which they knew was from God. Matthew proclaims that the Lord performed a vast number of Miracles in this area, which were not recorded by Mark (Mat. 15:29-31).

To try to describe Christ is impossible. How can imperfect ones, such as ourselves, describe perfection? How can we describe One Who never sinned, not even one time! So, the word *"astonishment"* pretty well describes the response!

There is no one like Jesus!

CHAPTER 8

(1) "IN THOSE DAYS THE MULTITUDE BEING VERY GREAT, AND HAVING NOTHING TO EAT, JESUS CALLED HIS DISCIPLES UNTO HIM, AND SAID UNTO THEM."

The diagram is:

Spiritually speaking, outside of Christ, the world *"has nothing to eat."*

NOTHING TO EAT

The phrase, *"In those days, the multitude being very great,"* speaks of anywhere from 8,000 to 10,000 people, counting women and children. Exactly where Jesus was, Mark does not specify. Wuest says the words, *"In those days,"* indicate Mark's inability or purpose to assign to this incident a precise historical place. I think it is obvious that the rejection of Christ pertained basically to the religious leaders of Israel. In fact, Mark will later say, *"The common people heard Him gladly,"* even as the following incident will prove (Mk. 12:37).

While it is certainly true that many will not follow Christ, even though their shepherds are Godly, still, some will! However, with ungodly leaders, such as those in Israel, the people are left with no shepherd, no one to point the True Way. In fact, Mark had previously stated that Jesus *"was moved with compassion toward them, because they were as sheep not having a shepherd"* (Mk. 6:34). Consequently, Israel would go to her doom, exactly as the apostate Church presently is going to its doom.

The phrase, *"And having nothing to eat,"* has a spiritual, as well as a physical, meaning. The later Text will show that many of these people had been following Christ for three days and nights, sleeping where they could, and eating what little they had brought with them, which had, no doubt, long since run out.

THE TRUE BREAD OF LIFE

As their physical provisions had run out, likewise, the spiritual. Outside of Christ, the world *"has nothing to eat."* He Alone is the True Bread of Life. This is what makes Bible Christianity so different than all else. Bible Christianity is a Person, and that Person is Christ. Christianity, even by the greatest stretch of imagination, is not a system of *"do's"* and *"don'ts,"* which characterizes religions, but is Faith and confidence in a Person. Upon accepting Christ, men do not accept a creed, dogma, theory, doctrine, or system, but instead a Man, *"The Man Christ Jesus."*

The phrase, *"Jesus called His Disciples unto Him, and said unto them,"* proclaims His care and concern for the people. To be sure, He is no less to all who seek unto Him.

(2) "I HAVE COMPASSION ON THE MULTITUDE, BECAUSE THEY HAVE NOW BEEN WITH ME THREE DAYS, AND HAVE NOTHING TO EAT."

The composition is:

The terminology portrays the Love of God; it would be the same as saying, *"My heart goes out to them."*

COMPASSION

The phrase, *"I have compassion on the multitude,"* portrays the Love of God. If one is to notice, the word *"compassion"* is used of Christ constantly, and actually denotes His Character. His entire Life was spent for others; consequently, the example He set is that which the Church should follow. In fact, if we are properly *"in Christ,"* that we will do (Jn. 14:20).

The phrase, *"Because they have now been with Me three days, and have nothing to eat,"* shows their hunger for Him, and His concern for them.

"Nothing to eat" did not mean they had not had anything at all during the past three days and nights, but what little they had, if anything, had long since been exhausted.

(3) "AND IF I SEND THEM AWAY

FASTING TO THEIR OWN HOUSES, THEY WILL FAINT BY THE WAY: FOR DIVERS OF THEM CAME FROM FAR."

The diagram is:

The hunger for Christ overrode even their most powerful physical hunger.

THE NEED OF THE PEOPLE

The idea of this Verse is that the Lord would not send them away without first meeting their need. As well, this is characteristic of Him. When coming to Christ, men receive that for which they come. All of these people who had been sick have been gloriously healed. As well, they had heard the Word of God as they had never heard it before. Now they will receive physical food, and produced by a Miracle, as well!

In effect, the Gospel of Jesus Christ is the whole Gospel for the whole man! Jesus saves, Jesus heals, Jesus Baptizes with the Holy Spirit, and Jesus is coming again. It meets every need, spiritually, physically, financially, and domestically.

The phrase, *"Divers of them came from far,"* characterizes that which will happen in the coming Kingdom Age. In fact, they will come from all over the world at that time, and will have every need met, with prosperity for all!

(4) "AND HIS DISCIPLES ANSWERED HIM, FROM WHENCE CAN A MAN SATISFY THESE MEN WITH BREAD HERE IN THE WILDERNESS?"

The overview is:

The insensibility of the natural heart appears in this Verse. The Disciples apparently learned nothing from the previous feeding of the multitudes, as recorded in Chapter 6.

THE WILDERNESS

The phrase, *"And His Disciples answered Him,"* with an answer which speaks of unbelief. This is the second time that Jesus had fed a great multitude of people, and yet the Disciples seemed to have learned little or nothing from the previous Miracle. This blindness is recorded in Mark 6:5 and 8:17. They seemed to resort, almost to the word, to their previous position, attempting to address the problem in the natural sense.

In effect, the very tenor of their question

NOTES

actually answered it. Jesus furnished bread in the wilderness for the Children of Israel upon their Deliverance from Egypt. This the Disciples knew, and yet they still walked in unbelief. There was a reason for it, which Verse 17 portrays.

(5) "AND HE ASKED THEM, HOW MANY LOAVES HAVE YOU? AND THEY SAID, SEVEN."

The exposition is:

Before, they had *"five"* loaves, which is God's number of Grace, while now they have *"seven,"* which is God's perfect number of completion.

SEVEN LOAVES

Whether the *"seven loaves"* were theirs or that which they had borrowed, as the *"five"* of the previous example, is anyone's guess. At any rate, this is the amount they had, which is almost nothing considering the vast number of people to be fed. However, as in Chapter 6, so here, the lesson to be learned is that we should have Faith in God, not looking at the natural, but the supernatural. Those loaves in the Disciples' hands were nothing, but in the Hands of Christ they will multiply into astounding proportions.

(6) "AND HE COMMANDED THE PEOPLE TO SIT DOWN ON THE GROUND: AND HE TOOK THE SEVEN LOAVES, AND GAVE THANKS, AND BROKE, AND GAVE TO HIS DISCIPLES TO SET BEFORE THEM; AND THEY DID SET THEM BEFORE THE PEOPLE."

The synopsis is:

We will find that the action is not in the loaves, but rather in Him.

IN HIS HANDS

The phrase, *"And He commanded the people to sit down on the ground,"* once again concerns what He is about to do. As well, He now takes charge. In fact, He is always in charge; however, the result of His Authority will now be brought out. They were to *"sit down"* in order to be served!

The phrase, *"And He took the seven loaves,"* represents them now in His Hands, and consequently will become a Miracle. In the Disciples' hands they were nothing. In His Hands, they are everything! The action, as stated, is not in the loaves, but rather in Him.

THANKSGIVING

The phrase, *"And gave thanks,"* is with Him a habit. It should be our habit, as well! He *"gave thanks"* to His Heavenly Father, Who is the Source of all Blessings.

The phrase, *"And gave to His Disciples to set before them,"* seems to proclaim the actual time of the multiplication. The giving was a continual act until all were filled.

The phrase, *"And they did set them before the people,"* presents the Disciples acting as the agents of Christ in serving the people. As then, so now, at least as it is supposed to be.

(7) "AND THEY HAD A FEW SMALL FISHES: AND HE BLESSED, AND COMMANDED TO SET THEM ALSO BEFORE THEM."

The composition is:

The actual number of the fish wasn't given.

THE BLESSING

The phrase, *"And they had a few small fishes,"* does not give the number, only *"a few,"* and small ones, at that! The phrase, *"And He blessed,"* refers to Him giving thanks for these, as He did for the bread. In other words, there seems to have been two *"Blessings."* When we offer the blessing at the table before meals, we do what the Lord did at this time. The phrase, *"And commanded to set them also before them,"* makes it seem as if the fish came a little after the bread, and was passed out accordingly to the people.

(8) "SO THEY DID EAT, AND WERE FILLED: AND THEY TOOK UP OF THE BROKEN MEAT THAT WAS LEFT SEVEN BASKETS."

The diagram is:

Once again, the Lord will perform an astounding Miracle!

THEY WERE FILLED

The phrase, *"So they did eat, and were filled,"* of course speaks of this great Miracle performed, but also speaks of the multiplicity of millions who have partaken of the Bread of Life, who, to be sure, *"were filled."* In Truth, it is the only Bread that will satisfy.

Everything else falls far short. As we have repeatedly stated, Jesus is that Bread.

SEVEN BASKETS

The phrase, *"And they took up of the broken meat that was left seven baskets,"* is in contrast to the twelve of the last Miracle of this nature. As we have stated, *"seven"* speaks of perfection and completion, and rightly typifies all that which the Lord does. It proclaims that the whole world could partake of this Gospel, and to their fill, and there would still be more to receive, if needed. Actually, it is impossible to exhaust the Gospel, or one's understanding of it.

The learning of every philosophy in this world can be exhausted in a short period of time; however, with the Gospel of Jesus Christ, because it is the Living Word of God, if one studied it for an entire lifetime, one still would not even have scratched the surface. Its depth, height, breadth, and width are absolutely inexhaustible.

The *"baskets"* spoken of in this Passage are different than the word *"basket"* used in the record of the other Miracle (Mk. 6:43). Those baskets were small hand-baskets of wickerwork. The baskets here spoken of are much larger baskets, actually large enough to hold a man. This, along with a great deal of other evidence, records the fact that this Miracle of multiplication was different than the other, and took place on a different occasion.

(9) "AND THEY WHO HAD EATEN WERE ABOUT FOUR THOUSAND: AND HE SENT THEM AWAY."

The overview is:

It is not known if the women and children were included in the 4,000 or not. At any rate, it was an astounding Miracle!

FOUR THOUSAND

The phrase, *"And they who had eaten were about four thousand,"* proclaims the fact that whatever needs to be done, Jesus could get it done. Believers need to learn to look to Him more and more, in order for our needs to be met, and irrespective as to what those needs might be. Whatever it was in His earthly Ministry, whether physical, financial, domestic, or spiritual, the need was always met.

What He did then, He can do now, and, in fact, will do, if we will only believe Him.

The phrase, *"And He sent them away,"* but only after they were filled, and in every capacity. The Gospel containing the Words of Life had been spoken unto them, as well as their sick having been healed. Also, they were fed physically. Consequently, nothing was left undone. I think the two incidents respecting the multiplication of the loaves and fishes proclaim to all that Jesus is concerned about our material welfare also!

(10) "AND STRAIGHTWAY HE ENTERED INTO A SHIP WITH HIS DISCIPLES, AND CAME INTO THE PARTS OF DALMANUTHA."

The exposition is:

Dalmanutha was on the western shore of the Sea of Galilee.

THE SHIP

The phrase, *"And straightway He entered into a ship with His Disciples,"* probably refers to the same ship which brought Him. As stated, it probably belonged to Zebedee. It was probably quite large, having ample room for all the Disciples, etc.

The phrase, *"And came into the parts of Dalmanutha,"* has Matthew calling it the *"coast of Magdala,"* which is a few miles south of Capernaum (Mat. 15:39).

(11) "AND THE PHARISEES CAME FORTH, AND BEGAN TO QUESTION WITH HIM, SEEKING OF HIM A SIGN FROM HEAVEN, TEMPTING HIM."

The synopsis is:

They were standing before the Creator of the Ages, Who had the answer to all things, but yet they are so spiritually stupid that they will ply Him only with silly questions.

THE PHARISEES

The phrase, *"And the Pharisees came forth,"* once again proclaims the opposition of the religious leaders of Israel. Matthew said the Sadducees were present, as well (Mat. 16:1).

Why is it that religious leaders are almost always opposed to Christ?

In the first place, there really is no such thing as a religious leader or even a spiritual leader. While it is true that men love to refer to themselves as such, still, the only True Spiritual Leader is Jesus Christ, Who is the Head of the Church (Col. 1:18). Whenever individuals attempt to abrogate the position of Christ, Paul addressed them as *"not holding the Head,"* in other words, taking the position of Christ as the Head of the Church (Col. 2:19).

So, even though the Lord has given, for the benefit of the Church, *"Apostles, Prophets, Evangelists, Pastors, and Teachers,"* still, these Offices pertain to particular Ministries and not designations of authority except in the spiritual realm (Eph. 4:11). Consequently, this means that all the man-made offices in the Church, which many refer to as offices of spiritual leadership, are not recognized as such by God. In many cases, these offices are in direct opposition to the Lord.

These man-devised offices are not necessarily wrong, as long as men understand that they carry no spiritual authority and are administrative only; however, most do not leave it at that, but rather become *"puffed up in their fleshly mind"* (Col 2:18). Most of these individuals who occupy these particular offices, whether Catholic or Protestant, and which includes most of Christianity, claim their position as God-ordained. Therefore, whatever they say must be obeyed. If wrong is committed, they say, it will not be the fault of the people, but the so-called spiritual leader.

CONTROL

In effect, *"control"* is the key word in most religious leadership. These individuals desire to control what is said, what is done, and every aspect of the religious community; consequently, the Headship of Christ is abrogated in almost all of Christianity. The Truth is that multiple millions have died eternally lost because they believed error as propagated by these individuals, be they Catholic or Protestant. It is the same as with the Pharisees and Scribes of old!

In Truth, the Lord demands responsibility of every single individual. This means that every person must learn the Word of God for themselves, and consequently be led by the Spirit accordingly. This is the same for the layman as the Preacher, with none being excluded.

While Preachers of the Gospel, and in various Ministries, are given by the Holy Spirit *"for the perfecting of the Saints, for the Work of the Ministry, for the edifying of the Body of Christ"* (Eph. 4:12), still, every person must know the Word of God well enough that if error is presented, it immediately will be recognized and rejected.

It is sad that men desire to control other men. But many, if not most, surprisingly enough, desire to be controlled. It is somewhat like a select few saying, *"Leave the driving to us."* Many arrive at the erroneous conclusion that if error is presented, it will not be their responsibility, but rather these religious leaders.

RESPONSIBILITY!

While these religious leaders, whoever they may be, will certainly be held accountable, those who look to them also will be responsible! Men love to shift responsibility to others; however, the responsibility for one's soul cannot be shifted to others, with God demanding accountability from each and every one (Ezek. 18:4).

QUESTIONING CHRIST

The phrase, *"And began to question with Him,"* concerns questions designed to get Him to say the wrong thing, which He never did. It is ironical! These men were standing before the Creator of all things; consequently, He knew the answer to anything that could be asked, irrespective of its nature. And yet, they did not have enough spiritual sense to know Who He was; consequently, they plied Him with arcane, inane questions, which really had no bearing on anything.

How many modern Believers miss the Lord, and do so badly, simply because they do not approve of the Messenger? In other words, they don't like God's choice, as it regards the Messenger, thinking it ought to be someone else. As a result, they entirely miss the Message. I have watched that as it regards the Message of the Cross.

THE MESSAGE OF THE CROSS

It is impossible to refute the Message of the Cross Scripturally. While it might be ignored or rejected, it is never rejected on Scriptural grounds. So, upon hearing the Message, if the person is truly Born-Again, they will instinctively know that what they are hearing is Truth. So, Satan takes another tact by casting aspersions and reflections on the Messenger.

How many people went to Hell simply because they didn't personally like Isaiah, Jeremiah, or Ezekiel, or Peter, James, and John, for that matter? How many disliked the Apostle Paul, so they missed entirely the great Message which God gave him, which, in reality, was the Message of the Cross?

This is one of Satan's greatest tricks. The person finds fault with the Messenger, and thinks that justifies them in rejecting the Message. It doesn't!

THE RIGHT MESSAGE, THE RIGHT MESSENGER!

I think it can be said, and without fear of Scriptural contradiction, that if a man (or woman) is proclaiming the right Message, then they themselves are right, as well! The Lord is not going to give the *"right Message"* to someone who is not living right, and who, in fact, is going in a wrong direction himself. The two, the right Message and the wrong person, simply don't go together. The Lord doesn't entrust His great Word to wrong individuals.

The people of Jerusalem didn't like Jeremiah; however, what they truly didn't like was his Message. Many didn't particularly like the Apostle Paul; however, once again, it was his Message that they really didn't like. Millions are in Hell because of these excuses. They justified their actions of refusing the Message because they rejected the Messenger.

A SIGN

The phrase, *"Seeking of Him a sign from Heaven, tempting Him,"* was not the first time such had been engaged. They had already asked from Him a sign from Heaven (Mat. 12:38). In effect, they were questioning Him in respect to His Miracles, wanting to know if He claimed to be the Messiah of Israel. Their questions were not sincere, inasmuch as they had already made up their minds that He was not the Messiah; consequently, what

He was doing had to be of Satan, at least in their thinking.

It is ironical that they would ask for a *"sign,"* when the signs were abundant! His Miracles were in fulfillment of the Prophecies of old. As well, His genealogy was perfect. Actually, there was nothing they could put their finger on respecting wrongdoing on His part, with the exception of some of their silly rules, which He ignored — rules which had no foundation in the Word of God.

So, the words, *"tempting Him,"* mean that their inquiry was not honest, with their sole motive being to snare Him in some way. Of course, they never were able to do so, because His Intelligence was so far beyond theirs. Moreover, His Knowledge of the Word of God far exceeded that of anyone who had ever lived, as would be obvious (Ps. 119:99-100).

WHY DID THE PHARISEES NOT KNOW THAT JESUS WAS THE MESSIAH?

The reasons are varied and many. These men were not right with God and, in fact, did not know God, despite speaking of Him constantly! As such, self-will ruled them, which caused them to twist the Word of God to their own selfish ends. Their self-righteousness would not allow them to admit their need of anything, much less to heed this *"Peasant,"* as He was thought to be!

The same situation presents itself now. Most in the modern Church little know what is of the Lord or not of the Lord. The reason is that they know the Word of God so little, and are so taken up with self-will, and lifted up in their own self-righteousness, because of religious activity, they little know the Spirit of God at all! Consequently, they follow that which is the most showy, ostentatious, entertaining, and boastful. Only those who are truly Spirit-led, which are few, truly follow the Lord and recognize that which is of the Lord. Regrettably, that number is small — very small!

(12) "AND HE SIGHED DEEPLY IN HIS SPIRIT, AND SAID, WHY DOES THIS GENERATION SEEK AFTER A SIGN? VERILY I SAY UNTO YOU, THERE SHALL NO SIGN BE GIVEN UNTO THIS GENERATION."

The structure is:

NOTES

No more signs would be given than what had already been given, which were astounding, to say the least, regarding healings and Miracles, etc.

A WOUNDED SPIRIT

The phrase, *"And He sighed deeply in His spirit,"* actually means He groaned in His spirit. As well, this groan, or *"sigh,"* came from deep within Him. This *"sigh"* pertained to several things:

1. He groaned because of the apostate rejection of His Ministry, knowing that it would bring doom to the rejecters. Jesus is not one of several solutions to the human dilemma; He is, in fact, the only solution. Consequently, to refuse Him is to refuse Life.

2. As well, this rejection came from the religious leaders of Israel, who, entrenched in their ecclesiasticism, later crucified the Lord of Glory, having recognized Him as such, and having seen the attesting Miracles He had performed, even attempting to break the force of these attesting Miracles by attributing them to Satan (Mat. 12:22-24; 21:37-39 — Wuest).

3. His rejection not only spelled doom for the religious leaders and their followers, but also for the entirety of the nation.

4. In this statement, we are given the Heart of God respecting the attitude of rejecters. In other words, it affects Him deeply!

THIS GENERATION

The question, *"And said, Why does this generation seek after a sign?"* speaks, in effect, of their terrible unbelief. In truth, it is impossible for unbelief to see a *"sign,"* even though it be given! Actually, there were *"signs"* galore; therefore, they were without excuse.

The great Miracles performed by Jesus were so astounding that a mere mortal, at least within himself, obviously could not do such things! The blind were made to see, the lame made to walk, the deaf made to hear, lepers were cleansed, and even the dead were raised. Israel and the world had never seen, even remotely, such an outstanding display of the Power of God; therefore, the religious leaders of Israel had either to admit that it was of God or else come up with another reason. Consequently, they said He did these things by the power of Satan.

Of course, such an accusation was preposterous, to say the least! In all of history, Satan had never been known to do such things. Actually, such works of healing and life were in direct contrast to his works of sickness and death. To be sure, men always reject God from a position of stupidity. Even though my statement is blunt, it cannot be explained any other way. Rationally, men cannot reject Christ; therefore, they must do so from a position of absurdity.

So, in effect, Jesus says that *"this generation"* has had more signs than any other generation that has ever been. Why are these not sufficient? Why are they seeking more?

The phrase, *"Verily I say unto you, There shall no sign be given unto this generation,"* says, in effect, *"I will perform the sign of miracles in healing the sick and casting out demons, etc., but I will not give a sign of performing miracles at the demand of apostates, who will not accept their attesting value, even if given!"*

His denial of their demand is powerfully firm; it left absolutely no doubt as to the reason for His refusal. In fact, they later refused to be convinced, even after He had risen from the dead (Acts 3:15).

(13) "AND HE LEFT THEM, AND ENTERING INTO THE SHIP AGAIN DEPARTED TO THE OTHER SIDE."

The exegesis is:

Spiritually speaking, He left them to their doom.

HE LEFT THEM

The phrase, *"And He left them,"* is of far greater import than just geographical location. He, in truth, left them, because of their unbelief, to their doom. Little did they realize that it was to be the most significant departure they would ever know or witness. And yet, these Pharisees were so spiritually dull, so spiritually stupid, that they had no idea what was happening. They were signing the death warrant for their nation.

CHRIST, THE ONLY HOPE

The phrase, *"And entering into the ship again departed to the other side,"* even though speaking of the other side of the lake, portends the darkening gloom which was beginning to settle over Israel. The only hope for this country, as any country, is Christ! However, the religious leadership did not believe this; as a consequence, they opposed Christ greatly!

As the Covenant people, Israel was of far greater significance than any other country. Actually, their rejection of Christ would postpone the material/physical advent of the Kingdom of God; the *"times of the Gentiles"* has been lengthened now for nearly 2,000 years. During this time, the world has been bathed in blood as the result of countless wars; in addition, starvation, disease, and plagues have characterized the planet — all because of Israel's rejection of Christ.

Thank the Lord that this will soon be rectified, with Israel ultimately coming to Christ, but not without Great Tribulation (Jer. 30:7; Rev., Chpts. 6-19).

(14) "NOW THE DISCIPLES HAD FORGOTTEN TO TAKE BREAD, NEITHER HAD THEY IN THE SHIP WITH THEM MORE THAN ONE LOAF."

The structure is:

Now another lesson is about to be taught!

THE DISCIPLES

They were on their way from the western shore to the northeastern side of the Sea of Galilee. The short journey would take approximately six hours. The statement about the *"one loaf"* is given only to set up the coming exchange between Jesus and the Disciples.

The Lord often used mundane things, actually everyday things of life, to teach most valuable lessons, as will here again be done.

(15) "AND HE CHARGED THEM, SAYING, TAKE HEED, BEWARE OF THE LEAVEN OF THE PHARISEES, AND OF THE LEAVEN OF HEROD."

The composition is:

In the Greek Text, it means that He kept on speaking to them, making certain they understood that of which He was speaking.

THE CHARGE

The phrase, *"And He charged them,"* means that as He began His teaching, He, in essence, was saying the same thing over and over, in order that they would finally understand its meaning.

Through His Word, He charges us no less presently! Consequently, each of us must take this to heart just as much as the warning to the Disciples.

To help you, the Reader, more fully understand the Word of God, we would strongly recommend THE EXPOSITOR'S STUDY BIBLE and also THE EXPOSITOR'S NEW TESTAMENT. These are both the King James Version, but designed in the most unique way of any Bibles that have ever been produced, at least according to our knowledge. The expository notes are given after each Scripture, and sometimes after each phrase, or even each word. I think I can say, without fear of contradiction, that I know, beyond the shadow of a doubt, that these Bibles will help you to understand the Word of God to a greater degree than you have previously known. If that, in fact, is true, the worth to you will be incalculable.

TAKE HEED, BEWARE

The phrase, *"Saying, Take heed, beware of the leaven of the Pharisees, and of the leaven of Herod,"* presented not only the dangers of that time, but of the present, as well! Jesus is speaking of false doctrine, for that is what *"leaven"* represents.

The words, *"Take heed"* and *"beware,"* speak of extreme caution, and that the teachings of these particular ones were to be put to the acid test. It speaks of the mind's eye, discerning mentally, understanding what is being said and done. It means that every Believer is to look at Doctrine carefully, inspecting it minutely according to the Word of God, before it is accepted. How so much trouble would be avoided if this were heeded!

Regrettably, most Believers so little know the Word of God that they readily bite into any bait offered. With many, it is almost like a child being mesmerized by the glitter of a brightly-colored object.

LEAVEN

Wuest says that *"leaven"* embodies the principle of fermentation which makes it the symbol of corruption, for fermentation is the result of the Divine curse upon the material universe because of sin. In the Bible, it always speaks of evil in some form, Matthew 13:33 being no exception, for the Kingdom of Heaven here refers to Christendom, in which is the true and the false, the evil and the good.

As well, in I Corinthians 5:5-8, *"leaven"* speaks of malice and wickedness as contrasted to sincerity and truth. In Matthew 16:12, it speaks of evil doctrine in its threefold form of Pharisaism, which is externalism in religion; of Sadduceeism, which is skepticism as to the supernatural and as to the Scriptures; and of Herodianism, which is worldliness.

In effect, the Pharisees taught some things concerning the Law of Moses which were right. This was not to be disregarded, but only so far as they corrupted the Law by their own vain traditions, which were contrary to the Law.

However, the mixture of truth and error, which the Pharisees did, and which is common today, is probably the greatest danger of all. Leaven has this property, that however small it may be in quantity, it spreads its influence rapidly through the mass. Thus, even if only a little spark of heretical doctrine be admitted into the soul, speedily a great flame arises and envelopes the whole man (Bickersteth).

EXAMPLES

As an example, the unscriptural doctrine of Unconditional Eternal Security, as leaven, which it is, has ultimately taken over the entirety of the Denomination(s) which teach and believe it. In other words, this unscriptural doctrine overshadows everything that is taught.

The teaching that one has to speak in tongues to be saved falls into the same category. Even though *"tongues"* are certainly Scriptural, even as Conditional Eternal Security is Scriptural, still, making such a part of Salvation is error, in fulfillment of the little leaven which leavens the whole lump (I Cor. 5:6).

The same can be said for Seventh Day Adventism, respecting the keeping of Saturday, etc. This leaven of the Mosaic Law, which, in effect, was fulfilled in Christ, now overshadows the entirety of that particular Denomination.

At the same time, it does not mean that all who believe these particular erroneous doctrines are lost. For, in Truth, many of them are truly saved. If one truly trusts Christ for one's Salvation, one is saved, irrespective of other types of error. Nevertheless, if allowed to remain, which proclaims a failure to heed the admonitions of the Holy Spirit as given in the Word of God, ultimately the Christian life will be seriously hindered and weakened. The Holy Spirit always leads one toward Truth and Christ (Jn. 16:13-14).

The Holy Spirit can never bless or anoint error. To be sure, He will, at times, bless and anoint us, even though error is present, but such is done because of a sincere heart. But, He never blesses the error, as should be obvious. Furthermore, His help and anointing will gradually subside if we fail to heed His admonitions respecting our walk in proper Scriptural Light.

TRUTH

The greatest sign of Truth being properly lived and preached is the fruit that it bears (Jn. 15:1-2). If the Word of God is properly practiced and taught, it will bring forth the Fruit of changed lives and Christian growth. If this is little present or not present at all, it is a sure sign that one of two things is taking place:

1. The Truth is not being preached, or else it is a mixture of Truth and error.
2. The Truth is being preached, but with no Anointing of the Holy Spirit, a practice which is all too prevalent, especially at this present time (I Thess. 1:5).

As is obvious, the Ministry of Christ brought forth much Fruit, even though it also garnered much opposition. The same could be said for the Apostle Paul. To be sure, the same holds true for all who truthfully proclaim the Gospel of Christ. That which is corrupted with *"leaven"* will greatly oppose that which is True.

The doctrine of the *"leaven,"* as it is taught throughout the Bible, also shoots down the theory propagated by the world and much of the Church, that man is getting better and better, with the world ultimately to be ushered into a utopian paradise.

Even though Bible Christianity has had a tremendous positive effect on the Earth, still, most of humanity rejects the Gospel of Jesus Christ; consequently, and despite thousands of years of education and technological advancement, especially in the last 100 years, man is not getting better, but rather worse. Despite intellectualism, the evil heart of man is not changed, actually because the *"leaven process"* is getting worse; and, were it not for the Second Coming of Christ, man would ultimately destroy himself and the world.

THE POLITICAL MESSAGE

The *"political message,"* as propagated by much of the modern Church, flies in the face of the leavening of the whole, as taught in the Word of God. The various cultures of the world are not and, in fact, will not be, Christianized, with the world getting better and better, ultimately ushering in the Millennium. As stated, such teaching flies in the face of the Word of God.

The sin problem cannot be educated out of people, neither can proper politics curtail the terrible problem of evil. Only the Coming of Jesus Christ, which will be in great power, will solve this problem. When He comes, it will not be to a world that has been Christianized, but instead to a world that is on the brink of total destruction. The account is given in Revelation, Chapter 19.

As we've already explained, the *"leaven of the Pharisees"* was the mixture of tradition with the True Word of God. As a consequence, there was not much of the True Word of God left, with the leaven, as is the manner of leaven, having taken over the whole.

The *"leaven of Herod"* concerned the Herodians, and spoke of worldliness. This party followed Herod, with some even claiming that he was the Messiah, and did all within its power to accommodate Rome, even at the expense of compromising the entirety of the Word of God.

Both, the *"leaven of the Pharisees"* and the *"leaven of Herod,"* are also prominent in the modern Church. So the admonition of Christ to His Disciples so long ago was an admonition to us, as well!

(16) "AND THEY REASONED AMONG THEMSELVES, SAYING, IT IS BECAUSE WE HAVE NO BREAD."

The diagram is:

At this stage, the Disciples had not the slightest idea what Jesus was talking about.

THE BREAD

The phrase, *"And they reasoned among themselves,"* concerned them discussing back and forth among themselves what He had said about the leaven. As the next phrase shows, they had not the slightest idea what He was speaking about.

The phrase, *"It is because we have no bread,"* concerns them having their minds on the *"one loaf,"* thinking He was upset because they had not brought more. His statement was spiritual, while their thinking and conversation were the opposite.

I'm afraid we presently, because of the same problem, miss so much of what the Holy Spirit tells us. Our thinking is too much in the carnal realm, and not enough in the spiritual.

The erroneous statement, that some *"are so spiritually minded that they are of no earthly use,"* has taken root in many Christian lives. In Truth, it is impossible to be too spiritually minded. Paul said, *"For to be carnally minded is death; but to be Spiritually minded is life and peace"* (Rom. 8:6).

One of the greatest truths they would ever hear was being given to them, but to this point, they missed it altogether!

(17) "AND WHEN JESUS KNEW IT, HE SAID UNTO THEM, WHY REASON YE, BECAUSE YE HAVE NO BREAD? PERCEIVE YE NOT YET, NEITHER UNDERSTAND? HAVE YE YOUR HEART YET HARDENED?"

The overview is:

They were thinking too much in the physical, not at all in the spiritual.

FAULTY REASON

The phrase, *"And when Jesus knew it,"* means, *"When Jesus perceived it"*! It was not so much a matter of Him overhearing the Disciples, but instead that the Spirit of God witnessed their confusion to His Spirit.

The question, *"He said unto them, Why reason ye, because ye have no bread?"* concerns the first of nine questions which will be asked. In fact, the Jews were very strict about the kind of leaven to be used in bread, of which the Pharisees, no doubt, had much to say. The amount of leaven in the one loaf they had may have been on their minds, in addition to the fact that the supply of bread was not ample.

Their thoughts concerning not having enough bread, to which His question pointed, was of far greater import than meets the eye. Not only were the Disciples forgetting His Miracle-working Power, but they also wanted this multiplication of bread to springboard Jesus to the Throne of Israel as King, with Rome consequently being overcome. The entirety of their perception was wrong, as He will later say.

UNDERSTANDING

The question, *"Perceive ye not yet, neither understand?"* concerns a wrong understanding of what the Miracles of the multiplication were all about. As a result of them misunderstanding, which was a total misconception of the Plan and Will of God, neither did they understand His statement concerning the *"leaven of the Pharisees,"* etc.

Once again, we see the leaven at work concerning their understanding, which, if not corrected, will ultimately corrupt the whole of their thinking. It is like a rotten apple in a barrel of good apples. The good apples do not make whole the bad one; but the bad one will definitely corrupt all the others, unless it is removed.

This is a lesson we should well learn. As we have repeatedly stated, if erroneous doctrine is allowed to continue in our thinking, our understanding concerning what Truth we do know will ultimately be affected. Actually, it is impossible to have any leaven at all, no matter how small, without it ultimately corrupting the whole, unless it is removed.

THE HARDENED HEART

The question, *"Have ye your heart yet hardened?"* goes back to Mark 6:52. Because this subject is so very important and affects so many people, please allow us to repeat what was previously given in commentary on Mark 6:52.

The Disciples misunderstood the reason for the multiplication of the loaves and fishes. The did not understand that Jesus, by doing this, was, in essence, telling the world that He was the Bread of Life, and that He Alone could satisfy the spiritual hunger of the human family. They saw the multiplication of the loaves and fishes as a springboard to power. He would be made King, and Israel would once again rule the world. Consequently, their thinking, which was contrary to the Will of God, hardened their hearts. The product of self-will, which this was, is always the hardened heart.

This means that every single individual who does not follow the Word of God, but who instead puts his own gloss on it, as the Pharisees of old, concludes with a hardened heart. Regrettably, almost all of the modern Church falls into this category.

As self-will intrudes, the heart ceases to be pliable in the Hands of the Lord and becomes hardened toward God. For one to be tender toward God, to be able to hear His Voice, and to be able to be led accordingly, one must be in the Will of God, which will always be according to the Word of God.

(18) "HAVING EYES, SEE YE NOT? AND HAVING EARS, HEAR YE NOT? AND DO YE NOT REMEMBER?"

The exposition is:

The statement of Christ refers to spiritual eyes and ears they were not using.

SPIRITUAL EYES AND SPIRITUAL EARS

The question, *"Having eyes, see ye not?"* pertained to spiritual eyes they were not using. Once again, they were seeing things in the carnal, which was a result of self-will. They were not seeing things in the spiritual sense; most today follow in their train.

The question, *"And having, ears, hear ye not?"* is the same as the *"eyes."* As they could not *"see"* correctly, neither could they *"hear"* correctly.

The question, *"And do ye not remember?"* proclaims their understanding, regarding what had happened regarding the multiplication of the loaves, as being faulty. So, they *"saw"* wrong; they *"heard"* wrong; they *"understood"* wrong!

When one considers that these men to whom Jesus was speaking were His chosen Disciples, who had the privilege of being under His tutelage constantly, one begins to understand how absolutely deadly this *"leaven"* actually is. Thank the Lord some personal problems, such as Peter's denial, along with the Day of Pentecost, would help cure these problems.

(19) "WHEN I BROKE THE FIVE LOAVES AMONG FIVE THOUSAND, HOW MANY BASKETS FULL OF FRAGMENTS TOOK YE UP? THEY SAY UNTO HIM. TWELVE."

The synopsis is:

Jesus will now draw their attention back to the Miracle of the multiplication of the loaves.

TWELVE BASKETS

Jesus will now direct the attention of the Disciples back to the first multiplication of the loaves and the fish by reminding them that they had *"twelve baskets"* of fragments left over, even after feeding multiple thousands of people. Therefore, the amount of bread they had in the boat should have been of no consequence to them.

Just how much do we act in the same fashion presently?

We get all concerned about a current problem, which, at times, is relatively insignificant, completely forgetting the many times in the recent past that the Lord has done great things for us. So, we shouldn't be too hard on the Disciples!

(20) "AND WHEN THE SEVEN AMONG FOUR THOUSAND, HOW MANY BASKETS FULL OF FRAGMENTS TOOK YE UP? AND THEY SAID, SEVEN."

The synopsis is:

We find here that the Lord uses both incidents; but, regrettably, they didn't seem to properly grasp the significance of those two mighty Miracles.

BASKETS FULL OF FRAGMENTS

As He reminded them of the first Miracle of multiplication, He now reminds them of the second Miracle. In other words, if one was not enough to prove His Power, surely two were enough. So, they had no reason to misunderstand His statements regarding the *"leaven of the Pharisees,"* etc., thinking He was speaking of their forgetting to bring more bread.

Why is it that we so easily forget the past, regarding what the Lord has done for us? I think the greatest reason is that we become overwhelmed by present circumstances, with what seems to be no way out.

Regarding my personal experiences, even after all of these years, I seem to be just now coming to the place, and only timidly it seems, of the knowledge that the Lord will supply the need, irrespective of the size of the need. The impossibilities (in the natural) still seem to overwhelm me, after a fashion. And yet, deep down in my heart, I know the Lord is going to meet that need, whatever it might be.

SATURDAY MORNING

As I dictate these notes in November of 2004, my mind goes back to a Saturday morning, approximately four or five years ago. I had awakened before daylight, with over $1,000,000 of bills pressing on my mind, and not knowing how in the world they could be paid.

I went into the bathroom to take a shower, and switched on SonLife Radio. And then it happened! For well over an hour, the oppressive powers of darkness had, it seems, screamed at me for the entire period of time. But the moment the Spirit of God came, the spirit of oppression instantly left. And then the Lord began to speak to my heart.

He said: *"I have brought you through demons, through Satan himself, through troubles, through problems, through false brethren, and through all types of difficulties. You don't think I'm going to drop you now, do you?"*

I stood there weeping and praising God, and, Oh Yes, somehow the bills were paid.

Any number of times since then, facing the same type of difficulties, the Lord has brought me back to that Saturday morning, and renewed it to my mind, in order to let me know that what He then said also holds now.

(21) "AND HE SAID UNTO THEM, HOW IS IT THAT YE DO NOT UNDERSTAND?"

The exegesis is:

The question would have been better translated, *"Do you yet not understand?"* There is a hint in the Greek Text that they did, in fact, finally begin to understand; actually,

NOTES

Matthew tells us this was the case (Mat. 16:12).

DO WE UNDERSTAND?

They now know that He was not speaking of earthly leaven, or earthly bread, but rather Spiritual Doctrine.

It is the business of the Holy Spirit to so renew our minds that we think like Christ at all times. Admittedly, in this body of flesh, it's not easy to do that, but yet it can be done.

Everything that comes our way, every problem, every difficulty, every circumstance, must be thought of in the sense of the Promises of God.

I firmly believe our being brought to this place is predicated on the proper object of our Faith, which must be the Cross. From experience, I personally believe that properly understanding the Cross provides an illumination that nothing else can give. In fact, this is the purpose of the strange vision of the Throne of God given to John the Beloved, in which he saw the slain lamb with seven horns and seven eyes (Rev. 5:6). The *"seven eyes"* represent the total and perfect illumination, all tendered by the Holy Spirit, but yet totally connected to the slain lamb.

Even as we've already stated regarding commentary on a previous Chapter, the *"seven horns"* represent total dominion over Satan and all the powers of darkness, and I'm speaking of dominion on our part, all made possible by the slain lamb. As just stated, the *"seven eyes"* speak of total illumination, which keeps the Believer from false doctrine, instantly pointing it out, which, before a proper understanding of the Cross, was not so simple.

(22) "AND HE COMES TO BETHSAIDA: AND THEY BRING A BLIND MAN UNTO HIM, AND BESOUGHT HIM TO TOUCH HIM."

The structure is:

The place probably refers to Bethsaida Julias, which was situated on the northeast shore of the Sea of Galilee.

THE BLIND MAN

The phrase, *"And He comes to Bethsaida, and they bring a blind man unto Him,"* represents the fact that they believed that Jesus could open this man's eyes, which He most definitely could.

I think it's impossible for us to fully understand and comprehend such power. If it is to be noticed, even though the Pharisees and the Scribes hated him, at least most of them, still, they never questioned the veracity of His healings and Miracles. They claimed that He was doing these things by the power of Satan, but they never questioned the validity of the Miracles.

How could they? The evidence was obvious for all to see.

The phrase, *"And besought Him to touch him,"* seems to indicate that they imagined that healing could not come forth from Christ except by actual contact. Therefore, they will plead with Him to *"touch Him."*

Jesus always met anyone and everyone according to their Faith. Whatever their faith called for (in this instance, Him touching the man), that's what He would do.

(23) "AND HE TOOK THE BLIND MAN BY THE HAND, AND LED HIM OUT OF THE TOWN; AND WHEN HE HAD SPIT ON HIS EYES, AND PUT HIS HANDS UPON HIM, HE ASKED HIM IF HE SAW OUGHT."

The exegesis is:

Jesus had already placed a curse on this city because of their refusal to repent; consequently, He would not perform another Miracle in its confines (Mat. 11:21).

THE CURSE

The phrase, *"And He took the blind man by the hand, and led him out of the town,"* was done for reason. As stated, due to so many Miracles being performed in this city, and still the city refusing to repent, Jesus, in essence, placed a curse upon the town (Mat. 11:21). Light refused is light cancelled.

This means that America and Canada just possibly might be entering into the most dangerous period of their existence as nations. One could say, without fear of contradiction, that more Gospel has been proclaimed in these two countries than possibly any other country or countries in the world. As a result, America and Canada have been blessed in an unprecedented way.

And yet, both nations are fastly hardening themselves against God. No longer do they know or realize the Source of their blessings. They are as Israel of old!

NOTES

Why?

Peter said (which is the answer), *"For the time is come that Judgment must begin at the House of God: and if it first begin at us, what shall the end be of them that obey not the Gospel of God?"* (I Pet. 4:17).

The horror of September, 11, 2001 (9/11), with nearly 4,000 American lives snuffed out, was, in effect, a declaration of war by the Muslim religion against Christianity. Our politicians may disavow such a statement; however, anyway one looks at the thing, one has to come to the conclusion, at least if they are truthful, that the war we are presently fighting is a religious war.

Two Preachers, both well known, were on one of the Television Networks almost immediately after 9/11. They were asked if the Lord had done this thing, or rather allowed it, against America. Both Preachers chimed in, claiming that the Lord did allow the 9/11 declaration of war, and the reason was because of the liberal abortion laws in this country, plus the problem of homosexuality and gay marriages, so-called.

I beg to disagree!

While these two sins mentioned are grievous, wicked, filthy, and diabolical, that is not the reason the Lord allowed such to happen against our nation. The reason is the Church! I have just quoted the Scripture to you, where Peter said, *"Judgment must begin at the House of God."*

Pure and simple, the Lord allowed this thing against the United States simply because of the spiritual condition of the Church. It has never been worse, at least since the Reformation.

The reason that Jesus placed a curse upon Bethsaida is not because of the alcoholics in the city, or such like, but rather because of the spiritual condition of the Church, so to speak. That was the problem then, and it is the problem now!

For the nation to have Revival, the Church must first have Revival!

REFORMATION

However, I'm concerned that before the Church can have Revival, that it first must have a Reformation. In other words, we must get our doctrine straight, which means that the Church must come back to the Cross. That and that alone will get the Church ready for Revival. Nothing else will!

THE UNUSUAL METHOD OF HEALING

The phrase, *"And when He had spit on his eyes, and put His Hands upon him, He asked him if he saw ought,"* has, in the Greek Text, that He kept on asking him. This is the second time that Jesus had done this thing, and I refer to the spittle (Mk. 7:33). The first concerned a malformed tongue of a man which caused an impediment in his speech, with this case being blindness.

The cause for the *"spittle"* is the same as in the previous incident. The saliva, which came from a Perfect Body, which had no taint of sin about it and was, therefore, perfectly free of germs, was a symbol of His Life, which was perpetual and eternal.

Exactly how the spittle was applied to his eyes, Mark does not say. He could have spat on His Fingers, as He probably did before, and then applied it to the man's eyes. Or He could have spat fully on his eyes, which seems to be the case.

Incidentally, He put His Hands upon the man, exactly as the friends of the blind man had requested.

(24) "AND HE LOOKED UP, AND SAID, I SEE MEN AS TREES, WALKING."

The composition is:

The Greek Text actually says, *"I see men; for I behold them as trees, walking,"*; the word *"walking"* refers to the men and not to the trees. There seemed to be a mist of sorts over his eyes, which disfigured things.

A MIRACLE

It is impossible for us to fully comprehend such Miracle-working Power as the opening of blinded eyes; however, the Miracle is of even greater magnitude than that of which we have mentioned.

Every Miracle performed by Christ not only dealt with the issue at hand (in this case, the blindness of the man), but also dealt with a great spiritual problem. In this case, it speaks not only of man's spiritual blindness, but the weight of the emphasis focuses on the change that takes place in a life and the fact that it is a progressive work,

NOTES

hence, Jesus putting His Hands on the man's eyes again.

(25) "AFTER THAT HE PUT HIS HANDS AGAIN UPON HIS EYES, AND MADE HIM LOOK UP: AND HE WAS RESTORED, AND SAW EVERY MAN CLEARLY."

The composition is:

This is the only incident in the four Gospels of Jesus dealing with someone the second time in this fashion. Why did Jesus have to lay His Hands on him a second time? The next Verse possibly tells us.

SYMBOLIC OF A PROGRESSIVE WORK

The phrase, *"After that He put His Hands again upon his eyes, and made him look up,"* addresses the progressive work of Sanctification carried out in the lives of all True Believers. It is not something that happens immediately, at least in practice, but that which is, as stated, progressive.

One of the problems with believing man is that he did not know just exactly how lost we was; presently, he does not know just how saved he now is.

The Text does not lend any credence to the idea that the person is only partially saved when they come to Christ. The moment an individual accepts Christ, they are just as saved as they will ever be, which means totally, completely, perfectly, and absolutely. However, as Jesus *"put His Hands again upon the man's eyes, and made him look up,"* such has to be done again and again with us in our progressive walk. It is not that the first touch was insufficient, but it's that we keep slipping away from the true path of Faith, which then requires another touch, so to speak.

RESTORATION

The phrase, *"And he was restored, and saw every man clearly,"* records the place and position to which the Holy Spirit desires to bring us and, in fact, will bring us, if we will only cooperate with Him. The *"restoration"* is to be complete, until we can come to the place that we *"see clearly."*

The Holy Spirit Alone can carry out this great work within our lives, and this is where the problem materializes. We keep trying to sanctify ourselves. In fact, every fad which comes down the spiritual pike, and which takes the Church by storm, is nothing but another effort by Satan to push us to the place of trying to sanctify ourselves. As soon as one fad dies, another rises to take its place. As stated, each fad is, it seems, eagerly accepted by the Church.

However, if it is to be noticed, the Message of the Cross, through which alone the Holy Spirit works, which is the only way that the Sanctification process can be enjoined and carried out (Rom. 6:3-14; 8:1-2, 11), is looked at with precious little excitement. And yet, every single thing the Believer needs is found exclusively in the Cross, for it was there that Jesus paid the total price. And it is there, consequently, by and through which the Holy Spirit works.

(26) "AND HE SENT HIM AWAY TO HIS HOUSE, SAYING, NEITHER GO INTO THE TOWN, NOR TELL IT TO ANY IN THE TOWN."

The diagram is:

This refers to the fact, as stated, that Jesus had placed a curse on this town for their refusal to repent (Mat. 11:21); due to this, Christ seemed unwilling to give Bethsaida any more evidence of the visitation of God. This could well be the reason why Jesus had to lay His Hands on the man a second time. The curse had been pronounced and the die cast; consequently, it was as if the door was shut.

INSTRUCTIONS

The phrase, *"And He sent him away to his house,"* implies that he was not a native to Bethsaida Julias. The phrase, *"Saying, Neither go into the town, nor tell it to any in the town,"* refers, as we have mentioned, to the curse He had placed on this town for their refusal to repent. He had said, *"Woe unto you, Bethsaida! for if the mighty works, which were done in you, had been done in Tyre and Sidon, they would have repented long ago in sackcloth and ashes"* (Mat. 11:21). Due to this, Christ seemed unwilling to give Bethsaida any more evidence of the visitation of God.

Many have claimed that the Lord led the man outside of town in order to avoid the crowds, etc. However, it is very doubtful that was the case. It was more likely because of the pronounced Judgment. The town had seen a display of the Power of God as only a few others had seen, namely, Capernaum and Chorazin. Still, all refused to repent, with all consequently being cursed.

THE CURSE

The man not being healed instantly when Christ first laid hands on him certainly was not because of a lack of power on the part of Christ, but rather that no more power would be displayed in this place; consequently, the man had to be led out of town and, even then, hands laid on him twice. As well, Jesus telling the man not to even relate the account of his healing to the people in Bethsaida tells us at least two things:

1. No more Light was to be given to them, because they had firmly rejected that already given.

2. If the man had said anything about it to the occupants, more than likely they would have ridiculed the Miracle. When men resist the Holy Spirit, He, by a just Judgment, abandons them to Wrath.

UNBELIEF

The mother of all evils is *"unbelief,"* and it has a mysterious power; consequently, and as stated here, it is useless to give evidence to unbelief. Had Jesus given the most overwhelming proofs of His Messiahship, they would not have believed upon Him, and for the reason that Faith waits for Repentance and the sense of sin against God, for the need of pardon and for a desire to escape from the defilement of sin.

Inasmuch as Faith is the foundation of the Gospel, Jesus threw the responsibility upon the cities of Israel, calling upon them to repent and believe the Gospel. His whole mission rested upon this moral foundation; and the satisfactory evidence He gave of His Deity could only be perceived by those who had spiritual eyesight. The demonstration that the Scribes demanded had no value; it would not have affected the heart and produced Repentance, even if done!

Is it possible that there are cities in America and Canada, or elsewhere in the world, for that matter, which have been cursed by God, and will, consequently, receive no further visitation?

SPIRITUAL BLINDNESS

As a spiritual lesson derived from this episode, Bede, the great Scholar of long ago, says, *"Christ teaches us how great is the spiritual blindness of man, which only by degrees, and by successive stages, can come to the light of Divine knowledge."*

Bickersteth says, *"The experiences of this blind man in gradually recovering his eyesight show as in a parable the stages of the spiritual change from absolute darkness to glimmering light, and thence to bright and clear vision."*

Back to the mysterious power of unbelief, such cannot be registered until Light is first given and rejected. Richards says, *"At heart, unbelief is staggering back from God's Revelation of Himself, refusing to respond, as Abraham, with trust"* (Rom. 4:20). Thus, unbelief exhibits a sinful heart *"that turns away from the Living God"* (Heb. 3:12).

LIGHT

If Light is rejected, darkness can be the only result! However, it is a darkness that ever deepens. While it is possible for one to be pulled back from unbelief, it can only be done by the Power of the Risen Christ.

Paul Rader experienced that Power.

It is said that he had a great experience with the Lord as a young Preacher, winning many souls and seeing great success; however, things happened which brought a bitterness to his soul, resulting in Him turning his back on God. He entertained great depths of sin, but with the greatest sin of all being that of unbelief, which disavowed even the fact of God's existence.

But, Miracle of miracles, the Holy Spirit was able to reach through the gloom of that stygian night and awakened the Light, though covered, that still resided in his soul. To be sure, it is not easy at all to turn out the Light that God has hung up in one's soul since infancy.

By the Power of God, he was brought back, and performed an even greater work for God. As well, he wrote the song:

"Only believe, only believe,
"All things are possible, only believe,
"Only believe, only believe,
"All things are possible, only believe!"

In the depths of his failure, he had had great difficulty in believing, because unbelief, with its mysterious power, destroys every vestige of Faith; however, even a shred of Faith is stronger than all unbelief. Consequently, Paul Rader was brought back to Jesus. Now the reason for this song becomes all the more obvious!

(27) "AND JESUS WENT OUT, AND HIS DISCIPLES, INTO THE TOWNS OF CAESAREA PHILIPPI: AND BY THE WAY HE ASKED HIS DISCIPLES, SAYING UNTO THEM, WHOM DO MEN SAY THAT I AM?"

The overview is:

The question asked by Christ constitutes Who Jesus really was, and the drawing out of the Disciples, as to Who they thought He was. The Greek Text says, *"He kept on asking,"* meaning that the question so startled them that, at first, they did not answer.

REJECTION

The phrase, *"And Jesus went out, and His Disciples,"* represents Jesus leaving Bethsaida, but in a much greater way than a mere physical departure. He left it spiritually, even as He had left the *"parts of Dalmanutha"* (Mk. 8:13). Even though the Text speaks of a geographical change, still, it has, as stated, great spiritual implications, as well! They had rejected Him, so He *"went out"*!

The phrase, *"Into the towns of Caesarea Philippi,"* places Him about 40 miles north of the Sea of Galilee, and about 40 miles south of Damascus. By the use of the word *"towns,"* He probably did not go into Caesarea Philippi proper, but rather to the towns which were nearby.

Scholars have suggested that as the name *"Jesus"* is here expressly mentioned, it refers to something very important about to be narrated, which closely concerned His Disciples, because they are mentioned, as well!

This is approximately six months before His Crucifixion. If one is to notice, Jesus spent more and more time away from Galilee and Judaea proper, because of the tremendous opposition. By now, He was welcome in very few Synagogues. At least as far as Judaea was concerned, the people were threatened with excommunication from the Synagogue if they followed Him (Jn. 9:22).

Despite His Miracles, despite His Teaching and Preaching, which were the most enlightening that man had ever heard, and despite the fact that He was the Messiah, the Son of the Living God, He was no longer welcome in their Churches, so to speak.

Were He on Earth presently, and under the same circumstances, I suspect He would be no better received. In Truth, He is not welcome in most Churches at present. While it is true that He is spoken of and talked about constantly, still, if there is the slightest manifestation of His Power through the Holy Spirit, such is instantly stopped!

While most Preachers and Priests speak favorably of Him, still, if they truly loved Him, and thereby served Him, He would not be a stranger in their Churches.

WHO IS JESUS?

The question, *"And by the way He asked His Disciples, saying unto them, Whom do men say that I am?"* constitutes Who He really was, and the drawing out of the Disciples as to Who they thought He was.

The Greek Text says, *"He kept on asking,"* meaning that the question so startled them that, at first, they did not answer.

The answer to the question as to Who He actually is constitutes the entirety of His Ministry. If the Disciples had a misunderstanding about this great Truth, that Jesus is God manifested in the flesh, then they would misunderstand everything else, as well.

(28) "AND THEY ANSWERED, JOHN THE BAPTIST; BUT SOME SAY, ELIAS (Elijah); AND OTHERS, ONE OF THE PROPHETS."

The exposition is:

They were answering the question He had asked, concerning Who Israel thought He was. Even though the answers were strange, yet this reflected the thinking of much of Israel at that particular time.

THE MISDIRECTION OF ISRAEL

The answers that many in Israel gave at that time concerning Christ proclaim the fact that they really did not believe, at least as a whole, that He was the Messiah.

NOTES

Concerning this, Bickersteth says, *"The great body of them were offended at His poverty and humility; for they thought that the Messiah would appear among them with royal state as a temporal King."* So, if He was not the Messiah, they reasoned, then He must be one of the great Prophets of old risen from the dead. Even though the Sadducees denied a Resurrection, the great body of the Jews believed in it.

Probably most of them thought He was Elijah, insomuch that Elijah had not died, but had been translated. As well, Malachi had prophesied that this Prophet would return. Some thought, therefore, that Elijah had returned, and that the Lord was Elijah the Prophet.

Their unbelief stemmed, in effect, from the fact that they would not believe the Word of God. The people were not altogether to blame for this situation, inasmuch as the religious leaders of Israel gave no credence at all to Biblical interpretation by the peasantry, with whatever they thought being passed off as inconsequential. The people were encouraged strongly to look to these so-called great scholars, who would interpret the Bible for them; consequently, most of the common people in Israel of that day simply did not know the Bible.

(29) "AND HE SAID UNTO THEM, BUT WHOM SAY YE THAT I AM? AND PETER ANSWERED AND SAID UNTO HIM, YOU ARE THE CHRIST."

The synopsis is:

Peter actually said, *"You are the Messiah,"* because that's what the Word *"Christ"* actually means; it was the Great Confession.

BUT WHOM DO YOU SAY THAT I AM?

The question, *"And He said unto them, But Whom say ye that I am?"* concerns the greatest question that anyone could be asked! Actually, it is a question that all must ultimately answer.

Hundreds of millions presently say that He was a Prophet, but no more than a Prophet, consequently, denying His Deity. Others say He was a great Man, and a Miracle-worker, but He was somewhat deluded respecting Himself being the Son of God. Of course, it is difficult to understand how someone could be great and, at the same time, a liar!

Actually, very few presently deny that He actually lived, because the evidence of His Life and Ministry is overwhelming; therefore, at least by most, He is passed off as merely a Great Man among other great men.

WHAT THE WORLD THINKS OF CHRIST

Years ago, I happened to read an article in Reader's Digest regarding the ten greatest men who ever lived. Jesus Christ was mentioned as One of the ten. Possibly, the editors of this magazine felt very kindly toward themselves for including Jesus in this august group; however, what they did was tantamount to blasphemy.

While it is certainly true that Jesus was a Man, still, as Peter proclaimed, He is much more, actually the Son of the Living God. He is Emmanuel, God manifest in the flesh. Even though He had a beginning as Man, as God He had no beginning, having always existed, and will always exist. He said, *"I am Alpha and Omega, the beginning* (of all things) *and the end* (of all things), *the first and the last"* (Rev. 22:13).

YOU ARE THE CHRIST

The phrase, *"And Peter answered and said unto Him, You are the Christ,"* is the English spelling of the Greek word, *"Christos,"* which means *"The Anointed One."* In the English, it is translated *"Messiah."* Some scholars feel that Peter actually said, *"You are the Messiah,"* with the word *"Christos"* translated accordingly. In Psalms 2:2, the kings of the Earth are said to take counsel against the Lord and His Anointed, the word *"Anointed"* being *"Messiah"* in the original.

Wuest says, "The word designates that King Whom God will provide for Israel, Who will occupy the Throne of David forever."

It should also be noticed that Mark omits the Great Blessing pronounced by the Lord upon Peter for this confession; however, Matthew did record it (Mat. 16:17-19). This is probably because Peter related this account to Mark; Peter probably was not comfortable in relating such Blessing, although He would relate in full the rebuke that Christ gave him

NOTES

(Vs. 33). Again, such proclaims the fact that the boastful Peter no longer exists, but only the Peter of humility!

(30) "AND HE CHARGED THEM THAT THEY SHOULD TELL NO MAN OF HIM."

The structure is:

The *"charge"* here given relates the fact that it was now obvious that Israel had rejected Him; consequently, there was no point in projecting the issue further.

THE CHARGE

The word *"charged"* is a strong one, meaning that He admonished or charged them sharply. It is almost a threatening tone. The phrase, *"That they should tell no man of Him,"* relates the fact that it was now obvious that Israel did not want Him; consequently, there was no point in further projecting the point. He was very concerned about His Disciples; He, therefore, made sure they knew Who He was. At all costs, they must not be pulled under by unbelief. Of course, the horror of the Crucifixion, which was only a few months away, would try their Faith to the fullest; however, the Resurrection, with the exclaimed, *"He's alive again,"* would instantly clear that up.

(31) "AND HE BEGAN TO TEACH THEM, THAT THE SON OF MAN MUST SUFFER MANY THINGS, AND BE REJECTED OF THE ELDERS, AND OF THE CHIEF PRIESTS, AND SCRIBES, AND BE KILLED, AND AFTER THREE DAYS RISE AGAIN."

The exegesis is:

The word *"rejected"* means that the religious leaders of Israel put Jesus to the test. He did not, however, meet their specifications. He was not the kind of a Messiah the Jews wanted. They wanted a military leader who would liberate them from the yoke of Rome, not a Saviour Who would free them from their bondage of sin.

TEACHING

The phrase, *"And He began to teach them,"* proclaims an explanation as to what was to happen, despite the fact that He was the Messiah. Consequently, Peter's confession, although correct, was not given in the correct posture. Peter, as the others, thought surely that the Throne of David would be occupied now. This is proven by Peter's rebuke of Him in the following Verse. Consequently, He begins to prepare them!

THE SUFFERING SAVIOUR

The phrase, *"That the Son of Man must suffer many things,"* proclaimed that they believed otherwise! While Jesus was speaking of suffering, they were thinking of Glory. Even though His Disciples believed Him, and also believed in Him, still, they had a totally erroneous view of His Mission.

In fact, the Fifty-third Chapter of Isaiah told them exactly what His Mission was, with the entirety of the Old Testament telling them why this Mission of death was necessary. But, once again, they had a very imperfect understanding of the Word of God, so they believed things which were wrong.

"Suffering" did not enter into their thinking; Glory did! In their minds, Jesus would use His great Power to take the Throne of Israel, overthrow the Roman yoke, and make Israel once again the greatest nation in the world, as it had been under David and Solomon. There are, in fact, untold numbers of Scriptures in the Old Testament which point to this very conclusion. However, there are also untold numbers of Scriptures which point to Israel's rejection of Christ and then her ultimate Restoration.

The problem with the Disciples, as is the problem, presently, is that they had an improper understanding of the Word of God. It was all there — His rejection and Israel's destruction, plus, as stated, her coming Restoration. However, the Disciples, as so many presently, evidently saw in the Scriptures what they wanted to see, instead of what they should have seen.

REJECTION

The phrase, *"And be rejected of the Elders, and of the Chief Priests, and Scribes,"* concerned the entirety of the religious leadership of Israel. In other words, He was, one might say, rejected totally, fully, and completely by the Church! These religious leaders rejected Jesus even though He fulfilled every Prophecy and, in Truth, met every specification; however, these were Biblical specifications and not specifications of self-will.

Their vision of the Messiah was not what the Bible projected. Their tradition, however, would not allow them to believe the Bible, but rather twist its words to their own unbelief. Jesus will, in Truth, one day take the Throne of Israel; consequently, He will put down every enemy and make Israel once again the greatest nation in the world. However, it will be only after Israel has accepted Christ as her Messiah, after having first made Him her Saviour (Zech. 12:10-13:1).

As we all know, this did not take place at the First Advent. It will take place at the Second Advent!

THE CRUCIFIXION

The phrase, *"And be killed,"* was something the Disciples, especially Peter, could not grasp or even believe. In their minds, how could such be? They still did not realize how evil the religious leaders of Israel actually were, and neither did they realize the true mission of Christ. He did not come to catapult Israel to greatness and glory as they thought, but rather to lift man from the terrible bondage from sin which had enslaved him. At that time, they did not understand this!

All of this tells us that the very purpose of Christ was to go to the Cross. In fact, even as Peter himself would later write, all of this was decided, and I speak of God becoming man and dying on the Cross, thereby shedding His Life's Blood in order that man might be saved, from before the foundation of the world (I Pet. 1:18-20). So, even though Christ did many great, good, and wonderful things during His earthly Ministry, still, His destination was ever the Cross.

There, the terrible sin debt of man would be forever settled! There, eternal life for all Believers would be made possible. There, Satan and all his minions of darkness would be totally and completely defeated! There, the way to Heaven's Gate would be forever opened for all who will believe! There, due to the great Plan of Redemption being consummated, the Holy Spirit could now come into the hearts and lives of Believers to dwell permanently! There, all guilt would be removed, with all condemnation taken away! There, that which had been planned before the foundation of the world would be carried out in its totality! There, is the Cross!

THE RESURRECTION

The phrase, *"And after three days rise again,"* was completely lost upon them. It was as if they did not hear what He said. Not only did they not believe it then, they had trouble believing it after the Resurrection. In this statement by Christ, the two great principles of Faith are presented:

1. The Divinity and the Humanity of Christ.

2. His Cross and Passion, whereby He redeemed the world.

At this time, the Disciples were not clear on these things, but, after the Day of Pentecost, they would be. As this statement by Christ makes obvious, due to the great Victory which will be won at the Cross, the Resurrection is a given. Therefore, the idea that Jesus had to fight and struggle to be raised from the dead is not actually found in Scripture. Calvary truly paid it all, which means that Satan was totally and completely defeated (Col. 2:14-15).

So, when Jesus went down into the underworld of departed spirits and walked into Paradise, there to liberate every single person who had been incarcerated since their death, and we speak of Believers, He did not go down there as a defeated victim, but rather as a great and glorious conqueror. At the Cross, He had conquered death, Hell, and the grave. In other words, all of the effects of sin were totally addressed, and forever (Eph. 4:8).

The Resurrection, of course, is of extreme significance, as should be overly obvious; still, it was at the Cross where the victory was won (I Cor. 1:17-18, 23; 2:2; Gal. 6:14). In fact, the Death, Resurrection, Ascension, and Exaltation of Christ should be looked at as one great Work, but all made possible by what Christ did at the Cross, hence, the Cross ever being the Object of our Faith.

When one makes the Cross the Object of one's Faith, and the Cross exclusively, at the same time, the Resurrection, Ascension, and Exaltation are included. However, if one makes the Resurrection or the Exaltation the object of one's faith, which means the Cross is eliminated, then it becomes a faith that God will not, and actually cannot, accept (Eph. 2:13-18). It is the Cross alone which the Holy Spirit projects, doing so from Genesis 1:1 through Revelation 22:21.

(32) "AND HE SPOKE THAT SAYING OPENLY. AND PETER TOOK HIM, AND BEGAN TO REBUKE HIM."

The composition is:

This means that Peter spoke with force, in effect, denying what Jesus had just said.

THE MESSAGE

The phrase, *"And He spoke that saying openly,"* actually has three meanings:

1. In the Greek Text, the idea is that Jesus didn't say this one time, but actually several times. In other words, He kept saying it over and over, so they would not miss it.

2. Concerning Him being killed and rising again on the third day, it was said *"openly,"* in that each Disciple heard Him, and unmistakably so; as well, it was not said as a Parable. The idea is that the Disciples should know exactly what He was saying, what it meant, and would have no questions about the matter.

3. The statement given by Christ proclaims the fact that the Cross was ever His destination. That was the reason that God became Man and came down to this world. God cannot die; therefore, in order for this terrible price to be paid regarding the sin of humanity, God would have to become Man, and fully Man! As a Man, He would face every power of darkness, would suffer every temptation, would meet Satan on his own ground, which was the domain of this world, and do so without failing even one single time. In other words, He kept the Law in every respect, and did so in perfection.

Moreover, when He went to the Cross — in fact, the very reason He went to the Cross — He there dealt with the broken Law, of which every man was guilty. Every man being guilty, this meant that every man was doomed to eternal darkness; however, by atoning for all sin, which He did at the Cross through His Death, which, of course, spoke of the shedding of His Precious Blood, the debt was then paid, at least for all who will believe, with the death sentence being eternally lifted (Eph. 2:13-18).

SIMON PETER

The phrase, *"And Peter took Him,"* means that the words hit the Disciples like a bombshell. Inasmuch as Peter had just made the great confession, he, as the leader, pulls the Lord aside, as it is implied in the Greek Text, in order to speak to Him privately. It's the same as someone taking another by the shoulders, which is probably what happened!

The idea that Jesus must be killed was not at all in their plans. Unfortunately, the Cross is not in the plans of most people, not even most Christians.

But let everyone know and understand:

In order to live the *"Resurrection Life,"* which so many speak of, first of all, one must fully understand that such is gained by the fact that *"we have been planted together in the likeness of His Death"* (Rom. 6:5). So, all Resurrection Life is predicated totally upon Calvary Death. If the *"Death"* is ignored, or misunderstood, Resurrection Life becomes impossible, with the person actually being put in the place of rebuking Christ, exactly as did Simon Peter!

THE REBUKE!

The phrase, *"And began to rebuke Him,"* means that Peter was speaking with force, but, above that, denying what Jesus had said. Even though Mark does not relate what Peter said, Matthew did record his statement. He said, *"Be it far from You, Lord: this shall not be unto You"* (Mat. 16:22). The terrible trials, and even His Death, expressed by Christ, flew in the face of what the Disciples were thinking. In their minds, He was going to be the King of Israel, making David's Throne the centerpiece of the world. Israel would once again regain her glory as under David and Solomon. Rome would be thrown off, and this hated subservience would end.

Furthermore, they (the Disciples), considering their association with Him, obviously would be His Chief Lieutenants in this New Kingdom. Actually, this is what caused their *"hardness of heart"*! Their position was not one of Faith, but rather of presumption, therefore, of self-will. Anyone out of the Will of God, whoever they may be, even the Disciples, takes unto himself the hardened heart.

NOTES

They did not understand the Mission of Christ, and neither did they properly understand the Scripture. While the Prophets had certainly spoke, as stated, of a coming Kingdom, their assumption that it was coming now was entirely wrong. Had they properly read Isaiah 53, Daniel 9, or Zechariah 11, they would have known better. But they, as so many others, read into the Word of God what they desired the Word of God to be.

(33) "BUT WHEN HE HAD TURNED ABOUT AND LOOKED ON HIS DISCIPLES, HE REBUKED PETER, SAYING, GET THEE BEHIND ME, SATAN: FOR YOU SAVOUR NOT THE THINGS THAT BE OF GOD, BUT THE THINGS THAT BE OF MEN."

The diagram is:

Jesus did not at all take lightly what Peter had said; and now He makes sure that His Disciples understand His reaction. This Passage presents Jesus speaking directly to Satan, and not Peter; however, the Words of our Lord brand Peter's words as Satanic; the Words, *"behind Me,"* say, in effect, *"Get out of My Face!"*

THE LOOK

The phrase, *"But when He had turned about,"* proclaims a sudden motion on the part of the Master upon hearing Peter's rebuke. He did not at all take lightly what Peter had said, as will be obvious! The phrase, *"And looked on His Disciples,"* means that what He will say must be heard also by them!

More than likely, the Disciples had heard Peter's rebuke, and now they must hear Jesus' answer. To be sure, it was not a pleasant time at all for our Lord. Even though they had been with Him constantly for about three years, still, they had little understanding as to what His True Mission was all about. Instead of Salvation for the world, they saw power, position, riches, and glory. Regrettably, many in the modern Church see the same thing instead of the True Purpose of Christ.

Every Believer should ask himself the question, *"How is the Lord looking at me?"* To be sure, this look that the Lord gave to Peter, actually to all of His Disciples, was not a look of approval, but rather of reprobation. We should all remind ourselves that He is still *"looking"*! So the great question is, *"What* type of look is it that He is giving to us?"

THE REBUKE GIVEN BY CHRIST

The phrase, *"He rebuked Peter,"* did not, at least at that time, obtain its intended result. Concerning the answer of Jesus, Mark uses the same word for *"rebuke"* as he did for Peter's answer to Christ. Peter's rebuke did not cause Jesus to change His Mind, because it should not have; however, the *"rebuke"* given to Peter and the Disciples of Christ should have brought Peter to Repentance, but sadly it did not!

It was not that Peter was stubbornly rebelling against the Lord, but that he simply did not understand; however, ignorance, although not as bad as open rebellion, still brings about the same results — the hardened heart (Mk. 8:17).

SATAN

The phrase, *"Saying, Get thee behind Me, Satan,"* presents Jesus speaking directly to Satan, and not Peter. He spoke directly to the Tempter, including Peter, in the rebuke; consequently, the Lord, in His utterance, brands Peter's words as Satanic. Jesus' rebuke has the same flavor as the temptation in the wilderness. At that time, Satan had said to Jesus, speaking of the great Roman Empire, *"All these things will I give You, if You will fall down and worship me"* (Mat. 4:9).

This time Satan does not ask Jesus to fall down and worship him, as he did previously, but instead he tempted the Lord to go around the Cross. To do this, he would use Jesus' most trusted Disciples. The words, *"behind Me,"* demand, in essence, that Satan cease his temptations, saying, in effect, *"Get out of My Face!"* The temptations of Christ were always in this capacity. Satan tempted Him to move outside of the Will of God, which is, in essence, the foundation of all temptation. Consequently, the question must be asked, *"What type of temptations did Jesus actually suffer?"*

TEMPTATION

Concerning Christ's temptations, the Scripture tells us, *"For we have not an High Priest which cannot be touched with the feeling of our infirmities* (being Very Man as well as Very God, He can do such); *but was in all points tempted like as we are, yet without sin"* (Heb. 4:15).

What exactly does it mean, *"in all points tempted like as we are"*?

Does this mean that Jesus was tempted to commit adultery? Homosexuality? To steal? To lie?

No!

For a person to be tempted to commit adultery, or anyone of the things we have listed, or things we have not listed, such must first be in the heart of that person. As we certainly should know, nothing like that was in the heart of Christ. So what was the type of temptation He suffered?

If one reads carefully the first ten Verses of the Fourth Chapter of Matthew, which concern the temptation of Christ, one will find the manner in which Jesus was tempted. As stated, in each case, He was tempted to step outside of the revealed Will of God, thereby taking another tact. That's where the real temptation was, and that's where the real temptation is.

God's revealed Will is found in His Word. But tragically, most modern Christians do not know the revealed Will of God, simply because they don't know the Word. Oftentimes, they take someone else's thoughts for the Word, which prove to be false.

The Holy Spirit sums all of this up in the phrase, *"Whatsoever is not of faith is sin"* (Rom. 14:23). This, in essence, pinpoints exactly what the revealed Will of God is, summing up the entirety of the Bible in this one phrase.

It means:

If our Faith is not anchored completely in Christ and the Cross, but rather in something else, the Holy Spirit constitutes such as *"sin."* If it's not Faith in Christ and the Cross, this means we have left God's Prescribed Order, exactly as Adam and Eve in the Garden, exactly as every person has done since. God's order has always been, *"Jesus Christ and Him Crucified"* (I Cor. 1:23).

Now, I realize that most would not think that faith improperly placed, which means it's placed in something other than the Cross of Christ, constitutes sin; however, if we understand the Cross as we should understand the Cross, then it actually becomes very easy to see why, and we then truly begin to understand the origination of all sin. The only way that *"sin"* will not have dominion over us is by the Believer understanding Romans 6:3-5, and making it a daily practice in his life (Lk. 9:23).

THE THINGS OF GOD AND THE THINGS OF MEN

The phrase, *"For you savour not the things that be of God, but the things that be of men,"* is addressed to both Satan and Peter. Satan, as is obvious, did not want the things which were of God, and Peter was wanting the things which were *"of men."* Actually, there was no difference in the two desires.

This is perhaps one of Satan's great ploys. If he can get men to follow other men, even religious men, he will have succeeded in his purpose. The reasons are obvious. The Lord through Isaiah said, *"For as the Heavens are higher than the Earth, so are My ways higher than your ways, and My Thoughts than your thoughts"* (Isa. 55:9).

"There is a way which seems right unto a man, but the end thereof are the ways of death" (Prov. 14:12).

At the moment of conversion, the Holy Spirit sets about to direct the ways of man toward God. This is done through the Word of God and by the leading of the Holy Spirit. Actually, there is not a single way which the Holy Spirit will lead a man that is not found first in the Word.

At the same time, Satan sets about to lead men away from the Word. To be sure, his efforts are subtle, smart, religious, and, to the carnal mind, plausible! To follow that way will reap the applause of men, and especially religious men, but the frown of God. To follow the Lord, and the Lord exclusively, will reap no applause from men, but rather their opposition, and especially from religious men. However, such will meet with the approval of God. This is what Jesus was speaking of when He said, *"Blessed are they which are persecuted for Righteousness' sake: for theirs is the Kingdom of Heaven"* (Mat. 5:10).

To follow the Lord as one should, one must follow very closely in order to hear His Voice. If one lags too far behind, the siren call of the world, and especially the religious world, will gradually drown out that Voice. It also should be understood that if Peter was so used by Satan, so can any Believer be thus used.

(34) "AND WHEN HE HAD CALLED THE PEOPLE UNTO HIM WITH HIS DISCIPLES ALSO, HE SAID UNTO THEM, WHOSOEVER WILL COME AFTER ME, LET HIM DENY HIMSELF, AND TAKE UP HIS CROSS, AND FOLLOW ME."

The exposition is:

This Verse implies that Jesus cannot be successfully followed unless it's by the way of the Cross.

FOLLOWING JESUS

The phrase, *"And when He had called the people unto Him with His Disciples also,"* speaks of an interval of some period of time between His rebuke of Peter and this present statement. In the previous exchange, only the Disciples were included; but others are now also addressed! What Jesus will say will be the very heartbeat of what it means to a Christian; consequently, the Message is given not only to the Disciples, but also to the people, because it is a requirement for all!

The phrase, *"Whosoever will come after Me,"* refers to those who accept the call. It means to be Born-Again, to become His Disciple, to follow His Teachings, and to enter into His fellowship. If one is to notice, Jesus didn't say, *"Come after the Church,"* or *"Preacher,"* or *"Priest,"* or *"Prophet,"* but rather Christ Himself (*"Me"*). Christianity without Christ is no more than any other philosophy. Such produces the moralist, of which there is an abounding number, but does not produce a changed life. The moralist reduces Christianity to a mere religion, which makes it little different than the other religions of the world. Actually, Christianity, within itself, cannot change anything or anyone. Only Christ can change hearts and lives! He actually makes a new creature of all who come to Him.

A CHRISTLESS CHRISTIANITY

Regrettably, Christianity, in most circles, is Christless and, by that, we mean that while

Christ is accepted, at least in some fashion, He is accepted minus the Cross. Of course, the Lord will not recognize such acceptance. When that happens, the Church becomes the Saviour, or something else, which, in effect, is no Saviour at all!

As a result, Jesus is the center of controversy. The argument is not with God, because God, at least to most, is merely an abstract. He can be labeled anything, and usually is, which consequently offends no one. However, Jesus is a Person Who functioned and lived among men, Who actually claimed to be God, and Who claimed to be the Way to the Father — to be sure, the only Way! As such, He stands in contrast to Muhammad and a host of other false luminaries. So the argument is with Jesus.

The Bible teaches that no man can come to the Father but by Jesus. It is only through His Name that one can be saved (Jn. 14:6; Acts 4:12). Even though we've given this elsewhere in this Volume, due to its significance, please bear with us again:

1. The only way to the Father is through the Son (Jn. 14:6).

2. The only way to the Son, the Lord Jesus Christ, is through the Cross (Lk. 9:23). This means that the way to Christ is not through Mary, or any Saint, etc. Only the Cross!

3. The only way to the Cross is by a denial of self (Lk. 9:23-24).

The Bible clearly teaches that which we have just addressed. So, why is it so hard for people, especially Preachers, to believe it?

Perhaps the next phrase will give us the reason why.

THE DENIAL OF SELF

The phrase, *"Let him deny himself,"* hits at the very crux of man's problem, which is *"self."* As we have previously stated, when man fell in the Garden of Eden, he lost God-consciousness, falling to the far lower level of self-consciousness. Before the Fall, his eyes were exclusively on God, from Whom he drew sustenance, life, and strength. Now, it is on *"self,"* which breeds acute selfishness, which causes all the misery in the world.

THE GOSPEL OF SELF-ESTEEM

To correct this situation, man (not God) has come up with the false gospel of *"self-esteem."* This false way basically teaches that man's problem is that he does not readily know his self-worth; man consequently needs his self-esteem elevated. If this can be done, they teach, man's problems will be solved.

One of the foremost proponents of the self-esteem gospel, Robert Schuller, has called for a *"new reformation,"* stating that the Sixteenth Century movement (under Martin Luther and John Calvin) was a *"reactionary movement"* because it emphasized that men are sinners. Schuller goes on to say, *"Once a person believes he is a 'unworthy sinner,' it is doubtful he can honestly accept the Saving Grace God offers in Jesus Christ."*

Schuller then offers his blueprint for bringing sinners to Salvation:

"If you want to know why I make people laugh once in a while, I am giving them sounds and strokes, sounds and strokes, like you would a baby.

"It's a strategy. People who don't trust need to be stroked. People are born with a negative self-image. Because they do not trust, they cannot trust God."

Of course, if this man is right, accepted Evangelistic practices, which have brought millions to Christ, are wrong. We should then stop telling people they're sinners who need Jesus Christ as their Saviour. We must no longer convince them of their sin and rebellion against a Holy God. We must never speak of Hell, nor warn of the terrible, eternal consequences of rejecting the wonderful offer of Salvation as an unmerited gift from God.

Instead we should begin to stroke men and women into faith, smile them into the kingdom of God, and elevate their self-esteem. If one knows his Bible, he will agree that this is a major change in Christian perspective. However, the proponent of this false gospel has an even broader concept in mind. He goes on to say:

"A theology of self-esteem also produces a theology of social ethics and a theology of economics — and these produce a theology of government. It all rises on one foundation: the dignity of a person who is created in the image of God."

Basically, this self-esteem theology states that we need a new reformation and a new theology. What it also suggests — but does not openly state — is that we need a new Bible. But, truthfully, without openly saying so, it is now giving the Church a new Bible. I speak of the many new interpretations which are now on the market, such as *"The Message Bible,"* and scores of others of similar perversion. By no stretch of the imagination can these interpretations be called the *"Bible."* Pure and simple, they constitute no more than mere prattle, one might even say drivel, of man.

Concerning this new gospel of self-esteem, it strikes at the very heart of the Gospel of Jesus Christ. The True Gospel states that man is a lost sinner, who cannot save himself, and who thus desperately needs a Redeemer.

WHERE DID THIS *"OTHER GOSPEL"* OF SELF-ESTEEM COME FROM?

In order to place this new teaching into proper perspective, we should realize that so-called *"Christian"* psychologists and psychiatrists transplanted it from outside the Church and from outside the Bible, and I speak of that which is truly the Bible, preferably the King James Version.

A leading evangelical psychologist, who vigorously promotes self-worth teaching, explains, in one of his books, *"You're someone special:"*

"Under the influence of humanistic psychologists, like Carl Rogers and Abraham Maslow, many of us Christians have begun to see our need for self-love and self-esteem."

Satan's threefold humanistic plan for world domination is basically simple, and you might be surprised how well it correlates with this new theology:

1. Darwinism (Darwin) — the concept of evolution, as it affects the social man, resulting in abortion, humanism, and the *"survival of the fittest."*

2. Marxism (Communism and Socialism) — Satan's economic foundation, which has been proven the world over to be an unworkable philosophy. It results in nothing but poverty.

3. Freudianism (Psychology) — a profound influence on the morals of man, and leading, one might say, toward immorality.

And there you have it! Satan's three-pronged assault — social, economic, and moral. The self-esteem philosophy comes directly from Freudian principles, and it does demand an entirely different theology.

ALL TRUTH IS GOD'S TRUTH?

The statement, *"All truth is God's truth,"* is a standard quote offered by *"Christian psychologists"* to justify the *"self-help"* philosophies and *"new-speak"* theologies. It is an *"answer"* in sloganized format.

"It doesn't matter," we are told, *"if Adler and Maslow* (psychologist) *were humanists. If they stumbled upon truth, so be it. We must accept truth — no matter its source."*

One *"Christian psychologist"* told me that Jesus used psychology in His Ministry. In other words, Jesus was *"a great psychologist."* Does he understand the blasphemy of such a statement?

"What kind of psychology did Jesus use?" we might ask. Was it Freudian? That is somewhat difficult to imagine, since Freud wasn't born until the 1800's. It also should be noted that Freud was a narcotics addict, a sexual pervert, and an unmitigated liar who falsified his medical results to make them conform to what he had already postulated as theory. These are well-known and accepted facts — admitted by even the most faithful of Freud's devotees.

Freud himself stated, in regard to his psychiatric method, *"I would trash the whole business, but I don't know what else to turn to."* How tragic that he never read John 14:6, which states, *"I am the Way, the Truth, and the Life."* Jesus is Truth. Without Him, there is no truth. Jesus does not merely contain truth, He is Truth, which is a vast difference!

Truth is not a philosophy, it actually is a Person, the Man Christ Jesus!

All that purports to be truth without Him is a lie. Psychotherapy — the wellspring of the self-esteem philosophy — is a lie. And, basically, what is being touted as truth today (*"All truth is God's truth"*) is little more than disconnected facts taken out of context.

Pavlov's dogs were trained to respond by salivating at the ringing of a bell — and huge segments of the *"science"* of psychology are built on this minor point. In keeping with this same policy of building great precepts on flimsy evidence, we are asked to accept this principle: *"Even though it's not in the Bible, it can still be truth. And anything that is truth is God's truth, because all truth comes from God. We must, therefore, avail ourselves of any and all 'helps' that fall into our hands, whatever their source is."*

Allow us, however, once again, to state this Truth! There is no truth outside of Christ! Anything else which looks like truth, but which comes from another source, actually comes from the *"angel of light,"* Satan himself (II Cor. 11:13-15). We must, as well, quickly add, as Jesus is Truth, likewise, Satan is a lie. He does not merely lie, but he is, in fact, the father of the lie (Jn. 8:44); consequently, Truth related by a liar becomes a lie.

IS MAN'S TRUE PROBLEM ONE OF LOW SELF-ESTEEM?

To be completely objective, this much-touted philosophy is the precise opposite of reality. When man fell in the Garden of Eden, he did so at the suggestion of Satan, because he fell for the idea of wanting to be a god.

"And the serpent said unto the woman, You shall not surely die:

"For God does know that in the day you eat thereof, then your eyes shall be opened, and you shall be as gods, knowing good and evil" (Gen. 3:4-5).

Yes, you shall be as gods. . . .

And there is the problem. It is the ancient temptation Satan used to beguile Eve, and he is still using the same, tired ruse today. This is why there are so many dictators around the world. They see themselves as gods. It is the foundation for humanism. Man is the focal point, replacing God. The whole world is now fascinated and beguiled by the false god of man's self-importance.

Socialism and Communism follow hard on the heels of humanism. They are all man-centered concepts — and Satan is the author of all such worldly systems. Regrettably, this is the basic source of all man-made philosophies which are permeating Pentecostal and Charismatic circles today — philosophies such as *"Christian"* psychology, sociology, possibility thinking, positive thinking, the fourth dimension, dream your own dream, inner healing, self-esteem, etc. Man wants to play God.

THE PURPOSE DRIVEN LIFE THEORY

The craze that is now sweeping the world of religion, *"The Purpose Driven Life"* philosophy, is based 100 percent on humanistic psychology. Over and over again, I have said that psychology is the religion of humanism. Now it has a more religious face in the form of *"The Purpose Driven Life/Church,"* which makes it even more acceptable to the modern Church. Having already accepted psychology, which is the total opposite of what the Word of God teaches, it is now easy for the Church to buy into *"The Purpose Driven Life"* scheme.

"The Purpose Driven Life" theory is, in fact, merely an extension of the self-esteem program. Whether they realize it or not, they (the self-esteem teachers and the proponents of the Purpose Driven Life) are saying that Jesus does not hold the answer to man's problems, and new concepts are, therefore, needed.

In some Pentecostal and Charismatic circles, statements such as the following are being made:

"We are little gods. As Adam was formerly god of this world and lost it, we have now regained it. And we are now little gods under the Lord Jesus Christ."

This is a dangerous, man-centered philosophy, which has no foundation in the Bible whatsoever, and will undermine and grossly cheapen the magnificent Gospel of the Lord Jesus Christ.

"Because you say, I am rich, and increased with goods, and have need of nothing; and knowest not that you are wretched, and miserable, and poor, and blind, and naked:

"I counsel you. . . .

"As many as I love, I rebuke and chasten: be zealous therefore, and repent" (Rev. 3:17-19).

In preaching to millions around the world of their need of a Saviour, I can state with assurance that at least one of the biggest problems the True Preacher of the Gospel finds in leading men to Christ is the *"god syndrome."*

"What do you mean, I need a Saviour?" say many! *"I'm not a sinner, I'm doin' just fine."*

Truly, the hardest thing in the world is to

get a man to admit that he is a sinner. And one must admit to himself that he is lost before he can be saved. One must admit that he needs a Saviour before he can be introduced to one. And the reason this matter of human pride is such a successful tool of Satan's is that man's basic problem is not one of low self-esteem, it is rather one of inflated self-esteem. Ultimately, this single fact is causing millions to perish.

SELF-CENTERED

Sometime back, I was listening to a Charismatic Preacher over Television, and I heard him espouse the Dominion Teaching theory. He said:

"We are going to take over the world.... We are going to solve the problems of mankind." It was *"we this"* and *"we that."* If Jesus Christ was mentioned, it was only in passing. I doubt very seriously that the proponents of this false gospel even remotely suspect the evil of that of which they are promoting. But at the core of it is the fact that Jesus Christ is relegated to a an inferior position, if any position at all, with man occupying the Throne.

Dominion teaching, Government of Twelve Teaching, Purpose Driven Life Teaching, Denominationalism, and Word of Faith Teaching are all doomed to failure, not only because they are unscriptural, but also because they are man-centered. Whenever any philosophy ceases to be Christ and Cross focused, it becomes unscriptural and heretical. It is easy to see the slimy trail of the serpent in all of this teaching as it parrots his original lie, *"You shall be as gods."*

A. W. Tozer said, *"If self occupies any part of the Throne, we cannot say that Jesus Christ is on the Throne of our heart. Self is man's greatest enemy. It embodies selfishness, greed, and all that opposes God. If Jesus Christ is centered on the Throne, self-will is eradicated. And until self-will is totally eradicated, there can be no Christ-centered Throne in our lives."*

To the statement made by Tozer, I might quickly add: *"Unless Jesus Christ is understood and accepted regarding the Cross, it is not possible for one to make Him the Center of all things, and especially of ourselves. As someone has well said, 'Jesus died on the Cross not only to save us from sin, but also to save us from self.'"*

Self-esteem, in which the Government of Twelve philosophy, the Purpose Driven Life philosophy, and the Word of Faith philosophy are all embedded, caters to man's basic nature. It first became apparent at the Fall in the Garden. It will lead no one to Christ. It will lead instead to the enshrinement of self. And the tragic fact is that thousands of Pentecostal and Charismatic Preachers are falling all over each other to embrace these errant doctrines.

Sadly, the old-line Churches have long since embraced it, at least for the most part.

THE BIBLE AND SELF-ESTEEM

Jay E. Adams, in his book, The Biblical View of Self-Esteem, says:

"Any system that proposes to solve human problems apart from the Bible and the Power of the Holy Spirit (as all of these pagan systems do, including the self-worth system) *is automatically condemned by Scripture itself. Nor does the system in any way depend upon the Message of Salvation. Love, joy, and peace are discussed as if they were not the Fruit of the Spirit but merely the fruit of right views of one's self, which anyone can attain without the Bible and the Work of the Spirit in his heart.*

"For these reasons, the self-worth system, with its claims of Biblical correspondences, must be rejected. It does not come from the Bible. Any resemblance between Biblical teaching and the teaching of the self-worth originators is either contrived or coincidental."

Actually, the only thing the Bible says about self-esteem can be found in Philippians 2:3:

"Let nothing be done through strife or vainglory; but in lowliness of mind let each esteem other better than themselves."

This teaches the precise opposite of puffed-up self-opinions. It clearly tells us to have a humble view of ourselves, being ever aware of our own secret faults and shortcomings. This does not state that man's crying need is enhanced self-esteem. It says that man needs less emphasis on ego and self-gratification.

J. I. Packer said:

"Modern Christians spread a thin layer of Bible teaching over their mixture of popular psychology and common sense. But their overall approach clearly reflects the narcissism — the 'selfism' or 'me-ism,' as it is sometimes called — that is the way of the world in the modern west."

The Apostle Paul plainly tells us that the person who fails to love others is *"nothing"*:

"Though I speak with the tongues of men and of Angels, and have not charity (love) *. . . I am nothing"* (I Cor. 13:1-2).

One of the foremost proponents of self-esteem claims that to glorify God, we must first love ourselves. This is not Biblical! As we have stated, the Lord through Paul said that man is nothing — unless and until he loves others. It says nothing, incidentally, about loving one's self first.

In Psalm 8, the Psalmist expresses amazement that God visits man. *"What is man?"* he asks. Then in Psalm 62, we have the answer to this question: Nothing! Man is nothing! Obviously, God does not love man because of his moral traits; He loves him despite them. This is why the Psalmist expressed amazement. It is a testimony to God's greatness — not man's.

Actually, in the statement of Christ in Mark 8:34, Jesus is saying, in effect, *"You must treat yourself — with your sinful ways, priorities, and desires — like a criminal. Your sins must be condemned and utterly done away with."*

This certainly says something about the self-image Christ expects us to have — and it is a far cry from the elevated self-esteem being promoted today.

THE WORK OF THE HOLY SPIRIT

John 16:8 tells us that the Work of the Holy Spirit is to *"reprove the world of sin and of* (self) *righteousness, and of judgment."* This means that, under the teaching of the Gospel (as in I Cor. 1:21), the Holy Spirit convicts men of sin — not of low self-esteem. It clearly states, furthermore, that man is a sinner.

When, according to the Gospel, an individual is convicted (reproved) of sin, he is brought to a place of Repentance. He suddenly sees himself as he is — which is *"lost, undone, and without God."*

In Peter's sermon on the Day of Pentecost (Acts, Chpt. 2), some 3,000 were saved. Read this Passage and you will search in vain for any reference to the elevation of the listener's self-esteem, as claimed by Robert Schuller and others of like ilk. Instead Peter said, *"Therefore let all the House of Israel know assuredly, that God has made that same Jesus, Whom you have crucified, both Lord and Christ"* (Acts 2:36). Peter did not, by any means, appeal here to their vanities in an effort to raise their self-esteem.

And what happened?

"Now when they heard this, they were pricked in their heart, and said unto Peter and to the rest of the Apostles, Men and brethren, what shall we do?" (Acts 2:37).

This is Holy Spirit conviction in fact. In Peter's second great sermon, as quoted in Acts, Chapter 3, he once more ignored the matter of the listeners' self-esteem. Instead, he refocused on the darker side of their natures.

"But you denied the Holy One and the Just, and desired a murderer to be granted unto you;

"And killed the Prince of Life, Whom God has raised from the dead; whereof we are witnesses" (Acts 3:14-15).

Again, what happened? This time 5,000 were saved.

I think it is by now clearly obvious that this is the God-approved principle of confronting men with the fact that they are sinners and lost without God. It then becomes the responsibility of the Holy Spirit to convict them and bring them to Jesus Christ. And where does all of this leave the gospel of self-esteem?

The two, the gospel of self-esteem and the Way the Holy Spirit used Simon Peter, are certainly hard to reconcile. In Truth, even though Jesus is mentioned (and given lip-service as Lord), the self-esteem gospel does not bring Biblical Salvation. It instead brings people to a man-centered philosophy.

As a result, individuals who respond to this siren song of deceit (and that's what it is) are not Born-Again. They do not turn to the Lord Jesus Christ as their Saviour, but instead to a vain philosophy. To be frank, it is impossible for them to be Born-Again, because the Gospel has not been preached to them. A vain philosophy has been tendered in its place. They are confronted with the impossible, the task of saving themselves.

"And if the blind lead the blind, both shall fall into the ditch" (Mat. 15:14).

THE FOOT-WASHING SPIRIT

The self-esteem spirit was the hardest spirit to purge out of the Disciples. It was a battle that raged in their lives and Ministries up until the time of the Crucifixion of Christ. *"And there was also a strife among them, which of them should be accounted the greatest"* (Lk. 22:24 — the account of the Last Supper).

The mother of James and John also evidenced this spirit, along with her sons, when she desired to have her sons seated at either side of Christ. The spirit of self-esteem is capable of invading any situation, no matter how holy in concept; once there, it can threaten the very future of that situation. *"What it really amounts to is that man's standard of greatness lies in obtaining the position where he will be served, while God's standard involves serving."*

Man's standard is to humble others, while God's standard is to humble self (Lk. 9:23-24). Failure to observe these Godly principles led to the downfall of both Lucifer and Adam. It was, as stated, the *"you shall be gods"* principle in action, and this is again being promoted by way of the self-esteem gospel. If this spirit of high self-esteem had not been purged from the Disciples, the entire Work of God would have been destroyed. The only way this could be accomplished was for the Master to demonstrate the foot-washing spirit, which He did at the Last Supper.

"After that He poured water into a bason, and began to wash the Disciples' feet, and to wipe them with a towel wherewith He was girded" (Jn. 13:5).

(And we should note that Judas' feet were also washed!)

Jesus then asked them:

"Do you know what I have done to you?" (Jn. 13:12).

No! The Lord was not instituting some new form of Church ritual; He was instead demonstrating the principle of humility that He wanted them to adopt, one that they, in fact, must adopt in their Ministry.

THE ANSWER TO SELF

Man is a *"self,"* so it is not possible for self to be eliminated. It is, however, definitely possible for self-will, self-aggrandizement, and self-righteousness to be eliminated. Christ and the Cross are the answer to self, whether it is low-self or high-self.

Some time ago, a man said to me, *"Well, then, you do believe that a person can have low self-esteem?"* I answered him in the affirmative; however, the answer to that individual is not in elevating their self-esteem, but rather taking their problem to Christ and the Cross. The answer is the exact opposite of what we think. Jesus said:

"If any man will come after Me (the criteria for Discipleship), *let him deny himself* (not asceticism, as many think, but rather that one denies one's own willpower, self-will, strength, and ability, depending totally on Christ), *and take up his cross* (the benefits of the Cross, looking exclusively to what Jesus did there to meet our every need) *daily* (this is so important, our looking to the Cross; that we must renew our Faith in what Christ has done for us, even on a daily basis, for Satan will ever try to move us away from the Cross as the object of our Faith, which always spells disaster), *and follow Me* (Christ can be followed only by the Believer looking to the Cross, understanding what it accomplished, and by that means alone [Rom. 6:3-5, 11, 14; 8:1-2, 11; I Cor. 1:17-18, 21, 23; 2:2; Gal. 6:14; Eph. 2:13-18; Col. 2:14-15]).

"For whosoever will save his life shall lose it (try to live one's life outside of Christ and the Cross)*: but whosoever will lose his life for My sake, the same shall save it"* (Lk. 9:23-24).

When we place our Faith entirely in Christ and the Cross, looking exclusively to Him and what He did for us at the Cross, we have just found *"more abundant life"* (Jn. 10:10). By trying to *"save self,"* we lose it, which means that we are taken over by evil passions. When we place self entirely in Christ, and that is the secret, we then actually find our life. However, *"self"* cannot be placed into Christ unless it is done by the means of the Cross. That is the only way (Lk. 9:23-24; Rom. 6:3-14; 8:1-2, 11).

THE CARNAL MIND

Attempting to get a person with low self-esteem into a mode of high self-esteem only exacerbates the problem. They are exchanging one problem for another. All the self-help philosophies in the world are, in fact, of no avail! Self, whether low or high, is evil, demented, perverted, wrong, and, in effect, of the flesh.

Paul said, *"For to be carnally* (self) *minded is death; but to be Spiritually minded* (Christ) *is life and peace"* (Rom. 8:6). Paul also said, *"Because the carnal mind* (self mind) *is enmity* (hatred) *against God: for it is not subject to the Law of God, and neither indeed can be."*

He then went on to say, *"So then they who are in the flesh* (trying to change self by their own efforts) *cannot please God"* (Rom. 8:7-8). So, all of this self-help effort in the realm of self-esteem, etc., is roundly condemned by the Holy Spirit.

The age in which we live could probably be labeled as the age of self-help. All type of programs, efforts, fads, many of them with religious overtones, are all designed to improve self. In fact, *"The Government of Twelve"* falls into this category, as well as *"The Purpose Driven Life."* One can also add *"The Word of Faith"* to that list.

While self definitely needs to be improved, it cannot be improved except by one way. That way is:

The Believer must place his faith exclusively in Christ and the Cross, which then gives the Holy Spirit latitude to work within our lives, and then He will improve our *"self"*; however, it is done strictly through the Cross, and no other way.

Paul said, *"I am crucified with Christ* (as the foundation of all victory; Paul here takes us back to Romans 6:3-5)*: nevertheless I live* (have new life)*; yet not I* (not by my own strength and ability) *but Christ lives in me* (by virtue of me dying with Him on the Cross and being raised with Him in newness of life)*: and the life which I now live in the flesh* (my daily walk before God) *I live by the Faith of the Son of God* (the Cross is ever the Object of my Faith)*, Who loved me and gave Himself for me* (which is the only way that I could be saved).

"I do not frustrate the Grace of God (if we make anything other than the Cross of Christ the object of our Faith, we frustrate the Grace of God, which means we stop its action, and the Holy Spirit will no longer help us)*: for if Righteousness come by the Law* (any type of Law)*, then Christ is dead in vain."* (If I can successfully live for the Lord by any means other than Faith in Christ and the Cross, then the death of Christ was a waste [Gal. 2:20-21].)

WHY DO MANY WHO CLAIM CHRIST INSIST ON THESE VAIN PHILOSOPHIES?

Especially considering that no human being has been successful in these self-help efforts, why does man continue trying? I am speaking of Believers!

He does so because he is deceived. Deception is Satan's greatest weapon. He used this tactic in the Garden of Eden, which caused the Fall of man; consequently, man comes quickly to the lie, but slowly to the Truth.

Self-esteem sounds good to the carnal mind. However, because it is doomed to failure, it does not sound good to the spiritual mind. Consequently, the propagators of this false gospel, and a false gospel it is, will help no one, but rather lead them to destruction.

Allow me to say it again:

THE CROSS

The only answer is Christ and Him Crucified, and not Christ plus some new philosophy dreamed up out of vapid minds.

The phrase, *"And take up his cross,"* is the central focus of the activity of Bible Christianity.

First of all, the *"Cross"* spoke of death. Death of what?

The death of *"self,"* or, more perfectly, *"selfishness."* As we have attempted to bring out, the greatest enemy of man is self! Self-will is always opposed to God's Will; consequently, self must be brought into Christ, for there alone can it realize its true worth.

To be sure, and as Jesus will say even in this short Message, man is extremely important. Actually, more important than all the things of the world. So important, in fact, that Jesus came from Heaven and died on a cruel Cross in order that man may be saved. However, the way for man properly to know his true worth can never be found in self, or its efforts at betterment, but only in Christ. Man is important not in what he is, but only in what Christ can make of him.

WHAT DOES IT MEAN TO BEAR THE CROSS?

First of all, many Christians are confused about bearing the Cross, thinking that difficulties and problems fall into this category; however, anything which can happen to the unsaved cannot be looked at by the Christian as bearing the Cross. In other words, poverty is not a Cross, inasmuch as most of the world lives in poverty. Neither is sickness, for much of the world falls into that category. The ill will of one's own family is not bearing the Cross, as that also happens to the worldling!

Bearing the Cross is simply looking to Christ and what He did for us at the Cross, understanding that everything we receive from the Lord is all, without exception, made possible at the Cross. As we've repeatedly stated, Christ is the *"Source,"* while the Cross is the *"Means,"* by which all things are done.

DAILY

Luke added the word *"daily"* (Lk 9:23), showing this is a decision we must make on a daily basis. In other words, the temptation will always present itself for the Cross to be aborted; consequently, the Believer, on a *"daily"* basis, must resolve to take up the Cross, ever looking to that Finished Work. It is something that continues through the entirety of life.

It is somewhat like the Manna, which fell each day, with the exception of the Sabbath. The people were admonished to get only enough for one day, because a fresh supply would fall, with the exception of the Sabbath, the next morning. On the day preceding the Sabbath, they were to gather twice as much, so they would have enough for the Sabbath.

To their amazement, they found that if they disobeyed the Lord by gathering more Manna than was needed, it would breed

NOTES

worms and stink. Likewise, we are to believe the Lord for the fresh benefits of the Cross, even on a daily basis. By doing so, we can rest assured that there will be a fresh supply for tomorrow. Furthermore, *"taking up the Cross daily"* teaches us Faith and Trust. It helps us to *"fight the good fight."*

Taking up the Cross is the only thing in the Bible which we are commanded to do on a *"daily"* basis. That should tell us something!

Verse 34 presents the conditions of Discipleship:

1. The attitude of the Disciple to himself — *"Let him deny himself."*
2. The attitude of the Disciple to the world — *"and take up his cross."*
3. The attitude of the Disciple to Christ — *"and follow Me."*

(35) "FOR WHOSOEVER WILL SAVE HIS LIFE SHALL LOSE IT; BUT WHOSOEVER SHALL LOSE HIS LIFE FOR MY SAKE AND THE GOSPEL'S, THE SAME SHALL SAVE IT."

The exposition is:

Placing one's life entirely in Christ can be done only by way of the Cross; doing so saves one's life, and does so forever.

THE SAVING OF ONE'S LIFE

The phrase, *"For whosoever will save his life shall lose it,"* actually constitutes Jesus' philosophy of life. In this statement, Christ is not telling one how to be saved from sin, for that can only be brought about by Faith in the shed Blood of Jesus. Jesus is here giving, as stated, His Word concerning life, in effect, telling one how to live.

To be sure, it is the opposite of self-gratification, which characterizes the world.

Wuest says, *"God has so created man that he does not find complete rest and satisfaction until his entire being is swallowed up in the sweet Will of God."*

The word *"life,"* as Jesus uses it here, is not referring to one's physical existence and its needs. It is rather referring to one's purpose for living.

I read the other day of the passing of one of the Noblemen of England, who was a very wealthy man. The only thing they could say of him was his love for his butterfly collection.

Whenever a Hollywood actor or actress dies, their films and Broadway appearances are extolled. Respecting the far greater majority, and even those who gain fame and notoriety, their lives are a waste. They simply lived and died without ever really knowing what true living actually is.

Solomon is a perfect example of what I say. In all of history, no one ever had the wisdom or riches to indulge his passions and appetites as Solomon. Nothing, at least as far as self-gratification is concerned, was out of his reach. Nothing was illegal, and nothing was too expensive. And yet, after he did it all, his answer was, *"All is vanity and vexation of spirit"* (Eccl. 1:14).

Actually, the entirety of the Book of Ecclesiastes exposes the emptiness of earthly wisdom in hastening after impossible satisfaction, whether sensual, industrial, or philosophic. In effect, in Ecclesiastes and the Song of Solomon, Christ and the world are contrasted. In the one Book, the heart is too large for the portion; in the other, the portion is too large for the heart.

WHAT DOES CHRIST MEAN BY ONE LOSING ONE'S LIFE?

The next phrase tells us:

"But whosoever shall lose his life for My sake and the Gospel's, the same shall save it."

When Jesus spoke of *"losing one's life,"* He was not speaking of physical death. He was speaking of one ceasing to depend on his own ability, strength, efforts, accomplishments (so-called), and ability, and doing so *"for My sake."* Actually, He presents two conditions:

1. *"My sake"*: This means to trust His Way, which is the Way of the Cross. Our Lord paid a terrible price for these benefits. Considering the price that He paid, it is a shame, if nothing else, for us not to avail ourselves of all that He has done for us. That should go without saying!

2. *"And the Gospel's"*: In this statement, the Lord is not speaking only of Preachers, but actually of every single Believer. The *"Gospel"* is *"good news."* It's the good news that Jesus died on the Cross, thereby making it possible for sinful man to be made righteous, and thereby to have eternal life.

NOTES

If Preachers do not look exclusively to Christ and the Cross, ever preaching the Cross (I Cor. 1:21, 23; 2:2), they will not be preaching the Gospel, but, in effect, something else entirely. As a result, very few precious people will be saved, and very few precious lives will be changed.

When it comes to Believers, we are to live the Christ life, which is to live the Cross life, which is to have *"more abundant life"* (Jn. 10:10). Only then can we live a victorious life, which, within itself, serves as a beacon of life to a lost world.

In this manner, *"the same shall save it,"* i.e., *"save one's life."*

(36) "FOR WHAT SHALL IT PROFIT A MAN, IF HE SHALL GAIN THE WHOLE WORLD, AND LOSE HIS OWN SOUL?"

The synopsis is:

The simple equation of profit and loss states that one's soul is worth more than the whole world.

PROFIT

The phrase, *"For what shall it profit a man,"* proclaims Christ bringing this all-important subject down to the level of the businessman. He now speaks of profit and loss!

The great question of the world is *"What's is in for me?"* Consequently, Jesus addresses the world on their own level. The conclusion of the question, *"If he shall gain the whole world, and lose his own soul?"* puts everything in stark contrast. In essence, our Lord states that one soul is worth more than the entirety of the riches of planet Earth.

How can that be?

The profit and loss equation is placed in each individual realm.

What do we mean by that?

If a man (or woman) gains the whole world, and then dies without God, thereby losing Eternal Life for his (her) soul, thereby being condemned to Hell forever and forever, it certainly should stand to reason that there is no profit in that. Our life on this Earth, at least when compared to eternity, is very short. So whatever we have here, whether it's greatness and grandeur, or suffering and poverty, it's only for a season. And then we face eternity, and eternity is a long, long time — forever. So, now, I think we can see that even if a person gains the whole world, but loses his own soul, then he's really gained nothing.

WHAT IS THE SOUL OF MAN?

First of all, the soul is one's personal existence. It is the life or self of an individual, as marked by vital drives and desires. It is the seat of emotion and feelings. The *"soul"* and *"spirit"* of man are indestructible. They were created by God to live forever, and actually make up the being of man. Man, in a sense, is a trinity, consisting of *"spirit, soul, and body"* (I Thess. 5:23).

By this trinity of being, the only part of man that dies physically is the body, and that because of the Fall in the Garden of Eden. (At the Resurrection, all Believers will be given new, Glorified Bodies, which cannot die [I Cor. 15:20-22, 51-57].) At the moment of death, the soul and spirit of the unbeliever, which are inseparable, are consigned to Hell to await the Second Resurrection of Death and Damnation, which will take place at the conclusion of the Kingdom Age. It will be the time of the *"Great White Throne Judgment"* (Lk. 16:19-31; Rev., Chpt. 20).

At the Second Resurrection of Damnation, all unbelievers also will be given an indestructible body, which will join their soul and spirit, and then will be cast into the Lake of Fire forever. This is called *"the second death"* (Rev. 20:14). At the moment of death, the soul and spirit of all Believers instantly go to be with Christ (Phil. 1:21-24). At the First Resurrection of Life, which will take place at the Rapture (I Thess. 4:13-18), the Believer will then, as stated, be given a Glorified Body, which will then join the soul and the spirit, and be with Christ forever (I Cor. 15:51-57).

1. With his body, man appeals to the world.
2. With his soul, man appeals to himself.
3. With his spirit, man appeals to God, or the spirit world of darkness.

(37) "OR WHAT SHALL A MAN GIVE IN EXCHANGE FOR HIS SOUL?"

The structure is:

Considering the forever of eternity, the soul is worth more than anything — far more!

EXCHANGE FOR THE SOUL

In Verse 36, the Lord used the entirety of the world by comparison to the soul. In this Thirty-seventh Verse, He goes beyond the world, and challenges man to think of anything that could be *"given in exchange for his soul."* Of course, looking at the soul in the light of eternity, which is the way and manner it is supposed to be addressed, the soul of man is more important than anything. And yet, virtually all of mankind, and for all time, do trade, and have traded, their soul for a mere trifle.

Why would they do so?

Man doesn't realize the value of his soul, simply because he is lost and undone without God, which means that he has no semblance of God, eternity, everlasting life, Heaven, or Hell. He does not believe and he little understands that he is created by God as an eternal being, which speaks of his soul and spirit. Not understanding that, he cannot understand the worth of the soul. Only when a man comes to God, making Jesus Christ the Lord of his life, thereby gaining an understanding of the Bible, and an understanding of eternity, as well, can he then understand the worth of the soul.

(38) "WHOSOEVER THEREFORE SHALL BE ASHAMED OF ME AND OF MY WORDS IN THIS ADULTEROUS AND SINFUL GENERATION; OF HIM ALSO SHALL THE SON OF MAN BE ASHAMED, WHEN HE COMES IN THE GLORY OF HIS FATHER WITH THE HOLY ANGELS."

The exegesis is:

The present conduct of the individual now determines Christ's future conduct with reference to that person.

SHAME

The phrase, *"Whosoever therefore shall be ashamed of Me and of My Words,"* actually proclaims a present tense, actually saying, *"Whosoever is ashamed."* Robertson says that this is not a statement concerning the future conduct of a person, but instead the person's present attitude toward Jesus. The present conduct of the individual now determines Christ's future conduct, as stated, with reference to that person. It speaks of *"shame"* respecting Christ and the Word of God.

Why would anyone be ashamed of Jesus?

Satan has made it his business to so insult

the Person of Christ, and in every conceivable way, that this spirit permeates the entirety of the world, and of mankind. Unbelievers allude to His peasant upbringing, thereby declaring that He must have been deluded. Moreover, the Jews, and from the time of their rejection of Him, have concocted the most evil lies about His Person, which could only have been spawned by Satan himself!

Islam, with its nearly one billion adherents, claims that He was a good man, but definitely not the Son of God. Consequently, to accept Christ as one's Saviour, and thereby openly proclaim Him to any and all, as one must do, requires an attitude and spirit that flies in the face of world thinking.

One Nashville entertainer said the other day, *"I am a silent witness"*! I don't know exactly what he meant by that statement; however, there is no such thing as a *"silent witness"* when it comes to Jesus Christ. One either confesses Him boldly, or not at all!

THE CROSS

However, the cause of the greatest opposition to Christ pertains to the manner in which He died in order to redeem humanity from the grip of Satan and sin. The Cross of Christ appears to the great body of mankind to be shameful and contemptible. To the Jews, it is a stumblingblock; to the Greeks (Gentiles), foolishness. Hence, vast numbers, whether through shame or fear, do not dare to confess it, and still less to preach it.

Therefore, it is that Paul says, *"I am not ashamed of the Gospel of Christ"* (Rom. 1:16).

AN ADULTEROUS AND SINFUL GENERATION

The phrase, *"In this adulterous and sinful generation,"* pertains to the character of Israel at the time of Christ, and also to every generation which has followed. Mankind is ashamed of Him because it is *"adulterous and sinful."* The word *"adulterous,"* although pertaining to immorality, pertains more in this instance to the worship of that which is not of God. That means that those who put the Church ahead of Christ, as do the whole of Catholicism, and many Protestants, are, according to Christ, *"adulterous."*

Paul said, *"Who changed the Truth of God into a lie, and worshipped and served the creature more than the Creator, who is blessed forever"* (Rom. 1:25).

THE SON OF MAN

The phrase, *"Of him shall also the Son of Man be ashamed,"* means that such attitude will be reciprocated in like kind. In other words, no one can be saved and be ashamed of Christ at the same time!

Considering what Christ has done to save mankind, and I speak of the Cross and the price which He paid, one then can well understand how *"shame"* will come back on the heads of those who hold Christ in disdain. Yes, He is *"the Son of Man,"* but He is also *"the Son of God."* The reason that men think of Him in the realm of shame is because they see Him only in the position of *"Son of Man."* As such, *"there is no beauty that we should desire Him"* (Isa., Chpt. 53). But if we see Him also in the realm of Deity, meaning that He is God, and that He never ceased to be God, even while on this Earth, then His Splendor and Glory outshine the Sun.

GLORY

The phrase, *"When He comes in the Glory of His Father with the Holy Angels,"* speaks of the Second Coming, and not the Rapture (Rev., Chpt. 19).

The idea is this:

All the reasons for which man presently seems to be ashamed of Christ will be proven baseless at the Second Coming. The Lord will come with such Splendor and Glory that there will be absolutely no doubt as to Who and What He is! In fact, His Coming will be with such Glory that *"the sun shall be darkened, and the Moon shall not give her light, and the stars shall fall from Heaven, and the powers of the Heavens shall be shaken"* (Mat. 24:29).

No one will be *"ashamed"* of Him then.

All who are Born-Again, and thereby not ashamed of Christ, will actually come back with Him at this time of Glory and Splendor. Conversely, those who have been ashamed of Him will not be with Him at the Second Coming.

CHAPTER 9

(1) "AND HE SAID UNTO THEM, VERILY I SAY UNTO YOU, THAT THERE BE SOME OF THEM WHO STAND HERE, WHICH SHALL NOT TASTE OF DEATH, TILL THEY HAVE SEEN THE KINGDOM OF GOD COME WITH POWER."

The composition is:

The statement of Jesus did not mean that they would not ultimately die, but that before they died, they would see beyond the veil into the Kingdom. It was an anticipatory picture of the coming Millennium.

THE GREAT EXPERIENCE

The phrase, *"And He said unto them, Verily I say unto you,"* presents, by its manner, a tremendously important statement that is about to be made. Some feel, and are probably correct, that the First Verse of this Ninth Chapter should have been the last Verse of the previous Chapter, because it speaks of the coming Kingdom of God, which is alluded to in Verse 38 of Chapter 8.

Concerning this, A.T. Robertson said that the first rule of Scripture interpretation is that one should ignore Chapter and Verse divisions as one studies the Word. Moreover, the Verse and Chapter divisions are not inspired by the Lord, as is the original Text.

The phrase, *"That there be some of them who stand here,"* referred, at least in this instance, to Peter, James, and John. The phrase, *"Which shall not taste of death,"* did not mean, as we've already stated, that they wouldn't die. It did mean they would be given a very important experience concerning the coming *"Kingdom of God."* This would happen some six days later.

THE KINGDOM OF GOD

The phrase, *"Till they have seen the Kingdom of God come with power,"* referred, according to Wuest, to an anticipatory picture of the Millennium. Matthew uses the phrase, *"Till they see the Son of Man coming in His Kingdom"* (Mat. 16:28). Luke said, *"Till they see the Kingdom of God"* (Lk. 9:27).

Actually, the terms *"Kingdom of God"* and *"Kingdom of Heaven"* are somewhat interchangeable, and have somewhat the same meaning. This is also the *"Kingdom of Heaven"* of Matthew 3:2 and 4:17, announced by John the Baptist and the Messiah Himself, but rejected by Israel at that time; however, it will be accepted by Israel at the Second Advent (Second Coming).

The reason for these terms being used differently, but yet referring to the same thing, is probably because Matthew was writing for the Jews and, therefore, used the phrase, *"Kingdom of Heaven."* Mark and Luke were writing for the Gentiles and, therefore, used the term *"Kingdom of God."*

In the strict sense of the word, the term *"Kingdom of God"* refers to the entirety of the Creation of God, some of it which has been corrupted, such as the kingdom of darkness, etc. The term *"Kingdom of Heaven"* could be said to be *"the Kingdom from Heaven,"* which will ultimately be transplanted to this Earth, which will take place in the coming Kingdom Age.

At the conclusion of the Kingdom Age, with Satan cast into the Lake of Fire, along with all of his fallen angels and demons (Rev. 20:7-15), John then said, *"Then comes the end, when He* (Jesus) *shall have delivered up the Kingdom to God, even the Father; when He shall have put down all rule and all authority and power"* (I Cor. 15:24).

This conclusion, with the Kingdom of God rid of all opposition, which refers to Satan and his kingdom of darkness, will then make *"the Kingdom of God"* and *"the Kingdom of Heaven"* one and the same.

POWER

This *"Kingdom"* of which Jesus spoke will come with great power, and will commence at the Second Coming. This was the Kingdom that Nebuchadnezzar saw in his dream, with the *"Stone"* coming from Heaven, which represents Christ, and smiting *"the image upon his feet that were of iron and clay, and broke them to pieces."* It then says, concerning these earthly kingdoms, *"that no place was found for them: and the Stone that smote the image became a great mountain, and filled the whole Earth"* (Dan. 2:34-35).

As stated, this represents Jesus and the

Second Coming, when He will come with great Power.

This completely refutes the Kingdom Now teaching, which states that we are either now living in the Millennium, or that society is getting better and better, due to the influence of Christianity, which will shortly usher in the Millennium. The *"Greed Message"* and *"Political Message"* are, by and large, a large part of this Kingdom Now philosophy, and consequently eagerly embraced by many Christians.

In truth, the world is not getting better and better, but actually worse. In fact, Satan, in the very near future, is going to make his great bid for world dominion by the advent of the Antichrist. The world, at that time, which is just ahead of us, and according to Revelation, Chapters 6 through 19, is going to experience turmoil, suffering, war, and judgment as it has never known before. Actually, the coming times of the near future are going to see *"tribulation"* as the world has never seen in all of its history. These are the very Words of Christ (Mat. 24:21).

No! Jesus was not speaking of the conflict of A.D. 70, when Jerusalem was destroyed, as many teach.

The Disciples of Christ had asked Him the question as to the sign of His Coming and of the end of the age (Mat. 24:3). Consequently, that is the question Jesus was answering. As should be obvious, Jesus did not come in A.D. 70. Furthermore, that date certainly did not mark the end of the age.

When the *"Kingdom of God comes with power,"* even as Jesus stated, He, in fact, will come back to this Earth, because, without Him, there can be no Kingdom. At that time, Israel will accept Him as Saviour, Messiah, and Lord (Zech. 13:6; 14:1-21). Then Israel will become the greatest nation in the world, with Christ reigning Personally and Supremely from Jerusalem.

(2) "AND AFTER SIX DAYS JESUS TOOK WITH HIM PETER, AND JAMES, AND JOHN, AND LED THEM UP INTO AN HIGH MOUNTAIN APART BY THEMSELVES: AND HE WAS TRANSFIGURED BEFORE THEM."

The diagram is:

Luke says *"eight days"* (Lk. 9:28); there is no discrepancy. In Luke, the Greek phrase is inclusive, meaning that all the time was addressed, while in Mark, it is exclusive, meaning that all the days and time were not included.

PETER, JAMES, AND JOHN

The phrase, *"And after six days Jesus took with Him Peter, and James, and John,"* speaks of the second experience in which they, but not the other Disciples, were included. Actually, there would be three experiences of this nature. They are as follows:

1. These three are taken with Jesus at the raising of Jairus' daughter (Mk. 5:37). In this instance, they saw the *"Power"* of Christ.

2. This incident of the Transfiguration: Here they saw the *"Glory"* of Christ.

3. These three were taken even further with Christ in Gethsemane (Mat. 26:37). Here they saw His *"Suffering."*

Why Peter, James, and John, relative to the other nine?

It was not an arbitrary decision on the part of Christ; therefore, there had to be a reason.

Inasmuch as the Bible does not say, we have to surmise that these three had a greater hunger for God and, therefore, a greater love for Christ, despite their faults and failings. As they drew near to Him, He drew near to them (James 4:8).

THE TRANSFIGURATION

The phrase, *"And led them up into an high mountain apart by themselves, and He was transfigured before them,"* refers to the act of giving outward expression of one's inner character, that outward expression coming from and being truly representative of that inner character.

The outward expression of the Lord was obvious to all. He was a travel-stained itinerant Preacher, a Peasant, if you will! As such, there was no evidence concerning His outward expression as to Who He actually was.

Wuest says, *"But now, that outward expression was changed. Out from within the inmost being of the Son of God, there shone that dazzling glory of the essence of Deity which He possesses co-eternally with God the Father and God the Spirit."*

As such, it shone right through the clay walls of His Humanity and through the clothing He wore.

Wuest goes on to say, *"It was that same dazzling radiance which the Angels saw in His pre-incarnate state* (Phil. 2:6), *but given through His physical Body, and not in the spiritual sense, as in the case of the Angels."*

(3) "AND HIS RAIMENT BECAME SHINING, EXCEEDING WHITE AS SNOW; SO AS NO FULLER ON EARTH CAN WHITE THEM."

The overview is:

This was the radiance of Glory shining from within Him.

SHINING

The phrase, *"And His raiment became shining,"* was a result of the Glory of God, which did shine from Him, and consequently made His clothing translucent. Matthew also said, *"His Face did shine."*

It should quickly be added that the Glory that shone on His clothing and Face was not merely a reflection or borrowed radiance, as the reflection of sunlight, but rather the effulgence of Glory which came from within Him.

The word *"shining"* is *"stilbo"* in the Greek, which indicates that the shining was active, or rather *"a living light."*

This is a picture of what He will be like in the coming Kingdom Age, i.e., Millennium.

The phrase, *"So as no fuller on Earth can white them,"* means that whatever color His garment was, due to the powerful effect of the light which shone from within Him, it took on a radiating white.

(4) "AND THERE APPEARED UNTO THEM ELIAS (Elijah) WITH MOSES: AND THEY WERE TALKING WITH JESUS."

The exposition is:

The Greek Text indicates that the conversation was a protracted one.

MOSES AND ELIJAH

The phrase, *"And there appeared unto them Elijah with Moses,"* proclaims a far greater portend than their mere appearance, as startling as that was. Their appearance had to do with the coming Kingdom Age, as did the Transfiguration of Christ.

NOTES

Moses represents the Law, and consequently all those who died in the Faith, which was before the Cross, looking forward to the coming Promise, Who was Christ. Elijah represents Grace.

Moses points to the Saints from Adam's time to the First Advent of Christ and, more particularly, the Cross. These who were under the Law, or before, will have as great a part in the Millennial Kingdom as those under Grace. Elijah speaks of the Saints, dead or alive, under Grace, who, at the Rapture, will also be glorified and translated and be a part of the Millennial Kingdom.

There will actually be no difference in the two groups.

Peter, James, and John represent Israel, cleansed and restored at the Second Advent. The great multitude, which was at the foot of the mountain, as spoken of in Verse 14, speaks of the entirety of the world at the beginning of the coming Kingdom Age, in desperate need of the Ministry of the Messiah.

The Transfiguration, consequently, is a picture, briefly given, of the coming Millennial Kingdom.

THE CONVERSATION

The phrase, *"And they were talking with Jesus,"* has the emphasis, in the Greek Text, that the conversation was a protracted one. Luke says they *"spoke of His decease which He should accomplish at Jerusalem"* (Lk. 9:31). So, from what Luke says, we find that while this glorious appearance of Moses and Elijah on the Mount of Transfiguration, with Jesus being transfigured, represented the coming Kingdom Age, the mechanics of that appearance, so to speak, pertain to what would make it all possible, which is what Jesus would do on the Cross. This should tell us just how important the Cross actually is.

As someone has well said, *"The number 'twelve' no longer represents the great Plan of God, nor the number 'forty,' as in forty days of Purpose, etc., but rather 'one,' which is the Cross."* In other words, the Cross of Christ is the one emblem of the great Plan of God.

What were Peter's thoughts as he saw and overheard this conversation concerning the coming death of Christ in Jerusalem, especially after he had rebuked the Lord concerning this very thing? (Mk. 8:31-32).

But yet, this tremendous experience of the Transfiguration would not give the Disciples, or even Peter, the Faith needed for that trying hour. Peter was still lifted up within his boastful self, and he would not be deterred without bitter humiliation.

In fact, experiences, as wonderful and desirous as they are, will never effect the change that is needed in one's life. That can only come about by Faith and, more particularly, it must be Faith in a specified object, which is Christ and the Cross (Rom. 6:3-14; I Cor. 1:17-18, 21, 23; 2:2; Gal. 6:14; Col. 2:14-15).

(5) "AND PETER ANSWERED AND SAID TO JESUS, MASTER, IT IS GOOD FOR US TO BE HERE: AND LET US MAKE THREE TABERNACLES; ONE FOR YOU, AND ONE FOR MOSES, AND ONE FOR ELIJAH."

The synopsis is:

We find here that Peter compounds his error by placing Moses and Elijah in the same category as Jesus.

PETER

The phrase, *"And Peter answered and said to Jesus,"* refers to him answering something that he had not been asked. However, it is easy to criticize Peter, when I suspect we would not have done any better, or even as well!

The phrase, *"Master, it is good for us to be here,"* certainly is true; however, it completely begs the point. If any response is warranted at all, which was doubtful, at the very most it would have been Praise to the Lord.

THREE TABERNACLES

The phrase, *"And let us make three Tabernacles, one for You, and one for Moses, and one for Elijah,"* is, in the strict sense of the word, not as off-the-wall, so to speak, as it at first seems. There is a possibility that Peter had the Feast of Tabernacles in mind, which will be continued in the coming Kingdom Age (Zech. 14:16). As such, and if that is what he thought, he surmised that it was now beginning, hence, the *"three Tabernacles,"* etc. Having overheard the conversation concerning the coming Crucifixion in Jerusalem, perhaps he thought that the Kingdom Age would commence immediately after this time.

This is evidenced by the question asked of Jesus immediately before the Ascension:

"Lord, will You at this time restore again the Kingdom to Israel?"

"And He said unto them, It is not for you to know the times or the seasons, which the Father has put in His Own Power" (Acts 1:6-7).

However, even if Peter had the Feast of Tabernacles in mind, still, his statement made little sense. Actually, it tells us several things:

1. First of all, Peter was not properly evaluating the Mission of Christ, because he had not properly evaluated the Word of God, i.e., of Christ. As such, his understanding of future events was skewed. He had, like many presently in the modern Church, little understanding as to what the Bible teaches concerning events at the end of this age, which, in fact, are immediately ahead. Christ was not, at this moment, preparing for His Second Coming; He was rather preparing for the great suffering He was to endure on the Cross.

2. As Peter, religious men are so prone to erect shrines where a great spiritual event has taken place. As such, and due to the penchant of man to worship, which actually is given by the Lord, in his carnality, he worships the gift instead of the Giver. Hence, millions worship the Church instead of the One Who builds the Church, i.e., Christ Jesus.

3. Whatever his error, Peter compounds it by placing Moses and Elijah in the same category as Jesus. This will be sharply rebuked by the Voice from Heaven, as outlined in Verse 7. The modern Church, especially Catholicism, also has the tendency to place Mary on a par with Christ. Such is blasphemy!

(6) "FOR HE DIDN'T KNOW WHAT TO SAY; FOR THEY WERE SORE AFRAID."

The structure is:

The word *"afraid"* means that they were actually *"terrified."*

FEAR

The phrase, *"For he didn't know what to say,"* is obvious by what he said, which means it would have been better for him not to have said anything.

The phrase, *"For they were sore afraid,"* speaks of them being terrified. No wonder!

All of a sudden, Jesus, even as He stands before them, begins to shine with such a brightness that the Disciples are hard put to describe it. And then two men appear, one who has been dead for hundreds of years, with the other (Elijah) having never died, but translated. Finally, there was the Voice from Heaven!

These three Disciples are here given a glimpse into the spirit world of Righteousness. The appearance of both Moses and Elijah tells us a number of things.

First of all, it tells us that the human being actually never dies, at least as far as the soul and the spirit are concerned. At death, the soul and the spirit, if redeemed, instantly go to be with the Lord (Phil. 1:23). If unredeemed, the soul and the spirit go to Hell (Lk. 16:19-31).

Second, these Passages completely refute the idea, as held by some that, at the time of death, not only does the body sleep, which actually goes back to dust, but the soul and spirit also sleep. Nowhere in the Bible does the Word of God teach *"soul sleep."*

Last of all, the soul and the spirit without the physical body, although not complete, still, have every appearance of a human being, as evidenced by Moses, who had died many centuries before. To be complete, however, a Glorified Body will be given to every Saint, which will take place at the First Resurrection of Life (I Cor., Chpt. 15; I Thess. 4:13-18).

(7) "AND THERE WAS A CLOUD THAT OVERSHADOWED THEM: AND A VOICE CAME OUT OF THE CLOUD, SAYING, THIS IS MY BELOVED SON: HEAR HIM."

The exegesis is:

This cloud was the Shekinah Glory Cloud, which guided Israel out of Egypt, and which rested above the Mercy Seat in the Holy of Holies in the Tabernacle.

THE CLOUD

The phrase, *"And there was a cloud that overshadowed them,"* presents that which is totally different than the clouds of which we normally think. As stated, this was the Shekinah Glory Cloud, the same one which led Israel out of Egypt (Ex. 13:21-22). It was also the same cloud which resided above the Mercy Seat, beneath the Golden Cherubim in the Holy of Holies, whether in the Tabernacle or Temple (Ex. 40:34; I Ki. 8:10-11).

The word that Mark used for *"cloud"* is *"nephele,"* which speaks of a cloud which has definite form and is of a certain size. Had he been speaking of a cloud which is a shapeless collection of vapor, which makes up the clouds in the Heavens, he would have used the word *"nephos."* So this *"Cloud"* was the Glory of the Lord!

THE VOICE

The phrase, *"And a Voice came out of the cloud,"* proclaims the actual Voice of God the Father. So here we once again see the Trinity. God the Father speaks from Heaven, God the Son is on the Mount, and God the Holy Spirit effects the Transfiguration of Christ and inspires Mark to give this account.

MY BELOVED SON

The phrase, *"Saying, This is My Beloved Son: hear Him,"* actually says, in the Greek Text, *"This is My Son, The Beloved One."* According to Wuest, this places emphasis equally upon two facts:

A. That the Messiah is God's Son; and,

B. That He is the Beloved One.

The phrase, *"Hear Him,"* refers to *"Christ."* In other words, Moses and Elijah are not to be placed on the same par with Christ, which should be obvious. Jesus is the One to Whom we must *"hear"* and *"listen."* It actually means, *"Be constantly hearing Him."*

Wuest says that it does not merely refer to the act of hearing, in the sense of listening, but also to the act of obeying what is heard. In a sense, these Words of God signify the abolition of the Old Covenant and the establishment of the New Covenant in Christ. The entire portrayal of the Transfiguration is meant to proclaim, along with its symbolism of the coming Kingdom Age, the price that would be paid for Redemption, and we speak of the Cross, and the Deity of Christ.

Consequently, He Alone was transfigured, not Elijah and Moses. They did not have within them that which He had within Him, because He, although Very Man, was also Very God.

(8) "AND SUDDENLY, WHEN THEY HAD LOOKED ROUND ABOUT, THEY SAW NO MAN ANY MORE, SAVE JESUS ONLY WITH THEMSELVES."

The exegesis is:

These three Disciples had just witnessed something that no other human beings had ever seen.

THE NATURAL BY COMPARISON WITH THE SUPERNATURAL

The words, *"And suddenly, when they had looked round about,"* proclaims, as is obvious, a change in this situation. Matthew seems to explain it a little more fully when he says, *"And when the Disciples heard it* (the Voice of God out of Heaven), *they fell on their face, and were sore afraid"* (Mat. 17:6). As if the Transfiguration of Jesus wasn't enough, and with the sudden appearance of two of the great Prophets of the distant past, the Voice of God coming from the Cloud, which overshadowed them, placed them in a position just short of terror.

Peter's foolish request concerning the Tabernacles are suddenly forgotten in the Glory of the moment. They hide their faces on the ground, with Matthew saying, *"And Jesus came and touched them, and said, Arise and be not afraid"* (Mat. 17:7).

JESUS ONLY

The phrase, *"They saw no man anymore, save Jesus only with themselves,"* proclaims the conclusion of this great happening.

Let it be known: This was not a Dream or even a Vision, at least as a Vision is commonly thought of, but rather an actual happening, which was as literal as possible for anything to be. They had witnessed the Glory of God in a way that no human being had ever witnessed before. While it is true that the Prophets of the past, such as Isaiah (Isa. 6:1-7) and Ezekiel (Ezek., Chpt. 1), etc., had seen great manifestations of the Glory of God, still, none had seen Jesus as did Peter, James, and John.

In truth, all the manifestations of Glory in the Old Testament were not an end within themselves, but rather pointed to that which was to come, namely Jesus. And yet, that which was seen by these Disciples, as glorious and wonderful as it was, was only a preview of that which is even yet to come.

The fulfillment of the great Plan of God will be the coming down out of Heaven of the New Jerusalem, which will take up its abode on this Earth. John the Beloved wrote, *"And the city had no need of the sun, neither of the moon, to shine in it: for the Glory of God did lighten it, and the Lamb is the Light thereof"* (Rev. 21:23).

> *"There's a country far beyond the starry sky.*
> *"There's a city where there never comes a night.*
> *"If we're faithful, we shall go there bye and bye.*
> *"'Tis the city where the Lamb is the Light."*

(9) "AND AS THEY CAME DOWN FROM THE MOUNTAIN, HE CHARGED THEM THAT THEY SHOULD TELL NO MAN WHAT THINGS THEY HAD SEEN, TILL THE SON OF MAN WERE RISEN FROM THE DEAD."

The structure is:

In the first place, they didn't understand it then well enough to properly explain what they had actually seen and heard. That would await the Day of Pentecost and the Advent of the Holy Spirit.

THE CHARGE

The phrase, *"And as they came down from the mountain, He charged them that they should tell no man what things they had seen,"* referred even to their fellow Disciples.

Spiritual things cannot be explained solely by natural means. That's the reason that Paul said, *"But the natural man receives not the things of the Spirit of God* (speaks of the individual who is not Born-Again)*: for they are foolishness unto Him* (a lack of understanding)*: neither can he know them* (fallen man cannot understand spiritual truths), *because they are spiritually discerned* (only the regenerated spirit of man can understand the things of the Spirit)" (I Cor. 2:14). He also said, *"But God has revealed them unto us by His Spirit: for the Spirit* (Holy Spirit) *searches all things, yes, the deep things of God"* (I Cor. 2:10).

Due to the fact, as stated, that the Holy Spirit had not yet come in order to abide permanently in hearts and lives of the redeemed, Who would then give all Believers understanding, it would be best that these three Disciples wait until then before trying to explain this great happening, which they did (Jn. 14:17).

THE RESURRECTION

The phrase, *"Till the Son of Man were risen from the dead,"* means that things would begin to fall into place at that time! They had truly seen much, but had understood little. The Cross, Resurrection, Ascension, and the Day of Pentecost, when they all would be baptized with the Holy Spirit, would then bring everything into proper focus.

That's why Jesus, just hours before His Crucifixion, said, *"I have yet many things to say unto you* (pertained to the entirety of the New Covenant, which meaning would be given to the Apostle Paul, and which foundation had already been laid by Christ), *but you cannot bear them now.*

"Howbeit when He, the Spirit of Truth, is come (which He did on the Day of Pentecost), *He will guide you into all Truth* (if our Faith is properly placed in Christ and the Cross, the Holy Spirit can then bring forth Truth to us; He doesn't guide into 'some' truth, but rather 'all Truth'): *for He shall not speak of Himself* (tells us not only What He does but Whom He represents); *but whatsoever He shall hear, that shall He speak* (doesn't refer to lack of knowledge, for the Holy Spirit is God, but rather He will proclaim the Work of Christ only, which refers to the Cross): *and He will show you things to come* (pertains to the New Covenant, which would shortly be given)" (Jn. 16:12-13).

(10) "AND THEY KEPT THAT SAYING WITH THEMSELVES, QUESTIONING ONE WITH ANOTHER WHAT THE RISING FROM THE DEAD SHOULD MEAN."

The composition is:

They still did not understand the purpose and reason for His coming to this world, which was to redeem man, which would necessitate His going to the Cross; in other words, the Cross was ever His destination.

NOTES

THE GREAT QUESTION

The phrase, *"And they kept that saying with themselves,"* means that they faithfully obeyed what the Lord had told them respecting what they had seen. They told no one!

The phrase, *"Questioning one with another what the rising from the dead should mean,"* presents two problems:

1. The manifestation of the Glory of God they had experienced was so startling, so unreal, so unexplainable, that the implication is that they discussed it very little among themselves. It was almost as if they were fearful of doing so, which they probably were. In other words, they really didn't understand the Transfiguration, at least not at this time.

2. They did, however, discuss intently the statement of Jesus about Him dying and rising from the dead. Despite His plain statements, they still did not understand what He was talking about. The Power He manifested in healing the sick, cleansing the lepers, and even raising the dead, was, within itself, so absolutely astounding that they could not begin to see how anyone could take His Life.

In their reasoning, *"How can you take the Life of One Who can walk on water, or speak the Word and a mighty storm instantly subsides, and Who can even raise the dead?"* In their minds, they cannot put it all together. Jesus is the Messiah, and of that they are sure! While it was true that the opposition of the Pharisees and Sadducees was severe, still, there was really nothing they could do against such Power.

As we have repeatedly stated, they did not understand that His True Mission was so much greater than bringing back once again the Glory to Israel. He rather had come to break the terrible grip that Satan had on humanity, a grip so severe, in fact, that man, within himself, could not break it. They looked at Him as a King, not a Sacrifice. In Truth, He was a King, and more than a King, in Truth, The King, but yet The Sacrifice!

They had heard Elijah and Moses speak with Jesus concerning His coming death, and now they hear Jesus speak of His rising from the dead. It should have been an encouragement to them, which, in reality, Christ intended it to be; however, they simply did not understand.

(11) "AND THEY ASKED HIM, SAYING, WHY SAY THE SCRIBES THAT ELIJAH MUST FIRST COME?"

The diagram is:

They were referring to Malachi 4:5.

ELIJAH

Their question concerning the coming of Elijah was based on his appearance before them on the Mount of Transfiguration. They were speaking of what the Scribes taught concerning the coming of Elijah, as prophesied by Malachi some 400 years earlier, *"Behold, I will send you Elijah the Prophet before the coming of the great and dreadful day of the LORD"* (Mal. 4:5).

The Scribes, however, even as the Disciples, had the time element somewhat confused. They did not distinguish the First Coming of Christ in the flesh from His Second Advent of Judgment, which is even yet to come.

WRONG THINKING!

The thinking of the Disciples seems to have been that immediately after the Resurrection of Christ, He would then set up the Kingdom; consequently, they thought the appearance of Elijah on the Mount of Transfiguration pertained to that event. In their minds, in view of the Kingdom soon to come, Elijah should have remained. This is also evidenced by their question to Christ immediately before the Ascension, *"Lord, will You at this time restore again the Kingdom to Israel?"* (Acts 1:6). Even at that late moment, they continued to hold to Jesus ushering in the Kingdom and once again making Israel great.

Actually, however, the difference between the First and Second Advents of Christ was amply outlined in the Old Testament; nevertheless, it seems that all of Israel confused them. As we have stated, Isaiah 53 and Daniel 9 adequately describe His First Coming in the flesh, and Him being *"cut off,"* as Daniel put it. Basically all the Prophets spoke of His Second Advent, which would be in Glory and Power (Ezek., Chpts. 38-39; Zech., Chpt. 14, Isa. 9:6-7). Actually, the religious leaders rejected Jesus as the Promised One, and the Disciples accepted Him, but confused His Coming and His Purpose.

(12) "AND HE ANSWERED AND TOLD THEM, ELIJAH VERILY COMES FIRST, AND RESTORES ALL THINGS; AND HOW IT IS WRITTEN OF THE SON OF MAN, THAT HE MUST SUFFER MANY THINGS, AND BE SET AT NOUGHT."

The overview is:

Jesus is speaking of Elijah coming as one of the two witnesses not long before the Second Advent (Rev. 11:3-12).

THE ANSWER

The phrase, *"And He answered and told them,"* proclaims Him explaining the situation, but with them still lacking in understanding. The phrase, *"Elijah verily comes first, and restores all things,"* refers to this Prophet, as stated, coming as one of the two witnesses, not long before the Second Advent (Mal. 4:5-6; Rev. 11:3-12).

Jesus is saying that the Scribes are correct in their statement about Elijah coming first, but that they are confusing the time. Many of the Scribes, no doubt, disclaimed Christ because Elijah had not come. They completely misunderstood the Mission of John the Baptist, who came in the spirit and power of Elijah (Mat. 17:13).

The phrase, *"Restores all things,"* did not mean that Elijah would do this personally, but that shortly after his appearance all things would be restored, which pertained to Israel and the Kingdom Age, which will affect the entirety of the world.

THE CROSS

The phrase, *"And how it is written of the Son of Man, that He must suffer many things, and be set at nought,"* pertains to the First Coming (birth of Christ and His Ministry), of which Elijah, at least in a personal sense, would have no part. By the words, *"it is written,"* Jesus is plainly saying that His Present Coming is when He will *"suffer,"* which pertains to the Cross, exactly as He has been telling the Disciples, and as is revealed in Isaiah 53, among other places; consequently, and as we have stated, there was no reason for the Scribes or the Disciples to confuse the issue.

Why didn't the Scribes understand these Prophecies as they should have?

The Pharisees, of which the Scribes were a part, so added to the Word of God that they no longer knew its true meaning. Self-will had degenerated into self-righteousness, which clouded their understanding of the Word of God. In other words, they simply no longer understood the Bible; however, and as should be obvious, it was a willful rejection of the Word. Inasmuch as they did not want its true meaning, the Lord took from them what little understanding they did have (Mat. 13:12).

(13) "BUT I SAY UNTO YOU, THAT ELIJAH IS INDEED COME, AND THEY HAVE DONE UNTO HIM WHATSOEVER THEY LISTED, AS IT IS WRITTEN OF HIM."

The exposition is:

This refers to John the Baptist, who came in the spirit and power of Elijah (Lk. 1:17).

ELIJAH

The phrase, *"But I say unto you, That Elijah is indeed come,"* presents Christ referring to John the Baptist, who came in the spirit and power of Elijah (Lk. 1:17). He would do, and did, before the First Advent what Elijah will do before the Second Advent (Isa. 40:3; Mal. 3:1; Mat. 17:12-13).

Concerning this, Wuest says, *"We are not to understand that John the Baptist was the actual Elijah of the Old Testament, nor that his appearance and Ministry to Israel fulfilled the Prophecy of the future coming and Ministry of Elijah, but that John came in the spirit and power of Elijah to prepare the hearts of Israel for the First Advent of the Messiah, as Elijah will do for His Second Advent."*

Revelation, Chapter 11, proclaims this event. Elijah will be one of two witnesses, with the other probably being Enoch. The two will make their appearance during the last half of the Great Tribulation. They will minister from Jerusalem, with the Antichrist unable to stop them until near the end of that Great Tribulation period. I wonder what the world will think of these two men at that time, considering that they are two individuals who actually lived on this Earth thousands of years before, and who were translated that they should not see death, at least until they are both killed at the end, as we have stated. They will not be overcome until *"they have finished their testimony"* (Rev. 11:7). The world, no doubt, will not in any way believe that these are what and who they claim to be — Enoch and Elijah.

JOHN THE BAPTIST

The phrase, *"And they have done unto him whatsoever they listed, as it is written of him,"* refers to John's execution by Herod. Elijah was persecuted by Jezebel, as John the Baptist was persecuted by Herodias. Further, Elijah, as we have stated, will, in the future, be killed by the Antichrist (Rev. 11:8), as John the Baptist was killed by Herod.

And yet, John the Baptist wasn't stopped until he had finished his Ministry; likewise, Elijah will not be stopped until he has finished his Ministry. Even though Mark did not mention it, Matthew said, *"Then the Disciples understood that He spoke unto them of John the Baptist"* (Mat. 17:13).

(14) "AND WHEN HE CAME TO HIS DISCIPLES, HE SAW A GREAT MULTITUDE ABOUT THEM, AND THE SCRIBES QUESTIONING WITH THEM."

The exposition is:

Jesus now joins the other nine Disciples at the foot of the mountain after the Transfiguration.

THE SCRIBES

The phrase, *"And when He came to His Disciples,"* refers to the Nine, because Peter, James, and John had been with Him. The phrase, *"He saw a great multitude about them,"* speaks of the crowd which had assembled, due to the argument that was now taking place between the Scribes and the nine Disciples. It concerned the Disciples attempting to cast a demon out of a boy, but without success.

The phrase, *"And the Scribes questioning with them,"* meant they were taunting the Disciples with their failure, and suggesting that it was because the Power of Jesus was waning. No doubt, the Disciples had used the Name of Jesus in attempting to cast the demon out of the boy. What the Disciples were answering is not recorded, but it is possible they were saying very little, if anything!

RELIGION

Regrettably, the world of religion at present, as then, has no regard for Christ. They may speak of Him, but most of the time it is in an unbelieving manner. They also have no regard or concern for those who are pitifully held captive by Satan, as was this boy, and who can be set free only by Christ.

Religion is a cold, calculating business! While it speaks of God, it is devised totally by man. Its task is the control of people and the taking in of money. Absolutely no one is helped by its efforts, but only hurt, and greatly so! God is not in it, so no one can be helped. When one looks at these Scribes, as they ridiculed the Disciples, one is also looking, by and large, at the modern Church!

In addition, the True Remnant, whoever they might be, is too often as the Disciples were — powerless. They use the Name of Jesus, but seemingly to little avail! Verses 28 and 29 tell us why.

(15) "AND STRAIGHTWAY ALL THE PEOPLE, WHEN THEY BEHELD HIM, WERE GREATLY AMAZED, AND RUNNING TO HIM SALUTED HIM."

The synopsis is:

The people greeted Jesus with great warmth and admiration — but the Scribes did not!

GREAT AMAZEMENT

The phrase, *"And straightway all the people, when they beheld Him,"* proclaims the sudden, unexpected arrival of Jesus. The word *"beheld"* denotes something more than mere recognition. It is also more than Him coming at this particular time, in the midst of the sarcasm of the Scribes. Quite possibly, traces of Glory, which He had just experienced on the Mount of Transfiguration, still lingered on Him.

The phrase, *"Were greatly amazed,"* means *"were utterly amazed."* The Greek expositors express something more than mere recognition. There was something about Him that stood out, which must have come as a shock to the Scribes, as well! Their sarcasm must have stuck in their throats at this point.

The phrase, *"And running to Him saluted Him,"* pertained to His popularity among the people. This is what angered the religious leaders of Israel.

(16) "AND HE ASKED THE SCRIBES, WHAT QUESTION YE WITH THEM?"

The structure is:

The Scribes were the supposed experts in the Law of Moses; consequently, Jesus addresses His question directly to them.

THE QUESTION

The question was actually directed to the entirety of the multitude who came to Christ upon His arrival, but which eventually concluded with the Scribes. More than likely, when the question was asked, the people turned and looked at the Scribes, who really did not answer. The next Verse gives us the reason!

(17) "AND ONE OF THE MULTITUDE ANSWERED AND SAID, MASTER, I HAVE BROUGHT UNTO YOU MY SON, WHICH HAS A DUMB SPIRIT."

The structure is:

The correct analysis of the situation is: A demon spirit had bound the boy's tongue and vocal organs, and had also tried to kill him several times.

THE DUMB SPIRIT

The phrase, *"And one of the multitude answered and said,"* concerned the man who had brought his son to Jesus. The Scribes were probably very pleased that the man quickly answered, so they would not have to answer. They desired no confrontation with Christ.

The phrase, *"Master, I have brought unto You my son, which has a dumb spirit,"* pertains to him hearing that Jesus was in the vicinity and, therefore, he brought his son for Deliverance. However, he found only nine of the Disciples, but Jesus was not present.

The *"dumb spirit"* was a correct analysis of the situation. The boy was demon-possessed, with the demon having bound his tongue and vocal organs. It seems that knowledge of demon spirits was more pronounced at that time even than presently. Inasmuch as the Holy Spirit did not contradict the findings of many, if any, of these people, this proclaims the truth of the situation.

DISCERNMENT

While it is certainly true that modern Disciples can overemphasize the presence of evil spirits, still, I am persuaded that these spirits are just as active today as then, and are the cause of far more problems that one realizes. If Satan cannot get one to become overly preoccupied with evil spirits, he will go in the other direction, tempting the Believer to ignore them altogether, thereby not correctly analyzing the situation in a true spiritual sense.

The modern Church, however, little depending on the Holy Spirit, with but few exceptions, rather recommends such cases to Psychologists. In fact, one of the greatly used terms in the modern Church, at least in situations similar to this of which we speak, is *"You need professional help."* Of course, neither the world of humanistic psychology, nor any other type of effort, holds any help for people who are demon-possessed.

We may think it strange for a child to be demon-possessed; but, most definitely, it can happen, even as here recorded. When children are raised in an atmosphere of ungodliness, as most are, to be frank, in the spiritual sense, anything can happen.

The only answer for this is the Lord Jesus Christ, and what He did at the Cross. In fact, at Calvary, He defeated Satan, every demon spirit, and every fallen angel (Col. 2:14-15).

Concerning Believers, millions of Christians are seriously demon-oppressed; they also are referred to the world of psychology. What they truly need is to be taught the veracity of the Cross as it refers to our Sanctification; they will then find that victory can be theirs, totally and completely, with all demon-oppression vanquished and stopped.

But again, regrettably, virtually all of Christendom has been referred to the *"Word of Faith"* camp, which doesn't believe in the Cross at all, or to the *"Purpose Driven Life"* fad, which also holds no answer whatsoever. The *"Government of Twelve"* could be thrown into this also! Sadly, the lot of the Christian in these false ways will fall out to great hurt in their hearts and lives, with many of them losing their souls.

And how do I know these things are wrong?

NOTES

I know they are wrong because the emphasis of their Faith is not Christ and Him Crucified, but something else altogether. As such, there can be no victory, because the Holy Spirit, Who Alone can bring about that which we need, simply will not function in such a capacity. He functions only within the parameters of the Finished Work of Christ (Rom. 8:1-2, 11).

(18) "AND WHERESOEVER HE TAKES HIM, HE TEARS HIM: AND HE FOAMS, AND GNASHES WITH HIS TEETH, AND PINES AWAY: AND I SPOKE TO YOUR DISCIPLES THAT THEY SHOULD CAST HIM OUT; AND THEY COULD NOT."

The exegesis is:

The Disciples tried repeatedly to cast the demon out, but without success; hence, the taunts of the Scribes.

DEMON POSSESSION

The phrase, *"And wheresoever he takes him,"* refers to the demon spirit *"seizing upon"* or *"taking possession of."* The power of the demon spirit is greater than the willpower or the strength of the individual; consequently, the control by the one possessed, as this boy, is limited, if any at all. In other words, such a person, as this boy, cannot control himself.

While one certainly should not give too much credit to Satan, still, at the same time, one also must not underestimate his power. To give the Reader an example of how great God's Power is, when the Lord wanted light, He simply spoke it into existence (Gen. 1:3). Moreover, the entire restoration of planet Earth, which was *"without form, and void; and darkness was upon the face of the deep,"* was brought about simply by the Word of God (Gen. 1:2).

Concerning this Restoration, the phrase, *"And God said,"* was used five times in order to bring it about, and it was accomplished in four days (Gen. 1:3-19); however, when time came to redeem man from the terrible horror of the Fall which resulted in destruction, this power of Satan, as it gripped humanity, was so great that God could not merely speak Redemption into existence, as He did Restoration.

Actually, God, Who is Almighty, could

have, in fact, spoken Redemption into existence, but His Nature would not allow such to happen. God's Almighty Power will never circumvent His Nature. His Nature demanded that sin be addressed, with the price properly paid. In order to do that, He had to come down to this Hell-bound world, taking upon Himself the frame of man, and then die on Calvary in order that the terrible bondage of sin could be completely broken.

Understanding this, at least somewhat, we then begin to see how powerful sin actually is. To be sure, only Jesus Christ has overcome Satan, defeating the powers of darkness, because He is stronger. Yet He did so by and through the Cross (Gal. 6:14). As a result, He entered into Satan's house and spoiled his goods — in fact, the entirety of his house (Mk. 3:27). Consequently, to depend on anything other than Christ and what He has done for us at the Cross is foolishness indeed!

Let's lay aside demon-possession and even demon-oppression for the moment, and deal with the struggle every Christian faces in his effort to live an overcoming life.

CAN SATAN OVERRIDE A BELIEVER'S WILL?

In a word, Yes! That is, if the Believer doesn't understand his place and position in Christ, and rather tries to live for God in all the wrong ways, which, regrettably, fits the vast majority of the modern Church. While many Preachers may deny that Satan can override a Believer's will, the Word of God says differently.

Paul said, *"For I know that in me (that is, in my flesh,) dwells no good thing: for to will is present with me; but how to perform that which is good I find not"* (Rom. 7:18). In this Passage and, in fact, in the entirety of the Seventh Chapter of Romans, which we will look at more fully momentarily, it plainly tells us that Satan can override the will of an individual.

Let's break this Scripture down for analysis.

"For I know that in me (that is, in my flesh,) dwells no good thing (speaks of man's own ability, or rather the lack thereof, in comparison to the Holy Spirit, at least when it comes to spiritual things)*: for to will is present with me* (Paul is speaking here of his willpower. Regrettably, most modern Christians are trying to live for God by means of willpower, thinking falsely that since they have come to Christ, they are now free to say *'No'* to sin. That is the wrong way to look at the situation; the Believer cannot live for God by the strength of willpower. While the will is definitely important, it alone is not enough. The Believer must exercise Faith in Christ and the Cross, and do so constantly. Then he will have the ability and strength to say *'Yes'* to Christ, which automatically says *'No'* to the things of the world)*; but how to perform that which is good I find not* (outside of the Cross, it is impossible to find a way to do good)."

WILLPOWER

Most Christians think that the Lord greatly strengthens their willpower once they come to Christ. That is not the case! He doesn't!

The will of the individual is definitely important, as should be overly obvious; however, if we try to live for God by means of willpower, the Holy Spirit labels such as the *"flesh."* To be sure, such a Believer is going to fail, and no matter how hard he tries otherwise.

The Believer must understand that Satan is stronger than we are. Trying to oppose him on the wrong ground cannot have any conclusion but defeat, and I speak of defeat regarding ourselves, and not Satan.

We must first come to the conclusion that no true Christian wants to sin. In fact, sin is abhorrent to the true Child of God. And yet, millions of Christians find themselves being ruled by the sin nature, despite all their efforts to do otherwise (Rom. 7:15).

Let's look at another Biblical example of this of which I speak.

SIMON PETER

Jesus said to Peter, *"Simon, Simon, behold, Satan has desired to have you, that he may sift you as wheat:*

"But I have prayed for you, that your Faith fail not: and when you are converted, strengthen your brethren" (Lk. 22:31-32).

To that statement by Christ, Peter said, *"Lord, I am ready to go with You, both into prison, and to death"* (Lk. 22:33).

Was Peter serious concerning his affirmation? At that time, was he really serious about going to prison with Christ, should that arise, or even death?

Yes, he was! I believe he meant every word he said; however, his affirmation, or boast, was in his own strength, and not true Faith, as given by Christ.

If one is to notice, Jesus did not tell Peter He would pray for him that his strength fail not, but instead *"that your Faith fail not."*

Did Peter want to do what he did? I believe it is obvious he did not want to deny Christ. However, Satan overrode his will. In truth, Peter's strength failed, but his Faith did not fail. He lost a battle, but he did not lose the war.

The Believer must understand:

Every attack Satan directs against us is, in one way or the other, designed to weaken and to ultimately destroy our Faith.

If Satan can maneuver the Believer into a position where he has tried his hardest and still lost, Satan will then tell the Believer any lie he can get him to believe. He will tell him that Christianity does not work, or the Word of God doesn't work, etc.! That's when our Faith is at stake. At that time, it's not really a question of our strength; it is a question of our Faith.

Can our Faith fail?

It can fail, as it has failed in the hearts and lives of many. Now we are coming close to the answer to this dilemma.

FAITH

If the Believer places his Faith exclusively in Christ and what Christ has done at the Cross, understanding that what Jesus there did was totally for me and you, he will then have the help of the Holy Spirit, which means that he's not relying on his own strength. The answer to the Christian dilemma of living a Godly life, victorious over the world, the flesh, and the Devil, is simply Christ and What He has done for us at the Cross.

That's why Paul said, *"But God forbid that I should glory* (boast), *save in the Cross of our Lord Jesus Christ, by Whom the world is crucified unto me, and I unto the world"* (Gal. 6:14).

The Believer must come to the place, and

NOTES

exclusively, that he understands that all victory was won at the Cross, and that our Faith must be anchored securely in that Finished Work. When this is done, the Holy Spirit, Who Alone can make us what we ought to be, will then work mightily on our behalf (Rom. 8:1-2, 11). In fact, this is God's Prescribed Order of Victory. He has no other, because He needs no other.

AS SIMPLE AS IT IS, WHY IS IT THAT SO MANY CHRISTIANS FIND IT SO DIFFICULT TO BELIEVE WHAT WE'VE JUST SAID?

To get at the root cause, the problem definitely is *"unbelief."*

Why?

First and foremost, the great victory of the Cross is precious little preached behind most pulpits. Considering that *"faith comes by hearing, and hearing by the Word of God,"* a lack of proper preaching and teaching is the basic cause of the problem (Rom. 10:17).

Along with Preachers preaching the wrong thing, there is something in every Believer, which Paul labels as *"the flesh,"* which desires to try to live this life by the means of our own ability, strength, and power. We like to think, *"We can do it!"* But the truth is, we can't. And it doesn't matter who we are or how strong we might think we are.

To try to live for God by the means of one's own willpower and strength, no matter how strong that willpower might be, failure will be the end result of such a person, just the same as the weakest individual who has ever lived. The problem is *"spiritual adultery."*

SPIRITUAL ADULTERY

In Romans 7:1-4, Paul tells the Believer that we are *"married to Christ."* He uses the analogy of a woman who is unfaithful to her husband. Then he says that she shall be called *"an adulteress."* In these four Verses, he says that if her husband has died, then she is free to remarry; otherwise, she is not!

He likens all of this to Christ and the Law. As stated, the Believer is married to Christ; but if the Believer tries to live for God by means of particular laws, which, regrettably, most try to do, such a Believer is, in effect, being unfaithful to Christ. The Believer is actually committing — in fact, living in a state of — *"spiritual adultery."*

Let us say it again: They are being unfaithful to Christ.

Let's say it even in a stronger way:

If the Believer places his faith in anything except Christ and the Cross, and I mean anything, such a Believer is, in effect, committing spiritual adultery, and the Holy Spirit emphatically will not help such a person. The Holy Spirit is not going to help the Believer commit spiritual adultery and live in such a state. While He will love the Believer, and will do all that He can to help him otherwise, when the Believer attempts to live for Christ outside of God's Prescribed Order, which is *"Christ and the Cross,"* such direction greatly limits the Holy Spirit.

There are millions of Christians who know that the Word says, *"There has no temptation taken you but such as is common to man* (refers to the limitations God has placed upon Satan respecting that which he can or cannot do)*: but God is faithful, Who will not suffer you to be tempted above that you are able; but will with the temptation also make a way to escape, that you may be able to bear it"* (I Cor. 10:13).

But yet, despite all the strength they can muster, they have not been able to overcome, which leaves them confused. In other words, they have *"not"* been able to bear it.

So what is wrong?

The wrong is that they have placed their faith in something other than Christ and the Cross, which means they have abrogated God's *"way of escape."* The Cross of Christ is the only escape route. There is none else!

The terrible truth is, the vast majority of Christians are living in a state of *"spiritual adultery."* They don't want to do this, and don't, in fact, mean to do this, but that's exactly what is happening.

Let it ever be understood: Whether doing such through ignorance or otherwise, the end result will be the same — failure. The tragedy is, the failure will become worse and worse as it goes along.

PAUL'S VICTORY

The Seventh Chapter of Romans presents the personal experience of the Apostle Paul, which should be looked at very closely by every Believer. Unfortunately, many Preachers have attempted to conclude that the Seventh Chapter of Romans has to do with Paul's experience before conversion. They say that simply because they cannot imagine the great Apostle living a life of spiritual failure. However, even a cursory examination of this Chapter proves, and beyond the shadow of a doubt, that Paul is relating his experience after conversion, and not before.

To be sure, when Paul wrote the information contained in this particular Chapter, he then readily understood God's Prescribed Order of Victory. He is relating his own personal experience, in order that we may know and understand that we will repeat his experience, if we do not adhere to the Truth that the Holy Spirit gave us in Romans, Chapter 6.

It was, in fact, to Paul that the meaning of the New Covenant was given, which, in effect, is the meaning of the Cross. And until Paul understood this great Truth, despite how hard he tried, Paul simply couldn't live a victorious life.

Listen carefully to his statements. All too often, you will see yourself in each Verse.

I will not deal with the entire Chapter, but only a few salient Verses. I would advise the Reader to secure for yourself our Commentary on Romans, which goes into detail regarding this Chapter.

Let's begin with Romans 7:8.

THE SIN NATURE

Paul said, *"But sin* (the sin nature), *taking occasion by the Commandment, wrought in me all manner of concupiscence* (*'concupiscence'* is *'evil desire,'* meaning if the Believer attempts to live for God by means other than the Cross, he will be ruled by *'evil desires'*; and no matter how dedicated he might be otherwise, he will not be able to stop the process in that manner, with it getting worse and worse)."

Paul did not understand God's Prescribed Order of Victory; and, in Paul's defense, no one else in the world at that time understood it either, because this great Truth had not yet been given. Irrespective, the sin nature ruled in Paul's life, because he was trying to live for God by means of his own strength and willpower. As a result, *"concupiscence,"* which is *"evil desires and evil thoughts,"* ruled his heart, despite all he could do otherwise.

Paul then said, *"For without the Law sin was dead."* What did he mean by that?

When most Christians look at this word *"Law,"* they automatically dismiss it, because they are interpreting it incorrectly. While Paul was talking about the *"Law of Moses,"* it could refer to any law. However, irrespective of whether it's laws that we make up ourselves, or someone else devises, still, whether realized or not, the Law of Moses, and we speak of the moral part of that Law, which is found in Exodus, Chapter 20, is the foundation of every moral law.

When the Believer sets himself out to live for God by means of keeping laws, whether devised by himself or someone else, which is the state, sad to say, of most modern Christians, such a Christian is going to fail every time. The reason is simple:

First of all, due to the Fall, no human being, even the greatest Christian among us, even Paul, could, within himself, keep the Law. However, we within ourselves do not have to keep the Law. To be sure, the moral law definitely is to be kept, but we have to understand how it is done before it can be done.

JESUS CHRIST, OUR SUBSTITUTE

We must ever look at Christ as our Substitute, in effect, our Representative Man. In other words, He came to this world to do for us what we could not do for ourselves. It's hard for us to admit that, but that is the truth.

First of all, He kept the Law perfectly in every respect, and did so on our behalf.

Let us say it again: He became our Substitute.

After walking perfectly before God, and living this life perfectly for some 33 years, once again, all on our behalf, He then went to the Cross in order to satisfy the demands of the broken Law. In fact, every human being who had ever lived had broken the Law, and had incurred upon himself the death penalty. And by that, we mean eternal separation from God. In fact, due to original sin, man is born in sin, which means he is born with a sin nature. So, in effect, he is shot down before he even begins.

On the Cross, Jesus satisfied every demand of the broken Law, doing so on our behalf, which means that He atoned for all sin, past, present, and future, at least for those who will believe (Jn. 3:16; Gal. 1:4).

Simple Faith in Christ and what He did for us at the Cross gives to us every benefit of Who Jesus is and what He did. With Faith evidenced in Christ and the Cross, and done so on a daily basis (Lk. 9:23-24), without even worrying about the Law, or even thinking about the Law, and again, we speak of the moral law, we will then fully keep the Law, because we're doing so through Christ (Gal. 2:20-21).

However, if we make up laws, and no matter how good they may sound, we will then find that the sin nature will come alive, and we are once again in trouble.

That's the reason we warn Christians about the wrong direction of the *"Purpose Driven Life,"* so-called, the *"Government of Twelve,"* and the *"Word of Faith,"* etc. That's the reason we warn people against *"Denominationalism,"* etc. All of these things are but laws, which will have the opposite effect on the Believer than he thinks.

In other words, when one adopts one of these fads, instead of getting closer to the Lord, the opposite effect will be the result. Instead of getting victory over sin, one will find the sin nature raging within his or her life. It is because, as we have repeatedly stated, our faith is in something other that Christ and the Cross.

Paul then said, *"For I was alive without the Law once: but when the Commandment came sin revived, and I died"* (Rom. 7:9).

What did Paul mean by this?

When he said that he was *"alive without the Law once,"* he is referring to his conversion to Christ. The Law, he states, had nothing to do with that conversion; neither did it have anything to do with his life in Christ. In fact, this was his Damascus Road experience.

But then he said, *"but when the Commandment came."* And what did he mean by that?

He meant, not knowing then how to properly live for God, he set out to try to keep the

Commandments, which is the only thing he knew at the time. When that happened, the sin nature *"revived,"* and then he said, *"and I died."* He did not mean that he physically died, as would be obvious, but that he died regarding the Commandment. In other words, he failed to obey, no matter how hard he tried.

Let all Believers understand: if the Apostle Paul couldn't live for God in this manner, neither can you!

Now don't misunderstand, even as he will say in the Tenth Verse, it's not the Commandments which are at fault, but rather the fact that the Believer simply cannot keep the Commandments, at least not in his own willpower and strength. He may think he can; millions of Christians actually think that. However, Paul also said, *"If Righteousness come by the Law, then Christ is dead in vain"* (Gal. 2:21).

In other words, if you as a Believer can live for God, and do so successfully, outside of God's Prescribed Order, which is the Cross of Christ, then Jesus didn't need to come down here and die. But, truthfully, no Believer can properly live for God outside of simple Faith in Christ and the Cross.

DOING WHAT I DON'T WANT TO DO

Trying to live for God by the keeping of Commandments, which means that the Apostle was not evidencing Faith in the Cross, he then said, *"For that which I do I allow not: for what I would, that do I not; but what I hate, that do I"* (Rom. 7:15).

The word *"allow,"* as used by the King James translators, should have been translated, *"I understand not."* In other words, Paul actually said, *"For that which I do I understand not."* He meant that he was doing all that he knew to do to live for God, but still was not being successful. What he wanted to do, which was to live a righteous, Godly, holy life, he found himself not able to do; and that which he hated, namely, to fail the Lord in any matter of sin, that he found himself doing.

Now, once again, sadly and regrettably, that's the lot of most modern Christians. This very Scripture proves that a Christian, and I speak of one who is truly a Christian, doesn't want to sin. So, what was happening to Paul?

As stated, he was trying to live for God in the wrong way, and despite all of his efforts otherwise, he couldn't live the life he wanted to live, and was being forced to live a life he didn't want to live.

If the modern Believer doesn't place his faith exclusively in the Cross of Christ, and not allow it to be moved elsewhere, the modern Believer is going to repeat the lifestyle of failure of which Paul here addresses.

In fact, there are millions of Christians who are trying with great strength to live for God, but doing so in the wrong way, and thereby failing. In fact, their failure is getting worse and worse, which puts them into a position of not understanding what is happening. They simply don't understand why they are failing, considering that they are trying so hard not to fail. But despite all their efforts, failure is the end result of all they are doing.

We've already dealt with the Eighteenth Verse (Rom., Chpt. 7) concerning willpower, and even though every single Verse is of great significance, we will instead skip down to Verse 24.

THE WRETCHED MAN

The great Apostle then says, *"O wretched man that I am! Who shall deliver me from the body of this death?"* In effect, he is saying, *"Any Believer who attempts to live for God outside of God's Prescribed Order, which is 'Jesus Christ and Him Crucified' will, in fact, live a wretched and miserable existence. This life can only be lived in one way, and that way is the Cross."*

When Paul used the pronoun *"Who"* in this Verse, he is now coming close to the path of Victory, for he is now calling upon a Person for help, and that Person is Christ; actually, the Greek Text is masculine, indicating a Person. It is never *"what"* but rather *"Who"*!

How long Paul lived in this state of spiritual failure, we aren't told; however, it probably was several years. Now please understand: this was a man who was genuinely saved, baptized with the Holy Spirit, with the evidence of speaking with other tongues, and even called to be an Apostle, but still living a life of spiritual failure.

It was to this very man that the Lord gave the great Truth of the New Covenant, which, as stated, was, and is, the meaning of the Cross.

After the Lord gave the Apostle the meaning of all this, which was intended that he then give it to us, we find this great Revelation throughout his fourteen Epistles, but, more particularly, in Romans, Chapters 6, 7, and 8. In other words, if we do not understand what the Apostle taught us in Romans, Chapter 6, we are bound to repeat Romans, Chapter 7, which no sane person desires to do. If we understand Romans, Chapter 6, and apply this great Word of God to our lives, even as it was given to Paul by the Lord Jesus Christ (Gal. 1:12), then we will enjoy the victory of Romans, Chapter 8.

THE POWER OF SATAN TO DESTROY

Going back to the Eighteenth Verse, the phrase, *"He tears him, and he foams, and gnashes with his teeth, and pines away, and I spoke to Your Disciples that they should cast him out; and they could not,"* presents the man bringing his son to Jesus, but, regrettably, Jesus was not there. Consequently, he asked help of the Nine Disciples.

They were not successful in their efforts to cast out this demon; and yet, at other times, they were. This is a picture of the modern Church, and I speak of the True Church. Sometimes it is able to effect amazing results, all by the Power of God, and sometimes it doesn't. But during the coming Kingdom Age, when Jesus will rule and reign Personally from Jerusalem, there will be no failure then. When He came on that memorable day of so long ago, the work was instantly done. When He comes again the second time without sin unto Salvation, it will be nothing but victory.

This means that as powerful as the True Church in Christ may be, still, until Jesus comes, and we speak of the Second Coming, Satan will not be completely cast out.

(19) "HE ANSWERED HIM, AND SAID, O FAITHLESS GENERATION, HOW LONG SHALL I BE WITH YOU? HOW LONG SHALL I SUFFER YOU? BRING HIM UNTO ME."

NOTES

The exegesis is:

This Passage implies that the boy was not immediately with the father, but was being held by others a short distance away.

FAITHLESS GENERATION

The phrase, *"He answered him, and said, O faithless generation,"* means *"without Faith, unbelieving"*; the Disciples definitely were also included in the rebuke. The unbelief of the Pharisees, which included the Scribes, had so ingrained itself in the entirety of Israel that all were affected by it, even including the choice Disciples of Christ, as is here obvious.

I wonder if this present generation doesn't fall into the same category. The closer to the end, the less true faith there will be. Jesus said, *"Nevertheless, when the Son of Man comes, shall He find Faith on the Earth?"* (Lk. 18:8).

The question, *"How long shall I be with you?"* in effect, asks if His time spent with them will be enough. The question, *"How long shall I suffer you?"* means *"to bear with, or endure."* Once again, this includes the Disciples. Jesus is saying that they should not be so slow to learn, especially considering that they were constantly in His Presence and constantly under His Teaching. But yet, bringing it up to the present, I'm afraid that all of us fall into the same category. We are *"slow to learn,"* and the Lord has to repeat His great Promises to us over and over again.

(20) "AND THEY BROUGHT HIM UNTO HIM: AND WHEN HE SAW HIM, STRAIGHTWAY THE SPIRIT TORE HIM AND HE FELL ON THE GROUND, AND WALLOWED FOAMING."

The composition is:

ACTIVITY OF THE DEMON SPIRIT

The phrase, *"And they brought him unto Him,"* proclaims them obeying Christ, with the boy being brought into the Presence of the Lord.

The phrase, *"And when he saw Him,"* refers to the evil spirit within the boy seeing Christ. In the phraseology, the idea presents itself of this evil spirit seeing the Disciples and being affected accordingly; however, when he saw Christ, He knew his time was up.

The phrase, *"Straightway the spirit tore him,"* presents the demon's final effort, possibly even to kill the boy. The phrase, *"And he fell on the ground, and wallowed foaming,"* means he kept rolling on the ground and foaming at the mouth. This sight had to be terrible to behold! However, this parent had undergone this suffering for quite some time.

(21) "AND HE ASKED HIS FATHER, HOW LONG IS IT AGO SINCE THIS CAME UNTO HIM? AND HE SAID, OF A CHILD."

The diagram is:

This incident tells us that children can be oppressed or even possessed by demon spirits.

THE CHILD

The phrase, *"And He asked his father,"* presents the beginning of a question which proclaims the humanity of Christ. As all men, He only knew what the Holy Spirit told Him, or by asking for information; however, and to be sure, the Holy Spirit was much more conversant with Him than with any other man (Ps. 45:7).

The question, *"How long is it ago since this came unto him?"* was for a purpose! I feel the asking of the question had nothing to do with the casting out of the demon, but rather to ascertain how young the boy was when this thing happened. It seems that Jesus sensed the answer given by the father, *"Of a child."*

HOW COULD A DEMON SPIRIT ENTER INTO A CHILD?

A child is innocent and would not be able, at least within himself, to yield or resist. Therefore, the cause had to be other than the child himself. Demons were rampant at this time in Israel. Some have suggested that they were there to oppose Christ. While that possibly may have played some part, still, it was not the main cause.

The True Word of God held no sway in Israel at that time. The *"leaven"* of the Pharisees ruled the land. In any country where religion rules, demon spirits abound. Hinduism rules India; therefore, demon spirits are rampant. The same can be said for Muslim countries, etc. Catholicism is another example!

NOTES

Judaism within itself was not a religion, because it was originally given by God; however, the Pharisees had made the Word of God noneffective by their tradition; consequently, religion ruled, i.e., demons ruled. As well, any home that does not know Christ is open to the demon powers of darkness, even upon children; therefore, the possibility definitely exists, and probably was the case, that this family did not know the Lord. They, no doubt, knew this corrupt form of Judaism, but not the True Word of God. Consequently, their son was an open target for the powers of darkness.

If one could pull back the cover and find the true cause of the terrible problems that beset America, and the entirety of the world for that matter, one would, no doubt, be shocked at the operation of demon spirits as the original cause. Many homes in modern America know the Lord not at all; they, consequently, are as susceptible as this family of our Text.

WHAT WOULD BE THE SPIRITUAL CONDITION OF THE CHILD SHOULD HE DIE IN THAT CONDITION?

As previously stated, a child is not able to resist or accept, at least with understanding; consequently, every child, and even one in the condition of our discussion, is protected by the Lord, at least regarding their soul, until they reach the age of accountability, whatever that may be. In fact, the age of accountability varies from child to child.

I believe that the Bible teaches that no child dies lost. Jesus verified this by saying, *"Verily I say unto you, Except you be converted, and become as little children, you shall not enter into the Kingdom of Heaven"* (Mat. 18:3). So, the Salvation experience, among other things, makes one guileless *"as little children."*

Remembering back, at least as far as I can, I was eight years old when the Lord began to deal with me about my soul. In fact, I was saved under very strange circumstances, actually standing in front of a Movie Theatre on a Saturday afternoon.

I was standing there in line with other children, waiting for the ticket window to open; and then, without warning, the Spirit of God spoke to my heart. He said, *"Do not go into this place. Give your heart to Me. I want to use you as a chosen vessel, used exclusively in My service."* Those may not have been the exact words, but they are as close as I can remember.

I was startled, to say the least. Even though I knew very little about the Lord, my parents only having been saved a short time, still, I knew it was the Lord Who had spoken to me. I made no move, remaining in the line. About that time, the ticket window opened, the kids began to buy their tickets, and the line began to move forward. And then the Lord spoke again, saying, in effect, the same thing.

By this time, I was standing at the ticket window, with my quarter on the counter, in order to purchase the ticket. About that time, the spool of tickets jammed, which occupied the attention of the ticket lady. I'll always believe that it was the Lord Who did this. At any rate, it gave me just a moment more. And in that moment, I said *"Yes"* to the Lord. I grabbed my quarter, ran away, and did not go back.

A few moments later, standing on the corner in front of Vogt's drugstore, I knew that I was saved. Even though I was only eight years old, and knew very little about sin, it felt like a hundred pound weight had been lifted off my shoulders.

I've often wondered how a person must feel, who has lived a life of gross sin, and who then comes to the Lord. There is, in fact, nothing like the *"Born-Again"* experience. If every child could experience what I experienced, juvenile delinquency would be at an end and, in fact, the situation would be changed overall, and completely. But unfortunately, most homes do not know the Lord. If the truth be known, more children are demon possessed than one would ever begin to contemplate or think.

(22) "AND OFTTIMES IT HAS CAST HIM INTO THE FIRE, AND INTO THE WATERS, TO DESTROY HIM: BUT IF YOU CAN DO ANY THING, HAVE COMPASSION ON US, AND HELP US."

The overview is:

The man's faith was weak, due to the failure of the Disciples.

NOTES

SUICIDE

The phrase, *"And ofttimes it has cast him into the fire, and into the waters, to destroy him,"* reflects suicidal tendencies, as promoted by this spirit. Consequently, the parents had to watch him constantly, in view of these terrible impulses. From this we know that this spirit had attempted to kill him again and again, but without success.

Even though it is impossible for us to go too deep into this scenario, could it be that Jehovah kept this child alive, despite the efforts of Satan, until he could be brought to Jesus? How much hand does the Lord take in matters of this nature, knowing that ultimately the Gospel will be brought to particular areas?

A PERSONAL EXPERIENCE

I was born into a home that did not know God. In fact, my Dad, until he was 25 years old, had never seen a Bible, heard a Gospel Message, heard a Gospel song, or darkened the doors of any type of Church. My mother was pretty much the same, having only attended a funeral at a Church once or twice. In fact, as far as I know, not a single member of our family, whether immediate or otherwise, knew the Lord before my parents came to Christ.

When I was two years old, my Dad had an experience that can only be credited to the Lord, even some four years before they gave their hearts to Christ. My mother and Dad were in a particular place working at a certain job. Times were hard in those days (1937), as economic depression ravaged America and the world.

During the few days of this particular work, they were staying at a small cabin, which consisted of one room containing a bed and one or two chairs. The accommodations were very Spartan, and the lock on the door was little more than a latch.

Sometime after midnight, my Dad awakened, or rather was awakened. Even though he was fully awake, he felt somewhat strange. He looked to his right, and he saw me sitting on the floor. I was, as stated, only two years old. He wondered what I was doing out of the bed, especially sitting on the floor.

About that time, he heard someone attempting to undo the latch on the door! He then shouted loudly to my mother to get the gun, even though they owned no gun. The action with the door stopped immediately. Moreover, strangely enough, I was no longer sitting on the floor, but I was asleep in the bed with my parents, and I had actually been there all the time. My Dad had seen a vision.

The next morning, it was discovered that two people had been murdered and robbed about two cabins down. Even though one cannot say for sure, quite possibly, and most probably, the robbers who murdered the two people had also attempted to come into our room. If so, they would have killed my parents and me. As stated, my parents were unsaved at this time, but yet the Lord knew that in a short time the Gospel would be brought to them, with them wondrously and gloriously accepting Christ as their Saviour.

The year my parents were saved, if I remember correctly, was 1941. I came to Christ in 1943 at 8 years of age, which account, in brief, I have just related. Did the Lord purposely give my Dad a vision, even though he was unsaved, in order to keep him alive until the Gospel could be brought to him? I believe He did!

And I believe He has worked accordingly in the lives of millions of others. And yet, my heart breaks for the multiple millions of others who never have an opportunity to accept or reject.

ANOTHER EXPERIENCE

In the mid-1980's, Frances and I, along with Donnie and others, were in Communist China, where we did a Television Special. Even though we visited several cities, one particular scene stands out in my mind. It was on the docks of Shanghai. Being Westerners, we quickly drew a crowd. Many of the Chinese desired to practice their English on us.

One young man, about 14 years old, stands out. He was a very handsome young fellow, and very personable. He attempted to speak to us in his broken English. At one point, Frances asked him, very slowly so he would understand, *"Do you know Jesus?"*

For a few moments, he stood there, slowly repeating the Name *"Jesus"*! Then he asked, *"Who is Jesus? I know not Jesus!"* In fact, most Chinese do not know Jesus, with many having never even heard of Him.

However, something else happened at that moment, which gave us hope. Two young Chinese men were overhearing our conversation with the boy. Even though the crowd was large, they got our attention. With raised eyebrows, they pointed to their hearts and let us know they were Believers. They then pointed to the boy and nodded their heads in the affirmative, letting us know that they would witness to him after we left.

COMPASSION

The phrase, *"But if You can do anything,"* portrays the man weak in Faith, and shaken by the failure of the Disciples. The severity of the case was also an obstacle!

The phrase, *"Have compassion on us, and help us,"* does not question the *"compassion"* of Christ. The structure of the sentence in the Greek Text proclaims that the man saw compassion all over Christ, and especially in His Face. He wasn't questioning the *"compassion,"* only the ability of Jesus to do what the Disciples could not do.

By using the pronoun *"us,"* he also identified himself with the misery of his son. Wuest reminds us that the Syro-Phenician woman also said, *"Have mercy on me,"* making her daughter's affliction her own. To be sure, this scenario, as it unfolds, is so beautiful as to defy all description, even though it begins so ugly.

(23) "JESUS SAID UNTO HIM, IF YOU CAN BELIEVE, ALL THINGS ARE POSSIBLE TO HIM WHO BELIEVES."

The exposition is:

If the Lord has promised it and you can believe it, you can have it.

BELIEVING

The phrase, *"Jesus said unto him,"* addressed itself to the unbelief, due to the recent events, of the man. Jesus will preach him a very short Message, which will build his Faith.

The phrase, *"If you can believe,"* addresses itself to all the things which have happened.

The man had been faced with the powerless Disciples, and Jesus is telling him to rise above that. The man has also heard the taunts of the Scribes, which further weakened him. Jesus is telling him to rise above that, as well!

In truth, this should be a valuable lesson to all of us. Faith is constantly battered by adverse circumstances. As we have just stated, every attack by Satan, and in whatever direction, is but for one purpose, to weaken or even destroy our Faith.

So, Jesus is telling him that he must believe despite these things. He is saying the same to us as well!

THE POSSIBILITY

The phrase, *"All things are possible to him who believes,"* is the second part of this short Message preached by Christ. As always, the Lord could say so much in so few words. This Promise is an open invitation for Believers to have Faith in God. As a result, the Lord has allowed Believers to enter into His Plan, helping to bring it to pass, and according to our Faith.

That He would allow us to do this is a privilege indeed! The Lord doesn't have to have us in order to get anything done. He is complete within Himself. And yet, He has allowed us this privilege!

Sometime ago, the Lord graphically spoke to my heart, saying this to me:

"You have believed I can, but you are not believing that I will."

And then He said, *"I want you to believe not only that I can, but also that I will!"*

Even before then, the Holy Spirit had been strongly dealing with my heart about Faith in God. It has been as if the Holy Spirit constantly has urged me to *"believe"*! To be sure, whatever He does is always for purpose and reason.

(24) "AND STRAIGHTWAY THE FATHER OF THE CHILD CRIED OUT, AND SAID WITH TEARS, LORD, I BELIEVE; HELP THOU MY UNBELIEF."

The exegesis is:

TEARS

The phrase, *"And straightway the father of the child cried out,"* speaks of a loud cry that comes from the very depths of the man's soul. The phrase, *"And said with tears, Lord, I believe,"* proclaims belief, but yet imperfect belief! The *"tears"* proclaim the consternation of the battle that is raging in the man's soul.

These *"tears"* also denote his helplessness; he is desperate. As someone has well said, *"Desperation always precedes Revelation."* This man was desperate, and very shortly he would have a Revelation that he would never forget.

UNBELIEF

The phrase, *"Help Thou my unbelief,"* proclaims the deficiency of his Faith. In other words, he is asking the Lord to help him in this deficiency. It is a prayer the Lord will always answer. Perhaps if the Truth be known, this man's statement, *"Lord, I believe; help Thou my unbelief,"* is indicative of every Believer. Our Faith is not perfect. There are areas in which we fall down. And in those areas, we miss some of the things which would have been *"possible"* otherwise! So, this is a prayer that every Believer ought to pray.

It also should be noted that this man did not, and, in fact, could not, confess this unbelief away. Neither was his *"unbelief"* caused by a bad confession. It was rather caused by adverse circumstances, which seemed to be impossible and insurmountable.

Even though one may habitually confess such away, still, the matter will not change unless the Lord helps us in this, for which we are encouraged to pray. One will also find that when the help comes, it will always be through the Word of God, for *"Faith comes by hearing, and hearing by the Word of God"* (Rom. 10:17).

IS EVERYTHING POSSIBLE ACCORDING TO OUR DEGREE OF FAITH?

While everything is possible, and the degree of faith certainly is important, still, the Will of God must be brought to bear, as well! Of course, it is always the Will of God for someone to be delivered, even as this boy. As well, it is always the Will of God for souls to be saved. But when it comes to some things, it is not definite that the answer will always be *"Yes."*

If the Lord allowed His Will to be ignored, people very soon would be using the Word of God against God. In other words, they would bring things into existence which would hurt the Kingdom of God, and even hurt them, if allowed to come to pass. So, the Lord will not allow His Word to be used against Himself. We must never forget that the Word of God is always predicated on the Will of God.

While a Believer definitely does not have to implore the Will of God as it regards Deliverance, even as here proclaimed, there definitely are many things for which we must seek the Will of God.

James said, *"Go to now, you who say, Today or tomorrow we will go into such a city, and continue there a year, and buy and sell, and get gain:*

"Whereas you know not what shall be on the morrow. For what is your life? It is even a vapor, that appears for a little time, and then vanishes away.

"For that you ought to say, If the Lord will, we shall live, and do this, or that" (James 4:13-15).

(25) "WHEN JESUS SAW THAT THE PEOPLE CAME RUNNING TOGETHER, HE REBUKED THE FOUL SPIRIT, SAYING UNTO HIM, YOU DUMB AND DEAF SPIRIT, I CHARGE YOU, COME OUT OF HIM, AND ENTER NO MORE INTO HIM."

The structure is:

This spirit came out and was to never come back again.

THE FOUL SPIRIT

The phrase, *"When Jesus saw that the people came running together,"* no doubt, concerns the crowd overhearing the loud cries of the boy's father. It seems that Jesus and the man were somewhat away from the crowd, and the boy was near them, as well. How He managed this is anyone's guess! Quite possibly, the Disciples held the crowd back for a period of time, but now they will wait no longer.

The phrase, *"He rebuked the foul spirit,"* concerns, seemingly, Him desiring to deliver this boy before the multitude came upon them. The word *"rebuke"* is not the type of rebuke offered to one desired to be brought to Repentance, but instead one who cannot repent, commanded, therefore, to cease and desist operations, for this demon could not repent; therefore, this *"rebuke"* was not meant in that fashion.

Wuest says that the word *"rebuke"* here used is, in the Greek, *"epitimao."* He goes on to say that normally the Greek word would have been *"elegcho,"* which is meant to lead one to Repentance. Consequently, by the use of this word, one is able to observe the meticulous accuracy with which the Holy Spirit leads the Bible writers in their choice of words or synonyms.

Truly this demon was *"foul,"* which may lend some credence to the idea that this evil spirit possessed more than ordinary power and malignity, and that this was the reason the Disciples could not cast him out. This expulsion needed the mighty arm of One stronger than the strong (Bickersteth).

The phrase, *"Saying unto him, You dumb and deaf spirit,"* refers to what this spirit brought about in this boy, as well as other things.

THE CHARGE

The phrase, *"I charge you, come out of him,"* is a powerful term which means *"to order or change."* The order was powerful and firm, leaving absolutely no room for disobedience. It is a military term.

The phrase, *"And enter no more into him,"* means that he was to leave out and never again come back. Hallelujah! It also seems from the Greek Text that this type of demon-possession was of the intermittent kind, which means it came and went! Quite possibly, when it went, the child was able to speak and hear, with the problem reoccurring upon the entrance of the spirit. Jesus is telling the demon spirit to *"Go, and stay gone!"*

(26) "AND THE SPIRIT CRIED, AND RENT HIM SORE, AND CAME OUT OF HIM: AND HE WAS AS ONE DEAD; INSOMUCH THAT MANY SAID, HE IS DEAD."

The composition is:

The boy lay motionless and pallid as a corpse.

THE EVIL SPIRIT

The phrase, *"And the spirit cried, and rent him sore, and came out him,"* concerns the last gasp of this spirit, in that he attempted to kill the boy as he came out. Quite possibly it is correct that this spirit was of greater power than most, because the description given here by the Holy Spirit through Mark is of greater portent than hardly any other Deliverance.

The phrase, *"And he was as one dead; insomuch that many said, he is dead,"* concerned the terrible ordeal he had just experienced, and the last gasp of this spirit. Wuest says that he *"lay motionless and pallid as a corpse."*

(27) "BUT JESUS TOOK HIM BY THE HAND, AND LIFTED HIM UP; AND HE AROSE."

The diagram is:

This concerned more than just a helping hand; healing power flooded the boy's body, healing that which the demon had damaged.

JESUS

The phrase, *"But Jesus took him by the hand,"* concerned more than just a helping hand. When Jesus touched him, whatever damage the demon had done was, no doubt, instantly healed by the Power of God. The phrase, *"And lifted him up,"* means that He gave him help in getting up.

How many millions has Jesus lifted up? How many millions has Satan almost destroyed, but Jesus changed them instantly, totally, and completely!

The phrase, *"And he arose,"* spoke of strength flooding his body, even as he stood to his feet.

We do not know if the boy's mother was alive or not, or if he had brothers and sisters! However, this we do know: whatever home he entered upon returning was not the same home he left. The father took from that house a demon-possessed wretch, but brought back a young man who was delivered, well, healed, and free. There would be joy in that house that night!

(28) "AND WHEN HE WAS COME INTO THE HOUSE, HIS DISCIPLES ASKED HIM PRIVATELY, WHY COULD NOT WE CAST HIM OUT?"

The diagram is:

They had been successful at other times, so why not now? There is evidence that this demon was more powerful than any that Jesus had addressed.

WHY THE FAILURE OF THE DISCIPLES?

The phrase, *"And when He was come into the house,"* spoke of lodging nearby, where they could escape the crowd. The question His Disciples asked Him privately, *"Why could not we cast him out?"* presented that which they could not wait to ask. They had been successful in the past, so why did they fail in this instance? Perhaps all of us should ask the same question.

It is the business of the Church to be His Hand extended. We are to use His Name to *"cast out demons"* (Mk. 16:17). But sadly and regrettably, the far greater majority of the modern Church is too busy referring such to the psychologists and psychiatrists, who offer no help whatsoever. The Church has, in fact, become one giant referral system.

Why?

The answer is that which Mark did not give, but Matthew included, *"Because of your unbelief"* (Mat. 17:20). Such unbelief leads to further unbelief! Today in most modern Churches, the Lord is not addressed at all, even in a negative sense; rather He is completely ignored. This is sad, considering the Church is the only real force against the powers of darkness. But yet, the modern Church at present exerts little force at all in this respect.

(29) "AND HE SAID UNTO THEM, THIS KIND CAN COME FORTH BY NOTHING, BUT BY PRAYER AND FASTING."

The exposition is:

"Fasting" includes not only doing without food, but also denying one's own strength and ability, looking exclusively to the Cross (I Cor. 1:17-18).

The phrase, *"And He said unto them,"* proclaims the answer. It is twofold:

1. *"Because of your unbelief"* (Mat. 17:20).
2. Their lack of prayer and fasting.

UNBELIEF

Two Greek words express unbelief, *"apistia"* and *"apeitheia."* Disobedience springs from *"apistia,"* a want of Faith and Trust. *"Apeitheia"* connotes disobedience, rebellion, and contumacy. *"Apistia"* is a state of mind; *"apeitheia"* is an expression of it. Unbelief towards Himself was the prime sin of which Christ said that the Spirit would convict the world (Jn. 16:9). Unbelief in all its forms is a direct affront to the Divine veracity (I Jn. 5:10), which is why it is so heinous a sin.

The Children of Israel did not enter into God's Rest (Grace) for two reasons. They lacked Faith (*"apistia"* [Heb. 3:19]) and they disobeyed (*"apeitheia"* [Heb. 4:6]). As stated, unbelief finds its practical issue in disobedience.

PRAYER AND FASTING

The phrase, *"This kind can come forth by nothing, but by prayer and fasting,"* presents the emphasis being on the two words, *"This kind,"* and denoting a particularly powerful demon spirit. As well, prayer and fasting are addressed. Prayer by man is communion with God and God with man. If it is according to the Word, which it definitely will be if it's in the Spirit, the results are staggering.

When coupled with *"fasting,"* its power is manifold. Actually, *"fasting"* concerns two aspects:

A. Abstaining from food for a protracted period of time.

B. Living a fasted life. This speaks of being immersed in God and not the world. The Believer in this state is *in* the world, but not *of* it. He is not moved by the things of the world, neither does he plan his course of action according to the direction of the world. His total sustenance is God, drawing nothing from the world save natural food, etc.

SALT AND LIGHT

However, this in no way means a withdrawal from fellow citizens, even the unsaved. Actually, true Christianity serves as *"salt"* and *"light."* Consequently, it is, as stated, to be *in* the world system, but not *of* it. This proclaims a vast difference!

Paul used the word *"separate."* He said, *"Wherefore come out from among them, and be ye separate, saith the Lord"* (II Cor. 6:17). He also said of Jesus, *"separate from sinners"* (Heb. 7:26). It should however be noted that the *"fasted life"* is not asceticism, which refers to a rigorous abstention from self-indulgence, which means that through the renunciation of the desires of the flesh and of pleasure in worldly things, and through self-mortification and self-denial, one can subdue his appetites and discipline himself so as to reach a high spiritual state.

This, in fact, is the opposite of the *"fasted life."* Asceticism is man-devised and consequently man-controlled. It has its roots in Eastern mystic religions. The *"fasted life"* is in Christ and Christ alone! It is actually in Christ by and through the means of the Cross, which is the only way that a person can be in Christ (Rom. 6:3-5). Such a life is led by the Spirit. As such, it's power is not in *"do's"* and *"don'ts,"* but rather in the Holy Spirit.

In fact, as Paul said, it has nothing to do with *"Touch not; taste not; handle not; Which all are to perish with the using; after the commandments and doctrines of men."* Paul went on to say, *"Which things have indeed a show of wisdom* (worldly wisdom) *in will worship* (worship which is not of God) *and humility* (which is not true humility), *and neglecting of the body* (asceticism); *not in any honor to the satisfying of the flesh* (powerless to deal with sin and the old man)*"* (Col. 2:21-23). Such only feeds self-righteousness and pride and does not change the heart.

So, Jesus told His Disciples, both then and now, that it was *"unbelief"* and a lack of *"prayer and fasting"* which brought about their lack of power. (In fact, fasting at that time was not enjoined, because Jesus was still with them. When He left, they would then fast [Mat. 9:15].)

(30) "AND THEY DEPARTED THENCE, AND PASSED THROUGH GALILEE; AND HE WOULD NOT THAT ANY MAN SHOULD KNOW IT."

The composition is:

By now there was a terrible opposition against Him from the religious leaders of the area; in fact, this would get progressively worse.

OPPOSITION TO CHRIST

The phrase, *"And they departed thence,"* concerns them leaving the area totally different than they had found it. God had moved mightily in this place, wherever it was. (Its location is unclear.)

Here, three of the Disciples had witnessed the Transfiguration of Jesus, plus the appearance of Elijah and Moses, and had heard the Voice of God. As well, a most powerful demon had been cast out of a boy, bringing joy, Salvation, and happiness to this family, and forevermore! So, they departed from it, leaving it much greater than when they found it. This will be the result of every God-called Preacher.

The phrase, *"And passed through Galilee; and He would not that any man should know it,"* was done for two reasons:

1. It is only months before He will die for the sin of the world; therefore, He desires to use as much time as possible in teaching His Disciples.

2. The opposition by now had become so fierce in Galilee, especially in Judaea, that any activity spurred a confrontation. The Church, so to speak, was now His greatest enemy! I'm afraid it is also His greatest enemy presently! In fact, the most dangerous place in town (spiritually speaking) is often the Church!

(31) "FOR HE TAUGHT HIS DISCIPLES, AND SAID UNTO THEM, THE SON OF MAN IS DELIVERED INTO THE HANDS OF MEN, AND THEY SHALL KILL HIM; AND AFTER THAT HE IS KILLED, HE SHALL RISE THE THIRD DAY."

The synopsis is:

This means that His betrayal in the heart of Judas had already begun.

TEACHING

The phrase, *"For He taught His Disciples,"* had as its main direction the coming Crucifixion. This event would be so shattering that the possibility of them losing their Faith was ever present. It was very difficult for them to understand that the Messiah would die and, in fact, how He could die! It should be remembered that notwithstanding these repeated warnings from their Lord, when these events actually took place, *"they all forsook Him and fled."*

They, no doubt, reasoned in their minds that inasmuch as *"he who is hanged is accursed of God,"* the one so executed consequently could not be the Messiah! (Deut. 21:23). They did not understand that Jesus actually was to be made a curse, which is different than being cursed by God, and that He did not experience that because of His Own sin, but rather for the sin of the world (Gal. 3:13).

As we have stated, had they known Isaiah 53 and Daniel 9, they would have understood; however, they really did not know the Word of God as they should have!

THE BETRAYAL OF CHRIST

The phrase, *"And said unto them, The Son of Man is delivered into the hands of men,"* means that His betrayal in the heart of Judas had already begun. It was imminent and in the process of accomplishment. Actually, at that time Judas possibly did not have such in his mind; however, this seedbed of thoughts, which was the opposite of the Will of God, was already germinating.

There is an excellent possibility that the thoughts of all the Disciples were in a direction foreign to Scripture. They felt the *"Kingdom"* was now coming, with Jesus at its head, and with them as His Chief Lieutenants. The only difference in the thoughts of Judas and the others was that Judas, it seems, pursued it more vigorously; however, with Jesus talking about being killed, such terminology confused and discouraged them.

In effect, this was one of the reasons that the Nine were powerless to cast the demons out of the boy. Thinking Jesus was going to establish the Kingdom at that time, and with them pushing hard for this purpose, they were actually out of the Will of God. Opposition to the Will of God always fosters unbelief. Jesus had answered them, that they could not cast the demon out *"because of your unbelief"* (Mat. 17:20).

Consequently, we presently have a powerless Church, which stems from unbelief, and which is caused by being out of the Will of God, i.e., man-led instead of God-led!

THE CRUCIFIXION

The phrase, *"And they shall kill Him,"* is bitter and to the point! It implies murder, which it actually was. And yet, they did not really take His Life, meaning that it was not an assassination or execution, but rather a Sacrifice. For He would say, *"No man takes it from Me, but I lay it down of Myself"* (Jn. 10:18).

Because Jesus was born without original sin, He was not tainted by the Fall; He, therefore, had not suffered the curse of the Fall, which was death. Consequently, had He not laid down His Life freely, He would not and, in fact, could not, have died. However, He was not going to the Cross by constraint, but, as stated, as a willing Sacrifice, that He might do the Will of His Father, and so redeem mankind (Bickersteth).

THE RESURRECTION

The phrase, *"And after that He is killed, He shall rise the third day,"* pronounces a Miracle of such proportions that it is beyond the comprehension of the Disciples. That He would be *"killed"* was not in their thinking at all, but to come from the tomb *"in three days"* was beyond the realm of plausibility, to say the least!

Also, this announcement given by Christ plainly tells us that the Resurrection was never in doubt. In fact, the Resurrection would have been impossible, had Jesus failed to atone for even one sin. The Bible clearly tells us that the *"wages of sin is death"* (Rom. 6:23). However, every single sin was atoned, past, present, and future, at least for those who will believe, which means that the Resurrection was a foregone conclusion.

Let the Reader understand: your Salvation, your Victory, your Healing, the Baptism with the Holy Spirit, your eternal life, your overcoming glory and, in fact, every single thing we receive from the Lord, all, and without exception, are made possible by the Cross. While the Resurrection is of vast importance, as anyone should realize, still, it was not the Resurrection which atoned for all sin, but rather the Cross (I Cor. 1:17-18, 23; 2:2; Eph. 2:13-18; Col. 2:14-15).

(32) "BUT THEY UNDERSTAND NOT THAT SAYING, AND WERE AFRAID TO ASK HIM."

The composition is:

Their fear stemmed back to Peter rebuking Him when He had previously made this announcement, and His response, which had been strong indeed!

NOTES

A LACK OF UNDERSTANDING

In the natural, what Jesus said really was quite difficult to understand. However, the Disciples, especially after being with Jesus for about three years, had seen Him time and time again do the impossible! Consequently, in that light, the *"rising on the third day"* was something they should have known He was able to do. Once again, *"they understood not"* because of their unbelief. It was not unbelief in His Power, or that He was able to do it; instead, it was unbelief regarding direction.

They had heard Him, as well as John the Baptist, say, *"The Kingdom of Heaven is at hand"*; therefore, they could see nothing else (Mat. 3:2; 4:17). They seemed to not realize that Israel had rejected the *"Kingdom."* Even though it would come in the spiritual, at least to all who would believe, still, its material and physical aspect would consequently be delayed. Actually, it has not come still, awaiting the Second Coming!

FEAR

The phrase, *"And were afraid to ask Him,"* stemmed back, no doubt, to Mark 8:33. Peter had flatly refused to believe Christ when the Lord at that time spoke of dying and then rising the third day. Being roundly rebuked by Christ, they are loath now to ask Him for more information.

(33) "AND HE CAME TO CAPERNAUM: AND BEING IN THE HOUSE HE ASKED THEM, WHAT WAS IT THAT YOU DISPUTED AMONG YOURSELVES BY THE WAY?"

The diagram is:

His question concerned a very serious problem in their lives.

THE QUESTION

The phrase, *"And He came to Capernaum,"* referred, as is known, to His Headquarters. The phrase, *"And being in the house He asked them,"* probably refers to the house of Simon Peter. Evidently, all the Disciples were there with Him. The question, *"What was it that you disputed among yourselves by the way?"* would concern something very serious — something that would wreck them, that is, if it was not addressed properly. The Lord will now address it.

Actually, He already knew what they were disputing, because the Holy Spirit had told Him.

(34) "BUT THEY HELD THEIR PEACE: FOR BY THE WAY THEY HAD DISPUTED AMONG THEMSELVES, WHO SHOULD BE THE GREATEST."

The overview is:

It is not unlikely that the preference given by our Lord to Peter, James, and John may have given occasion for this contention.

SELF-PROMOTION

The phrase, *"But they held their peace,"* means they were ashamed to relate to Him what they actually had been discussing. The phrase, *"For by the way they had disputed among themselves, who should be the greatest,"* constituted a problem in their lives, which, if not eradicated, would completely destroy the Work of God. Unfortunately, this problem rears its ugly head no less today!

Quite possibly, Peter, James, and John played a part in this contention, because Jesus had chosen them over the others on at least two occasions. However, even though that may have played a part in the dispute, with the word *"dispute"* meaning they were arguing forcibly, still, the wrongheaded course they were taking constituted the major offense.

As we have repeatedly stated, the entirety of their thinking was wrong respecting what Christ was doing, and why He had actually come! They knew He was the *"Messiah,"* with Peter having confessed it (Mk. 8:29). Therefore, at least in their thinking, the *"Messiah"* would take the Throne of David. Their contention was right, but their date was wrong!

Irrespective, Jesus will address not their wrongheadedness, referring to their direction, but instead their own disposition of heart, which was the true cause.

(35) "AND HE SAT DOWN, AND CALLED THE TWELVE, AND SAID UNTO THEM, IF ANY MAN DESIRE TO BE FIRST, THE SAME SHALL BE LAST OF ALL, AND SERVANT OF ALL."

The exposition is:

Jesus' statement means to think of one's self last, with all others first, to minister to others, which is the very opposite of the spirit of the world.

THE SERVANT PRINCIPLE

The phrase, *"And He sat down, and called the Twelve, and said unto them,"* reflects His posture, but, more so, that what He is about to say is extremely important! The phrase, *"If any man desire to be first,"* is in response to their question as to *"who should be the greatest?"* As well, He does not reprimand them for desiring to be *"first."* However, the direction to that position, as He will portray, is directly opposed to the direction of the world.

The phrase, *"The same shall be the last of all, and servant of all,"* is, as stated, the opposite of the way of the world; it is also the most revolutionary concept ever heard by man concerning *"greatness."* In other words, God's definition of *"greatness"* is totally opposite to that of the world. To be *"last of all"* means to think of one's self last, with all others first. To be *"servant of all"* means to minister to others.

By comparison, this short statement by Christ places Bible Christianity so far ahead of the religions of the world that there is no comparison; however, and sadly so, there are not many who practice this concept of greatness as looked at by the Lord. Too often the concept of the world, which is bloated egos and self-exaltation, is brought into the Church.

I have met thousands of people on this life's journey, and it's been my privilege to meet two or three who, in my opinion, so exemplified Christ that you left their presence not entertained by, nor desiring to emulate, their abilities, but instead to be like Christ. That is, perhaps, the greatest compliment that could be paid to anyone.

(36) "AND HE TOOK A CHILD, AND SET HIM IN THE MIDST OF THEM: AND WHEN HE HAD TAKEN HIM IN HIS ARMS, HE SAID UNTO THEM."

The synopsis is:

A child is now used as an example.

THE CHILD

The phrase, *"And He took a child, and set him in the midst of them,"* will be used as an example. Some say this child might have been Peter's. Another tradition, not earlier than the Ninth Century, says that this child was Ignatius. Irrespective, he will be the example!

Why a child?

First, a child is totally dependent on others. Such demonstrates the total dependency on the Lord that one of true greatness should have. Second, a child is trustful, the least self-conscious, and the least self-sufficient. Third, a child does not hold grudges, is quick to forgive, and retains anger only for a very short time.

The phrase, *"And when He had taken him in his arms, He said unto them,"* refers to Christ holding the child in such a way, literally embracing it, which says that He will do the same for all who place their total trust in Him, even as this child is now doing.

(37) "WHOSOEVER SHALL RECEIVE ONE OF SUCH CHILDREN IN MY NAME, RECEIVES ME: AND WHOSOEVER SHALL RECEIVE ME, RECEIVES NOT ME, BUT HIM WHO SENT ME."

The structure is:

The way to Christ is through a childlike spirit, and the way to the Father is through Christ (Jn. 14:6).

RECEPTION

The phrase, *"Whosoever shall receive one of such children in My Name, receives Me,"* says, in effect, that if the person is not of such posture (as a little child), he should not be received. As well, one who is truly of this posture is the same as Christ and, in effect, witnesses in His stead; consequently, to receive such a one is to receive Christ.

The phrase, *"And whosoever shall receive Me, receives not Me, but Him Who sent Me,"* proclaims the entirety of the foundation of Heaven and its government being tied to this doctrine. To receive such a person is to receive Christ; to receive Christ is to receive the Father; and to receive the Father is to receive the Government of God; consequently, blessings on such are freely given!

As well, those who fail to receive one who fits the description here outlined fails, at the same time, to receive Christ. We should look at that statement very carefully. In fact, such a position is very, very serious!

NOTES

To fail to receive one who has definitely been sent by Christ, is to fail to receive what Christ is sending. That can be tantamount to destruction!

(38) "AND JOHN ANSWERED HIM, SAYING, MASTER, WE SAW ONE CASTING OUT DEVILS IN YOUR NAME, AND HE FOLLOWS NOT US: AND WE FORBAD HIM, BECAUSE HE FOLLOWS NOT US."

The synopsis is:

Such portrays the sectarianism that is beginning to creep in.

SECTARIANISM

The phrase, *"And John answered Him,"* respects what Jesus has said, and occasions the only remark attributed by the synoptists (the Books of Matthew, Mark, and Luke) specifically to John. The phrase, *"Saying, Master, we saw one casting out devils* (demons) *in Your Name, and He follows not us,"* registers conviction on John's part, especially considering what Christ has said about receiving such a one.

We can see in this the beginning of sectarianism, which refers to a monopoly, so to speak. In other words:

"You have to belong to us, and meet all of our rules and specifications, before we will recognize you. And if you don't meet our requirements, we will do everything we can to stop you."

That, in brief, is the meaning of sectarianism.

The casting out of evil spirits was one of the foremost signs of Apostleship; consequently, John was somewhat nonplussed that one could do such a thing, even though he was not a member of the elite group. He admitted that the man was doing such in the Name of Jesus. But due to his lack of selective association, John felt he had no right to exercise this power or use this Name.

Justin Martyr said, *"While exorcism, as practiced by the Jews, often failed when it was attempted 'by the God of Abraham, Isaac, and Jacob,' it was eminently successful when administered 'by the Name of the Son of God,' Who was born of a Virgin and was crucified under Pontius Pilate."*

Consequently, it is given knowledge that this Name, the Name of Jesus, has power over evil spirits in such way that science has not yet been able to explain.

SCIENTIFIC?

Of course, it cannot be explained scientifically because it is not scientific, but instead spiritual. It was Jesus Who defeated Satan and all his minions at Calvary's Cross and, therefore, the Name that Satan fears the most. The phrase, *"And we forbad him, because he follows not us,"* seems to mean that such was not done out of envy or jealousy, but rather out of zeal for Christ, as though they were thus serving His Cause and upholding His Honor; however, this was *"a zeal, not according to knowledge."* It seems they did such without first taking counsel with Jesus.

(39) "BUT JESUS SAID, FORBID HIM NOT: FOR THERE IS NO MAN WHICH SHALL DO A MIRACLE IN MY NAME, THAT CAN LIGHTLY SPEAK EVIL OF ME."

The exegesis is:

Jesus did not say, *"Receive him,"* for the man's motive did not appear; however, he does say that the attitude toward such a one should at least be neutral.

ACCEPTANCE

The phrase, *"But Jesus said, Forbid him not,"* presents a striking Command that should be and, in fact, must be, the criteria of all Believers, that is, if one is to truly do the Work of the Lord.

Swete says, *"Whatever his intention, the man is for the time practically committed to a course of action which at least cannot be unfriendly. Therefore, do not forbid him."*

The phrase, *"For there is no man which shall do a Miracle in My Name, who can lightly speak evil of Me,"* proclaims many things! First of all, if the Miracle is performed by the use of the Name of Jesus, this automatically places the seal of legitimacy on the act, and the man, for that matter! Second, there is at least some relationship with Christ, or else such power would not be possible! So, in a sense, to forbid him is to forbid Christ, which no one desires to do, that is, if they are sane!

(40) "FOR HE WHO IS NOT AGAINST US IS ON OUR PART."

NOTES

The structure is:

The marks of false teachers are numerous in Scripture, so that no mistake need be made in detecting them (Mat. 7:15-20; 23:1-33; Acts 8:9; 13:8; Rom. 1:18-32; 16:17; I Cor. 1:18-31; I Tim. 4:1-8; II Tim. 3:1-13; 4:3-4; II Pet., Chpt. 2; III Jn. 9-10; Jude, Vss. 4-19; Rev. 2:14, 20).

JUDGMENT ON OTHERS

Regarding this statement, Morrison says, *"Regarding applied morals and sitting in judgment on ourselves, we should in ordinary circumstances apply the law strongly and stringently, 'he who is not with Christ is against Him.' But when we are sitting in judgment on others, into whose hearts we cannot look directly, we should in ordinary circumstances apply the law with generosity and largeness of heart, 'he who is not against Christ is with Him.'"*

In other words, when forced to make a judgment, we should be hard on ourselves but lenient on others, especially concerning their Work for the Lord, that is, providing their doctrine is Biblical. False doctrine, as should be obvious, cannot be supported (II Cor. 11:13-15).

(41) "FOR WHOSOEVER SHALL GIVE YOU A CUP OF WATER TO DRINK IN MY NAME, BECAUSE YOU BELONG TO CHRIST, VERILY I SAY UNTO YOU, HE SHALL NOT LOSE HIS REWARD."

The synopsis is:

This refers to helping take the Gospel to others; all help respecting this will be rewarded, no matter how small that help might be.

SUPPORT

The phrase, *"For whosoever shall give you a cup of water to drink in My Name,"* says three things:

1. Such knows Christ, because the act is being done in His Name.

2. The person has a spirit of giving, which is the Spirit of Christ.

3. No gift is to be looked at as unworthy or too small.

While it certainly may be true that the person could do more, still, the recipient is to be thankful for that given, even if it is only *"a cup of water."*

The phrase, *"Because you belong to Christ,"* indicates that not only is it done in His Name, but, in effect, for Him; consequently, it is to be received accordingly! The phrase, *"Verily I say unto you, he shall not lose his reward,"* means that the spiritual significance of help offered to a brother for Christ's sake is independent of the material value of the gift. If sincerely given, it will be duly noted by the Lord, with the giver *"not losing his reward."*

The Believer here is taught that small gifts, especially considering it is the best some can do, are looked at very highly by the Lord, and should be noted accordingly by other Believers.

(42) "AND WHOSOEVER SHALL OFFEND ONE OF THESE LITTLE ONES WHO BELIEVE IN ME, IT IS BETTER FOR HIM THAT A MILLSTONE WERE HANGED ABOUT HIS NECK, AND HE WERE CAST INTO THE SEA."

The composition is:

As the smallest help will be rewarded, likewise, the smallest offense will be also addressed; these admonitions had better be taken seriously.

OFFENSE

The phrase, *"And whosoever shall offend one of these little ones who believe in Me,"* refers to Believers who, following the admonition of Christ, conduct themselves as *"little children,"* at least regarding the temperament of the child. As a child is defenseless and absolutely dependent on someone else to protect it, likewise, the Believer who has the *"child spirit,"* who consequently will not defend himself, is here boldly proclaimed to be defended by the Lord.

The phrase, *"It is better for him that a millstone were hanged about his neck, and he were cast into the sea,"* is a reference to Greek and Roman punishment; consequently, one should well heed these words, for the punishment stated here is awful. Contrasts are presented here; great reward for even the smallest kindness and great punishment for even the slightest offense.

(43) "AND IF YOUR HAND OFFEND YOU, CUT IT OFF: IT IS BETTER FOR YOU TO ENTER INTO LIFE MAIMED, THAN HAVING TWO HANDS TO GO INTO HELL, INTO THE FIRE THAT NEVER SHALL BE QUENCHED."

The diagram is:

This Verse proves the reality of Hell, and of it being the destiny of those who oppose true Believers, who are truly doing the Work of God.

HELL

The phrase, *"And if your hand offend you, cut it off,"* presents a symbolic statement. It is not meant literally that the hand should be cut off, for sin does not originate with the hand, but rather with the heart. The *"hand,"* at least in this instance, figures power. It relates to one's power to do things, and especially if that power is used against a true Child of God.

The phrase, *"It is better for you to enter into life maimed, than having two hands to go into Hell,"* means that rather than offending a Believer, one would be far better off to be reduced to half of his power, i.e., ability to do things. Jesus is proclaiming the need for extreme caution on the part of all when it comes to His Children. (This pertains to fellow Believers or unbelievers who attempt to hinder or hurt.)

These *"little ones"* (humble Believers) are doing the Work of God on Earth, which is the only Work that really matters and, therefore, nothing must be done to hinder them, with everything done, in fact, to help them. This is the lesson being taught by Christ.

The phrase, *"Into the fire that never shall be quenched,"* proclaims two things:

1. Hell is a literal place, with literal fire, which will literally burn forever, in which the person will literally be eternally imprisoned.

2. Considering the punishment, the loss of one's soul meted out to those who *"offend one of these little ones,"* one should understand just how seriously the Lord holds the value of the *"little ones"* and their work.

(44) "WHERE THEIR WORM DIES NOT, AND THE FIRE IS NOT QUENCHED."

The overview is:

Christ is proclaiming what one faces who opposes true Believers; the punishment is eternal.

THE WORM THAT DOESN'T DIE AND THE FIRE THAT'S NOT QUENCHED

The metaphor used here is striking as well as terrible.

Ordinarily, the *"worm"* feeds upon the disorganized body and then dies. The fire consumes the fuel, and then itself expires. But here, the *"worm"* never dies; the fire never goes out. The words of Cornelius Lapide regarding this Passage are well worth repeating:

"I beseech you, O Reader, by the mercies of our God, by your own Salvation, by that one little life entrusted to you and committed to your care, that you will ever keep before your eyes the living memory, as of eternity and of eternal torments, so also of the eternal joys on the other side offered to you by God, concerning which you here cast the die, and that irrevocable.

"Let these two things never depart from your mind. In this world, 'vanity of vanities, and all is vanity.' Oh, what a void there is in earthly things! Oh, how vain is all our life without Christ! In the world to come, Truth of Truths and all is Truth; stability of stabilities and all is stability; eternity of eternities, and all is eternity.

"An eternity in Heaven most happy, in Hell most miserable, 'where the worm dies not, and the fire is not quenched.'"

(45) "AND IF YOUR FOOT OFFEND YOU, CUT IT OFF: IT IS BETTER FOR YOU TO ENTER HALT INTO LIFE, THAN HAVING TWO FEET TO BE CAST INTO HELL, INTO THE FIRE THAT NEVER SHALL BE QUENCHED."

The composition is:

In essence, the Lord is saying the same thing that He did in Verse 43. This shows the tremendous significance of the statement.

EVERY PRECAUTION TAKEN

The phrase, *"And if your foot offend you, cut it off,"* refers to self-will. It speaks of one's will which is apart from God's Will, which always leads one astray. As such, it will offend, and easily so, *"one of these little ones who believe in Me."*

The phrase, *"It is better for you to enter halt into life, than having two feet to be cast into Hell,"* refers to the stupidity of self-will. The idea is that any measure which can be taken in order to miss Hell must be taken. It is not the idea that such will save one's soul, for that comes about only by Faith in Christ. What it does refer to are things which keep us from accepting Christ. As well, if one refuses Christ, much of the time one will persecute those who follow Jesus. To do so only exacerbates the problem.

The phrase, *"Into the fire that never shall be quenched,"* is said now the second time, which gives added emphasis. Jesus desires that no mistake be made about it, referring to the certitude of the place called Hell.

(46) "WHERE THEIR WORM DIES NOT, AND THE FIRE IS NOT QUENCHED."

The overview is:

Christ makes this ominous statement for the second time.

THE WARNING CONTINUED

A Communications Baron, we are told, made this statement:

"I want to go to Hell when I die, because that's where all the fun is!"

I don't know where he is getting his information regarding the *"fun"* in Hell, because the Words of Jesus state otherwise! It is a place too dreadful for human language to describe or human thought to conceive. No! There is no *"fun"* there!

Even though the term *"Hell"* is bandied about as a joke, in Truth, *"Hell is no joke!"*

Again, let us state:

Hell is a literal place, and it is reserved for Satan and his angels and all who follow the Evil One. As well, it is eternal!

(47) "AND IF YOUR EYE OFFEND YOU, PLUCK IT OUT: IT IS BETTER FOR YOU TO ENTER INTO THE KINGDOM OF GOD WITH ONE EYE, THAN HAVING TWO EYES TO BE CAST INTO HELL FIRE."

The composition is:

This figures covetousness, or the wealth gained by covetousness.

THE OFFENSE OF THE EYES

The phrase, *"And if your eye offends you, pluck it out,"* figures the *"lust of the eyes."* In fact, the hands could well speak of the *"lust of the flesh,"* and the feet could well speak of *"the pride of life"* (I Jn. 2:16).

As we have previously stated, Jesus is not meaning that one should literally pluck out one's eye. He is speaking of the severity of the situation. Even if drastic measures must be taken, and in whatever capacity, such should be done without hesitation in order to gain victory over the powers of darkness.

Of course, such victory can be gained only by Faith evidenced in Christ and what He has done for us at the Cross (I Cor. 1:18; Gal. 6:14).

HELL FIRE

The phrase, *"It is better for you to enter into the Kingdom of God with one eye, than having two eyes to be cast into Hell fire,"* lets us know the reason that Jesus is saying this, i.e., *"Hell fire."* I think the analogy could be drawn in this manner:

If a man and his family live in a certain area, and that area has some serious spiritual drawbacks (of whatever capacity), which are dragging down this family, even though their economic welfare may be excellent in this particular place, still, if the situation can be bettered spiritually by moving elsewhere, even counting great economic loss, by all means it should be done, and instantly.

First of all, a good, spiritual Church is absolutely necessary, at least if it's possible to find and attend one like that. Regrettably, many Christians put money first and Church last. If the income is improved in a particular area, irrespective as to the spiritual condition of the Churches in that area, many opt for the money. Jesus is plainly saying in these Passages that such a move is foolish. In effect, His admonition is far stronger, as is obvious, than that of which we have just stated.

Even though they are not meant to be taken literally, still, for Jesus to use the examples of *"cutting off one's hand,"* or *"foot,"* or *"plucking out one's eye,"* they should portray, as they are meant to do, the utter seriousness of the situation.

PUT GOD FIRST

This means to put the things of God first in any and all situations. It means that every other consideration, such as economic welfare, geographical location, education, or likes and dislikes, should be last. Moreover, inasmuch as Jesus gave three examples, each almost identical to the others, such is done by design. The Believer is meant to understand the severity of the situation; therefore, it is repeated three times for effect.

The suggested acute measures recommended are given that we may know how strongly the powers of darkness may come against us. It is with both Believer and unbeliever in mind that Jesus makes these statements. Consequently, the Believer is told, in effect, that if the practicing of sin is allowed to continue, Hell fire could be the result.

This shoots down the unscriptural doctrine of Unconditional Eternal Security. As well, the unbeliever is told that his punishment is certain and increased, if a *"little one"* is hindered or hurt.

(48) "WHERE THEIR WORM DIES NOT, AND THE FIRE IS NOT QUENCHED."

The overview is:

This is the third time the Lord affirms the fact of the Lake of Fire and the conscious suffering of those cast into it.

THE DOCTRINE OF HELL

The Gehenna outside Jerusalem, on which these statements are based, was not eternal. Its fire was quenched and its worm died, because the corruption on which they fed ceased to exist. But the terrible words, *"their worm,"* reveals the eternal existence of the moral corruption that is *"to go into Hell."*

Regrettably, the doctrine of *"Hell"* is little taught and preached from behind most pulpits. The world and the Church have become so psychologized that the idea of a future Judgment and a eternal Hell are anathema to most; however, the failure to believe this doctrine in no way negates its reality. The Bible teaches that there is such a place called Gehenna, *"Hell,"* which Jesus graphically describes in these Passages.

The Rabbis used the word *"Gehenna"* to indicate the place of final punishment. Jesus maintained this meaning in the Gospels, but with a difference. Whereas, and as we have stated, the *"Gehenna"* was a place nearby Jerusalem where refuse and garbage were burned, still, at times, the fires would go out;

however, Jesus maintains that the fire will never go out in this place called *"Hell."* Consequently, the phrase *"Eternal fire"* is used of Hell; human beings will be punished there in a fire prepared for *"the devil and his angels"* (Mat. 25:41).

The most striking picture of eternal punishment is found in the Book of Revelation. There the state of the condemned is described. They are in a *"fiery lake of burning sulfur"* (Rev. 19:20; 20:10), a *"Lake of Fire"* (Rev. 20:14-15), where they will *"be tormented day and night forever and ever"* (Rev. 20:10).

FIRE

As we have stated, the fire of Hell that Jesus mentioned is literal. The word *"fire"* is found 542 times in Scripture; it is used figuratively only a few times. Moreover, it is always clear when it is used figuratively. The same words which are translated *"eternal,"* *"everlasting,"* and *"forever and ever,"* which are used to state the eternity of God, Christ, the Holy Spirit, Life, etc., are also used of Hell and punishment. Therefore, if these Persons and things are eternal, then Hell and punishment are also eternal.

Some teach that *"forever"* means *"age-long."* This may be true when used in a limited and qualified sense of temporary things, as in Exodus 21:6. But when used literally of God's Plan, it always means *"eternal."* The Hebrew word *"ololam"* and the Greek word *"aionios"* both mean *"time out of mind, past or future; eternity; always; forever; everlasting; perpetual; without end."*

In view of these great Truths, which leave no room for misinterpretation, one would do well to graphically heed what Jesus said concerning Hell and its eternal consequence. To be sure, He meant what He said and He said what He meant! As someone has said, *"There is a Heaven to gain and a Hell to shun!"* It makes no difference if man does not even believe in its existence or that some Preachers refuse to preach this Biblical Doctrine; still, Hell exists; at this very moment, most of humanity who have ever lived have gone to this horrible place.

This is one of the reasons that the Church is commanded to take the Gospel to the world. The eternal consequences of not being saved are so awful that they defy description. Here and hence the Scripture says, *"How shall we escape if we neglect so great Salvation"* (Heb. 2:3).

(49) "FOR EVERY ONE SHALL BE SALTED WITH FIRE, AND EVERY SACRIFICE SHALL BE SALTED WITH SALT."

The overview is:

Salt is a type of the Word of God.

SALTED WITH THE FIRE OF TESTING

The phrase, *"For every one shall be salted with fire,"* pertains, as stated, to the fire of testing, and has to do with our works. Jesus said, *"Now if any man build upon this foundation gold, silver, precious stones* (symbolic of the Word of God, which is the Standard), *wood, hay, stubble* (which will not stand the test of fire);

"Every man's work shall be made manifest (at the Judgment Seat of Christ): *for the day shall declare it* (the time of the Judgment Seat of Christ), *because it shall be revealed by fire* (the fire of God's Word); *and the fire shall try every man's work of what sort it is"* (I Cor. 3:12-13).

As is obvious, wood, hay, and stubble will not stand the test of fire, so they will be burned. Gold, silver, and precious stones will stand the test; all of this is used as a symbol.

THE SALTED SACRIFICE

The phrase, *"And every Sacrifice shall be salted with salt,"* refers, once again, to *"salt"* as symbolic of the Word of God. In the old Levitical Law, Sacrifices were offered with salt, which was a symbol of preservation (Lev. 2:13). The idea is this:

The Sacrifice must be according to the Word of God, of which *"salt,"* as stated, is a symbol. In fact, untold numbers of Sacrifices are offered up to the Lord constantly. To be frank, most all of these things will never be looked at as a Sacrifice by those who offer them, but, in reality, God labels them as such. However, the only *"Sacrifice"* that will stand the *"salt"* test, which means that it is entirely according to the Word of God, is the Cross. Any other Sacrifice is condemned out of hand. In other words, every sacrifice is put to the salt test, and the only one that will pass that test is the Cross of

Christ. It alone fulfills the Word of God, of which *"salt"* is a type.

(50) "SALT IS GOOD: BUT IF THE SALT HAVE LOST HIS SALTNESS, WHEREWITH WILL YOU SEASON IT? HAVE SALT IN YOURSELVES, AND HAVE PEACE ONE WITH ANOTHER."

The diagram is:

Abiding by the Word will guarantee peace.

SALT IS GOOD

The phrase, *"Salt is good,"* refers to the Word of God. If one abides by the Word, of course, such is *"good."* The Word is meant to serve as the Judge of one's life. The result will be peace, and not the disputation of Verse 34.

The Word of God is always the criteria for everything.

SALTNESS LOST

The phrase, *"But if the salt have lost his saltness, wherewith will you season it?"* has to do with the Sacrifice of service (Lev. 2:13), which must be seasoned with salt, i.e., judged by the health-giving, purifying, and preservative Word of God. Fire and salt are both symbols of purifying and preservative judgment. For the Christian, the fire is chastening in its action and only consumes the flesh (I Cor. 11:31-32).

Salt expresses fellowship and affection. It signifies an inward sweetening and preservative energy binding the heart to Christ and to His Service — an energy of holiness that judges everything contrary to His Nature and Will. Hence, Christians are the salt of the Earth, because, living in fellowship with Him and judging evil in themselves, they purify society.

The phrase about losing saltness means that if we who are of Christ fail in our testimony, where shall anything be found to restore this loss of the Word of God? The salt will have lost its savor, and what can season it, i.e., preserve society?

It is the Believer, as the salt of the Earth, which preserves society from total corruption and its consequent destruction.

Were it not for the family of Abraham before Jesus and all Believers thereafter, this world would have long since been destroyed

NOTES

of its own corruption. God would have had to destroy it, or man would have destroyed himself. Actually, this is what caused the destruction of the world by water during the time of Noah. The Scripture says, *"And God saw that the wickedness of man was great in the Earth, and that every imagination of the thoughts of his heart was only evil continually"* (Gen. 6:5).

Actually, until Noah, a period of about 1,600 years, the only recorded Believers during that period of time were *"Abel"* and *"Enoch."* There may have been others, but the Bible does not say; consequently, there was no *"salt,"* because there were no Believers, and consequently the world went to its doom.

To be sure, at this moment, and despite the United Nations, the great universities of the world, governments, etc., were it not for the Believers on this Earth, the world would have long since been destroyed.

That is the reason Judgment is going to come quickly after the Rapture of the Church.

Paul said, *"And then shall that Wicked (Antichrist) be revealed... Even him, whose coming is after the working of Satan with all power and signs and lying wonders,*

"And with all deceivableness of unrighteousness in them who perish; because they received not the love of the Truth, that they might be saved" (II Thess. 2:8-10).

At that time, the coming Great Tribulation, the world will *"have lost his saltness";* with nothing left to *"season it,"* it will be destroyed.

SALT AS SEASON

Actually, the conclusion of the question, *"wherewith will you season it?"* tells us in no uncertain terms that there is no alternative to the Christlike Believer. All of man's vaunted knowledge, education, ability, money, talent, state, and position cannot serve as a preservative, only the *"Believer seasoned with salt,"* i.e., the Word of God.

THE SALTNESS OF THE BELIEVER

The phrase, *"Have salt in yourselves,"* refers to the Word of God having free course within one's life, thereby preserving the Believer. The only way that one can successfully do this is for one to place their faith exclusively, as we've said over and over again, in Christ and the Cross, and not allow our faith to be moved elsewhere. Then the Holy Spirit, Who works entirely within the framework of the Finished Work of Christ, which is within the framework of the Word of God, can have free course in our lives, thereby bringing about that which we ought to be.

But let it ever be understood:

The Holy Spirit Alone can do what needs to be done. And He always, and without exception, works entirely within and according to the Word of God. If the Believer makes the Cross of Christ the Object of his Faith, he will *"have salt in himself."*

PEACE

The phrase, *"And have peace one with another,"* means that one will be at peace with his brethren, if the *"salt"* is present with all. This *"peace"* is afforded, at least in part, because the Believer understands the struggle of another, due to the struggle within himself; *"for every one shall be salted with fire."*

One of the most beautiful movings of the Holy Spirit I have ever experienced occurred relative somewhat to this word *"salt."*

A PERSONAL EXPERIENCE

If I remember correctly, it was November of 1991. Our Ministry was in crisis, to say the least; the only thing I knew to do was pray. I felt that the Lord had told me to call two prayer meetings a day, which I did, and which I personally continue unto this hour. Actually, I do not believe I could have survived the onslaught of darkness without this constant fellowship with the Lord.

At that time, we were having the nightly prayer meetings in our home, which would later be changed to the Church. At any rate, the time in question was a Friday night. Frances and I had gone with friends the earlier part of the evening to the home of another family in the Church, where we enjoyed fellowship and a good meal. We arrived back home in time for the evening prayer meeting.

There were not many people present that particular Friday night, possibly only seven or eight, if that.

NOTES

THE WORD OF GOD

Before we went to prayer, I read the short story of the healing of the waters at Jericho from II Kings 2:19-22. I made a few remarks, and then we went to prayer. This beautiful illustration speaks of Elisha being in Jericho, with the men of that city coming to him and telling him of the bad water which had made the ground barren. This evidently was a well which bubbled out of a stream. It was, in fact, called the *"spring of the waters"* (II Ki. 2:21). (Sometime ago I was in Jericho, and was shown this spring, which was said to be the same spring of Elisha.)

When the men of the city came to Elisha, telling him of this problem, he told them to bring unto him *"a new cruse, and put salt therein."* The *"new cruse,"* as Bible teachers know, was a Type of the Humanity of Christ. The *"salt"* was a type of the Word of God, which filled the life of Christ as no other.

Elisha walked to the *"spring of the waters"* and *"cast the salt in there."* He then said, *"Thus saith the LORD, I have healed these waters; there shall not be from thence any more death or barren land"* (II Ki. 2:21).

Of course, the salt in the natural had nothing to do with the healing of the waters, but simply served as a symbol of the Word of God, which emanates from the *"Living Word,"* i.e., *"New Cruse,"* the Lord Jesus, and is the solution to any problem.

(The *"Cruse"* was made of clay, which symbolizes, as stated, the Humanity of Christ. The word *"new"* symbolizes the fact that there had never been One like Jesus. He was solely unique, because He was Virgin-born, therefore, born without the sin nature.)

THE SPIRIT OF GOD

After I made some remarks concerning Elisha and the healing of the waters, we then went to prayer. After a few moments, the Spirit of God came over me in one of the greatest ways ever. Actually, the Presence of God lingered all night long, even into the next day. The Holy Spirit began to bring to my spirit what the healing of these waters meant, and how this Ministry would be healed.

The Lord not only told me that this

Ministry would be healed, but He also delineated the various departments of the Ministry. *"The Telecast will be healed!"* *"Family Worship Center will be healed!"* *"Your finances will be healed!"* *"Your Missions Program will be healed!"* *"Family Christian Academy will be healed!"* *"The Bible College will be healed!"*

As the Lord gave this to me, the Spirit of God washed over me in powerful waves of glory. As stated, the Spirit of the Lord lingered all night long, even until nearly noon of the following day. From that time until this, to be sure, it has not been easy. However, exactly that which the Lord said is now beginning to come to pass.

Time and time again, I have refreshed myself by going back to that moment when the Spirit of God spoke to me that Friday night and told me, *"I have healed these waters."* At times, my Faith has weakened, but then I know and realize that the Word of God will not fail.

From that time I have literally lived in the Word of God. I have applied the *"salt"* to every single problem. I have attempted to fill my life with the Word of God. I have tried to make certain that the salt does not lose its savor. And, by the Grace of God, I believe I can say, without fear of contradiction, it hasn't! The Lord said it, and I believe it!

"Thus saith the LORD, I have healed these waters; there shall not be from thence any more death or barren land" (II Ki. 2:21).

CHAPTER 10

(1) "AND HE AROSE FROM THENCE, AND COMETH INTO THE COASTS OF JUDAEA BY THE FARTHER SIDE OF JORDAN: AND THE PEOPLE RESORT UNTO HIM AGAIN; AND, AS HE WAS WONT, HE TAUGHT THEM AGAIN."

The composition is:

They so much needed His teaching, but it was His Death that would set them free.

THE JOURNEY

The phrase, *"And He arose from thence,"* refers to Jesus quitting Galilee and going to Jerusalem. The words are sadder than one may realize, because He is on the way to His Crucifixion, which will take place in a very short time. Consequently, the greatest Move of God the world has ever known, which took place in Galilee (called *"Galilee of the nations"* by the Prophet Isaiah [Isa. 9:1-2]) would be no more.

In describing this time, Matthew quotes Isaiah, saying, *"The people which sat in darkness saw great Light; and to them which sat in the region and shadow of death light is sprung up"* (Mat. 4:16). The *"Light"* he speaks of here in the Greek Text is *"phos,"* which means *"underived and absolute Light — the opposite of all darkness."*

However, the religious leaders of Galilee rejected this *"Light"*; consequently, Jesus said of them, *"Woe unto you Chorazin! . . . Bethsaida! . . . And thou, Capernaum, which are exalted unto Heaven, shall be brought down to Hell"* (Mat. 11:21-23).

REJECTION

So, they would not accept Him, despite the fact that blinded eyes were opened, lame legs made to walk, lepers cleansed, and even the dead raised, in effect, and as stated, the greatest Move of God ever known by any people anywhere. No wonder Jesus said of them, *"Woe. . . ."*

The ability of man to resist Light and to rebel against God, even in the face of such a witness as none other than the Son of God, is amazing, to say the least! So His departure, even though spoken in few words, is a happening of eternal consequence. To be sure, as He left Galilee, He has been forced to leave others. They did not want Him, never realizing they were sealing their own doom.

However, I want all to know that I want Him, and with every fiber of my being. I realize I have nothing to offer Him, while, at the same time, He has everything to offer me. On that basis, I can only throw myself at His Feet, as the *"woman of Canaan"* so long ago. Even though she was not a child of the Promise, still, by taking the position of a mere *"dog,"* she could then appeal to His Mercy and Grace, which He gladly supplied to her; instead of the crumbs which she sought, she was given everything (Mk. 7:24-30).

I, too, and in whatever capacity, bow at His Feet. I have caught a glimpse of His Grace and Glory, and nothing else will ever satisfy.

THE PEOPLE

The phrase, *"And cometh into the coasts of Judaea by the farther side of Jordan,"* means that He came to Judaea on the east side of the Jordan River, and would then cross over at Jericho. The phrase, *"And the people resort unto Him again,"* means that, on this journey from Galilee to Judaea, many other people on their way to the Feast of Passover would take up step with Him. Many, no doubt, had been healed by Him, with others being kindly disposed toward Him. These journeyed with the Lord and the Disciples along the road.

If the *"people"* had had qualified, spiritual leadership, Christ would have been totally and completely accepted; however, they didn't have such leadership. They would consequently go to their doom. About 37 years later, Rome would completely denude this part of Israel, totally destroying Jerusalem, with over one million Jews being slaughtered in the carnage, and other hundreds of thousands being sold as slaves.

If that wasn't enough, most of these people would die lost, which means that the hands of the religious leaders of Israel would drip with blood (Ezek. 3:17-21).

Is the situation any different presently?

I think not! At least as far as the United States is concerned, the people have too few true shepherds. There are many, many wolves in sheep's clothing (Mat. 7:15-20). In fact, the Laodicean Church portrays perfectly the modern Church, which, no doubt, it was meant to portray (Rev. 3:14). That Church said, *"I am rich, and increased with goods, and have need of nothing."*

Then Jesus said, *"Knowest not that you are wretched, and miserable, and poor, and blind, and naked"* (Rev. 3:17).

The Church cannot rise any higher than the pulpit; regrettably, the pulpit presently is running after fads — in fact, anything and everything except the Cross of Christ.

Isaiah described it perfectly:

NOTES

"The whole head is sick, and the whole heart faint."

"From the sole of the foot even unto the head there is no soundness in it; but wounds, and bruises, and putrifying sores: they have not been closed, neither bound up, neither mollified with ointment" (Isa. 1:5-6).

Yes, there is a Godly Preacher here and there; but, if the truth be known, the number is abysmally small!

THE TEACHING

The phrase, *"And, as He was wont, He taught them again,"* means that He taught them, and kept on teaching them. Of all the times these people had made this journey to Jerusalem to keep the Passover, this would be the most momentous occasion. How blessed they were to have had Jesus to teach them along the way! Even though the Scripture does not say, any sick among them were, no doubt, healed, as well! It would be a journey to remember!

And yet, they could little know or understand that He was on His way to His Crucifixion. Little did they realize that the One Whom the Passover represented, and had represented since its institution in Egypt some 1,500 years before, when Israel was delivered, was actually walking among them. In other words, Jesus was the Passover; He would fulfill its type and symbolism.

While many of them loved Him, there were probably few, if any, who knew exactly Who He was!

(2) "AND THE PHARISEES CAME TO HIM, AND ASKED HIM, IS IT LAWFUL FOR A MAN TO PUT AWAY HIS WIFE? TEMPTING HIM."

The diagram is:

The question of divorce and remarriage was the great controversy at that time in Israel.

DIVORCE AND REMARRIAGE

The question, *"And the Pharisees came to Him, and asked Him, Is it lawful for a man to put away his wife?"* presents the burning question of that particular day and time.

About 75 or so years before Christ, a learned Rabbi named Hillel, a native of Babylon who afterwards came to Jerusalem, studied the Law of Moses with great success, and became the head of the chief school in that city. One of his Disciples, named Shammai, separated from his master, and set up another school; so, in the time of our Lord, the Scribes and Doctors of the Law were ranged in two parties — namely the followers of Hillel, the most influential, and the followers of Shammai.

So this question put to the Lord was meant to bring Him into collision with one or the other of the two opposing parties. For if He had said that it was not lawful for a man to put away his wife, He would have exposed Himself to the hostility of many of the wealthy class, who put away their wives for any and every cause. But if He had allowed the lawfulness of divorce at all, they would have found fault with His Doctrine as imperfect and carnal, although He professed to be a Spiritual Teacher of a Perfect System sent down from Heaven.

Therefore, their question was crafted perfectly respecting one of the most controversial subjects ever discussed — the subject of divorce.

TEMPTING HIM

The phrase, *"Tempting Him,"* means that they were putting Him to the test as a Teacher, hoping to show that He was unorthodox, and thereby putting Him in an unfavorable light with the people. In other words, they had little interest at all in what the Word of God actually taught about divorce, in effect, knowing the truth about the matter. They only wished to embroil Him in controversy so that they would be able to accuse Him.

It seems they never learned! Irrespective as to what they asked Him, and how much time and thought had gone into the craftiness of their questions, every single time, and without fail, He bested them, and did so in totality. This time would be no exception.

(3) "AND HE ANSWERED AND SAID UNTO THEM, WHAT DID MOSES COMMAND YOU?"

The overview is:

He took them to the Word, but not as they thought. While He mentioned the Law of Moses, He would supercede that.

MOSES

The question, *"And He answered and said unto them, What did Moses command you?"* takes them to the place where they feel comfortable, because they professed much reverence for Moses. His answer, however, would take them to a degree of Bible knowledge that they had never known or heard before. They did not know how to rightly divide the Word. He knew how to rightly divide it, because He was the *"Living Word."* In fact, had they known the Word, they would have known Who He was!

However, the Expositors tell us that Jesus had in view not what Moses allowed in Deuteronomy 24:1, but what he in Genesis enjoined as the ideal state of things. (Moses was the writer of the Pentateuch — Genesis through Deuteronomy — and all its legislation. The Holy Spirit was the Author.)

When He mentioned Moses, they naturally supposed He had in view Moses' Commandment. As well, by Jesus using the word *"command,"* He showed the correctness of Moses' position; but yet He would take them to the ideal in Genesis instead of the permissible. Man is always attempting to make allowances for his failures, instead of coming up to the ideal as commanded by the Lord.

(4) "AND THEY SAID, MOSES SUFFERED TO WRITE A BILL OF DIVORCEMENT, AND TO PUT HER AWAY."

The exposition is:

The Pharisees misinterpreted Moses, even as many do.

A BILL OF DIVORCEMENT

The phrase, *"And they said,"* present them giving the statement of Moses, but still improperly interpreting it. The phrase, *"Moses suffered to write a bill of divorcement, and to put her away,"* is found in Deuteronomy 24:1. From this statement by Moses, the school of Hillel concluded that it was proper to obtain a divorce for *"every cause"* (Mat. 19:3). As a result of this liberal interpretation, which, by the way, was error, divorce was now being permitted on many frivolous grounds, such as a wife's careless seasoning of food, the wife going into the street with loose or uncombed hair, loud talk, constant talking in the home, etc. Actually, a husband, if he so desired, not satisfied with his wife, could use any of these things as an excuse.

So, by the time of the Christ, divorce was easily obtained in Israel, with the sanctity of the home being greatly threatened.

As stated, the other school, under Shammai, contended that divorce must be permitted only in the case of moral defilement, which was correct.

(5) "AND JESUS ANSWERED AND SAID UNTO THEM, FOR THE HARDNESS OF YOUR HEART HE WROTE YOU THIS PRECEPT."

The exposition is:

The Lord did not deny that Moses permitted divorce; but command it, he did not. Consequently, for the Pharisees to shelter themselves under the temporary recognition of a necessary evil was to confess that they had not outgrown the moral stature of their fathers.

THE HARDNESS OF THE HEART

The phrase, *"And Jesus answered and said unto them,"* will constitute an answer they had not expected. The phrase, *"For the hardness of your heart he wrote you this precept,"* means two things:

1. *"Hardness of the heart"*: This had to do with unbelief on the part of the people, and, above all, being outside the Will of God, to which unbelief will always lead. In other words, doing that which is not according to the Word of God, which is the Will of God! Such causes a *"hardness of heart"* in individuals. It even happened in the very hearts of the Disciples when they misunderstood the Mission of Christ, attempting to make Him King instead of Lord (Mk. 6:52).

Therefore, for the Pharisees to shelter themselves under the temporary recognition of a necessary evil was to confess that they had not outgrown, as stated, the moral stature of their fathers.

2. *"He wrote you this precept"*: Swete says, *"The Lord does not deny that Moses permitted divorce; command it, he did not."* The commandment given by Moses, which was allowed by the Holy Spirit, consisted of *"regulations tending to limit it and preclude its abuse."* No such regulations would have been necessary but for the hardness of heart in the Jews.

If this had not been permitted, many women and children would have been placed in an intolerable situation, the occasion for much suffering. The more sinful man became, the more sin changed and corrupted his nature; consequently, the institution of marriage became corrupted, as well!

Even then, Moses put particular legal steps into the act of divorce, which made it somewhat difficult. Thus, this legislation was adapted to the imperfect moral condition of the people, who were as yet quite unprepared for a higher moral code.

(It should also be obvious that the women at this time did not have much, if any, equality; consequently, this ruling by Moses, which, as stated, was allowed by the Holy Spirit, was primarily to protect them.)

(6) "BUT FROM THE BEGINNING OF THE CREATION GOD MADE THEM MALE AND FEMALE."

The diagram is:

The Lord did not mean from the beginning of Creation per se, but rather from the beginning of the Creation of humankind.

CREATION

The phrase, *"But from the beginning of the creation,"* refers to the beginning of the creation of man and woman. The phrase, *"God made them male and female,"* is the only type of creation made in this fashion respecting living beings. Adam was created first, and then Eve was created second, but with a distinction. She was created from Adam; both, therefore, were created from one (Gen. 2:21-23).

(7) "FOR THIS CAUSE SHALL A MAN LEAVE HIS FATHER AND MOTHER, AND CLEAVE TO HIS WIFE."

The overview is:

This statement completely debunks the homosexual lifestyle.

WIFE

The phrase, *"For this cause,"* contains a powerful statement within itself. It has reference to the nuclear family, which means *"a family group that consists of father, mother, and children."* It has to do with the way man and woman were created and, therefore, meant to live.

The phrase, *"Shall a man leave his father

and mother," constitutes a strong inclination. In other words, the inborn instinct is to ultimately be weaned away from one's parents and be joined to a wife or husband. Even though it does not constitute sin for one not to do this, but rather to remain single, still, the former is the natural order intended by God.

The phrase, *"And cleave to his wife,"* pertains to the initial command of a man joining himself to a wife and then remaining thus joined. As well, and as should be obvious, this condemns all homosexuality, including, and by all means, so-called homosexual marriages. Such is a serious affront to God and His Plan of Creation, which should be glaringly obvious!

Homosexuality is a sin against society, against nature, against the human body (which should be a temple of the Holy Spirit), and against God.

Paul said this:

"For this cause God gave them up unto vile affections: for even their women did change the natural use into that which is against nature:

"And likewise also the men, leaving the natural use of the woman, burned in their lust one toward another; men with men working that which is unseemly, and receiving in themselves that recompense of their error which was meet" (Rom. 1:26-27).

IS HOMOSEXUALITY THE WORST SIN?

Whether it is the worst sin or not, one cannot answer. All sin, in the eyes of God, is terribly wrong, with some sins, of course, worse than others. Jesus spoke of the religious leaders of Israel and said they had committed *"the greater sin"* (Jn. 19:11). We do know that the destruction of Sodom and Gomorrah was at least in part because of the sin of sodomy. *"The LORD said ... their sin is very grievous"* (Gen. 18:20).

"Then the LORD rained upon Sodom and upon Gomorrah brimstone and fire from the LORD out of heaven" (Gen. 19:24).

It seems these twin cities had become so evil, at least with a part of this evil being the sin of sodomy, that the Lord Personally took a hand and rained fire and brimstone upon these places, destroying them from the face of the Earth, until there is left no record of their former position and place.

The sins of homosexuality and lesbianism are Satan's diabolical thrust against God's choice Creation — namely man. Satan hates man because man was originally created in God's Image. The Breath of God is actually in him. His body should be the temple of the Holy Spirit. God has chosen man to rule and reign under Christ Jesus over His Creation forever and forever. God deemed man's Salvation so important that He paid a price so staggering it is impossible for our imagination to conceive of its significance.

The sin of homosexuality is Satan's strongest and most conscientious effort to destroy the human family; since man is favored by God, this would be a great victory for the forces of evil. If this terrible sin became pandemic, Satan's effort would be fastly achieved, for humanity would cease to exist. But Satan has not succeeded, and he never will. This is what he was attempting in Sodom and Gomorrah.

THE CAUSE OF HOMOSEXUALITY

The homosexual claims he is born this way, that it was God Who made him so and, therefore, his lifestyle is not wrong, or so he claims. Consequently, society is encouraged by some sociologists and some psychologists, etc., to accept this lifestyle, even to the point of sanctioning homosexual marriages. Courts in some places are allowing homosexual marriage partners to adopt children and demanding that these *"marriages"* be given the same rights as marriages between men and women.

Powerful political lobbies are working virtually day and night to bring about legislation that would make it a crime to refuse to hire a person because of their sexual orientation, i.e., homosexuality and lesbianism. Actually, there already are laws of this nature on the books in America and Canada, although, at the present time, exempting certain professions, at least in the United States.

President Clinton attempted to lower the standards of the Armed Forces respecting homosexuality. He was not altogether, thank the Lord, successful. At any rate, the homosexual lobby in Washington is so powerful that every effort is being made, with ground steadily being gained, to not only guarantee homosexuals the rights of everyone else, which they already have, but rather to give them rights above everyone else.

Once again, the idea is that inasmuch as these people are born the way they are, and their sexual orientation is not their fault, but rather God's, they, therefore, must be treated as everyone else, with a special place made for their lifestyle.

GENES

It is true that, due to the Fall, which brought about the sin nature, that every type of evil is engrained in the human soul and spirit, even homosexuality. From studying the Scriptures, and observing that even children can be demon-possessed, the terrible degeneration in the human family is obvious respecting wickedness. Consequently, due to the manner in which man fell, babies are born with original sin.

In that original sin, some could very well have and, no doubt, do have, propensities toward particular wickednesses, which are literally born in them, such as: criminal leanings, excessive rebellion, alcoholism, drug addiction, hatred, perversion — and, yes, homosexuality. This does not mean that one is born a *"criminal,"* or an *"alcoholic,"* or a *"homosexual,"* etc., but that certain tendencies are stronger in some children than in others. Science, whether medical or otherwise, continues to look for these *"causes"* in brain cells, with even a suggestion that the problem could be in the *"genes."*

Respecting the *"genes,"* they are closer to the truth than they realize. (Genes are an element of the germ plasm that controls transmission of a hereditary character by specifying the structure of a particular protein or by controlling the function of other genetic material. In plain language, it has to do with our physical and mental make-up, which we have inherited from our forefathers.)

However, the reason for those *"genes"* being the way they are is not physical or mental, neither is it sociological, etc. It is spiritual! It was caused by the Fall of man and original sin. Man fell from total God-consciousness to the far lower level of total self-consciousness.

NOTES

So, these terrible problems, be they homosexuality or whatever, are, in a sense, hereditary, and are the result, as we have stated, of original sin. This means that a baby is born a sinner, with all type of propensities toward evil, some with different and more perverse leanings than others.

Due to this, many psychologists, sociologists, and anthropologists have attempted to claim that man is not to blame for the predicament he is in, etc., which is the main argument of the homosexual. However, God did not leave man in this perilous condition, but sent His Son, the Lord Jesus Christ, to lift man out of this terrible fallen state, and to give him New Life. Jesus called it *"born again"* (Jn. 3:3-8).

When one is *"born again"* in Christ, and by the Power of Christ, and due to Faith in Christ, one is literally *"regenerated,"* i.e., *"re-gened."* This is why the *"born again"* experience changes a person so radically. Actually, it only by this experience that one can truly change. All the other efforts of man are doomed to failure (Tit. 3:5).

THE DOCTRINE OF REGENERATION

This doctrine must be considered in the context of man and sin (Jn. 3:6; Eph. 2:1-3, 5). The effects of sin on human nature are considered to be so serious that without the new birth, the sinner cannot see, let alone enter into the Kingdom of God (Jn. 3:3, 5; I Cor. 2:6-16).

The initiative in regeneration is ascribed to God (Jn. 1:13); it is from above (Jn. 3:3, 7), and of the Holy Spirit (Jn. 3:5, 8). The same idea occurs in Ephesians 2:4-5 and I John 2:29 and 4:7. This Divine act is decisive and once-for-all. The way the language is structured in these Scriptures indicates that this single, initial act of Regeneration (Born-Again) carries with it far-reaching effects (I Jn 2:29; 3:9; 4:7; 5:1, 4, 18).

The abiding results given in these Passages are doing Righteousness, not committing sin, loving one another, believing that Jesus is the Christ, and overcoming the world. These results indicate that in spiritual matters man is not altogether passive. He is somewhat passive, one might say, in the New Birth; God acts on him. But the result of such an act is far-reaching activity; he actively repents, believes in Christ and what Christ did at the Cross, and henceforth walks in newness of life (Rom. 6:3-5).

Actually, the question must be asked, *"What actually happens to the individual in the New Birth?"* I think one would be safe to say that there is no great change in the personality itself; the person is still the same. But now he is differently controlled, and that is the secret of the New Birth.

Before the New Birth, the sin nature controlled the man and made him a rebel against God; now the Spirit of God controls him and directs him toward God, or at least that's the way it's supposed to be, and can be, if the Believer anchors his faith completely and absolutely in Christ and what Christ has done for us at the Cross, not allowing it to be moved to something else (Rom. 6:3-14; I Cor. 1:17-18, 23; 2:2).

The regenerate man walks after the Spirit, lives in the Spirit, is led by the Spirit, and is commanded to be filled with the Spirit (Rom. 8:4, 9, 14; Eph. 5:18). And yet, the Holy Spirit is either hindered or given latitude to work within our lives according to our Faith having as its correct Object Christ and the Cross (Rom. 8:1-2); however, even though his Faith is properly placed, and there properly remains, this does not mean that he is perfect, for he is not. He must grow in Grace and progress in the Lord (I Pet. 2:2), but, in every department of his personality, he is directed towards God.

Thus, Regeneration may be defined as a drastic act by the Holy Spirit on fallen human nature which leads to a change in the person's whole outlook, who can now be described as a new man who seeks, finds, and follows God in Christ, leaving the old life and actually becoming a new Creation in Christ Jesus (II Cor. 5:17).

HOW DOES REGENERATION COME?

First, as stated, it is God Who always takes the initiative respecting Salvation tendered toward man. Man in his natural state is so fallen he cannot receive the things of the Spirit of God, at least within himself; consequently, within himself, he makes no overt act toward God. Therefore, all initiative must be from the Lord, and, in fact, is from the Lord.

Within himself, man is dead in trespasses and sins; to be sure, *"dead is dead."* This speaks of total depravity, meaning that man cannot, within himself, direct any proper response toward God, neither can he understand God. So, the initiative, as stated, must be from the Lord.

The Word of God is the vehicle used by the Holy Spirit to awaken man to his need (James 1:18; I Pet. 1:23). As the Word of God, delivered by whatever means, comes to the heart of man, man is awakened to his fallen condition, and made to realize his need for Redemption. Regrettably, many, if not most, spurn this clarion call, but some accept and receive.

As the Holy Spirit, using the Word of God, makes man aware of his need, a *"measure of faith"* is given to the individual by the Lord, making it possible for him to believe, that is, if he desires to do so (Rom. 12:3). Even though man's understanding of God at that time is extremely limited, still, because of the action of the Holy Spirit upon the Word of God, the individual knows enough to accept the Lord as his Saviour, which, if done, brings about an immediate, even miraculous, change (II Cor. 5:17).

THE ANSWER IS THE LORD JESUS CHRIST

Consequently, when medical science attempts to solve man's problems in the physical, it is a fruitless exercise. It has already been solved, and by Jesus Christ; however, man, as always, keeps seeking to find a way out of his dilemma without going God's Way. In this effort, he will ever fail, as ever fail he must!

In answer to the question:

No! Man is not born a homosexual, nor a criminal, etc., but definitely can be born with and, no doubt, is born with, proclivities or tendencies toward certain predispositions. Addressing this, the Holy Spirit through Peter says, *"Forasmuch as you know that you were not redeemed with corruptible things, as silver and gold, from your vain lifestyle received by tradition from your fathers"* (I Pet. 1:18). The only answer to this problem is the Lord Jesus Christ and what He did for us at the Cross of Calvary (Jn. 3:16).

So, for man to claim that God made him the way he is, due to his birth or any other tendency, is blasphemy against God. Man is in the condition he is because of his own sin and failure, or others, not because of God. To blame God for our problem only exacerbates the problem, making it even more difficult to solve. James said: *"Let no man say when he is tempted* (tempted to do evil), *I am tempted of God: for God cannot be tempted with evil, neither tempts He any man:*

"But every man is tempted, when he is drawn away of his own lust, and enticed.

"Then when lust has conceived, it brings forth sin: and sin, when it is finished, brings forth death.

"Do not err, my beloved Brethren" (James 1:13-16).

From this Passage we learn that a person is born with *"his own lust,"* and then when Satan sets the stage by tempting the individual, he yields to the temptation and then becomes snared and bound by the horrible thing. The word *"enticed"* is an interesting word, as well. While it is *"his own lust"* which *"entices"* him, still, once recruited, the homosexual tends to recruit others; consequently, multiple thousands of young boys and girls are enticed into this web of deceit, as the lust continues to work within and upon itself, as a result of this malignity of darkness.

Many of these enticed eventually become homosexuals, because some have a predisposition towards this evil.

THE RECOMPENSE OF THEIR ERROR

The Scripture tells us that those who walk in this deception of darkness, and we continue to speak of homosexuality, will receive in themselves the *"recompense of their error"* (Rom. 1:27). The Greek word for *"error"* means *"wandering, wrong action, wickedness."* This means that once the person is fully bound by the sin of homosexuality, their mind and body become debilitated to receive in themselves the penalty of their wickedness. Consequently, a homosexual is usually known by his mannerisms, actions, personality, and even facial expressions. The sordid lifestyle actually changes the individual's personality.

Some may refer to professional athletes and others who are homosexuals and do not seem to be changed in this manner presently; however, to be sure, if they continue in this dreadful path of darkness, it will change them just as surely as the Scripture says it will. It is impossible for them not to change, and for the worse!

THE CURE

Many have asked me, *"Can a homosexual be saved?"* The answer is obvious!

Of course a homosexual can be saved, as well as an alcoholic, drug addict, or good Church member, for that matter. When Jesus came and died on Calvary for the sins of lost humanity, the homosexual definitely was included. However, once the homosexual is brought to Christ, he will cease being a homosexual, as the alcoholic will cease being an alcoholic, etc.

Now this is where the controversy begins. As always, men desire to continue in their sin and have Salvation at the same time.

Let it ever be known:

Jesus does not save *in* sin, but *from* sin. Jesus came to destroy the works of Satan, not to perpetuate them. John said, *"And you know that He was manifested to take away our sins; and in Him is no sin"* (I Jn. 3:5).

So, when the homosexual comes to Christ, he ceases to be a homosexual. Consequently, the homosexual churches and homosexual preachers, etc., are an abomination in the eyes of God. One might as well have *"alcoholic churches"* or *"drug addict churches,"* etc.

Please allow us to say it again:

Jesus does not save *in* sin, but *from* sin!

There is not a power of darkness that the Power of Almighty God cannot break. There is not a darkened stain of sin that His Blood cannot cleanse. When Jesus died on the Cross, He addressed every single sin, atoning for all (Col. 2:14-15).

ABUSERS

The Bible speaks of *"abusers of themselves with mankind"* (I Cor. 6:9). The Greek word for *"abusers"* is *"arsenoloites."* It means *"a person guilty of unnatural offenses: a sodomite, a homosexual, a sexual pervert."*

Paul, in writing to the Church at Corinth, said, *"And such were some of you: but you are washed, but you are sanctified, but you are justified in the Name of the Lord Jesus, and by the Spirit of our God"* (I Cor. 6:11). In other words, the Lord Jesus Christ can deliver a person from this dreadful sin of homosexuality.

The Devil's tactics are according to the following:

He will first of all try to make a person believe such perversion is normal. If that does not work, he will tell him that he cannot be free, and that he cannot be normal, attempting to make him believe there is no hope. Consequently, many homosexuals have committed suicide, as many others caught in a terrible web of Satan's lies. However, let it ever be known, there is absolutely no sin that the Blood of Jesus Christ cannot cover and cleanse.

Trying to normalize sin to make it acceptable will not work — it only makes it worse. Turning from sin to the Lord Jesus Christ is the only answer.

> *"What can wash away my sin?*
> *"Nothing but the Blood of Jesus.*
> *"What can make me whole again?*
> *"Nothing but the Blood of Jesus."*

In respect to the phrase, *"God made them male and female,"* let us say that *"God created Adam and Eve, not Adam and Steve!"*

(8) "AND THEY TWAIN SHALL BE ONE FLESH: SO THEN THEY ARE NO MORE TWAIN, BUT ONE FLESH."

The synopsis is:

This is one of the reasons that adultery and fornication are so wicked.

ONE FLESH

The phrase, *"And they twain shall be one flesh,"* means that the *"two"* shall be *"one."* In other words, the man and his wife, at least in a sense, become what God originally created them, *"one flesh."* This is evident in every capacity of the marriage bond, that is, if it is a marriage as God intended. The union becomes such a union that it becomes *"one flesh."* Ideally, it should be *"one"* spiritually, mentally, and physically. It becomes *"one"* spiritually by a union with God in the Salvation process.

NOTES

The marriage becomes *"one"* mentally, because both, in Christ, have a renewed mind (Rom. 12:2). It becomes *"one"* physically by the sexual union. This is what makes adultery so sinful and wicked!

The phrase, *"So then they are no more twain, but one flesh,"* proclaims the action of the union. The first phrase proclaims the Will of God, with the second phrase proclaiming the Will of God carried out to its logical and beautiful conclusion.

(9) "WHAT THEREFORE GOD HAS JOINED TOGETHER, LET NOT MAN PUT ASUNDER."

The structure is:

This places the seal of God's approval on the marriage union; and we speak of the nuclear family of husband, wife, and children.

DIVORCE

The phrase, *"What therefore God has joined together,"* places the seal of God's approval on the marriage union. As stated, this refers to the nuclear family (husband, wife, and children), which is His Divine Will. It means that for every young man in the world there is a young lady who is God's Will for his wife. This means that marriage is not a random selection, but rather an order of the Will of God; consequently, every young man and young lady should seek the Lord extensively regarding this all-important life choice — for it is meant to be for life.

If a mate is chosen on looks alone, or other considerations other than the Will of God, the stage is already set for disaster. If the young man and young lady earnestly seek the Lord about this all-important matter, to be sure, the Lord will give Divine guidance and direction. He will give that boy or girl the one He wants them to have, and it will be the perfect choice.

However, this does not mean that marriage is trouble-free, for actually it is not. But, if a few simple directions are followed, marriage can be a little bit of Heaven on Earth.

ONLY IN CHRIST

1. All the needs of a person cannot be fulfilled by their husband or wife. This is the cause of many, if not most, divorces. The husband demands more of the wife, or

the wife of the husband, than it is possible to give.

Why?

There are many needs in every individual, be they spiritual, physical, or mental. While it is true that the husband or the wife can meet some of these needs, and they are, in fact, supposed to do so, still, the ultimate needs of any individual can only be met in Christ. This is the reason that people get disillusioned with their mates, with their jobs, country, etc. They try to make these things fulfill the inherent needs within their lives which only God can meet.

The husband demands more and more of the wife, or the wife of the husband, until the person is consumed, with the marriage ultimately falling apart. Therefore, if the husband and wife will have a true relationship with Jesus Christ, the crying needs within their lives, which can only be met by Him, will be met. Then the demands upon the mate are greatly lessened.

SELF-WILL

2. If self is hidden in Christ, self-will, which is the cause of so many marriage problems, will be eradicated. Self-will is really selfishness. It is the opposite of Christlikeness. It wants its way, irrespective of what it does to others. If the husband, in Christ, will seek to please the wife, and the wife seeks to please the husband, the servant mentality, which Jesus demands, will solve most marriage problems (Mk. 9:35).

If the Believer has the servant mentality, he will be kind and gracious toward his wife, and she toward her husband.

The servant mentality comes about only through true Christlikeness, which, regrettably, is lacking in many Believers. If one is to notice, the entirety of the success of any marriage is wrapped up in Christ. A marriage without Christ is no marriage at all; consequently, about 50 percent of all marriages conclude in the divorce courts. Many, if not most, of the other 50 percent are marriages in name only.

FORGIVENESS

3. Be quick to forgive, which is another command of Christ (Mat. 6:14-15).

NOTES

Irrespective of our Christlikeness, and even though we attempt to do our very best, still, at times, and due to the fact that we are human, things will be said or done which are wrong. When this happens, the wronged party should be quick to forgive the one who has committed the wrong. As well, the one who has committed the wrong should be quick to admit that, if, in fact, he (or she) is in the wrong. The matter is then settled, with God's Way making it right.

BIBLICAL DIRECTIVES

4. The two shall be *"one."* And yet there are distinctions! The husband is meant by God to be the head of the family (Eph. 5:23). Consequently, the husband is to love the wife *"even as Christ also loved the Church, and gave Himself for it"* (Eph. 5:25). I think it is obvious that if the husband obeys the Lord in loving his wife, even as Christ loves the Church, this would be love unexcelled. It would not then be difficult for the wife to submit to such a husband, as the Lord commands (Eph. 5:22).

Some have argued that wives are to submit to their husbands, even unsaved husbands, irrespective as to what they want them to do. This is an incorrect interpretation of this Passage. The wives are to submit only as long as it is *"unto the Lord,"* meaning that the Lord would be pleased with the action.

As long as the husband conducts himself as the Lord, then the wife can be subject to her husband *"in everything"* (Eph. 5:24). If one is to notice, everything is based on the Lord as the example.

GODLY FAMILIES

Actually, as is obvious in Ephesians, Chapter 5, the Godly family is to be a symbol of the Lord and His Church. Consequently, if there are strong, Godly families, likewise, the Church is strong. Conversely, if the families begin to break apart, because of their weak relationship with Christ, the Church, as well, becomes fragmented.

Even though it should not have to be mentioned, the subject of money, because it causes so many problems in marriages, should be addressed.

MONEY

The *"two becoming one"* refers to money, as well as all else. Even though the husband is the head of the family, the wife is the head of the house (I Tim. 5:14). That means she has authority in this domain, which covers much. While every viewpoint should be considered and taken into consideration, still, where the family lives should be more decided by the wife than the husband. The order of the house and its routine also should be guided by the wife! The last decision, concerning style, furnishings, and routine should be hers.

In this capacity, most husbands would be very wise to let their wives take care of the money. The wife generally pays more attention to detail and can generally make the money go further. She will generally take better care of it than the husband. That refers to paying bills, savings accounts, checking accounts, budgets, etc.

While, at times, some wives are not turned in this direction, still, I think, generally most are, and can do a better job than the husband in this department.

If the wife is capable of handling the money (and many are), this solves the problem of the wife having to go to the husband for every dollar she has to have, with him parceling it out to her as he would an allowance to a child. Such is not proper, and does not constitute the *"one"* as designed by the Lord. Even though the husband is the head, and as such should serve as a type of Christ, still, he is not the master. There is only one Master, and that is Jesus Christ.

If these simple directions laid out in the Word of God are adhered to, marriage can be a little bit of Heaven on Earth. All is tied to Christ. All is in Christ. If marriage is attempted without Christ, it can quickly become a Hell on Earth.

GROUNDS FOR DIVORCE

The phrase, *"Let not man put asunder,"* means that the marriage should be for life, with no thought of divorce, etc. In fact, God hates divorce, even though it is, at times, unavoidable (Mal. 2:16).

There are only two Scriptural grounds for divorce, one given by Jesus and the other by Paul. They are as follows:

1. *"Fornication"*: (Mat. 5:32). All fornication is adultery, but all adultery is not fornication. Many erroneously think that fornication pertains to unmarried people, while adultery pertains to married people. That is incorrect!

The meaning of *"fornication"* is several-fold:

A. Repeated adultery, going from one partner to the next (I Cor. 7:2; 10:8; I Thess. 4:3; Rev. 9:21).

B. Incest (I Cor. 5:1; 10:8).

C. Homosexuality: (Rom. 1:24-29; I Cor. 6:9-11; II Cor. 12:21; Gal. 5:19; Eph. 5:3).

2. Desertion because of the Gospel, or on spiritual grounds: (I Cor. 7:14-15).

In some cases, a husband or wife who doesn't want to live for God will leave their redeemed partner, thereby severing the marriage bonds. If such a thing happens, and it has happened countless times, the Christian is not held responsible for the divorce, or punished by a requirement to remain single for the rest of his or her life. In fact, the Christian has to submit to the breaking of the marriage covenant, simply because, under the circumstances, he (or she) has no choice.

(10) "AND IN THE HOUSE HIS DISCIPLES ASKED HIM AGAIN OF THE SAME MATTER."

The exposition is:

They evidently had stopped for the night on the way to Jerusalem.

THE SAME MATTER

The phrase, *"And in the house His Disciples,"* refers to them leaving the crowd and the Pharisees, and going into someone's house. Quite possibly, on their way to Jerusalem, they had stopped for the night. The phrase, *"Asked Him again of the same matter,"* proclaims the Disciples continuing to ply Jesus with questions concerning divorce, etc. In other words, they asked Him over and over!

(11) "AND HE SAID UNTO THEM, WHOSOEVER SHALL PUT AWAY HIS WIFE, AND MARRY ANOTHER, COMMITS ADULTERY AGAINST HER."

The synopsis is:

This Passage refers to having no Scriptural grounds; in doing such, such a person commits sin, not only against God, but also against his wife.

ADULTERY

The phrase, *"And He said unto them,"* evidently concerns marriage after divorce. Jesus had spoken plainly about divorce as He dealt with the Pharisees; however, at that time, He said nothing about marriage after divorce. Consequently, the Disciples ply Him with questions concerning this.

The phrase, *"Whosoever shall put away his wife,"* refers to divorce. The phrase, *"And marry another,"* refers to doing so without Scriptural grounds, which are fornication and/or desertion, as we have said, and as Jesus and Paul affirmed (Mat. 5:32; I Cor. 7:14-15).

The phrase, *"Commits adultery against her,"* means that if they have no Scriptural grounds, at the time of the union of the second marriage, etc., *"adultery"* is committed. The words, *"against her,"* mean *"in reference to her."* If the man leaves his wife (or the wife leaves the husband) without Scriptural grounds, he commits sin not only against God, but against his wife (or against her husband, as the case may be). The marriage bond instituted by God, and by which the partner was selected, has now been broken, which is in direct contradiction to the original command *"What therefore God has joined together, let not man put asunder"* (Vs. 9).

(12) "AND IF A WOMAN SHALL PUT AWAY HER HUSBAND, AND BE MARRIED TO ANOTHER, SHE COMMITS ADULTERY."

The structure is:

Again, this refers to divorce which has no Scriptural grounds; such constitutes the sin of adultery.

THE WOMAN

The phrase, *"And if a woman shall put away her husband,"* places the woman in the same position as the man, and holds her just as responsible.

The phrase, *"And be married to another, she commits adultery,"* indicates, and according to the Lord, that wives and husbands have equal rights in reference to divorce, and equal responsibility.

Consequently, these simple words of Jesus gave the woman more rights than she had ever had in history. Josephus makes it evident that in his time, which was the time of Christ, the wife by no means had equal rights with the husband; consequently, the Words of Christ make it clear that the lesser rights given to the woman were not pleasing to God.

(13) "AND THEY BROUGHT YOUNG CHILDREN TO HIM, THAT HE SHOULD TOUCH THEM: AND HIS DISCIPLES REBUKED THOSE WHO BROUGHT THEM."

The synopsis is:

This presents a paradox; the Disciples were strongly rebuking the people for bringing their children to Jesus, while Jesus was strongly blessing those brought to Him.

YOUNG CHILDREN

The phrase, *"And they brought young children to Him, that He should touch them,"* refers to Jesus and His Disciples being in the house, probably having stopped for the night on the way to Jerusalem. As there were great crowds on the road on their way to keep the Passover in Jerusalem, parents desired that Jesus lay His Hands on their children, who were traveling with them, and pray for them (Mat. 19:13).

This was, no doubt, a beautiful scene, with little children crowding around Jesus and Him laying His Hands on them, praying for them and, no doubt, even taking some on His knee.

Swete says, *"The custom of laying on of hands with prayer upon children, for the purpose of blessing, finds its symbolism in Genesis 48:14-15. Generally, the rulers of the Synagogues performed this task; however, to have Jesus do this was of the highest magnitude. How many of them actually knew that the God of all Creation was blessing their children?"*

A MISTAKEN ASSUMPTION

The phrase, *"And His Disciples rebuked those who brought them,"* proclaims this situation quickly developing into a paradox. The Disciples were strongly rebuking the people for bringing their children to Jesus, while Jesus was strongly blessing those brought to Him. No doubt, the motives of the Disciples were right. After walking, teaching, and even healing all day, Jesus was undoubtedly very tired; therefore, in looking out for Him, they probably felt that the children were an imposition. They quickly were to find out otherwise!

(14) "BUT WHEN JESUS SAW IT, HE WAS MUCH DISPLEASED, AND SAID UNTO THEM, SUFFER THE LITTLE CHILDREN TO COME UNTO ME, AND FORBID THEM NOT: FOR OF SUCH IS THE KINGDOM OF GOD."

The composition is:

To start a child out right is to insure their Salvation (Prov. 22:6).

THE DISPLEASURE OF CHRIST

The phrase, *"But when Jesus saw it, He was much displeased,"* concerns His perception respecting this activity, almost as quickly as the Disciples were doing such; therefore, it seems that none of the children were turned away.

The words, *"Much displeased,"* are strong; they mean *"to be moved with indignation."* In other words, there was some anger in Christ because of what the Disciples were doing.

Wuest says, *"The very fact that our sinless Lord manifested such feeling is enough to show that under proper circumstances it is not only right, but its absence would show a serious defect in Christian character."*

LITTLE CHILDREN

The phrase, *"And said unto them, Suffer the little children to come unto Me, and forbid them not,"* means that the Disciples were to stop forthwith! This simple narrative portrays to us the responsibility of parents in educating their children respecting the Word of God. Basically, this has to do with Solomon's statement, *"Train up a child in the way he should go: and when he is old, he will not depart from it"* (Prov. 22:6).

Consequently, a child should be encouraged in the Ways of the Lord at the tenderest of age. The moment they can grasp or understand, which is very early, should be the time their training begins. Nothing in the world is more important.

In dedicating babies at Family Worship Center in Baton Rouge, Louisiana, I constantly remind the parents that they are actually holding the eternal destiny of their child in their hands. In other words, if they obey Solomon's command, and train that child in the Ways of the Lord, they have the Promise of God that the child will not depart from it.

What a Promise!

This also means that the parents must live for God as an example to the child.

SYMBOLIC OF THE KINGDOM OF GOD

The phrase, *"For of such is the Kingdom of God,"* has powerful meanings. Some are as follows:

1. The innocence of *"little children"* is typical of *"the Kingdom of God."* Inasmuch as children are innocent, they are, at the same time, free of prejudice, bias, unforgiveness, anger, and hate.

2. Children, as Christ here affirms, can be saved at an early age, which not only saves the soul, but the life. As such, this would bring to a sudden halt all juvenile delinquency, gang warfare, drug addiction, and alcoholism, which are so prevalent among teenagers today. This terrible drain on society would be completely stopped.

3. The tremendous significance of the child in the eyes of God is portrayed here; consequently, if the spiritual direction of these children is that important to Jesus, it certainly should be that important to us!

4. And most of all, little children are totally dependent on their parents, which is symbolic of the dependence that we as Believers should have on the Lord.

(15) "VERILY I SAY UNTO YOU, WHOSOEVER SHALL NOT RECEIVE THE KINGDOM OF GOD AS A LITTLE CHILD, HE SHALL NOT ENTER THEREIN."

The exegesis is:

The simplicity of the little child is the model and the rule for everyone who desires, by the Grace of Christ, to obtain the Kingdom of God.

THE KINGDOM OF GOD

The phrase, *"Verily I say unto you,"* is meant to portray an extremely significant statement. Of course, anything Christ says is of extreme importance; however, some statements, as this, are of utmost importance, simply because they tie together all that has gone before.

The phrase, *"Whosoever shall not receive the Kingdom of God as a little child,"* proclaims the manner in which the Kingdom is to be received, which means to give up ambitious aims and earthly contests, and imitate the simple unworldly ways of little children.

Of course, Christ is not speaking of doing so literally, but figuratively. A child is generally trusting; he will believe whatever he is told. Likewise, regarding the Word of God, the seeker must have the same attitude.

Actually, as this refusal to *"receive the Kingdom of God as a little child"* keeps millions of unbelievers out, likewise, the refusal to believe and trust *"as a little child"* keeps many Believers from receiving from God.

The term *"childlike Faith"* is derived from this Fifteenth Verse.

QUALIFICATIONS FOR ENTERING THE KINGDOM OF GOD

The phrase, *"He shall not enter therein,"* presents a double negative in the Greek; consequently, it presents an emphatic denial. In other words, there is no way that one will receive the Kingdom of God unless he does so with the same spirit and attitude of a *"little child."* As we have repeatedly stated, this is the main reason why many never accept Christ. They are not willing to humble themselves, nor trust the Word of the Lord; therefore, because of this prideful attitude, they die lost!

And yet, when one finally does break before the Lord, he finds what he receives to be so much more than what he has lost. Actually, what was lost was a prideful deceit, which was merely a facade covering his insecurities. Once this facade is stripped away, with Christ taking its place, the prideful deceit is no longer needed, with Christ absorbing self.

It actually comes down to the person recognizing God as his Creator, i.e., his True Parent. For some reason, men are loath to admit this, rather claiming, *"I did it my way,"* which somehow makes them feel self-made. However, that which is self-made is also, ultimately, self-destroyed.

Jesus wants the person to believe Him exactly as the child believes its parent. The only way a child will not believe its parent is that the parent has lied to him several times. Otherwise, a child will believe a parent without fail.

Of course, the Lord has never lied to anyone, and His Word can be trusted implicitly. He simply desires that we believe Him exactly as we believed our Earthly parents when we were little children.

(16) "AND HE TOOK THEM UP IN HIS ARMS, PUT HIS HANDS UPON THEM, AND BLESSED THEM."

The diagram is:

The Greek Text lends emphasis to the fact that He blessed them fervently.

THE BLESSING

The phrase, *"And He took them up in His Arms, put His Hands upon them, and blessed them,"* was of far greater magnitude than the parents had at first envisioned.

Wuest says that the very word *"blessed"* is intensive in its force, meaning that He *"blessed them fervently."* Moreover, He *"kept on blessing them."* In addition, this Passage, although intending to express an action by Christ respecting these little children, still, expresses far, far more!

Spiritually speaking, Christ takes the trusting Believer in His Arms, thereby signaling love, devotion, attention, and protection. This emphasizes the *"security"* craved by the soul since the Fall of man, with every attempt made to secure it elsewhere, but without success.

Once the individual comes to Christ, he has come home, i.e., to his rightful Parent. As such, the craving for *"security"* will finally be realized; therefore, the individual needs no more the things of the world, such as alcohol, gambling, drugs, immorality, love of money, or worldly ambitions, etc. All of these things were a false security; they could never really satisfy. Only Christ can do that.

This is the reason that religion, which is always a work of man, is so damnable. It continues to promise but it never delivers; it cannot, in fact, deliver. Consequently, the

Preacher of the Gospel who does not *"preach Christ and Him Crucified"* is, in effect, committing *"spiritual high treason."*

THE IMAGE OF CHRIST

When Christ takes us up in His Arms, spiritually speaking, He also *"puts His Hands on us,"* in order to mold us in His Image. It is a Work He commences at our conversion, which continues throughout our life.

Regrettably, many Believers really do not allow Him this freedom of action, because they misunderstand what He is doing. His entire purpose is to *"bless us,"* exactly as He blessed these little children. Actually, all things Christ does for the person, even the times of *"chastisement,"* prove to be *"blessings."* If we obey His Word, He never curses, but rather blesses!

A long time ago, Balaam prophesied saying, *"God is not a man, that He should lie; neither the son of man, that He should repent: has He said, and shall He not do it? or has He spoken, and shall He not make it good?*

"Behold, I have received Commandment to bless: and He has blessed; and I cannot reverse it" (Num. 23:19-20).

One can only shout, *"Hallelujah!"*

(17) "AND WHEN HE WAS GONE FORTH INTO THE WAY, THERE CAME ONE RUNNING, AND KNEELED TO HIM, AND ASKED HIM, GOOD MASTER, WHAT SHALL I DO THAT I MAY INHERIT ETERNAL LIFE?"

The exegesis is:

In the first place, one cannot inherit Eternal Life. It is a free gift, which comes with the acceptance of Christ (Rom. 10:9-10, 13).

THE INQUIRY

The phrase, *"And when He was gone forth into the way,"* means that He was leaving the house on His way to Jerusalem. The phrase, *"There came one running, and kneeled to Him,"* proclaims a person of note. Luke called him, *"a certain ruler,"* which refers to one of preeminence. The term *"ruler,"* as used by Luke, was understood by Josephus as applying to a member of the Sanhedrin. At any rate, it was a general term for a great man or prince.

NOTES

Quite possibly, as indicated by the sentence structure, he had been waiting for Jesus to come out of the house. At that moment, he ran to Christ *"and kneeled to Him."*

Swete says that the homage paid Jesus by this man is remarkable because he is not asking for material or physical help. He is asking for spiritual help.

ETERNAL LIFE

The question, *"And asked Him, Good Master, what shall I do that I may inherit Eternal Life?"* is basically the question of most all humanity, at least in one form or the other! However, several things are wrong with this request. They are as follows:

GOOD MASTER

In the Greek Text, the words are reversed; they actually say, *"Teacher, Good One."* The man regarded Jesus as merely a *"good Teacher"* and not the Son of God. Consequently, he was looking for advice — what Christ could give, instead of Who Christ was!

He misunderstood, as most of the world misunderstands. Salvation is not a philosophy, but rather a Person. That Person is Christ Jesus! Men seek Salvation in Buddhism, Hinduism, Islam, Shintoism, Mormonism, Catholicism, and Humanism. They never find it in these sources, because basically all of these religions are a form of *"Humanism"*; they are devised by humans and not God. God's Salvation is Jesus and what He has done for us at the Cross (Eph. 2:13-18). He Alone says, *"I am the Way, the Truth, and the Life"* (Jn. 14:6).

HOW MAY I INHERIT ETERNAL LIFE?

The question, *"What shall I do that I may inherit Eternal Life?"* in the Greek actually says, *"What good things shall I do that I may inherit Eternal Life?"* Men ever seek to *"do"* something, especially something good. This is indicative not only with the religions of the world, which we have just named, but also much of Christianity.

In effect, no one can *"do"* anything which will give them *"Eternal Life,"* for no matter what they do, it would never be enough! In Truth, one does not have to *"do,"* because all that is needed has already been *"done."*

So, to *"inherit Eternal Life,"* all one has to do is to simply *"confess with your mouth the Lord Jesus, and shall believe in your heart that God has raised Him from the dead...."*

The Apostle then said, *"you shall be saved"* (Rom. 10:9).

However, inasmuch as what the Lord demands is so simple, most will not do it, or simply will not believe it. The religions of the world are constantly saying, *"Do,"* when, in Truth, Bible Christianity says, *"Done."* That simply means that Christ has already done at the Cross all that needs to be done regarding one's Salvation. When He died on Calvary, then the *"doing"* was *"done"*! Consequently, all one has to *"do"* is simply believe that, thereby accepting Christ as their Saviour (Jn. 3:16).

WHAT IS ETERNAL LIFE?

Christ is *"the True God, and Eternal Life"* (Jn. 1:4; 14:6; I Jn. 5:20). He is also the *"Prince* (Author) *of Life"* (Acts 3:15), to Whom the Father has granted *"to have Life in Himself"* (Jn. 5:26). He is *"the Resurrection and the Life"* (Jn. 11:25), *"the Bread of Life"* (Jn. 6:35), and His Words are *"Spirit and Life"* (Jn. 6:63).

Consequently, one receives this *"Eternal Life"* by receiving Christ and what He did for us at the Cross. He not only bestows *"Eternal Life"* on all who believe, but He *"is,"* as stated, *"Eternal Life,"* which was portrayed in His Resurrection.

In the Resurrection of Christ, immortal life has been actualized on the plain of history. His Resurrection becomes the basis of all Resurrection, and all Resurrection is to be understood in terms of His Resurrection (I Cor., Chpt. 15; Col. 3:4; I Jn. 3:2). In fact, when Lazarus died and Martha, the sister of Lazarus, went to meet Jesus, she said to Him, *"If You had been here, my brother had not died."*

Jesus then said to her, *"Your brother shall rise again."*

Martha answered Him, and said, *"I know that he shall rise again in the Resurrection at the last day."*

Jesus said unto her, *"I am the Resurrection, and the Life"* (Jn. 11:21-25).

In effect, Jesus was saying to her, *"Martha, look at Me. You are looking at the Resurrection. I am the Resurrection, and the Life."*

No longer does the hope of Resurrection rest, as in the Old Testament, merely upon prophetic vision or upon inferences from God's Covenant relationships. Resurrection Life now finds its meaning in the Image of Jesus Christ, all made possible by what He did for us at the Cross (Rom. 8:29).

HOW THE RESURRECTION OF CHRIST RELATES TO MAN

For man, then, True Life is grounded in Jesus Christ and what He did for us at the Cross, Who *"became a Life-giving Spirit"* (Jn. 6:63; I Cor. 15:45; II Cor. 3:17). The core of the Gospel proclamation is that He Who was dead is *"alive forevermore"* (Acts 2:31; I Cor. 15:3-4; Rev. 1:5, 18), and that He gives life to the world by the power of an indestructible Life (Jn. 6:33; Heb. 7:16).

If Christ had not been raised from the dead, *"Finished,"* must be written over the Christian dead (I Cor. 15:18, 32). But Christ is risen from the dead and has the *"keys to Hell,"* because Hell could not conquer Him, neither can it prevail against His Church (Mat. 16:18; Rev. 1:18).

His Life is given to the Believer through Repentance and Faith.

Paul said, *"Repentance toward God, and Faith toward our Lord Jesus Christ"* (Jn. 3:16; 11:25; Acts 20:21); by such, one is *"saved"* and given *"Eternal Life"* (Rom. 5:10). In Christ's Death and Resurrection, God pierces radically into the world of man to make him see the fatality of sin and the utter Grace of the New Life from God — an unfathomable, unexpected, and freely-bestowed act of Salvation.

This New Life is a Resurrection and New Birth, a sovereign and gracious act of the Creator-God (Jn. 1:13; 5:24; Rom. 6:4; Eph. 2:1; Col. 3:1).

A PRESENT POSSESSION

Resurrection Life is viewed as a present possession of the Believer. One passes *"from death to life"* at conversion (Jn. 5:24; Eph. 2:1; I Jn. 3:14), and one may even speak in the past tense of having been crucified (in Christ), raised to life, brought into Christ's

Kingdom, glorified and made to sit in Heavenly Places (Rom. 6:3-5; 8:30; Gal. 2:20; Eph. 2:5; Col. 1:13); however, this is always viewed as a corporate participation in Christ's Death and Resurrection (Jn. 6:33, 51; Rom. 6:4; 8:2; II Tim. 1:1). All of this is a *"down payment"* of the New Life we now have in Christ, but which will be realized in its fullness at the Resurrection (II Cor. 4:12; 5:5). Our life is hid with Christ (Col. 3:3); to have life simply means to have Christ (I Jn. 5:11).

At present, this *"Eternal Life"* is actualized personally only in Jesus Christ, *"the Firstfruits of those who have fallen asleep"* and *"the Firstborn among many brethren"* (I Cor. 15:20; Rom. 8:29).

(The statements on *"Eternal Life"* were derived from The New Bible Dictionary.)

(18) "AND JESUS SAID UNTO HIM, WHY CALLEST THOU ME GOOD? THERE IS NONE GOOD BUT ONE, THAT IS, GOD."

The synopsis is:

The statement is not meant to imply that Christ Himself wasn't good, but rather that the word *"good"* be placed in its proper perspective; Christ is God!

THE TEACHING MINISTRY OF CHRIST

The phrase, *"And Jesus said unto Him,"* concerns the greatest words this rich young ruler will ever hear. If one scans the Gospels, and without diligence, even though he knows that Jesus is God, still, the simple directives given in the teaching of Jesus will, by and large, escape the Reader. In the first place, their utter simplicity, which, of course, was designed by the Holy Spirit, causes many to miss the exceptional height and depth of their wisdom.

Further, the teaching given by Christ, which is the foundation of all knowledge and wisdom, little addresses itself to many things men are searching for, such as scientific achievements, economic power, or a host of other such pursuits. Jesus does not address these things, because those things do not in any way constitute the true problem of mankind.

Man's problem is not in knowing how to build an automobile that will give 100 miles to a gallon of gasoline, but rather how to live. Due to the Fall, which brought about the sin nature, man simply does not know to live; consequently, the lives of many brilliant scientists are but shambles. The same could be said for billionaires, educators, etc. Irrespective of one's knowledge in the field of science, or the billions of dollars that one may possess, if he does not know how to live, very little has actually been accomplished. Moreover, those things do not teach people how to live.

Knowing that something is wrong, man searches, but most of the time in all the wrong places. Only Christ can tell one how to live!

When Christ asked His Disciples the question, *"Will you also go away?"* Peter was quick to respond, *"Lord, to whom shall we go? You have the Words of Eternal Life"* (Jn. 6:67-68).

Let it be said again that Peter's affirmation is not only true, but, in fact, Jesus is the only One Who has these Words! He is not one of several choices, but, in fact, the only choice! Therefore, if one takes the time to explore the teaching of Christ, one will find the answer to every perplexing problem of life. Absolutely nothing is left unaddressed, with a simple but yet all-wise answer given to man's quest for life.

THE PERSON OF CHRIST

And yet, the mere study of the teaching of Christ will reap little harvest if divorced from the Person of Christ. The moralist has attempted to do this, but without success! Christ must be accepted, not merely as a great Teacher, as this rich young ruler thinks, but rather as the Son of the Living God. Furthermore, a mere affirmation of that is not enough. Man must accept Christ as his Saviour and Lord, which will then bring about an impartation of the Holy Spirit, Who leads into all Truth (Jn. 16:13). Then, and only then, will these all-wise Words of Christ become what they are intended — *"more abundant life"* (Jn. 10:10).

THAT WHICH IS GOOD

The question, *"Why callest thou Me good?"* is not meant to state that Christ is not *"good,"* but rather that the word *"good"* be placed in its proper perspective. Man's label of that which he calls *"good"* is predicated on many factors. Almost all come from the *"good side"* of *"The Tree of the Knowledge of Good and Evil"* (Gen. 2:17); consequently, it is *"good"* that God, because of its source, can never accept.

The concept that links all the uses of the word *"good"* is evaluation. To determine the good, one compares things, qualities, and actions with other things, qualities, and actions. One must contrast the beneficial and the right with other things, qualities, and actions that are not beneficial or which are wrong.

The account of the Creation introduces Biblically the manner in which God viewed each day's work and pronounced it *"good"* (Gen., Chpt. 1). Consequently, God evaluates, just as we are to evaluate. Actually, it is because God has shared His Image and Likeness with mankind that human beings have the capacity to make value judgments.

VALUE JUDGMENTS

However, man's value judgments are skewed because sin has distorted humanity's perceptions of what *"good"* really is! As a result, man is unable to properly evaluate as he should. Only God can perfectly evaluate. In view of this, the Prophets of old proclaim that God was the Giver and Measure of good, but also that He Alone knows what is truly beneficial for us and what is morally right. We who rely on Him are able to affirm with confidence that a certain thing, quality, or course of action is beneficial, i.e., *"good,"* only because God has shared His evaluation of the good in His Word.

Whatever is truly good is free from flaw, in full balance and harmony with the ideal, Who is God. Sin, as stated, has warped the Divine pattern to where man's evaluation is no longer trustworthy.

In the ultimate sense, as Jesus will here say, only God is good. Although human beings may be *"good"* in comparison with one another (Lk. 6:45; 19:17), nothing in any human action can be beneficial to God in the sense that it will merit Salvation.

Man is constantly comparing his standard of *"good"* with other men's standard of *"good."* However, even though such may satisfy man, it can never satisfy God. For the obvious reasons, He can never accept man's standard. The only standard for proper measurement is God's standard, which is *"The Word of God."* If men do not accept that as the standard, they are left only with their own standard, which can murder millions of unborn babies in their mother's womb and call it *"good"*!

JESUS IS GOD

The rich young ruler, by addressing Jesus as *"Good Master,"* was disavowing the true position of Christ as the Messiah, God manifest in the flesh. Consequently, the efforts of the Lord are not meant to instigate an argument, but, hopefully, to put this man on the right track.

The phrase, *"There is none good but One, that is, God,"* places everything in its proper perspective. If man does not begin with this premise, the entire fabric of his philosophy becomes unworkable. In fact, almost all of mankind falls into this trap. Man thinks he is good within himself, because he performs a so-called good deed on an occasional basis. Or, he thinks he is *"good,"* because he doesn't do certain bad things, etc. However, man's standard of goodness simply will not work. This is the reason wars continue to be fought, and jails continue to be filled, and marriages continue to be broken.

SPIRITUAL LAWS

Fortunately for man, there are particular laws of science, designed by God, which force man into a certain mode respecting engineering, etc. In other words, these laws must be adhered to, or airplanes will not fly, bridges will not hold up, and machinery will not function. Irrespective of what man likes or doesn't like, these laws must be obeyed.

However, concerning Spiritual Laws which God has laid down, which we find in God's Word (and in God's Word alone), man, due to his fallen nature, will not obey. As a result, using the vernacular, his spiritual airplanes will not fly, nor will his spiritual bridges hold up, so to speak!

As we have stated, man is loath to admit that he is not good, and also that most all he does falls into the same category. And yet, man, even unconverted man, is capable of doing some good things, because he was originally made in the Image of God. So, man equates being a *"good man"* with the *"good things"* he occasionally does.

However, the occasional good things done by unconverted man in no way mean that he, within himself, constitutes that which is *"good."* In fact, he is not *"good,"* and nothing he does can make him *"good"*! And this is where the great problem arises.

GOOD THINGS

Almost all of humanity equate their lives with these so-called good things they have done, or the bad things they have not done. Such is a false premise, and in no way can be accepted by God. Man must come to the conclusion that he is not *"good,"* and also that there is absolutely nothing he can do that will make him *"good,"* no matter how good on the surface it seems to be. But yet, he keeps trying!

Only God can make one *"good,"* and He does so through Faith exhibited in His Son, the Lord Jesus Christ. Upon Faith in Christ and what He did at the Cross, one can be *"bad"* one minute, even *"notoriously bad,"* and the very next minute be *"good."* This is called *"Imputed Righteousness."* Regrettably, it is a *"goodness,"* i.e., *"Righteousness,"* neither the world nor much of the Church will accept.

(19) "YOU KNOW THE COMMANDMENTS, DO NOT COMMIT ADULTERY, DO NOT KILL, DO NOT STEAL, DO NOT BEAR FALSE WITNESS, DEFRAUD NOT, HONOUR YOUR FATHER AND MOTHER."

The composition is:

Jesus draws the young man to the Word of God, in both a positive and negative sense — positive, because the Word alone holds the answer; negative, because it will show him, as a mirror, where he is wrong.

THE COMMANDMENTS

The phrase, *"You know the Commandments,"* draws attention to all of the Commandments, and not just one. And yet, of the Ten Commandments, Jesus will only deal with six, i.e., those which pertain to man's dealings with his fellowman. The remaining four pertain to man's dealings with God, which actually constitute the first four.

(Some feel, and it is probably correct, that the fifth Commandment, *"Honor your father and mother,"* actually pertains to man's dealings with God. The idea is: If a person does not properly *"honor his father and mother,"* he, at the same time, will not properly honor God. If that, in fact, is correct, then the first five Commandments pertain to man's dealings with God, with the remaining five pertaining to his dealings with his fellowman.)

THE DELINEATION OF SOME OF THE COMMANDMENTS

If man properly loves God, he, at the same time, will love his fellowman.

1. *"Do not commit adultery"*: This is the Seventh Commandment, with all Ten listed in Exodus, Chapter 20. This speaks of sexual relations between a man and woman before marriage, or unfaithfulness on the part of man or woman after marriage. The man claimed he had not broken this Commandment, and he was undoubtedly correct concerning the actual physical act of carrying out the deed.

2. *"Do not kill"*: This is the Sixth Commandment. This was kept, as well, he says!

3. *"Do not steal"*: This is the Eighth Commandment — also claimed as kept!

4. *"Do not bear false witness"*: He claimed he had not broken this Commandment; however, it is extremely doubtful that he was correct in this claim.

5. *"Defraud not"*: This is the Tenth Commandment, *"You shall not covet."* He claims obedience to this one, as well; his claim, no doubt, is false!

6. *"Honor your father and mother"*: This is the Fifth Commandment, to which he claims obedience.

Concerning the man's question as to how he may obtain or inherit Eternal Life, why did Jesus, by quoting a list of Commandments, answer him as He did?

In Truth, there is no Salvation, i.e., *"Eternal Life,"* in the Commandments.

Jesus answered him in this manner, because to have done otherwise would have been fruitless. The man, as most, had an entirely erroneous concept of what obtaining *"Eternal Life"* actually meant. So, Jesus set out to show him that his way was wrong, and would do so by dealing with him in the very area which he prized, and which he thought he had accomplished, i.e., the *"keeping of the Commandments."* Most of the world falls into the same category, thinking that by the doing of certain good things, and by not doing certain bad things, *"Eternal Life"* will be theirs.

(20) "AND HE ANSWERED AND SAID UNTO HIM, MASTER, ALL THESE HAVE I OBSERVED FROM MY YOUTH."

The composition is:

There is no Eternal Life in the keeping of Commandments, as wonderful as that is; had there been, he would not be seeking the satisfaction of the conscience.

A FOOLISH ANSWER

The phrase, *"And he answered and said unto Him,"* constitutes the reaction of most of humanity. Because he did not know Who Jesus was (the Son of God), he consequently did not know What Jesus was (the Saviour of mankind). He will answer accordingly!

The phrase, *"Master, all these have I observed from my youth,"* states his claim of perfection (Mat. 19:21). The word *"observed,"* as used by this man, is a military term meaning *"to guard, watch."* It was used of sentinels keeping guard.

According to Wuest, the word, as it is used here, refers not only to the act of obeying them, but to that preciousness and honor which belong to them. And yet, the very fact of this young man's question, i.e., concerning the obtaining of *"Eternal Life,"* portrays the emptiness of his heart that precipitates such a question in the first place. Whatever he was doing was not satisfying the thirst of his soul. Consequently, every single individual who claims Salvation should take a lesson from him.

If one truly wants Salvation and is trusting in the Church to provide it, one will find an emptiness exactly as this rich young ruler. The Church cannot provide Salvation. Only Jesus can do such!

For those who are depending on their good works, they too will find an emptiness in their hearts, because such cannot save! If one is truly saved, one will not thirst again (Jn. 4:13-14).

(21) "THEN JESUS BEHOLDING HIM LOVED HIM, AND SAID UNTO HIM, ONE THING YOU LACK: GO YOUR WAY, SELL WHATSOEVER YOU HAVE, AND GIVE TO THE POOR, AND YOU SHALL HAVE TREASURE IN HEAVEN: AND COME, TAKE UP THE CROSS, AND FOLLOW ME."

The overview is:

Without explanation, Christ tells the young man here, and all others for that matter, that Salvation is in the Cross alone; and it is only by and through the Cross that we can truly follow Christ.

LOVE

The phrase, *"Then Jesus beholding him loved him,"* means that Jesus fixed His Eyes on the young man, which saw to the very depths of his soul. Seeing, He *"loved him,"* not because He saw good things, but because He saw a desire for good things, i.e., *"Eternal Life."* In fact, and his answer showed, this man was not honest, not even with himself. He had not truly kept these Commandments! In Truth, no man, except Christ, ever kept them all the time. Jesus will now show him that even in that which he rashly claims, he is, in fact, woefully deficient.

THAT WHICH THE HUMAN RACE LACKS

The phrase, *"And said unto him, one thing you lack,"* will put its finger on the very heart of this man's problem. This phrase is not used by Christ in the sense that He believes the young man has kept these Commandments, but instead to show him that he does not have *"Eternal Life,"* and the reason why! In Truth, the *"one thing"* he lacked was the *"one thing"* which really mattered!

The keeping of Commandments is not the cause of one's Salvation, but rather the result of one's Salvation, which can only be done by one placing one's faith in Christ and what Christ has done for us at the Cross. Jesus, as our Substitute, has already kept all the Commandments, and kept them perfectly. As well, He addressed the broken Law at Calvary's Cross by shedding His Life's Blood, thereby giving His Life, which atoned for the broken Law, which means that every sin was washed clean, that is, for all who will believe (Jn. 3:16).

So, while the Moral Law most definitely must be kept, it can only be kept by our Faith placed exclusively in Christ, Who as our Substitute, kept the Law in every respect, doing it all on our behalf. Then our Faith in Him and what He did at the Cross makes us a Lawkeeper instead of a Lawbreaker. The Holy Spirit then works mightily within our lives, in order to actually bring us to the position to where the Law is perfectly kept; again, we are speaking of the Moral Law (Ex., Chpt. 20).

As that young man of so long ago, most modern Christians think they can keep the Law, i.e., keep the Commandments, and can do so, they think, because they are Believers.

KEEPING THE COMMANDMENTS

Most Christians presently, exactly as that young man of some 2,000 years ago, measure their Christian experience by the keeping of Commandments. When it comes to obeying the moral Commandments, and we continue to speak of the Ten Commandments outlined in Exodus, Chapter 20, there is no disagreement with what I'm teaching and those who extol the keeping of such. The contention comes in as to *"How?"* it is to be done. That's where the disagreement is.

The keeping of the moral Commandments can be done and, in fact, must be done, but can be done in only one way, and that is by Faith. When we use that term, *"by Faith,"* we are speaking of Faith in Christ and what Christ has done for us at the Cross. As we've said over and over in this Volume, Christ is the Source of everything that we receive from God, and the Cross is the Means by which it is done (Gal., Chpt. 5).

If one tries to keep the Commandments by his own strength, ability, power, efforts, willpower, etc., no matter how hard he tries, he will fail every single time. And of course, the question begs to be asked, *"Why will he fail?"*

He will fail simply because the course on which he has embarked, which is the course of self-effort, is one which the Holy Spirit can never sanction, because it is a course of spiritual adultery.

And what do we mean by that?

SPIRITUAL ADULTERY

As we've already stated elsewhere in this Volume, in the first four Verses of Romans, Chapter 7, Paul uses the analogy of a woman who leaves her husband and marries another. Paul says she shall be called *"an adulteress."* The Apostle then states that we, as Believers, are *"married to Christ."* As such, Christ is to meet our every need, whatever that need might be. He does so through our placing our faith exclusively in Him and His Atoning Work on the Cross (Rom. 6:3-14).

However, if we start to look elsewhere, no matter how *"righteous"* the elsewhere might seem to be, if it's not Christ and the Cross, in effect, we are being unfaithful to Christ, which constitutes *"spiritual adultery."* As should be obvious, the Holy Spirit is not going to sanction such behavior. To be sure, without the help of the Holy Spirit, there is no way that we can function properly as Christians. It simply cannot be done.

No matter how hard one tries to keep the moral commandments, if he doesn't do so by explicit faith in Christ and the Cross, not taking from that or adding to that, he will fail, as fail he must! Truthfully, the man of our illustration who came to Christ had it backwards, as do most presently!

THE HEART OF THE MATTER

The phrase, *"Go your way, sell whatsoever you have, and give to the poor,"* is, in effect, saying, *"If what you're saying is true, you will do this which I ask of you."* Truly, this man's possessions were his god. As we have stated, all the Commandments listed by Christ pertained to one's conduct toward one's fellowman. So, if he really loved his fellowman as he claimed, what Jesus asked of him readily would be done.

No! Jesus was not making the selling of one's goods and giving all to the poor a criteria for Salvation. He was merely putting His finger on what was keeping this young man from having *"Eternal Life."* Without coming out and saying it publicly, He was portraying the man's hypocrisy and deceit. And yet, He *"loved him,"* exactly as He loves us.

Keeping Commandments won't save one, and neither will giving everything to the poor; however, when one comes to Christ, everything one has then belongs to Christ. If that is not the case, then such a Believer is going to find great difficulties for himself.

TREASURE IN HEAVEN

The phrase, *"And you shall have treasure in Heaven,"* concerned the True Treasure. Even though the subject matter is not *"treasure in Heaven,"* it is a valid subject which must be addressed. Jesus had previously said, in the Sermon on the Mount, *"For where your treasure is, there will your heart be also"* (Mat. 6:21). So, we learn from this exchange that this man's heart was not with God, and consequently was not right with God, but instead was with the world. Consequently, this scenario tells us what the Lord expects of all, both rich and poor!

The *"treasure in Heaven"* consists of our life lived for Jesus, and our resources used for His Work. I have watched the Lord bless some Christians, and do so exceedingly, and I am speaking of material things. As well, I have watched only a few of these who truly use their resources for the Work of God. Most give God a pittance, at least as it regards what they really could give.

It is a shame, but the Muslim world gives far more to the spreading of their false way, even a demonic way, than Christians give to portray the grandest story ever told. In fact, of all the Christians, more than likely, it is only about 5 percent to 10 percent who really do all they can monetarily for the cause of Christ.

The reason?

They are confused about their *"treasure."* They do not quite understand the *"treasure in Heaven"* aspect. Therefore, they give a token amount to the Lord and His Work.

THE ALTAR CALL

The phrase, *"And come, take up the cross, and follow Me,"* refers to the dying to self-will, which was actually this young man's problem, with his attitude toward his possessions being but a symptom. A *"cross"* is made on which to die, which pertains to self,

NOTES

where lies the Believer's greatest struggle. Millions claim to follow Christ, but refuse the Cross of self-denial, consequently refusing the abrogation of self-will.

What did this young man think, and even the Disciples of Christ, when Jesus mentioned the Cross?

The *"Cross"* was the instrument of torture and death employed by Rome, on which it executed criminals who were not citizens of the Roman Empire. In fact, at busy intersections of every town and city in the Roman Empire, it was almost always possible to see crosses placed in a very obvious position, with people dying on those crosses, and dying a most horrible death.

It was Rome's way of telling the general public, *"This is what we do to criminals."* Consequently, the Cross, as it was viewed then, was one of the most horrifying, despicable things that one could even begin to imagine. And yet Jesus says that if one is to follow Him, one must take up their Cross.

I don't think that any one at that time understood at all what He was talking about. But, of course, He knew, and now we also know; or, we most definitely should know!

WHAT DO WE MEAN BY SELF-DENIAL?

While it definitely includes everything we are and everything we have, as should be obvious, even as is evidenced in this particular scenario given to us by Mark concerning the rich young ruler coming to Christ, still, self-denial more so pertains to our own self-efforts. And what do we mean by that?

I'm speaking of one attempting to live for God by any means other than Faith exclusively placed in Christ and the Cross. Anything else constitutes the glorification of self instead of self-denial. When one does that, and I'm speaking of placing one's faith exclusively in Christ and the Cross, then there will be no problem with one's personal possessions; everything will be dedicated exclusively to Christ. The key always is faith in Christ and what Christ has done for us at the Cross.

(22) "AND HE WAS SAD AT THAT SAYING, AND WENT AWAY GRIEVED: FOR HE HAD GREAT POSSESSIONS."

The composition is:
The only possession that really matters is Eternal Life, which can only be found in Christ.

POSSESSIONS

The phrase, *"And he was sad at that saying,"* constitutes the attitude of multiple millions. They, as he, desire Salvation, but on their own terms!

Why was he sad?

The price was too high, or so he thought!

The phrase, *"And went away grieved: for he had great possessions,"* pertained to his treasure, which captured his heart. And yet, he did not have the greatest possession of all, the only possession, in fact, that really matters, *"Eternal Life."*

CAN ONE HAVE BOTH, *"POSSESSIONS"* AND *"ETERNAL LIFE"*?

Actually, the possessions were not his problem, only the occasion of it. The problem was his heart. It was fastened onto these possessions, and would not let go in order to follow Christ. The answer to the question is twofold:

1. If the *"possessions"* are anything which capture the heart, then they have to go before Christ can be followed.

2. If the *"possessions"* do not capture the heart, they are of no consequence, and Christ can be adequately followed.

The idea is that one cannot follow both! Jesus addressed Himself to this by saying, *"No man can serve two masters: for either he will hate the one, and love the other; or else he will hold to the one, and despise the other. You cannot serve God and mammon"* (Mat. 6:24).

As an example, Zacchaeus *"was rich,"* and said to Jesus, *"Behold, Lord, the half of my goods I give to the poor; and if I have taken anything from any man by false accusation, I restore him fourfold."*

Jesus did not tell him to give the other half also, but rather said, *"This day is Salvation come to this house"* (Lk. 19:1-9).

So, the criteria is not the giving of all, or half, but rather the *"heart."*

Paul summed it up by saying, *"But what things were gain to me, those I counted loss for Christ."*

"Yea doubtless, and I count all things but loss for the excellency of the knowledge of Christ Jesus my Lord: for Whom I have suffered the loss of all things, and do count them but dung, that I may win Christ" (Phil. 3:7-8).

The only *"possession"* that really matters is *"Eternal Life,"* and that can only be found in Jesus. If we allow anything to come between Him and us, whatever it is, it must be put away.

Let no one think that the Message given to this *"rich young ruler"* was for him alone; actually, it is for all!

(23) "AND JESUS LOOKED ROUND ABOUT, AND SAID UNTO HIS DISCIPLES, HOW HARDLY SHALL THEY WHO HAVE RICHES ENTER INTO THE KINGDOM OF GOD."

The overview is:

It's not the riches which constitute the sin, but one's attitude toward them.

RICHES

The phrase, *"And Jesus looked round about,"* means that as Jesus previously *"beheld"* the young man, He now beholds His Disciples. As He looked searchingly then, He looks searchingly now!

The phrase, *"And said unto His Disciples, How hardly shall they who have riches enter into the Kingdom of God,"* comes as a bombshell to the Disciples! It was something they had never heard before and, in fact, the very opposite of what they believed. Jesus did not say that it was impossible for one who had riches to be saved, but rather that it was more difficult for them.

Why?

Many who have riches tend to trust those riches. In other words, their dependence and faith are not in God, but instead in the things of this world. As such, they think they can buy whatever they need! However, Salvation cannot be bought, though millions have tried!

As well, many who are rich place themselves, because of their riches, in a different category than others. They don't want to hear that they must come to Christ in the same manner and with the same heart attitude as the poorest of the poor. Many desire to be treated as a special case, which God will not do. As a result of their riches, they are loath to humble themselves.

Actually, and as stated, it is not the *"riches"* which constitute the sin, but one's attitude toward those riches.

(24) "AND THE DISCIPLES WERE ASTONISHED AT HIS WORDS. BUT JESUS ANSWERED AGAIN, AND SAID UNTO THEM, CHILDREN, HOW HARD IS IT FOR THEM WHO TRUST IN RICHES TO ENTER INTO THE KINGDOM OF GOD?"

The synopsis is:

The Jews at that time considered riches to be the approval of God; at the same time, they considered poverty to be His disapproval.

ASTONISHMENT

The phrase, *"And the Disciples were astonished at His Words,"* concerns the attitude of the Disciples, and for reason.

Why were they astonished?

Jews equated riches with the favor and blessing of God. In other words, if one had riches, that meant he was right with God, and consequently greatly blessed by Him. Conversely, poverty, at least in the eyes of the Jews, meant God's disfavor, or even His curse. So, the more riches one had, the closer to God he was, or so they thought! The less riches, the less close to God. The poverty-stricken were thus deemed to be under the curse of God and, therefore, eternally lost, or at least under the frown of God.

Jesus has just turned their theology upside down, or rather right side up, which astonished them.

CHILDREN

The phrase, *"But Jesus answered again, and said unto them, Children,"* adds another condition to Salvation, while, at the same time, clarifying what He has just said about riches. He uses the word *"children,"* taking them back to the dissertation He has just given concerning *"receiving the Kingdom of God as a little child."*

A child does not grasp after things, nor does it seek to own great numbers of things. In effect, *"riches"* mean nothing to a child.

NOTES

Children who are poor really do not know it, at least if they have enough to eat. Children who are rich pretty well fall into the same category.

So, Jesus is telling His Disciples, as well as all others, that one must have the attitude of a child toward these things.

TRUST

The phrase, *"How hard is it for them who trust in riches to enter into the Kingdom of God,"* proclaims Him explaining His statement concerning *"riches."* As we have stated, it was not the *"riches"* per se which constituted the wrong, but rather *"trust in riches"*! In effect, the Lord is saying that it is *"hard"* for anyone to *"enter into the Kingdom of God,"* and *"especially hard"* for those who had added encumbrances, such as *"riches"*!

He will explain it further by the following statement:

(25) "IT IS EASIER FOR A CAMEL TO GO THROUGH THE EYE OF A NEEDLE, THAN FOR A RICH MAN TO ENTER INTO THE KINGDOM OF GOD."

The diagram is:

The word that Jesus uses here for *"needle"* doesn't refer to a small hole in the wall, as some think, but rather the type of needle used with thread.

THE NEEDLE

The phrase, *"It is easier for a camel to go through the eye of a needle,"* spoke of an ancient Jewish proverb. Most cities in those days were encircled by walls for protection, with the gates being closed at night; however, for late-comers there was a small opening cut in the gate (an actual smaller gate), which would admit a man, or even a camel, if it were stripped of all baggage and got down on its knees. The idea of the proverb is that it would be easier to get a camel through this small opening than it would be for a *"rich man"* to be saved.

It is not too difficult to get all the baggage off a camel, but it borders on the impossible for a rich person to purposely strip themselves of all the baggage which accompanies riches. That baggage concerns itself with *"trusting riches,"* which Jesus has just mentioned.

Wuest, however, says that the *"needle"* spoken of here was the type of needle used with thread; consequently, it meant the tiny eye of a sewing needle. Actually, whether the small opening in the large gate, or the actual eye of a sewing needle, the impossibility continues to present itself regarding Salvation, that is, if one trusts in riches.

THE RICH MAN

The phrase, *"Than for a rich man to enter into the Kingdom of God,"* is a blunt statement! It leaves absolutely no room for misinterpretation. The absolute impossibility of such a thing, as Jesus momentarily will state, is not the idea of the statement, but rather the infrequency of it. In fact, there are rich people who have come to Christ, and who faithfully serve Him. That number, however, is infinitesimally small. Most, as we have stated, trust their riches, consequently refusing to admit they need a Saviour like all others do.

Due to the Fall, the nature of man is such that he tends to puff himself up, if given even the slightest opportunity; consequently, if he is adept at making large sums of money, he has a tendency to believe that he is a cut above others. The idea that he is a poor lost sinner, with a spiritual need just as desperate as the poorest pauper, is totally foreign to his thinking.

Actually, this is the reason for class distinction and racism. Men love to think of themselves as better than others. They reason that their state in life brought on by economic opportunity and educational privilege negates their need for Christ.

As I have mentioned elsewhere in these Volumes, I have had the opportunity to have dialogued, in whatever capacity, with some who consider themselves to be intellectually superior. They are the individuals, or at least they think they are, who mold the thinking of the common people. They are the political pundits of the news media.

Concerning Christ, their attitude, at least for the most part, places them at a position totally different, at least they think, from the mainstream of society. They feel that accepting Christ may be necessary as a crutch for the intellectually inferior; however, they, the intellectually superior, are above this need. In other words, only the ignorant, at least in their thinking, would bother with such foolishness. Their intellectual cleverness, therefore, becomes their god.

Most of these, in whatever category they fall, do not know or believe the Bible. If they did, they would realize how intellectually superior the Word of God is to all philosophies of man. They would also understand that true riches and true fulfillment are found only in loving and serving God.

(26) "AND THEY WERE ASTONISHED OUT OF MEASURE, SAYING AMONG THEMSELVES, WHO THEN CAN BE SAVED?"

The structure is:

The words of Jesus completely overturned their theology.

ASTONISHED BEYOND MEASURE

The phrase, *"And they were astonished out of measure,"* takes them a step beyond the astonishment of Verse 24. If they were astonished then, their astonishment now is beyond measure. They are totally flabbergasted at the Words of Christ!

If most Church people who claim Christ today had the truth of the Cross preached to them, exactly as Jesus proclaimed the great Truth of Salvation and who can be saved, they would be just as astonished now as the Disciples were then. In fact, as the Disciples were so off-base at that time, likewise, most modern Christians fall into the same category. The difference is that whereas the Disciples truly believed Christ, even though they understood not at all what He was saying, most presently will not believe the Truth, even when it is presented unto them.

WHO CAN BE SAVED?

The question, *"Saying among themselves, Who then can be saved?"* presents, as stated, their theology being completely turned over. The Jews, as we have previously mentioned, including the Disciples, thought that riches were a Blessing of God, and consequently the rich person was the most saved of all. Those in poverty were thought to have the curse of God upon them, and consequently lost! In other words, they equated riches, i.e., material possessions, as a barometer of one's Salvation.

Now Jesus proclaims the very opposite of what they have studiously believed. Hence, they begin to converse among themselves in acclimated surprise, finally blurting out the question, *"Who then can be saved?"*

But the belief of Israel at that time concerning Salvation was not so different from their modern counterparts respecting Faith. The propagators of the Greed gospel judge a person's faith, by and large, by the amount of worldly possessions they own, etc. Such is just as wrongheaded as the belief of the Disciples concerning Salvation. Material possessions were the criteria then, and, regrettably, material possessions are the criteria now, at least in these erroneous doctrines.

(27) "AND JESUS LOOKING UPON THEM SAID, WITH MEN IT IS IMPOSSIBLE, BUT NOT WITH GOD: FOR WITH GOD ALL THINGS ARE POSSIBLE."

The exposition is:

Only through God is the Salvation process possible.

IMPOSSIBLE

The phrase, *"And Jesus looking upon them said,"* presents Him gazing steadfastly at them, knowing that His statement would produce this type of reaction. If the truth be known, as stated, most of the theology in modern Christendom is just as skewed as the theology of the Disciples. And yet, despite this wrong thinking, as serious as it was, these men were definitely saved.

This means that one can be wrong in the head and right in the heart, as we all, I must quickly add, have been at one time or the other.

The phrase, *"With men it is impossible, but not with God,"* puts everything into a different perspective. Jesus was not saying that rich men could not be saved, but that, because of their riches, it was more difficult to bring them to a place of Repentance. Actually, Salvation is impossible with all men respecting their own efforts and abilities, etc. The idea of the Text is that none of man's machinations, be he rich or poor, will afford him Salvation.

This means that all the efforts of men to save themselves, whatever those efforts might be, are to no avail. Moreover, if we Believers fail to understand the Word of God properly, we can still cause ourselves great problems. But sadly, most Christians spend little time and make little effort to understand the Word. That is tragic, because the Bible holds every answer for life and living, i.e., when we as Believers go wrong, we have violated, in some way, the Word of God.

WITH GOD ALL THINGS ARE POSSIBLE

The phrase, *"For with God all things are possible,"* presents God as Omnipotent (all-powerful), Omniscient (all-knowing), and Omnipresent (everywhere). The Miracle of the New Birth, and a Miracle it is, presents all being saved by Grace, through Faith, without works of the Law and human merit (Eph. 2:8-9).

As such, the rich must humble themselves and meet God's terms exactly as the poor. As we have stated, there is no difference! All have sinned and come short of the Glory of God (Jn. 3:16-18; I Tim. 2:4; II Pet. 3:9; Rev. 22:17).

Being rich does not have to be a barrier in finding the Lord if one will humble oneself and renounce all human sins and human merits (Rom. 3:24-31; 5:1-11; 10:9-10; Eph. 2:8-9; I Jn. 1:9). To be sure, however, riches can definitely prove to be, as here explained by Christ, a great barrier to Salvation, as they are most of the time. But, as stated, if the rich will meet God's terms in the same manner as all others, they will be saved as all others.

Furthermore, a rich man does not necessarily have to give up all he possesses to be a Disciple, but he must become willing to do so if God would require it of him. The riches, in effect, must become the property of the Lord before such a one can be saved.

The reason the Salvation process is impossible with man, whether rich or poor, is because the spiritual rebirth Believers experience does not come through any natural process. God is the Initiator of Salvation, i.e., the One Who effects the New Birth in those who believe and receive the Son (Jn. 1:12-13). The New Birth, consequently, makes us Children of God, and leads us to moral transformation. As stated, only God can do this, and not man.

So, the Salvation process in the rich is identical to that in the poor. The process of which Jesus speaks is not in question, but rather the barrier to that process, which can be riches or many things. Therefore, just because a person is rich, or famous, or powerful, etc., doesn't mean we are not to pray for their Salvation. We should pray for them irrespective of who they are, believing that *"with God all things are possible."*

(28) "THEN PETER BEGAN TO SAY UNTO HIM, LO, WE HAVE LEFT ALL, AND HAVE FOLLOWED YOU."

The exegesis is:

By this statement, it seems that Peter and the other Disciples are still thinking in terms of material, rather than spiritual, riches.

PETER

The phrase, *"Then Peter began to say unto Him,"* respects Peter, as usual, the spokesman of the group. The statement Peter will make means that all the Disciples, concerned with what Jesus had said about riches, had been avidly discussing this subject. As stated, their theology had been completely upended.

The phrase, *"Lo, we have left all, and have followed You,"* in effect, says, *"We have abandoned all in order to follow You. What reward will we get for becoming poor for Your sake?"* Actually, several of the Disciples had left what seemed to be a lucrative fishing business, and Matthew had left his tax-collector's office, all to follow this poor, itinerant Preacher; consequently, Peter, as spokesman for the Disciples, showed by his question that they were still thinking in terms of material, rather than spiritual, riches.

In fact, as the following exchange proclaims, their eyes continued to be on an earthly Kingdom, with Jesus as its King, and they as His chosen lieutenants. Of course, at least in their thinking, this would bring great riches and power.

However, one is not to mistake Peter's statement as a proclamation of second thought. The Disciples had made an irrevocable decision to leave all they had, and forever, and follow with the Lord permanently (Wuest). There was no thought of going back, even if

NOTES

the answer given by Jesus was not according to their thinking.

While it was true that they had things somewhat confused about the Mission of Christ, they were not confused concerning His Person. They knew He was the Messiah! Of that, there was no doubt! So, wherever He led, they were determined to follow; but, still, they also wanted to know where all of this was leading. As of yet, they had not learned their lesson respecting the *"servant ministry"* (Mk. 9:35), but continued to exhibit the self-will of *"What's in it for me?"*

If one is to notice, while Jesus did definitely promise great things, as the following Verses proclaim, nevertheless, what He said was somewhat vague concerning material possessions. What He actually did say is a lesson we must learn if we are to properly understand His Purpose, which must become our purpose.

(29) "AND JESUS ANSWERED AND SAID, VERILY I SAY UNTO YOU, THERE IS NO MAN WHO HAS LEFT HOUSE, OR BRETHREN, OR SISTERS, OR FATHER, OR MOTHER, OR WIFE, OR CHILDREN, OR LANDS, FOR MY SAKE, AND THE GOSPEL'S."

The structure is:

Regarding many, Jesus is just a means to an end, in other words, to get what they want in the realm of material things. Here Jesus completely debunks that; contrary to that, He says here that everything must be placed secondary to Christ.

THE ANSWER AS GIVEN BY CHRIST

The phrase, *"And Jesus answered and said, Verily I say unto you,"* concerns itself with the lesson which must be learned by all!

The phrase, *"There is no man who has left,"* concerns not only what one has, but also what one desires to have. This is a great Truth which must be understood by all followers of the Lord. It is the reason that some continue and some don't.

Many are not willing to leave all, with many attempting to use Christ to get what they want, as was the spirit of the Disciples, at least at this present time. To them, Jesus was a means to an end, just as He is with millions today. Thankfully, the Disciples would climb out over this, but many, sadly, never do.

THE WORD OF FAITH DOCTRINE

Actually, most of those, if not all, who adhere to the *"Greed Message"* are made up of this premise. Jesus is the way to earthly riches and material possessions. It is a heady doctrine chased by many devotees because of the inherent greed in most hearts.

It must ever be understood that Jesus is not a means to an end. This is blatant self-will, and such will never be honored by God. When men follow Jesus, they are to leave all, with Him Alone charting the course. It is somewhat the same as the military.

When one joins the Service, or is drafted, one does not tell the military what one wants to do; rather, one does what the military wants him to do, whatever that may be. Men have their way, but the Service has its way. To be sure, it is the *"Army Way"* which will be done. This is somewhat akin to following Jesus, but with one great difference.

The military forces its way, while Jesus does the opposite, desiring, even demanding, that those who follow Him do so out of their own freewill and volition.

HOME, RELATIVES, AND PROPERTY

The phrase, *"House, or brethren, or sisters, or father, or mother, or wife, or children, or lands,"* places everything under the three headings given above. In effect, Jesus is saying that if all of this is not given up, *"he cannot be My Disciples"* (Lk. 14:26-27).

What does it mean to give up this of which Jesus speaks?

It simply means that Christ is to be placed before everyone and everything. To be frank, when this is done, loved ones are loved more than ever and treated better than ever. Jesus has to come first in everything; but, to be sure, He never asks anything of us that will diminish us or those we love. Of that, one can be certain.

FOR CHRIST'S SAKE

The phrase, *"For My sake, and the Gospel's,"* speaks as to the reason. Many have done these things, but for other purposes and reasons. Many declare a vow of poverty, but not for the sake of Christ or the Gospel. In effect, many in the world, if not most, give up these things, or at least put them in a secondary position, in order that they may do certain things. Those things may be the pursuit of money, fame, power, or position. Then, again, it may be alcohol or drugs, etc.

This is the reason there are so many broken homes, alienation of affection, and anger and hatred! So what Christ is demanding is not all that unusual, at least regarding leaving all. Most just do it for the wrong reason; consequently, they reap a bitter harvest.

What does Jesus mean by leaving all for His sake and the Gospel's?

He definitely does not mean that a person should desert his parents, wife, husband, children, or responsibilities in these areas. Nor does He mean that one should necessarily sell everything he owns, etc. What He does mean is this:

Everything, as stated, must be subservient to Christ, in effect, placed in Christ. Many people boast that Christ is first in their lives, with other things taking second or third place, etc. That too is improper! Jesus not only must have first place, but also second, third, etc. Everything else, irrespective as to what it is, must have no place at all except in Him.

However, when this is done, and properly so, the true meaning and purpose of all these things become readily obvious, with a greater love or appreciation for them than ever, but in the proper perspective. In other words, a husband cannot truly love his wife, at least as he ought to, until she is properly placed in Christ. The same would hold for all else! True love, respect, appreciation, and worth are found only as these things, as dear as they may be, are properly placed in Christ. It is a matter of God's Will in relationship to man's will.

If one is to notice, Jesus said, *"For My sake and the Gospel's."*

Why did He say it in this manner?

SELF-WILL OR GOD'S WILL

If one has truly given up all these things to follow Jesus, the evidence will portray itself regarding the direction it takes. If the course is true and the direction straight, meaning that Jesus is truly being followed, every effort will be made on the part of the follower to proclaim the Good News of the Gospel to others. This is the criteria of following Jesus.

If one is to notice, the one great thrust of the followers of Christ, especially headed up by the Apostle Paul in the Book of Acts, is the taking of the Gospel to those who had never heard it. This alone constituted the true following of Jesus Christ.

Those who claim to be following Jesus, but have little or no concern for the lost, are, in effect, following their own self-will. If they truly follow Christ, the Gospel and its proclamation will be first and foremost. Everyone has his part to play. All can pray, and all can give, and some can go. Nevertheless, as stated, all are to have their part. The Great Commission is not the obligation of a few, but all (Mk. 16:15).

(30) "BUT HE SHALL RECEIVE AN HUNDREDFOLD NOW IN THIS TIME, HOUSES, AND BRETHREN, AND SISTERS, AND MOTHERS, AND CHILDREN, AND LANDS, WITH PERSECUTIONS; AND IN THE WORLD TO COME ETERNAL LIFE."

The composition is:

The world to come is eternal, and one must have eternal life to enter into that world. That alone is what counts!

HUNDREDFOLD

The phrase, *"But he shall receive an hundredfold now in this time,"* refers to this present life.

What did Jesus mean by the hundredfold return?

Some have made a doctrine of this, claiming that if one gives a dollar to the Work of the Lord, or whatever amount, he will receive back a hundred times what he gave.

Is this what Jesus meant?

Concerning our giving to the Lord, whether money or otherwise, the Lord may in turn give back a hundredfold, or even greater. At times, it may even be a thousandfold!

However, if that is our purpose and reason for giving, then our giving has been reduced to the level of a gamble, which God will never honor. In other words, our giving will be fueled by greed. This means that almost all given to that which I refer to as the *"Greed Gospel"* is not looked at by the Lord as *"giving"* at all, but rather some type of investment or gamble. Such will never be honored by God, and will receive no return whatsoever.

If one is to notice, in the Twenty-ninth Verse, Jesus says, *"has left,"* meaning that it is given with no thought of getting it back. The person *"has left"* it! This should be the same and, in fact, must be the same, in our giving to God. If it is done with any other motive, it is the wrong motive and will garner no favorable response.

If one gives to *"prove the sincerity of one's love,"* as the Holy Spirit demands, one can then expect the Lord to *"open you the windows of Heaven, and pour you out a Blessing, that there shall not be room enough to receive it"* (Mal. 3:10; II Cor. 8:8).

MATERIAL BLESSINGS AND RELATIONSHIPS

The phrase, *"Houses, and brethren, and sisters, and mothers, and children, and lands,"* covers the waterfront, so to speak!

If, in fact, we do have to give up loved ones because they do not agree with our acceptance of Christ, then, in turn, the Lord will give us others to take their place. Actually, at times, Believers are much closer to other Believers even than to members of their own family, especially if those family members are unsaved. This is what Jesus meant.

While many may understand this, still, others may wonder, how this could be fulfilled (the hundredfold return) respecting *"houses and lands."*

Please allow me to give an example from my own experience.

PERSONAL

For years, a dear friend furnished Frances and me with two new cars, for which we were so very thankful. While we did not own them, at the same time, we had the use of them, exactly as if we did own them. Isn't this what Jesus was saying?

As another example, when I was eight years old, I asked the Lord to give me the talent to play the piano, etc. He was gracious and kind to do what I asked. In 1961, if I remember correctly, I made my first recording. During those early times of Evangelistic Work, had it not been for the income from the sale of this product, our income would have been meager indeed! Consequently, the recordings were a blessing to the people and to us.

In 1969, and according to the leading of the Lord, I went on Radio with our daily program called, *"The Campmeeting Hour."* The Lord greatly blessed it, with us quickly developing a very large daily audience. (The program was a 15-minute daily, aired Monday through Friday.)

In 1970, even before the program became popular, the Lord began to deal with me about our Recordings. He asked me to give all the proceeds to Him. As stated, Frances and I previously kept the profits from these sales for our own use. However, those profits were very small at that particular time.

The Lord, in His dealings with me, did not explain at all, but simply, as is His Method, told me that He desired that we place these Recordings in the name of the Ministry, and for all proceeds to be used in His Work. During this time we were struggling to pay for the Radio Program, and the Devil also made certain that I remembered the very difficult times we had had financially in getting started. At times, the finances were so lean that we did not even have the money to buy the bare necessities. Consequently, when we began making the Recordings, the extra help this gave was a lifesaver.

THE LORD AND THE RECORDINGS

At any rate, I asked the Lord if He would allow me to take half the profits, such as they were, with me giving Him the other half. There was no answer! I came to the place that I asked the Lord to allow me to keep 10 percent, with me giving Him 90 percent. I remember that time of prayer very vividly. I felt somewhat pleased with myself in making this particular offer, that is, until the Lord spoke to me again.

He said, *"If you insist, you can have all of it, if that is what you really want! However, if you want My Will, you will do as I have asked!"*

At that moment, I broke before Him, gladly pledging it all. Within days, Frances and I called in a lawyer to draw up the papers, designating all Recordings as belonging to the Ministry, with none of the profits accruing to us personally, but all going to the Work of God. To be sure, at that particular time, the sales were very small; however, the Lord knew what they would ultimately be. In fact, to this day (2005), we have sold approximately fifteen million (15,000,000) Recordings.

I am glad I can say that every dollar of the money has gone to the Work of God. Neither Frances and I nor any members of our family have been enriched from the sales of these products. Actually, all that we personally own in this world is our home, with even that fully mortgaged.

LOOK WHAT THE LORD HAS DONE!

However, along with the home I have spoken of, for which we are so thankful to the Lord, He has given us, as stated, beautiful cars to drive, good clothes to wear, and good food to eat. On top of all that, we have multiple thousands of people around the world who love us dearly, and who are a part of our *"family"* in Christ. What more could anyone ask?

Have I ever regretted consigning all these Recording profits over to the Work of the Lord, especially considering the tremendous number sold?

A million times *"No"*! God's Ways are always, and by far, the best ways. Actually, there are no suitable ways but His!

In the first place, the Lord is the One Who gave me the talent that I have. As well, I believe the great Blessings the Lord gave us, respecting the acceptance of our music all around the world, have been because of our obedience to Him. To be sure, as stated, He gave me the talent that I possess; consequently, He has every right to ask what He did. Of course, He has every right anyway!

A hundredfold return? It is that and more!

PERSECUTIONS

The short phrase, *"With persecutions,"* is added by the Lord for purpose and reason.

Even though the Lord does bless abundantly, still, the *"persecutions"* will come because of the animosity of the world and the apostate Church. When one totally sells out to the Lord, such consecration will never be met by approval, but only sarcasm, and even hurt, if possible.

Let no one think that such can be avoided or evaded. If the person truly follows the Lord, he will always travel against the current and, therefore, be greatly opposed. The implication given by Christ proclaims that if *"persecutions"* do not come, it is a good sign that one is not truly following the Lord.

So, we have the second sign of such consecration, with the first being the priority of the spread of the Gospel.

ETERNAL LIFE

The phrase, *"And in the world to come Eternal Life,"* is the second, and by far the greater, reward.

What did Jesus mean by *"the world to come"*?

He was speaking of the coming Kingdom Age, when all Believers shall rule and reign with Him for a thousand years on this Earth (Rev. 20:1-6). This coming time will present a world as it has never been seen before. Jesus will rule Personally from Jerusalem, with Satan and all his minions of darkness locked away in the bottomless pit. For the first time, the world will know peace, safety, and worldwide prosperity. War will cease, and even the nature of the animal kingdom will be changed (Isa. 11:6-7; 65:25).

Immediately after the *"thousand years are expired, Satan shall be loosed out of his prison."* For a short period of time, he will be allowed the attempt at another overthrow, of which we are given very little information. The Scripture simply says, *"And fire came down from God out of Heaven, and devoured them"* (Rev. 20:7-9).

At that time, Satan and all his followers will be *"cast into the Lake of Fire and brimstone . . . and shall be tormented day and night forever and ever"* (Rev. 20:10). This will write *"Finished"* for Satan and his efforts to overthrow the *"Kingdom of God."* To be sure, this effort has resulted in the loss of uncounted millions of souls, as well as suffering and heartache unparalleled. But, at long last, it is now over!

At that time, there will be *"a new Heaven and a new Earth,"* meaning the purging of such, and not their destruction. The Greek word is *"parerchomi,"* which means *"to pass from one condition to another"* (Rev. 21:1). At that time, the Lord will transfer His Capital City, *"The New Jerusalem,"* from Heaven to Earth (Rev. 21:2-3).

"And there shall be no more curse: but the Throne of God and of the Lamb shall be in it; and His servants shall serve Him . . . And they shall reign forever and ever" (Rev. 22:3-5).

Also, if one is to notice, the last two Chapters of Revelation, which proclaim this coming eternal Kingdom, refer to Christ some seven times as the *"Lamb"* (Rev. 21:9, 14, 22, 23, 27; 22:1, 3).

Why would Jesus be referred to now as the *"Lamb,"* especially considering that Satan and all sin is forever done away with?

He is referred to as the Lamb seven times to portray to us the fact that this New Jerusalem, including the participation of every Saint in that city, is all because of what Jesus did at the Cross.

This is what is meant by *"the world to come."*

"Eternal Life" is something the Saint of God now has and, in Truth, will have forever. It is the *"Life"* imparted by Christ at conversion, which is consequently *"eternal"*!

I do not know what the thoughts of Peter and the Disciples were upon hearing this; however, what Jesus promised them so far eclipsed their petty thoughts that no comparison is possible. Let it every be understood that the Believer must not plan and then ask God's Blessings on the plan. He should instead let God plan and the Blessings will automatically come, and of far greater magnitude than anyone could ever think possible.

(31) "BUT MANY WHO ARE FIRST SHALL BE LAST; AND THE LAST FIRST."

The overview is:

Israel, although first, will be last because of rejection of Christ; the Church, although last, will be first because of acceptance of Christ.

THE FIRST AND THE LAST

When Jesus comes the second time, most who will accompany Him will be those who were the *"last"* to be offered the Gospel and the first to receive, i.e., the Church. However and, as well, all who believed Christ from the very beginning, including the Children of Abraham, will also be in that number; but, that number will be few, with the greater part being made up of the Church.

If it is to be noticed, Jesus used the word *"many,"* meaning that most before the Church refused the Gospel, which pertains to the majority of Israel, and from its beginning.

Paul tells us that despite the great Move of God in the midst of Israel, and for many centuries, still, there was only a *"Remnant"* which were truly saved (Rom. 11:5). This means that, despite that great Move of God, most Jews died lost. Of course, since their rejection of Christ, virtually all of the Jewish people have staggered through the centuries in unbelief and consequently have died lost. However, at the Second Coming, Israel will finally come home, thereby making Jesus their Saviour, their Lord, and their Messiah (Zech., Chpts. 12-14).

(32) "AND THEY WERE IN THE WAY GOING UP TO JERUSALEM; AND JESUS WENT BEFORE THEM: AND THEY WERE AMAZED; AND AS THEY FOLLOWED, THEY WERE AFRAID. AND HE TOOK AGAIN THE TWELVE, AND BEGAN TO TELL THEM WHAT THINGS SHOULD HAPPEN UNTO HIM."

The exegesis is:

He had already related to them several times what would happen to Him, but still they did not understand.

JERUSALEM

The phrase, *"And they were in the way going up to Jerusalem,"* contains in the Greek Text little inference respecting the road, but rather the Lord and His Disciples, and, more importantly, the Mission that Jesus would carry out, the Redemption of mankind by dying on Calvary. This is the moment of which the Prophets had spoken, and to which everything had led in the great Plan of God. It was awful in more ways that one (Isa., Chpt. 53).

Israel had been raised up from the loins of Abraham for the express purpose of bringing the Messiah into the world (Gen. 15:6). This they did, but with all hatred, refusing to recognize Him. Ever more horrible still, they would kill the Lord of Glory. Jerusalem was the city chosen by God in which to place His Name (II Chron. 6:6). And yet, this city which He had chosen would be the site of His Murder, and by His Own people, at that!

(As an aside, the road from all points did lead *"up,"* because Jerusalem stands near the highest point of the backbone of Palestine, namely, the line of hills running north and south between the Mediterranean Sea and the Jordan River. The city cannot be approached from any direction without an ascent — Wuest.)

JESUS

The phrase, *"And Jesus went before them,"* speaks of a habitual practice. Jesus often walked alone, ahead of His Disciples. He, no doubt, did this in order that He may have solitude and privacy with the Father. The evidence points to the fact that Jesus lived a life of constant prayer. Not that He stayed on His knees constantly, but that He was in a constant state and attitude of prayer, as alluded to here.

AMAZEMENT

The phrase, *"And they were amazed,"* speaks of His manner, and even of His Countenance. In other words, there was something about Him and this particular time that spoke of impending doom. Even though the Disciples little understood what He had been telling them respecting His coming Death, still, this Text proclaims the fact that they sensed around Him, strongly, the spirit of this terrible moment.

I think in His Spirit it was not so much the thought of dying which produced this aura, but instead the thought of His Own people doing this, and thereby sealing their doom. So, the word *"amazed"* lends credence to the thought that the Disciples, as well as the crowd going up to the Passover, were so struck by His Manner that they did not disturb Him.

FEAR

The phrase, *"And as they followed, they were afraid,"* speaks not only of the Disciples, but also of all who were near Him. As stated, the roads were filled with people going to Jerusalem for the Passover, and the occasion, which normally would have been joyful, was, at this time, the very opposite! Even the people who did not personally know Him sensed the awe of this moment.

There is no way that one could properly describe this time. The Heart of the Master was so heavy that it could not be hidden.

The phrase, *"And He took again the Twelve,"* refers to Him slowing His pace until the Disciples caught up with Him. The word *"again"* stresses that He will relate to them that which previously had been related.

The phrase, *"And began to tell them what things should happen unto Him,"* is an attempt to prepare them for the horror of these coming events. And yet, even though it would be plainly spoken, they would little understand!

(33) "SAYING, BEHOLD, WE GO UP TO JERUSALEM; AND THE SON OF MAN SHALL BE DELIVERED UNTO THE CHIEF PRIESTS, AND UNTO THE SCRIBES; AND THEY SHALL CONDEMN HIM TO DEATH, AND SHALL DELIVER HIM TO THE GENTILES."

The exposition is:

The Sanhedrin, the ruling body of Israel, would pass sentence upon Him, and then deliver Him to the Romans.

THE CHIEF PRIESTS AND SCRIBES

The phrase, *"Saying, Behold, we go up to Jerusalem,"* is proclaimed in the manner that says, *"Now is the time."* They had been to Jerusalem several times, but this time would be different. The phrase, *"And the Son of Man shall be delivered unto the Chief Priests, and unto the Scribes,"* speaks of the betrayal by Judas unto these apostates. It is ironical, and yet awful, that the very ones, *"the Chief Priests and the Scribes,"* who should have been heralding His Name would instead kill Him. Such is religion!

The plural *"Chief Priests"* describes members of the high-priestly families who served in the Sanhedrin. This was the highest court of the Jews which met in Jerusalem. Traditionally it is said to have originated with the seventy Elders who assisted Moses (Num. 11:16-24). Ezra is supposed to have reorganized this body after the Exile. It appears that the High Priest presided over this ruling body.

The jurisdiction of the Sanhedrin at the time of Christ was wide. It exercised not only civil jurisdiction according to Jewish Law, but also criminal jurisdiction in some degree. It had administrative authority and could order arrests by its officers of justice (Mat. 26:47; Mk. 14:43). It was empowered to judge cases which did not involve capital punishment (Acts, Chpts. 4-5). Capital cases required the confirmation of the Roman Procurator (Jn. 18:31), hence, Jesus using the phrase, *"And shall deliver Him to the Gentiles."*

SCRIBES

The Scribes were supposed to be Scholars in the Mosaic Law. They were the originators of Synagogue service. Some of them even sat as members of the Sanhedrin (Mat. 16:21; 26:3). Their duty was to preserve the Mosaic Law and to apply it to daily life. Most of them were Pharisees, and they claimed the oral law was more important even than the written Law (Mk. 7:5). By their efforts, religion was reduced to heartless formalism. They were at times referred to as *"lawyers"* or *"teachers of the Law."*

CONDEMNED TO DEATH

The phrase, *"And they shall condemn Him to death,"* concerns the attitude of the Church of that day to the Person and Ministry of Christ.

The word *"condemned"* means that they could not themselves carry out the act of execution, but would seek to get their sentence carried out by the Roman authorities, which they did!

Even though the following statements are strong, still, I believe them to be true:

If the Time and Plan of God had been changed, and Jesus were to come presently, the modern Church, at least for the most part, would take the same attitude toward Him as their counterparts of some 2,000 years ago. Religion is Satan's most fertile field. It alone has caused more people to die eternally lost than every vice in the world put together. Up beside religion, alcohol, drugs, immorality, etc., are but beginners.

As these Chief Priests and Scribes had reduced the Law of Moses to mere formalism, likewise, the modern Church has so added to, taken from, or ignored the Word of God that its true meaning, at least for most, has long since been lost. Most worship has been reduced to ceremony and formalism. Most Churches have denied the veracity and Power of the Holy Spirit, even those which claim to be Full Gospel. Psychology has replaced the Holy Spirit; consequently, instead of being Preachers of the Word, many, if not most, Preachers are no more than amateur psychologists.

THE MODERN CHURCH

In one of the major Pentecostal Denominations, the crowning achievement of education for their Ministers is a degree in psychology. The Word of God is given lip service, while the Holy Spirit and His Ways have all but been abandoned. As a result, Full Gospel and Charismatics run hither and yon seeking for some type of demonstration, which is quickly labeled as spiritual, and which is too often readily accepted. Prayer and the study of the Word are all but ignored. Much of the Charismatic community claims that prayer is, by and large, a wasted effort, with confession having taken its place. The convicting Power of the Holy Spirit is ridiculed, if believed at all!

As well, the Church has abandoned the Cross of Christ, until it little knows any more where it's been, where it is, or where it's going. It falls for every wind of doctrine, because its foundation, which should be the Cross, has been abandoned.

Most modern Christians have no idea whatsoever as to the part the Cross plays in the Sanctification process. In fact, the very word *"Sanctification"* is little heard any more in modern Churches. Most Christians don't even know what it is, when, in reality, it is one of the great Doctrines of the Faith.

And yet, even though the modern Church little knows what it's doing, it reaches out after every fad and scheme that's conjured up by angels of light, trying, in effect, to sanctify itself, which, of course, is impossible! As a result, modern Christians simply do not know how to live for God. They have abandoned the Word, so they drift aimlessly, like a person without a soul. Furthermore, Hollywood has invaded the Church, with the *"star"* syndrome paramount, primarily through Television.

Even though I say what I say with sorrow, I believe it to be true; the Church in America and Canada is in worse condition spiritually than it has been at any time since the Reformation. Its only hope is Revival, and yet it is far from admitting such need! In fact, it actually cannot have Revival until it first has a Reformation, which pertains to the Church coming back to its proper foundation, which is the Cross of Christ.

In spirit, and exactly as the religious leaders of old, the Church is either killing Christ or ardently serving Him. There is no middle ground!

The phrase, *"And shall deliver Him to the Gentiles,"* proclaims the action that would follow their condemnation. They demanded He be crucified, so the Roman Government must carry out this ghastly detail!

(34) "AND THEY SHALL MOCK HIM, AND SHALL SCOURGE HIM, AND SHALL SPIT UPON HIM; AND SHALL KILL HIM: AND THE THIRD DAY HE SHALL RISE AGAIN."

The structure is:

He here predicts His Resurrection, even as He had already done several times before; but they actually didn't believe it.

THE MOCKING, THE SCOURGING, AND THE SPITTING

The phrase, *"And they shall mock Him,"* refers to both Jews and Gentiles (Mat. 26:68; 27:29). The phrase, *"And shall scourge Him,"* refers to the soldiers of Pilate carrying out this dreadful act (Jn. 19:1). This punishment of scourging was so awful, so terrible, that at times the victim did not survive it. It was implemented by a whip made with a wooden handle, with leather cords extended from the handle containing pieces of bone or metal, or any other type of sharp object; consequently, when the blow landed, the flesh was torn and ripped.

While the Jews also administered flogging, it was limited to 40 stripes (Deut. 25:3). However, Jesus endured the Roman flogging, which had no limit. In other words, the one wielding the lash would continue to strike the victim until he was ordered to stop.

The phrase, *"And shall spit upon Him,"* constituted the highest form of insult. This was done by the Temple guards, and possibly even by members of the Sanhedrin (Mk. 14:65).

CRUCIFIXION

The phrase, *"And shall kill Him,"* spoke of His Death by Crucifixion, the most horrible form of death one could begin to imagine. Consequently, both the Jews and Gentiles were guilty of this horrid crime.

Why did they do such to Him?

They did so because their hearts were evil and wicked! The Jews did not know God, despite the fact that they spoke constantly of Him! So, instead of serving Him, they would *"kill Him"*!

THE RESURRECTION

The phrase, *"And the third day He shall rise again,"* plainly proclaims to the Disciples what will happen. Therefore, there was absolutely no excuse for their not understanding that He would be raised from the dead, and the exact time it would happen; however, despite what He said, none believed that He would actually come from the dead. Thomas said he would not believe it, *"Except I shall see in His Hands the print of the nails, and put my finger into the print of the nails, and thrust my hand into His side"* (Jn. 20:25).

Why didn't they believe Him?

It goes back to Mark 6:52 and 8:17, where it says, *"For their heart was hardened."* There *"heart"* was hardened because self-will had taken the place of God's Will. In their minds, Jesus was going to be King of Israel, consequently overthrowing the Roman yoke, and they would be His Chief Lieutenants and have great power and riches. This is evident even at this late date by the request of James and John, as recorded in Verses 35 through 37.

Any time self-will is promoted, which of necessity abrogates God's Will, the hardened heart is the result! Consequently, the person will not believe anything that contradicts his self-will; therefore, the Disciples little believed what Jesus said concerning His Death and Resurrection.

NOTES

(35) "AND JAMES AND JOHN, THE SONS OF ZEBEDEE, COME UNTO HIM, SAYING, MASTER, WE WOULD THAT YOU SHOULD DO FOR US WHATSOEVER WE SHALL DESIRE."

The exegesis is:

Matthew claims Salome, the mother of James and John, evidently traveling with them, made this request; however, it seems that the sons prompted her to do such (Mat. 20:20).

JAMES AND JOHN

The phrase, *"And James and John, the sons of Zebedee, come unto Him, saying, Master,"* proclaims a request that is totally opposite of what Jesus has just said. Combining both the remarks of Matthew and Mark, both accounts are correct, with the sons prompting their mother to make this request.

The phrase, *"We would that You should do for us whatsoever we shall desire,"* constitutes a most selfish request! Jesus was going to the Cross, while they had their thoughts centered on self-advancement in the Kingdom.

I think the attitude of the modern Church is little different, in that it is what *"we desire"* instead of what *"He desires"*! This episode will proclaim the difference in the two.

The request reeks with selfish ambition. Even though Jesus had just made the most solemn announcement that could ever be made, they took little note, rather thinking of themselves. They would use Jesus to get what they wanted.

Sounds familiar, doesn't it?

One can tell from the tenor of their request that they knew Jesus had the power to do whatever was needed; consequently, they could not see Him being delivered to death.

(36) "AND HE SAID UNTO THEM, WHAT WOULD YOU THAT I SHOULD DO FOR YOU?"

The synopsis is:

In effect, Jesus is asking every Believer this same question!

THE GREAT QUESTION

Even with a heavy heart, He will speak kindly unto them, even asking what they desired. How patient He is with us! And yet, in the tenor of His question to them, one can sense that He knew the wrongness of what their request would be. The Text implies that they should have been warned, by the tone of His Voice, of the wrongness of their desires. His question should have been a rebuke, which it was intended to be, even though mild. But yet, self-will very seldom is slowed in its quest for gratification.

(37) "THEY SAID UNTO HIM, GRANT UNTO US THAT WE MAY SIT, ONE ON YOUR RIGHT HAND, AND THE OTHER ON YOUR LEFT HAND, IN YOUR GLORY."

The diagram is:

They were speaking of *"glory,"* while He was speaking of *"death."*

POSITION

The phrase, *"They said unto Him, Grant unto us that we may sit . . ."* refers to a position of honor, as well as power.

They are actually referring back to Peter's statement as to how they had left all to follow Him, and because of that, what would their reward be? (Vss. 28-31).

The phrase, *"One on Your right hand, and the other on Your left hand,"* concerns the greatest positions of all! They wanted to get in their request first of all, even before the other Disciples; consequently, the jockeying for position is taking place in His Own ranks. This spirit, the political spirit of self-will, did not die with the request of James and John. Unfortunately, it plagues the Church even unto this hour.

In fact, the modern Church is far more political than it is spiritual. That is unfortunate but true! Its members are little content to let the Lord promote them. They instead promote themselves, and too often use any and all means to carry out selfish ambition.

I remember years ago when Frances and I first began in Evangelistic Work. We were attending a particular meeting concerning the Denomination with which we were then associated. I happened to pass a group of Preachers standing in the hall and overheard one say to another, *"I will vote for you and get several others to do so, if you will thus and so,"* or words to that effect.

In this scenario, even though insignificant, one can readily see the jockeying for power, with little thought as to what the Lord wanted or desired. In truth, and with some exceptions, most offices in religious Denominations are purely political, and consequently carry no spiritual content.

Considering how close to Jesus these men were, how could they be of such mind? This shows us that *"association," "participation,"* and *"environment"* do not guarantee a close walk with God. In fact, the association, participation, and environment could not have been better! But, still, self-will, even at this late date, prevailed.

As we have said elsewhere in these Volumes, Jesus died on Calvary to save man from sin and self. Many understand the *"sin"* problem, but they little understand the *"self"* problem. In fact, sin can be easily forgiven in a few moments time upon proper confession and Repentance; however, *"self"* is not so easily subdued and placed in its proper position, i.e., in Christ (Rom. 8:1).

One can easily see in the Disciples that even though their sins have been washed, cleansed, and forgiven, still, they had a long way to go respecting *"self."*

THE GLORY

The phrase, *"In Your Glory,"* shows that they understood the coming Glory and Kingdom of the Messiah (Mat. 16:27-28); however, their timing, as with so many, was wrong. They still had in their minds that Jesus was about to set up His earthly Kingdom, and His statements concerning Death and Resurrection did not deter their thinking. If anything, His statement concerning being raised on the *"third day"* only fueled their wrong thoughts.

In fact, this Kingdom Age has not even yet come, but will do so at the Second Coming (Rev., Chpt. 19).

(38) "BUT JESUS SAID UNTO THEM, YOU KNOW NOT WHAT YOU ASK: CAN YOU DRINK OF THE CUP THAT I DRINK OF? AND BE BAPTIZED WITH THE BAPTISM THAT I AM BAPTIZED WITH?"

The synopsis is:

Both of these questions signify the Cross!

THE CUP

The phrase, *"But Jesus said unto them,*

You know not what you ask," characterizes so many petitions made by Believers. Any time one prays after self-will instead of *"after the Spirit,"* one falls into this category (Rom. 8:1, 6). Knowing how susceptible all of us are to the flesh, it is my practice when engaging in prayer to ask the Lord that the Holy Spirit may guide my petitions along with my worship that I may not pray wrongly.

The question, *"Can you drink of the cup that I drink of?"* implies that they will indeed have to do so. The *"Cup"* in Scripture signifies a man's portion, which is determined for him by God and sent to him. The figure is derived from the ancient custom at feasts by which the ruler of the feast tempered the wine according to his own will, and appointed to each guest his own portion, which it was his duty to drink (Bickersteth).

The *"Cup"* spoken of by Jesus was the Cross and all that it meant.

Even though the Disciples and all others would not be asked to bear the Cross to this extent, still, it must be borne by all, at least those who follow Christ, as determined by the Lord.

THE BAPTISM

The question, *"And be baptized with the Baptism that I am baptized with?"* had to do with the Baptism of His Sufferings. (The statement has nothing to do with Water Baptism, or even the Baptism with the Holy Spirit.) This *"Baptism"* actually refers to the Crucifixion and our part in that Crucifixion, which on our part is by Faith.

Paul said, *"Know ye not, that so many of us as were baptized into Jesus Christ were baptized into His Death?*

"Therefore we are buried with Him by baptism into death: that like as Christ was raised up from the dead by the Glory of the Father, even so we also should walk in newness of life.

"For if we have been planted together in the likeness of His Death, we shall be also in the likeness of His Resurrection" (Rom. 6:3-5).

As we've already stated, this has absolutely nothing to do with Water Baptism. In fact, every person must be Baptized with this Baptism, which is the Baptism of the Crucifixion, in order to be saved. After the person is saved, their faith is to remain in Christ and the Cross, because, as we've already stated, Christ is the Source and the Cross is the Means. This refers to the *"Baptism into Christ"* and, more particularly, the way this is done, i.e., we are baptized into His Crucifixion by Faith (Eph. 2:8-9).

(39) "AND THEY SAID UNTO HIM, WE CAN. AND JESUS SAID UNTO THEM, YOU SHALL INDEED DRINK OF THE CUP THAT I DRINK OF; AND WITH THE BAPTISM THAT I AM BAPTIZED WITHAL SHALL YOU BE BAPTIZED."

The overview is:

This was a mere profession of moral courage, not a claim to spiritual power; they really didn't know what they were saying.

THE ANSWER OF THE DISCIPLES

The phrase, *"And they said unto Him, We can,"* concerns itself with a brash reply. In fact, all of them would desert Him at the Crucifixion. But yet, the later years would prove the veracity of the prediction of Jesus concerning them. At this particular time, despite nearly 3-1/2 years of teaching, and by the greatest Teacher of all, they still had a very imperfect view of what this was all about. Not until the Day of Pentecost, when they would be baptized with the Holy Spirit, would they then begin to understand. Jesus would tell them, *"But when the Comforter (Helper) is come* (the Holy Spirit), *Whom I will send unto you from the Father* (presents Jesus as the Baptizer with the Holy Spirit [Mat. 3:11; Jn. 1:31-33]), *even the Spirit of Truth* (concerns the veracity of the Word of God; the Holy Spirit superintended its writing all the way from Moses, who began with Genesis, to the closing as given to John on the Isle of Patmos), *which proceeds from the Father* (proclaims the Father sending the Holy Spirit in the Name of Jesus and by the Authority of Jesus), *He shall testify of Me* (Who Christ is [God] and what Christ has done — the Cross):

"And you also shall bear witness (the Apostles), *because you have been with Me from the beginning* (speaks of them observing all He did and all He said [Eph. 2:20])" (Jn. 15:26-27).

THE ANSWER GIVEN BY CHRIST

The phrase, *"And Jesus said unto them, You shall indeed drink of the Cup that I drink of; and with the Baptism that I am baptized withal shall you be baptized,"* concerned not only the Disciples, but all who follow Christ, and for all time!

As we have stated, every Believer is appointed a *"Cup"* by the Lord, and of it they must drink. Always, it is a portion of some type of suffering. These twin appointments for the Child of God are guaranteed, for Jesus said, *"You shall indeed drink. . . ."*

In the last few years, a major part of the Charismatic community has attempted to abrogate this statement by Christ, claiming that a proper confession will remove all difficulties and sufferings. Many have even gone so far as to remove any and all songs from their repertoire that speak of such, even songs about the Cross. They claim that the Cross is *"past miseries"* and is not applicable to the modern Believer.

Such shows a complete misunderstanding of the Scriptures and also of the Mission of Christ. As distasteful as they are, these things are necessary for every Believer. The primary objective is the eradication of self-supremacy in favor of Christ, which can only be brought about by this method. Unfortunately, self-will cannot be confessed away. It is brought to its place only by this *"Baptism into Christ,"* which pertains to the Crucifixion.

However, once the Believer embraces the Cross, which is the Biblical way, to be sure, he will find quickly enough that the Cross contains an offense (Gal. 5:11). This *"offense"* is the *"Cup"* all of us must drink.

(40) "BUT TO SIT ON MY RIGHT HAND AND ON MY LEFT HAND IS NOT MINE TO GIVE; BUT IT SHALL BE GIVEN TO THEM FOR WHOM IT IS PREPARED."

The composition is:

Jerome says, *"Our Lord does not say, 'You shall not sit,' lest He put to shame these two; neither does He say, 'You shall sit,' lest the others should be envious; but by holding out the prize to all, He animates all to contend for it."*

PLACES AND POSITIONS

The phrase, *"But to sit on my right hand and on my left hand is not Mine to give,"* proclaims such being given in accordance with the Father's Disposition. In fact, Christ is indeed the anointed Distributor of all eternal rewards (II Tim. 4:8; Rev. 22:12); however, He seeks and determines the Father's Will in all that He does (Jn. 4:34). Consequently, in making this statement, Jesus proclaims to His Disciples that even He does not seek to carry out His Will, but rather the Will of the Father; therefore, it should not be *"whatsoever we shall desire,"* but instead *"whatsoever He shall desire"*!

PREPARATION

The phrase, *"But it shall be given to them for whom it is prepared,"* says several things:

1. Actually, someone will occupy these positions; the Father, in fact, is preparing them for it, whoever they may be.

2. The way that Jesus answers this question, He, in effect, holds the positions open for all, at least whom the Father selects.

3. As well, the Lord is careful to point out that he who humbles himself shall be exalted; in other words, this goal is not attained by the ways of the world, i.e., self-promotion, but instead by the road of humility, which is the very opposite (Mat. 23:12; Lk. 14:11).

(41) "AND WHEN THE TEN HEARD IT, THEY BEGAN TO BE MUCH DISPLEASED WITH JAMES AND JOHN."

The composition is:

The sons of Zebedee want to be first, and the Ten were unwilling to be last! Such was the energy of the carnal nature in all Twelve.

STRIFE

Political quests in the Church always lead to strife. Such is always the result of self-made plans. The Believer is to let God plan for him, and then walk in the way laid out. Too many Believers make their own plans and then ask God to bless them. Such is never to be! Actually, this is what James and John were doing.

(42) "BUT JESUS CALLED THEM TO HIM, AND SAID UNTO THEM, YOU KNOW THAT THEY WHICH ARE ACCOUNTED TO RULE OVER THE GENTILES EXERCISE LORDSHIP OVER THEM; AND THEIR GREAT ONES EXERCISE AUTHORITY UPON THEM."

The diagram is:
In the world, the greater the position, the greater the authority, which is, however, the opposite of the Way of the Lord.

LORDSHIP

The phrase, *"But Jesus called them to Him, and said unto them,"* expresses itself in a very serious discussion. If the spirit of self-will had continued, it would have destroyed the very fabric of all that Jesus taught. Quite possibly, this problem of self-aggrandizement, as evidenced here by the Disciples, which is the opposite of the *"Servant Principle,"* is the greatest danger to the Body of Christ; consequently, Jesus would call the Disciples close to Him in order to give them this most important teaching concerning this Principle.

The phrase, *"You know that they which are accounted to rule over the Gentiles exercise lordship over them,"* points out the way of the world. So, Christ will show the Disciples the difference between that which is esteemed great in the Gentile world system and the standard of greatness in the spiritual kingdom which He was inaugurating.

The great danger in the Church has always been the tendency to bring the world's system into the Work of God, which can never be accepted by the Lord.

THE AUTHORITY OF THE WORLD

The phrase, *"And their great ones exercise authority upon them,"* speaks of pomp and circumstance, privilege and power, position and authority in the Gentile world, which was esteemed great, and the greatness of the individual came from his place in the system. Jesus is teaching that Bible Christianity is the very opposite. Were that not the case, Jesus would have never chosen these men to be His Disciples. There was no greatness about them, at least as far as the world was concerned.

However, the Lord does not choose on the basis of greatness, but rather on the basis of what He can do through an individual's life. In fact, none of what the world calls *"great"* can be used at all by the Lord. Should such a person come to Christ, all of this *"husk"* has to be stripped from him before the Way of Christ can become evident in such a life.

This is what John the Baptist was speaking of when he spoke of Jesus Baptizing *"you with the Holy Spirit, and with fire."* Further he said, *"Whose fan is in His Hand, and He will thoroughly purge His Floor, and gather His Wheat into the garner; but He will burn up the chaff with unquenchable fire"* (Mat. 3:11-12).

The *"chaff"* He speaks of is that which is of the world!

When He called Paul, who was probably the most educated man ever called by the Lord, dependence on these things of the world had to be stripped from the Apostle. Of that, Paul was speaking when he said, *"But what things were gain to me, those I counted loss for Christ"* (Phil. 3:7).

This is the reason that *"not many wise men after the flesh, not many mighty, not many noble, are Called"* (I Cor. 1:26).

WISDOM AFTER THE FLESH

Paul was one of the few who would allow the Lord to strip him of all this *"wisdom after the flesh"* in order to use him mightily. This in no way meant to imply that God uses ignorance, etc. He doesn't! In fact, He can definitely use talent, education, ability, etc., exactly as He did in Paul; however, these things must be totally dedicated to Him, and the person must be led entirely by the Holy Spirit. Again, we emphasize, the Holy Spirit will use nothing which pertains to the ways of the world, but only that which is of His origin and design (Zech. 4:6).

Through the years I have had many Christians speak to me of particular entertainers, etc., saying that if they were saved, how God could use them. They were implying that their talent or ability would be greatly used by the Lord, and because of such talent and ability.

However, such thinking is totally unscriptural. In fact, God cannot use such talent and ability, etc., unless it is totally dedicated to Him, as we have stated! Unfortunately, the Church has repeatedly attempted to bring such into its bosom, but always without any positive spiritual results.

Recently on one of the major news programs over Television, I witnessed and observed a *"Christian rock group,"* who was supposedly winning many young people to their banner. Allow me to quickly state that while this group may be drawing many young people to their banner, they are not drawing them to the Lord.

And how do I know that?

My statement is not based on musical preference, but rather the *"ways of the world."* This group, as all others of similar ilk, attempts to copy the rock or rap groups of the world, using their mannerisms, style, etc. To be sure, the Lord will have none of it, with no work of the Spirit being performed in any heart and life. God's Ways are not man's ways, and the attempt to pull man's ways into God's Ways only leads to spiritual death (Prov. 16:25).

Consequently, this teaching by Christ, concerning the ways of the world versus the *"Ways of God,"* is of supreme significance.

(43) "BUT SO SHALL IT NOT BE AMONG YOU: BUT WHOSOEVER WILL BE GREAT AMONG YOU, SHALL BE YOUR MINISTER."

The diagram is:

The way of the world is not the Way of the Lord.

MINISTER

The phrase, *"But so shall it not be among you,"* proclaims the necessity of the Church in expelling all that which is not of God, but rather of the world.

The phrase, *"But whosoever will be great among you, shall be your Minister,"* proclaims God's standard of greatness. It is, as we have stated, the *"Servant Principle."* The word *"Minister"* in the Greek is *"diakonos,"* which means *"one who runs errands"* or *"a waiter on tables or other menial duties."* It does not literally mean that one is to do these things, but that one must be willing to do them, looking at no task for the Lord as menial. If one thinks he is too good to do such things, the Christlike spirit is obviously missing.

(44) "AND WHOSOEVER OF YOU WILL BE THE CHIEFEST, SHALL BE SERVANT OF ALL."

The overview is:

In the Kingdom of God, the greatness of the individual comes from the lowly place he takes as a servant of all.

NOTES

THE SERVANT

The phrase, *"And whosoever of you will be the chiefest,"* proclaims that the Lord does not condemn the desire for greatness, but only the wrong way of it being achieved. The phrase, *"Shall be servant of all,"* shows in the Kingdom of God that the greatness of the individual comes from the lowly place he takes as a servant.

So, the Believer can desire to be great before other men, or great before God. He cannot have both!

To be sure, if he takes the place of the *"servant,"* as the Lord demands, in no way will he be acclaimed great or *"Chief"* from those in the world, and, sadly, neither from most in the Church. However, with God, Who Alone matters, humility assures greatness.

(45) "FOR EVEN THE SON OF MAN CAME NOT TO BE MINISTERED UNTO, BUT TO MINISTER, AND TO GIVE HIS LIFE A RANSOM FOR MANY."

The overview is:

Christ is Very God of Very God, but became Incarnate in human flesh and a Servant to mankind. What a rebuke to His Disciples, and to us, as well!

THE RANSOM

The phrase, *"For even the Son of Man came not to be ministered unto,"* proclaims Christ as the example. The phrase, *"But to minister, and to give His Life a ransom for many,"* proclaims that the resplendent beauty of the Son of Man came from the fact that He, as Very God of Very God, became Incarnate in human flesh and a Servant to mankind.

As *"Minister"* referred to the activity of serving, likewise, the word *"Servant,"* in Verse 44 and pertaining to Verse 45, is, in the Greek, *"doulos,"* which means *"a slave."* The word *"ransom"* in the Greek is *"lutron,"* which means *"the price for redeeming, the ransom paid for slaves."* It refers to substitution. The Lord paid the ransom for sinners who could not pay it themselves, namely, His Own Precious Blood; consequently, Christ served as the greatest example of all respecting the *"Servant Principle."*

The phrase, *"A ransom for many,"* does not teach *"limited atonement,"* as some claim.

The word *"many"* is used here in the sense of the whole of mankind, and for all time, which, of course, was, and is, *"many."* It does not mean that Jesus died for some, but not for others. He died for the entirety of the world, and, as stated, for all time (Jn. 3:16).

Consequently, He once again refers to the Death He will die, which will be to set the captive free from sin; however, the Disciples little understood it at the time.

RANSOM AND SACRIFICE

Sacrifice is linked with ransom. Sacrifice was the Divinely appointed cover for sin. The ransom for the Deliverance of the sinner was to be by Sacrifice. Both the typical testimony of the Law and the prophetic testimony gave prominence to the thought of Redemption. The Coming One was to be a Redeemer. Redemption was to be the great work of the Messiah.

The people seemed to have looked for the Redemption of the soul to God Alone through the observance of their appointed ritual, but they linked Redemption in the more general sense of deliverance from all enemies and troubles with the Advent of the Messiah. It required a spiritual vision to see that the two things would coincide, that the Messiah would effect Redemption in all its phases and fullness by means of ransom, of Sacrifice, of expiation.

JESUS, WHO PAID THE RANSOM

Jesus appeared as the Messiah in Whom all the old economy was to be fulfilled. He knew perfectly the meaning of the typical and prophetic testimonies; with that fully in view, knowing that His Death was to fulfill the Old Testament types and accomplish its brightest prophetic anticipations, He deliberately uses this term, *"lutron,"* to describe it (Mat. 20:28). Speaking of His Death as a ransom, He also regarded it as a Sacrifice, an expiatory offering. The strong preposition used intensifies the idea of ransom and expiation, even to the point of substitution. In the Greek, it is *"anti,"* which means *"instead of,"* and also the idea of exchange, equivalence, and substitution, which cannot be removed from it.

In Numbers 3:45, *"Take the Levites instead of all the firstborn,"* the Greek interpretation uses *"anti,"* which, like the English *"instead of,"* exactly represents the Hebrew *"tahath"*; and all three convey most unmistakably the idea of *"substitution."*

SUBSTITUTION

And as the Levites were to be substituted for the firstborn, so for the surplus of the firstborn the *"ransom money"* was to be substituted, that idea, however, being clearly enough indicated by the use of the genitive. Indeed, the simpler way of describing a ransom would be with the genitive, the ransom of many; or as our version renders, *"a ransom for many"*; but just because the ransom here is not simply a money payment, but is the actual sacrifice of the life, the substitution of His soul for many, He is appropriately said *"to give His soul a ransom 'instead of' many."*

The Kingdom of God which Christ proclaimed was so diverse in character from that which Salome and her sons anticipated that, so far from appearing in dazzling splendor, with distinguished places of power for eager aspirants, it was to be a spiritual home for redeemed sinners. Men held captive by sin needed to be ransomed that they might be free to become subjects of the Kingdom, and so the ransom work, the sufferings and death of Christ, must lie at the very foundation of that Kingdom. The need of ransom supposes life forfeited; the ransom paid secures life and liberty; the life which Christ gives comes through His ransoming Death.

APOSTOLIC TEACHING CONCERNING RANSOM

The great utterance of the Saviour found in Mark 10:45, *"And to give His Life a ransom for many,"* may well be considered as the germ of all the Apostolic teaching concerning Redemption, but it is not for us to show its unfolding beyond noting that in Apostolic thought the Redemption was always connected with the Death, the Sacrifice of Christ.

Thus Paul says, *"In Whom we have Redemption through His Blood"* (Eph. 1:7). Thus, Peter says, *"You were not Redeemed with corruptible things . . . But with the*

Precious Blood, as of a Lamb without blemish and without spot, even the Blood of Christ" (I Pet. 1:18-19). So, in Hebrews 9:12, it is shown that Christ *"by His Own Blood entered in once for all into the Holy Place, having obtained Eternal Redemption"*; and, in the Book of Revelation, the song is: *"You were slain, and did purchase unto God with Your Blood men of every Tribe"* (Rev. 5:9).

In all but the last of these Passages, there is an echo of the very word used by Christ.

In I Timothy 2:5-6, Paul has a still closer verbal coincidence when he says, *"Christ Jesus, Who gave Himself a ransom for all."* The word used here is *"agorazo,"* which means *"to buy in the open market,"* a word which is frequently used of the redeeming Work of Christ (Rev. 14:3-4; II Pet. 2:1; I Cor. 6:20; 7:23). In the two places where Paul uses it, he adds the means of purchase: *"You were bought with a price,"* which from his point of view would be equivalent to ransom. In the Passages in Galatians 3:13 and 4:5, Paul uses the compound *"exagorazo,"* which is equivalent to *"redeemed, buy off, deliver by paying the price."*

TO WHOM WAS THE RANSOM PAID?

The question, *"Who receives the ransom?"* is not directly raised in Scripture, but it is one that not unnaturally occurs to the mind. Theologians have answered it in varying ways.

First of all, it definitely was not paid to Satan.

The idea entertained by some of the Early Church Fathers that the ransom was given to Satan, who is conceived of as having, through the sin of man, a righteous claim upon him which Christ recognizes and meets, is grotesque, and not in any way countenanced by Scripture. God owes Satan nothing, and the thought of such is ridiculous!

Christ paid the ransom to satisfy Divine justice. All that has been said goes to show that, in no mere figure of speech, but in tremendous reality, Christ gave *"His Life a ransom."* If our mind demands an answer to the question to Whom the ransom was paid, it does not seem at all unreasonable to think of the justice of God, or God in His Character of Moral Governor, as requiring and receiving it.

NOTES

In all that Scripture asserts about propitiation, sacrifice, and reconciliation in relation to the Work of Christ, it is implied that there is Wrath to be averted, Someone to be appeased or satisfied. While it may be enough simply to think of the effects of Christ's redeeming Work in setting us free from the penal claims of the Law — the just doom of sin — it does not seem to go beyond the spirit of Scripture to draw the logical inference that the ransom price was paid to the Guardian of the Holy Law, the Administrator of Eternal Justice.

"Christ has redeemed us from the curse of the Law, being made a curse for us" (Gal. 3:13). This essential, fundamental phase of Redemption is what theologians, with good Scriptural warrant, have called Redemption by Blood, or by price, as distinguished from the practical outcome of the Work of Christ in the life which is Redemption by power.

REDEMPTION BY PRICE

As to Satan's claims, whatever they might be, Christ, by having paid the ransom price and having thus secured the right to redeem, exercises His Power on behalf of the believing sinner. He does not recognize the right of Satan. Satan is the *"strong man"* holding his captives lawfully because of sin, but Christ is *"stronger than he"* and overcomes him and spoils him, thereby setting the captives free (Lk. 11:21-22). In one sense, men may be said to have sold themselves to Satan, but they have no right to sell, nor he to buy, and Christ ignores that transaction and brings *"to naught him who had the power of death, that is, the Devil"* (Heb. 2:14), and so is able to *"deliver all them who through fear of death were all their lifetime subject to bondage"* (Heb. 2:15).

REDEMPTION BY POWER

Many of the Old Testament Passages about the Redemption wrought on behalf of God's people illustrate this Redemption by power, and the Redemption by power is always founded on the Redemption by price; the release follows the ransom. In the case of Israel, there was first the Redemption by Blood — the sprinkled blood of the Paschal Lamb, which sheltered from the destroying

Angel (Ex., Chpt. 12) — and then followed the Redemption by power, when, by strength of hand, Jehovah brought His people out from Egypt (Ex. 13:14), and in His Mercy led forth the people which He had redeemed (Ex. 15:13).

So, under the Gospel, when He *"has visited and wrought Redemption for His people"* (Lk. 1:68), He can *"grant unto us, that we being delivered out of the hand of our enemies should serve Him without fear"* (Lk. 1:74). It is because we have in Him our Redemption through His Blood that we can be delivered out of the power of darkness (Col. 1:13). In other words, Jesus paid it all!

(Material on the *"Ransom"* was supplied by a conglomerate of authors, Weiss, Schmid, Stevens, M' Caig, etc.)

(46) "AND THEY CAME TO JERICHO: AND AS HE WENT OUT OF JERICHO WITH HIS DISCIPLES AND A GREAT NUMBER OF PEOPLE, BLIND BARTIMAEUS, THE SON OF TIMAEUS, SAT BY THE HIGHWAY SIDE BEGGING."

The exposition is:

This is the only record of Jesus being in Jericho; it was to be a red letter day for some.

JERICHO

The phrase, *"And they came to Jericho,"* denotes something of great significance which is to happen here. In effect, and as we shall see, it is the healing of Bartimaeus. The phrase, *"And as He went out of Jericho with His Disciples and a great number of people,"* proclaims this incident exactly as Matthew, *"And as they departed from Jericho"* (Mat. 20:29-34).

Luke says, *"As He was come near unto Jericho,"* (Lk. 18:35-43).

Is there a discrepancy?

No! There is no discrepancy. Some have claimed two entirely different incidents are recorded, and this may be correct; however, it is probably that all, Matthew, Mark, and Luke, are speaking of the same incident. As well, Matthew mentions *"two blind men,"* while Mark and Luke mention only one.

THE EXPLANATION

Only one, Bartimaeus, is mentioned by Mark and Luke, because, in some way, he

NOTES

stands out; however, this does not mean that the other one, as recorded by Matthew, was not present, or healed. In fact, he was!

When giving an account of a particular incident, many times an individual will highlight certain things and leave out entirely other things. This happens constantly, and with purpose; however, it does not mean that the situations left unmentioned did not happen. In fact, they did happen, but, for some particular reason, they just were not mentioned.

The way it is given by all three is the way the Holy Spirit desired that it be given, and for purpose and reason. Perhaps the reason in Matthew, where two blind men were healed, was because Jesus was portrayed in that account as King. As such, the two could have represented the Hebrew nation in its two divisions of Israel and Judah. Their both receiving sight could illustrate the light that will ultimately shine on them when they accept Jesus as their Lord and Saviour at the Second Coming, when He will then be crowned *"King of kings and Lord of lords"*! (Rev. 19:16).

THE LOCATION

Luke just simply made mention that they were *"coming near unto Jericho,"* and then gave the account of the healing of the *"blind man."* His account merely states that it was Jericho where this great Miracle took place, and not the location, whether coming in or going out.

If one is to notice, Mark mentions both. He spoke of them coming to Jericho, as Luke, and then he gave the place of the healing, *"as He went out of Jericho,"* which Luke did not give. As stated, there is no discrepancy.

BARTIMAEUS

The phrase, *"Blind Bartimaeus, the son of Timaeus,"* suggests, because of its careful description, that Bartimaeus may have come from a family of some note. Of course, there is no way this can be ascertained, but we do know that Mark's careful description was not without purpose. More than likely, Peter informed Mark of this situation, as of most of the experiences in this Book. Consequently, there was a reason he gave to Mark the name of the father of Bartimaeus.

A BEGGAR

The phrase, *"Sat by the highway side begging,"* denotes the low station in life to which Bartimaeus had fallen. If, in fact, it was true that Bartimaeus came from a family of note, he would serve as a perfect example of the Fall of mankind. As we have repeatedly stated, every Miracle performed by Christ was meant not only to meet the need of the person or persons involved, but also to serve as a teaching vehicle or example to the whole of humanity.

God was the Father of Adam and, as obvious, of great note. Nevertheless, man fell from this lofty position, and was reduced to spiritual blindness, in effect, the low station of a beggar. Consequently, Bartimaeus epitomizes the whole of humanity. Some would object to such a comparison, claiming that much of mankind is far above the station of *"begging."* However, the richest and most educated of men can be labeled as none other than *"beggars"* in comparison to what man was before the Fall. Man was intended to be a *"son of God,"* but, due to the Fall, he is now reduced to the place and position of a *"son of Adam"* (Gen. 5:3). As such, he is encumbered with all the terrible baggage of that terrible state. The term *"beggar"* affixed to *"blind Bartimaeus,"* therefore, is an apt description of man in his fallen state, irrespective of his financial, social, or educational status.

(47) "AND WHEN HE HEARD THAT IT WAS JESUS OF NAZARETH, HE BEGAN TO CRY OUT, AND SAY, JESUS, THOU SON OF DAVID, HAVE MERCY ON ME."

The exposition is:

This blind beggar knew that Jesus was the Messiah, but the religious leaders of Israel didn't!

JESUS OF NAZARETH

The phrase, *"And when he heard that it was Jesus of Nazareth,"* does not proclaim to us how he heard, but only that he did hear. He probably heard the great commotion of the crowd and asked someone who it was! They would have said, *"Jesus of Nazareth."*

The Name, *"Joshua of Nazareth,"* is the Name Bartimaeus would have heard because that is the Hebrew derivative of *"Jesus,"* which is Greek. Joshua, the namesake of Christ, came through this very area about 1,500 years before. At that time, God would perform a Miracle and open Jordan. Now He will open the eyes of a blind beggar.

Then, Joshua would defeat every enemy on the soil of the Promised Land. Now, Jesus will defeat *"the enemy"* of men's souls, Satan himself. Then, Joshua took the land, and it became the habitation of God's people. Now, Jesus will take Salvation, and it too will become the habitation of God's people. Then, the physical battle was won! Now, the spiritual battle will be won!

(There were many named *"Jesus,"* or *"Joshua,"* at that time; therefore, Jesus was designated by *"Nazareth"* being affixed to His Name, as that was the place of His upbringing.)

HOW DID BARTIMAEUS KNOW ABOUT JESUS?

This is the only time it is recorded that Jesus visited Jericho; however, no doubt, as His fame spread throughout all of Israel, the great Power of Christ came to the ears of this blind beggar. He, no doubt, asked, thinking of his own terrible situation, *"Can He open the eyes of the blind?"*

Of course, the answer would have been in the affirmative! From that moment, whenever it was, he undoubtedly dreamed of the time Jesus would pass this way. As well, he doubtless prayed extensively for this coming moment. To be sure, God would answer this prayer, as He will answer all prayers of such desperation.

The Scripture says that he *"heard"*! What would have happened, had he not heard? The answer is obvious.

What about the hundreds of millions in the world today who have not had the privilege to *"hear"*? Whereas Jesus could only be in one place at one time during His earthly sojourn, now, He is everywhere, at least where men will tell about Him.

Paul said, *"How shall they hear without a Preacher?"* (Rom. 10:14).

Consequently, it is the task of every Believer, with none excluded, to do all within his power, whether through prayer, giving, and witnessing, that others may hear about Jesus. As the blind beggar of so long ago, they too deserve that opportunity!

SON OF DAVID

The phrase, *"He began to cry out, and say, Jesus, Thou Son of David,"* means, in the Greek, that he kept crying over and over to Jesus. This is a *"cry"* from the soul of this man. In the *"cry"* is desperation, because he senses that this will be the only opportunity he will ever have.

Let it ever be known that anyone who will *"cry,"* as Bartimaeus cried, will be heard by our Lord.

"Son of David" was a title that referred to the Messiah. All Jews thought of David as their King, and of the Messiah as the Son of David in a special sense. So, Bartimaeus had already made up his mind that anyone who could perform the Miracles they said Jesus was performing had to be the *"Messiah."* He was right! He knew it, even though he was only a blind beggar, but the religious leaders of Israel did not know.

MERCY

The phrase, *"Have mercy on me,"* in the Greek indicates that he desired Jesus to heal him at once. The idea is that he felt that Christ may not pass this way again and, if he was to receive his eyesight, it had to be now.

The horror of living in darkness cannot even be remotely understood unless one has experienced such. The knowledge that Jesus could do it seems to have been implanted in the beggar's mind. The problem, in his imprisoned world of darkness, was to get to Him.

(48) "AND MANY CHARGED HIM THAT HE SHOULD HOLD HIS PEACE: BUT HE CRIED THE MORE A GREAT DEAL, THOU SON OF DAVID, HAVE MERCY ON ME."

The synopsis is:

The word *"charged"* is strong, meaning to *"censure severely"*; in other words, they, in no uncertain terms, were telling Bartimaeus to *"Shut up!"*

THE CHARGE

The phrase, *"And many charged him that he should hold his peace,"* proclaims the crowd attempting to stop him from getting to Jesus.

NOTES

Why were they doing this?

Perhaps they felt that Jesus, the Great Prophet, should not be troubled by this beggar; however, if these, in fact, were their thoughts, they completely misunderstood Christ and His Mission. Perhaps at the moment other things were demanding His attention, and they felt the cry of Bartimaeus was an intrusion.

At any rate, they, as we, should learn a lesson from the quest of this blind beggar.

THE CRY

The phrase, *"But he cried the more a great deal,"* proclaims their demand as having the opposite effect on him. The One Who could open his eyes was within shouting distance, and he had absolutely no intention of letting this moment pass.

This should be an example to all, inasmuch as most of the time when one truly seeks the Lord, there will be very little encouragement, if any! The crowd will mostly say, and for any number of reasons, that we cannot have for which we seek. So, if Bartimaeus had listened to the crowd, he would have remained blind. Likewise, if we listen to those who tell us we cannot reach Christ, and for whatever reason, our need also will never be met. However, if we take a lesson from this blind beggar, incidentally, who was very soon to no longer be blind, we can, as he, receive what is needed.

HAVE MERCY ON ME

The phrase, *"Thou Son of David, have mercy on me,"* proclaims such being cried with even more vigor! He did not change his petition because change was not necessary. The rich young ruler called Him *"Good Master"*; he did not receive what he asked for, because he felt the price was too high. The beggar called Him *"Son of David"*; he received everything for which he asked.

The former labeled Jesus only as a Teacher, while the latter labeled Him as *"God."* In fact, he continued to do it and did not care who heard him.

(49) "AND JESUS STOOD STILL, AND COMMANDED HIM TO BE CALLED. AND THEY CALL THE BLIND MAN, SAYING, UNTO HIM, BE OF GOOD COMFORT,

RISE; HE CALLS YOU."

The composition is:

Faith caused Jesus to stop; it will do the same presently!

JESUS STOOD STILL

The phrase, *"And Jesus stood still,"* is a beautiful and precious statement. Bartimaeus had Faith, as is evident in his continued petition. Even though Jesus was on His way to Calvary, which was the very reason for which He came, and which was the culmination of the Great Plan of God regarding the Redemption of humanity, still, on this journey which had taken so very long, actually from before the foundation of the world (I Pet. 1:18-20), and which was now coming to a climax, He would stop! This shows us the great power of Faith in God. This man, a blind beggar exhibiting his Faith, would cause Christ to stop, even though He was on His way to redeem the whole of humanity.

Among all the lessons we should learn from this episode, the lesson of Faith in God boldly stands out. No one could be in a worse position than blind Bartimaeus! It seems that very few people cared if he lived or died. He certainly had nothing going for him except one thing — his Faith in Jesus. And that is enough!

There are very few in worse shape than this man. And yet, because of his Faith, which is expressed in his determination, he received everything for which he asked. Cannot we do the same?

THE COMMAND

The phrase, *"And commanded him to be called,"* constitutes the greatest moment in the life of this blind beggar. Everything he had dreamed about, no doubt praying himself to sleep many nights, is about to be realized. The One Who spoke the worlds into existence now sends for him!

The phrase, *"And they call the blind man, saying unto him, Be of good comfort, rise; He calls you,"* proclaims the crowd obeying Christ and giving the good news to Bartimaeus.

Someone has said, *"Defeat is an orphan, while victory has many fathers."* Before Jesus recognized him, the crowd had no interest, only that he *"Shut up!"* Now that Jesus has recognized him, the mood of the crowd changes. In Truth, the Message, *"Be of good comfort, rise; He calls you,"* should be the Message of every single Believer to every lost soul. Sadly, most of the world has a misconception of God. They do not realize that His purpose is to bring *"comfort."* He also will *"pick up"* (i.e., *"rise"*) all found in His *"call."*

While it is true that tomorrow He will be the Judge, still, at the present He is the Saviour. Consequently, His *"call"* is for healing, health, happiness, joy, peace, and, above all, Salvation.

(50) "AND HE, CASTING AWAY HIS GARMENT, ROSE, AND CAME TO JESUS."

The structure is:

This was a type of garment worn only by beggars. During the day, he would spread it out for people to throw coins on it; at night, he would use it as a blanket. Bartimaeus knew he would never need it again.

CAST AWAY THE GARMENT

The two words, *"And he,"* refers to Bartimaeus receiving the Message as given by Christ, meaning that of all the people in Israel, the attention of Jesus was now solely upon him.

The phrase, *"Casting away his garment,"* has a far greater meaning than just the fact of leaving behind a garment. It is said that many beggars in those days used this outer garment for several purposes. First of all, it denoted their status as a beggar. Moreover, and as stated, it was removed during the day and used somewhat as a receptacle for gifts, being positioned on the ground accordingly. At night it was used for a covering.

When Bartimaeus *"cast away"* this garment, he was saying, in effect, that he would no longer need it. He was this sure of his healing! One can only shout, *"Hallelujah!"* The single word *"rose"* actually means that he *"leaped up"* upon hearing the call of Christ.

The phrase, *"And came to Jesus,"* was the greatest short distance he had ever traversed. His joy must have known no bounds!

(51) "AND JESUS ANSWERED AND SAID UNTO HIM, WHAT WILL YOU THAT I SHOULD DO UNTO YOU? THE BLIND MAN SAID UNTO HIM, LORD, THAT I

MIGHT RECEIVE MY SIGHT."

The exegesis is:

The question that Jesus asked is actually asked of all Believers. Our answer reveals our spiritual condition.

WHAT DO YOU WANT?

The phrase, *"And Jesus answered and said unto him,"* refers to the cry, *"Thou Son of David, have mercy on me."* The question, *"What will you that I should do unto you?"* constitutes a question that is open-ended, which could apply to anything. In other words, Jesus is saying to him, *"Whatever you need, that will I do!"*

Quite possibly, and more than likely, Jesus knew exactly what he wanted and needed, but He would ask this question in order to bring Faith to its highest pinnacle.

THE GREAT REQUEST

The phrase, *"The blind man said unto Him, Lord that I might receive my sight,"* constitutes what he was (blind), and what he wanted (sight). He minced no words! What were Bartimaeus' thoughts when he answered Christ? His heart must have been racing out of his breast. No doubt, the anticipation of the moment caused his breath to come in short gasps. The implication in the Greek is that he had at one time been able to see. He now desires to *"recover his sight."*

The word *"Lord"* is *"Rabboni"* in the Greek Text, which means *"My Master."* It was a term of reverent respect. It in no way meant to lessen his belief in Jesus as the Messiah.

(52) "AND JESUS SAID UNTO HIM, GO YOUR WAY; YOUR FAITH HAS MADE YOU WHOLE. AND IMMEDIATELY HE RECEIVED HIS SIGHT, AND FOLLOWED JESUS IN THE WAY."

The composition is:

Tradition says that Bartimaeus followed Jesus to Jerusalem and became an ardent Disciple in the Early Church.

FAITH

The phrase, *"And Jesus said unto him,"* should be an example of what Jesus says to all! To those who believe, and despite their past or present circumstances, His Words are always Words of help and healing. What a wonderful Lord we serve!

The phrase, *"Go your way; your Faith has made you whole,"* was Jesus' answer to the plea of Bartimaeus. It is said that the word *"whole"* in the Greek is in the perfect tense, and consequently speaks of a permanent cure. In other words, whatever had caused Bartimaeus to become blind would never return. He would retain his eyesight until the day he died.

The word *"whole"* in the Greek is *"sozo,"* which means *"to save."* It is used either of physical healing or spiritual Salvation. Consequently, the implication is that Bartimaeus was not only healed, but saved, as well!

As an aside, we should add that *"personal Faith"* must always be according to the Will and Word of God. Moreover, sometimes it is His *"Will"* but not His *"Wisdom"*!

THE MIRACLE

The phrase, *"And immediately he received his sight,"* means exactly what it says, i.e., that his sight returned instantly. I wonder what he did upon the opening of those blinded eyes. We do not know how many years he had remained in this condition; however, the joy that filled his heart upon his eyesight immediately being restored must have known no bounds. One can well imagine, but imagine only, such joy!

It is also very similar to the moment a person turns to Christ. Instantly, the load of sin is lifted, with the terrible guilt instantly removed. Possibly the Miracle of Jesus opening blinded eyes is the greatest example of the Born-Again experience.

The phrase, *"And followed Jesus in the way,"* is said by some to mean that he followed Jesus to Jerusalem and became a Disciple in the Early Church. If this is correct, it might explain why Mark and Luke mentioned only him and did not speak of the second blind man who was healed, whom Matthew does mention.

"Love Divine, all loves excelling,
"Joy of Heaven, to Earth come down;
"Fix in us Your humble dwelling;
"All Your faithful mercies crown."

"Jesus, You are our compassion,
"Pure, unbounded love You are;

"Visit us with Your Salvation;
"Enter every trembling heart."

"Come, Almighty, to deliver,
"Let us all Your Life receive;
"Suddenly return and never,
"Never more Your Temple leave."

"Thee we would be always blessing,
"Serve You as Your Host above,
"Pray and praise You without ceasing,
"Glory in Your Perfect Love."

CHAPTER 11

(1) "AND WHEN THEY CAME NEAR TO JERUSALEM, UNTO BETHPHAGE AND BETHANY, AT THE MOUNT OF OLIVES, HE SENT FORTH TWO OF HIS DISCIPLES."

The composition is:

Tradition says the ones sent were Peter and John.

JERUSALEM

The phrase, *"And when they came near to Jerusalem,"* concerns the last time they will visit this city before the Crucifixion. It must have been with heavy heart that Jesus drew near. Jesus was a King, but yet not just a King, but *"The King."* And yet, precious few there recognized Him as such! However, as is the manner of God, the opportunity will be given Israel, as recorded in this Chapter, to recognized her King. It is called the *"Triumphant Entry."* Even though the Person of Christ will be triumphant as always, still, it would be anything but such for Israel.

They would deny their King, and consequently go to their doom. To accept Christ is to accept life; to refuse Christ is to refuse life and to, therefore, accept death!

There are only two ways to go: *"Life"* or *"death."* The only way to *"Life"* is through Jesus Christ (Jn. 14:6). And, of course, the *"Life"* addressed is *"Eternal Life,"* referring to the Life of God.

The *"death"* addressed here is spiritual death, which is eternal separation from God, which means eternal separation from Life.

BETHPHAGE AND BETHANY

The phrase, *"Unto Bethphage and Bethany,"* concerns two villages close to Jerusalem, east of the city. They would have been on the way from Jericho to Jerusalem, a distance of about 17 miles. From Jericho to Jerusalem was about a day's journey. The road is winding, through a hilly, rugged, even desolate area. It was often plagued by robbers and bandits. But today, the Son of God would traverse its distance.

"Bethphage" means *"house of figs,"* while *"Bethany"* means *"house of dates."* As stated, they were very close together, approximately a mile separating the two. It appears from John 12:1 that Jesus arrived in this area *"six days before the Passover,"* i.e., six days before His Crucifixion.

Bethany was the home of Jesus' beloved friends, Mary, Martha, and Lazarus. Its most central role in the Gospel history is as the place of Jesus' Anointing, as Mark will later relate (Mk. 14:3-9).

MOUNT OF OLIVES

The phrase, *"At the Mount of Olives,"* figures a very prominent place in the Gospel narrative. It is a small range of four summits, the highest being about 3,000 feet. This high summit overlooks Jerusalem and the Temple Mount from the east across the Kidron Valley and the Pool of Siloam.

It was thickly wooded in Jesus' day, rich in olives which occasioned its name. It was stripped of trees when Titus, the Roman General, invaded Jerusalem. On a clear day, its summit can be seen from the Jordan River near Jericho, where tradition says Jesus was baptized, a distance of approximately 20 miles.

This Mount is the site of Gethsemane, and from its tallest peak the place of the Ascension of Jesus, where Zechariah said He would also touch down at the Second Coming (Zech. 14:4). It is also the area from which Jesus made the triumphant entry into Jerusalem.

Approximately a thousand years before, after Solomon completed the Temple, the Mount of Olives was famous for observing this beautiful edifice. It is said that pilgrims, travelers, and merchants, on their way into the city, would purposely spend the night on Olivet in order that they might see the rising of the Sun the following morning. As the Sun rose in the east, it would burst above Olivet, casting its rays on the two Temple columns, which were made of brightly polished copper. The Sun's rays striking these pillars, it is said, produced an amazing array of light. Now the greatest Light of all, the Lord Jesus Christ, of which the other was only a symbol, will grace its summit.

TWO OF HIS DISCIPLES

The phrase, *"He sent forth two of His Disciples,"* does not tell us which two, but many suppose they were Peter and John, because a little after this Christ sent these two to prepare for the Passover. Their Mission will pertain to the Triumphant Entry. From that day until the present, He is still *"sending forth His Disciples"* to tell the world of another Triumphant Entry soon to come, the Second Coming of Jesus Christ. Linked with the great Salvation Message (so Great a Salvation), it is the greatest story ever told!

(2) "AND SAID UNTO THEM, GO YOUR WAY INTO THE VILLAGE OVER AGAINST YOU: AND AS SOON AS YOU BE ENTERED INTO IT, YOU SHALL FIND A COLT TIED, WHEREON NEVER MAN SAT; LOOSE HIM, AND BRING HIM."

The diagram is:

This village was probably Bethphage, because it was nearer.

THE COLT

The phrase, *"And said unto them, Go your way into the village over against you,"* was probably, as just stated, Bethphage. The phrase, *"And as soon as you be entered into it, you shall find a colt tied,"* refers to a Word of Knowledge given to Jesus by the Holy Spirit, because the Master would not have known this otherwise (I Cor. 12:8).

All nine Gifts of the Spirit, as would be obvious, were possessed by Christ. Due to the Advent of the Holy Spirit, certain Gifts can be had by modern Believers, as well (Acts 2:1-4; I Cor. 12:8-10); however, I think no one can say that these Gifts of the Spirit work in the lives of Believers as they did in Christ, not even remotely so! He walked so after the Spirit that the Communion was constant.

NOTES

As well, He always did the Father's Will, which even the most consecrated Believer cannot claim.

JESUS, THE SERVANT

The phrase, *"Whereon never man sat,"* presents another unique situation in the Life and Ministry of Christ. He was born of one who *"did not know a man"* and was buried where *"no one was ever yet laid."* Now He will ride an animal *"whereon never man sat."*

The phrase, *"Loose him, and bring him,"* means it is to be done at once! Matthew not only mentions the colt, but also the mother of the animal. Mark, Luke, and John only mention the one animal. According to Matthew, the mother of the colt will accompany them. The two animals spoken of by Matthew could well have represented both Israel and the Gentiles. The mother of the colt, which probably trod alongside, would denote Israel, who would not accept Christ. The unbroken *"colt"* ridden by Christ could denote the Gentile Church, which would, in effect, accept Christ.

Inasmuch as Matthew presented Jesus as King, the mentioning of both animals would have been appropriate for Him, whereas it would not have served any consequence with Mark, Luke, and John, due to the manner in which they presented Christ in their Gospels. (Matthew presented Jesus as King; Mark, as Servant; Luke, as Man; and John presented Him as God. However, there would have been some of all in each presentation.)

(3) "AND IF ANY MAN SAY UNTO YOU, WHY DO YE THIS? SAY YE THAT THE LORD HAS NEED OF HIM; AND STRAIGHTWAY HE WILL SEND HIM HITHER."

The overview is:

The Holy Spirit revealed to Christ that the man would give permission for the colt to be used.

JESUS AS KING

The question, *"And if any man say unto you, Why do ye this?"* represents the possible contingency of such, which did happen, the idea being that if the owners objected, the Lord would not use the animal. If one is to notice, there is a strong authority presented by Christ throughout the entirety of this scenario. Jesus, at least at this time, is functioning as King, and King's little ask permission; consequently, there is no evidence that preparation had been made at all for the borrowing of this animal, but only the sudden request, with the instant approval by the owners.

THE LORD HAS NEED OF HIM

The phrase, *"Say ye that the Lord has need of him,"* represents a remarkable statement. Is it proper to say that presently the Lord *"has need"* of certain things in order that His Work be carried out?

As God, the Lord needs nothing! However, inasmuch as He has allowed Believers to be a part of His Work on Earth, in that context He does *"need"* certain things. For the Holy Spirit to do what must be done, and I speak of the taking of the Gospel to the world, the Lord *"needs"* consecration on the part of Believers. As well, He *"needs"* Believers to exhibit their Faith, trusting Him for the Work to be done.

In the consecration of Believers, He *"needs"* Believers to pray and intercede on behalf of the lost. As well, He *"needs"* Believers to give generously of their income in order that this Work be accomplished. Furthermore, the Lord *"needs"* Preachers to not fail to preach the Cross, without which there is no True Gospel. That being the case, we can easily see just how important this is (I Cor. 1:17-18, 21, 23; 2:2). So, the scenario of this *"colt,"* i.e., the manner in which Jesus secured him, is to be a lesson to all Believers everywhere, and for all time.

The phrase, *"And straightway he will send him hither,"* proclaims the Lord knowing in advance that the owners of this animal would immediately acquiesce to the request of the two Disciples.

Do all Believers obey that quickly?

(4) "AND THEY WENT THEIR WAY, AND FOUND THE COLT TIED BY THE DOOR WITHOUT IN A PLACE WHERE TWO WAYS MET; AND THEY LOOSE HIM."

The exposition is:

"Their way" was *"His Way."*

THE WORD OF THE LORD IS ALWAYS SURE

The phrase, *"And they went their way,"* proclaims the obedience of the Disciples. The phrase, *"And found the colt tied by the door without in a place where two ways met,"* referred to an intersection where two streets crossed. The *"colt"* was exactly where Jesus said it would be.

The phrase, *"And they loose him,"* concerns their doing exactly what Jesus had said! They did not at first ask permission, but proceeded to take the animal. They were then questioned by the owners.

No! Jesus would not have allowed the animal to have been taken without permission. However, the Disciples were instructed in this manner as to what to do, because Jesus knew the owners would be nearby and would give permission. The entire scenario speaks of a prearranged plan, which it was — arranged by the Holy Spirit.

This is the reason that Believers should seek the Lord incessantly, in order that they may know His Mind. To follow and obey Him is an exciting journey! To be sure, He continues to do the same presently, as He did 2,000 years ago.

A PERSONAL EXPERIENCE

Back in about 1970, if I remember the year correctly, we applied to the F.C.C. (Federal Communications Commission) in Washington, D.C., for the right to purchase a bankrupt radio station in Baton Rouge, Louisiana, WLUX-AM. At that time, Baton Rouge had no Christian Radio whatsoever, and I felt the Lord wanted this Station in this city, which would broadcast Gospel constantly.

The securing of the Station was not easy or simple, due to Satan doing everything possible to hinder all along the way; however, it eventually became ours, which proved to be a blessing to the greater Baton Rouge area.

One particular episode in the securing of this facility stands out, which is somewhat similar to the Disciples sent to fetch the colt. The F.C.C. had ruled that all who desired the Station could bid on it, with the highest bidder being awarded the Station. There were to be only two bidders, myself and another man, who desired to air a Rock-'n'-Roll format. We were to meet at the office of a particular lawyer in the city, who had been appointed as the referee by the F.C.C. The meeting was scheduled for 10 a.m.

That morning in prayer the Lord spoke to my heart and told me to go to the bank and get the sum of $250,000, which I did. It was not in cash, but in Certificates of Deposit, which are as good as cash. At that time, the Lord did not tell me why I was to do this, but just to do it. I obeyed; I went to the bank and secured the Certificates, putting them in my inside coat pocket. No one knew I had these funds, not even my lawyer.

THE MEETING

At 10 a.m. sharp, several of us met at the appointed place. A lawyer from Washington was present, representing our side, as well as the lawyer I had secured from Baton Rouge. The other man also was there to bid against me and, of course, the referee was present, as well.

For some unknown reason, which I think was orchestrated by the Holy Spirit, the referee had ruled that the bid could go no higher than $80,000. As the bidding began, both of us quickly arrived at the $80,000 level. The bidding then stopped, per the instructions. (I think that was the amount the Station owed its creditors, etc.)

Now, we faced an impasse, with both of us bidding the same amount. How could this deadlock be broken? The lawyers began to propose several things, when the Spirit of the Lord spoke to me again, telling me to ask the referee to make the other bidder prove that he actually had $80,000. I immediately ventured the question, and the other bidder quickly became uncomfortable. He stated that we was certain he could borrow the money if the bid were awarded to him.

I then remonstrated by saying, *"Your honor, what happens if he cannot borrow the money? It seems to me that whoever is awarded the bid to purchase the Station today should be able to prove that he has the money to do so!"*

The referee thought for a moment, and surmised that my remarks were correct. The other man obviously could not prove at that moment that he could secure the necessary funds, and I now knew why the Holy Spirit had told me that morning to bring the Certificates, without telling anyone about it.

THE CRITICAL MOMENT!

All the time, both of my lawyers were whispering in my ear, telling me to *"Shut up!"* As stated, they did not know what I knew, namely, that I had the CD's in my inside coat pocket. My own lawyers were quickly growing exasperated with me, with one of them saying to me, *"If you don't be quiet, we're going to lose this Station."*

I kept wondering when the referee (the judge) would turn from the other bidder to me to ask me if I could produce the funds. Finally, it happened! The referee looked at me and stated, *"You have been questioning this man about his ability to get the funds should he be awarded the bid. Can you produce the funds, or prove that you can obtain them?"*

I heard one of my lawyers groan, and the room grew deathly quiet. I reached into my inside coat pocket, pulled out the CD's totaling $250,000, and laid them on the table. For a moment you could have heard the proverbial pin drop. The referee, plus one of my lawyers, picked up the negotiable instruments, looked carefully at them, and realized they were CD's and were consequently as good as cash.

My lawyer then began to jump up and down, saying, *"Your honor, we obviously have the money, so you must award us the bid!"*

The referee turned to the opposing bidder and said, *"Can you match this?"*

Of course, he could not!

I remember him grabbing his brief case and suddenly leaving the room, saying, *"I am in the wrong business."*

The referee turned to me and said, *"I award you the Station."*

We operated WLUX for over twenty years, constantly proclaiming the Gospel of Jesus Christ to the city of Baton Rouge and surrounding areas. It was sold in 1995 to another Church in Baton Rouge, after the Lord gave us a twenty-four hour FM Station (WJFM-FM).

(The AM Station was a day-timer, with the FM Station giving around-the-clock coverage.)

If the Lord had not spoken to my heart that morning about securing those Certificates, there is a possibility I would not have been awarded the Station; however, to follow Him is to guarantee success. Consequently, the colt was secured, and the Radio Station was secured, all because of leading and direction by the Lord.

(5) "AND CERTAIN OF THEM WHO STOOD THERE SAID UNTO THEM, WHAT DO YE, LOOSING THE COLT?"

The synopsis is:

This represents that no prior arrangements had been made for securing the colt.

THE QUESTION

The phrase, *"And certain of them who stood there said unto them,"* represents the owners, as Luke identifies them (Lk. 19:33).

The question, *"What do ye, loosing the colt?"* represents, as stated, that no prior arrangements had been made.

What must have been the thoughts of these men as they saw the Disciples, who they probably did not know, taking the colt? Little did they realize that this animal which belonged to them was about to be used by the Creator of the ages. How blessed and honored they were!

How blessed and honored is anyone who is privileged to have a part in the Work of God!

Would they have been privileged to have loaned their colt to the Chief Priests, who crucified Christ? I think the answer to that would be obvious! And yet, millions of Believers support that which is not of God and which, in effect, opposes the Lord, while all the time they think they are supporting the Lord and His Work.

We need to know to whom we are loaning our *"colt"*!

(6) "AND THEY SAID UNTO THEM EVEN AS JESUS HAD COMMANDED: AND THEY LET THEM GO."

The structure is:

What a privilege these men had to lend their colt to Christ!

THE REQUEST HONORED

The phrase, *"And they said unto them even as Jesus had commanded,"* were the words, *"The Lord has need of him."* The phrase, *"And they let them go,"* respects an instant obedience. This shows that they knew Jesus, although possibly not being personally acquainted with Him. His Name, Fame, and Reputation had spread throughout all of Israel, causing all to know Him.

There is no record that the owners questioned the Disciples further, not actually knowing for what purpose the animal was to be used. As stated, how honored they were to be privileged to have a part in the *"Triumphant Entry."* Little did they realize that this simple act of loaning their colt to Christ would be preached about, sung about, talked about, and prayed about for thousands of years, actually for eternity.

As someone has well said, *"This life will soon be past, and only what is done for Christ will last!"*

How privileged all of us are to have a part in the Work of God.

(7) "AND THEY BROUGHT THE COLT TO JESUS, AND CAST THEIR GARMENTS ON HIM; AND HE SAT UPON HIM."

The exegesis is:

This proclaims the beginning of the Triumphal Entry; this was a fulfillment of the Prophecy given by Zechariah (Zech. 9:9).

THE TRIUMPHANT ENTRY

The phrase, *"And they brought the colt to Jesus,"* shows that the Disciples did not, at least at this time, know the purpose of the animal. Consequently, if the owners had asked them, they would not have been able to give an answer beyond *"The Lord has need of him"*! What that *"need"* was, they did not at that time know.

The phrase, *"And cast their garments on him,"* proclaims Jesus finally telling them He is to ride the animal. Even now, they probably did not know why He would ride him. The Disciples probably took extra garments they had brought with them, placing them on the animal's back.

The phrase, *"And He sat upon him,"* proclaims the beginning of the Triumphant Entry.

Several things should be noted:

THE FULFILLMENT OF ZECHARIAH'S PROPHECY

This was in fulfillment of the Prophecy as given by Zechariah, *"Rejoice greatly, O daughter of Zion; shout, O daughter of Jerusalem: behold, your King comes unto you: He is just, and having Salvation; lowly, and riding upon an ass, and upon a colt the foal of an ass"* (Zech. 9:9).

Had Israel accepted her King at that time, the Kingdom of God would have come, physically, materially, and spiritually. Inasmuch as Israel rejected her King, the *"Times of the Gentiles"* were lengthened; whereas, had Jesus been accepted, they would have been brought to an end. As a result, the world, and for some 2,000 years, has been afflicted by war, poverty, famine, plagues, and pestilence. As well, Israel has suffered horribly so, which all could have been avoided upon acceptance of Christ.

When Jesus comes again, which He certainly shall, Israel will then accept Him, with the *"Times of the Gentiles"* coming to an end, and with Israel finally taking her place as the conduit of the Blessings of God, which the Lord intended from the beginning (Lk. 21:24).

PEACEFUL INTENTIONS

Jesus sitting on the back of this colt, the foal of an ass, portrayed to any and all that His intentions were peaceful and consequently carried no threat, as he was later accused (Lk. 23:2). In fact, in times of old, the riding of an *"ass"* denoted leadership and great importance (Judg. 5:10; 10:4); however, all of this changed with the advent of Alexander the Great, about 300 years before Christ. Then the war-horse replaced the lowly *"ass"* as a symbol of pomp, power, and majesty.

So, if Jesus had intended to do that of which they accused Him, namely insurrection against Rome, He would not have ridden this lowly *"colt,"* but rather a war-horse. In truth, at the Second Coming, when He will come in Power and Glory, He then will be riding a war-horse (Rev. 19:11).

THE DESTRUCTION OF ISRAEL

The rejection of Israel of the presentation by Jesus of Himself as King of Israel would seal the doom of that nation. Their rejection of Him caused to be thrown aside the only protection they had, which was God. Without Him, they would be left to the mercy of the world, which would show little mercy, as the last 2,000 years have verified.

During this time, Israel has wandered as a people all over the world, scattered as outcasts and, regrettably, despised by most all. Only since 1948 have they had a place they could call home, once again the sacred land of Israel. And yet, they are in constant turmoil respecting their claim, with even now (as I dictate these words) portions of it being given to the Palestinians.

Sadly, their times of sorrow and trouble have not ended, with the coming of the Great Tribulation, as proclaimed by Jesus, to be the worst of all (Mat. 24:21). Nevertheless, they will yet accept Christ, which will be at the Second Coming, with this scenario, i.e., the Triumphant Entry, being played out once again, but then with a different conclusion.

(8) "AND MANY SPREAD THEIR GARMENTS IN THE WAY: AND OTHERS CUT DOWN BRANCHES OFF THE TREES, AND STRAWED THEM IN THE WAY."

The composition is:

This was His formal presentation of Himself as the Messiah; as is obvious, it would be rejected.

JESUS' PRESENTATION OF HIMSELF AS THE MESSIAH

The phrase, *"And many spread their garments in the way,"* represents the crowd understanding what Jesus was doing. Of course, the Disciples also understood it now, as well!

Robertson says that the deliberate conduct of Jesus here could have but one meaning, namely, that this was His formal presentation of Himself as the Messiah. The crowds realized this and entered into the spirit of the occasion. However, the attitude of the people would have been the same as that of the Disciples, expecting the Lord to set up His rule in opposition to that of Rome, and consequently to deliver them from the yoke of their oppressors.

Jesus definitely would have delivered them; however, it would be from a far greater oppressor, Satan himself! But this they did not know or understand; furthermore, it was a deliverance that most of them did not believe they needed. Observing Jesus on the animal riding toward Jerusalem, the people, as the

Disciples, began to throw their garments on the road in order to make a grand procession.

The phrase, *"And others cut down branches off the trees, and strawed them in the way,"* probably referred to palm fronds, as well as olive branches, etc. At any rate, it was a sign of their approval, but certainly did not include the Chief Priests and Scribes, etc. In fact, this very action by Christ would arouse the anger of the Sadducees, who occupied the High Priestly offices of Israel, which had actually been given to them by Rome. They saw this as a threat to their position, which brought them much power and money. (The office of the High Priest at that time was appointed by Rome, and consequently was not occupied by a descendant of Aaron, as it should have been.)

(9) "AND THEY WHO WENT BEFORE, AND THEY WHO FOLLOWED, CRIED, SAYING, HOSANNA: BLESSED IS HE WHO COMES IN THE NAME OF THE LORD."

The diagram is:

This acclamation was taken from Psalms 118:25-26.

HOSANNA

The phrase, *"And they who went before, and they who followed, cried, saying,"* represented crowds at both the back and front of Jesus. The crowds could well have numbered into the thousands, with possibly hundreds among them who had been healed by Christ; most of the them, consequently, knew Him, with many of them believing He was actually the Messiah.

The phrase, *"Hosanna; Blessed is He Who comes in the Name of the LORD,"* is taken from Psalms 118:25-26. The word *"Hosanna"* means *"O say."* The word *"Blessed"* means *"to eulogize"* or *"to praise."* This acclamation was given at the *"Feast of Tabernacles,"* as the Priests marched once daily for seven days around the Altar, with palm branches in their hands, etc.

On the eighth day, they marched seven times, which was the *"Great Hosanna,"* somewhat reminiscent of Jericho.

THE FEAST OF TABERNACLES

Even though this was now the time of the Passover, still, these people knew from the Prophecies of Zechariah that *"The Feast of Tabernacles"* would be kept in the coming Kingdom Age (Zech. 14:16). Believing that Jesus was now about to take the Throne, they felt the great Kingdom Age was now beginning, hence, the *"Hosannas,"* and also the garments and branches being spread on the road.

Some would say that these same people who were now shouting the praises of Christ would, some five days later, clamor for His life; however, that is untrue! The trial of Jesus took place at night, when these people would have been in bed. The ones who clamored for His Life were, by and large, the Chief Priests, Scribes, Pharisees, and the rabble of the city.

(10) "BLESSED BE THE KINGDOM OF OUR FATHER DAVID, WHO COMES IN THE NAME OF THE LORD: HOSANNA IN THE HIGHEST."

The exposition is:

This means that they were saying that Jesus was the Highest One, i.e., the only One Who could save them.

THE KINGDOM OF OUR FATHER DAVID

The phrase, *"Blessed be the Kingdom of our Father David,"* should have been translated, *"Blessed be the Kingdom that comes, the Kingdom of our Father David."* As we have stated, Israel looked at David as their Father, and likewise the Messiah as his Son, which He actually was (II Sam., Chpt. 7). The *"Kingdom"* spoken of is the *"Kingdom Age,"* when Jesus will rule and reign Personally from Jerusalem. The crowd thought this was the time; however, the religious leaders did not!

In truth, the *"Kingdom Age"* has not even yet come, but most assuredly will, upon the Second Advent of Christ.

JESUS

The phrase, *"Who comes in the Name of the Lord,"* should have been translated, *"Who cometh...."* Jesus was that Person!

The phrase, *"Hosanna in the highest,"* meant that He was the Highest One, and consequently the only One Who could save them. In that, they were correct, but did not fully understand His Mission. They thought only of themselves and their nation, actually giving very little consideration to the Gentiles, if any at all!

They really did not fully understand what the *"Kingdom Age"* actually meant. They saw only greatness and glory for themselves, not really realizing that their great need was Deliverance from sin, which could only be brought about by Calvary. Regrettably, the Church has by and large followed suit, never quite understanding the real need.

Even at the present time, much of the modern Church is busily engaged in pursuits which have little true bearing on the True Purpose of God. Jesus is attempting to pull the Church to Himself, while the Church is busily engaged in *"get rich quick"* schemes. While the Church should be confessing *"The Lord Jesus,"* it is instead busily confessing prosperity and such like, which, of course, the Lord will never honor (Rom. 10:9-10).

So, as the *"Kingdom"* was denied Israel at that time, likewise, it presently is denied to many in the modern Church.

(11) "AND JESUS ENTERED INTO JERUSALEM, AND INTO THE TEMPLE: AND WHEN HE HAD LOOKED ROUND ABOUT UPON ALL THINGS, AND NOW THE EVENTIDE WAS COME, HE WENT OUT UNTO BETHANY WITH THE TWELVE."

The overview is:

It was probably Sunday. If so, one week later Jesus would rise from the dead; consequently, the intervening week would be one of such magnitude of sorrow as to defy description.

THE TEMPLE

The phrase, *"And Jesus entered into Jerusalem, and into the Temple,"* represents a visit not recorded by Matthew. At this time, He will not cleanse the Temple, but will do so the next day. It would not have been the proper time at the moment, due to the fact that He had just concluded the Triumphant Entry, with, no doubt, many of these people near Him presently.

The part of the Temple into which Jesus went was probably the *"Court of the Gentiles."* He would not have gone into the inner structure containing the Holy Place and Holy of Holies, because He was not a Priest after the Order of Aaron, but rather after the Order of Melchizedek.

The phrase, *"And when He had looked round about upon all things,"* presents a searching, penetrating gaze, which was a comprehensive inspection. He observed all the haggling, bartering, and arguing over prices, etc. The *"Court of the Gentiles"* was more than likely where this action took place, which would have kept any Gentiles from worshipping God, for which it was originally intended.

The entire situation would have grieved Him to no end; however, that which was taking place in the *"Court of the Gentiles"* was indicative of all of Israel. Judaism had degenerated into religion, which was no more than a business. Regrettably, the religion business is just as rampant presently as then!

The phrase, *"And now the eventide was come, He went out unto Bethany with the Twelve,"* probably refers to the home of Lazarus, which He often visited when in this vicinity. However, it could well have referred to the open air on the Mount of Olives. This momentous day was drawing to a close and Jesus would retire for the night. It was probably Sunday. If so, one week later Jesus would rise from the dead; consequently, the intervening week would be beyond comprehension.

(12) "AND ON THE MORROW, WHEN THEY WERE COME FROM BETHANY, HE WAS HUNGRY."

The exposition is:

This suggests it was Monday. Matthew says it was early, probably before 6 a.m.

THE MAN, JESUS CHRIST

The phrase, *"And on the morrow,"* suggests, as stated, that it was Monday. The phrase, *"When they were come from Bethany, He was hungry,"* suggests one of two things:

1. He and His Disciples spent the night at the home of Lazarus, arose before dawn, and slipped out without breakfast before the host arose; or,

2. They had spent the night in the open air on Mount Olivet; consequently, they would have had nothing for breakfast.

Many do not quite understand the Incarnation of Christ. They think of Him as somewhat half-God and half-Man. This is totally incorrect. Jesus was Very God and Very Man. In other words, He was 100 percent God and 100 percent Man. However, He did not at all use His attributes of Deity while in the Incarnate state. As someone has said, *"He lost, or freely laid aside, His expression of Deity, while never losing the possession of Deity."*

Paul said, *"But made Himself of no reputation, and took upon Him the form of a servant, and was made in the likeness of men"* (Phil. 2:7).

The word *"made"* in the Greek is *"keno,"* which means *"to empty out"* or *"to make void."* In other words, Christ *"emptied Himself."*

OF WHAT DID CHRIST EMPTY HIMSELF?

It could not have been His Divine Nature, for He was God not only from all eternity (Mic. 5:1-2; Jn. 1:1-2; Heb. 1:8; Rev. 1:8-11), but also God manifest in the flesh during His Life on Earth (Isa. 7:14; 9:6-7; Mat. 1:18-25; Jn. 1:1-2, 14; I Tim. 3:16).

Concerning the self-emptying of Christ, Wuest says, *"He did not empty Himself of His Deity, since Paul says that the expression of His Deity was a fact after His Incarnation, that expression implying the possession of the essence of Deity* (Phil. 2:7). *He set aside the outward expression of His Deity when expressing Himself as a bondslave. It was the outward expression of the essence of His Deity of which our Lord emptied Himself during the time when He was giving outward expression of Himself as a bondslave.*

"But the emptying Himself of the expression of Deity is more implied by the context than stated specifically by the verb 'emptied.' When our Lord set aside the expression of Deity in order that He might express Himself as a bondslave, He was setting aside His legitimate and natural desires and prerogatives as Deity. The basic, natural desire and prerogative of Deity is that of being glorified.

"But when Deity sets these aside, it sets its desires aside, and setting its desires aside, it sets Self aside. The pronoun 'Himself' is in the accusative case. The action of the verb terminates in the thing expressed by that case. The act of emptying terminated in the Self-life of the Son of God. Our Lord emptied Himself of Self. This agrees perfectly with the context which is an example of humility and self-abnegation for the benefit of others. This setting aside of 'Self' by the Son of God was the example that Paul held before the Saints at Philippi."

Wuest goes on to say, *"Our Lord's humanity was real. He was really a Man, but He was not a real man in the sense that He was like others of the human race, only a man. He was always in His Incarnation more than man. There was always that single personality with a dual nature. His Deity did not make Him more or less than a Man, and His humanity did not make Him less than absolute Deity. He became in the likeness of man, and He was found and fashioned as a man.*

"'Likeness' states the fact of His real resemblance to men in mode of existence, and 'fashioned' defines the outward form as it appeared in the eyes of men. But He was not found and fashioned as a man. In fact, the indefinite article 'a' should not be in the translation. He was found in outward guise as man, not 'a' man. He was not a man, but God, although He had assumed human nature, yet without its sin."

UNDERSTANDING THE INCARNATION

We, as mortals, have some understanding of the Incarnation of Christ, i.e., God becoming Man, but only up to a point. Beyond that point, our comprehension falls down. In other words, we simply do not understand the Incarnation totally. And the wonder of all of this is that Jesus, as a result of the Incarnation, will forever have a human body, albeit Glorified.

And yet, in a sense, He is greater now than He was before the Incarnation. Before the Incarnation, all during eternity past, He was the Creator. He remains the Creator, but now He also is the Saviour. So, this makes Him greater!

(13) "AND SEEING A FIG TREE AFAR OFF HAVING LEAVES, HE CAME, IF HAPLY HE MIGHT FIND ANY THING THEREON: AND WHEN HE CAME TO IT, HE FOUND NOTHING BUT LEAVES; FOR THE TIME OF FIGS WAS NOT YET."

The overview is:

The last phrase means that despite its appearance, which suggested fruit (and there should have been fruit), it was barren.

THE BARREN FIG TREE

The phrase, *"And seeing a fig tree afar off having leaves,"* constituted the variety which bore early figs (Isa. 28:4; Jer. 24:2). *"Fig trees"* probably were plentiful in the area of Bethphage, because its very name means *"the house of figs."* Consequently, seeing such a tree growing at random on public property was nothing unusual. This would answer the question of the critics of Christ who decry His right to curse this tree.

The phrase, *"He came, if haply He might find anything thereon,"* means that according to all appearances, there should have been figs. The phrase, *"And when He came to it, He found nothing but leaves,"* means it was absolutely fruitless. The phrase, *"For the time of figs was not yet,"* means something different than the phrase sounds. In fact, there should have been fruit, but there was none.

(14) "AND JESUS ANSWERED AND SAID UNTO IT, NO MAN EAT FRUIT OF YOU HEREAFTER FOR EVER. AND HIS DISCIPLES HEARD IT."

The synopsis is:

The barren fruit tree was symbolic of the Jewish nation. A curse was placed on the fig tree, not necessarily for being barren, but for being false. Moreover, the word *"forever"* should have been translated *"for the age,"* that is, until the Times of the Gentiles would be fulfilled. This will be at the Second Coming.

THE CURSE

The phrase, *"And Jesus answered and said unto it,"* proclaims the Lord forgetting his natural hunger in the thought of the spiritual figure which the sight of this tree began to present to His mind. No doubt, as He looked at the tree, He also saw Israel, which had the leaves of a great profession, but yielded no fruit. The phrase, *"No man eat fruit of you hereafter forever,"* speaks of the Jewish nation. It promised much, but delivered nothing, exactly as this fig tree.

The phrase, *"And His Disciples heard it,"* somewhat lends credence to the thought that Jesus at that time did not necessarily do this thing concerning the fig tree for the benefit of the Disciples. But yet, the Holy Spirit saw to it that they were witnesses.

Concerning this, Bickersteth says, *"This Miracle would show His Disciples how soon He could have withered His enemies who were about to crucify Him; but He waited with longsuffering for their Salvation, by Repentance and Faith in Him."* Even though the Repentance has not yet materialized, one can rest certain that most assuredly it shall. We speak of the Restoration of Israel at a Coming Glad Day.

(15) "AND THEY COME TO JERUSALEM: AND JESUS WENT INTO THE TEMPLE, AND BEGAN TO CAST OUT THEM WHO SOLD AND BOUGHT IN THE TEMPLE, AND OVERTHREW THE TABLES OF THE MONEYCHANGERS, AND THE SEATS OF THEM WHO SOLD DOVES."

The exegesis is:

This refers to the fact that the condition of the Temple, spiritually speaking, had been on His Mind all night; He was probably in the Court of the Gentiles.

THE CLEANSING OF THE TEMPLE

The phrase, *"And they come to Jerusalem,"* should have constituted the city utterly joyous because the One Who had chosen Jerusalem, that His Name might be there, was in their midst (II Chron. 6:6). Instead, in a matter of hours, the city would find its religious leaders scheming as to how they could put to death the very One Whom they claimed to serve, but yet did not know Him. The Holy Spirit, in giving us this phrase, does so with the sob of a broken heart. The actions of Jerusalem would seal its own doom!

The phrase, *"And Jesus went into the Temple, and began to cast out them who sold and bought in the Temple,"* concerned this area minutely overseen by the High Priest. The booths of this market are mentioned in the Rabbinical Writings as the booths of the son of Hanan, or Annas; however, this market is never mentioned in the Old Testament, and seems to have sprung up after the captivity.

The phrase, *"And overthrew the tables of*

the moneychangers," concerned traders who exchanged money, in other words, exchanging Jewish coins for foreign coins. Many of the foreign coins had idols on them and, therefore, were not acceptable by the Jews, at least for Temple usage. As a result of the exchange, some of these moneychangers grew very wealthy.

ARE THERE MONEYCHANGERS IN THE MODERN CHURCH?

Unfortunately, yes! For instance, the Catholic doctrine of Purgatory, a place which does not, in fact, even exist, takes in untold amounts of money, as people pay to get their loved ones extricated. Moneychangers!

Furthermore, some of the schemes promoted in order to raise money in some Pentecostal and Charismatic efforts can only be labeled as *"moneychangers"*! A particular *"Brother"* looks into a Television camera, telling the people that the Spirit of the Lord has just come upon him and told him that everything given in the next fifteen minutes, etc., will be returned a hundredfold. Moneychangers! Or, the Preacher says, *"If you will give a thousand dollars, every bill you have will be paid in six months, even including the mortgage on your house."* Moneychangers!

Under such gimmickry, the people will not receive a hundredfold return. They will, in fact, lose what they give, as well as having the dubious honor of aiding and abetting Satan! In fact, the entirety of the *"Prosperity Message"* scheme, so-called, falls under the same category. One could say the same for money spent on the promotion of false doctrine. Somebody raised those funds under the pretext of promoting the Gospel. Maybe they were sincere, but being sincerely wrong in no way changes the outcome.

POINTS TO PONDER

The following should be some things we should consider, as it regards our giving:

1. Are we supporting the preaching of the Cross? If the Gospel that is being supported is not the *"Cross,"* i.e., *"Jesus Christ and Him Crucified,"* then we are supporting something that is false (I Cor. 1:17-18, 21, 23; 2:2). Supporting that which is not the True Gospel can never be sanctioned by the Lord!

2. Are we sure the Preacher we are supporting is honest? The reason dishonest Preachers can survive, even prosper, and even greatly so, is because they appeal to the flesh, and the flesh responds. In other words, we support what we are, which means that we need to read that line very carefully. In other words, larceny supports larceny, even as fraud supports fraud.

3. Millions support certain Denominations simply because that is their Denomination. Never mind that the Denomination quit preaching the Gospel many decades ago. If, in fact, that it correct, it should not be supported.

When we give money, we are actually giving of ourselves. As well, we are giving to that which proposes to be the Work of God, which makes it very, very important! As a result, we should know where our money is going, what it is supporting, and the results.

Tragically, the modern Temple is filled with moneychangers!

THE COURT OF THE GENTILES

The phrase, *"And the seats of them who sold doves,"* concerned those used in Sacrifices, that is, if the person could not afford a lamb or a bullock. Not only were the animals sold, but also *"wine, oil, salt, etc., and whatever else was used in the ritual."* This area was quite large; some say it was as big as three football fields. As the Lord began to cast out these traffickers, He made no distinction between sellers and buyers.

This *"Court of the Gentiles"* was supposed to be a place where Gentiles could come to pray. However, who could pray in a place which was both a cattle-market and an exchange, where the lowing of oxen mingled with the clinking of silver and the haggling of the dealers and those who came to purchase?

(16) "AND WOULD NOT SUFFER THAT ANY MAN SHOULD CARRY ANY VESSEL THROUGH THE TEMPLE."

The overview is:

Christ would have the whole of His Father's House regarded as sacred.

NO GOSPEL OF UNITY HERE!

The idea of this statement regarding Christ

concerned people on their everyday duties taking a shortcut through the Temple, as they went from one side of the city to the other. Such saved distance and time. So the Priests permitted servants and laborers, laden with goods, to take the shorter way through the great court of the Temple.

Jesus, if one could imagine this scenario, would have held up His Hand, and with an authority which could not be denied, compelled these individuals to go back. He would have the whole of His Father's House regarded as sacred. Consequently, when Jesus upset the tables of the moneychangers, and the *"seats of them who sold doves,"* etc., especially that it was at the Passover, i.e., the height of activity for the year, the anger of the High Priest would have known no bounds. It hit them in the pocketbook, because a large profit was made from these activities, especially at this time of the year.

(17) "AND HE TAUGHT, SAYING UNTO THEM, IS IT NOT WRITTEN, MY HOUSE SHALL BE CALLED OF ALL NATIONS THE HOUSE OF PRAYER? BUT YOU HAVE MADE IT A DEN OF THIEVES."

The exposition is:

This signified, as stated, that He was in the Court of the Gentiles, which had been turned into a marketplace. His statement is derived from Isaiah 65:7 and Jeremiah 7:11.

THE TEACHING OF CHRIST

The phrase, *"And He taught, saying unto them,"* no doubt pointed to a large crowd of people which, it seems, had gathered and were watching with open-mouthed astonishment! The question, *"Is it not written. . . ?"* proclaims Jesus giving Scripture as foundation for that which He has just done, i.e., the cleansing of the Temple. If one is to notice, everything He did always had Scripture as foundation. The Bible at that time would have consisted of Genesis through Malachi.

It is my contention that if one does not know and understand the Old Testament, one cannot know and understand the New Testament. Someone has said that the Old Testament is the New Testament concealed, while the New Testament is the Old Testament revealed. One of the reasons that many Charismatics, plus all types of other Church members, go into false doctrine is because many of them do not know the Old Testament; consequently, the foundation is removed from some of what they teach.

For that matter, and as we have previously stated, the entirety of the Bible is under attack today, possibly as never before. It is not so much a denial of the Scriptures as it is the substitution of very untrustworthy editions, such as The Message Bible, etc. In fact, there are probably more editions out presently than ever before. One cannot call them translations, because they aren't translations. More so than anything, they are interpretations, and sometimes not even that.

While there are a few translations which hold to the original Text, personally I still like the King James Version. In fact, that's all that I use.

THE HOUSE OF GOD

The continuing of the question, *"My House shall be called of all nations a House of Prayer?"* is derived, as stated, from Isaiah 56:7 and Jeremiah 7:11. Under the Old Economy of God, the Lord dwelt between the Mercy Seat and the Cherubims in the Holy of Holies (Ex. 25:22). In truth, this was the only place on Earth where God dwelt. This was first in the Tabernacle in the wilderness and then in Solomon's Temple.

Inasmuch as the Ark of the Covenant was lost (or spirited away) at the invasion of Nebuchadnezzar, there is no record that God resided in Zerubbabel's Temple, or Herod's at the time of Christ. In fact, Ezekiel saw the Holy Spirit leave the Temple not long before it was destroyed by Nebuchadnezzar (Ezek. 11:22-23), and He will not return until the Millennial Temple is built in the coming Kingdom Age (Ezek. 43:1-5).

Israel, as a beneficiary of the Word, was obligated to give it to the Gentiles, hence, the phrase, *"Of all nations."* But Israel failed! What they had done to the *"Court of the Gentiles"* in Herod's Temple amply illustrated the entirety of the nation. They had no interest in taking the Great Message of the Lord to others. They preferred instead to make money. Is the present Church any different?

There is presently very little interest in World Evangelism, and I speak primarily of

America and Canada. Conversely, there is great interest in the *"Greed Gospel,"* which promises great riches to its devotees. If Jesus cleansed the Temple now, I wonder how many would be left!

ROBBERS

The phrase, *"But you have made it a den of thieves,"* should have been translated *"robbers."* The *"robber"* conducted his operations on a large and systematic scale. He had the aid of bands or helpers, and is thus to be distinguished from the thieves who purloined or pilfered whatever comes to hand (Vincent).

Swete says: *"No bandit's cave along the Jericho Road* (Lk. 10:30), *by which our Lord had lately come, was the scene of such wholesale robbery as the Mountain of His House."*

Under the Old Economy of God, as stated, the Temple was the *"House of God."* Since the New Covenant, God no longer dwells in a house made with hands, but rather in the human heart.

Paul said, *"Know ye not that you are the Temple of God, and that the Spirit of God dwells in you?"* (I Cor. 3:16).

So, instead of God dwelling in one place, as in days of old, He now resides in the human heart, at least those who will have Him. However, the principle outlined in the cleansing of the Temple is just as apropos presently as then.

JESUS

The occupant of the House is to be Jesus, even as Jesus came into the Temple of old! It is *"His House,"* and consequently He is to be free to do whatever He desires. If Jesus is not Lord of all, He is not Lord at all! So, for the Temple to be a true Temple of the Lord, Jesus must reside there. He does so in the Power and Person of the Holy Spirit (Eph. 2:22). This means that every house (heart) which does not have Jesus as its Lord is no House of God. This would exclude Islam, Buddhism, Hinduism, Shintoism, and Mormonism. It would also exclude Catholicism and much of what is called *"Christianity."*

THE UNDESIRABLE

When He comes in, He will *"cast out"* everything that is undesirable. It is the business of the Spirit of God to take the Believer from the *"image of the earthy"* to the *"image of the Heavenly"* (I Cor. 15:49). Everything not of the Spirit must be *"cast out"*!

HOUSE OF PRAYER

It is to be a *"House of Prayer."* In other words, *"prayer"* should be the constant exercise of every Believer. If this is to be taken literally, and it certainly should, intercession and travail should be the major focus of the Child of God. Regrettably, in many religious circles, prayer is a lost art!

If one is to notice, Jesus did not say, *"A house of good confession,"* as important as that may be! Regrettably, *"confession"* has taken the place of *"prayer"* in many hearts and lives.

Please allow me to say the following:

It is impossible to confess a lost loved one to Jesus Christ, even though proper confession certainly does play an important part. The Believer must intercede before God in earnest travail for the unsaved to be truly brought under the convicting Power of the Holy Spirit.

Moreover, no revival has ever begun by *"confession."* Every revival has begun with Intercession and Prayer.

ALL NATIONS

"Of all nations" suggests the worldwide scope of the Gospel intended by the Lord. The Scripture says, *"For God so loved the world,"* and that doesn't mean just a part of it! It has been suggested that the phrase, *"Of all nations,"* would have been better translated *"for all nations."* This translation is double-barreled, and consequently proclaims two directions. *"All nations"* are intended to come, and prayer is to be made *"for all nations."*

(18) "AND THE SCRIBES AND CHIEF PRIESTS HEARD IT, AND SOUGHT HOW THEY MIGHT DESTROY HIM: FOR THEY FEARED HIM, BECAUSE ALL THE PEOPLE WERE ASTONISHED AT HIS DOCTRINE."

The overview is:

The Scribes and Chief Priests were actually the *"robbers,"* because they were in charge of what was taking place there, actually profiting personally from what was being done.

So they hated Christ!

THE SCRIBES AND CHIEF PRIESTS

The phrase, *"And the Scribes and Chief Priests heard it,"* proclaims for the first time both groups combined against Jesus. They *"heard"* about the Temple cleansing, instantly realizing how much money they had lost. Wuest says that the Lord's attack against the Temple-market incensed them.

MURDER

The phrase, *"And sought how they might destroy Him,"* meant not only kill Him, but to utterly destroy His influence as a great spiritual energy in the world. To do this, they would accuse Him of many things, including insurrection against Rome, blasphemy respecting the Law of Moses, performing miracles by the power of Satan, etc.

Of course, all these charges were false; however, their biggest ploy was the Crucifixion, at least if they could persuade Pilate to carry out this act. They knew, and they knew also that the people knew, that the Law of Moses said, *"For he that is hanged is accursed of God"* (Deut. 21:22-23). That spoke of a sin that was worthy of such death. Consequently, if they could manage to have Him crucified, it would speak to the people that their accusations of Him were correct, and that God had *"cursed Him"* by allowing Him to be crucified. In their minds, this would destroy His influence among the people.

They reasoned that if God allowed Him to be crucified, this would mean that He definitely was not the Messiah, or at least this is what they wanted the people to believe.

CURSED?

In truth, He would be *"made a curse,"* not for His Own sins, but instead for the sins of the world. That is when He would cry, *"My God, My God, why have You forsaken Me?"* (Mk. 15:34). At this moment, He would be bearing the sin penalty of the world, suffering as the *"Lamb of God, which would take away the sin of the world"* (Jn. 1:29).

THE DOCTRINE

The phrase, *"For they feared Him,"* expresses the idea that their authority and interest had been attacked. In other words, they were loosing control of the people. Religion majors on two specifics:

A. Control and
B. Money.

Jesus had hurt them severely in both areas.

The phrase, *"All the people were astonished at His Doctrine,"* refers to the teaching of the Lord being in such contrast to that of the Jewish leaders, which caused the people to see the difference at once. The difference was that the teaching of the Lord sparkles with life, because it was anointed by the Holy Spirit, whereas the type of teaching they had been receiving from the Pharisees, etc., was a dry, formal, stereotyped, powerless garble, which was above their heads and made little sense! (Wuest)

(19) "AND WHEN EVENING WAS COME, HE WENT OUT OF THE CITY."

The exposition is:

There is no indication that Jesus ever spent a night in Jerusalem, with the exception of the night that He was on trial.

JESUS WAS NOT WELCOME IN HIS OWN CITY

In this statement, two things are said:

1. It seemed as if the Lord attempted to cram everything possible into these final hours. Swete remarks that hunger and fatigue were forgotten in the Work of God, and that only the approach of the hour when the gates were closed induced Him to retire for rest.

2. There is no indication that Jesus, as stated, ever spent a night in Jerusalem. There are indications that He did not desire to visit the city at all, day or night; however, on the times when He felt He had to be there, at nightfall He would retreat to the environs of the city, whether to Bethany or the Mount of Olives.

The sadness knows no bounds concerning the city which should have welcomed Him with open arms, the city that, in fact, was His city, but which instead crucified Him!

(20) "AND IN THE MORNING, AS THEY PASSED BY, THEY SAW THE FIG TREE DRIED UP FROM THE ROOTS."

The overview is:

The fig tree had completely withered away; in a short time Israel would do the same, actually ceasing to be a nation.

THE WITHERED FIG TREE

The phrase, *"And in the morning,"* probably refers to Tuesday. The phrase, *"As they passed by,"* proclaims the morning light making plainly visible the fig tree and what had happened to it. When Jesus and the Disciples had left the city late the previous afternoon, the possibility existed that the twilight hindered the visibility of the tree at that time, which may have already withered. Another possibility is that they had returned by another route.

The phrase, *"They saw the fig tree dried up from the roots,"* means that it had completely withered away. Sadly and regrettably, the withered fig tree was a type of Israel, which was soon to be destroyed.

(21) "AND PETER CALLING TO REMEMBRANCE SAID UNTO HIM, MASTER, BEHOLD, THE FIG TREE WHICH YOU CURSED IS WITHERED AWAY."

The synopsis is:

Had He so desired, Jesus could have done the same thing with His enemies; but He never used His Power except in the way that the Heavenly Father told Him to use it.

SIMON PETER

The phrase, *"And Peter calling to remembrance said unto Him,"* seems to indicate that Peter was shocked by the condition of the tree, which, some twenty-four hours earlier, had been alive and vibrant.

The phrase, *"Master, Behold, the fig tree which You cursed is withered away,"* proclaims a startled Apostle! He has difficulty understanding how the mere words of Jesus, *"No man eat fruit of you hereafter forever,"* could bring about this obvious and almost instant result! However, it was not so much the words spoken, but rather Who spoke them.

(22) "AND JESUS ANSWERING SAID UNTO THEM, HAVE FAITH IN GOD."

This indicates Jesus dealing with what happened rather than why it happened; they were not yet able to grasp the fig tree as a symbol of Israel. That would come later!

HAVE FAITH IN GOD

The phrase, *"And Jesus answering said unto them,"* indicates the Master pulling them from what happened to why it happened. Due to the Disciples thinking so strongly about the prospect of supremacy of Israel, despite what Jesus had constantly taught them, perhaps the Master thought it would be pointless at this time to point out the fruitless tree as a type of Israel, i.e., of no value. In a short time, they would understand.

The phrase, *"Have Faith in God,"* literally says, *"Have the Faith of God."* The structure of the Greek shows *"God"* as the Object of Faith.

WHAT DOES IT MEAN TO HAVE FAITH IN GOD?

God has chosen to operate His Work from the basis of Faith. It follows in two directions:

1. Paul wrote: *"Through Faith we understand that the worlds were framed by the Word of God, so that things which are seen were not made of things which do appear"* (Heb. 11:3). Actually, neither this Verse nor Hebrews 11:1 is a definition of Faith so much as it is a declaration of its action. It makes promises present and real, and unseen things visible.

God's vast creation of *"worlds"* was created, not by existing materials, but rather by Faith. This means that God spoke these things into existence; consequently, His Word carries not only Power, but also creativity.

2. God desires, and actually insists, that man accept everything done for him on the premise of Faith. This refers to Faith in Christ and what Christ has done for us at the Cross. In other words, Christ must not be separated from the Cross, nor the Cross from Christ (I Cor. 1:17-18, 23; 2:2; Gal. 6:14; Col. 2:14-15).

This doesn't mean that Jesus is still on the Cross. In fact, Christ is seated by the Father in Heavenly Places; in essence, He will be there forever (Heb. 1:3). Furthermore, as Believers, He *"has raised us up together, and made us sit together in Heavenly Places in Christ Jesus"* (Eph. 2:6). It's the benefits of the Cross of which we speak, that which the Cross made possible, which actually is everything that comes from God.

Considering all of this, the idea is that man, at times, may little understand what God is doing, but nevertheless is to accept His Word at face value. His Word is all-important! It is so important that the simple fact of Abraham believing Him, that is, believing God's Word, caused Righteousness to be accounted unto him (Gen. 15:6). God's method of imputed Righteousness has not differed from that time until the present. Actually, it was the same at the very beginning, although not as clearly defined (Gen. 4:3-5). Consequently, the Jews' constant demand for *"signs"* from Jesus showed that they had no confidence in the Word of God (Mat. 12:38-39).

Faith in God insures Salvation, and produces Miracles, as Jesus will portray here. It is so important that Paul wrote, *"Without Faith it is impossible to please Him: for he who comes to God must believe* (have faith) *that He is* (able), *and that He is a rewarder of them who diligently seek Him"* (Heb. 11:6).

So, the ingredient to God, and that which will please God, is *"Faith in God,"* i.e., His Word.

(23) "FOR VERILY I SAY UNTO YOU, THAT WHOSOEVER SHALL SAY UNTO THIS MOUNTAIN, BE THOU REMOVED, AND BE THOU CAST INTO THE SEA; AND SHALL NOT DOUBT IN HIS HEART, BUT SHALL BELIEVE THAT THOSE THINGS WHICH HE SAID SHALL COME TO PASS; HE SHALL HAVE WHATSOEVER HE SAYS."

The exposition is:

THE WORDS OF CHRIST

The phrase, *"For verily I say unto you,"* is used often by Christ, and is meant to announce a Truth of unusual consequence. This great Truth concerns Faith in God. In this one Scripture, with even added emphasis given in the next one, Jesus tells us what Faith in God will do, and also the manner in which it is to be used. As the Holy Spirit generally does, the information given for such a weighty subject is couched in very simple terminology, and is very brief in content. But yet, it is the greatest form of teaching in the world, as should be obvious. Hopefully, the Lord will help us in dissecting this great Passage, to rightly divide it in such a way as to make it applicable to the hungry, seeking heart.

NOTES

Let's take it step by step:

WHOSOEVER

"That whosoever": First of all, the word *"whosoever"* puts mountain-moving Faith in reach of anyone. It is not limited to Bible Scholars, nationality, or race. It is open to all! That means that whatever problem may be besetting you, the Reader, if proper Faith in God is enjoined, the first step to the road of victory can begin instantly. When Jesus said, *"whosoever,"* the Believer should say in his heart, *"That means me!"* This was not for the Disciples only, or Preachers only, but includes any and all Believers.

CONFESSION

"Shall say": These two words proclaim to us the power of proper Scriptural confession. God has given each person a tongue, which is fueled by the mind and heart; consequently, whatever we *"say"* shows where our Faith actually is, and the direction we are heading. Faith speaks, and does not remain silent.

What does it say?

It actually says two things:

A. What the Word of God says; and,

B. How it applies to one's particular need, which incorporates the Will of God.

In other words, even though Faith can move mountains, the Lord will not allow a mountain to be moved in such a way that it will hurt or harm others. So, the Believer is to confess the Word of God and the Will of God. If we are led by the Spirit, we will never confess anything but that which the Lord desires.

So, one cannot move mountains by speaking doubt. One must speak that which one wants and believes to be the Will of God.

MOUNTAINS

"Unto this mountain": Jesus chose about the hardest thing that could be thought of, i.e., a mountain, in order to describe the utter and unlimited Power of Faith in God. As well, Jesus constantly used everyday situations and things, such as this mountain, to proclaim a spiritual point.

Whatever problem that you, the Reader, may have, cannot be any larger than a mountain. So, automatically, the Lord places every single problem in the world, irrespective of its situation, in the context of its possible solution. In other words, *"All things are possible with God."* If Satan can get the Believer to think that his or her problem is beyond solution, he has won the battle.

Please allow me to give a personal illustration.

A PERSONAL EXPERIENCE

If I remember correctly, it was 1990. Our situation was such, especially regarding our Ministry, that, little by little, I had come to believe it was hopeless. Satan is a genius at maneuvering certain things into place to make one believe such a lie. How in the world could we overcome the prejudice and bias of almost all the Church world? With almost every Preacher in the land turned against us, how would be it be possible to have any effective Ministry? These questions of such magnitude filled my mind, with Satan constantly fueling this train of thought.

On top of all of that, I was personally to blame for the situation. And yet, at the same time, at least then, I did not know what I could have done to have changed my personal situation. I had tried to overcome Satan in all the wrong ways. Looking back now, I readily see the reason. But then, in 1990, the reason was not at all understandable to me.

Under those circumstances, there seemed to be no hope, with Faith little by little giving way to despair. However, the Lord does not leave His people without a witness. He loves us dearly and will bring things to pass to increase our Faith, if we will only love Him and trust Him.

THE WITNESS OF A PREACHER FRIEND

During this time, a Preacher called me, a man whom I had known for years, but not in a direct way. If I remember correctly, this was the first time I had spoken with him. He called the office and asked if he and his wife could have lunch with Frances and me. He felt that God had given him something for me. So a date was set.

As the four of us met on that particular day, I enjoyed the fellowship extensively so, and I wondered in my mind exactly what he was going to say. After the meal was finished, he looked at me and said, *"Brother Swaggart, what I'm about to say sounds foolish. It seems so trivial that I'm ashamed to claim that God gave it to me to give to you. And yet, I can't shake it. I must obey the Lord."*

He sat there for a few moments, saying nothing. Finally, he said, *"The Lord told me to tell you these two words, 'God can!'"* That was the entirety of the Message, *"God can!"*

Almost immediately upon saying these words, he began to apologize, saying, *"I really don't know what it means, but that's what the Lord said to say to you."*

For a few moments I said nothing; however, when those two words, *"God can!"* were given to me, I sat there stunned for a few moments, and then the tears began to roll down my cheeks. Actually, it was a few moments before I could say anything. Then I said, *"My Brother, maybe you don't understand what you've said, but I understand it perfectly."* Then I added, *"Thank you so much for obeying God."*

It doesn't matter what it is or how large the mountain is, *"God can!"*

Further still, Jesus did not put a limit on the size of the *"mountain."* To be frank, it is actually no more difficult to move a large mountain than a small mountain, as should be obvious. Both in the natural are impossible. However, with God, there is no impossibility.

REMOVE THE MOUNTAIN

"Be thou removed": This proclaims the Word of Faith. It doesn't ask how it can be done, or whether it is possible for it to be done. It just simply says, *"Be done!"* This is actually the proper confession of the words, *"shall say."* Conversely, most will say it cannot be removed. However, Jesus tells us otherwise; consequently, one can believe doubters or one can believe Christ. I prefer to believe the Lord.

Concerning my own personal Ministry, I have seen the mountain of difficulties, even impossibilities, removed little by little. It has not been removed all at once; but, as stated, it is being removed. At this present time, November of 2004, it has been removed, it is being removed, and it shall be removed. So much has been done, the greatest of all being the Revelation of the Cross, which the Lord has been so kind and gracious to give to me, and which was given, or at least began to be given in 1997. I say, *"began to be,"* simply because He just keeps on giving and giving.

I personally believe, in fact, I can say I personally know, that the entirety of this mountain is going to be removed, and that which the Lord desires will be done totally and completely. As stated, one can believe doubters or one can believe the Lord. I prefer to believe the Lord.

BE CAST INTO THE SEA

Consequently, such Faith in God not only moves the mountain, it puts it in a place where it can hurt or harm no one else. That is the reason we say that God will not bring something to pass for the Believer that will harm others. This *"mountain"* is thrown into the sea where it will do no one any harm. In effect, it is totally removed.

This is somewhat the opposite of that which is known as Hamilton's Law. This Law states that for anything to be constructed, something must first be destroyed. It means that if one builds a house, trees have to be cut down, and other things have to be used in order to provide the materials from which the house is to be built. Consequently, things are destroyed in order to construct other things. That is Hamilton's Law.

However, when Jesus builds something, He does not deplete things elsewhere to get it done. Moreover, if He removes something for us, as this mountain, He does not make our gain someone else's loss. That is the reason the mountain is thrown into the *"sea."*

DOUBT

"And shall not doubt in his heart": The word *"doubt"* in the Greek is *"diakrino,"* which means *"to judge between two."* In this case, it means to judge whether Faith in God can, or whether it cannot! Everything within the Believer is to understand that God can, and that He not only can, but will. Many Believers agree that He can, but they are not sure if He will. It is not enough to believe that He can. One must also believe that *"He will"*!

When the Lord sent Moses to the Children of Israel in Egypt, He did not tell Moses to tell them, *"I can has sent me unto you,"* but rather *"I AM has sent me unto you"* (Ex. 3:14). There is a vast difference in *"I can"* and *"I Am,"* i.e., *"I will."* Actually, *"I Am"* is even stronger than *"I will"*! *"I will"* treats it in the sense of being done in the future; however, True Faith, as *"I Am"* represents, calls it done, even though it has not yet happened.

In the Mind of God, True Faith says that whatever is needed is already done, even though not yet carried out.

BELIEVE

"But shall believe": Not only does the person not doubt, but he also *"believes"* what Jesus has said here. Jesus said if we have the proper Faith in God, we can say to a mountain, *"Be thou removed into the sea,"* and it shall be done. We are to believe that. Once again, He is using the word *"mountain"* as a symbol for difficulties, severe difficulties, etc.

THOSE THINGS

"Those things": This speaks of our particular needs, whatever they may be! As we've already stated, the Lord is using the word *"mountain"* as a symbol of our problems, even severe problems, as should be obvious. In other words, we are to take everything to the Lord in prayer. We are also not to ask silly things of the Lord.

What do I mean by that?

Many have read this Passage, and others which are similar, and have stated, *"Lord, make me a millionaire by tomorrow,"* or *"by next week,"* etc.

First of all, the Lord hasn't promised that He's going to make you, or anyone else for that matter, a millionaire. He has promised to meet our needs, and, under that context, we are free to ask Him for His help. He has promised to give it, if we will evidence Faith.

CONFESSION

"Which he says": Once again, we are told to *"say"* what we want. Actually, this is the second of three times this phrase, in one way or the other, is used. Consequently, the Holy

Spirit is showing us the significance of a proper confession. That which we need, and which we believe the Lord will give to us, we are to *"say it,"* i.e., *"confess it."*

However, that needs to be qualified. For instance, husbands and wives who are unable to have a child have tried to carry this Promise by the Lord to absurd lengths. Even though the wife was not pregnant, she would wear a maternity smock and confess that she was pregnant. *"Lying"* is not Faith. Neither does it bring Glory to God. It's best to say, *"We are believing the Lord,"* or something to that effect.

RESULTS

"Shall come to pass": These words are present tense in the Greek Text. Consequently, it more accurately translates, *"comes to pass."* The idea is that it may not happen instantly, but happen it shall! We are to keep believing and continue confessing, at least confessing in the right way. It is what some refer to as a *"futuristic present,"* which has to do with the word *"believing."*

However, this is the hard part. It is called the *"trying of your Faith* (which) *works patience"* (James 1:3). Many Believers continue to believe for a while, but then grow weary and quit, losing that for which they are seeking. An excellent example for the opposite is the Patriarch Isaac. The Scripture says, *"And Isaac entreated the LORD for his wife, because she was barren"* (Gen. 25:21).

Many people do not realize how long Isaac entreated the Lord. Rebekah, his wife, was barren for 19 years; consequently, Isaac continued to entreat the Lord for this period of time. If Jesus were to come into the world, it was imperative that a little boy be born to Rebekah; consequently, Satan would make it as hard as possible. But Isaac did not quit. Regrettably, many, if not most, Christians quit after one or two petitions, much less 19 years. But Isaac continued to *"entreat the Lord,"* and the Scripture says, *"and Rebekah his wife conceived"* (Gen. 25:21).

The mountain of her *"barrenness"* had to be removed. Since so much was at stake, actually the Salvation of the world, Satan would fight horrendously so! Nevertheless, the Patriarch did not discontinue his entreaty of the Lord. He kept believing, and I think he kept confessing. Every indication is that he did! Actually, it would have been impossible for Rebekah to conceive if Isaac had been confessing that it was impossible for her to conceive.

Satan, no doubt, taunted him constantly, telling him any lie that seemed plausible at the moment. But Isaac kept believing, asking, and confessing. Ultimately, he received what he wanted!

OWNERSHIP

"He shall have": Jesus did not say, *"Maybe,"* but emphatically states, *"he shall have. . . ."* If it is the Will of God and we keep believing, asking, and confessing, the outcome is certain.

I realize that many object to me using the phrase, *"The Will of God."* They claim that *"The Word of God"* is *"The Will of God,"* which certainly is correct; however, many err in claiming that the Promises of the Word of God apply to them on a personal basis in any and all circumstances. In other words, if God gave Abraham and Sarah a child when he was 100 years old and she was 90, He will do the same for them because *"God is no respecter of persons,"* they say!

While it is certainly true that God is no respecter of persons, still, He does have respect according to His Promises. In other words, some of the Promises He gave were personal, and not meant to apply to everyone. Actually, despite all the Faith that has been exhibited throughout the thousands of years since Abraham and Sarah, I have never heard of another couple who has experienced the birth of a child at 100 and 90 years old respectively.

DON'T TRY TO USE THE WORD OF GOD AGAINST GOD

God gave a particular Promise to Abraham, which applied to him only, and had to do with the Great Plan of God in the world. To be sure, He has given great Promises to others that He never gave to Abraham, and which Abraham could not have had, because they did not apply to him. So, the Believer must be very careful that he does not try to use the Word of God against God, in other words, to try to force God to do certain things when it may not be the Will of God or the Wisdom of God, and for the obvious reasons, and, in some cases, for reasons which are not so obvious.

Some Promises in the Bible are applicable to all. This refers to Salvation, healing, and prosperity. In other words, these things are promised to all. And yet, healing and prosperity must be taken in proper context. What would be prosperity to one would not necessarily be such to another. So we must allow God to decide what type of *"prosperity"* He wants us to have. Furthermore, the Promise of Healing for all, as I believe the Scripture proclaims, also has limitations. Such will not stop the aging of the human body and the attendant problems which accompany such. In other words, irrespective of how much Faith in God a person has, a 70-year-old man does not have the reflexes of a 20-year-old. So things must be looked at in their proper context.

When asking the Lord for something, every Believer must first settle it in his mind that what he is asking is according to the Word of God and according to the Will of God. God's Will is an extraordinary thing. It is predicated not only on His Word, but is also according to His Wisdom in dealing with us as individuals.

THE WILL OF GOD

Please allow me to give an example:

I have had many people through the years come up to me and say, *"I am going to believe God to give me the talent to play the piano exactly as He did you!"* Probably they had heard me relate how I had asked the Lord for this talent when I was eight years old, and He had answered my childlike Faith, giving me this talent.

And yet, even though God is no respecter of persons, still, it may not be God's Will to give this particular talent to all who would ask Him. I realize that some will not agree with that statement, claiming that if we have enough Faith in God, we can have anything we desire. But that is incorrect! In the first place, our degree of faith does not guarantee us an answer from God. If that were the case, a person would be stronger than God. While the degree of faith is important, it is important only to a limited degree.

Many have thought that if they had enough Faith, they could do this, that, or the other. Again, I say, *"Not so!"* As we've already stated, God will not allow His Word to be used again Himself. God's Promises are always predicated on His particular Will for our life and ministry, whatever that may be.

If we have concluded that what we're asking for is according to God's Word, and also is His Will for our lives, not just something we have pulled out of the blue, then we should set our mind and heart to it, refusing to take *"No"* for an answer, believing that God ultimately will give us what we are seeking. We should not allow circumstances to hinder us or obstacles to impede our progress. We must not let doubters turn us aside, or unbelievers to deter us from that which the Lord has promised us. We must attack that mountain with Faith in God, believing that it ultimately will be removed, and not stop until it is done.

CONFESSION

"Whatsoever he says": This represents the third time this phrase, in one way or the other, is used. So here is what the Lord is telling us to do:

A. Shall say;
B. Shall not doubt;
C. Shall believe;
D. He says;
E. Shall have; and,
F. He says.

(24) "THEREFORE I SAY UNTO YOU, WHAT THINGS SOEVER YOU DESIRE, WHEN YOU PRAY, BELIEVE THAT YOU RECEIVE THEM, AND YOU SHALL HAVE THEM."

The composition is:

As is obvious in the above Text, the receiving of these things, whatever they might be, requires relationship, and that is the key.

WHATEVER YOU DESIRE

The phrase, *"Therefore I say unto you,"* is meant to serve as an enlargement on this profound Truth regarding Faith. It is the most important Truth, without which the result of Faith can never be realized.

The phrase, *"What things soever you desire,"* is a profound promise, but yet misunderstood by most people. It means, *"Whatsoever things we desire in the Will of God."* As should be obvious, these Promises are given to mature Believers. And by mature, we do not necessarily mean Believers of longstanding, but rather Believers who truly and fully understand that one is to desire the Will of God in all matters, irrespective as to how long one has been a Believer.

The Believer is to desire only what the Lord wants him to have. Paul said, *"And be not conformed to this world: but be ye transformed by the renewing of your mind, that you may prove what is that good, and acceptable, and perfect, Will of God"* (Rom. 12:2). In other words, nothing is *"acceptable"* to God but the *"Perfect Will of God,"* which negates any idea of that which sometimes is referred to as a *"permissive will."* On our part, God cannot accept a *"permissive will,"* only a *"Perfect Will."*

ERROR

Many Believers, immature in the Ways of the Lord, after reading Mark 11:24, have automatically made themselves a shopper's list of things they *"desire,"* and then set about to confess those things into existence. Such is foolishness!

Some time back, I heard of a Preacher confessing for himself a Mercedes, and some such like thing for his wife. As stated, this is foolishness, and has absolutely no relationship to this Promise, as given here by Christ. Such requests reek of selfishness. Regrettably, the so-called *"Faith Ministry,"* which in reality is no Faith at all, has pretty much deteriorated to the sub-strata levels. And yet, it continues to have a wide following, because such appeals to greed.

JESUS

In the Garden of Gethsemane, Jesus epitomizes the hunger and desire for the Will of God. Concerning His coming Crucifixion, He said, *"All things are possible unto You; take away this Cup from Me"* (Mk. 14:36). In other words, this statement by Christ proclaims that it was possible with God for the Plan of Salvation to be carried out in another fashion; however, Jesus only wanted that other way if it is what the Father wanted. His statement, *"Nevertheless not what I will, but what You will,"* is the criteria for every Believer.

Is it possible for God to do any and all things for me?

Of course it is!

However, that is not the point or the desire. The Will of God for my immediate life is what I desire, and it is what every Believer should want and desire. So, if the Believer majors only in what God can do, he completely misses the point. We must be careful that we seek only that which we know is His Will for our lives (Mk. 14:36).

Concerning the *"Will of God,"* I want to give you some teaching from a personal experience that takes us to the other side of the spectrum. We must not want things which aren't the Will of God; but, at that same time, once the Will of God has been made known to us, we should not hinder His Will from being brought about in our lives by praying incorrectly.

PRAYER

The phrase, *"When you pray,"* has been misunderstood by many, as well! Most have shortened the act of *"praying"* to merely *"confession."* While *"confession"* certainly will play a part in prayer, still, it is only a part. *"Prayer"* is not only to receive *"what things soever we desire,"* but also that we make certain that we desire the right things. Prayer is consecration to the Will of God, or it is not really prayer at all. By that we mean that we seek to consecrate ourselves to the highest, which is the noble Will of God. Nothing else will be satisfactory.

The word *"pray"* is *"proseuchomai,"* which means *"to offer prayer addressed to God, to Him as the Object of Faith and the One Who will answer one's prayer."* If God is the Object of Faith, which He must be, then His Will will be paramount. Otherwise, the petition will not and, in fact, cannot, be granted. So, Faith must be the constant attitude of the mind when one prays, with the object in view that we want to please God.

Paul wrote, *"But without Faith it is impossible to please Him"* (Heb. 11:6).

It is obvious that we must have Faith in God to please God. And yet, Faith used for that which is not His Will could not be pleasing to Him, as should be obvious. Neither is it pleasing to Him for us to refuse to evidence Faith in that which He has already promised us. As stated, it is somewhat a double-edged sword.

A PERSONAL EXPERIENCE

Having served the Lord for some 60 years, I've learned a few things. Sometimes, I think not many, but at least a few. I've learned that it's His Will that we want, and nothing else. I've learned that I cannot make it without His total and complete guidance in all things. In other words, I need Him in everything I do, whether it's small or large. In fact, the Lord has stated, and unequivocally so, *"For without Me, you can do nothing"* (Jn. 15:5).

If I remember correctly, the year was 2000. Along with Television, the Lord had given me a Vision concerning Radio. To make the story brief, He told me several things. The Ministry then owned two Radio Stations, one in Baton Rouge, Louisiana, and the other in Bowling Green, Ohio. The Lord informed me that I was to change the programming immediately. All the Programming in its entirety must come from Family Worship Center, at least in one form or the other.

Second, we were to acquire Stations all over the country.

Third, the Lord told me that the emphasis of this Radio Network was to be the Cross of Christ.

We instantly set about to carry out this which the Lord had said; however, to acquire Stations was not going to be easy, simply because we had no money.

The Lord told me how to start increasing the Network; He then told me how to acquire Full-power Stations, which we began to do. (At the time of this writing, November of 2004, the Ministry owns 70 Radio Stations, scattered all over the United States. It is our intention, according to that which we believe the Lord has told us to do, to fill this nation with Stations.)

Now the Lord had told me to fill the nation with Stations, but yet that did not mean that we were recklessly to plunge the Ministry into debt, which could endanger the entire process. I was to seek His Face about every acquisition, which we do.

PALM SPRINGS, CALIFORNIA

We heard of an F.M. Station which might be available in Palm Springs, California. To be sure, it is almost impossible to find an available F.M. in California, especially in a reasonable price range. At any rate, we made efforts to get the Station, but simply didn't have the money to swing the deal. We had to let it go.

Nearly a year passed, and then the Lord placed it into my mind to check on that Station again. I did so! The owners told me, *"We've just sold the Station, and the contracts have just been signed."* Upon hearing that news, I wondered why the Lord had put it into my mind again to try to obtain the Station. I felt a strong inclination in my spirit to continue to pray about the matter, which I did.

In praying, I was imploring the Lord to give us the Station, despite its present circumstances, *"if it be Your Will."* One particular afternoon, after a few days of praying like that, the Lord spoke to me very forcibly. It was while I was engaged in prayer, and praying about the Station in Palm Springs.

He said to me, *"You have already told me that you want nothing but My Will. I know your heart, and I know that you mean what you say. So, in praying about this Station, you don't have to ask Me to give you the Station 'if it's My Will,' because when you do that, you are hindering your Faith. You already know that it's My Will for you to have this Station."*

And then the Lord said to me, *"Concerning Radio Stations, don't ask Me anymore to give you a Station 'if it's My Will.' If it's not My Will, I will step in and stop the situation. You rather claim the Station, and do so without reservation or fear."*

When the Lord spoke that to me, it was done so forcibly, so powerfully, that I had no doubt as to what He was telling me.

THE LORD GAVE US THE STATION

And then it happened! The Brother who owned the Station called me and stated,

"Brother Swaggart, the people who signed the contract to buy the Station cannot go through with their desires. Are you still interested?"

Yes, we were, and the transaction was completed that day.

Now, truthfully, we didn't have any more money now than we had had a year ago. So, how were we to buy the Station?

While it was true that I didn't have any more money now than then, still, I had more Faith.

GREATER FAITH, GREATER UNDERSTANDING

Whenever our Faith is increased, our understanding is increased, as well.

What do I mean by that?

The Lord in the intervening year told me how to raise the funds. As stated, with greater Faith comes greater understanding. Furthermore, now when I pray about a Station, I don't ask the Lord to give us the Station, *"if it be Your Will,"* but rather I claim the Station. With some, the Lord has stepped in and stopped the transaction, using different means to do so. With others, He has given us the Stations, exactly as He said that He would do.

So, while we must strongly desire the Perfect Will of God in all things, at the same time, once we ascertain what the Will of God is, we must not hinder our Faith by questioning that Will, exactly as I have attempted to teach you in the above paragraphs.

BELIEVING

The phrase, *"Believe that you receive them,"* is the test of faith, the kind that sees the fulfillment before it happens. This Passage brings out the great Truth that we previously addressed. Most of the time what we ask for is not given immediately. A test of Faith results. Actually, sometimes the answer is long in coming. But, through it all, we must continue to *"believe,"* with the assurance that if this is properly done, we will ultimately *"receive."*

The word *"believe"* in the Greek is *"pisteuo,"* which means *"to put in trust with."* It means that we have to trust not only for our request to be granted, but also in God's time.

NOTES

The phrase, *"And you shall have them,"* refers to a present tense with a futuristic conclusion. He doesn't say exactly when we *"shall have them,"* but that it will be done, that is, if we keep believing, and in due time. *"The timing"* is that which we entrust to Him.

(25) "AND WHEN YOU STAND PRAYING, FORGIVE, IF YOU HAVE OUGHT AGAINST ANY: THAT YOUR FATHER ALSO WHICH IS IN HEAVEN MAY FORGIVE YOU YOUR TRESPASSES.

(26) "BUT IF YOU DO NOT FORGIVE, NEITHER WILL YOUR FATHER WHICH IS IN HEAVEN FORGIVE YOUR TRESPASSES."

The diagram is:

Unforgiveness breaks down relationship, which destroys the whole program of God. In such a case, our sins are not forgiven, and neither can we expect God to answer prayer. These are extremely serious implications.

FORGIVENESS

The phrase, *"And when you stand praying, forgive,"* is only meant to point to the standing posture when praying, as it was a practice among the Jews. It in no way means that it is the only posture allowed.

As the previous two Verses are some of the most powerful in the Word of God, likewise Verses 25 and 26 fall into the same category. Irrespective of what someone has done to us, whether they have asked forgiveness or not, the Scriptural Command is to *"forgive"*! It is to be an automatic thing with every Child of God. Failure to do so carries an awesome penalty.

WHAT DOES IT MEAN TO FORGIVE?

The New Testament places considerable stress on the importance of forgiving others. In Matthew, Chapter 18, Jesus tells three stories to illustrate forgiveness. He portrays human beings as sheep, prone to go astray. When this happens, we are to seek the straying. We are to bring the straying home, bearing them in our arms, rejoicing. The image is of a forgiveness that frees us from bitterness or recrimination and provides a joy that is able to heal every hurt (Mat. 18:10-14).

Jesus then spoke of the hurts and sins that mar family relationships. *"If your brother sins against you"* (Mat. 18:15), He began. Then He went on to explain that we are to take the initiative when we are hurt and we should seek reconciliation. As well, we should understand that Jesus is here speaking of personal problems between two or more individuals. He is not speaking of addressing Doctrine.

Peter, hearing Jesus teach this, recognized the difficulty of such teaching, and objected. He asked how often such hurts should be forgiven. Jesus answered, *"Seventy times seven"* (Mat. 18:22) — a phrase indicating unlimited forgiveness.

Following this, Jesus told a Parable about a servant with a debt equivalent to a staggering sum of money (possibly billions of dollars in 2004 rates). When the servant could not pay and begged for time, the ruler to whom he owed the sum simply forgave the entire obligation. But the same servant later demanded the minor amount which was owed to him by a fellow servant (equivalent to a few hundred dollars). He actually went so far as to throw the fellow servant into prison for nonpayment. Jesus' intention is clear: we who are forgiven an unimaginable debt by God (as all of us have been) surely must be so moved by gratitude that we treat our fellows as we have been treated.

This theme — forgive as you are forgiven — is often stressed in the New Testament, and the theme has two applications.

First, God's treatment of us provides an example that we are to follow in our relationships with other persons. We are to be *"kind and compassionate to one another, forgiving one another, just as in Christ God forgave us"* (Eph. 4:32).

Now, this is so important, please allow me to say it again:

Whenever the need for forgiveness enters the picture, we are to always use as an example, irrespective of the situations involved, God's forgiveness of us, of which we'll have more to say momentarily. This application, as presented by our Lord, seems to introduce a conditional aspect to the promise of forgiveness.

In Matthew 6:14-15, we read, *"For if you forgive men their trespasses, your Heavenly Father will also forgive you:*

NOTES

"But if you forgive not men their trespasses, neither will your Father forgive your trespasses."

Mark 11:25 expresses the same thought in the same way. These Passages seem to trouble many; however, there is a reason they should!

FORGIVENESS AFFECTS OUR PERSONALITY

Just as every coin has two sides, never only one, so forgiveness has two aspects which can never be separated. These two sides of forgiveness are accepting and extending. The person who accepts forgiveness becomes deeply aware of his own weakness and need. Pride is ruled out as we take our place as supplicants before the Lord. This basic attitude releases us from our tendency to become angry with, or judgmental of, others. We begin to see others as creatures who are, like us, flawed by weakness. Rather than react with enflamed pride (*"He can't do this to me!"*), we are freed to respond as God does, with loving concern and forgiveness.

It isn't that God will not forgive the unforgiving. It is simply that the unforgiving lack the humble attitude that both permits them to accept forgiveness and frees them to extend forgiveness.

THE INNER DYNAMICS OF FORGIVENESS

The foregoing discussion should demonstrate something of the transforming impact of forgiveness. One who accepts forgiveness from God adopts an attitude toward himself that transforms his or her attitude toward others. The person who accepts forgiveness becomes forgiving.

But there are other aspects of forgiveness, as well. Jesus once confronted a critical Pharisee who observed with contempt the tearful devotion for Jesus of a woman who seemed to be fallen. The Pharisee thought, *"This Man, if He were a Prophet, would have known who and what manner of woman this is who touches Him: for she is a sinner"* (Lk. 7:39).

Jesus responded to the Pharisee's unexpressed thought. He told a story of two men in debt to a moneylender. The one owed $200 and the other owed $2,000. If the moneylender should cancel both debts, asked Jesus, what man would love him more? The Pharisee answered, *"I suppose that he, to whom he forgave most"* (Lk. 7:43). Jesus then nodded toward the weeping woman and confirmed the principle. Her sins were many, but when she was forgiven, she knew the wonder of God's Gift of Love, and she responded with love. As we meditate on God's forgiveness and realize how much we have been forgiven, love for the Lord is nurtured in our hearts.

WHAT TYPE OF FORGIVENESS DOES GOD EXTEND TO THE REPENTANT SINNER?

The Book of Hebrews develops the type of forgiveness offered to us by Christ as perhaps no other Book in the Bible. Paul compares the Sacrifice of Jesus with the Old Testament Sacrifices that prefigured Him. If the earlier Sacrifices had the power to make the worshippers perfect, then *"would they not have ceased to be offered? Because that the worshippers once purged should have had no more conscience of sins"* (Heb. 10:2).

But Jesus' Sacrifice does make us perfect! Through Jesus all our sins are actually taken away! Thus, the Believer who realizes that he is truly forgiven is released from a sense of guilt and from bondages to past mistakes. Because God has forgiven our sins (Heb. 10:17), we can forget our past. Forgiven, we can concentrate all our energies on living a Godly life.

That is the reason Paul also said, *"Forgetting those things which are behind, and reaching forth unto those things which are before,*

"I press toward the mark for the prize of the high calling of God in Christ Jesus" (Phil. 3:13-14).

He also wrote, *"There is therefore now no condemnation to them which are in Christ Jesus, who walk not after the flesh, but after the Spirit"* (Rom. 8:1).

This means that all the past is washed and cleansed by the Precious Blood of Jesus Christ. It is what John was speaking of when he said, *"Behold the Lamb of God, which takes away the sin of the world"* (Jn. 1:29).

When Jesus *"takes our sin away,"* they can no longer be brought against us; consequently, we are treated by the Lord as if the sin or sins never had been committed. It is called *"Justification by Faith."*

Paul wrote, *"Therefore being justified by Faith, we have peace with God through our Lord Jesus Christ"* (Rom. 5:1).

Consequently, the sins which once marred that *"peace"* have been taken away, and *"peace"* has now been restored. It is called *"Justifying Peace."* The Believer should never go back and drag up sins which have been washed and cleansed by the Blood of Jesus, and actually should not even mention these sins any more. As we have stated, and as Paul wrote, *"Forgetting those things. . . ."*

HOW SHOULD FELLOW BELIEVERS CONDUCT THEMSELVES TOWARD A PENITENT ONE?

I think we have been replete in giving example after example where Jesus demanded that we understand just how much we have been forgiven by God, and that we treat others accordingly. In other words, the same type of forgiveness that God extends to the penitent Believer must be extended to others by us, or else it is no forgiveness at all! Anything less is not constituted by God as forgiveness.

However, for the Believer to conduct himself accordingly toward a fellow Believer, this necessitates the fellow Believer being truly repentant, as well! If he is not repentant, while in our hearts we should forgive him, fellowship is necessarily curtailed; however, even then Paul said, *"Yet count him not as an enemy, but admonish him as a Brother,"* in other words, continuing to make every effort to bring him to a place of Repentance (II Thess. 3:15).

As it regards someone who has wronged us, and there is no Repentance on their part, even though we should definitely forgive them, still, as would be obvious, and as we have stated, there can be no fellowship in such a situation.

Joseph of the Old Testament is an excellent example. His brothers did him a terrible injustice. They actually sold him into slavery, and then told their father Jacob that Joseph had been killed by an animal. As the

Scripture tells us, Joseph, enjoying the Blessings of the Lord, became the Viceroy of Egypt, then, more than likely, the most powerful nation on Earth. In other words, Joseph was second only to Pharaoh.

Joseph was appointed Viceroy simply because he had been able to interpret a dream given to Pharaoh which had tremendous implications. There was to be seven years of plenty regarding the harvests of Egypt, and then seven years of famine. When the time of famine came, Joseph's brothers back in Canaan journeyed to Egypt in order to secure grain, because there was none in Canaan. Of course, they had absolutely no idea that their brother Joseph, whom they had sold into slavery, was now Viceroy of Egypt.

When they saw Joseph, they did not recognize him; however, Joseph immediately recognized them. But yet, Joseph, not knowing if they had repented or not, did not go and introduce himself to them. In fact, he tested them greatly to make certain that there had been a change in their lives before he revealed himself to them (Gen., Chpts. 37-45).

The lesson we are to learn from this is that even though we truly forgive people who have wronged us, if they have not repented of that action, as stated, there can be no fellowship.

FORGIVENESS BY GOD

The phrase, *"If you have ought against any, that your Father also which is in Heaven may forgive you your trespasses,"* constitutes a tremendously important principle, which should be obvious. The word *"trespasses"* in the Greek is *"paraptoma,"* which means *"a fall from the right course"* or *"a false step."* It is foolish to think that such will not occur in our own lives. Therefore, considering our own weakness, we must also consider the weakness of others.

So, the implication is clear: if we want forgiveness for our *"trespasses,"* we must forgive others and be quick to do so.

REFUSAL TO FORGIVE

The phrase, *"But if you do not forgive, neither will your Father which is in Heaven forgive your trespasses,"* puts the unforgiving one in a terrible state. If one, because of his lack of forgiveness toward others, is in the posture in which his sins cannot be forgiven, if the situation is not somewhere rectified, the individual will die lost. No one can continue in this state until they die and still be saved. To be sure, the Holy Spirit will deal with them, making it abundantly clear that they must obey the Word of God; however, if they refuse to do so, i.e., forgive others, there is no alternative but eternal darkness.

Considering the seriousness of what our Lord is saying, every Believer must constantly search his heart in order that no unforgiveness be found to lodge there. And yet, I suspect that many little heed these dire admonitions. Because so little attention is given to the Word of God, many Believers have little or no knowledge of these statements. However, ignorance is no excuse!

(27) "AND THEY COME AGAIN TO JERUSALEM: AND AS HE WAS WALKING IN THE TEMPLE, THERE CAME TO HIM THE CHIEF PRIESTS, AND THE SCRIBES, AND THE ELDERS."

The composition is:

These were the religious leaders of Israel.

CHIEF PRIESTS, SCRIBES, AND ELDERS

The phrase, *"And they come again to Jerusalem,"* is thought by some to represent the third day in which He visits this edifice. The Crucifixion is drawing ever closer.

The phrase, *"And as He was walking in the Temple,"* probably spoke of the colonnades. He was probably teaching the people as He walked slowly among them. A great crowd had, no doubt, gathered, as it always did when He was present.

The phrase, *"There came to Him the Chief Priests, and the Scribes, and the Elders,"* represents three different groups or orders and, as well, leaders in these particular orders.

1. Chief Priests: These were members of the vaunted Sanhedrin, which was the ruling body of Israel. These could well have been the High Priests or former members who held that highest office. They were, at times, called *"Chief Priests."* These could have been representatives of these particular groups; however, inasmuch as the definite

article in the Greek is used in each case, quite possibly these were not representatives, but rather the High Priests themselves, whether current or former.

This group opposed Christ greatly, and as His claims and mission became more clear, their opposition increased, as here. As well, He strongly denounced them in His Parables, etc. Considering the cleansing of the Temple and the great crowds which flocked to Him, such fueled their opposition. It would reach its bitter climax only in the arrest and trial of the Saviour.

(The term *"Chief Priests"* might have described not only members of the High-Priestly families who served in the Sanhedrin, but the title could also have included Temple Officers, such as the Treasurer and Captain of Police.)

2. Scribes: These, in effect, were to be the Pastors of the people, and were supposed to be scholars of the Law of Moses.

3. Elders: These were members also of the Sanhedrin, and shared with the Chief Priests the power of determining religious affairs and, if necessary, of expulsion from the Synagogue. These were actually the religious leaders of Israel, and they bitterly opposed Christ. They saw in Him a threat to their position, and would not recognize Him as being sent from God. In truth, they would not have recognized anyone truly sent from God. These individuals were religious but exceedingly evil, so evil, in fact, that they would murder the Lord of Glory!

RELIGION!

When one reads these Passages, one is reading the greatest thrust of Satan, which has caused more people to die eternally lost than possibly anything else. I speak of religion! It has always opposed God, and consequently has ever attempted to stop His True Work. In truth, and sadly so, most of modern Christendom falls into the same category. This would include virtually all of Catholicism and most of that which calls itself *"Protestant."* Most of the old-line Churches, such as Baptist, Methodist, Presbyterian, etc., little believe at all in the Holy Spirit; consequently, precious little, if anything, can be done for the Lord in these circles. They have a *"form of Godliness, but deny the power thereof"* (II Tim. 3:5).

Regrettably, those who go under the Holiness banner, such as Nazarenes, etc., fall into the same category. Most have rejected the Holy Spirit; consequently, they have sunk into the quagmire of legalism. Sadder still, the Pentecostal Denominations, such as the Assemblies of God, Church of God, Pentecostal Holiness, etc., have pretty much abandoned the Holy Spirit in favor of the knowledge of this world, i.e., psychology, etc. (The old-line Churches have long since embraced these philosophies.)

Charismatics, which probably number approximately 100,000 Churches in America alone, are, for the most part, mired in false doctrine, such as the *"Greed Gospel"* or the *"Political Message."* And yet, there are some few exceptions to each group stated, with some Godly Preachers and people in any and all of these particular Churches, etc. But, for the far greater majority, if the situation presented itself now, as then, almost all would fall into step with the religious leaders in opposition to Christ. Even though many of these speak favorably of Him presently, still, He is window dressing in most Churches.

(28) "AND SAY UNTO HIM, BY WHAT AUTHORITY DO YOU THESE THINGS? AND WHO GAVE YOU THIS AUTHORITY TO DO THESE THINGS?"

The diagram is:

These who questioned Jesus were the custodians of the Temple. Our Lord, by forcibly ejecting those who were engaged in business in the Temple, was claiming a superior jurisdiction.

AUTHORITY

The phrase, *"And say unto Him,"* constitutes the very opposite of what they should have said and done. They should have fallen on their knees before Him, worshipping Him, but instead they will do the very opposite!

The question, *"By what authority do You these things?"* was reasonable in their minds. They were the custodians of the Temple. Our Lord, by forcibly ejecting those who were engaged in business activities in the Temple, had greatly encroached upon their authority and, in effect, was claiming a superior position; consequently, they asked Him in public now to produce His credentials: first, to state the nature of His authority; and second, to name the person from whom He had received it.

They were highly angered for a number of reasons: first of all, His action concerning cleansing the Temple had cost them a considerable amount of money, especially since it was Passover, which enjoyed the greatest crowds of the year. As well, in His Parables He was teaching the massive crowds particular things which greatly incriminated these religious leaders. Inasmuch as it was clearly obvious as to the identity of those of whom He was speaking, they are now placed in a very awkward position. Furthermore, they greatly resented His popularity, especially considering the healings and Miracles.

As stated, they in no way considered Him to be the Messiah, but instead to be far beneath them, socially, spiritually, and in every way, especially since He was but a peasant. Were it not for the accolades of the crowds and His vast popularity, they would long since have taken Him in hand. They had not done so simply because they felt they could not do so; however, the situation was now becoming desperate, at least in their eyes.

THE EXERCISE OF AUTHORITY

By the use of the word *"authority,"* they were speaking of delegated power, the liberty and right to act. Such authority as men have is delegated to them by God, whether directly or indirectly, to Whom they must answer for the way they use it. God's Authority is an aspect of His unalterable, universal, and eternal dominion over His world (Ex. 15:18; Ps. 29:10; 93:1; 146:10; Dan. 4:34).

Throughout the Bible, the reality of God's Authority is proved by the fact that all who ignore or flout this claim incur Divine Judgment. The Royal Judge has the last word, and so His Authority is vindicated. In Old Testament times, which were still in force as recorded in the Gospels, God exercised authority over His people through the agency of Prophets, Priests, and Kings, whose respective work it was to proclaim His Messages (Jer. 1:7), teach His Laws (Deut. 31:11; Mal. 2:7), and rule in accordance with those Laws (Deut. 17:18). In doing so, they were to be respected as God's representatives, having authority from Him.

AUTHORITY FROM GOD AND AUTHORITY FROM MAN

The authority held by these religious rulers who questioned Jesus was not derived from God but rather from Rome; consequently, it was man-devised authority, which the people were to obey up to a point, providing it did not abrogate the Word of God, which it often did. However, Jesus in no way was subject to the laws of Rome, or anyone else, for that matter, even though He willingly and Personally subjected Himself to such authority, providing it did not abrogate the Word of God.

The Authority of Jesus Christ is an aspect of Kingship, which these religious leaders would not recognize. It is both personal and official, for Jesus is both Son of God and Son of Man (the Messiah). As Man and Messiah, His Authority is real because it is delegated to Him by the God at Whose Command He does His Work (Christ applauded the centurion for seeing and recognizing this — Mat. 8:9).

As the Son, His Authority is real because He is Himself God. Authority to judge has been given Him, both that He may be honored as the Son of God (for judgment is God's Work), and also because He is the Son of Man (for judgment is the Messiah's Work [Jn. 5:22, 27]).

CHRIST JESUS AND AUTHORITY

The authority of the Son of God is that of a Divine Messiah; of a God-Man, doing His Father's Will in the double capacity of:

A. Human Servant, in Whom meet the saving offices of Prophet, Priest, and King; and,

B. Divine Son, Co-Creator and Sharer in all the Father's Works (Jn. 5:19).

The more-than-human Authority of Jesus was manifested during His Ministry in various ways, such as the finality and independence of His Teaching (Mat. 7:28); His Power to cast out devils (Mk. 1:27); His mastery over storms (Lk. 8:24); His forgiving of sin (a thing which, as the bystanders rightly pointed out, only God can do), which, when challenged, proved His claim (Mat. 9:8; Mk. 2:5-12).

After His Resurrection, He declared that He had been given *"All Power in Heaven and Earth"* — a Messianic Dominion to be exercised in such a way as effectively to bring the elect into His Kingdom of Salvation (Mat. 28:18; Jn. 12:31; 17:2; Acts 1:8-9; 5:31). The New Testament proclaims the exalted Jesus as *"both Lord and Christ"* (Acts 2:36) — Divine Ruler of all things, and Saviour-King of His people. The Gospel is in the first instance a demand for ascent to this estimate of His Authority.

In short, He did the things He did by Divine Authority from His Heavenly Father. He said, *"The Son can do nothing of Himself, but what He sees the Father do: for what things soever He does, these also does the Son likewise"* (Jn. 5:19).

The question, *"And who gave You this authority to do these things?"* concerned the Source. The first question pertained to His Authority being Divine, and the second question pertained to its Source, God the Father. It would have done Him no good to have answered them outright, for they would not have accepted His answer; consequently, He must address their questions from another angle.

(29) "AND JESUS ANSWERED AND SAID UNTO THEM, I WILL ALSO ASK OF YOU ONE QUESTION, AND ANSWER ME, AND I WILL TELL YOU BY WHAT AUTHORITY I DO THESE THINGS."

The overview is:

This Passage actually means that the correct response to His question will provide the answer to their questions.

THE WORD OF GOD

The phrase, *"And Jesus answered and said unto them,"* pertains to the Holy Spirit telling Him how to answer these questions; however, it must be understood that the Holy Spirit only helped Him respecting information that was already in His Heart. He knew the Word of God as no one had ever known it, and for several reasons.

First of all, He had never sinned, not even one time. Consequently, His Mind was not dulled in any manner regarding the debilitating effects of sin. He said, *"I have refrained my feet from every evil way, that I might keep Your Word"* (Ps. 119:101). We, therefore, learn from this that sin (the evil way) dulls the sense perception and Spirit perception of the Word of God.

Further, Christ had a love for the Word that no one else had ever had. He said, *"O how I love Your Law! It is my meditation all the day"* (Ps. 119:97). There is no one who has devoted the time and attention to the Word of God as Christ. It must also be remembered that the attention devoted was not in the form of Deity, but rather the Man, Christ Jesus. In other words, He had to learn the Word exactly as we learn the Word, but with the exception that He was not plagued, as we are, by the drawbacks of the Fall.

The phrase, *"I will also ask of you one question, and answer Me,"* points to only one question which will address their two. It will greatly simplify the issue. The phrase, *"And I will tell you by what authority I do these things,"* actually means that the correct response to His question will provide the answer.

(30) "THE BAPTISM OF JOHN, WAS IT FROM HEAVEN, OR OF MEN? ANSWER ME."

The exposition is:

John had introduced Christ as the Messiah; if they claimed the Prophet to be of God, then they would have to acknowledge the One Whom he had introduced. They had tried to put Jesus on the spot, but now they instead are on the spot.

THE BAPTISM OF JOHN

The question, which begins with the phrase, *"The Baptism of John,"* concerned the Ministry of John the Baptist, with its Baptism of Repentance demanded of Israel (Mk. 1:4). John was the one who *"prepared the Way of the Lord,"* i.e., Messiah, the Lord Jesus Christ (Mk. 1:3). John also introduced Jesus as the Messiah by saying, *"Behold the Lamb of God, which takes away the sin of the world"* (Jn. 1:29).

The question, *"Was it from Heaven, or of*

men?" puts these religious leaders on the spot. In effect, their answer, that is, if they would give one, must either proclaim John as being of God or of the Devil! The words, *"answer Me,"* are asked before the crowd, which, no doubt, had assembled. They had tried to put Him on the spot, but now the tables are turned.

(31) "AND THEY REASONED WITH THEMSELVES, SAYING, IF WE SHALL SAY, FROM HEAVEN; HE WILL SAY, WHY THEN DID YOU NOT BELIEVE HIM?"

The synopsis is:

It refers to believing what John said about Jesus.

THE HORNS OF A DILEMMA

The phrase, *"And they reasoned with themselves,"* means, in essence, that they went into a huddle. It would have been somewhat embarrassing with the crowd looking on awaiting their answer. They are thrown on the horns of a dilemma.

The phrase, *"Saying, If we shall say, From Heaven,"* proclaims them having no regard for who John really was, only for an answer which would get them out of this dilemma. The question, *"He will say, Why then did you not believe Him?"* means they would have to believe John, at least if this admission is made regarding John's introduction of Jesus as the Messiah.

(32) "BUT IF WE SHALL SAY, OF MEN; THEY FEARED THE PEOPLE: FOR ALL MEN COUNTED JOHN, THAT HE WAS A PROPHET INDEED."

The structure is:

The respect for John by the people had even deepened since his martyrdom; they feared if they denied John's calling, the people might stone them then and there.

FEAR

The phrase, *"But if we shall say, of men; they feared the people,"* presents the only thing that stopped them from claiming John the Baptist was *"of men,"* i.e., the Devil. The phrase, *"For all men counted John, that he was a Prophet indeed,"* means that the respect for John by the people was even greater now than when he was alive. These religious leaders feared that if they said what they really believed, which was to deny John, they might very well suffer the anger of the people, even then and there.

(33) "AND THEY ANSWERED AND SAID UNTO JESUS, WE CANNOT TELL. AND JESUS ANSWERING SAID UNTO THEM, NEITHER DO I TELL YOU BY WHAT AUTHORITY I DO THESE THINGS."

The exegesis is:

In effect, Jesus said: *"I will not answer you, because your answer to My question is the answer to your own."* Jerome says, *"He thus shows that they knew, but would not answer; they saved themselves from this dilemma by professing ignorance."*

IGNORANCE?

The phrase, *"And they answered and said unto Jesus, We cannot tell,"* concerns them giving an answer before the crowd which was ridiculous, to say the least. They were the very ones who were supposed to know, and yet they say, *"We cannot tell."* These were supposed to be the scholars of the Mosaic Law. They were the spiritual guides of the people. They were supposed to know if something was of God or of men! Their weak, tepid answer shows what they really were! They did not know God, and had no knowledge of spiritual things, and yet they considered themselves *"spiritual leaders."*

To be sure, many, if not most, modern religious leaders presently fall into the same category!

The phrase, *"And Jesus answering said unto them, Neither do I tell you by what authority I do these things,"* says, in effect, that they actually knew. Of course they did! They had no regard or concern for the spiritual authority which now presents itself, which means they had no regard for God. They were concerned about two things — the loss of the money, and their hatred for Christ.

> *"I love to tell the story of unseen things above,*
> *"Of Jesus and His glory, of Jesus and His love.*
> *"I love to tell the story, because I know 'tis true;*
> *"It satisfies my longings as nothing else can do."*

CHAPTER 12

(1) "AND HE BEGAN TO SPEAK UNTO THEM BY PARABLES. A CERTAIN MAN PLANTED A VINEYARD, AND SET AN HEDGE ABOUT IT, AND DUG A PLACE FOR THE WINEFAT, AND BUILT A TOWER, AND LET IT OUT TO HUSBANDMEN, AND WENT INTO A FAR COUNTRY."

The composition is:

The tower would contain a watchman, who was to guard the vineyard from plunderers; it spoke of the spiritual leaders of Israel.

THE PARABLE

The phrase, *"And He began to speak unto them by Parables,"* represents the first time our Lord had used this method in Jerusalem, although it had been used plentifully in Galilee. Many of the Parables of Jesus are not merely illustrations of general principles; instead they embody messages which cannot be conveyed any other way, at least to present the desired Truth. Parables are the appropriate form of communication for bringing to men the Message of the Kingdom, since their function is to jolt them into seeing things in a new way. They are means of enlightenment and persuasion, intended to bring the hearers to the point of decision.

Jesus, as it were, stands where his hearers stand, and uses imagery familiar to them to bring new and unfamiliar insights to them. Just as a betrothed finds himself restricted by common expression and must resort to poetry to express his feelings, so Jesus expresses the Message of the Kingdom in the appropriate forms of language.

Parables, and especially those given by Jesus, have a tendency to enlighten the Believer, while, at the same time, confusing the unbeliever. Actually, Isaiah prophesied that the preaching of the Word of God would do the same thing. The truth is that Jesus' Parables are unique.

Parables of other teachers can, to some extent, be separated from the teachers themselves, but Jesus and His Parables are inseparable. To fail to understand Him is to fail to understand His Parables.

PARABLE OF THE HOUSEHOLDER

In this *"Parable of the householder,"* Jesus is accusing the religious leaders of Israel, even in the presence of the crowds, of being the future murderers of the Messiah. His Purpose was to expose the true character of the hostility of the Sanhedrin.

The phrase, *"A certain man planted a vineyard,"* constitutes no other than God Himself. The *"Vineyard"* also was a recognized symbol of Israel as the Covenant people, and both the members of the Sanhedrin and the better-taught among the crowd could not but understand the symbolism (Wuest).

As the *"Church"* belongs to Jesus, likewise, the *"Vineyard"* belongs to God (Mat. 16:18). This *"Vineyard"* sprang from the loins of Abraham. The members of each of the Twelve Tribes also sprang from the twelve sons of Jacob. In the midst of a sinful, wicked, idol-worshipping world, God formed a people unto Himself, who would do three things:

1. Give the world the Word of God, which they did. Every writer of the Bible is Jewish, with possibly the exception of Luke; however, I personally think that Luke also was Jewish.

2. To be the womb of the Messiah, consequently bringing the Redeemer into the world, the Last Adam.

3. To evangelize the world, hence, the *"Temple being a house of prayer for all nations"* (Mk. 11:17). However, as we shall see, the *"Husbandmen,"* i.e., Israel, little attended the Vineyard as the Owner desired.

THE HEDGE

The phrase, *"And set an hedge about it,"* actually refers to the manner in which Israel is situated in the Middle East. The nation was somewhat guarded on the east by the River Jordan, and on the west by the Mediterranean Sea. On the north lay the mountains of Lebanon, and down south was the desert. So, in a sense, there was a physical *"hedge about it."*

Furthermore, and of far greater significance, there was a *"hedge"* of the Power of God about the nation. Consequently, when Israel conducted herself according to the Word of God, no nation or group of nations in the world could conquer her. Only when Israel forsook the Lord did the *"hedge"* come down. Ultimately, as the Parable will proclaim, the hedge would be torn down completely.

THE FRUIT

The phrase, *"And dug a place for the winefat,"* would have been better translated *"winevat."* The *"winevat"* referred to the receptacle into which the wine ran after it had been pressed out of the grapes. As is obvious, this speaks of the product of the Vineyard, and also speaks of the *"fruit"* which came from Israel. At times, there was *"much fruit,"* because of strong spiritual leadership such as David, Jehoshaphat, Hezekiah, Josiah, and others!

The manner in which the wine is produced by the crushing of the grapes spoke of the suffering and opposition that Israel underwent from other nations. It was allowed by God, with no intention of destruction, but rather that Israel would run to Him.

As well as this Parable applying to Israel of old, it can, by symbolism, also apply to the Church, and even to the individual.

Entire religious Denominations have experienced the results of this Parable, simply because they ultimately set Jesus aside; consequently, their *"Vineyard"* was given to others.

Every Believer should read this Parable, not only with Israel in mind, but with the understanding that its lesson applies to all, even, as stated, to the individual Believer.

THE TOWER

The phrase, *"And built a tower,"* referred to the watchtower, where a watchman was placed to guard the Vineyard from plunderers. It spoke of the spiritual leaders of Israel. It also speaks of the modern Ministry. Every Preacher of the Gospel, along with the type of Ministry that God has given him (Eph. 4:11), is likewise called to be a *"watchman."*

Jude said, *"That you should earnestly contend for the Faith which was once delivered unto the Saints"* (Jude, Vs. 3).

As well, Paul said, *"Preach the Word; be instant in season, out of season; reprove, rebuke, exhort with all longsuffering and doctrine.*

"For the time will come when they will not endure sound Doctrine; but after their own lusts shall they heap to themselves teachers having itching ears;"

He then said, *"And they shall turn away their ears from the Truth, and shall be turned unto fables."*

And then, *"But watch thou in all things,"* means to serve as a *"watchman"* (II Tim. 4:2-5).

Sadly and regrettably, the modern *"watchtower"* is occupied too much by those who little care regarding the encroachment of enemies, exactly as Israel of old.

THE HUSBANDMEN

The phrase, *"And let it out to husbandmen,"* refers to the teachers of the people, as well as the people. Each member of the Church, then, as now, is required to seek the welfare of the whole body (Bickersteth). All Believers are responsible; and yet, the leaders are always the far more responsible!

The Church, despite the fact of being stronger numerically and financially than maybe ever before, is weaker, regarding the spiritual sense, at this present time that it has been since the Reformation. It perfectly fits the scenario of the Church at Laodicea. Jesus said of that Church, *"So then because you are lukewarm, and neither cold nor hot, I will spue you out of My mouth.*

"Because you say, I am rich, and increased with goods, and have need of nothing; and knowest not that you are wretched, and miserable, and poor, and blind, and naked" (Rev. 3:16-17).

There is a powerful effort presently being made to shift the Church away from the Biblical model of Preaching and Teaching the Word. In fact, the *"new wave"* is probably spearheaded more than anything else by the *"Purpose Driven Church"* model. To be sure, the *"Government of Twelve* (G-12)" teaching is not far behind. Both of these models completely abrogate the leading of the Holy Spirit, with man taking the place of the Spirit. Probably one could say that the Purpose Driven model is far more worldly, with the G-12 model functioning greatly in the realm of superstition.

To be frank, both are fueled by psychology,

heavily laced with that philosophy. In essence, both of these genres fall under the heading of *"law."* To be sure, it's not the Law of Moses, but rather laws made up by individuals, under the guise of Revelation. While it definitely may be revelation, to be sure, it is revelation from *"angels of light"* (II Cor. 11:13-15).

HOW DO I KNOW THAT THESE REVELATIONS ARE THE PRODUCT OF ANGELS OF LIGHT?

Of course, as every Bible student knows, *"angels of light"* constitute that which is Satan. It means that he crafts his wares to look like God, sound like God, and claim to be of God, when, in reality, their father is Satan. As Paul said, those who propagate these false messages can be construed as none other than *"Satan's ministers"* (II Cor. 11:15).

I know that these *"revelations,"* so-called, are from angels of light simply because their message is anything but *"Jesus Christ and Him Crucified."*

A few days back, Frances asked me to read the book, *"The Purpose Driven Life."* She had read it, and commented on its absolute worthlessness, despite the fact it was being heralded far and wide, etc.

At any rate, I consented to read it, or at least I began to read it. But, after going through a few pages, I stopped, because it was useless to continue.

Why?

It quickly became very obvious that the Message was not *"Jesus Christ and Him Crucified,"* but something else altogether. And I personally know, as any serious Bible student knows, that if the Message is not *"Jesus Christ and Him Crucified,"* then whatever kind of message it is, it's not going to do anyone any good. It's just that simple.

That's the reason I know, and can be so certain of my position, that these *"new revelations"* are totally unscriptural; consequently, they will not fall out to the good of their adherents. In other words, no one will get saved by believing these false doctrines. No one will be delivered. No one will grow in Grace and the Knowledge of the Lord. In truth, the very opposite will be the end result.

As an example, Joel Osteen, who pastors Lakewood Church in Houston, Texas, boasts that even though he believes in the Cross, it will seldom, if ever, be mentioned in his messages; and, furthermore, no one will see any symbol of the Cross in his Church, because it might be offensive to some. And of course, the message of the *"Purpose Driven Church,"* which Joel Osteen's church advocates, is that no one be offended. And most definitely, the Cross of Christ is an offense (Gal. 5:11).

But what did Paul say?

He said, *"Christ sent me not to baptize, but to preach the Gospel: not with wisdom of words, lest the Cross of Christ should be made of none effect.*

"For the preaching of the Cross is to them who perish foolishness; but unto us which are saved it is the Power of God.

"But we preach Christ Crucified.

"For I determined not to know anything among you, save Jesus Christ and Him Crucified" (I Cor. 1:17-18, 23; 2:2).

Finally, Paul said, *"But God forbid that I should glory, save in the Cross of our Lord Jesus Christ, by Whom the world is crucified unto me, and I unto the world"* (Gal. 6:14).

Now, if the Bible is to be our guide, this means that our dear Brother in Houston is not preaching the Gospel, and neither are any of those who subscribe to the *"Purpose Driven Life/Church"* model.

To be sure, the Cross of Christ is definitely an offense; however, it must also quickly be said that every single person in this world who has ever been saved, and then delivered, had their life changed, etc., every single one, and without exception, has received what they did receive from the Lord, all by the means of the Cross. As we say constantly, Christ is the Source, while the Cross is the Means (Jn. 3:16; Rom. 6:3-5).

THE CROSS AND SUPERSTITION

Many Christians are being deceived into believing their Pastor is preaching the Cross, when, in reality, he only mentions it. In other words, about the only thing he knows about the Cross is as it refers to Salvation; consequently, the knowledge of most in that capacity is mostly in the sentimental vein.

In other words, they hardly know or understand what the Cross means in respect to the benefits, which pertain to every single thing we receive from the Lord. Consequently, most such Preachers, as sincere as they might be, although believing the Cross as it regards Salvation, look to other means as it regards Sanctification, and that's where the great problem comes in.

The whole of society favors as its greatest pastime the improvement of self. Whether Christian or otherwise, everyone is trying to *"improve self,"* which is actually the major thrust of these false revelations. But no matter how hard one tries, or what technique is used, self cannot be improved by self. By his own machinations, irrespective as to what they might be, man simply cannot improve himself.

While it is certainly true that *"self"* can be improved and, in fact, must be improved, it can only be done by and through the Ministry, Person, and Power of the Holy Spirit. He Alone can develop His Fruit (the Fruit of the Spirit) in our lives (Gal. 5:22-23). And the clincher is, He works exclusively within the boundaries of the Finished Work of Christ, i.e., the Cross (Rom. 8:2). In other words, He demands that our Faith be exclusively in the Cross, and remain exclusively in the Cross, before He will carry out His Work. That is the only way, and I mean the only way, that self can be improved.

Unfortunately, many Preachers are addressing themselves to the Cross in a totally unscriptural manner. In other words, it is mostly in the realm of superstition, which falls out to *"white magic."* Black magic is an attempt to manipulate the world of spiritual darkness, i.e., *"demon spirits,"* etc. White magic is an attempt to manipulate the world of light, i.e., that of the Lord, by doing certain things, etc.

One of those *"certain things"* is the superstition of the Cross.

Whenever the Catholic Priest lays a crucifix on someone, proposing to cast demons out of that person, that is no more than superstition, i.e., *"white magic."* It is an attempt to use something legitimate, such as the Cross, to overcome the powers of darkness, but doing it in all the wrong ways.

NOTES

Demons cannot be cast out in that manner. There is no magic about the Cross, etc. There are astounding benefits, but only if understood correctly.

Others think that by wearing a Cross around their neck as a necklace, or putting Crosses in their houses, or even on their Churches, that such are proclaiming the veracity of the Cross. They aren't! While there is nothing wrong with someone wearing a Cross on a necklace, or putting one on a Church, etc., the wrong comes in when one thinks that such carries with it some type of power. It doesn't!

The other day I heard of a Preacher who was attempting to bring about Deliverance for a homosexual. I'm told that he brought the man into his office, had him lay down on a large wooden Cross which he had in his office, stretching his arms out across the Cross beams, and then visualizing the terrible suffering experienced by Christ. He then, I'm told, poured water over him, which was supposed to symbolize some type of cleansing.

This is rank superstition; to be sure, the poor homosexual definitely did not experience any type of Deliverance.

Jesus said, *"And you shall know the Truth, and the Truth shall make you free"* (Jn. 8:32).

The Lord works exclusively by Faith, and that rules out all of these superstitious incantations. If the Preacher had sat the poor homosexual down and explained to him what Jesus did at the Cross, and that he is supposed to place his faith entirely in Christ and what Christ did at the Cross, he then would have been given the Truth, and if properly believing, could have been totally and completely delivered. In fact, that is the only way that anyone can be delivered of anything. But yet, many are trying to manipulate the Cross into some type of ceremony, etc., which, incidentally, is not found at all in the Word of God. And to be sure, if something is not in the Word, at least as it refers to a Doctrine, the Believer had better throw it aside.

VISUALIZATION AND THE SUFFERINGS OF CHRIST ON THE CROSS

Another favorite method of the G-12 and

others is the visualization of Christ suffering on the Cross. This, according to their thinking, is supposed to bring about some type of victory in one's life.

What do we mean by visualization?

First of all, visualization is not of God. Again, you won't find it in the Word of God any place. Visualization is an effort by the individual to place oneself in a trance of sorts, and doing so by visualizing the object desired, in this case, the sufferings of Christ and the Cross.

Let the Reader understand that even though the suffering and pain of Christ was extremely real, that's not what delivered humanity. While visualization of such may produce some type of trance or emotional experience and, no doubt, will, it will not be of God. In fact, when a person opens themselves up to visualization, which, incidentally is one of the methods of psychology, one opens oneself up to the spirit world, and not the spirit world of light, but rather darkness.

Let us put it in this way:

Paul said, *"For whatsoever is not of faith is sin"* (Rom. 14:23). In effect, *"visualization"* is sin! By no stretch of the imagination can it be labeled as *"Faith."* Faith is simply believing in something and, in this case, Christ and what He did for us at the Cross. That's the reason we constantly state that Christ and what He did at the Cross must ever be the Object of our Faith. In fact, this is where the great fight and struggle with the Christian commences. Satan endeavors to push the faith of the Believer onto something else other than Christ and the Cross, and he doesn't too very much care what the something else actually is. In fact, visualization will do just fine!

So, while a person may have an emotional experience regarding visualization of Christ on the Cross and His sufferings, it definitely will not fall out to any victory on the part of that person, but rather the very opposite. Again, you will look in vain in your Bible for anything that even remotely resembles visualization, especially visualization of Christ and the Cross. It simply isn't there. And if it isn't there, it should not, by any stretch of the imagination, be included in our way and worship.

WHAT ARE THE BENEFITS OF THE CROSS?

In effect, and as stated, every single thing that the Believer receives from the Lord, and I mean everything, is made possible, and exclusively, by the Cross. This was true from day one, is true at the present time, and will be forever true. The first thing that the Lord did with the First Family after their Fall was to tell them how they could have forgiveness of sins and communion with Him. It would be by virtue of an Altar, which symbolized the Cross, and the slain lamb, which symbolized Christ dying on the Cross. This is found in Genesis, Chapter 4.

And there the battle commences. It has raged ever since.

Of the two brothers of our illustration, Cain and Abel, there is no difference. They are both corrupt branches of a decayed tree, both born outside Eden, both guilty, both sinners, no moral difference, and both sentenced to death.

The words, *"By faith"* (Heb. 11:4), teach that God had revealed a way of approach to Himself (Rom. 10:17). Abel accepts this way, which is the Way of the Cross; Cain rejects it. As stated, while there was no difference between the brothers, there was an eternal difference between their sacrifices.

Abel's Altar speaks of Repentance, of Faith, and of the Precious Blood of Christ, the Lamb of God without blemish. Cain's altar tells of pride, unbelief, and self-righteousness, which, in effect, characterize the modern altars of the so-called new revelations. Abel's Altar is beautiful to God's Eye and repulsive to man's; Cain's altar, beautiful to man's eye and repulsive to God's.

These *"altars"* exist today: around the one, that is, Christ and His atoning Work, few are gathered; around the other, many. God accepts the slain lamb and rejects the offered fruit; and the offering being rejected, so, of necessity, is the offeror (Williams).

Today we have this scene being repeated all over, exactly as it has been repeated innumerable times from then until now. Abel's Altar, the Cross of Christ, is beautiful to God's Eye, but repulsive to man's. Cain's altar, while beautiful to man's eye, and accepted by man, is nevertheless repulsive to God's Eye.

As one follows the Bible Story, and all the way from the beginning, it becomes obviously clear that the Bible is the Story of Christ and Him Crucified. That is the Message, and it has not changed. And when someone, anyone, comes up with a Message which claims to be of God, which is something other than Christ and the Cross, irrespective as to how religious it may seem to be, it simply is not of God; it has, in fact, as its father, Satan himself. That is blunt, but true.

Let me say it again:

This means that the Purpose Driven Life message is from Satan! It means that the Government of Twelve teaching is from Satan! It means that the Word of Faith doctrine is from Satan! Actually, the Word of Faith doctrine openly repudiates the Cross, referring to it as *"past miseries"* and *"the greatest defeat in human history."*

But let the Believer understand that irrespective as to what these false directions promise, every single thing received by anyone from the Lord, ever, has always been by the means of Christ and the Cross.

THE CROSS, THE MEANING OF THE NEW COVENANT

It was to the Apostle Paul that the meaning of the New Covenant was given, which, in effect, is the meaning of the Cross.

Paul said, *"But I certify you, Brethren* (make known), *that the Gospel which was preached of me* (the Message of the Cross) *is not after man.* (Any Message other than the Cross is definitely devised by man.)

"For I neither received it of man (Paul had not learned this great Truth from human teachers), *neither was I taught it* (he denies receiving instruction from other men), *but by the Revelation of Jesus Christ.* (Revelation is the mighty act of God whereby the Holy Spirit discloses to the human mind that which could not be understood without Divine intervention)" (Gal. 1:11-12).

And if anyone halfway studies the Apostle Paul, the conclusion must be reached that his message was *"Jesus Christ and Him Crucified"* (Rom. 6:3-14; 8:1-2, 11; I Cor. 1:17-18, 23; 2:2; Gal., Chpt. 5; 6:14; Eph. 2:13-18; Col. 2:14-15).

NOTES

Concerning all who oppose the Cross, the Apostle said, *"Brethren, be followers together of me* (be 'fellow-imitators'), *and mark them which walk so as you have us for an example* (observe intently).

"(For many walk (speaks of those attempting to live for God outside of the victory and rudiments of the Cross of Christ), *of whom I have told you often, and now tell you even weeping* (this is a most serious matter), *that they are the enemies of the Cross of Christ* (those who do not look exclusively to the Cross of Christ must be labeled 'enemies'):

"Whose end is destruction (if the Cross is ignored, and continues to be ignored, the loss of the soul is the only ultimate conclusion), *whose God is their belly* (refers to those who attempt to pervert the Gospel for their own personal gain), *and whose glory is in their shame* (the material things they seek, God labels as 'shame'), *who mind earthly things.)* (This means they have no interest in Heavenly things, which signifies they are using the Lord for their own personal gain)" (Phil. 3:17-19).

The Apostle also said, *"I marvel that you are so soon removed from Him* (the Holy Spirit) *Who called you into the Grace of Christ* (made possible by the Cross) *unto another gospel* (anything which doesn't have the Cross as its Object of Faith):

"Which is not another (presents the fact that Satan's aim is not so much to deny the Gospel, which he can little do, as to corrupt it); *but there be some who trouble you, and would pervert the Gospel of Christ* (once again, to make the object of faith something other than the Cross of Christ).

"But though we (Paul and his associates), *or an Angel from Heaven, preach any other gospel unto you than that which we have preached unto you* (Jesus Christ and Him Crucified), *let him be accursed* (eternally condemned; the Holy Spirit speaks this through Paul, making this very, very serious)" (Gal. 1:6-8).

This doesn't mean that the Epistles written by Peter and John, etc., are less than those written by Paul. All are the Word of God, and equally important; however, it was to Paul, as stated, that this great Word of Faith was given; consequently, everything that

Peter and John and others said, as it regards the Cross, complements what Paul had already given.

Paul charted the course, as designed by the Holy Spirit. In fact, the Holy Spirit referred to him as the *"Masterbuilder"* of the Church.

He said, *"According to the Grace of God which is given unto me, as a wise masterbuilder* (in essence, Paul, under Christ, founded the Church), *I have laid the foundation* (Jesus Christ and Him Crucified), *and another builds thereon* (speaks of all Preachers who follow thereafter, even unto this very moment, and have built upon this foundation). *But let every man take heed how he builds thereupon.* (All must preach the same Doctrine Paul preached, in essence, *"Jesus Christ and Him Crucified"* [I Cor. 3:10].)

So, if what we preach is not that which Paul preached, then what we are preaching is not the Gospel, and must be shunned at all costs.

HEAVEN

The phrase, *"And went into a far country,"* refers to God's residence as being in Heaven. While He was here with His people in Spirit, still, the responsibility of the *"Vineyard"* was that of the Husbandmen. As it was with Israel then, it is the same with the Church presently! Due to what Jesus did at the Cross, the modern Believer has a far greater Presence of the Lord than Israel of old. Then He dwelt in a house made with hands, while now He dwells in every individual Believer (I Cor. 3:16).

However, if that house is defiled, whether the Temple of old or the individual Temple of the Holy Spirit, it will be destroyed, exactly as the old Temple was destroyed (I Cor. 3:17). This means that even with the greater Presence of the Lord in the modern Church, still, the responsibility lies with the *"Husbandmen,"* i.e., *"Preachers."*

The Lord is now in Heaven, seated by the Right Hand of the Father, because His Work is completed and accepted (Heb. 1:3). He has given us, as stated, the responsibility of carrying forth this great Message of Christ and Him Crucified, which is the only hope for a lost world.

NOTES

Jesus said, *"And I, if I be lifted up from the Earth* (refers to His Death at Calvary; He was *'lifted up'* on the Cross; the *'Cross'* is the foundation of all victory), *will draw all men unto Me* (refers to the Salvation of all who come to Him, believing what He did, and trusting in its atoning work).

"This He said, signifying what death He should die (Reynolds says, *'In these Words, we learn that the attraction of the Cross of Christ will prove to be the mightiest and most sovereign motive ever brought to bear on the human will, and, when wielded by the Holy Spirit as a Revelation of the matchless love of God, will involve the most sweeping judicial sentence that can be pronounced upon the world and its prince')"* (Jn. 12:32-33).

But let me quickly say that the Cross of Christ is proved mighty in the hearts and lives of those who accept it. Tragically, the far greater majority will reject it.

Jesus also said, *"Enter you in at the strait gate* (this is the Door, Who is Jesus [Jn. 10:1]): *for wide is the gate, and broad is the way, that leads to destruction, and many there be which go in thereat* (proclaims the fact of many and varied religions of the world, which are false and lead to eternal Hell-fire):

"Because strait is the gate, and narrow is the way, which leads unto life, and few there be that find it (every contrite heart earnestly desires to be among the *'few'*; the requirements are greater than most are willing to accept)" (Mat. 7:13-14).

(2) "AND AT THE SEASON HE SENT TO THE HUSBANDMEN A SERVANT, THAT HE MIGHT RECEIVE FROM THE HUSBANDMEN OF THE FRUIT OF THE VINEYARD."

The composition is:

This speaks of Old Testament Prophets.

THE SERVANT

The phrase, *"And at the season He sent to the Husbandmen a servant,"* speaks, as stated, of the Old Testament Prophets. In fact, the Lord guided Israel through the Ministry of *"Prophets."* Their Ministry was to a far greater degree the proclamation of Righteousness, rather than foretelling coming events. While the Lord definitely used them in the latter, still, their greater Ministry was always to preach Righteousness, and to whip Israel back into line.

Prophets still function in this capacity under the New Covenant; however, there is a difference, in that the Church today is led by the Office and Ministry of the Apostle, which was not brought about under the Old Covenant. The Ministry of the Apostle has to do with the *"Message"* which the Lord has given him. That *"Message,"* which will always coincide perfectly with the Word of God, is meant to serve as direction for the Church.

It doesn't mean that others are not preaching the same message, but it does mean that there is a far greater emphasis on whatever Message the Lord desires to give to the Apostle. Furthermore, the Apostle, with the evidence being the Early Church, can function in any of the fivefold Callings (Eph. 4:11).

Despite the fact that many of the leaders of modern religious Denominations have attempted to usurp the place and position of the Apostle, even claiming to be Apostles themselves, the Lord continues to drive the Church through the Ministry of the True Apostle.

It should be understood that Apostles aren't elected by popular ballot, and neither are they appointed by men. In fact, such an idea borders on the ridiculous. Man has ever sought to usurp God's True Government, which always constitutes His Word, thereby inserting their own type of government, which is unscriptural.

While it's not wrong to have religious Denominations, and neither is it wrong to belong to one or have offices in those Denominations, still, it is to be ever understood that all of that we have named constitutes that which has been devised by men, which means that, at best, it can only serve as a ministry of helps. Those offices, irrespective of the names given to them, and I continue to refer to those which are elected by popular ballot or appointed by men, can never be construed as being Scriptural offices. As stated, some of them can be useful, but only some!

THE HARVEST

The phrase, *"That He might receive from the husbandmen of the fruit of the vineyard,"* respects the harvest, and that which

NOTES

is rightly His. All of this refers to the fact that God has *"seasons"* for the outpouring of His Holy Spirit.

In my own lifetime, I have seen two of these *"seasons."* The first was in the 1950's, with the great Divine Healing Revivals taking place all over the world. It was the Move of God which brought the Pentecostal Message from obscurity to the limelight. Concerning the Assemblies of God, with which we then were associated, they were planting, on average, one new Church a day and three on Sunday, in other words, nearly ten per week. Many of the other Pentecostal Movements were doing the same.

At that time, giant tents, seating as many as 10,000 people, were being stretched all over America and other parts of the world, housing great Salvation-Healing Revivals. Even though the Lord continued to heal the sick all the way from the time of Pentecost, still, it was not until this great Move of God that the God of Might and Miracles once again was introduced to the world.

The second great Move took place in the 1980's. Frances and I had the privilege and opportunity of being a part of this great Outpouring. Our Telecast then was aired all over the United States, Canada, and Central and South America. We also aired in the Philippines, parts of Africa, Europe, Australia, and other parts of the world. The program was translated into the languages of the people, and resulted in hundreds of thousands being brought to a saving knowledge of Jesus Christ.

Our Crusades in various countries saw some of the largest crowds ever recorded in these respective countries, with multiple thousands of people responding to the Altar Calls. In the Stadium in Santiago, Chile, the Stadium manager said that 28,000 people responded to the Altar Call on the closing Sunday of the meeting. This was a Move of God which touched almost the entirety of the world of that time.

Even in the early 1990's, our Telecast, translated into the Russian language, aired in Russia and covered all fifteen Republics of the former Soviet Union. Untold thousands were brought to Christ. Actually, I think one can say, without fear of exaggeration, that everywhere the Telecast aired, tremendous numbers of souls were saved. We give the Lord Alone the Praise and the Glory!

ANOTHER SEASON

And yet, I feel that another great *"season"* of the Moving of the Holy Spirit is coming, a Move so powerful that it will eclipse all others. I believe this *"season"* is referred to in the Promise, *"And it shall come to pass in the last days, saith God, I will pour out of My Spirit upon all flesh"* (Acts 2:17).

I realize that many conclude the *"last days"* to refer to the entirety of the time from the Day of Pentecost until the present hour; however, Acts 2:19-21 lets us know that while this may be the case, still, a greater Move will take place at the end, which, I believe, is near! I also believe this Ministry (Jimmy Swaggart Ministries) will have a part in this great Move, even as we were privileged to have a part in the previous Move.

(3) "AND THEY CAUGHT HIM, AND BEAT HIM, AND SENT HIM AWAY EMPTY."

The diagram is:

The failure to receive fruit points to the failure of Israel to heed the preaching of the Prophets.

MALTREATMENT OF THE PROPHETS

The phrase, *"And they caught him,"* refers to them coming to the Prophets, not to heed the Message, but instead to stop the Message. The phrase, *"And beat him,"* means *"to beat severely, to scourge."* The phrase, *"And sent him away empty,"* means, according to Wuest, that the failure to receive fruit points to the failure of Israel to heed the preaching of the Prophets.

This is what Jesus was addressing when He said, *"O Jerusalem, Jerusalem,* (presents Jesus standing in the Temple when He gave this sorrowing account), *you who kill the Prophets, and stone them which are sent unto you* (presents the terrible animosity tendered toward the Messengers of God), *how often would I have gathered your children together, even as a hen gathers her chickens under her wings, and you would not!* (Proclaims every effort made by the Lord, and made often, to bring Israel back to her senses).

NOTES

"Behold, your house (the Temple and Jerusalem are no longer God's habitation) *is left unto you desolate* (without God, which means they were at the mercy of Satan)*"* (Mat. 23:37-38).

(4) "AND AGAIN HE SENT UNTO THEM ANOTHER SERVANT; AND AT HIM THEY CAST STONES, AND WOUNDED HIM IN THE HEAD, AND SENT HIM AWAY SHAMEFULLY HANDLED."

The overview is:

The Church has been the primary source of the ill-treatment of God's Messengers.

ANOTHER SERVANT

The phrase, *"And again He sent unto them another servant,"* does not so much point to the act, as to the patience in dealing with these recalcitrant rebels. Once again, these who were being sent were the Prophets.

The phrase, *"And at him they cast stones,"* refers to the opposition becoming increasingly more severe.

The phrase, *"And wounded him in the head,"* means two things:

1. They were trying to kill him.
2. The projectiles aimed at his head were meant to stop the Message.

SHAMEFULLY HANDLED

The phrase, *"And sent him away shamefully handled,"* refers more to their attitude than the condition of the one sent. In Truth, the True Message of God is seldom met with approval. Actually, if there is widespread approval, as there is with the modern Purpose Driven Life Message, that is a sure sign that it's not of the Lord.

However, the greatest opposition to the True Message will always come from the *"Church."* For Israel was the *"Church,"* so to speak, of that day! So, as one reads these statements, one is also reading the present response of the modern Church to the Gospel of Jesus Christ. They try to stop the Message, hence, the striking of the *"head"* and the *"shameful handling"* of the Messenger.

Were it not for the laws of the land, and I speak of the separation of Church and State, this scene would be repeated in most countries today. It is not lack of evil in the heart which stays the hand, but lack of opportunity.

There is nothing in the world more evil than religion. It is far more evil than the vices, such as alcohol, drugs, immorality, etc. Many may blanch at that; however, they must remember that it was not the vices, as sordid as they are, which nailed Jesus to the tree, but rather the Church of His day.

To be frank and blunt, many of the leaders of modern religious Denominations fall into a far worse spiritual category, at least in the Eyes of God, than the promoters of vice, as wicked as the latter may be.

Let us say it again:

It was the Pharisees, who considered themselves to be the religious leaders of Israel, the Chief Priests, and the Scribes, who were supposed to be the Pastors of the people, who crucified Christ. By way of contrast, those who were embroiled in vices, as sordid as that may have been, held little or no animosity against Christ. It is the same presently!

(5) "AND AGAIN HE SENT ANOTHER; AND HIM THEY KILLED, AND MANY OTHERS; BEATING SOME, AND KILLING SOME."

The exposition is:

All of this proclaims an increase in the rebellion and its obvious results; barring Repentance, sin never slows, but instead increases.

AN INCREASE IN REBELLION

The phrase, *"And again He sent another,"* proclaims patience, love, and longsuffering, such as no mortal could ever have. Such is God!

The phrase, *"And him they killed, and many others; beating some, and killing some,"* proclaims an increase in their rebellion and its obvious results. As Jesus said, they killed the Prophets, and stoned them which the Lord sent to bring them to Repentance. The word *"many"* emphasizes the constant efforts to bring the *"Husbandmen"* to their senses, but all to no avail!

(6) "HAVING YET THEREFORE ONE SON, HIS WELLBELOVED, HE SENT HIM ALSO LAST UNTO THEM, SAYING, THEY WILL REVERENCE MY SON.

(7) "BUT THOSE HUSBANDMEN SAID AMONG THEMSELVES, THIS IS THE HEIR; COME, LET US KILL HIM, AND THE INHERITANCE SHALL BE OURS."

NOTES

The synopsis is:
This refers to the Lord Jesus Christ.

THE HEIR

The phrase, *"But those Husbandmen said among themselves, This is the heir,"* in this case refers to the Sanhedrin, the ruling body of Israel. The phrase, *"This is the Heir,"* means that these religious leaders recognized the Lord for what and Who He was, the Son of God, the Messiah of Israel.

How did the religious leaders think they could kill the Lord of Glory and not suffer horrifying consequences?

Sin and rebellion against God warps one's mind, until one does not think straight. Sin and rebellion are extremely selfish acts; consequently, these individuals saw only their selfish desires. They wanted nothing and no one to interfere with their self-will, even God; consequently, they were willing to go to any lengths to insure their desires, even the murdering of the Son of God.

Regarding how they thought they could succeed in such a task, the question might well be asked, *"How does Satan think he can succeed against God?"* God is Omnipotent (all-powerful), Omniscient (all-knowing), and Omnipresent (everywhere), whereas Satan is only a created being.

DECEPTION

The answer lies in deception. Satan is deceived, and so are all his followers, which included the religious leaders of Israel.

The phrase, *"Come, let us kill Him,"* addresses itself to the words of Paul, *"But we speak the Wisdom of God in a mystery, even the hidden wisdom, which God ordained before the world unto our glory:*

"Which none of the princes of this world knew: for had they known it, they would not have crucified the Lord of Glory" (I Cor. 2:7-8).

The reason the religious leaders of Israel did what they did, even with full knowledge as to Who Jesus was, is the same reason the whole world conducts itself as it does toward Christ. Most people probably know that Jesus is the Son of God, even though they will not admit it; however, being deceived, unbelief concerning His Redemption Plan causes their opposition.

The phrase, *"And the inheritance shall be ours,"* actually constitutes the plan of Satan from the beginning. Satan said, *"I will ascend above the heights of the clouds; I will be like the Most High"* (Isa. 14:14). Satan maneuvered against Israel through these religious leaders in order to steal the *"inheritance,"* i.e., that which belonged to God. In fact, Satan constantly endeavors to take the *"inheritance"* even from the individual. And unless the Believer has, as the Object of his Faith, Christ and the Cross, Satan will succeed, or else come very close to doing so.

I keep saying it because I must keep saying it:

There is only one way to live for God, only one way to walk in victory, only one way to have the *"more abundant life"* which Jesus promised (Jn. 10:10), and that is for the Believer to ever make Christ and the Cross the Object of his Faith, which then guarantees the help of the Holy Spirit, without Whom we, as Believers, cannot know victory in any capacity (Rom. 8:1-2, 11).

(8) "AND THEY TOOK HIM, AND KILLED HIM, AND CAST HIM OUT OF THE VINEYARD."

The structure is:

This was the last effort of Divine Mercy — the sending of the Incarnate God, Whom the Jews put to death without the city.

THEY KILLED THE LORD OF GLORY, AND DID SO IN THE NAME OF THE LORD

The phrase, *"And they took Him, and killed Him,"* refers to the Sanhedrin, the ruling body of Israel, crucifying the Lord. The phrase, *"And cast him out of the Vineyard,"* means they excommunicated the Lord. In other words, and in today's terminology, He was thrown out of the Church. He was condemned as a blasphemer and handed over to the Romans for Crucifixion.

Wuest says that His Crucifixion outside the walls of Jerusalem symbolized His expulsion from the community of Israel.

Tragically, this horrible spectacle of what Israel did to Christ, their Messiah and our Saviour, sets the example for much of that which is called *"Church"* down through the ages. In other words, the *"Church"* has, by and large, *"cast out"* that which is truly of God. By its very nature, organized religion is man-controlled and consequently man-centered. If it is man-controlled, it cannot be God-controlled! Therefore, anything truly of the Lord ultimately will be *"cast out"* of such an arrangement.

Let me give an example:

CAST OUT OF THE VINEYARD

Some years ago I had the opportunity to help a young man through to the Baptism with the Holy Spirit. He was a celebrated baseball player who had recently played (at the time) in one of the World Series. At any rate, not long after he came to Christ, the Lord helped me to explain the Baptism with the Holy Spirit to him, which he ultimately received.

In those days, Frances and I were away from Baton Rouge almost constantly in Evangelistic Meetings; however, sometime later, when we were back in town, I happened to see him and asked him how his present relationship with his Church, which I knew to be one of the prominent old-line Churches in the city, was coming along since he had been baptized with the Holy Spirit.

He smiled, and then said, *"Brother Swaggart, I no longer attend that Church.*

"The Pastor called me into his office and told me that I would probably be happier elsewhere.

"As long as I was getting drunk, gambling, and being unfaithful to my wife, I was welcome in the Church. But once I found Jesus as my Saviour, and was baptized with the Holy Spirit, with the evidence of speaking with other tongues, I was no longer welcome."

Now let's look at that again:

As long as he was drinking, cursing, carousing, being unfaithful to his wife, in other words, living an ungodly lifestyle, he was perfectly welcome in that Church. But now that he has quit those things and is praising the Lord and loving Jesus intently, he is no longer welcome!

Why?

It was because he had been baptized with the Holy Spirit, with the evidence of speaking with other tongues. This particular

Church didn't believe in that, so they *"cast out"* all in their ranks who did.

Regrettably, this type of scenario is not limited to the Doctrine just mentioned, but basically covers almost anything that is truly of God. It is indicative of many, if not most, of the Churches in the United States and Canada, and elsewhere in the world, for that matter! Even among the Churches which claim to believe in the fullness of the Spirit, many of them have become so man-controlled that they cannot at all tolerate anything that is Christ-controlled.

The scenario is somewhat strange. Many, if not most, of present religious Denominations had their beginning as they were *"cast out"* of other religious Denominations. They grew hungry for God, and their hunger was rewarded by *"excommunication."* However, almost invariably after two or three generations, the same religious Denominations, by now large and rich, begin to practice the same thing. In other words, the fires of Revival are lost, with the new generation coming on that little knows or understands the Moving of the Holy Spirit, consequently becoming man-controlled, where they once were Spirit-controlled. It is almost a vicious circle.

However, I believe that, in these last days, the situation with organized religion is going to become even more anti-Christ. The Scriptural evidence is plentiful that the apostate Church will aid and abet the Antichrist, at least in his rise to power (II Tim. 3:12-13; 4:3-4; Rev. 13:11-15).

(9) "WHAT SHALL THEREFORE THE LORD OF THE VINEYARD DO? HE WILL COME AND DESTROY THE HUSBANDMEN, AND WILL GIVE THE VINEYARD UNTO OTHERS."

The structure is:

This speaks of the Church, made up mostly of Gentiles, being the channel through which God is operating temporarily while Israel is in dispersion, and until Israel is re-gathered at the Second Advent and restored to fellowship and usefulness to God.

THAT WHICH THE LORD DOES

The question, *"What shall therefore the Lord of the Vineyard do?"* constitutes the question of questions! Matthew said that the Scribes thus answered Jesus (Mat. 21:41), and probably He repeated their answer. As well, they knew He was speaking of them. First of all, the *"Lord"* has the power to do whatever He desires, although they treated Him as if He had no power at all!

The phrase, *"He will come and destroy the Husbandmen,"* constitutes exactly what happened! In A.D. 70, the Roman General Titus, who commanded the Roman Tenth Legion, and who served as the instrument of the Lord, although unwittingly, totally destroyed Jerusalem, slaughtering over one million Jews, and selling hundreds of thousands as slaves. At that time, the nation was effectively *"destroyed"*!

Some may argue that this was done by Rome; however, while that is true, it was the Lord Who allowed it to be done. God uses men, nations, empires, and all things, for that matter, to carry out His Will. Rome was the instrument, but God was the Director.

THE GENTILES

The phrase, *"And will give the vineyard unto others,"* speaks of the Church, made up mostly of Gentiles, being the channel through which God is operating temporarily while Israel is in dispersion. So, the portend of the question was weighty, to say the least!

As we have stated, while this Parable pointed directly to Israel, still, it can pertain in principle to certain segments of the Church, as it has through the ages, and even to individuals. While it is not possible presently for men to kill Christ, as did Israel of old, nevertheless, it is done, at least in a spiritual sense, every day.

When the Early Church finally did apostate itself, eventually, over several centuries, sinking to the level of what is now known as the *"Catholic Church,"* the *"Vineyard"* was taken from them and *"given unto others."* This would have involved the Reformation under Martin Luther, as well as other giants of the Faith.

Out of this came the Baptist and Methodist Churches, among others, which had such great and positive influence on the United States and the world; actually, the great Methodist move in the 1800's steered this nation, without a doubt, toward freedom and prosperity. As well, Methodism pulled England out of the Dark Ages, and very well could have saved that nation from the slaughter that engulfed France.

However, as with so many religious Denominations, the flames of Revival began to wane and die in these respective Churches, with the *"Holiness"* movements then springing up to take their place. Again, God gave the *"Vineyard"* to *"others"*!

The flame burned brightly under the *"Holiness"* banner for some time, and then began to dim low. Ultimately, the flame degenerated into legalism, with God then raising up another group called *"Pentecostals."* Once again, the *"Vineyard"* was given to *"others."*

The mighty Pentecostal Move shook the world in the 1900's, and especially in the 1950's and '80's. It was a worldwide move, with tens of millions being brought to Christ and baptized with the Holy Spirit, with the evidence of speaking with other tongues. Truly, Bible Days were here again! (Acts 2:4).

But sadly, in the 1990's, that flame, as others before, began to dim low. At the present, only about one-third of the people in Pentecostal Churches even claim to be baptized with the Holy Spirit, with the evidence of speaking with other tongues; consequently, by all rights, these once-mighty Pentecostal Denominations can no longer rightly call themselves *"Pentecostal."* As Jesus said of Sardis so long ago, *". . . you have a name that you live, and are dead"* (Rev. 3:1).

Will the *"Vineyard"* now be taken from them and given to *"others"*? Or has it already been taken from them?

Some may argue that it has been given to the Charismatics; however, I do not think that one can legitimately say that a genuine Move of God has come about in this sector. While some Charismatic Churches have been used, and are presently being used, greatly by the Lord, still, for the most part, that sector is so freighted with false doctrine respecting the *"Greed Message"* and *"Political Message,"* that precious little is actually being done for Christ.

(In effect, the Government of Twelve teaching is a part of the *"Political Message."* They have actually segmented the entirety of the world, appointing *"apostles"* over these particular segments. To be brief, their efforts are more political than spiritual, even though the political spectrum is not wholly visible, at least at all times.)

So, if the Rapture holds for any time at all, and if there is not a Revival in the Pentecostal ranks, or even others, to whom shall this *"Vineyard"* be given?

(10) "AND HAVE YOU NOT READ THIS SCRIPTURE; THE STONE WHICH THE BUILDERS REJECTED IS BECOME THE HEAD OF THE CORNER."

The exegesis is:

The *"Corner"* represents the Cornerstone, which is the pivot point for the structure; Christ is the Head of the Church, and of the Work of God, due to what He did at the Cross (Zech. 4:7).

THE STONE

The phrase, *"And have you not read this Scripture,"* refers to Psalms 118:22-23; it is quoted again in Acts 4:11 and I Peter 2:4, 7. The phrase, *"The Stone which the builders rejected is become the Head of the Corner,"* refers to Christ. He is the *"Stone"* and *"The Head of the Corner."* The *"builders"* are the spiritual leaders of Israel.

The word *"rejected"* means that *"something is put to the test for the purpose of approving."* This tells the story of the Messiah's rejection by Israel. Israel was looking for its Messiah, especially since Daniel had prophesied that He would come at this time (Dan., Chpt. 9)! Jesus of Nazareth claimed to be the Messiah.

The leaders of Israel investigated His claims and found them to be true, substantiated by the Miracles which He performed (Jn. 3:2); yet, with all this evidence, they rejected Him as the Messiah because He did not meet their specifications. They were looking for a Messiah who would deliver Israel from the despotism of Rome, not from the dominion of sin (Wuest).

However, this same Messiah, the One murdered by Israel, rose from the dead and will one day become King of kings and Lord of lords over the Earth, as the Head of the Millennial Empire, the *"Headstone of the Corner."* The Prophet Zechariah said, *"He shall bring forth the Headstone thereof with shoutings, crying, Grace, grace unto it"* (Zech. 4:7).

As well, the idea of the phrase, *"The Head of the Corner,"* means that as long as Jesus is the *"Head"* and recognized as such, the blessings continue to flow; however, the moment He is replaced, as with Israel of old and many in the modern Church, He simply gives the *"Vineyard"* to others who will recognize Him as the *"Head of the Corner."*

It must ever be remembered that Christ is an active Head, and not a passive Head. Religious Denominations have the tendency to abrogate His Position and replace it with man-devised offices. In the Kingdom of God, this can never be tolerated!

(11) "THIS WAS THE LORD'S DOING, AND IT IS MARVELOUS IN OUR EYES?"

The exegesis is:

It wasn't marvelous in the eyes of the Israel of Jesus' day, and the results were awful. As the Church, we should take a lesson from what He has done. It had better be marvelous in our eyes.

THE LORD'S DOING!

The phrase, *"This was the LORD's doing,"* comes from Psalms 118:23. It refers to the great Plan of God, which necessitated God becoming flesh and dwelling among men in order to bring about the Redemption of man; consequently, Israel rejected that which was of God, i.e., *"the LORD's doing."* To fight against God is an untenable situation. Israel would be totally destroyed as a result of her action, and so also will anyone who does such a thing. I have seen major religious Denominations fight against God and bring spiritual death upon themselves.

At approximately the turn of the Twentieth Century, the Latter Rain outpouring of the Holy Spirit exploded upon the world. Even though many, if not most, of the people baptized with the Holy Spirit were actually out of old-line Churches, still, these Churches as a whole, at least for the most part, rejected the Holy Spirit. In the 1960's and '70's, the Holy Spirit began to be poured out in an even stronger measure on these hungry hearts in these particular Churches, including Catholics.

NOTES

THE CAMPMEETING HOUR

On January 1, 1969, according to the leading of the Holy Spirit, we went on the air with our Daily Radio Program, *"The Campmeeting Hour."* It was a fifteen minute, daily Radio Program, Monday through Friday. To be sure, our beginnings were of small moment; nevertheless, God began to bless until we had one of the largest daily Gospel audiences in Radio. This is remarkable, considering that our Program was only fifteen minutes in duration.

Almost from the beginning of this effort, the Lord began to deal with me about teaching on the many and varied attributes of the Holy Spirit. His speaking to me about this matter went on for a period of time; however, it came to a head, I believe, early one morning sometime before daylight. This would have been, I think, during the latter part of 1969.

I had awakened that early morning hour at approximately 2 a.m. or 3 a.m. I slipped out of bed and went outside to my prayer room, which also doubled as my office, etc. As I began to seek the Lord, I sensed a mighty Moving of the Holy Spirit, which was one of the greatest experiences, at least up to that time, I had ever known.

The Lord began to deal strongly with me about the teaching format of the Radio Program. I remember remonstrating to the Lord how unqualified I was, reminding Him that I was an Evangelist and not a Teacher. (What foolish things we sometimes say when the Lord deals with us!)

Even though this was many years ago, I still have a vivid memory of those early morning hours and what transpired at that time. I knew what the Lord was telling me, but yet fear gripped my heart because I realized that I actually was woefully inadequate as a Bible Teacher. The thought entered my mind to attend Bible College, but I realized that would take years and would not fit into that which the Lord was telling me to do.

Knowing what I was thinking, the Lord spoke to me and said, *"I will give you the gift of teaching, if you will obey Me."* It was just that simple! And yet, I wondered exactly how the Lord would do this. To me, it seemed impossible, at least for it to be done in a short period of time. I knew the Lord was moving upon me to begin teaching on the Holy Spirit immediately. But yet, and as stated, I also knew that I was woefully unprepared.

THE TEACHING MINISTRY

A few days later, it happened! I realize that many would say that such is impossible, and, in the natural, it is; nevertheless, in a short time, actually, in a matter of an hour or so, the Lord showed me what to do with respect to this all-important subject of teaching on the Holy Spirit, plus other subjects! When it fell into place, it seemed so simple and easy. Of course, the Holy Spirit always knows exactly what He is doing.

To be sure, I had excellent Bible knowledge, at least concerning the Light I had at that time. But, as stated, I had served as an Evangelist all of these years and had made little attempt to teach the Word. Many have questioned me as to what the Lord told me to do with respect to this all-important aspect of our Ministry. Once or twice I attempted to explain, but I soon realized that those to whom I was attempting to explain this matter didn't have the slightest idea what I was talking about. Consequently, I have not attempted that since.

At any rate, I immediately began to teach on the Holy Spirit over our daily Radio Program. I taught on the Gifts of the Spirit, the Fruit of the Spirit, and other attributes of the Holy Spirit. I taught for weeks on how to receive the Holy Spirit, also about speaking with other tongues, plus many other things relating to this all-important subject. I suppose I must have taught several months without a break.

Thousands of letters began to pour into our office in Baton Rouge, many of them from Baptists, Methodists, Presbyterians, and even Catholics! Most were hungry for the Holy Spirit, and readily drank in that which the Lord gave to me for them. I even received letters addressed to *"Mr. Pentecost, Baton Rouge, Louisiana,"* which were promptly delivered!

During this time, the Lord also instructed me to dedicate at least one Service in each of our City-wide Crusades to Believers being baptized with the Holy Spirit. We did this for a period of several years, and multiple thousands were baptized with the Holy Spirit, with the evidence of speaking with other tongues (Acts 2:4).

Most of these people, as stated, were former Baptists, Methodists, Lutherans, etc. Many Preachers in these Denominations also were filled; however, as a whole, and as stated, these Denominations strongly resisted the Holy Spirit, and even strongly fought against it. During this time, strong efforts were made by particular individuals, whoever they may have been, to get our Radio Program off the air. To take the time to enumerate all the incidents would be a fruitless exercise; however, suffice it to say that every effort was made that could be made, but, thankfully, to no avail! The Lord preserved the Program, despite the efforts of these Preachers who seemed to despise anything about the Holy Spirit, especially speaking with other tongues.

At that time, I believe the Lord strongly dealt with the leadership of these Denominations. But sadly, they rejected it. However, *"This was the Lord's doing,"* and they found themselves fighting against God. As a result, there presently is very little, if any, Moving and Operation of the Holy Spirit in these particular Denominations.

To be sure, anything done for the Lord will be by and through the Person and Agency of the Holy Spirit. However, if He is not wanted, then nothing is accomplished, at least for God. Church degenerates into *"dead Preachers preaching dead sermons to dead congregations."* It is only the Holy Spirit Who makes the difference in our lives. If He does not do it, it is not done!

Furthermore, to reject a part of what He does is to reject all of what He does. Many claim they want the Holy Spirit, but they don't want tongues. I do not think it is possible to have one without the other (Acts 2:4).

MARVELOUS!

The question, *"And it is marvelous in our eyes?"* probably would have been better translated as an exclamation! The idea is this:

It is marvelous in the Eyes of God, this great Work of Redemption wrought by the

Holy Spirit through Jesus Christ. As well, it is *"marvelous"* in the eyes of all Believers, and it should have been *"marvelous"* in the eyes of Israel. But tragically, it wasn't, and Israel died.

Anything done by the Lord should be *"marvelous"* in the eyes of all who are privileged to behold its wonders! If it isn't, that which happened to Israel will also happen to others. These Denominations which I have mentioned, with possibly some few exceptions among certain Churches, have all but died spiritually. While they are rich regarding material things, and while they are large regarding numbers of people, still, spiritually they have died. I realize that is a strong statement, but I believe it to be true.

Once again, allow us to say:

If *"it is the Lord's doing,"* it should also be *"our doing,"* and it should be *"marvelous in our eyes"*!

(12) "AND THEY SOUGHT TO LAY HOLD ON HIM, BUT FEARED THE PEOPLE: FOR THEY KNEW THAT HE HAD SPOKEN THE PARABLE AGAINST THEM: AND THEY LEFT HIM, AND WENT THEIR WAY."

The exegesis is:

He predicted that they would kill Him and also what would happen to them. God would destroy them! But still, they wouldn't turn around.

THEY SOUGHT TO KILL HIM

The phrase, *"And they sought to lay hold on Him,"* refers to the fact that they knew beyond the shadow of a doubt that this Parable was directed at them; however, their response was according to the evil of their own hearts, and not because of the Parable. The Parable should have brought them to Repentance, which the Word of God always is designed to do, at least when it is directed at men, which, most of the time, it is. (At times, it is directed at Satan, with whom there can be no repentance.)

The word *"sought"* means that these religious leaders immediately began to make plans to stop Christ, and by whatever means! At this point, Matthew records that Jesus then gave the *"Parable of the Marriage Feast,"* which Mark does not record, and which again pointed to these hypocrites. So, they are now casting about for any means at their disposal in order to silence the Lord; they actually will not stop until they have succeeded with their evil plans.

FEAR

The phrase, *"But feared the people,"* shows the true heart of religion. The true man of God fears God, and not people; but religion fears people, and not God! At this Passover time, Jerusalem was filled with people, perhaps as many as half a million or more. Josephus, the Jewish Historian, said that approximately 250,000 lambs were offered at this time, which would have necessitated a half million or more people in the city.

Some of these people had been healed by Christ; in effect, their lives had been given back to them. Consequently, they loved Him dearly! So, whatever would be done must be done undercover so as not to arouse the ire of the people. The foul deed would have to be crafted in such a way that the people would think the worst of Him; and, more importantly, it must be done quickly.

The phrase, *"For they knew that He had spoken the Parable against them,"* referred to the fact that if this got out among the people, their situation (the religious leaders) might quickly become perilous. The phrase, *"And they left Him, and went their way,"* refers to their taking a position that Jesus must be stopped, and at whatever price. They were now determined to find a way to bring it about. Regrettably, in a matter of hours, Judas will offer them the opportunity.

(13) "AND THEY SEND UNTO HIM CERTAIN OF THE PHARISEES AND OF THE HERODIANS, TO CATCH HIM IN HIS WORDS."

The composition is:

They wanted something for which they could incriminate Him, irrespective as to what it was, false or otherwise!

PHARISEES AND HERODIANS

The phrase, *"And they send unto Him certain of the Pharisees,"* referred to their most brilliant minds. The phrase, *"And of the Herodians,"* concerns a sect of Jews who supported the house of Herod, and who were in favor of giving tribute to Rome. This began with Herod the Great, who, some 30 years earlier, had put to death the infants at Bethlehem that he might thus get rid of Christ, lest any other than himself might be regarded as Christ, i.e., *"The Anointed."*

Tertullian, St. Jerome, and others say that these Herodians believed, or claimed to do so, that Herod was the Promised Messiah, because they saw that in him the scepter had departed from Judah (Gen. 49:10). This refers to the fact that the scepter of power had departed from Judah, due to Rome now ruling that country. They said it was on this account that he rebuilt the Temple with such magnificence.

The Herod who now ruled was called *"Herod the Tetrarch,"* and was the youngest son of *"Herod the Great."* Jesus is recorded as having once described him as *"that fox"* (Lk. 13:32). He, like his father, was a great builder; the city of Tiberias on the Lake of Galilee was built by him in A.D. 22, and named in honor of the Emperor Tiberias. (*"Herod the Tetrarch"* was also called *"Herod Antipas."*) The Herodians thought of him as the Messiah, as they had of his father, *"Herod the Great."*

The Pharisees, on the other hand, claimed to be defenders of the Law of Moses, to which the Herodians gave no credence. In fact, the Pharisees and Herodians hated each other, but would now join together, temporarily laying aside their hatred in order to stop Christ; consequently, the Church would join the world in their attempt to destroy Christ. They did this even though they hated each other, because they both had the same father, the Devil.

THE APOSTATE CHURCH

On a personal basis, I am well acquainted with this spirit of the apostate Church joining with the world in their efforts to destroy the Work of God; consequently, the perfidiousness of this action of the Pharisees and Herodians would probably have a greater sting for me personally than for most! I think one could probably say, without fear of contradiction, that in this union, the apostate Church and the world, the depths of evil are reached. I personally think no vice or work of the flesh, as sinful as they may be, can remotely compare with the evil here enjoined.

It is Satan's masterstroke; it is reserved for his greatest efforts. All other evil is subservient to this evil. This is the reason that the greatest enemy to the Work of God is not alcohol, drugs, immorality, etc., as evil as these things may be, but the greatest enemy is the Church, i.e., the apostate Church, which includes almost all of organized religion and almost all of that which is not organized, so to speak!

Yes! There is a *"True Church,"* made up of Born-Again, Blood-washed Believers who love Jesus with all of their hearts, and who seek to please Him exclusively of all else. But in comparison to the whole, this number is few. Jesus Himself said, *"Because strait is the gate, and narrow is the way, which leads unto life, and few there be who find it"* (Mat. 7:14).

SPIRITUAL INTELLIGENCE

The phrase, *"To catch Him in His Words,"* is somewhat humorous, to say the least! First of all, Jesus was the most intelligent human being who has ever lived. The world has never seen such a level of intelligence, because He is the only One Who has lived absolutely free from sin. Actually, He was born without the sin nature; as a result, He was not subject to the terrible debilitations of the Fall. His intelligence regarding Life and Godliness was perfect, plus anything else He needed to know (II Pet. 1:3).

Moreover, He directed that super-intelligence strictly toward the Word of God. He did not use it in the realm of economics, personal aggrandizement, or power. It was used in the realm of learning the Word of God, applying it to His Heart and Life, and teaching it to others.

The Psalmist said of Him, *"I have more understanding than all my teachers: for Your testimonies are my meditation.*

"I understand more than the ancients, because I keep Your Precepts" (Ps. 119:99-100).

He also said, *"Through Your Precepts I get understanding: therefore I hate every false way"* (Ps. 119:104).

As stated, these Passages were spoken of Christ. So, for these hypocrites to think they could entangle or snare Christ *"in His Words"* was facetious indeed! Knowing that a great crowd would be gathered, they planned to pose a question to Him that, either way He answered it, would place Him in a position of incriminating Himself. He would then lose face in front of the people and be humiliated in their eyes; consequently, whatever they then desired to do to Him would be made easier.

(14) "AND WHEN THEY WERE COME, THEY SAY UNTO HIM, MASTER, WE KNOW THAT YOU ARE TRUE, AND CARE FOR NO MAN: FOR YOU REGARD NOT THE PERSON OF MEN, BUT TEACH THE WAY OF GOD IN TRUTH: IS IT LAWFUL TO GIVE TRIBUTE TO CAESAR, OR NOT?"

The diagram is:

This question rages in Israel at that time. The Jews were not necessarily discussing the legality of paying a poll tax to Caesar, but whether a Jew should do so in view of his theocratic relationship to God.

NO RESPECTER OF PERSONS

The phrase, *"And when they were come,"* concerns them ready to spring their trap. It is so sad, He could have given them Eternal Life, but instead they seek to destroy Him. And yet, doesn't almost the entirety of the world follow in their train?

The phrase, *"They say unto Him, Master,"* means *"Teacher."* The word is not used without design. As the great crowd looks on, they call Him *"Teacher,"* so that the people will think of Him in the same way; therefore, He must answer the question which will now be posed.

The phrase, *"We know that You are true, and care for no man: for You regard not the person of men,"* is skillfully arranged with the view of disarming suspicion, and, at the same time, preventing escape. So independent and fearless a Teacher of Truth could, from fear of consequences, neither refuse an answer to honest and perplexed inquiries nor conceal His real Opinion. Consequently, there is veiled irony in their words.

Jesus had shown little consideration for men of learning and hierarchical rank; doubtless, at least in their minds, He would be equally indifferent to the views of Rome, even the Emperor himself; when the Truth was concerned, His independence would assert itself with fearless impartiality.

THE PARADOX

The phrase, *"But teach the Way of God in Truth,"* presents a paradox. Every evidence is that these Pharisees and Herodians, especially the Pharisees, knew that what He taught was indeed Truth, i.e., *"the Way of God,"* and that He, in fact, was the *"Son of God."* The word *"know,"* in *"Master, we know,"* in the Greek is *"oida,"* which refers to positive knowledge. In other words, they were absolutely convinced of the fact. And yet, they would not publicly admit to the nation that He indeed was the Messiah and that all of Israel should accept Him as such.

Why?

There are a thousand excuses and ways to be wrong, while there is only one reason and way to be right. One is to do right because it is right, and because it is the Way of the Lord, and according to His Word. In order to do right, one must make a determination that one is going to obey the Lord irrespective of the price, or what other people say. In other words, there is no self-agenda, but only the desire to carry out the Will of the Lord.

The religious leaders of Israel, as most, had no desire to obey God. To them, religion was a business in which they did very well financially, socially, and in other ways. Jesus was a threat to this; therefore, they would oppose Him, even though the evidence was irrefutable as to Who He was.

They, as most, did not know or realize that truly serving God is the most rewarding and fulfilling thing that could ever be, far surpassing anything the world or the Devil has to offer. As someone has said, *"The worst day I have ever had in serving Jesus by far surpasses the very best Satan has to offer."*

TRIBUTE

The question, *"Is it lawful to give tribute to Caesar or not?"* presented an argument that was then raging in Israel. The *"tribute"* referred to the poll tax which the Jews paid the Emperor. This payment was objectionable to them for two reasons:

First, the coin with which the tribute was to be paid, the denarius, bore the Emperor's effigy stamped upon it. As well, and to make matters worse, Rome demanded that this Emperor be thought of and worshipped as a god. Consequently, many Jews were incensed at this intrusion into their religion by a foreign religion and into their daily lives.

The word *"lawful,"* as here used, means *"Is it permissible? Is it allowed? permitted?"*

They pressed for an answer from Him regarding this question, feeling they had Him trapped either way it went.

Actually, they hoped he would say, *"No,"* to their question, because this would involve Him at once with the Roman authorities. He might even be charged with treason (Lk. 23:2). On the other hand, if He said, *"Yes,"* such an answer would incur the displeasure of the Jewish people. So they had Him on the horns of a dilemma, or so they thought!

(15) "SHALL WE GIVE, OR SHALL WE NOT GIVE? BUT HE, KNOWING THEIR HYPOCRISY, SAID UNTO THEM, WHY TEMPT YE ME? BRING ME A PENNY, THAT I MAY SEE IT."

The diagram is:

He knew they had no desire for the true answer; they only were attempting to embarrass Him before the crowd, or to have something in order to accuse Him to Rome.

HYPOCRISY

The question, *"Shall we give, or shall we not give?"* places the situation in strictly a *"Yes"* or *"No"* mode, or so they thought! As they reasoned, this was a trap which would snare Him either way He answered.

Once again, allow us to allude to His Intelligence — an intelligence, we might add, which was far superior to theirs, or anyone else in the world, for that matter! Also, the Holy Spirit was constantly informing Him of what He should say.

Concerning Him, Isaiah said, *"The Lord GOD has given Me the tongue of the learned, that I should know how to speak a Word in season to him who is weary: He wakens morning by morning, He wakens My ear to hear as the learned.*

"The Lord GOD has opened My ear, and I was not rebellious, neither turned away back" (Isa. 50:4-5).

This means that the Lord GOD spoke into His ear that which He wanted Him to know, and that *"morning by morning,"* or day-by-day.

So, the instant communication He had with the Father was of such a direct manner, which no other human being has ever had or known; consequently, their trying to snare Him was a task doomed to failure!

The phrase, *"But He, knowing their hypocrisy, said unto them,"* means that He knew they had no desire for the true answer; they only wanted to embarrass Him before the crowd, or, as stated, have something in order to accuse Him to Rome. The Holy Spirit spoke into His ear exactly who and what these religious leaders were!

THE TEMPTING OF CHRIST

The question, *"Why tempt ye Me?"* proclaims Him relating to them that He knew what their subtle trap was all about. As someone has said, *"It is necessary for one who finds himself in the place of Jesus to know the mind of the questioner, and to adapt his answer accordingly."* This Jesus would do!

THE PENNY

The phrase, *"Bring Me a penny, that I may see it,"* referred to the Roman denarius, the coin with which the tax was to be paid. For the obvious reasons, there would not have been a coin of that nature in the Temple. Therefore, it was necessary for them to send for one. During this pause, it is easy to imagine the tension aroused by this breathless wait.

What would Jesus say when the coin was finally brought?

Furthermore, why did He want such a coin?

(16) "AND THEY BROUGHT IT. AND HE SAID UNTO THEM, WHOSE IS THIS IMAGE AND SUPERSCRIPTION? AND THEY SAID UNTO HIM, CAESAR'S."

The overview is:

They referred to the image of Tiberius Caesar, the then reigning Roman Emperor; consequently, the coin of the country proved the subjection of the country to him whose image was upon it, in this case, Caesar.

CAESAR

The phrase, *"And they brought it,"* refers to a period of time which lapsed as the coin was being obtained.

The question, *"And He said unto them, Whose is this image and superscription?"* probably was perplexing to these religious leaders, even though the answer was obvious.

The phrase, *"And they said unto him, Caesar's,"* referred to the image of Tiberius Caesar, the then reigning Roman Emperor. The very fact of this coin proved the subjection of Israel to the Roman power.

(17) "AND JESUS ANSWERING SAID UNTO THEM, RENDER TO CAESAR THE THINGS THAT ARE CAESAR'S, AND TO GOD THE THINGS THAT ARE GOD'S. AND THEY MARVELED AT HIM."

The overview is:

The Jewish leaders had used the word *"give"* respecting tribute or taxes paid to Caesar, while Jesus used the word *"render,"* which speaks of paying something as a debt; in other words, He was saying that Israel owed Rome certain obligations, such as taxes, etc. It also means that Believers are obligated to pay taxes, and also to submit to civil government in every respect, providing its demands do not abrogate the Word of God.

TAXES

The phrase, *"And Jesus answering said unto them,"* would refer to far more than they had asked. Actually, in a sense, Jesus, by His Answer, placed His Approval on the separation of Church and State. Heretofore, Israel's government, by Divine design, had united Church and State, so to speak, into one. In other words, the Mosaic Law was also the Civil Law. In effect, if they had thought through what Jesus was saying, they would have realized that Israel was not about to regain dominion. Actually, Roman power would continue for some time, even destroying the nation in A.D. 70.

When the founding Fathers of the United States drew up the Constitution, which guaranteed freedom of religion, they were following direction already laid down by Christ about 1,800 years earlier. It has proven to be one of the greatest foundations of freedom ever enjoyed by any nation.

The phrase, *"Render to Caesar the things that are Caesar's, and to God the things that are God's,"* says it all. Jesus was saying, *"The coin is Caesar's; let him have his own. The fact that it circulates in Judaea shows that it is in the ordering of God's providence."* Israel should have known that Rome could not have subjected them without the approval of Jehovah. Consequently, they must recognize these facts and submit.

THE PAYING OF TAXES BY CHRISTIANS

The *"rendering unto Caesar that which is his"* means that Believers are obligated to pay taxes, and also to submit to civil government in every respect, providing its demands do not violate the conscience of the Believer, or abrogate the Word of God. This means that we obey even those laws which we do not like, that is, if our conscience or the Word of God are not violated; however, we must understand that there will definitely be a price to pay for not obeying laws, whether they are righteous or not. This is something that Christians have had to face since the days of the Early Church, with many dying for their testimony.

Paul addressed the Christian's responsibility to government in Romans 13:1-7. That which is owed to God must also be paid.

TITHES AND OFFERINGS

On the material side, this would speak of our Tithes and Offerings. It also speaks of consecration and dedication, plus obedience to God's Word. The question posed by these religious leaders rested on an implied incompatibility of the payment of tribute with the requirements of the Law of God; but the Lord replies that there is no such incompatibility. Debts to man and debts to God are both to be discharged; the two spheres of duty are at once distinct and reconcilable.

The phrase, *"And they marveled at Him,"* refers not only to His Answer, but also at His Person, Which contained perfect wisdom. He vaulted over the trap set for Him, leaving them entangled in it. He lifted up the question far above the petty controversy of the hour and affirmed a great principle of natural and spiritual obligation which belongs alike to all times, persons, and places (Bickersteth).

In truth, they could have been beneficiaries of this great wisdom, had they only accepted Him for Who He actually was, the Messiah. In fact, every Believer is presently a beneficiary of such wisdom; however, so few take advantage of it, simply because so few truly know His Word. His Word, as should be obvious, is His Wisdom!

If this made his enemies *"marvel,"* how much more should it make His followers! That is the reason every Believer should do all within his power to master the Word of God. It alone contains the wisdom of the ages, because it is the Word of God. But sadly, many Believers have not read the Bible completely through even once, much less diligently sought to understand it.

The Word of God alone must be the standard for Life and Godliness. If anything intrudes into this sacred precinct, the results are always disastrous. Actually, this is Satan's greatest effort, whether taking from, or adding to, the Word of God.

(18) "THEN COME UNTO HIM THE SADDUCEES, WHICH SAY THERE IS NO RESURRECTION; AND THEY ASKED HIM, SAYING."

The exposition is:

This denial was their major platform; it was a denial of the possibility of such a thing as a Resurrection from the dead.

THE SADDUCEES

The phrase, *"Then come unto Him the Sadducees,"* concerns the third major party in Israel, after the Pharisees and Herodians. The Sadducees denied the doctrines which connect us more immediately with another world, such as the existence of spirits and Angels, and the Resurrection of the physical body.

Under Roman authority, the Sadducees controlled the High Priesthood of Israel. Caiaphas, the High Priest, was a Sadducee, as was his father-in-law, Annas, who had preceded Caiaphas as High Priest.

The Sadducees had little following among the people, but were more restricted to the well-to-do. Many, but not all, Priests were Sadducees; nearly all Sadducees, however, appear to have been Priests, especially of the most powerful Priestly families.

Under the Herods and Romans, the Sadducees dominated in the Sanhedrin. The party died out with the destruction of the Temple in A.D. 70.

DENIAL!

The phrase, *"Which say there is no Resurrection,"* means that this denial was their major platform. It was a denial of the possibility of such a thing as a Resurrection from the dead. Inasmuch as the Pharisees strongly believed in a Resurrection, the contention between the two parties was sharp; however, they would join together, temporarily laying aside their animosity, in order to ensnare Christ, or at least attempt to do so.

The phrase, *"And they asked him, saying,"* refers to a question they are certain He cannot answer. For each group quieted by our Lord, another ignorant group takes their place. They seemed unable to learn that they cannot best Him with their trick questions.

Once again, allow me to make this statement:

Standing before them is the Creator of the Ages, Who can answer any question, Who knows everything of life and living, and everything concerning eternity, and yet they are so spiritually stupid, so spiritually dull, even so spiritually dumb, that they do not know to Whom they are speaking, despite all the evidence to the contrary. So, they will remain in darkness. So goes most of the world!

(19) "MASTER, MOSES WROTE UNTO US, IF A MAN'S BROTHER DIE, AND LEAVE HIS WIFE BEHIND HIM, AND LEAVE NO CHILDREN, THAT HIS BROTHER SHOULD TAKE HIS WIFE, AND RAISE UP SEED UNTO HIS BROTHER."

The composition is:

This is quoted from Deuteronomy 25:5-6; this law was given, among other things, to prevent the family inheritance from being broken up.

MOSES

The title, *"Master,"* is no way meant that they considered Jesus to be a great teacher, which this title implied! Their use was purely formal. Their question was not posed in order that they may learn, but that hopefully they may ensnare Him.

The phrase, *"Moses wrote unto us,"* proclaims them quoting the Scripture, but attempting, as many, to subvert it. While they truly believed in an historical Moses, they did not believe all that Moses taught in the Pentateuch.

The statement, as given by Moses and inspired by the Holy Spirit, had nothing to do with Resurrection, but something else entirely; however, these hypocrites, ignorant of the Word of God, even as all hypocrites are, would attempt to use this Passage from Deuteronomy to prove their pet theory regarding no Resurrection.

The phrase, *"And raise up seed unto his brother,"* as stated, pertained to the prevention of the family inheritance from being broken up.

(20) "NOW THERE WERE SEVEN BRETHREN: AND THE FIRST TOOK A WIFE, AND DYING LEFT NO SEED.

(21) "AND THE SECOND TOOK HER, AND DIED, NEITHER LEFT HE ANY SEED: AND THE THIRD LIKEWISE.

(22) "AND THE SEVEN HAD HER, AND LEFT NO SEED: LAST OF ALL THE WOMAN DIED ALSO."

The Text of Verses 20 through 22 is not found in the Law of Moses; it is all a made-up story in order to prove, they think, their argument against the Resurrection. These skeptics will have a good laugh at Jesus' expense, or so they think!

THE PRATTLE OF MAN

This question is asked in the same spirit concerning where Cain got his wife (Gen. 4:17). Ignorant skeptics ask such questions thinking to disprove the Bible. Incidentally, Cain was over 100 years old when he took his wife and went into the land of Nod, where enough people already existed and lived to build and form a city. There he knew his wife, that is, had relationships with her and started his family (Gen. 4:16-26).

Inasmuch as Adam and Eve were the first and only people on Earth immediately after the six days' work of re-creation, they were commanded to multiply and replenish the Earth with their own kind (Gen. 1:26-28). They had sons and daughters (Gen. 4:1; 5:4; 6:1); however, the Bible does not tell us exactly how many sons and daughters Adam and Eve had. One tradition says that Adam had 30 sons and 30 daughters; another says 300 sons and 300 daughters.

At any rate, in order to get the race started, the first marriages had to be between brothers and sisters. After that, marrying close relatives was forbidden (Lev., Chpt. 18). By the time Cain married his wife, it is possible that there were from 250,000 to 500,000 people on the Earth.

So, these skeptics will ply Jesus with a question they think He cannot answer and, at the same time, prove the fallacy of the Resurrection.

(23) "IN THE RESURRECTION THEREFORE, WHEN THEY SHALL RISE, WHOSE WIFE SHALL SHE BE OF THEM? FOR THE SEVEN HAD HER TO WIFE."

The overview is:

This question is the pivot point of their trap.

THE RESURRECTION

The Sadducees were characterized by their denial, as stated, of the Resurrection. They had posed the question according to the Mosaic Law, therefore, thinking it repudiated the Doctrine of the Resurrection. Their hypothetical story of seven brothers who had been married to one wife will prove to be, at least in their thinking, a great confusion in the afterlife, should there be one.

The phrase, *"In the Resurrection, therefore, when they shall rise,"* is presented in sarcasm! As stated, they did not believe there was such a thing as a Resurrection. The question, *"Whose wife shall she be of them?"* is the question of their trap.

The Sadducees had absolutely no knowledge, at least properly so, of God or His Plan for the human family. They did not understand that God had originally *"breathed into the nostrils of man the breath of life,"* and, as a result, *"man became a living soul"* (Gen. 2:7). By its very definition, the word *"living"* refers to *"life without end."* Consequently, man was created by God to live forever.

The original intention by God was that man reside with Him forever; however, due to the Fall, even though man's companionship and position were changed, at least for those who will not accept Christ, the eternal consequence was not. Man continues to live forever, whether with the Lord or with Satan (Rev. 20:10-15).

WHAT IS THE DOCTRINE OF THE RESURRECTION?

The Doctrine of the Resurrection is pivotal in the Christian Faith. Paul wrote, *"If in this life only we have hope in Christ, we are of all men most miserable"* (I Cor. 15:19).

What does this *"hope"* mean?

The New Testament speaks decisively concerning this matter. It is not simply the continuation of existence. It is Resurrection, with all that Resurrection implies!

Even though the Old Testament is not as defined as the New, still, there are salient Passages which delineate the Resurrection. Isaiah said, *"He will swallow up death in victory; and the Lord GOD will wipe away tears from off all faces"* (Isa. 25:8). He also said, *"Your dead men shall live, together with my dead body shall they arise. Awake and sing, ye who dwell in dust: for your dew is as the dew of herbs, and the Earth shall cast out the dead"* (Isa. 26:19).

Daniel said, *"And many of them who sleep in the dust of the Earth shall awake, some to everlasting life, and some to shame and everlasting contempt"* (Dan. 12:2). The Doctrine of the Resurrection is not fully developed in the Old Testament, even as Salvation is not fully developed; still, the foundation is adequately laid.

The Pharisees, who held to the Doctrine of Resurrection (and they were right) and the Sadducees, who denied it, might argue about the Old Testament's implications for the Resurrection, but Jesus, as we shall see, justly condemned the denial of the Sadducees, saying, *"You are in error, because you know neither the Scriptures nor the Power of God."*

THE RESURRECTION OF JESUS

Jesus is called the *"Firstfruits of those who have fallen asleep"* (I Cor. 15:20). His Resurrection is the guarantee that the death which grips the human race because of Adam has been conquered and that life is now our destiny; consequently, the significance of Jesus' Resurrection is beyond imagination. Just a few of the New Testament themes associated with Resurrection show the central place that His Resurrection must play in our Faith.

First, Paul points out that Jesus *"through the Spirit of Holiness was declared with Power to be the Son of God by His Resurrection from the dead"* (Rom. 1:4). The Resurrection is proof of all of Christ's claims and a solid foundation for our Faith.

Next, Jesus' Resurrection to endless life guarantees that *"because He continues ever, has an unchangeable Priesthood. Wherefore He is able also to save them to the uttermost who come unto God by Him, seeing He ever lives to make intercession for them"* (Heb. 7:24-25).

Finally, Jesus' Resurrection is the key to fulfillment of all the Old Testament and New Testament Promises about the future. God's Purposes will be achieved only when Jesus returns.

Consequently, the Resurrection of Jesus was a keystone in Apostolic proclamation of the Gospel (Acts 2:24-36; 3:15-26; 4:10; 5:30; 10:40; 13:34, 37; 17:18-32).

THE RESURRECTION OF THE BELIEVER

The New Testament makes it clear that the dead must appear before God for Judgment (Heb. 9:27; Rev. 20:11-15). But Resurrection, as transformation to a different state of being, is for Believers only.

What do we know of Resurrection as transformation?

John wrote that God has made us His Own Children (I Jn. 3:1); he then added, *"And it does not yet appear what we shall be: but we know that, when He* (Jesus) *shall appear, we shall be like Him"* (I Jn. 3:2).

In I Thessalonians, Chapter 4, Paul provides the broad outline. When Jesus returns, *"those who have fallen asleep"* will come with Him, and those left alive will meet them in the air. The *"dead in Christ"* (I Thess. 4:16) will be raised before the living Believers are caught up, and together the whole family will meet Jesus in the air. Paul concludes by saying, *"So shall we ever be with the Lord"* (I Thess. 4:17).

There are more details in I Corinthians, Chapter 15. To the questions, *"How are the dead raised?"* and *"With what kind of body do they come?"* (I Cor. 15:35), Paul simply notes that the Resurrection Body will correspond to our present body; but, in contrast, it will be imperishable, glorious, and infused with power — spiritual rather than natural (I Cor. 15:42-44).

It will also be in *"the image of the Heavenly"* (I Cor. 15:49), through a transformation that will happen *"in the twinkling of an eye, at the last trump"* (I Cor. 15:52). Then the *"dead shall be raised incorruptible, and we* (those alive at the time) *shall be changed."*

In the asking of these questions, some of the Corinthians did not understand what the Resurrection Body of the dead would be like, considering that the Body had gone back to dust. Paul answered that by saying, *"But God gives it a body as it has pleased Him, and to every seed his own body"* (I Cor. 15:38).

In other words, God will give a new body, which is indestructible and very similar to our former body (but without its imperfections), which will be joined to the soul and spirit of the individual already with Him. Males will continue to be males in the Resurrection, and females will continue to be females, i.e., *"every seed his own body."*

WHAT DO WE KNOW ABOUT THE RESURRECTION STATE?

Actually, not very much! As stated, John said that we should be *"like Him"* (I Jn. 3:2). For instance, the Resurrected Jesus had a body of *"flesh and bones"* (Lk. 24:39). That means it was not of *"flesh and blood,"* as is our present bodies. Presently, *"the life of the flesh is in the blood"* (Lev. 17:11). Then the Resurrected person will be infused with a different kind of life, the Spirit of God. Furthermore, Jesus could appear and disappear at will, with doors and walls being no barrier to Him in His Resurrected State (Jn. 20:26).

It seems that in the Resurrected State the limitations of our physical nature will be gone. Whereas we are now corruptible, or rather perishable, we will then be imperishable.

NOTES

Power will replace weakness; immortality will end mortality. As it regards travel, it will then be at the *"speed of thought."* In other words, the Glorified Believer will think the thought regarding a particular place he desires to be and he will instantly be there. That, to be sure, is far, far greater even than the speed of light, which is, within itself, approximately 186,000 miles per second. So, the *"speed of thought"* will greatly transcend even that, even immeasurably so.

WHAT IS RESURRECTION POWER?

Resurrection Power now resides within the lives of Believers as an earnest or downpayment of the Resurrection that is to come. This Resurrection Power which we presently have is given to us in order that we may live an overcoming life. Paul writes, *"But if the Spirit* (Holy Spirit) *of Him* (from the Father) *Who raised up Jesus from the dead dwell in you, He Who raised up Christ from the dead shall also quicken your mortal bodies* (give us power in our mortal bodies that we might live a victorious life) *by His Spirit Who dwells in you"* (we have the same power in us, through the Spirit, that raised Christ from the dead, and is available to us only on the premise of the Cross and our Faith in that Sacrifice)" (Rom. 8:11).

The point Paul makes is that the Holy Spirit, the Agent of Jesus' Resurrection, lives within the Believer. This means that Resurrection Power is available to us presently even in our mortal bodies. Through the Holy Spirit, we are raised beyond our human limitations and enabled to live a righteous life. This Doctrine is sometimes overlooked, and certain Biblical Passages are, therefore, misinterpreted. For instance, in Philippians, Chapter 3, Paul is not expressing uncertainty about his own Resurrection when he yearns, *"If by any means I might attain unto the Resurrection of the dead"* (Phil. 3:11). The entire sentence reads, *"That I may know Him* (referring to what Christ did at the Cross), *and the power of His Resurrection* (refers to being raised with Him in *'newness of life'* [Rom. 6:3-5]), *and the fellowship of His sufferings* (regarding our Trust and Faith placed in what He did for us at the Cross), *being made conformable unto His death* (to conform to what He did for us at the Cross, understanding that this is the only means of Salvation and Sanctification)" (Phil. 3:10).

Paul's thought in this statement is focused on the present — living a Resurrected kind of life now by the Power of the Resurrected Christ, all made possible by the Cross (Rom. 6:3-5). However, he did not discount the Resurrection of the coming day when he said, *"If by any means I might attain unto the Resurrection of the dead"* (Phil. 3:11).

By that statement, he means that even though the Power of the Resurrected Christ presently resides in the Believer, still, we have not yet *"attained unto the Resurrection of the dead,"* which refers to that coming day when all the Saints will be Resurrected and given Glorified Bodies (I Thess. 4:16-17).

FINALLY

The New Testament makes clear the Doctrine of the Resurrection, which is only in shadow in the Old Testament; however, Jesus' Own Resurrection appeals to the Old Testament (Mk. 12:26-27), and shows sometimes-overlooked evidence.

The Bible makes it clear that there is an Eternal Destiny, a life beyond this life. Resurrection lies ahead. As well, it is the Resurrection of Jesus that is the final proof. Jesus' Resurrection not only declared Him to be what He claimed to be, the Son of God, but also provided a guarantee for us who believe. Because Jesus lives, we too shall live. We will share His Destiny. As John said, *"When He shall appear* (the Rapture), *we shall be like Him* (speaks of being glorified)*; for we shall see Him as He is* (physical eyes in a mortal body could not look upon that glory, only eyes in glorified bodies)*"* (I Jn. 3:2).

The question, *"Whose wife shall she be of them? for the seven had her to wife,"* shows, as Jesus will say, a complete misunderstanding of the Scriptures.

(24) "AND JESUS ANSWERING SAID UNTO THEM, DO YOU NOT THEREFORE ERR, BECAUSE YOU KNOW NOT THE SCRIPTURES, NEITHER THE POWER OF GOD?"

The overview is:

They assumed either that God could not raise the dead or that He could raise them only to a life which would be a counterpart of the present. Their failure to know *"the Power of God"* stems from unbelief.

THE SCRIPTURES

The phrase, *"And Jesus answering said unto them,"* proclaims an answer they had never yet received, even though having argued about this matter with the Pharisees for many years. The question, *"Do you not therefore err, because you know not the Scriptures . . . ?"* points to their ignorance, which was inexcusable, seeing that most Sadducees were members of the Priesthood. All error regarding *"Life and Godliness"* is because of not knowing the Scriptures (II Pet. 1:3).

This is the reason for the acceptance by the Church of the modern philosophy of psychology. The Christian propagators of this error simply do not know the Word of God. If they did, there would be no question in their minds concerning this matter.

Or else they know the Word, but they simply do not believe the Word, which I am concerned is the case in many religious circles.

THE CROSS OF CHRIST

The answer for every dilemma concerning man, as it regards *"Life and Godliness,"* is found entirely in Christ and what He did at the Cross. Every sin was there atoned, every question answered, and every problem presented with a solution, with nothing, in fact, left out. In other words, the Cross presents a *"Finished Work"* (I Cor. 1:17-18, 23; 2:2; Gal. 6:14).

As well, the Message of the Cross is not difficult to understand. In fact, even a child can understand this great thing that Jesus has done for humanity. This means that there is not a single bondage that has not been addressed, not a single sin that has not been atoned, not a single perversion that has not been answered.

So why does the far greater majority of the modern Church opt for humanistic psychology as an answer to the ills, sins, and perversions of humanity?

THE REASON IS NOT THEOLOGICAL, BUT RATHER MORAL

The reason that the modern Church

doesn't embrace the Cross is not theological. It's not something that's difficult to understand, which closes the door. It is rather a moral problem!

What do we mean by it being a moral problem?

It comes straight back to unbelief, even as Paul outlined in Hebrews, Chapters 3 and 4. It is not that they cannot believe the Cross, it's simply that they don't want to believe the Cross. Or else they will claim to place their faith and trust in what Christ did at the Cross, while, at the same time, embracing humanistic psychology or one of its religious off-shoots, such as the *"Purpose Driven Life"* or the *"Government of Twelve,"* etc.

BELIEF PATTERNS

The word *"moral"* is that which relates to principles of right and wrong in behavior. Behavior patterns will soon begin to follow belief patterns. In other words, what one believes, which is all-important, actually the single most important thing, will fall out sooner or later to the positive or negative, all according to right or wrong believing.

The Cross of Christ sets the Standard; the Cross, in fact, is the Standard. Righteousness can only come by and through a proper faith evidenced in Christ and what Christ did at the Cross. Paul emphatically said, *"If Righteousness come by the Law, then Christ is dead in vain"* (Gal. 2:21).

Inasmuch as *"Law"* covers everything other than the Cross, this means that Righteousness comes exclusively by and through what Christ did at the Cross (Rom. 6:3-14). This means that we can attain to what the Lord wants us to be and, in fact, demands that we be, only by placing our faith entirely in Christ and what He has done for us at the Cross, which then gives latitude to the Holy Spirit, Who Alone can develop Righteousness within our lives. The Holy Spirit works entirely within the parameters of the Finished Work of Christ (Rom. 8:1-2, 11). He will not work outside of those premises. So, if the Church is going to have the Operation and Moving of the Holy Spirit, which it must have, that is, if it's to do anything for the Lord, then it must come back to the Cross.

NOTES

Perhaps it would be better said, *"Go up to the Cross."* When the Church abandoned the Cross, it fell to the far lower level of human endeavor, which caused it to lose its way.

THE POWER OF GOD

The continuing of the question asked by Jesus, when He spoke of the Sadducees living in error because of not knowing the Scriptures *"neither the Power of God,"* portrays this group as incapable of conceiving of a power which could produce that outlined in the Scriptures concerning the Resurrection. Swete says, *"They assumed either that God could not raise the dead, or that He could raise them only to a life which would be a counterpart of the present, etc."* This gives rise to the wild intentions of reincarnation, etc.

The failure to know the *"Power of God,"* even as we have just addressed, stems from unbelief. This was characteristic not only of the Sadducees, but is also characteristic of their modern counterparts. Truthfully, most of the modern Church does not believe in the *"Power of God."* As alluded to, this is the reason for belief in psychology. Men who call themselves Believers simply do not believe that God delivers people, hence, they doubt His Power.

In truth, the entirety of life is wrapped up in the *"Scriptures,"* consequently in the *"Power of God."* If one truly knows the Scriptures, and one truly believes the Scriptures, then one truly knows and understands the Power of God. The two are inseparable.

A FORM OF GODLINESS

The Apostle Paul said, *"This know also, that in the last days* (the days in which we now live) *perilous times shall come."* The Apostle then listed a long line of sins and concluded by saying, *"Having a form of Godliness, but denying the power thereof"* (II Tim. 3:1-5).

Paul also told us that the *"power"* was in the Cross. He said, *"For the preaching of the Cross is to them who perish foolishness, but unto us who are saved it is the power of God"* (I Cor. 1:18). Actually, the *"power"* resides in the Holy Spirit (Acts 1:8). However, the Holy Spirit works exclusively, as stated, by and through the means of the Cross. This is what gives Him the legal right to do all the things which He Alone can do.

So, when the modern Church denies the Cross, they are denying the Power of God. Emphatically, and even dogmatically, the Holy Spirit tells us to *"turn away"* from them.

(25) "FOR WHEN THEY SHALL RISE FROM THE DEAD, THEY NEITHER MARRY NOR ARE GIVEN IN MARRIAGE; BUT ARE AS THE ANGELS WHICH ARE IN HEAVEN."

The exposition is:

Marriage was instituted by God to bring forth and perpetuate the human race; due to having Glorified Bodies in Heaven, which will take place in the Resurrection, there will be no death and, therefore, no need to perpetuate the race, therefore, no need for marriage.

MARRIAGE

The phrase, *"For when they shall rise from the dead,"* proclaims the guarantee by Christ of the Resurrection. The pronoun *"they"* speaks not only of the Sainted dead, but also of unbelievers. In other words, all will ultimately *"rise,"* whether in the First Resurrection of Life or the Second Resurrection of Damnation (Jn. 5:29), sometimes called *"The Second Death"* (Rev. 20:14).

The phrase, *"They neither marry nor are given in marriage,"* has to do with one of the reasons for marriage, the bringing of offspring into the world, i.e., the propagation of the human race. In the Resurrection, there will be no marriages, simply because none of the Resurrected Saints will ever die; consequently, it will not be necessary any longer to bring children into the world, at least by this method.

This sentence by Christ also tells us that husband and wife relationships as on Earth will not be continued in the Resurrection; this consequently blows to pieces the hypotheses of the Sadducees concerning the one woman and seven husbands, etc. It also eliminates the Mormon claims.

While recognition will, no doubt, be continued, and even relationship, still, relationship will be different in that Christ will be the focal point and not a husband or wife, etc.

ANGELS

The phrase, *"But are as the Angels which are in Heaven,"* is used in a limited context, which is what Christ intended! Every evidence is that all Angels were originally created at the same time. Due to them not dying, there are the same number of Angels in existence today as when they were created. They do not propagate their kind; consequently, human beings in the next life will be like Angels in this respect. They will not propagate their kind, nor will they need to, because death will be eliminated.

This does not mean that human beings will be Angels, for they will not. Human beings will continue to be human beings. As Paul said, *"every seed his own body"* (I Cor. 15:38).

(26) "AND AS TOUCHING THE DEAD, THAT THEY RISE: HAVE YOU NOT READ IN THE BOOK OF MOSES, HOW IN THE BUSH GOD SPOKE UNTO HIM, SAYING, I AM THE GOD OF ABRAHAM, AND THE GOD OF ISAAC, AND THE GOD OF JACOB?"

The synopsis is:

God did not say, *"I was the God of Abraham . . . ,"* referring to someone who was dead, out of existence, and was no more. He instead said, *"I am the God of Abraham . . . ,"* meaning that these individuals continued to be alive at the time of Moses, even though their bodies were dead.

THE DEAD

The phrase, *"And as touching the dead, that they rise,"* refers to dead bodies, not the soul and spirit. When death is addressed in the Bible, at least in this fashion, it is always referring to the death of the physical body, and never of the soul and spirit, which, in fact, cannot die. They are immortal.

While the Bible does say, *"The soul that sins, it shall die"* (Ezek. 18:4), it is speaking of separation from God, and not physical death, as we know of such. In fact, the soul and the spirit of each and every individual lives forever, and will do so in either Heaven or Hell — in Heaven, if the individual has accepted Christ as his Saviour (Jn. 3:3; 14:6); in Hell, if Christ is rejected!

In the coming Resurrection, it is the body

alone which will be resurrected, and refashioned into a glorified state. The soul and the spirit will not be resurrected, because they have never died, and will never die.

MOSES

The phrase, *"Have you not read in the Book of Moses, how in the bush God spoke unto him,"* takes the Sadducees to the Scriptures, but, more importantly, to the very part of the Bible they claimed to believe, i.e., the Pentateuch. The idea that Jesus would prove the Doctrine of the Resurrection from this part of the Word of God was something they did not count on, to say the least! (Jesus is referring to Exodus 3:5-6).

The continuing of the question, *"Saying, I am the God of Abraham, and the God of Isaac, and the God of Jacob?"* proves the validity of the Doctrine of the Resurrection. As we've already stated, God did not say, *"I was,"* as it regards Abraham, etc., but rather *"I am the God of Abraham . . . ,"* meaning that these individuals continued to be alive at the time of Moses, even though their bodies were dead; in truth, they are alive even at the present time. In soulish form, they are now with Christ, awaiting the Resurrection.

Jehovah was their God when they were here on this Earth; He continued to be their God during the time of Moses, hence, saying *"I am,"* because they were still alive; they were still alive as Jesus spoke; and, in truth, they will be alive forevermore. As Jehovah is the God of these Patriarchs, likewise, He is the God of all who believe and trust Him, who, therefore, have Eternal Life!

(27) "HE IS NOT THE GOD OF THE DEAD, BUT THE GOD OF THE LIVING: YOU THEREFORE DO GREATLY ERR."

The structure is:

This Scripture means that no individual goes out of existence at death, but actually lives forever, whether redeemed or in a fallen state; the soul and the spirit of man are eternal.

THE GOD OF THE LIVING

The phrase, *"He is not the God of the dead,"* as Jesus is using it, referring to the erroneous belief of the Sadducees, means that which no longer exists. The Sadducees were claiming that when a person dies, they are no more, ceasing to exist, and will never be resurrected. This is what Jesus is referring to by His use of the word *"dead"* in this instance.

The phrase, *"But the God of the living,"* means that the Doctrine of the Sadducees is wrong, in that no individual goes out of existence, but actually lives forever. The Lord is saying that God is not presiding over people who do not exist, for what use would that be? He is rather presiding over those who continue to live even though their bodies are dead. This speaks of the soul and spirit, which live forever, and which, in fact, cannot die.

Actually, at this moment in Heaven, if one could go to that blessed abode for observation, one would see Abraham, Isaac, and Jacob, and also every other Believer who has ever lived, and would recognize them, even though they were only in the form of their soul and spirit. In the Resurrection, which is soon to come, a Glorified Body will be given to every Believer now in Heaven, and also to those Believers who are alive on Earth at that time. They (those who are alive) will be *"changed"* (I Cor. 15:51-57).

For there not to be a Resurrection of the Body (for God to give a new body) would leave Believers in an imperfect condition. The living soul must, in due time, recover its partner (the body), and this will happen at the Resurrection.

The phrase, *"You therefore do greatly err,"* proclaims this Doctrine of the Sadducees as not only error, but *"great error."* For men not to believe in the coming Resurrection is to undermine the entirety of the Plan of God for the human race. It shows a gross misunderstanding, even ignorance, of Who God is and what God is doing!

Tragically, and despite some 2,000 years of access to the Bible, for most of the Church, and concerning many Doctrines, Jesus would probably continue to say to many, *"You therefore do greatly err"*!

A PERSONAL EXAMPLE

Our oldest grandson Gabriel was saved when he was five years old and baptized with the Holy Spirit when he was eight years old. He is now one of the Pastors at Family

Worship Center, actually in charge of the young people's group, *"Crossfire."*

When he was seven years old, the Lord gave him a Vision. At that time, he saw Satan, as the Evil One entered his room, with the room filled with an oppressive spirit. Satan made a bid for his soul, actually asking him to serve him. Being only a child, and not knowing what to do, he pulled the covers of the bed over his head. But then the room changed, with light filling it to such an extent that all the darkness of Satan was instantly gone. A Voice spoke to him, which he knew to be the Lord.

In the Vision, he was then taken to Heaven, where he saw my mother, who was his great-grandmother. In fact, he had never seen her, because she had passed away many years before he was born. In relating the Vision to his Dad, he described her perfectly, even though he had never seen her.

And then he related how he saw King David and actually spoke to him. As a child, he asked a question that would be indicative of a child. He asked, *"Did you really kill that giant?"*

David spoke very kindly to him, saying, *"Gabriel, it wasn't really me who killed the giant. It was the Lord."*

In the Vision my grandson then saw a great mass of people and heard me preaching to them. However, he couldn't understand the language I was using. The Lord explained to him that I was speaking in Russian, and that the people gathered before me were Russians.

The year my grandson Gabriel had this Vision was 1986. In the early part of 1989, we were able to go on Television in what was then the Soviet Union. At first we only covered a small part of that vast country, which then consisted of fifteen Republics, covering well over one-sixth of the world's land surface. A short time later, we were able to go on TV-1, which covered every town, village, and city in the former Soviet Union. The programs were interpreted into Russian, exactly as Gabriel had seen in the Vision.

(28) "AND ONE OF THE SCRIBES CAME, AND HAVING HEARD THEM REASONING TOGETHER, AND PERCEIVING THAT HE HAD ANSWERED THEM WELL, ASKED HIM, WHICH IS THE FIRST COMMANDMENT OF ALL?"

The exegesis is:

This question was not asked in sarcasm, but sincerely. This man is one of the few who took advantage of the Perfect Knowledge of Christ. He was not really referring to the single most important Commandment of the Ten, but rather asking which was the most important, the ritual or the ethical.

THE ANSWER

The phrase, *"And one of the Scribes came, and having heard them reasoning together,"* no doubt, spoke of a Pharisee. The implication is that this exchange took place a short time after the exchange with the Sadducees. Possibly this *"Scribe"* related to the Pharisees what Jesus had said concerning the Resurrection. Greatly impressed by Jesus' answer, he will now pose a question himself.

There is no indication that his question was framed with deceit, but rather was an earnest, sincere desire for Bible knowledge. He is one of the few who took advantage of the Perfect Knowledge of Christ. What a shame that so few took this advantage!

The phrase, *"And perceiving that he had answered them well,"* could be said of every answer given by Jesus. To which we have alluded, the religious leaders of Israel, plus anyone else for that matter, could have asked Jesus the deepest questions concerning Life and Godliness, and it would forthrightly have been answered. The wisdom of the ages was in their presence and they did not know it. Sadly, the religious leaders too often sought to trap Him instead of seeking answers which they desperately needed.

Their pride would not allow them to admit Who and What He was. The idea that this *"Peasant"* had perfect knowledge of the Bible, and furthermore was *"The Messiah,"* was a Truth with which they could not come to grips. Consequently, they opposed Him, thereby missing Eternal Life.

Is it any different presently?

Jesus is no less today and, in Truth, because of Calvary and the Resurrection, even more! And yet, the world as a whole ignores Him, or else bitterly opposes Him.

If anyone will seek Him, He will, without

fail, *"answer them well."*

THE FIRST COMMANDMENT

The question, *"Asked him, Which is the first Commandment of all?"* was not really referring to the single most important Commandment of the Ten Commandments. This argument concerning the *"first"* or *"greatest"* Commandment then raged in Israel. The idea was the distinction between the ritual and ethical. Which was the most important?

The Pharisees were hung up on the many rituals of the Mosaic Law, which they attempted to fastidiously keep, while others, and rightly so, were more concerned about the ethical, or moral, principles of the Law.

In a sense, it is no different at the present!

Most of the modern Church, steeped in self-righteousness, will bitterly oppose anyone who embarrasses them. I speak of sins of the flesh. Admittedly these sins are very grievous, as should be overly obvious; however, the greatest sins are not those sins, but rather sins of pride and unbelief, which characterize all too many, and which wreck the Work of God.

Jesus addressed this very thing by saying to the Chief Priests and the Elders, *"Verily I say unto you, That the publicans and the harlots go into the Kingdom of God before you* (He said this to their faces, and before the people; He could not have insulted them more, putting them beneath publicans, whom they considered to be traitors, and even harlots).

"For John (John the Baptist) *came unto you in the way of righteousness, and you believed him not* (speaking of the religious leaders): *but the publicans and the harlots believed him: and you, when you had seen it, repented not afterward, that you might believe him* (they saw the changed lives as a result of John's Gospel, but still wouldn't believe)" (Mat. 21:31-32).

Was Jesus condoning thievery and harlotry?

God forbid, no! He was, in fact, saying two things:

1. While the sins of the publicans and the harlots were very grievous, they were not as bad as the sin of unbelief, which characterized the religious leaders of Israel.

2. There is a terrible deception to all sin; however, the sin of unbelief carries the greatest deception.

(29) "AND JESUS ANSWERED HIM, THE FIRST OF ALL THE COMMANDMENTS IS, HEAR, O ISRAEL; THE LORD OUR GOD IS ONE LORD."

The structure is:

The word *"one,"* in the Hebrew, is *"echad,"* which means *"to be united as one, one in number."*

ONE LORD

The phrase, *"And Jesus answered him,"* is typical of the Lord. Every legitimate question, and even many of the previous ones, which were not legitimate, received answers, and, above all, *"the answer."*

The phrase, *"The first of all the Commandments is,"* proclaims an instant response respecting the correct interpretation of the Bible. The phrase, *"Hear, O Israel: The LORD our God is one LORD,"* is taken from Deuteronomy 6:4-5. It is said that it was recited daily by every Jew, and even written on a miniature roll, which every Scribe carried in his phylactery. This was a small case, made of parchment and bound to the forehead or arm, in which was placed small pieces of parchment inscribed with Scripture portions (Wuest).

The word *"one,"* in the Hebrew, as stated, is *"echad,"* which means *"to be united as one, one in number."* In Greek, it is *"heis,"* and has the same meaning.

God, as taught in the Bible, is Triune, existing as God the Father, God the Son, and God the Holy Spirit. Although three in number, they are One in unity and, above all, One in Essence. In other words, there aren't three Gods, just One, but manifested in Three Persons (Mat. 28:19; Mk. 1:1; I Cor. 1:1; II Cor. 1:2; Gal. 1:1; etc.).

(30) "AND YOU SHALL LOVE THE LORD YOUR GOD WITH ALL YOUR HEART, AND WITH ALL YOUR SOUL, AND WITH ALL YOUR MIND, AND WITH ALL YOUR STRENGTH: THIS IS THE FIRST COMMANDMENT."

The structure is:

This is the type of *"love"* which the world doesn't have and, in fact, cannot have, which only a Believer can have, and which can only be given by the Lord. It is *agape* love, the God-kind of love.

LOVE

The phrase, *"And you shall love the Lord your God with all your heart,"* refers to *"agape"* love, which speaks of Holy Spirit-generated love in the heart of the yielded Saint. It is a Divine Love, which is due God from his creatures. So, we are speaking of a type of *"love"* that the world cannot have and, in fact, only Believers can have, and which can only be given by the Lord.

Among the Pharisees, there was great profession of love to God, but little practice of love to man. Today, there seems to be great evidence of love to man, i.e., philanthropy, social schemes, and such like, but little evidence of love to God (Williams).

The *"heart,"* as spoken of here, does not refer to the physical organ, but instead to the seat of all affections and desires, and must be centered on God. The idea is not, as some think, that God is to be first, with other things being second, third, etc., but that God is to be all-in-all, and with every desire and affection brought into this sphere.

In other words, God does not occupy the largest portion of our affections and desires, but instead all of our affections and desires. When this is done, other things, such as family, etc., will enjoy the proper type of love, which makes for the happiest relationships and home life that one could ever have! It is all found in God, and not found at all outside of God.

THE SOUL

The phrase, *"And with all your soul,"* has to do with feelings and emotions. If we love the Lord with all our *"soul,"* then our emotions will be healthy, instead of a runaway engine, as they are in many people. When feelings and emotions are not anchored in Christ, they fuel psychological problems, which, in reality, are spiritual problems. Consequently, in this short statement given by Christ, we find the answer to these problems. Feelings and emotions must be centered in Christ, as stated, and must give vent through Praise and Worship.

NOTES

THE CROSS

Concerning this, Jesus said, *"Come unto Me* (is meant by Jesus to reveal Himself as the Giver of Salvation, and all that this means), *all you who labor and are heavy laden* (trying to earn Salvation and victory by works), *and I will give you rest* (this *'rest'* can only be found by placing one's Faith in Christ and what He has done for us at the Cross [Gal. 5:1-6]).

"Take My yoke upon you (the *'yoke'* of the *'Cross'*), *and learn of Me* (learn of His Sacrifice [Rom. 6:3-5]); *for I am meek and lowly in heart* (the only thing that our Lord Personally said of Himself): *and you shall find rest unto your souls* (the soul can find rest only in the Cross).

"For My yoke is easy, and My burden is light (what He requires of us is very little — just to have Faith in His Sacrificial Atoning Work)" (Mat. 11:28-30).

Now Jesus tells us how to do these things, to which we have already alluded in the expository notes.

TAKING UP THE CROSS DAILY

Jesus said, *"If any man will come after Me* (the criteria for Discipleship), *let him deny himself* (not asceticism, as many think, but rather that one denies one's own willpower, self-will, strength, and ability, depending totally on Christ), *and take up his cross* (the benefits of the Cross, looking exclusively to what Jesus did there to meet our every need) *daily* (our looking to the Cross is so important that we must renew our Faith in what Christ has done for us, even on a daily basis, for Satan will ever try to move us away from the Cross as the Object of our Faith, which always spells disaster), *and follow Me* (Christ can be followed only by the Believer looking to the Cross, understanding what it accomplished, and by that means alone [Rom. 6:3-5, 11, 14; 8:1-2, 11; I Cor. 1:17-18, 21, 23; 2:2; Gal. 6:14; Eph. 2:13-18; Col. 2:14-15]).

"For whosoever will save his life shall lose it (try to live one's life outside of Christ and the Cross): *but whosoever will lose his life for My sake, the same shall save it* (when we place our Faith exclusively in Christ and

the Cross, looking entirely to Him, we have just found *'more abundant life'* [Jn. 10:10])" (Lk. 9:23-24).

Taking up the Cross daily is the means by which we are able to properly follow the Lord, and only by that means.

THE MIND

The phrase, *"And with all your mind,"* concerns the will and the intellect. In essence, the *"mind"* is the gateway to the spirit. So, if the *"mind"* wills love for God and worship of God, as it must, the spirit of man will also be fed and nurtured.

The *"heart"* is mentioned first, because the desire must be generated in the heart first of all, and can only come from the heart. As the desire for God comes from the heart, the emotions are then stirred through the *"soul."* Then the will to love and worship God comes into play through the *"mind."*

The mind is the last to really be brought to bear, and is the reason that many begin correctly, but do not follow through. The desire is there and the emotions are in play, but the *"will"* is lacking.

STRENGTH

The phrase, *"And with all your strength,"* means that whatever strength is shown for the procurement of other things is to always be secondary to our efforts made respecting love for God. *"Strength"* refers to effort, and speaks of determination.

But yet, we must understand that our *"strength"* is exerted only in the capacity of our Faith. In fact, the commodity which spends in God's economy is Faith, and, I might quickly say, that alone! While all of these things are brought into play, and I speak of the heart, the soul, the mind, and our strength, still, all of this is to put our Faith into motion. This, as would be obvious, is very, very important. Without these things in play, even as our Lord proclaims, Faith cannot be put in motion.

THE FIRST COMMANDMENT

The phrase, *"This is the First Commandment,"* leaves no room for doubt! Succinctly and specifically, even dogmatically, the Lord proclaims the answer to this man's question; consequently, mere ritual, which was followed so minutely by the Pharisees, was given no credence at all by the Lord. He went far beyond the ritual and the ceremony, going to the very seat of man's being, which generates the true state of the individual.

Consequently, this *"First Commandment"* completely abrogates all religious ceremony, religion, rules, and works. These things (ceremonies, etc.) can be done without any change of heart, while this of which Jesus speaks must involve a change of heart, which can only be done by the Lord, and must come from within a person. This is the reason the *"born again"* experience, which generates these things, is the only Power on Earth which can change a person.

This alone is the answer to marriage problems, social problems, economic problems, and even most physical problems.

(31) "AND THE SECOND IS LIKE, NAMELY THIS, YOU SHALL LOVE YOUR NEIGHBOUR AS YOURSELF. THERE IS NONE OTHER COMMANDMENT GREATER THAN THESE."

The exegesis is:

If we truly love God, we will also *"love our neighbor"*; this is the answer to all war, prejudice, hate, bias, racism, etc.

THE SECOND COMMANDMENT

The phrase, *"And the second is like, namely this,"* gives the man that for which he did not ask; however, it is impossible to separate the two, hence, Jesus including the *"second."* The phrase, *"You shall love your neighbor as yourself,"* is, in effect, telling us the following:

If we truly love God as we should love Him, we will also *"love our neighbor."* This is the answer to man's inhumanity to man and, in fact, the only answer! If one says he loves God, but accommodating love is not shown to one's own neighbor, then his claims of love for God are obviously false; however, and as stated, philanthropic efforts, as engaged in by many, are not exactly what Jesus is speaking of here. It does not refer to action toward one's neighbor as a result of works, but instead of *"love."* There is a vast difference!

So, there would be no mistake as to what

Jesus was saying, He added the words, *"as yourself."* The love we have for ourselves is to be the barometer respecting love for others.

THE GREATEST COMMANDMENTS

The phrase, *"There is none other Commandment greater than these,"* has just explained the entirely of the Bible. It is so simple that a child can understand it, and yet the answer to all the problems which plague humanity. As one must quickly add, it is the only answer.

In writing these Commentaries on the four Gospels, the Words of Christ have intrigued me in a manner that I really cannot properly express. The wisdom He gave so far eclipses anything else known to man that all else pales by comparison. But yet, it is ignored by most all the world, and even by much of the Church! He beautifully takes complex questions and reduces them to the lowest common denominator, making them so simple, but yet they remain profound! Anyone can understand the answers He gives, and yet the most brilliant intellectuals could never begin to plumb their depths or scale their heights. Truly He is *"The Way, The Truth, and The Life"* (Jn. 14:6).

(32) "AND THE SCRIBE SAID UNTO HIM, WELL, MASTER, YOU HAVE SAID THE TRUTH: FOR THERE IS ONE GOD; AND THERE IS NONE OTHER BUT HE."

The composition is:

This refers to a Pharisee, who, for a change, spoke kindly to, and of, Jesus.

THE SCRIBE

The phrase, *"And the Scribe said unto Him,"* refers to the man who had asked the question to begin with. The phrase, *"Well, Master, You have said the Truth,"* refers to a Pharisee, who spoke graciously to Jesus, which was unusual! The word *"Well"* means *"good,"* which means that the Scribe was greatly blessed and instructed by the answer. And yet, by him calling Jesus *"Master,"* he merely referred to Him as a Teacher. There is no evidence that He recognized Jesus as the Messiah.

It would seem that the tremendous answers given by Christ would have made the man realize that, while Jesus was definitely a great Teacher, actually the greatest, more than all He was *"The Messiah."* Jesus not only spoke *"Truth,"* but also He was, in fact, *"Truth."*

The phrase, *"For there is One God; and there is none other but He,"* was certainly true; however, it is obvious that the man did not fully understand this *"Truth."* In effect, he was standing in front of God, i.e., the Son of God, but did not know it!

(33) "AND TO LOVE HIM WITH ALL THE HEART AND WITH ALL THE UNDERSTANDING, AND WITH ALL THE SOUL, AND WITH ALL THE STRENGTH, AND TO LOVE HIS NEIGHBOUR AS HIMSELF, IS MORE THAN ALL WHOLE BURNT OFFERINGS AND SACRIFICES."

The diagram is:

The answer proclaims the fact that this Pharisee understood what the Sacrifices actually were all about; in other words, they were not mere rituals.

MORE THAN ALL WHOLE BURNT OFFERINGS AND SACRIFICES

This man's recital of the First Commandment, *"And to love Him . . . ,"* and the Second, *"To love his neighbor as himself,"* proclaims that he understood what Christ had said. He did not add or take away from them; consequently, this portrays the rightful dividing of the Word.

The phrase, *"Is more than all Whole Burnt Offerings and Sacrifices,"* proclaims him going beyond most Pharisees, in that he now understands what the Law was all about. While the *"Whole Burnt Offerings"* and *"Sacrifices"* were important, still, many, if not the majority, engaged in these rituals and ceremonies, but received no spiritual benefit.

It is the same presently, as people who belong to Churches are baptized in water and frequently take the Lord's Supper, but, in reality, do not know Jesus as their personal Saviour. And yet, as most of Israel fell into this ceremonial trap, likewise, most in modern Christendom, sadly, follow suit.

A PERSONAL TESTIMONY

Some time ago, I received a letter from a dear lady who had been saved as a result of watching our Telecast. She said she was a member of a well-known Church, and she actually taught a Sunday School Class, which she had done for several years. She knew the Doctrine of this particular Denomination backwards and forwards; she even taught Doctrine Classes from time to time.

On the Sunday morning in question, as she began to watch the Telecast, the Spirit of God began to deal with her soul, convicting her of her lost condition. She was religious, but lost! In a few moments time, the Spirit of God let her know that she really did not know Jesus as her personal Saviour, and that she had never really been truly *"born again."* In a few moments time, as the Holy Spirit dealt with her, this was rectified, and she truly accepted Christ as her Saviour.

In the past, she had made some type of mental affirmation toward Christ, even as millions have, but really did not know Him. As stated, she was religious, but lost! In truth, her situation (like that of multiple millions of others) falls into the same category as Israel at the time of Christ, which was busily engaged in *"Whole Burnt Offerings and Sacrifices,"* but, in reality, did not know God, Whom these Sacrifices represented. In other words, they thought they were saved simply because they were Jews and engaged in these rituals. They were, as the lady, religious, but lost!

(34) "AND WHEN JESUS SAW THAT HE ANSWERED DISCREETLY, HE SAID UNTO HIM, YOU ARE NOT FAR FROM THE KINGDOM OF GOD. AND NO MAN AFTER THAT DID ASK HIM ANY QUESTION."

The overview is:

"Not there yet, but close!" The distance from the *"Kingdom of God"* is measured neither by miles, nor by ceremonial standards, but by spiritual conditions; however, being close is not enough; and regrettably, millions fall into this category.

THE KINGDOM OF GOD

The phrase, *"And when Jesus saw that he answered discreetly, He said unto him,"* represents Christ not only taking stock of his answer, but also seeing into the very depths of this man's heart. The word *"discreetly,"* in the Greek Text, is *"nounechos,"* which means *"intelligence, as one who has a mind*

NOTES

of his own." This is far more significant than meets the eye.

Most of the people in Jesus' day, as now, blindly followed religious leaders, believing what they were told; consequently, to meet someone who searched the Word of God himself, and who also formed conclusions on what he found rather than blindly following others, was refreshing, to say the least!

Most people presently, as always, are either on their way to Heaven or Hell because of what someone else has told them. In other words, most little search the Word of God and form their own conclusions, but rather blindly take the word of others. Furthermore, this is strongly encouraged in both Catholic and Protestant circles.

In a sense, Catholic Bishops claim infallibility, at least regarding interpretation of Scripture; consequently, the people are taught to blindly follow and not question. *"If a mistake is made,"* they are told, *"it will be the problem of the Priest and not the person."* Tragically, most Catholic Priests do not know the Word of God; therefore, the entire scenario points to double jeopardy for Catholic adherents. Let not the Reader think, however, that Catholics alone are in this category. Many, if not most, Protestants are hard on their heels.

For instance, the Pentecostal Denomination with which I formerly was associated pretty much espouses the same terrible error. One of their leading Officials called a Pastor acquaintance of mine, of that Denomination, demanding that he do a particular thing, which obviously was unscriptural. The Pastor quickly remonstrated by declaring the lack of Scriptural foundation for such action. The Official quickly answered, *"That is of no concern of yours. If it's wrong, I will be responsible, not you. It is your duty to obey me, irrespective of what I ask"*!

When the conversation ended, the Pastor hung up the phone, stunned, to say the least! He related the incident to his wife, who answered by saying, *"Surely you misunderstood him."* So he picked up the telephone and called the Official, asking him to again state what he had just said.

"No, you did not misunderstand," said the Official, *"you heard me exactly right. You*

are to do exactly what I say, whether it is right or wrong, and the responsibility will be mine."

Of course, anyone who has even a rudimentary knowledge of the Word of God knows the absolute fallacy of such thinking. Millions have gone to Hell, eternally losing their souls, because of such error.

I do not know if the Pastor obeyed this unscriptural command or not. However, this I do know:

THE CORRECT RESPONSE

The Pastor should have immediately rebuked this man, and then immediately disassociated himself from this religious Denomination. To continue to associate with such error, and especially after it has become so blatantly obvious, makes one a part and parcel of the error. Blindly closing one's eyes, and then making the lame excuse that all in that Denomination are not of that belief, can only be labeled as compromise of the highest sort!

Paul said, *"Be not unequally yoked together with unbelievers."*

He also said, *"Wherefore come out from among them, and be ye separate, saith the Lord, and touch not the unclean thing; and I will receive you"* (II Cor. 6:14, 17).

Some may argue that this religious Official of my illustration is not an unbeliever! And yet, I think one must conclude that the Pharisees of Jesus' day were unbelievers; consequently, those who follow in their train, as this man, can only be labeled accordingly. One either follows the Word of God, or one doesn't! While it certainly is true that no Believer has all the light on every subject in the Bible, still, to be in error on such a fundamental question as personal Salvation is, basically, to be in error regarding all.

NOT FAR FROM THE KINGDOM OF GOD

The phrase, *"You are not far from the Kingdom of God,"* constitutes one of the most positive recorded statements offered by Christ to a Pharisee. The distance from the *"Kingdom of God"* is measured neither by miles nor by ceremonial standards, but by spiritual conditions; however, being close is not enough. Millions fall into this category.

Expositors commented that it would be interesting to work out a comparison between this Scribe and the ruler of Mark 10:17. In both cases, something was wanting to convert admiration into Discipleship. If wealth was the bar in one case, pride of intellect may have been fatal in the other. In the tragedy of human life, the mental acumen which detects and approves spiritual Truth may keep its possessor from entering the Kingdom of God.

As this man, millions attend Churches presently, even making professions of Faith; however, many of these millions have never really had a heartfelt experience with Christ. They are religious and active in the Church; and they also give mental assent to the acceptance of Christ, but do not, in truth, know the Lord as their own personal Saviour.

What a tragedy! They are *"near the Kingdom of God,"* but not *"in the Kingdom of God."*

The phrase, *"And no man after that did ask Him any question,"* proclaims all three groups of religious leaders — Pharisees, Sadducees, and Herodians — as being unable to match wits with Jesus. It is tragic that they approached Christ in this fashion and not in worship and adoration. However, most today approach Christ in the same fashion. He is used and abused, but seldom proclaimed for Who He really is, *"The Son of God."* The man was so near, but yet so very far away.

(35) "AND JESUS ANSWERED AND SAID, WHILE HE TAUGHT IN THE TEMPLE, HOW SAY THE SCRIBES THAT CHRIST IS THE SON OF DAVID?"

The exposition is:

This concerns the Incarnation, i.e., God becoming Man and dwelling among men.

THE INCARNATION

The phrase, *"And Jesus answered and said,"* is presented by Matthew as Jesus talking with the Pharisees (Mat. 22:41-42). The phrase, *"While He taught in the Temple,"* presents Him only hours before the Crucifixion. The question, *"How say the Scribes that Christ is the Son of David?"* concerned the Incarnation, i.e., God becoming Man and dwelling among men.

The title *"Christ,"* in the Greek, is *"Christos,"* which means *"the Anointed One."* In the Hebrew, it is translated *"Messiah."* Consequently, the question asked by Christ carries all types of implications.

The word *"Son"* refers to a descendant, which Jesus was of David.

Both the Scribes and the people believed that the Jewish Messiah would come from the Royal Line of David. David was human, so the Messiah likewise would be human. Thus, He would be David's Son.

Actually, the Lord had promised David, *"The LORD tells you that He will make you an house.*

"And when your days be fulfilled, and you shall sleep with your fathers, I will set up your Seed after you, which shall proceed out of your bowels, and I will establish His Kingdom.

"He shall build an house for My Name, and I will establish the Throne of His Kingdom forever" (II Sam. 7:11-13).

The word *"Seed,"* as used, refers to all of David's lineage, which spoke of the Kings of Judah who followed David, but more specifically, the Lord Jesus Christ, the fulfillment of these Prophecies, Who was in the direct lineage of David, and Who would have been, had He been accepted, King of Israel at this time. Actually, the lineage of Jesus went through David all the way back to Adam. Paul, in fact, called Him, *"The Last Adam"* (I Cor. 15:45).

Why was the Incarnation so important?

Even though the word *"Incarnation"* is not found in the Bible, its meaning is found in some important New Testament statements about the Person and Work of Jesus Christ.

Paul said, *"God* (Jesus) *was manifest in the flesh* (I Tim. 3:16).

John ascribed the spirit of Antichrist to any denial that Jesus Christ has *"come in the flesh"* (I Jn. 4:2; II Jn., Vs. 7).

Paul says that Christ did His reconciling work *"in His Body of flesh"* (Eph. 2:15; Col. 1:22), and that, by sending His Son *"in the likeness of sinful flesh,"* God *"condemned sin in the flesh"* (Rom. 8:3).

Peter speaks of Christ dying for us *"in the flesh"* (I Pet. 3:18; 4:1).

All these Texts are enforcing the same Truth, but from different angles: that it was precisely by coming and dying *"in the flesh"* that Christ secured our Salvation. Theology calls His Coming the *"Incarnation,"* and His dying the *"Atonement."*

(The word *"Incarnation,"* in its simplest form, means that Deity, Who has no physical body, takes upon Himself a physical body, and lives among men, hence the phrase, *"God manifest in the flesh,"* or *"God with us"* (Isa. 7:14). The word *"Immanuel"* in Isaiah 7:14 means *"God with us."* Thus was Jesus.)

As a result of the Incarnation, Jesus, Who is God, and Who became flesh at the same time, is *"Very God"* and *"Very Man."* In other words, He is 100 percent God and 100 percent Man. He is not, as some teach, half God and half Man, etc. The New Testament writers never attempted to dissect the mystery of His Person; it is enough for them to proclaim the Incarnation as a fact, one of the sequence of mighty works whereby God has wrought Salvation for sinners.

Basically, the only sense in which the New Testament writers ever attempt to explain the Incarnation is by showing how it fits into God's overall Plan for redeeming mankind (Jn. 1:18; Rom. 8:3; Phil. 2:6-11; Col. 1:13-22; Heb. 1:2; 4:14-5:10; 7:1-10:18; I Jn. 1:1-2:2). The basic explanation and understanding of the Incarnation concerns Jesus as *"The Last Adam."*

THE FIRST ADAM

Adam was created, or formed, as a *"Son of God"* (Lk. 3:38). God, in His Creation, gave Adam and Eve the power, or ability, of procreation, which means to *"bring offspring into the world."* Had Adam not fallen, their offspring would, in fact, have been *"sons of God"* (Lk. 3:38).

As it was, due to the Fall, they could not bring *"sons of God"* into the world, but rather *"sons of Adam,"* in other words, after Adam's image instead of after the *"Image of God"* (Gen. 1:26; 5:3). The Fall, with all its resultant action, is the cause of all the pain, suffering, sickness, and death in the world; consequently, men must be redeemed from this fallen state or else all is lost.

How could this be done?

The penalty for disobedience by Adam was

death, which meant separation from God, which consequently is the cause of all death (Gen. 2:17). The price of Redemption was *"Life,"* i.e., a perfect Life, which could be offered in Sacrifice, which alone would satisfy the claims of Heavenly Justice (Jn. 3:16); however, there was a catch to all of this:

Adam, under Christ, was the federal head of the entirety of the human family. As a result, when Adam sinned, he, in effect, sinned for the entirety of the human race, even all who were to come, and for all time. Consequently, when Adam fell, the entirety of the human race fell. Every baby born would be born *"in sin,"* i.e., lost! (Ps. 51:5; Rom. 3:10-18; 5:17)

So, this meant there were no uncontaminated human beings, at least that God would accept, who could redeem fallen humanity. Angels could not redeem man, because they were of another creation. So, the only way that man could be redeemed was for God to become a Man, live a perfect, spotless life, free and uncontaminated by sin, and then die on Calvary, thereby paying the price for man's Redemption. As stated, He is called *"The Last Adam"* (I Cor. 15:45). What the First Adam failed to do, the Last Adam would have to do.

The only way that God could fulfill this task, thereby redeeming man, was to become Man, hence, the Incarnation.

THE VIRGIN BIRTH

However, for God to simply become flesh was not enough. Were He to be born in the manner of all other babies, He, as well, would be born *"in sin,"* and, therefore, unacceptable as a Perfect Sacrifice. And yet, to be the *"Last Adam,"* He had to be Man in every respect. As stated, He could not be half God and half Man. So, how was it is possible to do this?

Inasmuch as Adam, under Christ, was the federal head of the human family, the seed of procreation (bringing offspring into the world) was contained in man. In effect, the woman has no seed. Therefore, if Jesus was born of a Virgin, which means a woman who has never had sexual relations with a man, He would not be born *"in sin"* as all other babies; consequently, this is exactly what happened!

The Scripture says, *"Now the Birth of Jesus Christ was on this wise: When as His Mother Mary was espoused* (engaged) *to Joseph, before they came together, she was found with Child of the Holy Spirit"* (Mat. 1:18). Inasmuch as the First Adam was not born of woman, but instead formed by God, Jesus, being born of the Virgin Mary in the fashion that He was, did not violate the type. So, since man had nothing to do with His conception and Mary His Mother was a Virgin, He consequently was born without sin and, therefore, a fit subject for the Perfect Sacrifice.

However, He must, as well as the Last Adam, walk perfect before God, never failing or sinning. If He failed, even one time, He also would be fallen, just as the original Adam. He had to live a fully human life, just as all other men. As such, He had to face very temptation that man faces, at least as far as the root of temptation is concerned. This He did, and did so perfectly sinless, which is several times asserted in the Bible (Mat. 3:14-17; Jn. 8:46; II Cor. 5:21; Heb. 4:15; I Pet. 2:22; I Jn. 2:1); consequently, when He died on Calvary, He did not die for sins of His Own, for He had none, but for others. He died Vicariously (as our Substitute) and representatively (representing the entirety of the human race), the Righteous taking the place of the unrighteous (Rom. 5:16; II Cor. 5:21; Gal. 3:13; I Pet. 3:18).

WHAT EXACTLY WAS THE INCARNATE STATE?

It was a state of *"dependence and obedience."* The Incarnation did not change the relationship between the Son and the Father. They continued in unbroken fellowship, the Son saying and doing what the Father gave Him to say and do, not going beyond the Father's Will at any single moment.

During the time of the Incarnation, He emptied Himself of the qualities of Deity, while never ceasing to be Deity. As the Son, He did not wish or seek to know more than the Father wished Him to know (Phil. 2:5-8). As well, and as we have already stated, His Life was a state of sinlessness and impeccability. It had to be this way in order for Him to die as *"a Lamb without blemish and without spot"* (I Pet. 1:19).

He had to keep the Law of Moses in every respect, which He did, and which no other man ever did, even Moses; consequently, by keeping the Law, He became our Representative Man of Victory; Faith in Him guarantees the Believer the victory by Jesus. He was our Substitute, and a Perfect One at that; upon identification with Him, all that He gained, which is what Adam lost, which Christ did all for us, is now given to us.

The Incarnation was also a state of temptation and moral conflict. It had to be in order to be a true entry into the conditions of man's moral life. Being man, as the original Adam, it was necessary for Him to fight temptation and do it God's Way in order to overcome it. This He did, and never failed in even one point.

Paul, in his Epistle to the Hebrews, stresses that, by virtue of Christ's firsthand experience of temptation and the costliness of obedience, He is able to extend effective sympathy and help to tempted and distraught Christians (Heb. 2:18; 4:14; 5:2, 7).

THE PERFECT SACRIFICE

So, as the Perfect Man, the Last Adam, He did what the First Adam failed to do and, therefore, redeemed humanity. To fulfill the requirements of Heavenly Justice, His Perfect Life, which was ensconced in His Perfect Body, was offered as a Perfect Sacrifice — a Sacrifice which God, to be sure, could and would accept; therefore, as the Last Adam, He met Satan on even worse terms than the First Adam, but nevertheless overcame him in every respect. He came to the end of His human life and said, *"The prince of this world* (Satan) *comes, and has nothing in Me"* (Jn. 14:30).

So, the Incarnation was an absolute necessity if man was to be redeemed. Thank God that, even when we did not love Him, He loved us enough that He would come down to this world, taking upon Himself the wrappings of human flesh, living in humiliation as a Man, in order to pay the price for our Redemption. Such is incomprehensible to the human mind; it is simply beyond the ability of man to fully grasp. And yet, He did it for you and me.

As the Last Adam, He won back, or rather purchased, with His Own Precious Blood that which we had lost — that and more! As a Man, he faced Satan in every respect, and in every respect overcame Him. As well, He satisfied the claims of Heavenly Justice; nothing is left owing on man's ledger, at least for those who will believe (Jn. 3:16).

(36) "FOR DAVID HIMSELF SAID BY THE HOLY SPIRIT, THE LORD SAID TO MY LORD, SIT THOU ON MY RIGHT HAND, TILL I MAKE YOUR ENEMIES YOUR FOOTSTOOL."

The composition is:

The first *"LORD"* is the august title of God in the Hebrew Old Testament, i.e., *"Jehovah"*; so the first *"LORD"* refers to God the Father, with the second *"Lord"* referring to God the Son; in effect, the entirety of the Trinity is here addressed; the Holy Spirit makes up the Third Person, the One Who inspired what was said.

THE LORD

The phrase, *"For David himself said by the Holy Spirit,"* affirms by Christ that David wrote Psalm 110. It also proclaims that it was inspired by the Holy Spirit.

The phrase, *"The LORD said to my Lord,"* refers to *"LORD"* as the translation of the Greek word *"kurios,"* which is the august title of God in the Hebrew Old Testament, i.e., *"Jehovah."* As we have stated, the first *"LORD"* in this phrase refers to God the Father, with the second *"Lord"* referring to God the Son; consequently, this phrase proclaims two *"Lords"* in the Deity. Actually, there are three, with the *"Holy Spirit"* mentioned in the first phrase; therefore, there are Three Persons in the Trinity, *"the Father," "the Son,"* and *"the Holy Spirit"* (Mat. 3:16-17; 28:19; Jn. 14:16, 26; 15:26; 16:7-15; Acts 2:33; 7:55; II Cor. 13:14; Eph. 4:4-6; I Jn. 5:7; Rev. 1:4; 4:2-5; 5:7).

THE RIGHT HAND OF GOD

The phrase, *"Sit Thou on My Right Hand,"* refers to the time after the Death and Resurrection of Christ, when the Father will have exalted Him far above all principality and power, actually placing Him next to Himself in Heaven, that He may reign with supreme Power and Glory over all. As should be obvious, Christ is there at this very moment (Heb. 1:3).

THE FOOTSTOOL

The phrase, *"Till I make Your enemies Your footstool,"* does not imply that Christ will then cease to reign, but that He will then formally deliver up the Kingdom to God, even the Father. The defeating of these *"enemies,"* which refer to Satan and his kingdom of darkness, began with the Life of Christ, especially Calvary. It has continued through the Church Age, and will continue through the Millennial Reign. At the end of the Millennial Reign, Satan, along with all his minions of darkness, will be *"cast into the Lake of Fire and brimstone"* (Rev. 20:10). At that time, the *"last enemy,"* which is *"death,"* will also be destroyed (I Cor. 15:26).

Paul then said, and to which we have referred, *"Then comes the end, when He shall have delivered up the Kingdom to God, even the Father; when He shall have put down all* (evil) *rule and all* (evil) *authority and power"* (I Cor. 15:24). When all enemies are subdued, as they shall be, and the Kingdom is delivered to *"God the Father,"* then God will transfer His Headquarters from Heaven to Earth. John gives us that description in Revelation, Chapters 21 and 22.

The Scripture then says, *"And there shall be no more curse: but the Throne of God and of the Lamb shall be in it; and His servants shall serve Him:*

"And they shall see His Face; and His Name shall be in their foreheads.

". . . and they shall reign forever and ever" (Rev. 22:3-5).

(37) "DAVID THEREFORE HIMSELF CALLED HIM LORD, AND WHENCE IS HE THEN HIS SON? AND THE COMMON PEOPLE HEARD HIM GLADLY."

The diagram is:

The last phrase means that the common people believed Him respecting His claim to be the Messiah, but the religious leaders did not; with this statement about David, He brings them face-to-face with His claim to be Messiah, a claim they could not deny; so they said nothing (Mat. 22:46).

DAVID

The phrase, *"David therefore himself called Him Lord,"* recognizes Christ as Deity, the Jehovah of the Old Testament.

The question, *"And whence is He then His Son?"* refers to Him, the Messiah, not only as God, but human as well! This question is posed to these religious leaders as to how the Messiah, as Jehovah, can also be human. At once, the Incarnation is brought before them. Wuest says, *"One of the charges brought against the Lord Jesus was that He called God His* (His private and unique) *Father, making Himself equal with God, thus Deity"* (Jn. 5:18).

Plainly and clearly, Jesus tells these religious leaders exactly Who and How the Messiah would be; consequently, His statement cleared up misunderstanding and outright false interpretation. In view of what the Scripture plainly said, there was no reason for them to be confused. They were in this state because of their self-will; they would reject Jesus because of self-will.

They knew that the Messiah would come from the Royal Line of David. As well, they, no doubt, checked the genealogy in the Temple, where such of every family in Israel was kept, and knew that Joseph, the foster father of Jesus, was in the direct lineage of David. In fact, had the Davidic dynasty continued, Joseph would now be King.

Whereas Joseph's lineage traced back to David through Solomon, they also knew that Mary's lineage, the Mother of Jesus, traced back to David through Nathan, another son of David, a brother of Solomon. Consequently, the lineage of Jesus was perfect, which, of course, would characterize the Messiah.

They are, therefore, faced with a dilemma. Jesus is Who He says He is, of which there is incontrovertible proof, or else He is an impostor, but there is no evidence whatsoever of the latter! Sadly, despite the proof otherwise, they branded Him as an impostor.

This appeal to them just hours before the Crucifixion was another effort by Christ to bring them to their senses in order that they may not do this dastardly thing. The killing of Him was bad enough; however, He would rise from the dead in three days. The worst thing of all was that, in their killing of Him, they would destroy themselves, for they would not rise from the dead!

THE COMMON PEOPLE

The phrase, *"And the common people heard Him gladly,"* means that they, the common people, heard Him and believed Him respecting His claim to be the Messiah, but the religious leaders did not! Regrettably, such continues to the present!

The fault of most spiritual declension is not the pew, but rather the pulpit. One Methodist layman once told me, *"Brother Swaggart, it was not the Methodist people who destroyed the Methodist Church, but rather the Seminaries, which turned out Preachers who not longer believed in God or the Bible. They destroyed the Methodist Church!"*

(38) "AND HE SAID UNTO THEM IN HIS DOCTRINE, BEWARE OF THE SCRIBES, WHICH LOVE TO GO IN LONG CLOTHING, AND LOVE SALUTATIONS IN THE MARKETPLACES,

(39) "AND THE CHIEF SEATS IN THE SYNAGOGUES, AND THE UPPERMOST ROOMS AT FEASTS:

(40) "WHICH DEVOUR WIDOWS' HOUSES, AND FOR A PRETENCE MAKE LONG PRAYERS: THESE SHALL RECEIVE GREATER DAMNATION."

The overview is:

The latter phrase teaches degrees of punishment in the coming Judgment.

HIS DOCTRINE

The phrase, *"And He said unto them in His Doctrine,"* refers to these religious leaders, who had denied His claims.

The phrase, *"Beware of the Scribes,"* does not demean their official character, but rather their conduct. These *"Scribes"* were, in effect, the Pastors of the people. They were supposed to be experts in the Law of Moses, and consequently guide the people in the Ways of the Lord. Jesus' condemnation of this group proclaims them doing anything and everything totally opposite of the Ways of God.

As we shall see, He did not condemn them all, but only those who fit His following description, which, sadly, included the vast majority.

Presently, would He say, *"Beware of the Preachers"*?

I think it can be said, without any fear of contradiction, that, without a doubt, He would!

The scene is very little different now than then. As there were only a few *"Scribes"* then who truly followed the Lord, likewise, there are only a few Preachers today who truly follow. Consequently, concerning most Preachers standing behind modern pulpits, Jesus would say, *"Beware!"*

Why?

Paul said it well, when he was looking for a Preacher to send to Philippi:

"For I have no man like-minded, who will naturally care for your state.

"For all seek their own, not the things which are Jesus Christ's" (Phil. 2:20-21).

As Scribes then sought their own *"will and way,"* likewise, modern Preachers too often do the same!

A PRIDEFUL SPIRIT

The phrase, *"Which love to go in long clothing,"* spoke of Priestly or Royal robes. What the Lord was condemning was ostentatious display, not necessarily the type of clothing itself. In other words, they wanted to look important!

The phrase, *"And love salutations in the marketplaces,"* referred to them being fond of being called *"Rabbi," "Doctor,"* or *"Master."* Once again, He was not condemning these titles, but only the greedy grasping after them. To be called by these titles in public places, in the hearing of many people, made these people feel important.

The phrase, *"And the chief seats in the Synagogue,"* referred to seats or benches up front, which faced the congregation and which were reserved for officials and persons of distinction. Wuest says, *"The Scribes claimed these places of honor also at social gatherings."*

The phrase, *"And the uppermost rooms at feasts,"* referred to the place reserved for the most honored guests at a feast. At meals, the custom at that time was not to sit in chairs, as we do now, but rather to recline on couches around the table. Whoever the host was, the *"Scribes"* desired the uppermost room, or place, beside him.

The phrase, *"Which devour widows' houses,"* referred to money. People often left their entire fortunes to the Temple, and a good part of the money finally went to the Scribes and Pharisees. They would spend much time with wealthy widows, in order to get them to make out a will in which the money and property seemingly went to the Temple, but which was worded in such a way that most of the funds came to the Scribe himself.

The phrase, *"And for a pretence make long prayers,"* referred to the Scribes praying long and loud for these widows, and in their presence, which helped to ultimately influence them to make out a will in favor of the Scribe, etc.

The phrase, *"These shall receive greater damnation,"* means that God holds them more guilty than He does a dishonest man who makes no pretense of piety. In other words, to the sentence of the hypocrite, which these Scribes were, would be added in their case the sentence of the robber. This phrase also teaches degrees of punishment in the coming Judgment.

(41) "AND JESUS SAT OVER AGAINST THE TREASURY, AND BEHELD HOW THE PEOPLE CAST MONEY INTO THE TREASURY: AND MANY WHO WERE RICH CAST IN MUCH."

The exposition is:

They made an ostentatious display of their gift in order that all may know how much it was.

THE TREASURY

The phrase, *"And Jesus sat over against the treasury,"* pertained to the court of the women, which was situated immediately behind the Court of Israel, sometimes called the court of men. In the women's court, there were receptacles labeled for special purposes regarding offerings.

The phrase, *"And beheld how the people cast money into the treasury,"* would be used by Him to present a great lesson. I think it can be said, and beyond the shadow of a doubt, that our Lord does the same presently!

The phrase, *"And many who were rich cast in much,"* pertains not so much to the amount, but the manner in which it was given. With some of the rich, they made a display of their gift, i.e., the large amount of

NOTES

the gift was made known to the bystanders, and the givers would then receive accolades and well wishes for these large gifts.

If one is to notice, Jesus constantly condemned ostentatious display, whether in clothing, gifts, or public appearances. As stated, it was not the clothing or the gifts that were condemned, but rather the showy displays. It was the grasping for recognition and praise.

(42) "AND THERE CAME A CERTAIN POOR WIDOW, AND SHE THREW IN TWO MITES, WHICH MAKE A FARTHING."

The exposition is:

The *"farthing"* was a *"lepton,"* which was the smallest Greek copper coin, with both of them presently being worth about one dollar, if that, in 2004 currency.

THE POOR WIDOW

The phrase, *"And there came a certain poor widow,"* proclaims her being little noticed, if at all, by others, but greatly noticed by the Lord.

When will we ever learn that this is the only notice that really matters?

The word *"poor"* in the Greek Text is *"ptochos,"* which is used to designate a pauper rather than a mere peasant. The woman actually was destitute, and yet she gave from her meager income, actually *"all that she had, even all her living."*

The phrase, *"And she threw in two mites, which make a farthing,"* referred, as stated, to the *"lepton,"* which was the smallest Greek copper coin. It is very difficult to ascertain the worth of money in those days. So the idea that these two mites were probably worth about one dollar in present value is an educated guess, at best!

(43) "AND HE CALLED UNTO HIM HIS DISCIPLES, AND SAID UNTO THEM, VERILY I SAY UNTO YOU, THAT THIS POOR WIDOW HAS CAST MORE IN, THAN ALL THEY WHICH HAVE CAST INTO THE TREASURY."

The synopsis is:

Jesus will now teach His Disciples the motive for proper giving to the Lord.

THE GIVING OF MONEY

The phrase, *"And He called unto Him His*

Disciples," concerns an important lesson about to be taught to them. The phrase, *"And said unto them, Verily I say unto you, That this poor widow has cast more in, than all they which have cast into the treasury,"* proclaims the manner in which God looks at our giving.

First of all, the motive is pointed out. Many of the rich gave for show, while she gave because she loved God.

How do we know that?

As little as it was, she gave all she had. To be sure, such would not have been done unless she deeply loved the Lord.

Second, it's not so much what we give, but how much we have left. Someone who gives a dollar and then only has a little left is looked at with much higher regard by the Lord than someone who gives $10,000, who has hundreds of thousands left. However, at times, it is easier for some people to give from a meager income than it is when they come into large sums of money. Somehow, the giving of small amounts does not trouble them and they remain faithful in this endeavor; however, some balk at giving large amounts if such comes into their hands.

Then again, there are many who, unlike this *"poor widow,"* will not give their small amounts, claiming they cannot afford to. I think Christ lays that to rest. Anyone can afford to give to the Lord; and no amount, no matter how small, is looked at by Him with disdain, which this illustration proves. Actually, it is looked at with great favor; to be sure, it will garner great blessing (II Cor. 9:6).

One cannot imagine that Jesus allowed this woman to go unblessed. I believe that He saw to it that her needs were met, and abundantly so!

(44) "FOR ALL THEY DID CAST IN OF THEIR ABUNDANCE; BUT SHE OF HER WANT DID CAST IN ALL THAT SHE HAD, EVEN ALL HER LIVING."

The synopsis is:

The Holy Spirit evidently related this information to the Lord, because there is no record that He even spoke to the woman Personally.

CONSECRATION

The phrase, *"For all they did cast in of their abundance,"* was not necessarily criticized by the Lord, except in the showy display. Neither was it praised at all, because, in His Eyes, which are the only eyes that count, these rich men had not given very much, simply because of the *"abundance"* they had left. In other words, there was no sacrifice at all on their part.

The phrase, *"But she of her want did cast in all that she had, even all her living,"* means that, in the eyes of God, Who sees not as man sees, she gave more than all the others put together. God does not weigh the gift so much as the mind of the giver. This *"poor widow's"* gift was a sacrifice of tremendous proportions, because she gave all she had.

St. Ambrose says, *"That which God esteems is not that which you proudly present, but what you offer with humility and devotion."*

A PERSONAL EXPERIENCE

If I remember correctly, the year was 1970. I was at Brightmoor Tabernacle in Detroit, Michigan, in a Revival Meeting. One particular night after the Service, a dear lady came up to me and pressed a roll of bills into my hand. That night, as well as several other nights, I had received an offering for our Radio Program, *"The Campmeeting Hour."*

After she gave the money, I did something that I seldom do. I looked at the worn appearance of her coat and asked her, *"How much money is this?"*

She dropped her eyes and answered, *"Thirty-two dollars."*

Then I asked her, *"What do you do for a living?"* As stated, this was something I seldom ever did, but I asked for purpose and reason. I did not feel she could afford to give the money she had placed in my hands.

In reply to my question, she said, *"I work in an office building, and I scrub floors for a living."*

Then I asked her, *"How much money do you make each week?"*

She replied, *"Thirty-two dollars."*

"So you," I said, *"have given everything you worked for this week!"* I then attempted to put the money back into her hands, saying, *"Sister, the Lord does not need these funds this badly. I want you to take the money back."*

For the first time, she looked up at me. Her eyes literally flashed with fire. She said, *"I'm not giving this money to you. I'm giving it to the Lord. The Lord told me to do it. If you don't want to take it, I'll leave it laying on the floor!"*

I thanked her. In a few moments, she turned and walked away. It is very difficult for me to express exactly how I felt at that moment. I sensed somewhat the tremendous love that God has for those who will give so sacrificially.

THE WORD OF THE LORD

During this exchange, I was standing on the platform, and she was standing down on the main floor. After she left, I walked over to the corner of the platform. I could not hold back the tears. The Lord, I believe, spoke to me at that time. This is what He said:

"Much money will come into your hands to be used for My Work. Much of it will come from people just like this woman. Let it be a lesson to you: if you misuse it, you will not only answer to Me in the Judgment, but you will also answer to the people who gave!"

I have never forgotten that moment, or that dear lady. True enough, since that time, the Lord has placed large sums of money into my hands, respecting His Work. It has been used to pay for Television airtime and production, the building of schools for children, Churches, Bible Schools, and other efforts for the Cause of Christ, including SonLife Radio. I have tried my best that this lesson given to me on that cold January night in 1970 in Detroit, Michigan, be a lesson that I learned well. I have tried my best to remember exactly what the Lord spoke to my heart.

I have also seen that woman's face, so to speak, in the faces of countless thousands since then, realizing how precious their gifts are in the sight of God, especially those who give so sacrificially, as some do!

What a wonderful illustration the Lord gave us concerning this *"poor widow."* How little did she know that day, when she went into the Temple, possibly with much concern and anxiety on her mind respecting her poverty-stricken state, that the Lord of Glory would be there, that He would observe her, and that her story would be known for time and eternity.

But the Lord was observing, even as He observes presently. Moreover, His observation includes not only that which is done outwardly, but also the very motives of our hearts.

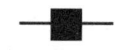

CHAPTER 13

(1) "AND AS HE WENT OUT OF THE TEMPLE, ONE OF HIS DISCIPLES SAID UNTO HIM, MASTER, SEE WHAT MANNER OF STONES AND WHAT BUILDINGS ARE HERE."

The structure is:

This concerns a conversation held, no doubt, on the Mount of Olives, as Jesus and the Disciples overlooked the Temple and surrounding area. Josephus said that this building was one of the wonders of the world.

THE TEMPLE

The phrase, *"And as He went out of the Temple,"* portrays a far greater meaning than the mere act itself. He will not return except at His arrest and trial. Consequently, when He went out, its protection left as well! As He, the Lord of the Temple, was not wanted, there remained no more use for the Temple. In effect, He left the Temple and the City (Mat. 23:39; 24:1).

About 600 years before, through the Person of the Holy Spirit, Christ had left the Temple reluctantly and in stages, withdrawing to the Mount of Olives; the Prophet Ezekiel saw Him as the God of Glory (Ezek. 9:3; 10:4, 19; 11:23). When men saw Him now leaving the second Temple and withdrawing to the Mount of Olives, they saw in Him neither beauty nor glory, but only a Man, the Carpenter of Nazareth!

When Israel finally does accept Him, which they shall at the Second Coming, the Temple will be rebuilt. Ezekiel also in a Vision saw Him at that time, through the Person of the Holy Spirit, return as the God of Glory, which is even yet future (Ezek. 43:1-7). This will signal the beginning of the coming Kingdom Age.

THE DISCIPLES

The phrase, *"One of His Disciples said unto Him,"* concerns a conversation probably held on the Mount of Olives, which took place not long after Jesus had left the Temple. It seems that Matthew, Chapters 24 and 25, along with Mark, Chapter 13, were spoken after Luke, Chapter 21, which seems to have been uttered *"in the Temple"* (Lk. 21:1-5, 37-38). As stated, this later discourse (Mk., Chpt. 13; Mat., Chpt. 24) was spoken on the Mount of Olives. Both Prophecies are similar down to Luke 21:12; they should be studied together.

(The Prophecy in Luke, Chapter 21, gives information concerning the near destruction of Jerusalem in A.D. 70, which is not given in either Matthew or Mark.)

The phrase, *"Master, see what manner of stones and what buildings are here,"* spoke of the beauty and grandeur of the Temple. It is said that this building was one of the wonders of the world. Josephus says that it lacked nothing that the eye and the mind could admire. Built of white marble, it shone with a fiery splendor; when the eye gazed upon it, it turned away as from the rays of the sun.

The size of the foundation-stones was enormous. Josephus speaks of some of the stones being nearly 70 feet long, 7-1/2 feet in height, and 9 feet wide. However, all this magnificence had no effect upon our Lord, Who only repeated the sentence of its downfall.

(2) "AND JESUS ANSWERING SAID UNTO HIM, DO YOU SEE THESE GREAT BUILDINGS? THERE SHALL NOT BE LEFT ONE STONE UPON ANOTHER, THAT SHALL NOT BE THROWN DOWN."

The structure is:

This prediction was fulfilled in exact totality, in A.D. 70, by the Roman General Titus.

DESTRUCTION

The phrase, *"And Jesus answering said unto Him,"* presents a response concerning the grandeur of the Temple and its coming destruction. It is obvious that the Disciple who pointed out the glory of the Temple to Jesus did not at all have in mind the destruction of which Jesus would now speak.

NOTES

Despite Him telling them several times that He would be killed and rise on the third day, they could not grasp such a statement. On the minds of the Disciples was the grandeur of the Temple and Jerusalem. Jesus would use His Power, they thought, to overthrow Rome, with Israel once again becoming the greatest nation in the world. The glory of the times of David and Solomon would now return. Until the Advent of the Holy Spirit on the Day of Pentecost, they seemingly could not grasp the Truths which He repeatedly told them; hence, the necessity of the Holy Spirit in the modern Church!

THE TEMPLE PROPER

The question, *"Do you see these great buildings?"* was probably uttered with a sweep of His Hand. In fact, the buildings were great!

The word *"buildings"* referred to the mass of separate edifices, enclosures, colonnades, halls, and sanctuaries composing the Temple enclosure.

Herod the Great had commenced work on the Temple in 19 B.C., over 50 years before. His building of the Temple was an attempt to reconcile the Jews to him, who was Idumaean, rather than to glorify God. Even though the main structure was finished in approximately 10 years, work continued until A.D. 64.

The plan of the shrine somewhat copied Solomon's. The porch, it is said, was 150 feet wide and 150 feet high; however, the height seems to be excessive, so that possibly this is a misquote. It is said that a doorway some 30 feet wide and 60 feet high gave entry, and one-half that size led into the Holy Place. The Holy Place was about 60 feet long and 30 feet wide. A curtain divided the Holy Place from the Inner Sanctuary called *"the Veil"* (Mat. 27:51; Mk. 15:38). Actually, this was the same *"Veil"* that ripped from the top to the bottom when Jesus died on Calvary (Mat. 27:51).

Josephus said this Veil was 60 feet high from the ceiling to the floor, 4 inches thick, and was so strong that four yoke of oxen could not pull it apart. And yet, it was torn from top to bottom, showing that it was God Alone Who did this thing, signifying that the way is now open for all who will believe, the way to the Holy of Holies, and all made possible by the Lord Jesus Christ and what He did at the Cross.

The Inner Sanctuary, referred to as the Holy of Holies, was 30 feet square; like the Holy Place, it was 60 feet high. An empty room above the Holy Place and the Inner Sanctuary rose to the height of the porch — 150 feet, if that was the correct height — thus making a level roof.

NOT ONE STONE UPON ANOTHER

The phrase, *"There shall not be left one stone upon another, that shall not be thrown down,"* was fulfilled in totality in A.D. 70. The soldiers of the Roman General Titus had heard that gold was in the mortar between the stones, which they pulled apart with teams of oxen. There was no gold in the mortar; nevertheless, in their search they pulled down all the stones, fulfilling the Prophecy of Christ. Thus, this magnificent structure of cream stone was barely finished (A.D. 64) before it was destroyed by the Roman Army.

The Golden Candelabrum, the Table of Shewbread, and other objects were carried in triumph to Rome, as depicted on the Arch of Titus in that city. Consequently, the destruction of the Temple signaled the destruction of the nation. Over a million Jews died in that carnage, with hundreds of thousands of others sold as slaves at trifling prices. The burning fires of rebellion against Rome burned in the hearts of zealots; they attempted to overthrow the Roman yoke. Of course, they were no match for Roman power. Even though the Roman Army suffered some losses in the several years it took to quell this rebellion, nevertheless, it ultimately succeeded, with the nation being totally destroyed.

Even though an attempt was made to hold the nation together somewhat, the future destruction about 65 years later, in A.D. 135, completely destroyed Israel as any semblance of a nation. They were then scattered all over the world, where they wandered as outcasts, even as the Prophets had proclaimed, until finally once again becoming a nation, such as it was, in 1948.

NOTES

Even yet, their most difficult time is ahead, with the nation of Israel and its people then coming close to total destruction. It will be the time of the Great Tribulation, which Jesus also predicted in Verse 19 of this Chapter. Coming close to annihilation by the Antichrist, Israel will be saved at the last moment by the Second Coming of the Lord Jesus Christ.

So, when the Temple was *"thrown down,"* the nation was also *"thrown down"* — all because of their rejection of Jesus Christ!

(3) "AND AS HE SAT UPON THE MOUNT OF OLIVES OVER AGAINST THE TEMPLE, PETER AND JAMES AND JOHN AND ANDREW ASKED HIM PRIVATELY."

The exegesis is:

It was extremely dangerous to speak of the destruction of the Temple, or anything that even resembled such, for fear of the Scribes and Pharisees, who would consider it as insurrection. So, the Disciples would *"ask Him privately."*

A PRIVATE CONVERSATION

The phrase, *"And as He sat upon the Mount of Olives over against the Temple,"* proclaims the occasion when the Disciples will question Him further concerning these momentous events.

The phrase, *"Peter and James and John and Andrew asked Him privately,"* proclaims these four pulling Him aside, not only from the multitude, but even from the other Disciples. As Jesus was leaving the Temple, He, with the Disciples, crossed the brook Kidron, ascended the steep road over the Mount of Olives which led to Bethany, and was now seated and resting on the top of the mountain overlooking the Temple and City.

Hearing Jesus mention the destruction of the Temple, even as they walked, they now pull Him aside to a place of privacy to ply Him with more questions.

It was extremely dangerous to speak of the destruction of the Temple, or anything that resembled such, for fear of the Scribes and Pharisees. It was this accusation that led to the stoning of Stephen. The Temple authorities considered such discussion as high treason against Israel; consequently, the four would *"ask Him privately."*

It is ironical, and yet planned by the Holy Spirit, that Jesus opened His Ministry with a Sermon on the Mount (Mat., Chpt. 5) and closed it with a Sermon on the Mount. The first was near the Sea of Galilee, and signaled Grace, while this, as is obvious, was on Mount Olivet, and signaled Judgment.

(4) "TELL US, WHEN SHALL THESE THINGS BE? AND WHAT SHALL BE THE SIGN WHEN ALL THESE THINGS SHALL BE FULFILLED?"

The composition is:

They were speaking, more than likely, of the near future. His answer would incorporate the future of Israel, in essence, forever.

BIBLE PROPHECY

The question, *"Tell us, when shall these things be?"* proclaims the first of two questions asked by these Disciples. These things spoken by Christ were startling, to say the least. So the Disciples want to know *"when"* they will happen.

The question, *"And what shall be the sign when all these things shall be fulfilled?"* is the question Christ will actually answer. *"All these things"* referred to far more than what the Disciples had in mind. They were thinking, no doubt, of the near future, while Jesus will give them an account of the entirety of the future of Israel. The span of time He covered now has been nearly 2,000 years, and has not concluded yet. Even though He answered what they asked, still, they would have little understood what He was saying, at least at that time. The future, as the evidence portrays, would greatly improve their understanding of this momentous Message given by Christ.

Furthermore, they would ask for a *"sign"* concerning the near fulfillment of these predictions, which Jesus would adequately give. There is even a possibility that one or two of the four took down notes while Jesus was speaking. Of course, there is no evidence of that; the idea is only speculation. However, their accounts are so similar (Matthew, Mark, and Luke) that such certainly may have been the case. Inasmuch as their accounts are very similar, but not identical, this shows that little, if any, collaboration was engaged before the writing of the Gospels.

NOTES

(5) "AND JESUS ANSWERING THEM BEGAN TO SAY, TAKE HEED LEST ANY MAN DECEIVE YOU."

The diagram is:

Jesus begins His discourse with a warning against deception; this is Satan's greatest weapon.

DECEPTION

The phrase, *"And Jesus answering them began to say,"* proclaims the beginning of this momentous answer, which has come, and shall come, to pass, exactly as predicted. Due to Israel rejecting Jesus as her Messiah, the *"Kingdom of God,"* which was then ready to be given, and which would have brought unprecedented peace and prosperity, was instead postponed, resulting in the terrible predictions which have come to pass, and which shall yet come to pass. Untold sorrow and heartache have been the result.

Man has ever attempted to rebuild the Garden of Eden, but without the Tree of Life. Such is not to be done and, in fact, cannot be done! Jesus is the *"Tree of Life,"* and unless He is in the Garden, it cannot be rebuilt. While the intelligence of man has increased greatly since the turn of the Twentieth Century, as prophesied by Daniel (Dan. 12:4), still, man has not succeeded in learning how to live. Actually, the increase of this vast intelligence has only given man the ability to become more destructive. He has little learned the words of Christ, that *"a man's life consists not in the abundance of things which he possesses"* (Lk. 12:15).

As we study this Chapter, much of that predicted by Christ is even yet to come to pass; however, its fulfillment is even at the door. As such, we should study it minutely, prayerfully, and with dedication. How momentous the occasion, considering that we are living on the very eve of the fulfillment of the most cataclysmic happenings the world has ever known! Such happenings, we might quickly add, will usher in the Second Coming of Christ!

Furthermore, as we study this Chapter, we must keep in mind that the predictions concern Israel, even though they will affect the entirety of the world. They do not pertain to the Church, except in an ancillary way.

For instance, the Rapture of the Church is not mentioned in these predictions, because the Church will have been raptured away when most are brought to fulfillment. Even though spanning the entirety of the last 2,000 years, still, the greatest bulk of these predictions pertain to the final seven years before the Second Coming, the time referred to as *"Daniel's 70th Week"* (Dan. 9:25-27).

TAKE HEED

The phrase, *"Take heed lest any man deceive you,"* has several implications. They are as follows:

1. Jesus began this discourse with a warning against *"deception,"* simply because Satan is so successful in this effort. Man fell in the Garden of Eden because of deception; consequently, deception continues to be man's greatest problem. If it is to be noticed, men would rather believe a lie than the Truth.

2. The greatest deception of all will come to Israel upon her acceptance of the Antichrist. Thinking he is the Messiah, she will be lulled to sleep by his promises. The awakening, however, will be traumatic, to say the least! She will then face her hardest time, called by Jesus *"affliction, such as was not from the beginning of the creation . . ."* (Vs. 19).

3. Even though Jesus is speaking of Israel, still, the warnings should not go unheeded respecting individual Christians. In effect, deception is just as great in the Church at present as it was in Israel of old.

The only defense against deception is a correct knowledge of the Word of God, which can only be brought about by the Believer ever having Christ and the Cross as the Object of his Faith (Rev. 5:6).

(6) "FOR MANY SHALL COME IN MY NAME, SAYING, I AM CHRIST; AND SHALL DECEIVE MANY."

The overview is:

After the Ascension of Christ, a number of Jews appeared on the scene, claiming to be the Messiah, who would lead Israel out from under the dominion of the Romans; those false Messiahs, however, led Israel to her destruction in A.D. 70.

FALSE MESSIAHS

The phrase, *"For many shall come in My Name,"* has to do with false claims. While there were many who came after the Ascension of Christ, there will be many more in the coming Great Tribulation. But the crowning claim of all will be that of the Antichrist, the one Israel will accept. He will deceive not only Israel, but much of the world.

I AM OF CHRIST!

The phrase, *"Saying, I am Christ, and shall deceive many,"* portrays not only the claim of Messiahship, but with even a deeper deception. The word *"deceive"* in the Greek is *"planao,"* which means *"to lead astray."* Our Lord warns the Disciples, not only against the deceptions of those who claim to be the Messiah, but against following them, thus being led astray.

The phrase, *"In My Name,"* is literally *"upon the basis of My Name,"* which means *"basing their claims on the use of My Name."* The idea presents itself, not only to Israel, but also as a bleed-over to the Church. It holds the idea of individuals claiming to be *"of"* the Lord, or *"sent from"* the Lord. Actually, this is a problem that has raged in the Church from the very beginning.

As an example, the Judaizers claimed they were sent from the Lord; however, Paul called them *"false apostles, deceitful workers, transforming themselves into the Apostles of Christ"* (II Cor. 11:13).

Concerning the Church, most all Preachers claim to be *"of"* the Lord, or *"sent from"* the Lord. Truthfully, some few are, but most aren't! Tragically, those who aren't oftentimes are successful in leading many astray. As stated, having a proper understanding of Christ and the Cross, which guarantees a proper understanding of the Word, presents the only protection against deception (I Cor. 1:17-18, 23; 2:2; Gal., Chpt. 5).

The Name *"Christ"* means *"The Anointed"*; it refers to the Messiah. However, He is truly the only One of such distinction, the only One of Whom it can be said *"I,"* in contradistinction to all others, *"am He."*

(7) "AND WHEN YOU SHALL HEAR OF WARS AND RUMORS OF WARS, BE YE NOT TROUBLED: FOR SUCH THINGS MUST NEEDS BE; BUT THE END SHALL NOT BE YET."

The composition is:

The Verse has to do with the mission at hand of evangelizing the world; our Lord exhorts the Disciples, and all who would follow, not to permit political and national upheavals to distract them from their work of Evangelism.

WARS AND RUMORS OF WARS

The phrase, *"And when you shall hear of wars and rumors of wars,"* has to do with the State of Israel and the world, which would begin after the Ascension, and actually continues unto this day, and will exacerbate in the near future. When Christ was born, peace reigned for one of the few times in history. There is also evidence that it continued throughout His Life and Ministry; however, with His rejection by Israel, the *"Times of the Gentiles"* continued, with its baggage of *"wars and rumors of wars."* Because of that rejection, the world has been bathed in blood from that time until now, and will continue to be so until the Second Coming.

After the Ascension of Christ, three Roman Emperors, Caligula, Claudius, and Nero, almost immediately began to threaten or wage war against the Jews. That continued until Jerusalem was destroyed in A.D. 70; the entire nation was destroyed totally in A.D. 135. As well, by no means were the *"wars and rumors of wars"* limited to Israel, with almost the entirety of the world bathed in blood, in one way or the other, from then until now.

WORLD EVANGELISM

The phrase, *"Be ye not troubled,"* has to do with the mission at hand of evangelizing the world.

Wuest said, *"Our Lord exhorts the Disciples not to permit political troubles and national upheavals to distract them from their work of Evangelism. There are two kingdoms on this Earth moving along side-by-side, the world's system of evil, headed up by Satan, in which the nations are constantly at sword's points, and the Kingdom of God.*

"No matter what happens in the former kingdom, the people of God must carry on toward the God-ordained and predicted conclusion.

NOTES

"The Disciples were already troubled about the political unrest in Israel. Our Lord says, 'Stop being troubled.'"

The total depravity of the human race is the root of all war, and that is the nature of the case that makes war inevitable.

Because of its vast significance, please allow us to say it again:

Nothing, as here proclaimed by Christ, must stop World Evangelism. Whatever happens on the world scene, the Leading and Guidance of the Holy Spirit must be sought, in order that the thrust of Evangelism continue unabated.

Perhaps my own particular burden in this area is much more emphasized than most. World Evangelism is a part, at least, of my calling. By and large, the instruments of Radio and Television are the major thrusts of our activities.

Through Radio and Television, the Lord has helped us to take the Gospel to vast regions of the world, with our Programs being translated into the various languages of the people. By the Grace of God, we have been able to see hundreds of thousands brought to a saving knowledge of Jesus Christ, and I exaggerate not! To be sure, I am not on Television or Radio simply because I have seen a need and have responded to that need. I am on these mediums of communication because of an Apostolic Call in respect to World Evangelism. That is the reason we see so many people brought to Christ, and that is the reason we seek God constantly respecting His Leading and Guidance; above all, we seek the Anointing of the Holy Spirit upon our efforts.

THE END OF THIS AGE

The phrase, *"For such things must needs be,"* pertains to the course of evil which fills the world, which, of necessity, brings about wars, etc. As stated, the Person of Christ was rejected; therefore, this is the alternative.

The phrase, *"But the end shall not be yet,"* means, in effect, that the *"end"* will not be brought about until the Second Coming. When Jesus used the term, *"the end,"* He was not talking about the end of the world, but rather the end of this particular Church Age, when Israel will once again be restored.

As stated, the Restoration will take place at the Second Coming.

Jesus gave, as men say, a sad interpretation of the future. His forecast was very dark: deception, conflict, suffering, family division, and universal hatred! Such is the experience of the world during His absence. He predicted that His Coming would be preceded by religious movements (Vs. 6), political movements (Vss. 7-8), and physical movements (Vs. 8). He warned against religious deception (Vss. 5-6), spiritual failure (Vss. 9-13), and against negligence (Vs. 23).

(8) "FOR NATION SHALL RISE AGAINST NATION, AND KINGDOM AGAINST KINGDOM: AND THERE SHALL BE EARTHQUAKES IN DIVERS PLACES, AND THERE SHALL BE FAMINES AND TROUBLES: THESE ARE THE BEGINNINGS OF SORROWS."

The exposition is:

Famines and troubles will be the natural product of the course taken by the human race and its rejection of Jesus Christ; and this problem will not be made right until Israel accepts Christ, which she will at the Second Coming.

NATION RISING AGAINST NATION

The phrase, *"For nation shall rise against nation, and kingdom against kingdom,"* constitutes the lot of the human family down through the ages. As well, thousands of years of education, culture, and experience have not ameliorated the problem. This is what makes the modern *"Kingdom Philosophy"* so ridiculous!

This philosophy in the modern Church, which I sometimes refer to as the *"Political Message,"* claims that Christianity is going to invade every culture, coming to terms with the religions of the world, thereby making things better and better, and finally ushering in the Millennium. Actually, some misguided souls claim that we are already in the Millennium. Such foolishness is proclaimed for two reasons:

1. Ignorance of the Word of God.
2. This erroneous Message appeals to the pride of man.

The modern Church, even more and more, in cutting across all Denominational lines, is focusing attention on this world instead of focusing attention on Heavenly things. The modern *"Faith Message,"* which, in reality, is no faith at all, has greatly exacerbated this error. The *"Purpose Driven Life"* scheme, which, again, is no *"purpose"* at all, at least which God will recognize, is already thrusting toward the entirety of the world. The *"Government of Twelve"* (G-12) philosophy has already partitioned the world off into sections. All of these efforts greatly compromise the Word in order that more people can be attracted to its siren call!

In these *"schemes,"* sin is no more mentioned, because it may offend some people. And if sin is mentioned, it is done in a setting which has little to do with the True Gospel, but rather directions made up by men. I speak of the *"Encounter Sessions"* fomented by the *"Government of Twelve"* philosophy.

The *"New Order"* claims that the Bible way is not sufficient for the modern times in which we live; therefore, the Church must be brought into the New Order, with new methods and ways. Regrettably, these *"new methods and ways"* do not correspond with the Word of God; they do not, in fact, correspond at all! While the Church is being glutted with people, these are not people who are Born-Again, but rather individuals who have embraced some type of moral religiosity.

THE HOLY SPIRIT

It must be understood that the Holy Spirit will not work outside of the Word of God. Moreover, the Word of God is the Story of Jesus Christ and Him Crucified, and that exclusively. In other words, in some way, the entirety of the Word of God, all the way from Genesis 1:1 through Revelation 22:21, presents the Story of Christ and the Cross. The Holy Spirit works entirely within the parameters of the Finished Work of Christ, which, in essence, is the Word of God.

That's why Paul said, *"We preach Christ Crucified"* (I Cor. 1:23). That's why he also said, *"I determined to know nothing among you, save Jesus Christ and Him Crucified"* (I Cor. 2:2). That's why he further said, *"For the preaching of the Cross is to them who perish foolishness, but unto us who are saved, it is the Power of God"* (I Cor. 1:18).

This *"new wave,"* while filling Churches with people, is not truly filling the hearts of the people with the Gospel, but with something else entirely. As a result, these people will die eternally lost, or else they will be spiritually stunted!

I personally believe that the Lord has raised up this Ministry (Jimmy Swaggart Ministries), no doubt, along with others around the world, to proclaim the Message of the Cross, and to do so without reservation. Until the Church comes back to the Cross, the Holy Spirit can have nothing to do with its efforts, inasmuch as He works entirely, as stated, within the framework of the Finished Work of Christ (Rom. 8:2).

As Jesus plainly says, and as we have also proclaimed, these end times are going to see things getting worse and worse instead of better and better. Admittedly, this is not the gospel that men want to hear. Doom and gloom are not an heady message! However, it does have one thing going for it; it happens to be the Truth (II Tim. 3:1-5).

NATURAL DISASTERS

The phrase, *"And there shall be earthquakes in divers places,"* proclaims disturbance at the very foundation of the Earth. The idea is that *"the whole Creation groans and travails in pain together until now"* (Rom. 8:22). Even though there have been *"earthquakes"* from the very beginning, still, the idea is that the closer to the end, the greater the frequency and intensity of these disturbances.

The phrase, *"And there shall be famines and troubles,"* proclaims the natural product of the course taken by the human family in their rejection of Jesus Christ. Some may argue that all did not do this, only the religious leaders of Israel. While that may be true, still, as the leaders of the chosen people, chosen for the purpose of bringing the Messiah into the world, they, in effect, acted for the world. Their rejection of Christ not only brought about their own destruction, but also sentenced the world to a long period of continued war, famine, and pestilence.

Furthermore, the problem cannot be remedied until Israel accepts Christ, faithfully serves God, and regains her place as the leading nation of the world, which will be done at the Second Coming. The tremendously important part Israel plays in the entirely of the Plan of God is little understood by the world, and not even by most Believers. Even by their rejection of Christ, Israel has not abrogated its position, except temporarily, although they have suffered terribly!

The great Promises made by the Lord to the Prophets of old will be ultimately realized in totality; hence, all of these predictions concerning the Endtime, as asked by the Disciples, and portrayed by Matthew, Mark, and Luke, pertain almost exclusively to Israel. Also, if anyone even halfway understands the Word of God, it quickly becomes obvious that these predictions were not fulfilled in A.D. 70, as some claim, but are even yet future.

THE BEGINNINGS OF SORROWS

The phrase, *"These are the beginnings of sorrows,"* is meant to impress upon all that these *"sorrows"* are not short-lived, but of duration. As stated, they have lasted now for nearly 2,000 years, which, of course, does not even count the thousands of years before Christ. The phrase is also meant to point to the greatest *"sorrow"* of all, the coming Great Tribulation, where the possibility exists that over half of the planet Earth's population could die in a seven-year period of time (Rev., Chpts. 6-19).

As we have already stated, these are not pleasant predictions, but they are true predictions.

(9) "BUT TAKE HEED TO YOURSELVES: FOR THEY SHALL DELIVER YOU UP TO COUNCILS; AND IN THE SYNAGOGUES YOU SHALL BE BEATEN: AND YOU SHALL BE BROUGHT BEFORE RULERS AND KINGS FOR MY SAKE, FOR A TESTIMONY AGAINST THEM."

The exposition is:

The last line of the Verse should have been translated, *"for a testimony to them."*

PERSECUTION

The phrase, *"But take heed to yourselves,"* takes these predictions from a national scope and puts them on a personal basis. The Lord is speaking directly to His Disciples, and also to every Believer, and for all time.

The phrase, *"For they shall deliver you up to councils,"* speaks of the Sanhedrin, or Elders, of Israel. This happened in the Early Church; it, no doubt, also will take place in the coming Great Tribulation.

The phrase, *"And in the Synagogues you shall be beaten,"* was experienced personally by the Apostle Paul; the cause was his strong advocacy of the great Covenant of Grace, which replaced the Covenant of Law. Of course, it was not limited to Paul, with countless others being included, as well!

The phrase, *"And you shall be brought before rulers and kings for My sake,"* actually pertains to all Believers for all time.

Wuest says, *"Paul faced Nero, or at least his representative in the court at Rome, and proclaimed the Gospel to the assembled audience.*

"But the language goes beyond this, even to the Jewish Remnant in the Great Tribulation."

The phrase, *"For a testimony against them,"* should have been translated *"for a testimony to them."*

Wuest says that the setting is Jewish, even though it could include all! However, it basically expresses two particular times:

A. The Early Church; and,

B. The coming Great Tribulation.

At the beginning, the Early Church was made up entirely of Jews, who experienced tremendous persecution from their own because of their stand for Christ, as here predicted. During the coming Great Tribulation, it will include all Believers, Jew and Gentile. This Passage tells us that quite a number of Jews will be saved during the coming Great Tribulation. Considering the powerful testimony of the two witnesses and the conversion of the 144,000, it is obvious that a powerful Move of the Holy Spirit will take place in Israel at that time (Rev. 11:3-12; 14:1-5).

(10) "AND THE GOSPEL MUST FIRST BE PUBLISHED AMONG ALL NATIONS."

The synopsis is:

It doesn't say *"every person,"* but it does say *"all nations"*; to a great degree this has been done, and is being done. But yet there is so much more to be done.

THE GOSPEL

Several things are said in this short Verse:

1. First of all, this speaks of the Church, albeit in shadow. It has been the task of the Church, even from the Day of Pentecost, to take the Gospel to the world.

2. The Jews did not do this; therefore, this tells us that these predictions were not fulfilled in A.D. 70, as great segments of the modern Church insist.

3. To take the Gospel to the world was the Plan of God for Israel; however, they failed. It was the Church, therefore, which had to accomplish the task.

4. The *"Gospel"* is Good News. Actually, it is the only truly good news on the face of the Earth. All else which men refer to as good news is merely an absence of bad news. This *"Good News"* tells us that Jesus died on Calvary and paid the price that man may be saved; therefore, due to what Jesus did at Calvary, man can now be reconciled to God. It is truly the *"Greatest Story ever told."*

5. This *"Gospel"* must be the same type as preached by Jesus, Peter, and Paul. It is the whole Gospel for the whole man: Jesus saves, Jesus heals, Jesus baptizes with the Holy Spirit, and Jesus is coming again. Any Gospel which compromises any one of these four points is no Gospel at all! For it to be the *"Gospel,"* it must be that which is given in the Word of God.

We are told in the Word of God exactly as to what the Gospel truly is.

Paul said, *"Christ sent me not to baptize, but to preach the Gospel, not with wisdom of words, lest the Cross of Christ should be made of none effect"* (I Cor. 1:17). Plainly and clearly, we are here told that the Gospel is the *"preaching of the Cross."* So, that means that if the Preacher doesn't *"preach the Cross,"* no matter what he actually does preach, it's not the Gospel.

6. If it is the True Gospel of Jesus Christ, it will bring forth fruit, which will be obvious to all.

7. This Verse does not say that the Gospel will have to go to every single person, but it does say that it will have to go to *"all nations."* Quite possibly that has been fulfilled.

However, it is the responsibility and task of every single Believer to do what he or she can to take the Gospel to every single person. None are to be excluded. Jesus died for all!

8. If one truly studies the Word of God and fully understands what Jesus did at Calvary, he cannot help but know that priority with God is the taking of the Gospel to the world. For every single person who does not know what Jesus has done for him, as far as that person is concerned, Jesus died in vain.

The hard part was done by Heaven; we are given the smaller part of simply telling the story. Regrettably, the proclamation of the Gospel is a non-priority with many, if not most, Christians. And if the Gospel is priority, all too often it is not the True Gospel, which speaks of the preaching of the Cross, but rather something else entirely.

THE JUDGMENT SEAT OF CHRIST

At the Judgment Seat of Christ, I firmly believe that every single Believer is going to have to give account for his or her actions respecting this all-important task. Did we do what we could? In truth, did we do anything at all? Many would ask, *"What exactly can I do?"*

PRAYER

There is not a single Believer who cannot pray. Jesus said, *"Pray you therefore the Lord of the Harvest, that He will send forth laborers into His Harvest"* (Mat. 9:38). Our prayers, consequently, should be twofold:

First of all, we should ask the Lord to give us a burden for a certain part of the world, in order that we may intercede for that particular place. It doesn't really matter where it is, or that we have little knowledge of the place. Those things are not important. The important thing is that the Holy Spirit burden our heart for a specific area or people, which He certainly shall, if we will only ask Him.

I believe every single Move of God that has ever taken place has been preceded by travailing intercession.

Second, in our intercession, we should seek the Lord that He would move on individuals to go to these respective places, wherever they may be. These should be persons who are definitely touched by the Holy Spirit, and who have a burning Message within their heart.

MONEY

Every Believer can not only pray, but every Believer can also give of their finances for this all-important task. The Believer should seek the Lord earnestly respecting where this tremendously important money should be given. If the Lord is earnestly sought, He will earnestly lead and direct.

To be sure, when He directs, the money will be given to someone who truly preaches the Gospel (preaches the Cross), and who preaches with the Anointing of the Holy Spirit, which is obvious by the fruit it produces. Tragically, most money given by Believers for the spread of the Gospel is, by and large, wasted. This will not only not be rewarded by the Lord, but, at the Judgment Seat of Christ, the Believer who supported that which is not of God is going to have to give account.

Due to its vast significance, please allow me to state it again:

The spreading of the Gospel is the responsibility of every single Believer; consequently, considering what Jesus did at Calvary, all of us must be diligent, giving time and attention to this task. In essence, it should be the most important thing in our lives.

If one is to notice, of all the things done in the Early Church, as recorded in the Book of Acts, the major thrust outlined by the Holy Spirit was that of taking the Gospel of Jesus Christ to a lost world. If He set this example for us, and He certainly did, then we should follow that example.

It is a wonderful fact that within 100 years after the Ascension of Christ, Churches had been planted, by and large, in almost every district of the Earth then known to the Romans. It is even more wonderful when one considers that this was done without the aid of the printing press or modern methods of communication and transportation. It was all done by the Power of the Holy Spirit!

(11) "BUT WHEN THEY SHALL LEAD YOU, AND DELIVER YOU UP, TAKE NO THOUGHT BEFOREHAND WHAT YOU SHALL SPEAK, NEITHER DO YE PREMEDITATE: BUT WHATSOEVER SHALL

BE GIVEN YOU IN THAT HOUR, THAT SPEAK YE: FOR IT IS NOT YOU WHO SPEAK, BUT THE HOLY SPIRIT."

The exposition is:

The Lord does not mean that we are not to premeditate a prudent and wise answer, seeking His Face for guidance, but that we are not to be anxious about it. He is speaking of fear, and that it is not to beset us.

DO NOT FEAR!

The phrase, *"But when they shall lead you, and deliver you up,"* refers to persecution. The idea is this:

To those who take the Gospel, and who do so by the Power of the Holy Spirit, Satan is going to do everything within his power to hinder this. Such was evident in the life and Ministry of the Apostle Paul and others in the Early Church. Satan will oppose; the world will oppose; and the apostate Church will oppose.

But, if the true presentation of the Gospel stops, as it has in many circles, then the persecution will stop.

Paul addressed this by saying, *"And I, Brethren, if I yet preach Circumcision, why do I yet suffer persecution? (Any message other than the Cross draws little opposition.) Then is the offense of the Cross ceased"* (Gal. 5:11).

Paul used the Rite of Circumcision to explain his stand and position; however, it could mean anything other than the Cross. In other words, Paul is saying that if he preached works of any nature, as most Preachers in the modern Church do, then the persecution would cease, because the offense of the Cross would cease. And, to be sure, there is an offense, as it regards the Cross. Man doesn't enjoy believing that he is so evil that it took the Cross for him to be saved; he is loath to admit that God loves him so much that He would become Man and die on a Cross that humanity might be saved.

This is one of the reasons, primarily the greatest reason, that the *"Purpose Driven Life"* message is so readily accepted. It is a gospel of works, which means it is not the Gospel of the Cross. As a result, the world readily embraces it and so does the Church.

That which is truly of the Lord, which means that it's going to be the proper Message, is always going to be greatly opposed by the world and greatly opposed by the Church, as well! One can understand the opposition of the world, but the opposition of the Church is something else altogether. Actually, there will be greater opposition from the Church than even from the world. It must not be forgotten that it was the *"Church"* which crucified Christ, and not the world per se, at least as we think of such.

LOOK TO THE LORD!

The phrase, *"Take no thought beforehand what you shall speak, neither do ye premeditate,"* has nothing to do with the preaching of the Gospel. Many have taken this Passage to mean that Preachers should not study, but rather go into the pulpit without any preparation. Such thinking is not only unscriptural, it is ludicrous!

The Passage rather speaks of Believers who are taken before hostile judges, officials, or magistrates. By this statement, the Lord does not mean that we are not to premeditate a prudent and wise answer, but that we are not to be anxious about it. He is speaking of fear, and that it is not to beset us.

The phrase, *"But whatsoever shall be given you in that hour, that speak ye,"* implies that if we look to the Lord, He will serve as our Defense, giving us what to say.

THE HOLY SPIRIT

The phrase, *"For it is not you who speak, but the Holy Spirit,"* concerns His constant Leading, Guidance, Companionship, and Counsel.

Let me give a minor example:

In 1985, I believe it was, Frances and I, along with others, were in the Soviet Union preaching a series of meetings. In every city, we first had to go to the Commissar of Religion for an interview of sorts. This particular city in Siberia would be no exception.

Almost immediately upon being introduced to the man, who spoke fairly good English, he began to accuse me of preaching against Communism.

"You preach over Television," he said, *"and you say some very strong and negative things about our form of Government!"*

I didn't feel that we were in any type of danger, but still, I didn't know where this was going to lead. The man was correct! I had preached very strongly against Communism, and these Messages had been carried by Television over a great part of the world. Obviously, it had come to his ears, even in the far north of Siberia.

One of my Associates was with me, and several Communist officials were also standing in the room. The tension mounted, to say the least! One could look at the man's face and tell that he was very sincere about what he was saying.

Very quietly I breathed a prayer to the Lord, asking Him to tell me what to say.

AN ANSWER FROM THE LORD

As we walked into the room, I had noticed that this man, the Commissar of Religion, walked with a slight limp. He also had a row of medals pinned to the tunic of his coat, which evidently had been given to him for service rendered in World War II. If I remember correctly, one medal was larger than the others and stood out.

As he stood there awaiting an answer to his charge respecting my opposition to Communism, I instead asked him what this particular medal represented.

Very quickly and curtly, he said, *"It was the Battle of Kursk!"*

I am sure he thought I had never heard of the place. It just so happened, however, that I had heard of it; I actually had just read the account of the battle fought there in World War II.

I said to him, *"Sir, do you mean that you fought in this battle, which was the largest tank battle in the history of the world up to that time?"* (It was between the Germans and the Russians.)

In a moment, his face softened, and then he asked, *"You mean you have heard of this battle?"*

"Oh yes," I replied. *"But there are a lot of things I would like to ask you, if you don't mind. You are the only person I have ever met who actually participated in this particular engagement."*

All his thoughts about my preaching against Communism seemed to be forgotten

instantly. For a good period of time, I plied him with questions and he answered eagerly. He told me how he was wounded, and his eyes lit up as he related this experience to me.

When we got ready to leave, he put his arm around my shoulder, and he told me that his office was at my disposal. Furthermore, he would do anything he could to help us in our visit to his city.

As I have stated, even though this was not a dangerous situation, still, I believe the Holy Spirit brought to my mind the question concerning his medal. The discussion which followed eased the tension completely. In fact, only the Holy Spirit could do such a thing!

(12) "NOW THE BROTHER SHALL BETRAY THE BROTHER TO DEATH, AND THE FATHER THE SON; AND CHILDREN SHALL RISE UP AGAINST THEIR PARENTS, AND SHALL CAUSE THEM TO BE PUT TO DEATH."

The composition is:

Beginning with Verse 11, and even though the admonition holds true for other times, it mostly speaks of the coming Great Tribulation; during that time, some Jews will come to Christ, and many of them will lose their lives, betrayed by even their close loved ones.

BETRAYAL

This Passage, as given by Christ, has been fulfilled countless times in the past 2,000 years. It was true in the Early Church, and it was especially true during the Catholic Inquisition.

Some time ago, Frances and I, along with friends, were in Toledo, Spain. This was the center of the Spanish Inquisition, which saw untold thousands put to death in the most tortuous ways by Catholic authorities. If there was any hint that anyone had less than total allegiance to the Pope, they were placed on the torture racks. Those instruments of torture are still there today, visible for all to see.

Countless times, brother was betrayed by brother, father was betrayed by son, etc., which brought about these horrible tortures, which ultimately led to death. Multiple thousands died, tortured to death, because of their allegiance to Jesus Christ, and not to the Pope of Rome.

For the Reader's enlightenment, *"Fox's Book of Martyrs"* should be read. A tremendous price was paid for the freedoms we now enjoy!

Even in modern times, multiple thousands, if not millions, died under Communism for their testimony of Jesus Christ. At times, the betrayals would be brought about by relatives, exactly as Jesus here predicted.

THE GREAT TRIBULATION

In the coming Great Tribulation, this treachery will be exacerbated manyfold. No doubt, at that time hundreds of thousands will have to die for their testimony of their faithfulness to Christ. It will include both Jews and Gentiles, as the Antichrist declares all-out war on those who profess the Name of Jesus.

Even though the fact of this prediction is obvious, still, it should be noted that Bible Christianity alone draws this type of persecution. The religions of the world, such as Islam, Buddhism, Hinduism, etc., draw little negative response. The reason is simple! These religions are fostered and nurtured by Satan; most of the time, therefore, he does not oppose his own efforts.

On the other hand, Bible Christianity, for all the obvious reasons, is opposed greatly by Satan. It alone lays waste his kingdom of darkness! It alone snatches souls from the edge of the burning pit. It alone offers Jesus!

Someone has said that if a person is not ready to die for Jesus, then he is not ready to live for Him!

As a case in point, multiple millions in the United States see little harm in the religion of Islam; some, in fact, hold up Islam above Christianity, even though the nation suffered the loss of nearly 4,000 lives on September 11, 2001 (9/11), all caused by the religion of Islam. These untold millions in this nation literally hate Christianity.

Why?

They hate it because Bible Christianity is true Righteousness, but these religions are the opposite. In fact, both the millions mentioned and Islam have the same father, Satan! That is the reason for the animosity toward Christ and those who follow Him.

(13) "AND YOU SHALL BE HATED OF ALL MEN FOR MY NAME'S SAKE: BUT HE WHO SHALL ENDURE UNTO THE END, THE SAME SHALL BE SAVED."

The diagram is:

While Israel has been hated for so very long, that hatred will intensify in the coming Great Tribulation — and all because of Christ. It is ironic; Israel hates the Name of Jesus, and they are hated for His Name's sake!

THE NAME OF JESUS

The phrase, *"And you shall be hated of all men for My Name's sake,"* proclaims the reason for this hatred and resultant persecution. It is *"the Name of Jesus"*!

Why is He hated so much?

The reason should be obvious. Jesus is God, and yet God Who became Man, and Who died on Calvary, thereby satisfying the claims of Heavenly Justice; as well, He defeated Satan and his powers of darkness, and did so at the Cross (Col. 2:14-15). He is the One Who overcame death, Hell, and the grave.

He, and He Alone, is the One Who opens the door to the Heavenly Father (Jn. 10:7). *"Neither is there Salvation in any other: for there is none other name under Heaven given among men, whereby we must be saved"* (Acts 4:12).

That is the reason Jesus is hated so much!

It is natural that Satan's children would hate Him. It is also natural that an apostate Church would follow suit!

ENDURE TO THE END

The phrase, *"But he who shall endure unto the end, the same shall be saved,"* actually has two meanings:

First of all, it refers to the tremendous number of Jews which will be slaughtered during the coming Great Tribulation. Actually, the Prophet Zechariah said that during this time two-thirds of the population of Israel will die (Zech. 13:8-9). Those who survive this terrible time will come to Christ at the Second Coming and be saved.

The second meaning has to do with the Salvation process. Persecution at that time, the time of the Great Tribulation, will be so severe, especially for Israel, that those who accept Christ will, for the most part, have to give their lives. So, in essence, the Lord is saying that if they can endure unto the end, that is, unto death, which means that despite torture and the threat of death, they will not deny Christ, they *"shall be saved."* It has to do with this Promise, *"Be thou faithful unto death, and I will give you a Crown of Life"* (Rev. 2:10).

(14) "BUT WHEN YOU SHALL SEE THE ABOMINATION OF DESOLATION, SPOKEN OF BY DANIEL THE PROPHET, STANDING WHERE IT OUGHT NOT, (LET HIM WHO READS UNDERSTAND,) THEN LET THEM WHO BE IN JUDAEA FLEE TO THE MOUNTAINS."

The overview is:

This refers to the time that the Antichrist will show his true colors and invade Israel; she will be defeated for the first time since becoming a nation again in 1948.

THE ABOMINATION OF DESOLATION

The phrase, *"But when you shall see the abomination of desolation, spoken of by Daniel the Prophet,"* speaks of the coming Great Tribulation. This is found in Daniel 9:27. It speaks of the seven-year Covenant that the Antichrist will make with Israel, with them thinking he is the Messiah. Either immediately before the seven-year period begins, or at its beginning, he will make it possible for the Jews to rebuild their Temple on its ancient site.

That site is presently occupied by the Muslim *"Dome of the Rock,"* the second most holy place in Islam. The nearness of the Great Tribulation period is indicated by articles in both *"Newsweek"* and *"Time"* magazines, which tell of young men, supposedly of the Tribe of Levi, now training in Jerusalem for Temple duties. I am told that plans have been drawn, or else are being drawn, for the construction of this edifice. To be sure, it must be rebuilt, because Bible Prophecy says that it shall (Dan. 9:27; Mat. 24:15; II Thess. 2:4; Rev., Chpt. 13; 14:9-11; 15:2-4; 16:10; 20:4-6).

At the midpoint of the seven-year period, the Antichrist will break his Covenant with Israel, actually invading the country, with Israel suffering her first defeat since becoming a nation in 1948 (Dan. 9:27; Rev. 12:6). At that time, the Antichrist will set up an image of himself in the Temple in Jerusalem, even in the Holy Place, where it is to be worshipped. This is the *"abomination of desolation"* spoken of by Christ (Dan. 9:27; II Thess. 2:4).

THE TEMPLE

The phrase, *"Standing where it ought not,"* refers to the Holy Place in the Temple, where nothing of this sort should ever be. In the Holy Place in the Temple, the only items were to be the Table of Shewbread, the Golden Lampstand, and the Altar of Worship. Quite possibly, the Antichrist will replace the Altar of Worship with his image, demanding that it be worshipped.

CORRECT UNDERSTANDING

The phrase, *"Let him who reads understand,"* means that there is no reason to misunderstand. Many claim that this was fulfilled when Antiochus Epiphanes set up the statue of Jupiter on the Great Altar of Burnt Sacrifice in Jerusalem; however, this is incorrect, because all of this happened about 200 years before Christ made these predictions.

What Antiochus did was truly an *"abomination"*; however, it was not *"the abomination of desolation"* spoken of by Daniel and referred to by Christ.

FLEE TO THE MOUNTAINS

The phrase, *"Then let them who be in Judaea flee to the mountains,"* refers to the Antichrist breaking his seven-year Covenant with Israel at the midpoint, actually invading this country. At that time, Israel is to *"flee to the mountains,"* which will actually be *"Petra."* In fact, hundreds of thousands of Jews will make this ancient hidden city of Petra their home for the last half of the Great Tribulation. The place, incidentally, is now empty.

While the Antichrist could definitely defeat Israel handily at that time, Daniel also said that instead of following up his victory by slaughtering these hundreds of thousands, he instead will hear *"tidings out of the east and out of the north* (which) *shall trouble him: therefore he shall go forth with great fury to destroy, and utterly to make away many"* (Dan. 11:44). In other words, at that time the Antichrist will have bigger fish to fry; he will, therefore, save Israel for a later time. That later time will be, in fact, the Battle of Armageddon. So, Israel will live to fight another day, all predicted by the Prophets (Ps. 60:6-12; Isa. 16:1-5; 26:20-21; 63:1-6; Ezek. 20:43-44; Dan. 11:40-45).

(15) "AND LET HIM WHO IS ON THE HOUSETOP NOT GO DOWN INTO THE HOUSE, NEITHER ENTER THEREIN, TO TAKE ANY THING OUT OF HIS HOUSE:

(16) "AND LET HIM WHO IS IN THE FIELD NOT TURN BACK AGAIN FOR TO TAKE UP HIS GARMENT.

(17) "BUT WOE TO THEM WHO ARE WITH CHILD, AND TO THEM WHO GIVE SUCK IN THOSE DAYS!

(18) "AND PRAY YE THAT YOUR FLIGHT BE NOT IN THE WINTER."

The exposition is:

Christ is portraying the time when the Antichrist will attack Israel, which will be at the midpoint of the Great Tribulation. In other words, He is telling Israel, some 2,000 years in advance, that they must, at this time, flee.

GREAT TRIBULATION

The idea of these Passages is several-fold:

1. The betrayal of Israel by the Antichrist will be sudden. Without warning, he will break his seven-year treaty with Israel by attacking her with his army. Israel will suffer her first defeat since her formation again as a nation in 1948. Inasmuch as the attack is sudden and without warning, Israel will be caught completely by surprise. The Antichrist will then show himself to be, not the reputed friend and protector of Israel he has claimed to be, but, in reality, its bitter enemy.

In fact, were it not for a series of events, Israel would be totally destroyed at this time; however, these events, as described in Daniel 11:44 and Revelation 12:15-16, will turn the attention of the Antichrist elsewhere, at least for the time being.

2. This attack will be so sudden that Israel will not have time to prepare her retreat. The haste required will be so great that Jesus warns them that if they are on the housetops, they should not take the time to go in the house and retrieve things needed for the retreat. (Houses then, and even now, in Israel had a flat roof, which was used for various activities. So, the admonishment given, i.e., concerning not going into the house, lets us know how much haste will be required at that time.)

For those who are working in the fields, they are not to even go a few yards to retrieve a garment; they are immediately to flee.

As should be obvious, women who are pregnant, and those with small children, would have a difficult time fleeing as speedily as is suggested.

The *"winter"* has to do with the possibility of adverse weather conditions, which could impede progress.

The entirety of the statements, as used by Christ, are merely symbolisms, reflecting the suddenness of the invasion and the necessary haste required to escape.

3. This will begin the last three and a half years of the Great Tribulation, which will bring Israel close to annihilation. Jeremiah calls it *"the Time of Jacob's Trouble"* (Jer. 30:7). It will be worse than any tribulation they have ever experienced; it is necessary to bring them to the place that they will plead for the Messiah to come to save them, which He will. They will then find that the One Who has come is none other than the Lord Jesus Christ, the very One Whom they crucified (Zech. 13:6).

(19) "FOR IN THOSE DAYS SHALL BE AFFLICTION, SUCH AS WAS NOT FROM THE BEGINNING OF THE CREATION WHICH GOD CREATED UNTO THIS TIME, NEITHER SHALL BE."

The synopsis is:

The last half of the Great Tribulation will be worse than the Earth has ever seen, so bad, in fact, that such will never be seen again.

AFFLICTION

The phrase, *"For in those days,"* refers, as stated, to the last three and a half years of the coming Great Tribulation. It is regrettable that the far greater majority of the modern Church has such little knowledge of futuristic events that it little believes in this of which Jesus spoke. This lack of knowledge is inexcusable for the simple reason that the

Bible clearly outlines that which is coming. Consequently, this lack of knowledge pertains to rabid unbelief.

If people believed the Bible, they would read it and study it more. They neglect and ignore it because they little believe it or they simply have no interest in it. And then again, the foolish teaching of *"Kingdom Now"* fills the hearts of many. This teaching claims, as we have previously stated, that the world, due to the influence of Christianity, is going to get better and better, ultimately ushering in the Millennium.

The truth is the very opposite (II Tim. 3:1-5). The Bible teaches that on all fronts the world situation is not going to be better, but progressively worse, and regrettably so!

The phrase, *"Shall be affliction,"* proclaims a dogmatic certitude of such action. In other words, Jesus is not saying that it may come, but, for a certainty, it shall come!

Wuest says that the correct translation should be, *"Those days will be a tribulation."* He goes on to say, *"The Judgments of God which will fall upon unbelieving Israel and the Gentile nations will have no precedent in all past history, no counterpart in all succeeding history."*

Even though it will affect the entirety of the world, still, its greatest concentration will be in the Middle East, and, more specifically, in Israel. The cause of this tribulation, as brought by God, will be twofold:

THE WRATH OF GOD

It is called *"The Great Day of His Wrath"* (Rev. 6:17). It is a time of God's Judgment poured out on a world which has forgotten Him days without number. Millions have asked the question, *"When will the Lord do something about the sin and the wickedness in this world?"* The Great Tribulation will be His answer to that question. Chapters 6 through 19 of the Book of Revelation give us the account.

ISRAEL

The cause of the Great Tribulation is to bring Israel to a state of Repentance. As stated, she will come close to annihilation, and actually would be annihilated, were it not for the Second Coming of the Lord.

NOTES

Perhaps it would be helpful to comment on Israel's present position.

Despite the present problems in Israel, this tiny nation is still the most prosperous country in the Middle East. Actually, it is predicted that by the year 2020, the present land area of Israel will be completely filled with businesses and housing, with the possible exception of the very heart of the desert.

But yet, the nagging problem with the Palestinians remains, which, unjustly, causes the animosity of much of the world toward Israel. The bombings by the Palestinians in the last few years have caused this tiny nation to suffer much. In spite of what the world thinks, the Palestinians actually have not really wanted a nation per se. Perhaps their people do, but the leaders don't. They want the status quo to remain in order to garner the support of most of the world. In fact, about the only friend that Israel truly has is the United States.

The Palestinians, as stated, are really not interested in any particular part of Israel as a nation for their own; they rather desire the entirety of the land of Israel and the death of every Jew. The world community should realize, that is, if they care to, that the Arabs have invaded Israel some five times since her inception as a nation in 1948. Israel won every one of these wars, but allowed the Palestinians to remain in her land; and it is her land, all of it!

Let it be understood: If the Arabs had won any one of these wars, unless the United States had intervened, there would have been no more Israel. They would have massacred every Jew down to the last woman and child. But yet Israel, despite winning all of these wars provoked against them, has allowed the Palestinians to remain; the world community, however, does not seem to understand that. Or perhaps the world community doesn't really care.

We must go back to the Words of Christ when He stated, *"And you shall be hated of all men for My Name's sake."*

THE DEATH OF ARAFAT

I think it should be obvious that Yasser Arafat really did not want peace. Perhaps the real reason was that if he had signed any type of peace accords, he would have been assassinated by the radicals among the Palestinians. With his death, the question is open to debate as to exactly what the future holds. But yet it doesn't require too much debate to understand that the same radicals among the Palestinians, of which there are many, have not changed their ways, and will not change their ways.

It really doesn't matter too very much as to who heads up the Palestinian state, so-called. The bombings will continue.

So, what is the answer?

Of course, the only answer is the Coming of the Lord; however, before that time, some momentous things will have to happen.

THE ANTICHRIST

In the very near future, a strong man is going to make his appearance in the Middle East. He will have an economic and diplomatic intelligence as no one has ever had. He will come in by flattery, seemingly increasing the stability and prosperity of the region.

Daniel wrote: *"And through his policy also he shall cause craft* (deceit) *to prosper in his hand; and he shall magnify himself in his heart, and by peace shall destroy many"* (Dan. 8:25).

In this great amalgamation of economic and diplomatic prosperity, this man, who is actually the Antichrist, will endear himself to the world, and, more specifically, to Israel. They will actually think he is the Messiah. During this time, he may well be instrumental in helping Israel build her Temple. If, in fact, he is involved in this effort, which it seems he shall be, he will find a way to satisfy both Israel and the Muslims regarding the Temple site, where the Muslim Dome of the Rock presently sits.

Some time during these happenings, he will sign a seven-year agreement with Israel and other nations, guaranteeing prosperity and growth (Dan. 9:27). In Bible terminology, it is called *"Daniel's 70th Week"* (Dan. 9:24-27).

In the midst of this seven-year Covenant, the Antichrist, as we have stated, will show his true colors, attacking Israel, and breaking the Covenant. Then will begin this time of *"affliction,"* which will be the worst the

NOTES

world has ever known.

THE GREATEST TRIBULATION

The phrase, *"Such as was not from the beginning of the creation which God created unto this time, neither shall be,"* is a startling proclamation! To be sure, the world has seen some bad times in its recorded history of approximately 6,000 years. One thinks of World War II, with some 50 million dead, including 6 million Jews dying in the horror known as the *"holocaust,"* as being beyond compare, as it was! However, the coming time of the Great Tribulation, because of the Wrath of God, will be even worse. War and its Hell are bad enough; however, compared to what the anger of God can bring about, there is no comparison. This is what the world is facing. To be certain, it will happen!

THE RAPTURE OF THE CHURCH

Before this time, the Church will have been raptured away, because this period refers basically to Israel, and not the Church (I Thess. 4:16-18; II Thess. 2:7-8). In fact, the Church (the True Church) will be raptured away before the advent of the Antichrist.

Concerning this, Paul said, *"For the mystery of iniquity does already work* (concerns false teaching by false teachers): *only he* (the Church) *who now lets* (who now hinders evil) *will let* (will continue to hinder), *until he* (the Church) *be taken out of the way.* (The pronoun 'he' confuses some people. In Verses 4 and 6, the pronoun 'he' refers to the Antichrist, while in Verse 7, the pronoun 'he' refers to the Church.)

"And then (after the Rapture of the Church) *shall that Wicked* (the Antichrist) *be revealed* (proving conclusively that the Rapture takes place before the Great Tribulation [Mat. 24:21]) . . ."* (II Thess. 2:7-8).

In truth, the Rapture will be the Salvation of the Church, as the Second Coming will be the Salvation of the world. The Church presently is apostatizing at a frightful pace; however, it is an apostasy that is very subtle. Much of the modern Church does not even bother to deny the Bible or Jesus Christ. It just ignores them, at least as to their rightful place. The Bible is set aside in favor of modern psychology. Jesus Christ is used as a means of *"getting rich,"* etc., i.e., *"the Greed Message."* The Holy Spirit is all but ignored, if not outright denied, or else made a part of nefarious activities.

So, if the Bible Doctrine of the Rapture is not true, as many claim, it is doubtful that even a True Remnant would survive. Even though presently faith is much talked about, still, True Faith has never been in shorter supply.

Jesus said, *"Nevertheless, when the Son of Man comes, shall He find Faith on the Earth?"* (Lk. 18:8).

Because of the coming activities of the Antichrist, especially the Battle of Armageddon, were it not for the Second Coming, not only would Israel be completely lost, but the world, as well!

So, these twin happenings, the *"Rapture"* and the *"Second Coming,"* are of vast significance, as should be obvious.

(20) "AND EXCEPT THAT THE LORD HAD SHORTENED THOSE DAYS, NO FLESH SHOULD BE SAVED: BUT FOR THE ELECT'S SAKE, WHOM HE HAS CHOSEN, HE HAS SHORTENED THE DAYS."

The structure is:

The Lord chose Israel, actually raising them up from the loins of Abraham and the womb of Sarah.

THE WORST TIME THE WORLD HAS EVER KNOWN

The phrase, *"And except that the Lord had shortened those days, no flesh should be saved,"* is startling indeed! Even though the world, and even much of the Church, pay little attention to this statement, its horror, without fail, is going to break upon this world.

This statement could well apply to the entirety of the world, and not just to Israel, as many believe! The great plagues and judgments referred to in Revelation, Chapters 6 through 19, while centered in the Middle East, still, because of the moon and planetary bodies being affected, all the world will suffer, as well (Rev. 6:12-17). The possibility actually exists that half or more of the world's population at that time could die. What is being spoken of is of such consequence that it beggars description.

In miniscule, the world witnessed what the elements can do in a few minutes time, regarding the earthquake and resultant tidal wave which killed upwards of 200,000 people in the far east, which took place in the last days of 2004. Multiply that any number of times, and Chapters 6 through 19 of the Book of Revelation become more readily understood.

THE TIME OF JACOB'S TROUBLE

The phrase, *"But for the elect's sake, whom He has chosen,"* refers to Israel, not the Church. The Church will by now have been raptured away (II Thess. 2:6-8).

What does the word *"chosen"* mean?

Wuest says, *"The verb 'eklego' means 'to choose out from a number' and refers to the act of God, Who in sovereign grace, chooses certain from among mankind for Himself, and for a specific purpose."*

God raised up Israel, choosing them for three particular reasons:

1. To be the womb of the Messiah (Gen. 12:3).

2. To give the world the Word of God: All of the Word of God was written by Jews. (Some think that Luke, who wrote the Gospel that bears his name and the Books of Acts, was a Gentile. This may be true; however, there is also some evidence that he was a Jew.)

3. To evangelize the world: In this, Israel failed miserably, but will yet succeed in the coming Kingdom Age (Isa. 66:18-19).

In the context of which Israel was chosen, they were to be a holy people and have a close relationship with God. Actually, they were the only people on the face of the Earth who had such a relationship. As such, they were to convey this Message to the Gentiles. Perhaps they came closer to doing this under the administration of David and the first years of Solomon than at any other time; however, by and large, they failed, and failed greatly, in this respect.

Being the people of God, they were to be the premier nation in the world, showing the world the way. Whenever Judah was defeated by Nebuchadnezzar and Jerusalem was destroyed, the scepter of power passed from the faltering hands of the *"chosen"* to the Gentiles, where it has remained ever since. When Jesus came, their great opportunity was lost in them not recognizing Him as the Messiah and consequently rejecting Him. In rejecting Him, they, in effect, rejected themselves, which brought about their destruction.

The entirety of their purpose, in one way or the other, was Christ. Without Him, they were of no consequence; they were, therefore, destroyed.

However, the Promises to the Prophets included a Restoration, which will be brought about at the Second Coming (Ezek., Chpt. 37; Hos., Chpt. 14; Joel Chpt. 3; Amos 9:14-15; Obad. 19-21; Mic., Chpt. 4; Zeph. 3:18-20; Zech., Chpts. 12-14; Rev., Chpt. 19).

The phrase, *"He has shortened the days,"* means that the Lord will limit the most destructive times of the Great Tribulation, or else the entirety of Israel would be destroyed. Even then, as stated, Zechariah prophesied that two-thirds of the population of Israel will die during that time (Zech. 13:8).

(21) "AND THEN IF ANY MAN SHALL SAY TO YOU, LO, HERE IS CHRIST; OR, LO, HE IS THERE, BELIEVE HIM NOT."

The exegesis is:

The Lord is actually speaking here of the Antichrist, who will make great claims.

THE TIME ELEMENT

The two words, *"And then,"* lets us know the time element of which Jesus is speaking. From Verses 24 through 27, we know that these warnings do not pertain to the time preceding the destruction of Jerusalem by Titus, which took place about 37 or so years after the Ascension of Christ. Actually, these warnings apply to the coming Great Tribulation. As a result, they have not yet been fulfilled.

THE ANTICHRIST

The phrase, *"If any man shall say to you, Lo, here is Christ; or, lo, He is there,"* records the fact that the Antichrist will be heralded as the Messiah. Jesus plainly warns concerning the acclamations of this deceiver. He said, *"Believe him not!"* Consequently, there will be no excuse for Israel accepting this fraud, especially considering the warnings given here by Christ; however, Israel does not believe the New Testament, and, truthfully, precious little of the Old. These warnings, consequently, fall on deaf ears, at least for most!

As we have stated, the word *"Christ"* is the English spelling of the Greek *"Christos,"* which means *"The Anointed One."* It refers to the promised and coming King of Israel, Who comes in the dynasty of David to rule over Israel in the Messianic Kingdom. Thus, our Lord was speaking of false messiahs. This false christ does not deny the Being of a Christ. He builds on the world's expectation of such a Person. He appropriates to himself the title and identity, claiming that he is the foretold One (Wuest).

(22) "FOR FALSE CHRISTS AND FALSE PROPHETS SHALL RISE, AND SHALL SHOW SIGNS AND WONDERS, TO SEDUCE, IF IT WERE POSSIBLE, EVEN THE ELECT."

The composition is:

The word *"elect"* refers normally to the Jews, at least as it's used in the Book of Revelation. But as it is used here, it refers to all who have accepted Christ, whoever they might be.

FALSE CHRISTS AND FALSE PROPHETS

The phrase, *"For false Christs and false Prophets shall rise,"* proclaims the certitude of those coming at that particular time, claiming to be the *"real thing."* Above all, the *"Antichrist"* and the *"False Prophet"* will be included in this group. They, in fact, will be accepted by Israel and much of the world, despite these warnings given here by Christ.

The phrase, *"And shall show signs and wonders,"* proclaims the working of miracles by these false ones, especially the Antichrist and False Prophet.

(Before the Antichrist, many others may arise claiming to be the Messiah. Upon the advent of the Antichrist, however, all other claimants thereafter quickly will be put down, with the field left exclusively to the Antichrist and the False Prophet. In other words, the Antichrist will not tolerate anyone, at least under his domain, claiming to be what he alone claims to be.)

The *"signs and wonders"* spoken of here are fulfilled in the Passage, *"And deceives them who dwell on the Earth by the means of those miracles which he had power to do in the sight of the beast"* (Rev. 13:14). These miracles will be performed by the False Prophet, whom John described as *"another beast."*

It also says, *"And he does great wonders, so that he makes fire come down from Heaven on the Earth in the sight of men"* (Rev. 13:11-13).

The word *"signs,"* in the Greek Text, is *"semeon,"* which means *"a miracle whose purpose is that of attesting the claims of the one performing the miracle to be true."* The word *"wonders,"* in the Greek Text, is *"teras,"* which means *"a miracle whose purpose it is to awaken amazement in the beholder,"* typified by calling fire down from Heaven, and such like!

SEDUCTION

Israel is warned, and all others, as well, against accepting the claims of one who performs miracles solely upon the basis of the fact that he performs miracles. The person and his message must also be taken into consideration.

The phrase, *"To seduce, if it were possible, even the elect,"* proclaims the powerful force of Satanic seduction. The word *"seduce"* means *"to stray from Truth."* Regrettably, this problem is going to increase as we near the end, even as Jesus is saying.

The words, *"If it were possible,"* leave the possibility undetermined.

THE CROSS AND MIRACLES

As we've just stated, Preachers should not be accepted as genuine solely on the base of the performance of miracles, or that which claims to be miracles. The person and the message proclaimed must be looked at even more closely than the miracles, so-called.

I use the word *"so-called,"* simply because the word *"miracles"* is bandied about presently in wholesale lots, with many things claiming to be miracles, when, in fact, no miracle has been performed. If the Message is not the Cross, I seriously doubt the miracle is genuine; or, if it is genuine, it is coming from the wrong source. Satan can perform miracles, as well, even as we are now studying.

NOTES

The Message of the Cross is the True Gospel. Anything based on any other type of message cannot be right, irrespective of the *"signs"* and *"wonders."*

THE ELECT

Even though the Jews, as a whole, are referred to by the Lord as the *"elect,"* the word is here used in a slightly different manner. It refers not just to Jews in general, but instead to those Jews who have accepted Christ as their Saviour in the coming Great Tribulation. The idea is that the force of this seduction, as a result of the *"signs"* and *"wonders,"* will be so powerful that even those who truly know the Lord and His Word can be swayed in the wrong direction.

Even though this does not exactly pertain to the Church, still, the principle is the same. The closer to the end, the more powerful the seduction. Satan is presently pulling out all stops in order to seduce the Church.

Speaking of the very time in which we now live, Paul said, *"And they shall turn away their ears from the Truth, and shall be turned unto fables"* (II Tim. 4:4).

FABLES

The word *"fables"* has the idea of *"a mystery,"* or, in other words, a superior knowledge. Most of the modern fads, such as the *"Faith Ministry,"* the *"G-12,"* and the *"Purpose Driven Life,"* all come, in fact, under the heading of *"fables."* Every single Message, irrespective as to what it might be, that's not totally and completely that of which Paul preached, and I speak of the Message of the Cross, must be labeled as a *"fable."*

As stated, many of these false directions claim a superior knowledge, which actually is no more than ancient gnosticism under a new label. The modern Church is inundated with this type of teaching, which pulls people from the foundation of the Faith, making them think they have some *"new revelation,"* etc.

(23) "BUT TAKE YE HEED: BEHOLD, I HAVE FORETOLD YOU ALL THINGS."

The synopsis is:

The admonishment to take heed is repeated four times in this Chapter (Vss. 5, 9, 23, 33).

TAKE HEED

The phrase, *"But take ye heed,"* proclaims as emphatic the pronoun *"ye"* (you), specifically meaning that each individual must take heed. This places a far greater emphasis on the warning. Many take these admonitions as directions to the entirety of Israel and the Church, which they certainly are; however, the Greek Text emphasizes the fact that each individual must be very cautious, realizing that this attack by Satan is not only directed at the Church as a whole, but also toward each individual.

THE WARNING

The phrase, *"Behold, I have foretold you all things,"* proclaims Jesus clearly giving this information, which leaves no one with an excuse.

How can the modern Believer keep himself from being seduced by Satan, especially considering the tremendous power of this evil of darkness?

As we have stated, spiritual seduction is rampant at present, and speedily growing worse. In truth, much, if not most, of the modern Church has been seduced by Satan. It supports false doctrine; for the most part, it has its priorities wrong; it also has gotten its eyes off Jesus.

This is obvious by the type of *"fruit"* presently being born.

What is the *"fruit"* of the modern Church?

With some exceptions, it is entertainment, fads, and philosophies.

Hundreds of millions of dollars are presently pouring into certain Television programming which claims to be *"Christian,"* but, in reality, is not. It is, without a doubt, doing greater harm to the Body of Christ than words could ever begin to express. Much of the money even goes to what could be better labeled *"entertainment."* Regrettably, this is, by and large, financed by Pentecostals and Charismatics, who should know better. They are, however, *"seduced."* I speak primarily of T.B.N.

Great segments of the modern Church are also running after *"fads,"* which, because they are not truly of the Lord, loom big for a while and then fade. They have little or no Scriptural foundation. To be sure, Satan does not care how *"spiritual"* we become, providing it's not Scriptural. Almost all the Church has accepted the humanistic philosophy of psychology, which is as opposed to Scripture as is humanly possible.

Regrettably, that is the *"fruit"* of much of the modern Church. As stated, there are some exceptions, but those exceptions are few and far between! The *"fruit"* ought to be souls saved, Believers baptized with the Holy Spirit, the sick truly healed, and bondages broken. Such will result in *"love, joy, peace, longsuffering, gentleness, goodness, Faith, meekness, and temperance"* (Mk. 16:15; Gal. 5:22-23).

Sadly, there isn't much of this type of *"fruit"* presently being produced.

(24) "BUT IN THOSE DAYS, AFTER THAT TRIBULATION, THE SUN SHALL BE DARKENED, AND THE MOON SHALL NOT GIVE HER LIGHT."

The structure is:

This pertains to the fifth time the planets will be affected in part or in whole, which will take place during the Great Tribulation.

THE DAYS OF TRIBULATION

The phrase, *"But in those days,"* refers to the time *"immediately after that Tribulation,"* when Christ comes, i.e., *"the Second Coming"* (Zech., Chpt. 14; Mat. 24:29-31; Rev. 19:11-21).

The phrase, *"After that Tribulation,"* refers to the seven-year Tribulation, which is to take place in the very near future. It will come about after the Rapture of the Church, and will affect the entirety of the world, but will have its greatest impact in the Middle East. At the very end of the Great Tribulation, certain phenomenon will take place in the Heavens, as outlined here by Christ. It pertains, as stated, to the Second Coming.

The phrase, *"The sun shall be darkened, and the moon shall not give her light,"* pertains to the fifth time the planets will be affected in part or in whole, which will take place throughout the seven-year Tribulation period.

(25) "AND THE STARS OF HEAVEN SHALL FALL, AND THE POWERS THAT ARE IN HEAVEN SHALL BE SHAKEN."

The exegesis is:

The latter phrase of the Verse refers to the Satanic hosts that now rule the air (Eph. 2:1-3; 6:12).

THE STARS OF HEAVEN

The phrase, *"And the stars of Heaven shall fall,"* pertains to a meteorite display, which will take place at the Second Coming, which will occasion, no doubt, the greatest display of such that the world has ever known. The entirety of the creation was affected adversely at the Fall.

Concerning this, Paul said, *"For we know that the whole Creation groans and travails in pain together until now,"* which tells us that the very creation itself is waiting for the Redemption of all things, which will have its beginning at the Second Coming (Rom. 8:22).

When Jesus comes back, and does so in a display of glory such as the world has never seen before, the very Heavens will dance in glee, knowing that the effects of the Fall are now about to be eradicated. In other words, everything that Jesus did at the Cross is now about to be realized, at least all that can be realized up to this present time. The total result of the Cross will not be realized until the Lord changes His Headquarters from Planet Heaven to Planet Earth, which is proclaimed by Revelation, Chapters 21 and 22.

THE POWERS OF HEAVEN

The phrase, *"And the powers that are in Heaven shall be shaken,"* refers to Satan's domain in the Heavenlies, which will now be shattered (Eph. 2:1-3; 6:12). To be sure, the Second Coming will proclaim the total defeat in every capacity of Satan and his minions of darkness. The Evil One and all of his fallen angels and demon spirits will be thrown into the bottomless pit and will remain there throughout the entirety of the Kingdom Age (Rev. 20:1-3).

They will be loosed for a short period of time at the end of the Kingdom Age, when they again will be soundly defeated, and then thrown into the Lake of Fire, where they will remain forever and forever (Rev. 20:7-10).

As an aside, some people think of Satan as being in Hell; however, there is no Biblical record that he has ever been there. Satan will not be there until he is forced there, as given to us in Revelation 20:10.

(26) "AND THEN SHALL THEY SEE THE SON OF MAN COMING IN THE CLOUDS WITH GREAT POWER AND GLORY."

The composition is:

When Christ truly comes back, no one will have to ask the question, *"Is this really Him?"* It will be overly obvious that it is.

THE SON OF MAN

The two words, *"And then,"* refer to the time of the stars, or meteorites, falling from Heaven, as well as the Satanic powers of Heaven being shaken.

The phrase, *"Shall they see the Son of Man coming,"* refers to the Second Coming. At the beginning of this Chapter, as well as the Twenty-fourth Chapter of Matthew, Jesus warned against believing reports of the Messiah being in *"the desert"* or *"secret chambers,"* etc. (Mat. 24:26). As we have stated, this refers to the beginning of the Great Tribulation; however, His Coming will be at the end of the Great Tribulation, actually during the Battle of Armageddon.

In essence, the Lord is saying that the time of His Coming will be so glorious, even cataclysmic, that there will absolutely be no doubt as to Who He actually is. The very heavens will announce His Coming by a display of meteorite activity and other Heavenly phenomenon, which, when coupled with the Glory of Christ, will present a display of power such as the world never before has known.

So, no one will have to wonder if this is the Messiah! It will be very obvious to the entirety of the world that it is the Messiah, and He is the Lord Jesus Christ.

THE CLOUDS

The phrase, *"In the clouds,"* does not speak of clouds as we think of such, but rather a great multitude of people who will be with Him, namely all the Saints who have ever lived (Rev. 19:14). Not only will all the Saints of God accompany the Lord at the Second Coming, but also an innumerable company of Angels.

It will be a *"cloud of Saints"* and a *"cloud of Angels."*

POWER AND GLORY

The phrase, *"With great Power and Glory,"* proclaims that of which we have been speaking. It will be a display such as the world has never seen. Quite possibly, at least if the atmospheric conditions do not knock out satellite transmission, Television will record this event, portraying it all over the world.

This will happen at the Battle of Armageddon. Undoubtedly, every major Television Network in the world will be there to record this event. With the Antichrist pressing Jerusalem, actually with half of it falling, and with total annihilation of Israel seeming certain, Television transmission will be going into most of the homes of the world, portraying what is happening on the battlefield. It will be news as it happens!

The world, however, eagerly observing this battle of all battles, will little expect what is about to transpire. It is the Second Coming!

The very Creation, as stated, which has groaned for Deliverance (Rom. 8:22), now realizes that Deliverance is at hand. Jesus Christ, the Creator of the ages, is coming back, and the powers of darkness, which have caused so much heartache, death, and trouble, are about to be totally defeated. It is the times of which the Prophets spoke; it is the fulfillment of all the Prophecies.

As meteorites crisscross the heavens in a display of Glory and, one might quickly add, of ecstatic joy, Jesus, with all the Glorified Saints and Angels, will present a display of Glory which will be a scene totally eclipsing anything that man could ever begin to imagine. Hollywood has faked these scenes for years; however, this one is for real!

At that time, the Antichrist will be totally defeated, defeated to such an extent that Satan's power will be completely broken.

TELEVISION

One might very well imagine the Television Networks of the world reporting the scenes from the Battle of Armageddon, as they announce to the world that Jerusalem has just about fallen. The Antichrist, who is called *"Gog"* (Ezek. 38:1-2, 14), is about to claim his prize. As stated, every single Television Network in the world, no doubt, will be represented at this battle of all battles.

But when it seems that all hope is gone for Israel, something will be noticed in the heavens that is speedily growing larger and larger. The Networks, no doubt, will point their Television cameras toward the heavens, thinking this is another new weapon that the Antichrist is bringing to bear upon Jerusalem. But, to their surprise, as this great *"cloud"* comes closer and closer, instead of it being a weapon, they will see horses, millions of them, all being ridden by men and women and Angels.

Furthermore, the Leading One, so Glorious as to defy description, will be riding a *"white horse,"* with the *"armies of Heaven following Him* (also) *upon white horses"* (Rev. 19:11, 14).

The Television announcers will attempt to explain what they are seeing, but they really can't believe what they are seeing. But yet, their cameras are portraying it, so it cannot be denied. One can well imagine the newscasters attempting to explain this phenomenon in the Heavens, but who could explain it?

More than likely, somebody will begin to understand that this actually is *"The Second Coming."*

Concerning the Lord's defeat of the Antichrist, which all of these hundreds of Television cameras will record, Ezekiel says, *"And I will plead against him with pestilence and with blood; and I will rain upon him, and upon his bands, and upon the many people who are with him, an overflowing rain, and great hailstones, fire, and brimstone.*

"Thus will I magnify Myself, and sanctify Myself; and I will be known in the eyes of many nations, and they shall know that I am the LORD" (Ezek. 38:22-23).

(27) "AND THEN SHALL HE SEND HIS ANGELS, AND SHALL GATHER TOGETHER HIS ELECT FROM THE FOUR WINDS, FROM THE UTTERMOST PART OF THE EARTH TO THE UTTERMOST PART OF HEAVEN."

The composition is:

All the Jews then alive on Earth will be brought to the land of Israel; they will gladly come, even helped by Angels, simply because they finally have accepted their Messiah, the

Lord Jesus Christ, Whom they rejected so long ago.

THE GATHERING OF ISRAEL

This Verse of Scripture proclaims the fulfillment of all the Prophecies concerning the Restoration of Israel. Israel's Salvation is omitted here, with Jesus portraying the Second Coming and then the Regathering of Israel, which will be after their acceptance of Christ.

The Prophet Zechariah proclaims this moment of Israel's Salvation graphically. He says, *"In that day there shall be a fountain opened to the House of David, unto the inhabitants of Jerusalem for sin and for uncleanness"* (Zech. 13:1).

About that time, Zechariah also prophesied, *"And one shall say unto Him, What are these wounds in Your Hands? Then He shall answer, Those with which I was wounded in the house of My friends"* (Zech. 13:6). They will then know that Jesus, the One Whom they crucified, was indeed the Messiah, the Son of God, the Saviour of the world.

When this information is known, Zechariah also said, *"And they shall look upon Me Whom they have pierced, and they shall mourn for Him, as one mourns for his only son"* (Zech. 12:10).

THE GATHERING

The phrase, *"And then shall He send His Angels, and shall gather together His elect from the four winds,"* refers to the regathering of Jews from all over the world at the beginning of the Kingdom Age, after they have accepted Christ (Isa. 11:11-12; 60:8-9; 65:9, 22; 66:19-21; Jer. 31:36-40; 33:17-26; Ezek. 36:8-24; 37:21-28; 39:25-29; Amos 9:11-15; Acts 15:13-18).

The phrase, *"From the uttermost part of the Earth to the uttermost part of Heaven,"* has a double meaning:

THE JEWS AND ISRAEL

Knowing that Jesus is now reigning in Jerusalem, with Israel once again the premier nation in the world, especially that Israel now has a different spirit since her acceptance of Christ, most every Jew in the world will now want to relocate to Israel. They will be aided and abetted in this endeavor by Angels. More than likely, the Angels will be visible.

Irrespective as to who these Jews are, whether rich or poor, the evidence from Scripture is that even the various governments of particular nations will help in their endeavor, in order that the expense to the Jews be minimal, if any.

It is difficult to imagine the feelings which will fill the hearts of Jews all over the world when they come to the realization that Jesus is the Messiah and actually reigns in Jerusalem. No doubt, everything Jesus does and says will be heralded all over the world by Television and every other type of Media. Consequently, the new order of things will be known by the entirety of the world. It will unparalleled in all history. Now the great Promises of God for blessing will fill the entirety of the Earth, even as this Planet begins its Kingdom Age, all because of Christ and what He did at the Cross.

ISRAEL AND THE PLAN OF GOD

As we have repeatedly stated, many in the modern Church have little understanding as to the tremendous part played by Israel in the great Plan of God. While it is true that she, due to her rejection of Christ, has suffered terribly, still, the Prophecies given by the Prophets of old continue to hold true!

When Nebuchadnezzar, the Babylonian Monarch, defeated Judah approximately 600 years before Christ, the scepter of world power passed at that time from the faltering hands of the Kings of Judah, the sons of David, and was given to the Gentiles. There it has remained ever since.

At this particular time, however, that scepter will be returned to the House of David. Israel will once again be the greatest nation in the world. Its greatness will be totally different than the greatness of the Gentile nations of the past. The Glory of God will be its strength. The Power of God will be its Salvation. As such, it will rule the world in Righteousness.

It will be a rulership of fairness and equity, resulting in such prosperity as the world has never known. Poverty will be eliminated; man's inhumanity to man will be over; racism will end; in Christ, all will be equal. Sickness, disease, death, and sorrow will be things of the past. It will be that for which the righteous human heart has longed! Then, spiritually speaking, the Garden of Eden will be brought back, an effort, incidentally, that man constantly has made, but without success. At this time, however, the *"Tree of Life"* will be in its midst, i.e., the Lord Jesus Christ.

All is in Christ, as all must be in Christ!

GLORIFIED SAINTS

Not only will every Jew be gathered from the entirety of the Earth, but every son of Jacob who went to be with the Lord in all the intervening centuries will return to this Earth, even as all the Saints of the Church, all with Glorified Bodies. These will help administer the affairs, not only of Israel, but the entirety of the world.

There will, therefore, be two types of Jews and Gentiles in the world at that time. There will be Jews with Glorified Bodies, as well as Gentiles with Glorified Bodies, which incorporates every single Believer who has ever lived and had part in the First Resurrection. This will be all those who accepted Christ as their personal Saviour, even from Adam's day unto the Second Coming of the Lord (Rev. 20:1-6).

There will also be all the Jews, plus all the Gentiles, who will be alive after the Second Coming, who will accept Jesus as their personal Saviour. These will not have Glorified Bodies. They will have normal human bodies, but will be kept alive indefinitely by virtue of eating the *"fruit"* which grows on the Trees beside the River, which will flow from the Temple in Jerusalem (Ezek. 47:1-12).

These from the *"uttermost part of Heaven"* will include all the Bible Greats, such as Abraham, Moses, David, etc. At stated, it will include every believing Jew, for all time, who died in Christ or was taken in the Rapture.

(28) "NOW LEARN A PARABLE OF THE FIG TREE; WHEN HER BRANCH IS YET TENDER, AND PUTS FORTH LEAVES, YOU KNOW THAT SUMMER IS NEAR."

The overview is:

This Passage, uttered nearly 2,000 years ago by Christ, refers to the rebirth of Israel as it began in 1948; for about 1,900 years, this *"fig tree"* produced nothing. Now, this tree, taking life from the roots, is beginning to *"put forth leaves."*

Israel is God's prophetic time clock; looking at Israel, we now know that summer is near, i.e., *"the Endtime Prophecies are about to be fulfilled."*

PARABLE OF THE FIG TREE

The phrase, *"Now learn a Parable of the Fig Tree,"* is used in the same sense as the vine and the olive, with which is associated in God's Promises of prosperity and in prophetic warnings (Jer. 5:17; Hos. 2:12; Joel 1:7, 12; Hab. 3:17).

Actually, the fig tree is often planted with the vine (Lk. 13:6), so that its branches and the vine's foliage led to the well-known expression, *"to sit down under one's own vine and fig tree,"* as a symbol of long-continued well-being and prosperity (I Ki. 4:25; II Ki. 18:31; Isa. 36:16; Mic. 4:4; Zech. 3:10).

So, the *"fig tree"* is here as a symbol of Israel, and, more particularly, the Second Coming of Christ.

THE PUTTING FORTH OF LEAVES

The phrase, *"When her branch is yet tender, and puts forth leaves,"* has a double meaning:

1. It refers to the rebirth of Israel, and it began in 1948. As we've already stated, for about 1,900 years, this *"fig tree"* was barren. Now, this tree, taking life from the roots, is beginning to *"put forth leaves."*

Even though completely devoid of any type of spirituality, the rebirth of Israel as a nation is a fulfillment of Bible Prophecy of such proportions as to defy all description. Never before has a nation such as Israel, which was scattered all over the world, been brought back to a place of viability. It has never happened before, and it has only happened this time because it is the Will of God.

How anyone could see the many Scriptures in the Word of God concerning the coming Restoration of Israel, and we speak of spiritual Restoration, and see what is happening now with Israel, especially considering her past, and not understand that Israel is still viable in the great Prophetic Plan of

God, is beyond me!

As we have stated, Israel is God's Prophetic time clock. Not only do the Prophets of old proclaim her Restoration, but the Apostle Paul, in the Eleventh Chapter of the Book of Romans, graphically predicts her Restoration, and by the Holy Spirit, as is all of the Word of God, which means that the predictions are infallible.

Despite Israel's problems with the Palestinians, still, she is, hands down, the most powerful State in the entirety of the Middle East and, in fact, one of the most powerful in the world.

2. The second meaning merely concerns the fig tree used here by Jesus as a symbol of the Second Coming. When it puts forth leaves, it is about ready to bear fruit, i.e., *"Jesus is soon to come!"* We speak of the Second Coming. And if Israel's present state and position is a sign of the soon-to-happen Second Coming, how close must the Rapture of the Church be!

The phrase, *"You know that summer is near,"* refers to the fig tree about to bring forth fruit, and, consequently, the advent of *"summer."*

(29) "SO YOU IN LIKE MANNER, WHEN YOU SHALL SEE THESE THINGS COME TO PASS, KNOW THAT IT IS NEAR, EVEN AT THE DOORS."

The exegesis is:

Instead of being translated, *"It is near,"* it should have stated, *"He is near,"* because it refers to Christ.

LIKE MANNER

The phrase, *"So you in like manner, when you shall see these things come to pass,"* is referring to all the predictions of the preceding Verses, i.e., *"false messiahs," "signs and wonders," "the putting forth of the fig tree,"* etc.

The phrase, *"Know that it is near, even at the doors,"* tells us, presently, that *"It is late!"*

This Parable of the Fig Tree pertains to Israel and the Second Coming, and is meant to explain the time of that world-shaking event. No doubt, many Jews, who, during the coming Great Tribulation, accept Christ as their Saviour, will read these very words with encouragement. There is no reason for the world to be in ignorance concerning this all-important event; however, ignorance prevails because most people simply do not believe the Bible, hence, they do not believe these Words.

But worse yet, where does the Church stand in all of this?

THE CHURCH

Only a small number are rightly interpreting these Passages referring to Endtime events, and most in the modern Church have little interest in Endtime Prophecies. The reason is simple:

The modern Church, at least for the most part, little cares about Endtime Prophecy, because their treasure is in this world and not in Heaven. And where your treasure is, that is where your heart will be (Mat. 6:19-21).

When I was a young Preacher just getting started (now about 50 years ago), there were Preachers who traveled from Church to Church teaching on Bible Prophecy. Actually, I preached Campmeetings with some of these Preachers, whose teaching was very much needed, as should be obvious; however, for the reason mentioned, that is little done anymore. Most Christians have their attention, their heart, and their thinking on the things of this world; they have, therefore, little interest in that which pertains to eternity. It is sad, but true!

THE CROSS

The simple reason is that the Church is abandoning the Word of God; however, that which says too much concludes by saying very little. While it is certainly true that the Church, with some few exceptions, is no longer attempting to abide by the Word, still, the basic reason is that the Church has abandoned the Cross. The Cross of Christ is the Gospel of Christ.

Paul said so: *"For Christ sent me not to baptize, but to preach the Gospel: not with wisdom of words, lest the Cross of Christ should be made of none effect"* (I Cor. 1:17).

Emphatically, and even dogmatically, the Holy Spirit through Paul here tells us exactly what the Gospel is. It is the Cross of Christ. That's the reason that Paul also said, *"We preach Christ Crucified"* (I Cor. 1:23). And *"I determined to know nothing among you, save Jesus Christ and Him Crucified"* (I Cor. 2:2).

Unless the Cross of Christ, is properly understood, which, in essence, is the meaning of the New Covenant, then nothing else about the Bible will be properly understood, either. Every Doctrine must be built upon the Foundation of the Cross, because this is the foundation first laid, even before the foundation of the world (I Pet. 1:18-20). If our Doctrine is not built squarely on the Cross of Christ, then, in some way, it will be a house built on sand, which means it has no proper foundation, and the end result is inevitable (Mat. 7:24-27).

(30) "VERILY I SAY UNTO YOU, THAT THIS GENERATION SHALL NOT PASS, TILL ALL THESE THINGS BE DONE."

The exposition is:

This concerns the generation in existence at the time of these happenings, which will be the time of the Great Tribulation. It is the events of Revelation, Chapters 6 through 19.

THIS GENERATION

"This generation" spoken of by Jesus concerns the generation in existence at the time of the happenings of these predictions. Actually, this will be the last generation living on Earth at the time all these things will be fulfilled — the last generation before the beginning of the Kingdom Age.

This proves that all these things will be fulfilled in one generation only, actually in less than one generation. The Great Tribulation, called *"Daniel's 70th Week,"* will last for seven years (Dan. 9:27). All of the predictions in Revelation, Chapters 6 through 19, will take place during this seven years; consequently, as is obvious, that is much shorter than a generation, but yet many things will undoubtedly take place leading up to the Great Tribulation. (It is possible that the *"generation"* of which Jesus spoke is this present generation. That should be a sobering thought.)

Once again, there is no excuse for Israel's rebellion and their acceptance of the Antichrist, especially considering that Jesus plainly tells them what will take place; however, sadly, the nation of Israel gives no credence at all to the New Testament, especially Christ and His Words. To be sure, this unbelief will cost them dearly!

Sadder still, even much of the Church, as stated, has little knowledge of futuristic events, as they are predicted in the Bible. The reason, as with Israel, is unbelief!

(31) "HEAVEN AND EARTH SHALL PASS AWAY: BUT MY WORDS SHALL NOT PASS AWAY."

The synopsis is:

It would have been better translated, *"Heaven and Earth shall pass from one condition to another."*

THE CHANGING OF HEAVEN AND EARTH

The phrase, *"Heaven and Earth shall pass away,"* actually refers to a change, a change from one condition to another. The Greek Word for *"pass away"* is *"parerchomai,"* which means *"to change from one condition or state to another."* It does not carry the idea of obliteration or annihilation.

Peter addressed this when he said, *"But the Day of the Lord will come as a thief in the night* (the conclusion of the Millennium; what will happen at that time will be unexpected, and for a variety of reasons); *in the which the Heavens shall pass away with a great noise, and the elements shall melt with fervent heat, the Earth also and the works that are therein shall be burned up"* (II Pet. 3:10).

(This does not speak of annihilation, but rather, as stated, passing from one condition to another.)

THE WORD OF GOD

The phrase, *"But my words shall not pass away,"* means that Heaven and Earth may change, and, in fact, will change, but *"My Words shall never change."* In other words, what He is saying is going to pass, and without fail! It will not and, in fact, cannot, be changed by world events, unbelief in God's Word, or other machinations of evil men.

In fact, God's Word is always unchangeable; in Truth, it is the only thing that is unchangeable. God said, *"For I am the LORD, I change not"* (Mal. 3:6).

Perfection cannot change, because perfection does not need to change!

(32) "BUT OF THAT DAY AND THAT HOUR KNOWS NO MAN, NO, NOT THE ANGELS WHICH ARE IN HEAVEN, NEITHER THE SON, BUT THE FATHER."

The exegesis is:

The Son of Man, under the self-imposed limitations of the Incarnation, says that even He Himself did not, at that time, know the hour of the Second Advent and of the time of the fulfillment of these other things grouped around that event; without a doubt, He now knows. I'm sure the Angels now know, as well. But then, they didn't!

THE FATHER

The phrase, *"But of that day and that hour knows no man,"* refers to the exact time these things will happen. In fact, since Christ uttered these Words, it has been nearly 2,000 years. However, if, in fact, the *"fig tree"* typifies Israel, we know these events are not far off, simply because Israel, so to speak, is *"putting forth leaves."*

The phrase, *"No, not the Angels which are in Heaven, neither the Son,"* means they did not then know, but definitely do know now. I speak of this present time as my notes are written, the year 2004.

The Lord Jesus, then speaking in the capacity of the Son of Man and under the self-imposed limitations of the Incarnation, says that even He Himself did not, at that time, know the hour of the Second Advent, and of the time of the fulfillment of these other things grouped around that event. There were many things, in fact, that Christ, at that time, did not know; again, this was because of self-imposed limitations. That is no longer the case; it changed instantly when He was raised from the dead and glorified. Now, He is Omniscient, even as He was before His Incarnation.

The phrase, *"The Father,"* means that, at that time, the time when Christ was speaking these Words, only the Father knew the exact time of the fulfillment of these coming events. This tells us that our Lord sought to know only the things the Father then desired that He know. This spoke of total submission to the Father, which serves as our example, and which was meant to serve as our example, i.e., leaving all in the Father's Hands.

Now that He is seated at the Right Hand of the Father, the limitations of the Incarnation, as stated, have now passed. As such, He is now *"Omnipotent"* (all-powerful), *"Omniscient"* (all-knowing), and *"Omnipresent"* (everywhere), and has been since his Glorification and Ascension (Acts 1:9; Eph. 1:20-23).

(33) "TAKE YE HEED, WATCH AND PRAY: FOR YOU KNOW NOT WHEN THE TIME IS."

The structure is:

The *"time"* itself is not that important, but *"watchfulness"* is!

WATCH AND PRAY

The phrase, *"Take ye heed, watch and pray,"* is an admonition given not only to Israel, but to the Church, as well! The idea is a state of watchfulness, which is seasoned by prayer. If the Believer does not have a strong prayer life, these predictions will grow more and more dim, such as is happening in the modern Church!

The phrase, *"For you know not when the time is,"* is not meant to draw our attention to the *"time"* itself, but rather to the *"watchfulness."* In other words, we are to be ready at all times. Even though the Rapture is not mentioned here, still, the same principle applies. No one knows when that important event will take place. However, we are admonished to be ready at all times, living as if it will happen at any time (I Thess. 1:10; 5:6).

Concerning the Rapture, John said, *"And every man who has this hope in Him purifies himself, even as He is pure"* (I Jn. 3:3). The idea is, as is obvious, that the *"hope"* of the Rapture, as we realize it could happen at any time, causes us, hopefully, to draw closer to Jesus Christ.

(34) "FOR THE SON OF MAN IS AS A MAN TAKING A FAR JOURNEY, WHO LEFT HIS HOUSE, AND GAVE AUTHORITY TO HIS SERVANTS, AND TO EVERY MAN HIS WORK, AND COMMANDED THE PORTER TO WATCH."

The synopsis is:

Christ is speaking of Himself when He will go back to Heaven, which He did.

A FAR JOURNEY

The phrase, *"For the Son of Man is as a Man taking a far journey,"* refers to the Lord speaking of Himself. He left this Earth and went back to Heaven, where He resides even at this present time, seated by the Right Hand of the Father, making intercession for the Saints (Eph. 1:20-23; Heb. 7:25).

HIS HOUSE

The phrase, *"Who left His House,"* refers to the Work He established on Earth, constituted as the *"Church"* (Mat. 16:18). We must never forget that it is *"His Church"* and not our Church. This means that Christ is a very active Head and not a passive Head, as some think. In other words, He is very much involved in His Church through the Person and Office of the Holy Spirit. He purchased the Church, so to speak, with His Own Precious Blood. Considering the price that has been paid, and we speak of the Cross, which made the Church possible, He, to be sure, is very actively involved. Due to the spiritual declension of the modern Church, however, John the Beloved gives us the status of Christ presently, as it regards the Church.

When John had his Vision nearly 2,000 years ago, he saw *"Seven Golden Candlesticks,"* which presents the symbolism for the seven Churches which typified the entirety of the Church Age through its Dispensation. Jesus was standing in the midst of those *"Seven Golden Candlesticks,"* meaning that He was in the midst of the Church (Rev. 1:12-13).

However, when John, in his Vision, saw the Church at Laodicea, which portrays the Church at the end of this Age, in other words, this present time, Christ, instead of being in the Church, is rather outside the door knocking, trying to get in. In fact, as the Message to the Church of Laodicea implies, Christ is no longer dealing with the institutionalized Church, but rather with individuals only (Rev. 3:14-22).

If, in fact, the Rapture did not take place, the entirety of the Church would be totally corrupted. It is almost that now.

AUTHORITY TO HIS SERVANTS

The phrase, *"And gave authority to His servants,"* concerns those to whom belongs the responsibility of guarding the house and being ready to open the door to the Master at His return. In a sense, this stands for every Believer, but, more particularly, for every full time Christian worker, such as the fourfold Calling of Apostle, Prophet, Evangelist, Pastor and Teacher (Eph. 4:11).

The phrase, *"And commanded the porter to watch,"* is a little different than the word *"watch"* in Verse 33. That *"watch"* speaks of a sleeping man arousing himself, while this *"watch"* conveys the idea of wakefulness.

(35) "WATCH YE THEREFORE: FOR YOU KNOW NOT WHEN THE MASTER OF THE HOUSE COMES, AT EVENING, OR AT MIDNIGHT, OR AT THE COCKCROWING, OR IN THE MORNING."

The synopsis is:

Christ is not speaking here of the Rapture of the Church, but specifically to Israel; but yet, the admonition can definitely apply to modern Believers, and should apply, as it regards the Rapture.

DILIGENCE

The phrase, *"Watch ye therefore,"* is used again to portray the seriousness of the matter, referring to the Coming of the Lord. The phrase, *"For you know not when the Master of the house comes, at evening, or at midnight, or at the cockcrowing, or in the morning,"* pertains, according to Vincent, to Preachers, and, in a sense, every Believer, who are thus compared with the doorkeepers of Verse 34. The night season, as here represented, is an apt description. In the Temple, during the night, the Captain of the Temple made his rounds. At his approach, the guards had to rise and salute him in a particular manner. Any guard found asleep on duty was beaten, or his garments were set on fire. One can compare this illustration with Revelation 16:15: *"Blessed is he who watches, and keeps his garments."*

The preparations for the morning service required all to be early astir. The superintending Priest might knock at the door at any moment.

(36) "LEST COMING SUDDENLY HE FIND YOU SLEEPING."

The exposition is:

Regrettably, most of the modern Church is spiritually asleep; most little know and realize the lateness of the hour.

SLEEPING ON WATCH

After the establishment of Roman power in Judaea, the Jews copied the Roman method of dividing the night into four watches. Jesus continues with that custom in Verse 35. The first watch would have begun at 6 p.m. and continued until 9 p.m. The second watch would have begun at 9 p.m. and ended at midnight. The third watch began at midnight and concluded at 3 a.m., i.e., *"at cockcrowing,"* which was the first crowing of the rooster. The fourth watch began at 3 a.m. and concluded at 6 a.m., i.e., the *"last cockcrowing"* (the roosters crowed twice, at approximately 3 a.m. and 6 a.m.)

"Sleeping on watch," of course, was a serious offense. With the Romans, it was punishable by death, and, with the Temple guards, it could result in a severe beating, etc. Once again, the constant vigilance respecting the Coming of the Lord is here intoned.

(37) "AND WHAT I SAY UNTO YOU I SAY UNTO ALL, WATCH."

The overview is:

This is the last Word of Christ respecting this dissertation; we should take it very seriously.

WATCH

This was said to the Apostles, but was meant for all Israel; it also pertains to the Church. For Jesus to be as elaborate as He was in this explanation, to even repeat Himself several times, one should realize the seriousness of His Words.

What does He mean by the word *"Watch"*?

1. The certitude of His Coming is portrayed here. Nothing can stop this; it is a foregone conclusion.

2. The time of that Coming is not given; even He, at least at that time, did not know the date (Vs. 32).

3. The idea of this short Message concerning the Second Coming is *"Watchfulness."* The Believer is importuned to stay ready at all times. Even though Jesus is not, as stated, speaking here of the Rapture, still, it definitely could apply in principle to that event.

The manner in which Jesus spoke of this event, referring to the guards and each watch of the night, is an excellent example. No guard would want to be found sleeping at his post, or even conducting himself in a way that spoke of lack of diligence. During the time of his watch, he was to remain alert, realizing that the Priest could show up at any time.

The principle of these statements, as they pertain to modern Believers, concerns the attitude and consecration of our everyday life before the Lord. We are to live as if Jesus may come at any moment. This is the thrust of what Christ is saying.

If the Believer thought the Trump of God would sound tomorrow morning at daybreak, I greatly suspect that many Christians would hurriedly attempt to right wrongs, pay back tithe, ask forgiveness, and call out to God in prayer and worship. The idea is that we live in this manner of consecration at all times.

Were this truly the case, how different the Church would be!

CHAPTER 14

(1) "AFTER TWO DAYS WAS THE FEAST OF THE PASSOVER, AND OF UNLEAVENED BREAD: AND THE CHIEF PRIESTS AND THE SCRIBES SOUGHT HOW THEY MIGHT TAKE HIM BY CRAFT, AND PUT HIM TO DEATH."

The diagram is:

The Passover was the greatest Feast of the Jewish year, celebrating the deliverance from Egypt; it lasted one day.

The second Feast, that of *"Unleavened Bread,"* began on the day of the Passover, and continued for seven days; during that time, no leaven was to be placed in bread or anything else. The *"Passover"* symbolized the price that Christ would pay on Calvary's Cross; *"Unleavened Bread"* symbolized His Perfect Life and Perfect Body, which would be offered in Sacrifice.

THE PASSOVER

The phrase, *"After two days was the Feast*

of the Passover," pertained to the Pascal Lamb, which was offered for Sacrifice by the ancient Israelites in Egypt, with the Blood being sprinkled on the doorposts of their dwellings in Egypt so that the destroying Angel might pass over their homes without entering and taking the life of the firstborn.

Moses wrote: *"And the Blood shall be to you for a token upon the houses where you are: and when I see the Blood, I will pass over you, and the plague shall not be upon you to destroy you, when I smite the land of Egypt"* (Ex. 12:13).

After that, they were instructed to *"keep this Ordinance in his season from year to year"* (Ex. 13:10). Consequently, for nearly 1,500 years it had been kept, with the exception of the time spent in dispersion in Babylon and times of spiritual declension.

The Passover is very significant to Christians, as well as to Jews. To God's Old Testament, the Passover recalled a Redemption linked with death and the shedding of blood. To the Christian, the Passover speaks of Jesus, for He actually was the Passover Lamb, fulfilling the symbolism which the slain lambs represented.

As the symbolic Passover was about to be celebrated at this time in Israel, the actual Passover Lamb was entering Jerusalem to fulfill the type by dying on the Cross. As Israel's Redemption and Victory were linked to their trust in what the Passover Lamb represented, namely Jesus, likewise, our Redemption is linked in totality to what Jesus did at Calvary, which not only saves us, but also protects us from the ultimate destroyer.

So, the Passover was a Type of Christ shedding His Life's Blood on Calvary's Cross, in order that men might be redeemed; therefore, inasmuch as the Passover could be proclaimed as the focal point of the entire worship system of Judaism, which all prefigured the coming Redeemer, we are led to understand just how important the Cross of Christ actually is. In fact, any Jew, or any Gentile for that matter, who was saved in Old Testament times, was saved by looking forward to the Cross, which is what the Sacrifices and the Passover represented. Presently, anyone who is saved today is saved by looking back to the Cross, the Cross being the pivot point of history. Believers in Old Testament times looked forward to a prophetic Jesus, while Believers now look backward to an historical Jesus.

UNLEAVENED BREAD

The phrase, *"And of Unleavened Bread,"* refers to the second Feast which began on the day of the Passover and continued for seven days, during which time only Unleavened Bread was used. The killing of the Passover Lamb and the celebration of that Feast, as stated, took place on the first of these seven days. As the Passover Lamb typified Jesus, Who would shed His Blood, likewise, the *"Unleavened Bread"* typified His Perfect Life and Perfect Body, which would be given in a Perfect Sacrifice, which was necessary, that is, if man was to be redeemed.

The Feast of *"Unleavened Bread"* symbolized what Jesus had to be in order to serve as a Sacrifice on the Cross of Calvary. He had to be perfect in every respect, hence, no *"leaven"* being used for these seven days. Leaven in Bible times was sourdough, which, with added juices, served as a fermenting agent to leaven (make it rise) new dough. It is used in a figurative and symbolic sense in the New Testament.

So, inasmuch as leaven was used as a symbol for sin, when it was removed from all bread during this seven-day period, this symbolized, as stated, the pure and spotless Life and Body of our Lord. This Feast pointed, therefore, to the Cross, exactly as did the Passover.

THE RELIGIOUS LEADERS OF ISRAEL

The phrase, *"And the Chief Priests and the Scribes sought how they might take Him by craft, and put Him to death"* spoke of representatives of each order of the Sanhedrin, who were gathered together in council to discuss ways and means of killing Christ.

Actually, they were assembled in the house of Caiaphas, the High Priest, who had for some time been advocating the policy of sacrificing Jesus to the Roman power (Jn. 11:49). They were not divided as to whether to do such a thing, but only as to how it should be done. The point under consideration was the strategic, opportune, safe time to give

Jesus over to the Roman authorities.

As sordid as it sounds, we have before us what was, in effect, the *"Church"* of that day plotting the death of Christ. In Truth, the Church has always been the biggest enemy of the Lord. Of course, I speak of the apostate Church, which makes up the far greater majority. The most dangerous place in town is oftentimes the Church. Where a person attends Church is, therefore, extremely important.

Inasmuch as the leaders of most Churches do not follow the Lord and do not preach the Bible, they consequently do not have the Power of the Holy Spirit; and, for one to associate with one of these Churches, whatever their names may be, is tantamount to spiritual death.

There are some few good Churches led by Spirit-filled Preachers, but not many! The person who has the privilege to attend such a Church is privileged indeed!

(2) "BUT THEY SAID, NOT ON THE FEAST DAY, LEST THERE BE AN UPROAR OF THE PEOPLE."

The composition is:

The Feast Day of which they spoke was the Day of the Passover.

THE FEAST DAY

The phrase, *"But they said, not on the Feast Day,"* was not done because of respect for this particular Day, but rather that their perfidious action not be known. Little did they know or understand that they were murdering the One Whom the Passover had symbolized for all of these centuries. They were plotting the murder of the Lord of Glory!

The phrase, *"Lest there be an uproar of the people,"* concerned the vast population of Jerusalem, which swelled during the Passover Feast, and could have numbered as many as 500,000 or more. Scores of these people had experienced Healings and even Miracles at the Hand of Christ. Moreover, many considered Jesus to be a great Prophet, if not the Messiah. These Church leaders consequently felt that if this matter, i.e. the matter of murdering Him, was not handled delicately, it could cause severe problems, even a riot, should the people rise in His defense. Their first intention, therefore, was not to destroy Him until after the close of the Passover Feast.

They were, however, overruled by events, all ordered by God's never-failing providence. The sudden betrayal by Judas led them to change their minds; Jesus would be handed over to the Roman authorities and would die on the Passover Day, even at 3 p.m., which was the exact time the Pascal Lamb was offered.

Thus, the Divine Purpose was fulfilled that Christ should suffer at that particular time so that the type would be satisfied, which it was.

(3) "AND BEING IN BETHANY IN THE HOUSE OF SIMON THE LEPER, AS HE SAT AT MEAT, THERE CAME A WOMAN HAVING AN ALABASTER BOX OF OINTMENT OF SPIKENARD VERY PRECIOUS; AND SHE BROKE THE BOX, AND POURED IT ON HIS HEAD."

The overview is:

She broke the seal that kept the fragrance preserved; the pouring upon Him spoke of her anointing Him for His Burial. Since anointing was generally done after death, by her anointing Him now, she testified to her belief in the Resurrection; she seems to have been the only one who did believe in His Resurrection before the fact.

This woman probably was Mary, the sister of Lazarus (Jn. 11:1-2).

SIMON THE LEPER

The phrase, *"And being in Bethany,"* spoke of the small village where Jesus and His Disciples spent much time when they were in the vicinity of Jerusalem. Actually, there is no evidence that Jesus ever spent the night in Jerusalem, with the exception of the night He was arrested. He had close friends in Bethany, including Lazarus and his sisters, Mary and Martha. It seems that *"Simon the Leper"* was also in this favored group.

The phrase, *"In the house of Simon the Leper,"* probably referred to a man whom Jesus had healed. Oftentimes, something was linked, as here, to the name of a person, and done so for recognition.

The phrase, *"As He sat at meat,"* referred, more than likely, to the evening meal. The meals in those days were not taken as presently, with people sitting in chairs, but instead reclining on cushions or couches on the floor.

The phrase, *"There came a woman,"* probably refers to Mary, the sister of Lazarus. Some have claimed it was another woman, thereby another anointing; however, there is little evidence of such!

THE ALABASTER BOX

The phrase, *"Having an alabaster box of ointment of spikenard very precious,"* referred to a perfume which came from India, which was well known to the Greeks and Romans, and which was procured from the hills on the banks of the Ganges River.

The Greek word *"pistikos"* is used, meaning that it was genuine, not imitation or adulterated. The Greek word *"boluteles"* (precious) tells us that it was very costly.

The phrase, *"And she broke the box,"* means that she broke the seal that kept the fragrance preserved. It did not mean that the container was smashed or broken.

THE ANOINTING

The phrase, *"And poured it on His Head,"* spoke of her anointing Him for His Burial.

Of this anointing, Williams says, *"Her action denoted affection and intelligence. Having heard that He was to die, she purchased a costly spikenard to assist in the embalming of His Body; but instructed by the Resurrection of her brother Lazarus, hearing that Jesus was Himself the Resurrection and the Life, learning that He was to rise on the third day, and recognizing that embalmment would be needless, she poured it upon His Living Body, and so testified her belief in the Resurrection."*

It seems that she was the only person who believed and understood the Lord's teaching as to His Death and Resurrection. None of the Disciples seems to have understood what He said to them on that matter until after Pentecost.

As recorded in John, she anointed both the Lord's Feet and His Head.

(Some believe that Martha was the wife of Simon the Leper; Lazarus and Mary, therefore, would be brother-in-law and sister-in-law to Simon.)

(4) "AND THERE WERE SOME WHO HAD INDIGNATION WITHIN THEMSELVES, AND SAID, WHY WAS THIS WASTE OF THE OINTMENT MADE?"

The exposition is:

It is believed by some that this ointment would have been worth approximately $10,000 in 2004 currency. Truthfully, however, nothing given to Christ is wasted, while much of the world's resources used otherwise are, in fact, wasted.

INDIGNATION

The phrase, *"And there were some who had indignation within themselves,"* pertained to some of the Disciples, but Judas Iscariot, it seems, took the lead. This shows how fault-finding can quickly spread. It is the same in a local Church. One individual finds fault, and then attempts to peddle it to others. This usually succeeds!

Continuing in the vein of the local Church, no one should be a party to such action. If false doctrine is being presented, it should be examined according to Scripture, and then confronted. If it seems the situation or direction will not change, the individual should leave that particular Church body and go elsewhere. He should not remain, at least in those circumstances, and become a part of a Church fight.

It is obvious why Judas did as he did. His affections had already found root other than Christ. He would, therefore, grow *"indignant"* at what he considered a *"waste."* Regrettably, the minds and hearts of some of the other Disciples also were more carnal than spiritual. It was, therefore, very easy for these to join Judas. Other than Judas, how saddened they must have been when they thought back on this situation! Jesus was about to die. The anointing He received would be the only such anointing. Mary anointed His *"Head,"* signifying His Death; she also anointed His *"Feet"* (Jn. 12:3), signifying, whether she understood it at that time or not, that He would walk out of that tomb.

WASTE?

The question, *"And said, Why was this waste of the ointment made?"* proclaims the carnal attitude of some of the Disciples, which is still prevalent, regrettably, in the modern Church.

First of all, to refer to this as *"waste"* shows, as stated, a woeful lack of spiritual knowledge! Such must have been grievous to the heart of Jesus. Actually, the entirety of the spirit of the world follows in this train. Anything done for God, including anything spent for the Work of the Lord, is termed *"waste."*

Through the years, I have dealt often with the media along these very lines. They greatly complain about our appealing to people for funds to help us take the Gospel to the world. They professed to be extremely agitated at elderly people on fixed incomes giving for this cause and purpose. I have not, however, noticed the media saying anything negative concerning the scores of elderly and destitute poor buying lottery tickets, which they can ill afford.

To give to God is the most noble thing that one could ever do, irrespective of one's status or position in life. To throw away one's money on lottery tickets is truly the biggest *"waste"* in which one could ever engage.

Why is it that the media says nothing about that sort of *"waste,"* i.e., gambling. The answer is simple! Their spirit and the gambling spirit are one and the same. In other words, it all comes from the same parent, Satan! Actually, the only thing in this world that is not a *"waste"* is that which is done for God! Of course, that would also include the care of one's family.

(5) "FOR IT MIGHT HAVE BEEN SOLD FOR MORE THAN THREE HUNDRED PENCE, AND HAVE BEEN GIVEN TO THE POOR. AND THEY MURMURED AGAINST HER."

The exposition is:

Murmuring has never been justified or sanctioned by God in Scripture, irrespective as to how right the cause may seem to be.

THE POOR

The phrase, *"For it might have been sold for more than three hundred pence,"* represented, as stated, approximately $10,000 in 2004 currency. The phrase, *"And have been given to the poor,"* originated with Judas (Jn. 12:4-6). Actually, Judas did not care for the poor, but only that this money could be brought within his reach. The Scripture says of him, *"This he said, not that he cared for the poor; but because he was a thief, and had the bag, and bore what was put therein"* (Jn. 12:6).

MURMURING

The phrase, *"And they murmured against her,"* concerned whichever Disciples had joined in with Judas in complaining about this *"anointing"*! Murmuring and complaining are sins; these sins are probably committed by Christians more than any other. In the first place, when we murmur and complain, we are, in effect, finding fault with the Lord. If there is, in fact, a problem, it is not the Lord's fault that the problem exists, but ours, or else others, but not the Lord!

I'm absolutely certain the Lord doesn't enjoy being blamed for something which He has not done.

Second, whatever our problem may seem to be, there are untold numbers of others in the world that have it much worse — in fact, much more worse, as should be obvious.

Murmuring about particular situations and circumstances, as bad as that is, is one thing; however, to murmur against someone else, when we have little knowledge as to what is actually happening, is the greatest sin of all. And this also is a sin that so many Christians commit, and do so constantly.

One of the favorite pastimes of Christians is to form conclusions and to generate opinions about something of which they have no knowledge. If they don't like the person, or if they are jealous of the person, they seize on something which has taken place, knowing nothing about what happened or why it happened. All of this comes under the heading of *"judging one's motives,"* of which we are specifically warned against by Christ.

Christ, in fact, said, *"For with what judgment you judge, you shall be judged: and with what measure you mete, it shall be measured to you again"* (Mat. 7:1-2). Judas and the Disciples who joined in with him in their murmuring against the particular woman had no idea as to what she did or why she did it. In fact, this *"anointing"* would be so sanctioned by the Holy Spirit that He would have this act placed in the Word of God, where it will remain forever. He also was so displeased by what Judas and the other

Disciples did, regarding murmuring against her, that He had this account placed in the Word, as well. I'm sure it was a great embarrassment to the other Disciples who did the murmuring. Thankfully, the Holy Spirit didn't call their names, because they soon saw the wrong of their actions and repented.

(6) "AND JESUS SAID, LET HER ALONE; WHY TROUBLE YE HER? SHE HAS WROUGHT A GOOD WORK ON ME."

The overview is:

Even though these Disciples didn't understand it, her actions showed her Faith in His Resurrection.

JESUS

The phrase, *"And Jesus said, Let her alone,"* proclaims the same Word He says to all who would attempt to hinder that done for Him. It appears from John 12:7 that Jesus here addressed Himself pointedly to Judas in these Words.

The question, *"Why trouble ye her?"* concerned itself with the *"murmuring."* What she did was not the business of Judas, or anyone else. So, what right did any of them have in saying anything? Judas was accusing her of *"waste,"* which, in reality, was no waste at all, while he would be guilty of the largest *"waste"* ever perpetrated by a human being. He would *"waste"* himself, all of Israel, and, most of all, the Lord Jesus Christ.

Actually, almost all the world falls into this category. They waste themselves, their families, all of humanity in which they come in contact, and, above all, the Plan of God for their lives.

No! The anointing of Jesus with this costly *"box of ointment"* was no waste. What Judas did, was!

People waste their time, talent, and money on that which is of no use or consequence; conversely, anything done for the Lord, in whatever capacity, that is, if our motives are right, is not only not a *"waste,"* but, in reality, a profit of incalculable proportions.

The phrase, *"She has wrought a good work on Me,"* is epitomized in the following statement:

"One life will soon be past, only what's done for Christ will last."

(7) "FOR YOU HAVE THE POOR WITH YOU ALWAYS, AND WHENSOEVER YOU WILL YOU MAY DO THEM GOOD: BUT ME YOU HAVE NOT ALWAYS."

The synopsis is:

The two, Himself and the poor, are equivalent in His sight (Mat. 25:40-45).

THE POOR

The phrase, *"For you have the poor with you always,"* portrays, regrettably, a condition resulting from the Fall in the Garden of Eden. While it is certainly no sin to be poor, still, poverty is a crushing, debilitating weight on humanity. The word *"always"* speaks of the time up to the Second Coming. At that time, the beginning of the Kingdom Age, poverty will be completely eliminated.

To be poor often means the lack of adequate basic necessities. The poor are always in need of the resources that provide for an improved quality of life. But more than material need is implied by poverty. Poverty assumes a low social status and a terrible vulnerability to the abuses of those with power. Because the poor lack resources, they are defenseless against those in society who are above them. They are also likely to be treated unfairly in the courts (Deut. 15:1-4).

When defrauded by the well-to-do, they have no recourse but to appeal to the Lord. Because of their powerlessness, the poor are the most easily robbed in any society (Ps. 35:10). Poverty strips the individual of rights, respect as a human being, and a place in society.

THE CAUSE OF POVERTY

In the Old Testament, and especially in Proverbs, there is sometimes strong emphasis on individual responsibility. Solomon said, *"He becomes poor who deals with a slack hand: but the hand of the diligent makes rich"* (Prov. 10:4). He also said, *"Drunkards and gluttons become poor, and drowsiness clothes them in rags"* (Prov. 23:21; 24:34).

However, the Book of Proverbs also recognizes causes of poverty over which an individual has no control. Solomon said, *"Much food is in the tillage of the poor: but there is that is destroyed for want of judgment"* (Prov. 13:23).

Clearly, it is the injustice of those who

oppress the poor and the helpless that the Old Testament portrays as the most common cause of poverty. Although certain Laws in the Law of Moses were intended to guard the poor, Israel's failure in this regard is reflected both in history and in the Old Testament Prophets' pronouncements.

Calling for a return to God, Isaiah communicated God's Message that His people are to stop their practice of empty ritual and begin to live a life acceptable to the Lord: *"Is not this the fast that I have chosen? to loose the bands of wickedness, to undo the heavy burdens, and to let the oppressed go free, and that you break every yoke?*

"Is it not to deal your bread to the hungry, and that you bring the poor who are cast out to the house? when you see the naked, that you cover him; and that you hide not yourself from your own flesh?" (Isa. 58:6-7).

The Lord through the Prophet Zechariah said, *"Thus speaks the LORD of Hosts, saying, Execute true judgment, and show mercy and compassions every man to his brother:*

"And oppress not the widow, nor the fatherless, the stranger, nor the poor; and let none of you imagine evil against his brother in your heart" (Zech. 7:9-10).

Solomon also said, *"He who oppresses the poor reproaches his Maker: but he who honors Him has mercy on the poor"* (Prov. 14:31).

ISRAEL AND THE POOR

Even though the Laws of God were strong respecting the poor, none of the mechanisms worked on a society-wide scale in Israel's entire history! God's people remained hardened. Although individuals may have approached the ideal, no generation of Israelites ever achieved it. This may be the one reason why commitment to God is closely associated in Scripture with concern for the poor and oppressed. Only by putting God and His Way first would someone exhibit compassion by surrendering material possessions to meet the needs of others.

However, in the Old Testament, there is a strong linkage between sin entrenched in society and practice by individuals and the crushing poverty that many suffered. God Himself sometimes brought the nation of Israel to a state of poverty. This came as a Judgment to those generations that would not serve the Lord in times of prosperity. Such Judgment brought hunger and thirst, nakedness and dire poverty (Deut. 28:48).

THE POOR WITHIN THE CHURCH

Regarding the teaching on poverty, the Epistles differ in several striking ways from the Old Testament.

First, the Old Testament links poverty in society with oppression and establishes social mechanisms that people of good will can use to reduce poverty. The New Testament does not explore the relationship between social oppression and the state of the lower classes. Nor does it suggest social mechanisms by which a society can deal with poverty. This is primarily because Israel was a nation as well as community of Faith. Old Testament Law was civil as well as ethical in nature.

The New Testament Church, by contrast, exists as a community of Faith within a variety of societies and cultures. The Christian may influence his or her society, but the Church is never envisioned as a State. Thus, no New Testament writer felt that it was his mission to set up the constitution of an ideal society.

Second, social class differences are assumed in the New Testament. But these differences are not to be considered within the fellowship of those who follow Jesus. James warns against showing favoritism to the rich (James 2:1-7). He reminds us that early Christianity was a movement of the lower classes and that the rich were exploiting the Believers.

Paul makes a similar point of view to the Corinthians: *"For you see your calling, Brethren, how that not many wise men after the flesh, not many mighty, not many noble, are Called"* (I Cor. 1:26). But instead, the Holy Spirit through Paul labels us as *"the lowly things of this world"* (I Cor. 1:28). Paul insisted that those now clothed with Christ *"are all one in Christ Jesus,"* and not to be categorized as slave or free, male or female (Gal. 3:28).

It follows, then, that class distinctions are to be rejected in the Body of Christ. As Paul says to the Romans, and I paraphrase,

"Do not be proud, but be willing to associate with people of low position. Do not be conceited" (Rom. 12:16).

THE RESPONSE OF THE CHURCH TO THE POOR

The New Testament definitely focuses on the plight of the poor and on the way in which the Church and the individual Believer are to respond. The New Testament records that when one part of the ancient world suffered famine or persecution, Believers in more prosperous areas responded by sending funds to meet the survival needs of their Brothers and Sisters. However, due to the influence of Christianity for the last 2,000 years, Governments are now very much involved respecting needs as a result of famine or catastrophe. Thankfully, this relieves the burden on the Church, which then may use its funds for World Evangelism, or at least that's where they should be used.

Individual Believers are also to respond to the immediate needs of others whom he or she knows (James 2:14-16; I Jn. 3:16-18); however, this is done only if the individual truly cannot help himself. Paul also said, *"That if any would not work, neither should he eat"* (II Thess. 3:10).

This statement was given, no doubt, because of lazy busybodies and shiftless individuals in the Church who had become professional moochers. The New Testament does not command the distribution of wealth to bring about a level society, but the rich are to see their wealth as a gift God has given them for them to help alleviate the needs of Brothers and Sisters, whether physically or spiritually.

Generosity is to be the basic principle as a sharing modeled after Christ, Who sacrificed Himself to meet our needs (II Cor. 8:8-9). Because God ultimately is the One Who supplies our needs, we can give generously, knowing that He will care for us when we have need. Then, having all that you need, you will abound in every good work (II Cor. 9:8-11).

Although Believers are exhorted to *"do good to all people,"* they are to do so *"especially to those who belong to the family of Faith"* (Gal. 6:10). Regarding the poor, someone,

NOTES

however, has well said, *"If every person in the world was given one million dollars, at the end of twelve months or less, 1 percent would have all the money, with the other 99 percent having little or none."* Regrettably, that is true! Consequently, we *"have the poor with us always,"* or at least until the Kingdom Age.

The phrase, *"And whensoever you will you may do them good,"* was in no way an intention on the Lord's part to contrast services rendered to Himself in Person with services rendered to the poor for His sake — the two are equivalent in His sight (Mat. 25:40-45).

The phrase, *"But Me you have not always,"* is meant to point out that this privilege would very soon be impossible, while opportunity for the poor would abound to the end of this age.

(8) "SHE HAS DONE WHAT SHE COULD: SHE IS COME AFOREHAND TO ANOINT MY BODY TO THE BURYING."

The overview is:

His Body had been prepared by God for Sacrifice (Heb. 10:5).

PREPARATION

The phrase, *"She has done what she could,"* pertained to Mary. She had been moved upon by the Holy Spirit, because of its great significance, to do this. She did *"what she could"*! Are we doing what we can? As a result, her unselfish act has been spoken of for 2,000 years. Of the millions of Believers who have praised her, not one True Believer has taken the position that Judas took.

The phrase, *"She is come aforehand to anoint My Body to the burying,"* represented something so very important that it defies all description. Sadly, Judas and some of the other Disciples did not see or understand this extremely important event.

The *"Body"* of Jesus was to be the Sacrifice that would redeem humanity from the terrible grip of sin. His Sacrifice would satisfy the claims of Heavenly Justice in that the debt owed by mankind would be paid in full. For this cause, Jesus came into the world. The Prophet had said, *"A Body You have prepared Me"* (Heb. 10:5).

So, Mary was anointing this Body of Christ, which had been prepared by God for this very purpose. Inasmuch as the embalming process was never really carried out, since the Resurrection prevented the fulfillment of this purpose, the only anointing which the Lord received was the anticipatory one by Mary.

What an honor that God chose a woman to do this! Another woman, Mary Magdalene, was the first to announce the Resurrection (Mk. 16:9-10).

(9) "VERILY I SAY UNTO YOU, WHERESOEVER THIS GOSPEL SHALL BE PREACHED THROUGHOUT THE WHOLE WORLD, THIS ALSO THAT SHE HAS DONE SHALL BE SPOKEN OF FOR A MEMORIAL OF HER."

The synopsis is:

This act of anointing is connected with Mary and will never be forgotten.

THIS GOSPEL

The phrase, *"Verily I say unto you, wheresoever this Gospel shall be preached throughout the whole world,"* tells us several things:

1. This tells us that the Gospel was to be preached *"throughout the whole world."* And so it has! Admittedly, it has been preached much more in some places than others, but, in a sense, it has come close to covering the world. We, in fact, have helped carry this out with our Telecast.

2. It will be *"This Gospel,"* the Gospel of Jesus Christ, which, in effect, is the Gospel of the *"Cross of Christ"* (I Cor. 1:17). Even though false prophets abound, propagating their false message, still, there are some few Preachers who are still preaching the Truth. While that number is few, still, the Power of the Spirit with these Preachers, whoever they might be, can get much done.

3. This which Mary did, which was so very important, will ever be heralded, because anything and everything done for Christ bears eternal consequences.

A MEMORIAL

The phrase, *"This also that she has done shall be spoken of for a memorial of her,"* has been fulfilled in totality, and will continue to be fulfilled. If one is to notice, it says, *"a memorial of her,"* signifying that this act is connected with her and will never be forgotten.

NOTES

I believe one could say, without fear of Scriptural contradiction, that every single thing done for Christ, by anyone, is written down in a *"Memorial Book"* in Heaven. The *"Books"* are mentioned in Revelation 20:12 and proclaim that everything is noted, whether good or bad; however, upon trust in the shed Blood of Jesus Christ and because of Justification by Faith, all of that which is negative or bad is erased. Only the good remains!

(10) "AND JUDAS ISCARIOT, ONE OF THE TWELVE, WENT UNTO THE CHIEF PRIESTS, TO BETRAY HIM UNTO THEM."

The overview is:

By design it is noted by the Holy Spirit that all may know it is Judas who did this, and that he forfeited one of the most important offices ever given to a human being in the history of mankind.

JUDAS ISCARIOT

The phrase, *"And Judas Iscariot, one of the Twelve,"* presents the Holy Spirit specifying who this is. He desires all to know that Judas was chosen by the Lord as one of the *"Twelve,"* consequently one of the Twelve most important offices ever given to a human being in history.

What Judas lost is incalculable! But, at the same time, every single person in the world who refuses to accept Christ falls, in some way, into the same category. That's why Jesus said, *"What does it profit a man if he gain the whole world and lose his own soul?"* (Mk. 8:36-37).

THE CHIEF PRIESTS

The phrase, *"Went unto the Chief Priests,"* means that he had lost one opportunity of gain; he would now seek another. Judas had entered such a state of rebellion that the rebuke tendered by Christ caused the other Disciples to be brought to their senses, but not Judas. Whereas it softened them, it only served to harden him.

Such is the Gospel! It is like the sun; it hardens clay, but softens wax. The fault is not in the sun, as it not in the Gospel, but in the material.

As we have repeatedly stated, it was not the world that was opposed to Christ so very much, but rather the *"Church"* of that day. In fact, the greatest opposition to the True Gospel of Jesus Christ has always been the religious establishment. That should not come as a surprise, seeing that Satan himself is a very religious being; as such, he knows how to infiltrate, deceive, and promote his way. As stated, he does most of it through the Church.

BETRAYAL

The phrase, *"To betray Him unto them,"* proclaims the most perfidious act ever carried out by any human being. Any wrong thing done to anyone is always censured by the Lord, and stringently so! However, nothing can compare with that which was done to Christ, for He was absolutely sinless, therefore, Perfect. He had never done anything to anyone but be kind and gracious to them. He had never made a leg become lame, but made many lame legs walk. He had never caused an eye to become blind, but had opened many blinded eyes. So, why would anyone want to betray Him?

That question could be asked concerning the rejection of Christ by almost the entirety of the world.

Why?

Unbelief! (Jn. 16:9)

Judas would fall into the same category. He simply did not believe in the Mission of Christ regarding the Salvation of humanity, but instead placed his own self-will in the forefront. When it looked as if Christ was not going to use His Power to bring about the selfish desires of Judas, namely the supremacy of Israel, he consented to betray Him.

The word, *"Betray"* is *"paradidomai"* in the Greek, which means *"to hand over or alongside"* or *"sell Him down the river."* The pronoun *"them,"* referring to the *"Chief Priests,"* is said with some sarcasm by the Holy Spirit. They were supposed to be *"Priests"* of God; however, they were *"Priests"* of man, actually, lackeys of Rome. To this level the Church had fallen!

(11) "AND WHEN THEY HEARD IT, THEY WERE GLAD, AND PROMISED TO GIVE HIM MONEY. AND HE SOUGHT HOW HE MIGHT CONVENIENTLY BETRAY HIM."

The composition is:

NOTES

The word *"conveniently"* refers to the fact that Judas would attempt to carry it out in a manner in which his part and activity would be concealed; however, it was not to be!

MONEY

The phrase, *"And when they heard it, they were glad,"* proclaims these evil religious leaders more delighted than they cared to show. Swete remarks: *"The burden of finding a way to do away with Jesus so that the Passover crowds would not see, now was definitely on the shoulders of Judas. His position in the inner circle of Disciples gave him an advantage which the Chief Priests did not have."*

The phrase, *"And they promised to give him money,"* proclaims the amount given by Matthew as *"30 pieces of silver"* (Mat. 26:15). Some 500 years earlier, the Prophet Zechariah had prophesied the exact amount (Zech. 11:12). Some commentators think that this was only an installment of what they promised him if he completed his treasonable design.

THE FOUL DEED

The phrase, *"And he* (Judas) *sought how he might conveniently betray Him* (Christ),*"* proclaims the devilish deed about to be carried out. He betrayed Him at night, when He was alone with His Disciples in the Garden of Gethsemane. As a result, a night of eternal darkness would settle over Judas' soul, which is there today, and will, in fact, ever be there. For Judas is now in Hell!

The word *"conveniently"* is interesting! Judas would betray Him, but he would attempt to carry it out in a manner in which his part and activity would be concealed. It was, however, not to be! It would be observed by all the Disciples, plus all the Temple Guards, and would be written in all four Gospels. Judas' perfidious act would not be covered, but rather would be known to all, and for all time!

(12) "AND THE FIRST DAY OF UNLEAVENED BREAD, WHEN THEY KILLED THE PASSOVER, HIS DISCIPLES SAID UNTO HIM, WHERE WILL YOU THAT WE GO AND PREPARE THAT YOU MAY EAT THE PASSOVER?"

The overview is:

A place had to be prepared, and so it was!

THE PASSOVER

The phrase, *"And the first day of Unleavened Bread, when they killed the Passover,"* presents the fact that the first day of the week of Unleavened Bread actually began on the Day of the Passover, at least as far the Jews were concerned. Actually, it began the day after, but the Jews began to observe it on the Day of Passover.

The question, *"His Disciples said unto Him, Where will You that we go and prepare that You may eat the Passover?"* concerns, in effect, the greatest Passover of all! The Sacrifice had to be eaten in Jerusalem; therefore, the question was in what *"house"* it was to be prepared.

For it to be prepared, a lamb would have to be killed, and prepared in a certain way, with every family eating the Passover in their respective houses, or wherever they happened to be. Of course, tens, if not hundreds, of thousands of Jews had come in from all over Judaea, but, more specifically, from all over the Roman world to *"keep the Passover."*

While this Celebration was meant to portray their deliverance from Egypt approximately 1,500 years earlier, still, and more importantly, it prefigured Christ, Who would be the actual Passover, with the Lamb typifying His Death on Calvary's Cross, in order that man might be redeemed.

(Some claim that the first day of Unleavened Bread was the evening of Thursday, actually the beginning of the Jewish Friday; however, the evidence points to that being incorrect. It actually was on a Wednesday, with the next day, a Thursday, actually being a *"high day,"* which was a special Sabbath, not the Saturday Sabbath, as many have been led to believe (Lev. 23:6-7; Jn. 19:30-31). Jesus would be in the tomb three full days and nights, which means that He was in the tomb Thursday, Friday, and Saturday; He was raised from the dead some time after sunset Saturday evening.

The Jewish reckoning of time was not like ours presently. Our days end at midnight, with the new day beginning at 12:01 a.m. The Jewish time, at least as it was then reckoned, actually had the new day beginning at sunset. In other words, at approximately 6 p.m., or at least when the sun went down, the next day began. For instance, if it was Tuesday, whenever the sun did set that Tuesday evening, it then became Wednesday, etc. [Mat. 12:40].)

(13) "AND HE SENT FORTH TWO OF HIS DISCIPLES, AND SAID UNTO THEM, GO YE INTO THE CITY, AND THERE SHALL MEET YOU A MAN BEARING A PITCHER OF WATER: FOLLOW HIM."

The exegesis is:

In a spiritual sense, this man they were to follow was a Type of the Holy Spirit.

THE SENDING OF TWO

The phrase, *"And He sent forth two of His Disciples,"* refers to Peter and John (Lk. 22:8). The phrase, *"And said unto them, Go ye into the city,"* proclaims the identical way in which the Lord continues to deal with His people. Although He is not here physically, still, through the Agency and Person of the Holy Spirit, Christ is here now in an even greater way than when He was here physically.

THE HOLY SPIRIT

The Holy Spirit does *"not speak of Himself,"* but instead Christ. Jesus said of Him, *"He shall glorify Me: for He shall receive of Mine, and shall show it unto you"* (Jn. 16:13-14).

Some time ago, while speaking with a noted Preacher of one of the major religious Denominations in America, he made mention to me that this organization, which claims to be fundamental in their beliefs (believe all the Bible), does not believe that God speaks to people in this day and time. To be sure, I was somewhat nonplussed when he said this to me.

I asked him, *"How do they carry on their work?"*

His answer was revealing, and yet typical of most of that which today refers to itself as *"Christian."*

"Men direct it," he said, *"making decisions as they think best."*

In other words, there is no leading of the Holy Spirit whatsoever! What is done, and in every capacity, is consequently man-originated, man-led, and man-directed. While there may be much religious machinery, there is, under these circumstances, absolutely nothing done for the Lord.

Anything that is truly done for the Lord on this Earth is done by the Unction, Guidance, Power, Leading, and Person of the Holy Spirit (Zech. 4:6). As stated, He shows to the Believer what Jesus wants, Who always carries out the Will of the Heavenly Father. Any Believer who attempts any type of work for the Lord without being led by the Holy Spirit is *"in the flesh"*; he, consequently, *"cannot please God"* (Rom. 8:8).

THE MANNER OF THE HOLY SPIRIT

The leading of the Holy Spirit is not an automatic process. To be led by the Spirit one must be filled with the Spirit and also must have his faith firmly anchored in Christ and the Cross. This is the way, and absolutely the only way, in which the Holy Spirit works.

Paul said, *"For the Law* (a Law generated by the Godhead in eternity past) *of the Spirit* (Holy Spirit) *of Life* (all life flows from Christ by virtue of the Cross, and through the Holy Spirit to the individual in question) *in Christ Jesus* (refers to Christ and what He did for us at the Cross) *has made me free from the Law of Sin and Death.* (In this one Verse is presented to us the two most powerful laws in the universe. The only Law that is greater and more powerful than *'the Law of Sin and Death'* is *'the Law of the Spirit of Life in Christ Jesus')"* (Rom. 8:2).

The Holy Spirit demands that our Faith be anchored firmly in the Cross of Christ. When the Holy Spirit gave to Paul God's Prescribed Order of Victory in the life of the Child of God, i.e., the manner and the way in which we obtain victory and maintain victory, He took us straight to the Cross, as is given to us in Romans 6:3-5.

So, we have two particulars here before us.

First of all, it is absolutely imperative that the Believer be baptized with the Holy Spirit, which will always, without exception, be accompanied by speaking with other tongues, as the Spirit of God gives the utterance (Acts 2:4; 10:45-46; 19:1-7).

Second, the Spirit-filled Believer also must

NOTES

have, as stated, his Faith anchored firmly in Christ and the Cross. Regrettably, there are multiple millions of modern Christians who are genuinely baptized with the Holy Spirit, but who have anchored their faith in something other than Christ and the Cross. As a result, they cannot walk in victory.

While it is true that every person who gets saved (Born-Again) instantly receives the Holy Spirit (without which they cannot be saved), that is different than being baptized with the Spirit. There is a world of difference in being *"born of the Spirit,"* which always takes place at conversion, than being *"baptized with the Spirit,"* which is given to us for power (Acts 1:8; 2:4). To which we have already alluded, it is virtually impossible for the Believer to properly yield to the Spirit, to look to the Spirit, and to depend on the Spirit, even as we all must, without being baptized with the Holy Spirit. And being baptized with the Holy Spirit will always be, as we have also already stated, accompanied by the speaking with other tongues.

By these statements, we are not implying that one is more saved when one is baptized with the Holy Spirit. In fact, it is not possible to be more saved than one's initial conversion, which is always by Faith, even as being baptized with the Holy Spirit is by Faith (Eph. 2:8-9). As stated, the Baptism with the Spirit is for power, which also generates leading and guidance, etc.

PENTECOSTAL?

The last two or three years I was associated with a major Pentecostal Denomination, I began to notice things which sounded strange to my ears. I would mention the Anointing of the Holy Spirit, and some of the Preachers in that particular Denomination would ridicule my statement, saying, in effect, *"What is that?"*

Their questions and sarcasm confused me at first, because I could not imagine anyone calling himself *"Pentecostal"* and not knowing that of which I spoke! However, they did not know! Actually, these particular Preachers were no more led by the Spirit of God than their counterparts in the Denomination of which I originally spoke, who did not even believe in the leading of the Spirit.

(The Denomination of which I spoke concerning the leading of the Spirit was the Baptist Denomination. The Pentecostal Denomination was the Assemblies of God. Of course, there certainly are some few Preachers in the Baptist Denomination who believe in the leading of the Spirit, or rather that the Lord speaks to people in this day and age, as there are some few Preachers in the Assemblies of God who know what the anointing is. But still, the greater thrust of these two Denominations, sadly and regrettably, is not toward the Spirit, but away from the Spirit.)

Furthermore, when it comes to the Lord speaking to people, that which He says will always be exactly according to the Word of God. It will never add to the Word nor take from the Word, but will always be anchored centrally in the Word. To be sure, if someone claims the Lord has given them something, and it's not according to the Word, that's a sure sign that it isn't from God, but rather from an angel of light (II Cor. 11:13-15).

That's the reason that we emphatically state that the *"Word of Faith Doctrine,"* the *"Purpose Driven Life Doctrine,"* and the *"Government of Twelve Doctrine,"* are not from the Lord. These doctrines do not match up with the Word of God, so they must be dismissed out of hand as being a product of *"angels of light."*

RESIDENCE OF THE HOLY SPIRIT

There is a Verse in James that may help explain this all-important subject a little better. James said, *"Do you think that the Scripture says in vain, The Spirit Who dwells in us lusts to envy?"* (James 4:5).

The Greek Scholars say that the verb *"dwell"* is not from the Greek word which means *"to take up one's residence,"* but from a closely allied verb meaning *"to cause to take up residence, to send or bring to an abode."* In other words, the Holy Spirit does not, of Himself, take up His Residence in the heart of the Believer. He is caused to do so by God the Father.

In the outworking of the Plan of Salvation, there is a subordination among the members of the Godhead. Here the Holy Spirit, very God Himself, the Third Person of the Triune God, is sent by God the Father and caused to take up His Residence in our hearts and lives.

But that is not all. The simple verb means, as we have stated, *"to cause to take up residence."* The idea is one of permanency. Thus, the Holy Spirit has been caused to take up His permanent Residence in our hearts. This agrees with I John 2:27, where the word translated *"abide"* means *"to abide,"* in the sense of *"to remain."* Thus, the Holy Spirit never leaves the Believer, that is, not on His Own! He will only leave if the Believer no longer trusts Christ, because trusting Christ and what He has done for us at the Cross is the requirement. When that requirement is abandoned, the Holy Spirit cannot remain (Heb. 6:4-6; 10:26-31).

Concerning this statement by James, the words, *"lusts to envy,"* have been confusing to many. The word *"lusts"* is the translation of the Greek word which means *"to earnestly or passionately desire."* The meaning, consequently, is that the indwelling Holy Spirit within our lives, possessing all the potential power and help a Saint needs, has a passionate desire to the point of envy.

Of what is He envious, and what does He passionately desire?

The context makes this clear.

James is speaking of Christians who are not separated unto God, but, in reality, are playing false with their Lord and fellowshipping with the world. They are allowing their evil natures to control them, those evil natures from which they had been delivered when God saved them. The Holy Spirit is envious of any control which that fallen nature might have over the Believer. He is passionately desirous that He Himself control the thoughts, words, and deeds of the Believer. He is desirous of having the Believer depend upon Him for His Ministry to him, in order that He might discharge His responsibility to the One Who sent Him, namely the Heavenly Father, which is to cause the Believer to grow in his Christian Life.

GIVING THE HOLY SPIRIT LIBERTY

The help given to the Believer by the Holy Spirit, which Jesus would make possible (Jn. 16:7-15), forms the basis of all His Ministry to and on behalf of the Believer. Let us remember, however, that this *"help"* is *"potential"* in its nature. In other words, the mere indwelling of the Spirit, as important as that may be within itself, does not guarantee the full Efficacy of His Work in us, since that indwelling is not automatic in its nature.

God's ideal for the indwelling of the Spirit is found in the word translated *"cause to take up His residence."* Its root is in the word *"home."* In other words, the Holy Spirit has been sent by the Father to the Believer's heart to make His home there. This means that the Christian must make Him feel at home. He can do that by giving the Holy Spirit absolute liberty of action in his heart, the home in which he lives. This means that the Believer is to yield himself, all of himself, to the Spirit's control, depending upon the Spirit for guidance, teaching, and strength.

And how, exactly, is this done?

The vehicle through which this *"yielding"* is done is strictly by Faith, and Faith alone (Rom. 5:1; Eph. 2:8-9; I Cor. 2:5).

And what do we mean by that?

FAITH

When we speak of *"Faith,"* we are speaking of the Believer having Faith in Christ and what Christ has done for us at the Cross. The Believer must always look to Jesus, and Jesus Alone. The business of the Holy Spirit is, in fact, to glorify Jesus (Jn. 16:14-15). In this Passage from the Gospel of John, we are told that the Holy Spirit glorifies Christ. He glorifies Christ, because it is Christ Who died on the Cross, paying the price in order that the lost sons of Adam's fallen race might be redeemed.

Furthermore, as that Passage also states, the Holy Spirit takes that for which Christ has paid such a price and gives it to the Believer. In other words, while Christ is the Source and the Cross is the Means, it is the Holy Spirit Who Alone can make possible to us that which Christ has done. It only requires that we exhibit Faith in Christ and the Cross at all times (Rom. 6:3-14).

Someone has well said, *"Romans, Chapter 6, presents the mechanics of the Holy Spirit, in other words, 'how' things are done, and Romans, Chapter 8, presents the dynamics of the Spirit, in other words, 'what' He does for us, after we understand 'how' He does it."* He does it all through the Cross (Rom. 8:1-2,11).

Only when this is done, i.e., the Believer ever evidencing Faith in Christ and the Cross, will the potential power resident in the presence of the Spirit in the heart of the Believer be operative in one's life.

FELLOWSHIP OF THE SPIRIT

Some think that *"fellowship of the Spirit"* means *"companionship with the Spirit."* To think such leaves the path of sound doctrine and practice. Such individuals seek the Holy Spirit and His fullness for His sake alone. They seek intercourse with Him as an end in itself. Thus, they lay themselves open to the snares of Satan, even to be controlled by evil spirits, etc.

There is no such thing in Scripture as the Believer's fellowship or companionship with the Spirit comparable to the Believer's fellowship and companionship with the Lord Jesus. The Ministry of the Holy Spirit, as stated, is to glorify the Son; in doing that, He always calls the Believer's attention to the Lord Jesus, never to Himself. He keeps Himself always in the background. The Lord Jesus must always be central in the life of the Saint. He is the One with Whom we have fellowship in the commonly accepted usage of the word today. The Holy Spirit makes all of this possible (Jn. 16:13-14).

One might say, *"In proportion, therefore, as mind and heart are fixed on Christ and what He has done for us at the Cross, we may count on the Spirit's Presence and Power, but if we make the Holy Spirit Himself the object of our aspirations and worship, some false spirit may counterfeit the true and take us for a prey."*

The association which the correctly instructed Saint has with the Holy Spirit is in the form of a moment-by-moment conscious trust and dependence upon Him for His Guidance and Strength, and a yielding to Him for His Ministry of putting sin out of the life, keeping it out, and radiating the beauty of the Lord Jesus through our every thought, word, and deed. This, together with a cooperation with Him and a constant Faith in

Christ and the Cross, if carried out in this manner, takes the form of mutual interest and active participation in the things of God.

G. D. Watson said this: *"The Holy Spirit will put a strict watch over you with a jealous love, will rebuke you for little words and feelings, or for wasting your time, which other Christians never seem distressed over. So make up your mind that God is an infinite Sovereign, and has a right to do as He pleases with His Own.*

"He may not explain to you a thousand things which puzzle your reason in His dealings with you, but if you absolutely sell yourself to be His loveslave, He will wrap you up in a jealous love, and bestow upon you many blessings which come only to those who are in the inner circle.

"Settle it forever, then, that you are to deal directly with the Holy Spirit, and that He is to have the privilege of tying your tongue or chaining your hand or closing your eyes, in ways that He does not seem to use with others. Now when you are so possessed with the Living God that you are, in your secret heart, pleased and delighted over this peculiar, personal, private, jealous guardianship and management of the Holy Spirit over your life, you will have found the vestibule of Heaven."

And let us say in again, commenting on what was said by our dear Brother: One can have such leading and guidance by the Holy Spirit only as one understands that it is all made possible by Christ and what Christ has done for us at the Cross. As I hope by now the Reader understands, Christ cannot be separated from the Cross and the Cross cannot be separated from Christ.

That's why Paul said, *"We preach Christ Crucified"* (I Cor. 1:23). That's why Paul also said, *"I determined to know nothing among you, save Jesus Christ and Him Crucified"* (I Cor. 2:2).

1. Christ is the only way to the Father (Jn. 14:6).

2. The Cross is the only way to Christ, meaning that He cannot be found by any other method (Lk. 9:23).

3. The only way to the Cross is by and through self-abnegation (Lk. 9:23-24).

4. The only way to self-abnegation is by Faith in Christ and the Cross, which then gives the Holy Spirit latitude to work within our lives (Rom. 8:1-2, 11).

CONTROL BY THE SPIRIT

The Believer is exhorted to *"Be filled with the Spirit"* (Eph. 5:18), or, as we have translated it, *"Be controlled by the Spirit."* Thus, the expression, *"Filled with the Holy Spirit,"* speaks of the Spirit possessing the mind and heart of the Believer. This possession implies His control over that mind and heart. Thus, the words, *"full"* and *"filled,"* refer to the control which the Spirit exerts over the Believer, who is said to be filled with Him. Thus, the *"Spirit"* exerts the control.

We must not think of the Holy Spirit filling our hearts as water fills a bottle, or air a vacuum, or a bushel of oats an empty basket, etc. The heart of a Christian is not a receptacle to be emptied in order that the Holy Spirit may fill it. The Holy Spirit is not a substance to fill an empty receptacle. He is a Person to control another person, the Believer. He does not fill a Christian's life with Himself. He controls that person, or rather He desires to do so!

The heart is a symbol used to refer to the passions. Thus, the Holy Spirit possesses, or controls, the volitional, rational, and emotional activities of the Believer, who is said to be filled with Him. He brings all these into the place of obedience and conformity to the Word of God. Therefore, when we speak of a Christian filled with the Spirit, we are referring to the control which a Divine Person, the Holy Spirit, has over a human being, the Believer.

It is the business of the Holy Spirit, among other things, to maintain the actual experience of the Christian, which God did for him the moment He saved him. The Holy Spirit suppresses the activities of the evil nature whose power was broken at the Cross, and produces His Fruit in the life. The very fact that an individual is exhorted by the Spirit to do something, demands, as a logical accompaniment, that person's exercise of his will in the doing of that thing. That is, the Believer here is not automatically controlled by the Spirit just because the Spirit indwells him.

The control which the Spirit exercises over

the Believer is dependent upon the Believer's active and correct adjustment to the Spirit. More than all, such control is dependent upon the Believer's Faith ever being registered in Christ and the Cross. We must always understand that the Holy Spirit will never take control; He must freely and willingly be given control.

THE WILL OF THE BELIEVER

As an example, the Lord Jesus did not save us until we recognized Him as the Saviour, thereby putting our trust in Him for Salvation. We had to *"will"* that to happen (Jn. 3:16; Rev. 22:17). Just so, the Holy Spirit does not control us in the sense of permeating our will, reason, and emotions until we recognize Him as the One Who has been sent by the Father to sanctify our lives and trust Him to perform His Ministry in and through us.

There must be an ever-present conscious dependence upon and definite subjection to the Holy Spirit, a constant yielding to His Ministry and leaning upon Him for guidance and power, that is if He is to control the Believer in the most efficient manner and with the largest and best results. The Lord Jesus waited for you and me to recognize Him as Saviour before He saved us. The Holy Spirit indwelling a Believer also is waiting to be recognized as the One to come to that Believer's aid.

Salvation is by Faith from start to finish. We speak of Faith in Christ and what He did for us at the Cross. It is a Work of God for man. But God waits for man, unsaved or saved, as the case may be, to avail himself of the Salvation he needs by means of faith. One of the reasons why the Holy Spirit has so little control over many Christians is because they think He works automatically in their hearts.

TWO REQUIREMENTS

In John 7:37-38, our Lord lays down two simple requirements for the fullness of the Spirit: a thirst for His control; and, a trust in the Lord Jesus for the Spirit to take control. As we have stated, there are millions of Pentecostals, who have been baptized with the Holy Spirit, with the evidence of speaking with other tongues (Acts 2:4), but who, because their faith is misplaced, actually receive very little help from the Spirit, which we will address again in the following paragraphs.

As it regards the Believer, there is nothing more important than the Truth we are about to give you. I ask, therefore, that you would be open to the Word of God, even asking the Lord to reveal to you the Truth of what we say.

FIRST

The first requirement for perpetual control by the Holy Spirit is, as stated, that you thirst after Him. Jesus said, *"If any man thirst, let him come unto Me and drink."* This refers to a desire on the part of the Believer that the Holy Spirit be the One Who controls his every thought, word, deed. We do not take a drink of water unless we are thirsty. We do not appropriate the control of the Spirit unless we desire Him to control us.

A desire for His control will include, among other things, a desire that He call us to judge sin in our lives, a desire that He put sin out of our lives and keep it out, a desire that He separate us from all the ties we might have with the system of evil called the world, a desire that He dethrone our self-life and enthrone the Lord Jesus as absolute Lord and Master, a desire that He produce in us His Own Fruit, a desire that He make us Christlike, a desire that He lead us and teach us.

Such a desire is a serious thing. It involves crucifixion of self, and self dies hard. The Spirit-controlled life is a crucified life. And yet, desire on our part, as necessary as it is (Rev. 22:17), even as absolutely necessary as it is, is, within itself, not enough. We must always remember that with everything the Lord requires of us, which speaks of something we must do, Faith, at the same time, is required.

And what does that mean?

As important as having faith and exhibiting same, the object of our faith must be correct or else our efforts will be in vain. And that is the problem with most Christians presently. The Object of Faith must ever be the Cross of Christ, through which the Spirit works, and works exclusively. Most Christians, however, have made other things the object of their faith.

WHAT DOES IT MEAN TO MAKE THE CROSS OF CHRIST THE OBJECT OF ONE'S FAITH?

Within itself, the making of the Cross the Object of one's Faith is a very simple thing. It is so simple, in fact, that a child can easily carry out such. But the problem is that Satan has been very successful in pushing other things into our path which demand our faith, or else we are told they demand our faith, and, because it seems so religious and right, those things, whatever they might be, are made the object of our faith.

While I could name specific things, I will merely say that irrespective as to what it is, or how right it may seem to be on the surface, if it's not the Cross of Christ, then it's wrong. And remember this: one cannot have one's Faith in the Cross of Christ and something else at the same time. That produces a double-minded man, of whom James said, *"Let not that man think that he shall receive anything of the Lord"* (James 1:7-8).

That means that the Word of Faith Doctrine must go, simply because it's not anchored at all in the Christ and the Cross. That means the G-12 Doctrine must go, that means the Purpose Driven Life Doctrine must go, that means all Denominationalism must go, or anything of this nature. All of these things constitute Satan attempting to push our Faith from Christ and the Cross to other things.

All of these things which we have mentioned, plus scores we haven't mentioned, constitute faith in one's self. As we've already stated, control by the Spirit involves crucifixion of self, and self dies hard.

Paul addressed this, and I continue to speak of the incorrect object of faith, by saying, *"Christ sent me not to baptize, but to preach the Gospel: not with wisdom of words* (intellectualism is not the Gospel), *lest the Cross of Christ should be made of none effect.* (This tells us in no uncertain terms that the Cross of Christ must always be the emphasis of the Message)" (I Cor. 1:17).

So, the *"satisfied thirst"* of which we have mentioned can only be brought to a successful conclusion by our faith being properly placed.

TRUST

The other requirement is trust. Our Lord said, *"He who believes on Me* (it is not *'doing'* but rather *'believing'*) *as the Scripture has said* (refers to the Word of God being the story of Christ and Him Crucified; all the Sacrifices pointed to Christ and what He would do at the Cross, as well as the entirety of the Tabernacle and Temple and all their appointments), *out of his innermost being shall flow rivers of Living Water* (speaks of Christ directly, and Believers indirectly)" (Jn. 7:38).

The trust here in this context is not only trust in Christ as Saviour, but trust in Him as the One Who fills with the Spirit. The Spirit-controlled life is a matter of trust. Salvation is by Faith. We receive our Justification by Faith (Rom. 5:1). We also are to receive our Sanctification by Faith. It is this constant *"desire"* for the Spirit's control and a *"trust"* in the Lord Jesus for the Spirit's control that result in the Spirit-controlled life, providing one's faith is properly placed, as we've already stated.

When one faces a new day, it is well to include in our prayers thanksgiving for the Presence of the Holy Spirit in our hearts, the expression of our desire for His control, and a definite assertion of our trust in the Lord Jesus and what He did for us at the Cross, all for the Spirit's constant control during each particular day. When we are faced with temptation, our faith is to be exclusively in Christ and the Cross, which will then give us the help of the Holy Spirit, with Whose help we can find total victory, and without Whose help there can be no victory. That help is forthcoming by our constant attention to our Faith and where it is placed.

That is why Jesus said, *"If any man will come after Me* (the criteria for Discipleship), *let him deny himself* (not asceticism, as many think, but rather than one denies one's own willpower, self-will, strength, and ability, depending totally on Christ), *and take up his cross* (the benefits of the Cross, looking exclusively to what Jesus did there to meet our every need) *daily* (this is so important, our looking to the Cross, that we must renew our Faith in what Christ has done for us, even on a daily basis, for Satan will ever try to move us away from the Cross as the object of our Faith, which always spells disaster), *and follow Me* (Christ can be followed only by the Believer looking to the Cross, understanding what it accomplished, and by that means alone [Rom. 6:3-5; 11, 14; 8:1-2, 11; I Cor. 1:17-18, 21, 23; 2:2; Gal. 6:14; Eph. 2:13-18; Col. 2:14-15])" (Mk. 8:34; Lk. 9:23).

The Holy Spirit always comes to our aid when we avail ourselves of His help, which means that we do it in the right way; therefore, in the *"desire"* and the *"trust,"* faith must ever be properly placed, which will then guarantee the leading, guidance, help, and aid of the Holy Spirit, without which we simply cannot live for God.

Now let me say that again, because it's so very, very important:

THE BELIEVER CANNOT LIVE FOR GOD WITHOUT THE HELP OF THE HOLY SPIRIT

It's just that simple! But the problem is that virtually the entirety of the modern Church world attempts to just that — live for God without the aid, the means, the power, and the help of the Holy Spirit.

Let us state it again: It simply cannot be done!

That's the reason that we come down so hard on these modern fads, such as the *"Purpose Driven Life,"* *"G-12,"* etc. These particular doctrines attempt to replace the Holy Spirit with man's aid, which guarantees defeat.

Of course, they would deny that, but it is true.

And how do I know it's true?

I know it's true because the very ingredient that one must have for the Holy Spirit to work within our lives, which is our Faith in the Cross of Christ, these particular fads do not stress at all. In fact, the *"Word of Faith Doctrine"* repudiates the Cross, actually referring to it, as previously stated, as *"the greatest defeat in human history."*

Anything that doesn't stress the Cross, and I mean stress it totally, completely, and absolutely, must be rejected out of hand.

THE MAN WITH THE PITCHER OF WATER

The phrase, *"And there shall meet you a man bearing a pitcher of water,"* was not as difficult as it might at first seem. Inasmuch as Jerusalem was thronged with people during the Passover time, it would seem that such a task might be impossible; however, the carrying of water was usually a woman's work, and was seldom done by men. Hence, a man carrying out this activity would be very noticeable.

The words, *"Shall meet you,"* express a design by the Holy Spirit. In other words, the Holy Spirit told Jesus exactly what to do and what to tell the Disciples to look for. There seemed to be no further directions than *"Go ye into the city."* Consequently, the Holy Spirit would bring about the meeting, which He did.

This example beautifully portrays the manner in which the Holy Spirit works. He very seldom gives total information, only part. We are expected to trust and believe that He will provide the balance as we proceed.

As another example, the Lord told Samuel to go the house of Jesse in order to anoint one of his sons as King; however, He did not tell him which son; Jesse, in fact, had seven. Samuel was to trust the Lord for that information after he arrived, which he did, and which ultimately was given (I Sam. 16:1, 6-13).

Such teaches trust and dependence.

FOLLOW HIM

The words, *"Follow him,"* present another beautiful symbolism. The entirety of this episode can serve as a beautiful example of that which Jesus does for the Believer. It is as follows:

1. The Passover speaks of Salvation, and the sinner's acceptance of Christ as Saviour.

2. Immediately upon finding Christ, the Lord *"sends"* the Believer to *"meet the Man bearing a pitcher of water,"* Who here is a symbol of the Holy Spirit.

The last Words Jesus gave to His Disciples before His Ascension were, *"Wait for the Promise of the Father...."*

"You shall be baptized with the Holy Spirit" (Acts 1:4-5).

In other words, these followers were not to go build Churches, witness, or do anything for the Lord until they were first Baptized with the Holy Spirit. That Command continues to be apropos unto this moment.

3. *"Follow him"*: Once the Believer is Baptized with the Holy Spirit (Acts 2:4), the Spirit will then *"guide you into all Truth"* (Jn. 16:13). His business will be to *"glorify Me,"* i.e., Jesus.

4. *"He will show you a large upper room furnished"*: This *"upper room,"* spiritually speaking, to which the Holy Spirit will lead the trusting Believer, is thoroughly furnished with everything the Believer needs pertaining to *"Life and Godliness"* (II Pet. 1:3-4).

5. *"And prepared"*: This means that the furnishings are prepared by the Spirit, and not by man. This one word, *"prepared,"* is the bane of the modern Church. Instead of allowing the Holy Spirit to prepare, religious man attempts to prepare of his own abilities, which God cannot accept. Let Him *"prepare"* for us and the preparation will be perfect.

6. *"And they sat and did eat"*: This speaks of fellowship, not only with other Disciples, but, above all, with Jesus. Although service for Him is definitely important, still, fellowship with Him is the most important. Without that fellowship, there can be no proper service. And, to be sure, it is the Holy Spirit Alone Who can provide all of this; He has, in effect, already provided it all. It remains only for us to be properly led by the Spirit.

(14) "AND WHERESOEVER HE SHALL GO IN, SAY YE TO THE GOODMAN OF THE HOUSE, THE MASTER SAYS, WHERE IS THE GUESTCHAMBER, WHERE I SHALL EAT THE PASSOVER WITH MY DISCIPLES?"

The composition is:

This house is believed to have been owned by John Mark, or his family, in fact, the one who wrote this Gospel.

THE GUESTCHAMBER

The phrase, *"And wheresoever he shall go in,"* refers to the man bearing the pitcher of water, whom they were to follow, and where they would eat the Passover. As stated, only the Holy Spirit could have orchestrated all of this. Considering how large this room must have been to accommodate Jesus and all the Disciples, John Mark must have been a man of some substance, if, in fact, this was his house.

The phrase, *"Say ye to the goodman of the house,"* referred to the owner, who, as stated, could have been John Mark. The question, *"The Master says, Where is the guestchamber, where I shall eat the Passover with My Disciples?"* actually says, *"My guestchamber."* The indication is that there seems to have been some type of previous understanding between the Lord and the owner of this house, who, undoubtedly, was a follower of Christ.

What an honor for the owner to have had Jesus and His Disciples partake of the Last Supper in his house!

(15) "AND HE WILL SHOW YOU A LARGE UPPER ROOM FURNISHED AND PREPARED: THERE MAKE READY FOR US."

The overview is:

This Passage has to do with the preparation of the Passover ingredients.

PREPARATION

The phrase, *"And he will show you a large upper room furnished and prepared,"* means that he himself (maybe Mark) personally conducted Peter and John to the room. The room being *"furnished"* means that it was in a state of readiness. It was furnished with carpets and hall couches around the table properly spread. The room was prepared for the eating of the Passover, speaking of the removal of all leaven, also possibly of the Master of the house sharing his Passover Lamb with our Lord and His Disciples, as the custom was in Israel in the case of small families.

The phrase, *"There make ready for us,"* has to do with the preparation of the Passover ingredients, as the room itself was already prepared.

(16) "AND HIS DISCIPLES WENT FORTH, AND CAME INTO THE CITY, AND FOUND AS HE HAD SAID UNTO THEM: AND THEY MADE READY THE PASSOVER."

The exposition is:

This meant that Peter and John took the

Pascal Lamb to the Temple, where it was there killed, with the Priests officiating, and the blood poured out at the base of the Brazen Altar; the carcass of the lamb would have been brought back to this house, where it would have been roasted and prepared by the Disciples.

MAKING READY THE PASSOVER

The phrase, *"And His Disciples went forth and came into the city,"* refers to Peter and John obeying the Lord implicitly. The phrase, *"And found as He had said unto them,"* is a beautiful expression! Of all the countless things He has said to His many followers, everything has always been exactly as He said it would be.

The phrase, *"And they made ready the Passover,"* meant that Peter and John took the Passover Lamb to the Temple, where it was there killed. They would have then brought the lamb to the house, and then prepared the Unleavened Bread, the bitter herbs, the wine, and water for purification.

Exactly what Peter and John personally did in this case is not stated; however, they either prepared the Passover themselves or saw to it that it was done. Our Lord partook of the Passover a day early, inasmuch as He would be offered up as a Sacrifice on the actual day it was to be eaten, which was the next day (Jn. 13:1).

(17) "AND IN THE EVENING HE COMES WITH THE TWELVE."

The synopsis is:

He would be arrested that night, after He had eaten the Passover.

THE TWELVE

The *"evening"* mentioned here referred to the same day. Because of Him being arrested that night, and being unable to eat the Passover the next day when it was supposed to be observed, they would, as stated, eat it a day early. The phrase, *"He comes with the Twelve,"* means that Peter and John evidently went back to Bethany in order to inform Christ that all was ready. Then Jesus and the entirety of the Twelve, which included Judas, would come for the purpose of eating the Passover, i.e., *"The Last Supper."*

(18) "AND AS THEY SAT AND DID EAT, JESUS SAID, VERILY I SAY UNTO YOU, ONE OF YOU WHICH EATS WITH ME SHALL BETRAY ME."

The synopsis is:

The words, *"Eats with Me,"* are not merely to point to the individual who would betray Christ, but to the enormity of the offense.

THE BETRAYAL

The phrase, *"And as they sat and did eat,"* refers, as is obvious, to the partaking of the Passover. Of all the approximate 1,500 years in which the Passover had been observed, this was the most important of all. As stated, Jesus would literally become the Passover, Whom this solemn and beautiful Feast was meant to portray.

On the first Passover in Egypt, they were to eat standing, because they had not yet been delivered; now in the Promised Land, their inheritance, they were to eat *"sitting,"* signifying that the work had been done. It is a *"type"* of the *"rest"* that one has in Christ, which is obtained by constantly making Christ and the Cross the Object of one's Faith.

The phrase, *"Jesus said, Verily I say unto you, one of you which eats with Me shall betray Me,"* narrows down the prediction to the point where the traitor is said to be one of the Disciples. The words, *"Eats with Me,"* are not meant merely to point to the individual who would betray Christ, but, as stated, to point to the enormity of the offense.

Partaking of food together, at least in those times, was of far greater consequence than presently. Then, and especially in the type of setting as the Last Supper, such fellowship denoted deep friendship. Actually, this very moment had been prophesied by David approximately 1,000 years earlier:

"Yea, My Own familiar friend, in whom I trusted, which did eat of My bread, has lifted up his heel against Me" (Ps. 41:9). Actually, Jesus would quote this very Verse in John 13:18. It was at this time that Satan entered into Judas and impelled him onwards to this terrible sin. It was considered an act of utmost severity among eastern nations of those days for one to do an evil deed against those who had given of such hospitality and friendship as Jesus.

(19) "AND THEY BEGAN TO BE SORROWFUL, AND TO SAY UNTO HIM ONE BY ONE, IS IT I? AND ANOTHER SAID, IS IT I?"

The structure is:

None had any idea that it was Judas. The evil that was in his heart had been concealed from all except Christ.

THE QUESTION

The phrase, *"And they began to be sorrowful,"* speaks of the opposite of that which this occasion, the Passover, should have enjoyed. It was normally a festive time, especially considering that it was to commemorate the great deliverance of the Children of Israel from Egyptian bondage. However, the Words of Christ cast a pall over the entire proceedings.

The phrase, *"And to say unto Him one by one,"* speaks of each understanding the significance of the accusation. It was a moment of heart-searching for each.

The question, *"Is it I? and another said, Is it I?"* would have probably been better translated, *"It is not me, is it?"* from each of them!

(20) "AND HE ANSWERED AND SAID UNTO THEM, IT IS ONE OF THE TWELVE, WHO DIPS WITH ME IN THE DISH."

The exegesis is:

All were dipping with Him in the dish, so that statement really did not tell them very much.

ONE OF THE TWELVE

The phrase, *"And He answered and said unto them,"* now presents a scenario of tremendous proportions. As we shall see, the Lord made every effort to appeal to Judas not do this thing, but to no avail!

The phrase, *"It is one of the Twelve, who dips with Me in the dish,"* little answered the question, because all, as stated, were partaking. The *"dish"* referred to a sauce made of dates, raisins, and vinegar, into which each dipped pieces of the unleavened bread with bitter herbs. To which we have alluded, this further statement is meant to point to the seriousness of the act which Judas was even then contemplating.

Even though Mark does not take the situation further, John records that Peter hinted to John, who was *"reclining on Jesus' bosom,"* that John should ask Him to say definitely by name who it was that should betray Him. Our Lord then said to John, *"He it is to whom I shall give a sop, when I have dipped it"* (Jn. 13:23-26). The Lord then dipped the sop and gave it to Judas Iscariot. That is when Jesus said unto Judas, *"That you do, do quickly"* (Jn. 13:27).

It was now that Judas repelled all efforts by Christ for him not to do this dastardly thing, which pushed him over the edge.

(21) "THE SON OF MAN INDEED GOES, AS IT IS WRITTEN OF HIM: BUT WOE TO THAT MAN BY WHOM THE SON OF MAN IS BETRAYED! GOOD WERE IT FOR THAT MAN IF HE HAD NEVER BEEN BORN."

The structure is:

This predestined purpose of God did not make the guilt any the less of those who brought the Saviour to His Cross. The *"Woe"* is not of vindictiveness, or even in the nature of a curse, but rather *"reveals a misery which love itself could not prevent."*

THE SON OF MAN

The phrase, *"The Son of Man indeed goes, as it is written of Him,"* refers to Psalm 22 and Isaiah 51, as well as Genesis 3:15. Actually, the tenor of the entirety of the Old Testament points to Christ giving His Life as a ransom for many, even to which all the Sacrifices pointed. However, this predestined purpose of God did not, as stated, make the guilt any less of those who brought the Saviour to His Cross.

The phrase, *"But woe to that man by whom the Son of Man is betrayed,"* refers to the fact that, because it was predestined, it had to be and, in fact, would be. However, it was only the act itself which was predestined, not the individual who would perform the act. The Lord never violates the free moral agency of any individual. He will deal with people, but He never forces the issue.

So, what Judas did was by his own willful desire!

AN ANNOUNCEMENT OF DOOM

The phrase, *"Good were it for that man if he had never been born,"* is one of the saddest pronouncements of doom in Scripture.

Williams says (and to which we have already alluded), *"Obedient to the Divine purpose, Christ must die as a Sacrifice for sin, but that necessity did not excuse the free agent who brought it about."*

Bickersteth says, *"Existence is no blessing, but a curse, to him who consciously and willfully defeats the purpose of his existence."*

The statement, *"Good were it for that man if he had never been born,"* was said of Judas; but tragically, the same can been said for all of the human family who do not accept Christ as their Saviour.

The scenario of Jesus' pointing out Judas as the one guilty of the betrayal seems to have been done with only Judas fully hearing and understanding, at least at that moment, that it was him. Had the conversation and act been fully heard and understood by others, such as Peter and John, they might have risen at once to inflict vengeance upon the apostate traitor.

THE DOCTRINE OF PREDESTINATION

Many who hold to an erroneous concept of the Doctrine of Predestination mistakenly think that Judas was predestined to do what he did and consequently had no choice. This, however, is incorrect. Judas did what he did of his own free will.

It is true that Satan moved upon him regarding this evil. The Holy Spirit, through the Person of Christ, also moved upon him for the opposite effect. But the choice belonged to Judas alone.

Many Believers misunderstand the foreknowledge of God regarding predestination. God, foreknowing that Judas would do this thing, which he certainly did, in no way means that God forced this action. In other words, Judas was not elected by God to do this thing, as many suggest!

When it comes to *"predestination,"* which is a viable, Biblical Doctrine, it is only the act or the Plan that is predestined, not the one who participates in the Plan. For instance, Paul said, *"For whom He* (God) *did foreknow* (God's foreknowledge), *He also did predestinate to be conformed to the Image of His Son, that He* (Jesus) *might be the Firstborn among many Brethren"* (Rom. 8:29).

NOTES

Predestination has to do with what the individual is to become, which is *"the Image of His Son."* In no way does this insinuate that the individual personally is predestined, only the Plan. Each individual is free to accept or reject God's Call for Salvation; but those who accept are predestinated to be justified and ultimately glorified (Rom. 8:30).

The words, *"elect," "election,"* and *"predestination,"* are basically the same.

Peter said, *"Elect* (those who elect to favorably respond to the Call of the Holy Spirit are the elect of God) *according to the foreknowledge of God the Father* (refers to God seeing ahead that He would have to send a Saviour to redeem man from the Fall; all who accept the Saviour are the *'elect'*), *through Sanctification of the Spirit, unto obedience and sprinkling of the Blood of Jesus Christ . . ."* (I Pet. 1:2).

Those who accept Christ are elected to be sanctified by the Spirit. But who accepts is up to each person's own free moral agency.

The Bible teaches the free moral agency of man. In fact, one of the themes of the Word of God is *"whosoever will"* (Jn. 3:16; Rev. 22:17). But if the person, of his own free will, accepts the Lord as Saviour, several things are predestined to take place within his heart and life.

Again, we state, it is not the person who is elected, or predestinated, but rather the Plan of Action. The idea that humanity is born either to go to Heaven or Hell, and there is nothing they can do about it, i.e., *"the die is cast,"* is not taught anywhere in the Word of God. Such teaching, in fact, is a doctrine of devils. It is *"whosoever will"*!

(22) "AND AS THEY DID EAT, JESUS TOOK BREAD, AND BLESSED, AND BROKE IT, AND GAVE TO THEM, AND SAID, TAKE, EAT: THIS IS MY BODY."

The structure is:

This is typical of what the Lord has to do with us; He takes us, blesses us, and then breaks us. Only then can we be given to others.

THE LORD'S SUPPER

The phrase, *"And as they did eat,"* pertained to the Passover, but out of this was instituted that which we know as *"The Lord's Supper."* Up to this point in the Pascal meal, only unleavened cakes and bitter herbs, along with the sauce, as mentioned, were consumed. The Lamb would be reserved for the end. However, at this Passover, the Lord would use the ingredients of the *"Bread"* and the *"Cup"* to institute *"The Lord's Supper,"* which is sacred to the Church.

The meanings of both, the Passover and the Supper, are similar, but yet totally different. The *"Passover"* represented something which was to come; the *"Supper"* represents something which has already come, namely Christ. The *"Passover"* represented a work not yet finished, while the *"Supper"* represents a work completely finished.

THE ORDER OF EVENTS IN THE CHRISTIAN EXPERIENCE

The phrase, *"Jesus took bread, and blessed, and broke it, and gave to them,"* represents the first step in *"The Lord's Supper,"* and pertains to His Body. Once again, the order is maintained, even as Jesus multiplied the loaves and the fishes, which, in a sense, was a Type of Christ being given to the world (Mk. 6:41; 8:6). The order is as follows:

HE TOOK

This represents His Body, which was offered at Calvary's Cross for the Redemption of humanity. It also represents the Believer, who comes to Christ, who, in effect, is *"taken"* by Christ.

BLESSED

Jesus blesses the bread, which is a Type of Himself being given to humanity. Jesus' offering of Himself for the Salvation of humanity was *"blessed"* by God. Once the sinner comes to Christ, he, likewise, is *"blessed"* by the Lord in many and varied ways.

BROKE IT

For Jesus to be a blessing, His Body must be broken, as it was at Calvary. Likewise, for the Believer to be a blessing, the self-life must be *"broken"* in order that it become Christlike. This is what Jesus was speaking of when He gave the command to *"take up your cross and follow Me"* (Mk. 8:34-35).

NOTES

Many Believers want only the *"blessing"* and not the *"breaking."* However, if we are to be a blessing to others, we, as Christ, must be *"broken."* It is not something that is easily or quickly done. It can, in fact, only be done by the Holy Spirit. And the Holy Spirit works exclusively within the parameters of the Finished Work of Christ, which demands that our Faith ever be in Christ and the Cross.

THE GIFT

The phrase, *"And gave to them,"* refers to Jesus giving the bread to the Disciples. Jesus, before Calvary, could not save anyone except by Faith in that which was to come, namely His Death and Resurrection. Even though the Incarnation was necessary, still, it did not, within itself, save anyone. The same can be said for His Miracles, etc. Unfortunately, much of the modern Church is attempting to give to the world the Miracles of Christ, etc. It is only the Crucified Christ Who will save.

That is the reason Paul said, *"I determined not to know anything among you, save Jesus Christ and Him Crucified"* (I Cor. 2:2).

Even though all the other things are very important, still, we must never forget that it is only the Crucified Christ Who saves! Likewise, far too many Believers are attempting to give themselves to the world instead of giving Christ. It is only Christ within us which can accomplish the desired task.

The phrase, *"And said, Take, eat: this is My Body,"* could be translated, *"This represents My Body."* It is said in the same sense that Jesus also said, *"I am the Door of the sheep"* (Jn. 10:7). He did not mean that He was the literal, actual door or gate of the sheepfold, but that He, as Saviour, constituted the Way whereby a sinner could enter into Salvation. Just as the actual sheep gate pictured, illustrated, and symbolized our Lord in His Position and Work as Saviour, so the bread symbolized Him as the Spiritual Nourishment upon which a sinner may feed and have Eternal Life (Wuest).

Salvation is a gift; hence, the word *"take."*

(For a full commentary on the erroneous conclusion of the Catholic Church regarding the Mass, or what we refer to as *"The Lord's Supper,"* please see the Jimmy Swaggart

Bible Commentary on the Book of Matthew, Chapter 26.)

(23) "AND HE TOOK THE CUP, AND WHEN HE HAD GIVEN THANKS, HE GAVE IT TO THEM: AND THEY ALL DRANK OF IT."

The structure is:

The cup signifies the shedding of the Saviour's Blood at Calvary, and that which it afforded, i.e., Eternal Life, at least to those who will take Christ as Saviour.

THE CUP

The phrase, *"And He took the cup,"* probably represents the third cup; the Talmud says four cups were consumed during the Pascal Feast. The third was known as the *"cup of blessing,"* which adequately described that which the Lord would do for the human family at Calvary's Cross.

The phrase, *"And when He had given thanks, He gave it to them,"* proclaims two extremely important attributes of Christ. They are as follows:

1. He lived a life of perpetual thanksgiving to the Lord, as is epitomized in the last five Psalms. Even though He was facing Calvary with all its darkness, still, He was thanking the Lord that He had the privilege to do this for humanity, even though humanity loved Him not at all. However, His thanksgiving and praise had nothing to do with the attitude of those for whom He was dying; His thanksgiving was centered in the Will of God.

What a lesson for us!

If one is in the Will of God, such is the highest attainment of life. It gives occasion for all Praise and Thanksgiving. Everything else is of small consequence.

2. His Life poured out for humanity, typified by the *"Cup,"* was done for others, hence, (He) *"gave it to them."* Inasmuch as it was freely given, it is to be freely received.

THE EATING OF THE BREAD AND THE DRINKING OF THE CUP

The *"eating of the Bread,"* signifying His Body offered in Sacrifice, and the *"drinking of the Cup,"* signifying His *"Blood,"* which signified His Life being poured out in that Sacrifice, are perfect portrayals of accepting Christ and the fulfillment of John 6:54. Salvation is not a ceremony, creed, dogma, theory, Church, or philosophy. It is rather a Person — more particularly, a Man, *"The Man, Jesus Christ."*

Millions desire to accept Him as a good Man, but not as the Son of God and, consequently, the Saviour; however, unless He is accepted as the Saviour, which refers to Who He is and what He did at the Cross, He cannot be accepted as anything. The Born-Again experience is totally unlike anything else in which man engages. It is a Work of the Spirit, with man furnishing only the small amount of Faith given to him by God, with the Lord doing everything else (Jn. 3:16).

This is what Jesus was speaking of when He said, *"At that day you shall know that I am in My Father, and you in Me, and I in you"* (Jn. 14:20).

Someone has rightly called it *"the Divine Entanglement."*

Furthermore, *"they all drank of it,"* and not just the Priests, as maintained by the Catholic Church.

(24) "AND HE SAID UNTO THEM, THIS IS MY BLOOD OF THE NEW TESTAMENT WHICH IS SHED FOR MANY."

The composition is:

His Blood was shed for the whole world (Jn. 3:16).

THE NEW COVENANT

The phrase, *"And He said unto them, This is My Blood of the New Testament,"* speaks of the Sacrifice of our Lord on the Cross, constituting the *"New Testament,"* i.e., *"New Covenant."* The First Testament was spoken of as the Old Testament, which referred to the system of symbolic Sacrifices known as the Levitical economy (Heb. 8:7).

Just as the Bread was not literally His Body, the grape juice was also not literally His Blood, but rather symbolic of His Blood. As the Lamb, symbolic of Christ, did not turn into the literal Body of Christ under the Old Covenant, likewise, the Bread and Grape Juice do not now turn into the literal Body and Blood of Christ, as claimed by the Catholic Church.

The phrase, *"Which is shed for many,"* refers to the whole world, and for all time, which is *"many."* The Lord's Supper is, in effect, symbolic of the Covenant cut at Calvary. This New Covenant (Testament) was cut between God and man, exactly as the Covenants of old, but with one major difference.

Jesus Christ was both God and Man; this produced a New Covenant, unlike the First Covenant, which cannot fail. He, as God, spilled His Blood, for *"God was in Christ, reconciling the world unto Himself, not imputing their trespasses unto them; and has committed unto us the Word of Reconciliation"* (II Cor. 5:19).

Jesus was the Substitute Man, Who did all the things that God demanded that man do, but which man was never able to do. In Christ, it was all done. He is our Substitute, and, consequently, when we identify with Him, we become everything He is. Paul called it *"joint-heirs with Christ"* (Rom. 8:17).

(25) "VERILY I SAY UNTO YOU, I WILL DRINK NO MORE OF THE FRUIT OF THE VINE, UNTIL THAT DAY THAT I DRINK IT NEW IN THE KINGDOM OF GOD."

The structure is:

Jesus is speaking here of the coming Kingdom Age.

THE KINGDOM AGE

The phrase, *"Verily I say unto you,"* is meant to portray several things:

1. *"I will drink no more of the fruit of the vine"*: After saying, *"This is My Blood,"* He now says, *"It is the fruit of the vine,"* proclaiming that it was not literal blood, and neither does it turn into literal blood, as claimed by the Catholics in the Doctrine of Transubstantiation.

The words, *"no more,"* speak of the one Sacrifice of Christ at Calvary, performing and accomplishing all that was needed for the Salvation of mankind. No repeat performance is needed, and no repeat performance is necessary.

2. *"Until that day"*: This refers to His Second Coming.

3. *"That I drink it new"*: The word *"new"* does not refer to time, but *"new"* as to quality. His drinking it at that time simply refers to His Personal Presence, and not that Calvary is needed all over again.

4. *"In the Kingdom of God"*: This refers

NOTES

to the coming Millennial Kingdom, which will begin at the Second Coming, when the Messiah and His cleansed and restored Israel will drink, in a new and glorious way, the fruit of the mystical Vine (Jn. 15:1) in the worldwide Kingdom, where He will reign as a King upon the Throne of His Father David.

In respect to this coming time, the Holy Spirit through the Apostle Paul said, *"For as often as you eat this bread, and drink this cup, you do show the Lord's Death till He come"* (I Cor. 11:26).

(26) "AND WHEN THEY HAD SUNG AN HYMN, THEY WENT OUT INTO THE MOUNT OF OLIVES."

The composition is:

The Mount of Olives is where He would be betrayed.

THE HYMN

The phrase, *"And when they had sung an hymn,"* refers, no doubt, to Psalm 118.

When we read this Psalm, it gives it an added preciousness to the heart to know that the Lord and His Disciples sang this immediately before setting out for Gethsemane. As the True Israel, He could perfectly sing it, and, as the High Priest of His people, thus express His Faith in her Faith and make real and bring near the joys of the morning, which are predicted to follow the sorrows of that dark night and the affliction of Jacob's long exile.

This Psalm will be sung by Israel on the happy morning of her renewed espousal, as Jesus alluded to in the previous Verse. In Psalm 117, Israel will invite the nations of the world to trust Jehovah and to praise Him. She will testify that the Messiah is her One and Efficient Saviour. In Psalm 118, that Praise is offered (Williams).

THE MOUNT OF OLIVES

The phrase, *"They went out into the Mount of Olives,"* refers to the moment of His betrayal being carried out. His hour had come, so He voluntarily put Himself in the way of the traitor (Jn. 18:2). There is no evidence at all that the Disciples had any idea what awaited them that night. The things Jesus would say, as outlined in the following Verses, and Peter's answer (Vs. 29), portray their spiritual insensitivity.

(27) "AND JESUS SAID UNTO THEM, ALL YOU SHALL BE OFFENDED BECAUSE OF ME THIS NIGHT: FOR IT IS WRITTEN, I WILL SMITE THE SHEPHERD, AND THE SHEEP SHALL BE SCATTERED."

The diagram is:

This referred to His betrayal and subsequent arrest by the Romans; *"offended"* means to *"find occasion of stumbling."*

THE OFFENSE

The phrase, *"And Jesus said unto them,"* is to be an announcement the Disciples do not desire to hear, and actually do not believe. The phrase, *"All you shall be offended because of Me this night,"* refers to His betrayal and what would happen to Him regarding His arrest and ultimate Crucifixion. All of this should not have been a surprise to them, as He had related to them several times that this was coming.

The word *"offended,"* in the Greek, is *"skandalizo,"* which means *"to find occasion of stumbling"* or *"to see in another what is disapproving and what hinders one from acknowledging authority."* The Disciples deserted their Lord and fled. This was their act of stumbling. The occasion for their stumbling was in the fact that our Lord's arrest and treatment by Rome might involve them in the same kind of treatment. In other words, they were out to save themselves (Wuest).

The tone of the announcement of the desertion by the Disciples was not made as a reproach, nor intended as such, but is intended to point to a better moment when their Faith would return.

THE SHEPHERD AND THE SHEEP

The phrase, *"For it is written, I will smite the Shepherd, and the sheep shall be scattered,"* is quoted from Zechariah 13:7. Even though Israel and the Romans were the instruments, still, the Hand was God's. At the same time, this does not mean, as we have already stated, that they were destined to do this, but that God will use their wicked desires to carry out His Plan.

The *"sheep"* being scattered proclaims a weakening of their Faith. They felt doubtful

NOTES

for the moment whether He was indeed the Son of God. *"They trusted that it was He Who should redeem Israel,"* but now saw that such would not be, at least in the manner in which they had thought, with their hopes giving way to fear and doubt.

The word *"scattered"* describes it perfectly, with Peter and John coming to the empty tomb on the testimony of Mary Magdalene, with the other Disciples elsewhere. Moreover, He appeared unto the Ten without Thomas (Jn. 20:19-24). However, they were not to remain *"scattered"* very long.

(28) "BUT AFTER THAT I AM RISEN, I WILL GO BEFORE YOU INTO GALILEE."

The synopsis is:

This would occur after His Resurrection and the two appearances in Jerusalem.

THE RESURRECTION

The phrase, *"But after that I am risen,"* although a startling announcement, fell on deaf ears. His Death was so horrible that not one single Disciple remembered these words, or else they failed to believe them.

The phrase, *"I will go before you into Galilee,"* was fulfilled as recorded in John 21:1. However, there were first two other appearances in Jerusalem, the first being to the Ten, which was without Thomas, and the second appearance being to the Eleven, which, of course, included Thomas (Jn. 20:19-24, 26).

(29) "BUT PETER SAID UNTO HIM, ALTHOUGH ALL SHALL BE OFFENDED, YET WILL NOT I."

The diagram is:

The statement by Peter constitutes presumption on his part and also an insult toward the others.

SIMON PETER

The phrase, *"But Peter said unto Him,"* portrays, as we shall see, a disavowal of what Christ has just said respecting *"all being offended."* After three and a half years of walking by the side of Christ, Peter should have known that whatever Jesus said was going to happen, would, in fact, happen exactly as He had said it. But he was, as we are, slow to learn!

The phrase, *"Although all shall be offended, yet will not I,"* constitutes presumption on

Peter's part and a position that he found he could not maintain. Peter's statement contains the idea that he felt the other Disciples most probably would stumble, but he considered himself to be far above them and, therefore, above such weakness. His answer, if anything at all, should have been, *"I know that through my own infirmity this may easily happen, but, nevertheless, I trust to Your Mercy and Goodness to save me"* (Bickersteth).

Bickersteth further says, *"The true remedy against temptation is the consciousness of our own weakness, and supplication for Divine strength."*

Anyone who would read these words uttered by Peter, and who would think lightly of him in his heart, would, by such an attitude, be proclaiming a moral weakness even greater than that shown by the fisherman.

IS OUR FAITH ANY STRONGER?

We often think that we are strong in Faith, strong in purity, and strong in patience. But when temptation arises, we often falter and fail. Many who criticize Peter have never faced the onslaught of Satan as Peter did face. In truth, most who criticize, at least in this capacity, have never faced the same type of oppression and, in fact, probably never will. The few who have faced such and have come out victorious have no criticism whatsoever.

Many years ago, the following statement was made in a particular sermon:

1. Upon hearing that a Brother or Sister in the Lord has failed, one should realize they are hearing gossip and treat it accordingly. An accusation should not be received against an Elder except before two or three witnesses (I Tim. 5:19).

2. If, in fact, one feels they actually do have inside information respecting a failure by a fellow Christian, still, they have little or no knowledge of the spiritual warfare involved.

3. If placed in the same circumstances as the one who failed, would we do any better, or even as well?

(30) "AND JESUS SAID UNTO HIM, VERILY I SAY UNTO YOU, THAT THIS DAY, EVEN IN THIS NIGHT, BEFORE THE COCK CROW TWICE, YOU SHALL DENY ME THRICE."

The overview is:

As we shall see, Peter wouldn't even have the strength to last out the night.

A PROPHECY

The phrase, *"And Jesus said unto him, Verily I say unto you,"* is meant to proclaim a very solemn announcement. The phrase, *"That this day, even in this night,"* means that Peter would not even have the strength to last out the night. Despite what he thought, his strength was small.

The phrase, *"You shall deny Me thrice,"* speaks of three times. In other words, Peter would deny Christ, not once, but again and again. At the very time he thought he was so very strong, he was, in fact, so very weak. It is regrettable, but the far greater majority of the modern Church think of themselves as Peter first thought of himself.

And how do I know that?

The modern Church would not be so critical, as Peter was at first, if it did not think of itself so very highly. As stated, Peter not only boasted of his own strength, but he also criticized the small strength, at least as he saw it, in the remaining Ten. However, most boasting is done in this manner. The putting down of someone else somehow makes us feel superior.

(31) "BUT HE SPOKE THE MORE VEHEMENTLY, IF I SHOULD DIE WITH YOU, I WILL NOT DENY YOU IN ANY WISE. LIKEWISE ALSO SAID THEY ALL."

The exposition is:

Peter was so carried away by the fervor of his zeal and love for Christ that he regarded neither the weakness of his own flesh nor the truth of his Master's Word.

THE BOAST OF SIMON PETER

The phrase, *"But he spoke the more vehemently,"* has a double meaning:

A. Peter kept on speaking, disavowing that he would ever fail Christ.

B. He said it strongly, loudly, and repeatedly!

The phrase, *"If I should die with You, I will not deny You in any wise,"* was uttered before all the other Disciples and also Christ. The words, *"any wise,"* mean that whatever happens, even to the forfeiting of his life, he will not deny Christ; however, his strength was so small that he began to deny long before his life was even close to being threatened. He never made it past the little servant girl, much less the Sanhedrin or the Romans (Vs. 66).

PRESUMPTION

The phrase, *"Likewise also said they all,"* proclaims the other Disciples being carried forth by Peter's bold declaration, with them joining their voices. All of them minutes before had heard Jesus state that *"all would be offended because of Me this night."* He even quoted the Prophecy given by the Holy Spirit through the Prophet Zechariah, which proclaimed what they would do, but still they denied it.

How so typical of most of us! When we should be on our knees crying to God for strength, instead we are boldly proclaiming what we will or won't do.

The modern Faith Message, which, in reality, is no Faith at all, perhaps fosters this presumptuous spirit more than anything else. To admit that one is weak and must have the help and strength of the Lord is considered by these people to be a bad confession. But the so-called *"good confession"* too often proclaims, not the strength of Christ, but more so the spiritual ignorance of the individual.

While a *"good confession"* certainly is important, still, we must be very careful that we see ourselves as we really are, thereby extolling the Power and Strength of Christ.

(32) "AND THEY CAME TO A PLACE WHICH WAS NAMED GETHSEMANE: AND HE SAID TO HIS DISCIPLES, SIT YE HERE, WHILE I SHALL PRAY."

The synopsis is:

This was a Garden at the foot of the Mount of Olives. *"Gethsemane"* means *"the place of the Olive-press."*

GETHSEMANE

The phrase, *"And they came to a place which was named Gethsemane,"* spoke of a Garden at the foot of the Mount of Olives. John called it a *"Garden"* or *"Orchard"* (Jn. 18:1). Gethsemane is the place where olives were brought in order that the oil contained in them might be pressed out. Gethsemane also would *"press out"* the self-will of the Disciples, or at least would begin the process. Sooner or later every Believer comes, spiritually speaking, to Gethsemane. The conclusion of its effect is that we might say, as did Christ, *"Not My will, but Yours, be done"* (Lk. 22:42).

PRAYER

The phrase, *"And He said to His Disciples, sit ye here, while I shall pray,"* proclaims the prescription for every Believer. It is sad, but, for such times and circumstances, much of the modern Church recommends the services of the psychologist. Much of the remaining Church claims that if a proper confession is maintained, there never will have to be a Gethsemane.

Precious few recommend prayer, as the Holy Spirit did to Jesus. James said, *"Is any among you afflicted? Let him pray"* (James 5:13).

Once again, we must understand that it is the Holy Spirit Who gives us strength to do what we ought to do and to be what we ought. Without Him, we simply cannot function, at least in a position of victory.

Again, the Holy Spirit works exclusively within the framework of the Finished Work of Christ. We as Believers, therefore, must ever anchor our Faith in Christ and the Cross, which then gives the Holy Spirit latitude to work. Then our praying will take on a brand-new complexion. Personally, I do not feel that, without a proper understanding of the Cross, any Believer can have the type of prayer life that one ought to have. Most definitely they can have a prayer life, and the Lord most definitely will bless to a certain degree. However, due to the fact that Faith is an ingredient that is required in all that we do, and, more particularly, Faith in Christ and the Cross, and inasmuch as this involves the Sanctification of the Saint, a proper understanding of Faith is here required (Rom. 6:3-14; 8:1-2, 11).

(33) "AND HE TOOK WITH HIM PETER AND JAMES AND JOHN, AND BEGAN TO BE SORE AMAZED, AND TO BE VERY HEAVY."

The exegesis is:

Concerning this, Swete says, *"The Lord was overwhelmed with sorrow, but His first feeling was one of terrified surprise; His foreseeing the Passion was one thing, but when it came clearly into view, its terrors, it seems, exceeded His anticipations"* (Heb. 5:7-8).

THE TERRIBLE TRIAL OF GETHSEMANE

The phrase, *"And He took with Him Peter and James and John,"* proclaims the third time such a thing was done in reference to the other Disciples.

1. First of all, these Three witnessed the *"Power"* of Christ when He raised the daughter of Jairus from the dead (Mk. 5:37-43).

2. These three were chosen to witness the Transfiguration of Christ, thereby witnessing His *"Glory"* (Mk. 9:1-10).

3. Last of all, these Three witnessed His Passion and, therefore, His *"Sufferings"* (Mk. 14:32-42).

Some have claimed that the Three Disciples here chosen had been fortified to endure the sight of the Passion of Christ by the glories of the Transfiguration. It has been suggested that it would have been too much for the Faith of the others. But these Three witnessed it that they themselves might learn and be able to teach others that the way to Glory is, sometimes, by Suffering.

Regarding the phrase, *"And began to be sore amazed,"* the Greek word for *"sore amazed"* is *"ekthanbeo,"* which means *"to throw into terror, alarm, and distress."* All of this means that Jesus learned upon the basis of the things He suffered, and the last lesson of obedience began with a sensation of inconceivable awe.

The phrase, *"And to be very heavy,"* is, in the Greek, *"ademoneo,"* which means *"an experience of which one is not familiar, and in which one does not feel at home, that is, at rest, and which distresses him."*

(34) "AND SAID UNTO THEM, MY SOUL IS EXCEEDING SORROWFUL UNTO DEATH: TARRY YE HERE, AND WATCH."

The overview is:

Jesus was so overwhelmed by grief that He was close to death. Satan definitely tried to kill Him at this time!

NOTES

DEATH

The phrase, *"And said unto them,"* has to do with Peter, James, and John. They were called upon to witness His Sufferings, even though at the time they little understood it, if at all!

The phrase, *"My soul is exceeding sorrowful unto death,"* means that grief so overwhelmed Him that He was close to death. Satan definitely tried to kill Him at this time!

That which caused this had to be *"this Cup,"* which He spoke of in Verse 36. What this *"Cup"* contained was horrible beyond belief.

First of all, He, Who knew no sin, will be forced to take upon Himself the penalty for every sin that ever had been, or would be, committed. This was the Judgment and Anger of God which would smite Him instead of us (Isa. 53:4). Even worse, during this time, He would be separated from the Father. This agony is described in Psalm 22.

There is no way that mere human mortals could ever begin to realize the extent of the price that was paid for our Redemption. Into this *"price"* it is possible for man to go so far, but no further! The full brunt of what He suffered will never be known or understood by the human heart and mind. We can only surmise. Even then, the greatest stretch of our imagination cannot begin to encompass what He did, what He, in fact, had to do, to bring about our Redemption.

TARRY AND WATCH

The phrase, *"Tarry ye here, and watch,"* was addressed, as stated at the beginning, to Peter, James, and John. Of this third expression, which was Suffering, it is my personal belief that these Three learned more at this time than at the other two times combined. The lessons of all the experiences would never be lost upon them, but what they witnessed in Gethsemane has never been witnessed by other human mortals. They saw a side of Christ that they did not know existed. They were taken to a depth of human suffering, at least as far as observation was concerned, that no one else has ever experienced.

What were their thoughts at this particular

time? Were they even halfway able to comprehend what they were seeing?

I think not, and neither could we! They saw it, but they did not understand it. They could not understand it, at least at this time!

Quite possibly at a later time, the Holy Spirit helped them to more fully grasp what they had seen and experienced.

Why these Three, and not the others?

The only answer that could be given, I think, is that Jesus undoubtedly saw a degree of hunger in their hearts for God that the others did not quite possess. And that, despite their present weaknesses! The Lord never looks at us as we are, but instead as to what He can make of us, at least if the desire is present in the soul.

Peter would ultimately be the spokesman for the Early Church, at least in its beginning stages. He would mightily be used of God. He would write two of the Epistles in the New Testament.

John would outlive all of the Apostles, and would write five Books in the New Testament. The depth of John's writing reached a level that is truly beyond comprehension. In the Book of Revelation, which would close out the Canon of Scripture, he would be given the greatest Revelation of all.

Not much is known about James, even though he was one of the chosen Three. He was martyred about ten or eleven years after the Day of Pentecost (Acts 12:1-2). He was the brother of John the Beloved.

(35) "AND HE WENT FORWARD A LITTLE, AND FELL ON THE GROUND, AND PRAYED THAT, IF IT WERE POSSIBLE, THE HOUR MIGHT PASS FROM HIM."

The overview is:

It actually means that He fell on the ground repeatedly; it portrays the desperation of the struggle.

THE TERRIBLE TRIAL

The phrase, *"And He went forward a little, and fell on the ground,"* actually means, from the Greek Text, that He fell on the ground repeatedly. In other words, He would fall, arise, then fall again. More than anything else, this portrays the desperation of the struggle in which our Lord was engaged at the time. Quite possibly it was at this time that, as Luke reported it, *"His sweat was as it were great drops of blood falling down to the ground"* (Lk. 22:44).

It is medically known that, under extreme mental pressure, the pores may become so dilated that blood may issue from them, producing a bloody sweat. Even though the Disciples a little later are shown sleeping, the indication is that they were eyewitnesses of these particular happenings.

The phrase, *"And prayed that, if it were possible, the hour might pass from Him,"* means that He continued to pray and put forth the same petition, saying it over and over. The *"hour"* spoken of here pertains to the Cross and His terrible death in this fashion, which pertained to the bearing of the sin penalty of the entirety of the world, past, present, and future. Even though He had looked ahead to this hour (Jn. 2:4; 7:30; 8:20; 12:23, 27; 13:1), still, as it now draws near, the horror of it, along with the terrible opposition by Satanic powers, produced an oppression, or spectacle, if you will, such as no human being has ever had to face.

His going *"forward"* means that this action probably took place about 100 feet from the Three Disciples.

(36) "AND HE SAID, ABBA, FATHER, ALL THINGS ARE POSSIBLE UNTO YOU; TAKE AWAY THIS CUP FROM ME: NEVERTHELESS NOT WHAT I WILL, BUT WHAT YOU WILL."

The structure is:

The first sentence of the Verse is actually the expression of two languages. He thus in His agony cried to God in the name of the whole human family, the Jew first, and also the Gentile.

ABBA, FATHER

The phrase, *"And He said, Abba, Father,"* is actually the expression of two languages. Some feel that Mark only added the word *"Father,"* which was the Greek, with Jesus using the Aramaic word *"Abba,"* which actually means *"Father."* However, it is far more natural to conclude that Mark is taking his narrative from an eye and ear witness, Peter, and that both the words were uttered by the Lord; so that He thus in His agony cried to God in the name of the whole human family, the Jew first, and also the Gentile.

The address to the Heavenly Father, as used by Christ, portrays a relationship which no one else has, or actually could have! It seems this relationship between the Father and the Son even deepens at this terrible time of suffering, if it would be possible to deepen more than it already was! This tells us that our relationship with the Heavenly Father cannot be deepened without, in some way, being deepened through suffering. This was, no doubt, the major lesson, among others, that was taught to Peter, James, and John.

It is certainly true that no one desires suffering for the sake of suffering; but still, if one truly takes up the Cross, and thereby truly follows Christ, due to the fact that there is an offense to the Cross, suffering from without will definitely come to the Believer (Gal. 5:11).

This is the reason that the Cross is ignored or even opposed by much of the modern Church. It doesn't desire the suffering of opposition that goes along with the Cross.

Paul said, *"If so be that we suffer with Him, that we may be also glorified together"* (Rom. 8:17; I Cor. 4:12; Gal. 5:11; 6:12; Phil. 1:29; I Tim. 4:10; II Tim. 2:12; 3:12; Heb. 11:25).

ALL THINGS ARE POSSIBLE

The phrase, *"All things are possible unto You,"* tells us that God, being Omnipotent and Omniscient, could have effected the Salvation and Redemption of humanity in another way. Such was possible! But such was not His Will!

The phrase, *"Take away this Cup from Me,"* refers to the lot or portion, whether good or evil, which is appointed for us by God. In the case of Christ, it was a bitter Cup, from which He naturally and sinlessly shrank.

Wuest says, *"If He had not offered this petition, He would not have been Who and What He was."*

A part of this Cup was to be made sin and to be charged by the High Court of Heaven with the guilt of all human sin. From that, the Holy Son of God drew back with all the infinite hatred of sin that was His. Knowing that sin was the cause of all the hurt and harm in the Creation of God, the horror of it overwhelmed Him, as it should have.

The other was the agony of being deprived of the fellowship of the Father from 9 o'clock in the morning until 3 in the afternoon (Ps. 22:1-2). The fellowship between Father and Son had no beginning.

Wuest further says, *"For a sinner, who has never known the bliss of the Father's fellowship, to be deprived of it all through eternity is bad enough. But for the Holy Son of God, Who knew nothing else up to that moment, the loss of that fellowship meant infinite suffering."*

To most, even Believers, the loss of six hours of fellowship may not seem like a large thing. However, only spiritual ignorance would think such a thing. Even though the relationship with the Heavenly Father by the Believer is of necessity far less than between Jesus and His Father, still, for the Believer to have to do without the Presence of God, even for a minute, is an appalling thought. The Lord is everything to us, and in every capacity. Even the weakest Believer enjoys a relationship that is supernatural, to say the least. The longer one lives for the Lord, the deeper that relationship becomes.

To view it in that light lets us know the horror that overwhelmed Christ by that relationship being broken. Even though it was only approximately six hours, still, the horror of that filled Christ will revulsion, which is understandable once we comprehend the seriousness of the matter.

THE WILL OF GOD

The phrase, *"Nevertheless, not what I will, but what You will,"* proclaims far more than the acquiescence of Christ to the Will of God, but instead proclaims the principle of Faith for all Believers. His Will was subject to the Will of the Father, as our wills must be subject.

In this one Passage is found the cause of all spiritual declension, disobedience, suffering, and problems experienced by the Believer. It is God's Will versus our will. Even though it was possible for the Heavenly Father to have carried out Redemption in another fashion, still, it was not His Will to do so. This Way was the Best Way, and it was the business of Christ, as He wondrously did, to acquiesce His Will to the Father's Will.

Most, if not all, Believers would automatically agree with the statements I have just made; however, the great error is in erroneously interpreting the Will of God. The modern Faith teaching, which, in reality, is precious little faith at all, claims, for the most part a life free of disturbances, hindrances and difficulties, at least if one has the proper faith and confession. Such teaching is attractive and draws many adherents. To be the master of our fate, and not have to depend on anyone, even God, is attractive indeed! The truth is that there aren't many who desire a Gethsemane. Actually, no one would desire such. However, one must understand the certitude of a personal Gethsemane, at least in a limited way, that is, if we are to be what we should be in Christ.

AN EXPERIENCE

Some time back, I was listening to the News, and heard the announcer say that Tommy Dorsey had died the day before. The announcer also mentioned that Thurgood Marshall, another African American, had passed away on the same day. Mr. Marshall was the first Black to grace the august Supreme Court of the United States. The announcer went on to say that Mr. Marshall had influenced America. But then he said, *"Tommy Dorsey influenced the world."*

What did he mean?

Tommy Dorsey wrote many songs for the cause of Christ. However, one stands out, and it was that song of which the announcer spoke. The song was, *"Take my hand, Precious Lord, and lead me on."* That one song has blessed the world.

Tommy Dorsey lost his wife and six children in a fire. He was away preaching a meeting in a distant city when he received the news.

Is it possible to imagine how one would feel at being given this type of message?

Out of that trial and heartache came the song, *"Take my hand, Precious Lord, and lead me on."* Most, if not all, who, in Christ, truly bless the world come out of a Gethsemane. This, I think, is evident in the Word of God from Genesis through Revelation.

It is not that the suffering itself, and of whatever direction it may take, has any special cleansing or redemptive power, for it doesn't. What is does do is to drive a person to his knees, thereby closer to God. At least that is the intention by the Holy Spirit! Then the work that Christ desires can be accomplished in our hearts and lives, out of which comes the Blessing.

Perhaps David said it best when he said, *"Neither will I offer Burnt Offerings unto the LORD my God of that which does cost me nothing"* (II Sam. 24:24).

(37) "AND HE CAME, AND FOUND THEM SLEEPING, AND SAID UNTO PETER, SIMON, ARE YOU SLEEPING? COULD YOU NOT WATCH ONE HOUR?"

The structure is:

Jesus addresses Peter by his old name.

ONE HOUR

The phrase, *"And He came, and found them sleeping,"* presents, as Luke explained it, a sleep from the exhaustion produced from their deepening realization of what was really happening all around them — that Jesus was really going to die (Lk. 22:45). The question, *"And said unto Peter, Simon, are you sleeping?"* presents Jesus addressing Peter by his old name.

Wuest says, *"For the time he is 'Peter' no more; the new character which he owes to association with Jesus is now in abeyance. He who was ready to die with the Master has been proved not to possess the strength of will requisite for resisting sleep during the third part of a single watch."*

The question, *"Could you not watch one hour?"* pertains to the struggle between the flesh and the spirit.

Swete explains the flesh and the spirit here as follows: *"The flesh is man as he belongs to the sphere of the material life, under the limitations of a corporeal nature, frail, mortal, and, in fact, impure* (Gen. 6:12). *The spirit is the vital force* (Gen. 6:17) *which, in man, is directly dependent on the Spirit of God* (Gen. 2:7), *and is the organ or communication with God and the spiritual world."*

THE FLESH AS EXPLAINED BY THE APOSTLE PAUL

In Paul's Epistles, a number of Passages

expand implications of the Old Testament view of human nature expressed regarding the *"flesh."* According to Paul, human nature is not just frail and weak; human nature is also twisted and tangled. Human perspectives, human understanding, and human efforts are actually hostile to the perspective, understanding, and Plan of God. In other words, we are morally inadequate, and we are driven toward rebellion.

The contrasts are drawn between human powers, perspectives, and abilities and the powers, perspectives, and abilities of God, most importantly, His Ability to enable people to do His Will. The whole of human nature, not merely a *"part"* of human beings, is in view when Scripture uses *"flesh"* in a moral or theological sense to make statements about human nature.

ISOLATION FROM GOD

The Scripture presents human beings in isolation from God. Human beings are cut off from the Lord because they are morally inadequate (Rom. 6:19; 7:7-11, 15-20; 8:3). To live according to the *"flesh"* is completely different from living according to God's Spirit (Rom. 8:4-13; Gal. 5:16-26). Living in accordance with God's Spirit is the only manner by which one can walk in victory. This is done by the Believer evidencing Faith exclusively in Christ and what Christ has done for us at the Cross, which is the sphere in which the Holy Spirit works (Rom. 8:1-2, 11).

Apart from the Holy Spirit, humanity is characterized by a complex web of thoughts, desires, values, and actions that are in opposition to God's intended pattern for us. This is what is meant by the *"flesh."* Several Passages in Paul's letters explore the nature and meaning of the flesh.

THE STRUGGLE WITH SIN

Exploring his own struggle with sin, Paul faced his moral inadequacy. The Law of God is spiritual, but Paul was attempting to overcome by the flesh, thereby failing and, therefore, trapped in sin. One must also realize that this was Paul's experience after he was saved and baptized with the Holy Spirit (Acts, Chpt. 9).

With the revelation of the Cross not yet given, the Apostle (and he definitely was then an Apostle) simply did not know how to live for God. Therefore, he tried to live the best way he knew how, which was by keeping Commandments, which the Holy Spirit could not honor. It was, in fact, to Paul that this great Revelation of the New Covenant was given, which is, in effect, the Revelation of the Cross (Gal., Chpt. 1).

In his efforts before the understanding of the Cross was given to him, Paul realized that *"nothing good"* lived in him, that is, in his *"flesh,"* i.e., *"in my sinful nature."* Trapped by his moral frailty, which characterizes all of us, Paul, at least in the flesh, could not live the righteous life that is revealed in God's Law, even though he acknowledged its beauty, and no matter how hard he tried (Rom. 7:4-25).

And let me quickly add: Neither can you! Nor can anyone else, for that matter! No one can live for God as one should live for the Lord without knowing and understanding the great Revelation which the Lord gave to Paul, which is found in Romans, Chapter 6. When one understands Romans, Chapter 6, then one will find the secret to victory in the Holy Spirit, which Paul then gave us in Romans, Chapter 8.

As we've already stated in this Volume, Romans, Chapter 6, gives us the mechanics of the Holy Spirit, i.e., *"how"* He does things, while in Romans, Chapter 8, we have the dynamics of the Holy Spirit, i.e., *"what"* the Holy Spirit does in our hearts and lives after we learn *"how"* He does it.

THE SIN NATURE

In Galatians 5:16-26, the *"flesh"* could be translated *"sinful nature."* Paul here describes the flesh as energized and motivated by desires that find expression in a number of actions, ranging from sexual immorality to jealousy and fits of rage. In contrast, as Believers are called on to *"live by the Spirit,"* God Himself becomes the Source of transformed desires that can motivate a new life. What's more, He is also the Source of Power for such a life. When we keep in step with the Spirit rather than the flesh, God will fill us and our actions with love, joy, peace, and the other aspects of the Fruit of the Spirit.

Because it's so important, let us say it again: This can be done, and I continue to speak of *"keeping in step with the Spirit rather than the flesh,"* only by the Believer understanding that the price for everything we need was paid at Calvary. Our faith, consequently, is to rest in the Finished Work of Christ, i.e., within the sphere in which the Holy Spirit works, which then guarantees our victory.

If one is to notice, Paul constantly told us to look to the Cross of Christ, for it is in the Cross where the solution to every spiritual problem is found, and where every victory is won. That victory is now ours, but only if we evidence and maintain faith in Christ and what He did for us at the Cross (Rom. 6:3-14; 8:1-2, 11; I Cor. 1:17-18, 23; 2:2; Eph. 2:13-18; Col. 2:14-15).

THE BEHAVIOR OF CHRISTIANS

In I Corinthians 3:1-4, Paul alludes to the behavior of the Christians at Corinth. Their bickering and factions show that, despite their relationship with Jesus, the Corinthians were acting like *"mere men,"* meaning that their outlook was human, i.e., *"the flesh,"* rather than being shaped by God's perspective on the issues they found so important.

We Christians do have the potential to live beyond the possibilities of our *"sinful human nature."* But such an enabled life is not guaranteed, at least it is not guaranteed if we do not function according to God's Prescribed Order. We must make the choice to place our faith and our trust exclusively in Christ and what Christ has done for us at the Cross, never separating Christ from the Cross. If our Faith is there properly placed, and there properly maintained, this will always guarantee the help of the Holy Spirit, without Whom we simply cannot live for God, at least as we ought to live.

To break out of this pattern of the flesh, these Corinthians had to return to God's Word and search out His Perspective.

GOD'S REMEDY

Release from the limits of our human nature is possible. Romans 8:3-14 explains God's remedy for the limitations and sin of the flesh. That remedy is not found in the Law. Law was unable to lift us to Righteousness because it was *"weakened by our sinful nature,"* in other words, dependent upon the strength of mere man, which is woefully insufficient. While the Mosaic Law could show us what we are, as a mirror shows the reflection of our face, it had no power to change what we are.

So God, through Christ, provided the Holy Spirit to Believers, all made possible by the Cross (Jn. 14:17). Now we have the possibility of being controlled by the Spirit and not by the flesh. It is the Spirit Whose life-giving power raised Jesus from the dead. It is the Spirit Who can bring us life and power despite our mortality. Consequently, we are now raised to a new level entirely.

If we choose to rely on the Spirit, which is the only way of Victory, and which can only be done by the Believer placing his faith exclusively in Christ and the Cross (Rom. 8:2), we will experience a Resurrection kind of life, and do so now! The limits imposed by our fleshly human nature will no longer contain us or restrain us, and we will be freed from the mastery of the flesh.

Listen again to Paul:

"But if the Spirit (Holy Spirit) *of Him* (from God) *Who raised up Jesus from the dead dwell in you* (and He definitely does, that is, if you are saved), *He Who raised up Christ from the dead shall also quicken your mortal bodies* (give us power in our mortal bodies that we might live a victorious life) *by His Spirit Who dwells in you.* (We have the same power in us, through the Spirit, that raised Christ from the dead, and He is available to us only on the premise of the Cross and our Faith in that Sacrifice)" (Rom. 8:11).

Paul is not speaking here of the Resurrection of Life that is ultimately going to come, which will be accompanied by the Trump of God (I Thess. 4:17-18), but rather the Resurrection life we are meant to live as Believers doing the Will of God. The key to this is found in Romans 6:3-5. There we are told that we are baptized into the Death of Christ, buried with Him by Baptism into death, and raised with Him in Newness of Life.

Now, please understand. Paul is not speaking here of Water Baptism, but rather the Crucifixion of Christ, and our part in that Crucifixion, which we obtain by Faith.

Paul then said: *"For if we have been planted together* (with Christ) *in the likeness of His Death* (Paul proclaims the Cross as the instrument through which all Blessings come; consequently, the Cross must ever be the Object of our Faith, which then gives the Holy Spirit latitude to work within our lives), *we shall also be in the likeness of His Resurrection.* (We can have the *'likeness of His Resurrection,'* i.e., *'live this Resurrection life,'* only as long as we understand the *'likeness of His Death,'* which refers to the Cross as the means by which all of this is done)" (Rom. 6:5).

That is God's Remedy.

THE OLD AND THE NEW TESTAMENTS

The Old Testament emphasized the frailty of human beings. Because of our weakness, we must look to God for everything good. He Alone is the Source of our help. To recognize His Power brings us release from fear of other persons, who are ultimately as powerless as we are.

The New Testament took the explanation of the flesh further by emphasizing humanity's moral inadequacy, even of Believers. When humans are isolated from God, they become energized by evil desires and guided by perceptions that distort God's Will and His Nature. The word *"flesh"* reminds us that we are caught in the grip of sin. Even a desire for Righteousness cannot enable us to actually become Righteous, as Paul's experience teaches us (Rom., Chpt. 7).

THE MANNER IN WHICH GOD DEALS WITH OUR FLESH

God deals with our *"flesh"* in a surprising way. He does not free us now from the fleshly nature (sin nature). Instead, He provides a source of power that will release us from the domination of that sin nature. Jesus has paid for sins generated by our flesh, whether sins of the past or those yet in our future. But, Christ has also provided us with His Holy Spirit.

The Holy Spirit now lives within us as Believers, and He is the Source of new desires and a new perspective. Even more, the spiritual power unleashed in the Resurrection of Christ is made available to us in the Spirit by the means of the Cross.

The bonds of our mortality and all that mortality implies can be shattered if we live according to the Spirit, with our desires and motives shaped by Him, with His Power enabling us to do what is truly good. Through Romans, Chapter 3, we are made to see just how important the Holy Spirit is within the life of the Believer. Without Him, the victorious life is impossible, and that despite all our good intentions. With Him, the unlawful passions of the sin nature can be defeated.

THE REVELATION

Some time early in 1997, the Lord began to open up to me the Revelation of the Cross. It was so startling, so eye-opening, so revolutionary, at least to me, that I noticed an immediate change in my life. The first thing the Lord showed me was the cause of spiritual failure in the hearts and lives of Believers. It is not knowing how to address the sin nature. And if we do not know how to address the sin nature, then the sin nature will dominate us in some way, exactly as it did before we came to Christ. While it may not be as all-encompassing as it was before we were saved, it will still rule us in some way.

Listen again to Paul:

"Let not sin (the sin nature) *therefore reign* (rule) *in your mortal body* (showing that the sin nature can once again rule in the heart and life of the Believer, if the Believer doesn't constantly look to Christ and the Cross; the *'mortal body'* is neutral, which means it can be used for Righteousness or unrighteousness), *that you should obey it in the lusts thereof* (ungodly lusts are carried out through the mortal body, if Faith is not maintained in the Cross [I Cor. 1:17-18].)

"Neither yield you your members (of your mortal body) *as instruments of unrighteousness unto sin* (the sin nature): *but yield yourselves unto God* (we are to yield ourselves to Christ and the Cross; that alone guarantees victory over the sin nature), *as those who are alive from the dead* (we have been raised with Christ in *'newness of life'*), *and your members* (the members of our physical body) *as instruments of Righteousness unto God* (this can be done only by virtue

of the Cross and our Faith in that Finished Work and Faith which continues in that Finished Work from day-to-day [Lk. 9:23-24].)

"For sin shall not have dominion over you (the sin nature will not have dominion over us if we Believers continue to exercise Faith in the Cross; otherwise, the sin nature most definitely will have dominion over the Believer): *for you are not under the Law* (means that if we try to live this life by any type of law, no matter how good that law might be in its own right, we will conclude by the sin nature having dominion over us), *but under Grace.* (The Grace of God flows to the Believer on an unending basis only as long as the Believer exercises Faith in Christ and what He did at the Cross; Grace is merely the Goodness of God exercised by and through the Holy Spirit, given to undeserving Saints)" (Rom. 6:12-14).

I realize that some Preachers claim that Believers no longer have a sin nature, that being separated from us at conversion; however, if that is the case, then the Holy Spirit went to a great deal of trouble and used up a great deal of space to explain something that doesn't exist. In this Sixth Chapter of Romans, in fact, the word *"sin"* is mentioned seventeen times. Fifteen of those times, it carries the definite article in front of the word *"sin,"* which actually then reads *"the sin,"* which refers to the principle of sin instead of acts of sin.

Yes, the Christian most definitely has a sin nature; it can, however, be controlled by the Power of the Holy Spirit, that is, if our faith is correctly placed in Christ and the Cross. Otherwise, the sin nature will control us, as it does most Christians, because of their lack of understanding respecting the Cross and how the Holy Spirit works.

THE CROSS

Whenever the Lord showed me the cause of spiritual failure in the hearts and lives of Believers, which is not knowing how to control the sin nature, He did not really tell me the solution to the problem, at least at that time! A few days later, while I was in one of the morning prayer meetings, the Holy Spirit immediately opened up to me the solution to the problem. I had found out the cause, but I had not yet found out the solution. Now the Holy Spirit gave me the solution.

He spoke emphatically to my heart and said, *"The solution for which you seek is found in the Cross, and is found in the Cross alone!"* When you study Paul's writings, this will become amazingly clear. If you wonder why I emphasize the Cross so much, well then, that's the reason. It and it alone is the answer to the sin problem. This means that our faith must ever be anchored in Christ and what He has done for us at the Cross.

I've said it over and over in this Volume, but let me say it again:

"Christ is the Source, while the Cross is the Means."

THE HOLY SPIRIT

Once again, allow me to restate the role of the Holy Spirit in all of this of which we have stated.

After the Lord began to open up to me the Revelation of the Cross and how it worked, in my heart I wondered, *"Exactly how does the Holy Spirit come into all of this?"* I knew that He definitely did, but I just simply did not know how.

And then, a few weeks later, the Lord opened up to me this great Truth. Even though it is very simple, actually that which Paul taught, still, I personally believe it is a Truth that has been little known in the Church up until this time.

The Lord told me that the Holy Spirit works exclusively within the framework of the Finished Work of Christ. This means that the Cross of Christ is His sphere of operation. We are told this in Romans 8:2.

Paul said, *"For the Law* (a law devised by the Godhead in eternity past) *of the Spirit* (Holy Spirit) *of Life* (all life flows from Christ, but through the Holy Spirit) *in Christ Jesus* (refers to what Christ did for us at the Cross) *has made me free from the Law of Sin and Death."*

Tragically, most Believers, even Pentecostals, little know and understand how the Holy Spirit works. Many Pentecostals think if they speak in tongues that's the answer. While that is very valuable, that is not the answer to overcoming sin.

All sin was overcome at the Cross. To

have that overcoming power, the Believer, as we have stated any number of times, must place and maintain his Faith in the Finished Work of Christ. The Holy Spirit requires this, at least if we are to have His help, which we must have if we are going to live a holy life.

It is sad, but most Believers, because they do not understand the Cross, get so little help from the Holy Spirit, but, in reality, the Lord has made provision for us to have all the help we need. The bonds of our mortality and all that mortality implies can be shattered if we live according to the Spirit, with our desires and motives shaped by Him, with His Power enabling us to do what is truly good.

Through Romans, Chapter 8, we are made to see just how important the Holy Spirit is within the life of the Believer. Without Him, the victorious life is impossible, and that, despite all of our good intentions. With Him, the unlawful passions of the sin nature can be defeated.

(38) "WATCH YE AND PRAY, LEST YOU ENTER INTO TEMPTATION. THE SPIRIT TRULY IS READY, BUT THE FLESH IS WEAK."

The exegesis is:

As we've already stated, the *"flesh"* pertains to our own personal strength, ability, and willpower. Within themselves, these things are insufficient for the task. Unless the Believer properly understands the Cross, as it regards Sanctification, he will inevitably fall back on the flesh, which spells disaster.

WATCH AND PRAY

The phrase, *"Watch ye and pray, lest you enter into temptation,"* provides us with the true remedy against temptation of every kind. *"Prayer"* teaches us reliance on the Holy Spirit and also creates within us a *"watchfulness"* able to recognize the craft and subtlety of the devil or man.

Incidentally, this was not a suggestion by Christ, but actually a Command! The Believer who does not *"watch and pray"* will not only be subject to temptation, but also will have no means to overcome its pull. This is a problem that is constant and, therefore, requires continuous *"watchfulness and prayer."*

I am certain that Peter, along with the other Disciples, learned this valuable lesson, even from this very experience in Gethsemane. When the Early Church began to grow, *"The Twelve,"* no doubt, headed up by Peter, advised the large number of Believers to *"look ye out among you seven men of honest report, full of the Holy Spirit and wisdom, who we may appoint over this business."* They then said, *"But we will give ourselves continually to prayer, and to the Ministry of the Word"* (Acts 6:3-4).

The *"entering into temptation"* has the meaning of being pulled into a trap laid by Satan. The *"watching and praying"* circumvents those traps. However, there is something else here which must be said, which our Lord did not at this time mention, but which is a great truth given to the Apostle Paul.

Along with *"watchfulness and prayer,"* one's Faith must be exclusively in Christ and the Cross, even as we've already, even laboriously, explained. If our faith is not in Christ and the Cross, then our faith will be in our prayer life, etc., which the Lord can never accept.

This confuses many Christians. Understanding that prayer is one of the highest forms of worship in which one can engage, they cannot understand how it alone cannot solve the problem. Jesus did not give here all the information, simply because the Cross was yet in the future, and His statements could very well have been misconstrued. He had told them to take up the Cross and follow Him; however, He never really explained it, at least not at that time.

One can well imagine the thoughts that entered into the minds of the Disciples when they heard Him state that Believers must bear their Cross! At that time, the Cross was the most despicable form of punishment and death known throughout the entirety of the world.

Our Lord told His Disciples, *"I have yet many things to say unto you, but you cannot bear them now.*

"Howbeit when He, the Spirit of Truth, is come, He will guide you into all Truth" (Jn. 16:12-13).

So, after the Cross, the Lord gave His Prescribed Order of Victory to the Apostle Paul, and Paul then gave it to us in his Epistles.

But let the Reader understand:

Even though Faith is placed exclusively in the Cross, exactly as it ought to be, which then gives the Holy Spirit latitude to work, still, our prayer life is very, very important. We must never forget that. Without a proper prayer life, we simply cannot have the relationship with Christ we ought to have.

A READY SPIRIT AND A WEAK FLESH

The phrase, *"The spirit truly is ready, but the flesh is weak,"* could be translated, *"the spirit* (of man) *truly is ready, but the flesh* (of man) *is weak."* The *"spirit"* here refers to the spirit of man. In the Believer, the regenerated spirit is willing, i.e., has the desire to obey God, but has no power within itself to do so, and certainly cannot override the evil passions and desires of the *"flesh,"* i.e., *"the sin nature."* However, as we have stated, the Lord has given us the Holy Spirit with all His great Power, Who can easily override the sin nature, and will do so, if our Faith is placed properly in Christ and the Cross (Rom. 6:3-14). This is the reason the Holy Spirit is so absolutely important (Rom. 8:2).

THE BAPTISM WITH THE HOLY SPIRIT

Does the Spirit of God come into the life of the Believer at conversion with the power needed to overcome the *"flesh"*?

The answer is: *"Yes"* and *"No"*!

While the Spirit of God definitely does come into the heart and life of the Believer at conversion, without the Baptism with the Holy Spirit, the Believer, at least for the most part, simply will not look to Christ as he or she should. There is a modicum of power that accompanies the Baptism with the Holy Spirit, which, incidentally, is always accompanied with the initial physical evidence of speaking with other tongues (Acts 2:4).

It must be understood that the people who gathered in the Upper Room definitely were saved. Jesus had *"Commanded them that they should not depart from Jerusalem, but wait for the Promise of the Father"* (Acts 1:4). The *"Promise of the Father"* is the *"Baptism with the Holy Spirit"* (Acts 1:5).

NOTES

As stated, it should be obvious that these people to whom Jesus was speaking, which included the Disciples, definitely were saved; however, they had not yet been baptized with the Holy Spirit.

Jesus told them not to evangelize, build Churches, preach the Gospel, etc. until they first were *"Baptized with the Holy Spirit."* And it was not a suggestion, but a command!

The reason is found in Acts 1:8, *"But you shall receive power, after that the Holy Spirit is come upon you."* However, the word *"power"* here needs to be looked at more closely.

THE POWER OF THE HOLY SPIRIT

The Greek word for *"power"* is *"dunamis,"* which means *"ability, abundance, might, strength, mighty."* This *"power"* is to be used by the Child of God in many and varied ways. It is available for every Believer and in every capacity. But yet, this *"power"* must be accompanied by Faith, and it must be Faith that is in the correct object, which is Christ and the Cross (Rom. 8:1-2, 11).

Unfortunately, there are millions of people who have been baptized with the Holy Spirit, with the evidence of speaking with other tongues, which is the only way one can be baptized, who, nevertheless, do not walk in victory, but rather in defeat. Regrettably, this is the case with virtually the entirety of the Pentecostal and Charismatic worlds, and simply because most little understand the victory of the Cross. Not understanding that, which means they place their faith in something else other than the Cross of Christ, this, in effect, ties the hands of the Holy Spirit. Inasmuch as the Holy Spirit works exclusively within the framework of the Finished Work of Christ, i.e., *"the Cross,"* He demands that our Faith ever be placed in the Atonement.

If our faith is placed in something else, such a Believer is guilty of *"spiritual adultery"* (Rom. 7:1-4). To be sure, the Holy Spirit definitely will not help any Believer commit spiritual adultery. So that leaves such a Believer without much help from the Holy Spirit.

The Holy Spirit will definitely work in the heart and life of any Believer as much as He can. In other words, He will do all that He can do, irrespective as to where our faith might be; nevertheless, we limit Him greatly when we have misplaced faith.

A PERSONAL EXPERIENCE

I am very thankful to the Lord for the way and manner in which He has used me to touch this world for Christ. By His help and Grace, we have seen hundreds of thousands, and I exaggerate not, brought to a saving knowledge of the Lord Jesus Christ. We have seen tens of thousands baptized with the Holy Spirit. Through our Telecast, we have seen entire nations touched by the Power of God and, of course, for that we are eternally grateful. But yet, all the while the Lord was using me, as it regards the Salvation of many souls, I did not know or understand God's Prescribed Order of Sanctification. If the truth be known, during those years, even as I look back, I didn't know a single other Preacher who knew and understood this of which I speak. Of course, I'm certain there were some few, but, from what I know now, that number was small indeed. Even at the present time, there isn't one Preacher out of ten thousand, I think, who can properly relate to a congregation of people as to how, according to the Bible, one can successfully live for the Lord. That means that all the myriads of books and tapes being offered by Television and Radio Preachers are, for the most part, simply a waste of time.

Let me say it again:

If the Preacher doesn't understand the Cross, and I'm referring to the Cross as it refers to Sanctification, then that Preacher simply cannot tell anyone how to live.

As stated, there was a day that I did not understand the Cross in this fashion. No matter how hard I tried, it simply was not possible to walk victoriously in the manner in which my efforts were extended. One can look at the Seventh Chapter of Romans, where Paul plainly and clearly spells it out.

Paul said, *"For that which I do* (the failure) *I allow not* (should have been translated, *'I understand not'*; these are not the words of an unsaved man, as some claim, but rather a Believer who is trying and failing): *for what I would, that do I not* (refers to the obedience he wants to render to Christ, but rather fails. Why? As Paul explained, the Believer is married to Christ, but is being unfaithful to Christ by spiritually cohabiting with the Law, which frustrates the Grace of God; that means the Holy Spirit will not help such a person, which guarantees failure [Gal. 2:21]); *but what I hate, that do I* (refers to sin in his life, which he doesn't want to do, and, in fact, hates, but finds himself unable to stop; unfortunately, due to the fact of not understanding the Cross as it refers to Sanctification, this is the plight of most modern Christians)" (Rom. 7:15).

No Believer on the face of the Earth, no matter how zealous or sincere that he might be, can successfully live for God if he doesn't understand the Sanctification process. It simply cannot be done. Paul answered this by saying, *"I do not frustrate the Grace of God* (if we make anything other than the Cross of Christ the object of our Faith, we frustrate the Grace of God, which means we stop its action, and the Holy Spirit will no longer help us): *for if Righteousness come by the Law* (any type of Law), *then Christ is dead in vain.* (If I can successfully live for the Lord by any means other than Faith in Christ and the Cross, then the Death of Christ was a waste)" (Gal. 2:21).

I know what it is to weep before the Lord, asking Him why He wouldn't help me. He was helping me to win untold thousands to Christ, but seemingly that help was lacking in my own personal life, no matter how hard I tried otherwise. However, the Lord actually couldn't help me in this particular, simply because my faith wasn't in His Finished Work, but in something else.

True, my situation was one of Scriptural ignorance; nevertheless, the results were the same. However, there came an hour in 1997 that the Lord opened up to me the Word of the Cross, which completely revolutionized my life, my Ministry, every single thing I am, and every single thing I do.

Furthermore, the Lord did not give me this Revelation solely for myself, but also for the entirety of the Church. As the Lord helps me to give this Message to others, and I continue to speak of the Message of the Cross, if they will receive it and believe it, then my suffering was not in vain.

WALKING AFTER THE FLESH AND WALKING AFTER THE SPIRIT

Romans 8:1 tells us that it is possible to be *"in Christ Jesus,"* in other words, *"born again,"* but still continue to *"walk after the flesh."* In fact, millions of Christians, as stated, experience this defeat on a daily basis. Every single Believer, in fact, even as Paul, has at times walked *"after the flesh."*

At the time, Jesus did not fully explain what He meant by the statement, *"The spirit truly is ready, but the flesh is weak."* There really was little point in explaining it then because the Cross was not yet a fact, which means the Holy Spirit was not yet given, at least as He would be given on the Day of Pentecost, all made possible by the Cross (Jn. 7:39; 14:17).

Jerome said, and rightly so, *"In whatever degree we trust to the Power of the Spirit, in the same degree ought we to fear because of the infirmity of the flesh."* In other words, it is a constant struggle, with the *"flesh"* ready to take the upper hand the moment we relax our vigil. The Lord has designed this Christian walk so that we constantly need to depend upon the Spirit. Yesterday's blessings, as wonderful as they were, will not suffice for today. Consecration and yielding to the Spirit must be fresh, even on a daily and constant basis, which can come about only by the constant placing of our faith in Christ and the Cross (Lk. 9:23; Eph. 5:18).

(39) "AND AGAIN HE WENT AWAY, AND PRAYED, AND SPOKE THE SAME WORDS."

The overview is:

Many times we have to pray the same thing over and over; this is not a sign of lack of faith, but can be rather of great faith.

PRAYING AGAIN

The phrase, *"And again He went away, and prayed,"* is meant to portray to us a valuable lesson. First of all, He felt the necessity of more prayer. He set the example for us by continuing to seek the Face of the Heavenly Father, in order that the Will of God be carried out. This, and this alone, was His concern.

If these words are studied closely, we learn that they abrogate the teaching of many who claim that we should not pray or ask about something more than once. These false teachers claim that such shows a lack of faith. I think this Passage tells us the very opposite.

The phrase, *"And spoke the same words,"* does not show lack of faith, but, as stated, great faith. Of His statement, *"Nevertheless, not what I will, but what You will,"* there must not be any doubt. Consequently, He will repeat this all-important Doctrine. In effect, He was saying it was not just for Himself, but for all Believers.

(40) "AND WHEN HE RETURNED, HE FOUND THEM ASLEEP AGAIN, (FOR THEIR EYES WERE HEAVY,) NEITHER WIST THEY WHAT TO ANSWER HIM."

The synopsis is:

The Greek Text means that they were literally *"weighed down."* Their sleep was not deliberate, but the result of an oppressive sorrow.

SLEEP

The phrase, *"And when He returned, He found them asleep again, for their eyes were heavy,"* means literally, in the Greek Text, they were *"pushed down"* or *"weighed down."* Their sleep was not deliberate, but rather the result of an oppressive sorrow that enveloped them. They didn't understand all that was happening, but they knew it was very foreboding.

At the time of the Transfiguration, these three had experienced the same overpowering drowsiness and the same inability to give expression to their thoughts. Then their situation was the result of fear; here, the result of grief.

The phrase, *"Neither wist they what to answer Him,"* concerns the question He previously had asked, and now probably had asked again, *"Could not you watch one hour?"* They did not know what to answer, so they said nothing!

Peter had claimed that he would even die for Christ, and *"likewise also said they all,"* but they cannot even *"watch one hour."* The lesson should be well taken for all. Within the spiritual arena, without the Power of God, we have no strength against the Evil One. How foolish for man, therefore, to say what he will or will not do!

(41) "AND HE CAME THE THIRD TIME AND SAID UNTO THEM, SLEEP ON NOW, AND TAKE YOUR REST: IT IS ENOUGH, THE HOUR IS COME; BEHOLD, THE SON OF MAN IS BETRAYED INTO THE HANDS OF SINNERS."

The exposition is:

The word *"sinners"* refers not only to Judas, but also to the religious leaders!

THE THIRD TIME

The phrase, *"And He came the third time, and said unto them, Sleep on now, and take your rest,"* is actually said in irony. There would, in fact, be no more rest! The implication is that all of these terrible scenes of the agony of Christ were repeated three times. If we are to take the Thirty-seventh Verse literally, this entire scenario lasted approximately three hours; however, we have no way of knowing if the last two times of the Passion of Christ were as long as the first.

As an aside, and observing the effect all of this had on Peter, James, and John, who were, no doubt, in excellent physical shape, we are made to realize how prime actually was the manhood of Christ. Such oppression would have killed a normal human being. His Manhood, which had never been touched by sin, sickness, or disease, was of such excellence that it defies description. I think this is evident considering the torture He would undergo up to and during the Crucifixion.

THE HOUR

The phrase, *"It is enough, the hour is come,"* is a statement so important that it beggars description. This is the *"hour"* which had been planned even before the foundation of the world (I Pet. 1:18-20; Rev. 13:8). Even though this *"hour"* would be one of absolute horror for Him, it would be, on the other hand, an *"hour"* of triumph for the entirety of the world, at least for those who will place their faith and confidence in Christ. The price would be paid for man's Redemption. The door would be opened for all to enter in, with Jesus Himself being the *"Door"* (Jn. 10:7).

SINNERS

The phrase, *"Behold, the Son of Man is betrayed into the hands of sinners,"* reflects the perfidiousness of Judas. The word *"sinners"* not only expresses Judas, but the Pharisees, the Sadducees, and even the Scribes, all religious leaders of Israel. The reputations of the Pharisees in Israel at that time were literally impeccable, at least as far as man was concerned; however, Jesus calls them *"sinners"*!

Moreover, concerning this very thing, Jesus said to Pilate, *"You could have no power at all against Me, except it were given you from above: therefore he who delivered Me* (the religious leaders of Israel) *unto you has the greater sin"* (Jn. 19:11).

The world does not recognize at all, and the Church but little, the reputation which Christ Alone can give. That which He cleanses by His Blood is cleansed indeed! However, precious few recognize and honor His Finished Work in the lives of those who truly trust Him. Nevertheless, it is not what man thinks that counts, but what God knows!

Ironically, these Pharisees were so deceived that they would kill the Lord in the Name of the Lord.

(42) "RISE UP, LET US GO; LO, HE WHO BETRAYS ME IS AT HAND."

The composition is:

This was His hour, and He was there to meet it.

THE BETRAYAL

The two words, *"Rise up,"* mean that the Disciples were still lying on the ground, and Jesus was standing. The phrase, *"Let us go,"* refers to the approach of Judas and those with him, and that Jesus and the Disciples would meet them. There is no idea here of Jesus contemplating flight.

Wuest says, *"This was His hour and He was there to meet it."*

The phrase, *"Lo, he who betrays Me is at hand,"* means that the Holy Spirit had informed Christ of their immediate arrival. So, it is obvious that even at this tremendously trying time, with Satan trying to kill Him, the Holy Spirit was watching over Him constantly. Luke said, *"And there appeared an Angel unto Him from Heaven, strengthening Him"* (Lk. 22:43). His Father would not forsake Him until He actually hung on the Cross, which, as stated, was from approximately 9 a.m. until 3 p.m. Even then, the Father forsook Him only in a limited way. God could not at this time look upon Him, because He was bearing the sin penalty of mankind, and for all time.

(43) "AND IMMEDIATELY, WHILE HE YET SPOKE, CAME JUDAS, ONE OF THE TWELVE, AND WITH HIM A GREAT MULTITUDE WITH SWORDS AND STAVES, FROM THE CHIEF PRIESTS AND THE SCRIBES AND THE ELDERS."

The diagram is:

Sadly, this was the *"Church"* of that day!

JUDAS

The phrase, *"And immediately, while He yet spoke, came Judas, one of the Twelve,"* proclaims their arrival, even while Jesus was speaking. The Holy Spirit is careful to delineate the fact that it was *"Judas, one of the Twelve,"* who betrayed Christ. The implication is dark indeed!

No man had any greater opportunity than Judas. He was shoulder-to-shoulder with Christ, the Son of God, for a period of approximately three and a half years; however, *"association"* does not bring Salvation, neither does *"environment"* or *"participation."* There must be a heart-changing work of Repentance that takes place in the life, and there must also be an ongoing relationship.

I think the evidence is clear that Judas once had an experience with the Lord. Luke wrote of him, *"Which Judas by transgression fell, that he might go to his own place"* (Acts 1:25). It is impossible to *"fall"* from something that one has not previously had; consequently, this refutes the erroneous Doctrine of Unconditional Eternal Security.

Judas, as many, allowed his relationship with Christ to wane and weaken until he became grist for Satan's mill. Judas did what he did of his own free will; consequently, he would reap the bitter results! Luke says that Judas *"went before them,"* in other words, eager to accomplish his hateful task (Lk. 22:47). Primarily, Judas traveled this course because he rejected the way of the Cross (Jn. 6:53, 60-71).

NOTES

THE RELIGIOUS LEADERS OF ISRAEL

The phrase, *"And with him a great multitude with swords and staves,"* consisted of some of the members of the vaunted Sanhedrin, members of the Temple Police, and some of the regular Roman soldiers, along with some of the personal servants of the High Priest. Thus, Gentiles and Jews were united in the daring act of arresting the Son of God. John 18:3 says they had *"lanterns and torches."*

The phrase, *"From the Chief Priests and the Scribes and the Elders,"* constituted the entirety of the religious order of Israel. Truly, *"He came unto His Own, and His Own received Him not"* (Jn. 1:11). As we have previously stated, it was not the thieves, drunks, or gamblers who killed Christ, but actually the *"Church"* of that day. It is my firm belief that if time and the Plan of God were changed, and Jesus came now as He did then, the modern Church would do the same to Him as the did the Church of old! There is no evil like religious evil!

A PERSONAL EXPERIENCE

If my memory is correct, the year was 1982. It was a Saturday morning, and I had left the house to go to a particular place close to the Mississippi River where I often went, and where I would spend much of the day in prayer and study of the Word. That morning was to present a momentous occasion.

I suppose I had been there an hour of so when the Spirit of God began to come upon me very heavily. It was so heavy that I doubled over, as a deep spirit of intercession gripped me. I remember looking around to see if anyone was watching me, inasmuch as I was walking back and forth in the open air. (It was on the levee beside the Mississippi River, which normally afforded a place of privacy.)

That morning the Lord spoke some things to my heart which would come to pass in amazing clarity. He said to me, *"I have a Message I want you to deliver to the Catholics, the Denominational Churches, and to your own,"* which referred to the Pentecostals. At that time, we had the largest Television audience in the world, at least regarding

Christian programming.

Concerning the Catholics, the Message was simple. The Lord simply told me to tell them, *"The just shall live by faith."* I was to find, however, that that Message, although it saw multiple thousands of Catholics brought to Christ, would not meet with approval from most of the Church world, and especially from my own, the Pentecostals.

To the Denominational world, the Lord told me to proclaim to them the *"necessity of the Holy Spirit."* That Message resulted in multiple thousands of these people being baptized with the Holy Spirit, but also saw, at the same time, tremendous opposition.

To the Pentecostals, the Lord told me to tell them, *"Your own* (as the Lord had put it) *must return to the Holy Spirit."* If the opposition from Catholicism and the Denominational world had been strong, it was nothing in comparison to the opposition from *"my own."* They reacted to my Message with great anger.

Actually, the Lord told me that if I obeyed Him and preached what He told me to preach, we would suffer great loss. He said, *"Your own will turn against you."* Then He asked, *"Will you do what I ask you to do?"*

MY ANSWER!

I did not immediately answer. As I have stated, the Spirit of God was on me to such an extent that I could barely stand. The word spoken to me by the Lord weighed heavily, extremely so, upon my heart. The implication was clear. He also told me, if I did what He said, we might lose everything.

At that time, as I have stated, our Telecast had the largest audience in Christendom in the world. We were even at that moment constructing Family Worship Center, which would grow to some 7,000 in attendance. The Bible College was also under construction, and would shortly begin its first semester.

Our Missions works of building Churches, Bible Schools, and schools for children were in high gear all over the world, and would grow to very large proportions. All of this streamed before my eyes, with the word of the Lord, *"You could lose it all,"* constantly flashing before me.

After a period of time, I said to the Lord,

NOTES

"I will do my best, no matter what the cost." Actually, even though the Lord had spelled it out to me, I little knew or understood just what that *"cost"* would be. The opposition, I was to find out, would be fierce, even to the place that I was, at times, concerned for my life. But when the time came that my enemies, which seemed to be many, had something they could use against me, they lost no time and spared no expense in doing so. Exactly as the Lord had said, *"My own turned against me,"* and in a way that I could not even have begun to imagine. The hatred was so intense that, in some small measure, I know and understand what the Lord experienced. That hatred and opposition also were worldwide, and regrettably, continue unto this hour!

THE MESSAGE

I realize that many think that the action taken against me by the religious world was because of what happened; however, that was only an excuse. They hated me for two reasons: because of the *"Message"* I preached, and because of the *"Anointing"* of the Holy Spirit upon that Message, which garnered tremendous results.

In the last year of Jesus' public Ministry, He was banned from most all Synagogues. I have also suffered that same opposition, as it regards Churches. As we will soon see, when Christ was condemned and rendered helpless, or so they thought, with men able to do anything to Him they so desired, then the real wickedness of these *"Chief Priests, Scribes, and Elders"* became obvious.

I also know the feeling of total helplessness, with anyone permitted to do any negative thing they so desired, which would not be censured, but rather applauded. Then one sees how many true Believers there really are! Now, as then, regrettably, there aren't many!

However, as the songwriter said, *"Through it all I have learned to depend upon the Lord."*

What a person suffers is designed by Satan and allowed by the Lord. Satan means for it to destroy us, while the Lord means for it to draw us closer to Him. As it regards spiritual failure, I take the blame for everything; but thankfully, this that Frances and

I have faced, along with our entire family, has drawn us closer to the Lord — much, much closer!

No! The Lord never gets glory out of sin, but He does get glory out of victory over sin.

(44) "AND HE WHO BETRAYED HIM HAD GIVEN THEM A TOKEN, SAYING, WHOMSOEVER I SHALL KISS, THAT SAME IS HE; TAKE HIM, AND LEAD HIM AWAY SAFELY."

The overview is:

This proclaims the most perfidious act in human history; Judas had told his co-conspirators that the One Whom he kissed would be Jesus (Ps. 109:5-20).

THE JUDAS KISS

The phrase, *"And he who betrayed Him had given them a token,"* proclaims the scheme that had been perpetrated by Judas and the religious leaders. The phrase, *"Saying, Whomsoever I shall kiss, that Same is He,"* portrays the most perfidious act in human history. The *"kiss"* was the customary mode of saluting a Rabbi. So, Judas had told his co-conspirators that the One Whom he would kiss would be Jesus. Now, the strong words spoken of Judas in Psalm 109 take on completely new meaning. Before the terrible curse concerning Judas was rendered through the lips of David by the Holy Spirit (Ps. 109:6-20), the reason was given, *"And they have rewarded Me evil for good, and hatred for My love"* (Ps. 109:5).

The phrase, *"Take Him, and lead Him away safely,"* is a somewhat ridiculous statement! First of all, Judas had seen Jesus walk through hate-filled mobs several times, when they were bent on killing Him. He had seen Him raise the dead and perform miracles of unprecedented proportions. How did he think they could *"take Him,"* unless He would simply allow them to do so?

Actually, John recorded that when Judas and these brigands approached, Jesus *"said unto them, Whom seek ye?"*

The Scriptures says, *"They answered Him, Jesus of Nazareth."*

Then *"Jesus said unto them, I am He."*

John then said, *"As soon as He had said unto them, I am He, they went backward, and fell to the ground"* (Jn. 18:4-6).

At this time, the Power of God on Him was so strong that His mere words caused all of them to fall backward to the ground. There is consequently no way they could have taken Him unless He allowed them to do so, which He did! This portrays how insensitive and dull these religious leaders were to the Moving and Operation of the Holy Spirit. In truth, they did not know God at all, despite all their religious claims! In fact, many of them had blasphemed the Holy Spirit! This means they actually were children of Satan, despite all their religious claims. To be sure, the worst child of Satan in the world is the religious child of Satan. This evil is unequalled, whether then or now!

(45) "AND AS SOON AS HE WAS COME, HE WENT STRAIGHTWAY TO HIM, AND SAID, MASTER, MASTER; AND KISSED HIM."

The exposition is:

The foul deed of betrayal is now carried out.

THE DEED IS DONE!

The phrase, *"And as soon as he was come, he went straightway to Him,"* proclaims Judas carrying out this perfidious action. The words, *"as soon as he was come,"* seems to imply that he was in a hurry to carry out this ungodly act.

The phrase, *"And said, Master, Master; and kissed Him,"* means that the traitor gave the Lord an affectionate, fervent kiss, but, as obvious, it was hypocritical. The words, *"Master, Master,"* mean *"Rabbi, Rabbi"* or *"Teacher, Teacher"*!

Chrysostom says, *"Judas felt assured by the gentleness of Christ that He would not repel him, or, if He did, the treacherous action would have answered its purpose."*

(46) "AND THEY LAID THEIR HANDS ON HIM, AND TOOK HIM."

The synopsis is:

They could only lay their hands on Him because He allowed them to do so (Jn. 10:17-18).

HANDS OF ANGER

The phrase, *"And they laid their hands on Him,"* portrays, in glaring detail, the difference between the action of Christ and the action of these hypocrites. The Hands of Jesus were used to heal the sick and cast out devils. Not one time did those hands ever minister sickness, suffering, heartache, disappointment, or failure. Every single time, when His Hands touched anyone, it was for blessing.

Conversely, the only time it is recorded that the Church of that day used their hands to touch Him, it was for the purpose of hurt and harm. The contrast should be obvious!

FRUIT!

Jesus had said, *"You shall know them by their fruits"* (Mat. 7:16). The *"fruits"* of His Life and Ministry were saved souls, changed lives, broken bondages, and the sick brought to health. In other words, the *"fruits"* were obvious!

What were the *"fruits"* of the lives and ministries of these religious leaders, etc.? No lives were changed, no souls were saved, no bondages broken, and no sick were healed. All they could do was kill. This was all they could do, because their master was Satan, who can only *"steal, kill, and destroy"* (Jn. 10:10).

The Reader should take a lesson from this. That which is not of God has no good *"fruits."* And yet, most of the money goes to support that which produces nothing, at least nothing good.

The phrase, *"And took Him,"* was, as John recorded, after they had all fallen back to the ground. Their hypocrisy was overshadowed only by their ignorance! There was no way they could have *"taken Him,"* unless He had allowed them to do so!

(47) "AND ONE OF THEM WHO STOOD BY DREW A SWORD, AND SMOTE A SERVANT OF THE HIGH PRIEST, AND CUT OFF HIS EAR."

The synopsis is:

The servant's name was *"Malchus"*; Luke is the only one who mentions the healing of the wound by our Lord (Lk. 22:51).

SIMON PETER

The phrase, *"And one of them who stood by drew a sword,"* refers to Peter (Jn. 18:10). The phrase, *"And smote a servant of the High Priest,"* proclaims, as recorded by John, that the servant's name was *"Malchus."* The phrase,

NOTES

"And cut off his ear," pictures Peter attempting, no doubt, to cleave his skull. Luke is the only one who mentions the healing of the wound by our Lord (Lk. 22:51).

Of all the thousands of healings performed by Christ in His public Ministry, the last healing He performed before His Death, at least that is recorded, was performed on an enemy. How so much He lived and proclaimed His Own Message, *"Bless them who curse you"* (Mat. 5:44).

Incidentally, if the authorities had desired to press charges against Peter, they would have had difficulty, since no evidence remained. The man's ear was whole. In a way, this is a picture of *"Justification by Faith."* No evidence is left of the sin. Jesus not only forgives, but cleanses and heals until no trace remains. Satan, in his attempt to press charges, finds no evidence.

(48) "AND JESUS ANSWERED AND SAID UNTO THEM. ARE YOU COME OUT, AS AGAINST A THIEF, WITH SWORDS AND WITH STAVES TO TAKE ME?"

The composition is:

The Lord protests the manner in which this act is carried out. He was not a thief, so why were they treating Him as one?

THE TAKING OF CHRIST

The phrase, *"And Jesus answered and said unto them,"* is spoken after the Lord had rebuked His Disciples for their resistance, after which He proceeded to rebuke those who were bent upon apprehending Him (Mat. 26:52).

The question, *"Are you come out, as a against a thief, with swords and with staves to take Me?"* proclaims the Lord protesting the manner in which this act is carried out. All of this shows that they completely misunderstood Him, even as the world continues to misunderstand Him.

The question might be asked, *"Why were they armed, inasmuch as He led no rebellion?"*

(49) "I WAS DAILY WITH YOU IN THE TEMPLE TEACHING, AND YOU TOOK ME NOT: BUT THE SCRIPTURES MUST BE FULFILLED."

The diagram is:

They did not take Him in the Temple because they did not have any legitimate charge to bring against Him. They also feared the people.

THE SCRIPTURES

The phrase, *"I was daily with you in the Temple teaching, and you took Me not,"* proclaims the wickedness of their act. Jesus had appeared in the Temple some three times in the last few days. He had taught and healed, so why didn't they take Him then?

They did not take Him then because they had no legitimate charge to level against Him. Moreover, had they tried to arrest Him in the Temple, there could have been an insurrection among the people. So they would carry out their perfidious act by night. Never was anything done in such an underhanded, ungodly, wicked, demeaning manner.

The phrase, *"But the Scriptures must be fulfilled,"* spoke of Prophecies given to the Prophets of old, as the Lord through foreknowledge saw what would happen (Isa., Chpt. 53; Zech. 11:13; 13:7).

As we have previously stated, this does not mean that these individuals were foreordained to do these dastardly deeds, but simply that God saw what they would do of their own free choice, and then foretold it through the Prophets. It is not predestination, but rather foreknowledge.

(50) "AND THEY ALL FORSOOK HIM, AND FLED."

The overview is:

This refers to the Eleven Disciples. Not being allowed to fight, they fled. The flesh will fight or flee, but it will not *"trust."*

THE FORSAKING OF CHRIST

Even though all of His Disciples fled at this time, Peter and John, to their credit, did take courage and followed Him to the house of the High Priest, where Peter was to deny Him. This is the beginning of the fulfillment of the Prophecy of David, *"I looked on My Right Hand, and, behold, but there was no man who would know Me: refuge failed Me; no man cared for My soul"* (Ps. 142:4).

It is too awful to contemplate, but, at this time, not a single individual, not even His chosen Disciples, stood up for Him. He had healed thousands, but none were there to speak up for Him. He had taught tens of thousands, even with Words of Life, which they had never before heard, and yet there is no one at this terrible time to speak a word of kindness to Him!

Even those He had purposely chosen now refused to choose Him.

(51) "AND THERE FOLLOWED HIM A CERTAIN YOUNG MAN, HAVING A LINEN CLOTH CAST ABOUT HIS NAKED BODY; AND THE YOUNG MEN LAID HOLD ON HIM."

The exposition is:

Even though it is not known for sure, most think that this *"young man"* was Mark, who wrote this Gospel.

JOHN MARK?

The phrase, *"And there followed Him a certain young man,"* is given only here.

Who was this young man?

Inasmuch as the Scripture is silent regarding identity, no one knows for sure; however, Hahn says, *"In this curious incident, we have the monogram of the painter* (Mark) *in a dark corner of the picture."*

The phrase, *"Having a linen cloth cast about his naked body,"* tells us several things:

1. Whoever this young man was, he must have been in bed when news was given to him of the arrest of Christ.

2. The *"linen cloth"* spoken of here was that which people of poor circumstances could have not have owned. Therefore, he belonged to a family of means.

3. This was a kind of light cloak frequently worn in hot weather.

The phrase, *"The young men laid hold on him,"* means the soldiers were setting about to arrest him.

(52) "AND HE LEFT THE LINEN CLOTH, AND FLED FROM THEM NAKED."

The synopsis is:

This probably means that he was left only with his undergarments; there is no evidence that they pursued him.

THE LINEN CLOTH

This incident portrays to us the great hatred of the Jews against Jesus, inasmuch as they endeavored to seize a young man who was merely following at a distance. The idea of the Verse is that the soldiers grabbed him, but he struggled to get away. In the struggle, his *"linen cloth garment"* was pulled from him.

In the idea that this may have been John Mark, some suggest that his may have been the house in which the Lord celebrated the Passover, from whence He went out to the Mount of Olives. If this is correct, and it probably is, there is even a possibility that Mark was present at the Last Supper. If that is true, Mark may have sensed that something was about to happen to Christ.

There is even a possibility that after the arrest of Christ, the group passed by the house of Mark, awakening him, which occasioned this scenario.

(53) "AND THEY LED JESUS AWAY TO THE HIGH PRIEST: AND WITH HIM WERE ASSEMBLED ALL THE CHIEF PRIESTS AND THE ELDERS AND THE SCRIBES."

The structure is:

The High Priest was Caiaphas; however, we learn from John 18:13 that Jesus was first brought before Annas, the father-in-law of Caiaphas.

THE HIGH PRIEST

The phrase, *"And they led Jesus away to the High Priest,"* refers, as stated, to Caiaphas. Annas and his five sons held the High Priesthood in succession. Caiaphas, his son-in-law, stepped in between the first and the second sons and held the office for twelve years.

It is supposed that it was at the house of Annas where the price of the betrayal was paid to Judas. Annas, although not then High Priest, must have had considerable influence in the councils of the Sanhedrin. This probably explains why our Lord was first taken to him.

The High Priesthood of Israel was now bought and sold like a commodity. In other words, whoever gave Rome the most money was appointed the High Priest, with most of these coming from the party of the Sadducees.

CHIEF PRIESTS, ELDERS, AND SCRIBES

The phrase, *"And with Him were assembled all the Chief Priests and the Elders and the Scribes,"* proclaims the religious hierarchy of Israel. It is very difficult, if not impossible, for all organized religion not to fall into this category of wickedness. Most of the laity do not realize it, but organized religion is just as political, if not more so, than its worldly counterpart. As such, the Will of God is totally abrogated, and the will of man becomes paramount. As such, it becomes Satanic!

This does not mean that everyone associated with organized religion is Satanic, for there were even two members of the Jewish Sanhedrin who were Godly, i.e., Nicodemus and Joseph of Arimathaea. However, as particular Church groups begin to apostatize, the idea is almost always ventured forth that association with that particular Denomination or group plays a part in one's Salvation. An elitist attitude develops, which is indicative of self-righteousness. As the spiritual deterioration becomes more and more acute, however, less and less people in such a particular Denomination truly know Christ. This happens to almost all religious Denominations.

Many Denominations begin with true Holy Spirit Revival; however, if the following generation does not experience the same Moving of the Spirit, the spiritual deterioration begins. Most Denominations do not survive spiritually after three generations. They become more and more man-led, and, consequently, less and less God-led. Unless there is a Move of God, the end result is identical to that which crucified Christ.

(54) "AND PETER FOLLOWED HIM AFAR OFF, EVEN INTO THE PALACE OF THE HIGH PRIEST: AND HE SAT WITH THE SERVANTS, AND WARMED HIMSELF AT THE FIRE."

The exegesis is:

The Holy Spirit delineates the *"afar off."* This is meant to call our attention to the boasts of Peter, which this following at a distance occasioned.

FOLLOWING AFAR OFF

The phrase, *"And Peter followed Him afar off,"* now begins the saga of the big fisherman. At this time, a great turmoil, no doubt, is going on in the heart of Peter. The Holy Spirit delineates the *"afar off."*

What would have happened if Peter had followed in the very Presence of Christ instead of *"afar off"*?

To be sure, nothing would have happened to him because Christ would have seen to it that he would have been spared. However, it is a moot point!

The phrase, *"Even into the palace of the High Priest,"* actually refers to the court of the palace, where the guards and servants of the High Priest were assembled. Jesus had been taken inside the palace to be arraigned before the Council. John tells us that inasmuch as he (John) was known to the High Priest, he had been the means of bringing in Peter, who had been standing outside at the door leading into the court (Jn. 18:15).

WARMING AT SATAN'S FIRE

The phrase, *"And he sat with the servants, and warmed himself at the fire,"* proclaims the coolness of the early spring, especially considering that it was now after midnight. The glow of the fire would have clearly outlined Peter's features as he crouched to warm himself.

The idea of having a trial at this ridiculous time of the night is indicative of the perverseness of this action. Such action was clearly opposed to Mosaic Law, which the religious leaders of Israel so loudly claimed to keep. To be honest, the worst criminal would not have been tried at this time of night; however, among other things, they were fearful that if Jesus had been tried during the day, the vast crowds filling Jerusalem for the Passover would have come to His aid. Even above that, Jesus must die at the same time as the Passover lambs were killed, regarding the evening Sacrifice, which took place at 3 o'clock each afternoon.

Once again, we emphasize that these evil men did this of their own free will, not at all coerced by God. While it is true that they would fulfill Bible Prophecy, still, it is not true that they were predestined to do so. The predestination only pertained to Christ and how and when He would die, and not who would bring about this evil process.

(55) "AND THE CHIEF PRIESTS AND ALL THE COUNCIL SOUGHT FOR WITNESS AGAINST JESUS TO PUT HIM TO DEATH; AND FOUND NONE."

The composition is:

They were attempting to legalize their vile action.

A WITNESS AGAINST CHRIST?

The phrase, *"And the Chief Priests and all the Council,"* refers to the vaunted Sanhedrin, the great Council of the Jews of Jerusalem, which consisted of 71 members, made up of Scribes, Elders, and prominent members of the High Priestly families. The High Priest, Caiaphas, was the president of this body. The most important cases in the land were brought before this tribunal, inasmuch as Rome had left it in the power of this group to try such cases, and also to pronounce the sentence of death; however, a capital sentence of death was not valid unless it was confirmed by the Roman Procurator, in this case, Pilate.

The word *"all"* indicates that it was a full meeting of this body of men; however, it is not known whether Nicodemus or Joseph of Arimathaea, both members of this body, were present. The word *"all"* could very well refer to those opposed to Christ, which pertained to all except the two mentioned.

The phrase, *"Sought for witness against Jesus to put Him to death,"* proclaims this group attempting to legalize their action. They were attempting to find a way to kill the Lord in the Name of the Lord! Deception is a cruel thing!

How could these religious leaders have sunk so low until they, who were supposed to know God more than anyone in the world, didn't even recognize Him, even though He stood before them?

Even though my statement is strong, I feel it must be said. If the truth were known, many, if not most, of present religious leaders of modern Christendom fall into the same category. Jesus said as much concerning the Church in the last days.

THE MODERN CHURCH

Jesus said, *"The Kingdom of Heaven is like unto leaven, which a woman took, and hid in three measures of meal, till the whole was leavened"* (Mat. 13:33). This means that in these last days, which are now upon us, the *"whole"* of the modern Church would become so corrupted by false doctrines and unscriptural programs that its entirety would be *"leavened,"* i.e., corrupted.

Paul said, *"Now the Spirit* (Holy Spirit) *speaks expressly* (pointedly), *that in the latter times* (the times in which we now live, the last of the last days, which begin the fulfillment of Endtime Prophecies) *some shall depart from the Faith* (any time Paul uses the term *'the Faith,'* in short, he is referring to the Cross; so we are told here that some will depart from the Cross as the means of Salvation and Victory), *giving heed to seducing spirits* (evil spirits, i.e., *'religious spirits,'* making something seem like what it isn't) *and doctrines of devils* (should have been translated, *'doctrines of demons'*; the *'seducing spirits'* entice Believers away from the True Faith, causing them to believe *'doctrines inspired by demon spirits')"* (I Tim. 4:1).

NO EVIDENCE

The phrase, *"And found none,"* refers to the emptiness of their accusations. There was nothing they could legally or morally put their hands on by which to condemn Him; consequently, He was arraigned before this Court, not because He had done something wrong, but simply because they hated Him.

The Psalmist had prophesied some 1,000 years before, saying, *"For the mouth of the wicked and the mouth of the deceitful are opened against Me: they have spoken against Me with their lying tongues.*

"They compassed Me about also with words of hatred; and they fought against Me without a cause" (Ps. 109:2-3).

(56) "FOR MANY BORE FALSE WITNESS AGAINST HIM, BUT THEIR WITNESS AGREED NOT TOGETHER."

The diagram is:

This Passage proclaims such being contrary to the Law of Moses, which required a trial to begin with those things which would acquit the accused instead of condemning Him.

FALSE WITNESSES

The phrase, *"For many bore false witness against Him,"* proclaims such being contrary to the Law of Moses. Under that Law, the individual was judged to be innocent until proven guilty. In this case, not one thing was sought that could acquit Christ. They were determined to kill Him, so they looked for every excuse possible, not realizing they were fulfilling Bible Prophecy.

The phrase, *"But their witness agreed not together,"* proclaims them not even being able to find one honest witness against Him, much less two, which were required before charges could legally be brought.

Whatever things these witnesses brought forward were either false or self-contradictory. In other words, the trial was a farce!

(57) "AND THERE AROSE CERTAIN, AND BORE FALSE WITNESS AGAINST HIM, SAYING,

(58) "WE HEARD HIM SAY, I WILL DESTROY THIS TEMPLE THAT IS MADE WITH HANDS, AND WITHIN THREE DAYS I WILL BUILD ANOTHER MADE WITHOUT HANDS."

The overview is:

They had added the words, *"That is made with hands, and I will build another made without hands."* They tried to make it seem as if Jesus was talking about the Jerusalem Temple, when actually what He did say was speaking of His physical body; He really said, *"Destroy this Temple* (speaking of His Own Body) *and in three days I will raise it up."*

THE TEMPLE OF HIS BODY

The phrase, *"And there arose certain,"* speaks of two men, as given in Matthew 26:60. The phrase, *"And bore false witness against Him, saying,"* proclaims the Sanhedrin thinking they finally had a proper accusation against Him; however, they were to see that this was false, as well!

The phrase, *"We heard Him say,"* constitutes a lie, because He did not say what they accused Him of saying.

First of all, He was not speaking of Herod's Temple, as they were accusing Him, but His Own Body. He also was not speaking of destroying His Body Himself, but that they, the Jews, even this very Sanhedrin, would destroy it, i.e., kill Him. It was a Prophecy concerning the way He would die, and that He would raise it up, hence, the Resurrection.

The phrase, *"That is made with hands, and within three days I will build another made without hands,"* is not, as we have stated, what He said! They had added the words, *"that is made with hands"* and *"I will build another made without hands,"* to make it seem as if Jesus was talking about the Temple in Jerusalem. This is a favorite method of Satan, especially when he is successful in getting religious people to do his work, which he often is! Words are twisted to make it seem as if something else altogether is said.

Those who do such things have no regard or concern for the truth, but just the lying accusation. This court, as is obvious, was not seeking Truth, as Satan never seeks Truth. Likewise, those in the religious world who follow in Satan's train also do not seek Truth!

(59) "BUT NEITHER SO DID THEIR WITNESS AGREE TOGETHER."

The structure is:

In the Greek Text, the idea is that they made repeated attempts to bring testimony that would warrant conviction, but without success.

NO AGREEMENT

As they began to venture forth this accusation, they found themselves opposing each other. One was saying that He said thus and so, while another was saying, *"No, He said this...."* Consequently, their testimony falls down.

To which we have alluded, according to the Law of Deuteronomy 19:15, the testimony of two witnesses was required for a conviction. No two witnesses could be found who agreed on essential points. The idea in the Greek Text, as stated, is that they made repeated attempts to bring testimony that would warrant conviction, but they were not able to do so.

(60) "AND THE HIGH PRIEST STOOD UP IN THE MIDST, AND ASKED JESUS, SAYING, DO YOU ANSWER NOTHING? WHAT IS IT WHICH THESE WITNESS AGAINST YOU?"

The exegesis is:

The High Priest had become exasperated by their inability to bring forth a credible witness, and sought by bluster to make up the lack of evidence.

THE HIGH PRIEST

The phrase, *"And the High Priest stood up in the midst,"* suggests that this man had become exasperated. He would try to ramrod an accusation through, even though there was no evidence. They had no regard for Truth, but only their determination to kill him in order to silence him, which they were determined to do at whatever cost. To be sure, the price would be high, i.e., the destruction of their nation and their banishment among the nations of the world, to wander as outcasts for nearly 2,000 years.

NO ANSWER!

The question, *"And asked Jesus, saying, Do you answer nothing?"* now presents a change of tactics. Unable to get credible witnesses, Caiaphas will now attempt to trap Jesus by getting Him to say something which will give them grounds for some type of condemnation. They are, by now, desperate! With this tactic, they will succeed; however, Jesus will say nothing wrong, but they will claim that He has!

Jesus did not answer these accusations made by these false witnesses because such was pointless. Silence, in fact, was the greatest answer of all! Had they been seeking Truth, that would have been a different story; however, they had no interest in truth!

The question, *"What is it which these witness against You?"* proclaims Caiaphas demanding an answer from Christ concerning the accusations, but Jesus says nothing, at least to that charge.

(61) "BUT HE HELD HIS PEACE, AND ANSWERED NOTHING. AGAIN THE HIGH PRIEST ASKED HIM, AND SAID UNTO HIM, ARE YOU THE CHRIST, THE SON OF THE BLESSED?"

The structure is:

This Passage actually means, *"Are You the Messiah, namely, The Anointed of God?"*

CHRIST, THE SON OF GOD!

The phrase, *"But He held His peace, and answered nothing,"* means, in the Greek Text, that He kept on maintaining His silence. To answer these foolish questions would have been admitting the authority of this assembly, which had been illegally brought together by an unjust arrest and by the employment of perjured witnesses; consequently, Christ would lend no credence to this unlawful assembly. The efforts of Caiaphas to force Jesus to incriminate Himself were, within themselves, unlawful in jurisprudence; however, this wicked assembly had long since ceased to abide by any degree of honesty and integrity.

The phrase, *"Again the High Priest asked Him,"* will now present another tactic. Caiaphas already knows the answer to the question he now asks, because Jesus had made clear Who He actually was on several occasions.

The question, *"And said unto Him, Are You the Christ, the Son of the Blessed?"* actually was asking Him if He was the *"Messiah?"* The word *"Blessed,"* in the Greek Text, is *"Eulogetos,"* which is used as a Name for God.

Josephus, the Jewish Historian, gave this statement concerning Jesus and Who He was:

"Now there was about this time Jesus, a wise man, if it be lawful to call Him a man; for He was a doer of wonderful works, a Teacher of such men as received the Truth with pleasure. He drew over to Him both many of the Jews and many of the Gentiles. He was the Christ. And when Pilate, at the suggestion of the principle men among us, had condemned Him to the Cross, those who loved Him at the first did not forsake Him; for He appeared to them alive again the third day, as the Divine Prophets had foretold these and ten thousand other wonderful things concerning Him. And the Tribe of Christians, so named from Him, are not extinct at this day" (Josephus, Ant. of the Jews, page 535, 3).

(62) "AND JESUS SAID, I AM: AND YOU SHALL SEE THE SON OF MAN SITTING ON THE RIGHT HAND OF POWER, AND COMING IN THE CLOUDS OF HEAVEN."

The composition is:

Jesus' statement constitutes a bold declaration of Who He was. The pronoun *"I"* is used for emphasis; it is *"as for Myself, in contradistinction to all others, I am."* His answer left absolutely no doubt (Ex. 3:14).

I AM

The phrase, *"And Jesus said, I am,"* constitutes a bold declaration of Who He was. Christ either deceived men by conscious fraud, He deceived Himself, or He was God. It is impossible to get out of this dilemma.

Wuest says, *"The pronoun 'I' is used for emphasis. It is 'as for Myself, in contradistinction to all others, I am.'"* In other words, the answer given by Jesus left absolutely no doubt about Who He claimed to be; Who, in Truth, He actually was!

Jesus had refused to answer the false accusations; but to this question concerning His Divinity, He must answer! To refuse to do so would have been a denial of Who He was.

Furthermore, as Chrysostom says, *"Our Lord answered thus that He might leave without excuse all those who listened to Him, who would not hereafter be able to plead in the Day of Judgment that, when our Lord was solemnly asked in the Council whether He was the Son of God, He had refused to answer, or had answered evasively. The answer of our Lord is full of majesty and sublimity."*

Not only must He answer Who He was, but these men also must know, and without doubt, that they are condemning the Messiah, the Holy One of God, even the *"I am"* of the Old Testament.

THE IMPACT OF HIS STATEMENT

When Jesus gave this solemn witness as to His Divinity, it must have hit like a bombshell. There is no way it could have been otherwise. Grown men must have trembled, and yet they refused to heed this, the last appeal to their hearts and consciences, which would have saved them and their nation. Instead they pressed on, even to their own doom.

Considering the three and a half years of Miracles, even to the raising of the dead, even in a manner the world never before had seen, and even with the fulfilling of all Prophecy, still, they would not believe! Truly, as the Prophet Jeremiah said, *"The heart is deceitful above all things, and desperately wicked: who can know it?"* (Jer. 17:9).

The phrase, *"And you shall see,"* proclaims that Caiaphas, as well as the entirety of the Jewish Sanhedrin, would ultimately *"see"* that what Jesus had just said was absolutely true.

It is as if Jesus said, *"You, O Caiaphas, and you, the Chief Priests and Elders of the Jews, are now unjustly condemning Me as a false Prophet and a false Christ. But the day is at hand when I, Who am now a prisoner at your judgment seat, shall sit on the Throne of Glory as the Judge of you and of all mankind. You are now about to condemn Me to the death of the Cross. But I shall then sit in Judgment upon you, and condemn you for this terrible guilt of slaying Me, Who am the True God and the Judge of the world"* (Bickersteth).

THE RIGHT HAND OF POWER

The phrase, *"The Son of Man sitting on the right hand of power, and coming in the clouds of Heaven,"* is a reference to Psalms 110:1 and Daniel 7:13. These two statements were considered as a claim to Messiahship by the Jews, as these Old Testament Passages were looked upon as Messianic.

Consequently, these words, uttered by Christ at this trial before the Sanhedrin, were, as we have alluded, a final, but ineffective, summons to Repentance and Faith, in that the Jewish leaders, instead of repenting of their rejection of Jesus as Messiah and accepting Him as such, caused Him to be crucified.

Jesus is saying, *"You are judging Me now, but, one day, I will judge you. And even though you will now kill Me, still, I will rise again and one day come back to this Earth in Power and Glory.*

"That which you now deny Me, I will have at the Second Coming."

The answer of Jesus was so ringing and so declarative that there was absolutely no way of misunderstanding what He had said. To be sure, that which He said will one day come to pass, exactly as He said it.

Actually, the latter part concerning the Second Coming will be fulfilled first. At the conclusion of the Kingdom Age, which the Second Coming will precipitate, the Great White Throne Judgment will commence, with Jesus judging all, as He sits *"on the Right Hand of Power,"* i.e., God (Rev. 20:11-15).

It is also a solemn announcement to the world that Jesus is now the Saviour, but, at a point in time, He will become the Judge. As wonderful as He was, and is, as Saviour, likewise, He will be as Judge!

(63) "THEN THE HIGH PRIEST RENT HIS CLOTHES, AND SAID, WHAT NEED WE ANY FURTHER WITNESSES?"

The exegesis is:

In their minds, this was the sought-for evidence. The prisoner had incriminated Himself, or so they said!

THE ACTION OF THE RELIGIOUS LEADERSHIP OF ISRAEL

The phrase, *"Then the High Priest rent his clothes,"* signified the garment immediately under the outer robe. The Jewish tunic was open under the chin, whereby the wearer could seize the garment with both hands at this opening and violently tear it asunder down to the waist. The tearing of garments was an old sign of mourning or sorrow first mentioned in Genesis 37:29.

The Mosaic Law forbade the High Priest from rending his garments in the case of private troubles (Lev. 10:6; 21:10), but, when acting as judge, he was required by custom to express in this way his horror of that which he considered to be blasphemy, at least that uttered in his presence. Some of the Early Church Fathers think that, by this action, Caiaphas involuntarily typified the rending of the Priesthood from himself and from the Jewish nation.

As the abrogation of the Throne of David was carried out by Nebuchadnezzar some 600 years before, the Priesthood now also was destroyed, or soon would be, placing Israel in a position of having no more reason to exist. And that is exactly what happened!

For nearly 2,000 years the Jewish people have wandered from nation to nation as outcasts, because, by their rejection of Jesus Christ, they, during this time, have had no Divine purpose. As all know, in 1948 Israel once again became a nation. This was brought about by the Lord in order that they may fulfill Divine Prophecies and ultimately accept Jesus Christ as Messiah and Redeemer. They will then resume their role and place as originally intended by God (Zech., Chpt. 14).

The question, *"And said, What need we any further witnesses?"* proclaims the statement of Christ concerning His Deity being the sought-for evidence. The prisoner had incriminated Himself, or so they said!

The liars they had produced as *"witnesses"*

could not agree among themselves; Caiaphas consequently felt that this was the only opportunity of condemnation he would have. He, therefore, seized upon it.

(64) "YOU HAVE HEARD THE BLASPHEMY: WHAT DO YOU THINK? AND THEY ALL CONDEMNED HIM TO BE GUILTY OF DEATH."

The composition is:

This proclaims the High Priest rendering his conclusion even before testing the claims of Jesus; consequently, it becomes more and more obvious that this farce of a trial was not convened to seek for Truth, but instead to find any way to condemn Christ.

GUILTY OF DEATH?

The exclamation, *"You have heard the blasphemy,"* proclaims the High Priest rendering his conclusion even before testing the claims of Jesus. They wanted to condemn Christ at any cost. As previously stated, they would get their desires, but the price would be high — the destruction of themselves and their nation.

No! What they heard was not *"blasphemy,"* but rather a proclamation of the Son of God respecting His Deity. There was *"blasphemy"* all right, but it was on their part instead!

The question, *"What do you think?"* would be the single most important question ever asked of these men. Their answer would seal their eternal doom. The question, *"What do you think?"* asked by Caiaphas so long is a question that not only the Jewish Sanhedrin had to answer, but also every single human being who has ever lived. Actually, this is the question of the ages.

THE CONTROVERSY

The controversy is not so much with God as it is with His Son, the Lord Jesus Christ. Much of the world is steeped in heathenistic religion and does not believe that Jesus Christ is the Son of God and the Redeemer of the world. So, as Caiaphas and the Sanhedrin, they have given their answer.

Even in the ranks of that which purports to be *"Christian,"* this is the question of the hour. The world of Roman Catholicism claims to believe that Jesus is the Son of God, but almost altogether ignores Him in favor of His mother, Mary. She is lionized, even deified, whether they admit to such or not! By their actions, which center up in Mary-worship, they deny Jesus Christ, whether they realize it or not.

Even in Christian Protestant circles, a very great percentage do not believe that Jesus Christ is the Son of God. On this question hangs the Salvation of the entirety of mankind, and for all time. While no Salvation is afforded for the mere affirmation that Jesus is the Son of God, still, it is certain that one cannot be saved without embracing this cardinal doctrine. Believing that He is the Son of God is the first step in the Salvation process, and accepting Him as one's Lord and Saviour is the concluding step (Jn. 3:16).

So, *"What do you think?"*

CONDEMNATION

The phrase, *"And they all condemned Him to be guilty of death,"* thus fulfilled the Prophecy of 8:31. According to Luke 23:51, Joseph of Arimathaea was not present, since he did not consent to the death of Jesus. It seems that Nicodemus also was absent. He probably was not invited because of his sympathy with Christ. So, the *"all"* pertained to those present, and not to those absent.

Even though these two men were members of the highest ruling religious body in Israel, which spoke of unparalleled success, still, the emptiness in their hearts was not satisfied until they met Jesus. Then they found what the soul of man craves.

Salvation is not a philosophy or a set of rules and regulations. Neither is it a Church, but rather a Person — more particularly, a Man, The Man, Jesus Christ. There were only two of these seventy-one members of the vaunted Sanhedrin who knew and served the Lord and accepted Christ; this ratio would probably be very close to modern Christendom respecting those in religious hierarchy who are truly saved.

I am not saying that the Holy Spirit intended for this to serve as an example, but, I suspect, especially when one considers all of Christendom, that most modern Christian leaders, so-called, would fall into the category of those who condemned Christ to death. I realize this statement is strong, but I believe it to be true.

And how do I come to this conclusion?

FRUIT

Jesus said, *"You shall know them by their fruits"* (Mat. 7:16). Most in religious hierarchy oppose anything that is of God, exactly as their counterparts of 2,000 years ago. It is true that they are religious, even very religious, even as the Pharisees of old, but, still, it is religion and not Christlikeness. Actually, religion is the biggest business in the world, whether apostate Christendom or the other major religions, far eclipsing General Motors, Honda, Wal-Mart, Microsoft, etc. It actually enslaves much of the world.

When Lenin, the father of Communism, said, *"Religion is the opiate of the masses,"* he actually was correct. However, that in no way includes a true relationship with Jesus Christ. I have been in Russia, even in the services of the Russian Orthodox Church. I have watched the people kissing the feet of the Priests and kissing the religious icons on the walls or places of prominence in all of these Churches.

I know how the Apostle Paul felt as *"his spirit was stirred in him, when he saw the city* (Athens) *wholly given to idolatry"* (Acts 17:16). The Russian Orthodox Church, Catholicism, the Church of England, and much of Protestant Christendom can be labeled only as *"idolatry."* And yet, there is a True Remnant called the *"Body of Christ,"* which truly knows the Lord as their Saviour and Redeemer. To be sure, that group is small, at least in comparison to the whole. But, nevertheless, it is *"a Glorious Church, not having spot, or wrinkle, or any such thing; but that it should be Holy and without blemish"* (Eph. 5:27).

(65) "AND SOME BEGAN TO SPIT ON HIM, AND TO COVER HIS FACE, AND TO BUFFET HIM, AND TO SAY UNTO HIM, PROPHESY: AND THE SERVANTS DID STRIKE HIM WITH THE PALMS OF THEIR HANDS."

The overview is:

The *"some"* included members of the Sanhedrin, as well as the Temple guards and soldiers. Actually, the evidence is that the latter did not join in these indignities until they observed the members of the Sanhedrin engaging in these vile acts.

TERRIBLE PERSECUTION

The phrase, *"And some began to spit on Him,"* fulfilled Isaiah 50:6, *"I hid not My Face from shame and spitting."* There is no way the mind of man can adequately comprehend the depths to which the religious heart can sink. These Verses will show that it is the most vile of all. Even hardened Roman soldiers, who were pagans, were not this cruel. Such action is reserved for professors of religion.

The phrase, *"And to cover His Face,"* means they wrapped a covering around the Lord's Head so as to blindfold Him. This was for the purpose of asking Him, actually with great sarcasm, to identify the one who struck Him. The phrase, *"And to buffet Him,"* is, in the Greek Text, *"kolaphizo,"* which means *"to strike with the fist,"* i.e., *"to pummel."*

Isaiah, some 800 years before, had prophesied, *"His Visage was so marred more than any man"* (Isa. 52:14). The effect of the brutalities described here caused His Face to be so marred that His appearance was not that of a man, but rather like something not human. It also must be noted that modern religious leaders who do not know Christ will do the same to the true followers of Christ, if the law of the land did not prevent them. Actually, more blood has been spilled in this fashion than words ever could begin to describe.

As an aside, this one Scripture (Isa. 52:14) pretty well destroys the myth of the Shroud of Turin, which is alleged by some in Catholicism to be the cloth which covered the Face of Jesus after His Death. To be sure, whatever type of cloth it was which was placed over His Face at that particular time, it would have had no discernible imprint because of the disfigurement of His Features.

MOCKERY

The phrase, *"And to say unto Him, Prophesy,"* now adds the spiritual abuse to the physical abuse. The phrase, *"And the servants did strike Him with the palms of their hands,"* proclaims, as stated, them joining in after they see the religious leaders of Israel conducting themselves accordingly.

How could these people do such a thing?

Despite their religious activity, these men were wicked, vile reprobates. They claimed to know God, but actually were children of Satan. Had they known God, they would have known that which belonged to God, namely His Son, the Lord Jesus Christ.

People who truly know the Lord will know that which is of the Lord. If they oppose that which is truly of God, it is a sign that they do not know God, or at least have very little relationship with Him, if any!

(66) "AND AS PETER WAS BENEATH IN THE PALACE, THERE CAME ONE OF THE MAIDS OF THE HIGH PRIEST."

The synopsis is:

This speaks of the porch of the palace; the trial of Jesus was held in an upper story.

SIMON PETER

The phrase, *"And as Peter was beneath in the palace,"* speaks of a different location than where Jesus was being held. The phrase, *"There came one of the maids of the High Priest,"* concerns one of the domestics who had the very early morning shift, which evidently began sometime before daylight.

(67) "AND WHEN SHE SAW PETER WARMING HIMSELF, SHE LOOKED UPON HIM, AND SAID, AND YOU ALSO WERE WITH JESUS OF NAZARETH."

The composition is:

The very fact that Peter was there shows that he did not want to desert Jesus. His actions, however, would show that he does not desire to stand up for Him either.

THE MAID

The phrase, *"And when she saw Peter warming himself,"* now begins the saga which will prove hollow the boastings of Peter. Peter was in a spiritual twilight zone. He was, in fact, in the same position as multiple millions are presently; they want Christ, but not enough to stand up and be counted. They are neither here nor there. Almost all in such a position, when tested, which sooner or later will come about, will fail in the same manner as did Peter. There is no middle ground in serving Christ. One either serves Him with one's whole heart or serves Him not at all!

The phrase, *"She looked upon him and said,"* means, in the Greek Text, that she *"gazed intently at him."* The phrase, *"And you also were with Jesus of Nazareth,"* means that even though she possibly did not know his name, yet she knew he was a follower of Christ. Quite possibly she had seen him with Jesus at an earlier time. Her statement also suggests much more than this knowledge, but also that she was well aware of the proceedings concerning Jesus, which even then were taking place.

(68) "BUT HE DENIED, SAYING, I KNOW NOT, NEITHER UNDERSTAND I WHAT YOU SAY. AND HE WENT OUT INTO THE PORCH; AND THE ROOSTER CROWED."

The overview is:

Peter's test came in an unexpected form, which discovered a weak point — his lack of moral courage.

THE ROOSTER

The phrase, *"But he denied, saying, I know not, neither understand I what you say,"* proclaims Peter doing exactly what Jesus had said he would do!

Swete suggests:

"Had Peter been called to go with the Master to judgment and death, possibly he would have done so. However, his test came in an unexpected form, and it discovered a weak point — his lack of moral courage."

In simple terminology, Peter was attempting to act as if he was a stranger to Christ, not knowing or understanding what the girl was talking about.

The phrase, *"And he went out into the porch; and the rooster crowed,"* proclaims his consternation after he answered the girl. He was, no doubt, filled with guilt. He leaves the fire and walks away from the small crowd which had gathered, probably to get away from the girl more so than anything else.

Then he heard the rooster crow!

I wonder what was in Peter's mind when this happened. He, no doubt, recalled the Words of Jesus, *"That this day, even in this night, before the rooster crows twice, you shall deny Me thrice"* (Vs. 30).

Did he resolve not to deny again? Or was

he so caught up in the act of the moment that he momentarily forgot that Jesus said he would do this thing three times?

(69) "AND A MAID SAW HIM AGAIN, AND BEGAN TO SAY TO THEM WHO STOOD BY, THIS IS ONE OF THEM."

The diagram is:

This is a different maid.

ANOTHER MAID

The phrase, *"And a maid saw him again,"* implies that this is a different *"maid"* than the previous. The phrase, *"And began to say to them who stood by, this is one of them,"* probably means that Peter had by now returned to the fire and, once more, he was being pointed out.

(70) "AND HE DENIED IT AGAIN. AND A LITTLE AFTER, THEY WHO STOOD BY SAID AGAIN TO PETER, SURELY YOU ARE ONE OF THEM: FOR YOU ARE A GALILAEAN, AND YOUR SPEECH AGREES THERETO."

The synopsis is:

This occasions the third denial, exactly as Jesus said it would happen.

THE SECOND DENIAL

The phrase, *"And he denied it again,"* proclaims the second denial. He possibly said basically the same words that he previously had said. When the second maid pointed him out, quite possibly a man joined in with her, because Luke records Peter, concerning his association with Jesus, saying at this time, *"Man, I am not"* (Lk. 22:58).

The phrase, *"And a little after, they who stood by said to Peter, Surely you are one of them,"* proclaims the occasion for the third denial. The people standing around the fire, both men and women, began to pick up on what the *"maid"* had said.

The phrase, *"For you are a Galilaean, and your speech agrees thereto,"* is actually used in contempt. Many people in Jerusalem looked down on the Galilaeans for various reasons; their accent was one of the reasons. In other words, they were looked at somewhat like country bumpkins. It was commonly known that most of the Twelve, i.e., the chosen Disciples of Jesus, were from Galilee.

(71) "BUT HE BEGAN TO CURSE AND TO SWEAR, SAYING, I KNOW NOT THIS MAN OF WHOM YOU SPEAK."

The structure is:

This does not refer to profanity, but rather *"to declare anathema or a curse."* Peter thus declares himself subject to the Divine curse if he is not telling the truth when he disclaims all acquaintance with Jesus. What he did was, in fact, much worse than the use of profanity.

THE CURSE

The phrase, *"But he began to curse and to swear,"* proclaims Peter declaring himself subject to the Divine curse if he is not telling the truth when he disclaims all acquaintance with Jesus. The word *"swear"* is the same word found in Hebrews 3:11, where God is said to swear, that is, to put Himself under oath. Peter's sin was about as bad as could be imagined, inasmuch as he brought God into his lie. He was, in effect, calling on God to curse him to eternal damnation if he was not telling the truth concerning his disavowal of any association with Christ — and this at the very moment the Sanhedrin and others were striking Jesus repeatedly and were spitting on His Face.

The phrase, *"Saying, I know not this Man of Whom you speak,"* proclaims the third denial, which completely fulfilled the prediction of Christ.

(72) "AND THE SECOND TIME THE ROOSTER CROWED. AND PETER CALLED TO MIND THE WORD THAT JESUS SAID UNTO HIM, BEFORE THE ROOSTER CROWS TWICE, YOU SHALL DENY ME THRICE. AND WHEN HE THOUGHT THEREON, HE WEPT."

The exposition is:

The word *"wept"* refers to wracking sobs, which came from the depths of his being. This was the time of Peter's Repentance, which is portrayed by *"a broken and a contrite spirit"* (Ps. 51:17).

THE REPENTANCE OF SIMON PETER

The phrase, *"And the second time the rooster crowed,"* was probably pretty close to daylight. Some have suggested that the first time could have been as early as 1 a.m. At any rate, these several intervening hours were momentous, to say the least! All the Disciples forsook Jesus, and Peter even denied him. Furthermore, by their perfidious action, the religious leaders of Israel would seal the doom of themselves and their nation. They would condemn and crucify the Lord of Glory. No greater sin has ever been committed!

The phrase, *"And Peter called to mind the Word that Jesus said unto him,"* may have been the time that Jesus walked by and looked at him (Lk. 22:61). Since it was not yet daylight, the Sanhedrin would meet again to formally condemn Jesus, because it was not legal for them to do so during the night. Before they took Jesus to Pilate, they would, therefore, *"legalize"* their insidious activities.

When Jesus looked at Peter, it was probably as He was being led to the formal meeting place of the Sanhedrin. There is no record that Jesus said anything to Peter. That one look was enough to stamp on Peter's mind the things which Christ had said.

The phrase, *"Before the rooster crows twice, you shall deny Me thrice,"* proclaims exactly what Jesus had said. The phrase, *"And when he thought thereon, he wept,"* means, according to Matthew, he *"wept bitterly"* (Mat. 26:75). This refers to wracking sobs, which came from the depths of his being. This was the time of Peter's Repentance, which is portrayed by *"a broken and contrite heart"* (Ps. 51:17).

It is said that forever after, when Peter would hear the crowing of a rooster, he would fall to his knees. He never forgot this moment. And yet, the Lord would wondrously and graciously re-commission him (Jn. 21:15-17) and use him mightily. Despite his failure, he was one of the greatest men of God who ever lived.

DID PETER FALL?

Almost all would say he did. However, the Scripture is replete with the wonderful truth that, despite failure, one is never fallen who continues to trust in Christ (I Jn. 1:9). It is true that Peter did sin, and grievously so; but, still, he did not turn away from the Lord, but rather to Him. Sin in any form is a horrible and wicked thing; however, if sin is properly taken to Christ, if proper confession is made to Him, then the act is cleansed and canceled by the Precious Blood of Jesus (I Jn. 2:1-2).

Some may claim that such is too easy and provides a license for people to sin. Such thinking is foolishness, simply because no True Believer desires to sin. Sin is repugnant to him. If sin does happen, he is quick to take it to Christ. Only unbelievers practice sin (I Jn. 5:18).

Anyone who would suggest that Peter wanted and desired to do what he did knows little of the situation. No True Believer, as stated, desires to sin. Even the very thoughts of failing God are abhorrent to the soul. And yet, there is not a Believer who has ever lived, who has not had to go before the Lord quite a number of times to plead for Mercy and Grace.

Thank God such Mercy and Grace are available.

Furthermore, on such occasions, we are invited to *"come boldly unto the Throne of Grace, that we may obtain Mercy, and find Grace to help in time of need"* (Heb. 4:16).

No! Even though Peter failed, he did not fall!

CHAPTER 15

(1) "AND STRAIGHTWAY IN THE MORNING THE CHIEF PRIESTS HELD A CONSULTATION WITH THE ELDERS AND SCRIBES AND THE WHOLE COUNCIL, AND BOUND JESUS, AND CARRIED HIM AWAY, AND DELIVERED HIM TO PILATE."

The exposition is:

Sentences of condemnation might not be legally pronounced on the day of trial. Yet our Lord was tried, condemned, and crucified on the same day. As they took Him to Pilate, they continued to strike and beat Him.

THE RELIGIOUS LEADERSHIP OF ISRAEL

The phrase, *"And straightway in the morning,"* refers to the approximate time of daybreak. The phrase, *"The Chief Priests held a consultation with the Elders and Scribes and the whole Council,"* refers to the entire

Sanhedrin, with the possible exceptions of Nicodemus and Joseph of Arimathaea.

The proceedings recorded in the last Chapter probably terminated a little before daybreak. As stated, they were illegal. Now comes the more formal trial. But they continue to break their own Law. In capital cases, sentences of condemnation might not be legally pronounced on the day of trial. Yet our Lord was tried, condemned, and crucified, all on the same day.

The phrase, *"And bound Jesus,"* refers to the time they finished the second trial. By now, He must have been a grotesque sight! His Face would have been unrecognizable, but the torture had not ended; it had actually only begun!

The phrase, *"And carried Him away,"* means that even while they were taking Him to Pilate, they were doing so with violence and force. In other words, they continue to strike and beat Him, even while He is attempting to walk from one building to another.

He is by now *"fair game,"* a term used to denote that *"anything goes."*

Due to Roman control, the religious leadership of Israel was unable to carry out the death sentence on Him. They would, however, torture Him to near death. In these actions, their true hearts begin to show. When one is helpless, in a situation where anything can be done to that person without any fear of reprisal, but rather commendation, one quickly sees what people really are.

By His Own choice, Jesus was now helpless. The religious leaders, therefore, would be allowed to do whatever they desired. What they desired was exactly what Satan desired, *"to steal, and to kill, and to destroy"* (Jn. 10:10).

PONTIUS PILATE

The phrase, *"And delivered Him to Pilate,"* meant that knowing such action, within itself, and even their own charges against Him, would not guarantee His Death; therefore, they would put a political construction on the confession of Jesus regarding His claim of Deity. They would claim that He was a pretender to the Throne of Israel. They will force Pilate to deal with Jesus from a political stance instead of a religious stance, because failure to do so could involve Pilate in a dereliction of duty towards the Throne of the Caesars. The accusation would boil down to the Jews accusing Jesus of setting Himself up as a King in opposition to Caesar, which, of course, was a serious charge.

Judaea had now been added to the Province of Syria and was governed by Procurators, of whom Pontius Pilate was the fifth. It was necessary for the Jews to deliver Christ to Roman power, because, as stated, the power of life and death had been take from the Jews since they became subject to the Romans.

John recorded them saying, *"It is not lawful for us to put any man to death"* (Jn. 18:31). Pontius Pilate was a Roman of the upper middle-class order. Little is known of his career before A.D. 26. In that year, however, the Emperor Tiberius appointed him, as stated, to be the fifth Procurator.

Before A.D. 21, such Governors could not be accompanied by their wives. In A.D. 21, however, the Roman Senate reversed its policy on that issue. Consequently, Pilate has his wife with him in Judaea (Mat. 27:19). As Procurator (Governor), he has full control in the Province, being in charge of an army of approximately 5,000 men. They were stationed at Caesarea, with a detachment on garrison duty at Jerusalem and the fortress of Antonia.

Pilate had full powers of life and death; he could reverse capital sentences passed by the Sanhedrin, which had to be submitted to him for ratification. He also appointed the High Priests and controlled the Temple and its funds. The very vestments of the High Priest were in his custody and were released only for festivals, when the Governor took up residence in Jerusalem, consequently, bringing in additional troops to patrol the city, as he did at this Passover time.

It is somewhat ironical that even pagan historians mention Pilate only in connection with his authorization of the death of Jesus.

A WEAK MAN

Philo finds nothing good to say about Pilate. He describes him as *"by nature rigid and stubbornly harsh and of spiteful disposition and an exceeding wrathful man."* The verdict of the New Testament is that he was a weak man, ready to serve expediency rather than principle, whose authorization of the judicial murder of the Saviour was due less to a desire to please the Jewish authorities than the fear of imperial displeasure if Tiberias heard of further unrest in Judaea. This is made abundantly evident by his mockery of the Jews in the wording of the superscription on the Cross of Christ (Jn. 19:19-22).

Due to extensive trouble at Mount Gerazim, to which Pilate responded by executing the ringleaders, he was ultimately called to Rome, where he was to appear before the Emperor to answer the charges brought against him. However, Tiberius died while Pilate was on his way to Rome. This was in A.D. 37. Nothing is known of the outcome of this trial, as he appeared before Emperor Gaius, who succeeded Tiberius. Eusebius says that Pilate committed suicide shortly thereafter.

(2) "AND PILATE ASKED HIM, ARE YOU THE KING OF THE JEWS? AND HE ANSWERING SAID UNTO HIM, YOU SAY IT."

The overview is:

To Pilate, this was a political question. He had no regard or concern for the religious controversy.

Jesus answered in the affirmative. In effect, He said, *"You say that which is true."*

THE KING OF THE JEWS

The question, *"And Pilate asked Him, Are You the King of the Jews?"* proclaims the Governor going to the very heart of the matter, which to him was a political question. He had no regard or concern for the religious controversy. It seems the Jews had brought three charges against Jesus, at least as far as Pilate was concerned. They are as follows:

1. He perverted the nation.
2. He forbade to give tribute to Caesar.
3. He said He was Christ, a King.

It would have been virtually impossible for Pilate to have not heard of Jesus. He was no doubt familiar with His blameless Life, His pure Doctrine, and the many Miracles that He performed. As we have alluded, his disposition before Jesus portrayed Him as a weak man. He seemed to have enemies in Rome and elsewhere. As facts would later prove, his hold on his Governorship was weak to say the least! As a result, he saw in Jesus the possibility of another threat to his position, so he would yield to expediency, allowing these reprobates to have their way.

The phrase, *"And He answering said unto him, You say it,"* refers to Jesus answering in the affirmative. In effect, Jesus said, *"You say that which is true."*

(3) "AND THE CHIEF PRIESTS ACCUSED HIM OF MANY THINGS: BUT HE ANSWERED NOTHING."

The composition is:

Jesus knew that to refute their erroneous and ridiculous charges was a waste of time.

CHIEF PRIESTS

Even though He answered Pilate, He would not answer the accusations of the *"Chief Priests."*

Why?

Although they accused Him of many things, He said nothing, simply because their accusations were not only false, they were basely ridiculous! Pilate's question was legitimate; he thereby received a legitimate answer. Their accusations were not legitimate, so *"He answered nothing."*

(4) "AND PILATE ASKED HIM AGAIN, SAYING, ANSWEREST THOU NOTHING? BEHOLD HOW MANY THINGS THEY WITNESS AGAINST YOU."

The diagram is:

Pilate had never seen a man who would not defend himself. He did not understand Christ!

JESUS

The phrase, *"And Pilate asked Him again,"* proclaims the astonishment of the Governor at Jesus saying nothing, especially considering how serious these allegations were! To Pilate, this self-restraint was incomprehensible. Actually, he had never met anyone like Christ. In truth, no one else had ever met anyone like Christ.

The question, *"Answerest Thou nothing?"* refers to the puzzlement of the Governor. The Lord does not defend Himself and the Governor does not understand the reason why. It is obvious that he does not believe Jesus to be a political pretender, but he does not know quite what to make of Him!

The phrase, *"How many things they*

witness against You," proclaims, more so than anything else, the astonishment of the Governor. He has never seen a man who would not defend himself.

(5) "BUT JESUS YET ANSWERED NOTHING; SO THAT PILATE MARVELED."

The overview is:

The silence of a blameless life pleads more powerfully than any defense, however elaborate.

THE RESPONSE OF PILATE

The phrase, *"But Jesus yet answered nothing,"* proclaims the answer of Christ to the constant exclamation of Pilate. The answer was silence.

The phrase, *"So that Pilate marveled,"* proclaims the Governor startled and marveling about several things: the silence of Christ in the face of these vehement accusations by the leading men of the Jews; His contempt of death; and, His calmness. As stated, he had never met anyone even remotely like Jesus.

(6) "NOW AT THAT FEAST HE RELEASED UNTO THEM ONE PRISONER, WHOMSOEVER THEY DESIRED."

The exegesis is:

Immediately before the situation concerning Barabbas, Pilate sent Jesus to Herod, which is omitted by Mark (Lk., Chpt. 23). The origin of the custom of releasing a prisoner at this time is anyone's guess.

A CUSTOM

Immediately before the situation concerning Barabbas, even though Mark did not mention it here, Pilate sent Jesus to Herod. By this act, Pilate hoped to rid himself of the responsibility of Jesus. Herod, however, mockingly sent Him back to Pilate. So this strategy failed!

The phrase, *"Now at that feast he released unto them one prisoner,"* constitutes his second effort to rid himself of the responsibility of Christ. This strategy will succeed no better than the former.

In John 18:39, we read that Pilate said, *"You have a custom that I should release unto you one at the Passover."* There is no record in the Law of Moses where such a custom originated. Some maintain that the custom began with the Jews at some point in time to commemorate the deliverance of the Children of Israel from Egyptian bondage. Others claim that it was a practice engaged in by the Romans all over the world of that day, so they also instituted it in Israel. It was deemed to be a political ploy which would find favor with the people. The origin of this custom is anyone's guess.

The phrase, *"Whomsoever they desired,"* means, it seems, exactly what it says.

(7) "AND THERE WAS ONE NAMED BARABBAS, WHICH LAY BOUND WITH THEM WHO HAD MADE INSURRECTION WITH HIM, WHO HAD COMMITTED MURDER IN THE INSURRECTION."

The overview is:

This man had been arrested for homicidal political terrorism. There is some evidence that he was referred to as *"Jesus Barabbas."* If so, the Jews had the choice of *"Jesus Barabbas"* or *"Jesus Christ."*

BARABBAS

The phrase, *"And there was one named Barabbas,"* speaks of a leader of insurrection and a murderer. He was arrested for homicidal political terrorism. From the way Mark describes it, the incident in which Barabbas was engaged seemed to be well-known. His crime was insurrection against Rome, an insurrection which had the sympathy of many people. Actually, there were many insurrectionists at this particular time, and this problem continued to increase in one form or the other until Rome finally destroyed Jerusalem in A.D. 70.

The phrase, *"Which lay bound with them who had made insurrection with him,"* concerned the entire group, however large it was, which had been apprehended by Pilate. Rome was quick to put down any hint of insurrection, so Pilate was going to be thrown into another quandary.

He is going to be forced to make the choice between a murderous leader of insurrection and a pretender to the Throne of Israel. At first glance, it would seem that the choice should be easily made. Barabbas is a known enemy of Rome, while Jesus has expressed no tendency whatsoever in this direction. However, the weakness of Pilate would see him succumbing to the expediency of the moment.

The phrase, *"Who had committed murder in the insurrection,"* probably pertained to the murder of a Roman soldier, or at least someone favorable to Rome.

(8) "AND THE MULTITUDE CRYING ALOUD BEGAN TO DESIRE HIM TO DO AS HE HAD EVER DONE UNTO THEM."

The diagram is:

Their clamor concerned the releasing of a particular prisoner.

THE MULTITUDE

The phrase, *"And the multitude crying aloud,"* concerns this custom of releasing a prisoner at this time of the year and the loud clamor for this to be done. This activity would have had little or nothing to do with Jesus, but with Pilate attempting to take advantage of the interruption. He would be disappointed!

The phrase, *"Began to desire him to do as he had ever done unto them,"* concerned the releasing of a particular prisoner. At this stage, it does not seem as if the clamoring crowd had anything particular in mind respecting release. They seemed to be more concerned about the custom than the person.

(9) "BUT PILATE ANSWERED THEM, SAYING, WILL YOU THAT I RELEASE UNTO YOU THE KING OF THE JEWS?"

The diagram is:

Pilate is speaking of releasing Jesus, which is what he hoped the crowd would request. He used the title, *"King of the Jews,"* in sarcasm.

THE KING OF THE JEWS

The phrase, *"But Pilate answered them, saying,"* proclaims the Governor attempting to take advantage of this, which he sees as another opportunity to rid himself of the responsibility of Jesus. His efforts will be fruitless. The question, *"Will you that I release unto you the King of the Jews?"* refers to Jesus. Pilate hoped the crowd would want Jesus' release.

Pilate reasoned that inasmuch as Jesus had claimed such, he also was entitled to use the title, which, at least in his mind, was ludicrous, considering the present appearance of Christ. Whatever he thought of Jesus, he in no way thought of Him as being a King.

Consequently, he was to make the greatest mistake of his life. For Jesus was not only *"King of Jews,"* but also the *"Son of the Living God."*

(10) "FOR HE KNEW THAT THE CHIEF PRIESTS HAD DELIVERED HIM FOR ENVY."

The composition is:

The *"envy"* was so obvious that even this pagan could see it. This tells us to what level these religious leaders had sunk.

ENVY

The *"Chief Priests"* saw that Jesus was gaining popularity and increasing influence over the people as a result of His Person, His Miracles, and the Power of His Words. As they saw His influence gaining, they saw theirs lessening. Consequently, they must destroy Him.

This evil passion, *"envy,"* is the ruling factor of most, if not all, religion. Inasmuch as all religion is man-directed and man-led, it is extremely political in nature. As such, it cannot be God-directed. It must protect its interests at whatever cost! That which is God-directed is protected by the Lord, with His followers giving no consideration to place or position. However, place and position are everything to those who are man-led, and they will do anything to protect them. Such make up the world of religion, even to this present hour.

When men fight to hold on to whatever they think they presently have, at least in the realm of religion, one can be certain that it was not given by God. The Apostle Paul would greatly defend the Gospel, but he did little to defend himself, at least where the Gospel was not at stake.

Pilate now knows that the real offense of Jesus was His great influence with the people. Swete says, *"The pretense of loyalty to the Emperor was too flimsy to deceive a man of the world. And he detected under their disguise the vulgar vice of envy."*

(11) "BUT THE CHIEF PRIESTS MOVED THE PEOPLE, THAT HE SHOULD RATHER RELEASE BARABBAS UNTO THEM."

The diagram is:

The Chief Priests demanded the release of a murderer. Consequently, murderers have dominated the Jews from then until now.

BARABBAS

The phrase, *"But the Chief Priests moved the people,"* proclaims at least some interval of time after Pilate had asked, at least in a roundabout way, if they were requesting the release of Jesus. What these Chief Priests told the people is not known, at least respecting the choice of Barabbas. Whatever it was, it swayed the people.

The phrase, *"That he should rather release Barabbas unto them,"* presents them with a choice. As stated, *"Jesus Barabbas"* or *"Jesus Christ"*! The crowd which had gathered at this very early morning hour was probably the rabble of the city, which easily could be influenced, especially for evil. So they demanded the release of *"Barabbas,"* even though he was a murderer.

As a result of this demand, Israel has had murderers ruling over them for nearly 2,000 years. Only since 1948 have they gained some type of autonomy and safety. Even that is precarious, especially as it regards the Palestinian human bombers in Israel. Up until now Israel has been at the mercy of the world, which showed no mercy. They wanted a murderer, so they received a murderer. Adolf Hitler is but one example of the many!

Some would claim that whatever was done then should not apply to succeeding generations. But the succeeding generations of Jewish people, at least as a whole, have held Jesus Christ with the same contempt as their forefathers; as a result, even worse days lie immediately ahead (Jer. 30:7).

(12) "AND PILATE ANSWERED AND SAID AGAIN UNTO THEM, WHAT WILL YOU THEN THAT I SHALL DO UNTO HIM WHOM YOU CALL THE KING OF THE JEWS?"

The overview is:

The question asked by Pilate is the greatest question that Israel will ever hear. Regrettably, their answer destroyed them.

WHAT WILL YOU DO WITH JESUS?

The phrase, *"And Pilate answered and said again unto them,"* probably proclaims him not knowing at the moment whom the crowd will demand for release. It seems he still has hope that they will request Jesus Christ. But yet he will continue with his sarcasm!

The question, *"What will you then that I shall do unto Him Whom you call the King of the Jews?"* presents a slight twist from the first time he asked the question. Now he says, *"Whom you call . . ."* which curtailed his chances, even though, in reality, he had none at all. Some claim he was appealing to their national pride by adding the words, *"Whom you call."*

However, even though that may have been possible, it is doubtful! He seems to be more and more disgusted with the entire scenario. Even though he certainly does not give Jesus any credence as a King, he knows that the accusations of these religious leaders also have no credence. Jesus is harmless, as least as far as a threat to Rome is concerned.

So, whatever was in his mind did not work at all. The situation is now taken completely out of his hands, since he only desired to please the people.

(13) "AND THEY CRIED OUT AGAIN, CRUCIFY HIM."

The exposition is:

They wanted Him to be crucified, because they thought this would prove to the people that He was not the Messiah.

THE DEMAND FOR CRUCIFIXION

The phrase, *"And they cried out again,"* constituted a response that seemed to shock even Pilate. The phrase, *"Crucify Him,"* is not only what he did not expect, but he also knew there were no grounds for such action.

The Jews did not crucify people; crucifixion was a Roman form of execution. The Jews used stoning as their method of punishment. So this means that the *"Chief Priests"* had been working the crowd. What the crowd was told, which caused them to bring forth such a response, is not known.

This rabble probably could be easily persuaded to believe anything, at least if it would provide them some sort of entertainment, as disgusting as that may be. These, more than likely, were the drunks and thieves who prowled the city at night. Little did they realize that they were being used as pawns in the most horrifying spectacle the world had ever known. Their cry for crucifixion would come back to haunt them.

About 37 years later, when Titus laid siege to Jerusalem, so many Jews were crucified that literally there were no more places to put crosses. Tens of thousands, if not hundreds of thousands, died in this agonizing manner — quite possibly some who screamed these very words that very day.

(14) "THEN PILATE SAID UNTO THEM, WHY, WHAT EVIL HAS HE DONE? AND THEY CRIED OUT THE MORE EXCEEDINGLY, CRUCIFY HIM."

The exposition is:

It was not for *"evil"* that they wanted to crucify Him, but because of His *"good."*

WHAT EVIL HAS HE DONE?

The question, *"Then Pilate said unto them, Why, what evil has He done?"* rings out through the ages! In Truth, He has done no evil. He had never harmed anyone; He helped everyone. He had never caused sickness; He healed everyone. He had never brought disappointment or sorrow; He brought joy and more abundant life. He never added to the terrible weight of sin; He delivered men from sin. He, in Truth, is the only truly good Man Who ever has lived. He is the only One Who has ever walked perfectly in character, whether by word, thought, or deed.

It was not for *"evil"* that they wanted to crucify Him, but because of His *"good."* His Perfection and Goodness were a constant rebuke to their evil. To be sure, all who attempt to follow Him will face the same type of opposition. Moreover, it will come from the same sources: the world, the Devil, and the apostate Church.

The phrase, *"And they cried out the more exceedingly, Crucify Him,"* represents their intensified answer. Luke says they repeated the cry again and again (Lk. 23:23).

Pilate was attempting to reason with them. But a mob cannot be reasoned with, and this was a mob! Pilate's last half-hearted effort to free Christ has thus been thwarted.

(15) "AND SO PILATE, WILLING TO CONTENT THE PEOPLE, RELEASED BARABBAS UNTO THEM, AND DELIVERED JESUS, WHEN HE HAD SCOURGED HIM, TO BE CRUCIFIED."

The synopsis is:

Pilate was willing to content the people but not willing to content God. Untold thousands of Preachers do the same every week.

COMPROMISE

The phrase, *"And so Pilate, willing to content the people,"* shows what type of leader he actually was — weak and vacillating. A strong leader would have done what he felt was right, irrespective of the demands of the people. Pilate had approximately 5,000 soldiers to ensure his decision. Instead of acting like a statesman, he conducted himself like a politician. He would, consequently, destroy himself.

Who were these people he was willing to content?

Some have claimed that these were the same people who, some hours before during the triumphant entry, had cried, *"Hosanna to the highest!"* However, that is incorrect.

Those people who lined the roads during the momentous occasion were now in bed. These *"people"* were, no doubt, as we have previously stated, the rabble of the city. For the most part, they were the night prowlers, i.e., a baser sort. As is obvious, they were for sale to the highest bidder. The Chief Priests were the bidders, and these *"people"* would sell cheap!

What all of them did not know or realize was that this with Whom they were dealing was the Lord of Glory, the Creator of the ages. As a result, every action toward Him ultimately would be answered in kind.

Let it also ever be known that the treatment of those who are His equates to the treatment of Him.

Even though He had Power to call down any number of Angels, who would have come to His rescue at the slightest signal, He instead allowed evil to take its course. However, His allowing such in no way abrogated the penalty that all these participants would ultimately have to pay. In the Sermon on the Mount, He had plainly stated, *"For with what judgment you judge, you shall be judged: and with what measure you mete, it shall be measured unto you again"* (Mat. 7:2).

THE MEASUREMENT WE METE

That day the religious leaders of Israel, the mob, and Pilate *"measured Jesus"*; they, in turn, were measured! Caiaphas committed suicide not long thereafter, and so did Pilate. About 37 years later, when Titus the Roman General laid siege to Jerusalem at this very sight, blood ran in the streets, even the blood of those who had cried, *"Crucify Him!"*

The phrase, *"Released Barabbas unto them,"* is a study in irony! They accused Christ of being an insurrectionist, which He was not, and yet demanded Barabbas be released, who actually had made insurrection! Such is evil.

EVIL

In evil, as here, everything is upside down. Truth becomes a lie, and a lie becomes the Truth. Right becomes wrong, and wrong becomes right. Darkness becomes light, and light becomes darkness. Tragically, almost the entirety of the world operates on this basis, hence, the wars, insurrection, starvation, hate, etc.

The phrase, *"And delivered Jesus,"* is said by the Holy Spirit with a broken heart. It definitely was God's Will that His Son would die on a Cross in order that the terrible price of sin would be paid and that men would be saved. Still, it was not God's Will at all that these people do what they did. This terrible act, the condemnation of Christ, the most vile act in human history, was carried out by people who desired to do such a thing because their hearts were evil.

In the entirety of this scenario, Pilate, representing the world, is placed on one side, and the religious leaders of Israel are placed on the other. Although he was a pagan who knew nothing about God, still, Pilate had a far greater sense of fairness and integrity, such as it was, than the religious leaders of Israel. They had none at all! Their evil was the evil of refusing light and purposely accepting darkness. Pilate's evil, at least in part, was an evil of ignorance. Theirs was an evil of rebellion.

OPPOSITION TO THE WORK OF GOD

In this episode, a picture is drawn by the Holy Spirit of the true opposition against God and His Work. While the world definitely opposes that which is of God, still, the greater opposition by far comes from organized religion.

In conducting crusades in many foreign countries all over the world, there has never been much opposition from the secular part of society. Most of the Governments remain neutral, with little hindrance from that sector. However, organized religion, and from whatever source, always opposed our meetings in every conceivable way.

Why?

The reason then, and I speak of the Crucifixion of Christ, is the reason now! It didn't matter to these people that many souls were saved in my Crusades, which means lives were changed and the glory of the New Birth taking place, which is the greatest Miracle that one could ever know. To these people, it didn't matter that Love replaced hate, and Light replaced darkness, with all of its glorious results. They bitterly opposed it, even while all of the time claiming to be of God. The religious leaders of Israel also claimed to be of God, while all the time crucifying the Son of God.

Of course, it should be obvious that they were not of God, but rather of Satan! That which truly is of God will not oppose God. So, the Believer at present is placed in the same position as the people during the time of Christ.

Who was right, Jesus or the religious leaders? The people had to make a choice, just as the people today have to make a choice. That choice then was not hard to make, just as it is now not hard to make. The Fruit of Jesus' Ministry was obvious. The religious leaders had no fruit in their ministry.

So, why didn't the people readily choose Christ?

Many did, but many, even though they knew that Jesus was actually Who He said He was, would not follow Him, because they feared excommunication. Millions today fear the same!

RELIGION

Religion controls people. Actually, its power is in its *"control."* It controls their money and their minds. In doing so, it desires to do their thinking and make their decisions for them. This is the earmark of religion.

The religious leaders of Israel saw their control of the people slipping away, so they felt they must destroy, and at any cost, the One Who was undermining this control. The same spirit that killed Christ is alive and well today, attempting to do the same identical thing to all those who truly follow Him instead of religion.

As we have repeatedly stated, religion is that which is instituted by man, even though it constantly speaks of God. True Bible Christianity is not a religion, because it is instituted by God. Bible Christianity is a relationship with a Person, actually The Man, Christ Jesus. It is all of God and none of man.

Whenever man begins to add to, or take from, that which God has given, it then becomes *"religion."*

THE SUFFERING

The phrase, *"When he had scourged Him,"* spoke of something so terrible that many men did not survive it. Scourging was usually inflicted on slaves, but was also inflicted upon those who were condemned to death, even though free men. This scourging, which was a part of the punishment of Crucifixion, was of frightful severity. From John 19:1, however, it seems that the scourging of Jesus took place before His formal condemnation to be crucified.

Pilate may have used this tactic, hoping that the mob, upon seeing the brutally beaten Body of Jesus, would have their blood lust satisfied and would relent in their demand for Crucifixion. If that was his thought, he was again to be disappointed (Jn. 19:1-16).

Wuest says, *"The Roman scourge was a lash usually made of leather thongs loaded at intervals with bone or metal. Peter, using the phrase, 'By Whose stripes you were healed,' gives us a vivid portrayal of his recollection of how our Lord's back looked after the scourging* (I Pet. 2:24). *The word 'stripes' in the Greek Text is in the singular number. The word refers to a bloody wale trickling with blood that arises under a blow. Our Lord's back was so lacerated by the scourge that it was one massive, open, raw, quivering flesh, trickling with blood, not a series of stripes or cuts, but one mass of torn flesh."*

NOTES

The phrase, *"To be crucified,"* proclaims Mark omitting the details given by John of how Pilate once again tried to reason with the religious leaders of Israel concerning the release of Jesus, but to no avail. They would be satisfied with nothing except His Death, and that by Crucifixion. Then they could claim to the people that Rome demanded His execution because He pretended to be a King. So, their demands upon this weak, vacillating Governor would bring about the desired result, i.e., *"Crucifixion"*!

(16) "AND THE SOLDIERS LED HIM AWAY INTO THE HALL, CALLED PRAETORIUM; AND THEY CALL TOGETHER THE WHOLE BAND."

The structure is:

The Praetorium was actually the barracks of the soldiers, who could have numbered as many as 600.

FAIR GAME

The phrase, *"And the soldiers led Him away into the hall, called Praetorium,"* was actually, as stated, the barracks of the soldiers. The phrase, *"And they call together the whole band,"* referred to all the soldiers, which actually constituted Pilate's bodyguard. Jesus had been condemned by the religious leaders of Israel, and now He is also condemned by the State. As He was *"fair game"* then, He is *"fair game"* now! Anything these soldiers desired to do to Him, short of death, they could do without any fear of censure.

(17) "AND THEY CLOTHED HIM WITH PURPLE, AND PLATTED A CROWN OF THORNS, AND PUT IT ABOUT HIS HEAD."

The exegesis is:

The Greek word used here for *"crown"* is *"stephanos,"* which means *"the victor's crown."* In the Mind of God, the victory had already been won, because He knew that Calvary would pay the total price.

THE VICTOR'S CROWN

The phrase, *"And they clothed Him with purple,"* probably spoke of the cloak of one of the soldiers, possibly a cast-off and faded rag. The phrase, *"And platted a crown of thorns, and put it about His Head,"* spoke, some say, of *"victor's thorns,"* which were about six inches long. As they punctured the skin, they often created a festering wound.

The soldiers made this crude crown of sorts, which was meant to serve as a mockery of His claim to being King of the Jews. However, it also was meant to denote, again in mockery, His claim of Deity. The religious leaders had, no doubt, spread this bit of information, i.e., that Jesus claimed Divinity, to the mob. Now, as a result, this poor pathetic figure standing before the soldiers was mocked as God and King. To them, it was one big joke! However, despite His appearance and His refusal to defend Himself, He was God, the Creator of all things. Little did they know what they were doing!

It is known that the scalp quickly swells when struck or lacerated. As the thorns were pressed onto the brow of Christ, piercing the skin (for the soldiers would show no mercy), His Head must have looked grotesque, swollen as it was!

(18) "AND BEGAN TO SALUTE HIM, HAIL, KING OF THE JEWS."

The composition is:

He was the King of the Jews, even though they didn't know it. He also was the King of the whole world, which the world will recognize in the coming Kingdom Age.

KING OF THE JEWS

All was done in mockery, because they in no way knew Who and What He was! Cyril said that the purple cloak symbolized the Kingdom of the whole world, which Christ was about to receive, and which He was to obtain by the shedding of His Most Precious Blood. He would not receive the world at the hand of Satan, but He would receive it by the terrible price He paid; however, the possession of it is yet to be obtained. But, to be certain, it shall be obtained. The world awaits His Coming! As certainly as He paid the price, as certainly shall He come!

(19) "AND THEY SMOTE HIM ON THE HEAD WITH A REED, AND DID SPIT UPON HIM, AND BOWING THEIR KNEES WORSHIPPED HIM."

The diagram is:

That with which they smote Him was a stiff object, which would have driven the thorns deep within His scalp.

THE TORTURE!

The phrase, *"And they smote Him on the Head with a reed,"* spoke of a stiff object approximately two feet long, which would have driven the thorns deep within His scalp, possibly even creasing His Skull. The pain must have been unbearable! As stated, the swelling and shedding of blood would have made Him not only unrecognizable, but inhuman, respecting appearance, as well!

The phrase, *"And did spit upon Him,"* actually says they *"kept spitting."* This was a part of the contempt they showed Him. I suspect it would be impossible for one to imagine exactly what He looked like, with His Head swollen, as it was, and spittle mixed with blood covering His Face.

Concerning this, the Prophet Isaiah said, *"As many were astonied at You; His Visage was so marred more than any man, and His form more than the sons of men"* (Isa. 52:14). As we stated some pages back, this should forever settle the controversy regarding the *"Shroud of Turin,"* which claims to be the cloth that covered the Face of Jesus when He died. His disfigurement would have been to such an extent that no discernible imprint would have been left on any cloth.

The phrase, *"And bowing their knees worshipped Him,"* spoke to His claim of being God and King. In their *"worship,"* which actually was mockery, even as the next Verse proclaims, they, no doubt, were telling Him to perform a miracle, etc. When the impact of this horror is even in part comprehended, the Love of God takes on a completely different complexion.

How could He love people who would do such a thing? And yet, we know He does!

Paul wrote, *"But God commends His Love toward us, in that, while we were yet sinners, Christ died for us"* (Rom. 5:8). This is Love that is beyond the comprehension of man, but yet the Love that God gives to all who truly accept and follow Him.

(20) "AND WHEN THEY HAD MOCKED HIM, THEY TOOK OFF THE PURPLE FROM HIM, AND PUT HIS OWN CLOTHES ON HIM, AND LED HIM OUT TO CRUCIFY HIM."

The diagram is:

They would later gamble for His Robe!

THE INJUSTICE OF ALL INJUSTICES

The phrase, *"And when they had mocked Him,"* did not, sadly, conclude the *"mocking."* Men have been mocking Him ever since!

Let it be known, however, that the One Who is now the Saviour, is, at the same time, the Judge. Assuming these soldiers did not make this horrible thing right with God (which some of them may well have done), they will stand one day at the Great White Throne Judgment to give account for these actions. Their deeds, as vile as they were, were written down in Heaven and will be recalled in glaring detail (Rev. 20:11-15).

As we have repeatedly stated, the contention of the world and the Church is with Jesus Christ. He Alone is the Way to the Father (Jn. 10:7). Jesus said, *"No man comes unto the Father but by Me"* (Jn. 14:6). Hundreds of millions of people in the world claim to know God, but without Jesus Christ. Such claims are spurious; no man knows God, nor can he know God, without accepting Jesus Christ as his Saviour. Christ Alone is the Way to the Father.

A newsman once exclaimed to me that such was not fair because *"the Jews do not believe in Christ"*! If my memory is correct, I said, *"You don't believe in Him either!"* He looked somewhat startled, realizing that this subject has nothing to do with a class of people, but actually with Faith, or the lack thereof.

The phrase, *"They took off the purple from Him, and put His Own clothes on Him,"* referred to the seamless robe. The phrase, *"And led Him out to crucify Him,"* constitutes the injustice of injustices. Pilate had said, as recorded by Luke, that Jesus had done nothing worthy of death (Lk. 23:15). And yet, he will *"crucify Him"* for political expediency, or so he thinks!

(21) "AND THEY COMPEL ONE SIMON A CYRENIAN, WHO PASSED BY, COMING OUT OF THE COUNTRY, THE FATHER OF ALEXANDER AND RUFUS, TO BEAR HIS CROSS."

The overview is:

Due to the beatings, Jesus could no longer physically carry the Cross, which possibly weighed nearly 100 pounds. So they pressed this particular man to carry it for Him.

THE CROSS

The phrase, *"And they compel one Simon a Cyrenian,"* means they pressed him into service. It seems that Jesus carried the Cross toward Golgotha as long as He could. But, there is evidence that He, being exhausted from the beatings and torture, could not carry it further. That which was being carried was probably only the crossbar, which was probably about eight feet long and two or three inches thick. It could have weighed anywhere from 50 to 100 pounds.

The long part of the Cross, on which the body of the victim was placed, was normally left suspended in the ground. When arriving at the scene of the Crucifixion, the victim would have been laid on the ground, and the crossbar would have been laid under his back, with his arms extended on the crossbar beam on either side. The arms either were tied or nailed to the crossbar, in this case, nailed.

Once the hands were nailed to the crossbar, the victim was picked up, crossbar and all, and suspended on the upright portion of the cross. The crossbar was laid on top of the suspended portion, held in place either by being tied or nailed. The feet of the victim would then have been placed one on top of the other and nailed through the instep to the suspended portion of the cross. It was the most cruel form of death that one could ever begin to imagine.

Execution by crucifixion is supposed to have been invented by Semiramis, Queen of Nimrod, who founded the Babylonian system of mysteries. It was, as stated, reserved for slaves and the worst criminals. The weight of the body hung on nails through the hands and feet. The victim was left on the cross until he died of pain and shock.

(At times, victims carried the entire cross, while, at other times, the crossbar only. It is not known for certain which Jesus carried; however, most of the time, it seems, the victims carried only the crossbar.)

SIMON OF CYRENE

It is thought by some that Simon may

have been a black man, inasmuch as he lived on the north coast of Africa. There is, however, no proof of that. The name *"Simon"* actually lends credence to the possibility that he was a Jew who lived in Cyrene. The Cyrenians had a Synagogue in Jerusalem (Acts 6:9). Simon may well have come to Jerusalem at this time, making the long journey in order to keep the Passover, as many did!

Whether black or white, Simon had the distinct honor of helping Jesus at this crucial time. To be sure, there were precious few who did!

The phrase, *"Who passed by, coming out of the country,"* means that he was not a party in any way to these insidious proceedings. He just happened to be standing there when Jesus came by. Quite possibly, he saw the commotion and stopped to see what was happening.

In bearing the Cross, the Lord evidently became so exhausted that He could not proceed under the terrible weight, especially considering the torture He had already endured. His legs must have buckled and He could no longer carry the wooden beam. It all happened very close to where Simon was standing.

Probably a Roman soldier, riding a horse, was leading the procession. If, in fact, that was the case, the soldier would have wheeled around on seeing Jesus stumble and fall, spotted Simon, and then demanded that Simon carry the Cross. It may have been by chance, or so he thought, that he was standing there at that time. But it was not by chance as far as God was concerned. The Heavenly Father, no doubt, orchestrated this very moment. Even though it was an extremely sad occasion, still, it was to be the greatest day of Simon's life. He would meet Jesus.

ALEXANDER AND RUFUS

The phrase, *"The father of Alexander and Rufus, to bear His Cross,"* speaks of two who would give their hearts to the Lord and become well-known Disciples, all because of what happened here this day. By the time Mark wrote his Gospel, these two were well-known.

Paul, writing to the Romans, sends a special salutation to Rufus, *"chosen in the Lord,*

NOTES

and his mother, and mine," which, no doubt, spoke of some special care bestowed upon him by the mother of Rufus (Rom. 16:13). By the time Paul wrote this Epistle, it is probable that Simon had passed on, and maybe even Alexander also had died.

Rufus is honorably mentioned by Polycarp, a Disciple of John the Beloved, in one of his letters. There is also a tradition that Rufus became a Bishop (Pastor) in Spain and that his brother, Alexander, suffered martyrdom.

What an honor it was for Simon to bear the Cross of Jesus Christ! It was to change the entirety of his life and the lives of his children.

Even as I dictate these words, I sense the Presence of the Lord. Any contact with Jesus leaves one immeasurably bettered, and gloriously changed.

As the song says:

"What the world needs is Jesus,
"Just a glimpse of Him."

Simon had that glimpse, and it was to change his life forever.

(22) "AND THEY BRING HIM UNTO THE PLACE GOLGOTHA, WHICH IS, BEING INTERPRETED, THE PLACE OF A SKULL."

The composition is:

Some claim this is the place where Adam was buried and his skull later found. There is, however, no evidence whatsoever of this tradition. Others think the interpretation simply means that the rock face of the hill resembles a skull, which is probably the correct interpretation.

GOLGOTHA

The phrase, *"And they bring Him unto the place Golgotha,"* has been interpreted two ways. The word *"bring"* in the Greek Text is *"phero,"* which means *"to carry a burden"* or *"to lead."* Consequently, as stated, it can be interpreted two ways:

1. Some think that Jesus was being *"led"* as a prisoner to execution, or as a victim to the Sacrifice.

2. It also could mean that Jesus was so weak through the strain of the last few days, especially considering the scourging and torture, that, at a point in time, perhaps when He no longer could carry the Cross, He also became unable to walk. As a consequence,

He had to be helped, or half-carried.

Even though there is no definitive answer either way, I think my opinion would rest with this latter version. If Jesus had become so weak that He could not bear the Cross, He also, more than likely, was so weak that He needed help to even continue to walk.

There also has been disagreement on the actual site of *"Golgotha."* All that is known from Scripture is that it was outside Jerusalem, fairly conspicuous, probably not far from a city gate and a highway, and that a garden containing a tomb was nearby.

Two sites are pointed out presently as the location of the Cross and Tomb. The one is the Church of the Holy Sepulchre, claimed to be the correct site by the Catholics; the other is Gordon's Calvary, which has the Garden Tomb nearby. The Catholic site seems to indicate a tomb of slightly too late a date to be authentic. Calvary (Golgotha) and the Garden Tomb were first pointed out in 1849 by General Gordon of the British Army. The rock formation of Golgotha indeed resembles a skull. The site also accords with the Biblical data.

THE PLACE OF A SKULL

The phrase, *"Which is, being interpreted, The place of a skull,"* also has two or three meanings.

As we have stated, tradition says that *"Golgotha"* was the place where Adam was buried and his skull later found. There is no evidence, however, of that. Others think the interpretation simply means that the rock face of the hill resembles a skull, which probably is the correct interpretation.

It was here where Jesus redeemed lost humanity. It was here that the justice of God was satisfied in that the Perfect Sacrifice was offered in the Person of the Lord Jesus Christ. As such, even though it was an extremely sad spectacle, it was the most glorious in human history. The entirety of the world turns on this pivot — the Crucifixion of Christ and Calvary. There He bore the sin penalty of the world (Jn. 1:29).

(23) "AND THEY GAVE HIM TO DRINK WINE MINGLED WITH MYRRH: BUT HE RECEIVED IT NOT."

The overview is:

NOTES

This refers to a strong narcotic made of sour wine and mingled with bitter herbs. It was supposed to dull the sense of pain. Some think that Christ was offered the drink twice, but there is some indication that it was offered three times.

He would not, however, take of this drink. He sought no alleviation of the agonies of the Crucifixion by any drug potion which might render Him insensible. He would bear the full burden consciously.

THE DRUG POTION

The phrase, *"And they gave Him to drink wine mingled with myrrh,"* actually referred to a strong narcotic. It was supposed to dull the sense of pain. There is some evidence that Christ was offered this drink and another type of drink some three times. They are as follows:

1. On arrival at Calvary (Mat. 27:33-34; Mk. 15:22-23). There is evidence that this was offered to Him just before He was nailed to the Cross. This is the time of which Mark now speaks. Jesus refused it.

2. When He was on the Cross before the thief cried for mercy (Lk. 23:36). The Scripture does not say if He accepted it or not. This seems to have been a drink which was not drugged.

3. Just before He died (Mat. 27:48; Jn. 19:29). He, it seems, accepted this drink; however, there is no evidence that it was a narcotic.

The phrase, *"But He received it not,"* refers, as stated, to the first drink offered to Him upon arriving at the place of Crucifixion.

(24) "AND WHEN THEY HAD CRUCIFIED HIM, THEY PARTED HIS GARMENTS, CASTING LOTS UPON THEM, WHAT EVERY MAN SHOULD TAKE."

The overview is:

His garments, with the exception of the seamless robe, were divided among the soldiers. They did not want to tear apart the seamless robe, so they cast lots. The winner took ownership of the garment (Ps. 22:18).

THE CRUCIFIXION

The phrase, *"And when they had crucified Him,"* referred to them nailing Him to the Cross, which Mark omits. The religious leaders of Israel had their desires granted. Even though God had no part in their wickedness and evil, still, He would use it to further His Own Will, for it was His Will that Jesus die on Calvary. This must be done in order that the terrible sin debt of mankind may be paid. Man could not pay it himself, so God would have to pay it for man. This is the manner in which it was paid.

In truth, God uses everything, be it people or happenings, to ultimately carry out His Plan. He even uses Satan! In no way, however, does He involve Himself in the evil or wickedness, only using what transpires in whatever way He chooses. That is how Paul could say, *"And we know that all things work together for good to them who love God, to them who are the called according to His purpose"* (Rom. 8:28).

It should be noted, however, that *"all things working together for good"* applies only to those who:

A. *"Love God"*; and,

B. *"Are the called according to His purpose."*

THE SEAMLESS ROBE

The phrase, *"They parted His garments,"* means they divided them among the four soldiers employed for the Crucifixion. It was an unwritten rule that the clothing of the condemned belonged to the executioners. Unless Jesus had other clothing elsewhere, what is spoken of here is all He possessed in the world.

He owned no real estate, places of business, or anything else for that matter! That does not mean that it is wrong to own these things. It just simply means that He came for one purpose, which was to die for lost humanity and rise again on the third day.

These *"garments,"* however many they were, included the robe without seam (Jn. 19:23). Some have claimed this seamless robe was an undergarment, but others claim it was the outer robe.

The phrase, *"Casting lots upon them, what every man should take,"* basically refers to the seamless robe. The other garments were divided up among them. But the seamless robe was of such workmanship that they did not desire to rend it. Consequently, they gambled (cast lots), and the winner took ownership of the garment. This was the fulfillment of Psalms 22:18.

(25) "AND IT WAS THE THIRD HOUR, AND THEY CRUCIFIED HIM."

The exposition is:

It was 9 a.m. in the morning, the time of the morning Sacrifice.

THE THIRD HOUR

The *"third hour"* in Jewish time corresponds to our 9 a.m., which was the time of the morning Sacrifice. He died at 3 p.m., the time of the evening Sacrifice. It was not only the time of the evening Sacrifice, but the time the Passover Lambs were killed (Mat. 27:45-50; Lk. 23:44-46). So, Jesus fulfilled every Type in totality!

(26) "AND THE SUPERSCRIPTION OF HIS ACCUSATION WAS WRITTEN OVER, THE KING OF THE JEWS."

The structure is:

Out of anger, no doubt toward the Jews, Pilate wrote the title himself (Jn. 19:19). The Chief Priests were visibly angry over this and strongly requested that it be changed to read: *"He said, I am King of the Jews."* Pilate answered by saying: *"What I have written, I have written"* (Jn. 19:21-22).

So over Jesus' Head on the Cross was fitly placed the truth about Who and What He really was!

THE KING OF THE JEWS

The phrase, *"And the superscription,"* pertained to that which was written concerning Who and What Jesus was. John says this *"superscription"* was written in three languages, Hebrew, Latin, and Greek. It is spoken of in all four Gospels, but no two carry precisely the same words. By the comparison of them, it appears that the whole title was: *"This is Jesus of Nazareth, the King of the Jews."*

The difference in the wording in each Gospel account probably could be explained in the three languages in which the superscription originally was written by Pilate.

ACCUSATION

The phrase, *"Of His accusation was written over,"* normally pertained to the type of crime committed which occasioned the Crucifixion. In the case of remarkable prisoners, the accusation was written on a white tablet and carried before them as they went to the place of execution. It was then placed over their heads, fastened to the top of the cross.

In the case of Jesus, no accusation concerning any crime was attributed to Him, because He committed no crime. Out of anger, no doubt toward the Jews, Pilate, as stated, wrote the title himself (Jn. 19:19).

Bede says, *"He was crucified in weakness for us, yet He shone with the majesty of a King above His Cross. The Title proclaimed that He was, after all, a King; and that from henceforth He began to reign from His Cross over the Jews."* And over the entirety of the world, I might quickly add! Consequently, Pilate was Divinely restrained from making any alteration in the title, i.e., it should not mean anything less than Who, and What, Jesus actually was, and is.

The phrase, *"THE KING OF THE JEWS,"* is a title the Jews did not then recognize, but shall one day!

Zechariah prophesied about that moment: *"And one shall say unto Him, What are these wounds in Your Hands? Then He shall answer, Those with which I was wounded in the house of My friends.*

"And the LORD shall be King over all the Earth: in that day shall there be one LORD, and His Name One" (Zech. 13:6; 14:9).

That awaits the Second Coming and the Kingdom Age.

(27) "AND WITH HIM THEY CRUCIFY TWO THIEVES; THE ONE ON HIS RIGHT HAND, AND THE OTHER ON HIS LEFT."

The overview is:

He died that others might live!

TWO THIEVES

The phrase, *"And with Him they crucify two thieves,"* probably would have been better translated *"robbers."* These two robbers formed a part of the procession to Calvary; however, the evidence is they were crucified after Him.

The phrase, *"The one on His right hand, and the other on His left,"* proclaims Jesus being crucified in the middle. Luke tells us that one of the robbers was saved, and it appears the other died in his sins (Lk. 23:40).

Ambrose stated, *"Christ upon His Cross, between these two men, and with the title of King over His Head, presented a striking and awful picture of the final Judgment."*

Augustine said, *"This Cross, if you mark it well, was a Judgment Seat. For the Judge being placed in the midst, the one who believed was set free; the other, who reviled Him, was condemned. And thus He signified what He will do with the quick and the dead."*

(28) "AND THE SCRIPTURE WAS FULFILLED, WHICH SAID, AND HE WAS NUMBERED WITH THE TRANSGRESSORS."

The exposition is:

He took the place of the transgressors; His Death, its manner, and with whom He died, therefore, were fitting!

THE SCRIPTURE

The phrase, *"And the Scripture was fulfilled,"* proclaims the Holy Spirit, as always, going back to the Scripture. It was always fulfilled, because it was, and is, the Word of God.

How so much should the Believer take advantage of the Word of God to master its contents! How so few do!

As the *"Scripture"* was fulfilled concerning His First Coming, likewise, all will be fulfilled concerning His Second Coming. And yet the world pays precious little attention to these august Prophecies given concerning the days just ahead. Regrettably, most of the Church falls into the same category.

The phrase, *"Which said, And He was numbered with the transgressors,"* is taken from Isaiah 53:12. He was *"numbered with the transgressors,"* because He took the place of the transgressors. So, as stated, His Death, its manner, and with whom He died, therefore, were fitting!

(29) "AND THEY WHO PASSED BY RAILED ON HIM, WAGGING THEIR HEADS, AND SAYING, AH, YOU WHO WOULD DESTROY THE TEMPLE, AND BUILD IT IN THREE DAYS."

The exegesis is:

They were referring to the statement He did make, recorded in John 2:19-21, which referred to His Body as the Temple, and its Death and Resurrection in three days. He was not talking about the Temple in Jerusalem.

THE MOCKERS

The phrase, *"And they who passed by railed on Him, wagging their heads,"* is also a fulfillment of Prophecy. The Psalmist said, *"All they who see Me laugh Me to scorn: they shoot out the lip, they shake the head, saying,*

"He trusted on the LORD that He would deliver Him: let Him deliver Him, seeing He delights in Him" (Ps. 22:7-8).

The pronoun *"they"* referred to *"the Chief Priests, Scribes, and Elders,"* among others (Mat. 27:41). The *"railing"* would have included mockery, reproach, and insults. It is difficult to image human beings doing that to another.

Even if Jesus had been guilty of all they said, still, their actions and attitude were ungodly, to say the least! Considering that He was guilty of nothing and, in fact, was the Son of God, the very Personification of Goodness and Righteousness, their crime is beyond belief. Even the pagan Romans did not do such a thing. Such cruelty is reserved for professors of religion.

The phrase, *"And saying, Ah, You Who would destroy the Temple, and build it in three days,"* constitutes an error on their part. Jesus had never said such a thing. They were referring to the statement He did make in John 2:19-21, which referred to His Body as the Temple, and its Death and Resurrection in three days.

But, of course, they were not interested in what He really said or meant, only in their own devious designs.

(30) "SAVE YOURSELF, AND COME DOWN FROM THE CROSS."

The structure is:

This jest was the harder to endure since it appealed to a consciousness of power held back only by the self-restraint of a sacrificed will. Had He saved Himself, no one else could have been saved.

THE TAUNT

The phrase, *"Save Yourself,"* constituted that which He would not do! Had He saved Himself, which He certainly could have done, He could not have saved others. The entire purpose of His Coming was to give Himself. He was to serve as the Sacrifice! This He did, and in a manner in which no other ever has, or ever shall!

The phrase, *"And come down from the Cross,"* constituted the very opposite of the real purpose for which He came. His entire purpose was to die on a Cross as the Perfect Sacrifice, which would save the souls of men, at least those who will believe (Jn. 3:16).

Calvary was probably near one of the thoroughfares leading to the city. There would have been, therefore, a continual stream of persons passing to and fro, especially at this time, when Jerusalem was thronged with visitors who had come for the Passover.

(31) "LIKEWISE ALSO THE CHIEF PRIESTS MOCKING SAID AMONG THEMSELVES WITH THE SCRIBES, HE SAVED OTHERS; HIMSELF HE CANNOT SAVE."

The exegesis is:

They could not deny the fact that He saved others, but they attempted to turn that fact against Him by alleging that He performed these Miracles by the power of Satan rather than by the Power of God.

HIMSELF HE WILL NOT SAVE!

The phrase, *"Likewise also the Chief Priests mocking said among themselves with the Scribes,"* presents these two groups conversing among themselves. They watch Him die, even suffering an agony that is indescribable, and register no pity or sympathy whatsoever! Religion hardens the hearts of men until there is no sympathy for others. It is the product of acute self-righteousness.

The Lord helped us to build 176 schools for underprivileged children in third world countries during the 1980's. To be sure, these were not elaborate buildings. Each school cost approximately $50,000. Basically, they were walls and roof. However, from 200 to 1,000 children attended each school.

We also did our best to give each child a hot meal each day at noon. For many of these children it was the only meal they received all day, for there was nothing at home. For the most part, these schools only went through the elementary grades. Without this, however, the children would have received no education at all.

One of the men who was a part of the

religious Denomination with which we formerly were associated, who actually had been placed in charge of a particular area of the world, was greatly opposed to our building these schools, or anything else, for that matter. I did not know him too well, but I was shocked at his ideas.

He said (I am told), *"These people should not be educated. Better that they starve to death, because there are too many of them anyway,"* or words to that effect. In spite of the fact that he was a leader in that particular Denomination, I do not believe such a man knew the Lord. He died shortly thereafter. I do pray that he made his peace with God.

Even though there certainly were some Godly Preachers and Missionaries in that particular Denomination, still, there were far too many of the stripe just mentioned. They had no heart, no pity, no sympathy. In truth, they had the same spirit as these *"Chief Priests and Scribes."*

If it is to be noticed, the Holy Spirit constantly brings out who these individuals were and what they were. Remember, He is talking about the leaders of the Church of that day!

The phrase, *"He saved others; Himself He cannot save,"* is, in effect, the old charge that His Miracles of healing and Deliverance had been wrought by Beelzebub. If they had been wrought by God, they claim, then God would have interposed in this, His sore extremity, and have set Him free.

They would take advantage of this opportunity to publicly expose Him as an impostor. They must do everything within their power to destroy any influence He may have had.

How could they come to this terrible state of unbelief?

THE RELIGION OF SATAN

This was the Church of Israel, actually the very leaders who were supposed to lead the people to Righteousness. They were the ones who were to point people toward God. And yet, they did not even know God when He was in their very midst. They were not Children of God, but rather of Satan!

Jesus had said as much of them and to them, *"You are of your father the devil, and the lusts of your father you will do. He was a murderer from the beginning, and abode not in the truth, because there is no truth in him. When he speaks a lie, he speaks of his own: for he is a liar and the father of it"* (Jn. 8:44).

Exactly as Jesus said they were, that they did.

Their father Satan was a *"murderer"*; consequently, they also were murderers! Satan was a *"liar"*; consequently, his children are liars and would lie about Christ.

How could they be so blind that they did not recognize Jesus for Who He was?

Deception is a powerful thing; and they were deceived!

DECEPTION

The human family fell in the Garden of Eden through deception; consequently, deception plagues the human race. The very word *"deception"* means *"to lead astray by words or behavior."* If a person knows the Lord, deception can come from without, that is, if that individual does not know the Word of God as one should. For those who do not know the Lord, deception comes from within, as the desires impel in that direction.

To be sure, these religious leaders of Israel were not saved, and, in fact, had never been saved.

From the very beginning, men have made Truth relative. In other words, those who are deceived speak of something as being *"true for you"* (subjective) but not necessarily *"true for me."* In other words, they deny the existence of absolute truth, which always is objective.

The Bible clearly affirms objective Truth, and it grounds that belief in the Biblical concept of God. God is Truth. All that He says is in strict accord with reality. His Words are firm and trustworthy. By contrast, human beings, at least those who do not truly know God, are trapped in allusion. They struggle to understand the meaning of the world around them and of their experiences. Unaided, they cannot distinguish between the real and the counterfeit, the truth and the lie. It is, as stated, because they do not know the Lord, Who is Truth.

Only reliance on God's Word, which is

Truth, enables us to build our lives on a firm foundation.

These religious leaders did not know Truth, because they did not know God; consequently, they were very easily deceived, because, in truth, the entirety of their lives was deception. Everything they taught and believed was skewed until its true meaning was lost.

When Jesus came, they saw Him only in the light of their own wicked, ungodly hearts. In the state they were in, it was impossible for them to see Him as He truly was. Willful unrighteousness cannot see Righteousness! Willful ungodliness cannot see Godliness! So these religious leaders, despite all the proof in the world, actually believed that Jesus was an impostor.

In their deception, they reasoned that if He really was the Son of God, He would not be on a Cross, because it was known that only those who committed terrible sins were hanged, and thereby cursed of God (Deut. 21:22-23). Consequently, they deemed Jesus cursed by God. Had they truly known and understood the Fifty-third Chapter of Isaiah, they would have known exactly Who He was and His mission. But they did not know Isaiah 53, nor did they properly interpret any other part of the Bible.

They reasoned in their minds that if He were truly of God, God surely would not allow Him to remain in this position. They understood not at all! They truly were congratulating themselves on having rid the world of this impostor.

Such is deception!

They were, in a sense, right concerning the statement, *"He saved others; Himself He cannot save,"* because if He had saved Himself, He could not have saved others.

(32) "LET CHRIST THE KING OF ISRAEL DESCEND NOW FROM THE CROSS, THAT WE MAY SEE AND BELIEVE. AND THEY WHO WERE CRUCIFIED WITH HIM REVILED HIM."

The exegesis is:

These people who taunted Him were liars. He rose from the dead after the third day, and they still didn't believe.

UNBELIEF

The phrase, *"Let Christ the King of Israel,"* is said in mockery. They did not believe He was the *"King of Israel."* They believe now, but it is too late!

The phrase, *"Descend now from the Cross, that we may see and believe,"* constitutes a lie! He rose from the dead, which was far greater than coming down from the Cross while He was still alive, and they still would not *"believe."* While they were mocking Him, He, in His terrible torment, never said a word against these mockers. On the contrary, He proclaimed mercy. For as He hung there, He said, *"Father, forgiven them: for they know not what they do."*

They had seen Him open blinded eyes, but they would not believe. They had seen Him instantly cleanse lepers, but they would not believe. They had seen Him raise the dead, but they still would not believe. There was nothing that God could have done which would have brought them to a place of Faith. They, as stated, were woefully deceived.

The phrase, *"And they who were crucified with Him reviled Him,"* constitutes something unusual, for, most of the time, those in such circumstances will not mock others in the same plight. And yet, one of these very robbers, who at the time was reviling Him, would observe something about Jesus that he had never before witnessed. Before this horrible day was over, he would accept Christ as his Saviour (Lk. 23:40).

(33) "AND WHEN THE SIXTH HOUR WAS COME, THERE WAS DARKNESS OVER THE WHOLE LAND UNTIL THE NINTH HOUR."

The structure is:

It was dark from 12 noon until 3 p.m.

THE DARKNESS

The phrase, *"And when the sixth hour was come,"* denoted 12 noon. Jesus had now been on the Cross for three hours. The phrase, *"There was darkness over the whole land until the ninth hour,"* records this beginning at noon and ending at 3 p.m. This supernatural darkness, for that's what it was, came when the day was at its brightest. Since it was the Passover, the moon was now at the full, so the darkness could not have been caused by an eclipse. When the moon is full, it cannot intervene between the Earth and the Sun.

An account of it is given by Phlegon of Tralles, a man who was personally set free by the Emperor Andrian Eusebius. His records of the year A.D. 33 quoted at length from Phlegon, who says, *"In the fourth year of the Two hundred and second Olympiad, there was a great and remarkable eclipse of the Sun above any that had happened before."* (He said it was an eclipse, because that's actually what he thought it was, even though it wasn't.)

He went on to say that at the sixth hour, the day was turned into the darkness of night, so that the stars were seen in the heavens; and there was a great earthquake in Bithynia, which overthrew many houses in the city of Nicaea. His mention of an earthquake also brings into account the Sacred Narrative (Mat. 27:51-54). Exactly how far this darkness extended is not known.

Dionysius says that he saw this phenomenon at Heliopolis in Egypt. He is reported to have exclaimed, *"Either the God of nature, the Creator, is suffering, or the universe is dissolving."* Cyprian, when looking back at that time some years later, said, *"The Sun was constrained to withdraw its rays, and close its eyes, that it might not be compelled to look upon this crime of the Jews."*

THE BURNT OFFERING AND THE SIN OFFERING

Someone has said: *"God pulled the blinds on Earth at this time, so that neither He nor anyone else might have to look at His Son bearing the sin penalty of the world."* During this final three hours that Jesus hung on the Cross, there is no way the mind of man could even begin to comprehend that which He suffered. The physical pain was nothing in comparison to the spiritual agony.

"For He has made Him to be sin for us, Who knew no sin; that we might be made the Righteousness of God in Him" (II Cor. 5:21).

It was at this hour that He became the Burnt Offering (Lev., Chpt. 1) and the Sin Offering (Lev., Chpt. 4). Even then, with nature convulsing, darkness covering the land, an earthquake causing it to tremble, and even though the Roman Centurion said, *"Truly this Man was the Son of God,"* the religious leaders of Israel still would not believe!

(34) "AND AT THE NINTH HOUR JESUS CRIED WITH A LOUD VOICE, SAYING, ELOI, ELOI, LAMA SABACHTHANI? WHICH IS, BEING INTERPRETED, MY GOD, MY GOD, WHY HAVE YOU FORSAKEN ME?"

The exegesis is:

During this three hour period, when darkness covered that part of the world, if not the whole Earth, He bore the sin penalty of mankind, on which the Heavenly Father could not look (Hab. 1:13; I Pet. 2:24).

THE CRY OF JESUS

The phrase, *"And at the ninth hour,"* referred to 3 o'clock in the afternoon, which was the time, as stated, of the evening Sacrifice. It also was the time that the Passover Lamb was to be killed.

The phrase, *"Jesus cried with a loud voice,"* proclaims the fact that the torture and wounds did not kill Him, but rather He laid down His Own Life. When a person is very, very weak, the first thing that goes is *"the voice."* Jesus *"crying with a loud voice"* tells us that He did not die from weakness or from the brutal torture which He suffered, but rather that He purposely laid down His Life. In fact, the Holy Spirit told Him exactly when He could die (Heb. 9:14).

The death of Christ was a *"Sacrifice,"* not an execution or an assassination.

The question, *"Saying, Eloi, Eloi, lama sabachthani?"* seems not to explain exactly what language Jesus was speaking. Even though we have the interpretation given to us, still, it is not certain as to the original language He was using.

Some say that Jesus was speaking Aramaic, which Mark uses, and which probably was the case, with Matthew referring to the original Hebrew.

The question, *"Which is, being interpreted, My God, My God, why have You forsaken Me?"* is taken from Psalms 22:1. Some believe that He quoted the entirety of Psalm 22. At any rate, whether part or whole, His reciting this Psalm showed Himself to be the very Being to Whom the words refer, so that the Jewish Scribes and people might examine it and see the cause why He would not descend from the Cross; mainly, because this very Psalm showed that it was appointed that

He should suffer these things.

FORSAKEN?

The question, *"Why have You forsaken Me?"* actually proclaimed Him bearing the sin penalty of the world, on which the Heavenly Father could not look. The Prophet Habakkuk said, *"You are of purer eyes than to behold evil, and cannot not look on iniquity"* (Hab. 1:13).

Of course, God, being God, sees everything, even *"evil"*; however, He cannot countenance such, even though borne by His Only Son.

Was Jesus actually forsaken by God?

In a sense, He was, for some three hours, in that God the Father could not look upon Him while He was bearing the sin penalty of the world. The moment He died, He said, *"It is finished"* (Jn. 19:30). Then He said, *"Father, into Your Hands I commend My Spirit: and having said thus, He gave up the ghost"* (Lk. 23:46).

The point is:

If God had forsaken Him in totality, as some teach, He could not have committed Himself to the Father when He died. His doing this shows that God had turned His back on Him, so to speak, only for a short period of time, actually about three hours. During that time, God judged man's sin, which was upon Him; He also Personally judged Christ.

The sentence of death rested on man personally because of his sinful nature, and because of his sinful actions. If Christ, therefore, would redeem him from this doom, He must suffer it Himself, that is, must load Himself with the sinner's sins. He, Himself sinless, was constituted sin itself, which demanded the penalty of death, which Jesus paid (II Cor. 5:21; Gal. 3:13).

THE PRICE THAT WAS PAID

To deliver man, Christ became the Sin Offering. As such, He bore our sins in His Own Body on the tree (I Pet. 2:24). He abolished sin by the sacrifice of Himself (Heb. 9:26). He suffered the wrath of God due to disobedience: man's obedience; but not His disobedience (Eph. 5:6). The sword of that wrath awoke not only against the sins that were laid upon Him, but against Himself as being the Sin Offering, while, at the same, He was the Fellow of Jehovah (Zech. 8:7). He, therefore, was made a curse by God Personally (Gal. 3:10), i.e., condemned to death, the mysterious death of separation from God, which He experienced during the last three hours He was on the Cross.

Herein lies the mystery of Christ as the Burnt Offering and the Sin Offering of Leviticus, Chapters 1 and 4. Never was He more perfect and more precious to the Heart of God, more truly a Sweet Savor, than when hanging on the Tree. And yet, at that same moment, He was made a curse, which had to be in order for Him to suffer the full penalty as the Sin Offering, which had to be suffered. Hence, He Himself declared (Jn. 3:14) that the serpent on the pole, the similitude of the deadly stinging serpent, prefigured that which He must defeat, and which He did defeat on Calvary's Cross.

Jesus went to the Cross because of sin: not His sin, for, as stated, He had none; but for the sin of the world (Jn. 1:29). And the Cross is where Satan, i.e., *"that old serpent, the Devil,"* was defeated. He was defeated by Jesus atoning for all sin, past, present, and future, at least for those who will believe (Jn. 3:16). If we think that Jesus went to the Cross for any other reason, we are missing the point of the entirety of the Bible. The story of the Bible is the story of man's Fall and man's Redemption, a Redemption which came about solely through Jesus Christ and what He did at the Cross.

(35) "AND SOME OF THEM WHO STOOD BY, WHEN THEY HEARD IT, SAID, BEHOLD, HE CALLS ELIJAH."

The diagram is:

This was mockingly said by the religious leaders of Israel.

THE SEVEN SAYINGS OF CHRIST ON THE CROSS

The phrase, *"And some of them who stood by,"* refers to the Roman soldiers, and even possibly some of the religious leaders of Israel. The phrase, *"When they heard it,"* refers to the cry of Jesus. Actually, there were seven sayings of Christ on the Cross. The following is probably the order in which they were uttered:

1. *"Woman, Behold your son! . . . Behold your mother"* (Jn. 19:26-27).
2. *"Father, forgive them; for they know not what they do"* (Lk. 23:34).
3. *"Verily, I say unto you, Today shall you be with Me in Paradise"* (Lk. 23:43).
4. *"I thirst"* (Jn. 19:28).
5. *"My God, My God, why have You forsaken Me?"* (Ps. 22:1; Mat. 27:46; Mk. 15:34).
6. *"It is finished"* (Jn. 19:30).
7. *"Father, into Your Hands I commend My Spirit"* (Lk. 23:46).

The phrase, *"Said, Behold, He calls Elijah,"* proclaims them not understanding what He said, or else not understanding the language. Or else, they only pretended to misunderstand, and the statement by the Jews concerning Elijah was made in sarcasm, which was probably the case.

(36) "AND ONE RAN AND FILLED A SPONGE FULL OF VINEGAR, AND PUT IT ON A REED, AND GAVE HIM TO DRINK, SAYING, LET ALONE; LET US SEE WHETHER ELIJAH WILL COME TO TAKE HIM DOWN."

The overview is:

According to John, this was placed on hyssop (Jn. 19:29), which fulfilled Exodus 12:22. There is no record that He drank it.

THE HYSSOP

The phrase, *"And one ran and filled a sponge full of vinegar,"* was probably in response to the words of Jesus, *"I thirst"* (Jn. 19:28). Expositors differ as to whether this was a drugged potion or the ordinary drink of the soldiers, which contained no narcotics, called *"posca."* It doesn't actually say whether Jesus drank the *"vinegar"* or not, but, according to John, He *"received the vinegar"* (Jn. 19:30). At any rate, it touched His lips, whether He was able to consume any or not.

The phrase, *"And put it on a reed,"* was, according to John, *"hyssop"* (Jn. 19:29). This would have been a fitting symbol, as hyssop was used to apply the blood to the doorposts in Egypt, when the Children of Israel were delivered from Egyptian bondage (Ex. 12:22). When the *"hyssop"* touched His Lips, it came back, no doubt, stained with His Blood. As such, it fulfilled the Type in every way of

NOTES

what happened in Egypt so long ago.

As the blood was then applied to the doorposts by faith, likewise, it is applied to our hearts presently by faith. The glorious Promise that was then rich with life continues to hold true unto today:

"When I see the Blood, I will pass over you" (Ex. 12:13).

ELIJAH

The phrase, *"And gave Him to drink,"* may or may not have represented an act of kindness. If truly it was kindness, it was the only such kindness shown to Him at this horrible time.

It is not known if the phrase, *"Let alone,"* was uttered in kindness or not.

The phrase, *"Let us see whether Elijah will come to take Him down,"* was said, once again, either in jest or true kindness. If it was said in jest, of course, it was in sarcasm, meant only to mock. If it was said in compassion, the motive was to offer our Lord the liquid in an effort to prolong His Life so that Elijah would have an opportunity to work an effectual deliverance by taking Him down from the Cross.

Jews regarded Elijah as a deliverer in time of trouble. But, of course, the Word of God promised no such thing regarding Elijah, but only that his ministry will touch Israel in the coming Great Tribulation (Mal. 4:5-6).

It is almost positive this statement was meant to be a mockery and not a kindness!

(37) "AND JESUS CRIED WITH A LOUD VOICE, AND GAVE UP THE GHOST."

The exposition is:

It should have been translated, *"breathed out His Life."* He didn't die until the Holy Spirit told Him to die (Heb. 9:14).

THE DEATH OF JESUS

The phrase, *"And Jesus cried with a loud voice,"* portrays something very unusual for someone who is dying; it is recorded by Matthew, Mark, and Luke.

Usually the voice fails the dying one, more especially when the natural forces have been weakened by long agony, as in the case of our Lord. This tells that He did not die of necessity, but voluntarily, in accordance with what He had Himself said, *"No man takes My Life from Me . . . I have power to lay it down, and I have power to take it again"* (Jn. 10:18).

Antiochanus said, *"By this action the Lord Jesus proved that He had His whole Life, and His Death, in His Own free Power."*

In truth, had He not purposely laid down His Life, due to the fact that the Lord was not born of the seed of Adam, and consequently did not have a *"sin nature,"* His human Body would have lived forever, not seeing death, as God originally intended with Adam. If Adam and Eve had not fallen, all children born to them would have been born *"sons and daughters of God"* (Lk. 3:38). As such, they would not have died, nor were they intended to die; however, Adam and Eve, as is known, fell before a child was born to them.

After the Fall, all children born to Adam and his seed were not born in the likeness of God, but rather in the likeness of Adam (Gen. 5:3), therefore, subject to death, which passed upon all men (Rom. 5:12).

THE LAST ADAM

Thank God that Jesus came, serving as *"The Last Adam,"* purchasing back by His Own Precious Blood what the First Adam lost! Paul said, *"For as in Adam all die, even so in Christ shall all be made alive"* (I Cor. 15:22). When Jesus died, He purposely laid down His Own Life, for no man took it from Him. This is shown by the strength He exhibited, even at the last moment.

The phrase, *"And gave up the ghost,"* probably would have been better translated *"breathed out His Life,"* because the words, *"gave up,"* literally are *"breathed out."* At this moment, Jesus purposely gave up His Life, and thus ended that which had been planned before the foundation of the world (I Pet. 1:20).

The penalty for disobedience to God in the Garden of Eden had been death, spiritual death, i.e., separation from God. The price for Redemption had been death, but the death of a Perfect Sacrifice. That Perfect Sacrifice was the Lord Jesus Christ (Jn. 3:16). The Word of God makes it clear that Jesus' Life is the price of Redemption (Mat. 20:28; Mk. 10:45). The Redemption price, as stated, *"The Precious Blood of Christ, a Lamb without blemish or defect,"* was paid to release people from *"the empty way of life"* received from the forefathers (I Pet. 1:18-19).

Redemption is a release *"from all iniquity (wickedness)"* (Tit. 2:14). The Redemption that Jesus accomplished by His Blood is an eternal Redemption (Heb. 9:12), intended to cleanse us that *"we may serve the Living God."* Thus, Redemption in the New Testament focuses on the condition of the Believer, who had been locked in a wicked and empty way of life, and on the price of Redemption, the Blood of Christ. It also focuses on the results of Redemption, a commitment by the Believer to serve God.

ROMAN LAW

The last aspect of Redemption has a parallel in Roman law. If a person had been captured in war and then released through the payment of a ransom by another Roman citizen, the person was obligated to his ransomer until the price had been repaid. You and I, ransomed at incalculable cost, are forever in the debt of God and must rightfully surrender ourselves to Him (Rom. 6:12-14). But it is in bondage to Him that our true freedom lies.

Each person in the world is in the grip of sin. Sin's bondage can be broken only through Christ's Blood. Redeemed, the Believer is given a place in the Family of God and is called to live a life which reflects his new standing, which can be done only by the Believer looking steadfastly to Christ and the Cross.

Among all the world's religious writings, only the Bible, the Word of God, so portrays the relation between human beings and God in terms of Redemption. Redemption reveals a helpless humanity; and Redemption affirms a God Whose Love drives Him to take the part of the near kinsman. At His Own expense, He paid the price needed to win our release. That price was the Life of His Only Son, poured out at Calvary in the shedding of His Own Blood.

(38) "AND THE VEIL OF THE TEMPLE WAS RENT IN TWAIN FROM THE TOP TO THE BOTTOM."

The overview is:

The Veil being rent signified that the price had been paid, with all sin atoned; now, the way to the Holy of Holies was opened up that man might come, for the Veil hid the Holy of Holies.

THE TORN VEIL

The phrase, *"And the Veil of the Temple,"* referred to the curtain which separated the Holy Place and the Holy of Holies. The Holy Place contained the Table of Shewbread, the Golden Lampstand, and the Altar of Worship. The Holy of Holies contained the Ark of the Covenant, on which sat the Mercy Seat, over which were the Cherubim.

God dwelt between the Mercy Seat and the Cherubim, or rather He there was supposed to dwell. This room, the Holy of Holies in Herod's Temple, was empty, due to the fact that Ark of the Covenant had been lost when Nebuchadnezzar desecrated and destroyed Solomon's Temple some 600 years earlier. From that time, the Blood of the sacrificial Lamb could not be applied once a year to the Mercy Seat on the Great Day of Atonement.

This was fitting. Because of sinful rebellion, Israel had forfeited her right to be led by God, and since that time was now led by Gentile powers.

The phrase, *"Was rent in twain from the top to the bottom,"* signified the finish of the Old Mosaic Law, meaning that the Sufferer, Who had just died on the Cross, had fulfilled all the Levitical Offerings and had abrogated them. The rending of the *"Veil"* specified that, with Jesus' Death, the way into the Holiest — where God Himself dwelt — was open for all. Because of Jesus and what He did at Calvary, we can *"approach the Throne of Grace with confidence"* (Heb. 4:16).

All of this means that the entire price was paid at Calvary, with the entire victory there won. Inasmuch as all sin was atoned, the Resurrection was not in doubt. If there had been one sin left unatoned, Jesus could not have risen from the dead, because *"the wages of sin is death"* (Rom. 6:23). But, due to the fact that He atoned for all sin, past, present, and future, Satan and his cohorts were totally and completely defeated (Col. 2:14-15).

Sin is what gave Satan the legal right to hold mankind in bondage. With all sin atoned, that legal right is removed, at least for those who believe God (Jn. 3:16). So, at present, Satan is able to hold man captive only by man's consent, which refers to man refusing to accept Christ and what Christ has done at the Cross.

THE WAY IS NOW OPEN

Whereas under the Old Levitical Law, the Holy of Holies, which, in a sense, typified the Throne of God, could only be approached by the Great High Priest, and only once a year, and then only with blood. It can now be approached at any time by anyone who has Faith in the Lord Jesus Christ and what He did at Calvary. This Scripture is emphatically clear in this, saying, *"And the Spirit and the Bride say, Come. And let him who hears say, Come. And let him who is athirst come. And whosoever will, let him take the Water of Life freely"* (Rev. 22:17).

Even as I dictate these words, I sense the Presence of God. It is as if the Holy Spirit is saying (which He is saying) to any and all that this great Way of Salvation has been opened to any and all, and for all time!

Paul said it beautifully, *"But now in Christ Jesus you who sometimes were far off* (Gentiles, who were unable to approach God) *are made nigh* (now able to come) *by the Blood of Christ"* (Eph. 2:13).

The rending of this *"Veil"* at the time of the death of Jesus is of far greater significance than even the brightest spiritual mind could ever begin to comprehend. Because of the Blood of Jesus, the most sinful of men can approach, by Faith, with confidence that God will not strike him dead, but will, in Truth, wash and cleanse him from all sin.

The *"Veil"* signified that Heaven was closed to all until Christ, by His Death, rent this Veil in twain and laid open the Way. The Justice of God has been satisfied. The price has been paid. Now, unholy men can approach a thrice-Holy God, that is, if they approach by Faith in Christ and what He has done for us at the Cross.

THE VEIL

According to Josephus, the *"Veil"* was 60 feet high and 15 feet wide. It is said that it was 4 inches thick and so strong that four yoke of oxen could not pull it apart. The very moment Jesus died, however, the Hand of God immediately ripped this giant Veil from top to bottom, signifying that the Way was now open to all.

From this action, we can see the great Heart of God. He so desired the Way to be open, that not a second was lost after the price had been paid. Immediately, He ripped this barrier asunder, and with a violent action, signifying that all may come. Hallelujah!

He ripped it from the top, which would have been impossible for man to do, at least at that time. The rending it from the top portrayed that this action came from Heaven and was ordained by God. It was the duty of the officiating Priest on the evening of the day of preparation, which would have been at 3 p.m., to enter into the Holy Place, where he would open the Outer Veil, thus exposing the Holy Place to the people in the Outer Court. This time (3 p.m.) was the actual time of the evening Sacrifice, in this case the offering of the Passover Lamb, and the moment Jesus died. Without a doubt, as the Priest opened the Outer Veil, exposing the Inner Veil, this latter Veil hiding the Holy of Holies, he and many others saw something that was so startling it must have defied description.

To the shock and amazement of the Priest and the observers, they saw this giant Veil begin to rend from the top, slowly making its way to the bottom until it was completely rent asunder. There had been many strange happenings on this day: the darkness which had lasted from noon until 3 p.m., the earthquake, and now the strangest of all, the *"rending of the Veil."*

Did the Priest understand the significance of this momentous occasion?

More than likely, not! However, his lack of understanding, if so, in no way weakened the effectiveness of this which was wondrously done.

"*Saved by the Blood of the Crucified One!*
"*Now ransomed from sin and a new work begun,*
"*Sing praise to the Father and praise to the Son,*
"*Saved by the Blood of the Crucified One!*"

NOTES

(39) "AND WHEN THE CENTURION, WHICH STOOD OVER AGAINST HIM, SAW THAT HE SO CRIED OUT, AND GAVE UP THE GHOST, HE SAID, TRULY THIS MAN WAS THE SON OF GOD."

The synopsis is:

This Centurion was the first Gentile to render this testimony of faith; tradition affirms that his name was Longinus, and that he became a devoted follower of Christ, preached the Faith, and died a martyr's death.

CENTURION

The phrase, *"And when the Centurion, which stood over against Him,"* presents something which is somewhat unusual! A *"Centurion,"* who was in charge of 100 men, normally would not have officiated at a crucifixion. More than likely there were not 100 soldiers present. However, the possibility definitely exists that Pilate assigned this man this duty because of the unusual circumstances which surrounded the Crucifixion of Christ.

At any rate, a duty which, no doubt, repulsed him, and in which he probably had no desire to serve, turned out to be the greatest day of his life. For there he met Jesus; he would make a ringing declaration which would carry forth through the ages.

The evidence is that this man closely observed all the things that happened, such as the darkness and earthquake. But, more importantly, the evidence seems to be that he stood very near Jesus, closely observing Him, at least as much as one could in the darkness. What he would see would change his life.

THE MANNER IN WHICH JESUS DIED

The phrase, *"Saw that He so cried out, and gave up the ghost,"* concerns the manner in which Jesus died. This *"Centurion"* had, no doubt, seen many men die; however, he had never seen one die in the manner that Jesus did. He heard Jesus when He uttered the words, *"Father, forgive them, for they know not what they do!"* This was something he had never heard in all his life — someone forgiving one's tormentors, especially the kind of torment that Jesus had!

Then he heard Him cry, *"My God, My God,*

why have You forsaken Me?" The way that Jesus uttered these words proclaimed, at least to the Centurion's ears, a relationship unexplainable in the natural. How much knowledge he had of Jehovah is anyone's guess. However, he knew that this One hanging on the Cross was different from anyone he had ever known. The God to Whom He spoke was more, far more, than the superstitious pagan gods of Rome!

THE SON OF GOD

The phrase, *"He said, Truly this Man was the Son of God,"* presents a controversy in some circles. Some say that he actually said, *"'a' son of god"* instead of *"'the' Son of God."* However, tradition, as stated, affirms that the Centurion's name was Longinus, that he became a devoted follower of Christ, preached the Faith, and died a martyr's death.

If, in fact, this tradition is true, the evidence would conclude that he said, *"'the' Son of God,"* referring to Christ. If he used the word *"the,"* he was distinguishing Jesus from the many called by the Romans *"'a' son of god."* Even Caesar claimed to be god! So, in effect, the Centurion was saying, *"Many have claimed to be, but this is 'The One.'"*

The testimony of the Centurion also is conclusive proof that Jesus really died, for his testimony was impartial, as should be obvious.

(Some claim Jesus only swooned and then regained consciousness in the tomb. The lengths to which men will go, attempting to boast of their unbelief, are amazing!)

(40) "THERE WERE ALSO WOMEN LOOKING ON AFAR OFF: AMONG WHOM WAS MARY MAGDALENE, AND MARY THE MOTHER OF JAMES THE LESS AND OF JOSEPH, AND SALOME."

The synopsis is:

There is no record that Mary the mother of Jesus was there; no doubt, the strain was more than she could bear. John undoubtedly took her away.

THE WOMEN

The phrase, *"There were also women looking on afar off,"* spoke of women from Galilee, as the Text proclaims, and not women from Jerusalem. John 19:25 says these women stood near the Cross, which is no contradiction. Jesus was on the Cross for some six hours. The account given by John seems to point to those first hours. To be sure, the women could have come closer and then stood further away several times, depending on the immediate happenings. When He died, however, Mark says they were *"looking on afar off."*

The phrase, *"Among whom was Mary Magdalene, and Mary the mother of James the less and of Joseph, and Salome,"* proclaims some of the most ardent followers of Christ.

"Mary Magdalene" came from Magdala, a little village near Capernaum. Jesus cast seven demons out of her (Mk. 16:9; Lk. 8:2). The horror of that defies description, and the devotion this woman gave to Christ proclaims to all the great Deliverance effected by Christ. He literally gave her life back to her. The agony she underwent before Deliverance can only be measured by her love shown to Christ after her Deliverance. She had the honor of being the first person to herald the Resurrection.

The other *"Mary"* mentioned here is said to be the wife of Cleophas and sister of Mary the mother of Jesus (Jn. 19:25).

"James the less" is distinguished from the Apostle James, the brother of John, and James the half-brother of Jesus (Mat. 13:55).

"Salome" was the mother of James and John (Mat. 27:56), and wife of Zebedee (Mat. 4:21; 20:20; 27:56).

While the Scripture is clear that Mary the mother of Jesus was there, at least at the beginning of the Crucifixion, it is not clear whether or not she was there at the last! The evidence seems to indicate that she was not; undoubtedly, the horror of this was more than she could bear, so possibly John the Beloved took her away (Jn. 19:25-27).

(41) "(WHO ALSO, WHEN HE WAS IN GALILEE, FOLLOWED HIM, AND MINISTERED UNTO HIM;) AND MANY OTHER WOMEN WHICH CAME UP WITH HIM UNTO JERUSALEM."

The exposition is:

We aren't told who these women were!

MINISTERED UNTO CHRIST

The phrase, *"Who also, when He was in*

Galilee, followed Him," concerned the many meetings He conducted in this area. Other than the terrible opposition by the Pharisees, these were the most glorious days that the Earth had ever known. The crowds were tremendous in size, but, above all, the display of the Power of God was unlike anything anyone had ever seen before. In front of the very eyes of onlookers, the lame walked, the dumb spoke, and the blind saw.

When Jesus spoke, His Words were totally unlike anything anyone had previously ever heard. Above all, everything He did was accompanied by the Power of God and in a fashion never before experienced. Jesus Himself said, *"The Spirit of the Lord is upon Me . . ."* (Lk. 4:18).

No wonder they *"followed Him."*

Even though I was not privileged to be there at that time, nevertheless, it is my glorious privilege to follow Him now! Once you have *"followed Him,"* everything else fades into insignificance.

As Peter responded, *"Lord, to whom shall we go? You have the Words of Eternal Life.*

"And we believe and are sure that You are that Christ, the Son of the Living God" (Jn. 6:67-69).

MINISTRY

The phrase, *"And ministered unto Him,"* means they did the best they could to help with the various needs of His Humanity. This would, no doubt, speak of the washing of clothes, helping to arrange meals, or anything else they were able to do. What a privilege it was to have the opportunity to do anything for Christ, even that which seemed to be menial.

From this one phrase, which the Holy Spirit wanted us to know and remember, we learn that nothing is overlooked in our efforts for the cause of Christ. No one must ever think or believe that their task, no matter how small it may seem, is insignificant. All is dear and precious to the Heart of God, as this proclaims.

Mary Magdalene had been delivered from seven demons. She, no doubt, felt in her mind that what little she could do, although it would never serve as payment, would proclaim her love. It would be wonderful if every Believer felt the same way. To be sure, every Believer has been delivered, in one way or the other, exactly as was Mary Magdalene.

YOUR MINISTRY

The Lord has called me for Media Ministry. I speak of Radio and Television. I am not on these particular mediums simply because I have seen a need and have responded. I definitely have been called to do what I am doing. You also have been called to help us get this work completed. Anyone who has any real knowledge of our Ministry knows that the Lord, in the last few years, has laid it on my heart, and extensively so, to preach the Message of the Cross, to bring the Church back to the Cross, to proclaim the Cross of Christ as the answer for the ills, perversions, and, above all, the sins of man. There is, in fact, no other answer, only the Cross the Christ.

Paul wrote, *"But this Man* (this Priest, Christ Jesus), *after He had offered One Sacrifice for sins forever* (speaks of the Cross), *sat down on the Right Hand of God.* (This refers to the great contrast between the Priests under the Levitical System, who never sat down because their work was never completed, and the Work of Christ, which was a *'Finished Work,'* and which needed no repetition)" (Heb. 10:12). It answered sin in every capacity.

So, the only answer for sin is the Cross of Christ. There is no other answer, because no other answer is needed.

As I have been called, and called by Revelation, I might quickly add, to take this Message to the world, you also have been called to help us accomplish this work.

Concerning this, Paul said, *"How then shall they call on Him in Whom they have not believed?* (the great sin of mankind is the sin of *'unbelief'*) *and how shall they believe in Him of Whom they have not heard?* (Ignorance is not Salvation. It is the business of Believers to take the Gospel to the world.) *And how shall they hear without a Preacher?* (This reveals God's method of proclaiming His Message.)

"And how shall they preach, except they be sent? (Those who send the Preacher are just as important as the Preacher . . .)" (Rom. 10:14-15).

In this Text, Paul plainly tells us that the Lord calls some to be sent and some to do the sending. Both, as stated, are equally important in the great Plan of God.

God has called you to send me. He has given me the Message, but I cannot get it to others without your help. And the type of help of which I speak is prayerful help and financial help. Both are absolutely imperative. Don't ever let the Devil tell you that your call is less than mine. It isn't!

Let me say it again:

I have been called; I have been sent; but I cannot go unless you send me.

In the Fall of 2004, the Lord laid it on my heart to institute a simple, little program entitled *"SOLDIERS OF THE CROSS."* It simply means that each and every one of you who helps us carry out this great work, which refers to the taking of the Message of the Cross to a hurting world and a dying Church, is a SOLDIER OF THE CROSS. I believe the Lord gave me this program. I also believe that it is a tremendous privilege to be a part of this which the Lord is doing.

THE MESSAGE OF THE CROSS

The Church has drifted so far away from its Scriptural moorings that it hardly knows anymore where it has been, where it is, or where it is going. With some few exceptions, Church is no longer what it once was. Presently, it is strictly man-originated, man-guided, man-led, and man-organized. All of that means that it's not of God, no matter how religious it may seem.

Unscriptural programs, such as *"The Purpose Driven Life"* and the *"Government of Twelve* (G-12),*"* are sweeping the nation and the world. They, however, are not of the Lord.

How do I know that?

As I've already said, even several times, in this Volume, I know they are not of the Lord because *"Jesus Christ and Him Crucified"* is not the centerpiece of their Message. Since the Cross is not their theme, then this means that their Message is not of God.

What did Paul say concerning this?

"But though we (Paul and his associates), *or an Angel from Heaven, preach any other gospel unto you than that which we have preached unto you* (Jesus Christ and Him Crucified), *let him be accursed* (eternally condemned; the Holy Spirit speaks this through Paul, making this very serious).

"As we said before, so say I now again (at sometime past, Paul had said the same thing to them, making their defection even more serious), *If any man preach any other gospel unto you* (anything other than the Cross) *than that you have received* (which saved your souls), *let him be accursed* (*'eternally condemned,'* which means the loss of the soul)*"* (Gal. 1:8-9).

That's why Paul also said, *"For Christ sent me not to baptize* (presents to us a Cardinal Truth), *but to preach the Gospel* (the manner in which one may be saved from sin)*: not with wisdom of words* (intellectualism is not the Gospel), *lest the Cross of Christ should be made of none effect.* (This tells us in no uncertain terms that the Cross of Christ must always be the emphasis of the Message)*"* (1 Cor. 1:17).

Let me say it again:

If the Message is not *"The Cross of Christ,"* then it is not the Gospel! So this means that these fads, to which I have briefly alluded, simply aren't the Gospel. They won't help anyone, they won't save anyone, and they won't steer anyone correctly, which means they are worthless!

As these people helped Christ in His earthly Ministry, likewise, I am asking you also to help us, both prayerfully and financially. For every person who doesn't know what Jesus did for them at the Cross, as far as that person is concerned, Jesus died in vain. Considering the price that was paid, such a thought is unthinkable!

MANY OTHER WOMEN

The phrase, *"And many other women which came up with Him unto Jerusalem,"* gives us no indication as to who they were, but they had been, no doubt, recipients of great things from His Ministry and they desired to be in His Presence.

What a privilege they had, to be included at this particular time! Even though the Scripture leaves them nameless, they are noted as individuals who did what they could do to help the Lord.

That is the question:

Are you doing all that you can do?

(42) "AND NOW WHEN THE EVENING WAS COME, BECAUSE IT WAS THE PREPARATION, THAT IS, THE DAY BEFORE THE SABBATH."

The composition is:

This was the High Sabbath of the Passover Feast, which was Thursday, not the ordinary weekly Sabbath, which was Saturday (Lev. 23:6-7). Jesus was crucified on a Wednesday, not on Friday, as many think. He spent three full days and nights in the Tomb. He rose on the first day of the week, even as He had said He would do (Mat. 12:40).

THE HIGH SABBATH

The phrase, *"And now when the evening was come,"* referred to approximately 6 p.m., when the High Sabbath of the Feast would begin. It was now just after 3 p.m. in the afternoon, and much work still had to be done before the Passover Sabbath began, when all work had to stop. During this three-hour period of time, Joseph of Arimathaea had to go to Pilate and ask for the Body of Jesus. Jesus had to be taken down from the Cross, with some care given, and placed in the Tomb before sundown.

The phrase, *"Because it was the preparation,"* spoke of all the work being done in preparation for the Passover. This was the day the lambs were killed for the Passover. All activity had to cease, as stated, at sundown.

The phrase, *"That is, the day before the Sabbath,"* spoke, as stated, of the High Sabbath of the Passover Feast, which was Thursday, not the ordinary weekly Sabbath, which was Saturday (Lev. 23:6-7). The misinterpretation of this one Passage, i.e., most thinking it refers to the normal weekly Sabbath of Saturday, confuses many, causing them to think that Jesus died on a Friday. He actually was crucified on a Wednesday and spent three full days and nights in the Tomb, rising on Sunday morning, just as He had said He would do, which could have been any time after sundown on Saturday (Mat. 12:40).

The Jews then reckoned time a little differently than we do now. Our new day starts at 12:01 midnight. Theirs began at sundown. In other words, at approximately 6:01 p.m. on what we think of as Saturday evening, the Jews of that time would have reckoned this as the beginning of Sunday.

(43) "JOSEPH OF ARIMATHAEA, AN HONORABLE COUNSELOR, WHICH ALSO WAITED FOR THE KINGDOM OF GOD, CAME, AND WENT IN BOLDLY UNTO PILATE, AND CRAVED THE BODY OF JESUS."

The diagram is:

Joseph was a member of the Grand Council of Jerusalem, the Sanhedrin, which means that he was a very wealthy man.

JOSEPH OF ARIMATHAEA

The name, *"Joseph of Arimathaea,"* stands out boldly because of what he did for Christ at this time.

The Scripture says of him, *"he was a good man, and a just . . . who also himself waited for the Kingdom of God"* (Lk. 23:50-51).

He also was *"a Disciple of Jesus, but secretly for fear of the Jews"* (Jn. 19:38).

He also was a member of the Sanhedrin, but he had not voted for the death of Jesus. Whether he was present at the illegal trial of Jesus is not exactly known.

From what description is given of this man, it seems he struggled inwardly concerning his devotion to Christ before the Crucifixion. He was rich, respected, and occupied one of the highest offices in the land. It seems he had trouble openly declaring his devotion to Christ.

Sadly, there are many, even presently, who are secret Disciples of Christ. As with Joseph, sooner or later, either the *"secret"* will have to be divulged or Jesus will have to be denied.

The record is clear that all this man had, i.e., riches, office, place, and position, in no way satisfied the longing and craving in his heart. That was only stirred and satisfied when he first heard Jesus. What this occasion was is not known. But he would never again be the same.

Now, he will fulfill Bible Prophecy by giving Jesus his tomb (Isa. 53:9). Had he not done this, Christ would have been buried with criminals.

AN HONORABLE COUNSELOR

The phrase, *"An honorable Counselor,"* refers to him being a member of the Grand

Council of Jerusalem, the Sanhedrin. Even though he was a native of Arimathaea, every evidence is that he now lived in Jerusalem. Jerome says that his city, Arimathaea, was called Ramathaim-Zophim, and was where Samuel was born.

The Holy Spirit uses the word *"honorable"* for a specific reason. This man, although not as bold as he should have been, had a heart for God. The phrase, *"Which also waited for the Kingdom of God,"* spoke of this hunger. It was to be fulfilled in Jesus, as it can be fulfilled only in Jesus!

The phrase, *"Came, and went in boldly unto Pilate,"* means that what he did was not commonly done. Pilate consented, no doubt, to see him because of who he was, i.e., rich and a member of the Sanhedrin.

The phrase, *"And craved the Body of Jesus,"* means that he strongly requested that he be given the remains. He *"craved"* the *"Body"* simply because if such was not granted, Jesus would have been buried, as stated, in a common grave with criminals. Also, time was running out! What was done must be done quickly!

(44) "AND PILATE MARVELED IF HE WERE ALREADY DEAD: AND CALLING UNTO HIM THE CENTURION, HE ASKED HIM WHETHER HE HAD BEEN ANY WHILE DEAD."

The overview is:

It normally took several days for one to die on a Cross. Jesus had only been on the Cross for six hours, so Pilate was skeptical.

THE DEATH OF CHRIST

The phrase, *"And Pilate marveled if He were already dead,"* is understandable, because it normally took from two to three days, or even longer, for one to die on a cross. Inasmuch as Jesus had only been on the Cross for six hours, Pilate was skeptical. The time was probably a little bit after 3 p.m.

The phrase, *"And calling unto him the Centurion, he asked him whether He had been any while dead,"* pertained to the man who had said, *"Truly this Man was the Son of God."* Pilate was not satisfied that Jesus was dead. If He truly was dead, how long had it been since He expired? There is a possibility that the Centurion had come with Joseph but had not actually gone in before Pilate, remaining in a side room until he was called.

(45) "AND WHEN HE KNEW IT OF THE CENTURION, HE GAVE THE BODY TO JOSEPH."

The exposition is:

The word *"body"* in the Greek is *"ptoma,"* which means *"a corpse."* Jesus was dead!

THE BODY OF CHRIST

The phrase, *"And when he knew it of the Centurion,"* proclaims the fact that Pilate satisfied himself that Jesus truly was dead. The unprejudiced testimony of an unbiased witness, in this case, a Roman Centurion, placed the official stamp of Rome on the death of Jesus.

Some skeptics have attempted to claim that Jesus never actually died. But it is to be noticed, even the Jews, who thoroughly hated Christ, never claimed that He did not die, only that He did not rise from the dead. They knew He died, because they watched Him die. Furthermore, the uncontestable testimony of the Centurion, as stated, verified His Death.

The phrase, *"He gave the Body to Joseph,"* proclaims such being done, not so much out of a feeling of generosity, but so he would rid himself of this most inconvenient and troublesome affair.

(46) "AND HE (Joseph) BOUGHT FINE LINEN, AND TOOK HIM DOWN, AND WRAPPED HIM IN THE LINEN, AND LAID HIM IN A SEPULCHER WHICH WAS HEWN OUT OF A ROCK, AND ROLLED A STONE UNTO THE DOOR OF THE SEPULCHER."

The synopsis is:

The tomb was in the Garden adjacent to the place of Crucifixion, which most certainly was the property of Joseph.

THE TOMB

The phrase, *"And he bought fine linen,"* proclaims Joseph purchasing such on the way back from Pilate to Golgotha. The *"linen"* was not a garment, but rather a piece of cloth, fresh and unused. It would be used to wrap around the Body of Jesus.

The phrase, *"And took Him down,"* constituted one of the most touching and heart-rending moments in human history. From

John's account, it seems that Nicodemus was waiting for Joseph at the Crucifixion site. There may have been others present; even the Roman Centurion may have helped.

It would not have been simple or easy to take Him down from the Cross. Somehow they would have to remove the large nails from His Hands and from His Feet. Using some type of instrument to pull the nails out, they would have tried to be as gentle as possible so as not to enlarge the wound any more than it already was, whether in His Hands or His Feet. They would have been the first to look upon those wounds, which He will bear forever (Zech. 13:6).

When they finally were able to remove the nails, two or three of the men gently would have laid Him on the ground at the foot of the Cross. Even though the Scripture is silent, they undoubtedly attempted to cleanse the Blood from the wounds in His Hands, Feet, and Side. As they held His Hands, attempting to wipe away the Blood, their minds would have gone to the countless scores whom He had touched, instantly bringing healing.

They would have had little success in attempting to cleanse His Back, because there were too many wounds, with hardly any skin left intact. His Face also would have been unrecognizable. There would have been nothing they could do with His Face except close His Eyes.

THE STONE

The phrase, *"And wrapped Him in the linen,"* speaks of the cloth purchased by Joseph. The phrase, *"And laid Him in a sepulcher which was hewn out of a rock,"* pertained to Joseph's own tomb. The tomb was in the garden adjacent to the place of Crucifixion, most certainly the property of Joseph. Since Golgotha was as close as it was to the Garden Tomb, Joseph and Nicodemus, more than likely, carried the body that short distance, possibly with the help of others who were nearby.

The phrase, *"And rolled the stone unto the door of the sepulcher,"* refers to the tomb being new. If the tomb previously had been used, the opening would have been closed with a stone. The fact that they rolled the stone over the opening after the Body was carefully placed inside lets us know that it had never been used.

While our Lord died with the wicked (the thieves on the cross), He was with the rich in His Death, exactly as the Prophet had predicted nearly 800 years earlier (Isa. 53:9). Tradition says that Joseph of Arimathaea was sent by Philip from Gaul to Britain in A.D. 63 and founded the first Christian settlement in this country, afterward the site of Glastonbury.

(47) "AND MARY MAGDALENE AND MARY THE MOTHER OF JOSEPH BEHELD WHERE HE WAS LAID."

The structure is:

These women were evidently present when Jesus was first laid in the tomb.

WHERE HE WAS LAID

Evidently, these two women remained behind after the other women had left. No doubt, they watched as Joseph and Nicodemus prepared the Body, probably both at the Crucifixion site and at the Tomb. It is obvious that Mary Magdalene did not want to leave, even though there was nothing left but a corpse. The horror of this moment must have been indescribable. Little did she realize that approximately 72 hours later she would see Him standing near this tomb in all His Resurrection Power. At this time, however, despite what He had said, no one believed He would rise from the dead!

The song says,

"Were you there when they laid Him in the tomb?
"Were you there when they laid Him in the tomb?
"Sometimes it makes me to tremble, tremble, tremble,
"Were you there when they laid Him in the tomb?"

At this time, there was nothing but gloom that settled over the Disciples and those who followed Jesus. He was dead. Despite what He had said, there was no one, not even Simon Peter, who believed He would rise from the dead. That's all they could see, *"Jesus Christ was dead!"*

Evil, it seemed, had triumphed. The sun

would never rise again. There would never be the bloom of another flower, nor the chuckle of a baby. Darkness had prevailed, or so it seemed!

WATERLOO

Sometime ago, I stood on the field of Waterloo, where Napoleon, the French Emperor, was defeated by the British General, Wellington. On the memorable day of the battle, the world awaited the outcome. But especially in England did they wait. If the Corsican tyrant, as they referred to Napoleon, defeated Wellington, he easily could occupy England.

On the day in question, multiple tens of thousands gathered in London to await news from the battle front. Before modern communications, the method was to post the news on the top of the tallest building for all to see.

At last the news came, and the tens of thousands of people in the streets below held their breath as they watched the workmen on top of the building putting up the big block letters which would give the news.

The letters to the first word were placed on the giant backdrop. They spelled:

W – E – L – L – I – N – G – T – O – N

The crowd eagerly awaited the second word. What would it be?

Quickly, the workmen spelled it out:

D – E – F – E – A – T – E – D

About that time, one of those sinister London fogs rolled in and covered the top of the building. All the people could remember was what they had just read, *"Wellington defeated!"* A groan went up from the crowd. Women fainted; men wept! England was vanquished! But then, all of a sudden, the fog lifted. The crowd grew quiet, because the workmen were putting up another word. It read:

N – A – P – O – L – E – A – N

Now they had the total message, *"WELLINGTON DEFEATED NAPOLEON"*!

One can well imagine the joy that filled London as the news spread all over the British Empire. *"WELLINGTON DEFEATED NAPOLEON"*!

When they laid Jesus in that tomb, it seems as though the darkness shouted:

NOTES

J – E – S – U – S   D – E – F – E – A – T – E – D

That, however, is not the end of the story. Sunday morning is coming, and the message will then read:

J – E – S – U – S   D – E – F – E – A – T – E – D   S – A – T – A – N!

CHAPTER 16

(1) "AND WHEN THE SABBATH WAS PAST, MARY MAGDALENE, AND MARY THE MOTHER OF JAMES, AND SALOME, HAD BOUGHT SWEET SPICES, THAT THEY MIGHT COME AND ANOINT HIM."

The exposition is:

All of this proves that they really did not believe that Jesus would rise from the dead; if so, it would have been pointless to have wasted money on the purchase of these expensive items.

THE MEETING AT THE TOMB

The phrase, *"And when the Sabbath was past,"* spoke of the regular weekly Sabbath on Saturday. Jesus had been in the Tomb three full days and nights. This destroys the myth that Jesus was crucified on Friday. Were that the case, it would not have fulfilled His Own statement, *"For as Jonah was three days and three nights in the whale's belly; so shall the Son of Man be three days and three nights in the heart of the Earth"* (Mat. 12:40). There is no way that He could be crucified on Friday, be raised from the dead at sunset on Saturday, or near that time, and still fulfill His prediction.

Christ was crucified on a Wednesday and put in the Tomb just before sunset. He was resurrected three days later on Saturday evening, which was their beginning of Sunday. As we have stated, days then were reckoned from sunset to sunset.

People are confused about this simply because they misinterpret the *"Sabbath"* of Mark 15:42. They think that Sabbath was speaking of Saturday, but it wasn't. It was the High Sabbath of the Passover, which was on Thursday. They would not have been allowed to purchase the spices on that particular day, and so they would have purchased these items on Friday. With nothing being allowed to be done on Saturday, which was the regular weekly Sabbath, they would then have been at the Tomb early Sunday morning.

A WASTED PREPARATION BECAUSE OF UNBELIEF

The phrase, *"Mary Magdalene, and Mary the mother of James, and Salome,"* once again speaks of these three women who, in this case, had thought to finish the embalming process. The phrase, *"Had bought sweet spices, that they might come and anoint Him,"* proves that none of these thought He would rise from the dead. If so, it would have been pointless to have wasted money on the purchase of these items.

One is not to condemn Mary, the mother of Jesus, for not being there, due to what she had undergone the last three days and nights. The Prophecy of Simeon predicted the sorrow and heartache that Mary would undergo. As is obvious, the fulfillment was exactly as the aged Prophet had said (Lk. 2:34-35).

Joseph and Nicodemus had begun the embalming process late Wednesday afternoon. They had *"brought a mixture of myrrh and aloes, about an hundred pound weight"* (Jn. 19:39).

This was a compound of the gum of the myrrh tree and a powder of the fragrant aloe wood mixed together, with which they would completely cover the body, which was then swathed with linen. According to John, it seems that they finished this part of the embalming process, and the women would now complete the task.

(2) "AND VERY EARLY IN THE MORNING THE FIRST DAY OF THE WEEK, THEY CAME UNTO THE SEPULCHRE AT THE RISING OF THE SUN."

The structure is:

This was Sunday morning.

SUNDAY

The phrase, *"And very early in the morning the first day of the week,"* spoke of daybreak on Sunday morning. Why they came now was probably according to the following:

Jesus was placed in the tomb just before sunset on Wednesday evening. According to Jewish reckoning, Thursday would have begun at sunset. For all of that night and the next day, which was the High Sabbath of the Passover Feast, all businesses were closed and all work was condemned. This was the day that the Passover Feast, having been prepared the day before, was supposed to be eaten. (Jesus and His Disciples had eaten it a day early.)

The next day was Friday and all the businesses were open once again, with normal activity. On this day, the women had probably purchased the *"sweet spices,"* etc. Beginning at sunset Friday, the weekly Jewish Sabbath of Saturday began, and all activity ceased once again. Since the embalming process again could not be completed on this day, they came *"very early in the morning,"* which would have been Sunday, the *"first day of the week."* This would be the first time they would have the opportunity to apply these spices, due to the two Sabbaths which had fallen during the past three days.

The phrase, *"They came unto the sepulcher at the rising of the sun,"* proclaimed their first opportunity, as stated, to finish this process. However, the *"rising of the sun"* on this day also meant the *"Rising of The Son"*! It would be the greatest day in history!

Of course, as is obvious, without the Resurrection, Calvary would have been in vain. The Resurrection, consequently, was the ratification of what Jesus had done on the Cross. So, this day would not be one of sorrow, as these women and others had envisioned, but rather the happiest, the most joyful, the most wonderful day they would ever know. Jesus is alive again!

(3) "AND THEY SAID AMONG THEMSELVES, WHO SHALL ROLL US AWAY THE STONE FROM THE DOOR OF THE SEPULCHER?

(4) "AND WHEN THEY LOOKED, THEY SAW THAT THE STONE WAS ROLLED AWAY: FOR IT WAS VERY GREAT."

The exegesis is:

The stone, which was very heavy, would have to be rolled away so they could apply the spices to the corpse.

THE STONE

The phrase, *"And when they looked,"*

probably means they approached the tomb with downcast eyes. In no manner did they expect to see what awaited them. The phrase, *"They saw that the stone was rolled away,"* proclaims them staring intently at the scene that greeted them. The phrase, *"For it was very great,"* means it was not something which could be done easily or quickly.

If one carefully reads all four accounts of the Resurrection, one will see a diversity of testimony. Swete says, *"The very diversity of the accounts strengthens the certitude that the story rests upon the basis of Truth; the impressions of the witnesses differ, but they agree upon the main facts."*

Had it been a *"made-up"* story, as many suggest, the stories of all of them would have been identical. This account is identical to the accounts given by any of the several people who witness a traumatic happening. Each account differs a little bit, because one witness would see something that another did not see, etc. The evidence at this stage seems to be that upon seeing the stone rolled away from the door, Mary Magdalene immediately left to go tell Peter and John (Jn. 20:2). If that is the case, she would not have seen the Angel in the Tomb, as did *"Mary and Salome,"* who entered the Tomb.

In John's account, Mary Magdalene never mentions the Angel. It stands to reason that if she had seen him, she surely would have mentioned it. As it was, she only said, *"They have taken away the Lord out of the sepulcher, and we know not where they have laid Him"* (Jn. 20:1-2).

(5) "AND ENTERING INTO THE SEPULCHER, THEY SAW A YOUNG MAN SITTING ON THE RIGHT SIDE, CLOTHED IN A LONG WHITE GARMENT; AND THEY WERE AFRAID."

The diagram is:

He was sitting on the raised projection, which had contained the Body of Jesus; his *"sitting"* portrayed far more than posture. It meant that the work of the Resurrection was completed and death had been defeated.

THE ANGEL

The phrase, *"And entering into the sepulcher,"* spoke only, as stated, of Mary, the mother of James, and Salome. The phrase, *"They saw a young man sitting on the right side,"* speaks of one of the several Angels who were present (Jn. 20:12). He was *"sitting"* on the raised projection which had contained the Body of Jesus.

The phrase, *"Clothed in a long white garment,"* refers, in the Greek Text, to a long stately robe, reaching to the feet, even sweeping the ground. The word was used of any garment of special solemnity, richness, or beauty. Expositors remark that *"no such robe was worn by young men on Earth."* The implication is that the individual described was not a human being, but an Angel.

No doubt, this *"white garment"* of such beauty was worn especially to celebrate the Resurrection. If that is the case, what must have been taking place in Heaven at this time? It would have had to have been a time of unprecedented celebration and rejoicing. Jesus Christ had redeemed man and had defeated death, Hell, and the grave. Hallelujah!

FEAR

The phrase, *"And they were afraid,"* is no wonder! Matthew said, *"His countenance was like lightning"* (Mat. 28:3). They had come expecting to find a corpse, but instead found an empty tomb and an Angel sitting where the Body of Jesus had been, with the Glory of God displayed on his countenance in such a fashion that they were terrified.

By now they should have learned that anything pertaining to Jesus always resulted in the miraculous. Wherever He was, the sick were healed, lives were changed, Miracles performed, and Angels appeared! This is the Jesus Who is the Head of the Church. That is the reason Bible Christianity is a Miracle experience. Nothing in the world can even remotely compare with it!

Tragically and sadly, the Headship of Christ in the Church has been too often replaced by pitiful men; consequently, there are few miracles, few healings, few true Salvations, etc. When and where Jesus reigns, that which He does is obvious. When men reign, nothing happens!

(6) "AND HE SAID UNTO THEM, BE NOT AFRAID: YOU SEEK JESUS OF NAZARETH, WHICH WAS CRUCIFIED: HE IS RISEN; HE IS NOT HERE: BEHOLD

THE PLACE WHERE THEY LAID HIM."

The overview is:

The statement of the Angel signifies the empty tomb; in other words, He definitely was dead, but now definitely is alive!

HE'S ALIVE AGAIN!

The phrase, *"And he said unto them, Be not afraid,"* proclaims the very first words uttered by the Angel to the New Church, in effect, *"Fear not!"* In other words, this thing is not ending as you thought, but, in reality, just beginning.

The phrase, *"You seek Jesus of Nazareth, which was crucified,"* specifies exactly Who they were looking for, and also rendered an identification which left absolutely no doubt as to Who it was! It was *"Jesus of Nazareth"*!

For quite some time, *"Nazareth"* had been looked at with disdain. A Roman garrison was located nearby, which gave rise to Gentile contamination. So, up to now, to have *"Nazareth"* attached to one's name was not exactly complimentary. But now, all of this would change. The greatest happening the world has ever known, the Resurrection, has just taken place. It was *"Jesus of Nazareth"* Who was resurrected, which, consequently, proclaimed to the world that He was exactly Who and What He said He was, i.e., the Son of God and the Redeemer of mankind.

As He changed the complexion of *"Nazareth,"* likewise, He can, and will, if given the opportunity, change the complexion of any and all who come to Him.

THE RESURRECTION

The words, *"He is risen,"* comprise, without doubt, the greatest statement ever made in the annals of human history. Even though Calvary affected man's Redemption, and did so in totality, still, had Jesus not risen from the dead, all would have been in vain! But, of course, at the same time, the Resurrection was never in doubt. Jesus had even previously stated that while He would be crucified, still, He would rise again.

Also, and as stated, Jesus atoned for all sin, so Satan had no means nor way to even hinder His rising from the dead, much less stop it.

The phrase, *"He is not here,"* speaks of victory over death, Hell, and the grave.

I have visited the tomb of Lenin in Moscow. I have looked upon his waxen, cold face. The founder of Communism is dead! Likewise is every other pretender; however, no one ever found the Body of Jesus, because there was no Body, due to the Resurrection. To be sure, inasmuch as the Roman officials were greatly embarrassed, with the members of the Jewish Sanhedrin doing everything they could to secure the Tomb, if the Disciples had stolen Him away, as was claimed, no stone would have been unturned until that Body had been found. It was not found because it did not exist. As the Angel said, speaking of the Tomb, or anywhere else, for that matter, referring to a corpse, *"He is not here!"*

The phrase, *"Behold the place where they laid Him,"* signifies the empty tomb. In other words, He definitely was dead, but definitely is now alive!

It is sad, but multiple millions have visited that empty tomb in Jerusalem, but Israel still will not believe! Their greatest Son was denied; because of that, their suffering has lasted for nearly 2,000 years. Nevertheless, in the near future this will all change. The sons of Jacob will finally come home. And I speak of the acceptance of their Lord and Saviour, the Lord Jesus Christ.

(7) "BUT GO YOUR WAY, TELL HIS DISCIPLES AND PETER THAT HE GOES BEFORE YOU INTO GALILEE: THERE SHALL YOU SEE HIM, AS HE SAID UNTO YOU."

The exposition is:

There was no censure or reprimand concerning their unbelief; as well, *"Peter"* is added to let him know that he is included, despite his denial of Christ, because Peter had definitely repented.

PETER

The phrase, *"But go your way, tell His Disciples and Peter,"* presents a special comfort. As stated, there is no censure or reprimand concerning the unbelief of the Disciples. Only a proclamation that they should be told the Good News. *"Peter"* is added to let him know that he is included, because after his denial of Christ, he probably felt he was no longer a part of the Disciples. He was to find out differently. Actually, the Lord Personally appeared to Peter a very short time after this (Lk. 24:34).

The grief of failure, especially failure concerning one's commitment to the Lord, has no counterpart. It would kill one, at least one who, as Peter, is totally dedicated, were not Grace and Mercy extended, as it certainly was. The modern Church in no way would have said, *"and Peter,"* but the Angel did!

The modern Church, by and large, says that the words, *"And Peter,"* can be included after two years of probation, etc. In other words, the Protestant Church pretty much demands penance, exactly as the Catholics. As such, the Grace, Mercy, and Finished Work of Christ are denied. In the Bible, there is no such thing as probation, at least pertaining to the Mercy and Grace of the Lord.

THE CHURCH

Why does the modern Church insist on such?

It does so because of self-righteousness. Self-righteousness cannot abide failure of any nature, even though it, within itself, is the greatest failure of all. Jesus says that Ministry begins with Repentance (Rev. 2:5). Strangely enough, with the modern Church, Ministry ends with Repentance!

Tragically, most of the time in the modern Church, the ones doing the judging are in worse condition spiritually than the one they are judging! That is sad, but true. Such is done, because men have departed from the Word of God, instituting their own rules instead.

Every Believer in the world should be hilariously thrilled and overjoyed that the Angel said, *"And Peter,"* because, in one way or the other, he said it to all!

GALILEE

The phrase, *"That He goes before you into Galilee: there shall you see Him, as He said unto you,"* is exactly what Jesus had told them in Mark 14:28.

Why Galilee?

Even though He appeared to them immediately after the Resurrection several times in Jerusalem, still, Jesus did not re-commission them until He appeared to them in Galilee. John records this incident in his closing Chapter. Galilee is where He first commissioned them, and Galilee is where He will re-commission them.

There is every evidence that Jesus, during the entirety of His Ministry, did not visit Jerusalem unless it was on the Feast Days, when He had to come. There is no record that He ever spent the night in Jerusalem, except the night of His arrest and trial. Religious opposition in this city was so bitterly against Him that the rejection was felt almost immediately upon commencement of His public Ministry. In effect, the religious leaders hated Him!

Even though the major cities of Galilee did not repent and, in fact, would not repent, and even though they had been the recipients of the greatest visitation from God ever known, still, their opposition was not nearly as pronounced as that in Jerusalem. The arrest, trial, and Crucifixion attest to that. Knowing that there would be no acceptance of Him in Jerusalem, the Holy Spirit proclaimed hundreds of years before that Galilee should be the place primarily of His Ministry (Isa. 9:1-2). There He called them, and there, after the Resurrection, He let them know that call was still in force.

(8) "AND THEY WENT OUT QUICKLY, AND FLED FROM THE SEPULCHER; FOR THEY TREMBLED AND WERE AMAZED: NEITHER SAID THEY ANY THING TO ANY MAN; FOR THEY WERE AFRAID."

The overview is:

Among other things, they were fearful that they would be accused of stealing the Body.

FEAR

The phrase, *"And they went out quickly, and fled from the Sepulcher; for they trembled and were amazed,"* proclaims them seeing more than they could comprehend, digest, or even accept for the moment! They had come to finish the embalming of the Body of Christ, with the shock of the Crucifixion still ever much evident within and upon their persons. If they even thought of His Words, where He spoke of rising again, they dismissed them from their minds, or else felt that even though He did say such a thing, it must have a meaning to it that they did not understand. In no way did they expect Him to rise from the dead.

They had seen His Back cut to pieces by the whip and His Face so disfigured that He was unrecognizable. They had watched the nails driven into His Hands and Feet. Even though they did not actually face-to-face see Him die, there was no doubt that He had, in fact, died. The testimony of the Centurion attested to this fact. Moreover, Nicodemus and Joseph of Arimathaea had attended the corpse. So there was no doubt about His Death. It was final, so what more could be said!

THE CURSE

Perhaps of even greater magnitude, they knew that anyone who hung on a Cross was cursed by God (Deut. 21:22-23). Not only were their minds shattered by what they had seen, but their Faith was shattered as well! How could Jesus be the Messiah, which they at first had thought, and be cursed by God? They really had very little understanding as to Who He actually was, and especially His Mission.

While He was truly made a curse by God, it was not for any sin He had committed, but for the sin of the world. This, they did not understand, at least at that time! And now, these further developments are beyond comprehension! Jesus is not in the Tomb, but instead a Being of such startling appearance that they could scarcely look upon him. Furthermore, with their own ears they heard him say, *"You seek Jesus of Nazareth, Who was crucified: He is risen; He is not here: Behold the place where they laid Him."*

No doubt, they were wondering in their minds if what they had seen was actually real. These women do not want to mislead the Disciples, thereby making their hurt and pain even worse; therefore, they will say nothing!

THE WOMEN

The phrase, *"Neither said they anything to any man; for they were afraid,"* means that what these women had witnessed was too much for them to comprehend, at least at this time. They would say nothing! However, Mary Magdalene, who had not see the Angel, now heard of his announcement concerning the Resurrection of Christ. She, therefore, would tell Peter and John at least that the Tomb was empty. The two Apostles, according to John's Gospel, will come to investigate; they also will find the Tomb empty, but no Angel.

Matthew records the account of the women leaving the Tomb with *"fear,"* but also with *"great joy."* They were going to bring the Disciples word, but never were able to do so because *"Jesus met them, and they held Him by the Feet, and worshipped Him"* (Mat. 28:8-10). This was very shortly after Jesus had first appeared to Mary Magdalene. Later these two women related this incident, but, at the time, as Mark said, due to events, *"neither said they anything to any man."*

(9) "NOW WHEN JESUS WAS RISEN EARLY THE FIRST DAY OF THE WEEK, HE APPEARED FIRST TO MARY MAGDALENE, OUT OF WHOM HE HAD CAST SEVEN DEVILS."

The structure is:

Jesus appeared to Mary Magdalene even before appearing to His Disciples.

MARY MAGDALENE

The phrase, *"Now when Jesus was risen early the first day of the week,"* probably referred to sometime after sundown Saturday, which would have been the beginning of the Jewish Sunday, the first day of the week. The phrase, *"He appeared first to Mary Magdalene,"* constitutes an honor of unparalleled proportions. He appeared to her *"first,"* no doubt because of her love, devotion, and faith.

After she had told Peter and John about the Tomb being empty, they had immediately come to see for themselves. Finding it as she said, they left; however, she had lingered behind, which occasioned the appearance of Christ (Jn. 20:1-18). This was even before Jesus appeared to the other women, which must have been almost immediately after He appeared to Mary (Mat. 28:8-10).

The phrase, *"Out of whom He had cast seven devils,"* gives us at least a hint as to the cause of her love and devotion. As we have previously stated, the horror of this woman's life before Jesus delivered her, due to her being possessed by these demons, would be beyond imagination. As to how and when Jesus delivered her, the Scriptures are silent; it seems that from the moment of her Salvation, she immediately began to follow Christ and never stopped, even after the Crucifixion.

The terrible bondages binding humanity are of spiritual origin. As such, all the psychologists in the world cannot alleviate this terrible problem. Jesus is not only the Answer, but, in Truth, the only Answer! It is sad when much of the Church opts for other than Jesus.

(10) "AND SHE WENT AND TOLD THEM THAT HAD BEEN WITH HIM, AS THEY MOURNED AND WEPT."

The exegesis is:

As she told His Disciples what she had seen, the Scripture says, *"They mourned and wept."*

DESPAIR

The phrase, *"And she went and told them that had been with Him,"* referred to His Disciples. This was the second time she had left the Sepulcher; the first time she had gone to Peter and John. At that time, she only reported an empty Tomb, but this time she reported that she had seen Jesus.

The phrase, *"As they mourned and wept,"* expresses their grief, which was natural, but also expressed, as the next Verse shows, that they did not believe her. Mary Magdalene had the distinct privilege of being the first person to preach the Gospel. Actually, the first Preachers of a risen Saviour were women. No other speakers are mentioned as addressing the Church, so to speak, on that first Sunday morning. Many, misunderstanding the language of I Corinthians 14:34 and I Timothy 2:11-12, believe that the Scriptures forbid a woman to preach the Gospel; however, such is incorrect, as proved here.

(11) "AND THEY, WHEN THEY HAD HEARD THAT HE WAS ALIVE, AND HAD BEEN SEEN OF HER, BELIEVED NOT."

The composition is:

They flatly rejected her testimony. Luke said that it seemed to them *"as idle tales"* (Lk. 24:11); the repeated unbelief of the Apostles concerning the Resurrection destroys the theory that they invented the Resurrection.

NOTES

UNBELIEF

The words, *"And they,"* are said by the Holy Spirit in this fashion to denote their unbelief, which was inexcusable. They knew that Mary Magdalene was trustworthy, because they had witnessed her life in the last months. Possibly they thought she was overwrought with grief and had imagined that she had seen Him.

The phrase, *"When they had heard that He was alive, and had been seen of her,"* should have been enough to have awakened His Words in them, in which He had foretold concerning His Resurrection.

The words, *"Believed not,"* mean they flatly rejected her testimony.

They did not believe her story, for it seemed, as stated, *"as idle tales"* (Lk. 24:11). They did not seem to remember, even though they should have, what Christ had said on numerous occasions — that He would rise after the third day and would see them in Galilee (Mat. 16:21).

(12) "AFTER THAT HE APPEARED IN ANOTHER FORM UNTO TWO OF THEM, AS THEY WALKED, AND WENT INTO THE COUNTRY."

The exposition is:

"Another form," in the Greek Text, literally says *"in a different outward expression or appearance"*; this is given in detail in Luke 24:13-35.

ANOTHER FORM

This *"appearance"* pertains to that which is given in detail in Luke 24:13-15.

Even though the words, *"another form,"* in the Greek Text literally say, *"in a different outward expression or appearance,"* still, there is nothing in the Text which means that the Lord's appearance distinguished Him from any other wayfaring man.

With Mary Magdalene, He had seemed to her to be a gardener (Jn. 20:15). And now, these *"two,"* who were Cleophas and possibly Luke, thought He was just another traveler on the road. Mary did not instantly recognize Him, and neither did they!

Why?

There is really no way that any natural explanation will suffice. About the only thing that can be said is that after the Resurrection, He was known as He pleased, and not necessarily at once. It seems that a particular spiritual harmony with the Lord had to be entered into before He could be recognized. Mary Magdalene and the other *"two"* were preoccupied with their sorrow.

When the Disciples on the Lake failed to recognize Him (Jn. 21:4), they also were preoccupied with their grief and consternation. There undoubtedly is an excellent lesson to be learned from this.

I personally believe the lack of recognition, at least concerning the examples we give, was meant to portray *"recognition"* or the *"lack"* of it for all time. It is sad, but true, that most Believers presently, even the truly saved, as the Disciples of old, most of the time do not recognize the Lord, i.e., that which is truly of Him. The lack of recognition presently is, as then, the lack of spiritual harmony.

RECOGNITION

If a Believer, as the Disciples, is clouded by unbelief, and especially unbelief, I personally think that *"recognition"* is impossible. This could well account for many in the modern Church falling for whatever looks spiritual, even though it has precious little, if any, Scriptural, foundation.

Sometime back, while we were in the country of Brazil, some of the leading Believers (Preachers) in that country were questioning me concerning particular religious phenomena being accepted so readily in the United States and Canada. That which had been so readily accepted in the U.S. and Canada little was accepted in Brazil at all! If one has had the opportunity to preach in both the United States and Brazil, one will readily see the spiritual harmony with the Word of God, which seems to me to be far more pronounced in Brazil than in the United States or Canada. I take no delight in saying that, but I believe it to be true.

So, I think this lesson respecting *"recognition"* of Jesus after the Resurrection was not merely a spiritual quirk, but instead designed by the Holy Spirit concerning spiritual harmony with Christ, according to the Word of God.

NOTES

(13) "AND THEY WENT AND TOLD IT UNTO THE RESIDUE: NEITHER BELIEVED THEY THEM."

The overview is:

The Disciples are now placed in the position of disbelieving two different and distinct sources.

UNBELIEF CONTINUED

The phrase, *"And they went and told it unto the residue,"* speaks of Cleophas and possibly Luke giving the Grand Message of the Resurrection of Christ to the other Disciples. They met with no greater success than had Mary Magdalene!

The phrase, *"Neither believed they them,"* places the Disciples in the position of a continued unbelief. They had now disavowed two different and distinct sources. To not believe Mary Magdalene was bad enough, but to refuse the second witness, which came from two men, and in detail, is inexcusable. There was no spiritual harmony of Faith, which actually means they disbelieved the Words of Christ when He told them that He would rise from the dead. To not believe these individuals is one thing. To disbelieve Christ is to disbelieve the Word of God. All unbelief is wrapped up in this premise, a failure to know the Word or else to disbelieve the Word that is known. *"Faith comes by hearing and hearing by the Word of God"* (Rom. 10:17).

EARS TO HEAR

Millions *"hear"* the Word of God, exactly as the Disciples heard Jesus speak of His coming Death and Resurrection; however, they really don't *"hear it"*! They *"hear"* it with their ears, but do not *"hear"* with their hearts. The Disciples heard what Jesus said, but their hearing was superficial and, therefore, not really understood. To truly *"hear"* the Word of God is to truly believe the Word of God and to act upon what has been heard. The Disciples did not *"hear"* Jesus properly; therefore, they do not *"hear"* these testimonies properly!

Why didn't they *"hear"* Him as they should have concerning this all-important issue of His Death and Resurrection?

As it is unbelief now concerning the fact

of His Resurrection, it was unbelief then concerning the Truth of His Resurrection.

Their unbelief was a misinterpretation of the Word of God concerning the Mission and Work of Christ. In their minds, He was going to overthrow the Roman yoke and set up Israel as the premier nation as in the days of David and Solomon. They did not understand that His true Mission was to liberate the entirety of the world from the terrible grip of sin. Their thinking, as such thinking usually does, has some Scriptural validity, but was completely misplaced according to time and fulfillment.

So, when He spoke to them of Who He really was, the Messiah of Israel, they misinterpreted that. In their minds, He was the victorious Messiah, instead of the suffering Messiah. Isaiah 53 spelled it out to them perfectly, but they either did not know these Passages, or else they dismissed them. In their minds, Jesus was going to be King and they were going to be powerful men by His side; consequently, they only heard what they wanted to *"hear"* instead of what they should have heard. This was the cause of their unbelief; it is the cause of unbelief presently.

(14) "AFTERWARD HE APPEARED UNTO THE ELEVEN AS THEY SAT AT MEAT, AND UPBRAIDED THEM WITH THEIR UNBELIEF AND HARDNESS OF HEART, BECAUSE THEY BELIEVED NOT THEM WHICH HAD SEEN HIM AFTER HE WAS RISEN."

The composition is:

Our Lord rebuked His Disciples, and did so sharply!

JESUS UPBRAIDED HIS DISCIPLES

The phrase, *"Afterward He appeared unto the Eleven as they sat at meat,"* could have well referred to His Appearance to them by the Sea of Galilee (Jn. 21:4-23). The phrase, *"Upbraided them with their unbelief and hardness of heart,"* proclaims that which I have just said. Unbelief causes *"hardness of heart,"* which means hardness toward God. In this state, people do not know what is of God and what is not of God.

The words, *"Upbraided them,"* are strong, meaning *"He rebuked them."*

The phrase, *"Because they believed not

NOTES

them which had seen Him after He had risen,"* means there was no reason they should not have received the testimony of competent witnesses. They were in this state because of unbelief. In the true sense, *"hardness of heart"* comes about because of being out of the Will of God. However, this is also caused by unbelief.

Even as I dictate these words, in the last few months the Lord has given us some particularly good services in our Campmeetings and in the regular worship services at Family Worship Center, which have registered a powerful Moving and Operation of the Holy Spirit. When these types of programs are aired over Television, it would seem, surely, that they would have a positive effect on Believers. Despite the powerful Moving and Operation of the Holy Spirit, however, the effect is small.

To be sure, we will receive letters from people who have been saved as a result of the these programs, with ringing testimonies of such deliverances that defy description, but almost nothing from Believers. The reason then is the reason now.

UNBELIEF

As we have stated, unbelief among Believers, which is an oxymoron, stems from failing to adhere to the Word of God. As a consequence, many of these Believers, whoever they may be, simply do not recognize the Moving and Operation of the Holy Spirit when they see it.

In one of our prayer meetings sometime back, I had addressed our small group for a few minutes on Luke 24, where the account is given of the two Disciples who did not recognize Christ, even though He walked with them. I dealt with the subject very briefly, and then we went to prayer. As I began to seek the Lord that evening, the Holy Spirit brought back to my mind this account which I had just dealt with. The Lord began to speak to me, basically saying the following:

*"These two men could not have been convinced of My Resurrection, no matter how much proof, other than My appearance unto them. Likewise, you cannot convince people of what I have called you to do, nor can you make them see what I presently am doing,

no matter what argument you may use. However, I can make them see!"

From that day until this, I have lived on that Promise. Little by little, I am beginning to see it come to pass. I realize, at least at this present time, we have a long way to go. But, still, I believe with all my heart that the Lord has promised me that He will open their eyes. I cannot believe that the Lord would have given me this great Revelation of the Cross, and then not move accordingly that the Church have the opportunity to accept the Message. Most, as is usually the case, will reject it; but some will accept and receive. The Lord Alone can open their eyes. He did it then, and He can do it now!

(15) "AND HE SAID UNTO THEM, GO YE INTO ALL THE WORLD, AND PREACH THE GOSPEL TO EVERY CREATURE."

The diagram is:

The Gospel of Christ is not merely a western Gospel, as some claim. It is for the entirety of the world.

THE GREAT COMMISSION

The phrase, *"And He said unto them,"* constitutes the introduction of the Great Commission. Some think He spoke these words to the Disciples in Galilee. Some think the statement was given at Bethany immediately before the Ascension. I tend to think it was given immediately before the Ascension.

The phrase, *"Go ye into all the world,"* tells us several things:

As this Commission begins with the word *"Go,"* someone has pointed out that two-thirds of the Name of God is *"Go"*! The thrust of the Gospel is that it be taken to everyone. For the person who does not know of the Saving Grace of Christ, the Lord's Death on Calvary was in vain. Considering that, I think one should well understand the significance the Lord places on the taking of the Gospel to the world.

If one knows and properly understands the Bible, one will quickly recognize that the Lord places great stock in everyone having an opportunity to hear, whether they accept or not (Ezek. 3:17-21; Rom. 10:14-17). Every Believer should understand that the Lord requires that every person in each particular generation must be reached with the Gospel. If they are not reached, as He told Ezekiel, *"his blood will I require at your hand"* (Ezek. 3:18). The seriousness of taking lightly these Words of our Lord is great indeed!

THE RESPONSIBILITY OF EVERY BELIEVER

This Commission is intended to be the responsibility of every single Believer, not just a select few. Some have a greater calling of leadership in this capacity; still, all must do their part. The sad truth is, however, that only about 1 percent of those who call themselves *"born again"* truly take this burden to heart. Most Christians do absolutely nothing toward this all-important task.

What does the Lord expect of each Believer in this capacity?

First of all, whatever it is, He expects our best. He gave His best, and He requires the same of us. The following is something everyone can do:

PRAY

Jesus said, *"The harvest truly is great, but the laborers are few: Pray ye therefore the Lord of the harvest, that He would send forth laborers into His harvest"* (Lk. 10:2). So every Believer can pray. Each Believer should pray that the Lord would give him (or her) a spirit of intercession, as it regards what the Lord wants and desires.

Many would ask the question, *"Why is it necessary to do this? Doesn't the Lord already know what is needed and where it is needed?"*

That is certainly true, but He has given us the glorious privilege of entering into the carrying out of His Plan and participating in the harvest. However, with that privilege comes a great responsibility.

Many Believers have the erroneous idea that the Lord, being the Lord and able to do all things, will get His Work done, whether they do their share or not. That is totally incorrect! The Lord has a part for everyone to play. That part, whatever it may be, was decided in the High Councils of Heaven. If certain Believers do not carry out that which God has called them to do, that part of the Great Plan of God remains undone. Actually, that is what the Lord was speaking of when He gave the Parable of the Talents (Mat. 25:14-30). Tragically, most Believers not only do not do their part, but actually have no idea what their part is. In other words, they are not even close enough to God to discern His Will for their lives.

This I know: If the Believer, any Believer, will begin to seek the Lord on a daily basis concerning this all-important subject, soon the Holy Spirit will begin to deal with them concerning their part in the Great Plan of God.

What an honor to have a part! What an honor by the help of the Lord to carry out that part!

To be sure, when all of us one day stand before God, the only thing that is going to be remembered is that which we were supposed to do for the Lord, and whether we did it or not! At that time, it will not matter who won the World Series or what other things we did — only what was done for Christ.

GIVING

There is not a single individual who cannot give of their resources to God, as little as it may be. Many have the erroneous idea that their small amount will make no difference and they might as well keep it. That shows a total lack of understanding regarding the Lord and how He looks at our gifts.

When Jesus was ready to use, as an example, the giving of a particular individual, He chose a woman who gave only two mites, which, in today's money, would be worth about $1, if that. He judged her motives, not the amount. He also judged the sacrifice, because her giving was a sacrifice. Our Lord used this woman's giving as an example for all time (Mk. 12:42). She gave, in fact, everything she had! So, let not anyone think that their gift is too small.

On the other hand, those whom God has blessed with financial prosperity should be extremely generous with the Work of God. They should stop and think that this is the real reason the Lord has blessed them.

THE DESTINATION OF ONE'S MONEY

Every Believer ought to know exactly what his or her money is going for. I have had many years of experience in taking the Gospel of Jesus Christ to the world. In these years, I have learned a few things regarding what should or should not be done in this respect. Tragically, I have observed that the far greater amount of money given for that which is purported to be for the Work of God, much of the time, isn't! Regrettably, most Believers little seek the Lord for this all-important Work and Ministry. They blindly support particular religious Denominations, and most of the time their money is wasted.

So, not only is the giving important, but how and where it is given is just as important.

Many Believers are going to stand before the Judgment Seat of Christ and find out that their financial support to what they thought was the Work of God was, many times, not only not of God, but actually supported the work of the Devil. While such Believers will not lose their soul in such a situation, they definitely will lose their reward (I Cor. 3:11-15).

Each Believer should be concerned enough about the Work of God, realizing how important it actually is, to check the fruit of that which they support (Mat. 7:15-20). The fruit should be souls saved, lives changed, sick bodies healed, bondages broken, Believers baptized with the Holy Spirit, and the Fruit of the Spirit made evident in people's lives.

One should pray earnestly over what they give, and especially where it is given. If the Believer engages earnestly in prayer and sincerely seeks the Lord, the Holy Spirit will give direction (Jn. 16:13-15).

AN EXAMPLE OF WASTE

To give the Reader an example of a waste of God's money, please allow me to relate one incident.

Sometime ago, Frances and I were in a large U.S. city and happened to be visiting a Pastor, a dear friend. Very near his Church was a large, brand-new building which cost approximately $15 million. A particular Ministry, so-called, had raised the money to build this structure. The claim was made that, in this building, the Gospel would be translated into many languages and sent all over the world. Believers actually sent much more than the $15 million.

The building had been sitting there for approximately two years, unused for anything. Above all, no Gospel is being translated, as had been claimed, from English into other languages.

Why?

First of all, Preachers have to be called of God and given a special Ministry for this task. It is not something that just anyone can do. With many of the Preachers associated with that particular organization, even if their messages were translated, the results, if there would be any results at all, would be abysmally small. Due to the lack of anointing of the Holy Spirit as it regards this particular Ministry, very little would be done.

Furthermore, it costs a great deal of money to translate languages, and it is a continuous cost, occurring every week; most do not truly have the burden to continue to shoulder that expense. This building was constructed for this particular task, not because the Lord had instructed them to do so, but because it was an easy way to raise money. In other words, there never was any real intention to use this structure to take the Gospel to anyone. As stated, it was simply a money-raising tool!

Having said that, what happens to the multiple thousands of Christians who give to such a project?

SPIRITUAL DISCERNMENT

First of all, they are not truly supporting the Work of God as they think. Their money actually is being wasted. They give because they do not have enough spiritual discernment to know right from wrong. In other words, as we have previously stated, there is not enough spiritual harmony with the Lord to know what is of God and what is not of God. They are led by what their natural eyes see and what their natural ears hear instead of being led by the Holy Spirit.

Most of the giving of Christendom, sad to say, falls into the same category! Very little truly goes to help take the Gospel of Jesus Christ to a lost world. Satan is very successful in his efforts to deceive in order that things be grandly supported, things which have no Scriptural foundation whatsoever. As a result,

NOTES

most of the money in Christendom is siphoned off into worthless projects which accomplish nothing for the Lord. One day every Believer will answer. With that in mind, we should be more responsible with that which is so very, very important.

THE APOSTATE CHURCH

Satan, of course, will do everything possible within his power to oppose the taking of the Gospel to the world. This is where his greatest concentration is. Sadly and regrettably, to carry out this evil task, he uses the apostate Church more than anything else. It was that way with Paul, and it is that way presently. Rome little opposed Christ, but the apostate Church opposed Him greatly, even crucifying Him.

Paul, likewise, had little problem with Rome. His biggest opposition came from the Church. This is sad but true! In other words, the very thing the Church ought to be engaged in, they oppose the most. The modern Church does actually carry out extensive *"Missions Works,"* and some of it definitely is of the Lord, but, for the most part, it is not of the Lord. Religious Denominations desire to exert total control under the guise of proper management and administration, but, in reality, these efforts are Satanic. In the doing of this, the Headship of Christ is abrogated; the organization or Denomination, consequently, becomes man-led instead of God-led. This is Satan's greatest trump card, so to speak!

These religious leaders, with some exceptions, are not satisfied to preach their powerless gospel. They feel they also must use every method at their disposal to stop anything and anyone who does not have their seal of approval. To be sure, if one has the approval of the Lord, he will not have their approval, whoever they may be.

I realize the Reader may peruse these words with some astonishment. However, that which is hindering the Church and the carrying out of the Great Commission is not so much the sins of the flesh, as damnable as they may be, but instead this of which we speak. In other words, it is the Church which is hindering the Church!

I remind the Reader that it was not the

gamblers, harlots, or thieves who nailed Christ to the Cross, but rather the Church of His day. No! The Lord in no way condones the vile sins to which I have alluded! But, again, I emphasize that these have never truly hindered the Gospel. The true hindrance of the Gospel has always been *"religious control"*!

PREACH THE GOSPEL

The phrase, *"And preach the Gospel to every creature,"* likewise, is powerful indeed! Preaching is God's method of proclaiming His Word, of heralding the Good News, and calling attention to Truth. The method cannot be improved upon because it was given by the Holy Spirit. As the Church weakens and wanes spiritually, preaching does as well! One might well say that with the weakening of *"preaching,"* everything else in the Church also begins to weaken. Spiritually illiterate men attempt to take the place of preaching with *"singspirations,"* talk shows, symposiums, stage productions, or whatever fad has come along recently.

However, to accomplish that which the Lord demands, there must be Spirit-filled and Spirit-led Preachers of the Gospel, who strongly, and without fear or favor, proclaim the Truth. True Spirit-anointed preaching may anger, upset, threaten, minister, comfort, soothe, and inspire, but it never bores.

Paul wrote, *"It pleased God by the foolishness of preaching* (preaching the Cross) *to save them who believe"* (I Cor. 1:21).

"Because the foolishness of God is wiser than men" (I Cor. 1:25).

It is regrettable that true Bible Preaching in the United States and Canada is weaker today possibly than ever before. The energy of the Church has instead turned to secular means and ways, which means the Holy Spirit is eliminated, which means that whatever is being done, it is not Church — at least Church that God will recognize.

THE GOSPEL

The Gospel is Good News, the only truly Good News, in fact, that man could ever hear. Furthermore, only the Gospel which is truly the Word of God and truly anointed by the Holy Spirit will set the captive free. A compromised, watered-down gospel is of no positive consequence to anyone. Regrettably, most *"preaching"* today falls into that category.

The Holy Spirit through the Apostle Paul graphically told us just exactly what the Gospel is, and should be.

Paul said, *"Christ sent me not to baptize, but to preach the Gospel, not with wisdom of words, lest the Cross of Christ should be made of none effect"* (I Cor. 1:17). Here we are plainly told that the Gospel is the preaching of the Cross. That means that anything else is not really the Gospel.

Through the Apostle Paul, the Holy Spirit called it *"another gospel,"* and then turned right around and said, *"Which is not another,"* meaning that this fake gospel will not do anyone any good (Gal. 1:6-7).

If, in fact, that is correct, and we can rest assured that it is, this means that most of the *"Gospel"* being preached in the world at this present time is, in fact, *"another gospel."*

Let us say it again:

If the Preacher is not preaching the Cross, then he is not preaching the Gospel!

THE HOLY SPIRIT

If the True Gospel of Jesus Christ is being preached, it always will be accompanied by the Holy Spirit. The Holy Spirit will not, in fact, anoint anything that's not true or which is erroneous in any way. He will not be party to such. So, if the Holy Spirit is not present, that is a sure sign that it's not the true Gospel, and its not the true Church.

In virtually all of the modern schemes that plague the land and the world, and I speak of religious schemes, men have taken the place of the Holy Spirit. To be sure, it's a sorry trade! As a result, what they say, even when it's the Truth, carries little weight, because there is no unction by the Holy Spirit.

Tragically, most modern Christians are Christians little at all, at least by Bible standards, because they have accepted, at least for the most part, a philosophy instead of a Person. That Person of Whom I speak is Christ Jesus.

Through the years I have seen thousands of *"Christians"* give their hearts to the Lord, saying, after they truly were convicted by the

Holy Spirit, *"I thought I was saved, but I really was not!"* For the first time, they had truly come under the Word of God as it was preached under the anointing of the Holy Spirit. The Holy Spirit convicted them and truly brought them to a saving knowledge of Jesus Christ. They had previously been indoctrinated, but not truly *"born again."*

Regrettably, most of that which calls itself *"Christian"* falls into the category of mere indoctrination instead of true conversion. Two things must always be done before people can be truly brought to Christ. They are as follows:

A. The True Gospel must be preached, which is the Message of the Cross, and not a compromised version (Mat. 24:14).

B. It must be preached under the Anointing of the Holy Spirit (Acts 1:8).

(16) "HE WHO BELIEVES AND IS BAPTIZED SHALL BE SAVED; BUT HE WHO BELIEVES NOT SHALL BE DAMNED."

The overview is:

The believing pertains to believing in Christ and what He did for us at the Cross. The baptism concerns being baptized into Christ (Rom. 6:3-5), not Water Baptism.

BELIEVING

The phrase, *"He who believes and is baptized shall be saved,"* tells us how to be saved, and what Salvation actually means; however, it is probably one of the most misinterpreted Passages in the Word of God.

First of all the word *"believes"* pertains to believing in a Person, in this instance, the Lord Jesus Christ, and not a philosophy, etc. The simple meaning of the word in the Greek Text is *"to put in trust with."* More particularly, and even more importantly, it refers to believing in what Christ did for us at the Cross. To separate Christ from the Cross, or the Cross from Christ, is to miss the point altogether.

No! That doesn't mean that we put Jesus back on the Cross. In fact, He presently is seated on the right hand of the Father, and will be there forever (Heb. 1:3). What we mean by ever linking the Cross to Christ pertains to the benefits of the Cross. The Cross is something that happened nearly 2,000 years ago. It will never have to be repeated, simply because the Sacrifice was complete in every way, thereby totally accepted by the Lord (Heb. 10:12).

As we've also said repeatedly, Christ is the Source of all things, while the Cross is the Means of all things. So, our *"believing"* must be in Christ and the Cross.

Jesus said, *"For God so loved the world, that He gave His Only Begotten Son, that whosoever believes in Him should not perish, but have Everlasting Life"* (Jn. 3:16).

Regrettably, the faith of millions is not solely in Christ and the Cross, but rather in a Church, particular Doctrine, or Sacrament. Such affords no Salvation, because it constitutes *"Christ plus."* To believe in Christ and the Cross simply means to believe that He is the Son of God and that He died on Calvary in order to pay for the sin of man. In other words, He took upon Himself the penalty we rightly deserve. He literally died for us. On the third day, He rose from the dead, which, in effect, ratified, as should be obvious, all that He did at Calvary's Cross.

To be saved, one must believe this Truth, even though one may have very little understanding of all that it means, at least at the beginning. This is brought about by the correct teaching of the Word, which the Holy Spirit moves upon to convict the heart. Man is not brought to Christ by a mental affirmation, i.e., intellectualism, even though that also definitely is involved, but rather by heartfelt conviction. It is impossible for the person to come to a place of Faith, or the act of believing, otherwise!

Hundreds of millions believe, in one way or the other, but still are not saved. In other words, they mentally agree that Jesus is the Son of God, but that is as far as they go. Such does not bring Salvation. *"The devils also believe, and tremble,"* but they are not Saved (James 2:19).

WHAT DOES IT MEAN TO TRULY BELIEVE IN JESUS?

To truly believe in something or someone means to take upon oneself the thrust, action, and even nature and character of what is believed. It is not mere acquiescence to something, or affirmation of something, but rather a conviction. To believe in Jesus means not only to accept Him as one's Saviour, but as one's Lord, as well. This is what Jesus meant when He said, *"At that day* (the day one truly believes in Christ, thereby effecting the entrance of the Holy Spirit), *you shall know that I am in My Father, and you in Me, and I in you"* (Jn. 14:20).

Churches are filled with people who claim to *"believe,"* but who, in reality, have only mentally affirmed, instead of truly accepting.

Paul said, *"That if you shall confess with your mouth the Lord Jesus, and shall believe in your heart that God has raised Him from the dead, you shall be saved.*

"For with the heart man believes unto Righteousness; and with the mouth confession is made unto Salvation.

"For whosoever shall call upon the Name of the Lord shall be saved" (Rom. 10:9-10, 13).

If it is to be noticed, the Holy Spirit through Paul didn't say, *"If you shall 'do certain things'..."* but rather *"if you 'believe certain things'...."* Salvation is not *"doing"* but rather *"believing."*

BAPTIZED

The word *"baptized,"* as used here by Christ has nothing to do with Water Baptism, as is commonly believed.

Paul said, *"Know ye not, that so many of us as were baptized into Jesus Christ were baptized into His Death?"*

"Therefore we are buried with Him by baptism into death: that like as Christ was raised up from the dead by the Glory of the Father, even so we also should walk in newness of life" (Rom. 6:3-4).

As stated, this is Baptism into Christ which takes place at conversion and has nothing to do with Baptism by water (I Cor. 12:13; Gal. 3:28-29; Eph. 4:5; Col. 2:11-13). It actually refers to being baptized into Christ, which is done by Faith, and regards His Crucifixion. In other words, we believe what Jesus did for us at the Cross, i.e., He went to the Cross for us, and there paid the penalty for all of our sins, and then was buried.

In effect, when He died on the Cross, we died on the Cross with Him. When He was buried, we were buried with Him. When He rose from the dead, we rose from the dead with Him. It was all done for us. Our Faith places us in Him, in the very act of Crucifixion, Burial, and Resurrection. In other words, He became our Substitute; by our identifying with Him, we accrue to ourselves what He did for us.

The Holy Spirit through Paul used the word *"baptized"* and *"Baptism"* simply because those words, as no other words, explain our union with Christ in His Death, Burial, and Resurrection. In simple terms, the words mean that *"we are in something, and the something also is in us."* In this case, it is Christ. An excellent example is a sunken ship. The ship is in the water and the water is in the ship. That is a true symbol of the word *"Baptism."*

So, even though He didn't explain it here, our Lord is speaking of being baptized into His Death and Burial, in order that we might be raised with Him, that *"we also should walk in newness of life."*

WATER BAPTISM

To be sure, Water Baptism is meant to serve as a symbol of Baptism into Christ, but a symbol only. It is not that of which Jesus speaks in Mark 16:16. If Water Baptism is meant in this Verse, that means that Salvation is impossible without it. Consequently, the penitent thief is not now in Heaven; and the many tens of thousands who, through the ages, have truly believed but had no opportunity to be baptized for particular reasons, such as death-bed Repentance, etc., are perished.

But if Water Baptism is fundamental to Salvation or essential to obedience, the Apostle Paul could not possibly have rejoiced that he Saved so few or made so few obedient (I Cor. 1:14-17). And further, if Water Baptism is a necessity for Salvation, God would have so ordered the climate of the Earth that it would have been possible of performance in all countries, and in all seasons of the year. But in the Arctic and Antarctic regions and in the vast desert regions of Arabia, Central Asia, and Africa, immersion in water is, at times, impossible.

If Water Baptism saves, then all persons so baptized will be Saved, which is absurd. What proves too much, proves nothing.

If the ellipses in the Greek Text be fully

supplied, the Verse will become clearer to the Reader:

"He who believes on Me, and is Baptized in Me, shall be saved" (I Cor. 12:13).

Even though the following on Water Baptism and Infant Baptism has been given elsewhere in these Volumes, due to the manner in which Commentaries are generally studied, I think it would be profitable to again relate this information.

WATER BAPTISM ACCORDING TO THE BIBLE

As we have stated, Water Baptism is a symbol, although a very important symbol, but cannot save anyone. It is the answer of a clean conscience toward God, a conscience, incidentally, already cleansed by the Blood of the Lamb, and a symbol of the Birth, Death, and Resurrection of our Lord. In essence, it is a type of our birth (our Born-Again experience), death (our death to the old life and to the world), and Resurrection (risen in His likeness and His image).

Some people misunderstand when they read, *"The like figure whereunto even baptism does also now save us (not the putting away of the filth of the flesh, but the answer of a good conscience toward God,) by the Resurrection of Jesus Christ"* (I Pet. 3:21). Many people focus on the Passage, *"Baptism does also now save us,"* and consequently miss the point of what it actually does say, i.e., *"The like figure whereunto even Baptism does also save us."*

Is it the water that saves or the *"like figure"* that saves?

Water Baptism has never Saved any soul. It is a person's Faith in the Death, Burial, and Resurrection of Jesus Christ that saves the soul. In other words, it is the *"like figure,"* i.e., Baptism into Christ, even as Paul explained in Romans 6:3-5, that saves the soul. As we've previously stated, Jesus did not explain Himself when He gave this Word in Mark 16:16. There was no point in doing so, simply because the explanation of the Cross had not yet been given. Once the Cross was history, and He had ascended to the Father, with Him then sending back the Holy Spirit, then He gave the meaning of this Word, *"Baptism,"* as He used it at that particular time, to the Apostle Paul.

Water Baptism is a type or figure of what has already happened in the heart and the life of an individual. In other words, a person is baptized in water simply because they have already been Saved, and not in order to be Saved. A mere figure has no power to save, but the reality of the figure can, and that real figure is Jesus.

Lest anyone should trust in Water Baptism to save his soul, Peter made it clear that Water Baptism does not save a person from the filth or moral depravity of the flesh. That can only be done by one's Faith in Christ and what Christ did for us at the Cross. Water Baptism, as stated, is the answer of a good conscience toward God — a conscience that has been made clean by Faith in the Precious Blood of Jesus Christ.

WORKS

It is not possible for a person who trusts in the Lord Jesus to be only partially Saved until he is baptized with water, and then be completely Saved. Such thinking is foolishness! The moment an individual trusts Jesus Christ as his Saviour, at that moment the person is Saved, instantly, totally, and completely. He can never be more Saved, no matter what else he may or may not do.

Now we come back to the *"works syndrome."* I once heard a Preacher say, *"The water saves."* I wondered what kind of water he was talking about — river water, flowing water, deep water, shallow water, water from the River Jordan? What kind of water?

I don't mean to be facetious; but, still, if Water Baptism does, in fact, save, as many claim, what type of water is the best?

Water Baptism, in Truth, is a sacred, holy, and precious symbol that a person should, by all means, follow after, but he should partake of it for the reasons given, i.e., that he has already been Saved, and that the Water Baptism is an outward symbol of what has already taken place in his heart. Water Baptism does not save; it is a public confession of Faith in the Lord Jesus Christ, of that which has already been brought about in the heart by the acceptance of Christ as one's Saviour, which constitutes Salvation.

Regrettably, many people attempt to tack

some kind of works on to Salvation. Many claim that one has to join a particular Church, or be baptized in the manner of their Church, or take the Lord's Supper in their particular fashion, etc. However, such is nothing short of adding to the Great Price that Jesus Christ has already paid. Of course, that is not possible, much less needful! As wonderful as these symbols and sacraments are, they only represent the reality; they are not *the* reality. The reality *is* Jesus. The Scripture says, *"Looking unto Jesus the Author and Finisher of our Faith"* (Heb. 12:2), not Water Baptism, not the Lord's Supper, not Church membership, and not religious traditions, as important as some of these things might be, but Jesus!

INFANT BAPTISM

Infant Baptism is not a Scriptural doctrine. Moreover, Infant Baptism probably is responsible for causing more people to be eternally lost than perhaps any other doctrine or religious error. It is a terrible thing when a person has been erroneously led to believe that him being baptized as a baby constitutes his Salvation and that he consequently is on his way to Heaven.

JESUS AND THE CHILDREN

The fact that Jesus loves children very much was made evident when He stated, *"Suffer little children, and forbid them not, to come unto Me"* (Mat. 19:14). As we have said many times, we believe all babies and children below the age of accountability are protected by the Lord respecting their eternal souls. In other words, I do not believe any child who has died below the age of accountability has ever died lost. The age of accountability varies with children according to their environment. It could range anywhere from 5 years old to 8 or 9.

Accountability is when a child is able to understand and comprehend enough about the Salvation Message to accept Christ. Surprisingly enough, children are able to grasp these truths very early and very readily when they are presented unto them.

HISTORY OF INFANT BAPTISM

Infant Baptism appeared in Church History about the year A.D. 370. It came about as a result of the Doctrine of Baptismal Regeneration — the teaching that Water Baptism is essential to Salvation; or if one desires to turn it around, that Water Baptism saves the soul (or at least constitutes a part of one's Salvation). As the teaching of Baptismal Regeneration began to be propagated, it was natural for those holding to this doctrine to believe that everyone should be baptized as soon as possible. Thus, the Baptism of Infants, who are still in the innocent state (and as yet unaccountable for their actions), came into vogue among many of the Churches. Once again I state: these two grievous errors (Baptismal Regeneration and Infant Baptism) probably have caused more people to die lost than any other doctrine.

(Baptismal Regeneration simply means that one is regenerated spiritually at the time of Water Baptism, and that the act of Water Baptism, therefore, constitutes Salvation.)

EMPEROR CONSTANTINE

The professed conversion of Emperor Constantine (Emperor of the Roman Empire) in A.D. 313 was looked upon by many persons as a great triumph for Christianity; however, more than likely, it was the greatest tragedy in Church history, because it resulted in the union of Church and State and the establishment of a hierarchy that ultimately developed into the Roman Catholic system.

There is a great question as to whether or not Constantine was ever truly converted. At the time of his supposed vision of the sign of the Cross, he promised to become a Christian. But he was not baptized in water until he was near death. He postponed the act in the belief that baptism washed away all past sins, and he wanted all his sins to be in the past tense before he was baptized. Such thinking is indicative of a lack of knowledge of the Word of God, and, more specifically, of what true Bible Salvation really means.

In A.D. 416, Infant Baptism was made compulsory throughout the Roman Empire. Naturally, this filled the Churches with unconverted members who had only been *"baptized into favor."* So whatever power the Church had in the past relative to actual conversions was now null and void. The world consequently was plunged into the gloom of the Dark Ages, which endured for more than twelve centuries, until the Reformation.

During this time, God had a Remnant who remained faithful to Him; they never consented to the union of Church and State, Baptismal Regeneration, or Infant Baptism. The people were called by various names, but probably could be summed up by their generic name, *"Anabaptist,"* meaning re-baptizers. These people ignored Infant Baptism, and rightly so, and re-baptized those who had been saved through personal Faith. They also had a generic name for themselves, *"Antipedobaptists,"* meaning *"against Infant Baptism."*

ERROR

The strange thing about these two diabolical doctrines of Baptismal Regeneration and Infant Baptism is that the great reformers (Martin Luther, for one) brought with them out of Rome these two dreaded errors: the union of Church and State and Infant Baptism. Strangely enough, in those days not only did the Roman Catholic Church persecute those who would not conform to its ways, but, after the Lutheran Church became the established Church of Germany, it also persecuted the nonconformists — however, not as stringently so and not in such numbers as those before them.

John Calvin and Cromwell in England and John Knox in Scotland all stuck to the union of Church and State and Infant Baptism, using their power, when they had power, to seek to force others to conform to their own views. Unaware to many people, this thing came to the Americas well in the early days of this Republic. Before the Massachusetts Bay Colony was twenty years old, it was decreed by statute that *"if any person or persons within this jurisdiction shall either openly condemn or oppose the baptizing of infants, or go about secretly to seduce others from the approbation or use thereof, or shall purposely depart from the congregation at the administration of the ordinance — after due time and means of conviction — every such person shall be subject to banishment."*

So, religious persecution existed even in the early days of the United States of America. Roger Williams and others were banished (when banishment meant to go and live with the Indians), because they would not submit to the Doctrine of Baptismal Regeneration or the Baptizing of Infants. However, it was the Constitution of the Rhode Island Colony (founded by Roger Williams, John Clark, and others) that first established religious liberty by law in 1,300 years (over the world). Thus it was that Rhode Island, founded by a small group of Believers, was the first spot on Earth where religious liberty became the Law of the Land. This settlement was made in 1638 and the Colony was legally established in 1663. Virginia followed, becoming the second, in 1786.

As you can see, the Doctrine of Infant Baptism has a long and bloody history; it has been one of Satan's chief weapons to condemn untold millions of people to Hell.

FURTHER EXPLANATION

What does the above have to do with us today?

A great deal!

The union of Church and State continues today in many countries of the world, or else a particular Church is more readily recognized by the State. In these State Churches, or Churches recognized somewhat by the State, Pastors and Leaders christen babies, which means they make them *"Christians"* by baptizing them; thus the person who is christened as a baby believes he is on his way to Heaven simply because he was christened (or baptized) in infancy. Since he has been taught all his life that baptism has saved him, he naturally considers himself saved by the act of Infant Baptism.

The Roman Catholic Church, with its approximately one billion adherents, teaches Baptismal Regeneration and practices Infant Baptism. Its statement of Doctrine says, *"The Sacrament of Baptism is administered by the pouring of water and the pronouncement of the proper words, and cleanses from original sin."*

The Reformed Church says, *"Children are baptized as heirs of the Kingdom of God and of His Covenant."*

The Lutheran Church teaches that Baptism, whether of infants or adults, is a means of Regeneration.

Because of the following declaration, I believe the Episcopal Church teaches that Salvation comes with Infant Baptism. In his confirmation, the catechist answers a question about his baptism in infancy by saying:

"In my Baptism . . . I was made a member of Christ, a Child of God, and an Inheritor of the Kingdom of God." (This is printed in the prayer book and can be read by anyone interested enough to look for it.)

Most people who practice Infant Baptism believe the ceremony has something to do with the Salvation of the child. These are, however, merely traditions of men. We can follow the Commandments of God or follow after the traditions of men; we cannot follow both!

CLEAR BIBLE TEACHING

The Word of God is clear regarding the matter of Salvation. Jesus said, *"He who believes on the Son has Everlasting Life: and he who believes not the Son shall not see life; but the wrath of God abides on him"* (Jn. 3:36).

"He who believes on Him is not condemned: but he who believes not is condemned already, because he has not believed in the Name of the Only Begotten Son of God" (Jn. 3:18).

Basically, there are two groups of people in the world today: those who do believe on the Son and those who do not. Those who believe are not condemned; they have everlasting life (whatever Church to which they may or may not belong). Those who believe not on the Son are condemned already, and they shall not see life, but the Wrath of God abides on them. This is the clear, unmistakable teaching and language of the Bible.

If you will notice, the Word of God never says simply, *"Believe and be saved,"* but, *"Believe on the Lord Jesus Christ and be saved."* The Word of God always identifies the object of Faith, which is the Lord Jesus Christ. *"For God so loved the world, that He gave His Only Begotten Son, that whosoever believes in Him should not perish, but have Everlasting Life"* (Jn. 3:16). It is not enough to believe; a person must believe in Him.

When the Philippian jailer asked, *"Sirs, what must I do to be saved?"* Paul answered, *"Believe on the Lord Jesus Christ, and you shall be saved"* (Acts 16:30-31). It was not enough simply to believe; that belief, that trust, and that dependence had to be *"in Him."*

IN CHRIST ALONE

If a person is trusting in Baptism for Salvation, he cannot be trusting *"in Him."* Christ is not one way of Salvation; He is the only Way of Salvation (Jn. 10:1, 7, 9; 14:6). There is no promise in the Word of God to those who believe partially in Christ. In other words, a person cannot trust in the Lord Jesus 90 percent and trust in Baptism 10 percent, or Jesus 50 percent and Baptism 50 percent, or Jesus 95 percent and some Church 5 percent, etc. As a matter of fact, there is no such thing as partially trusting Christ. The man who is trusting partially is not trusting at all. Yet the sad fact is that the majority of people in Churches in the United States and the world today are not trusting Christ at all — they believe they are trusting Him, while only partially doing so.

It is even sadder to realize that more people are going to Hell through religious organizations than any other way. That is a shocking, startling, statement, but it is true.

Jesus said, *"Many will say to Me in that day, Lord, Lord, have we not Prophesied in Your Name? And in Your Name have cast out devils? And in Your Name done many wonderful works?*

"And then will I profess unto them, I never knew you: Depart from Me, you who work iniquity" (Mat. 7:22-23).

This Scripture makes it clear that any works offered to Christ for Salvation are called, by Jesus Himself, *"works of iniquity."*

There is an old song that expresses true Faith, which says:

"My hope is built on nothing less
"Than Jesus' Blood and Righteousness;
"I dare not trust the sweetest frame,
"But wholly lean on Jesus' Name.

"On Christ, the Solid Rock, I stand;
"All other ground in sinking sand;
"All other ground is sinking sand.

(Note: Portions of source material for the article on Infant Baptism were derived from a Message, entitled *"Infant Baptism,"* by the late Dr. William Pettingill.)

DAMNATION

The phrase, *"But he who believes not shall be damned,"* refers to the final damnation. This simply means, if one doesn't believe on the Lord Jesus Christ and what He has done for us at the Cross, in fact believing something else, even anything else, such a person will be eternally lost. As we have stated, *"believing in Christ"* is the manner in which one is *"Baptized into Christ,"* and thereby saved.

If one is to notice, Jesus did not say, *"But he who believes not, and is not baptized, shall be damned."* If, in fact, He was speaking of *"Water Baptism"* when He used the word *"baptized,"* He surely would have said that; however, He did not do so because He was not speaking of Water Baptism, but that which believing in Christ affords, *"Baptism into Christ,"* which was effected at the Cross, and our Faith in that Finished Work. If a person truly *"believes in Christ,"* at that moment the person is instantly and completely *"baptized into Christ."* It is a work of the Spirit and not of the flesh (Jn. 3:3, 16; Rom. 6:3-5; 10:9-10, 13; Rev. 22:17).

(17) "AND THESE SIGNS SHALL FOLLOW THEM WHO BELIEVE; IN MY NAME SHALL THEY CAST OUT DEVILS; THEY SHALL SPEAK WITH NEW TONGUES."

The exegesis is:

Our Lord said these *"signs"* would follow them who believe, and not *"sins."*

SIGNS

The phrase, *"And these signs shall follow them who believe,"* specifically tells us how it can be known if one is merely professing Salvation rather than truly possessing Salvation. The criteria is laid out in Verses 17 and 18. One of the reasons many claim that Verses 17 through 20 are not in the original Manuscripts is because these *"signs"* are not evident in their lives and ministries. Furthermore, the real reason is that most have strayed considerably from the Book of Acts criteria.

NOTES

If one studies the Book of Acts, which is given by the Holy Spirit and intended to be the criteria for the Church, one finds that these *"signs"* were common in that account. Knowing that to be true, many make up the excuses that such were to be in the Early Church but not intended to continue thereafter, or that such *"signs"* ceased with the Apostles, etc. Jesus, however, did not say, *"And these signs shall follow the Apostles"* or *"the Early Church,"* but *"shall follow them who believe,"* including any and all, and for all time!

One thing is certain, it is only through the Power of the Holy Spirit that these things can be carried out. If the Holy Spirit is denied, ignored, or misinterpreted, there will not be *"signs."* Consequently, since the modern Church is, at least for the most part, bereft of these *"signs,"* this tells us it is also bereft of the Holy Spirit.

The criteria is *"believing."* Sadly, most Christians simply do not *"believe."* The greatest oxymoron of all is *"Believers who don't believe."* Furthermore, one does not have to be an Apostle, an Evangelist, a Prophet, etc., to have these *"signs"*; one only has to *"believe"*!

THE CASTING OUT OF DEMONS

The phrase, *"In My Name shall they cast out devils,"* presents such Believers as the only authority against evil spirits. This is done in many and varied ways: at times, by the laying on of hands; and, at times, by the Word being preached to individuals, which, upon the acceptance of Christ, causes demons to depart.

It is regrettable that presently the modern Church has turned into a giant referral system. It refers the alcoholics to Alcoholics Anonymous, the drug addicts to psychological therapy, etc. But, in Truth, the Bible holds the answer to all of these problems, and the Bible alone, we might quickly add. However, most Preachers no longer believe the Bible. Even many who profess to do so really do not! Only Jesus Christ, by the Power of the Holy Spirit, can set the captive free from domination of evil spirits (Lk. 4:18).

As we have related elsewhere in this

Volume, what Jesus did at the Cross totally and completely defeated every power of darkness.

Paul wrote: *"Blotting out the handwriting of Ordinances that was against us* (pertains to the Law of Moses, which was God's Standard of Righteousness that man could not reach), *which was contrary to us* (Law is against us, simply because we are unable to keep its precepts, no matter how hard we try), *and took it out of the way* (refers to the penalty of the Law being removed), *nailing it to His Cross* (the Law with its decrees was abolished in Christ's Death, as if Crucified with Him, meaning that its claims were settled at the Cross);

"And having spoiled principalities and powers (Satan and all of his henchmen were defeated at the Cross of Christ, atoning for all sins; sin was the legal right Satan had to hold man in captivity; with all sin atoned, he has no more legal right to hold anyone in bondage), *He* (Christ) *made a show of them openly* (what Jesus did at the Cross was in the face of the whole universe), *triumphing over them in it.* (The triumph is complete, and it was all done for us, meaning we can walk in power and perpetual victory, due to the Cross)" (Col. 2:14-15).

When the sinner comes to Christ, at that time, if they are demon-possessed, and some are, demons leave. To be frank, upon the entrance of Christ, demons cannot remain. However, demon spirits will definitely come back to oppress the Christian, which, of course, is different than possession, but oppression can still cause the Believer many, many problems.

The answer to *"demon-oppression"* is Faith in Christ and the Cross, with the Believer realizing that every victory was won at the Cross; consequently, when we place our Faith exclusively in Christ and what He has done for us at the Cross, the Holy Spirit will then work mightily on our behalf, and the oppression will cease (Rom. 6:3-14; 8:1-2, 11).

That's what Jesus was talking about when He said, *"To preach deliverance to the captives"* (Lk. 4:18). If it is to be noticed, He didn't say, *"To deliver the captives,"* but rather *"to preach deliverance to the captives."* He also said, *"And you shall know the Truth, and the Truth shall make you free"* (Jn. 8:32).

Believers cannot be delivered from *"demon-oppression"* by hands being laid on them, although this might possibly help. They are delivered as the Truth is preached to them, which we are doing right here, which means they can then get their believing straight.

Many Christians, and I'm speaking of people who truly love the Lord, are prayed for, as it regards *"demon-oppression,"* and, at times, the Power of God will move on them greatly. Sometimes great manifestations will come about, such as *"falling out in the Spirit."* While this can be very real, and definitely from the Lord, if they do not know the Truth of the Cross, even though they have experienced a touch from the Lord, they very shortly will find that the problem is with them again. As someone has well said, *"Believers need the Truth a whole lot more than they need a touch."*

The only way the Believer can walk in victory is that Christ and the Cross ever be the Object of his Faith, which then gives the Holy Spirit latitude to work mightily in one's life. Otherwise, the Believer, although loving the Lord very much, is going to be plagued by demon spirits oppressing him in one way or the other for the entirety of his life.

SPEAKING WITH NEW TONGUES

The phrase, *"They shall speak with new tongues,"* refers to the Baptism with the Holy Spirit, in which the initial physical evidence is *"speaking with other tongues, as the Spirit of God gives the utterance"* (Acts 2:4; 10:46; 19:6).

In the policy section of a catalog outlining the Course Offerings of a particular *"Christian College,"* the statement was made that anyone who speaks with tongues is either mentally unbalanced or demon-possessed; consequently, those who believe in the Baptism with the Holy Spirit, with the evidence of speaking with other tongues, are not welcome at that school. Furthermore, anyone at that school who is caught *"speaking with tongues"* would be summarily dismissed.

Considering the statements made, one can easily see why there are few Biblical *"signs"* of Salvation registered in such an atmosphere, with even acute spiritual danger being engaged by referring to the Holy Spirit in the realm of *"demon-possession."* This is the same thing the Pharisees did concerning Christ, i.e., linking the Holy Spirit with demon powers (Mat. 12:24-32).

While there is much religious machinery manifested at this particular school and Ministry, there are few *"signs"* of true Salvation. Where that leaves these people is left up to the Lord; sadly and regrettably, most fall into the same category!

Considering the significance of the Baptism with the Holy Spirit, perhaps more detailed information on this all-important subject would be helpful at this point.

THE BAPTISM WITH THE HOLY SPIRIT

Salvation is God's greatest gift to the world. The Holy Spirit is God's greatest gift to His Children, the Church. The Baptism with the Holy Spirit might properly be called the Baptism of Power. As such, it is an invaluable asset to the Christian committed to seeking the furtherance of God's Plan for the world and his life.

As well, we believe that every Christian who is baptized with the Holy Spirit speaks with other tongues, as the Spirit gives the utterance. We believe there are no exceptions. We believe that speaking with other tongues is the initial evidence that one has been baptized with the Holy Spirit (Acts 2:4).

(While it certainly is not the only evidence, we definitely do believe it is the initial physical evidence.)

We believe (and teach) that any Preacher, Teacher, or Church which does not acknowledge and proclaim the mighty Baptism with the Holy Spirit (with the evidence of speaking with other tongues) is remiss in their teaching and will spiritually weaken those who depend on them for guidance. Sending a Christian into the world without the Holy Spirit Baptism and His full Operation in our lives is tantamount to sending a soldier into battle without a weapon. Admittedly, at the moment a person is Saved, he becomes a Christian, just as a person becomes a soldier the moment he is sworn into the Army. But the inductee is not ready for battle until he has basic training and has been issued his weapons.

The Christian is in the same condition at the time of Salvation. If he isn't encouraged to be baptized with the Holy Spirit, preparing him for the ever-continuing battle against Satan, he is being sent out onto a battlefield woefully unprepared. Out Lord Jesus Christ said (Acts 1:8), *"But you shall receive power, after that the Holy Spirit is come upon you."* We need power if we are to work effectively against the perverting, destructive conspiracy promoted by the enemy. Anyone hindering the Christian in any way as he enters this battle, by giving him wrong information as it regards the Baptism with the Holy Spirit, is tacitly working for Satan, even though he may not even be aware that he is doing such.

It is God's wish (and Command) that every Christian should be baptized with the Holy Spirit. Jesus said, *"And being assembled together with them* (speaks of the time He ascended back to the Father; this was probably the time of the *"above 500"* [I Cor. 15:6]), *commanded them* (not a suggestion) *that they should not depart from Jerusalem* (the site of the Temple, where the Holy Spirit would descend), *but wait for the Promise of the Father* (spoke of the Holy Spirit, which had been promised by the Father [Lk. 24:49; Joel, Chpt. 2]), *which, said He, you have heard of Me* (you have also heard Me say these things [Jn. 7:37-39; 14:12-17, 26; 15:26; 16:7-15]).

"For John truly baptized with water (merely symbolized the very best Baptism Believers could receive before the Day of Pentecost)*; but you shall be baptized with the Holy Spirit not many days hence* (spoke of the coming Day of Pentecost, although Jesus did not use that term at that time)*"* (Acts 1:4-5).

Understanding what Jesus said, it should be obviously clear that anyone working against that infilling, whether consciously or through erroneous doctrine, is, in effect, working at cross purposes to the Will of God.

WHO IS THE HOLY SPIRIT?

The Holy Spirit is a distinct but separate Member of the Divine Trinity. He works in association with, and in complete harmony with, the Father and the Son. They are all three of the same Essence. The Holy Spirit, however, should not be confused with either the Father or the Son. I John 5:7 tells us, *"There are Three Who bear record in Heaven, the Father, the Word, and the Holy Spirit."* Jesus Christ is the *"Word"* (Jn. 1:1-2). The Lord Himself said, *". . . teach all nations, baptizing them in the Name of the Father, and of the Son, and of the Holy Spirit"* (Mat. 28:19).

The Holy Spirit is God, just as the Father is God and the Son is God; there are, however, differences between the Father and the Son and the Holy Spirit. The Three are not carbon copies. They have individual characteristics which set Their roles apart, even though Their purposes and Their aims are inseparable.

Moreover, we must be careful to understand that even though there are Three Persons in the Godhead, there aren't three Gods, only One. And that is because They are One in Essence.

THE LAST MESSAGE JESUS PREACHED

The last Message Jesus preached before His Ascension (Acts 1:4-9) was confined to the subject of the Holy Spirit Baptism. This was an historic occasion. The Lord was leaving the Earth; His lifetime of work was completed. He was about to depart for Heaven. This would be the last time He would be physically present to advise His Disciples and other followers. This unique situation stamps His Words with unusual significance. He might have spoken of Prophecy, Salvation, Worship, or any number of other important subjects. But He mentioned none of these things, at least not directly!

Being God, Who knew (and knows) everything, He told them, in effect, that they should attempt nothing concerning the Salvation of the world until they would first receive the Promise of the Father (Acts 1:4). In view of the dramatic circumstances surrounding this pronouncement, we can assume that every Word contained within these Verses (Acts 1:4-9) was among the most important ever uttered by our Lord and Master.

RECEIVING THE HOLY SPIRIT AT SALVATION

There is controversy today as to whether one receives the Holy Spirit at the moment of conversion. Actually, the only proper answer to this question is, *"Most definitely, Yes!"* At the moment a person is Born-Again, that person receives the Holy Spirit; it is simply impossible to be saved without the Holy Spirit doing His Office Work and coming into the heart and life of the new Believer (Jn., Chpt. 3).

The responsibilities of the Holy Spirit, however, are many and varied. One of the most important of these responsibilities is that of Regeneration, which refers to the Born-Again experience. Paul states (I Cor. 12:3), *"No man can say that Jesus Christ is Lord, but by the Holy Spirit."* This demonstrates, without question, that the Holy Spirit plays a unique role in bringing a sinner to Conviction, Repentance, and Salvation.

As the responsibilities of the Spirit are many, likewise, the activities of the Holy Spirit also are many. He is a Comforter; He is a Leader; He is a Teacher; He is a Communicator; He is a Guide; and, He is the Director of all of God's activities on Earth today. So, when the sinner comes to the moment of Salvation, he certainly has received the Holy Spirit within the context of Regeneration. That is, however, not in the context of Acts 1:8 and 2:4.

While it is true that every Believer definitely has the Holy Spirit, it is not true that every Believer is baptized, according to Acts 2:4, with the Holy Spirit. The Work of the Holy Spirit, as stated, in the capacity of Regeneration is one thing altogether, with His Work in the capacity of Power, referring to the Baptism, being something else entirely. There is a difference in being *"born of the Spirit"* and being *"baptized with the Spirit."* They are two separate things altogether.

However, while all Believers, although truly Saved by the Blood of Jesus, are not baptized with the Holy Spirit, they certainly can be if they so desire and if they will *"ask, seek, and knock"* (Lk. 11:9-13). At Salvation, life is imparted to someone who was heretofore spiritually dead. At the Baptism with the Holy Spirit, power is imparted to the Christian who was previously weak and ineffectual. He is henceforth fitted for service to God, whether he utilizes it or not! It is clearly the mandate of God that every Christian should be Baptized with the Holy Spirit (Acts 1:4).

Salvation and the Baptism with the Holy Spirit are two separate and distinct experiences. They are different as to source, time, and nature. A person may experience Salvation without experiencing the Baptism with the Holy Spirit (Acts 2:4). They cannot, however, experience the Baptism without first experiencing Salvation. The Baptism with the Holy Spirit must be preceded by Regeneration (Salvation); only then can the Holy Spirit function within us as He so desires. It is this indwelling of the Holy Spirit, which, incidentally, is not automatic, that endows us with power and enables us to be of greater service to God.

THE WORD OF GOD

Are there Scriptures to support the contention that the Baptism with the Spirit and Salvation are not simultaneous? Let's look at the Word of God.

In Luke 10:20, Jesus said to the Disciples, upon their return from spreading the Gospel, *"Rejoice, because your names are written in Heaven."* What can we assume from this? We can assume that these men were Saved. If their names were written in Heaven (in the Lamb's Book of Life), they were unquestionably Saved. But they did not receive the Baptism with the Spirit until the Day of Pentecost, some time later!

And then there was Paul (Saul of Tarsus). Chapter 9 in the Book of Acts tells of the dramatic, glorious, and sudden conversion of Paul as he traveled toward Damascus. It also tells us that it was three days later before the Lord sent Ananias to Paul for the laying on of hands for healing and for the Baptism with the Holy Spirit! Obviously, Paul was not baptized with the Holy Spirit at the time of his Salvation on the road to Damascus.

In Acts 19:1-6, we are told of Paul's experience in Ephesus. Arriving there, he found a party of twelve. They were saved, water-baptized Believers. He said unto them,

NOTES

"Have you received the Holy Spirit since you believed?"

They answered him, *"We have not so much as heard whether there be any Holy Spirit."*

So Paul laid his hands upon them and the Holy Spirit came upon them; they spoke with tongues and prophesied.

The Bible states, without room for doubt, these men were Saved. They were Believers. Scripture refers to them as Disciples. But when Paul met them, he asked them, *"Have you received the Holy Spirit since you believed?"* Anyone reading this sentence cannot help but feel that *"since you believed"* stands out in bold type. It is almost as if Paul, anticipating the future debate over whether the Holy Spirit comes simultaneously with Salvation, would include this phrase to prove that these men were Believers (Saved) who had not yet been baptized with the Spirit. This should have laid the question to rest before it ever started.

Some, however, see what they want to see in Scripture, despite all the evidence to the contrary.

Was the Lord foreseeing this when He, in Mark 8:18, said, *"Having eyes, see ye not?"*

To those who desire additional proof that the Holy Spirit Baptism comes subsequent to Salvation, I would refer them to Acts 8:5-16. In this Passage, it tells how Philip went to Samaria where he held a Revival Meeting. During the course of the Meeting, many were delivered and many were healed. Upon seeing all these Miracles, the people were convicted, they accepted Jesus as their Saviour, and then they were baptized in the Name of Jesus Christ.

Read Verses 15 and 16 of the Eighth Chapter of Acts carefully: They say, *"When* (Peter and John) *came down* (to Samaria from Jerusalem at a later date), *they prayed that they might receive the Holy Spirit; for as yet He was not fallen upon them, they were only baptized in the Name of the Lord Jesus."* This is another definite Scriptural proof that the Baptism with the Holy Spirit is not simultaneous with Salvation.

Another aspect of this question of whether we are automatically baptized with the Holy Spirit at the time of Salvation is revealed in the Words of our Lord, as quoted in Luke

11:11-13. He says, *"How much more shall your Heavenly Father give the Holy Spirit to them who ask Him?"*

The simple fact of the matter is that we must seek the Baptism with the Holy Spirit. It is not something imposed unknowingly (or unwillingly) upon anyone at the moment they become Christians. The Baptism with the Spirit imparts power and fire to those who receive it. Anyone desirous of being a retiring, ineffectual Christian has the right to accept Salvation without accepting the next step, the Baptism with the Holy Spirit; however, they will be a powerless, and, by and large, ineffective Christian (Acts 1:8).

DOES EVERY RECIPIENT SPEAK
WITH OTHER TONGUES?

The Bible teaches that every recipient of the Holy Spirit, as it refers to Baptism, speaks with other tongues. But before we pursue this, let us clarify something in the beginning. One does not have to speak in tongues to be Saved. In fact, speaking in tongues has nothing to do with one being Saved. Such comes about by simple faith and trust in the Lord Jesus Christ.

A person is not Saved by seeing visions, delivering prophetic utterances, working miracles, or speaking in tongues. A person is Saved by confessing the Lord Jesus with his mouth and believing in his heart (Rom. 10:9-10, 13). A person can be Saved in a Church, in his home, on a street corner, or anywhere. It is not the place, it is the action. The person who believes in his heart and confesses with his mouth is Saved! And once he is Saved, he cannot be more Saved by speaking in tongues, or seeing visions, etc.

Some, therefore, ask the question, *"If I already have a complete gift of Grace in Salvation, why do I need the additional endowment of the Baptism with the Spirit?"*

First of all, if we did not need it, the Lord would not have commanded His followers to receive it (Acts 1:4). Furthermore, to be what one ought to be in Christ, the Baptism with the Holy Spirit is imperative. Also, for the Power to do the Work of the Lord, the Baptism with the Spirit is an absolute necessity. However, it must quickly be said that it is only the potential of all of this that is available to the Spirit-baptized Believer. Regrettably, there are millions of Spirit-baptized Christians who do little for the Lord, simply because they do not allow the Holy Spirit to have His way within their hearts and lives.

THE HELPER

During our Lord's Ministry here on Earth, the Disciples had Him as a Personal Advisor, Comforter, Leader, Helper, and Manager. Today we do not have Him on hand Personally to fill these essential roles. This is why, before He left, He said, *"I will send the Comforter* (Helper)*"* (Jn. 15:26). He knew His Personal time on Earth would be short; that He would Personally oversee only the beginning of the Great Salvation story; and that those committed to sharing the responsibility for bringing the Gospel to unsaved millions would need direction beyond their human capabilities. Basically, this is the inestimable value of the Baptism with the Spirit.

As well, every Believer, active or passive, is going to be forced to confront the powers of darkness described by the Apostle Paul in Ephesians 6:12. Satan has his army of demons committed to interfering with, and even destroying, Christian lives. The only way, as we've already stated, that the Christian can walk in victory and power, and perpetually, is by evidencing Faith in Christ and what Christ has done for us at the Cross, which then gives the Holy Spirit the latitude to work mightily within our lives.

Salvation equips us to enter into the Presence of God after mortal life is over. The Baptism with the Spirit equips us to live fruitfully during those years before we go to be with the Lord. To willingly eschew this God-given assistance is to handicap ourselves throughout our Christian lifetime.

SCRIPTURAL EVIDENCE
FOR TONGUES

Acts 2:4 says, *"And they were all filled with the Holy Spirit, and began to speak with other tongues, as the Spirit gave them utterance."* This is very clear and uncomplicated. It says, *"They began to speak with other tongues."*

Acts 9:17 describes the incident where

Paul was baptized with the Holy Spirit. Because this Passage gives no description as to exactly what happened when Paul was filled, it does not specifically say that he spoke with tongues at that time. But turning to his Epistle to the Corinthians (I Cor. 14:18), he said, *"I thank my God, I speak with tongues more than you all."*

Obviously, he spoke in tongues as the result of his Baptism with the Spirit, or he would not have mentioned it here. Furthermore, this has nothing to do with Paul being multilingual, as some have taught!

Acts 10 tells the story of Cornelius (the first of the Gentiles to come to the Lord) receiving Salvation. Verses 45 and 46 bear retelling, *"And they of the circumcision which believed were astonished, as many as came with Peter, because that on the Gentiles also was poured out the Gift of the Holy Spirit*

"For they heard them speak with tongues, and magnify God."

We mention the incident of Paul laying hands on the twelve at Ephesus and their being baptized with the Spirit some time after Salvation. This incident also enters into the question of the moment whether speaking in tongues is valid evidence of the Baptism with the Holy Spirit. Acts 19:6 says, *"And when Paul had laid his hands upon them, the Holy Spirit came on them; and they spoke with tongues, and prophesied."*

In the Eighth Chapter of Acts, Simon the Sorcerer offered money to the Apostles if they would teach him how to bring about the Baptism with the Spirit by laying on of hands. This indicates there was some observable manifestation to prove something definitive had happened. If there was no tangible demonstration (such as speaking in tongues), why would Simon have gone to the extreme of offering money to learn the secret? He could very easily have set up shop on his own, pretending to bring about the results.

Only a supernatural proof, like speaking in tongues, could have forced Simon to:

1. Believe there was some dramatic change taking place.

2. Make him greedy enough to offer money so he could share in the unique ability to produce this result.

3. As well, Peter told Simon, *"You have neither part nor lot in this matter"* (Acts 8:21). The word here translated *"matter,"* in the Greek, is *"logos,"* which means *"a word or speech."* So, in essence, Peter said, *"You have neither part nor lot in this speaking with tongues,"* proving that these Samaritans spoke with tongues when they were baptized with the Holy Spirit.

Without doubt, speaking with other tongues is the initial, physical evidence of the Baptism with the Spirit, as given throughout all of the accounts in the Book of Acts.

GREAT CONTROVERSY

Presently, great controversy swirls about the Baptism with the Holy Spirit with the evidence of speaking with other tongues. It is not surprising, perhaps, that this should be so. Satan, with all of his being, hates seeing individuals in Churches transformed and set on fire as a result of the Baptism with the Holy Spirit. It is not surprising that he would promote doctrines suggesting this *"is not for today,"* etc. Certainly, if the Devil had his say, it would not have been for any day.

But Scripture does not agree with what Satan is trying to promote with false doctrine. Misguided Christians, who admit tongues were an evidence of the Baptism with the Holy Spirit during Apostolic days, say, *"It ended when the last Apostle died. It is not for today."*

But what does Scripture say?

In Joel 2:28 and Acts 2:17-18, Almighty God makes a statement concerning this. He says, *"In the last days . . .*

"On My servants and on My handmaidens I will pour out in those days of My Spirit. . . ."

In Acts 2:38-39, our Heavenly Father further confirms this with the words, *". . . you shall receive the Gift of the Holy Spirit.*

"For the Promise is unto you, and to your children, and to all who are afar off, even as many as the Lord our God shall call." This does not sound like an offer with an expiration date stamped on it.

Why does Satan fight so hard to discredit this Biblical experience?

Because he knows far better than we ever could the frustration he faces when the mighty Holy Spirit Power falls on an individual or group. Ineffectual, Christ-denying *"Churches"* suddenly are turned around to become bastions of power for the Lord. Weak and frightened Christians become raging lions in the cause of Christ. People who could not be persuaded to tell others about their Saviour suddenly are turned into adept and dedicated witnesses. Backsliding Christians suddenly straighten out their lives and become examples of righteous Christian living.

The Holy Spirit is the single most important factor in the world today, as far as the Church is concerned. Without Him, Christ is not glorified and the Church is ineffectual. With Him, the Church becomes effective, dedicated, and productive, at least as long as they allow the Holy Spirit to have His way.

I thank God for the outpouring of the Holy Spirit in these last days. For those who look to His empowerment, who trust Him through Christ for leading and guidance, they will never be disappointed.

UNKNOWN TONGUES?

Too many people are confused about *"speaking with tongues."* They think speaking with tongues is an end in itself, or that speaking in tongues is the main manifestation of the Baptism with the Holy Spirit. Unfortunately, they are looking at things incorrectly. The mere act of speaking in tongues is not, in itself, life-changing or all-important. What is important is the yielding of our unruly member (James 3:1-8), the tongue, to the control of God's Spirit.

It is very similar to Salvation. The act of publicly confessing our acceptance of the Lord accomplishes nothing within itself; however, it is crucially important within the context of our acknowledging the Lordship of Christ. Jesus said, *"Whosoever therefore shall confess Me before men, him will I confess also before My Father which is in Heaven"* (Mat. 10:32).

I believe a willingness to yield our unruly member, the tongue, to the Holy Spirit is exactly parallel to publicly confessing Christ. Giving our tongues and voices to the use of God's Spirit is, I believe, the same principle.

"Speaking in tongues" sets one apart, not only from the unsaved, but from formal religion, as well!

Someone has well said, *"Salvation separates one from the world, while the Baptism with the Holy Spirit separates one from cold, dead, formal religion."* Relinquishing our will to God to allow this radical departure serves as a *"sign."* A sign not only to ourselves, but to God, as well, that we are ready to yield our will to His.

HOW DOES SPEAKING WITH OTHER TONGUES HELP ONE?

Let's see what the Bible says about this all-important matter.

First of all, if it was merely a matter of someone supernaturally speaking in a foreign language, as exciting as that, within itself, may be, it would be of little significance. The Lord, however, as we shall see, never does anything that is insignificant.

The benefits:

1. It is the Lord Who said that speaking with tongues would be a part of the Believer's experience. He said it, in fact, nearly 800 year before the fact. Through the Prophet Isaiah, He said, *"For with stammering lips and another tongue will He speak to this people"* (Isa. 28:11).

Paul quoted this Scripture when he said, *"In the Law it is written, With men of other tongues and other lips will I speak unto this people; and yet for all that will they not hear Me, saith the Lord"* (I Cor. 14:21). We had best understand that whatever the Lord gives is of supreme importance. So, when people ask, *"What good is it?"* they, in effect, are saying that the Lord doesn't know what He is doing.

2. Paul also said, *"Wherefore tongues are for a sign, not to them who believe, but to them who believe not"* (I Cor. 14:22).

What did he mean by that?

He meant that speaking with other tongues, especially in this Latter Rain outpouring, is a sign to the entirety of the world (unbelievers) that we are coming down to the end. Jesus is about ready to come.

3. When one speaks in tongues, one is speaking unto God. Paul said, *"For he who speaks in an unknown tongue speaks not*

unto men, but unto God" (I Cor. 14:2). To be sure, anything that one speaks to God, especially when controlled by the Holy Spirit, cannot be anything but beneficial.

4. Paul also said, *"Howbeit in the Spirit he speaks mysteries"* (I Cor. 14:2). The word *"mysteries"* actually means that the person speaks *"secrets"* unto God.

5. Luke wrote, *"We do hear them speak in our tongues the wonderful Works of God"* (Acts 2:11). So, when a person speaks in tongues, he is not only declaring secrets to the Lord, but also *"the wonderful Works of God"* (Acts 2:1-13).

6. Paul said, *"He who speaks in an unknown tongue edifies himself"* (I Cor. 14:4). I think it should go without saying that every Believer needs edification. We need encouragement, comfort, and strength; all of this can come through the Believer worshipping in tongues.

7. Tongues and interpretation are used to give Messages from the Lord to the people. Anything from the Lord is of great blessing (I Cor. 14:13). This is so important, in fact, that the Holy Spirit implored those to whom He had given the *"gift of tongues,"* and we speak of one of the nine gifts of the Spirit, to pray that they also may be given the gift of interpretation.

While all things from the Lord can be described as *"gifts,"* still, the nine Gifts of the Spirit are set aside as special (I Cor. 12:4-11).

8. Jude said, *"But you, beloved, building up yourselves on your most Holy Faith, praying in the Holy Spirit"* (Jude 20). This speaks of praying in tongues, and plainly tells us that when such is done, it builds up the Believer as it regards *"Faith."* This means that the Faith that one has is enlarged to its utmost capacity, which every Believer needs.

9. Isaiah, in predicting the coming time when Believers would be baptized with the Holy Spirit, with the evidence of speaking with other tongues (Isa. 28:11), also stated, *"This is the rest wherewith you may cause the weary to rest"* (Isa. 28:12). Understanding this, one might say that speaking with other tongues is God's way of replenishing the Believer's strength. And, to be sure, as one goes through this vale of life, weariness, at times, sets in, requiring rest. Speaking with other tongues will provide that *"rest."*

10. Isaiah also said in the same Verse, *"And this is the refreshing."* So, not only is *"rest"* provided, but speaking with other tongues rejuvenates the Believer. It is sad that the modern Church has, by and large, opted for humanistic psychology, which holds no answers whatsoever, when the Lord has plainly given us His solution for the wear and tear of life's journey (Isa. 28:11-12).

11. Concerning the episode involving Simon Peter and Cornelius, Luke wrote, *"For they heard them speak with tongues, and magnify God"* (Acts 10:46). We are plainly told here that speaking with other tongues magnifies God. Anything that magnifies God is beneficial, as should be readily understood.

12. Luke also wrote, concerning the Day of Pentecost, *"And they were all filled with the Holy Spirit, and began to speak with other tongues, as the Spirit gave them utterance"* (Acts 2:4). Anything which the Holy Spirit originates, as He does the *"speaking with other tongues,"* is beneficial — and in more ways than we will ever know.

13. Speaking with other tongues is the fulfillment of Bible Prophecy. Peter, quoting the Prophet Joel, said, *"And it shall come to pass in the last days, saith God, I will pour out of My Spirit upon all flesh: and your sons and your daughters shall Prophesy, and your young men shall see visions, and your old men shall dream dreams:*

"And on My servants and on My hand-maidens I will pour out in those days of My Spirit; and they shall Prophesy" (Acts 2:16-18).

So, every time a Believer speaks with other tongues, it is a fulfillment of Bible Prophecy. Anyone who is privileged to participate in such a Move of God is privileged indeed!

14. Concerning praying in tongues, Paul said, *"For if I pray in an unknown tongue, my spirit prays"* (I Cor. 14:14). One's spirit praying is the highest form of prayer and of worship, and that which every Believer ought to desire.

A REFRESHING AND REST

Even though we've already mentioned it, due to its vast significance, please allow us to go back to the prediction that Isaiah gave nearly 800 years before its fulfillment.

He said, *"For with stammering lips and another tongue will He speak to this people.*

"To whom He said, This is the rest wherewith you may cause the weary to rest; and this is the refreshing; yet they would not hear" (Isa. 28:11-12).

Let us look at the two attributes which the Holy Spirit brings out, and do so in a more detailed way. We speak of *"rest"* and *"refreshing."*

REST

In the Hebrew, this word speaks of comfort, ease, quiet, and a *"resting place."* It is the attribute of the Holy Spirit, through speaking with other tongues, which humanistic psychology attempts to fulfill, but cannot. Regrettably, most of the modern Church has opted for psychology instead of the Holy Spirit.

While many would argue that they have not forsaken the Holy Spirit by embracing psychology, still, it is impossible for one to trust in both God and man at the same time, and for the same help, especially considering that one originates with God and the other with Satan.

Speaking in tongues, as the Scripture plainly says, provides this *"rest,"* which the soul desperately needs. It does so because it *"speaks not unto men, but unto God"* (I Cor. 14:2). This is expressed by the words of Paul, as well, *"In the Spirit he speaks mysteries."* If the words could be understood, they, within themselves, would not be a mystery; however, it would certainly be a mystery to Satan, as the Lord uses them according to His Word to minister to the individual doing the speaking. This is the reason Paul also said, *"He who speaks in an unknown tongue edifies himself"* (I Cor. 14:4).

Even though *"edifying oneself"* is not the purpose of the Holy Spirit in a public service, still, it is definitely the purpose of the Holy Spirit respecting the individual in his own private devotions.

THE HUMAN MIND AND SPIRIT

The human mind and spirit are so constructed that they need rest and comfort. Such can only be truly received from the Lord.

Although *"speaking with other tongues"* is not the only way, still, it is certainly one way outlined by the Lord, and probably one of the greatest ways. Drugs, therapy, psychological counseling, etc., as well-intentioned as some of these may be, cannot in any way take the place of the Holy Spirit. I am persuaded if Believers who are Spirit-baptized would speak in tongues more as they go about their daily duties, even doing so in their mind and spirit, they would find stress levels falling, and nervous disorders lessened, which, in turn, would create a far healthier physical and emotional atmosphere — all generated by the Power and Operation of the Holy Spirit.

Incidentally, the Spirit-filled Believer can utilize this Gift of *"speaking with tongues"* as often or as much as he or she desires. One can even speak in tongues subconsciously, as stated, and, in fact, should do so as much as possible, which will help provide a needed *"rest."*

REFRESHING

The word in the Hebrew has the idea of a *"violent, stormy sea, with an oasis of repose in the very midst of the storm."* In essence, this tells us that *"speaking with other tongues"* gives the speaker a refreshing while storms are raging all about him. This is beautiful beyond description! Life is turbulent and seemingly more so by the day. Without this wonderful Gift, our ability to come into this beautiful *"refreshing,"* which is so desperately needed for body, soul, and spirit, is desperately impaired.

So, for one to ridicule *"tongues"* by asking, *"What good is it?"* only portrays one's Scriptural and Spiritual ignorance.

SOME ERRONEOUS CONTENTIONS

We have discussed some of the major arguments raised against the Baptism with the Holy Spirit (with the evidence of speaking with other tongues). I hope we have clarified the fact that God does not change His methods every few years, and that the methods employed during the Apostolic years are still operative today. As well, we would like to deal with some of the other arguments, Scriptural and otherwise.

DO ALL SPEAK WITH TONGUES?

Disputants love I Corinthians 12:29-30. Here Paul says, *"Have all the gifts of healing? Do all speak with tongues?"* Those who resist the testimony of millions, as well as the Word of God, use this line of Scripture to convince themselves they are on God's side when they refuse to be drawn into this business of *"glossolalia."* They say Paul was indicating that while some may receive the Gift of Tongues, it is certainly not mandatory that the Gift of Tongues be present to prove the Baptism with the Holy Spirit. They will be shocked to hear me say this, but they are right!

What they do not realize, however, is that, throughout this Chapter (I Corinthians 12), Paul is speaking about *"Spiritual Gifts."* Careful reading of this Chapter, beginning with Verse 8, will reveal that the *"Gifts of the Spirit"* include such things as the *"Word of Wisdom,"* the *"Word of Knowledge,"* the *"Working of Miracles,"* and so forth. Among these Gifts is the Gift of *"Diverse Tongues"*; that is, the ability, in the Spirit, to give an utterance in a tongue or tongues not known by the speaker, and, as would be obvious, without ever having studied or learned them, which is meant to be interpreted (I Cor. 14:27-28).

In Verses 28 through 30, Paul is explaining to the Church at Corinth, and all others, as well, that they must all pull together, using their individual Gifts in concert, in order to be a complete body, effective in the Lord's Work. Obviously, all do not have the Gift of Diversity of Tongues, as mentioned in Verse 30. Most have just one unknown tongue, given to them at the moment of Baptism with the Spirit, which is a prayer and worship tongue between that particular individual and God. Careful reading of the Epistle to the Corinthians makes this clear.

In Chapter 12, the Apostle is speaking of the *"Gift of Tongues,"* which is one of the nine Gifts of the Spirit, and which is used to give an utterance in a group, which, as stated, should be interpreted. He is <u>not</u> discussing speaking in tongues, which does accompany every Spirit-filled Believer, and which is a part of the Believer's worship. As stated, all obviously do not have *"Gifts of Healings"* or *"Gifts of Tongues,"* etc. While speaking, praying, and worshipping with tongues is certainly a Gift, as one is baptized with the Holy Spirit, and continues to use it thereafter, it is not one of the nine *"Gifts"* that Paul is speaking of in I Corinthians 12. Our unbelieving friends confuse this issue.

THE TONGUES OF MEN AND OF ANGELS

Paul is referring to I Corinthians 13:1 and 14:2. Some claim from this Passage that most have *"tongues of men,"* a language understood by all, while a few might have *"tongues of Angels."*

No! Paul is <u>not</u> saying this. He is saying that if we are able to speak in every type of *"tongues of men,"* and even possibly of *"Angels,"* still, if we have not *"love,"* we become as *"sounding brass, or a tinkling cymbal"* (I Cor. 13:1). He is not denigrating *"tongues"* in any capacity, but only a lack of love. As well, he is <u>not</u> saying that one must have love and not tongues. That is not the idea at all!

He is merely reminding the Corinthians, and all others, that Gifts of the Spirit, as worthwhile as they are in their own right, can never take the place of *"love."* Most of all, the Holy Spirit through him is saying that no matter how many *"Gifts"* we may have, if we don't have and show *"love,"* then the effectiveness of the Gifts will be greatly reduced.

WHETHER THERE BE TONGUES, THEY SHALL CEASE

Once again, this is an example of taking a few words out of context and building a doctrine on them. In order to put this statement in proper perspective, one must read all of I Corinthians 13:8-10 to get the full meaning of what Paul is saying. He is <u>not</u> saying, as some claim, that tongues would cease when the last Apostle died.

"Charity (love) *never fails,"* he said. *"But where there be Prophecies, they shall fail. Where there be tongues, they shall cease; where there be knowledge, it shall vanish away."*

Some, looking for a time frame in which to assign this day when tongues will cease, have claimed that *"when that which is perfect is come"* refers to the day in which all the Books of the Bible were collected into a single work. Actually, this error is so ridiculous as not to warrant serious discussion.

The One spoken of here as *"Perfect"* is the Lord Jesus Christ, and pertains to His Second Coming. When He comes back, many things will be changed, or no longer necessary, as should be obvious! But until He, the Perfect One, comes, we need everything the Holy Spirit gives us.

I HAD RATHER SPEAK FIVE WORDS WITH MY UNDERSTANDING, THAN TEN THOUSAND WORDS IN AN UNKNOWN TONGUE

This is a favorite Scripture for those who are antagonistic to the concept of speaking with tongues. This Passage is taken from I Corinthians 14:19. However, the careful reading of the whole of the Fourteenth Chapter tells us what Paul was actually saying.

The Church at Corinth had become somewhat unbalanced in their worship services, concentrating unduly on the matter of speaking in tongues during their services. Paul spends the whole Fourteenth Chapter teaching the proper place of tongues in a public service.

Obviously, if someone were opposed to speaking in tongues, he would hardly devote the amount of teaching encompassed in the Fourteenth Chapter to its proper utilization. He simply could have said, *"Don't speak with tongues."*

But does he say this?

Hardly! He says, *"I would that you all spoke with tongues."* He says, *"I thank my God, I speak with tongues more than you all."*

Why would those who stress the Nineteenth Verse completely ignore the Thirty-ninth?

The Thirty-ninth Verse says, *"Forbid not to speak in tongues."*

Paul is simply saying that when it comes time for the Preacher to deliver the Word of God, it would do no one any good to stand behind the pulpit (or wherever) and address the people in tongues. They would not know what he was talking about, and so would not be edified or helped; consequently, when it came time to teach the people, five words in a tongue they can understand would be of greater value than ten thousand words in a tongue which no one can understand. That should be obvious! That is what the Apostle is saying. The idea is *"teaching and instruction,"* not worship.

THE LEAST OF ALL THE GIFTS

Some say, since Paul placed tongues last in his list of Gifts in I Corinthians 12:28, that it might well be eliminated.

What a hornet's nest of Satanic confusion would be opened if we were to accept this proposal! Do we begin with the Ten Commandments and eliminate the Tenth because it is last? Then with the Tenth removed, do we strike out the Ninth? What about the Beatitudes? Do we ignore the last one, simply because it is last? I think one can see the foolishness of such thinking.

Obviously, any list has to have a first item and a last item. This does not imply, however, that items on the list become optional to a greater or lesser degree depending on their position. Nothing from God is insignificant. No statement from God is to be considered *"optional"* by man.

The Lord set up the roster of Spiritual Gifts. Evidently, He intended all the Gifts to be operational in the Church. Without all the Gifts, a body becomes less effective than it would be with all the Gifts.

Any man who takes over God's authority and begins picking and choosing from among those God-given Gifts is assuming an authority I would not want to assume. The mere fact that placement on the list might be above or below something else is small authority to remove anything instituted by God. I think the argument that *"Tongues"* is the least of all Gifts is a dangerous argument, and one belittling God's ability to decide whether or not something is of value to man and His Church.

IS THE BAPTISM WITH THE HOLY SPIRIT FOR US TODAY?

The question, ultimately, is this. Is the mighty Baptism with the Holy Spirit, with the evidence of speaking with other tongues, for every Believer today?

Yes, it is!

And more than that, I believe it is a *"must"* for every Christian. It isn't something to be placed on the *"optional"* shelf, where the Christian shopper can browse and debate whether or not it will be *"desirable."* Without the Baptism with the Spirit, the Christian will never be what he could be within God's Plan for his life. John the Baptist said (Lk. 3:16), *"He shall baptize you with the Holy Spirit and with fire!"* Anyone who has seen a lukewarm Christian transformed by the Holy Spirit knows what John was talking about.

All the arguments against the Baptism with the Spirit stem from unbelief. There is not a hint in the Word of God that such passed away, or was only for a certain period of time. Such thinking is ludicrous, to say the least!

To fall short of God's intentions is to fall short indeed. To be sure, He did not suggest that Believers be baptized with the Spirit, but rather commanded it (Acts 1:4). His Commands are not to be taken lightly, and no less presently!

The Church today, and in any age, for that matter, without the Holy Spirit, is lackluster, man-led, and, therefore, ineffective as far as the Work of God is concerned. To be sure, I have no interest whatsoever in what man wants or desires. I want what the Lord wants. Moreover, He has said I can have this mighty Holy Spirit Baptism. In obedience to His Word, I have received it, and so have multiple millions of others.

We must ever remember that it is *"Not by might* (human might), *nor by power* (human power), *but by My Spirit, saith the LORD of Hosts"* (Zech. 4:6).

(18) "THEY SHALL TAKE UP SERPENTS; AND IF THEY DRINK ANY DEADLY THING, IT SHALL NOT HURT THEM; THEY SHALL LAY HANDS ON THE SICK, AND THEY SHALL RECOVER."

The exposition is:

The Passage speaks of putting away demon spirits, and has nothing to do with reptiles (Lk. 10:19). The balance speaks of protection, and not presumption!

TAKING UP SERPENTS

The phrase, *"They shall take up serpents,"* has absolutely nothing to do with the handling of poisonous snakes, or any type of snakes, for that matter, etc. Actually, to do such is a sin, the sin of presumption. This is the same sin that Satan attempted to get Jesus to commit by throwing Himself off the pinnacle of the Temple (Mat. 4:6-7). Jesus answered by saying, *"You shall not tempt the Lord your God."* As stated, this is the sin of presumption.

The word, *"take up,"* is, in the Greek Text, *"airo,"* which means *"to remove, take away, put away, or kill."* So, the correct translation would have been, *"they shall remove serpents."* The word *"serpents"* has nothing to do with vipers, etc. It speaks of demon spirits. In other words, the proclamation of the Gospel drives out demon spirits from their control of people and even areas. Satan is called *"that old serpent, which is the Devil, and Satan"* (Rev. 20:2).

Jesus also said, *"Behold, I give unto you power to tread on serpents and scorpions, and over all the power of the enemy: and nothing shall by any means hurt you"* (Lk. 10:19). The seventy had been on a preaching mission and came back rejoicing that *"the devils were subject unto them through the Name of Jesus"* (Lk. 10:17).

The answer given by Jesus has nothing to do with vipers, etc., but rather with demon spirits. When Jesus used the word *"serpents,"* He was using a synonym, which refers to a symbolic or figurative name, given to explain something. He is explaining the fact that Satan is venomous like a poisonous serpent.

DRINKING SOMETHING DEADLY

The phrase, *"And if they drink any deadly thing, it shall not hurt them,"* simply speaks of protection. In no way does it speak of purposely drinking poison, etc., in order to prove one's Faith. The word *"if"* speaks of accidental ingestion. To do otherwise is the sin of presumption.

The idea of this statement comes from the previous phrase concerning the removal of serpents (demon spirits), and mastery over the world of darkness. Spirit-filled Believers alone have power over Satan. Education, money, or culture have no authority whatsoever in this arena.

Actually, the authority possessed by the Believer is that which is derived from the *"Name of Jesus."* The phrase, *"In My Name . . . ,"* as used in Verse 17, is implied in the other phrases. For instance, *"In My Name, they shall speak with new tongues,"* etc. So, it is the *"Name of Jesus"* which gives the Believer the authority and power to do the Works of Christ, which, incidentally, are never authority and power over other people, but rather authority and power over the spirit world of darkness. The idea is that the Ministry of Christ continues on in the lives and Ministries of Believers.

An example is given in the sending out of the *"seventy"* as recorded in Luke 10:17, which we mentioned a few paragraphs back. Regrettably, the modern Church, especially in the United States and Canada, is a far cry from True Christlike Ministry. The modern Church is little more than a glorified social club. For the most part, it impacts the world of spiritual darkness not at all. It is a social club and the Preacher is a social worker! God help us!

A powerless Church, bereft of the Holy Spirit, attempts to disavow these Verses. It does so because it in no way resembles this which Christ proclaimed. If we take Jesus' Words at face value, which we certainly should, and we look at the lack of *"signs"* which will follow True Believers, then we have to assume that most claiming Salvation are not, in fact, even Saved.

HEALING OF THE SICK

The phrase, *"They shall lay hands on the sick, and they shall recover,"* once again means to do so *"in the Name of Jesus."* Both the Old and the New Testaments proclaim the laying on of hands to both heal the sick and to bless (Gen. 48:14; Num. 8:10; 27:23; Deut. 34:9; Mat. 19:15; Mk. 5:23; Acts 5;12; 13:3; I Tim. 4:14; Heb. 6:2).

The *"laying on of hands in the Name of Jesus"* is meant to portray blessing. Actually, such is the only Blessing afforded in this world. Believers ought to be quick to lay hands on others for this purpose.

(19) "SO THEN AFTER THE LORD HAD SPOKEN UNTO THEM, HE WAS RECEIVED UP INTO HEAVEN, AND SAT ON THE RIGHT HAND OF GOD."

The exegesis is:

Our Lord's Ascension signifies that the Work of Redemption was total and complete, i.e., a Finished Work.

THE LORD HAS SPOKEN

The phrase, *"So then after the Lord had spoken unto them,"* refers to Verses 15 through 18. The Great Commission given at the conclusion of this Gospel according to Mark, as well as Matthew and Luke, is supposed to be carried out exactly as He said. If the True Gospel is preached, and not some watered-down, compromised version, *"these signs shall follow them who believe."* If they don't follow, it is because the Gospel is not truly being preached.

Sadly, many modern Missionaries are little more than glorified social workers. Many are amateur psychologists or sociologists, i.e., they are not Preachers of the Gospel at all. Many of these do not even believe in the Power of the Holy Spirit, which is obvious in their lack of *"signs."*

If the True Gospel of Jesus Christ is preached, with the complete Message being the *"Message of the Cross,"* and done so by the Power of the Holy Spirit, such will automatically dispel demon spirits, resulting in bondages being broken and darkness dispelled. This will result in people being Saved, baptized with the Holy Spirit, delivered from bondages, and healed by the Power of God. It is impossible for it to be otherwise!

These things *"spoken unto them"* are extremely important, as should be obvious, and were meant to be spoken to all. The Church has a choice to make. It can accept the doubt and skepticism of unbelievers or it can accept the Words of Christ, as recorded in the Bible. I will say, as Joshua of old, *"As for me and my house, we will serve the LORD"* (Josh. 24:15).

THE ASCENSION

The phrase, *"He was received up into Heaven,"* pertains, as should be obvious, to the Ascension. It speaks of the Mission of Christ to redeem humanity, which was done at the Cross, as finished and complete, and victorious in every capacity.

Christ was *"received"* by God the Father, and received in a manner that proclaims that the great work which He came to this Earth to do, was, in fact, done, with nothing left undone. In other words, the Cross defeated Satan and his minions of darkness in every capacity (Col. 2:14-15). There all sin was atoned, which removed Satan's legal right to hold mankind in bondage, at least for all who will believe (Jn. 3;16).

THE RIGHTFUL PLACE OF CHRIST

The phrase, *"And sat on the Right Hand of God,"* speaks of the rightful place of Christ. There He serves as our *"High Priest," "making Intercession for the Saints"* (Heb. 7:25; 8:1). As such, *"He is the Mediator of a Better Covenant, which was established upon better Promises"* (Heb. 8:6).

Even though Jesus resides literally on the *"Right Hand of God,"* even more so this speaks of the Power of God, which is resident in Christ. In other words, He has the Power to back up the use of *"His Name."* Actually, He said, *"All Power is given unto Me in Heaven and in Earth"* (Mat. 28:18). He gained this by what He did at the Cross, and totally by what He did at the Cross! Through the Agency and Person of the Holy Spirit, this *"Power"* is freely given to the Spirit-filled Believer (Acts 1:8). It is given, as stated, for many purposes and reasons, the least not being the Work and Ministry of Christ.

(20) "AND THEY WENT FORTH, AND PREACHED EVERY WHERE, THE LORD WORKING WITH THEM, AND CONFIRMING THE WORD WITH SIGNS FOLLOWING. AMEN."

The overview is:

If the *"signs"* are not *"following,"* the Gospel is not being preached, but rather something else.

THEY WENT FORTH

The phrase, *"And they went forth,"* refers to the entirety of the Early Church, and not just the Twelve Apostles. They did exactly what Jesus told them to do, *"Go"* (Mk. 16:15). If one is to carefully study the Book of Acts, as given by the Holy Spirit, which is meant to be a blueprint for the Church for all time, one will quickly ascertain the thrust that is intended.

The Church, as ultimately spearheaded by the Apostle Paul, was meant to take the Gospel to the entirety of the world, in obedience to Christ. Its Message was to be the Message of the Cross. This was priority. Without the aid of modern transportation or modern communications, they were able to touch much of the world of that day. They did so by the Power, Leading, and Operation of the Holy Spirit.

The Book of Acts alludes to the Holy Spirit, in one form or the other, over 50 times. He empowered, He led, He spoke. It is impossible to miss His Leadership in the Book of Acts, which is a continuation of the Gospels according to Matthew, Mark, Luke, and John.

PREACHING

The phrase, *"And preached everywhere,"* once again proclaims them doing exactly what Jesus said to do, *"And preach the Gospel to every creature"* (Mk. 16:15).

What did they preach?

They *"preached Christ unto them"* (Acts 8:5, 35).

And then a little later, the Lord gave to Paul the total meaning of the New Covenant, which is, in effect, the meaning of the Cross. Then Paul and all others would say, *"We preach Christ Crucified"* (I Cor. 1:23; 2:2).

Someone asked the question, and rightly so, *"Why didn't the Apostles, at the very beginning of the Book of Acts, preach the Cross?"*

The answer is simple!

They didn't preach the Cross at that time, because they didn't know anything about the Cross. That Revelation had not yet been given, and, as stated, would ultimately be given to the Apostle Paul, with the time frame being approximately fifteen years after the Day of Pentecost.

Why didn't the Lord give this Revelation to Simon Peter or John the Beloved?

Of course, the full answer to that is probably known only by the Lord. However, the Lord needed a certain type of man in order to fill this role, which would be most difficult, to say the least. Paul was that man.

First of all, Paul probably knew the Law of Moses greater than any human being on the face of the Earth. To fully understand the Cross, one had to fully understand the Law, because the Law pointed to Christ in every respect. In fact, when Paul desired to prove the Cross to the Jewish Christians, he used the Law, or at least the Tabernacle part of the Law, to prove his point, which is given to us in the Book of Hebrews.

It also took, as stated, a certain type of man to be able to stand the fiery opposition which would come against him, as it regards the Cross, in order to be given this Revelation. Paul was, as stated, that man!

This is, in no way, meant to take away from the powerful Ministries of Simon Peter, John the Beloved, or any of the original Twelve, for that matter. It is only meant, at least as far as we poor humans can do so, to put everything into proper perspective.

THE LORD WORKED WITH THEM

The phrase, *"The Lord working with them,"* proclaims such being done, and we speak of *"signs following,"* that is, if His Commands are followed. Otherwise, He will not *"work"*! As stated, He does so through the Power and Agency of the Holy Spirit. It hasn't changed from then until now.

The Lord can only work with those who truly seek to follow Him.

What did He Personally say about this?

He said, *"If any man will come after Me* (the criteria for Discipleship), *let him deny himself* (not asceticism, as many think, but rather that one denies one's own willpower, self-will, strength, and ability, depending totally on Christ), *and take up his Cross* (the benefits of the Cross, looking exclusively to what Jesus did there to meet our every need) *daily* (this is so important, our looking to the Cross, that we must renew our Faith in what Christ has done for us, even on a daily basis, for Satan will ever try to move us away from the Cross as the object of our Faith, which always spells disaster), *and follow Me.* (Christ can be followed only by the Believer looking to the Cross, understanding what it accomplished, and by that means alone [Rom. 6:3-5, 11, 14; 8:1-2, 11; I Cor. 1:17-18, 21, 23; 2:2; Gal. 6:14; Eph. 2:13-18; Col. 2:14-15])" (Lk. 9:23).

The Lord works with people according to the Light they presently have. However, when more Light is given, the Lord expects that individual, whoever they might be, to walk in that given Light. If not, that Light is not only withdrawn, but whatever else the person has is also removed.

Jesus said, *"For unto everyone who has shall be given, and he shall have abundance: but from him who has not shall be taken away even that which he has"* (Mat. 25:29).

SIGNS FOLLOWING

The phrase, *"And confirming the Word with signs following,"* is another clear reference to the New Testament program for the Church. If the *"signs"* are not *"following,"* the Gospel is not truly being preached.

In 1968, the Lord began to deal with my heart about going on Radio. In January of 1969, we aired our first program, which was a little fifteen minute daily we called *"The Campmeeting Hour."* It aired Monday through Friday. The Lord began to bless, and soon we were on approximately 600 stations daily.

In about 1975, the Lord also began to deal with me respecting Television. As a result, we began airing our Telecast that year. To be sure, all of it was a very simple beginning. However, the Lord began to bless that, as well.

In 1980, if I remember the year correctly, the Lord began to deal with me concerning the placement of our Telecast in foreign countries. This we did, translating from English to whatever language was necessary. We ultimately translated into Spanish, Portuguese, Japanese, Chinese, French, Arabic, and Russian. We even translated into Zulu, if I remember correctly. Translating is a very difficult process, but yet very effective, that is, if one has the proper Interpreter.

At any rate, the Lord began to bless immeasurably so, with our offices receiving literally millions of letters over a period of time. Many of these letters contained some of the greatest testimonies of Salvation and Deliverance that one could ever begin to imagine. To be sure, it was similar to the Book of Acts, and continues unto this very day. Perhaps the following illustration will serve as an example.

A TESTIMONY OF GRACE

One particular area of the country of Peru was noted for its lawlessness. It is said that even the Army was afraid to go into these locations. Drunkenness, dope, and crime were pretty much the agenda. In one particular area, there was one Television set, which the villagers would hook up to an automobile battery in order to bring in sporting events, or whatever they wanted to see. On a particular Sunday, the ringleader of the area was attempting to bring in a soccer match from Lima. As it so happened, he was unable to bring in the channel on which this sporting event was transmitted, but instead he was able to receive only the channel over which our program was being aired. Being in Peru, it was translated into Spanish. To be sure, he was not too happy about this arrangement, but inasmuch as they could not pull in any other channel, he and the others sat back to watch the Program.

The Spirit of God moved that day and in a great way. When I gave the Altar Call, the Lord began to move all over the world, at least everywhere the Program was being aired. He also moved in this group that we have just mentioned.

How many in this particular group in Peru accepted Christ, I have no way of knowing, but the ringleader, in fact, one of the greatest criminals of all in that area, was among those who did. He was said to be one of the meanest men in the area, and guilty of just about anything one could think of. But that day, he was gloriously and wondrously Saved by the Precious Blood of Jesus Christ.

Some time later, a Missionary came through Baton Rouge and told of going into that part of Peru. When he arrived, this dear brother who had been gloriously Saved thought I (Jimmy Swaggart) had sent the Missionary to build a Church. Even though I had not sent him, still, he preached the Gospel to these people, and a little later a Church was built.

This entire community changed. Men who formerly were drunkards and thieves now were sober and thieves no longer, because they had accepted Jesus Christ. As mean as this ringleader had previously been, now, because of the Gospel of Jesus Christ, he was totally opposite.

Soon, many in this area were baptized with the Holy Spirit. Of course, the power of demon spirits was broken in these hearts and lives that had come to Christ. Actually, the power of darkness was greatly weakened in the entirety of this area, as it always is when a Moving of the Holy Spirit takes place as a result of the Gospel being preached.

This is just one of the multiple thousands of examples of what has transpired, and is transpiring, as a result of the Gospel we preach over the Telecast and Radio. These *"signs"* have followed and continue to follow, simply because we believe. They will follow all who believe.

AMEN

The word *"Amen"* is meant to portray that what Jesus has said and done is to be continued. It is not to be changed.

"Down from the Glories of Heaven,
"Down to a world of woe,
"When there was no eye to pity,
"Jesus said 'I will go.'"

"Go, Go, Go, Go,
"Leave what He asks you to leave;
"Pray for your part in the harvest,
"Give what He asks you to give."

"Out in the dark they are dying,
"For them His Life He gave;
"Go, tell the lost of Salvation,
"Give them a chance to live."

"Uttermost part is His order,
"Dare any answer, 'No'?
"What will you do when you meet Him,
"If you refuse to go?"

BIBLIOGRAPHY

Dictionary Of New Testament Theology
Dictionary Of Paul And His Letters
Interlinear Greek-English New Testament
Josephus, The Essential Writings
New Bible Dictionary
Pulpit Commentary
Richard's Expository Dictionary Of Bible Words

Strong's Exhaustive Concordance Of The Bible

Student's Commentary On The Holy Scriptures — Williams

The Complete Word Study Dictionary

The International Standard Bible Encyclopedia

Vine's Expository Dictionary Of New Testament Words

Webster's New Collegiate Dictionary

Word Studies in the Greek New Testament — Kenneth Wuest

Young's Literal Translation Of The Holy Bible

Zondervan Pictorial Encyclopedia Of The Bible

NOTES

INDEX

The index is listed according to subjects. The treatment may include a complete dissertation or no more than a paragraph. But hopefully it will provide some help.

As well, even though extended treatment of a subject may not be carried in this Commentary, one of the other Commentaries may well include the desired material.

A READY SPIRIT AND A WEAK FLESH, 508
ABBA, FATHER, 500
ABOMINATION OF DESOLATION, 455
ABUSERS, 330
ACCEPTANCE, 316
ACCUSATION, 540
ACTION OF THE RELIGIOUS LEADERSHIP OF ISRAEL, 522
ACTIVITY OF THE DEMON SPIRIT, 304
ACTIVITY OF THE HEART, 60
ADULTERIES, 243
ADULTEROUS AND SINFUL GENERATION, 287
ADULTERY, 334
AFFLICTION, 456
AGAPE, 53
ALABASTER BOX, 474
ALEXANDER AND RUFUS, 538
ALL BLESSINGS ARE FROM HEAVEN, 205
ALL THINGS ARE POSSIBLE, 501
ALL TRUTH IS GOD'S TRUTH?, 278
ALTAR CALL, 344
ALTAR OF INCENSE, 231
AMAZEMENT, 354
AN APPARITION?, 221
AN ASTOUNDING MIRACLE, 209
AN HUNDREDFOLD, 124
ANDREW, 100
ANGELS, 21, 426, 559
ANGER, 86
ANNOUNCEMENT OF DOOM, 491
ANOINTING, 239, 474
ANOINTING OF THE HOLY SPIRIT, 113
ANOTHER FORM, 563
ANOTHER JESUS, ANOTHER SPIRIT, ANOTHER GOSPEL, 8, 162

ANSWER, 110, 295
ANSWER TO POVERTY, SICKNESS, AND SUFFERING, 156
ANSWER TO SELF, 282
ANSWER TO UNBELIEF!, 62
ANTICHRIST, 458, 460
APOSTATE CHURCH, 133, 416, 568
APOSTLES, 197
APOSTOLIC TEACHING CONCERNING RANSOM, 363
APPEARANCE OF OUR LORD, 221
ARE THERE MONEYCHANGERS IN THE MODERN CHURCH?, 380
ARE THERE PEOPLE WHO DESIRE TO GIVE THEIR HEART TO GOD, BUT CANNOT, BECAUSE THEY HAVE BLASPHEMED THE HOLY SPIRIT?, 107
ASCENSION, 589
ASK, SEEK, KNOCK, 216
ASTONISHMENT, 183, 184, 253, 346
ATTACK ON THE CROSS, 2
AUTHORITY, 33, 40, 396
AUTHORITY FROM GOD AND AUTHORITY FROM MAN, 397
AUTHORITY OF THE BELIEVER, 40
AUTHORITY OF THE WORLD, 361
AUTHORITY TO HIS SERVANTS, 470
BALL OF FIRE, 43
BAPTISM, 359
BAPTISM OF CHRIST, 16
BAPTISM OF JOHN, 398
BAPTISM WITH THE HOLY SPIRIT, 15, 508, 578
BAPTISMAL REGENERATION, 9
BAPTIZED, 571
BARABBAS, 530, 532

BARREN FIG TREE, 379
BARTHOLOMEW, 100
BARTIMAEUS, 365
BASICS OF FAITH, 172
BE CAST INTO THE SEA, 387
BE NOT AFRAID, ONLY BELIEVE, 181
BE OF GOOD CHEER, 221
BEELZEBUB, 103
BEGINNINGS OF SORROWS, 449
BEHAVIOR OF CHRISTIANS, 504
BELIEF PATTERNS, 425
BELIEVER CANNOT LIVE FOR GOD WITHOUT THE HELP OF THE HOLY SPIRIT, 488
BELIEVER IN TROUBLE, 34
BELIEVING, 307, 392, 570
BETHPHAGE AND BETHANY, 370
BETRAYAL, 453, 480, 490, 511
BETRAYAL OF CHRIST, 312
BIBLE, 35, 122
BIBLE AND SELF-ESTEEM, 280
BIBLE PROPHECY, 445
BIBLICAL DIRECTIVES, 332
BILL OF DIVORCEMENT, 325
BINDING THE STRONG MAN, 105
BIRTHDAY OF HEROD, 194
BLADE, THE EAR, THE FULL CORN IN THE EAR, 130
BLASPHEMIES?, 61
BLASPHEMING THE HOLY SPIRIT, 106
BLESSING, 206, 256, 336
BLESSINGS OF GOD, 236
BOAST OF SIMON PETER, 497
BODY OF CHRIST, 555
BONDAGE, 140
BREAD, 203, 263
BREAKING, 207
BRIDEGROOM, 75
BRIDEGROOM TAKEN AWAY, 76
BROKEN CHAINS AND FETTERS, 142
BURN OUT?, 198
BURNT OFFERING AND THE SIN OFFERING, 545
CAESAR, 419
CAIN AND ABEL, 11
CALL OF GOD, 237
CAN A PSYCHOLOGIST HELP PEOPLE IF HE LOVES GOD AND HAS A TRUE DESIRE TO BE OF SERVICE?, 150
CAN CHRISTIANS BE DEMON POSSESSED?, 34
CAN ONE HAVE BOTH, *"POSSESSIONS"* AND *"ETERNAL LIFE"*?, 345
CAN SATAN OVERRIDE A BELIEVER'S WILL?, 299
CANDLE, 125

CAPERNAUM, 30, 56
CARES OF THIS WORLD, 121
CARNAL MIND, 283
CARPENTER, 185
CAST OUT OF THE VINEYARD, 410
CASTING OF THE SEED, 129
CASTING OUT OF DEMONS, 99, 576
CAUSE OF HOMOSEXUALITY, 327
CAUSE OF POVERTY, 476
CAUSE OF TROUBLE, 140
CHANGING OF HEAVEN AND EARTH, 468
CHARGE, 183, 253, 260, 271, 293, 309
CHIEF PRIESTS, 479, 529
CHIEF PRIESTS AND SCRIBES, 355
CHIEF PRIESTS, SCRIBES, AND ELDERS, 395, 517
CHOICE, 238
CHOOSING OF THE TWELVE, 95
CHRIST AND THE PHARISEES, 85
CHRIST JESUS AND AUTHORITY, 397
CHRIST, THE ONLY HOPE, 260
CHRIST, THE SON OF GOD!, 520
CHRISTIAN TRADITION, 32
CHRISTIANITY, THE GREATEST RELIGION, 132
CHRISTLESS CHRISTIANITY, 276
CHURCH, 467, 561
CLEANSED, 55
CLEANSING OF THE LEPER, 49
CLEANSING OF THE TEMPLE, 379
CLEANSING POWER, 54
CLOUDS, 292, 463
COMMANDMENT OF GOD, 233
COMMANDMENTS, 341
COMMANDMENTS OF MEN, 232
COMMON PEOPLE, 439
COMPASSION, 52, 161, 200, 254, 307
COMPASSION AND THE MINISTRY, 201
COMPASSION AS A WORD, 200
COMPROMISE, 533
CONDEMNATION, 523
CONDEMNED TO DEATH, 355
CONDITION OF THE HEART, 242
CONDITION OF THE LEPER, 49
CONDITIONS FOR ANSWERED PRAYER, 216
CONFESSION, 385, 387, 389
CONSECRATION, 441
CONSTANT MISERY, 151
CONTEMPT, 184
CONTRARY WIND, 219
CONTROL, 257
CONTROL BY THE SPIRIT, 485
CONTROLLING SPIRIT, 97
CONTROVERSY, 523

CORBAN, 235
CORRECT UNDERSTANDING, 455
COUNSELING?, 145
COUNTRY, 155
COURT OF THE GENTILES, 380
COVENANT BLESSINGS, 206
COVETOUSNESS, 243
CREATION, 326
CROSS, 11, 17, 35, 283, 287, 295, 430, 467, 506, 537
CROSS AND MIRACLES, 461
CROSS AND SUPERSTITION, 402
CROSS AND THE BIBLE, vi (Introduction)
CROSS AND THE NEW COVENANT, vi (Introduction)
CROSS MUST BE THE OBJECT OF FAITH, 7
CROSS OF CHRIST, 162, 424
CROSS, THE MEANING OF THE NEW COVENANT, 405
CROSS, THE ONLY ANSWER FOR BURN OUT, 198
CROSS, THE PRIMARY MESSAGE, 2
CRUCIFIXION, 272, 312, 357, 539
CRUMBS FROM THE TABLE, 249
CRY OF DOOM, 35
CRY OF JESUS, 545
CULT OF MARY WORSHIP, 110
CULTURE, 229
CURSE, 235, 266, 268, 379, 526, 562
CURSED?, 383
DAILY, 284
DAMNATION, 576
DARKNESS, 544
DAVID, 79, 438
DAYS OF TRIBULATION, 462
DEAD, 426
DEAFNESS, 251
DEATH, 499
DEATH OF CHRIST, 555
DEATH OF JESUS, 547
DEBTOR, 247
DECAPOLIS, 251
DECEIT, 243
DECEPTION, 409, 445, 543
DEFILEMENT, 238, 241
DEITY OF CHRIST, 102
DELINEATION OF SOME OF THE COMMANDMENTS, 341
DELIVERANCE, 39, 156, 161, 245, 250
DELIVERANCE OF THE CHILDREN OF ISRAEL, 148
DEMAND FOR CRUCIFIXION, 532
DEMON POSSESSION, 34, 44, 139, 298
DEMON SPIRITS, 133
DEMON SPIRITS AND CHILDREN, 246

DEMON SPIRITS OBEY CHRIST, 37
DEMONIC REQUEST, 36
DEMONS, 156
DENIAL OF SELF, 277
DENOMINATIONALISM, 133
DEPENDENCE, 214
DESERT PLACES, 56, 202
DESPAIR, 563
DESTINATION OF ONE'S MONEY, 567
DESTROY THE WORKS OF THE DEVIL, 36
DESTRUCTION, 443
DESTRUCTION OF ISRAEL, 375
DID NOT JESUS, IN HIS EARTHLY MINISTRY, HEAL EVERYONE WHO CAME TO HIM?, 66
DID PETER FALL?, 527
DILEMMA OF THE UNREDEEMED, 151
DILIGENCE, 470
DIRECT REVELATION OF THE HOLY SPIRIT, 33
DISCERNMENT, 298
DISCIPLES, 91, 134, 260, 443
DISCIPLES OF JOHN, 74
DISCIPLES OF JOHN THE BAPTIST, 197
DISEASED, 44
DISOBEDIENCE, 56, 216
DIVINE HEALING, 92
DIVORCE, 331
DIVORCE AND REMARRIAGE, 324
DO ALL SPEAK WITH TONGUES?, 586
DO NOT FEAR!, 452
DOCTRINE, 32, 114, 383
DOCTRINE OF HELL, 319
DOCTRINE OF PREDESTINATION, 492
DOCTRINE OF REGENERATION, 328
DOES EVERY RECIPIENT SPEAK WITH OTHER TONGUES?, 581
DOES HE CARE THAT WE PERISH?, 135
DOGS, 248
DOING WHAT I DON'T WANT TO DO, 303
DON'T TRY TO USE THE WORD OF GOD AGAINST GOD, 388
DOUBLE MEANING OF THIS PARABLE, 131
DOUBT, 387
DOVE, 17
DRASTIC MEASURES, 58
DRINKING SOMETHING DEADLY, 588
DRUG ADDICTION, 142
DRUG POTION, 539
DUMB SPIRIT, 297
EARS TO HEAR, 116, 126, 239, 564
EATING OF THE BREAD AND THE DRINKING OF THE CUP, 494
ELECT, 461
ELIJAH, 296

ELIMINATION OF THE CROSS OF CHRIST, 50
EMPEROR CONSTANTINE, 573
END OF THIS AGE, 447
ENDURE TO THE END, 454
ENVY, 531
ERROR, 390, 574
ETERNAL LIFE, 337, 353
ETERNAL SIN, 107
EVIL, 534
EVIL EYE, 244
EVIL HEART, 230
EVIL ONE, vi (Introduction)
EVIL SPIRIT, 309
EVIL THINGS, 245
EVIL THOUGHTS, 243
EXAMPLE OF UNBELIEF, OR LACK OF FAITH, 172
EXAMPLE OF WASTE, 567
EXCHANGE FOR THE SOUL, 286
EXECUTION OF JOHN THE BAPTIST, 196
FABLES, 461
FAIR GAME, 535
FAITH, 59, 137, 149, 164, 170, 211, 300, 369, 484
FAITH AND LIFE, 174
FAITH AS EXPRESSED IN THE GOSPELS, 173
FAITH AS EXPRESSED IN THE NEW TESTAMENT, 173
FAITH AS LOOKED AT BY JOHN THE BELOVED, 173
FAITHLESS GENERATION, 304
FALSE CHRISTS AND FALSE PROPHETS, 460
FALSE MESSAGE, 232
FALSE MESSIAHS, 446
FALSE WITNESSES, 519
FAME, 41
FAME OF CHRIST, 246
FAMILY, 182
FAMILY CURSE, 139
FAMILY OF GOD, 112
FAR JOURNEY, 470
FASHION OF THE LORD, 65
FASTING, 75
FAULT!, 228
FAULTY REASON, 263
FEAR, 136, 158, 169, 291, 313, 354, 399, 415, 559, 561
FEAR OF CHRIST, 37, 137
FEAST DAY, 473
FEAST OF TABERNACLES, 376
FELLOWSHIP OF THE SPIRIT, 484
FETTERS AND CHAINS, 141
FIRE, 320
FIRST ADAM, 435
FIRST AND THE LAST, 353

FIRST COMMANDMENT, 429, 431
FISHERS OF MEN, 28
FLEE TO THE MOUNTAINS, 455
FLESH AS EXPLAINED BY THE APOSTLE PAUL, 502
FOCUS, 140
FOLLOWING AFAR OFF, 517
FOLLOWING HIM, 28, 69
FOLLOWING JESUS, 47, 276
FOOLISH DOCTRINES, 227
FOOTSTOOL, 438
FOOT-WASHING SPIRIT, 282
FOR CHRIST'S SAKE, 350
FOREGLIMPSE OF THE COMING KINGDOM AGE, 225
FORGIVEN SINS, 59
FORGIVENESS, 332, 392
FORGIVENESS AFFECTS OUR PERSONALITY, 393
FORGIVENESS BY GOD, 395
FORM OF GODLINESS, 425
FORNICATIONS, 243
FORSAKEN?, 546
FORSAKING OF CHRIST, 516
FOUL DEED, 480
FOUL SPIRIT, 309
FOUNDATIONS OF OLD TESTAMENT PRAYER, 210
FOURTH WATCH OF THE NIGHT, 220
FOWLS OF THE AIR, 132
FRUIT, 124, 130, 401, 515, 524
FRUSTRATING THE GRACE OF GOD, 239
FULFILLED TIME, 25
FULFILLMENT OF ZECHARIAH'S PROPHECY, 374
FUNCTIONING OF THE EROS-TYPE OF LOVE, 53
GALATIAN HERESY, 77
GALILEE, 22, 41, 561
GATHERING, 45, 69, 465
GATHERING OF ISRAEL, 465
GENES, 328
GENTILES, 411
GETHSEMANE, 498
GIVE YE THEM TO EAT, 203
GIVING, 207, 567
GIVING OF MONEY, 440
GIVING THE HOLY SPIRIT LIBERTY, 483
GLORIFIED SAINTS, 466
GLORIOUS PROMISE, 106
GLORY, 287, 358
GOD ALONE CAN FORGIVE SINS!, 61
GOD IS THE SOURCE, 206
GOD'S COMMITMENT, 214
GOD'S GOVERNMENT, 95
GOD'S ORDER, 205
GOD'S REMEDY, 504

GOD'S WAY, 65, 166
GOD'S WORD, 166
GODLINESS OF JOHN THE BAPTIST, 194
GODLY FAMILIES, 332
GOLGOTHA, 538
GOOD AND EVIL, 85
GOOD GROUND, 116
GOOD GROUND AND MUCH FRUIT, 124
GOOD NEWS, 1
GOSPEL, 450, 479, 569
GOSPEL OF SELF-ESTEEM, 277
GOSPEL OF THE KINGDOM OF GOD, 23
GOVERNMENT OF TWELVE, 95
GRAIN OF MUSTARD SEED, 132
GREAT AMAZEMENT, 297
GREAT COMMAND, 68
GREAT COMMISSION, 566
GREAT MOVE OF GOD, 12
GREAT PHYSICIAN, 71
GREAT QUESTION, 294
GREAT STORM, 135
GREAT STRUGGLE, 78
GREAT THINGS, 160
GREAT TRIBULATION, 454, 456
GREAT TRUTHS CONCEALED NOW REVEALED, vii (Introduction)
GREATER FAITH, GREATER UNDERSTANDING, 392
GREATEST ATTACK ON THE BIBLE, 123
GREATEST COMMANDMENTS, 432
GREATEST HINDRANCE TO THE WORK OF GOD, 84
GREATEST TRIBULATION, 458
GROUNDS FOR DIVORCE, 333
GROWTH OF THE SEED, 130
GUESTCHAMBER, 489
GUILTY CONSCIENCE, 192
GUILTY OF DEATH?, 523
HAMILTON'S LAW, 208
HANDS OF ANGER, 514
HARDENED HEART, 87, 223, 263, 326
HARVEST, 131, 407
HEALING, 83, 91
HEALING OF THE SICK, 589
HEALINGS AND DELIVERANCES, 45
HEART, 60, 242
HEAVEN, 406
HEDGE, 400
HEIR, 409
HELL, 317
HELL FIRE, 319
HELPER, 581
HEROD, 88
HERODIANS, 88
HERODIAS, 193
HIGH PRIEST, 79, 517, 520
HIGH SABBATH, 554
HIS DOCTRINE, 439
HIS HOUSE, 470
HISTORICAL ACCOUNT OF CHRIST, 103
HISTORY OF INFANT BAPTISM, 573
HOLY SPIRIT, 4, 448, 452, 506, 569
HOLY SPIRIT AND THE CROSS OF CHRIST, 97
HOLY SPIRIT COMING UPON CHRIST FOR MINISTRY, 17
HOLY SPIRIT CONTROL, 97
HOME, 246
HOME OF SIMON PETER, 41
HOME, RELATIVES, AND PROPERTY, 350
HONORING PARENTS, 235
HORNS OF A DILEMMA, 399
HOUSE, 181
HOUSE OF GOD, 381
HOUSE OF PRAYER, 382
HOW CAN I BE SO CERTAIN THAT IT IS NOT THE GOSPEL?, 152
HOW CAN THE BELIEVER HAVE SANCTIFYING PEACE?, 179
HOW COULD A DEMON SPIRIT ENTER INTO A CHILD?, 305
HOW DID BARTIMAEUS KNOW ABOUT JESUS?, 366
HOW DO I KNOW THAT THESE REVELATIONS ARE THE PRODUCT OF ANGELS OF LIGHT?, 402
HOW DOES REGENERATION COME?, 329
HOW DOES SPEAKING WITH OTHER TONGUES HELP ONE?, 583
HOW IS THE CROSS THE POWER OF GOD?, 198
HOW IS THE PREACHING OF THE CROSS THE POWER OF GOD?, 38
HOW MAY I INHERIT ETERNAL LIFE?, 337
HOW POWERFUL IS SIN?, 140
HOW SHOULD FELLOW BELIEVERS CONDUCT THEMSELVES TOWARD A PENITENT ONE?, 394
HOW THE HOLY SPIRIT WORKS, 99
HOW THE RESURRECTION OF CHRIST RELATES TO MAN, 338
HUMAN MIND AND SPIRIT, 585
HUMANISTIC PSYCHOLOGY, 37
HUMANITY HAS NO SOLUTION FOR SIN, 141
HUMILITY, 14, 249
HUNDREDFOLD, 351
HUSBANDMEN, 401
HYMN, 495

HYPOCRISY, 418
HYPOCRITES, 230
HYSSOP, 547
I AM, 521
I HAD RATHER SPEAK FIVE WORDS WITH MY UNDERSTANDING, THAN TEN THOUSAND WORDS IN AN UNKNOWN TONGUE, 587
IF IT'S THE WILL OF GOD FOR ALL BELIEVERS TO ENJOY HEALING, WHY AREN'T ALL HEALED AT THE MOMENT OF PRAYER?, 64
IGNORANCE?, 399
IMAGE OF CHRIST, 337
IMAGE OF THE VINE, 123
IMMACULATE CONCEPTION, 111
IMPERTINENCE?, 136
IMPOSSIBLE, 348
IN JESUS' NAME, 217
INCARNATION, 434
INCOMPLETE FAITH?, 65
INCREASE IN REBELLION, 409
INDIGNATION, 474
INFANT BAPTISM, 9, 573
INJUSTICE OF ALL INJUSTICES, 537
INNER DYNAMICS OF FORGIVENESS, 393
INSANE?, 101
INSTRUCTIONS, 188, 268
INSUFFICIENT PREPARATION, 120
INTERCESSORY PRAYER, 215
INTRUSION OF CHRIST, 36
IS A LACK OF HEALING ALWAYS CAUSED BY A LACK OF FAITH?, 64
IS EVERYTHING POSSIBLE ACCORDING TO OUR DEGREE OF FAITH?, 308
IS HOMOSEXUALITY THE WORST SIN?, 327
IS HUMANISTIC PSYCHOLOGY THE ANSWER?, 142
IS MAN'S TRUE PROBLEM ONE OF LOW SELF-ESTEEM?, 279
IS OUR FAITH ANY STRONGER?, 497
IS PSYCHOTHERAPY TRULY SCIENTIFIC AND, THEREFORE, NEUTRAL?, 145
IS THE BAPTISM WITH THE HOLY SPIRIT FOR US TODAY?, 587
IS THE PREACHER OF THE GOSPEL QUALIFIED TO DEAL WITH THE PROBLEMS OF MANKIND?, 150
IS THERE SUCH A THING AS A CHRISTIAN PSYCHOLOGIST?, 149
ISOLATION FROM GOD, 503
ISRAEL, 457
ISRAEL AND ROME, 70
ISRAEL AND THE PLAN OF GOD, 465
ISRAEL AND THE POOR, 477

IT IS BLASPHEMY TO ADD TO THE WORD OF GOD, 112
JAIRUS, 163
JAMES AND JOHN, 29, 100
JAMES, THE SON OF ALPHAEUS, 100
JERUSALEM, 227, 354, 370
JESUS AND BLESSINGS, 206
JESUS AND THE CALL!, 28
JESUS AND THE CHILDREN, 573
JESUS AS KING, 371
JESUS CHRIST AND HIM CRUCIFIED, 3
JESUS CHRIST, OUR SUBSTITUTE, 302
JESUS IS GOD, 340
JESUS OF NAZARETH, 102
JESUS ONLY, 293
JESUS' PRESENTATION OF HIMSELF AS THE MESSIAH, 375
JESUS, THE SERVANT, 371
JESUS, THE SON OF THE MOST HIGH GOD, 153
JESUS WAS NOT WELCOME IN HIS OWN CITY, 383
JESUS, WHO PAID THE RANSOM, 363
JEWS AND ISRAEL, 465
JOHN MARK?, 516
JOHN THE BAPTIST, 192, 195, 296
JOSEPH OF ARIMATHAEA, 554
JUDAS, 512
JUDAS ISCARIOT, 101, 479
JUDAS KISS, 514
JUDGMENT, 189
JUDGMENT IN THE NEW TESTAMENT, 190
JUDGMENT ON OTHERS, 316
JUDGMENT SEAT OF CHRIST, 451
KEEPING THE COMMANDMENTS, 343
KING HEROD, 192
KING OF THE JEWS, 529, 536, 540
KINGDOM, 104
KINGDOM AGE, 495
KINGDOM LIFE AND LIVING, 25
KINGDOM OF GOD, 129, 288, 335, 433
KINGDOM OF GOD IS AT HAND, 26
KNOWLEDGE OF THE WORD, 113
LASCIVIOUSNESS, 244
LAST ADAM, 548
LAST MESSAGE JESUS PREACHED, 579
LAW OF CLEANSING, 51
LEAST OF ALL THE GIFTS, 587
LEAVEN, 261
LEGION, 155
LEPER, 48
LEPER AND HIS CONDITION, 51
LESSON FOR THE DISCIPLES, 209
LET MY PEOPLE GO, 148
LICENTIOUS DANCE, 194

LIFE, 251
LIFE IN THIS KINGDOM, 24
LIGHT, 269
LINEN CLOTH, 516
LOOK, 274
LOOK WHAT THE LORD HAS DONE!, 213
LOOKING BACK AT FAITH, 176
LORD LOOKS FOR THOSE WHO EXHIBIT FAITH IN HIM, 169
LORD OF THE SABBATH, 81
LORD SEES OUR EVERY ACTION, 219
LORDSHIP, 361
LOVE, 52, 342, 430
LOW SELF-ESTEEM, 203
MAINTAINING OUR SALVATION, 175
MAKING READY THE PASSOVER, 490
MAKING THE WORD OF GOD OF NONE EFFECT, 237
MALTREATMENT OF THE PROPHETS, 408
MAN WITH THE PITCHER OF WATER, 488
MANNER IN WHICH GOD DEALS WITH OUR FLESH, 505
MANNER IN WHICH JESUS DIED, 550
MANNER IN WHICH THE NAME OF JESUS MUST BE USED, 217
MANNER OF CHRIST, 70, 71
MANNER OF THE GOSPEL, 119
MANNER OF THE HOLY SPIRIT, 482
MANNER OF THE LIGHT, 125
MANY MORE RULES AND REGULATIONS, 229
MARRIAGE, 426
MARY, 102, 186
MARY MAGDALENE, 562
MATERIAL BLESSINGS AND RELATIONSHIPS, 351
MATTHEW, 67, 100
MEASURE YOU METE, 127
MEASUREMENT WE METE, 533
MECHANICS AND DYNAMICS OF THE SPIRIT, 99
MEDIATOR, 111
MEETING AT THE TOMB, 557
MEMORIAL, 479
MERCY, 170, 367
MESSAGE, 273, 513
MESSAGE OF FAITH, 167
MESSAGE OF THE CROSS, v (Introduction), 90, 258, 553
MESSENGER, 6
MESSIAH, 192
MIGHT OF THE MAN, CHRIST JESUS, 14
MIND, 431
MINISTRY, 42, 552
MINISTRY OF JOHN THE BAPTIST, 22

MIRACLE, 63, 87, 183, 204, 208, 221, 252, 267, 369
MIRACLE OF REDEMPTION, THE ONLY SOLUTION FOR THE HUMAN DILEMMA!, 160
MIRACLE OF THE LOAVES, 223
MISDIRECTION OF ISRAEL, 270
MISSION OF MERCY, 138
MOCKERS, 542
MOCKERY, 524
MOCKING, THE SCOURGING, AND THE SPITTING, 356
MODERN CHURCH, 7, 13, 356, 518
MODERN PREACHERS, 236
MODERN PSYCHOLOGY, 7
MONEY, 122, 333, 451, 480
MORE THAN ALL WHOLE BURNT OFFERINGS AND SACRIFICES, 432
MOSES, 234, 325
MOUNT OF OLIVES, 370, 495
MOVE OF THE HOLY SPIRIT, 212
MURDER, 243, 383
MURMURING, 475
MUSICAL TALENT, 168
MUZZLE, 141
MY BELOVED SON, 18, 292
MYSTERY OF THE KINGDOM OF GOD, 118
NAME OF JESUS, 38, 454
NATION RISING AGAINST NATION, 448
NATURAL BY COMPARISON WITH THE SUPERNATURAL, 293
NATURAL DISASTERS, 449
NATURE OF FAITH, 175
NAZARETH, 184
NAZARETH OF GALILEE, 15
NEED OF THE PEOPLE, 255
NEEDLE, 346
NEW COVENANT, 76, 494
NEW DOCTRINE?, 40
NEW WINE AND OLD BOTTLES, 77
NEWS MEDIA, 225
NO GOSPEL OF UNITY HERE!, 380
NO RESPECTER OF PERSONS, 417
NOT ONE STONE UPON ANOTHER, 444
OATH, 195
OBEDIENCE, 68, 218
OBJECT OF FAITH, 140
OBJECT OF FAITH MUST EVER BE JESUS CHRIST AND HIM CRUCIFIED, 171
OCCASION OF BLASPHEMING THE HOLY SPIRIT, 107
OF WHAT DID CHRIST EMPTY HIMSELF?, 378
OFFENSE, 185, 317, 496
OFFENSE OF THE EYES, 318

OLD TESTAMENT CONCEPT OF PEACE, 178
OLD TESTAMENT TEACHING OF JUDGMENT, 190
OLD TESTAMENT VIEW OF FAITH, 171
ONCE AGAIN, CHRIST AND THE CROSS MUST EVER BE THE OBJECT OF OUR FAITH, 177
ONE FLESH, 331
OPEN HEAVEN, 16
OPPORTUNITY, 126
OPPOSITION TO CHRIST, 311
OPPOSITION TO THE WORK OF GOD, 534
ORAL LAWS, 237
ORDAINED, 96
OUR FAITH, 4
OWNERSHIP, 388
PARABLE, 114, 117, 240
PARABLE OF THE FIG TREE, 466
PARABLE OF THE HOUSEHOLDER, 400
PARADOX, 417
PARALYSIS, 58
PASSOVER, 471, 481
PAUL AND FAITH, 175
PAUL'S VICTORY, 301
PAYING OF TAXES BY CHRISTIANS, 419
PEACE, 177, 322
PEACE AND THE CROSS, 179
PEACE BE STILL, 136
PEACE IN THE EPISTLES, 178
PEACE OFFERING OF THE OLD TESTAMENT, 178
PEACE THAT JESUS BRINGS, 178
PENNY, 418
PENTECOSTAL, 482
PERFECT SACRIFICE, 437
PERSECUTION, 352, 449
PERSEVERE, 166
PERSON OF CHRIST, 339
PETER, 560
PHARISEES, 78, 257
PHARISEES AND HERODIANS, 415
PHARISEES AND THE SCRIBES, 226
PHILEO, 53
PHILIP, 100
PHYSICAL EXHAUSTION, 135
PHYSICIANS, 165
PLACE OF A SKULL, 539
PLAGUES, 91
PLANTING OF THE SEED, 130
PLEAD WITH ME, 213
POLITICAL MESSAGE, 262
PONTIUS PILATE, 528
POOR, 475, 476
POOR WIDOW, 440
POOR WITHIN THE CHURCH, 477
POSSESSIONS, 345

POWER, 62, 288
POWER AND GLORY, 464
POWER OF GOD, 166, 425
POWER OF SATAN TO DESTROY, 304
POWER OF THE HOLY SPIRIT, 508
POWER SOURCE, 140
POWER TO HEAL THE SICK, 99
POWERS OF HEAVEN, 463
PRAY, 566
PRAYER, 46, 94, 209, 390, 451, 498
PRAYER AND FASTING, 311
PRAYER AND THE HOLY SPIRIT, 215
PRAYER IN JESUS' NAME, 217
PRAYER IN THE NEW TESTAMENT, 214
PRAYER IN THE OLD TESTAMENT, 210
PRAYER MEETING, 212
PREACH DELIVERANCE, 38
PREACH THE GOSPEL, 569
PREACH THE WORD, 57
PREACHING, 14, 48, 96, 590
PREACHING AND DELIVERANCE, 48
PREACHING PLATFORM, 90
PREACHING THE CROSS, 105
PREDESTINATION, 116
PREPARATION, 6, 478
PRESENCE OF CHRIST, 57, 222
PRESENT ATTITUDES CONCERNING JUDGMENT, 190
PRESENT POSSESSION, 338
PRESUMPTION, 498
PRICE THAT WAS PAID, 546
PRIDEFUL SPIRIT, 439
PRIEST, 55
PRISON, 21
PROBATION, 19
PROFESSIONAL HELP, 144
PROFIT, 285
PROOFS OF DEITY, 103
PROPHECY, 497
PROPHETS, 5
PROSPERITY!, 68
PSYCHOLOGY, 202
PSYCHOTHERAPY AND THE PREACHING OF THE CROSS, 143
PURPOSE DRIVEN LIFE THEORY, 279
PUTTING FORTH OF LEAVES, 466
QUALIFICATIONS FOR ENTERING THE KINGDOM OF GOD, 336
QUESTION, 297, 313
QUESTIONING CHRIST, 258
RANSOM, 362
RANSOM AND SACRIFICE, 363
RAPTURE OF THE CHURCH, 458

REBUKE, 36, 274
REBUKE GIVEN BY CHRIST, 275
RECEIPT OF CUSTOM, 67
RECEIVING THE HOLY SPIRIT AT SALVATION, 579
RECEPTION, 315
REDEMPTION, 20
REDEMPTION BY POWER, 364
REDEMPTION BY PRICE, 364
REFORMATION, 266
REFRESHING, 585
REFRESHING AND REST, 584
REFUSAL TO FORGIVE, 395
REJECTION, 269, 272, 323
REJECTION OF CHRIST, 159
REJECTION OF THE WORD OF GOD, 234
RELATIONSHIP, 24
RELATIVES OF CHRIST, 109
RELIGION, 82, 297, 396, 534
RELIGION OF JUDAISM, 69
RELIGION OF SATAN, 543
RELIGIOUS LEADERS OF ISRAEL, 472, 512
RELIGIOUS LEADERSHIP OF ISRAEL, 527
REMEDY ALONE IS CHRIST, 170
REMISSION OF SIN, 10
REMOVE THE MOUNTAIN, 386
REPENTANCE, 10, 27, 72, 191
REPENTANCE AND FAITH, 191
REPENTANCE OF SIMON PETER, 526
REPLACEMENT OF BIBLICAL COUNSELING, 142
REQUEST, 42
REQUIREMENTS, 188
RESIDENCE OF THE HOLY SPIRIT, 483
RESPONSE OF THE CHURCH TO THE POOR, 478
RESPONSIBILITY!, 258
RESPONSIBILITY OF EVERY BELIEVER, 128, 566
RESPONSIBILITY OF THE GOSPEL, 129
REST, 197, 250, 585
RESTORATION, 267
RESURRECTION, 273, 294, 313, 357, 421, 496, 560
RESURRECTION OF JESUS, 422
RESURRECTION OF THE BELIEVER, 422
REVELATION, 505
RICH MAN, 347
RICHES, 345
RIGHT HAND OF GOD, 437
RIGHT HAND OF POWER, 522
RIGHTEOUS ANGER, 87
RIGHTFUL PLACE OF CHRIST, 590
ROBBERS, 382
ROMAN LAW, 548
ROOT OF COMPASSION, 200
RULES MADE UP BY MEN, 228
SABBATH, 80

SABBATH DAY, 78
SACRED DUTY, 236
SADDUCEES, 420
SALT AND LIGHT, 311
SALT AS SEASON, 321
SALTED SACRIFICE, 320
SALTED WITH THE FIRE OF TESTING, 320
SALTNESS LOST, 321
SALTNESS OF THE BELIEVER, 321
SANCTIFYING PEACE, 179
SATAN, 20, 104, 275
SATAN'S METHODS, 121
SATISFACTION OF CHRIST, 207
SAVING OF ONE'S LIFE, 284
SCIENTIFIC?, 316
SCORN, 182
SCRIBES, 60, 104, 296, 355, 432
SCRIBES AND CHIEF PRIESTS, 383
SCRIBES AND PHARISEES, 70
SCRIPTURAL EVIDENCE FOR TONGUES, 581
SCRIPTURES, 516
SEA OF GALILEE, 27
SEAMLESS ROBE, 540
SECOND COMMANDMENT, 431
SECOND DENIAL, 526
SECTARIANISM, 315
SEDUCTION, 461
SEEKING, 109
SEEKING JESUS, 47
SELF, 203
SELF-CENTERED, 280
SELF-CONSCIOUSNESS, 241
SELF-PROMOTION, 314
SELF-WILL, 332
SELF-WILL OR GOD'S WILL, 350
SEND THEM AWAY?, 202
SERVANT, 362, 406
SERVANT OF JEHOVAH, viii (Introduction)
SERVANT PRINCIPLE, 314
SEVEN BASKETS, 256
SEVEN HORNS AND SEVEN EYES, 106
SEVEN LOAVES, 255
SEVEN SAYINGS OF CHRIST ON THE CROSS, 546
SHAME, 286
SHAMEFULLY HANDLED, 408
SHEPHERD AND THE SHEEP, 496
SHEWBREAD, 80
SHINING, 290
SICK, 225
SICKNESS, 41
SIGNS, 258, 576
SIGNS FOLLOWING, 591
SIMON, 100

SIMON OF CYRENE, 537
SIMON PETER, 274, 496, 515, 525
SIMON THE CANAANITE, 101
SIMON THE LEPER, 473
SIMPLICITY, v (Introduction)
SIN NATURE, 34, 301, 503
SINNERS, 71, 72, 511
SINNER'S PRAYER, 74
SLAIN LAMB AND THE HOLY SPIRIT, 105
SLEEP, 182, 510
SLEEPING ON WATCH, 471
SODOM AND GOMORRHA, 189
SOLOMON, 26
SON OF GOD, 93
SON OF MAN, 287
SOUL, 430
SOURCE, 50
SOURCE OF EVIL, 242
SOWER, 114
SOWING THE WORD, 119
SPEAKING WITH NEW TONGUES, 577
SPIRIT OF GOD, 322
SPIRIT OF MAN, 61
SPIRITUAL ADULTERY, 300, 343
SPIRITUAL BLINDNESS, 269
SPIRITUAL DISCERNMENT, 568
SPIRITUAL EYES AND SPIRITUAL EARS, 264
SPIRITUAL INTELLIGENCE, 416
SPIRITUAL LAWS, 340
SPITTLE, 251
SPOIL SATAN'S GOODS, 105
SPOKEN WORD, 55
SPREAD OF THE GOSPEL, 47, 117
STARS OF HEAVEN, 463
STONE, 412, 556, 558
STONY GROUND, 115
STRAIGHT PATHS, 8
STRAIGHTFORWARD PREACHING, 193
STRENGTH, 431
STRIFE, 360
STRONG MAN, 105
STRUGGLE WITH SIN, 503
SUBSTITUTION, 363
SUFFERING, 535
SUFFERING SAVIOUR, 272
SUICIDE, 306
SUNDAY, 558
SUPERFICIAL BELIEF, 174
SWINE, 156
SYMBOL OF MAN'S HELPLESSNESS, 84
SYMBOL OF THE FORGIVEN, CLEANSED SINNER, 54
SYMBOLS OF THE HOLY SPIRIT, 18

SYNAGOGUE, 31
TAKE HEED WHAT YOU HEAR, 127
TAKING UP SERPENTS, 588
TAKING UP THE CROSS DAILY, 430
TARRY AND WATCH, 499
TAXES, 419
TEACHING, 31, 113, 271, 312
TEACHING MINISTRY OF CHRIST, 339
TEACHING MINISTRY OF THE MASTER, 201
TEACHING OF CHRIST, 67, 381
TEACHING OF THE CROSS, 240
TEARS, 308
TELEVISION, 464
TEMPLE, 377, 442, 455
TEMPLE OF HIS BODY, 519
TEMPTATION, 19, 275
TEMPTING OF CHRIST, 418
TERRIBLE PERSECUTION, 524
TERRIBLE TRIAL, 500
TERRIBLE TRIAL OF GETHSEMANE, 499
TESTIMONY, 56, 163
TESTIMONY OF GRACE, 592
TESTIMONY THAT WAS UNHEEDED, 159
THADDAEUS, 100
THANKSGIVING, 256
THAT IN WHICH GOD IS PLEASED, 18
THAT WHICH THE HUMAN RACE LACKS, 342
THE ANOINTED ONE, 1
THE CALL, 29, 95
THE CROSS IS THE ONLY ANSWER FOR SIN, 49
THE CUP, 494
THE EXERCISE OF AUTHORITY, 397
THE LORD'S SUPPER, 492
THE MAN, JESUS CHRIST, 377
THE REASON IS NOT THEOLOGICAL, BUT RATHER MORAL, 424
THE RIGHT MESSAGE, THE RIGHT MESSENGER!, 258
THE TWELVE, 490
THE WAY, 8
THE WORM THAT DOESN'T DIE AND THE FIRE THAT'S NOT QUENCHED, 318
THEFTS, 243
THEY KILLED THE LORD OF GLORY, AND DID SO IN THE NAME OF THE LORD, 410
THINGS OF GOD AND THE THINGS OF MEN, 276
THIRST, 98
THIS GENERATION, 259, 468
THOMAS, 100
THORNS, 115
THOSE WHO REFUSE TO SEE AND HEAR, 118
THREE TYPES OF ANGER, 86

TIME ELEMENT, 460
TIME OF JACOB'S TROUBLE, 459
TITHES AND OFFERINGS, 419
TO GLORIFY GOD, 64
TO OPPOSE THAT WHICH BELONGS TO GOD IS TO OPPOSE GOD!, 85
TO WHOM WAS THE RANSOM PAID?, 364
TOMB, 138, 555
TONGUES OF MEN AND OF ANGELS, 586
TORMENTING SATAN, 153
TORN VEIL, 549
TORTURE!, 536
TOUCH, 53
TOUCHING JESUS, 91, 225
TOWER, 401
TRADITION, 228
TRADITION OF MEN, 233
TRANSFIGURATION, 289
TREASURE IN HEAVEN, 344
TREASURY, 440
TRIBUTE, 417
TRIUMPHANT ENTRY, 374
TRUE BREAD OF LIFE, 254
TRUE GOSPEL, 47
TRUST, 98, 346, 487
TRUST IN RULES AND REGULATIONS, 228
TRUTH, 262
TRUTH OF LAW AND GRACE, 77
TWELVE, 187
TWELVE BASKETS, 264
TWISTING OF THE WORD OF GOD, 235
TWO THIEVES, 541
UNBELIEF, 153, 186, 268, 308, 310, 544, 563, 565
UNCLEAN SPIRIT, 33, 37, 93, 138, 154, 187, 246
UNCOMPROMISED PREACHING OF JOHN THE BAPTIST, 193
UNDERSTANDING, 240, 263
UNDERSTANDING THE INCARNATION, 378
UNDERSTANDING THE PARABLES, 119
UNFRUITFUL, 122
UNKNOWN TONGUES?, 583
UNLEAVENED BREAD, 472
UNUSUAL METHOD OF HEALING, 267
VAIN WORSHIP, 231
VALUE JUDGMENTS, 340
VICTOR'S CROWN, 535
VICTORY, 249
VIRGIN BIRTH, 436
VIRTUE, 167
VISUALIZATION AND THE SUFFERINGS OF CHRIST ON THE CROSS, 403
VOICE, 6, 292
VOICE FROM HEAVEN, 18

WALKING AFTER THE FLESH, 154
WALKING AFTER THE FLESH AND WALKING AFTER THE SPIRIT, 510
WALKING AFTER THE FLESH LEADS TO BURN OUT, 199
WALKING AFTER THE SPIRIT, 155
WARFARE, 187
WARMING AT SATAN'S FIRE, 518
WARNING, 462
WARS AND RUMORS OF WARS, 447
WASTE?, 474
WASTED PREPARATION BECAUSE OF UNBELIEF, 558
WATCH, 471
WATCH AND PRAY, 469, 507
WATER BAPTISM, 9, 15, 571
WATER BAPTISM ACCORDING TO THE BIBLE, 572
WATERLOO, 557
WAYS OF THE LORD, 73
WHAT ARE THE BENEFITS OF THE CROSS?, 404
WHAT DO WE KNOW ABOUT THE RESURRECTION STATE?, 423
WHAT DO WE MEAN BY SELF-DENIAL?, 344
WHAT DOES CHRIST MEAN BY ONE LOSING ONE'S LIFE?, 285
WHAT DOES IT MEAN TO BEAR THE CROSS?, 284
WHAT DOES IT MEAN TO FORGIVE?, 392
WHAT DOES IT MEAN TO HAVE FAITH IN GOD?, 384
WHAT DOES IT MEAN TO MAKE THE CROSS OF CHRIST THE OBJECT OF ONE'S FAITH?, 487
WHAT DOES IT MEAN TO REPENT OF THE GOOD?, 11
WHAT DOES IT MEAN TO TRULY BELIEVE IN JESUS?, 570
WHAT EVIL HAS HE DONE?, 533
WHAT EXACTLY WAS THE INCARNATE STATE?, 436
WHAT IS BLASPHEMING THE HOLY SPIRIT?, 108
WHAT IS COMPASSION?, 200
WHAT IS ETERNAL LIFE?, 338
WHAT IS FAITH?, 64
WHAT IS LIKE THE KINGDOM OF GOD?, 131
WHAT IS PSYCHOLOGY?, 144
WHAT IS RESURRECTION POWER?, 423
WHAT IS THE BIBLICAL SYSTEM FOR HELP?, 147
WHAT IS THE DOCTRINE OF THE RESURRECTION?, 422
WHAT IS THE GOSPEL?, 1
WHAT IS THE GOSPEL OF JESUS CHRIST?, 3
WHAT IS THE ORIGINATION OF PSYCHOLOGY?, 146

WHAT IS THE SOUL OF MAN?, 286
WHAT IS VICTORY!, 211
WHAT MANNER OF MAN IS THIS?, 137
WHAT THE CALL ACTUALLY MEANS, 29
WHAT THE SABBATH IS ALL ABOUT, 80
WHAT THE WORLD THINKS OF CHRIST, 271
WHAT TYPE OF FORGIVENESS DOES GOD EXTEND TO THE REPENTANT SINNER?, 394
WHAT WILL YOU DO WITH JESUS?, 532
WHAT WOULD BE THE SPIRITUAL CONDITION OF THE CHILD SHOULD HE DIE IN THAT CONDITION?, 305
WHATEVER YOU DESIRE, 389
WHERE DID THIS *"OTHER GOSPEL"* OF SELF-ESTEEM COME FROM?, 278
WHETHER THERE BE TONGUES, THEY SHALL CEASE, 586
WHO CAN BE SAVED?, 347
WHO CAN COMMIT THE SIN OF BLASPHEMING THE HOLY SPIRIT?, 107
WHO CAN HAVE COMPASSION?, 201
WHO IS JESUS?, 270
WHO IS THE HOLY SPIRIT?, 578
WHOLENESS OF MIND, BODY, AND SPIRIT, 180
WHOSOEVER WILL, 117
WHY DID THE PHARISEES NOT KNOW THAT JESUS WAS THE MESSIAH?, 259
WHY DO MANY WHO CLAIM CHRIST INSIST ON THESE VAIN PHILOSOPHIES?, 283
WHY DON'T YOU KEEP THESE RULES?, 230
WHY THE FAILURE OF THE DISCIPLES?, 310
WHY WAS THIS THE RIGHT TIME?, 25
WHY WOULD A CHRISTIAN NEED DELIVERANCE?, 245
WICKEDNESS, 243
WILD BEASTS, 20
WILDERNESS, 255
WILL OF GOD, 166, 389, 501
WILL OF THE BELIEVER, 486
WILL ONE KNOW HE HAS BLASPHEMED THE HOLY SPIRIT?, 108
WILLPOWER, 299
WISDOM AFTER THE FLESH, 361
WITH GOD ALL THINGS ARE POSSIBLE, 348
WITHERED FIG TREE, 384
WITHERED HAND, 81
WITNESS AGAINST CHRIST?, 518
WITNESS OF DEMONS NOT ACCEPTED, 45
WOLVES IN SHEEP'S CLOTHING, 201
WONDER OF THE WORD OF GOD, v (Introduction)
WORD OF FAITH DOCTRINE, 350
WORD OF GOD, 234, 322, 580
WORD OF THE LORD, 442
WORD OF THE LORD IS ALWAYS SURE, 372
WORK OF THE HOLY SPIRIT, 281
WORKS, 572
WORLD EVANGELISM, 447
WORLDLINESS, 229
WORLDLY WISDOM, 124
WORSHIP, 152
WORST TIME THE WORLD HAS EVER KNOWN, 459
WOUNDED SPIRIT, 259
WRATH OF GOD, 457
WRETCHED MAN, 303
WRONG THINKING!, 295
YOU FURNISH THE SINNER, AND GOD FURNISHES THE SAVIOUR, 74
YOUR OWN TRADITION, 234
ZEBEDEE, 30

For all information concerning the *Jimmy Swaggart Bible Commentary*, please request a Gift Catalog.

You may inquire by using Books of the Bible.

- Genesis (639 pages) (11-201)
- Exodus (639 pages) (11-202)
- Leviticus (435 pages) (11-203)
- Numbers
  Deuteronomy (493 pages) (11-204)
- Joshua
  Judges
  Ruth (329 pages) (11-205)
- I Samuel
  II Samuel (528 pages) (11-206)
- I Kings
  II Kings (560 pages) (11-207)
- I Chronicles
  II Chronicles (528 pages) (11-226)
- Ezra
  Nehemiah
  Esther *(will be ready Summer 2011)* (11-208)
- Job (320 pages) (11-225)
- Psalms (688 pages) (11-216)
- Isaiah (688 pages) (11-220)
- Jeremiah
  Lamentations (456 pages) (11-070)
- Ezekiel (508 pages) (11-223)
- Daniel (403 pages) (11-224)
- Hosea-Malachi (582 pages) (11-072)
- Matthew (625 pages) (11-073)

- Mark (606 pages) (11-074)
- Luke (626 pages) (11-075)
- John (532 pages) (11-076)
- Acts (697 pages) (11-077)
- Romans (536 pages) (11-078)
- I Corinthians (632 pages) (11-079)
- II Corinthians (589 pages) (11-080)
- Galatians (478 pages) (11-081)
- Ephesians (550 pages) (11-082)
- Philippians (476 pages) (11-083)
- Colossians (374 pages) (11-084)
- I Thessalonians
  II Thessalonians (498 pages) (11-085)
- I Timothy
  II Timothy
  Titus
  Philemon (687 pages) (11-086)
- Hebrews (831 pages) (11-087)
- James
  I Peter
  II Peter (730 pages) (11-088)
- I John
  II John
  III John
  Jude (377 pages) (11-089)
- Revelation (602 pages) (11-090)

For telephone orders you may call 1-800-288-8350 with bankcard information. All Baton Rouge residents please use (225) 768-7000. For mail orders send to:

Jimmy Swaggart Ministries
P.O. Box 262550
Baton Rouge, LA 70826-2550

Visit our website: www.jsm.org

NOTES

NOTES

NOTES

NOTES

NOTES

NOTES

NOTES